Sociology

"Dear Professor Henslin . . ."

The following are excerpts from letters and emails to Jim Henslin from students who have used various versions and editions of *Sociology: A Down-to-Earth Approach.*

Dear Dr. Henslin,

I am a nursing student in Broward Community College. I had to take sociology in the summer before I could start my RN program in August. I had a wonderful time reading *Sociology: A Down-to-Earth Approach.* I never thought sociology would interest me much. I thank you for spectacularly presenting different religions, caste, cultures, and their norms very tactfully. I read all the chapters that were on my syllabus entirely. I learned a lot from this book and hope it will make the rest of my education journey easier.

Sincerely,

Abuasad Haque

Hi Mr. Henslin,

I hope this is still your email address. I am a student at Greenville Technical College in Greenville, South Carolina. I am currently taking Introduction to Sociology here at Tech and I must tell you, your book rocks!!!! It is the most fun I have ever had reading any textbook in my life!

Sincerely,

Kim B

Dear Professor Henslin,

I am a student at Stony Brook University in New York and I'm working toward a major in Sociology. I just completed an introductory summer course in Sociology that was taught with your textbook. I found your book to be incredibly interesting—so much that I am now reading the chapters we skipped over in class.

Thanks again,

Anna Maria Huertas Kormoski

Mr. Henslin,

I am a student at Texas Pan American University in Edinburg, Texas. I just want to take the time to write and say how much I have enjoyed your book. Not only is it very simple to understand, it is also very interesting. I was reluctant to take the class but through the text, I enjoy the class so much more.

Sincerely,

Julissa Rodriguez

Dear Mr. Henslin,

My name is Sydney Conley. I'm a student at Midlands Technical College in Columbia, South Carolina. I'm studying for a test that I have tomorrow in Sociology and I just thought you might like to know that I find your book *Essentials of Sociology* very interesting. Thanks to your book, I'm considering continuing my study of Sociology.

Thanks again

Sydney Conley

Hello Professor Henslin,

My name is Marta Holiday and I am a student at Marymount College in Tarrytown, NY. I am taking Introduction to Sociology at Nassau Community College to earn extra credits and your text was required reading for our class. I just wanted to tell you how much I enjoyed your book. I found the chapters fun and interesting—especially how you opened each with a sketch or a personal vignette.

It was a pleasure to read your work. I felt as though I became acquainted with you through your words.

Sincerely,

Marta A. Holliday

I am currently a freshman at Dordt College, a liberal arts college in Sioux City, Iowa. I really enjoy your book so far. It is very easy to read and understand. I especially appreciate the "down-to-earthiness" of this book. I have found that I can apply the things I have learned [from your text] to my Psychology 201 class also. Thanks for your dedication to making the field of sociology more exciting to learn about.

Joya Gerritsma

My name is April and I live in West Virginia. I am currently reading the book that you wrote. I took Sociology classes in high school and none have made as much sense as this text. I just thought that I would write and let you know.
Sincerely,
April

Dear James,

Hey there, my name is Leo Chagolla. I attend the University of Toledo and I am a Pharmacy major. When I registered for classes in the beginning of the fall semester, I was told I would either need to take sociology or psychology as an elective. To tell you the truth, I only took sociology because I had to—and it sounded easier than psychology. What I have discovered is that sociology has become one of the most interesting subjects I have ever studied.

Your book, *A Down-to-Earth Approach*, is marvelously well written and constructed. I seriously believe that reading your book has made me a better person. I am only one chapter away from completing the book—my class was only supposed to read on to chapter 9—but I just cannot stop reading.

Leo Chagolla

Hello,

My name is Margaux Strawn and I have just signed up for Sociology 101. I had taken a course on Sociology in high school many moons ago. I felt very overwhelmed when first reading your textbook, but as I dug into the book, the reading became very easy and interesting. I would like to thank you for helping to produce a book that already has me looking up more information on DuBois.
Sociology potential,
Margaux Strawn

Dr. James Henslin,

I had acquired Essentials of Sociology: A Down-to-Earth Approach as part of my required liberal arts core classes (Sociology 101) at Marquette University. I am now in the middle of my senior year and would like to tell you that I have used this text in most of the subsequent classes that I enrolled in after that class.

I want to thank you for helping the rest of my educational journey to be a pleasant one. It may also interest you to know that I am an adult learner at age 41, who returned to college after 18 years of factory work.
Doug Bulson
East Troy, WI
MarquetteUniversity

Dear Mr. Henslin,

I just finished a Sociology class using your text, the fourth edition of Sociology, A Down-to-Earth Approach. Tomorrow, I will take my final exam. I just wanted to commend you on this book. I found it extremely fascinating, well-organized, easy to read and most of all, interesting.

If you want a profile of some of your readers (students), I am 60 years old, a Catholic writer, author of four books, and a late bloomer who is just now getting her college education. I will graduate in August from Ottawa U. with a degree in Religion and a concentration on Psychology.

Thank you again for your fine book. My college education would not have been complete without this course.
Sincerely,
Judy Esway
Mesa, AZ

Dear Mr. Henslin,

I just completed an Introduction to Sociology course at my local college (Lansing Community College in Lansing, Michigan). It was great! I especially enjoyed reading your textbook. It is one of the best textbooks I've come across yet! It was very engaging and easy to follow with current events which I could relate to.
Sincerely,
Julie Markham

Sociology
A DOWN-TO-EARTH APPROACH
ninth edition

James M. Henslin
Southern Illinois University, Edwardsville

PEARSON

Boston   New York   San Francisco
Mexico City   Montreal   Toronto   London   Madrid   Munich   Paris
Hong Kong   Singapore   Tokyo   Cape Town   Sydney

Senior Series Editor/Series Editor: Jeff Lasser
Development Editor: Jennifer Albanese
Series Editorial Assistant: Lauren Houlihan
Marketing Manager: Kelly May
Editorial Production Service: Nesbitt (Dusty Friedman)
Composition Buyer: Linda Cox
Manufacturing Buyer: Megan Cochran
Electronic Composition: Nesbitt Graphics, Inc. and
    Dusty Friedman
Interior Design: Carol Somberg
Photo Researcher: Katharine S. Cebik (interior)/
    Laurie Frankenthaler (chapter openers)
Cover Administrator: Linda Knowles

For related titles and support materials, visit our online catalog at
www.ablongman.com.

Between the time website information is gathered and then
published, it is not unusual for some sites to have closed. Also,
the transcription of URLs can result in typographical errors. The
publisher would appreciate notification where these errors occur
so that they may be corrected in subsequent editions.

ISBN-13: 978-0-205-57023-2 (college edition)
ISBN-10: 0-205-57023-2 (college edition)
ISBN-13: 978-0-13-135924-6 (high school binding)
ISBN-10: 0-13-135924-X (high school binding)

Printed in the United States of America
10 9 8 7 6 5 4 3   RRD-MO   11 10 09

Photo credits appear on page PC1, which constitutes an extension
of the copyright page.

Chapter Opener Art Credits:

Chapter 1: *Rainy Day Crowd* by Diana Ong, 1999. Computer graphics.
© Diana Ong/SuperStock.

Chapter 2: *Cakewalk* by Carmen Lomas Garza, 1987. Acrylic painting, 36 × 48
in. © 1987 Carmen Lomas Garza. Collection of Paula Maciel-Benecke and Norbert
Benecke, Aptos, CA. Photo by M. Lee Fatherree.

Chapter 3: *Orgullo de Familia (Family Pride)* by Simon Silva, 1997. Gouache.
From Gathering the Sun by Alma Flor Alda, illustrated by Simon Silva. Illustrations copyright © 1997 by Simon Silva, www.simonsilva.com. Used with permission of the illustrator and BookStop Literary Agency. All rights reserved.

Chapter 4: *Street Scene (Boy with Kite)* by Jacob Lawrence, 1962. Egg tempera
on hardboard, 23 7/8 × 30 in. Conservation Center of the Institute of Fine
Arts, New York University, NY, USA. Photo © The Jacob and Gwendolyn
Lawrence Foundation/Art Resource, NY. © 2009 The Jacob and Gwendolyn
Lawrence Foundation, Seattle/Artists Rights Society (ARS), New York.

Chapter 5: *Diverse Cross-Section* by Ivan Lee Sanford, 1991. Acrylic, 4 × 2.75
in. © Ivan Lee Sanford/Images.com.

Chapter 6: *Unity* by Bharati Chaudhuri. Acrylic/mixed medial on canvas.
© Bharati Chaudhuri/SuperStock.

Chapter 7: *Human Pyramid of Businesspeople* by David Tillinghast, 1998.
Acrylic. © David Tillinghast/Images.com.

Chapter 8: *Prisoners Exercising (After Gustave Dore's Print)* by Vincent van
Gogh, 1890. Oil on canvas, 80 × 64 cm. Pushkin Museum of Fine Arts,
Moscow. © Alinari Archives/CORBIS.

Chapter 9: *Farmers Work in Rice Paddies in Taiwan* by Franklin McMahon.
© Franklin McMahon/Corbis.

Chapter 10: *Have and Have Not* by Frank Freed, 1970. Oil on canvas, 101.6 × 61
cm. © Frank Freed (1906–1975), Private Collection/The Bridgeman Art Library
International. © The Eleanor and Frank Freed Foundation, Houston, TX.

Chapter 11: *Women in Burkah* by Pacita Abad, 1979. Oil on canvas, 125 × 88
cm. © Pacita Abad Art.

Chapter 12: *All Human Beings are Born Free and Equal in Dignity and Rights* by
Ron Waddams, 1998. Acrylic on board, 122 × 92 cm. © Ron Waddams (Contemporary Artist)/Private Collection/Bridgeman Art Library International.

Chapter 13: *Woman and Cello* by Deidre Scherer, 2003. Fabric and thread,
26 × 21 in. © Deidre Scherer 2003, www.dscherer.com.

Chapter 14: *Paperworkers* by Douglass Crockwell, 1934. Oil on canvas,
48 1/4 × 36 1/8 in. (91.7 × 122.4 cm.). WPA work. Smithsonian American
Art Museum, Washington, DC, USA. © Smithsonian American Art Museum,
Washington, DC/Art Resource, NY.

Chapter 15: *We The People* by Fred Otnes, 1978. Mixed media, collage, 24 × 20
in. © Fred Otnes/Images.com.

Chapter 16: *Circle of Love* by Michael Escoffery, 1996. Mixed media. Private
Collection. Photo © Michael Escoffery/Art Resource, NY. © 2009 Michael Es-
coffery/Artists Rights Society (ARS), New York.

Chapter 17: *Students* by Stephen Schildbach, 1999. Acrylic, 16 × 13 in.
© Stephen Schildbach/Images.com,.

Chapter 18: *Mural on South Street,* Philadelphia, PA, artist unknown. © James
Lemass/Index Stock Imagery.

Chapter 19: *Harlem Hospital* by Jacob Lawrence, 1953. Egg tempera on
hardboard, 20 × 24 in. Michael Rosenfeld Gallery: Photo © The Jacob and
Gwendolyn Lawrence Foundation/Art Resource, NY. © 2009 The Jacob and
Gwendolyn Lawrence Foundation, Seattle/Artists Rights Society (ARS), New York.

Chapter 20: *Feast of San Gennaro* by Sharon Florin, 1998. Oil on canvas, 30 ×
36 in. © 1998 Sharon Florin. Courtesy of the artist and PaintingsDIRECT, Inc.
(www.PaintingsDIRECT.com)

Chapter 21: *Demonstration* by Isaak Brodskij, 1930. © The State Russian Mu-
seum/CORBIS.

Chapter 22: *Exhaustive Fumes from Cars and Factories Contribute to Global
Warming* by Roy Scott. © Roy Scott/Images.com.

To my fellow sociologists, who do such creative research on social life and who communicate the sociological imagination to generations of students. With my sincere admiration and appreciation,

Jim Henslin

What's New?

Because sociology is about social life and we live in a changing global society, an introductory sociology text must reflect the national and global changes that engulf us, as well as new sociological research. In this revision of *Sociology: A Down-to-Earth Approach*, there are over 60 new suggested readings, 350 new references, 260 new instructional photos, and 115 updated illustrations. Here are some of the new topics, illustrations, tables, and boxed features.

CHAPTER 1
New topic: In light of the hanging of Saddam Hussein, the application of network analysis in his capture is recast as problematic for class discussion

CHAPTER 2
New Cultural Diversity box: Culture Shock: The Arrival of the Hmong

CHAPTER 3
New topic: *Anime* in the socialization of children

CHAPTER 4
New topics:
• Shooting deaths at an Amish school
• Cultural diversity in smiling
• Applied body language: training of airport personnel and interrogators
• Applied impression management: Helping women executives get promoted

CHAPTER 5
New topic: Billboards that display your name and a personal message by reading information from your car key.

CHAPTER 6
New topics:
• Torture warrants
• Groupthink applied to the acceptance of torture by U.S. officials
• No-Sneeze kittens mentioned as a new product

CHAPTER 7
New topic: "Corporate cook-offs" as the new fad in corporate team-building exercises

CHAPTER 8
New topic: Online shaming sites
New Cultural Diversity box: "What Kind of Prison Is This?"

CHAPTER 9
New topics:
• Enslavement of children to be jockeys in camel races.
• Canceling of debts of the poorest nations by G-8
• How ideology sets limits for a society's elite

CHAPTER 10
New illustration: Figure 10.9, illustrating births to single women by education

CHAPTER 11
New tables:
• Table 11.3 Age of Rape Victims
• Table 11.4 Relationship of Rapists to Victims

CHAPTER 12
New topics:
• New immigration bill
• First Latino to compete for the Democratic candidacy for President
• *Proposition 2* of the Michigan state constitution
• The Skywalk over the Grand Canyon, opened by the Hualapai
New Cultural Diversity box: The Illegal Travel Guide

CHAPTER 13
New topics:
• Creative aging
• Gerotranscendence theory

CHAPTER 14
New Cultural Diversity boxes:
• Child Workers
• China's New Capitalism

CHAPTER 15
New Down-to-Earth Sociology box: Child Soldiers

CHAPTER 16
New topics:
• Finding brides for dead sons (China)
• Housework, child care, and paid labor data from Bianchi et al. research
New Down-to-Earth Sociology boxes:
• Finding a Mate: Not the Same as It Used to Be
• Caught Between Two Worlds: The Children of Divorce

CHAPTER 17
New topic: More education increases life expectancy

CHAPTER 18
New Down-to-Earth Sociology box: The New Face of Religion: Pentecostals and the Spanish Immigrants
New Cultural Diversity box: Human Heads and Animal Blood: The Toleration of Religion

CHAPTER 19
New Down-to-Earth Sociology box: "Cry Baby! Cry Baby!": Childhood Social Experiences and Adult Physical Health
New topic: Circumcision and HIV/AIDS

CHAPTER 20
New topic: In 2007, for the first time in history, more people live in cities than in rural areas.

CHAPTER 22
New topic in box on space wars: "Rods from God" and China's challenge to U.S. dominance by shooting down one of its own orbiting satellites
New table: Table 22.2 Ogburn's Processes of Social Change
New topic: Russia's threat to aim its missiles at the cities of Europe in retaliation for the U.S. plan to put missiles in Poland

Brief Contents

Contents

2 Culture 36

3 Socialization 64

4 Social Structure and Social Interaction 96

THROUGH THE AUTHOR'S LENS

When a Tornado Strikes: Social Organization Following a Natural Disaster

When TV news announced that a tornado had ripped apart a town just hours from my own, not only destroying buildings but also taking lives, I wondered how the people were adjusting to their sudden loss. These photos, taken the next day, show a community in the process of rebuilding. (Page 122)

7 Bureaucracy and Formal Organizations   176

THROUGH THE AUTHOR'S LENS

The Dump People: Working and Living and Playing in the City Dump of Phnom Penh, Cambodia

I could hardly believe my ears when I learned that people were living in the city dump of Phnom Penh, the capital of Cambodia. This photo essay reveals their life far better than words ever could. These men, women, and children are not only scavenging trash, but also they are participating in a community. (Page 256)

10 Social Class in the United States 266

11 Sex and Gender 298

Work and Gender: Women at Work in India

Like women in the West, women in India are not limited to the home. Their work roles, however, stand in sharp contrast with those of women in the West. This photo essay illustrates some of the amazing differences I saw. (Page 310)

12 Race and Ethnicity 332

PART IV Social Institutions

THROUGH THE AUTHOR'S LENS

Small Town USA: Struggling to Survive

All across the nation, small towns are struggling to survive. How can small towns contend with cutthroat global competition when workers in some countries are paid a couple of dollars a day? Many small towns are left in a time warp as history shifts around them. This photo essay tells the story. (Page 414)

19 Medicine and Health   556

THROUGH THE AUTHOR'S LENS

A Walk Through El Tiro in Medellin, Colombia

One of the most significant changes in the world is the global rush of poor, rural people to the cities of the Least Industrialized Nations. Some of these settlements are dangerous. I was fortunate to be escorted by an insider through this section of Medellin, Colombia. (Page 604)

21 Collective Behavior and Social Movements 622

THROUGH THE AUTHOR'S LENS

Social Movements and Propaganda:
The Execution of Timothy McVeigh

When Timothy McVeigh, the Oklahoma bomber, was scheduled to be executed at the federal penitentiary in Terre Haute, Indiana, the media reported rumors that there was going to be a riot—and maybe even an insurrection. I couldn't resist going. This photo essay illustrates the use of propaganda by social movement activists. (Page 640)

22 Social Change and the Environment 650

Boxed Features

Thinking Critically

Guide *to* Social Maps

To the **Student** *from the* **Author**

WELCOME TO SOCIOLOGY! I've loved sociology since I was in my teens, and I hope you enjoy it, too. Sociology is fascinating because it is about human behavior, and many of us find that it holds the key to understanding social life.

If you like to watch people and try to figure out why they do what they do, you will like sociology. Sociology pries open the doors of society so you can see what goes on behind them. *Sociology: A Down-to-Earth Approach* stresses how profoundly our society and the groups to which we belong influence us. Social class, for example, sets us on a particular path in life. For some, the path leads to more education, more interesting jobs, higher income, and better health, but for others it leads to dropping out of school, dead-end jobs, poverty, and even a higher risk of illness and disease. These paths are so significant that they affect our chances of making it to our first birthday, as well as of getting in trouble with the police. They even influence our satisfaction in marriage, the number of children we will have—and whether or not we will read this book in the first place.

When I took my first course in sociology, I was "hooked." Seeing how marvelously my life had been affected by these larger social influences opened my eyes to a new world, one that has been fascinating to explore. I hope that you will have this experience, too.

From how people become homeless to how they become presidents, from why people commit suicide to why women are discriminated against in every society around the world— all are part of sociology. This breadth, in fact, is what makes sociology so intriguing. We can place the sociological lens on broad features of society, such as social class, gender, and race-ethnicity, and then immediately turn our focus on the small-scale level. If we look at two people interacting—whether quarreling or kissing—we see how these broad features of society are being played out in their lives.

We aren't born with instincts. Nor do we come into this world with preconceived notions of what life should be like. At birth, we have no concepts of race-ethnicity, gender, age, or social class. We have no idea, for example, that people "ought" to act in certain ways because they are male or female. Yet we all learn such things as we grow up in our society. Uncovering the "hows" and the "whys" of this process is also part of what makes sociology so fascinating.

One of sociology's many pleasures is that as we study life in groups (which can be taken as a definition of sociology), whether those groups are in some far-off part of the world or in some nearby corner of our own society, we gain new insights into who we are and how we got that way. As we see how *their* customs affect *them,* the effects of our own society on us become more visible.

This book, then, can be part of an intellectual adventure, for it can lead you to a new way of looking at your social world—and in the process, help you to better understand both society and yourself.

I wish you the very best in college—and in your career afterward. It is my sincere desire that *Sociology: A Down-to-Earth Approach* will contribute to that success.

Jim Henslin

James M. Henslin
Department of Sociology
Southern Illinois University, Edwardsville

P.S. I enjoy communicating with students, so feel free to comment on your experiences with this text. Because I travel a lot, it is best to reach me by e-mail: henslin@aol.com

To the Instructor from the Author

REMEMBER WHEN YOU FIRST GOT "HOOKED" on sociology, how the windows of perception opened as you began to see life-in-society through the sociological perspective? For most of us, this was an eye-opening experience. This text is designed to open those windows onto social life, so students can see clearly the vital effects of group membership on their lives. Although few students will get into what Peter Berger calls "the passion of sociology," we at least can provide them the opportunity.

To study sociology is to embark on a fascinating process of discovery. We can compare sociology to a huge jigsaw puzzle. Only gradually do we see how the intricate pieces fit together. As we begin to see these interconnections, our perspective changes as we shift our eyes from the many small, disjointed pieces to the whole that is being formed. Of all the endeavors we could have entered, we chose sociology because of the ways in which it joins together the "pieces" of society and the challenges it poses to "ordinary" thinking. To share with students this process of awareness and discovery called the sociological perspective is our privilege.

As instructors of sociology, we have set ambitious goals for ourselves: to teach both social structure and social interaction, and to introduce students to the sociological literature–both the classic theorists and contemporary research. As we accomplish this, we would also like to enliven the classroom, encourage critical thinking, and stimulate our students' sociological imagination. Although formidable, these goals *are* attainable, and this book is designed to help you reach them. Based on many years of frontline (classroom) experience, its subtitle, *A Down-to-Earth Approach,* was not proposed lightly. My goal is to share the fascination of sociology with students, and thereby make your teaching more rewarding.

Over the years, I have found the introductory course especially enjoyable. It is singularly satisfying to see students' faces light up as they begin to see how separate pieces of their world fit together. It is a pleasure to watch them gain insight into how their social experiences give shape to even their innermost desires. This is precisely what this text is designed to do—to stimulate your students' sociological imagination so they can better perceive how the "pieces" of society fit together—and what this means for their own lives.

Filled with examples from around the world as well as from our own society, this text helps to make today's multicultural, global society come alive for students. From learning how the international elite carves up global markets to studying the intimacy of friendship and marriage, students can see how sociology is the key to explaining contemporary life—and their own place in it.

In short, this text is designed to make your teaching easier. There simply is no justification for students to have to wade through cumbersome approaches to sociology. I am firmly convinced that the introduction to sociology should be enjoyable, and that the introductory textbook can be an essential tool in sharing the discovery of sociology with students.

The Organization of this Text

The text is laid out in five parts. Part I focuses on the sociological perspective, which is introduced in the first chapter. We then look at how culture influences us (Chapter

2), examine socialization (Chapter 3), and compare macrosociology and microsociology (Chapter 4). After this, we look at how sociologists do research (Chapter 5). Placing research methods in the fifth chapter is not the usual sequence, but doing so allows students to first become immersed in the captivating findings of sociology—then, after their interest is awakened, they learn how sociologists gather their data. This works very well, but if you prefer the more traditional order, simply teach this chapter as the second chapter. No content will be affected.

Part II, which focuses on groups and social control, adds to the students' understanding of how far-reaching society's influence is—how group membership penetrates even their thinking, attitudes, and orientations to life. We first examine the different types of groups that have such profound influences on us and then look at the fascinating area of group dynamics (Chapter 6). We then examine the impact of bureaucracy and formal organizations (Chapter 7). After this, we focus on how groups "keep us in line" and sanction those who violate their norms (Chapter 8).

In Part III, we turn our focus on social inequality, examining how it pervades society and how it has an impact on our own lives. Because social stratification is so significant, I have written two chapters on this topic. The first (Chapter 9), with its global focus, presents an overview of the principles of stratification. The second (Chapter 10), with its emphasis on social class, focuses on stratification in U.S. society. After establishing this broader context of social stratification, we examine gender, the most global of the inequalities (Chapter 11). Then we focus on inequalities of race and ethnicity (Chapter 12), and those of age (Chapter 13).

Part IV helps students to become more aware of how social institutions encompass their lives. We first look at economy, the social institution that has become dominant in U.S. society (Chapter 14), and then at politics, our second overarching social institution (Chapter 15). We then place the focus on marriage and family (Chapter 16), and education (Chapter 17). After this, we look at the significance of religion (Chapter 18), and, finally, that of medicine (Chapter 19). Throughout, we examine how these social institutions are changing, and how their changes, in turn, influence our orientations to life.

With its focus on broad social change, Part V provides an appropriate conclusion for the book. Here we examine why our world is changing so rapidly, as well as catch a glimpse of what is yet to come. We first analyze trends in population and urbanization, sweeping forces in our lives that ordinarily remain below our level of awareness (Chapter 20). Our focus on collective behavior and social movements (Chapter 21), and social change and the environment (Chapter 22) takes us to the "cutting edge" of the vital changes that engulf us all.

Themes and Features

Six central themes run throughout this text: down-to-earth sociology, globalization, cultural diversity, critical thinking, the new technology, and the growing influence of the mass media on our lives. For each of these themes, I have written a series of boxes. These boxed features are one of my favorite components of the book. They are especially useful for introducing the controversial topics that make sociology such a lively activity.

Let's look at these six themes.

Down-to-Earth Sociology

As many years of teaching have shown me, all too often textbooks are written to appeal to the adopters of texts rather than to the students who must learn from them. Therefore, a central concern in writing this book has been to present sociology in a way that not only facilitates understanding but also shares its excitement. During the course of writing other texts, I often have been told that my explanations and writing style are "down-to-earth," or accessible and inviting to students—so much so that I chose this phrase as the book's subtitle. The term is also featured in my introductory reader, *Down to Earth Sociology,* 14th edition (New York: Free Press, 2007).

This first theme is highlighted by a series of boxed features that explore sociological processes that underlie everyday life. The topics that we review in these **Down-to-Earth Sociology** boxes are highly diverse. In them, we analyze

- how sociology was used to capture Saddam Hussein (Chapter 1)
- the relationship between heredity and environment (Chapter 3)
- how football can help us understand social structure (Chapter 4)
- beauty and success (Chapter 4)
- improper and fraudulent social research (Chapter 5)
- facebooking (Chapter 6)
- how the United States is being "McDonaldized" (Chapter 7)
- serial killers in our midst (Chapter 8)
- what life is like after hitting it big at the lottery (Chapter 10)
- the lifestyles of the super-rich (Chapter 10)
- cold-hearted surgeons and their women victims (Chapter 11)
- the taken-for-granted privileges attached to being white (Chapter 12)
- how women navigate male-dominated corporations (Chapter 14)
- the life of child soldiers (Chapter 15)

- how people's views affect the outcome of cohabitation (Chapter 16)
- how technology is changing the way people find mates (Chapter 16)
- how the children of divorce are caught between two worlds (Chapter 16)
- why so many abused women don't leave their abusers (Chapter 16)
- home schooling (Chapter 17)
- terrorism in the name of God (Chapter 18)
- what we know and don't know about religion and health (Chapter 18)
- how childhood social experiences affect people's health as adults (Chapter 19)
- the international black market in human body parts (Chapter 19)
- the gentrification of Harlem (Chapter 20)
- how tsunamis can help us to understand world population growth (Chapter 20)
- mass hysteria (Chapter 21)
- corporate welfare (Chapter 22)

This first theme is actually a hallmark of the text, as my goal is to make sociology "down to earth." To help students grasp the fascination of sociology, I continuously stress sociology's relevance to their lives. To reinforce this theme, I avoid unnecessary jargon and use concise explanations and clear and simple (but not reductive) language. I also use student-relevant examples to illustrate key concepts, and I base several of the chapters' opening vignettes on my own experiences in exploring social life. That this goal of sharing sociology's fascination is being reached is evident from the many comments I receive from instructors and students alike that the text helps make sociology "come alive."

Globalization

The second theme, *globalization,* explores the impact of global issues on our lives and on the lives of people around the world. As our global economy increasingly intertwines the fates of nations, it vitally affects our own chances in life. The globalization of capitalism influences the kinds of skills and knowledge we need, the types of work available to us, the costs of the goods and services we consume, and even whether our country is at war. In addition to the strong emphasis on global issues that runs throughout this text, I have written a separate chapter on global stratification. I have also featured global issues in the chapters on social institutions and the final chapters on social change: population, urbanization, social movements, and the environment.

What occurs in Russia, Japan, Germany, and China, as well as in much smaller nations such as Afghanistan and Iraq, has far-reaching consequences on our own lives. Consequently, in addition to the global focus that runs throughout the text, the next theme, cultural diversity, also has a strong global emphasis.

Cultural Diversity in the United States and Around the World

The third theme, *cultural diversity*, has two primary emphases. The first is cultural diversity around the world. Gaining an understanding of how social life is "done" in other parts of the world often challenges our taken-for-granted assumptions of social life. At times, when we learn about other cultures, we gain an appreciation for the life of other peoples; at other times, we may be shocked or even disgusted at some aspect of another group's way of life (such as female circumcision) and come away with a renewed appreciation of our own customs.

To highlight this first subtheme, I have written a series of boxes called **Cultural Diversity around the World.** Among the topics in this subtheme are

- food customs that shock people from different cultures (Chapter 2)
- how Easterners and Westerners perceive the world differently (Chapter 3)
- where prisoners are allowed to work at outside-of-prison jobs—and to have guns (Chapter 8)
- human sexuality in Mexico and Kenya (Chapter 8)
- selling brides in China (Chapter 11)
- female circumcision in Africa (Chapter 11)

- child workers (Chapter 14)
- China's new capitalism (Chapter 14)
- the globalization of capitalism (Chapter 14)
- love and arranged marriage in India (Chapter 16)
- female infanticide in China and India (Chapter 20)
- the destruction of the rainforests and indigenous peoples of Brazil (Chapter 22)

In the second subtheme, **Cultural Diversity in the United States,** we examine groups that make up the fascinating array of people who comprise the U.S. population. The boxes I have written with this subtheme review such topics as

- the culture shock the Hmong experienced when they arrived in the United States (Chapter 2)
- the controversy over the use of Spanish or English (Chapter 2)
- the terms that people choose to refer to their own race-ethnicity (Chapter 2)
- the resistance to social change by the Amish (Chapter 4)
- social class and upward social mobility of African Americans (Chapter 10)
- how Tiger Woods represents a significant change in racial-ethnic identity (Chapter 12)

- the author's travels with a Mexican who transports undocumented workers to the U.S. border (Chapter 12)
- the Pentecostal religion among Spanish-speaking immigrants (Chapter 18)
- how human heads and animal sacrifices are testing the toleration of religion (Chapter 18)
- our shifting racial-ethnic mix (Chapter 20)

Looking at cultural diversity—whether it be in the United States or in other regions of the world—can challenge our own orientations to life. Seeing that there are so many ways of "doing" social life highlights the arbitrariness of our own customs—and our taken-for-granted ways of thinking. These contrasts provide a stimulating context that can help students to develop their sociological imagination. They also help students to see connections among key sociological concepts such as culture, socialization, norms, race-ethnicity, gender, and social class. As your students' sociological imagination grows, they can attain a new perspective on their own experiences—and a better understanding of the social structure of U.S. society.

Critical Thinking

The fourth theme, *critical thinking*, focuses on controversial social issues and engages students in examining the various sides of those issues. In these sections, titled **Thinking Critically,** I present objective portrayals of positions on social issues. I do not take a side—although I occasionally play the "devil's advocate" in the questions that close these topics. Like the boxed features, these critical thinking sections can enliven your classroom by stimulating a vibrant exchange of ideas. Among the issues addressed are

- our tendency to conform to evil authority, as uncovered by the Milgram experiments (Chapter 6)

- bounties paid to kill homeless children in Brazil (Chapter 9)

- *maquiladoras* on the U.S.-Mexican border (Chapter 9)

- whether it is desirable to live as long as Methuselah (Chapter 13)

- medically assisted suicide (Chapter 19)

- abortion as a social movement (Chapter 21)

These *Thinking Critically* sections are based on controversial social issues that either affect the student's own life or focus on topics that have intrinsic interest for students. Because of their controversial nature, these sections stimulate both critical thinking and lively class discussions. These sections can also be used as the basis for in-class debates and as topics for small discussion groups.

Small discussion groups can enliven a class and be an effective way to present sociological ideas. I describe the nuts and bolts of this teaching technique in the Instructor's Manual.

Sociology and the New Technology

The fifth theme, *sociology and the new technology*, explores an aspect of social life that has come to be central in our lives. We welcome these new technological tools, for they help us to be more efficient at performing our daily tasks, from making a living to communicating with others—whether those people are nearby or on the other side of the globe. The significance of the new technology, however, extends far beyond the tools and the ease and efficiency they bring to our lives. The new technology is better envisioned as a social revolution that will leave few aspects of our lives untouched. It even penetrates our being, shapes our thinking, and leads to changed ways of viewing life.

This theme is introduced in Chapter 2, where technology is defined and presented as a major aspect of culture. The impact of technology is then discussed throughout the text. Examples include how technology is related to cultural change (Chapter 2), how technology is used to control workers in order to produce the "maximum security" workplace (Chapter 7), the implications of technology for maintaining global stratification (Chapter 9), how the consequences of technology differ by social class (Chapter 10), and how technology is changing education (Chapter 17), religion (Chapter 18), and medicine (Chapter 19). The final chapter (22), "Social Change and the Environment," concludes the book with a focus on this theme.

To highlight this theme, I have written a series of boxes called **Sociology and the New Technology.** In these boxes, we explore how technology is changing society and affecting our lives. We examine

- the implications of cloning for our coming society (Chapter 6)

- cyberloafing and cybersleuthing (Chapter 7)

- how technology is aiding—and complicating–reproduction (Chapter 16)

- capitalism and distance learning (Chapter 17)

- how technology has created a controversy about rationing medical care (Chapter 19)

- the luddite reaction to new technology (Chapter 22)

The Mass Media and Social Life

In the sixth theme, we stress how the *mass media* affect our behavior and permeate our thinking. We consider how the media penetrate our consciousness to such a degree that they even influence how we perceive our own bodies. As your students consider this theme, they may begin to see the mass media in a different light, which should further stimulate their sociological imagination.

To make this theme more prominent for students, I have written a series of boxed features called **Mass Media in Social Life**. Among these are

- an analysis of why Native Americans like Westerns even though Indians are usually portrayed as victims (Chapter 2)

- the influence of computer games on images of gender (Chapter 3)

- the worship of thinness—and how this affects our own body images (Chapter 4)

- the issue of censoring high-tech pornography (Chapter 8)

- the reemergence of slavery in today's world (Chapter 9)

- stimulating greed to stimulate the economy (Chapter 14)

- the pros and cons of electronic voting (Chapter 15)

- God on the Net (Chapter 18)

New Topics

Because sociology is about social life and we live in a changing global society, the topics of an introductory text must reflect the national and global changes that engulf us, as well as new sociological research. Among the many new topics in this edition are *Anime* in the socialization of children (Chapter 3), the shooting deaths at an Amish school (Chapter 3), cultural diversity in smiling (Chapter 3), applied body language–training airport personnel and interrogators (Chapter 3), and applied impression management–helping women executives get promoted.

Other new topics include billboards that display your name and a personal message by reading information from your car key (Chapter 5), torture warrants (Chapter 6), how groupthink applies to the acceptance of torture by U.S. officials and to the President's evaluation of the war in Iraq (Chapter 6), no-sneeze kittens (Chapter 6), "corporate cook-offs" as a new fad in corporate team-building exercises (Chapter 7), online shaming sites (Chapter 8), the enslavement of children to be jockeys in camel races (Chapter 9), the canceling of debts of the poorest nations by G-8 (Chapter 9), births to single women by level of education (Chapter 10), the age of rape victims (Chapter 11), and the relationship of rapists to their victims (Chapter 11).

We also consider *Proposition 2* of the Michigan state constitution (Chapter 12), creative aging (Chapter 13), gerotranscendence theory (Chapter 13), child workers (Chapter 14), the excesses in China's new capitalism (Chapter 14), the dilemma and experiences of child soldiers (Chapter 15), a practice in China of finding brides for dead sons (Chapter 16), new data on housework, child care, and paid labor (Chapter 16), how technology is changing the way people find mates (Chapter 16), and the plight of children in divorce, how they are caught between two worlds (Chapter 16), and that the more education people get, the longer they live (Chapter 17).

Other new topics include the attraction of Pentecostalism to Spanish-speaking immigrants (Chapter 18), how human heads and animal sacrifices are testing the limits of religious toleration (Chapter 18), how being teased in childhood has negative effects on adults' health (Chapter 19), that the circumcision of males reduces the likelihood of contracting HIV/AIDS (Chapter 19), the Supreme Court's decision on partial birth abortion/intact dilation and evacuation (Chapter 19), "Rods from God" in the new space wars (Chapter 22), China's challenge to U.S. dominance by shooting down one of its own orbiting satellites (Chapter 22), divisions within G-8 that are showing up with Russia's threat to aim its missiles at the cities of Europe in retaliation for the U.S. plan to put missiles on European soil (Chapter 22), and the report of the United Nations' Intergovernmental Panel on Climate Change (Chapter 22).

Visual Presentations of Sociology

Through the Author's Lens   Using this format, students are able to look over my shoulder as I experience other cultures or explore aspects of this one. These six photo essays should expand your students' sociological imagination and open their minds to other ways of doing social life, as well as stimulate thought-provoking class discussion.

When a Tornado Strikes: Social Organization Following a Natural Disaster   When a tornado hit a small town just hours from where I lived, I photographed the aftermath of the disaster. The police let me in to view the neighborhood where the tornado had struck, destroying homes and killing several people. I was impressed by how quickly people were putting their lives back together, the topic of this photo essay (Chapter 4).

The Dump People of Phnom Penh, Cambodia   Among the culture shocks I experienced in Cambodia was not to discover that people scavenge at Phnom Penh's huge city dump— this I knew about—but that they also live there. With the aid of an interpreter, I was able to interview these people, as well as photograph them as they went about their everyday lives. An entire community lives in the city dump, complete with restaurants amidst the huge piles of garbage. This photo essay reveals not just these people's activities but also their social organization (Chapter 9).

Work and Gender: Women at Work in India   As I traveled in India, I took photos of women at work in public places. The more I traveled in this country and the more photos I took, the more insight I gained into gender relations. Despite the general submissiveness of women to men in India, women's worlds are far from limited to family and home. Women are found at work throughout the society. What is even more remarkable is how vastly different "women's work" is in India than it is in the United States. This, too, is an intellectually provocative photo essay (Chapter 11).

Small Town USA: Struggling to Survive   To take the photos for this essay, I went off the beaten path. On a road trip from California to Florida, instead of following the interstates, I followed those "little black lines" on the map. They took me to out-of-the-way places that the national transportation system has bypassed. Many of these little towns are putting on a valiant face as they struggle to survive, but, as the photos show, the struggle is apparent, and, in some cases, so are the scars (Chapter 14).

A Walk through El Tiro in Medellin, Colombia: One of the most significant social changes in the world is taking place in the Least Industrialized Nations. There, in the search for a better life, people are abandoning rural areas. Fleeing poverty, they are flocking to the cities, only to find even more poverty. Some of these settlements of the new urban poor are dangerous. I was fortunate to be escorted by an insider through a section of Medellin, Colombia (Chapter 20).

Social Movements and Propaganda: The Execution of Timothy McVeigh: Although McVeigh's execution is "old news," what is significant are the sociological principles that the demonstrators at McVeigh's execution exemplified. The national news had piqued my interest, especially the reports about a possible riot and perhaps even an insurrection. This was too much to resist, and I drove to Terra Haute, Indiana, where I was able to interview and photograph activists on both sides of the death penalty issue, and see how the police and military were handling the potential riot. Chapter 21 features my account of this media event, a study in propaganda and social movements.

Photo Essay on Subcultures   The photo essay in Chapter 2 is designed to help students better understand subcultures. Because this photo essay consists of photos taken by others, it is not a part of the series, *Through the Author's Lens.* The variety of subcultures featured in this photo essay, however, should be instructive to your students.

Photo Collages   Because sociology lends itself so well to photographic illustrations, this text also includes photo collages. In Chapter 2, students can catch a glimpse of the fascinating variety that goes into the cultural relativity of beauty. The collage in Chapter 6 illustrates categories, aggregates, and primary and secondary groups, concepts that students sometimes wrestle to distinguish. The photo collage in chapter 11 lets students see how differently gender is portrayed in different cultures.

Other Photos by the Author   Sprinkled throughout the text are photos that I took during travels to India and Cambodia. These photos illustrate sociological principles and topics better than photos available from commercial sources. As an example, while in the United States, I was told about a feral child who had been discovered living with monkeys and who had been taken to an orphanage in Cambodia. The possibility of photographing and interviewing that child was one of the reasons that I went to Cambodia. That particular photo is on page 67. Another of my favorites is on page 204.

Other Special Pedagogical Features

In addition to chapter summaries and reviews, key terms, and a comprehensive glossary, I have included several special features to aid students in learning sociology. **In Sum** sections help students review important points within the chapter before going on to new sections. I have also developed a series of **Social Maps,** which illustrate how social conditions vary by geography.

Chapter-Opening Vignettes   These accounts feature down-to-earth illustrations of a major aspect of each chapter's content. Some of these are based on my own experiences. Several come from my research with the homeless, the time I spent with them on the streets and slept in their shelters (Chapters 1, 10, and 19). Others recount my travels in Africa (Chapters 2 and 11) and Mexico (Chapter 20). I also share my experiences when I spent a night with street people at DuPont Circle in Washington, D.C. (Chapter 4). Other vignettes are based on current and historical events (Chapters 5, 7, 9, 12, 17, 18, 21, and 22), composite accounts (chapters 14 and 16), classical studies in the social sciences (Chapters 3, 8, and 13), and even novels (Chapters 6 and 15). Many students have told their instructors that they find these vignettes compelling, that they arouse their interest in the chapter.

Thinking Critically About the Chapters   I close each chapter with three critical thinking questions. Each question focuses on a major feature of the chapter, asking students to reflect on and consider some issue. Many of the questions ask the students to apply sociological findings and principles to their own lives.

On Sources   Sociological data are found in a wide variety of sources, and this text reflects that variety. Cited throughout this text are standard journals such as the *American Journal of Sociology, Social Problems, American Sociological Review,* and *Journal of Marriage and the Family,* as well as more esoteric journals such as the *Bulletin of the History of Medicine, Chronobiology International,* and *Western Journal of Black Studies.* I have also drawn heavily from standard news sources, especially the *New York Times* and the *Wall Street Journal,* as well as more unusual sources such as *El País.* In addition, I cite unpublished papers by sociologists.

Acknowledgments

The gratifying response to earlier editions indicates that my efforts at making sociology down to earth have succeeded. The years that have gone into writing this text are a culmination of the many more years that preceded its writing—from graduate school to that equally demanding endeavor known as classroom teaching. No text, of course, comes solely from its author. Although I am responsible for the final words on the printed page, I have received excellent feedback from instructors who have taught from the first eight editions. I am especially grateful to

Reviewers of the Eighth Edition

Christina Alexander, *Linfield College*

Larry Curiel, *Cypress College*

Arunas Juska, *East Carolina University*

Darina Lepadatu, *Kennesaw State University*

Rachel Stehle, *Cuyahoga Community College*

Marios Stephanides, *University of Tampa*

Reviewers of the First through Seventh Editions

Francis O. Adeola, *University of New Orleans*

Brian W. Agnitsch, *Marshalltown Community College*

Sandra L. Albrecht, *The University of Kansas*

Richard Alman, *Sierra College*

Gabriel C. Alvarez, *Duquesne University*

Kenneth Ambrose, *Marshall University*

Alberto Arroyo, *Baldwin–Wallace College*

Karren Baird-Olsen, *Kansas State University*

Rafael Balderrama, *University of Texas—Pan American*

Linda Barbera-Stein, *The University of Illinois*

Brenda Blackburn, *California State University, Fullerton*

Ronnie J. Booxbaum, *Greenfield Community College*

Cecil D. Bradfield, *James Madison University*

Karen Bradley, *Central Missouri State University*

Francis Broouer, *Worcester State College*

Valerie S. Brown, *Cuyahoga Community College*

Sandi Brunette-Hill, *Carrol College*

Richard Brunk, *Francis Marion University*

Karen Bullock, *Salem State College*

Allison R. Camelot, *California State University at Fullerton*

Paul Ciccantell, *Kansas State University*

John K. Cochran, *The University of Oklahoma*

James M. Cook, *Duke University*

Joan Cook-Zimmern, *College of Saint Mary*

Russell L. Curtis, *University of Houston*

John Darling, *University of Pittsburgh—Johnstown*

Ray Darville, *Stephen F. Austin State University*

Jim David, *Butler County Community College*

Nanette J. Davis, *Portland State University*

Vincent Davis, *Mt. Hood Community College*

Lynda Dodgen, *North Harris Community College*

Terry Dougherty, *Portland State University*

Marlese Durr, *Wright State University*

Helen R. Ebaugh, *University of Houston*

Obi N. Ebbe, *State University of New York—Brockport*

Cy Edwards, Chair, *Cypress Community College*

John Ehle, *Northern Virginia Community College*

Morten Ender, *U.S. Military Academy*

Rebecca Susan Fahrlander, *Bellevue University*

Louis J. Finkle, *Horry-Georgetown Technical College*

Nicole T. Flynn, *University of South Alabama*

Lorna E. Forster, *Clinton Community College*

David O. Friedrichs, *University of Scranton*

Bruce Friesen, *Kent State University—Stark*

Lada Gibson-Shreve, *Stark State College*

Norman Goodman, *State University of New York—Stony Brook*

Rosalind Gottfried, *San Joaquin Delta College*

G. Kathleen Grant, *The University of Findlay*

Bill Grisby, *University of Northern Colorado*

Ramon Guerra, *University of Texas—Pan American*

Remi Hajjar, *U.S. Military Academy*

Donald W. Hastings, *The University of Tennessee—Knoxville*

Lillian O. Holloman, *Prince George's Community College*

Michael Hoover, *Missouri Western State College*

Howard R. Housen, *Broward Community College*

James H. Huber, *Bloomsburg University*

Erwin Hummel, *Portland State University*

Charles E. Hurst, *The College of Wooster*

Nita Jackson, *Butler County Community College*

Jennifer A. Johnson, *Germanna Community College*

Kathleen R. Johnson, *Keene State College*

Tammy Jolley, *University of Arkansas Community College at Batesville*

David Jones, *Plymouth State College*

Ali Kamali, *Missouri Western State College*

Irwin Kantor, *Middlesex County College*

Mark Kassop, *Bergen Community College*

Myles Kelleher, *Bucks County Community College*

Mary E. Kelly, *Central Missouri State University*

Alice Abel Kemp, *University of New Orleans*

Diana Kendall, *Austin Community College*

Gary Kiger, *Utah State University*

Gene W. Kilpatrick, *University of Maine—Presque Isle*

Jerome R. Koch, *Texas Tech University*

Joseph A. Kotarba, *University of Houston*

Michele Lee Kozimor-King, *Pennsylvania State University*

Abraham Levine, *El Camino Community College*

Diane Levy, *The University of North Carolina, Wilmington*

Stephen Mabry, *Cedar Valley College*

David Maines, *Oakland University*

Ron Matson, *Wichita State University*

Armaund L. Mauss, *Washington State University*

Evelyn Mercer, *Southwest Baptist University*

Robert Meyer, *Arkansas State University*

Michael V. Miller, *University of Texas—San Antonio*

John Mitrano, *Central Connecticut State University*

W. Lawrence Neuman, *University of Wisconsin—Whitewater*

Charles Norman, *Indiana State University*

Patricia H. O'Brien, *Elgin Community College*

Robert Ostrow, *Wayne State*

Laura O'Toole, *University of Delaware*

Mike K. Pate, *Western Oklahoma State College*

Lawrence Peck, *Erie Community College*

Ruth Pigott, *University of Nebraska—Kearney*

Phil Piket, *Joliet Junior College*

Trevor Pinch, *Cornell University*

Daniel Polak, *Hudson Valley Community College*

James Pond, *Butler Community College*

Deedy Ramo, *Del Mar College*

Adrian Rapp, *North Harris Community College*

Ray Rich, *Community College of Southern Nevada*

Barbara Richardson, *Eastern Michigan University*

Salvador Rivera, *State University of New York—Cobleskill*

Howard Robboy, *Trenton State College*

Paulina X. Ruf, *University of Tampa*

Michael Samano, *Portland Community College*

Michael L. Sanow, *Community College of Baltimore County*

Mary C. Sengstock, *Wayne State University*

Walt Shirley, *Sinclair Community College*

Marc Silver, *Hofstra University*

Roberto E. Socas, *Essex County College*

Susan Sprecher, *Illinois State University*

Mariella Rose Squire, *University of Maine at Fort Kent*

Randolph G. Ston, *Oakland Community College*

Vickie Holland Taylor, *Danville Community College*

Maria Jose Tenuto, *College of Lake County*

Gary Tiederman, *Oregon State University*

Kathleen Tiemann, *University of North Dakota*

Judy Turchetta, *Johnson & Wales University*

Stephen L. Vassar, *Minnesota State University, Mankato*

William J. Wattendorf, *Adirondack Community College*

Jay Weinstein, *Eastern Michigan University*

Larry Weiss, *University of Alaska*

Douglas White, *Henry Ford Community College*

Stephen R. Wilson, *Temple University*

Anthony T. Woart, *Middlesex Community College*

Stuart Wright, *Lamar University*

Mary Lou Wylie, *James Madison University*

Diane Kholos Wysocki, *University of Nebraska—Kearney*

Stacey G. H. Yap, *Plymouth State College*

William Yoels, *University of Alabama Birmingham*

I couldn't ask for a more outstanding team than the one that I have the pleasure to work with at Allyn and Bacon. I want to thank Jeff Lasser, whose counsel continues to be excellent; Jenn Albanese, whose willingness to pursue leads in research has been an ongoing help in this formidable task; Judy Fiske, for constantly hovering over the many details—and for whole-heartedly supporting my many suggestions; Kathy Smith, for continuing her creative copy editing; Kate Cebik, for her creativity in photo research—and for her willingness to "keep on looking"; and Dusty Friedman, who while so capably overseeing both the routine and the urgent manages to exhibit an exemplary attitude.

I do so appreciate this team. It is difficult to heap too much praise on such fine, capable, and creative people. Often going "beyond the call of duty" as we faced non-stop deadlines, their untiring efforts coalesced with mine to produce this text. Students, whom we constantly kept in mind as we prepared this edition, are the beneficiaries of this intricate teamwork.

Since this text is based on the contributions of many, I would count it a privilege if you would share with me your teaching experiences with this book, including any suggestions for improving the text. Both positive and negative comments are welcome. It is in this way that I continue to learn.

I wish you the very best in your teaching. It is my sincere desire that *Sociology: A Down-to-Earth Approach* contributes to your classroom success.

James M. Henslin
Department of Sociology
Southern Illinois University, Edwardsville

I welcome your correspondence. E-mail is the best way to reach me: henslin@aol.com

A NOTE FROM THE PUBLISHER ON SUPPLEMENTS

▮▮ ▰▰▰ Instructor's Supplements

All of the teacher supplements and resources for this book are available electronically for preview and download on the Instructor Resource Center (IRC). Please go to pearsonschool.com/advanced and click "Online Teacher Supplements" for directions. You will be required to complete a one time registration subject to verification before being emailed access information to download materials.

Instructor's Manual *Jessica Herrmeyer, Hawkeye Community College*

For each chapter in the text, the Instructor's Manual provides a list of key changes to the new edition, chapter summaries and outlines, learning objectives, key terms and people, classroom activities, discussion topics, recommended films, Web sites, and additional references.

Test Bank *Anthony W. Zumpetta, West Chester University*

The Test Bank contains approximately 150 questions per chapter in multiple-choice, true-false, short answer, essay, vocabulary matching, and open-book formats. A recent addition is a section that challenges students to look beyond words and answer questions based on the text's figures, tables, and maps. All questions are labeled and scaled according to Bloom's Taxonomy.

Computerized Test Bank

The printed Test Bank is also available through Allyn and Bacon's computerized testing system, TestGen EQ. This fully networkable test-generating software is available on a multi-platform CD-ROM for Windows and Macintosh. The user-friendly interface allows you to view, edit, and add questions, transfer questions to tests, and print tests in a variety of fonts. Search and sort features allow you to locate questions quickly and to arrange them in whatever order you prefer.

PowerPoint Presentation *Dan Cavanaugh*

These PowerPoint slides on a CD, created especially for the Ninth Edition, feature lecture outlines for every chapter and many of the tables, charts, and maps from the text. PowerPoint software is not required, as a PowerPoint viewer is included.

Instructor's Resource CD

This CD contains electronic versions of all Instructor and Student Supplements in one convenient place. Print supplements are provided both in PDF format and as Word documents that can be edited. The CD includes the Instructor's Manual, Test Bank, Computerized Test Bank, PowerPoint Presentation, Study Guide Plus, Study Guide, and Telecourse Faculty Guide.

Transparencies to Accompany Introductory Sociology, by James Henslin

This package, updated for *Sociology: A Down-to-Earth Approach*, 9e, includes over 125 color acetates featuring illustrations from Henslin's introductory sociology texts.

Allyn and Bacon/ABC News Sociology Videos

This series of videos contains news footage and documentary-style programs from *Nightline*, *World News Tonight*, and *20/20* that illustrate sociological themes. Each video has an accompanying User's Guide (available electronically through Allyn and Bacon's Instructor's Resource

Center). Available titles are *Poverty and Stratification, Race and Ethnicity, Gender, Deviance,* and *Aging.* Available to qualified adopters.

The Video Professor: Applying Lessons in Sociology to Classic and Modern Films *Anthony W. Zumpetta, West Chester University*

This manual describes hundreds of commercially available videos that represent nineteen of the most important topics in Introductory Sociology textbooks. Each topic lists a number of movies, along with specific assignments and suggestions for class use. Available in print, and also electronically through the Instructor's Resource Center.

▮▮ ◢◣ Student Supplements

Exploring Social Life: Readings to Accompany Sociology: A Down-to-Earth Approach, Ninth Edition *James M. Henslin*

This brief reader, revised for the Ninth Edition, contains one reading for each chapter of the text, chosen and introduced by James M. Henslin. The reader can be purchased separately. An instructor's manual for the reader is available electronically through the Instructor's Resource Center.

Study Guide *Shelly Dutchin, Western Wisconsin Technical College*

This study guide is designed to help students prepare for quizzes and exams. For each chapter in the text, the guide contains a chapter summary, a list of key terms and people, a practice test with 25 multiple-choice questions and an answer key, and a set of PowerPoint lecture outlines. Available for purchase.

Study Guide Plus *Jessica Herrmeyer, Hawkeye Community College*

The Study Guide Plus is an expanded version of the Study Guide. For every chapter in the text, the Study Guide Plus contains a chapter summary; a list of learning objectives; a detailed chapter outline; a list of key terms and people; 3–5 student projects; and a practice test with 30 multiple-choice, 20 true/false, 15 short answer, 10 matching, and 5 essay questions. An answer key is provided for all questions. The Study Guide Plus also includes a section on successful study strategies. Available separately for student purchase.

Study Card for Introduction to Sociology

Compact, efficient, and laminated for durability, the Allyn and Bacon Study Card for Introductory Sociology condenses course information down to the basics, helping students quickly master fundamental facts and concepts or prepare for an exam. Available for purchase.

▮▮ ◢◣ Online Course Management

MySocLab

MySocLab is a state-of-the-art interactive and instructive solution for introductory sociology, delivered within CourseCompass, Allyn and Bacon's course management system (powered by Blackboard and hosted nationally on our server). MySocLab is designed to be used as a supplement to a traditional lecture course, or to completely administer an online course. Built around a complete e-book version of the text, MySocLab enables students to explore important sociological concepts by listening to interviews with prominent researchers and social scientists; listening to stories from the National Public Radio archives; reading current newspaper articles; completing activities based on maps and graphs in the text; and performing other hands-on activities. Self-scoring practice tests (in English and Spanish) help students prepare for quizzes and exams, and create a customized study plan for them. MySocLab also includes access to Research Navigator™ and a tutorial on Writing About Sociology. Customize your course or use the materials as presented. For more information visit www.mysoclab.com.

High school adopters should receive an access registration code with their textbook order. Directions on how to register for teacher and student access are available at pearsonschool .com/advanced by clicking on the Password Protected Web Site's link. If a teacher does not receive an access registration card with the textbook order or needs additional assistance, he or she should contact the local sales representative or email PHwebaccess@pearsoned.com <mailto:PHwebaccess@pearsoned.com>.

WebCT™ and Blackboard Test Banks

For high schools with **WebCT™** and **Blackboard** licenses, we have converted the complete Test Bank into these popular course management platforms. Adopters can download the electronic file by logging in to our Instructor Resource Center.

■■ ◢◢◣◣ Additional Supplements

New! The Allyn and Bacon Social Atlas of the United States *William H. Frey, University of Michigan, with Amy Beth Anspach, and John Paul DeWitt.*

This brief and accessible atlas uses colorful maps, graphs, and some of the best social science data available to survey the leading social, economic, and political indicators of American society. Available for purchase separately.

College and Society: An Introduction to the Sociological Imagination *Stephen Sweet, Ithaca College*

This supplemental text uses examples from familiar surroundings—the patterns of interaction, social structures, and expectations of conduct on a typical college campus—to help students see the ways in which the larger society also operates. Available for purchase separately.

About the Author

JAMES M. HENSLIN, who was born in Minnesota, graduated from high school and junior college in California and from college in Indiana. Awarded scholarships, he earned his Master's and doctorate degrees in sociology at Washington University in St. Louis, Missouri. After this, he won a postdoctoral fellowship from the National Institute of Mental Health, and spent a year studying how people adjust to the suicide of a family member. His primary interests in sociology are the sociology of everyday life, deviance, and international relations. Among his many books is *Down to Earth Sociology: Introductory Readings* (Free Press), now in its fourteenth edition. He has also published widely in sociology journals, including *Social Problems* and *American Journal of Sociology.*

While a graduate student, Jim taught at the University of Missouri at St. Louis. After completing his doctorate, he joined the faculty at Southern Illinois University, Edwardsville, where he is Professor Emeritus of Sociology. He says, "I've always found the introductory course enjoyable to teach. I love to see students' faces light up when they first glimpse the sociological perspective and begin to see how society has become an essential part of how they view the world."

Jim enjoys reading and fishing, and he also does a bit of kayaking. His two favorite activities are writing and traveling. He especially enjoys visiting and living in other cultures, for this brings him face to face with behaviors and ways of thinking that challenge his perspectives and "make sociological principles come alive." A special pleasure has been the preparation of the photo essays that appear in this text.

Jim is currently immersed in Eastern Europe, where he is observing first-hand the transition to capitalism of former Soviet-dominated countries.

Sociology

The Sociological Perspective

Diana Ong, *Rainy Day Crowd*, 1999

Even from the glow of the faded red-and-white exit sign, its faint light barely illuminating the upper bunk, I could see that the sheet was filthy. Resigned to another night of fitful sleep, I reluctantly crawled into bed.

The next morning, I joined the long line of disheveled men leaning against the chain-link fence. Their faces were as downcast as their clothes were dirty. Not a glimmer of hope among them.

No one spoke as the line slowly inched forward.

When my turn came, I was handed a cup of coffee, a white plastic spoon, and a bowl of semiliquid that I couldn't identify. It didn't look like any food I had seen before. Nor did it taste like anything I had ever eaten.

My stomach fought the foul taste, every spoonful a battle. But I was determined. "I will experience what they experience," I kept telling myself. My stomach reluctantly gave in and accepted its morning nourishment.

I was determined. "I will experience what they experience," I kept telling myself.

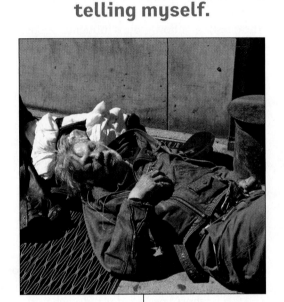

The room was strangely silent. Hundreds of men were eating, each one immersed in his own private hell, his head awash with disappointment, remorse, bitterness.

As I stared at the Styrofoam cup that held my coffee, grateful for at least this small pleasure, I noticed what looked like teeth marks. I shrugged off the thought, telling myself that my long weeks as a sociological observer of the homeless were finally getting to me. "This must be some sort of crease from handling," I concluded.

I joined the silent ranks of men turning in their bowls and cups. When I saw the man behind the counter swishing out Styrofoam cups in a washtub of murky water, I began to feel sick to my stomach. I knew then that the jagged marks on my cup really had come from a previous user's mouth.

How much longer did this research have to last? I felt a deep longing to return to my family—to a welcome world of clean sheets, healthy food, and "normal" conversations.

The Sociological Perspective

sociological perspective understanding human behavior by placing it within its broader social context

society people who share a culture and a territory

social location the group memberships that people have because of their location in history and society

Why were these men so silent? Why did they receive such despicable treatment? What was I doing in that homeless shelter? After all, I hold a respectable, professional position, and I have a home and family.

Sociology offers a perspective, a view of the world. The *sociological perspective* (or imagination) opens a window onto unfamiliar worlds—and offers a fresh look at familiar worlds. In this text, you will find yourself in the midst of Nazis in Germany and warriors in South America, as well as the people I visited who live in a city dump in Cambodia. But you will also find yourself looking at your own world in a different light. As you view other worlds—or your own—the sociological perspective enables you to gain a new perception of social life. In fact, this is what many find appealing about sociology.

The sociological perspective has been a motivating force in my own life. Ever since I took my introductory course in sociology, I have been enchanted by the perspective that sociology offers. I have thoroughly enjoyed both observing other groups and questioning my own assumptions about life. I sincerely hope the same happens to you.

Seeing the Broader Social Context

The **sociological perspective** stresses the social contexts in which people live. It examines how these contexts influence people's lives. At the center of the sociological perspective is the question of how groups influence people, especially how people are influenced by their **society**—a group of people who share a culture and a territory.

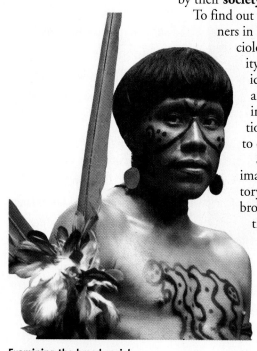

Examining the broad social context in which people live is essential to the *sociological perspective,* for this context shapes our beliefs and attitudes and sets guidelines for what we do. From this photo, you can see how distinctive those guidelines are for the Yanomamö Indians who live on the border of Brazil and Venezuela. How has this Yanomamö man been influenced by his group? How have groups influenced your views and behavior?

To find out why people do what they do, sociologists look at **social location,** the corners in life that people occupy because of where they are located in a society. Sociologists look at how jobs, income, education, gender, age, and race-ethnicity affect people's ideas and behavior. Consider, for example, how being identified with a group called *females* or with a group called *males* when we are growing up shapes our ideas of who we are and what we should attain in life. Growing up as a female or a male influences not only our aspirations but also how we feel about ourselves. It also affects the way we relate to others in dating and marriage and at work.

Sociologist C. Wright Mills (1959) put it this way: "The sociological imagination [perspective] enables us to grasp the connection between history and biography." By *history,* Mills meant that each society is located in a broad stream of events. Because of this, each society has specific characteristics—such as its ideas about the proper roles of men and women. By *biography,* Mills referred to each individual's specific experiences. In short, people don't do what they do because of inherited internal mechanisms, such as instincts. Rather, *external* influences—our experiences—become part of our thinking and motivations. The society in which we grow up, and our particular location in that society, lie at the center of what we do and how we think.

Consider a newborn baby. If we were to take the baby away from its U.S. parents and place it with a Yanomamö Indian tribe in the jungles of South America, you know that when the child begins to speak, his or her words will not be in English. You also know that the child will not think like an American. He or she will not grow up wanting credit cards, for example, or designer clothes, a car, a cell phone, an iPod, and the latest video game. Equally, the child will unquestioningly take his or her place in Yanomamö society—perhaps as a food gatherer, a hunter, or a warrior—and he or she will not even know about the world left behind at birth. And, whether male or female, the child will grow up assuming that it is natural to want many children, not debating whether to have one, two, or three children.

People around the globe take their particular views of the world for granted. Something inside us Americans tells us that hamburgers are delicious, small families are desirable, and designer clothing is attractive. Yet something inside some of the Sinai Desert Arab tribes tells them that warm, fresh camel's blood makes a fine drink and that everyone should have a large family and wear flowing robes (Murray 1935; McCabe and Ellis

1990). And that something certainly isn't an instinct. As sociologist Peter Berger (1963) phrased it, that "something" is "society within us."

Although obvious, this point frequently eludes us. We often think and talk about people's behavior as though it were caused by their sex, their race, or some other factor transmitted by their genes. The sociological perspective helps us escape from this cramped, personal view by exposing the broader social context that underlies human behavior. It helps us see the links between what people do and the social settings that shape their behavior.

This brings us to *you*—to how *your* social groups have shaped *your* ideas and desires. Over and over in this text, you will see that the way you look at the world is the result of your exposure to specific human groups. I think you will enjoy the process of self-discovery that sociology offers.

The Global Context—and the Local

As is evident to all of us—from the labels on our clothing that say Hong Kong, Brunei, or Macau, to the many other imported products that have become part of our daily lives—our world has become a global village. How life has changed! Our predecessors lived on isolated farms and in small towns. They grew their own food and made their own goods, buying some sugar, coffee, and a few other items that they couldn't produce. Beyond the borders of their communities lay a world they perceived only dimly.

And how slow communications used to be! In December 1814, the United States and Great Britain signed a peace treaty to end the War of 1812. Yet their armies fought a major battle in New Orleans two weeks *later*. The armed forces there had not yet heard that the war was over (Volti 1995).

Even though our world has changed so greatly that we can pick up a telephone or use the Internet to communicate instantly with people anywhere on the planet, we continue to occupy our own little corners of life. Like those of our predecessors, our worlds, too, are marked by differences in family background, religion, job, gender, race-ethnicity, and social class. In these corners, we continue to learn distinctive ways of viewing the world.

One of the beautiful—and fascinating—aspects of sociology is that it enables us to analyze both parts of our current reality: the changes that incorporate us into a global network *and* our unique experiences in our smaller corners of life. In this text, we shall examine both of these vital aspects of our lives.

Sociology and the Other Sciences

Just as humans today have an intense desire to unravel the mysteries around them, people in ancient times also attempted to understand their world. Their explanations were not based on observations alone, however, but were also mixed with magic and superstition.

To satisfy their basic curiosities about the world around them, humans gradually developed **science,** systematic methods to study the social and natural worlds and the knowledge obtained by those methods. *Sociology,* the study of society and human behavior, is one of these sciences.

A useful way of comparing these sciences—and of gaining a better understanding of sociology's place—is to divide them into the natural and the social sciences.

The Natural Sciences

The **natural sciences** are the intellectual and academic disciplines that are designed to explain and predict the events in our natural environment. The natural sciences are divided into specialized fields of research according to subject matter, such as biology, geology, chemistry, and physics. These are further subdivided into even more highly specialized areas. Biology is divided into botany and zoology; geology into mineralogy and geomorphology; chemistry into its organic and inorganic branches; and physics into biophysics and quantum mechanics. Each area of investigation examines a particular "slice" of nature.

science the application of systematic methods to obtain knowledge and the knowledge obtained by those methods

natural sciences the intellectual and academic disciplines designed to explain and predict events in our natural environments

The Social Sciences

People have not limited themselves to investigating nature. In the pursuit of a more adequate understanding of life, they have also developed fields of science that focus on the social world. The **social sciences** examine human relationships. Just as the natural sciences attempt to objectively understand the world of nature, the social sciences attempt to objectively understand the social world. Just as the world of nature contains ordered (or lawful) relationships that are not obvious but must be discovered through controlled observations, so the ordered relationships of the human or social world are not obvious, and must be revealed by means of repeated observations.

Like the natural sciences, the social sciences are divided into specialized fields based on their subject matter. These divisions are anthropology, economics, political science, psychology, and sociology. The social sciences are subdivided further into specialized fields. Thus, anthropology is divided into cultural and physical anthropology; economics has macro (large-scale) and micro (small-scale) specialties; political science has theoretical and applied branches; psychology may be clinical or experimental; and sociology has its quantitative and qualitative branches. Since our focus is sociology, let's contrast sociology with each of the other social sciences.

Anthropology   Anthropology, which traditionally focuses on tribal peoples, is closely related to sociology. The chief concern of anthropologists is to understand *culture,* a people's total way of life. Culture includes a group's (1) *artifacts,* such as its tools, art, and weapons; (2) *structure,* that is, the patterns that determine how its members interact with one another (such as positions of leadership); (3) *ideas and values,* especially how a group's belief system affects its members' lives; and (4) *forms of communication,* especially language.

Graduate students working on their doctorate in anthroplogy usually spend a period of time living with a tribal group. In their reports, they emphasize the group's family (kin) relationships. As there are no "undiscovered" groups left in the world, this focus on tribal groups is giving way to the study of groups in industrialized settings. When anthropologists study the same groups that sociologists do, they place greater emphasis on artifacts, authority (hierarchy), and language, especially kinship terms.

Economics   Economics concentrates on a single social institution. Economists study the production and distribution of the material goods and services of a society. They want to know what goods are being produced, what they cost, and how those goods are distributed. Economists also are interested in the choices that determine production and consumption; for example, they study what motivates people to buy a certain item instead of another.

Political Science   Political science focuses on politics and government. Political scientists examine how governments are formed, how they operate, and how they are related to other institutions of society. Political scientists are especially interested in how people attain ruling positions in their society, how they maintain those positions, and the consequences of their actions for the people they govern. In studying a constitutional government, such as that of the United States, political scientists also analyze voting behavior.

Psychology   The focus of psychology is on processes that occur *within* the individual, inside what they call the "skin-bound organism." Psychologists focus primarily on mental processes (what occurs in the brain, or the mind). They examine intelligence, emotions, perception, memory, even dreams. Some study how personality is formed. Others focus on personal adjustment and mental illness. Many psychologists work in private practice and as counselors in school and work settings, where they give personality tests, IQ tests, and vocational aptitude tests. As therapists, they focus on resolving personal problems, whether the need is to recover from trauma, such as abuse, or to get help with addiction to drugs, alcohol, or gambling.

Sociology   Sociology has many similarities to these other social sciences. Like anthropologists, sociologists study culture; they, too, have an interest in group structure and belief systems, as well as in how people communicate with one another. Like economists, sociologists are also concerned with the distribution of the goods and services of a society, especially how that distribution results in inequality. Like political scientists, sociologists study how people govern one another, especially how government affects people's lives. Like psychologists, sociologists are concerned with how people adjust to the difficulties of life.

Given these overall similarities, then, what distinguishes sociology from the other social sciences? Unlike anthropologists, sociologists focus primarily on industrialized societies. Unlike economists and political scientists, sociologists do not concentrate on a single social institution. And unlike psychologists, sociologists stress factors *external* to the individual to determine what influences people. These differences should become more apparent in the Down-to-Earth Sociology box below, in which we revisit an old tale about how members of different disciplines perceive the same subject matter.

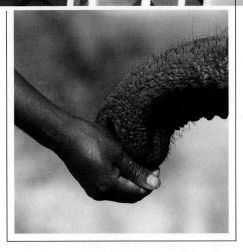

generalization a statement that goes beyond the individual case and is applied to a broader group or situation

patterns recurring characteristics or events

The Goals of Science

The first goal of each scientific discipline is to *explain* why something happens. The second goal is to make **generalizations,** that is, to go beyond the individual case and make statements that apply to a broader group or situation. For example, a sociologist wants to explain not only why Mary went to college or became an armed robber but also why people with her characteristics are more likely than others to go to college or to become armed robbers. To achieve generalizations, sociologists look for **patterns,** recurring characteristics or events. The third scientific goal is to *predict,* to specify what will happen in the future in the light of current knowledge.

To attain these goals, scientists do not rely on magic, superstition, or common beliefs, but, instead, they do systematic research. They explain exactly how they did

Down-to-Earth Sociology

An Updated Version of the Old Elephant Story

IT IS SAID THAT in the recent past, five wise men and women, all blindfolded, were led to an elephant and asked to explain what they "saw." The first, an anthropologist, tenderly touching the trunk and the tusks, smiled and said, "This is really primitive. I feel very comfortable here. Concentrate on these."

The second, an economist, feeling the mouth, said, "This is what counts. What goes in here is distributed throughout the body. Concentrate your research on how it is distributed."

The third, a political scientist, feeling the gigantic ears, announced, "This is the power center. What goes in here controls the entire beast. Concentrate your studies here."

The fourth, a psychologist, stroking the top of the elephant's head, broke into a huge grin and said, "This is the only thing that counts. All feeling and thinking take place inside here. To understand this beast, we'll study this part."

Then came the sociologist (of course!), who, after feeling the entire body, said, "You can't understand the beast by concentrating on only one part. Each is but part of the whole. The trunk and tusks, the mouth, the ears, the head—all are important. But so are the parts of the beast that you haven't mentioned. We must remove our blindfolds so we can see the larger picture. We have to see how everything works together to form the entire animal."

Pausing for emphasis, the sociologist added, "And we also need to understand how this creature interacts with similar creatures. How does its life in groups influence its behavior?"

I wish I could conclude this tale by saying that the anthropologist, the economist, the political scientist, and the psychologist were dazzled on hearing the wisdom of the sociologist, and, amidst gasps of wonderment, they tore off their blindfolds, joined together, and began to examine the entire animal. But, alas and alack! On hearing this sage advice, the specialists stubbornly bound their blindfolds even tighter so they could concentrate all the more on their particular part. And if you listened very, very carefully, you could even hear them mutter, "Don't touch the tusks." "Stay away from the mouth—that's my area." "Take your hand off the ears." "The top of the head is mine—stay away from it."

their research so it can be reviewed by others. Secrecy, prejudice, and other biases go against the grain of science.

Sociologists and other scientists also move beyond **common sense**—the prevailing ideas in a society, the things that "everyone knows" are true. "Everyone" can be misguided today just as easily as when common sense dictated that the world was flat or that no human could ever walk on the moon. As sociologists examine people's assumptions about the world, their findings may contradict commonsense notions about social life. To test your own "common sense," read the Down-to-Earth Sociology box on the next page.

The Risks of Sociology   Sometimes the explorations of sociologists take them into nooks and crannies that people would prefer remain unexplored. For example, a sociologist might study how people make decisions to commit a crime or to cheat on their spouses. Since sociologists want above all to understand social life, they cannot cease their studies because people feel uncomfortable. Sociologists consider all realms of human life legitimate avenues to explore, and their findings sometimes challenge cherished ideas.

As they examine how groups operate, sociologists often confront attempts to keep things secret. It seems that every organization, every group, nourishes an ideal image that it presents to others. Sociologists are interested in knowing what is really going on behind the scenes, however, so they peer beneath the surface to get past those sugar-coated images (Berger 1963; 2007). This approach sometimes brings sociologists into conflict with people who feel threatened by that information—which is all part of the adventure, and risk, of being a sociologist.

Origins of Sociology

Tradition Versus Science

Just how did sociology begin? In some ways, it is difficult to answer this question. Even ancient peoples tried to figure out social life. They, too, asked questions about why war exists, why some people become more powerful than others, and why some are rich but others are poor. However, they often based their answers on superstition, myth, or even the positions of the stars, and they did not *test* their assumptions.

Science, in contrast, requires the development of theories that can be tested by research. Measured by this standard, sociology only recently appeared on the human scene. It emerged about the middle of the 1800s, when social observers began to use scientific methods to test their ideas.

Sociology grew out of social upheaval. The Industrial Revolution had just begun. By the middle of the nineteenth century, Europe's economy was changing from agriculture to factory production. Masses of people were moving to cities in search of work. Their ties to the land—and to a culture that had provided them with ready answers to the difficult questions of life—were broken. The city greeted them with horrible working conditions: low pay; long, exhausting hours; dangerous work. For families to survive, even children had to work in these conditions; some children were even chained to factory machines to make certain they could not run away. Life no longer looked the same, and tradition, which had provided the answers to questions about social life, no longer could be counted on.

Tradition suffered further blows. The success of the American and French revolutions encouraged people to rethink social life. New ideas emerged, including the conviction that individuals possess inalienable rights. As this new idea caught fire, many traditional Western monarchies gave way to more democratic forms of government. People found the answers of tradition, including religion, inadequate.

When tradition reigns, it provides ready answers: "We do this because it has always been done this way." Tradition discourages original thinking. Since the answers already have been provided, why search for explanations? Sweeping change, however, does the opposite: By upsetting the existing order, it encourages questioning and demands new answers.

Enjoying A Sociology Quiz—Sociological Findings Versus Common Sense

SOME FINDINGS OF SOCIOLOGY support commonsense understandings of social life, but others contradict them. Can you tell the difference? To enjoy this quiz, complete *all* the questions before turning the page to check your answers.

1. **True/False** More U.S. students are killed in school shootings now than ten or fifteen years ago.
2. **True/False** The earnings of U.S. women have just about caught up with those of U.S. men.
3. **True/False** It is more dangerous to walk near topless bars than fast-food restaurants.
4. **True/False** Most rapists are mentally ill.
5. **True/False** Most people on welfare are lazy and looking for a handout. They could work if they wanted to.
6. **True/False** Compared with women, men make more eye contact in face-to-face conversations.
7. **True/False** Couples who live together before marriage are usually more satisfied with their marriages than couples who do not live together before marriage.
8. **True/False** Most husbands of employed wives who themselves get laid off from work take up the slack and increase the amount of housework they do.
9. **True/False** Because bicyclists are more likely to wear helmets now than just a few years ago, their rate of head injuries has dropped.
10. **True/False** Students in Japan are under such intense pressure to do well in school that their suicide rate is about double that of U.S. students.

Then there was the imperialism (empire building) of the time. The Europeans had conquered many parts of the world, and their new colonies stretched from Asia and Africa to North and South America. This exposed them to radically different ways of life, and they began to ask why cultures differ.

Another impetus for the development of sociology was the success of the natural sciences. Just as tradition was breaking down and people were questioning fundamental aspects of life, **the scientific method**—using objective, systematic observations to test theories—was being tried out in chemistry and physics. Many secrets that had been concealed in nature were being uncovered. With tradition no longer providing the answers to questions about social life, the logical step was to apply the scientific method to these questions. The result was the birth of sociology.

scientific method (the) using objective, systematic observations to test theories

positivism the application of the scientific approach to the social world

sociology the scientific study of society and human behavior

Auguste Comte and Positivism

This idea of applying the scientific method to the social world, known as **positivism,** apparently was first proposed by Auguste Comte (1798–1857). With the philosophical upheaval of the French Revolution still fresh in his mind, Comte left the small town in which he had grown up and moved to Paris. The changes he experienced in this move, combined with those France underwent in the revolution, led Comte to become interested in what holds society together. What creates social order, he wondered, instead of anarchy or chaos? And then, once society does become set on a particular course, what causes it to change?

As Comte considered these questions, he concluded that the right way to answer them was to apply the scientific method to social life. Just as this method had revealed the law of gravity, so, too, it would uncover the laws that underlie society. Comte called this new science **sociology**—"the study of society" (from the Greek *logos,* "study of," and the Latin *socius,* "companion," or "being with others"). Comte stressed that this new science not only would discover social principles but also would apply them to social reform. Sociologists would reform the entire society, making it a better place to live.

To Comte, however, applying the scientific method to social life meant practicing what we might call "armchair philosophy"—drawing conclusions from informal observations of social life. He did not do what today's sociologists would call research, and his

Auguste Comte (1798–1857), who is credited as the founder of sociology, began to analyze the bases of the social order. Although he stressed that the scientific method should be applied to the study of society, he did not apply it himself.

Sociological Findings Versus Common Sense— Answers to the Sociology Quiz

1. **False.** More students were shot to death at U.S. schools in the early 1990s than now (National School Safety Center 2007). See page 520.
2. **False.** Over the years, the wage gap has narrowed, but only slightly. On average, full-time working women earn less than 70 percent of what full-time working men earn. This low figure is actually an improvement over earlier years. See Figures 11.7 and 11.8 on pages 321 and 322.
3. **False.** The crime rate outside fast-food restaurants is considerably higher. The likely reason for this is that topless bars hire private security and parking lot attendants (Linz et al. 2004).
4. **False.** Sociologists compared the psychological profiles of prisoners convicted of rape and prisoners convicted of other crimes. Their profiles were similar. Like robbery, rape is a learned behavior. See pages 148–149.

5. **False.** Most people on welfare are children, the old, the sick, the mentally and physically handicapped, or young mothers with few skills. Less than 2 percent fit the stereotype of an able-bodied man. See page 288.
6. **False.** Women make considerably more eye contact (Henley et al. 1985).
7. **False.** The opposite is true. The likely reason is that many couples who cohabit before marriage are less committed to marriage in the first place—and a key to marital success is a strong commitment to one another (Larson 1988; Dush, Cohan, and Amato 2003).
8. **False.** Most husbands who have employed wives and who themselves get laid off from work *reduce* the amount of housework they do (Hochschild 1989; Brines 1994).
9. **False.** Bicyclists today are more likely to wear helmets, but their rate of head injuries is higher. Apparently, they take more risks because the helmets make them feel safer (Barnes 2001). (Unanticipated consequences of human action are studied by functionalists. See pages 26–27.)
10. **False.** The suicide rate of U.S. students is about double that of Japanese students (Lester 2003).

conclusions have been abandoned. Nevertheless, Comte's insistence that we must observe and classify human activities to uncover society's fundamental laws is well taken. Because he developed this idea and coined the term *sociology*, Comte often is credited with being the founder of sociology.

Herbert Spencer and Social Darwinism

Herbert Spencer (1820–1903), sometimes called the second founder of sociology, coined the term "survival of the fittest." Spencer thought that helping the poor was wrong, that this merely helped the "less fit" survive.

Herbert Spencer (1820–1903), who grew up in England, is sometimes called the second founder of sociology. Spencer disagreed profoundly with Comte that sociology should guide social reform. Spencer thought that societies evolve from lower ("barbarian") to higher ("civilized") forms. As generations pass, the most capable and intelligent ("the fittest") members of a society survive, while the less capable die out. Thus, over time, societies improve. To help the lower classes is to interfere with this natural process. The fittest members will produce a more advanced society—unless misguided do-gooders get in the way and help the less fit survive.

Spencer called this principle "the survival of the fittest." Although Spencer coined this phrase, it usually is attributed to his contemporary, Charles Darwin, who proposed that organisms evolve over time as they adapt to their environment. Because they are so similar to Darwin's ideas about the evolution of organisms, Spencer's views of the evolution of societies became known as *social Darwinism.*

Spencer's ideas that charity and helping the poor were wrong offended many. The wealthy industrialists of the time, however, liked these ideas: They saw themselves as "the fittest"—and therefore superior. Spencer's views also helped them avoid feelings of guilt for living like royalty while people around them went hungry.

Spencer did not conduct scientific studies. Like Comte, he simply developed ideas about society. Spencer gained a wide following in England and the United States, where he was sought after as a speaker, but eventually social Darwinism was discredited.

Karl Marx and Class Conflict

Karl Marx (1818–1883) not only influenced sociology but also left his mark on world history. Marx's influence has been so great that even the *Wall Street Journal,* that staunch advocate of capitalism, has called him one of the three greatest modern thinkers (the other two being Sigmund Freud and Albert Einstein).

Like Comte, Marx thought that people should try to change society. Marx, who came to England after being exiled from his native Germany for proposing revolution, believed that the engine of human history is **class conflict.** He said that the **bourgeoisie** (boo-shwa-zee) (the *capitalists,* those who own the means to produce wealth—capital, land, factories, and machines) are locked in conflict with the **proletariat** (the exploited workers, who do not own the means of production). This bitter struggle can end only when members of the working class unite in revolution and throw off their chains of bondage. The result will be a classless society, one free of exploitation, in which people will work according to their abilities and receive goods and services according to their needs (Marx and Engels 1848/1967).

Marxism is not the same as communism. Although Marx supported revolution as the only way that the workers could gain control of society, he did not develop the political system called *communism.* This is a later application of his ideas. Indeed, Marx himself felt disgusted when he heard debates about his insights into social life. After listening to some of the positions attributed to him, he shook his head and said, "I am not a Marxist" (Dobriner 1969b:222; Gitlin 1997:89).

Unlike Comte and Spencer, Marx did not think of himself as a sociologist. He spent years studying in the library of the British Museum in London, where he wrote widely on history, philosophy, and, of course, economics and political science. Because of his insights into the relationship between the social classes, especially the class struggle between the "haves" and the "have-nots," many sociologists claim Marx as a significant early sociologist. He also introduced one of the major perspectives in sociology, conflict theory, which is discussed on pages 29–30.

Karl Marx (1818–1883) believed that the roots of human misery lay in class conflict, the exploitation of workers by those who own the means of production. Social change, in the form of the overthrow of the capitalists by the workers (proletariat), was inevitable from Marx's perspective. Although Marx did not consider himself a sociologist, his ideas have influenced many sociologists, particularly conflict theorists.

The French Revolution of 1789 not only overthrew the aristocracy but also upset the entire social order. This extensive change removed the past as a sure guide to the present. The events of this period stimulated Auguste Comte to analyze how societies change. His writings are often taken as the origin of sociology. This engraving depicts the 1794 execution of Maximilien Robespierre, a leader of the Revolution.

class conflict Marx's term for the struggle between capitalists and workers

bourgeoisie Marx's term for capitalists, those who own the means of production

proletariat Marx's term for the exploited class, the mass of workers who do not own the means of production

Emile Durkheim and Social Integration

The primary professional goal of Emile Durkheim (1858–1917) was to get sociology recognized as a separate academic discipline (Coser 1977). Up to this time, sociology had been viewed as part of history and economics. Durkheim, who grew up in eastern France and was educated in both Germany and France, achieved his goal when he received the first academic appointment in sociology at the University of Bordeaux in 1887.

Durkheim also had another goal: to show how social forces affect people's behavior. To accomplish this, he conducted rigorous research. Comparing the suicide rates of several European countries, Durkheim (1897/1966) found that each country had a different suicide rate, and that these rates remained about the same year after year. He also found that different groups within a country had different suicide rates, and that these, too, remained stable from year to year. For example, Protestants, males, and the unmarried killed themselves at a higher rate than did Catholics, Jews, females, and the married. From this, Durkheim drew the insightful conclusion that suicide is not simply a matter of individuals here and there deciding to take their lives for personal reasons. Instead, *social factors underlie suicide,* and this is what keeps a group's rate fairly constant year after year.

Durkheim identified **social integration,** the degree to which people are tied to their social group, as a key social factor in suicide. He concluded that people who have weaker social ties are more likely to commit suicide. This, he said, explains why Protestants, males, and the unmarried have higher suicide rates. This is how it works, Durkheim said: Protestantism encourages greater freedom of thought and action; males are more independent than females; and the unmarried lack the ties and responsibilities that come with marriage. In other words, members of these groups have fewer of the social bonds that keep people from committing suicide. In Durkheim's term, they have less social integration.

Although strong social ties help protect people from suicide, Durkheim noted that in some instances strong bonds encourage suicide. An example is people who, torn apart by grief, kill themselves after their spouse dies. Their own feelings are so integrated with those of their spouse that they prefer death rather than life without the one who gave it meaning.

Despite the many years that have passed since its publication, Durkheim's study is still quoted. His research was so thorough that the principle he uncovered still applies: People who are less socially integrated have higher rates of suicide. Even today, those same groups that Durkheim identified—Protestants, males, and the unmarried—are more likely to kill themselves.

The French sociologist Emile Durkheim (1858–1917) contributed many important concepts to sociology. His comparison of the suicide rates of several counties revealed an underlying social factor: People are more likely to commit suicide if their ties to others in their communities are weak. Durkheim's identification of the key role of *social integration* in social life remains central to sociology today.

social integration the degree to which members of a group or a society feel united by shared values and other social bonds; also known as social cohesion

 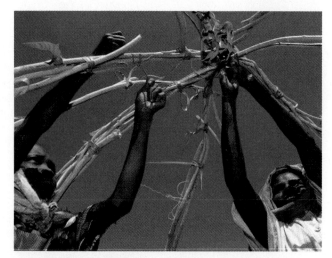

Durkheim believed that modern societies produce feelings of isolation, much of which comes from the division of labor. In contrast, members of traditional societies, who work alongside family and neighbors and participate in similar activities, experience a high degree of *social integration*. The Sudanese women in the photo on the right are building a house.

From Durkheim's study of suicide, we see the principle that was central in his research: *Human behavior cannot be understood only in individualistic terms; we must always examine the social forces that affect people's lives.* Suicide, for example, appears at first to be such an intensely individual act that it would seem that psychologists should study it, not sociologists. Yet, as Durkheim illustrated, if we look at human behavior (such as suicide) only in individualistic terms, we miss its *social* basis. For a glimpse of what Durkheim meant, look at Figure 1.1. That African Americans and whites commit suicide in such similar ways indicates something that goes far beyond the individual. Since these patterns are similar year after year, they reflect conditions in society, such as the popularity and accessibility of guns.

Max Weber and the Protestant Ethic

Max Weber (Mahx VAY-ber) (1864–1920), a German sociologist and a contemporary of Durkheim, also held professorships in the new academic discipline of sociology. Like Durkheim and Marx, Weber is one of the most influential of all sociologists, and you will come across his writings and theories in later chapters. Let's consider an issue Weber raised that remains controversial today.

Religion and the Origin of Capitalism Weber disagreed with Marx's claim that economics is the central force in social change. That role, he said, belongs to religion. Weber (1904/1958) theorized that the Roman Catholic belief system encouraged followers to hold on to traditional ways of life, while the Protestant belief system encouraged its members to embrace change. Protestantism, he said, undermined people's spiritual security. Roman Catholics believed that because they were church members, they were on the road to heaven. Protestants, however, did not share this belief. Protestants of the Calvinist tradition were told that they wouldn't know if they were saved until Judgment Day. Uncomfortable with this, they began to look for "signs" that they were in God's will. Eventually, they concluded that financial success was the major sign that God was on their side. To bring about this "sign" and receive spiritual comfort, they began to live frugal lives, saving their money and investing the surplus in order to make even more. This, said Weber, brought about the birth of capitalism.

Weber called this self-denying approach to life the *Protestant ethic.* He termed the readiness to invest capital in order to make more money the *spirit of capitalism.* To test his theory, Weber compared the extent of capitalism in Roman Catholic and Protestant

Max Weber (1864–1920) was another early sociologist who left a profound impression on sociology. He used cross-cultural and historical materials to trace the causes of social change and to determine how social groups affect people's orientations to life.

Figure 1.1   How Americans Commit Suicide

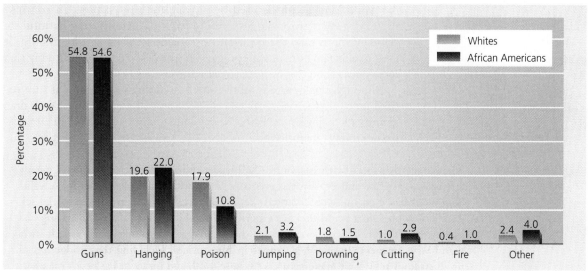

Note: The source lists no separate totals for Latinos.
Source: By the author. Based on Centers for Disease Control 2002.

value free the view that a sociologist's personal values or biases should not influence social research

values the standards by which people define what is desirable or undesirable, good or bad, beautiful or ugly

objectivity total neutrality

replication repeating a study in order to test its findings

countries. In line with his theory, he found that capitalism was more likely to flourish in Protestant countries. Weber's conclusion that religion was the key factor in the rise of capitalism was controversial when he made it, and it continues to be debated today (Wade 2007). We'll explore these ideas in more detail in Chapter 7.

Values in Sociological Research

Weber raised another issue that remains controversial among sociologists. He said that sociology should be **value free.** By this, he meant that a sociologist's **values**—beliefs about what is good or worthwhile in life and the way the world ought to be—should not affect his or her research. Weber wanted **objectivity,** total neutrality, to be the hallmark of social research. If values influence research, he said, sociological findings will be biased.

That bias has no place in research is not a matter of debate. All sociologists agree that no one should distort data to make them fit preconceived ideas or personal values. It is equally clear, however, that because sociologists—like everyone else—are members of a particular society at a given point in history, they, too, are infused with values of all sorts. These values inevitably play a role in the topics we choose to research. For example, values are part of the reason that one sociologist chooses to do research on the Mafia, while another turns a sociological eye on kindergarten students.

Because values can lead to unintended distortions in how we interpret our findings, sociologists stress the need of **replication,** researchers repeating a study in order to compare their results with the original findings. If an individual's values have distorted research findings, replication by other sociologists should uncover the bias and correct it.

Despite this consensus, however, values remain a hotly debated topic in sociology (Buroway 2007; Clawson et al. 2007). As summarized in Figure 1.2, the disagreement centers on the proper purposes and uses of sociology. Regarding its *purpose,* some sociologists take the position that their goal should be simply to advance understanding of social life. They should gather data on any topic in which they are interested and then use the best theory available to interpret their findings. Others are convinced that sociologists have the responsibility to investigate the social arrangements that harm people—the causes of poverty, crime, racism, war, and other forms of human exploitation.

Then there is the disagreement over the *uses* of sociology. Those who say that sociology's purpose is to understand human behavior take the position that there is no specific use for the knowledge gained by social research. This knowledge belongs to both the scientific community and the world, and it can be used by anyone for any purpose. In contrast, those who say that sociologists should focus on investigating harmful social conditions take the position that sociological knowledge should be used to alleviate human suffering and improve society. Some also say that sociologists should spearhead social reform.

Although this debate is more complicated than the argument summarized here—few sociologists take such one-sided views—this sketch does identify its major issues. Perhaps sociologist John Galliher (1991) best expresses today's majority position:

Figure 1.2 **The Debate over Values in Sociological Research**

Some argue that social scientists, unlike politicians and religious leaders, should merely attempt to describe and explain the events of the world but should never make value judgments based on those observations. Yet a value-free and nonjudgmental social science has no place in a world that has experienced the Holocaust, in a world having had slavery, in a world with the ever-present threat of rape and other sexual assault, in a world with frequent, unpunished crimes in high places, including the production of products known by their manufacturers to cause death and injury as has been true of asbestos products and continues to be true of the cigarette industry, and in a world dying from environmental pollution by these same large multinational corporations.

Verstehen and Social Facts

Weber and *Verstehen*

Weber also stressed that to understand human behavior, we should use *Verstehen* (vare-shtay-in) (a German word meaning "to understand"). Perhaps the best translation of this term is "to grasp by insight." By emphasizing *Verstehen,* Weber meant that the best interpreter of human behavior is someone who "has been there," someone who can understand the feelings and motivations of the people being studied. In short, we must pay attention to what are called **subjective meanings**—how people interpret their situation in life, how they view what they are doing and what is happening to them.

To better understand this term, let's return to the homeless in our opening vignette. Why were the men so silent? Why were they so unlike the noisy, sometimes boisterous college students who swarm dorms and cafeterias?

Verstehen can help explain this. When I interviewed men in the shelters (and, in other settings, homeless women), they revealed their despair. Because you know—at least on some level—what the human emotion of despair is, you can apply your understanding to their situation. You know that people in despair feel a sense of hopelessness. The future looks bleak, hardly worth plodding toward. Consequently, why is it worth talking about? Who wants to hear another hard-luck story?

By applying *Verstehen*—your understanding of what it means to be human and to face some situation in life—you gain insight into other people's behavior. In this case, you can understand these men's silence, their lack of communication in the shelter.

Granted their deprivation, it is not surprising that the homeless are not brimming with optimism. This scene at a homeless shelter in Los Angeles, California, is typical, reminiscent of the many meals I ate in soup kitchens with men like this.

Durkheim and Social Facts

In contrast to Weber's emphasis on *Verstehen* and subjective meanings, Durkheim stressed what he called **social facts.** By this term, he meant the patterns of behavior that characterize a social group. Examples of social facts in the United States include June being the most popular month for weddings, suicide rates being higher among the elderly, and more births occurring on Tuesdays than on any other day of the week.

Durkheim said that we must use social facts to interpret social facts. In other words, each pattern reflects some condition of society. People all over the country don't just coincidentally decide to do similar things, whether that is to get married or to commit suicide. If this were the case, in some years, middle-aged people would be the most likely to kill themselves, in other years, young people, and so on. *Patterns that hold true year after year indicate that as thousands and even millions of people make their individual decisions, they are responding to conditions in their society.* It is the job of the sociologist, then, to uncover social facts and to explain them through other social facts. In the following section, let's look at how the social facts I mentioned—weddings, suicide, and births—are explained by other social facts.

How Social Facts and *Verstehen* Fit Together

Social facts and *Verstehen* go hand in hand. As a member of U.S. society, you know how June weddings are related to the end of the school year and how this month, now locked in tradition, common sentiment, and advertising, carries its own momentum. As for suicide among the elderly (see Chapter 13), you probably already have a sense of the greater despair that many older Americans feel.

But do you know why more Americans are born on Tuesday than on any other day of the week? One would expect Tuesday to be no more common than any other day, and

Verstehen a German word used by Weber that is perhaps best understood as "to have insight into someone's situation"

subjective meanings the meanings that people give their own behavior

social facts Durkheim's term for a group's patterns of behavior

Cesarean deliveries used to be unusual, a last resort to prevent harm to the mother or to save the baby. Today, these deliveries have become routine in the United States. To understand this change, both social facts and *Verstehen* are useful.

that is how it used to be. But no longer. To understand this change, we need a combination of social facts and *Verstehen*. Four social facts are relevant: First, due to technology, the hospital has become a dominating force in the U.S. medical system. Second, medical technology has made delivery by cesarean section safer. Third, as discussed in Chapter 19 (page 564), doctors have replaced midwives for the delivery of babies. Fourth, medicine in the United States is a business, with profit a major goal. As a result of these social facts, an operation that used to be a last resort for emergencies has become so routine that more than one-fourth (27.5 percent) of all U.S. babies are now delivered in this manner (*Statistical Abstract* 2007:Table 86).

If we add *Verstehen* to these social facts, we gain insight that goes far beyond the cold statistics. We can understand that most mothers-to-be prefer to give birth in a hospital and that, under the influence of physicians at an emotionally charged moment, alternatives appear quite slim. We can also understand that physicians schedule births for a time that is most convenient for them. Tuesday is the day that fits their schedules the best.

Sexism in Early Sociology

Attitudes of the Time

As you may have noticed, all the sociologists we have discussed are men. In the 1800s, sex roles were rigid, with women assigned the roles of wife and mother. In the classic German phrase, women were expected to devote themselves to the four K's: *Kirche, Küchen, Kinder, und Kleider* (church, cooking, children, and clothes). Trying to break out of this mold meant risking severe disapproval.

Few people, male or female, received any education beyond basic reading and writing and a little math. Higher education, for the rare few who received it, was reserved for men. A handful of women from wealthy families, however, did pursue higher education. A few even managed to study sociology, although the sexism so deeply entrenched in the universities stopped them from obtaining advanced degrees or becoming professors. In line with the times, the writings of women were almost entirely ignored. Jane Frohock, Lucretia Mott, and Elizabeth Cady Stanton, for example, were little known beyond a small circle. Frances Perkins, a sociologist and the first woman to hold a cabinet position (as Secretary of Labor under President Franklin Roosevelt), is no longer remembered.

Harriet Martineau and Early Social Research

A classic example is Harriet Martineau (1802–1876), who was born into a wealthy family in England. When Martineau first began to analyze social life, she would hide her writing beneath her sewing when visitors arrived, for writing was "masculine" and sewing "feminine" (Gilman 1911:88). Martineau persisted in her interests, however, and eventually she studied social life in both Great Britain and the United States. In 1837, two or three decades before Durkheim and Weber were born, Martineau published *Society in America,* in which she reported on this new nation's customs—family, race, gender, politics, and religion. Despite her insightful examination of U.S. life, which is still worth reading today, Martineau's research met the same fate as the work of other early women sociologists and, until recently, was ignored. Instead, she is known primarily for translating Comte's ideas into English. The Down-to-Earth Sociology box below features selections from *Society in America.*

Down-to-Earth Sociology

Listening to an Early Feminist

IN SEPTEMBER OF 1834, Harriet Martineau, an early feminist sociologist from England, began a fascinating two-year journey around the United States. Traveling by stagecoach, she interviewed people living in poverty, as well as James Madison, the former President of the United States. She spoke with both slaveholders and abolitionists. She also visited prisons and attended sessions of the U.S. Supreme Court. Her observations on the status of U.S. women are taken from this research, published in her 1837 book, *Society in America.*

Concerning women not being allowed to vote:

One of the fundamental principles announced in the Declaration of Independence is that governments derive their just powers from the consent of the governed. How can the political condition of women be reconciled with this?

Governments in the United States have power to tax women who hold property . . . to fine, imprison, and execute them for certain offences. Whence do these governments derive their powers? They are not "just," as they are not derived from the consent of the women thus governed. . . .

The democratic principle condemns all this as wrong; and requires the equal political representation of all rational beings. Children, idiots, and criminals . . . are the only fair exceptions . . .

Concerning sex, slavery, and relations between white women and men in the South:

[White American women] are all married young . . . and there is ever present an unfortunate servile class of their own sex [female slaves] to serve the purposes of licen-

Interested in social reform, Harriet Martineau (1802–1876) turned to sociology, where she discovered the writings of Comte. She became an advocate for the abolition of slavery, traveled widely, and wrote extensive analyses of social life.

tiousness [as sexual objects for white slaveholders]. . . . [When most] men carry secrets which their wives must be the last to know . . . there is an end to all wholesome confidence and sympathy, and woman sinks to be the ornament of her husband's house, the domestic manager of his establishment, instead of being his all-sufficient friend. . . . I have seen, with heart-sorrow, the kind politeness, the gallantry, so insufficient to the loving heart, with which the wives of the south are treated by their husbands. . . . I know the tone of conversation which is adopted towards women; different in its topics and its style from that which any man would dream of offering to any other man. I have heard the boast of chivalrous consideration in which women are held throughout their woman's paradise; and seen something of the anguish of crushed pride, of the conflict of bitter feelings with which such boasts have been listened to by those whose aspirations teach them the hollowness of the system . . .

Concerning women's education:

The intellect of woman is confined by an unjustifiable restriction . . . As women have none of the objects in life for which an enlarged education is considered requisite, the education is not given . . . [S]ome things [are] taught which . . . serve to fill up time . . . to improve conversation, and to make women something like companions to their husbands, and able to teach their children somewhat. . . . There is rarely or never a . . . promotion of clear intellectual activity. . . . [A]s long as women are excluded from the objects for which men are trained . . . intellectual activity is dangerous: or, as the phrase is, unfit. Accordingly marriage is the only object left open to woman.

Sociology in North America

Early History: The Tension Between Social Reform and Sociological Analysis

Transplanted to U.S. soil in the late nineteenth century, sociology first took root at the University of Kansas in 1890, at the University of Chicago in 1892, and at Atlanta University (then an all-black school) in 1897. From there, academic specialties in sociology spread throughout North America. The growth was gradual, however. It was not until 1922 that McGill University gave Canada its first department of sociology. Harvard University did not open its department of sociology until 1930, and the University of California at Berkeley did not follow until the 1950s.

Initially, the department at the University of Chicago, which was founded by Albion Small (1854–1926), dominated sociology. (Small also founded the *American Journal of Sociology* and was its editor from 1895 to 1925.) Members of this early sociology department whose ideas continue to influence today's sociologists include Robert E. Park (1864–1944), Ernest Burgess (1886–1966), and George Herbert Mead (1863–1931). Mead developed the symbolic interactionist perspective, which we will examine later.

The situation of women in North America was similar to that of European women, and their contributions to sociology met a similar fate. Among the early women sociologists were Jane Addams, Emily Greene Balch, Isabel Eaton, Sophie Germain, Charlotte Perkins Gilman, Alice Hamilton, Florence Kelley, Elsie Clews Parsons, and Alice Paul. Denied faculty appointments in sociology, many turned to social activism (Young 1995).

Because some of these women worked with the poor rather than as professors of sociology, many sociologists classify them as social workers. Today's distinction between sociology and social work is fairly clear cut. There is a profession called social work; people train for it, they are hired to do it, and they call themselves social workers. They focus on aiding people in poverty and socially maladjusted members of society. They have jobs in hospitals and schools, and many work in the area of public aid. Others set up private practice and counsel patients. Earlier in the development of sociology, however, there often was little distinction between sociology and social work. This fuzziness lasted for generations, and many departments combined sociology and social work. Some still do.

Jane Addams and Social Reform

Although many North American sociologists combined the role of sociologist with that of social reformer, none was as successful as Jane Addams (1860–1935). Like Harriet Martineau, Addams came from a background of wealth and privilege. She attended the Women's Medical College of Philadelphia, but dropped out because of illness (Addams 1910/1981). On one of her many trips to Europe, Addams was impressed with work being done to help London's poor. From then on, she worked tirelessly for social justice.

In 1889, Addams cofounded Hull-House, located in Chicago's notorious slums. Hull-House was open to people who needed refuge—to immigrants, the sick, the aged, the poor. Sociologists from the nearby University of Chicago were frequent visitors at Hull-House. With her piercing insights into the social classes, especially the ways in which workers were exploited and how peasant immigrants adjusted to city life, Addams strived to bridge the gap between the powerful and the powerless. She worked with others to win the eight-hour work day and to pass laws against child labor. Her efforts at social reform were so outstanding that in 1931, she was a co-winner of the Nobel Prize for Peace, the only sociologist to win this coveted award.

W. E. B. Du Bois and Race Relations

Confronted by the racism of this period, African American professionals also found life difficult. The most notable example is provided by W. E. B. Du Bois (1868–1963), who, after earning a bachelor's degree from Fisk University, became the first African American to earn a doctorate at Harvard. After completing his education at the Univer-

Jane Addams, 1860–1935, a recipient of the Nobel Prize for Peace, worked on behalf of poor immigrants. With Ellen G. Starr, she founded Hull-House, a center to help immigrants in Chicago. She was also a leader in women's rights (women's suffrage), as well as the peace movement of World War I.

sity of Berlin, where he attended lectures by Max Weber, Du Bois taught Greek and Latin at Wilberforce University. He was hired by Atlanta University in 1897, and remained there for most of his career (Du Bois 1935/1992).

It is difficult to grasp how racist society was at this time. For example, Du Bois once saw the fingers of a lynching victim displayed in a Georgia butcher shop (Aptheker 1990). Although Du Bois was invited to present a paper at the 1909 meetings of the American Sociological Society, he was too poor to attend, despite his education, faculty position, and accomplishments. When he could afford to attend subsequent meetings, discrimination was so prevalent that restaurants and hotels would not allow him to eat or room with the white sociologists. Later in life, when Du Bois had the money to travel, the U.S. State Department feared that he would criticize the United States and refused to give him a passport (Du Bois 1968).

Each year between 1896 and 1914, Du Bois published a book on relations between African Americans and whites. Of his almost 2,000 writings, *The Philadelphia Negro* (1899/1967) stands out. In this analysis of how African Americans in Philadelphia coped with racism, Du Bois pointed out that some of the more successful African Americans were breaking their ties with other African Americans in order to win acceptance by whites. This, he said, weakened the African American community by depriving it of their influence. One of Du Bois' most elegantly written books, which preserves a picture of race relations immediately after the Civil War, is *The Souls of Black Folk* (1903). The Down-to-Earth Sociology box on the next page is taken from this book.

At first, Du Bois was content to collect and interpret objective data. Later, frustrated that racism continued, he turned to social action. Along with Jane Addams and others from Hull-House, Du Bois founded the National Association for the Advancement of Colored People (NAACP) (Deegan 1988). Continuing to battle racism both as a sociologist and as a journalist, Du Bois eventually embraced revolutionary Marxism. At age 93, dismayed that so little improvement had been made in race relations, he moved to Ghana, where he is buried (Stark 1989).

Until recently, the work of W. E. B. Du Bois was neglected in sociology, his many contributions unrecognized. As a personal example, during my entire graduate program at Washington University, I was never introduced to Du Bois' books and thought. Today, however, sociologists are rediscovering Du Bois, and he is beginning to receive some long-deserved respect.

W(illiam) E(dward) B(urghardt) Du Bois(1868–1963) spent his lifetime studying relations between African Americans and whites. Like many early North American sociologists, Du Bois combined the role of academic sociologist with that of social reformer. He was also the editor of *Crisis,* an influential journal of the time.

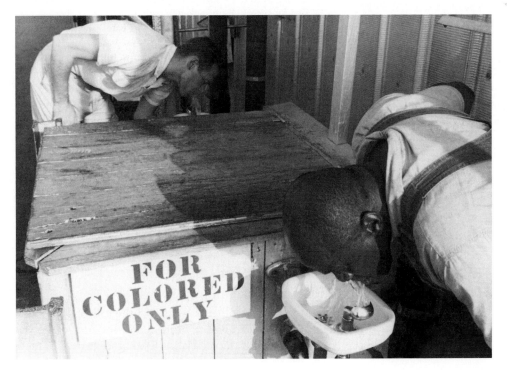

In the 1940s, when this photo was taken, racial segregation was a taken-for-granted fact of life. Although many changes have occurred since then—and since W. E. B. Du Bois analyzed race relations—race-ethnicity remains a significant factor in the lives of Americans.

Early Sociology in North America: Du Bois and Race Relations

THE WRITINGS OF W. E. B. Du Bois, who expressed sociological thought more like an accomplished novelist than a sociologist, have been neglected in sociology. To help remedy this omission, I reprint the following excerpts from pages 66–68 of *The Souls of Black Folk* (1903). In this book, Du Bois analyzes changes that occurred in the social and economic conditions of African Americans during the thirty years following the Civil War.

For two summers, while he was a student at Fisk, Du Bois taught in a segregated school housed in a log hut "way back in the hills" of rural Tennessee. The following excerpts help us understand conditions at that time.

In the 1800s, poverty was widespread in the United States. Most people were so poor that they expended their life energies on just getting enough food, fuel, and clothing to survive. Formal education beyond the first several grades was a luxury. This photo depicts the conditions of the people Du Bois worked with.

It was a hot morning late in July when the school opened. I trembled when I heard the patter of little feet down the dusty road, and saw the growing row of dark solemn faces and bright eager eyes facing me. . . . There they sat, nearly thirty of them, on the rough benches, their faces shading from a pale cream to deep brown, the little feet bare and swinging, the eyes full of expectation, with here and there a twinkle of mischief, and the hands grasping Webster's blue-black spelling-book. I loved my school, and the fine faith the children had in the wisdom of their teacher was truly marvelous. We read and spelled together, wrote a little, picked flowers, sang, and listened to stories of the world beyond the hill. . . .

On Friday nights I often went home with some of the children,—sometimes to Doc Burke's farm. He was a great, loud, thin Black, ever working, and trying to buy these seventy-five acres of hill and dale where he lived; but people said that he would surely fail and the "white folks would get it all." His wife was a magnificent Amazon, with saffron face and shiny hair, uncorseted and barefooted, and the children were strong and barefooted. They lived in a one-and-a-half-room cabin in the hollow of the farm near the spring. . . .

Often, to keep the peace, I must go where life was less lovely; for instance, 'Tildy's mother was incorrigibly dirty,

Reuben's larder was limited seriously, and herds of untamed insects wandered over the Eddingses' beds. Best of all I loved to go to Josie's, and sit on the porch, eating peaches, while the mother bustled and talked: how Josie had bought the sewing-machine; how Josie worked at service in winter, but that four dollars a month was "mighty little" wages; how Josie longed to go away to school, but that it "looked liked" they never could get far enough ahead to let her; how the crops failed and the well was yet unfinished; and, finally, how mean some of the white folks were.

For two summers I lived in this little world. . . . I have called my tiny community a world, and so its isolation made it; and yet there was among us but a half-awakened common consciousness, sprung from common joy and grief, at burial, birth, or wedding; from common hardship in poverty, poor land, and low wages, and, above all, from the sight of the Veil* that hung between us and Opportunity. All this caused us to think some thoughts together; but these, when ripe for speech, were spoken in various languages. Those whose eyes twenty-five and more years had seen "the glory of the coming of the Lord," saw in every present hindrance or help a dark fatalism bound to bring all things right in His own good time. The mass of those to whom slavery was a dim recollection of childhood found the world a puzzling thing: it asked little of them, and they answered with little, and yet it ridiculed their offering. Such a paradox they could not understand, and therefore sank into listless indifference, or shiftlessness, or reckless bravado.

*"The Veil" is shorthand for the Veil of Race, referring to how race colors all human relations. Du Bois' hope, as he put it, was that "sometime, somewhere, men will judge men by their souls and not by their skins" (p. 261).

Talcott Parsons and C. Wright Mills: Theory Versus Reform

Like Du Bois, many early North American sociologists combined the role of sociologist with that of social reformer. They saw society, or parts of it, as corrupt and in need of reform. During the 1920s and 1930s, for example, Robert Park and Ernest Burgess

(1921) not only studied crime, drug addiction, juvenile delinquency, and prostitution but also offered suggestions for how to alleviate these social problems.

During the 1940s, the emphasis shifted from social reform to social theory. Talcott Parsons (1902–1979), for example, developed abstract models of society that influenced a generation of sociologists. Parsons' models of how the parts of society work together harmoniously did nothing to stimulate social activism.

C. Wright Mills (1916–1962) deplored the theoretical abstractions of this period, and he urged sociologists to get back to social reform. He warned that an imminent threat to freedom was the coalescing of interests on the part of a group he called the *power elite*—the top leaders of business, politics, and the military. Shortly after Mills' death came the turbulent late 1960s and 1970s. This precedent-shaking era sparked interest in social activism, and Mills' ideas became popular among a new generation of sociologists.

C. Wright Mills was a controversial figure in sociology because of his analysis of the role of the power elite in U.S. society. Today, his analysis is taken for granted by many sociologists and members of the public.

The Continuing Tension and the Rise of Applied Sociology

The apparent contradiction of these two aims—analyzing society versus working toward its reform—created a tension in sociology that is still with us today. As we saw in Figure 1.2 on page 14, some sociologists believe that their proper role is to analyze some aspect of society and to publish their findings in sociology journals. This is called **basic** (or **pure**) **sociology.** Others say that basic sociology is not enough: Sociologists have an obligation to use their expertise to try to make society a better place in which to live and to help bring justice to the poor.

Somewhere between these extremes lies **applied sociology,** using sociology to solve problems. (See Figure 1.3, which contrasts basic and applied sociology.) One of the first attempts at applied sociology—and one of the most successful—was just mentioned: the founding of the National Association for the Advancement of Colored People. As illustrated in the Down-to-Earth Sociology box on the next page, today's applied sociologists work in a variety of settings. Some work for business firms to solve problems in the workplace. Others investigate social problems such as pornography, rape, environmental pollution, or the spread of AIDS. A new specialty in applied sociology is determining ways to disrupt terrorist groups (Ebner 2005). The Down-to-Earth Sociology box on page 23 presents a startling example of applied sociology. (For another example of applied sociology, see the Cultural Diversity box on page 32.)

basic or **pure sociology** sociological research whose purpose is to make discoveries about life in human groups, not to make changes in those groups

applied sociology the use of sociology to solve problems—from the micro level of family relationships to the macro level of crime and pollution

---

Figure 1.3 **Comparing Basic and Applied Sociology**

BASIC SOCIOLOGY
Audience: Fellow sociologists and anyone interested
Product: Knowledge

APPLIED SOCIOLOGY
Audience: Clients
Product: Change

| Constructing theory and testing hypotheses | Research on basic social life, on how groups affect people | The middle ground: criticisms of society and social policy | Analyzing problems, evaluating programs, and suggesting solutions | Implementing solutions (clinical sociology) |

Source: By the author. Based on DeMartini 1982.

theory a general statement about how some parts of the world fit together and how they work; an explanation of how two or more facts are related to one another

symbolic interactionism a theoretical perspective in which society is viewed as composed of symbols that people use to establish meaning, develop their views of the world, and communicate with one another

Applied sociology is not the same as social reform. It is an application of sociology in some specific setting, not an attempt to rebuild society, as early sociologists envisioned. Consequently, a new tension has emerged in sociology. Sociologists who want the emphasis to be on social reform say that applied sociology doesn't even come close to this. It is an application of sociology, but not an attempt to change society. Those who want the emphasis to remain on discovering knowledge say that when sociology is applied, it is no longer sociology. If sociologists use sociological principles to help teenagers escape from pimps, for example, is it still sociology?

At this point, let's consider how theory fits into sociology.

Theoretical Perspectives in Sociology

Facts never interpret themselves. To make sense out of life, we use our common sense. That is, to understand our experiences (our "facts"), we place them into a framework of more-or-less related ideas. Sociologists do this, too, but they place

Down-to-Earth Sociology

Careers in Sociology: What Applied Sociologists Do

MOST SOCIOLOGISTS TEACH IN colleges and universities, sharing sociological knowledge with college students, as your instructor is doing with you in this course. Applied sociologists, in contrast, work in a wide variety of areas—from counseling children to studying how diseases are transmitted. Some even make software more "user-friendly." (They study how people use software and give feedback to the programmers who design those products [Guice 1999].) To give you an idea of this variety, let's look over the shoulders of four applied sociologists.

Leslie Green, who does marketing research at Vanderveer Group in Philadelphia, Pennsylvania, earned her bachelor's degree in sociology at Shippensburg University. She helps to develop strategies to get doctors to prescribe particular drugs. She sets up the meetings, locates moderators for the discussion groups, and arranges payments to the physicians who participate in the research. "My training in sociology," she says, "helps me in 'people skills.' It helps me to understand the needs of different groups, and to interact with them."

Stanley Capela, whose master's degree is from Fordham University, works as an applied sociologist at HeartShare Human Services in New York City. He evaluates how children's programs—such as ones that focus on housing, AIDS, group homes, and preschool education—actually work, compared with how they are supposed to work. He spots problems and suggests solutions. One of his assignments was to find out why it was taking so long to get children adopted, even though there was a long list of eager adoptive parents.

Capela pinpointed how the paperwork got bogged down as it was routed through the system and suggested ways to improve the flow of paperwork.

Laurie Banks, who received her master's degree in sociology from Fordham University, analyzes statistics for the New York City Health Department. As she examined death certificates, she noticed that a Polish neighborhood had a high rate of stomach cancer. She alerted the Centers for Disease Control, which conducted interviews in the neighborhood. They traced the cause to eating large amounts of sausage. In another case, Banks compared birth certificates with school records. She found that problems at birth—low birth weight, lack of prenatal care, and birth complications—were linked to low reading skills and behavior problems in school.

Daniel Knapp, who earned a doctorate from the University of Oregon, decided to apply sociology by going to the dumps. Moved by the idea that urban wastes should not simply be buried, that they could be recycled and reused, he tested this idea in a small way—by scavenging at the city dump at Berkeley, California. Starting a company called Urban Ore, Knapp did studies on how to recycle urban wastes. He also campaigned successfully for changes in waste disposal laws (Knapp 2005). Knapp became a major founder of the recycling movement in the United States, with a goal of changing human behavior, and his application of sociology continues to influence us all.

From just these few examples, you can catch a glimpse of the variety of work that applied sociologists do. Some work for corporations, some are employed by government and private agencies, and others run their own businesses. You can also see that you don't need a doctorate in order to work as an applied sociologist.

Capturing Saddam Hussein: A Surprising Example of Applied Sociology

APPLIED SOCIOLOGY TAKES MANY twists and turns, but perhaps none as startling as capturing Saddam Hussein. After U.S.-led forces took over Baghdad, Hussein disappeared. His capture became a pressing goal with two purposes. The first was symbolic, a sign of the coalition's triumph. The second was practical: to prevent Hussein from directing resistance to the occupation of Iraq.

But Hussein was nowhere to be found. Rumors placed him all over the map, from neighboring countries to safe houses in Baghdad. To find him, U.S. intelligence officers began to apply sociology, specifically, a form known as *network analysis*. Analysts traced Hussein's tribal and family linkages (Hougham 2005). On a color-coded "people map," they placed Hussein's photo in a yellow circle, like a bull's-eye. They then drew links to people who were connected to Hussein, placing their photos closer to or farther from Hussein's photo on the basis of how close their relationship was with Hussein (Schmitt 2003).

The photos placed closest to Hussein represented an intimate and loyal group. These people were the most likely to know where Hussein was, but because of their close ties to him, they also were the least likely to reveal this information. Those who were pictured slightly farther away knew people in this more intimate group, so it was likely that some of them had information about Hussein's whereabouts. Because these people's social ties to Hussein were not as strong, they provided the weaker links to try to break.

The approach worked. Using software programs to sift through vast amounts of information gained from informants and electronic intercepts, the analysts drew the "people map" that pictured these social relationships. Identifying the weaker links led to the capture of Saddam Hussein.

for your Consideration

This unexpected application of sociology has made some sociologists uncomfortable (Hougham 2005). What they find especially bothersome is the specific result of this applied sociology, that Hussein was executed. What do you think?

---

their observations into a conceptual framework called a theory. A **theory** is a general statement about how some parts of the world fit together and how they work. It is an explanation of how two or more "facts" are related to one another.

Sociologists use three major theories: symbolic interactionism, functional analysis, and conflict theory. Let's first examine the main elements of these theories. Then let's apply each theory to the U.S. divorce rate, to see why it is so high. As we do this, you will see how each theory, or perspective, provides a distinct interpretation of social life.

Symbolic Interactionism

We can trace the origins of **symbolic interactionism** to the Scottish moral philosophers of the eighteenth century, who noted that individuals evaluate their own conduct by comparing themselves with others (Stryker 1990). In the United States, a long line of thinkers added to this analysis, including the pioneering psychologist William James (1842–1910) and the educator John Dewey (1859–1952), who analyzed how people use symbols to understand their experiences. This theoretical perspective was brought to sociology by Charles Horton Cooley (1864–1929), William I. Thomas (1863–1947), and George Herbert Mead (1863–1931). Cooley's and Mead's analyses of how symbols lie at the basis of the self-concept are discussed on pages 70–72.

Symbols in Everyday Life Symbolic interactionists study how people use *symbols*—the things to which we attach meaning—to develop their views of the world and to

George Herbert Mead (1863–1931) is one of the founders of symbolic interactionism, a major theoretical perspective in sociology. He taught at the University of Chicago, where his lectures were popular. Although he wrote little, after his death students compiled his lectures into an influential book, *Mind, Self, and Society*.

communicate with one another. Without symbols, our social life would be no more sophisticated than that of animals. For example, without symbols we would have no aunts or uncles, employers or teachers—or even brothers and sisters. I know that this sounds strange, but it is symbols that define what our relationships are. There would still be reproduction, of course, but no symbols to tell us how we are related to whom. We would not know to whom we owe respect and obligations, or from whom we can expect privileges—the stuff that human relationships are made of.

Look at it like this: If you think of someone as your aunt or uncle, you behave in certain ways, but if you think of that person as a boyfriend or girlfriend, you behave quite differently. It is the symbol that tells you how you are related to others—and how you should act toward them.

To make this clearer

Suppose that you have fallen head-over-heels in love and are going to marry. The night before your wedding, your mother confides that she had a child before she married your father, a child that she gave up for adoption. She then adds that she has just discovered that the person you are going to marry is this child. You can see how the symbol will change overnight!—and your behavior, too!

Symbols allow not only relationships to exist, but also society. Without symbols, we could not coordinate our actions with those of other people. We could not make plans for a future date, time, and place. Unable to specify times, materials, sizes, or goals, we could not build bridges and highways. Without symbols, there would be no movies or musical instruments. We would have no hospitals, no government, no religion. The class you are taking could not exist—nor could this book. On the positive side, there would be no war.

In short, symbolic interactionists analyze how our behaviors depend on the ways we define ourselves and others. They study face-to-face interaction, examining how people work out their relationships and how they make sense out of life and their place in it. Symbolic interactionists point out that even the *self* is a symbol, for it consists of the ideas we have about who we are. And the self is a changing symbol: As we interact with others, we adjust our views of who we are based on how we interpret the reactions of others to us. We'll get more into this later.

Applying Symbolic Interactionism   To better understand symbolic interactionism, let's see how changes in symbols (meanings) help to explain the high U.S. divorce rate. For background, you should understand that marriage used to be a lifelong commitment. Divorce was viewed as an immoral act, a flagrant disregard for public opinion, and the abandonment of adult responsibilities.

1. *Emotional satisfaction.* Slowly, the meaning of marriage began to change. In 1933, sociologist William Ogburn observed that personality was becoming more important in mate selection. In 1945, sociologists Ernest Burgess and Harvey Locke noted the growing importance of mutual affection, understanding, and compatibility in marriage. These sociologists had observed a fundamental shift in U.S. marriage: Husbands and wives were coming to expect—and demand—greater emotional satisfaction from one another.

   As this trend intensified, intimacy became the core of marriage, and Americans placed greater importance on a potential spouse's physical attractiveness (Bus et al. 2001). At the same time, as society grew more complex and impersonal, Americans came to view marriage as a solution to the tensions that society produced (Lasch 1977). This new form, "companionate marriage," contributed to divorce, for it encouraged people to expect that their spouse would satisfy "each and every need." As sociologists say, this helped to make marriage an "overloaded institution."

2. *The love symbol.* Our symbol of love also helps to "overload" marriage. Expecting "true love" to be a constant source of emotional satisfaction sets people up for crushed hopes, for when dissatisfactions enter marriage, as they inevitably do, spouses tend to blame one another for what they see as the other's failure. Being engulfed in the symbol of love at the time of marriage blinds them to the basic unreality of their expectations.

3. *The meaning of children.* Ideas about childhood have undergone a deep historical shift, with far-reaching consequences for the U.S. family. In medieval Europe, children were viewed as miniature adults, and there was no sharp separation between the worlds of adults and children (Ariés 1965). Boys were apprenticed at about age 7, while girls of the same age learned the homemaking duties associated with being a wife. In the United States, just three generations ago, children "became adults" when they graduated from eighth grade and went to work. Today's contrast is amazing: From miniature adults, children have been culturally fashioned into impressionable, vulnerable, and innocent beings who are not expected to assume adult responsibilities until their mid-twenties.

4. *The meaning of parenthood.* These changed ideas of childhood have had a deep impact on our ideas of good parenting. Today's parents are expected not only to provide unending amounts of love and tender care but also to help their children "reach their potential." Today's child rearing lasts longer and is more demanding. These greater responsibilities place heavier burdens on today's couples, and along with them, more strain on marriage.

5. *Marital roles.* In earlier generations, the responsibilities and privileges of husbands and wives were defined clearly. Newlyweds knew what they had a right to expect from each other. In contrast, today's more vague guidelines force couples to work out more aspects of their roles on their own. Many struggle to figure out how to divide up responsibilities for work, home, and children.

6. *Perception of alternatives.* As these changes were taking place, more and more women were taking jobs outside the home. As more wives earned paychecks of their own, many began to see alternatives to remaining in unhappy marriages. Symbolic interactionists consider the perception of an alternative to an unhappy marriage to be an essential first step to making divorce possible.

7. *The meaning of divorce.* Divorce increased as these changes came together—expecting more emotional satisfaction in marriage, new marital and parental roles, and a growing perception of alternatives to an unhappy marriage. As Figure 1.4 below shows, divorce went from practically zero in 1890 to our current 1.1 million divorces a year. (The plateau for both marriage and divorce since 1980 is probably due to increased cohabitation.)

Figure 1.4 **U.S. Marriage, U.S. Divorce**

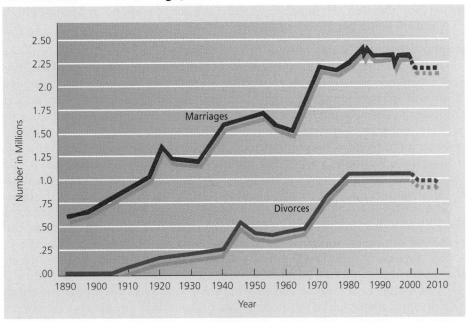

Source: By the author. Based on *Statistical Abstract of the United States* 1998:Table 92 and 2007:Table 119; earlier editions for earlier years. the broken lines indicate the author's estimates.

As divorce became more common, its meaning changed. Once a symbol of failure—and of immorality and irresponsibility—divorce came to indicate freedom and new beginnings. Removing the stigma from divorce shattered a barrier that had kept husbands and wives from breaking up, setting the stage for divorce on an even larger scale.

8. *Changes in the law.* As the law—itself a powerful symbol—began to reflect these changed ideas about divorce, it became an additional factor that encouraged divorce. Divorce previously had been granted only for severe reasons, such as adultery, but then legislators made "incompatibility" one of the grounds for divorce. After this came "no-fault" divorce, in which a couple could dissolve their marriage without accusing each other of wrongdoing. Most states even began to provide do-it-yourself divorce kits.

IN SUM Symbolic interactionists explain an increasing divorce rate in terms of the changing symbols (or meanings) associated with both marriage and divorce. Changes in people's ideas—about divorce, marital satisfaction, love, the nature of children and parenting, and the roles of husband and wife—have made marriage more fragile. No single change is *the* cause, but taken together, these changes provide a strong "push" toward divorce.

Are these changes good or bad? Central to symbolic interactionism is the position that to make a value judgment about change (or anything else) requires a value framework from which to view the change. Symbolic interactionism provides no such value framework. In short, symbolic interactionists, like other sociologists, can analyze social change, but they cannot pass judgment on that change.

Functional Analysis

The central idea of **functional analysis** is that society is a whole unit, made up of interrelated parts that work together. Functional analysis, also known as *functionalism* and *structural functionalism,* is rooted in the origins of sociology. Auguste Comte and Herbert Spencer viewed society as a kind of living organism. Just as a person or animal has organs that function together, they wrote, so does society. Like an organism, if society is to function smoothly, its various parts must work together in harmony.

Emile Durkheim also viewed society as being composed of many parts, each with its own function. When all the parts of society fulfill their functions, society is in a "normal" state. If they do not fulfill their functions, society is in an "abnormal" or "pathological" state. To understand society, then, functionalists say that we need to look at both *structure* (how the parts of a society fit together to make the whole) and *function* (what each part does, how it contributes to society).

Robert Merton and Functionalism Robert Merton (1910–2003) dismissed the organic analogy, but he did maintain the essence of functionalism—the image of society as a whole composed of parts that work together. Merton used the term *functions* to refer to the beneficial consequences of people's actions: Functions help keep a group (society, social system) in equilibrium. In contrast, *dysfunctions* are consequences that harm a society: They undermine a system's equilibrium.

Functions can be either manifest or latent. If an action is *intended* to help some part of a system, it is a *manifest function.* For example, suppose that government officials become concerned about our low rate of childbirth. Congress offers a $10,000 bonus for every child born to a married couple. The intention, or manifest function, of the bonus is to increase childbearing. Merton pointed out that people's actions can also have *latent functions;* that is, they can have *unintended* consequences that help a system adjust. Let's suppose that the bonus works and the birth rate jumps. As a result, the sale of diapers and baby furniture booms. Because the benefits to these businesses were not the intended consequences, they are latent functions of the bonus.

Of course, human actions can also hurt a system. Because such consequences usually are unintended, Merton called them *latent dysfunctions.* Let's assume that the government has failed to specify a "stopping point" with regard to its bonus system. To collect

functional analysis a theoretical framework in which society is viewed as composed of various parts, each with a function that, when fulfilled, contributes to society's equilibrium; also known as *functionalism* and *structural functionalism* more bonuses, some people keep on having children. The more children they have, however, the more they need the next bonus to survive. Large families become common, and poverty increases. Welfare is reinstated, taxes jump, and the nation erupts in protest. Because these results were not intended and because they harmed the social system, they would represent latent dysfunctions of the bonus program.

IN SUM From the perspective of functional analysis, society is a functioning unit, with each part related to the whole. Whenever we examine a smaller part, we need to look for its functions and dysfunctions to see how it is related to the larger unit. This basic approach can be applied to any social group, whether an entire society, a college, or even a group as small as a family.

Applying Functional Analysis Now let's apply functional analysis to the U.S. divorce rate. Functionalists stress that industrialization and urbanization undermined the traditional functions of the family. Let's see how each of the basic functions of the family has changed.

1. *Economic production.* Prior to industrialization, the family was an economic team. At that time, it was difficult to obtain the basic necessities of life, and to survive, family members had to work together to produce what they needed. When industrialization moved production from home to factory, it disrupted this family team. This weakened the bonds that tied family members to one another. Especially significant was the transfer of the husband-father to the factory, for this isolated him from the family's daily routine. Another result was that the wife-mother and children contributed less to the family's economic survival.

2. *Socialization of children.* While these sweeping changes were taking place, the government was growing larger and more powerful. As it expanded, it took over many family functions. To give just one example, schools took away from the family the education of children. In so doing, they assumed much of the responsibility for socializing children. To make certain that families went along with this change, states passed laws requiring school attendance and threatened parents with jail if they did not send their children to school.

Sociologists who use the *functionalist perspective* stress how industrialization and urbanization undermined the traditional *functions* of the family. Before industrialization, members of the family worked together as an economic unit, as in this painting by Leopoldo Romanach (1958–) of Havana, Cuba. As production moved away from the home, it took with it first the father and, more recently, the mother. One consequence is a major *dysfunction*, the weakening of family ties.

3. *Care of the sick and elderly.* As medical training and technology improved, care of the sick gradually shifted from the family to medical specialists. Government agencies multiplied, and care of the aged changed from being a family concern to a government obligation.

4. *Recreation.* As more disposable income became available to Americans, businesses sprang up to compete for that income. This cost the family a good part of its recreational function, for much entertainment and "fun" moved from home-based, family-centered activities to attendance at paid events.

5. *Sexual control.* The vast changes that swept the country also had an impact on the family's influence on sexuality. Traditionally, only sexual relations within marriage were considered legitimate. Although this value was more ideal than real—even the Puritans had a lot of sex outside marriage (Smith and Hindus 1975)—the "sexual revolution" opened many alternatives to marital sex.

6. *Reproduction.* The only family function that might seem to be untouched is reproduction. Yet even this function has been moving gradually away from the family. A prime example is the number of single women who bear children. Over one third (36 percent) of all U.S. babies are born to unmarried mothers (*Statistical Abstract* 2007:Table 84).

Even schools and doctors have taken over some of the family's control over reproduction. A married woman, for example, can get an abortion without informing her husband, and some U.S. high schools distribute condoms.

A Glimpse of the Past To see how sharply family functions have changed, it may be useful to take a glimpse of family life in the 1800s.

> When Phil became sick, he was nursed by Ann, his wife. She cooked for him, fed him, changed the bed linen, bathed him, read to him from the Bible, and gave him his medicine. (She did this in addition to doing the housework and taking care of their six children.) Phil was also surrounded by the children, who shouldered some of his chores while he was sick.
>
> When Phil died, the male neighbors and relatives made the casket while Ann, her mother, and female friends washed and dressed the body. Phil was then "laid out" in the front parlor (the formal living room), where friends, neighbors, and relatives viewed him, paying their last respects. From there, friends moved his body to the church for the final message, and then to the grave they themselves had dug.

As you can see, the family used to have more functions than it does now. Families handled many aspects of life and death that we now assign to outside agencies. Not only did caring for the sick take place almost exclusively within the family but also death was a family affair—from preparing the body to burying it. Today we assume that such functions *properly* belong to specialized agencies, and few of us can imagine ourselves preparing the body of a close relative for burial. Such an act may even seem grotesque, almost barbarous, for our current customs also guide our feelings, another fascinating aspect of social life. (On pages 76–78, we return to the topic of emotions.)

IN SUM The family has lost many of its traditional functions, and others are presently under assault. Especially significant are changes in economic production. No longer is this a cooperative, home-based effort, with husbands and wives depending on one another for their interlocking contributions to a mutual endeavor. Husbands and wives today earn individual paychecks, and increasingly function as separate components in an impersonal, multinational, and even global system. When outside agencies take over family functions, the family becomes more fragile and an increase in divorce is inevitable. The fewer functions that family members have in common, the fewer are their "ties that bind"—and these ties are what help husbands and wives get through the problems they inevitably experience.

Conflict Theory

Conflict theory provides a third perspective on social life. Unlike the functionalists, who view society as a harmonious whole, with its parts working together, conflict theorists stress that society is composed of groups that are competing with one another for scarce resources. Although alliances or cooperation may prevail on the surface, beneath that surface lies a struggle for power.

conflict theory a theoretical framework in which society is viewed as composed of groups that are competing for scarce resources

Karl Marx and Conflict Theory   Karl Marx, the founder of conflict theory, witnessed the Industrial Revolution that transformed Europe. He saw that peasants who had left the land to seek work in cities had to work for wages that provided barely enough to eat. Things were so bad that the average worker died at age 30, the average wealthy person at age 50 (Edgerton 1992:87). Shocked by this suffering and exploitation, Marx began to analyze society and history. As he did so, he developed **conflict theory.** He concluded that the key to human history is *class conflict*. In each society, some small group controls the means of production and exploits those who are not in control. In industrialized societies, the struggle is between the *bourgeoisie*, the small group of capitalists who own the means to produce wealth, and the *proletariat*, the mass of workers who are exploited by the bourgeoisie. The capitalists also control politics: If the workers rebel, the capitalists are able to call on the power of the state to subdue them.

When Marx made his observations, capitalism was in its infancy and workers were at the mercy of their employers. Workers had none of what we take for granted today—minimum wages, eight-hour days, coffee breaks, five-day work weeks, paid vacations and holidays, medical benefits, sick leave, unemployment compensation, Social Security, and, for union workers, the right to strike. Marx's analysis reminds us that these benefits came not from generous hearts, but from workers forcing concessions from their employers.

Conflict Theory Today   Some conflict sociologists use conflict theory in a much broader sense than Marx did. They examine how conflict permeates every layer of society—whether that be a small group, an organization, a community, or the entire society. When people in a position of authority try to enforce conformity, which they must do, this creates resentment and resistance. The result is a constant struggle throughout society to determine who has authority and how far that authority goes (Turner 1978; Bartos and Wehr 2002).

Sociologist Lewis Coser (1913–2003) pointed out that conflict is most likely to develop among people who are in close relationships. These people have worked out ways to distribute responsibilities and privileges, power and rewards. Any change in this arrangement can lead to hurt feelings, bitterness, and conflict. Even in intimate relationships, then, people are in a constant balancing act, with conflict lying uneasily just beneath the surface.

Feminists and Conflict Theory   Just as Marx stressed conflict between capitalists and workers, many feminists stress a similar conflict between men and women. A primary focus is the historical, contemporary, and global inequalities of men and women—and how the traditional dominance by men can be overcome to bring about equality of the sexes. Feminists are not united by the conflict perspective, however. They tackle a variety of topics and use whatever theory applies. (Feminism is discussed in Chapter 11.)

Applying Conflict Theory   To explain why the U.S. divorce rate is high, conflict theorists focus on how men's and women's relationships have changed. For millennia, men dominated women. Women had few alternatives other than accepting their exploitation. Today, in contrast, with industrialization, women can meet their basic survival needs outside of marriage. Industrialization has also fostered a culture in which females participate in social worlds beyond the home. Consequently, with the ability to refuse to bear burdens that earlier generations accepted as inevitable, today's women are much more likely to dissolve a marriage that becomes intolerable—or even unsatisfactory.

IN SUM | The dominance of men over women was once considered natural and right. As women gained education and earnings, however, their willingness to accept men's domination diminished, and they strived for more power. One consequence has been a higher divorce rate as wives grew less inclined to put up with relationships that they defined as unfair. From the conflict perspective, then, our increase in divorce is not a sign that marriage has weakened, but, rather, a sign that women are making headway in their historical struggle with men.

Levels of Analysis: Macro and Micro

A major difference between these three theoretical perspectives is their level of analysis. Functionalists and conflict theorists focus on the **macro level;** that is, they examine large-scale patterns of society. In contrast, symbolic interactionists usually focus on the **micro level,** on **social interaction**—what people do when they are in one another's presence. These levels are summarized in Table 1.1 below.

To make this distinction between micro and macro levels clearer, let's return to the example of the homeless, with which we opened this chapter. To study homeless people, symbolic interactionists would focus on the micro level. They would analyze what homeless people do when they are in shelters and on the streets. They would also analyze their communications, both their talk and their **nonverbal interaction** (gestures, silence, use of space, and so on). The observations I made at the beginning of this chapter about the silence in the homeless shelter, for example, would be of interest to symbolic interactionists.

Table 1.1 **Major Theoretical Perspectives in Sociology**

Perspective	Usual Level of Analysis	Focus of Analysis	Key Terms	Applying the Perspective to the U.S. Divorce Rate
Symbolic Interactionism	Microsociological: examines small-scale patterns of social interaction	Face-to-face interaction, how people use symbols to create social life	Symbols Interaction Meanings Definitions	Industrialization and urbanization changed marital roles and led to a redefinition of love, marriage, children, and divorce.
Functional Analysis (also called functionalism and structural functionalism)	Macrosociological: examines large-scale patterns of society	Relationships among the parts of society; how these parts are functional (have beneficial consequences) or dysfunctional (have negative consequences)	Structure Functions (manifest and latent) Dysfunctions Equilibrium	As social change erodes the traditional functions of the family, family ties weaken, and the divorce rate increases.
Conflict Theory	Macrosociological: examines large-scale patterns of society	The struggle for scarce resources by groups in a society; how the elites use their power to control the weaker groups	Inequality Power Conflict Competition Exploitation	When men control economic life, the divorce rate is low because women find few alternatives to a bad marriage. The high divorce rate reflects a shift in the balance of power between men and women.

This micro level, however, would not interest functionalists and conflict theorists. They would focus instead on the macro level. Functionalists would examine how changes in the parts of society have increased homelessness. They might look at how changes in the family (fewer children, more divorce) and economic conditions (inflation, fewer unskilled jobs, loss of jobs to workers overseas) cause homelessness among people who are unable to find jobs and who have no family to fall back on. For their part, conflict theorists would stress the struggle between social classes. They would be especially interested in how decisions by international elites on global production and trade affect the local job market, and along with it unemployment and homelessness.

Putting the Theoretical Perspectives Together

Which theoretical perspective should we use to study human behavior? Which level of analysis is the correct one? As you have seen, these theoretical perspectives produce contrasting pictures of human life. In the case of divorce, these interpretations are quite different from the commonsense understanding that two people are simply "incompatible." *Because each theory focuses on different features of social life, each provides a distinct interpretation. Consequently, it is necessary to use all three theoretical lenses to analyze human behavior. By combining the contributions of each, we gain a more comprehensive picture of social life.*

Trends Shaping the Future of Sociology

Two major trends indicate changing directions in sociology. Let's look again at the relationship of sociology to the reforming of society, and then at globalization.

Sociology Full Circle: Reform Versus Research

Three Stages in the Development of Sociology   A tension between social reform and social analysis has always run through sociology. To better understand this tension, some sociologists find it useful to divide sociology into three major time periods (Lazarsfeld and Reitz 1989). During the *first* phase, sociologists stressed the need to do research in order to improve society. One of the first presidents of the American Sociological Society, Albion Small, made this goal explicit. In 1912, Small said that the primary reason for sociology was its "practical application to the improvement of social life." He said that sociologists should use science to gain knowledge, and then use that knowledge to "realize visions" (Fritz 1989). This first phase of sociology lasted until the 1920s.

During the *second* phase, from the 1920s until World War II, the emphasis switched from making the world a better place to making sociology a respected field of knowledge. Sociologists emphasized *basic* or *pure sociology*, that is, research and theory aimed at making discoveries about life in human groups, but not directing that knowledge toward making changes in those groups. They achieved this goal within a generation, and almost every college and university in the United States added sociology to its course offerings. It is because of these efforts that you are able to take this introductory course in sociology.

We are now in a *third* phase, which began around the end of World War II. In 1954, the U.S. Supreme Court made a major ruling partially based on sociological research. The Court was deciding whether racially segregated public schools were constitutional. Up to this time, states followed a so-called "separate but equal" doctrine and had separate public schools for whites and blacks. (The schools, as many observers noted, were separate, but certainly not equal.) In this landmark ruling (*Brown v. the Board of Education of Topeka*), which banned segregated public schools, sociologists testified about the harmful effects of segregation.

This fundamental change in law had a direct impact on education across the country. It also made sociologists more aware of their potential to bring about social change. Just as sociologists switched from their initial concern with improving society to developing abstract knowledge, today they are seeking ways to apply their research findings. With the development of applied sociology, these efforts have gained momentum. Many sociology departments offer courses in applied sociology; some offer internships in applied sociology at both the graduate and undergraduate levels.

Public Sociology   The American Sociological Association (ASA) is promoting *public sociology*. By this term, the ASA refers to the public—especially politicians and policy makers—becoming more aware of the sociological perspective. This understanding can guide politicians as they make social policy. In the Cultural Diversity box below, you can see an example of public sociology—how data from basic sociological research can stimulate social policy.

Diversity of Orientations   I want to stress that sociology is filled with diverse opinions. Sociologists do not move in lock-step toward a single goal. To divide sociology into three separate phases overlooks as much as it reveals. Even during the first phase, Durkheim and Weber did research for the purpose of gaining academic respectability for sociology. Similarly, during the second phase, many sociologists who wanted to reform society chafed at the emphasis on understanding. And today, many sociologists want the emphasis to remain on basic sociology. Some do not even acknowledge that applied sociology is "real" sociology. They say that it is actually social work or psychology masquerading as sociology.

Cultural Diversity *in the* United States

Studying Job Discrimination: Another Surprising Example of Applied Sociology

SOMETIMES SOCIOLOGISTS DO BASIC sociology—research aimed at learning more about some behavior—and then someone else applies it.

Devah Pager was a graduate student at the University of Wisconsin in Madison. When she was doing volunteer work, homeless men told her how hard it was to find work if they had had been in prison.

Pager decided to find out just what difference a prison record made in getting a job. She sent pairs of college men to apply for 350 entry-level jobs in Milwaukee. One team was African American, and one was white. Pager prepared identical résumés for the teams, but with one difference: On each team, one of the men said he had served 18 months in prison for possession of cocaine.

Figure 1.5 shows the difference that the prison record made. Men without a prison record were two or three times as likely to be called back.

But Pager came up with another significant finding. Look at the difference that race-ethnicity made. White men with a prison record were more likely to be offered a job than African American men who had a clean record!

The application of this research? Pager didn't apply anything, but others did. After President Bush was told of these results, he announced in his State of the Union speech that he wanted Congress to fund a $300 million program to provide mentoring and other support to help former prisoners get jobs (Kroeger 2004).

As you can see, the distinction between basic sociology and applied sociology can be artificial. In some instances, as in this one, research and reform fit together well.

At this point, the prison part of the research has been applied. So far, the race-ethnicity findings have yet to be addressed by social policy.

Figure 1.5 **Call-Back Rates by Race-Ethnicity and Criminal Record**

Source: Courtesy of Devah Pager.

Each particular period, however, does have basic emphases, and this division of sociology into three phases pinpoints major trends. The tension that has run through sociology—between gaining knowledge and applying knowledge—will continue. During this current phase, the pendulum is swinging toward applying sociological knowledge.

Globalization

A second major trend, globalization, is also leaving its mark on sociology. **Globalization** is the breaking down of national boundaries because of advances in communication, trade, and travel. Currently, the United States dominates sociology. As sociologists William Martin and Mark Beittel (1998) put it, U.S. sociology is the "unrivaled center of the discipline on a world scale." One consequence of this dominance is an emphasis on studying groups in the United States. We U.S. sociologists tend to look inward, concentrating on events and relationships that occur in our own country. We even base most of our findings on U.S. samples. Globalization is destined to broaden our horizons, directing us to a greater consideration of global issues. This, in turn, is likely to motivate us to try more vigorously to identify universal principles.

Application of Globalization to This Text   With each passing year, the world becomes smaller as we become more connected to the global village. What occurs elsewhere has a direct impact on our lives, and, increasingly, our welfare is tied to that of people in other nations. To help broaden our horizons, in this book we will visit many cultures around the world, examining what life is like for the people who live in those cultures. Seeing how *their* society affects their behavior and orientations to life helps us to understand how *our* society influences what we do and how we feel about life.

Globalization is one of the most significant events in world history, and you and I are living through its development. Throughout this text, I will stress the impact of globalization on your life, especially how it is likely to shape your future. We will also examine the **globalization of capitalism,** focusing on implications of the triumph of this economic system. From time to time in the following pages, you will also confront the developing new world order, which appears destined to play a significant role in your future.

globalization the growing interconnections among nations due to the expansion of capitalism

globalization of capitalism capitalism (investing to make profits within a rational system) becoming the globe's dominant economic system

Summary *and* Review

The Sociological Perspective
What is the sociological perspective?
The **sociological perspective** stresses that people's social experiences—the groups to which they belong and their experiences within these groups—underlie their behavior. C. Wright Mills referred to this as the intersection of biography (the individual) and history (social factors that influence the individual). Pp. 4–5.

Sociology and the Other Sciences
What is science, and where does sociology fit in?
Science is the application of systematic methods to obtain knowledge and the knowledge obtained by those methods. The sciences are divided into the **natural sciences,** which seek to explain and predict events in the natural environment, and the **social sciences,** which seek to understand the social world objectively by means of controlled and repeated observations. **Sociology** is the scientific study of society and human behavior. Pp. 5–8.

Origins of Sociology
When did sociology first appear as a separate discipline?
Sociology emerged as a separate discipline in the mid-1800s in western Europe, during the onset of the Industrial Revolution. Industrialization affected all aspects of human existence—where people lived, the nature of their work, how they viewed life, and their interpersonal relationships. Early sociologists who focused on these social changes include Auguste Comte, Herbert Spencer, Karl Marx, Emile Durkheim, Max Weber, Harriet Martineau, and W. E. B. Du Bois. Pp. 8–14.

Values in Sociological Research
Should the purpose of social research be only to advance human understanding or also to reform society?
Sociologists agree that research should be objective, that is, that the researcher's **values** and beliefs should

not influence conclusions. But sociologists do not agree on the uses and purposes of social research. Some believe its purpose should be only to advance understanding of human behavior; others, that its goal should be to reform harmful social arrangements. P. 14.

Verstehen and Social Facts

How do sociologists use *Verstehen* and social facts to study human behavior?

According to Weber, to understand why people act as they do, sociologists must try to put themselves in their shoes. He used the German verb *Verstehen,* "to grasp by insight," to describe this essentially subjective approach. Although not denying the importance of *Verstehen,* Emile Durkheim emphasized the importance of uncovering **social facts,** social conditions that influence how people behave. Contemporary sociology uses both approaches to understand human behavior. Pp. 15–16.

Sexism in Early Sociology

What was the position of women in early sociology?

Sociology appeared during a historical period of deep sexism. Consequently, the few women who received the education necessary to become sociologists, such as Harriet Martineau, were ignored. Pp. 16–17.

Sociology in North America

When were the first academic departments of sociology established in the United States?

The earliest departments of sociology were established in the late 1800s at the universities of Kansas, Chicago, and Atlanta. During the 1940s, the University of Chicago dominated sociology. Today, no single university or theoretical perspective dominates. In sociology's early years, the contributions of women and minorities were largely ignored. Pp. 17–21.

What is the difference between basic (or pure) and applied sociology?

Basic (or **pure**) **sociology** is sociological research whose purpose is to make discoveries. In contrast, **applied sociology** is the use of sociology to solve problems. Pp. 21–22.

Theoretical Perspectives in Sociology

What is a theory?

A **theory** is a general statement about how facts are related to one another. A theory provides a conceptual framework for interpreting facts. Pp. 22–23.

What are sociology's major theoretical perspectives?

Sociologists use three primary theoretical frameworks to interpret social life. **Symbolic interactionists** examine how people use symbols to develop and share their views of the world. Symbolic interactionists usually focus on the **micro level**—on small-scale, face-to-face interaction. **Functional analysts,** in contrast, focus on the **macro level**—on large-scale patterns of society. Functional theorists stress that a social system is made up of interrelated parts. When working properly, each part fulfills a function that contributes to the system's stability. **Conflict theorists** also focus on large-scale patterns of society. They stress that society is composed of competing groups that struggle for scarce resources.

With each perspective focusing on select features of social life and each providing a unique interpretation, no single theory is adequate. The combined insights of all three perspectives yield a more comprehensive picture of social life. Pp. 23–31.

Trends Shaping the Future of Sociology

What trends are likely to have an impact on sociology?

Sociology has gone through three phases: The first was an emphasis on reforming society; the second, an emphasis on basic sociology. In today's third phase, we are swinging full circle, coming closer to our roots of applying sociology to social change. The influence of applied sociology is likely to increase. A second major trend, **globalization,** is likely to broaden sociological horizons, refocusing research and theory away from its concentration on U.S. society. Pp. 31–33.

Thinking Critically
about Chapter 1

1. Do you think that sociologists should try to reform society, or to study it dispassionately?

2. Of the three theoretical perspectives, which one would you like to use if you were a sociologist? Why?

3. Considering the macro- and micro-level approaches in sociology, which one do you think better explains social life? Why?

Additional Resources

What can you use MySocLab for? www.mysoclab.com

- **Study and Review:** Pre and Post-Tests, Practice Tests, Flash Cards, Individualized Study Plans.

- **Current Events:** *Sociology in the News,* the daily *New York Times,* and more.

- **Research and Writing:** *Research Navigator, Writing About Sociology,* and more.

Where Can I Read More on This Topic?

Suggested readings for this chapter are listed at the back of this book.

Culture

I had never felt heat like this before. This was *northern* Africa, and I wondered what it must be like closer to the equator. Sweat poured off me as the temperature climbed past 110 degrees Fahrenheit.

As we were herded into the building—which had no air conditioning—hundreds of people lunged toward the counter at the rear of the structure. With body crushed against body, we waited as the uniformed officials behind the windows leisurely examined each passport. At times like this, I wondered what I was doing in Africa.

When I first arrived in Morocco, I found the sights that greeted me exotic—not far from the scenes in *Casablanca, Raiders of the Lost Ark,* and other movies. The men, women, and even the children really did wear those white robes that reached down to their feet. What was especially striking was that the women were almost totally covered. Despite the heat, they wore not only full-length gowns but also head coverings that reached down over their foreheads and veils that covered their faces from the nose down. All you could see was their eyes—and every eye the same shade of brown.

And how short everyone was! The Arab women looked to be, on average, 5 feet, and the men only about three or four inches taller. As the only blue-eyed, blonde, 6-foot-plus person around, and the only one

Everyone stared. No matter where I went, they stared.

who was wearing jeans and a pullover shirt, in a world of white-robed short people I stood out like a creature from another planet. Everyone stared. No matter where I went, they stared. Wherever I looked, I found brown eyes watching me intently. Even staring back at those many dark brown eyes had no effect. It was so different from home, where, if you caught someone staring at you, that person would look embarrassed and immediately glance away.

And lines? The concept apparently didn't even exist. Buying a ticket for a bus or train meant pushing and shoving toward the ticket man (always a man—no women were visible in any public position), who took the money from whichever outstretched hand he decided on.

And germs? That notion didn't seem to exist here either. Flies swarmed over the food in the restaurants and the unwrapped loaves of bread in the stores. Shopkeepers would considerately shoo off the flies before handing me a loaf. They also offered home delivery. I watched a bread vendor deliver a loaf to a woman who was standing on a second-floor balcony. She first threw her money to the bread vendor, and he then threw the unwrapped bread up to her. Only, his throw was off. The bread bounced off the wrought-iron balcony railing and landed in the street, which was filled with people, wandering dogs, and the ever-present, urinating and defecating

(continued)

donkeys. The vendor simply picked up the unwrapped loaf and threw it again. This certainly wasn't his day, for he missed again. But he made it on his third attempt. The woman smiled as she turned back into her apartment, apparently to prepare the noon meal for her family.

Now, standing in the oppressive heat on the Moroccan-Algerian border, the crowd once again became unruly. Another fight had broken out. And once again, the little man in uniform appeared, shouting and knocking people aside as he forced his way to a little wooden box nailed to the floor. Climbing onto this makeshift platform, he shouted at the crowd, his arms flailing about him. The people fell silent. But just as soon as the man left, the shouting and shoving began again.

The situation had become unbearable. His body pressed against mine, the man behind me decided that this was a good time to take a nap. Determining that I made a good support, he placed his arm against my back and leaned his head against his arm. Sweat streamed down my back at the point where his arm and head touched me.

Finally, I realized that I had to abandon U.S. customs. So I pushed my way forward, forcing my frame into every square inch of vacant space that I could create. At the counter, I shouted in English. The official looked up at the sound of this strange tongue, and I thrust my long arms over the heads of three people, shoving my passport into his hand.

What Is Culture?

What is culture? The concept is sometimes easier to grasp by description than by definition. For example, suppose you meet a young woman from India who has just arrived in the United States. That her culture is different from yours is immediately evident. You first see it in her clothing, jewelry, makeup, and hairstyle. Next you hear it in her speech. It then becomes apparent by her gestures. Later, you might hear her express unfamiliar beliefs about relationships or about what is valuable in life. All of these characteristics are indicative of **culture**—the language, beliefs, values, norms, behaviors, and even material objects that are passed from one generation to the next.

In northern Africa, I was surrounded by a culture quite alien to my own. It was evident in everything I saw and heard. The **material culture**—such things as jewelry, art, buildings, weapons, machines, and even eating utensils, hairstyles, and clothing—provided a sharp contrast to what I was used to seeing. There is nothing inherently "natural" about material culture. That is, it is no more natural (or unnatural) to wear gowns on the street than it is to wear jeans.

I also found myself immersed in a contrasting **nonmaterial culture,** that is, a group's ways of thinking (its beliefs, values, and other assumptions about the world) and doing (its common patterns of behavior, including language, gestures, and other forms of interaction). North African assumptions that it is acceptable to stare at others in public and to push people aside to buy tickets are examples of nonmaterial culture. So are U.S. assumptions that it is wrong to do either of these things. Like material culture, neither custom is "right." People simply become comfortable with the customs they learn during childhood, and—as in the case of my visit to northern Africa—uncomfortable when their basic assumptions about life are challenged.

culture the language, beliefs, values, norms, behaviors, and even material objects that are passed from one generation to the next

material culture the material objects that distinguish a group of people, such as their art, buildings, weapons, utensils, machines, hairstyles, clothing, and jewelry

nonmaterial culture (also called *symbolic culture*) a group's ways of thinking (including its beliefs, values, and other assumptions about the world) and doing (its common patterns of behavior, including language and other forms of interaction)

Culture and Taken-for-Granted Orientations to Life

To develop a sociological imagination, it is essential to understand how culture affects people's lives. If we meet someone from a different culture, the encounter may make us aware of culture's pervasive influence on all aspects of a person's life. Attaining the same level of awareness regarding our own culture, however, is quite another matter. *Our* speech, *our* gestures, *our* beliefs, and *our* customs are usually taken for granted. We assume that they are "normal" or "natural," and we almost always follow them without question. As anthropologist Ralph Linton (1936) said, "The last thing a fish would ever notice would be water." So also with people: Except in unusual circumstances, most characteristics of our own culture remain imperceptible to us.

Yet culture's significance is profound; it touches almost every aspect of who and what we are. We came into this life without a language; without values and morality; with no ideas about religion, war, money, love, use of space, and so on. We possessed none of these fundamental orientations that are so essential in determining the type of people we become. Yet by this point in our lives, we all have acquired them—and take them for granted. Sociologists call this *culture within us.* These learned and shared ways of believing and of doing (another definition of culture) penetrate our beings at an early age and quickly become part of our taken-for-granted assumptions about what normal behavior is. *Culture becomes the lens through which we perceive and evaluate what is going on around us.* Seldom do we question these assumptions, for, like water to a fish, the lens through which we view life remains largely beyond our perception.

The rare instances in which these assumptions are challenged, however, can be upsetting. Although as a sociologist I should be able to look at my own culture "from the outside," my trip to Africa quickly revealed how fully I had internalized my culture. My upbringing in Western culture had given me assumptions about aspects of social life that had become deeply rooted in my being—appropriate eye contact, proper hygiene, and the use of space. But in this part of Africa these assumptions were useless in helping me navigate everyday life. No longer could I count on people to stare only surreptitiously, to take precautions against invisible microbes, or to stand in line in an orderly fashion, one behind the other.

As you can tell from the opening vignette, I found these unfamiliar behaviors upsetting, for they violated my basic expectations of "the way people *ought* to be"—and I did not even realize how firmly I held these expectations until they were challenged so abruptly. When my nonmaterial culture failed me—when it no longer enabled me to make sense out of the world—I experienced a disorientation known as **culture shock.** In the case of buying tickets, the fact that I was several inches taller than most Moroccans and thus able to outreach others helped me to adjust partially to their different ways of doing things. But I never did get used to the idea that pushing ahead of others was "right," and I always felt guilty when I used my size to receive preferential treatment.

Think of the cultural shock that people from a tribal culture would experience if they were thrust suddenly into the United States. This is the topic of the Cultural Diversity box on the next page.

An important consequence of culture within us is **ethnocentrism,** a tendency to use our own group's ways of doing things as a yardstick for judging others. All of us learn that the ways of our own group are good, right, proper, and even superior to other ways of life. As sociologist William Sumner (1906), who developed this concept, said, "One's own group is the center of everything, and all others are scaled and rated with reference to it." Ethnocentrism has both positive and negative consequences. On the positive side, it creates in-group loyalties. On the negative side, ethnocentrism can lead to discrimination against people whose ways differ from ours.

The many ways in which culture affects our lives fascinate sociologists. In this chapter, we'll examine how profoundly culture influences everything we are and do. This will serve as a basis from which you can start to analyze your own assumptions of reality. I should give you a warning at this point: You might develop a changed perspective on social life and your role in it. If so, life will never look the same.

culture shock the disorientation that people experience when they come in contact with a fundamentally different culture and can no longer depend on their taken-for-granted assumptions about life

ethnocentrism the use of one's own culture as a yardstick for judging the ways of other individuals or societies, generally leading to a negative evaluation of their values, norms, and behaviors

Cultural Diversity *in the* United States

Culture Shock: The Arrival of the Hmong

IMAGINE THAT YOU WERE A member of a small tribal group in the mountains of Laos. Village life and the clan were all you knew. There were no schools, and you learned everything you needed to know from your relatives. U.S. agents recruited the men of your village to fight communists, and they gained a reputation as fierce fighters. When the U.S. forces were defeated in Vietnam, to prevent your people from being killed in reprisal, your people were moved to the United States.

Here is what happened. Keep in mind that you had never seen a television or a newspaper, and that you had never gone to school. Your entire world had been the village.

They put you in a big house with wings. It flew.

They give you saniwipes with other strange food on a tray. The saniwipes were hard to chew.

After the trip, you were placed in a house. This was an adventure. You had never seen locks before, as no one locked up anything in the village. Most of the village homes didn't even have doors, much less locks.

You found the bathroom perplexing. At first, you tried to wash rice in the bowl of water, which seemed to be provided for this purpose. But when you pressed the handle, the water and rice disappeared. After you learned what the toilet was for, you found it difficult not to slip off the little white round thing when you stood on it. In the village, you didn't need a white thing when you squatted to defecate.

When you threw water on the electric stove to put out the burner, it sparked and smoked. You became afraid to use the stove because it might explode.

And no one liked it when you tried to plant a vegetable garden in the park.

Your new world was so different that to help you adjust the settlement agency told you (Fadiman 1997):

Children make the fastest adjustment to a new culture, although they remain caught between the old and new ones.

1. To send mail, you must use stamps.
2. The door of the refrigerator must be shut.
3. Do not stand or squat on the toilet since it may break.
4. Always ask before picking your neighbor's flowers, fruit, or vegetables.
5. In colder areas you must wear shoes, socks, and appropriate outerwear. Otherwise, you may become ill.
6. Always use a handkerchief or a tissue to blow your nose in public places or inside a public building.
7. Picking your nose or ears in public is frowned upon in the United States.
8. Never urinate in the street. This creates a smell that is offensive to Americans. They also believe that it causes disease.

To help the Hmong assimilate, U.S. officials dispersed them across the nation. This, they felt, would help them to adjust to the dominant culture and prevent a Hmong subculture from developing. The dispersal brought tremendous feelings of isolation to the clan- and village-based Hmong. As soon as they had a chance, the Hmong moved from these towns scattered across the country to the same areas, the major one being in California's Central Valley. Here they united, renewing village relationships and helping one another adjust to the society they had never desired to join.

for your Consideration

Do you think you would have reacted differently if you had been a displaced Hmong? Why did the Hmong need one another more than their American neighbors to adjust to their new life? What cultural shock do you think an American-born 19-year-old Hmong would experience if his or her parents decided to return to Laos?

IN SUM To avoid losing track of the ideas under discussion, let's pause for a moment to summarize, and in some instances clarify, the principles we have covered.

1. There is nothing "natural" about material culture. Arabs wear gowns on the street and feel that it is natural to do so. Americans do the same with jeans.
2. There is nothing "natural" about nonmaterial culture. It is just as arbitrary to stand in line as to push and shove.

3. Culture penetrates deeply into our thinking, becoming a taken-for-granted lens through which we see the world and obtain our perception of reality.
4. Culture provides implicit instructions that tell us what we ought to do and how we ought to think. It provides a fundamental basis for our decision making.
5. Culture also provides a "moral imperative"; that is, the culture that we internalize becomes the "right" way of doing things. (I, for example, believed deeply that it was wrong to push and shove to get ahead of others.)
6. Coming into contact with a radically different culture challenges our basic assumptions of life. (I experienced culture shock when I discovered that my deeply ingrained cultural ideas about hygiene and the use of personal space no longer applied.)
7. Although the particulars of culture differ from one group of people to another, culture itself is universal. That is, all people have culture, for a society cannot exist without developing shared, learned ways of dealing with the challenges of life.
8. All people are ethnocentric, which has both positive and negative consequences.

cultural relativism not judging a culture but trying to understand it on its own terms

Practicing Cultural Relativism

To counter our tendency to use our own culture as the standard by which we judge other cultures, we can practice **cultural relativism;** that is, we can try to understand a culture on its own terms. This means looking at how the elements of a culture fit together, without judging those elements as superior or inferior to our own way of life.

With our own culture embedded so deeply within us, however, practicing cultural relativism can challenge our orientations to life. For example, most U.S. citizens appear to have strong feelings against raising bulls for the purpose of stabbing them to death in front of crowds that shout "Olé!" According to cultural relativism, however, bullfighting must be viewed from the perspective of the culture in which it takes place—*its* history, *its* folklore, *its* ideas of bravery, and *its* ideas of sex roles.

You may still regard bullfighting as wrong, of course, if your culture, which is deeply ingrained in you, has no history of bullfighting. We all possess culturally specific ideas about cruelty to animals, ideas that have evolved slowly and match other elements of our culture. In the United States, for example, practices that once were common in some areas—cock fighting, dog fighting, bear–dog fighting, and so on—have been gradually eliminated.

None of us can be entirely successful at practicing cultural relativism. Look at the Cultural Diversity box on the next page. My best guess is that you will evaluate these "strange" foods through the lens of your own culture. Applying cultural relativism, however, is an attempt to refocus that lens so we can appreciate other ways of life rather than simply asserting, "Our way is right." As you view the photos on page 43, try to appreciate the cultural differences in standards of beauty.

Many Americans perceive bullfighting, which is illegal in the United States, as a cruel activity that should be abolished everywhere. To Spaniards and those who have inherited Spanish culture, however, bullfighting is a beautiful, artistic sport in which matador and bull blend into a unifying image of power, courage, and glory. *Cultural relativism* requires that we suspend our own perspectives in order to grasp the perspectives of others, something that is much easier described than attained.

You Are What You Eat? An Exploration in Cultural Relativity

The World

HERE IS A CHANCE TO TEST your ethnocentrism and ability to practice cultural relativity. You probably know that the French like to eat snails and that in some Asian cultures, chubby dogs and cats are considered a delicacy ("Ah, lightly browned with a little doggy sauce!"). But did you know that cod sperm is a delicacy in Japan (Raisfeld and Patronite 2006)?

Marston Bates (1967), a zoologist, noted this ethnocentric reaction to food:

I remember once, in the llanos of Colombia, sharing a dish of toasted ants at a remote farmhouse. . . . My host and I fell into conversation about the general question of what people eat or do not eat, and I remarked that in my country people eat the legs of frogs.

The very thought of this filled my ant-eating friends with horror; it was as though I had mentioned some repulsive sex habit.

Then there is the experience of the production coordinator of this text, Dusty Friedman, who told me:

When traveling in Sudan, I ate some interesting things that I wouldn't likely eat now that I'm back in our society. Raw baby camel's liver with chopped herbs was a delicacy. So was camel's milk cheese patties that had been cured in dry camel's dung.

You might be able to see yourself eating frog legs, toasted ants, perhaps cod sperm and raw camel liver, maybe even dogs and cats, but here's another test of your

What some consider food, even delicacies, can turn the stomachs of others. These little critters were for sale in a market in Laos.

ethnocentrism and cultural relativity. Maxine Kingston (1975), an English professor whose parents grew up in China, wrote:

"Do you know what people in [the Nantou region of] China eat when they have the money?" my mother began. "They buy into a monkey feast. The eaters sit around a thick wood table with a hole in the middle. Boys bring in the monkey at the end of a pole. Its neck is in a collar at the end of the pole, and it is screaming. Its hands are tied behind it. They clamp the monkey into the table; the whole table fits like another collar around its neck. Using a surgeon's saw, the cooks cut a clean line in a circle at the top of its head. To loosen the bone, they tap with a tiny hammer and wedge here and there with a silver pick. Then an old woman reaches out her hand to the monkey's face and up to its scalp, where she tufts some hairs and lifts off the lid of the skull. The eaters spoon out the brains."

for your Consideration

1. What is your opinion about eating toasted ants? About eating fried frog legs? About eating cod sperm? About eating puppies and kittens? About eating brains scooped out of a living monkey?
2. If you were reared in U.S. society, more than likely you think that eating frog legs is okay; eating ants is disgusting; and eating cod sperm, dogs, cats, and monkey brains is downright repugnant. How would you apply the concepts of ethnocentrism and cultural relativism to your perceptions of these customs?

Although employing cultural relativism helps us to avoid cultural smugness, this view has come under attack. In a provocative book, *Sick Societies* (1992), anthropologist Robert Edgerton suggests that we develop a scale for evaluating cultures on their "quality of life," much as we do for U.S. cities. He also asks why we should consider cultures that practice female circumcision, gang rape, or wife beating, or cultures that sell little girls into prostitution as morally equivalent to those that do not. Cultural values that result in exploitation, he says, are inferior to those that enhance people's lives.

Edgerton's sharp questions and incisive examples bring us to a topic that comes up repeatedly in this text: the disagreements that arise among scholars as they confront contrasting views of reality. It is such questioning of assumptions that keeps sociology interesting.

Standards of beauty vary so greatly from one culture to another that what one group finds attractive, another may not. Yet, in its *ethnocentrism,* each group thinks that its standards are the best—that the appearance reflects what beauty "really" is.

As indicated by these photos, around the world men and women aspire to their group's norms of physical attractiveness. To make themselves appealing to others, they try to make their appearance reflect those standards.

Peru

New Guinea

Thailand

China

Cameroon

United States

Kenya

Tibet

Components of Symbolic Culture

Sociologists sometimes refer to nonmaterial culture as **symbolic culture,** because its central component is the symbols that people use. A **symbol** is something to which people attach meaning and that they then use to communicate with one another. Symbols include gestures, language, values, norms, sanctions, folkways, and mores. Let's look at each of these components of symbolic culture.

Gestures

Gestures, using one's body to communicate with others, are shorthand ways to convey messages without using words. Although people in every culture of the world use gestures, a gesture's meaning may change completely from one culture to another. North Americans, for example, communicate a succinct message by raising the middle finger in a short, upward stabbing motion. I wish to stress "North Americans," for this gesture does not convey the same message in most parts of the world.

I was surprised to find that this particular gesture was not universal, having internalized it to such an extent that I thought everyone knew what it meant. When I was comparing gestures with friends in Mexico, however, this gesture drew a blank look from them. After I explained its intended meaning, they laughed and showed me their rudest gesture—placing the hand under the armpit and moving the upper arm up and down. To me, they simply looked as if they were imitating monkeys, but to them the gesture meant "Your mother is a whore"— the worst possible insult in that culture.

With the current political, military, and cultural dominance of the United States, "giving the finger" is becoming well known in other cultures. Following 9/11, the United States began to photograph and fingerprint foreign travelers. Feeling insulted, Brazil retaliated by doing the same to U.S. visitors. Angry at this, a U.S. pilot raised his middle finger while being photographed. Having become aware of the meaning of this gesture, Brazilian police arrested him. To gain his release, the pilot had to pay a fine of $13,000 ("Brazil Arrests" . . . 2004).

Gestures not only facilitate communication but also, because they differ around the world, can lead to misunderstanding, embarrassment, or worse. One time in Mexico, for example, I raised my hand to a certain height to indicate how tall a child was. My hosts began to laugh. It turned out that Mexicans use three hand gestures to indicate height: one for people, a second for animals, and yet another for plants. They were amused because I had ignorantly used the plant gesture to indicate the child's height. (See Figure 2.1.)

Figure 2.1 **Gestures to Indicate Height, Southern Mexico**

To get along in another culture, then, it is important to learn the gestures of that culture. If you don't, you will fail to achieve the simplicity of communication that gestures allow and you may overlook or misunderstand much of what is happening, run the risk of appearing foolish, and possibly offend people. In some cultures, for example, you would provoke deep offense if you were to offer food or a gift with your left hand, because the left hand is reserved for dirty tasks, such as wiping after going to the toilet. Left-handed Americans visiting Arabs, please note!

Suppose for a moment that you are visiting southern Italy. After eating one of the best meals in your life, you are so pleased that when you catch the waiter's eye, you smile broadly and use the standard U.S. "A-OK" gesture of putting your thumb and forefinger together and making a large "**O**." The waiter looks horrified, and you are struck speechless when the manager asks you to leave. What have you done? Nothing on purpose, of course, but in that culture this gesture refers to a part of the human body that is not mentioned in polite company (Ekman et al. 1984).

Is it really true that there are no universal gestures? There is some disagreement on this point. Some anthropologists claim that no gesture is universal. They point out that even nodding the head up and down to indicate "yes" is not universal, because in some parts of the world, such as areas of Turkey, nodding the head up and down means "no" (Ekman et al. 1984). However, ethologists, researchers who study biological bases of behavior, claim that expressions of anger, pouting, fear, and sadness are built into our biological makeup and are universal (Eibl-Eibesfeldt 1970:404). They point out that even infants who are born blind and deaf, who have had no chance to *learn* these gestures, express themselves in the same way.

Although this matter is not yet settled, we can note that gestures tend to vary remarkably around the world. It is also significant that certain gestures can elicit emotions; some gestures are so closely associated with emotional messages that the gestures themselves summon up emotions. For example, my introduction to Mexican gestures took place at a dinner table. It was evident that my husband-and-wife hosts were trying to hide their embarrassment at using their culture's obscene gesture at their dinner table. And I felt the same way—not about *their* gesture, of course, which meant nothing to me—but about the one I was teaching them.

Although most gestures are learned, and therefore vary from culture to culture, some gestures that represent fundamental emotions such as sadness, anger, and fear appear to be inborn. This crying child whom I photographed in India differs little from a crying child in China—or the United States or anywhere else on the globe. In a few years, however, this child will demonstrate a variety of gestures highly specific to his Hindu culture.

Language

The primary way in which people communicate with one another is through **language**—symbols that can be combined in an infinite number of ways for the purpose of communicating abstract thought. Each word is actually a symbol, a sound to which we have attached some particular meaning. Although all human groups have language, there is nothing universal about the meanings given to particular sounds. Like gestures, in different cultures the same sound may mean something entirely different— or may have no meaning at all. In German, for example, *gift* means poison, so if you give chocolate to a non-English speaking German and say, "Gift" . . .

Because *language allows culture to exist,* its significance for human life is difficult to overstate. Consider the following effects of language.

Language Allows Human Experience to Be Cumulative
By means of language, we pass ideas, knowledge, and even attitudes on to the next generation. This allows others to build on experiences in which they may never directly participate. Because of this, humans are able to modify their behavior in light of what earlier generations have learned. Hence the central sociological significance of language: *Language allows culture to develop by freeing people to move beyond their immediate experiences.*

Without language, human culture would be little more advanced than that of the lower primates. If we communicated by grunts and gestures, we would be limited to a

language a system of symbols that can be combined in an infinite number of ways and can represent not only objects but also abstract thought short time span—to events now taking place, those that have just taken place, or those that will take place immediately—a sort of slightly extended present. You can grunt and gesture, for example, that you want a drink of water, but in the absence of language how could you share ideas concerning past or future events? There would be little or no way to communicate to others what event you had in mind, much less the greater complexities that humans communicate—ideas and feelings about events.

Language Provides a Social or Shared Past   Without language, our memories would be extremely limited, for we associate experiences with words and then use words to recall the experience. Such memories as would exist in the absence of language would be highly individualized, for only rarely and incompletely could we communicate them to others, much less discuss them and agree on something. By attaching words to an event, however, and then using those words to recall it, we are able to discuss the event. As we talk about past events, we develop shared understandings about what those events mean. In short, through talk, people develop a shared past.

Language Provides a Social or Shared Future   Language also extends our time horizons forward. Because language enables us to agree on times, dates, and places, it allows us to plan activities with one another. Think about it for a moment. Without language, how could you ever plan future events? How could you possibly communicate goals, times, and plans? Whatever planning could exist would be limited to rudimentary communications, perhaps to an agreement to meet at a certain place when the sun is in a certain position. But think of the difficulty, perhaps the impossibility, of conveying just a slight change in this simple arrangement, such as "I can't make it tomorrow, but my neighbor can take my place, if that's all right with you."

Language Allows Shared Perspectives   Our ability to speak, then, provides us a social (or shared) past and future. This is vital for humanity. It is a watershed that distinguishes us from animals. But speech does much more than this. When we talk with one another, we are exchanging ideas about events; that is, we are sharing perspectives. Our words are the embodiment of our experiences, distilled into a readily exchangeable form, one that is mutually understandable to people who have learned that language. *Talking about events allows us to arrive at the shared understandings that form the basis of social life.* Not sharing a language while living alongside one another, however, invites miscommunication and suspicion. This risk, which comes with a diverse society, is discussed in the Cultural Diversity box on the next page.

Language is the basis of human culture around the world. The past decade has seen a major development in communication—the ease and speed with which we can "speak" to people across the globe. This development is destined to have vital effects on culture.

Miami—Language in a Changing City

Florida

Florida

WITH VAST IMMIGRATION FROM CUBA and other Spanish-speaking countries, the city of Miami has become a Latin American mecca. Nothing reflects Miami's changed character as much as its long-simmering feud over language: English versus Spanish. Half of the city's 385,000 residents have trouble speaking English. Only *one-fourth* of Miamians speak English at home.

As this chapter stresses, language is a primary means by which people learn—and communicate— their social worlds. Consequently, Miami's language differences reflect not only cultural diversity but also the separate social worlds of the city's inhabitants.

Although its ethnic stew makes Miami culturally one of the richest cities in the United States, the language gap sometimes creates misunderstandings and anger—in both directions. Anglo business owners, feeling excluded, have become fed up with people speaking Spanish. An employee at the Coral Gables Board of Realtors lost her job for speaking Spanish at the office, and a cashier at a Publix supermarket was fired for chatting with a friend in Spanish. The protests by Spanish speakers that followed these firings made headlines in Miami newspapers.

Latinos are now a majority in Miami, and many think that learning language should be a two-way street. Anglos, they feel, should try to learn at least some Spanish. Nicaraguan immigrant Pedro Falcon, for example, who is studying English, wonders why more people don't try to learn his language. "Miami is the capital of Latin America," he says. "The population speaks Spanish."

This, of course, as Anglos see it, is the problem. Miami is in the United States, not in Latin America.

This problem of the language of immigrants isn't new. The millions of Germans who immigrated to the United States in the 1800s brought their language with them. They operated schools in German, published German-language newspapers, held their religious services in German, and, of course, spoke German at home and in the taverns.

Mural from Miami.

Some of their Anglo neighbors didn't like this a bit. "Why don't those Germans assimilate?" they wondered. "Just whose side would they fight on if we had a war?"

This question was answered, of course, with the participation of German Americans in two world wars.

But what happened to all this German language? The first generation of immigrants struggled with English, but spoke German almost exlusively. The second generation assimilated, learning English well, but also speaking German with their parents at home. For the most part, the third generation knew German only as "that language" that their grandparents spoke.

This is also happening with Spanish speakers. Spanish, however, is being kept alive longer because Mexico borders the United States, and there is constant traffic between the countries. In addition, the vast migration from Mexico and other Spanish-speaking countries continuously feeds the language.

If Germany had bordered the United States, there would still be a lot of German spoken here.

With the continuing immigration from Spanish-speaking countries, Miami's percentage of non-English speakers will increase further. But, as sociologist Douglas Massey says, this "doesn't mean that Miami is going to end up being a Spanish-speaking city." Instead, Massey believes that bilingualism will prevail. He says, "The people who get ahead are not monolingual English speakers or monolingual Spanish speakers. They're people who speak both languages."

In the meantime, Miami officials have tried to resolve the controversy by delaring English to be the official language of Miami. In one small way, at least, they have succeeded. When we tried to get a photograph of "Bienvenidos a Miami" for this box, we discovered that such a sign would be illegal!

Source: Based on Sharp 1992; Usdansky 1992; Kent and Lalasz 2007.

Language Allows Complex, Shared, Goal-Directed Behavior Common understandings enable us to establish a *purpose* for getting together. Let's suppose you want to go on a picnic. You use speech not only to plan the picnic but also to decide on reasons for having the picnic—which may be anything from "because it's a nice day and it shouldn't be wasted studying" to "because it's my birthday." Language permits you to blend individual activities into an integrated sequence. In other words, through discussion you decide where you will go; who will drive; who will bring the hamburgers, the potato chips, the soda; where you will meet; and so on. Only because of language can you participate in such a common yet complex event as a picnic—or build roads and bridges, or attend college classes.

IN SUM The sociological significance of language is that it takes us beyond the world of apes and allows culture to develop. Language frees us from the present, actually giving us a social past and a social future. That is, language gives us the capacity to share understandings about the past and to develop shared perceptions about the future. Language also allows us to establish underlying purposes for our activities. As in the example of planning a picnic, each individual is able to perform a small part of a larger activity, aware that others are carrying out related parts. In this way, language enables a series of separate activities to become united into a larger whole.

In short, *language is the basis of culture.* Like most aspects of culture, its linguistic base is usually invisible to us.

Language and Perception: The Sapir-Whorf Hypothesis   In the 1930s, two anthropologists, Edward Sapir and Benjamin Whorf, became intrigued when they noted that the Hopi Indians of the southwestern United States had no words to distinguish among the past, the present, and the future. English, in contrast—as well as French, Spanish, Swahili, and other languages—distinguishes carefully among these three time frames. From this observation, Sapir and Whorf began to think that words might be more than labels that people attach to things. *Eventually, they concluded that language has embedded within it ways of looking at the world.* In other words, language not only expresses our thoughts and perceptions but also shapes the way we think and perceive. When we learn a language, we learn not only words but also ways of thinking and perceiving (Sapir 1949; Whorf 1956).

The **Sapir-Whorf hypothesis** reverses common sense: It indicates that rather than objects and events forcing themselves onto our consciousness, it is our language that determines our consciousness, and hence our perception of objects and events. Sociologist Eviatar Zerubavel (1991) gives a good example. Hebrew, his native language, does not have separate words for jam and jelly. Both go by the same term, and only when Zerubavel learned English could he "see" this difference, which is "obvious" to native English speakers. Similarly, if you learn to classify students as Jocks, Goths, Stoners, Skaters, and Preps, you will perceive students in an entirely different way from someone who does not know these classifications.

Although Sapir and Whorf's observation that the Hopi do not have tenses was inaccurate (Edgerton 1992:27), they did stumble onto a major truth about social life. Learning a language means not only learning words but also acquiring the perceptions embedded in that language. In other words, language both reflects and shapes cultural experiences (Drivonikou et al. 2007). The racial-ethnic terms that our culture provides, for example, influence how we see both ourselves and others, a point that is discussed in the Cultural Diversity box on the next page.

Values, Norms, and Sanctions

To learn a culture is to learn people's **values,** their ideas of what is desirable in life. When we uncover people's values, we learn a great deal about them, for values are the standards by which people define what is good and bad, beautiful and ugly. Values underlie our preferences, guide our choices, and indicate what we hold worthwhile in life.

Every group develops expectations concerning the right way to reflect its values. Sociologists use the term **norms** to describe those expectations (or rules of behavior) that develop out of a group's values. The term **sanctions** refers to the reactions people receive for following or breaking norms. A **positive sanction** expresses approval for following a norm, and a **negative sanction** reflects disapproval for breaking a norm. Positive sanctions can be material, such as a prize, a trophy, or money, but in everyday life they usually consist of hugs, smiles, a pat on the back, or even handshakes and "high fives." Negative sanctions can also be material—being fined in court is one example—but they,

Sapir-Whorf hypothesis Edward Sapir's and Benjamin Whorf's hypothesis that language creates ways of thinking and perceiving

values the standards by which people define what is desirable or undesirable, good or bad, beautiful or ugly

norms expectations, or rules of behavior, that reflect and enforce values

sanctions expressions of approval or disapproval given to people for upholding or violating norms

positive sanction a reward or positive reaction for following norms, ranging from a smile to a prize

negative sanction an expression of disapproval for breaking a norm, ranging from a mild, informal reaction such as a frown to a formal reaction such as a prison sentence or an execution

Race and Language: Searching for Self-Labels

THE GROUPS THAT DOMINATE society often determine the names that are used to refer to racial-ethnic groups. If those names become associated with oppression, they take on negative meanings. For example, the terms *Negro* and *colored people* came to be associated with submissiveness and low status. To overcome these meanings, those referred to by these terms began to identify themselves as *black* or *African American.* They infused these new terms with respect—a basic source of self-esteem that they felt the old terms denied them.

In a twist, African Americans—and to a lesser extent Latinos, Asian Americans, and Native Americans—have changed the rejected term *colored people* to *people of color.* Those who embrace this modified term are imbuing it with meanings that offer an identity of respect. The term also has political meanings. It indicates bonds that cross racial-ethnic lines, mutual ties, and a sense of identity rooted in historical oppression.

There is *always* disagreement about racial-ethnic terms, and this one is no exception. Although most rejected the term

The ethnic terms we choose—or which are given to us—are major self-identifiers. They indicate both membership in some group and a separation from other groups.

colored people, some found in it a sense of respect and claimed it for themselves. The acronym NAACP, for example, stands for the National Association for the Advancement of Colored People. The new term, *people of color,* arouses similar feelings. Some individuals whom this term would include claim that it is inappropriate. They point out that this new label still makes color the primary identifier of people. They stress that humans transcend race-ethnicity, that what we have in common as human beings goes much deeper than what you see on the surface. They stress that we should avoid terms that focus on differences in the pigmentation of our skin.

The language of self-reference in a society that is so conscious of skin color is an ongoing issue. As long as our society continues to emphasize such superficial differences, the search for adequate terms is not likely to ever be "finished." In this quest for terms that strike the right chord, the term *people of color* may become a historical footnote. If it does, it will be replaced by another term that indicates a changing self-identification in a changing historical context.

too, are more likely to be symbolic: harsh words, or gestures such as frowns, stares, clenched jaws, or raised fists. Getting a raise at work is a positive sanction, indicating that you have followed the norms clustering around work values. Getting fired, however, is a negative sanction, indicating that you have violated these norms. The North American finger gesture discussed earlier is, of course, a negative sanction.

Because people can find norms stifling, some cultures relieve the pressure through *moral holidays,* specified times when people are allowed to break norms. Moral holidays such as Mardi Gras often center on getting rowdy. Some activities for which people would otherwise be arrested are permitted—and expected—including public drunkenness and some nudity. The norms are never completely dropped, however—just loosened a bit. Go too far, and the police step in.

Some societies have *moral holiday places,* locations where norms are expected to be broken. Red light districts of our cities are examples. There, prostitutes are allowed to work the streets, bothered only when political pressure builds to "clean up" the area. If these same prostitutes attempt to solicit customers in adjacent areas, however, they are promptly arrested. Each year, the home town of the team that wins the Super Bowl becomes a moral holiday place—for one night.

One of the more interesting examples is "Party Cove" at Lake of the Ozarks in Missouri, a fairly straight-laced area of the country. During the summer, hundreds of boaters—from those operating cabin cruisers to jet skis—moor their vessels together in a highly publicized cove, where many get drunk, take off their clothes, and dance on the boats. In one of the more humorous incidents, boaters complained that a nude woman was riding a jet ski outside of the cove. The water patrol investigated but refused to arrest the woman because she

Many societies relax their norms during specified occasions. At these times, known as *moral holidays*, behavior that is ordinarily not permitted is allowed. From a functional standpoint, *moral holidays*, such as the Mardi Gras held at New Orleans, and spring break in Florida and Mexico, serve as safety valves, allowing a release of deviance. When the *moral holiday* is over, the usual enforcement of rules follows.

was within the law—she had sprayed shaving cream on certain parts of her body. The Missouri Water Patrol has even given a green light to Party Cove, announcing in the local newspaper that officers will not enter this cove, supposedly because "there is so much traffic that they might not be able to get out in time to handle an emergency elsewhere."

Folkways and Mores

Norms that are not strictly enforced are called **folkways.** We expect people to comply with folkways, but we are likely to shrug our shoulders and not make a big deal about it if they don't. If someone insists on passing you on the right side of the sidewalk, for example, you are unlikely to take corrective action, although if the sidewalk is crowded and you must move out of the way, you might give the person a dirty look.

Other norms, however, are taken much more seriously. We think of them as essential to our core values, and we insist on conformity. These are called **mores** (MORE-rays). A person who steals, rapes, or kills has violated some of society's most important mores. As sociologist Ian Robertson (1987:62) put it,

> A man who walks down a street wearing nothing on the upper half of his body is violating a folkway; a man who walks down the street wearing nothing on the lower half of his body is violating one of our most important mores, the requirement that people cover their genitals and buttocks in public.

It should also be noted that one group's folkways may be another group's mores. Although a man walking down the street with the upper half of his body uncovered is deviating from a folkway, a woman doing the same thing is violating the mores. In addition, the folkways and mores of a subculture (discussed in the next section) may be the opposite of mainstream culture. For example, to walk down the sidewalk in a nudist camp with the entire body uncovered would conform to that subculture's folkways.

A **taboo** refers to a norm so strongly ingrained that even the thought of its violation is greeted with revulsion. Eating human flesh and having sex with one's parents are examples of such behaviors. When someone breaks a taboo, the individual is usually judged unfit to live in the same society as others. The sanctions are severe, and may include prison, banishment, or death.

folkways norms that are not strictly enforced

mores norms that are strictly enforced because they are thought essential to core values or the well-being of the group

taboo a norm so strong that it often brings revulsion if violated

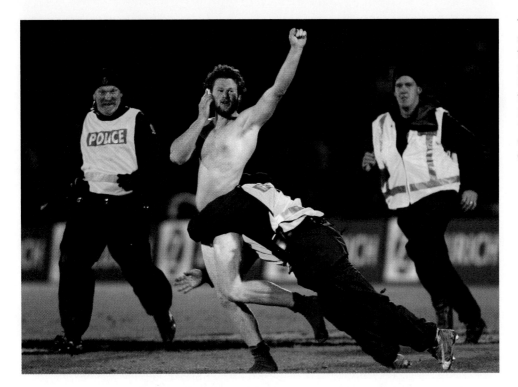

The violation of *mores* is a serious matter. In this case, it is serious enough that the police at this rugby match in Dublin, Ireland, have swung into action to protect the public from seeing a "disgraceful" sight, at least one so designated by this group.

Many Cultural Worlds

Subcultures

What common condition do you think this doctor is describing? Here is what he said:

> [It accompanies] diaphragmatic pleurisy, pneumonia, uremia, or alcoholism . . . Abdominal causes include disorders of the stomach, and esophagus, bowel diseases, pancreatitis, pregnancy, bladder irritation, hepatic metastases, or hepatitis. Thoracic and mediastinal lesions or surgery may be responsible. Posterior fossa tumors or infarcts may stimulate centers in the medulla oblongata. (Chambliss 2003:443)

My best guess is that you don't have the slightest idea what this doctor was talking about. For most of us, he might as well have been speaking Greek. Physicians who are lecturing students in medical school, however, talk like this. This doctor is describing hiccups!

Here's my favorite quote from a politician:

> There are things we know that we know. There are known unknowns; that is to say, there are things that we now know we don't know. But there are also unknown unknowns; there are things we do not know we don't know. (Dickey and Barry 2006:38)

Whatever Donald Rumsfeld, the former Secretary of Defense under George W. Bush, meant by his statement probably will remain a known unknown. (Or would it be an unknown known?)

Politicians and physicians form a **subculture,** *a world within the larger world of the dominant culture.* Subcultures consist of people whose experiences have led them to have distinctive ways of looking at life or some aspect of it. Even if we cannot understand the preceding quotes, they make us aware that the physicians' and politicians' views of life are not quite the same as ours.

U.S. society contains tens of thousands of subcultures. Some are as broad as the way of life we associate with teenagers, others as narrow as those we associate with body

subculture the values and related behaviors of a group that distinguish its members from the larger culture; a world within a world builders—or with doctors. Some U.S. ethnic groups also form subcultures: Their values, norms, and foods set them apart. So might their religion, language, and clothing. Occupational groups also form subcultures, as anyone who has hung out with artists (McCall 1980), construction workers (Haas 1972), or undertakers (Thompson 2007) can attest. Even sociologists form a subculture. As you are learning, they also use a unique language in their efforts to understand the world.

For a visual depiction of subcultures, see the photo montage on pages 54–55.

Countercultures

Consider this quote from another subculture:

> If everyone applying for welfare had to supply a doctor's certificate of sterilization, if everyone who had committed a felony were sterilized, if anyone who had mental illness to any degree were sterilized—then our economy could easily take care of these people for the rest of their lives, giving them a decent living standard—but getting them out of the way. That way there would be no children abused, no surplus population, and, after a while, no pollution. . . .
>
> Now let's talk about stupidity. The level of intellect in this country is going down, generation after generation. The average IQ is always 100 because that is the accepted average. However, the kid with a 100 IQ today would have tested out at 70 when I was a lad. You get the concept . . . the marching morons. . . .
>
> When the . . . present world system collapses, it'll be good people like you who will be shooting people in the streets to feed their families. (Zellner 1995:58, 65)

Welcome to the world of the Survivalists, where the message is much clearer than that of physicians—and much more disturbing.

The values and norms of most subcultures blend in with mainstream society. In some cases, however, such as these survivalists, some of the group's values and norms place it at odds with the dominant culture. Sociologists use the term **counterculture** to refer to such groups. Another example would be Satanists. To better see this distinction, consider motorcycle enthusiasts and motorcycle gangs. Motorcycle enthusiasts—who emphasize personal freedom and speed *and* affirm cultural values of success through work or education—are members of a subculture. In contrast, the Hell's Angels, Pagans, and Bandidos not only stress freedom and speed but also value dirtiness and contempt toward women, work, and education. This makes them a counterculture.

Countercultures do not have to be negative, however. Back in the 1800s, the Mormons were a counterculture that challenged the dominant culture's core value of monogamy.

An assault on core values is always met with resistance. To affirm their own values, members of the mainstream culture may ridicule, isolate, or even attack members of the counterculture. The Mormons, for example, were driven out of several states before they finally settled in Utah, which was then a wilderness. Even there, the federal government would not let them practice *polygyny* (one man having more than one wife), and Utah's statehood was made conditional on its acceptance of monogamy (Anderson 1942/1966).

Values in U.S. Society

An Overview of U.S. Values

As you know, the United States is a **pluralistic society,** made up of many different groups. The United States has numerous religious and racial-ethnic groups, as well as countless interest groups that focus on activities as divergent as collecting Barbie dolls and hunting deer. This state of affairs makes the job of specifying U.S. values difficult. Nonetheless, sociologists have tried to identify the underlying core values that are shared

counterculture a group whose values, beliefs, and related behaviors place its members in opposition to the broader culture

pluralistic society a society made up of many different groups by most of the groups that make up U.S. society. Sociologist Robin Williams (1965) identified the following:

1. *Achievement and success.* Americans place a high value on personal achievement, especially outdoing others. This value includes getting ahead at work and school, and attaining wealth, power, and prestige.

2. *Individualism.* Americans cherish the ideal that an individual can rise from the bottom of society to its very top. If someone fails to "get ahead," Americans generally find fault with that individual rather than with the social system for placing roadblocks in his or her path.

3. *Activity and work.* Americans expect people to work hard and to be busy doing some activity even when not at work. This value is becoming less important.

4. *Efficiency and practicality.* Americans award high marks for getting things done efficiently. Even in everyday life, Americans consider it important to do things fast, and they seek ways to increase efficiency.

5. *Science and technology.* Americans have a passion for applied science, for using science to control nature—to tame rivers and harness winds—and to develop new technology, from iPods to Segways.

6. *Progress.* Americans expect rapid technological change. They believe that they should constantly build "more and better" gadgets that will help them move toward some vague goal called "progress."

7. *Material comfort.* Americans expect a high level of material comfort. This comfort includes not only good nutrition, medical care, and housing but also late-model cars and recreational playthings—from Land Rovers to iPhones.

8. *Humanitarianism.* Americans emphasize personal kindness, aid in mass disasters, and organized philanthropy.

9. *Freedom.* This core value pervades U.S. life. It underscored the American Revolution, and Americans pride themselves on their personal freedom. The Mass Media in Social Life box on page 56 highlights an interesting study on how this core value applies to Native Americans.

10. *Democracy.* By this term, Americans refer to majority rule, to the right of everyone to express an opinion, and to representative government.

11. *Equality.* It is impossible to understand Americans without being aware of the central role that the value of equality plays in their lives. Equality of opportunity (part of the ideal culture discussed later) has significantly influenced U.S. history and continues to mark relations among the groups that make up U.S. society.

12. *Racism and group superiority.* Although it contradicts the values of freedom, democracy, and equality, Americans regard some groups more highly than others and have done so throughout their history. The slaughter of Native Americans and the enslaving of Africans are the most notorious examples.
    In an earlier publication, I updated Williams' analysis by adding these three values.

13. *Education.* Americans are expected to go as far in school as their abilities and finances allow. Over the years, the definition of an "adequate" education has changed, and today a college education is considered an appropriate goal for most Americans. Those who have an opportunity for higher education and do not take it are sometimes viewed as doing something "wrong"—not merely as making a bad choice, but as somehow being involved in an immoral act.

14. *Religiosity.* There is a feeling that "every true American ought to be religious." This does not mean that everyone is expected to join a church, synagogue, or mosque, but that everyone ought to acknowledge a belief in a Supreme Being and follow some set of matching precepts. This value is so pervasive that Americans stamp "In God We Trust" on their money and declare in their national pledge of allegiance that they are "one nation under God."

15. *Romantic love.* Americans feel that the only proper basis for marriage is romantic love. Songs, literature, mass media, and "folk beliefs" all stress this value. They especially love the theme that "love conquers all."

Looking at Subcultures

Subcultures can form around any interest or activity. Each subculture has its own values and norms that its members share, giving them a common identity. Each also has special terms that pinpoint the group's corner of life and that its members use to communicate with one another. Some of us belong to several subcultures simultaneously.

As you can see from these photos, most subcultures are compatible with the values of the dominant or mainstream culture. They represent specialized interests around which its members have chosen to build tiny worlds. Some subcultures, however, conflict with the mainstream culture. Sociologists give the name counterculture to subcultures whose values (such as those of outlaw motorcyclists) or activities and goals (such as those of terrorists) are opposed to the mainstream culture. Countercultures, however, are exceptional, and few of us belong to them.

Membership in this subculture is not easily awarded. Not only must **high-steel ironworkers** prove that they are able to work at great heights but also that they fit into the group socially. Newcomers are tested by members of the group, and they must demonstrate that they can take joking without offense.

The cabbies' subculture, centering on their occupational activities and interest, is also broken into smaller subcultures that reflect their experiences of race-ethnicity.

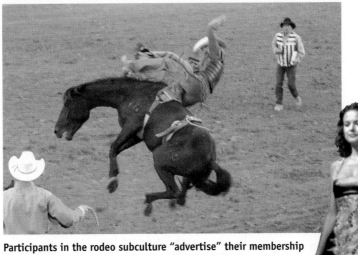

Participants in the rodeo subculture "advertise" their membership by wearing special clothing. The clothing symbolizes a set of values that unites its members. Among those values is the awarding of hyper-masculine status through the conquest of animals—or in this instance, the attempted conquest.

Values and interests are perhaps the two main characteristics of subcultures. What values and interests distinguish the modeling subculture?

This subculture, with its fierce traditions, used to consist of white men. The subculture's painful adjustment to changed times is evident in its name being changed from firemen to fire-fighters.

The subculture that centers around tattooing previously existed on the fringes of society, with seamen and circus folk its main participants. It now has entered the mainstream of society.

Each subculture provides its members with values and distinctive ways of viewing the world. What values and perceptions do you think are common among body builders?

People who raise champion rams belong to a small subculture, in which the norms are explicit and high conformity is expected.

Why would someone decorate themselves like this? Among the many reasons, one is to show their solidarity with the basketball subculture.

mass Media in social life

Why Do Native Americans Like Westerns?

U.S. audiences (and even German, French, and Japanese ones) devour Western movies. In the United States, it is easy to see why Anglos might like Westerns. It is they who are portrayed as heroes who tame the wilderness and defend themselves from the attacks of cruel, savage Indians who are intent on their destruction. But why would Indians like Westerns?

Sociologist JoEllen Shively, a Chippewa who grew up on Indian reservations in Montana and North Dakota, observed that Westerns are so popular that Native Americans bring bags of paperbacks into taverns to trade with one another. They even call each other "cowboy."

Intrigued, Shively decided to investigate the matter by showing a Western to adult Native Americans and Anglos in a reservation town. She matched the groups in education, age, income, and percentage of unemployment. To select the movie, Shively (1991, 1992) previewed more than seventy Westerns. She chose a John Wayne movie, *The Searchers,* because it not only focuses on conflict between Indians and cowboys but also shows the cowboys defeating the Indians. After the movie, the viewers filled out questionnaires, and Shively interviewed them.

She found something surprising: *All* Native Americans and Anglos identified with the cowboys; *none* identified with the Indians. Anglos and Native Americans, however, identified with the cowboys in different ways. Each projected a different fantasy onto the story. While Anglos saw the movie as an accurate portrayal of the Old West and a justification of their own status in society. Native Americans, in contrast, saw it as embodying a free, natural way of life. In fact, Native Americans said that they were the "real cowboys." They said, "Westerns relate to the way I wish I could live"; "He's not tied down to an eight-to-five job, day after day"; "He's his own man."

Shively adds,

What appears to make Westerns meaningful to Indians is the fantasy of being free and independent like the cowboy. . . . Indians . . . find a fantasy in the cowboy story in which the important parts of their ways of life triumph and are morally good, validating their own cultural group in the context of a dramatically satisfying story.

To express their real identity—a combination of marginality on the one hand, with a set of values which are about the land, autonomy, and being free—they

Although John Wayne often portrayed an Anglo who kills Indians, Wayne is popular among Indian men. These men tend to identify with the cowboys, who reflect their values of bravery, autonomy, and toughness.

(use) a cultural vehicle written for Anglos about Anglos, but it is one in which Indians invest a distinctive set of meanings that speak to their own experience, which they can read in a manner that affirms a way of life they value, or a fantasy they hold to.

In other words, values, not ethnicity, are the central issue. If a Native American film industry were to portray Native Americans with the same values that the Anglo movie industry projects onto cowboys, then Native Americans would identify with their own group. Thus, says Shively, Native Americans make cowboys "honorary Indians," for the cowboys express their values of bravery, autonomy, and toughness.

Value Clusters

As you can see, values are not independent units; some cluster together to form a larger whole. In the **value cluster** that surrounds success, for example, we find hard work, education, efficiency, material comfort, and individualism bound up together. Americans are expected to go far in school, to work hard afterward, to be efficient, and then to attain a high level of material comfort, which, in turn, demonstrates success. Success is attributed to the individual's efforts; lack of success is blamed on his or her faults.

Value Contradictions

value cluster values that together form a larger whole

value contradiction values that contradict one another; to follow the one means to come into conflict with the other

Not all values fall into neat, integrated packages. Some even contradict one another. The value of group superiority contradicts freedom, democracy, and equality, producing a **value contradiction.** There simply cannot be full expression of freedom, democracy, and equality along with racism and sexism. Something has to give. One way in which Americans sidestepped this contradiction in the past was to say that freedom, democracy, and equality applied only to some groups. The contradiction was bound to surface over time, however, and so it did with the Civil War and the women's liberation movement. *It is precisely at the point of value contradictions, then, that one can see a major force for social change in a society.*

Emerging Values

A value cluster of four interrelated core values—leisure, self-fulfillment, physical fitness, and youthfulness—is emerging in the United States. A fifth core value—concern for the environment—is also emerging.

1. *Leisure.* The emergence of leisure as a value is reflected in a huge recreation industry—from computer games, boats, vacation homes, and spa retreats to sports arenas, home theaters, extreme vacations, and luxury cruises.
2. *Self-fulfillment.* This value is reflected in the "human potential" movement, which emphasizes becoming "all one can be," and in magazine articles, books, and talk shows that focus on "self-help," "relating," and "personal development."
3. *Physical fitness.* Physical fitness is not a new U.S. value, but its increased emphasis is moving it into this emerging cluster. This trend is evident in the stress on nutrition and organic foods; obsessive attention to weight and diet; the growing number of joggers, cyclists, and backpackers; and the countless health clubs and physical fitness centers.
4. *Youthfulness.* Although valuing youth and disparaging old age are not new, some note a new sense of urgency. They attribute this to the huge number of aging baby boomers, who, aghast at the physical changes that accompany their advancing years, attempt to deny or at least postpone their biological fate. An extreme view is represented by a physician who claims that "aging is not a normal life event, but a disease" (Cowley 1996). It is not surprising, then, that techniques for maintaining and enhancing a youthful appearance—from cosmetic surgery to exotic creams and Botox injections—have become popular.

This emerging value cluster is a response to fundamental changes in U.S. society. Earlier generations of Americans were focused on forging a nation and fighting for economic survival. Today, millions of Americans are freed from long hours of work, and millions more are able to retire from work at an age when they anticipate decades of life ahead of them. This value cluster centers on helping people to maintain their health and vigor during their younger years and enabling them to enjoy their years of retirement.

5. *Concern for the environment.* During most of U.S. history, the environment was viewed as something to be exploited—a wilderness to be settled, forests to be cleared for farm land and lumber, rivers and lakes to be fished, and animals to be hunted. One result was the near extinction of the bison and the extinction in 1915 of the passenger pigeon, a bird previously so numerous that its annual migration would darken the skies for days. Today, Americans have developed a genuine and apparently long-term concern for the environment.

The many groups that comprise the United States contribute to its culture. With their growing numbers, Latinos are making a greater impact on U.S. art, entertainment, music, and literature. This is also true of other areas of everyday life, such as customized vehicles. These "tricked out" cars at a show at Sturgeon Bay, Wisconsin, feature bumping hydraulics and ornate paint jobs.

Values, both those held by individuals and those that represent a nation or people, can undergo deep shifts. It is difficult for many of us to grasp the pride with which earlier Americans destroyed trees that took thousands of years to grow, are located only on one tiny speck of the globe, and that we today consider part of the nation's and world's heritage. But this is a value statement, representing current views. The pride expressed on these woodcutters' faces represents another set of values entirely.

This emerging value of environmental concern is related to the current stage of U.S. economic development: People act on environmental concerns only after they have met their basic needs. At this point in their development, for example, the world's poor nations have a difficult time "affording" this value.

Culture Wars: When Values Clash

Challenges in core values are met with strong resistance by the people who hold them dear. They see changes as a threat to their way of life, an undermining of both their present and their future. Efforts to change gender roles, for example, arouse intense controversy, as does support for the marriage of homosexuals. Alarmed at such onslaughts to their values, traditionalists fiercely defend historical family relationships and the gender roles they grew up with. Today's clash in values is so severe that the term *culture wars* has been coined to refer to it. Compared with the violence directed against the Mormons, however, today's reactions to such controversies are mild.

Values as Blinders

Just as values and their supporting beliefs paint a unique picture of reality, so they also form a view of what life *ought* to be like. Americans value individualism so highly, for example, that they tend to see almost everyone as free to pursue the goal of success. This value blinds them to circumstances that keep people from reaching this goal. The dire consequences of family poverty, parents' low education, and dead-end jobs tend to drop from sight. Instead, Americans cling to the notion that everyone can make it—if they put forth enough effort. And they "know" they are right, for every day, dangling before their eyes are enticing stories of individuals who have succeeded despite huge handicaps.

"Ideal" Versus "Real" Culture

ideal culture the ideal values and norms of a people; the goals held out for them

Many of the norms that surround cultural values are followed only partially. Differences always exist between a group's ideals and what its members actually do. Consequently, sociologists use the term **ideal culture** to refer to the values, norms, and goals that a group considers ideal, worth aspiring to. Success, for example, is part of ideal culture. Americans glorify academic progress, hard work, and the display of material goods as signs of individual achievement. What people actually do, however, usually falls short of the cultural ideal. Compared with their abilities, for example, most people don't work as hard as they could or go as far as they could in school. Sociologists call the norms and values that people actually follow **real culture.**

Cultural Universals

With the amazing variety of human cultures around the world, are there any **cultural universals**—values, norms, or other cultural traits that are found everywhere?

To answer this question, anthropologist George Murdock (1945) combed through data that anthropologists had gathered on hundreds of groups around the world. He drew up a list of customs concerning courtship, marriage, funerals, games, laws, music, myths, incest taboos, and even toilet training. He found that although such activities are present in all cultures, *the specific customs differ from one group to another.* There is no universal form of the family, no universal way of toilet training children, nor of disposing of the dead.

Even incest is defined differently from group to group. For example, the Mundugumors of New Guinea extend the incest taboo so far that for each man, seven of every eight women are ineligible marriage partners (Mead 1935/1950). Other groups go in the opposite direction and allow some men to marry their own daughters (La Barre 1954). In certain circumstances, some groups *require* that brothers and sisters marry one another (Beals and Hoijer 1965). The Burundi of Africa even insist that, in order to remove certain curses, a son must have sex with his mother (Albert 1963). Such sexual relations are usually allowed only for special people (royalty) or in extraordinary situations (such as when a lion hunter faces a dangerous hunt). No society permits generalized incest for its members.

In short, although there are universal human activities (speech, music, games, storytelling, preparing food, marrying, child rearing, disposing of the dead, and so on), there is no universally accepted way of doing any of them. Humans have no biological imperative that results in one particular form of behavior throughout the world. As indicated in the following Thinking Critically section, although a few sociologists take the position that genes significantly influence human behavior, almost all sociologists reject this view.

Thinking Critically

Are We Prisoners of Our Genes? Sociobiology and Human Behavior

A controversial view of human behavior, called **sociobiology** (also known as neo-Darwinism and evolutionary psychology), provides a sharp contrast to the perspective of this chapter, that human behavior is primarily due to culture. Sociobiologists (evolutionary psychologists, evolutionary anthropologists) believe that because of natural selection, the basic cause of human behavior is biology.

Charles Darwin (1859), who developed the idea of natural selection, pointed out that the genes of a species—the units that contain the individual's traits—are not distributed evenly among the offspring. The characteristics passed on to some members make it easier for them to survive their environment, increasing the likelihood that they will pass their genetic traits to the next generation. Over thousands of generations, the genetic traits that aid survival tend to become common in a species, while those that do not aid survival tend to disappear.

Natural selection explains not only the physical characteristics of animals but also their behavior, for over countless generations, instincts emerged. Edward Wilson (1975), an insect specialist, claims that human behavior is also the result of natural selection. Human behavior, he asserts, is no different from the behavior of cats, dogs, rats, bees, or mosquitoes—it has been bred into *Homo sapiens* through evolutionary principles.

Wilson set out to create a storm of protest, and he succeeded. He went on to claim that competition and cooperation, envy and altruism, even religion, slavery, genocide, and war and peace can be explained by sociobiology. He provocatively added that because human behavior can be explained in terms of genetic programming, sociobiology will eventually absorb sociology—as well as anthropology and psychology.

real culture the norms and values that people actually follow

cultural universal a value, norm, or other cultural trait that is found in every group

sociobiology a framework of thought that views human behavior as the result of natural selection and considers biological factors to be the fundamental cause of human behavior

Obviously, most sociologists find Wilson's position unacceptable. Not only is it a direct attack on their discipline but also it bypasses the essence of what sociologists focus on: humans developing their own cultures, their own unique ways of life. Sociologists do not deny that biology underlies human behavior—at least not in the sense that it takes a highly developed brain to develop human culture and abstract thought, and that there would be no speech if humans had no tongue or larynx.

But most sociologists find it difficult to believe that anyone would claim that genetic programming causes human behavior. Pigs act like pigs because they don't have a cerebral cortex, and instincts control their behavior. So it is for spiders, elephants, and so on (Howe et al. 1992). Humans, in contrast, possess a self and are capable of abstract thought. They discuss the reasons that underlie what they do. They develop purposes and goals. They immerse themselves in a world of symbols that allow them to consider, reflect, and make reasoned choices.

This controversy has turned into much more than simply an academic debate among scientists. Homosexuals, for example, have a personal interest in its outcome. If homosexuality is a lifestyle *choice,* then those who consider that lifestyle to be immoral will use this as a basis for excluding homosexuals from full social participation. If, however, homosexuality has a genetic basis, then choice as a reason for social exclusion is eliminated. Sociologist Peter Conrad (1997) expresses the dominant sociological position when he points out that not all homosexuals have Xq28, the so-called "gay gene," and some people who have this gene are not homosexual. This gene, then, does not determine behavior. Instead, we must look for *social* causes (Bearman and Bruckner 2002).

In short, sociobiologists and sociologists stand on opposite sides, the one looking at human behavior as determined by genetics, the other looking at human behavior as determined by social learning, by experiences in the human group. Sociologists point out that if humans were prisoners of their genes, we would not have developed such fascinatingly different ways of life around the world—we would live in a monoculture of some sort.

technology in its narrow sense, tools; its broader sense includes the skills or procedures necessary to make and use those tools

new technology the emerging technologies of an era that have a significant impact on social life

Technology in the Global Village

The New Technology

The gestures, language, values, folkways, and mores that we have discussed—all are part of symbolic or nonmaterial culture. Culture, as you recall, also has a material aspect: a group's *things,* from its houses to its toys. Central to a group's material culture is its technology. In its simplest sense, **technology** can be equated with tools. In a broader sense, technology also includes the skills or procedures necessary to make and use those tools.

We can use the term **new technology** to refer to an emerging technology that has a significant impact on social life. People develop minor technologies all the time. Most are slight modifications of existing technologies. Occasionally, however, they develop a technology that makes a major impact on human life. It is primarily to these innovations that the term *new technology* refers. For people 500 or 600 years ago, the new technology was the printing press. For us, the new technology consists of computers, satellites, and the Internet.

The sociological significance of technology goes far beyond the tool itself. *Technology sets the framework for a group's nonmaterial culture.* If a group's technology changes, so do people's ways of thinking and how they relate to one another. An example is gender relations. Through the centuries and throughout the world, it has been the custom (the nonmaterial culture of a group) for men to dominate women. Today's global communications (the material culture) make this custom more difficult to maintain. For example, when Arab women watch Western television, they observe much freer gender relations. As these women talk to other women by e-mail and telephone, their communications both convey and create discontent, as well as feelings of sisterhood. These communications motivate some of them to agitate for social change.

In today's world, the long-accepted idea that it is proper to withhold rights on the basis of someone's sex can no longer be sustained. What is usually beyond our

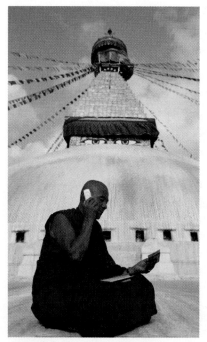

The adoption of new forms of communication by people who not long ago were cut off from events in the rest of the world is bound to change their *nonmaterial culture.*

How do you think the use of cell phones is changing this Buddhist monk's thinking and views of the world? (This photo was taken in Kathmandu, Nepal.)

awareness in this revolutionary change is the role of the new technology, which joins the world's nations into a global communications network.

Cultural Lag and Cultural Change

About three generations ago, sociologist William Ogburn (1922/1938), a functional analyst, coined the term **cultural lag.** By this, Ogburn meant that not all parts of a culture change at the same pace. When one part of a culture changes, other parts lag behind.

Ogburn pointed out that *a group's material culture usually changes first, with the nonmaterial culture lagging behind,* playing a game of catch-up. For example, when we get sick, we could type our symptoms into a computer and get an immediate diagnosis and a recommended course of treatment. In some tests, computers outperform physicians. Yet our customs have not caught up with our technology, and we continue to visit the doctor's office.

Sometimes nonmaterial culture never catches up. Instead, we rigorously hold onto some outmoded form—one that once was needed, but that long ago was bypassed by technology. A striking example is our nine-month school year. Have you ever wondered why it is nine months long, and why we take summers off? For most of us, this is "just the way it's always been," and we have never questioned it. But there is more to this custom than meets the eye, for it is an example of cultural lag.

In the late 1800s, when universal schooling came about, the school year matched the technology of the time, which was labor-intensive. Most parents were farmers, and for survival, they needed their children's help at the crucial times of planting and harvesting. Today, generations later, when few people farm and there is no need for the school year to be so short, we still live with this cultural lag.

Technology and Cultural Leveling

For most of human history, communication was limited and travel slow. Consequently, in their relative isolation, human groups developed highly distinctive ways of life as they responded to the particular situations they faced. The unique characteristics they developed that distinguished one culture from another tended to change little over time. The Tasmanians, who lived on a remote island off the coast of Australia, provide an extreme example. For thousands of years, they had no contact with other people. They were so isolated that they did not even know how to make clothing or fire (Edgerton 1992).

Except in such rare instances, humans have always had *some* contact with other groups. During these contacts, people learned from one another, adopting some part of the other's way of life. In this process, called **cultural diffusion,** groups are most open to changes in their technology or material culture. They usually are eager, for example, to adopt superior weapons and tools. In remote jungles in South America one can find metal cooking pots, steel axes, and even bits of clothing spun in mills in South Carolina. Although the direction of cultural diffusion today is primarily from the West to other parts of the world, cultural diffusion is not a one-way street—as bagels, woks, hammocks, and sushi in the United States attest.

With today's travel and communications, cultural diffusion is occurring rapidly. Air travel has made it possible to journey around the globe in a matter of hours. In the not-so-distant past, a trip from the United States to Africa was so unusual that only a few adventurous people made it, and newspapers would herald their feat. Today, hundreds of thousands make the trip each year.

The changes in communication are no less vast. Communication used to be limited to face-to-face speech, written messages that were passed from hand to hand, and visual signals such as smoke or light that was reflected from mirrors. Despite newspapers, people in some parts of the United States did not hear that the Civil War had ended until weeks and even months after it was over. Today's electronic communications transmit messages across the globe

"COOL! A KEYBOARD THAT WRITES WITHOUT A PRINTER."

Technological advances are now so rapid that the technology of one generation is practically unrecognizable by the next generation.

This Barbie doll, sold in Japan, is dressed in a stage costume of a Japanese singer. As objects diffuse from one culture to another, they are modified to meet the tastes of the adoptive culture. In this instance, the modification has been done intentionally as part of the globalization of capitalism.

cultural leveling the process by which cultures become similar to one another; refers especially to the process by which U.S. culture is being exported and diffused into other nations

in a matter of seconds, and we learn almost instantaneously what is happening on the other side of the world. During Gulf War II, reporters traveled with U.S. soldiers, and for the first time in history, the public was able to view live video reports of battles and deaths as they occurred.

Travel and communication unite us to such an extent that there is almost no "other side of the world" anymore. One result is **cultural leveling,** a process in which cultures become similar to one another. The globalization of capitalism is bringing both technology and Western culture to the rest of the world. Japan, for example, has adopted not only capitalism but also Western forms of dress and music. These changes have transformed Japan into a blend of Western and Eastern cultures.

Cultural leveling is occurring rapidly around the world, as is apparent to any traveler. The Golden Arches of McDonald's welcome today's visitors to Tokyo, Paris, London, Madrid, Moscow, Hong Kong, and Beijing. When I visited a jungle village in India—no electricity, no running water, and so remote that the only entrance was by a footpath—I saw a young man sporting a cap with the Nike emblem.

Although the bridging of geography and culture by electronic signals and the exportation of Western icons do not in and of themselves mark the end of traditional cultures, the inevitable result is some degree of *cultural leveling,* some blander, less distinctive way of life—U.S. culture with French, Japanese, and Brazilian accents, so to speak. Although the "cultural accent" remains, something vital is lost forever.

Summary *and* Review

What Is Culture?

All human groups possess **culture**—language, beliefs, values, norms, and material objects that are passed from one generation to the next. **Material culture** consists of objects (art, buildings, clothing, weapons, tools). **Nonmaterial** (or **symbolic**) **culture** is a group's ways of thinking and their patterns of behavior. **Ideal culture** is a group's ideal values, norms, and goals. **Real culture** is their actual behavior, which often falls short of their cultural ideals. Pp. 38–41.

What are cultural relativism and ethnocentrism?

People are naturally **ethnocentric;** that is, they use their own culture as a yardstick for judging the ways of others. In contrast, those who embrace **cultural relativism** try to understand other cultures on those cultures' own terms. Pp. 41–43.

Components of Symbolic Culture

What are the components of nonmaterial culture?

The central component is **symbols,** anything to which people attach meaning and that they use to communicate with others. Universally, the symbols of non-material culture are **gestures, language, values, norms, sanctions, folkways,** and **mores.** Pp. 44–45.

Why is language so significant to culture?

Language allows human experience to be goal-directed, cooperative, and cumulative. It also lets humans move beyond the present and share a past, future, and other common perspectives. According to the **Sapir-Whorf hypothesis,** language even shapes our thoughts and perceptions. Pp. 45–48.

How do values, norms, sanctions, folkways, and mores reflect culture?

All groups have **values,** standards by which they define what is desirable or undesirable, and **norms,** rules or expectations about behavior. Groups use **positive sanctions** to show approval of those who follow their norms, and **negative sanctions** to show disapproval of those who do not. Norms that are not strictly enforced are called **folkways,** while **mores** are norms to which groups demand conformity because they reflect core values. Pp. 48–50.

Many Cultural Worlds

How do subcultures and countercultures differ?

A **subculture** is a group whose values and related behaviors distinguish its members from the general culture. A **counterculture** holds some values that stand in opposition to those of the dominant culture. Pp. 51–52.

Values in U.S. Society

What are the core U.S. values?

Although the United States is a **pluralistic society,** made up of many groups, each with its own set of values, certain values dominate: achievement and success, individualism, activity and work, efficiency and practicality, science and technology, progress, material comfort, equality, freedom, democracy, humanitarianism, racism and group superiority, education, religiosity, and romantic love. Some values cluster together (**value clusters**) to form a larger whole. **Value contradictions** (such as equality and racism) indicate areas of tension, which are likely points of social change. Leisure, self-fulfillment, physical fitness, youthfulness, and concern for the environment are emerging core values. Core values do not change without opposition. Pp. 52–59.

Cultural Universals

Do cultural universals exist?

Cultural universals are values, norms, or other cultural traits that are found in all cultures. Although all human groups have customs concerning cooking, childbirth, funerals, and so on, because these customs vary from one culture to another, there are no cultural universals. Pp. 59–60.

Technology in the Global Village

How is technology changing culture?

William Ogburn coined the term **cultural lag** to describe how a group's nonmaterial culture lags behind its changing technology. With today's technological advances in travel and communications, **cultural diffusion** is occurring rapidly. This leads to **cultural leveling,** whereby many groups are adopting Western culture in place of their own customs. Much of the richness of the world's diverse cultures is being lost in the process. Pp. 60–62.

Thinking Critically
about Chapter 2

1. Do you favor ethnocentrism or cultural relativism? Explain your position.
2. Do you think that the language change in Miami, Florida, (discussed on page **47**) is an indicator of the future of the United States? Why or why not?
3. Are you a member of any subcultures? Which one(s)? Why do you think that your group is a subculture? What is your group's relationship to the mainstream culture?

Additional Resources

What can you use MySocLab for?   www.mysoclab.com

- **Study and Review:** Pre and Post-Tests, Practice Tests, Flash Cards, Individualized Study Plans.
- **Current Events:** *Sociology in the News,* the daily *New York Times,* and more.
- **Research and Writing:** *Research Navigator, Writing About Sociology,* and more.

Where Can I Read More on This Topic?

Suggested readings for this chapter are listed at the back of this book.

CHAPTER 3

Socialization

Simon Silva, *Orgullo de Familia* (*Family Pride*), 1997

The old man was horrified when he found out. Life never had been good since his daughter lost her hearing when she was just 2 years old. She couldn't even talk—just fluttered her hands around trying to tell him things. Over the years, he had gotten used to that. But now . . . he shuddered at the thought of her being pregnant. No one would be willing to marry her; he knew that. And the neighbors, their tongues would never stop wagging. Everywhere he went, he could hear people talking behind his back.

If only his wife were still alive, maybe she could come up with something. What should he do? He couldn't just kick his daughter out into the street.

After the baby was born, the old man tried to shake his feelings, but they wouldn't let loose. Isabelle was a pretty name, but every time he looked at the baby he felt sick to his stomach.

He hated doing it, but there was no way out. His daughter and her baby would have to live in the attic.

Her behavior toward strangers, especially men, was almost that of a wild animal, manifesting much fear and hostility.

Unfortunately, this is a true story. Isabelle was discovered in Ohio in 1938 when she was about 6½ years old, living in a dark room with her deaf-mute mother.

Isabelle couldn't talk, but she did use gestures to communicate with her mother. An inadequate diet and lack of sunshine had given Isabelle a disease called rickets. Her legs were so bowed that as she stood erect the soles of her shoes came nearly flat together, and she got about with a skittering gait. Her behavior toward strangers, especially men, was almost that of a wild animal, manifesting much fear and hostility. In lieu of speech she made only a strange croaking sound. (Davis 1940/ 2007:157-158)

When the newspapers reported this case, sociologist Kingsley Davis decided to find out what had happened to Isabelle after her discovery. We'll come back to that later, but first let's use the case of Isabelle to gain insight into human nature.

What Is Human Nature?

social environment the entire human environment, including direct contact with others

For centuries, people have been intrigued with the question of what is human about human nature. How much of people's characteristics comes from "nature" (heredity) and how much from "nurture" (the **social environment,** contact with others)? One way to answer this question is to study identical twins who were separated at birth and reared in different environments, such as those discussed in the Down-to-Earth Sociology box below. Another way is to examine children who have had little human contact. Let's consider such children.

Down-to-Earth Sociology

Heredity or Environment? The Case of Oskar and Jack, Identical Twins

IDENTICAL TWINS SHARE EXACTLY THE SAME GENETIC heredity. One fertilized egg divides to produce two embryos. If heredity determines personality—or attitudes, temperament, skills, and intelligence—then identical twins should be identical not only in their looks but also in these characteristics.

The fascinating case of Jack and Oskar helps us unravel this mystery. From their experience, we can see the far-reaching effects of the environment—how social experiences take precedence over biology.

Jack Yufe and Oskar Stohr are identical twins born in 1932 to a Jewish father and a Catholic mother. They were separated as babies after their parents divorced. Oskar was reared in Czechoslovakia by his mother's mother, who was a strict Catholic. When Oskar was a toddler, Hitler annexed this area of Czechoslovakia, and Oskar learned to love Hitler and to hate Jews. He joined the Hitler Youth (a sort of Boy Scout organization, except that this one was designed to instill the "virtues" of patriotism, loyalty, obedience—and hatred).

Jack's upbringing was a mirror image of Oskar's. Reared in Trinidad by his father, he learned loyalty to Jews and hatred of Hitler and the Nazis. After the war, Jack and his father moved to Israel. When he was 17, Jack joined a kibbutz, and later, served in the Israeli army.

In 1954, the two brothers met. It was a short meeting and Jack had been warned not to tell Oskar that they were Jews. Twenty-five years later, in 1979, when they were 47 years old, social scientists at the University of Minnesota brought them together again. These researchers figured that because Jack and Oskar had the same genes, any differences they showed would have to be the result of their environment—their different social experiences.

The question of the relative influence of heredity and the environment in human behavior has fascinated and plagued researchers. To try to answer this question, researchers have studied identical twins. Some human behaviors, such as beliefs, political and otherwise, are clearly due to the environment, but uncertainty remains about the origin of other behaviors.

Not only did Oskar and Jack hold different attitudes toward the war, Hitler, and Jews but also their basic orientations to life were different. In their politics, Oskar was conservative, while Jack was more liberal. Oskar enjoyed leisure, while Jack was a workaholic. And, as you can predict, Jack was very proud of being a Jew. Oskar, who by this time knew that he was a Jew, wouldn't even mention it.

That would seem to settle the matter. But there was another side. The researchers also found that Oskar and Jack had both excelled at sports as children, but had difficulty with math. They also had the same rate of speech, and both liked sweet liqueur and spicy foods. Strangely, both flushed the toilet both before and after using it and enjoyed startling people by sneezing in crowded elevators.

for your Consideration

Heredity or environment? How much influence does each one have? The question is not yet settled, but at this point it seems fair to conclude that the *limits* of certain physical and mental abilities are established by heredity (such as ability at sports and aptitude for mathematics), while attitudes are the result of the environment. Basic temperament, though, seems to be inherited. Although the answer is still fuzzy, we can put it this way: For some parts of life, the blueprint is drawn by heredity; but even here the environment can redraw those lines. For other parts, the individual is a blank slate, and it is up to the environment to determine what is written on that slate.

Sources: Based on Begley 1979; Chen 1979; Wright 1995; Segal and Hershberger 2005.

Feral Children

Over the centuries, people have occasionally found children living in the forests. Supposedly, these children could not speak; they bit, scratched, growled, and walked on all fours. They drank by lapping water, ate grass, tore ravenously at raw meat, and showed an insensitivity to pain and cold. These stories of what are called **feral children** sound like exaggerations, and it is easy to dismiss them as folk myth.

Because of what happened in 1798, however, we can't be so sure. In that year, a child who walked on all fours and could not speak was found in the forests of Aveyron, France. "The wild boy of Aveyron," as this child became known, would have been simply another of those legends, except that French scientists took the child to a laboratory and studied him. Like the earlier informal reports, this child, too, gave no indication of feeling the cold. Most startling, though, the boy would growl when he saw a small animal, pounce on it, and devour it uncooked. Even today, the scientists' detailed reports make fascinating reading (Itard 1962).

Ever since I read Itard's account of this boy, I've been fascinated by feral children, especially the seemingly fantastic possibility that animals could rear human children. In 2002, I received a report from a contact in Cambodia that a feral child had been found in the jungles. When I had the opportunity the following year to visit the child and interview his caregivers, I grabbed it. The boy's photo is on this page.

If animals really have raised children, the sociological question is: If we were untouched by society, would we be like feral children? By nature, would our behavior be like that of wild animals? Unable to study feral children, sociologists have studied children like Isabelle who were reared in isolation.

Isolated Children

Reports of isolated children have been well documented. What can they tell us about human nature? We can first conclude that humans have no natural language, for Isabelle and others like her are unable to speak.

But maybe Isabelle was mentally impaired, and she simply was not able to progress through the usual stages of development. When Isabelle was given her first intelligence test, she scored practically zero. But after a few months of intensive language training, she was able to speak in short sentences. In about a year, she could write a few words, do simple addition, and retell stories after hearing them. Seven months later, she had a vocabulary of almost 2,000 words. In just two years, Isabelle reached the intellectual level that is normal for her age. She then went on to school, where she was "bright, cheerful, energetic . . . and participated in all school activities as normally as other children" (Davis 1940/2005:139).

As discussed in the previous chapter, language is the key to human development. Without language, people have no mechanism for developing and communicating thought. Unlike animals, humans have no instincts that take the place of language. If an individual lacks language, he or she lives in an isolated world—a world of internal silence, without shared ideas, lacking connections to others.

Without language, there can be no culture—no shared way of life—and culture is the key to what people become. Each of us possesses a biological heritage, but this heritage does not determine specific behaviors, attitudes, or values. It is our culture that superimposes the specifics of what we become onto our biological heritage.

Institutionalized Children

Other than language, what else is required for a child to develop into what we consider a healthy, balanced, intelligent human being? We find part of the answer in an intriguing experiment from the 1930s. Back then, parents died a lot younger, and orphanages were more common throughout the United States. Children reared in orphanages often had difficulty establishing close bonds with others—and they tended to have low IQs. "Common sense" (which we noted in Chapter 1 is unreliable) told everyone that the cause of mental retardation is biological ("They're just born that way"). Two psychologists, H. M. Skeels and H. B. Dye (1939), however, began to suspect a social cause.

One of the reasons I went to Cambodia was to interview a feral child—the boy shown here—who supposedly had been raised by monkeys. When I arrived at the remote location where the boy was living, I was disappointed to find that the story was only partially true. During its reign of terror, the Khmer Rouge had shot and killed the boy's parents, leaving him, at about the age of two, abandoned on an island. Some months later, villagers found him in the care of monkeys. They shot the female monkey that was carrying the boy. Not quite a feral child—but the closest I'll ever come to one.

feral children children assumed to have been raised by animals, in the wilderness, isolated from other humans

For background on their experiment, Skeels (1966) provides this account of a "good" orphanage in Iowa during the 1930s, where he and Dye were consultants:

Until about six months, they were cared for in the infant nursery. The babies were kept in standard hospital cribs that often had protective sheeting on the sides, thus effectively limiting visual stimulation; no toys or other objects were hung in the infants' line of vision. Human interactions were limited to busy nurses who, with the speed born of practice and necessity, changed diapers or bedding, bathed and medicated the infants, and fed them efficiently with propped bottles.

Perhaps, thought Skeels and Dye, the absence of stimulating social interaction was the problem, not some biological incapacity on the part of the children. To test their controversial idea, they selected thirteen infants whose mental retardation was so obvious that no one wanted to adopt them. They placed them in an institution for the mentally retarded. Each infant, then about 19 months old, was assigned to a separate ward of women ranging in mental age from 5 to 12 and in chronological age from 18 to 50. The women were pleased with this arrangement. Not only did they take care of the infants' physical needs—diapering, feeding, and so on—but also they loved to play with the children. They cuddled them and showered them with attention. They even competed to see which ward would have "its baby" walking or talking first. Each child had one woman who became

particularly attached to him [or her] and figuratively "adopted" him [or her]. As a consequence, an intense one-to-one adult-child relationship developed, which was supplemented by the less intense but frequent interactions with the other adults in the environment. Each child had some one person with whom he [or she] was identified and who was particularly interested in him [or her] and his [or her] achievements. (Skeels 1966)

The researchers left a control group of twelve infants at the orphanage. These infants were also thought to have low IQs, but they were considered higher in intelligence than the other thirteen. They received the usual care. Two and a half years later, Skeels and Dye tested all the children's intelligence. Their findings were startling: Those assigned to the care of women in the institution had gained an average of 28 IQ points while those who remained in the orphanage had lost 30 points.

What happened after these children were grown? Did these initial differences matter? Twenty-one years later, Skeels and Dye did a follow-up study. Those in the control group who had remained in the orphanage had, on average, less than a third-grade education. Four still lived in state institutions, while the others held low-level jobs. Only two had married. In contrast, the average level of education for the thirteen individuals in the experimental group was twelve grades (about normal for that period). Five had completed one or more years of college. One had even gone to graduate school. Eleven had married. All thirteen were self-supporting or were homemakers (Skeels 1966). Apparently, then, one characteristic that we take for granted as being a basic "human" trait—high intelligence—depends on early, close relations with other humans.

A recent experiment in India confirms the Skeels and Dye research. Many of India's orphanages are similar to the ones that Skeels and Dye studied, dismal places where unattended children lie in bed all day. When experimenters added stimulating play and interaction to the

Under Communist rule, orphans in Romania received horrible treatment. The children will carry emotional scars into adulthood. In severe cases, their treatment is likely to affect their ability to reason and to function as adults.

children's activities, the children's motor skills improved and their IQs increased (Taneja et al. 2002). The longer that children lack stimulating interaction, though, the more difficulty they have intellectually (Meese 2005).

Let's consider one other case, the story of Genie:

> In 1970, California authorities found Genie, a 13-year-old girl who had been locked in a small room and tied to a chair since she was 20 months old. Apparently her father (70 years old when Genie was discovered) hated children, and probably had caused the death of two of Genie's siblings. Her 50-year-old mother was partially blind and frightened of her husband. Genie could not speak, did not know how to chew, was unable to stand upright, and could not straighten her hands and legs. On intelligence tests, she scored at the level of a 1-year-old. After intensive training, Genie learned to walk and use simple sentences (although they were garbled). As she grew up, her language remained primitive, she took anyone's property if it appealed to her, and she went to the bathroom wherever she wanted. At the age of 21, Genie went to live in a home for adults who cannot live alone. (Pines 1981)

IN SUM From Genie's pathetic story and from reports of institutionalized children, we can conclude that the basic human traits of intelligence and the ability to establish close bonds with others depend on early interaction with other humans. In addition, apparently there is a period prior to age 13 in which children must experience language and human bonding if they are to develop high intelligence and the ability to be sociable and follow social norms.

Deprived Animals

Finally, let's consider animals that have been deprived of normal interaction. In a series of experiments with rhesus monkeys, psychologists Harry and Margaret Harlow demonstrated the importance of early learning. The Harlows (1962) raised baby monkeys in isolation. They gave each monkey two artificial mothers, shown in the photo on this page. One "mother" was only a wire frame with a wooden head, but it did have a nipple from which the baby could nurse. The frame of the other "mother," which had no bottle, was covered with soft terrycloth. To obtain food, the baby monkeys nursed at the wire frame.

When the Harlows (1965) frightened the baby monkeys with a mechanical bear or dog, the babies did not run to the wire frame "mother." Instead, they would cling pathetically to their terrycloth "mother." The Harlows concluded that infant–mother bonding is not the result of feeding but, rather, of what they termed "intimate physical contact." To most of us, this phrase means cuddling.

The monkeys raised in isolation were never able to adjust to monkey life. Placed with other monkeys when they were grown, they didn't know how to participate in "monkey interaction"—to play and to engage in pretend fights—and the other monkeys rejected them. Neither did they know how to have sexual intercourse, despite futile attempts to do so. The experimenters designed a special device, which allowed some females to become pregnant. After giving birth, however, these monkeys were "ineffective, inadequate, and brutal mothers . . . [who] . . . struck their babies, kicked them, or crushed the babies against the cage floor."

In one of their many experiments, the Harlows isolated baby monkeys for different lengths of time. They found that when monkeys were isolated for shorter periods (about three months), they were able to overcome the effects of their isolation. Those isolated for six

Like humans, monkeys need interaction to thrive. Those raised in isolation are unable to interact satisfactorily with others. In this photograph, we see one of the monkeys described in the text. Purposefully frightened by the experimenter, the monkey has taken refuge in the soft terrycloth draped over an artificial "mother."

months or more, however, were unable to adjust to normal monkey life. As mentioned, they could not play or engage in pretend fights, and the other monkeys rejected them. In other words, the longer the period of isolation, the more difficult its effects are to overcome. In addition, a critical learning stage may exist: If that stage is missed, it may be impossible to compensate for what has been lost. This may have been the case with Genie.

Because humans are not monkeys, we must be careful about extrapolating from animal studies to human behavior. The Harlow experiments, however, support what we know about children who are reared in isolation.

IN SUM **Society Makes Us Human.** Apparently, babies do not develop "naturally" into human adults. Although their bodies grow, if children are reared in isolation they become little more than big animals. Without the concepts that language provides, they can't experience or even grasp relationships between people (the "connections" we call brother, sister, parent, friend, teacher, and so on). And without warm, friendly interactions, they don't become "friendly" in the accepted sense of the term, nor do they cooperate with others. In short, it is through human contact that people learn to be members of the human community. This process by which we learn the ways of society (or of particular groups), called **socialization,** is what sociologists have in mind when they say "Society makes us human."

Socialization into the Self and Mind

At birth, babies have no idea that they are separate beings. They don't even know that they are a he or she. How do we humans develop a **self,** our image of who we are? How do we develop our ability to reason? Let's see how this occurs.

Cooley and the Looking-Glass Self

About a hundred years ago, Charles Horton Cooley (1864–1929), a symbolic interactionist who taught at the University of Michigan, concluded that this unique aspect of "humanness" called the self is socially created. He said that *our sense of self develops from interaction with others.* Cooley (1902) coined the term **looking-glass self** to describe the process by which our sense of self develops. He summarized this idea in the following couplet:

> **Each to each a looking-glass**
> **Reflects the other that doth pass.**

The looking-glass self contains three elements:

1. *We imagine how we appear to those around us.* For example, we may think that others perceive us as witty or dull.
2. *We interpret others' reactions.* We come to conclusions about how others evaluate us. Do they like us for being witty? Do they dislike us for being dull?
3. *We develop a self-concept.* How we interpret others' reactions to us frames our feelings and ideas about ourselves. A favorable reflection in this *social mirror* leads to a positive self-concept; a negative reflection leads to a negative self-concept.

Note that the development of the self does *not* depend on accurate evaluations. Even if we grossly misinterpret how others think about us, those misjudgments become part of our self-concept. Note also that *although the self-concept begins in childhood, its development is an ongoing, lifelong process.* The three steps of the looking-glass self are a part of our everyday lives: As we monitor how others react to us, we continually modify the self. The self, then, is never a finished product—it is always in process, even into old age.

socialization the process by which people learn the characteristics of their group—the knowledge, skills, attitudes, values, and actions thought appropriate for them

self the unique human capacity of being able to see ourselves "from the outside"; the views we internalize of how others see us

looking-glass self a term coined by Charles Horton Cooley to refer to the process by which our self develops through internalizing others' reactions to us

Mead and Role Taking

Another symbolic interactionist, George Herbert Mead (1863–1931), who taught at the University of Chicago, added that play is crucial to the development of a self. In play, children learn to **take the role of the other,** that is, to put themselves in someone else's shoes—to understand how someone else feels and thinks and to anticipate how that person will act.

Only gradually do children attain this ability (Mead 1934; Coser 1977). Psychologist John Flavel (1968) asked 8- and 14-year-olds to explain a board game to some children who were blindfolded and to others who were not. The 14-year-olds gave more detailed instructions to those who were blindfolded, but the 8-year-olds gave the same instructions to everyone. The younger children could not yet take the role of the other, while the older children could.

As they develop this ability, at first children are able to take only the role of **significant others,** individuals who significantly influence their lives, such as parents or siblings. By assuming their roles during play, such as dressing up in their parents' clothing, children cultivate the ability to put themselves in the place of significant others.

As the self gradually develops, children internalize the expectations of more and more people. The ability to take on roles eventually extends to being able to take the role of "the group as a whole." Mead used the term **generalized other** to refer to our perception of how people in general think of us.

Taking the role of others is essential if we are to become cooperative members of human groups—whether they be our family, friends, or co-workers. This ability allows us to modify our behavior by anticipating how others will react—something Genie never learned.

Learning to take the role of the other entails three stages (see Figure 3.1):

1. *Imitation.* Children under age 3 can only mimic others. They do not yet have a sense of self separate from others, and they can only imitate people's gestures and words. (This stage is actually not role taking, but it prepares the child for it.)
2. *Play.* During the second stage, from the ages of about 3 to 6, children pretend to take the roles of specific people. They might pretend that they are a firefighter, a wrestler, a nurse, Supergirl, Spiderman, a princess, and so on. They also like costumes at this stage and enjoy dressing up in their parents' clothing, or tying a towel around their neck to "become" Spiderman or Wonder Woman.
3. *Team Games.* This third stage, organized play, or team games, begins roughly with the early school years. The significance for the self is that to play these games the individual must be able to take multiple roles. One of Mead's favorite

To help his students understand the term *generalized other,* Mead used baseball as an illustration. Why are team sports and organized games such excellent examples to use in explaining this concept?

taking the role of the other putting oneself in someone else's shoes; understanding how someone else feels and thinks and thus anticipating how that person will act

significant other an individual who significantly influences someone else's life

generalized other the norms, values, attitudes, and expectations of people "in general"; the child's ability to take the role of the generalized other is a significant step in the development of a self

Figure 3.1 **How We Learn to Take the Role of the Other: Mead's Three Stages**

Stage 1: Imitation
Children under age 3
No sense of self
Imitate others

Stage 2: Play
Ages 3 to 6
Play "pretend" others
  (princess, Spiderman, etc.)

Stage 3: Team Games
After about age 6 or 7
Team games
  ("organized play")
Learn to take multiple roles

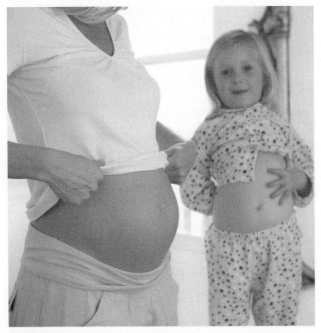

examples was that of a baseball game, in which each player must be able to take the role of all the other players. To play baseball, the child not only must know his or her own role but also must be able to anticipate who will do what when the ball is hit or thrown.

Mead also said there were two parts of the self, the "I" and the "me." The "*I*" is *the self as subject*, the active, spontaneous, creative part of the self. In contrast, the "*me*" is *the self as object.* It is made up of attitudes we internalize from our interactions with others. Mead chose these pronouns because in English "I" is the active agent, as in "I shoved him," while "me" is the object of action, as in "He shoved me." Mead stressed that we are not passive in the socialization process. We are not like robots, passively absorbing the responses of others. Rather, our "I" is active. It evaluates the reactions of others and organizes them into a unified whole. Mead added that the "I" even monitors the "me," fine-tuning our actions to help us better match what others expect of us.

Mead also drew a conclusion that some find startling: *Both the self and the human mind are social products.* Mead stressed that we cannot think without symbols. But where do these symbols come from? Only from society, which gives us our symbols by giving us language. If society did not provide the symbols, we would not be able to think, and thus would not possess what we call the mind. The mind, then, like language, is a product of society.

Mead analyzed *taking the role of the other* as an essential part of learning to be a full-fledged member of society. At first, we are able to take the role only of significant others, as this child is doing. Later we develop the capacity to take the role of the *generalized other*, which is essential not only for extended cooperation but also for the control of antisocial desires.

Piaget and the Development of Reasoning

An essential part of being human is the ability to reason. How do we learn this skill?

This question intrigued Jean Piaget (1896–1980), a Swiss psychologist who noticed that young children give similar wrong answers when they take intelligence tests. He thought that young children might be using some consistent, but incorrect, reasoning to figure out their answers. Perhaps children go through a natural process as they learn how to reason.

To find out, Piaget set up a laboratory where he could give children of different ages various problems to solve (Piaget 1950, 1954; Flavel et al. 2002). After years of testing, Piaget concluded that children go through four stages as they develop their ability to reason. (If you mentally substitute "reasoning skills" for the term *operational* in the following explanations, Piaget's findings will be easier to understand.)

Shown here is Jean Piaget with one of the children he studied in his analysis of the development of human reasoning.

1. **The sensorimotor stage** (from birth to about age 2) During this stage, understanding is limited to direct contact with the environment—sucking, touching, listening, looking. Infants do not "think" in any sense that we understand. During the first part of this stage, they do not even know that their bodies are separate from the environment. Indeed, they have yet to discover that they have toes. Neither can infants recognize cause and effect. That is, they do not know that their actions cause something to happen.
2. **The preoperational stage** (from about age 2 to age 7) During this stage, children *develop the ability to use symbols.* However, they do not yet understand common concepts such as size, speed, or causation. Although they can count, they do not really understand what numbers mean. Nor do they yet have the ability to take the role of the other. Piaget asked preoperational children to describe a clay model of a mountain range. They did just fine. But when he asked them to describe how the mountain range looked from where another child was sitting, they couldn't do it. They could only repeat what they saw from their view.

3. **The concrete operational stage** (from the age of about 7 to 12) Although reasoning abilities are more developed, they remain *concrete*. Children can now understand numbers, causation, and speed, and they are able to take the role of the other and to participate in team games. Without concrete examples, however, they are unable to talk about concepts such as truth, honesty, or justice. They can explain why Jane's answer was a lie, but they cannot describe what truth itself is.
4. **The formal operational stage** (after the age of about 12) Children are now capable of abstract thinking. They can talk about concepts, come to conclusions based on general principles, and use rules to solve abstract problems. During this stage, children are likely to become young philosophers (Kagan 1984). If shown a photo of a slave, for example, a child at the concrete operational stage might have said, "That's wrong!" However, a child at the formal operational stage is likely to add, "If our county was founded on equality, how could people have owned slaves?"

Global Aspects of the Self and Reasoning

Cooley's conclusions about the looking-glass self appear to be true for everyone around the world. So do Mead's conclusions about role taking and the mind as a social product, although researchers are finding that the self may develop earlier than Mead indicated. The stages of reasoning that Piaget identified probably also occur worldwide, although researchers have found that the stages are not as distinct as Piaget concluded and the ages at which individuals enter the stages differ from one person to another (Flavel et al. 2002). Even during the sensorimotor stage, for example, children show early signs of reasoning, which may indicate an innate ability that is wired into the brain. Although Piaget's theory is being refined, his contribution remains: *A basic structure underlies the way we develop reasoning, and children all over the world begin with the concrete and move to the abstract.*

Interestingly, some people seem to get stuck in the concreteness of the third stage and never reach the fourth stage of abstract thinking (Kohlberg and Gilligan 1971; Suizzo 2000). College, for example, nurtures the fourth stage, and most people without this experience apparently have less ability for abstract thought. Social experiences, then, can modify these stages. Also, there is much that we don't yet know about how culture influences the way we think, a topic explored in the Cultural Diversity box on the next page.

Learning Personality, Morality, and Emotions

Our personality, morality, and emotions are vital aspects of who we are. Let's look at how we learn these essential aspects of our being.

Freud and the Development of Personality

Along with the development of our mind and the self comes the development of our personality. Sigmund Freud (1856–1939) developed a theory of the origin of personality that has had a major impact on Western thought. Freud was a physician in Vienna in the early 1900s who founded *psychoanalysis,* a technique for treating emotional problems through long-term, intensive exploration of the subconscious mind. Let's look at his theory.

Freud believed that personality consists of three elements. Each child is born with the first element, an **id,** Freud's term for inborn drives that cause us to seek self-gratification. The id of the newborn is evident in its cries of hunger or pain. The pleasure-seeking id operates throughout life. It demands the immediate fulfillment of basic needs: food, safety, attention, sex, and so on.

The id's drive for immediate gratification, however, runs into a roadblock: primarily the needs of other people, especially those of the parents. To adapt to these constraints, a second component of the personality emerges, which Freud called the ego. The **ego** is

id Freud's term for our inborn basic drives

ego Freud's term for a balancing force between the id and the demands of society

Cultural Diversity *around the* World

Do You See What I See? Eastern and Western Ways of Perceiving and Thinking

WHICH TWO OF THESE ITEMS GO together: a panda, a monkey, and a banana? Please answer before you read further.

You probably said the panda and the monkey. Both are animals, while the banana is a fruit. This is logical.

At least this is the logic of Westerners, and it is difficult for us to see how the answer could be anything else. Someone from Japan, however, is likely to reply that the monkey and the banana go together.

Why? Whereas Westerners typically see categories (animals and fruit), Asians typically see relationships (monkeys eat bananas).

In one study, Japanese and U.S. students were shown a picture of an aquarium that contained one big, fast-moving fish and several smaller fish, along with plants, a rock, and bubbles. Later, when the students were asked what they had seen, the Japanese students were 60 percent more likely to remember background elements. They also referred more to relationships, such as the "the little pink fish was in front of the blue rock."

The students were also shown 96 objects and asked which of them had been in the picture. The Japanese students did much better at remembering when the object was

What do you see when you look at this aquarium? Perception depends not only on biology but also on culture.

shown in its original surroundings. The U.S. students, in contrast, had not noticed the background.

Westerners pay more attention to the focal object, in this case the fish, while Asians are more attuned to the overall surroundings. The implications of this difference run deep: Easterners attribute less causation to actors and more to context, while Westerners minimize the context and place greater emphasis on individual actors.

Differences in how Westerners and Easterners perceive the world and think about it are just being uncovered. We know practically nothing about how these differences originate. *Because these initial findings indicate deep, culturally based, fundamental differences in perception and thinking,* this should prove to be a fascinating area of research.

for your Consideration

In our global village, differences in perception and thinking can have potentially devastating effects. Consider a crisis between the United States and North Korea. How might Easterners and Westerners see the matter differently? How might they attribute cause differently and, without knowing it, "talk past one another"?

Source: Based on Nisbett 2003; Davies 2007.

---

the balancing force between the id and the demands of society that suppress it. The ego also serves to balance the id and the **superego,** the third component of the personality, more commonly called the *conscience.*

The superego represents *culture within us,* the norms and values we have internalized from our social groups. As the *moral* component of the personality, the superego provokes feelings of guilt or shame when we break social rules, or pride and self-satisfaction when we follow them.

According to Freud, when the id gets out of hand, we follow our desires for pleasure and break society's norms. When the superego gets out of hand, we become overly rigid in following those norms, finding ourselves bound in a straitjacket of rules that inhibit our lives. The ego, the balancing force, tries to prevent either the superego or the id from dominating. In the emotionally healthy individual, the ego succeeds in balancing these conflicting demands of the id and the superego. In the maladjusted individual, however, the ego fails to control the inherent conflict between the id and the superego. Either the id or the superego dominates this person, leading to internal confusion and problem behaviors.

Sociological Evaluation   Sociologists appreciate Freud's emphasis on socialization—that the social group into which we are born transmits norms and values that restrain our biological drives. Sociologists, however, object to the view that inborn and subconscious

superego Freud's term for the conscience, the internalized norms and values of our social groups motivations are the primary reasons for human behavior. *This denies the central principle of sociology:* that factors such as social class (income, education, and occupation) and people's roles in groups underlie their behavior (Epstein 1988; Bush and Simmons 1990).

Feminist sociologists have been especially critical of Freud. Although what we just summarized applies to both females and males, Freud assumed that what is "male" is "normal." He even said that females are inferior, castrated males (Chodorow 1990; Gerhard 2000). It is obvious that sociologists need to continue to research how we develop personality.

Kohlberg, Gilligan, and the Development of Morality

If you have observed young children, you know that they focus on immediate gratification and show little or no concern for others. ("Mine!" a 2-year-old will shout, as she grabs a toy from another child.) Yet, at a later age this same child will become considerate of others and concerned with moral issues. How does this change happen?

Kohlberg's Theory Psychologist Lawrence Kohlberg (1975, 1984, 1986; Walsh 2000) concluded that we go through a sequence of stages as we develop morality. Building on Piaget's work, he found that children begin in the *amoral stage* I just described. For them, there is no right or wrong, just personal needs to be satisfied. From about ages 7 to 10, children are in what Kohlberg called a *preconventional stage.* They have learned rules, and they follow them to stay out of trouble. They view right and wrong as what pleases or displeases their parents, friends, and teachers. Their concern is to avoid punishment. At about age 10, they enter the *conventional stage.* During this period, morality means following the norms and values they have learned. In the *postconventional stage,* which Kohlberg says most people don't reach, individuals reflect on abstract principles of right and wrong and judge a behavior according to these principles.

Gilligan and Gender Differences in Morality Carol Gilligan, another psychologist, grew uncomfortable with Kohlberg's conclusions, which didn't seem to match her own experience. Then she noted that Kohlberg had used only boys in his studies. By this point, more women had become social scientists, and they were questioning the assumption male researchers held that female subjects were not necessary because the results of research with boys would apply to girls as well.

Gilligan (1982, 1990) decided to find out if there were differences in how men and women looked at morality. After interviewing about 200 men and women, she concluded that women are more likely to evaluate morality in terms of *personal relationships*. Women want to know how an action affects others. They are more concerned with personal loyalties and with the harm that might come to loved ones. Men, in contrast, tend to think more along the lines of *abstract principles* that define right and wrong. As they see things, an act either matches or violates a code of ethics, and personal relationships have little to do with the matter.

Researchers tested Gilligan's conclusions. They found that *both* men and women use personal relationships and abstract principles when they make moral judgments (Wark and Krebs 1996). Although Gilligan no longer supports her original position (Brannon 1999), the matter is not yet settled. Some researchers have found differences in how men and women make moral judgments (White 1999; Jaffee and Hyde 2000). Others stress that both men and women learn cultural forms of moral reasoning (Tappan 2006).

As with personality, in this vital area of human development, sociological research is also notably absent.

Socialization into Emotions

Emotions, too, are an essential aspect of who we become. Sociologists who research this area of our "humanness" find that emotions also are not simply the results of biology. Like the mind, emotions depend on socialization (Hochschild 1975; 1983; Wang and Roberts 2006). This may sound strange. Don't all people get angry? Doesn't everyone cry? Don't we all feel guilt, shame, sadness, happiness, fear? What has socialization to do with emotions?

Global Emotions   At first, it may look as though socialization is not relevant. Paul Ekman (1980), an anthropologist, studied emotions in several countries. He concluded that everyone experiences six basic emotions: anger, disgust, fear, happiness, sadness, and surprise—and we all show the same facial expressions when we feel these emotions. A person from Zimbabwe, for example, could tell from just the look on an American's face that she is angry, disgusted, or fearful, and we could tell from the Zimbabwean's face that he is happy, sad, or surprised. Because we all show the same facial expressions when we experience these six emotions, Ekman concluded that they are built into our biology, "a product of our genes."

Expressing Emotions   The existence of universal facial expressions for these basic emotions does *not* mean that socialization has no effect on how we express them. Facial expressions are only one way in which we show emotions. Other ways vary with gender. For example, U.S. women are allowed to express their emotions more freely, while U.S. men are expected to be more reserved. To express sudden happiness, or a delighted surprise, for example, women are allowed to make "squeals of glee" in public places. Men are not. Such an expression would be a fundamental violation of their gender role.

Then there are culture, social class, and relationships. Consider culture. Two close Japanese friends who meet after a long separation don't shake hands or hug—they bow. Two Arab men will kiss. Social class is also significant, for it cuts across many other lines, even gender. Upon seeing a friend after a long absence, upper-class women and men are likely to be more reserved in expressing their delight than are lower-class women and men. Relationships also make a big difference. We express our emotions more openly if we are with close friends, more guardedly if we are at a staff meeting with the corporate CEO. A good part of childhood socialization centers on learning these "norms of emotion"—how to express our emotions in a variety of settings.

What We Feel   The matter goes deeper than this. Socialization not only leads to different ways of expressing emotions but even affects *what* we feel (Clark 1997; Shields 2002). People in one culture may even learn to experience feelings that are unknown in another culture. For example, the Ifaluk, who live on the Western Caroline Islands of Micronesia, use the word *fago* to refer to the feelings they have when they see someone

What emotions are these people expressing? Are these emotions global? Is their way of expressing them universal?

suffer. This comes close to what we call sympathy or compassion. But the Ifaluk also use this term to refer to what they feel when they are with someone who has high status, someone they highly respect or admire (Kagan 1984). To us, these are two distinct emotions, and they require separate words to express them.

Research Needed   Although Ekman identified only six emotions that are universal in feeling and facial expression, I suspect that other emotions are common to people around the world—and that everyone shows similar facial expressions when they experience them. I suggest that feelings of helplessness, despair, confusion, and shock are among these universal emotions. We need cross-cultural research to find out whether this is so. We also need research into how children learn to feel and express emotions.

Society Within Us: The Self and Emotions as Social Control

Much of our socialization is intended to turn us into conforming members of society. Socialization into the self and emotions is an essential part of this process, for both the self and our emotions mold our behavior. Although we like to think that we are "free," consider for a moment just some of the factors that influence how we act: the expectations of friends and parents, or neighbors and teachers; classroom norms and college rules; city, state, and federal laws. For example, if in a moment of intense frustration, or out of a devilish desire to shock people, you wanted to tear off your clothes and run naked down the street, what would stop you?

The answer is your socialization—*society within you.* Your experiences in society have resulted in a self that thinks along certain lines and feels particular emotions. This helps to keep you in line. Thoughts such as "Would I get kicked out of school?" and "What would my friends (parents) think if they found out?" represent an awareness of the self in relationship to others. So does the desire to avoid feelings of shame and embarrassment. Our *social mirror,* then—the result of being socialized into a self and emotions—sets up effective controls over our behavior. In fact, socialization into self and emotions is so effective that some people feel embarrassed just thinking about running nude in public!

IN SUM Socialization is essential for our development as human beings. From interaction with others, we learn how to think, reason, and feel. The net result is the shaping of our behavior—including our thinking and emotions—according to cultural standards. This is what sociologists mean when they refer to "*society within us.*"

Socialization into Gender

To channel our behavior—including our thinking and emotions—along expected avenues, society also uses **gender socialization.** By expecting different attitudes and behaviors from us *because* we are male or female, the human group nudges boys and girls in separate directions in life. This foundation of contrasting attitudes and behaviors is so thorough that, as adults, most of us act, think, and even feel according to our culture's guidelines of what is appropriate for our sex.

The significance of gender is emphasized throughout this book, and we focus specifically on gender in Chapter 11. For now, though, let's briefly consider some of the "gender messages" that we get from our family and the mass media.

Gender Messages in the Family

Our parents are the first significant others who teach us our role in this fundamental symbolic division of the world. Sometimes they do so consciously, perhaps by bringing into play pink and blue, colors that have no meaning in themselves but that are now associated with gender. Our parents' own gender orientations have become embedded so firmly that they do most of this teaching without being aware of what they are doing.

This is illustrated in a classic study by psychologists Susan Goldberg and Michael Lewis (1969), whose results have been confirmed by other researchers (Fagot et al. 1985; Connors 1996).

> Goldberg and Lewis asked mothers to bring their 6-month-old infants into their laboratory, supposedly to observe the infants' development. Covertly, however, they also observed the mothers. They found that the mothers kept their daughters closer to them. They also touched their daughters more and spoke to them more frequently than they did to their sons.
>
> By the time the children were 13 months old, the girls stayed closer to their mothers during play, and they returned to their mothers sooner and more often than the boys did. When Goldberg and Lewis set up a barrier to separate the children from their mothers, who were holding toys, the girls were more likely to cry and motion for help; the boys, to try to climb over the barrier.

Goldberg and Lewis concluded that in our society mothers subconsciously reward daughters for being passive and dependent, and sons for being active and independent.

These lessons continue throughout childhood. On the basis of their sex, children are given different kinds of toys. Boys are more likely to get guns and "action figures" that destroy enemies. Girls are more likely to get dolls and jewelry. Some parents try to choose "gender neutral" toys, but kids know what is popular, and they feel left out if they don't have what the other kids have. The significance of toys in gender socialization can be summarized this way: Almost all parents would be upset if someone gave their son Barbie dolls.

gender socialization the ways in which society sets children onto different courses in life *because* they are male or female

The *gender roles* that we learn during childhood become part of our basic orientations to life. Although we refine these roles as we grow older, they remain built around the framework established during childhood.

Parents also let their preschool sons roam farther from home than their preschool daughters, and they subtly encourage the boys to participate in more rough-and-tumble play. They expect their sons to get dirtier and to be more defiant, their daughters to be daintier and more compliant (Gilman 1911/1971; Henslin 2007). In large part, they get what they expect. Such experiences in socialization lie at the heart of the sociological explanation of male–female differences.

We should note, however, that some sociologists would consider biology to be the cause, proposing that Goldberg and Lewis were simply observing innate differences in the children. In short, were the mothers creating those behaviors (the boys wanting to get down and play more, and the girls wanting to be hugged more), or were they responding to natural differences in their children? It is similarly the case with toys. In an intriguing experiment with monkeys, researchers discovered that male monkeys prefer cars and balls more than do female monkeys, who are more likely to prefer dolls and pots (Alexander and Hines 2002). We shall return to this controversial issue of nature versus nurture in Chapter 11.

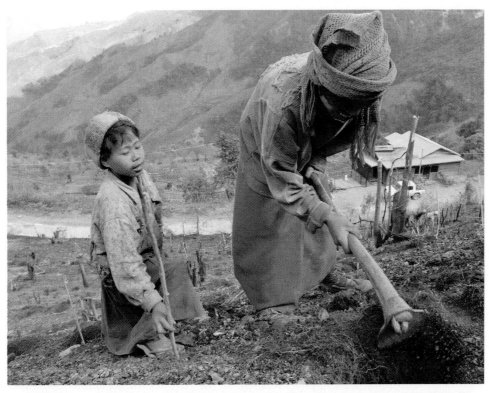

The family is one of the primary ways that we learn gender. Shown here is a woman of the Chin tribe in Myanmar as she farms her field. What gender messages do you think her daughter is learning?

Gender Messages from Peers

Sociologists stress how this sorting process that begins in the family is reinforced as the child is exposed to other aspects of society. Of those other influences, one of the most powerful is the **peer group,** individuals of roughly the same age who are linked by common interests. Examples of peer groups are friends, classmates, and "the kids in the neighborhood." Consider how girls and boys teach one another what it means to be a female or a male in U.S. society.

Let's eavesdrop on a conversation between two eighth-grade girls studied by sociologist Donna Eder (2007). You can see how these girls are reinforcing images of appearance and behavior that they think are appropriate for females:

CINDY: The only thing that makes her look anything is all the makeup . . .

PENNY: She had a picture, and she's standing like this. (Poses with one hand on her hip and one by her head)

CINDY: Her face is probably this skinny, but it looks that big 'cause of all the makeup she has on it.

PENNY: She's ugly, ugly, ugly.

Boys, of course, also reinforce cultural expectations of gender (Pascoe 2003). When sociologist Melissa Milkie (1994) studied junior high school boys, she found that much of their talk centered on movies and TV programs. Of the many images they saw, the boys would single out sex and violence. They would amuse one another by repeating lines, acting out parts, and joking and laughing at what they had seen.

If you know boys in their early teens, you've probably seen behavior like this. You may have been amused, or even have shaken your head in disapproval. As a sociologist, however, Milkie peered beneath the surface. She concluded that the boys were using media images to develop their identity as males. They had gotten the message: To be a "real" male is to be obsessed with sex and violence. Not to joke and laugh about murder and promiscuous sex would have marked a boy as a "weenie," a label to be avoided at all costs.

Gender Messages in the Mass Media

Another powerful influence is the **mass media,** forms of communication that are directed to large audiences. Let's look at how images in advertising, television, and video games reinforce **gender roles,** the behaviors and attitudes considered appropriate for our sex.

Advertising Advertising bombards us so greatly that the average U.S. child watches about 25,000 commercials a year (Moore 2006). Commercials aimed at children are more likely to show girls as cooperative and boys as aggressive. They also are more likely to show girls at home and boys in other locations (Larson 2001). Girls are also more likely to be portrayed as giggly and less capable at tasks (Browne 1998). When advertising directed at adults portrays men as dominant and rugged and women as sexy and submissive, it perpetuates similar stereotypes.

The result is a spectrum of stereotypical, culturally molded images. At one end of this spectrum are cowboys who roam the wide open spaces, while at the other end are scantily clad women, whose assets are intended to sell a variety of products, from automobiles to hamburgers. The portrayal of women with unrealistic physical assets makes female viewers feel inadequate (Kilbourne 2003). This, of course, creates demand for an array of products that promise physical enhancement and romantic success.

Television Television reinforces stereotypes of the sexes. On prime-time television, male characters outnumber female characters. Male characters are also more likely to be portrayed in higher-status positions (Glascock 2001). Sports news also maintains traditional stereotypes. Sociologists who studied the content of televised sports news in Los Angeles found that women athletes receive little coverage (Messner et al. 2003). When they do, they are sometimes trivialized by men newscasters

peer group a group of individuals of roughly the same age who are linked by common interests

mass media forms of communication, such as radio, newspapers, and television that are directed to mass audiences

gender role the behaviors and attitudes considered appropriate because one is a female or a male who focus on humorous events in women's sports or turn the woman athlete into a sexual object. Newscasters even manage to emphasize breasts and bras and to engage in locker-room humor.

Stereotype-breaking characters, in contrast, are a sign of changing times. In comedies, women are more verbally aggressive than men (Glascock 2001). The powers of the teenager *Buffy, The Vampire Slayer,* were remarkable. On *Alias,* Sydney Bristow exhibited extraordinary strength. In cartoons, Kim Possible divides her time between cheerleading practice and saving the world from evil, while, also with tongue in cheek, the Powerpuff Girls are touted as "the most elite kindergarten crime-fighting force ever assembled." This new gender portrayal continues in a variety of programs, such as *Totally Spies.*

The gender messages on these programs are mixed. Girls are powerful, but they have to be skinny and gorgeous and wear the latest fashions, too. This is almost impossible to replicate in real life.

Sports are a powerful agent of socialization. That suma wrestling teaches a form of masculinity should be apparent from this photo. What else do you think these boys are learning?

Video Games The popularity of video games has surged. Even one-fourth of 4- to 6-year-olds play them for an average of an hour a day (Rideout and Vandewater 2003). College students, especially men, relieve stress by escaping into video games (Jones 2003).

Although sociologists have begun to study how the sexes are portrayed in video games, their influence on the players' ideas of gender is still unknown (Dietz 2000; Berger 2002). Because these games are on the cutting edge of society, they sometimes also reflect cutting-edge changes in sex roles, the topic of the Mass Media in Social Life box on the next page.

Anime *Anime* is a Japanese cartoon form targeted at children. Because anime crosses boundaries of video games, television, movies, and books (comic), we shall consider it as a separate category. Perhaps the most recognizable feature of anime is the big-eyed little girls and the fighting little boys. Japanese parents are concerned about the depiction of violence and the antisocial heroes in anime, but to keep peace they reluctantly buy anime for their children (Khattak 2007). As anime becomes popular with U.S. children, it joins a scene in which targeting violence at children is taken for granted—and with its cute characters, anime is unlikely to cause a stir among Americans. Anime's depiction of active, dominant little males and submissive little females leads to the question, of course, of what gender lessons it is giving children.

IN SUM | "Male" and "female" are such powerful symbols that learning them forces us to interpret the world in terms of gender. As children learn their society's symbols of gender, they learn that different behaviors and attitudes are expected of boys and girls. First transmitted by the family, these gender messages are reinforced by other social institutions. As they become integrated into our views of the world, gender messages form a picture of "how" males and females "are." Because gender serves as a primary basis for **social inequality**—giving privileges and obligations to one group of people while denying them to another—gender images are especially important to understand.

social inequality a social condition in which privileges and obligations are given to some but denied to others

agents of socialization people or groups that affect our self-concept, attitudes, behaviors, or other orientations toward life

Agents of Socialization

People and groups that influence our orientations to life—our self-concept, emotions, attitudes, and behavior—are called **agents of socialization.** We have already considered how three of these agents—the family, our peers, and the

Lara Croft, Tomb Raider: Changing Images of Women in the Mass Media

The mass media reflect women's changing role in society. Portrayals of women as passive, as subordinate, or as mere background objects remain, but a new image has broken through. Although this new image exaggerates changes, it also illustrates a fundamental change in gender relations. Lara Croft is an outstanding example of this change.

Like books and magazines, video games are made available to a mass audience. And with digital advances, they have crossed the line from what is traditionally thought of as games to something that more closely resembles interactive movies. Costing an average of $10 million to produce and another $10 million to market, video games now have intricate subplots and use celebrity voices for the characters (Nussenbaum 2004).

Sociologically, what is significant is that the *content* of video games socializes their users. As they play, gamers are exposed not only to action but also to ideas and images. The gender images of video games communicate powerful messages, just as they do in other forms of the mass media.

Lara Croft, an adventure-seeking archeologist and star of *Tomb Raider* and its many sequels, is the essence of the new gender image. Lara is smart, strong, and able to utterly vanquish foes. With both guns blazing, she is the cowboy of the twenty-first century, the term *cowboy* being purposefully chosen, as Lara breaks stereotypical gender roles and dominates what previously was the domain of men. She was the first female protagonist in a

The mass media not only reflect gender stereotypes but also they play a role in changing them. Sometimes they do both simultaneously. The images of Lara Croft not only reflect women's changing role in society, but also, by exaggerating the change, they mold new stereotypes.

field of muscle-rippling, gun-toting macho caricatures (Taylor 1999).

Yet the old remains powerfully encapsulated in the new. As the photos on this page make evident, Lara is a fantasy girl for young men of the digital generation. No matter her foe, no matter her predicament, Lara oozes sex. Her form-fitting outfits, which flatter her voluptuous physique, reflect the mental images of the men who fashioned this digital character.

Lara has caught young men's fancy to such an extent that they have bombarded corporate headquarters with questions about her personal life. Lara is the star of two movies and a comic book. There is even a Lara Croft candy bar.

for your Consideration

A sociologist who reviewed this text said, "It seems that for women to be defined as equal, we have to become symbolic males—warriors with breasts." Why is gender change mostly one-way—females adopting traditional male characteristics? To see why men get to keep their gender roles, these two questions should help: Who is moving into the traditional territory of the other? Do people prefer to imitate power or powerlessness?

Finally, consider just how far stereotypes have actually been left behind. The ultimate goal of the video game, after foes are vanquished, is to see Lara in a nightie.

mass media—influence our ideas of gender. Now we'll look more closely at how agents of socialization prepare us to take our place in society. We shall first consider the family, then the neighborhood, religion, day care, school and peers, sports, and the workplace.

The Family

Around the world, the first group to have a major impact on us is our family. Our experiences in the family are so intense that their influence is lifelong. These experiences lay down our basic sense of self, establishing our initial motivations, values, and beliefs. The family gives us ideas about who we are and what we deserve out of life. It is in the family that we begin to think of ourselves as strong or weak, smart or dumb, good-looking or ugly—or somewhere in between. And as already noted, the lifelong process of defining ourselves as female or male also begins in the family.

The Family and Social Class Middle-class and working-class families socialize their children differently, a process that has life-long consequences on children. Sociologist Melvin Kohn (1959, 1963, 1976, 1977; Kohn et al. 1986) found that working-class parents are mainly concerned that their children stay out of trouble. They also tend to use physical punishment. Middle-class parents, in contrast, focus more on developing their children's curiosity, self-expression, and self-control. They are more likely to reason with their children than to use physical punishment.

This photo captures an extreme form of family socialization. The father seems to be more emotionally involved in the goal—and in more pain—than his daughter, as he pushes her toward the finish line in the Teen Tours of America Kid's Triathlon.

These findings were a sociological puzzle. Just why would working-class and middle-class parents rear their children so differently? Kohn knew that life experiences of some sort held the key, and he found that key in the world of work. Bosses usually tell blue-collar workers exactly what to do. Since blue-collar parents expect their children's lives to be like theirs, they stress obedience. At their work, in contrast, middle-class parents take more initiative. Expecting their children to work at similar jobs, middle-class parents socialize them into the qualities they have found valuable.

Kohn was still puzzled, for some working-class parents act more like middle-class parents, and vice versa. As Kohn probed this puzzle, the pieces fell into place. The key was the parents' type of job. Middle-class office workers, for example, are closely supervised, and Kohn found that they follow the working-class pattern of child rearing, emphasizing conformity. And some blue-collar workers, such as those who do home repairs, have a good deal of freedom. These workers follow the middle-class model in rearing their children (Pearlin and Kohn 1966; Kohn and Schooler 1969).

Working-class and middle-class parents also have different views of how children develop, which has interesting consequences for children's play (Lareau 2002). Working-class parents think of children as developing naturally, while middle-class parents think that children need a lot of guidance to develop correctly. As a result, working-class parents see their job as providing food, shelter, and comfort, with the child's development taking care of itself. They set limits ("Don't go near the railroad tracks"), and let their children play as they wish. Middle-class parents, in contrast, want to structure their children's play to help them develop knowledge and social skills. For example, they may want them to play baseball, not for the enjoyment of the sport, but to help them learn how to be team players.

The Neighborhood

As all parents know, some neighborhoods are better than others for their children. Parents try to move to those neighborhoods—if they can afford them. Their commonsense evaluations are borne out by sociological research. Children from poor neighborhoods are more likely to get in trouble with the law, to become pregnant, to drop out of school, and even to have worse mental health in later life (Brooks-Gunn et al. 1997; Sampson et al. 2001; Wheaton and Clarke 2003; Yonas et al. 2006).

Sociologists have also found that the residents of more affluent neighborhoods watch out for the children more than do the residents of poor neighborhoods (Sampson et al. 1999). This isn't because the adults in poor neighborhoods care less about children. Rather, the more affluent neighborhoods have less transition, so the adults are more likely to know the local children and their parents. This better equips them to help keep the children safe and out of trouble.

Religion

By influencing values, religion becomes a key component in people's ideas of right and wrong. Religion is so important to Americans that half of them belong to a local congregation, and during a typical week, two of every five Americans report that they attend a religious service (Gallup Poll 2007; *Statistical Abstract* 2007:Tables 73, 75). Religion is significant even for people who are reared in nonreligious homes; religious ideas pervade U.S. society, providing basic ideas of morality for us all.

The influence of religion extends to many areas of our lives. For example, participation in religious services teaches us not only beliefs about the hereafter but also ideas about what kinds of dress, speech, and manners are appropriate for formal occasions. Religion is so significant that we shall examine its influence in a separate chapter (Chapter 18).

Day Care

It is rare for social science research to make national news, but occasionally it does. This is what happened when researchers published their findings on 1,200 kindergarten children they had studied since their first month after birth. They had observed the children multiple times both at home and at day care. They had also videotaped and made detailed notes on the children's interaction with their mothers (National Institute of Child Health and Human Development 1999; Guensburg 2001). What caught the media's attention? Children who spend more time in day care have weaker bonds with their mothers and are less affectionate to them. They are also less cooperative with others and more likely to fight, to be cruel, and to be "mean." By the time they get to kindergarten, they are more likely to talk back to teachers and to disrupt the classroom. This holds true regardless of the quality of the day care, the family's social class, or whether the child is a girl or a boy (Belsky 2006). On the positive side, the children also scored higher on language tests.

Are we, then, producing a generation of "smart but mean" children? This question has come to bother many, especially since the study was designed so well and an even larger study of children in England has come up with similar findings (Belsky 2006). Some point out that the differences between children who spend a lot of time in day care and those who spend less time is slight. Others stress that with several million children in day care (*Sociological Abstract* 2007:Table 564), slight differences can be significant for society. The researchers are following these children as they continue in school. The most recent report on the children, when they were in the 6th grade, indicates that these patterns are continuing (Belsky et al. 2007).

The School

Part of the **manifest function,** or *intended* purpose, of formal education is to teach knowledge and skills, such as reading, writing, and arithmetic. The teaching of such skills is certainly part of socialization, but so are the schools' **latent functions,** their *unintended* consequences that help the social system. Let's look at this less visible aspect of education.

At home, children learn attitudes and values that match their family's situation in life. At school, they learn a broader perspective that helps prepare them to take a role in the world beyond the family. At home, for example, a child may have been the almost exclusive focus of doting parents, but in school, the child learns *universality*—that

manifest functions the intended beneficial consequences of people's actions

latent functions unintended beneficial consequences of people's actions the same rules apply to everyone, regardless of who their parents are or how special they may be at home. The Cultural Diversity box below explores how these new values and ways of looking at the world sometimes even replace those the child learns at home.

Cultural Diversity *in the* United States

Caught Between Two Worlds

IT IS A STRUGGLE TO LEARN a new culture, for its behaviors and ways of thinking contrast with the ones already learned. This can lead to inner turmoil. One way to handle the conflict is to cut ties with your first culture. This, however, can create a sense of loss, perhaps one that is recognized only later in life.

Richard Rodriguez, a literature professor and essayist, was born to working-class Mexican immigrants. Wanting their son to be successful in their adopted land, his parents named him Richard instead of Ricardo. While his English-Spanish hybrid name indicates the parents' aspirations for their son, it was also an omen of the conflict that Richard would experience.

Like other children of Mexican immigrants, Richard's first language was Spanish—a rich mother tongue that introduced him to the world. Until the age of 5, when he began school, Richard knew only fifty words in English. He describes what happened when he began school:

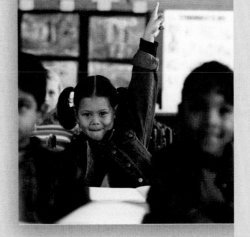

> The change came gradually but early. When I was beginning grade school, I noted to myself the fact that the classroom environment was so different in its styles and assumptions from my own family environment that survival would essentially entail a choice between both worlds. When I became a student, I was literally "remade"; neither I nor my teachers considered anything I had known before as relevant. I had to forget most of what my culture had provided, because to remember it was a disadvantage. The past and its cultural values became detachable, like a piece of clothing grown heavy on a warm day and finally put away.

As happened to millions of immigrants before him, whose parents spoke German, Polish, Italian, and so on, learning English eroded family and class ties and ate away at his ethnic roots. For him, language and education were not simply devices that eased the transition to the dominant culture. Instead, they slashed at the roots that had given him life.

To face conflicting cultures is to confront a fork in the road. Some turn one way and withdraw from the new culture— a clue that helps to explain why so many Latinos drop out of

U.S. schools. Others go in the opposite direction. Cutting ties with their family and cultural roots, they wholeheartedly adopt the new culture.

Rodriguez took the second road. He excelled in his new language—so well, in fact, that he graduated from Stanford University and then became a graduate student in English at the University of California at Berkeley. He was even awarded a prestigious Fulbright fellowship to study English Renaissance literature at the British Museum.

But the past wouldn't let Rodriguez alone. Prospective employers were impressed with his knowledge of Renaissance literature. At job interviews, however, they would skip over the Renaissance training and ask him if he would teach the Mexican novel and be an adviser to Latino students. Rodriguez was also haunted by the image of his grandmother, the warmth of the culture he had left behind, and the language and thought to which he had become a stranger.

Richard Rodriguez represents millions of immigrants—not just those of Latino origin but those from other cultures, too—who want to be a part of life in the United States without betraying their past. They fear that to integrate into U.S. culture is to lose their roots. They are caught between two cultures, each beckoning, each offering rich rewards.

for your Consideration

I saw this conflict firsthand with my father, who did not learn English until after the seventh grade (his last in school). German was left behind, but broken English and awkward expressions remained for a lifetime. Then, too, there were the lingering emotional connections to old ways, as well as the suspicions, haughtiness, and slights of more assimilated Americans. His longing for security by grasping the past was combined with his wanting to succeed in the everyday reality of the new culture. Have you seen anything similar?

Sources: Based on Richard Rodriguez 1975, 1982, 1990, 1991, 1995.

Schools are one of the primary agents of socialization. One of their chief functions is to sort young people into the adult roles thought appropriate for them, and to teach them the attitudes and skills that match those roles. What sorts of attitudes and adult roles do you think this 8-year old is learning from the 15-year old cheerleader? Are these attitudes and roles functions or dysfunctions—or both?

Sociologists have also identified a *hidden curriculum* in our schools. This term refers to values that, although not explicitly taught, are part of a school's "message." For example, the stories and examples that are used to teach math and English may bring with them lessons in patriotism, democracy, justice, and honesty. There is also a *corridor curriculum,* what students teach one another outside the classroom. Unfortunately, the corridor curriculum seems to emphasize racism, sexism, illicit ways to make money, and coolness (Hemmings 1999). You can determine for yourself which of these is functional and which is dysfunctional.

Conflict theorists point out that social class separates children into different worlds. Children born to wealthy parents go to private schools, where they learn skills and values that match their higher position. Children born to middle- and lower-class parents go to public schools, which further refine the separate worlds of social class. Middle-class children learn that good jobs, even the professions, beckon, while children from blue-collar families learn that not many of "their kind" will become professionals or leaders. This is one of the many reasons that children from blue-collar families are less likely to take college prep courses or to go to college. In short, schools around the world reflect and reinforce their nation's social class, economic, and political systems. We will return to this topic in the chapter on education (Chapter 17).

Peer Groups

As a child's experiences with agents of socialization broaden, the influence of the family decreases. Entry into school marks only one of many steps in this transfer of allegiance. One of the most significant aspects of education is that it exposes children to peer groups that help them resist the efforts of parents and schools to socialize them.

When sociologists Patricia and Peter Adler (1998) observed children at two elementary schools in Colorado, they saw how children separate themselves by sex and develop their own worlds with unique norms. The norms that made boys popular were athletic ability, coolness, and toughness. For girls, popularity was based on family background, physical appearance (clothing and use of makeup), and the ability to attract popular boys. In this children's subculture, academic achievement pulled in opposite directions: For boys, high grades lowered their popularity, but for girls, good grades increased their standing among peers.

You know from your own experience how compelling peer groups are. It is almost impossible to go against a peer group, whose cardinal rule seems to be "conformity or rejec-

Gradeschool boys and girls often separate themselves by gender, as in this lunchroom in Schenectady, New York. They generally also prefer to play all-girl and all-boy games. The socialization that occurs during self-segregation by gender is a topic of study by sociologists.

tion." Anyone who doesn't do what the others want becomes an "outsider," a "nonmember," an "outcast." For preteens and teens just learning their way around in the world, it is not surprising that the peer group rules.

As a result, the standards of our peer groups tend to dominate our lives. If your peers, for example, listen to rap, nortec, death metal, rock and roll, country, or gospel, it is almost inevitable that you also prefer that kind of music. It is the same for clothing styles and dating standards. Peer influences also extend to behaviors that violate social norms. If your peers are college-bound and upwardly striving, that is most likely what you will be; but if they use drugs, cheat, and steal, you are likely to do so, too.

Sports and Competitive Success

Sports are another powerful socializing agent. Everyone recognizes that sports teach not only physical skills but also values. In fact, "teaching youngsters to be team players" is often given as the reason for financing organized sports.

Sports have deep effects on the self-image. Boys who are successful in sports, especially combative sports such as football, are considered to be more macho or masculine (Pascoe 2003). Boys who fail at sports have to confront negative images of being less masculine, in some cases, even of being sissies. I am sure that this doesn't surprise you. It is likely that your own experiences in social life make this seem obvious. The implications of this aspect of sports, however, are far reaching. Sociologist Michael Messner (1990) points out that deriving such emotionally gratifying rewards from success in sports encourages boys to develop *instrumental* relationships—those based on what they can get out of people. (This would also apply to other areas of competitive success, not just to sports.)

I am sure you can see how being socialized into relating instrumentally affects gender relationships. Competitive success fosters the strong motivation that boys already have to see what they can get from girls. Girls, in contrast, have traditionally been socialized to construct more of their identities around meaningful relationships, not on instrumental ones. With sports and competitive success in other areas apparently becoming more important in the formation of female identities, it will be interesting to see what effects this has on women.

The Workplace

Another agent of socialization that comes into play somewhat later in life is the workplace. Those initial jobs that we take in high school and college are much more than just a way to earn a few dollars. From the people we rub shoulders with at work, we learn not only a set of skills but also perspectives on the world.

Most of us eventually become committed to some particular line of work, often after trying out many jobs. This may involve **anticipatory socialization,** learning to play a role before entering it. Anticipatory socialization is a sort of mental rehearsal for some future activity. We may talk to people who work in a particular career, read novels about that type of work, or take a summer internship in that field. This allows us to gradually identify with the role, to become aware of what would be expected of us. Sometimes this helps people avoid committing themselves to an unrewarding career, as with some of my students who tried student teaching, found that they couldn't stand it, and then moved on to other fields more to their liking.

An intriguing aspect of work as a socializing agent is that the more you participate in a line of work, the more the work becomes a part of your self-concept. Eventually you come to think of yourself so much in terms of the job that if someone asks you to describe yourself, you are likely to include the job in your self-description. You might say, "I'm a teacher," "I'm a nurse," or "I'm a sociologist."

Resocialization

What does a woman who has just become a nun have in common with a man who has just divorced? The answer is that they both are undergoing **resocialization;** that is, they are learning new norms, values, attitudes, and behaviors to

anticipatory socialization because one anticipates a future role, one learns parts of it now

resocialization the process of learning new norms, values, attitudes, and behaviors match their new situation in life. In its most common form, resocialization occurs each time we learn something contrary to our previous experiences. A new boss who insists on a different way of doing things is resocializing you. Most resocialization is mild—only a slight modification of things we have already learned.

Resocialization can also be intense. People who join Alcoholics Anonymous (AA), for example, are surrounded by reformed drinkers who affirm the destructive effects of excessive drinking. Some students experience an intense period of resocialization when they leave high school and start college—especially during those initially scary days before they find companions, start to fit in, and feel comfortable. To join a cult or to begin psychotherapy is even more profound, for these events expose people to ideas that conflict with their previous ways of looking at the world. If these ideas "take," not only does the individual's behavior change but also he or she learns a fundamentally different way of looking at life.

Total Institutions

Relatively few of us experience the powerful agent of socialization that sociologist Erving Goffman (1961) called the **total institution.** He coined this term to refer to a place in which people are cut off from the rest of society and where they come under almost total control of the officials who are in charge. Boot camp, prisons, concentration camps, convents, some religious cults, and some boarding schools, such as West Point, are total institutions.

A person entering a total institution is greeted with a **degradation ceremony** (Garfinkel 1956), an attempt to remake the self by stripping away the individual's current identity and stamping a new one in its place. This unwelcome greeting may involve fingerprinting, photographing, shaving the head, and banning the individual's *personal identity kit* (items such as jewelry, hairstyles, clothing, and other body decorations used to express individuality). Newcomers may be ordered to strip, undergo an examination (often in a humiliating, semipublic setting), and then to put on a uniform that designates their new status. (For prisoners, the public reading of the verdict and being led away in handcuffs by armed police are also part of the degradation ceremony.)

Total institutions are isolated from the public. The walls, bars, gates, and guards not only keep the inmates in but also keep outsiders out. Staff members closely supervise the day-to-day lives of the residents. Eating, sleeping, showering, recreation—all are standardized. Inmates learn that their previous statuses—student, worker, spouse, parent—mean nothing. The only thing that counts is their current status.

No one leaves a total institution unscathed, for the experience brands an indelible mark on the individual's self and colors the way he or she sees the world. Boot camp, as described in the Down-to-Earth Sociology box on the next page, is brutal but swift. Prison, in contrast, is brutal and prolonged. Neither recruit nor prisoner, however, has difficulty in pinpointing how the institution affected the self.

total institution a place in which people are cut off from the rest of society and are almost totally controlled by the officials who run the place

degradation ceremony a term coined by Harold Garfinkel to describe an attempt to remake the self by stripping away an individual's current identity and stamping a new one in its place

life course the stages of our life as we go from birth to death

Socialization Through the Life Course

You are at a particular stage in your life now, and college is a good part of it. You know that you have more stages ahead of you as you go through life. These stages, from birth to death, are called the **life course** (Elder 1975; 1999). The sociological significance of the life course is twofold. First, as you pass through a stage, it affects your behavior and orientations. You simply don't think about life in the same way when you are 30, are married, and have a baby and a mortgage, as you do when you are 18 or 20, single, and in college. (Actually, you don't even see life the same as a freshman and as a senior.) Second, your life course differs by social location. Your social class, race-ethnicity, and gender, for example, map out distinctive worlds of experience. Consequently, the typical life course differs for males and females, the rich and the poor, and so on. To emphasize this major sociological point, in the sketch that follows I will stress the *historical* setting of people's lives. Because of your particular social location, your own life course may differ from this sketch, which is a composite of stages that others have suggested (Levinson 1978; Carr et al. 1995; Quadagno 2007).

Down-to-Earth Sociology

Boot Camp as a Total Institution

THE BUS ARRIVES AT PARRIS ISLAND, South Carolina, at 3 A.M. The early hour is no accident. The recruits are groggy, confused. Up to a few hours ago, the young men were ordinary civilians. Now, as a sergeant sneeringly calls them "maggots," their heads are buzzed (25 seconds per recruit), and they are quickly thrust into the harsh world of Marine boot camp.

Buzzing the boys' hair is just the first step in stripping away their identity so that the Marines can stamp a new one in its place. The uniform serves the same purpose. There is a ban on using the first person "I." Even a simple request must be made in precise Marine style or it will not be acknowledged. ("Sir, Recruit Jones requests permission to make a head call, Sir.")

Every intense moment of the next eleven weeks reminds the recruits that they are joining a subculture of self-discipline. Here pleasure is suspect and sacrifice is good. As they learn the Marine way of talking, walking, and thinking, they are denied the diversions they once took for granted: television, cigarettes, cars, candy, soft drinks, video games, music, alcohol, drugs, and sex.

Lessons are bestowed with fierce intensity. When Sgt. Carey checks brass belt buckles, Recruit Robert Shelton nervously blurts, "I don't have one." Sgt. Carey's face grows red as his neck cords bulge. "I?" he says, his face just inches from the recruit. With spittle flying from his mouth, he screams, " 'I' is gone!"

"Nobody's an individual" is the lesson that is driven home again and again. "You are a team, a Marine. Not a civilian. Not black or white, not Hispanic or Indian or some hyphenated American—but a Marine. You will live like a Marine, fight like a Marine, and, if necessary, die like a Marine."

Each day begins before dawn with close-order formations. The rest of the day is filled with training in hand-to-hand combat, marching, running, calisthenics, Marine history, and—always—following orders.

"An M-16 can blow someone's head off at 500 meters," Sgt. Norman says. "That's beautiful, isn't it?"

"Yes, sir!" shout the platoon's fifty-nine voices.

"Pick your nose!" Simultaneously fifty nine index fingers shoot into nostrils.

The pressure to conform is intense. Those who are sent packing for insubordination or suicidal tendencies are mocked in cadence during drills. ("Hope you like the sights you see/Parris Island casualty.") As lights go out at 9 P.M., the exhausted recruits perform the day's last task: The entire platoon, in unison, chants the virtues of the Marines.

Recruits are constantly scrutinized. Subperformance is not accepted, whether it be a dirty rifle or a loose thread on a uniform. The subperformer is shouted at, derided, humiliated. The group suffers for the individual. If a recruit is slow, the entire platoon is punished.

The system works.

One of the new Marines (until graduation, they are recruits, not Marines) says, "I feel like I've joined a new society or religion."

He has.

for your Consideration

Of what significance is the recruits' degradation ceremony? Why are recruits not allowed video games, cigarettes, or calls home? Why are the Marines so unfair as to punish an entire platoon for the failure of an individual? Use concepts in this chapter to explain why the system works.

Sources: Based on Garfinkel 1956; Goffman 1961; Ricks 1995; Dyer 2007.

Childhood (from birth to about age 12)

Consider how different your childhood would have been if you had grown up in another historical era. Historian Philippe Ariès (1965) noticed that in European paintings from about 1000 to 1800 A.D. children were always dressed in adult clothing. If they were not depicted stiffly posed, as in a family portrait, they were shown doing adult activities.

From this, Ariès drew a conclusion that sparked a debate among historians: He believed that during this era in Europe, childhood was not regarded as a special time of life. He said that adults viewed children as miniature adults, and put them to work at very early ages. At the age of 7, for example, a boy might leave home for good to learn to be a jeweler or a stonecutter. A girl, in contrast, stayed home until she married, but by the age of 7 she was expected to assume her share of the household tasks. Historians do

In contemporary Western societies such as the United States, children are viewed as innocent and in need of protection from adult responsibilities such as work and self-support. Ideas of childhood vary historically and cross-culturally. From paintings, such as this 1642 British painting by the Le Nain brothers, "A Woman and Five Children," some historians conclude that Europeans once viewed children as miniature adults who assumed adult roles at the earliest opportunity.

not deny that these were the customs of that time, but some say that Ariès' conclusion is ridiculous. They say that other evidence of that period indicates that childhood was viewed as a special time of life (Orme 2002).

Having children work like adults did not disappear with the Middle Ages. It is still common in the Least Industrialized Nations. The photo on the upper left of page 257 provides a startling example of this custom—reflecting not just different activities but also a view of children different from the one common in the Most Industrialized Nations.

In earlier centuries, parents and teachers also considered it their moral duty to terrorize children to keep them in line. They would lock children in dark closets, frighten them with bedtime stories of death and hellfire, and force them to witness gruesome events. Consider this:

> A common moral lesson involved taking children to visit the gibbet [an upraised post on which executed bodies were left hanging from chains], where they were forced to inspect rotting corpses hanging there as an example of what happens to bad children when they grow up. Whole classes were taken out of school to witness hangings, and parents would often whip their children afterwards to make them remember what they had seen. (DeMause 1975)

Industrialization transformed the way we perceive children. With children having the leisure to go to school, they came to be thought of as tender and innocent, as needing more adult care, comfort, and protection. Over time, such attitudes of dependency grew, and today we view children as needing gentle guidance if they are to develop emotionally, intellectually, morally, even physically. We take our view for granted—after all, it is only "common sense." Yet, as you can see, our view is not "natural." It is, instead, rooted in geography and history.

Technology can also change the nature of childhood. When television shows images of murder, rape, war, and other violence, children of a tender age learn about a world that used to be kept hidden from them (Lee 2001).

In many societies, manhood is not bestowed upon males simply because they reach a certain age. Manhood, rather, signifies a standing in the community that must be achieved. Shown here is an initiation ceremony in Indonesia, where boys, to lay claim to the status of manhood, must jump over this barrier.

IN SUM | Childhood is more than biology. Everyone's childhood occurs at some point in history, and is embedded in particular social locations, especially social class and gender. *These social factors are as vital as our biology, for they determine what childhood will be like for us.* Although a child's *biological* characteristics (such as being small and dependent) are universal, the child's *social* experiences (the kind of life the child lives) are not. Because of this, sociologists say that childhood varies from culture to culture.

Adolescence (ages 13–17)

Adolescence is not a "natural" age division. It is a social invention. In earlier centuries, people simply moved from childhood into young adulthood, with no stopover in between. The Industrial Revolution brought such an abundance of material surpluses, however, that for the first time in history, millions of people in their teens were able to remain outside the labor force. At the same time, education became a more important factor in achieving success. The convergence of these two forces in industrialized societies created a gap between childhood and adulthood. In the early 1900s, the term *adolescence* was coined to indicate this new stage in life (Hall 1904), one that has become renowned for inner turmoil.

To ground the self-identity of children and mark their passage into adulthood, tribal societies hold *initiation rites.* In the industrialized world, however, adolescents must "find" themselves on their own. As they attempt to carve out an identity that is distinct from both the "younger" world being left behind and the "older" world that is still out of range, adolescents develop their own subcultures, with distinctive clothing, hairstyles, language, gestures, and music. We usually fail to realize that contemporary society, not biology, created this period of inner turmoil that we call *adolescence.*

Transitional Adulthood (ages 18–29)

If society invented adolescence, can it also invent other periods of life? As Figure 3.2 on the next page illustrates, this is actually happening now. Postindustrial societies are adding a period of extended youth to the life course, which sociologists call **transitional adulthood** (also known as *adultolescence*). After high school, millions of young adults go to college, where they postpone adult responsibilities. They are mostly freed from the control of their parents, yet they don't have to support themselves. Even after college, many return home, so they can live cheaply while they establish themselves in a career—and, of course, continue to "find themselves." During this time, people are "neither psychological adolescents nor sociological adults" (Keniston 1971). At some point during this period of extended youth, young adults gradually ease into adult responsibilities. They take a full-time job, become serious about a career, engage in courtship rituals, get married—and go into debt.

transitional adulthood a term that refers to a period following high school when young adults have not yet taken on the responsibilities ordinarily associated with adulthood; also called *adultolescence*

The Middle Years (ages 30–65)

The Early Middle Years (ages 30–49) During their early middle years, most people are more sure of themselves and of their goals in life. As with any point in the life course, however, the self can receive severe jolts. Common in this period are divorce

Figure 3.2 Transitional Adulthood: A New Stage in the Life Course

Who has completed the transition?

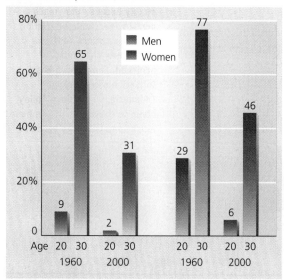

The data show the percent who have completed the transition to adulthood, as measured by leaving home, finishing school, getting married, having a child, and being financially independent.

Source: Furstenberg et al. 2004.

and losing jobs. It may take years for the self to stabilize after such ruptures.

The early middle years pose a special challenge for many U.S. women, who have been given the message, especially by the media, that they can "have it all." They can be superworkers, superwives, and supermoms—all rolled into one. The reality, however, usually consists of conflicting pressures—too little time and too many demands. Something has to give. Attempts to resolve this dilemma are often compounded by another hard reality—that during gender socialization, their husbands learned that housework and child care are not "masculine." In short, adjustments continue in this and all phases of life.

The Later Middle Years (ages 50–65)   During the later middle years, health issues and mortality begin to loom large as people feel their bodies change, especially if they watch their parents become frail, fall ill, and die. The consequence is a fundamental reorientation in thinking—*from time since birth to time left to live* (Neugarten 1976). With this changed orientation, people attempt to evaluate the past and come to terms with what lies ahead. They compare what they have accomplished with what they had hoped to achieve. Many people also find themselves caring not only for their own children but also for their aging parents. Because of this set of burdens, which is often crushing, people in the later middle years sometimes are called the "sandwich generation."

Life during this stage isn't stressful for everyone. Many find late middle age to be the most comfortable period of their lives. They enjoy job security and a standard of living higher than ever before; they have a bigger house (one that may even be paid for), newer cars, and longer and more exotic vacations. The children are grown, the self is firmly planted, and fewer upheavals are likely to occur.

As they anticipate the next stage of life, however, most people do not like what they see.

The Older Years (about age 65 on)

The Early Older Years   In industrialized societies, the older years begin around the mid-60s. This, too, is recent, for in agricultural societies, when most people died early, old age was thought to begin at around age 40. Industrialization brought about improved nutrition and public health, which prolonged life. Today, people in good health who are over the age of 65 often experience this period not as old age, but as an extension of the middle years. People who continue to work or to do things they enjoy are less likely to perceive themselves as old (Neugarten 1977). Although frequency of sex declines, most men and women in their 60s and 70s are sexually active (Denney and Quadagno 1992).

Because we have a self and can reason abstractly, we can contemplate death. Initially, we regard death as a vague notion, a remote possibility. But as people see their friends die and observe their own bodies no longer functioning as before, the thought of death becomes less abstract. Increasingly during this stage in the life course, people feel that "time is closing in" on them.

The Later Older Years   As with the preceding periods of life except the first one, there is no precise beginning point to this last stage. For some, the 75th birthday may mark entry into this period of life. For others, that marker may be the 80th or even the 85th birthday. For most, this stage is marked by growing frailty and illness; for all who reach this stage, it is ended by death. For some, the physical decline is slow, and a rare few manage to see their 100th birthday mentally alert and in good physical health.

The Sociological Significance of the Life Course

The sociological significance of the life course is that it does not merely represent biology, things that naturally occur to all of us as we add years to our lives. Rather, *social* factors influence our life course. As you just saw, *when* you live makes a huge difference in the course that your life takes. And with today's rapid social change, the difference in historical time does not have to be vast. Being born just ten years earlier or later may mean that you experience war or peace, an expanding economy or a depression—factors that vitally affect what happens to you not just during childhood but throughout your life.

Your *social location,* such as social class, gender, and race-ethnicity is also highly significant. Your experience of society's events will be similar to that of people who share your social location, but different from that of people who do not. If you are poor, for example, you likely will feel older faster than most wealthy people for whom life is much less demanding. Individual factors—such as your health, or marrying early or entering college late—may throw your life course "out of sequence," making it atypical.

For all these reasons, this sketch of the life course may not adequately reflect your own past, present, and future. As sociologist C. Wright Mills (1959) would say, because employers are beating a path to your door, or failing to do so, you are more inclined to marry, to buy a house, and to start a family—or to postpone these life course events, perhaps indefinitely. In short, changing times change lives, steering the life course into different directions.

This January 1937 photo from Sneedville, Tennessee, shows Eunice Johns, age 9, and her husband, Charlie Johns, age 22. The groom gave his wife a doll as a wedding gift. The new husband and wife planned to build a cabin, and, as Charlie Johns phrased it, "go to housekeepin'."

This photo illustrates the cultural relativity of life stages, which we sometimes mistake as fixed. It also is interesting from a symbolic interactionist perspective—that of changing definitions. Today, such a marriage would land the husband in jail and the wife in protective custody.

Are We Prisoners of Socialization?

 From our discussion of socialization, you might conclude that sociologists think of people as robots: The socialization goes in, and the behavior comes out. People cannot help what they do, think, or feel, for everything is simply a result of their exposure to socializing agents.

Sociologists do *not* think of people in this way. Although socialization is powerful, and profoundly affects us all, we have a self. Established in childhood and continually modified by later experience, the self is dynamic. It is not a sponge that passively absorbs influences from the environment, but, rather, a vigorous, essential part of our being that allows us to act on our environment.

Indeed, it is precisely because individuals are not robots that their behavior is so hard to predict. The countless reactions of other people merge in each of us. As the self develops, each person internalizes or "puts together" these innumerable reactions, producing a unique whole called the *individual.* Each individual uses his or her own mind to reason and to make choices in life.

In this way, *each of us is actively involved in the construction of the self.* For example, although our experiences in the family lay down the basic elements of our personality, including fundamental orientations to life, we are not doomed to keep those orientations if we do not like them. We can purposely expose ourselves to groups and ideas that we prefer. Those experiences, in turn, will have their own effects on our self. In short, although socialization is powerful, we can change even the self within the limitations of the framework laid down by our social locations. And that self—along with the options available within society—is the key to our behavior.

Summary *and* Review

What Is Human Nature?

How much of our human characteristics come from "nature" (heredity) and how much from "nurture" (the social environment)?

Observations of isolated, institutionalized, and **feral children** help to answer this question, as do experiments with monkeys that were raised in isolation. Language and intimate social interaction—aspects of "nurture"—are essential to the development of what we consider to be human characteristics. Pp. 66–70.

Socialization into the Self and Mind

How do we acquire a self?

Humans are born with the *capacity* to develop a **self,** but the self must be socially constructed; that is, its contents depend on social interaction. According to Charles Horton Cooley's concept of the **looking-glass self,** our self develops as we internalize others' reactions to us. George Herbert Mead identified the ability to **take the role of the other** as essential to the development of the self. Mead concluded that even the mind is a social product. Pp. 70–72.

How do children develop reasoning skills?

Jean Piaget identified four stages that children go through as they develop the ability to reason: (1) *sensorimotor,* in which understanding is limited to sensory stimuli such as touch and sight; (2) *preoperational,* the ability to use symbols; (3) *concrete operational,* in which reasoning ability is more complex but not yet capable of complex abstractions; and (4) *formal operational,* or abstract thinking. Pp. 72–73.

Learning Personality, Morality, and Emotions

How do sociologists evaluate Freud's psychoanalytic theory of personality development?

Freud viewed personality development as the result of our **id** (inborn, self-centered desires) clashing with the demands of society. The **ego** develops to balance the id and the **superego,** the conscience. Sociologists, in contrast, do not examine inborn or subconscious motivations, but, instead, how *social* factors—social class, gender, religion, education, and so forth—underlie personality development. Pp. 73–75.

How do people develop morality?

Children are born without morality, and, according to Kohlberg, they go through four stages in learning it: amoral, preconventional, conventional, and postconventional. As they make moral decisions, both men and women use personal relationships and abstract principles. Pp. 75–76.

How does socialization influence emotions?

Socialization influences not only *how we express our emotions* but also *what emotions we feel.* Socialization into emotions is one of the means by which society produces conformity. Pp. 76–78.

Socialization into Gender

How does gender socialization affect our sense of self?

Gender socialization—sorting males and females into different roles—is a primary means of controlling human behavior. Children receive messages about gender even in infancy. A society's ideals of sex-linked behaviors are reinforced by its social institutions. Pp. 78–81.

Agents of Socialization

What are the main agents of socialization?

The **agents of socialization** include the family, neighborhood, religion, day care, school, **peer groups,** sports, the **mass media**, and the workplace. Each has its particular influences in socializing us into becoming full-fledged members of society. Pp. 81–87.

Resocialization

What is resocialization?

Resocialization is the process of learning new norms, values, attitudes, and behavior. Most resocialization is voluntary, but some, as with residents of **total institutions,** is involuntary. Pp. 87–88.

Socialization Through the Life Course

Does socialization end when we enter adulthood?

Socialization occurs throughout the life course. In industrialized societies, the **life course** can be divided into childhood, adolescence, young adulthood, the middle years, and the older years. The West is adding a new stage, transitional adulthood. Life course patterns vary by social location such as history, gender, race-ethnicity, and social class, as well as by individual experiences such as health and age at marriage. Pp. 88–93.

Are We Prisoners of Socialization?

Although socialization is powerful, we are not merely the sum of our socialization experiences. Just as socialization influences human behavior, so humans act on their environment and influence even their self concept. P. 93.

Thinking Critically
about Chapter 3

1. What two agents of socialization have influenced you the most? Can you pinpoint their influence on your attitudes, beliefs, values, or other orientations to life?
2. Summarize your views of the "proper" relationships of women and men. What in your socialization has led you to have these views?
3. What is your location in the life course? How does the text's summary of that location match your experiences? Explain the similarities and differences.

Additional Resources

What can you use MySocLab for?

 www.mysoclab.com

- **Study and Review:** Pre and Post-Tests, Practice Tests, Flash Cards, Individualized Study Plans.
- **Current Events:** *Sociology in the News,* the daily *New York Times,* and more.
- **Research and Writing:** *Research Navigator, Writing About Sociology,* and more.

Where Can I Read More on This Topic?

Suggested readings for this chapter are listed at the back of this book.

Social Structure and Social Interaction

Jacob Lawrence, *Street Scene (Boy with Kite)*, 1962

My curiosity had gotten the better of me. When the sociology convention finished, I climbed aboard the first city bus that came along. I didn't know where the bus was going, and I didn't know where I would spend the night.

"Maybe I overdid it this time," I thought, as the bus began winding down streets I had never seen before. Actually, this was my first visit to Washington, D.C., so everything was unfamiliar to me. I had no destination, no plans, not even a map. I carried no billfold, just a driver's license shoved into my jeans for emergency identification, some pocket change, and a $10 bill tucked into my sock. My goal was simple: If I saw something interesting, I would get off the bus and check it out.

"Nothing but the usual things," I mused, as we passed row after row of apartment buildings and stores. I could see myself riding buses the entire night. Then something caught my eye. Nothing spectacular—just groups of people clustered around a large circular area where several streets intersected.

I climbed off the bus and made my way to what turned out to be Dupont Circle. I took a seat on a sidewalk bench and began to observe what was going on around me. As the scene came into focus, I noticed several streetcorner men drinking and joking with one another. One of the men broke from his companions and sat down next to me. As we talked, I mostly listened.

As night fell, the men said that they wanted to get another bottle of wine. I contributed. They counted their money and asked if I wanted to go with them.

Although I felt my stomach churning—a combination of hesitation and fear—I heard a confident "Sure!" come out of my mouth. As we left the circle, the three men began to cut through an alley. "Oh, no," I thought. "This isn't what I had in mind."

I had but a split second to make a decision. I found myself continuing to walk with the men, but holding back half a step so that none of the three was behind me. As we walked, they passed around the remnants of their bottle. When my turn came, I didn't know what to do. I shuddered to think about the diseases lurking within that bottle. I made another quick decision. In the semidarkness I faked it, letting only my thumb and forefinger touch my lips and nothing enter my mouth.

When we returned to Dupont Circle, we sat on the benches, and the men passed around their new bottle of Thunderbird. I couldn't fake it in the light, so I passed, pointing at my stomach to indicate that I was having digestive problems.

Suddenly one of the men jumped up, smashed the emptied bottle against the sidewalk, and thrust the jagged neck outward in a menacing gesture. He glared straight ahead at another bench, where he had spotted someone with whom he had some sort of unfinished business. As the other men told him to cool it, I moved slightly to one side of the group—ready to flee, just in case.

Suddenly one of the men jumped up, smashed the empty bottle against the sidewalk, and . . .

Levels of Sociological Analysis

macrosociology analysis of social life that focuses on broad features of society, such as social class and the relationships of groups to one another; usually used by functionalists and conflict theorists

microsociology analysis of social life that focuses on social interaction; typically used by symbolic interactionists

social interaction the ways that people interact with one another

On this sociological adventure, I almost got myself in over my head. Fortunately, it turned out all right. The man's "enemy" didn't look our way, the man put the broken bottle next to the bench "just in case he needed it," and my intriguing introduction to a life that up until then I had only read about continued until dawn.

Sociologists Elliot Liebow (1967/1999), Mitchell Duneier (1999), and Elijah Anderson (1978, 1990, 2006) have written fascinating accounts about men like my companions from that evening. Although streetcorner men may appear to be disorganized—simply coming and going as they please and doing whatever feels good at the moment—sociologists have analyzed how, like us, these men are influenced by the norms and beliefs of our society. This will become more apparent as we examine the two levels of analysis that sociologists use.

Macrosociology and Microsociology

The first level, **macrosociology,** focuses on broad features of society. Conflict theorists and functionalists use this approach to analyze such things as social class and how groups are related to one another. If they were to analyze streetcorner men, for example, they would stress that these men are located at the bottom of the U.S. social class system. Their low status means that many opportunities are closed to them: The men have few job skills, little education, hardly anything to offer an employer. As "able-bodied" men, however, they are not eligible for welfare–even for a two-year limit–so they hustle to survive. As a consequence, they spend their lives on the streets.

In the second level, **microsociology,** the focus is on **social interaction,** what people do when they come together. Sociologists who use this approach are likely to focus on the men's rules or "codes" for getting along; their survival strategies ("hustles"); how they divide up money, wine, or whatever other resources they have; their relationships with girlfriends, family, and friends; where they spend their time and what they do there; their language; their pecking order; and so on. With their focus on face-to-face interaction, it is primarily symbolic interactionists who use microsociology.

Because each approach has a different focus, macrosociology and microsociology yield distinctive perspectives, and both are needed to gain a fuller understanding of social life. We cannot adequately understand streetcorner men, for example, without using

Sociologists use both macro and micro levels of analysis to study social life. Those who use *macrosociology* to analyze the homeless—or any human behavior—focus on broad aspects of society, such as the economy and social classes. Sociologists who use the *microsociological approach* analyze how people interact with one another. This photo illustrates social structure—the disparities between power and powerlessness are amply evident. It also illustrates the micro level—the interaction of these homeless men.

macrosociology. It is essential that we place the men within the broad context of how groups in U.S. society are related to one another—for, as is true for ourselves, the social class of these men helps to shape their attitudes and behavior. Nor can we adequately understand these men without *microsociology,* for their everyday situations also form a significant part of their lives—as they do for all of us.

Let's look in more detail at how these two approaches in sociology work together to help us understand social life. As we examine them more closely, you may find yourself feeling more comfortable with one approach than the other. This is what happens with sociologists. For reasons that include personal background and professional training, sociologists find themselves more comfortable with one approach and tend to use it in their research. Both approaches, however, are necessary to understand life in society.

The Macrosociological Perspective: Social Structure

Why did the street people in the opening vignette act as they did, staying up all night drinking wine, prepared to use a lethal weapon? Why don't *we* act like this? Social structure helps us answer such questions.

The Sociological Significance of Social Structure

To better understand human behavior, we need to understand *social structure,* the framework of society that was already laid out before you were born. **Social structure** refers to the typical patterns of a group, such as its usual relationships between men and women or students and teachers. *The sociological significance of social structure is that it guides our behavior.*

Because this term may seem vague, let's consider how you experience social structure in your own life. As I write this, I do not know your race-ethnicity. I do not know your religion. I do not know whether you are young or old, tall or short, male or female. I do not know whether you were reared on a farm, in the suburbs, or in the inner city. I do not know whether you went to a public high school or to an exclusive prep school. But I do know that you are in college. And this, alone, tells me a great deal about you.

From this one piece of information, I can assume that the social structure of your college is now shaping what you do. For example, let's suppose that today you felt euphoric over some great news. I can be fairly certain (not absolutely, mind you, but relatively confident) that when you entered the classroom, social structure overrode your mood. That is, instead of shouting at the top of your lungs and joyously throwing this book into the air, you entered the classroom in a fairly subdued manner and took your seat.

The same social structure influences your instructor, even if he or she, on the one hand, is facing a divorce or has a child dying of cancer, or, on the other, has just been awarded a promotion or a million-dollar grant. Your instructor may feel like either retreating into seclusion or celebrating wildly, but most likely he or she will conduct class in the usual manner. In short, social structure tends to override personal feelings and desires.

Just as social structure influences you and your instructor, so it also establishes limits for street people. They, too, find themselves in a specific location in the U.S. social structure—although it is quite different from yours or your instructor's. Consequently, they are affected in different ways. Nothing about their social location leads them to take notes or to lecture. Their behaviors, however, are as logical an outcome of where they find themselves in the social structure as are your own. In their position in the social structure, it is just as "natural" to drink wine all night as it is for you to stay up studying all night for a crucial examination. It is just as "natural" for you to nod and say, "Excuse me," when you enter a crowded classroom late and have to claim a desk on which someone has already placed books as it is for them to break off the neck of a wine bottle and glare at an enemy.

social structure the framework that surrounds us, consisting of the relationships of people and groups, which gives direction to and sets limits on behavior

In short, people learn their behaviors and attitudes because of their location in the social structure (whether they be privileged, deprived, or in between), and they act accordingly. This is equally true of street people and ourselves. *The differences in behavior and attitudes are due not to biology (race, sex, or any other supposed genetic factors), but to people's location in the social structure.* Switch places with street people and watch your behaviors and attitudes change!

To better understand social structure, read the Down-to-Earth Sociology box on football below.

Because social structure so crucially affects who we are and what we are like, let's look more closely at its major components: culture, social class, social status, roles, groups, and social institutions.

Culture

In Chapter 2, we considered culture's far-reaching effects on our lives. At this point, let's simply summarize its main impact. Sociologists use the term *culture* to refer to a group's language, beliefs, values, behaviors, and even gestures. Culture also includes the material

Down-to-Earth Sociology

College Football as Social Structure

TO GAIN A BETTER IDEA OF WHAT *social structure* is, think of college football (see Dobriner 1969a). You probably know the various positions on the team: center, guards, tackles, ends, quarterback, running backs, and the like. Each is a *status;* that is, each is a social position. For each of these statuses, there is a *role;* that is, each of these positions has certain expectations attached to it. The center is expected to snap the ball, the quarterback to pass it, the guards to block, the tackles to tackle or block, the ends to receive passes, and so on. Those role expectations guide each player's actions; that is, the players try to do what their particular role requires.

Let's suppose that football is your favorite sport and you never miss a home game at your college. Let's also suppose that you graduate, get a great job, and move across the country. Five years later, you return to your campus for a nostalgic visit. The climax of your visit is the biggest football game of the season. When you get to the game, you might be surprised to see a different coach, but you are not surprised that each playing position is occupied by people you don't know, for all the players you knew have graduated, and their places have been filled by others.

This scenario mirrors *social structure,* the framework around which a group exists. In football, that framework consists of the coaching staff and the eleven playing positions. The game does not depend on any particular individual, but, rather, on *social statuses,* the positions that the individuals occupy. When someone leaves a position, the game can go on because someone else takes over that position or status and plays the role. The game will continue even though not a single individual remains from

one period of time to the next. Notre Dame's football team endures today even though Knute Rockne, the Gipper, and his teammates are long dead.

Even though you may not play football, you nevertheless live your life within a clearly established social structure. The statuses that you occupy and the roles you play were already in place before you were born. You take your particular positions in life, others do the same, and society goes about its business. Although the specifics change with time, the game—whether of life or of football—goes on.

Figure 4.1 **Team Positions (Statuses) in Football**

objects that a group uses. Culture is the broadest framework that determines what kind of people we become. If we are reared in Chinese, Arab, or U.S. culture, we will grow up to be like most Chinese, Arabs, or Americans. On the outside, we will look and act like them; and on the inside, we will think and feel like them.

Social Class

To understand people, we must examine the social locations that they hold in life. Especially significant is *social class,* which is based on income, education, and occupational prestige. Large numbers of people who have similar amounts of income and education and who work at jobs that are roughly comparable in prestige make up a **social class.** It is hard to overemphasize this aspect of social structure, for our social class influences not only our behaviors but even our ideas and attitudes. We have this in common, then, with the street people described in the opening vignette: We both are influenced by our location in the social class structure. Theirs may be a considerably less privileged position, but it has no less influence on their lives. Social class is so significant that we shall spend an entire chapter (Chapter 10) on this topic.

Social Status

When you hear the word *status,* you are likely to think of prestige. These two words are welded together in people's minds. As you saw in the box on football, however, sociologists use **status** in a different way—to refer to the *position* that someone occupies. That position may carry a great deal of prestige, as in the case of a judge or an astronaut, or it may bring little prestige, as in the case of a convenience store clerk or a waitress at the local truck stop. The status may also be looked down on, as in the case of a streetcorner man, an ex-convict, or a thief.

All of us occupy several positions at the same time. You may simultaneously be a son or daughter, a worker, a date, and a student. Sociologists use the term **status set** to refer to all the statuses or positions that you occupy. Obviously your status set changes as your particular statuses change. For example, if you graduate from college and take a full-time job, get married, buy a home, have children, and so on, your status set changes to include the positions of worker, spouse, homeowner, and parent.

Like other aspects of social structure, statuses are part of our basic framework of living in society. The example I gave of students and teachers who come to class and do what others expect of them despite their particular circumstances and moods illustrates how statuses affect our actions—and those of the people around us. Our statuses—whether daughter or son, worker or date—serve as guides for our behavior.

Ascribed and Achieved Statuses   An **ascribed status** is involuntary. You do not ask for it, nor can you choose it. You inherit some ascribed statuses at birth such as your race-ethnicity, sex, and the social class of your parents, as well as your statuses as female or male, daughter or son, niece or nephew. Others, such as teenager and senior citizen, are related to the life course discussed in Chapter 3, and are given to you later in life.

Achieved statuses, in contrast, are voluntary. These you earn or accomplish. As a result of your efforts you become a student, a friend, a spouse, a lawyer, or a member of the clergy. Or, for lack of effort (or for efforts that others fail to appreciate), you become a school dropout, a former friend, an ex-spouse, a debarred lawyer, or a defrocked member of the clergy. In other words, achieved statuses can be either positive or negative; both college president and bank robber are achieved statuses.

Each status provides guidelines for how we are to act and feel. Like other aspects of social structure, statuses set limits on what we can and cannot do. Because social statuses are an essential part of the social structure, they are found in all human groups.

Status Symbols   People who are pleased with their social status often want others to recognize their particular position. To elicit this recognition, they use **status symbols,** signs that identify a status. For example, people wear wedding rings to announce their marital status; uniforms, guns, and badges to proclaim that they are police officers (and not so subtly to let you know that their status gives them authority over you); and "backward" collars to declare that they are Lutheran ministers or Roman Catholic or Episcopal priests.

social class according to Weber, a large group of people who rank close to one another in wealth, prestige, and power; according to Marx, one of two groups: capitalists who own the means of production or workers who sell their labor

status the position that someone occupies in society or in a social group

status set all the statuses or positions that an individual occupies

ascribed statuses positions an individual either inherits at birth or receives involuntarily later in life

achieved statuses positions that are earned, accomplished, or involve at least some effort or activity on the individual's part

status symbols items used to identify a status

Some social statuses are negative, and so, therefore, are their status symbols. The scarlet letter in Nathaniel Hawthorne's book by the same title is one example. Another is the CONVICTED DUI (Driving Under the Influence) bumper sticker that some U.S. courts require convicted drunk drivers to display if they wish to avoid a jail sentence.

All of us use status symbols to announce our statuses to others and to help smooth our interactions in everyday life. You might consider what your own status symbols communicate. For example, how does your clothing announce your statuses of sex, age, and college student?

Master Statuses   A **master status** is one that cuts across the other statuses that you hold. Some master statuses are ascribed. An example is your sex. Whatever you do, people perceive you as a male or as a female. If you are working your way through college by flipping burgers, people see you not only as a burger flipper and a student but also as a *male* or *female* burger flipper and a *male* or *female* college student. Other master statuses are race and age.

Some master statuses are achieved. If you become very, very wealthy (and it doesn't matter whether your wealth comes from a successful invention or from winning the lottery—it is still *achieved* as far as sociologists are concerned), your wealth is likely to become a master status. For example, people might say, "She is a very rich burger flipper"—or, more likely, "She's very rich, and she used to flip burgers!"

Similarly, people who become disfigured find, to their dismay, that their condition becomes a master status. For example, a person whose face is scarred from severe burns will be viewed through this unwelcome master status regardless of his or her occupation or accomplishments. In the same way, people who are confined to wheelchairs can attest to how their handicap overrides all their other statuses and influences others' perceptions of everything they do.

Although our statuses usually fit together fairly well, some people have a contradiction or mismatch between their statuses. This is known as **status inconsistency** (or discrepancy). A 14-year-old college student is an example. So is a 40-year-old married woman who is dating a 19-year-old college sophomore.

These examples reveal an essential aspect of social statuses: Like other components of social structure, they come with built-in *norms* (that is, expectations) that guide our behavior. When statuses mesh well, as they usually do, we know what to expect of people. This helps social interaction to unfold smoothly. Status inconsistency, however, upsets our expectations. In the preceding examples, how are you supposed to act? Are you

Master statuses are those that overshadow our other statuses. Shown here is Stephen Hawking, who is severely disabled by Lou Gehrig's disease. For some, his *master status* is that of a person with disabilities. Because Hawking is one of the greatest physicists who has ever lived, however, his outstanding achievements have given him another *master status*, that of world-class physicist in the ranking of Einstein.

supposed to treat the 14-year-old as you would a young teenager, or as you would your college classmate? Do you react to the married woman as you would to the mother of your friend, or as you would to a classmate's date?

Roles

> All the world's a stage
> And all the men and women merely players.
> They have their exits and their entrances;
> And one man in his time plays many parts . . .
> (William Shakespeare, *As You Like It,* Act II, Scene 7)

Like Shakespeare, sociologists see roles as essential to social life. When you were born, **roles**—the behaviors, obligations, and privileges attached to a status—were already set up for you. Society was waiting with outstretched arms to teach you how it expected you to act as a boy or a girl. And whether you were born poor, rich, or somewhere in between, that, too, attached certain behaviors, obligations, and privileges to your statuses.

The difference between role and status is that you *occupy* a status, but you *play* a role (Linton 1936). For example, being a son or daughter is your status, but your expectations of receiving food and shelter from your parents—as well as their expectations that you show respect to them—are part of your role. Or, again, your status is student, but your role is to attend class, take notes, do homework, and take tests.

Roles are like a fence. They allow us a certain amount of freedom, but for most of us that freedom doesn't go very far. Suppose that a woman decides that she is not going to wear dresses—or a man that he will not wear suits and ties—regardless of what anyone says. In most situations, they'll stick to their decision. When a formal occasion comes along, however, such as a family wedding or a funeral, they are likely to cave in to norms that they find overwhelming. Almost all of us follow the guidelines for what is "appropriate" for our roles. Few of us are bothered by such constraints, for our socialization is so thorough that we usually *want* to do what our roles indicate is appropriate.

The sociological significance of roles is that they lay out what is expected of people. As individuals throughout society perform their roles, those roles mesh together to form this thing called *society.* As Shakespeare put it, people's roles provide "their exits and their entrances" on the stage of life. In short, roles are remarkably effective at keeping people in line—telling them when they should "enter" and when they should "exit," as well as what to do in between.

Groups

A **group** consists of people who regularly interact with one another. Ordinarily, the members of a group share similar values, norms, and expectations. Just as social class, statuses, and roles influence our actions, so, too, the groups to which we belong are powerful forces in our lives. In fact, *to belong to a group is to yield to others the right to make certain decisions about our behavior.* If we belong to a group, we assume an obligation to act according to the expectations of other members of that group.

Although this principle holds true for all groups, some groups wield influence over only small segments of our behavior. For example, if you belong to a stamp collector's club, the group's influence may center on your display of knowledge about stamps, and perhaps fairness in trading them. Other groups, in contrast, such as the family, control many aspects of our behavior. When parents say to their 15-year-old daughter, "As long as you are living under my roof, you had better be home by midnight," they show their expectation that their daughter, as a member of the family, will conform to their ideas about many aspects of life, including their views on curfew. They are saying that as long as the daughter wants to remain a member of the household, her behavior must conform to their expectations.

Let's look in greater detail at the next component of social structure, social institutions.

role the behaviors, obligations, and privileges attached to a status

group people who have something in common and who believe that what they have in common is significant; also called a *social group*

Social Institutions

social institution the organized, usual, or standard ways by which society meets its basic needs

At first glance, the term *social institution* may seem to have little relevance to your life. The term seems so cold and abstract. In fact, however, **social institutions**—the ways that each society develops to meet its basic needs—vitally affect your life. By weaving the fabric of society, social institutions shape our behavior. They even color our thoughts. How can this be? Look at what social institutions are: the family, religion, education, economics, medicine, politics, law, science, the military, and the mass media.

In industrialized societies, social institutions tend to be more formal; in tribal societies, they are more informal. Education in industrialized societies, for example, is highly structured, while in tribal societies it usually consists of children informally learning what adults do. Figure 4.2 on the next page summarizes the basic social institutions. Note that each institution has its own groups, statuses, values, and norms. Social institutions are so significant that Part IV of this book focuses on them.

The Sociological Significance of Social Institutions

To understand social institutions is to realize how profoundly social structure affects our lives. Much of the influence of social institutions lies beyond our ordinary awareness. For example, because of our economic institution, it is common to work eight hours a day for five days every week. There is nothing normal or natural about this pattern, however. This rhythm is only an arbitrary arrangement for dividing work and leisure. Yet this one aspect of a single social institution has far-reaching effects. Not only does it dictate how people divide up their days, but it also lays out a structure for their interaction with family and friends and for how they meet their personal needs.

Each of the other social institutions also has far-reaching effects on our lives. They establish the context in which we live, shaping our behavior and coloring our thoughts. Social institutions are so significant that if they were different, we would be different people. We certainly could not remain the same, for social institutions influence our orientations to the social world, and even to life itself.

An Example: The Mass Media as an Emerging Social Institution

Far beyond serving simply as sources of information, the mass media influence our attitudes toward social issues, the ways that we view other people, and even our self-concept. Because the media significantly shape public opinion, all governments attempt to influence them. Totalitarian governments try to control them.

The mass media are relatively new in human history, owing their origins to the invention of the printing press in the 1400s. This invention had profound consequences on all social institutions. The printing of the Bible altered religion, for instance, while the publication of political broadsides and newspapers altered politics. From these beginnings, a series of inventions—from radio and movies to television and the microchip—has made the media an increasingly powerful force.

One of the most significant questions we can ask about this social institution is: Who controls it? That control, which in totalitarian countries is obvious, is much less visible in democratic nations. Functionalists might conclude that the media in a democratic nation represent the varied interests of the many groups that make up that nation. Conflict theorists, in contrast, see the matter quite differently: The mass media—at least a country's most influential newspapers and television stations—represent the interests of the political elite. They give coverage to mildly dissenting opinions, but they

The mass media are a major influence in contemporary life. Until 1436, when Johann Gutenberg invented movable type, printing was a slow process, and printed materials were expensive. Today, printed materials are common and often cheap. "Cheap" has a double meaning, with its second meaning illustrated in this photo.

Figure 4.2 **Social Institutions in Industrial and Postindustrial Societies**

Social Institution	Basic Needs	Some Groups or Organizations	Some Statuses	Some Values	Some Norms
Family	Regulate reproduction, socialize and protect children	Relatives, kinship groups	Daughter, son, father, mother, brother, sister, aunt, uncle, grandparent	Sexual fidelity, providing for your family, keeping a clean house, respect for parents	Have only as many children as you can afford, be faithful to your spouse
Religion	Concerns about life after death, the meaning of suffering and loss; desire to connect with the Creator	Congregation, synagogue, mosque, denomination, charity; clergy associations	Priest, minister, rabbi, imam, worshipper, teacher, disciple, missionary, prophet, convert	Reading and adhering to holy texts such as the Bible, the Torah, and the Koran, honoring God	Attend worship services, contribute money, follow the teachings
Education	Transmit knowledge and skills across generations	School, college, student senate, sports team, PTA, teachers' union	Teacher, student, dean, principal, football player, cheerleader	Academic honesty, good grades, being "cool"	Do homework, prepare lectures, don't snitch on classmates
Economy	Produce and distribute goods and services	Credit unions, banks, credit card companies, buying clubs	Worker, boss, buyer, seller, creditor, debtor, advertiser	Making money, paying bills on time, producing efficiently	Maximize profits, "the customer is always right," work hard
Medicine	Heal the sick and injured, care for the dying	AMA, hospitals, pharmacies, insurance companies, HMOs	Doctor, nurse, patient, pharmacist, medical insurer	Hippocratic oath, staying in good health, following doctor's orders	Don't exploit patients, give best medical care available
Politics	Allocate power, determine authority, prevent chaos	Political party, congress, parliament, monarchy	President, senator, lobbyist, voter, candidate, spin doctor	Majority rule, the right to vote as a privilege and a sacred trust	One vote per person, be informed about candidates
Law	Maintain social order	Police, courts, prisons	Judge, police officer, lawyer, defendant, prison guard	Trial by one's peers, innocence until proven guilty	Give true testimony, follow the rules of evidence
Science	Master the environment	Local, state, regional, national, and international associations	Scientist, researcher, technician, administrator, journal editor	Unbiased research, open dissemination of research findings, originality	Follow scientific method, be objective, disclose findings, don't plagiarize
Military	Protection from enemies, support of national interests	Army, navy, air force, marines, coast guard, national guard	Soldier, recruit, enlisted person, officer, veteran, prisoner, spy	To die for one's country is an honor, obedience unto death	Follow orders, be ready to go to war, sacrifice for your buddies
Mass Media (an emerging institution)	Disseminate information, mold public opinion, report events	TV networks, radio stations, publishers, association of bloggers	Journalist, newscaster, author, editor, publisher, blogger	Timeliness, accuracy, large audiences, freedom of the press	Be accurate, fair, timely, and profitable

stand solidly behind the government. The most obvious example is the positive treatment that the media give to the inauguration of a president.

Since the mass media are so influential in our lives today, the answer to this question of who controls the media is of more than passing interest. This matter is vital to our understanding of contemporary society.

functional requisites the
major tasks that a society
must fulfill if it is to survive

Comparing Functionalist and Conflict Perspectives

Just as the functionalist and conflict perspectives of the mass media differ, so do their views of the nature of social institutions. Let's compare these views.

The Functionalist Perspective   Functionalists stress that social institutions perform such vital functions for human survival that no society is without them. A group may be too small to have people who specialize in education, but it will have its own established ways of teaching skills and ideas to the young. It may be too small to have a military, but it will have some mechanism of self-defense. To survive, every society must meet its basic needs (or **functional requisites**). According to functionalists, that is the purpose of social institutions.

What are those basic needs? Functionalists identify five *functional requisites* that each society must fulfill if it is to survive (Aberle et al. 1950; Mack and Bradford 1979).

Functionalist theorists have identified five *functional requisites* for the survival of a society. One, providing a sense of purpose, is often met through religious groups. To most people, snake handling, as in this church service in Kingston, Georgia, is nonsensical. From a functional perspective, however, it makes a great deal of sense. Can you identify its sociological meanings?

1. *Replacing members.* If a society does not replace its members, it cannot continue to exist. Because reproduction is so fundamental to a society's existence, and because every society has a vital need to protect infants and children, all groups have developed some version of the family. The family gives the newcomer to society a sense of belonging by providing a "lineage," an account of how he or she is related to others. The family also functions to control people's sex drive and to maintain orderly reproduction.
2. *Socializing new members.* Each baby must be taught what it means to be a member of the group into which it is born. To accomplish this, each human group develops devices to ensure that its newcomers learn the group's basic expectations. As the primary "bearer of culture," the family is essential to this process, but other social institutions, such as religion and education, also help meet this basic need.
3. *Producing and distributing goods and services.* Every society must produce and distribute basic resources, from food and clothing to shelter and education. Consequently, every society establishes an *economic* institution, a means of producing goods and services along with routine ways of distributing them.
4. *Preserving order.* Societies face two threats of disorder: one internal, the potential for chaos, and the other external, the possibility of attack. To defend themselves against external conquest, they develop a means of defense, some form of the military. To protect themselves from internal threat, they develop a system of policing themselves, ranging from formal organizations of armed groups to informal systems of gossip.
5. *Providing a sense of purpose.* Every society must get people to yield self-interest in favor of the needs of the group. To convince people to sacrifice personal gains, societies instill a sense of purpose. Human groups develop many ways to implant such beliefs, but a primary one is religion, which attempts to answer questions about ultimate meaning. Actually, all of a society's institutions are involved in meeting this functional requisite; the family provides one set of answers about the sense of purpose, the school another, and so on.

The Conflict Perspective   Although conflict theorists agree that social institutions were designed originally to meet basic survival needs, they do not view social institutions as working harmoniously for the common good. On the contrary, conflict theorists stress that powerful groups control society's institutions, manipulating them in order to maintain their own privileged position of wealth and power (Useem 1984; Domhoff 1999a, b, 2006).

Conflict theorists point out that a fairly small group of people has garnered the lion's share of the nation's wealth. Members of this elite sit on the boards of both the major corporations and the country's most prestigious universities. They make strategic campaign contributions to influence (or control) the nation's lawmakers, and it is they who make the major decisions in this society: to go to war or to refrain from war; to increase or to decrease taxes; to raise or to lower interest rates; and to pass laws that favor or impede moving capital, technology, and jobs out of the country.

Feminist sociologists (both women and men) have used conflict theory to gain a better understanding of how social institutions affect gender relations. Their basic insight is that gender is also an element of social structure, not simply a characteristic of individuals. In other words, throughout the world, social institutions divide males and females into separate groups, each with unequal access to society's resources.

IN SUM Functionalists view social institutions as working together to meet universal human needs. Conflict theorists, in contrast, regard social institutions as having a single primary purpose—to preserve the social order. For them, this means safeguarding the wealthy and powerful in their positions of privilege.

Changes in Social Structure

As you can see, this enveloping system that we call social structure powerfully affects our lives. This means that as social structure changes, so, too, do our orientations to life. Our culture is not static. It is continuously evolving as it responds to changing values, to new technology, and to contact with cultures around the world. As our culture changes, so do we. Similarly, as our economy responds to globalization, it either grows or stagnates. This opens or closes opportunities, changing our lives, sometimes brutally so. New groups such as the Department of Homeland Security come into being, wielding extraordinary power over us. In short, the corner in life that we occupy, though small and seemingly private, is not closed off; rather, it is pushed and pulled and stretched in different directions as our social structure changes.

What Holds Society Together?

With its many, often conflicting, groups and its extensive social change, how can a society manage to hold together? Let's examine two answers that sociologists have proposed.

Mechanical and Organic Solidarity Sociologist Emile Durkheim (1893/1933) found the key to **social integration**—the degree to which members of a society are united by shared values and other social bonds—in what he called **mechanical solidarity**. By this term, Durkheim meant that people who perform similar tasks develop a shared consciousness. Think of a farming community in which everyone is involved in planting, cultivating, and harvesting. Members of this group have so much in common that they know how almost everyone else in the community feels about life. Societies with mechanical solidarity tolerate little diversity in thinking and attitudes, for their unity depends on similar thinking.

As societies get larger, their **division of labor** (how they divide up work) becomes more specialized. Some people mine gold, others turn it into jewelry, while still others sell it. This division of labor makes people depend on one another—for the work of each person contributes to the well-being of the whole group.

Durkheim called this new form of solidarity based on interdependence **organic solidarity.** To see why he used this term, think about how you depend on your teacher to guide you through this introductory course in sociology. At the same time, your teacher needs you and other students in order to have a job. You and your teacher are *like organs in the same body.* (The "body" in this case is the college or university.) Although each of you performs different tasks, you depend on one another. This creates a form of unity.

The change to organic solidarity produced a new basis for solidarity—not similar views, but separate activities that contribute to the overall welfare of the group. As a result, modern societies can encompass many differences among people and still manage to work as a whole. Both past and present societies are based on social solidarity, but the types of solidarity differ remarkably.

social integration the degree to which members of a group or a society feel united by shared values and other social bonds; also known as social cohesion

mechanical solidarity Durkheim's term for the unity (a shared consciousness) that people feel as a result of performing the same or similar tasks

division of labor the splitting of a group's or a society's tasks into specialties

organic solidarity Durkheim's term for the interdependence that results from the division of labor; people depending on others to fulfill their jobs

Gemeinschaft and Gesellschaft Ferdinand Tönnies (1887/1988) also analyzed this fundamental shift in relationships. He used the term ***Gemeinschaft*** (Guh-MINE-shoft), or "intimate community," to describe village life, the type of society in which everyone knows everyone else. He noted that in the society that was emerging, the personal ties, kinship connections, and lifelong friendships that marked village life were being crowded out by short-term relationships, individual accomplishments, and self-interest. Tönnies called this new type of society ***Gesellschaft*** (Guh-ZELL-shoft), or "impersonal association." He did not mean that we no longer have intimate ties to family and friends, but, rather, that our lives no longer center on them. Few of us take jobs in a family business, for example, and contracts replace handshakes. Much of our time is spent with strangers and short-term acquaintances.

How Relevant Are These Concepts Today? I know that *Gemeinschaft, Gesellschaft,* and *mechanical* and *organic solidarity* are strange terms and that Durkheim's and Tönnies' observations must seem like a dead issue. The concern these sociologists expressed, however—that their world was changing from a community in which people are united by close ties and shared ideas and feelings to an anonymous association built around impersonal, short-term contacts—is still very real. In large part, this same concern explains the rise of Islamic fundamentalism (Volti 1995). Islamic leaders fear that Western values will uproot their traditional culture, that cold rationality will replace the informal personal relationships among families and clans. They fear, rightly so, that this will change even their views on life and morality. Although the terms may sound strange, even obscure, you can see that the ideas remain a vital part of today's world.

IN SUM Whether the terms are *Gemeinschaft* and *Gesellschaft* or *mechanical solidarity* and *organic solidarity,* they indicate that as societies change, so do people's orientations to life. *The sociological point is that social structure sets the context for what we do, feel, and think, and ultimately, then, for the kind of people we become.* As you read the Cultural Diversity box on the next page, which describes one of the few remaining *Gemeinschaft* societies in the United States, think of how fundamentally different you would be had you been reared in an Amish family.

The warm, more intimate relationships of *Gemeinschaft* society are apparent in this restaurant in Salzburg, Austria. The more impersonal relationships of *Gesellschaft* society are evident in this café in Bangkok, Thailand, where, ignoring one another, the customers engage in electronic interactions.

Cultural Diversity *in the* United States

The Amish: *Gemeinschaft* Community in a *Gesellschaft* Society

FERDINAND TÖNNIES' TERM, *Gesellschaft,* certainly applies to the United States. Impersonal associations pervade our everyday life. Local, state, and federal governments regulate many of our activities. Corporations hire and fire people not on the basis of personal relationships, but on the basis of the bottom line. And, perhaps even more significantly, millions of Americans do not even know their neighbors.

Within the United States, a handful of small communities exhibits characteristics that are distinct from those of the mainstream society. One such community is the Old Order Amish, followers of a sect that broke away from the Swiss-German Mennonite church in the 1600s, and settled in Pennsylvania around 1727. Today, about 150,000 Old Order Amish live in the United States. About 75 percent live in just three states: Pennsylvania, Ohio, and Indiana. The largest concentration, about 22,000, reside in Lancaster County, Pennsylvania. The Amish, who believe that birth control is wrong, have doubled in population in just the past two decades.

Because Amish farmers use horses instead of tractors, most of their farms are one hundred acres or less. To the five million tourists who pass through Lancaster County each year, the rolling green pastures, white farmhouses, simple barns, horse-drawn buggies, and clotheslines hung with somber-colored garments convey a sense of peace and innocence reminiscent of another era. Although just sixty-five miles from Philadelphia, "Amish country" is a world away.

Amish life is based on separation from the world—an idea taken from Christ's Sermon on the Mount—and obedience to the church's teachings and leaders. This rejection of worldly concerns, writes sociologist Donald Kraybill in *The Riddle of Amish Culture* (2002), "provides the foundation of such Amish values as humility, faithfulness, thrift, tradition, communal goals, joy of work, a slow-paced life, and trust in divine providence."

The *Gemeinschaft* of village life that has been largely lost to industrialization remains a vibrant part of Amish life. The Amish make their decisions in weekly meetings, where, by consensus, they follow a set of rules, or *Ordnung,* to guide their behavior. Religion and discipline are the glue that holds the Amish together. Brotherly love and the welfare of the community are paramount values. In times of birth, sickness, and death, neighbors pitch in with the chores. In these ways, they maintain the bonds of intimate community.

The Amish are bound by other ties, including language (a dialect of German known as Pennsylvania Dutch), plain clothing—often black, whose style has remained unchanged for almost 300 years–and church-sponsored schools. Nearly all Amish marry, and divorce is forbidden. The family is a vital ingredient in Amish life; all major events take place in the home, including weddings, births, funerals, and church services. Amish children attend church schools, but only until the age of 13. (In 1972, the Supreme Court ruled that Amish parents had the right to take their children out of school after the eighth grade.) To go to school beyond the eighth grade would expose them to values and "worldly concerns" that would drive a wedge between the children and their community. The Amish believe that violence is bad, even personal self-defense, and they register as conscientious objectors during times of war. They pay no Social Security, and they receive no government benefits.

The Amish cannot resist all change, of course. Instead, they try to adapt to change in ways that will least disrupt their core values. Because urban sprawl has driven up the price of farmland, about half of Amish men work at jobs other than farming, most in farm-related businesses or in woodcrafts. They go to great lengths to avoid leaving the home. The Amish believe that when a husband works away from home, all aspects of life change—from the marital relationship to the care of the children—certainly an astute sociological insight. They also believe that if a man receives a paycheck, he will think that his work is of more value than his wife's. For the Amish, intimate, or *Gemeinschaft*, society is essential for maintaining their way of life.

Perhaps this is the most poignant illustration of how the Amish approach to life differs from the dominant culture: When in 2006 a non-Amish man shot several girls at a one-room school, the Amish community raised money not only for the families of the dead children but also for the family of the killer.

Sources: Hostetler 1980; Aeppel 1996; Kephart and Zellner 2001; Kraybill 1989, 2002; Dawley 2003; Johnson-Weiner 2007.

The Microsociological Perspective: Social Interaction in Everyday Life

Whereas the macrosociological approach stresses the broad features of society, the microsociological approach has a narrower focus. Microsociologists examine *face-to-face interaction*—what people do when they are in one another's presence. Let's examine some of the areas of social life that microsociologists study.

Symbolic Interaction

For symbolic interactionists, the most significant part of life in society is social interaction. Symbolic interactionists are especially interested in the symbols that people use. They want to know how people look at things and how this, in turn, affects their behavior and orientations to life. Of the many areas of social life that microsociologists study, let's look at stereotyping, personal space, touching, eye contact, and smiling.

Stereotypes in Everyday Life   You are familiar with how strong first impressions are and the way they set the tone for interaction. When you first meet someone, you cannot help but notice certain features, especially the person's sex, race-ethnicity, age, and clothing. Despite your best intentions, your assumptions about these characteristics shape your first impressions. They also affect how you act toward that person—and, in turn, how that person acts toward you. These fascinating aspects of our social interaction are discussed in the Down-to-Earth Sociology box on the next page.

Personal Space   We all surround ourselves with a "personal bubble" that we go to great lengths to protect. We open the bubble to intimates—to our friends, children, parents, and so on—but we're careful to keep most people out of this space. In a crowded hallway between classes, we might walk with our books clasped in front of us (a strategy often chosen by females). When we stand in line, we make certain there is enough space so that we don't touch the person in front of us and aren't touched by the person behind us.

At times, we extend our personal space. In the library, for example, you may place your coat on the chair next to you—claiming that space for yourself even though you aren't using it. If you want to really extend your space, you might even spread books in front of the other chairs, keeping the whole table to yourself by giving the impression that others have just stepped away.

The amount of space that people prefer varies from one culture to another. South Americans, for example, like to be closer when they speak to others than do people reared in the United States. Anthropologist Edward Hall (1959; Hall and Hall 2007) recounts a conversation with a man from South America who had attended one of his lectures.

Social space is one of the many aspects of social life studied by sociologists who have a microsociological focus. What do you see in common in these two photos?

Beauty May Be Only Skin Deep, But Its Effects Go On Forever: Stereotypes in Everyday Life

MARK SNYDER, A PSYCHOLOGIST, wondered whether **stereotypes**—our assumptions of what people are like—might be self-fulfilling. He came up with an ingenious way to test this idea. He (1993) gave college men a Polaroid snapshot of a woman (supposedly taken just moments before) and told them that he would introduce them to her after they talked with her on the telephone. Actually, the photographs—showing either a pretty or a homely woman—had been prepared before the experiment began. The photo was not of the woman the men would talk to.

Stereotypes came into play immediately. As Snyder gave each man the photograph, he asked him what he thought the woman would be like. The men who saw the photograph of the attractive woman said that they expected to meet a poised, humorous, outgoing woman. The men who had been given a photo of the unattractive woman described her as awkward, serious, and unsociable.

The men's stereotypes influenced the way they spoke to the women on the telephone, who did not know about the photographs. The men who had seen the photograph of a pretty woman were warm, friendly, and humorous. This, in turn, affected the women they spoke to, for they responded in a warm, friendly, outgoing manner. And the men who had seen the photograph of a homely woman? On the phone, they were cold, reserved, and humorless, and the women they spoke to became cool, reserved, and humorless. Keep in mind that the women did not know that their looks had been

evaluated—and that the photographs were not even of them. In short, stereotypes tend to produce behaviors that match the stereotype. This principle is illustrated in Figure 4.3.

Although beauty might be only skin deep, its consequences permeate our lives (Katz 2007). Not only does beauty bestow an advantage in everyday interaction, but people who are physically attractive are likely to make more money. Researchers in both Holland and the United States found that advertising firms with better-looking executives have higher revenues (Bosman et al. 1997; Pfann et al. 2000). The reason? The researchers suggest that people are more willing to associate with individuals whom they perceive as good-looking.

for your Consideration

Stereotypes have no single, inevitable effect. They are not magical. People can resist stereotypes and change outcomes. However, these studies do illustrate that stereotypes deeply influence how we react to one another.

Instead of beauty, consider gender and race-ethnicity. How do they affect those who do the stereotyping and those who are stereotyped?

Physical attractiveness underlies much of our social interaction in everyday life. The experiment reviewed in this box illustrates how college men modified their interactions on the basis of attractiveness. How do you think men would modify their interactions if they were to meet the two women in these photographs? How about women? Would they change their interactions in the same way?

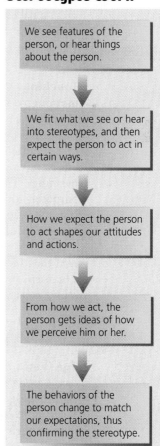

Figure 4.3 How Self-Fulfilling Stereotypes Work

We see features of the person, or hear things about the person.

⬇

We fit what we see or hear into stereotypes, and then expect the person to act in certain ways.

⬇

How we expect the person to act shapes our attitudes and actions.

⬇

From how we act, the person gets ideas of how we perceive him or her.

⬇

The behaviors of the person change to match our expectations, thus confirming the stereotype.

He came to the front of the class at the end of the lecture. . . . We started out facing each other, and as he talked I became dimly aware that he was standing a little too close and that I was beginning to back up. Fortunately I was able to suppress my first impulse and remain stationary because there was nothing to communicate aggression in his behavior except the conversational distance. . . .

By experimenting I was able to observe that as I moved away slightly, there was an associated shift in the pattern of interaction. He had more trouble expressing himself. If I shifted to where I felt comfortable (about twenty-one inches), he looked somewhat puzzled and hurt, almost as though he were saying, "Why is he acting that way? Here I am doing everything I can to talk to him in a friendly manner and he suddenly withdraws. Have I done anything wrong? Said something I shouldn't?" Having ascertained that distance had a direct effect on his conversation, I stood my ground, letting him set the distance.

As you can see, despite Hall's extensive knowledge of other cultures, he still felt uncomfortable in this conversation. He first interpreted the invasion of his personal space as possible aggression, for people get close (and jut out their chins and chests) when they are hostile. But when he realized that this was not the case, Hall resisted his impulse to move.

After Hall (1969; Hall and Hall 2007) analyzed situations like this, he observed that North Americans use four different "distance zones."

1. *Intimate distance.* This is the zone that the South American unwittingly invaded. It extends to about 18 inches from our bodies. We reserve this space for comforting, protecting, hugging, intimate touching, and lovemaking.
2. *Personal distance.* This zone extends from 18 inches to 4 feet. We reserve it for friends and acquaintances and ordinary conversations. This is the zone in which Hall would have preferred speaking with the South American.
3. *Social distance.* This zone, extending out from us about 4 to 12 feet, marks impersonal or formal relationships. We use this zone for such things as job interviews.
4. *Public distance.* This zone, extending beyond 12 feet, marks even more formal relationships. It is used to separate dignitaries and public speakers from the general public.

Touching   Not only does frequency of touching differ across cultures, but so does the meaning of touching within a culture. In general, higher-status individuals do more touching. Thus you are much more likely to see teachers touch students and bosses touch secretaries than the other way around. Apparently it is considered unseemly for lower-status individuals to put their hands on superiors.

An experiment with surgery patients illustrates how touching can have different meanings. The nurse, whose job it was to tell patients about their upcoming surgery, purposely touched the patients twice, once briefly on the arm when she introduced herself, and then for a full minute on the arm during the instruction period. When she left, she also shook the patient's hand (Thayer 1988).

Men and women reacted differently. Touching soothed the women patients. It lowered their blood pressure both before the surgery and for more than an hour afterward. The men's blood pressure increased, however. The experimenters suggest that the men found it harder to acknowledge dependency and fear. Instead of a comfort, the touch was a threatening reminder of their vulnerability. Perhaps. But the answer could be much simpler: Being touched by a pretty nurse aroused the men sexually, which increased their blood pressure. We don't know the reason. For this, we need more research.

Eye Contact   One way that we protect our personal bubble is by controlling eye contact. Letting someone gaze into our eyes—unless the person is our eye doctor—can be taken as a sign that we are attracted to that person, and even as an invitation to intimacy. Wanting to become "the friendliest store in town," a chain of supermarkets in Illinois ordered their checkout clerks to make direct eye contact with each customer. Women clerks complained that men customers were taking their eye contact the wrong way, as an invitation to intimacy. Management said they were exaggerating. The clerks' reply

"Eye encounters" are a fascinating aspect of everyday life. We use fleeting eye contact for most of our interactions, such as those with clerks or people we pass in the hall between classes. Just as we reserve our close personal space for intimates, so, too, we reserve lingering eye contact for them.

was, "We know the kind of looks we're getting back from men," and they refused to make direct eye contact with them.

Smiling   In the United States, we take it for granted that clerks will smile as they wait on us. But it isn't this way in all cultures. Apparently, Germans aren't used to smiling clerks, and when Wal-Mart expanded into Germany, it brought its American ways with it. The company ordered its German clerks to smile at their customers. They did—and the customers complained. The German customers interpreted the smiles as flirting (Samor et al. 2006).

Applied Body Language   The ways we use our bodies to give messages to others— from our facial expressions to our posture—are called **body language.** We all learn to interpret body language as part of our childhood lessons in culture, and we use this learning to help us get through everyday life. But now interpreting body language has become a tool in the government's fight against terrorism. Because many of the messages we give with our bodies lie beneath our consciousness, airport personnel and interrogators are being trained to look for tell-tale facial signs—from a quick downturn of the mouth to rapid blinking—that might indicate nervousness or that the individual is telling a lie (Davis et al. 2002).

Let's now turn to dramaturgy, a special area of symbolic interactionism.

Dramaturgy: The Presentation of Self in Everyday Life

It was their big day, two years in the making. Jennifer Mackey wore a white wedding gown adorned with an 11-foot train and 24,000 seed pearls that she and her mother had sewn onto the dress. Next to her at the altar in Lexington, Kentucky, stood her intended, Jeffrey Degler, in black tie. They said their vows, then turned to gaze for a moment at the four hundred guests.

That's when groomsman Daniel Mackey collapsed. As the shocked organist struggled to play Mendelssohn's "Wedding March," Mr. Mackey's unconscious body was dragged away, his feet striking—loudly—every step of the altar stairs.

"I couldn't believe he would die at my wedding," the bride said. (Hughes 1990)

Sociologist Erving Goffman (1922–1982) added a new twist to microsociology when he developed **dramaturgy** (or dramaturgical analysis). By this term he meant that social life is like a drama or a stage play: Birth ushers us onto the stage of everyday life, and our socialization consists of learning to perform on that stage. The self that we studied in the previous chapter lies at the center of our performances. We have ideas of how we want others to think of us, and we use our roles in everyday life to communicate those ideas. Goffman called these efforts to manage the impressions that others receive of us **impression management.**

Stages   Everyday life, said Goffman, involves playing our assigned roles. We have **front stages** on which to perform them, as did Jennifer and Jeffrey. (By the way, Daniel Mackey didn't really die—he had just fainted.) But we don't have to look at weddings to find front stages. Everyday life is filled with them. Where your teacher lectures is a front stage. And if you make an announcement at the dinner table, you are using a front stage. In fact, you spend most of your time on front stages, for a front stage is wherever you deliver your lines. We also have **back stages,** places where we can retreat and let our hair

body language the ways in which people use their bodies to give messages to others, much of which is done subconsciously

dramaturgy an approach, pioneered by Erving Goffman, in which social life is analyzed in terms of drama or the stage; also called dramaturgical analysis

impression management people's efforts to control the impressions that others receive of them

front stage where performances are given

back stage where people rest from their performances, discuss their presentations, and plan future performances

In *dramaturgy*, a specialty within sociology, social life is viewed as similar to the theater. In our everyday lives, we all are actors like those in this cast of *The George Lopez Show*. We, too, perform roles, use props, and deliver lines to fellow actors—who, in turn, do the same.

down. When you close the bathroom or bedroom door for privacy, for example, you are entering a back stage.

The same setting can serve as both a back and a front stage. For example, when you get into your car and look over your hair in the mirror or check your makeup, you are using the car as a back stage. But when you wave at friends or if you give that familiar gesture to someone who has just cut in front of you in traffic, you are using your car as a front stage.

Role Performance, Conflict, and Strain   Everyday life brings with it many roles. As discussed earlier, the same person may be a student, a teenager, a shopper, a worker, and a date, as well as a daughter or a son. Although a role lays down the basic outline for a performance, it also allows a great deal of flexibility. The particular emphasis or interpretation that we give a role, our "style," is known as **role performance.** Consider your role as son or daughter. You may play the role of ideal daughter or son—being respectful, coming home at the hours your parents set, and so forth. Or this description may not even come close to your particular role performance.

Ordinarily, our statuses are sufficiently separated that we find minimal conflict between them. Occasionally, however, what is expected of us in one status (our role) is incompatible with what is expected of us in another status. This problem, known as **role conflict,** is illustrated in Figure 4.4 on the next page, in which family, friendship, student, and work roles come crashing together. Usually, however, we manage to avoid role conflict by segregating our statuses, which in some instances requires an intense juggling act.

Sometimes the *same* status contains incompatible roles, a conflict known as **role strain.** Suppose that you are exceptionally well prepared for a particular class assignment. Although the instructor asks an unusually difficult question, you find yourself knowing the answer when no one else does. If you want to raise your hand, yet don't want to make your fellow students look bad, you will experience role strain. As illustrated in Figure 4.4, the difference between role conflict and role strain is that role conflict is conflict *between roles,* while role strain is conflict *within* a role.

role performance the ways in which someone performs a role, showing a particular "style" or "personality"

role conflict conflicts that someone feels *between* roles because the expectations attached to one role are incompatible with the expectations of another role

role strain conflicts that someone feels *within* a role

Figure 4.4 Role Strain and Role Conflict

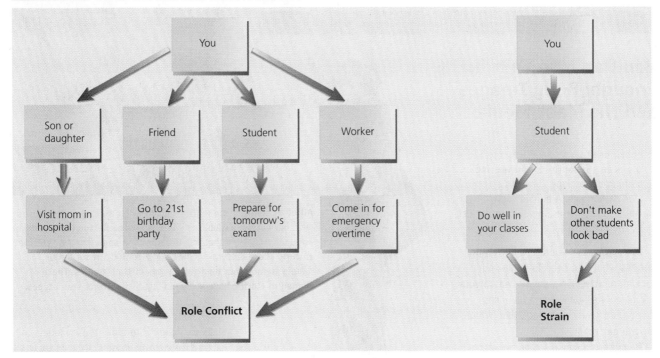

Source: By the author.

Sign-Vehicles To communicate information about the self, we use three types of **sign-vehicles:** the social setting, our appearance, and our manner. The *social setting* is the place where the action unfolds. This is where the curtain goes up on your performance, where you find yourself on stage playing parts and delivering lines. A social setting might be an office, dorm, living room, church, gym, or bar. It is wherever you interact with others. Your social setting includes *scenery,* the furnishings you use to communicate messages, such as desks, blackboards, scoreboards, couches, and so on.

The second sign-vehicle is *appearance,* or how we look when we play our roles. Appearance includes *props,* which are like scenery except that they decorate the person rather than the setting. The teacher has books, lecture notes, and chalk, while the football player wears a costume called a uniform. Although few of us carry around a football, we all use makeup, hairstyles, and clothing to communicate messages about ourselves. Props and other aspects of appearance give us cues that help us navigate everyday life: By letting us know what to expect from others, props tell us how we should react. Think of the messages that props communicate. Some people use clothing to say they are college students, others to say they are older adults. Some use clothing to say they are clergy, others to say they are prostitutes. Similarly, people choose brands of cigarettes, liquor, and automobiles to convey messages about the self.

Our body is an especially important sign-vehicle, its shape proclaiming messages about the self. The messages that are attached to various shapes change over time, but, as explored in the Mass Media box on the next page, thinness currently screams desirability.

The third sign-vehicle is *manner,* the attitudes we show as we play our roles. We use manner to communicate information about our feelings and moods. If we show anger or indifference, sincerity or good humor, for example, we indicate to others what they can expect of us as we play our roles.

Teamwork Being a good role player brings positive recognition from others, something we all covet. To accomplish this, we often use **teamwork**—two or more people working together to make certain that a performance goes off as planned. When a performance doesn't come off quite right, however, it may require **face-saving behavior.**

sign-vehicles the term used by Goffman to refer to how people use social setting, appearance, and manner to communicate information about the self

teamwork the collaboration of two or more people to manage impressions jointly

face-saving behavior techniques used to salvage a performance that is going sour

mass Media in social life

You Can't Be Thin Enough: Body Images and the Mass Media

An ad for Kellogg's Special K cereal shows an 18-month-old girl wearing nothing but a diaper. She has a worried look on her face. A bubble caption over her head has her asking, "Do I look fat?" (Krane et al. 2001)

When you stand before a mirror, do you like what you see? To make your body more attractive, do you watch your weight or work out? You have ideas about what you should look like. Where did you get them?

TV and magazine ads keep pounding home the message that our bodies aren't good enough, that we've got to improve them. The way to improve them, of course, is to buy the advertised products: hair extensions for women, hairpieces for men, hair transplants, padded bras, diet programs, anti-aging products, and exercise equipment. Muscular hulks show off machines that magically produce "six-pack abs" and incredible biceps—in just a few minutes a day. Female movie stars effortlessly go through their own tough workouts without even breaking into a sweat. Women and men get the feeling that attractive members of the opposite sex will flock to them if they purchase that wonder-working workout machine.

All of us contrast the reality we see when we look in the mirror with our culture's ideal body types. Mischa Barton represents an ideal body type that has developed in some parts of Western culture. These cultural images make it difficult for larger people to maintain positive images of their bodies. These women in Florida have struggled against cultural stereotypes.

Although we try to shrug off such messages, knowing that they are designed to sell products, the messages still get our attention. They penetrate our thinking and feelings, helping to shape ideal images of

how we "ought" to look. Those models so attractively clothed and coiffed as they walk down the runway, could they be any thinner? For women, the message is clear: You can't be thin enough. The men's message is also clear: You can't be muscular enough.

Woman or man, your body isn't good enough. It sags where it should be firm. It bulges where it should be smooth. It sticks out where it shouldn't, and it doesn't stick out enough where it should.

And—no matter what your weight is—it's too much. You've got to be thinner.

Exercise takes time, and getting in shape is painful. Once you do get in shape, if you slack off it seems to take only a few days for your body to sag into its previous slothful, drab appearance. You

---

We may, for example, ignore flaws in someone's performance, which Goffman defines as *tact*.

Suppose your teacher is about to make an important point. Suppose also that her lecturing has been outstanding and the class is hanging on every word. Just as she pauses for emphasis, her stomach lets out a loud growl. She might then use a *face-saving technique* by remarking, "I was so busy preparing for class that I didn't get breakfast this morning." It is more likely, however, that both class and teacher will simply ignore the sound, giving the impression that no one heard a thing—a face-saving technique called *studied nonobservance*. This allows the teacher to make the point, or as Goffman would say, it allows the performance to go on.

Becoming the Roles We Play We become so used to the roles we play in everyday life that we tend to think we are "just doing" things, not that we are like actors on a stage can't let up, you can't exercise enough, and you can't diet enough.

But who can continue at such a torrid pace, striving for what are unrealistic cultural ideals? A few people, of course, but not many. So liposuction is appealing. Just lie there, put up with a little discomfort, and the doctor will vacuum the fat right out of your body. Surgeons can transform flat breasts into super breasts overnight. They can lower receding hairlines and smooth furrowed brows. They remove lumps with their magical tummy tucks, and can take off a decade with their rejuvenating skin peels, face lifts, and Botox injections.

With impossibly shaped models at *Victoria's Secret* and skinny models showing off the latest fashions in *Vogue* and *Seventeen*, half of U.S. adolescent girls feel fat and count calories (Hill 2006). Some teens even call the plastic surgeon. Anxious lest their child violate peer ideals and trail behind in her race for popularity, parents foot the bill. Some parents pay $25,000 just to give their daughters a flatter tummy (Gross 1998).

With peer pressure to alter the body already intense, surgeons keep stoking the fire. A sample ad: "No Ifs, Ands or Butts. You Can Change Your Bottom Line in Hours!" Some surgeons even offer gift certificates—so you can give your loved ones liposuction or botox injections along with their greeting card (Dowd 2002).

The thinness craze has moved to the East. Glossy magazines in Japan and China are filled with skinny models and crammed with ads touting diet pills and diet teas. In China, where famine used to abound, a little extra padding was valued as a sign of good health. Today, the obsession is thinness (Rosenthal 1999; Prystay and Fowler 2003). Not-so-subtle ads scream that fat is bad. Some teas come with a package of diet pills. Weight-loss machines, with electrodes attached to acupuncture pressure points, not only reduce fat but also build breasts—or so the advertisers claim.

Not limited by our rules, advertisers in Japan and China push a soap that supposedly "sucks up fat through the skin's pores" (Marshall 1995). What a dream product! After all, even though our TV models smile as they go through their paces, those exercise machines do look like a lot of hard work.

Then there is the other bottom line: Attractiveness does pay off. U.S. economists studied physical attractiveness and earnings. The result? "Good-looking" men and women earn the most, "average-looking" men and women earn more than "plain" people, and the "ugly" earn the least (Hamermesh and Biddle 1994). In Europe, too, the more attractive workers earn more (Brunello and D'Hombres 2007). Then there is that potent cash advantage that "attractive" women have: They attract and marry higher-earning men (Kanasawa and Kovar 2004).

More popularity *and* more money? Maybe you can't be thin enough after all. Maybe those exercise machines are a good investment. If only we could catch up with the Japanese and develop a soap that would suck the fat right out of our pores. You can practically hear the jingle now.

for your Consideration

What image do you have of your body? How do cultural expectations of "ideal" bodies underlie your image? Can you recall any advertisement or television program that has affected your body image?

What is considered ideal body size differs with historical periods and from one ethnic group to another. The women who posed for 16th century European sculptors and painters, for example, were much "thicker" than the so-called "ideal" young women of today. (As I was looking at a painting in the Vatican, I heard a woman remark,"Look at those rolls of fat!") Why do you think that this difference exists?

Most advertising and television programs that focus on weight are directed at women. Women are more concerned than men about weight, more likely to have eating disorders, and more likely to be dissatisfied with their bodies (Honeycutt 1995; Hill 2006). Do you think that the targeting of women in advertising creates these attitudes and behaviors? Or do you think that these attitudes and behaviors would exist even if there were no such ads? Why?

who manage impressions. Yet every time we dress for school, or for any other activity, we are preparing for impression management. Have you ever noticed how some clothing simply doesn't "feel" right for certain occasions? Have you ever changed your mind about something you were wearing and decided to change your clothing? Or maybe just switch shirts or add a necklace? That is fine-tuning the impressions you want to make. Similarly, you may have noticed that when teenagers want to impress the opposite sex, they stand before a mirror for hours as they comb and restyle their hair, and then change and adjust their clothing as they try to "get it just right."

Although roles might be uncomfortable at first, after we get used to them *we tend to become the roles we play.* That is, roles become incorporated into the self-concept, especially roles for which we prepare long and hard and that become part of our everyday lives. When sociologist Helen Ebaugh (1988), who had been a nun, studied *role exit,* she interviewed people who had left marriages, police work, the military, medicine, and religious vocations. She found that the role had become so intertwined with the individual's self-concept that leaving it threatened the person's identity. The question these people struggled with was "Who am I, now that I am not a nun (or wife, police officer, colonel, physician, and so on)?" Even years after leaving these roles, many continue to perform them in their dreams.

A statement by one of my respondents illustrates how roles become part of the person and linger even after the individual leaves them:

> After I left the ministry, I felt like a fish out of water. Wearing that backward collar had become a part of me. It was especially strange on Sunday mornings when I'd listen to someone else give the sermon. I knew that I should be up there preaching. I felt as though I had left God.

Applying Impression Management   I can just hear someone saying, "Impression management is interesting, but is it really significant?" In fact, it is so significant that the right impression management can make a vital difference in your career. To be promoted, you must be perceived as someone who *should* be promoted. You must appear dominant. You certainly cannot go unnoticed. But how you manage this impression is crucial. If an executive woman tries to appear dominant by wearing loud clothing, using garish makeup, and cursing, this will get her noticed—but it will not put her on the path to promotion. How, then, can she exhibit dominance in the right way? To help women walk this fine line between femininity and dominance, career counselors advise women on fine details of impression management. Here are two things they recommend—that women place their hands on the table during executive sessions, not in their lap, and that they carry a purse that looks more like a briefcase (Needham 2006).

Ethnomethodology: Uncovering Background Assumptions

Certainly one of the strangest words in sociology is *ethnomethodology*. To better understand this term, consider the word's three basic components. *Ethno* means "folk" or "people"; *method* means how people do something; *ology* means "the study of." Putting them together, then, *ethno/method/ology* means "the study of how people do things." Specifically, **ethnomethodology** is the study of how people use commonsense understandings to make sense of life.

Let's suppose that during a routine office visit, your doctor remarks that your hair is rather long, then takes out a pair of scissors and starts to give you a haircut. You would feel strange about this, for your doctor would be violating **background assumptions**—your ideas about the way life is and the way things ought to work. These assumptions, which lie at the root of everyday life, are so deeply embedded in our consciousness that we are seldom aware of them, and most of us fulfill them unquestioningly. Thus, your doctor does not offer you a haircut, even if he or she is good at cutting hair and you need one!

The founder of ethnomethodology, sociologist Harold Garfinkel, conducted some interesting exercises designed to reveal our background assumptions. Garfinkel (1967) asked his students to act as though they did not understand the basic rules of social life. Some tried to bargain with supermarket clerks; others would inch close to people and stare directly at them. They were met with surprise, bewilderment, even anger. In one exercise Garfinkel

ethnomethodology the study of how people use background assumptions to make sense out of life

background assumptions deeply embedded common understandings of how the world operates and of how people ought to act asked students to act as though they were boarders in their own homes. They addressed their parents as "Mr." and "Mrs.," asked permission to use the bathroom, sat stiffly, were courteous, and spoke only when spoken to. As you can imagine, the other family members didn't know what to make of this (Garfinkel 1967):

> They vigorously sought to make the strange actions intelligible and to restore the situation to normal appearances. Reports (by the students) were filled with accounts of astonishment, bewilderment, shock, anxiety, embarrassment, and anger, and with charges by various family members that the student was mean, inconsiderate, selfish, nasty, or impolite. Family members demanded explanations: What's the matter? What's gotten into you? . . . Are you sick? . . . Are you out of your mind or are you just stupid?

In another exercise, Garfinkel asked students to take words and phrases literally. When a student asked his girlfriend what she meant when she said that she had a flat tire, she said:

> What do you mean, "What do you mean?"? A flat tire is a flat tire. That is what I meant. Nothing special. What a crazy question!

Another conversation went like this:

ACQUAINTANCE: How are you?

STUDENT: How am I in regard to what? My health, my finances, my schoolwork, my peace of mind, my . . . ?

ACQUAINTANCE: (red in the face): Look! I was just trying to be polite. Frankly, I don't give a damn how you are.

Students who are asked to break background assumptions can be highly creative. The young children of one of my students were surprised one morning when they came down for breakfast to find a sheet spread across the living room floor. On it were dishes, silverware, lit candles—and bowls of ice cream. They, too, wondered what was going on, but they dug eagerly into the ice cream before their mother could change her mind.

This is a risky assignment to give students, however, for breaking some background assumptions can make people suspicious. When a colleague of mine gave this assignment, a couple of his students began to wash dollar bills in a laundromat. By the time they put the bills in the dryer, the police had arrived.

All of us have *background assumptions*, deeply ingrained assumptions of how the world operates. How do you think the background assumptions of this Londoner differ from this Ecuadoran shaman, who is performing a healing ceremony to rid London of its evil spirits?

IN SUM | Ethnomethodologists explore *background assumptions*, the taken-for-granted ideas about the world that underlie our behavior. Most of these assumptions, or basic rules of social life, are unstated. We learn them as we learn our culture, and we violate them only with risk. Deeply embedded in our minds, they give us basic directions for living everyday life.

The Social Construction of Reality

Symbolic interactionists stress how our ideas help determine our reality. In what has become known as *the definition of the situation,* or the **Thomas theorem,** sociologists W. I. and Dorothy S. Thomas said "If people define situations as real, they are real in their consequences." Consider the following incident:

> On a visit to Morocco, in northern Africa, I decided to buy a watermelon. When I indicated to the street vendor that the knife he was going to use to cut the watermelon was dirty (encrusted with filth would be more apt), he was very obliging. He immediately

Thomas theorem William I. and Dorothy S. Thomas' classic formulation of the definition of the situation: "If people define situations as real, they are real in their consequences."

bent down and began to swish the knife in a puddle on the street. I shuddered as I looked at the passing burros that were urinating and defecating as they went by. Quickly, I indicated by gesture that I preferred my melon uncut after all.

For that vendor, germs did not exist. For me, they did. And each of us acted according to our definition of the situation. My perception and behavior did not come from the fact that germs are real but *because I grew up in a society that teaches they are real.* Microbes, of course, *objectively* exist, and whether or not germs are part of our thought world makes no difference as to whether we are infected by them. Our behavior, however, does not depend on the *objective* existence of something but, rather, on our *subjective interpretation,* on what sociologists call our *definition of reality.* In other words, it is not the reality of microbes that impresses itself on us, but society that impresses the reality of microbes on us.

Let's consider another example. Do you remember the identical twins, Oskar and Jack, who grew up so differently? As discussed on page 66, Jack was reared in Trinidad and learned to hate Hitler, while Oskar was reared in Germany and learned to love Hitler. Thus what Hitler meant to Oskar and Jack (and what he means to us) depends not on Hitler's acts, but, rather, on how we view his acts—that is, on our definition of the situation.

This is the **social construction of reality.** Our society, or the social groups to which we belong, holds particular views of life. From our groups (the *social* part of this process), we learn ways of looking at life—whether that be our view of Hitler or Osama bin Laden (they're good, they're evil), germs (they exist, they don't exist), or *anything else in life.* In short, through our interaction with others, we *construct reality;* that is, we learn ways of interpreting our experiences in life.

Gynecological Examinations   To better understand the social construction of reality, let's consider an extended example.

To do research on vaginal examinations, I interviewed a gynecological nurse who had been present at about 14,000 examinations. I focused on how doctors construct social reality in order to define this examination as nonsexual (Henslin and Biggs 1971/2007). It became apparent that the pelvic examination unfolds much as a stage play does. I will use "he" to refer to the physician because only male physicians were part of this study. Perhaps the results would be different with women gynecologists.

Scene 1 (the patient as person) In this scene, the doctor maintains eye contact with his patient, calls her by name, and discusses her problems in a professional manner. If he decides that a vaginal examination is necessary, he tells a nurse, "Pelvic in room 1." By this statement, he is announcing that a major change will occur in the next scene.

Scene 2 (from person to pelvic) This scene is the depersonalizing stage. In line with the doctor's announcement, the patient begins the transition from a "person" to a "pelvic." The doctor leaves the room, and a female nurse enters to help the patient make the transition. The nurse prepares the "props" for the coming examination and answers any questions the woman might have.

What occurs at this point is essential for the social construction of reality, for *the doctor's absence removes even the suggestion of sexuality.* To undress in front of him could suggest either a striptease or intimacy, thus undermining the reality so carefully being defined: that of nonsexuality.

The patient also wants to remove any hint of sexuality, and during this scene she may express concern about what to do with her panties. Some mutter to the nurse, "I don't want him to see these." Most women solve the problem by either slipping their panties under their other clothes or placing them in their purse.

Scene 3 (the person as pelvic) This scene opens when the doctor enters the room. Before him is a woman lying on a table, her feet in stirrups, her knees tightly together, and her body covered by a drape sheet. The doctor seats himself on a low stool before the woman and says, "Let your knees fall apart" (rather than the sexually loaded "Spread your legs"), and begins the examination.

social construction of reality the use of background assumptions and life experiences to define what is real

The drape sheet is crucial in this process of desexualization, for it *dissociates the pelvic area from the person:* Leaning forward and with the drape sheet above his head, the physician can see only the vagina, not the patient's face. Thus dissociated from the individual, the vagina is dramaturgically transformed into an object of analysis. If the doctor examines the patient's breasts, he also dissociates them from her person by examining them one at a time, with a towel covering the unexamined breast. Like the vagina, each breast becomes an isolated item dissociated from the person.

In this third scene, the patient cooperates in being an object, becoming, for all practical purposes, a pelvis to be examined. She withdraws eye contact from the doctor, and usually from the nurse, is likely to stare at the wall or at the ceiling, and avoids initiating conversation.

Scene 4 (from pelvic to person) In this scene, the patient becomes "repersonalized." The doctor has left the examining room; the patient dresses and fixes her hair and makeup. Her reemergence as a person is indicated by such statements to the nurse as, "My dress isn't too wrinkled, is it?" indicating a need for reassurance that the metamorphosis from "pelvic" back to "person" has been completed satisfactorily.

Scene 5 (the patient as person) In this final scene, the patient is once again treated as a person rather than as an object. The doctor makes eye contact with her and addresses her by name. She, too, makes eye contact with the doctor, and the usual middle-class interaction patterns are followed. She has been fully restored.

IN SUM To an outsider to our culture, the custom of women going to a male stranger for a vaginal examination might seem bizarre. But not to us. We learn that pelvic examinations are nonsexual. To sustain this definition requires teamwork—patients, doctors, and nurses working together to *socially construct reality.*

It is not just pelvic examinations or our views of microbes that make up our definitions of reality. Rather, *our behavior depends on how we define reality.* Our definitions (or constructions) provide the basis for what we do and how we feel about life. To understand human behavior, then, we must know how people define reality.

The Need for Both Macrosociology and Microsociology

As was noted earlier, both microsociology and macrosociology make vital contributions to our understanding of human behavior. Our understanding of social life would be vastly incomplete without one or the other. The photo essay on the next two pages should help to make clear why we need *both* perspectives.

To illustrate this point, let's consider two groups of high school boys studied by sociologist William Chambliss (1973/2007). Both groups attended Hanibal High School. In one group were eight middle-class boys who came from "good" families and were perceived by the community as "going somewhere." Chambliss calls this group the "Saints." The other group consisted of six lower-class boys who were seen as headed down a dead-end road. Chambliss calls this group the "Roughnecks."

Boys in both groups skipped school, got drunk, and did a lot of fighting and vandalism. The Saints were actually somewhat more delinquent, for they were truant more often and engaged in more vandalism. Yet the Saints had a good reputation, while the Roughnecks were seen by teachers, the police, and the general community as no good and headed for trouble.

The boys' reputations set them on distinct paths. Seven of the eight Saints went on to graduate from college. Three studied for advanced degrees: One finished law school and became active in state politics, one finished medical school, and one went on to earn a Ph.D. The four other college graduates entered managerial or executive training programs with large firms. After his parents divorced, one Saint failed to graduate from high school on time and had to repeat his senior year. Although this boy tried to go to

When a **Tornado Strikes:**
Social Organization Following a Natural Disaster

as I was watching television on March 20, 2003, I heard a report that a tornado had hit Camilla, Georgia. "Like a big lawn mower," the report said, it had cut a path of destruction through this little town. In its fury, the tornado had left behind six dead and about 200 injured.

From sociological studies of natural disasters, I knew that immediately after the initial shock the survivors of natural disasters work together to try to restore order to their disrupted lives. I wanted to see this restructuring process first hand. The next morning, I took off for Georgia.

These photos, taken the day after the tornado struck, tell the story of people who are in the midst of trying to put their lives back together. I was impressed at how little time people spend commiserating about their misfortune and how quickly they take practical steps to restore their lives.

As you look at these photos, try to determine why you need both microsociology and macrosociology to understand what occurs after a natural disaster.

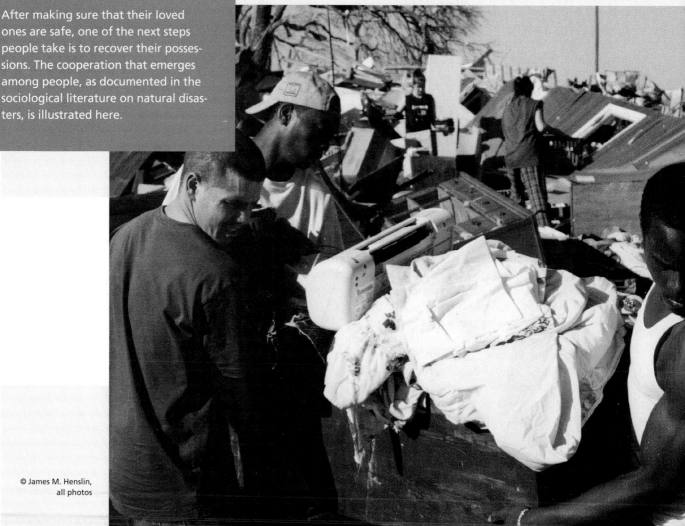

After making sure that their loved ones are safe, one of the next steps people take is to recover their possessions. The cooperation that emerges among people, as documented in the sociological literature on natural disasters, is illustrated here.

© James M. Henslin, all photos

In addition to the inquiring sociologist, television news teams also were interviewing survivors and photographing the damage. This was the second time in just three years that a tornado had hit this neighborhood.

The owners of this house invited me inside to see what the tornado had done to their home. In what had been her dining room, this woman is trying to salvage whatever she can from the rubble. She and her family survived by taking refuge in the bathroom. They had been there only five seconds, she said, when the tornado struck.

Just the night before, members of this church had held evening worship service. After the tornado, someone mounted a U.S. flag on top of the cross, symbolic of the church members' patriotism and religiosity—and of their enduring hope.

Personal relationships are essential in putting lives together. Consequently, reminders of these relationships are one of the main possessions that people attempt to salvage. This young man, having just recovered the family photo album, is eagerly reviewing the photos.

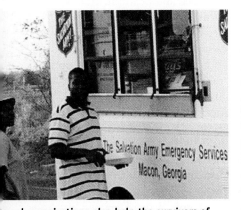

rmal organizations also help the survivors of tural disasters recover. In this neighborhood, I w representatives of insurance companies, the lice, the fire department, and an electrical co-. The Salvation Army brought meals to the ighborhood.

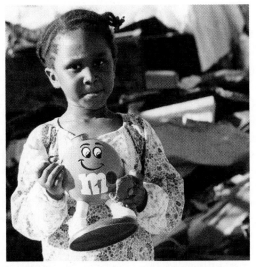

For children, family photos are not as important as toys. This girl has managed to salvage a favorite toy, which will help anchor her to her previous life.

A sign of the times. Like electricity and gas, cable television also has to be re-stored as soon as possible.

college by attending night school, he never finished. He was unemployed the last time Chambliss saw him.

In contrast, only four of the Roughnecks finished high school. Two of these boys did exceptionally well in sports and were awarded athletic scholarships to college. They both graduated from college and became high school coaches. Of the two others who graduated from high school, one became a small-time gambler and the other disappeared "up north," where he was last reported to be driving a truck. The two who did not complete high school were convicted of separate murders and sent to prison.

To understand what happened to the Saints and the Roughnecks, we need to grasp *both* social structure and social interaction. Using *macrosociology*, we can place these boys within the larger framework of the U.S. social class system. This reveals how opportunities open or close to people depending on their social class and how people learn different goals as they grow up in different groups. We can then use *microsociology* to follow their everyday lives. We can see how the Saints manipulated their "good" reputations to skip classes and how their access to automobiles allowed them to protect those reputations by transferring their troublemaking to different communities. In contrast, the Roughnecks, who did not have cars, were highly visible. Their lawbreaking, which was limited to a small area, readily came to the attention of the community. Microsociology also reveals how their respective reputations opened doors of opportunity to the first group of boys while closing them to the other.

It is clear that we need both kinds of sociology, and both are stressed in the following chapters.

Summary *and* Review

Levels of Sociological Analysis

What two levels of analysis do sociologists use?

Sociologists use macrosociological and microsociological levels of analysis. In **macrosociology,** the focus is placed on large-scale features of social life, while in **microsociology,** the focus is on **social interaction.** Functionalists and conflict theorists tend to use a macrosociological approach, while symbolic interactionists are more likely to use a microsociological approach. Pp. 98–99.

The Macrosociological Perspective: Social Structure

How does social structure influence our behavior?

The term **social structure** refers to the social envelope that surrounds us and establishes limits on our behavior. Social structure consists of culture, social class, social statuses, roles, groups, and social institutions. Our location in the social structure underlies our perceptions, attitudes, and behaviors.

Culture lays the broadest framework, while **social class** divides people according to income, education, and occupational prestige. Each of us receives **ascribed statuses** at birth; later we add **achieved statuses.** Our behaviors and orientations are further influenced by the **roles** we play, the **groups** to which we belong, and

our experiences with social institutions. These components of society work together to help maintain social order. Pp. 99–103.

Social Institutions

What are social institutions?

Social institutions are the standard ways that a society develops to meet its basic needs. As summarized in Figure 4.2 (page 105), industrial and postindustrial societies have ten social institutions—the family, religion, education, economics, medicine, politics, law, science, the military, and the mass media. From the functionalist perspective, social institutions meet universal group needs, or **functional requisites.** Conflict theorists stress how society's elites use social institutions to maintain their privileged positions. Pp. 104–107.

What holds society together?

According to Emile Durkheim, in agricultural societies people are united by **mechanical solidarity** (having similar views and feelings). With industrialization comes **organic solidarity** (people depend on one another to do their more specialized jobs). Ferdinand Tönnies pointed out that the informal means of control of *Gemeinschaft* (small, intimate) societies are replaced by formal mechanisms in *Gesellschaft* (larger, more impersonal) societies. Pp. 107–109.

The Microsociological Perspective: Social Interaction in Everyday Life

What is the focus of symbolic interactionism?

In contrast to functionalists and conflict theorists, who as macrosociologists focus on the "big picture," symbolic interactionists tend to be microsociologists who focus on face-to-face social interaction. Symbolic interactionists analyze how people define their worlds, and how their definitions, in turn, influence their behavior. P. 110.

How do stereotypes affect social interaction?

Stereotypes are assumptions of what people are like. When we first meet people, we classify them according to our perceptions of their visible characteristics. Our ideas about those characteristics guide our behavior toward them. Our behavior, in turn, may influence them to behave in ways that reinforce our stereotypes. Pp. 110–111.

Do all human groups share a similar sense of personal space?

In examining how people use physical space, symbolic interactionists stress that we surround ourselves with a "personal bubble" that we carefully protect. People from different cultures use "personal bubbles" of varying sizes, so the answer to the question is no. Americans typically use four different "distance zones": intimate, personal, social, and public. Pp. 110, 112.

What is dramaturgy?

Erving Goffman developed **dramaturgy** (or dramaturgical analysis), in which everyday life is analyzed in terms of the stage. At the core of this analysis is **impression management,** our attempts to control the impressions we make on others. For this, we use the **sign-vehicles** of setting, appearance, and manner. Our performances often call for **teamwork** and **face-saving behavior.** Pp. 113–118.

What is the social construction of reality?

The phrase **the social construction of reality** refers to how we construct our views of the world, which, in turn, underlie our actions. **Ethnomethodology** is the study of how people make sense of everyday life. Ethnomethodologists try to uncover **background assumptions,** our basic ideas about the way life is. Pp. 118–121.

The Need for Both Macrosociology and Microsociology

Why are both levels of analysis necessary?

Because each focuses on different aspects of the human experience, both microsociology and macrosociology are necessary for us to understand social life. Pp. 121–124.

Thinking Critically
about Chapter 4

1. The major components of social structure are culture, social class, social status, roles, groups, and social institutions. Use social structure to explain why Native Americans have such a low rate of college graduation. (See Table 12.2 on page 356.)

2. Dramaturgy is a form of microsociology. Use dramaturgy to analyze a situation with which you are intimately familiar (such as interaction with your family or friends, or in one of your college classes).

3. To illustrate why we need both macrosociology and microsociology to understand social life, consider a student getting kicked out of college as an example.

Additional Resources

What can you use MySocLab for?

 www.mysoclab.com

- **Study and Review:** Pre- and Post-Tests, Practice Tests, Flash Cards, Individualized Study Plans.
- **Current Events:** *Sociology in the News,* the daily *New York Times,* and more.
- **Research and Writing:** *Research Navigator, Writing About Sociology,* and more.

Where Can I Read More on This Topic?

Suggested readings for this chapter are listed at the back of this book.

How Sociologists Do Research

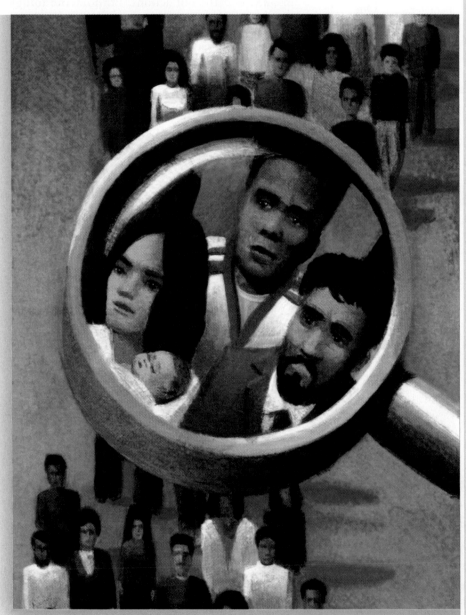

Ivan Lee Sanford, *Diverse Cross-Section*, 1991

Cindy Hudo, a 21-year-old mother of two in Charleston, South Carolina, who was charged with the murder of her husband, Buba, said:

I start in the car, and I get down the road, and I see Buba walking, and he's real mad . . . . I pull over, you know, and [I said] "I didn't know to pick you up. You know, I'm sorry." And he didn't even say nothing to me. He just started hitting on me. And that's all I wanted to do, was just get home, because I was just self-conscious. I don't want nobody to see him hitting me, because I didn't want him to look bad.

I had to go to work in a half-hour, because I was working a double-shift. And he told me I had forty minutes to get all my furniture out of the house and get my clothes and be out or he was going to throw them out. And I was sitting there, because I could talk him down. You know, because I didn't want to leave him. I just talked to him. I said, "Buba, I don't want to leave." I said, "This is my house." And then he told me . . . (unclear) . . . "my kids." And I said, "No, you're not taking my kids from

> **"I don't want nobody to see him hitting me, because I didn't want him to look bad."**

me. That's too much." And so I said, "Just let me leave. Just let me take the kids. And, you know I'll go, and you know, I won't keep the kids from you or nothing like that." And he said, "I'm going to take them, and you're getting out."

[After they went inside their trailer, Buba threatened to shoot Cindy. He loaded a shotgun, pointed it at her, and said]: "The only way you're going to get out of this is if you kill me, and I'll—I'll kill you." [Buba gave me the shotgun and] turned around and walked right down the hall, because he knew I wouldn't do nothing. And I just sat there a minute. And I don't know what happened. I just, you know, I went to the bedroom, and I seen him laying there, and I just shot him. He moved. I shot him again because I thought he was going to get up again . . . .

I loved him too much. And I just wanted to help him.

Source: ABC Television, *20/20*, October 18, 1979

What Is a Valid Sociological Topic?

Sociologists do research on just about every area of human behavior. On the macro level, they study such broad matters as race relations (Wilson and Taub 2006), the military (Moscos and Butler 1997), and multinational corporations (Kristensen and Morgan 2006). On the micro level, they study such individualistic matters as pelvic examinations (Henslin and Biggs 1971/2007), how people interact on street corners (Whyte 1989, 2001), and even shyness (Scott 2006). Sociologists study priests and prostitutes, cops and criminals, as well as all kinds of people in between. In fact, no human behavior is ineligible for sociological scrutiny—whether that behavior is routine or unusual, respectable or reprehensible.

What happened to Cindy and Buba, then, is also a valid topic of sociological research. But exactly *how* would you research spouse abuse? As we look at how sociologists do research, we shall try to answer this question.

Common Sense and the Need for Sociological Research

First, why do we need sociological research? Why can't we simply depend on common sense, on "what everyone knows"? As noted in Chapter 1 (pages 8–9), commonsense ideas may or may not be true. Common sense, for example, tells us that spouse abuse has a significant impact on the lives of the people who are abused.

Although this particular idea is accurate, we need research to test commonsense ideas, because not all such ideas are true. After all, common sense also tells us that if a woman is abused, she will pack up and leave her husband. Research, however, shows that the reality of abuse is much more complicated than this. Some women do leave right away, some even after the first incident of abuse. For a variety of reasons, however, some women suffer abuse for years. The main reason is that they feel trapped and don't perceive any viable alternatives.

This brings us to the need for sociological research, for we may want to know why some women put up with abuse, while others don't. Or we may want to know something entirely different, such as why men are more likely to be the abusers. Or why some people abuse the people they say they love.

In order to answer a question, we need to move beyond guesswork and common sense. We want to *know* what is really going on. To find out, sociologists do research on about every aspect of social life. Let's look at how they do their research.

A Research Model

As shown in Figure 5.1, scientific research follows eight basic steps. This is an ideal model, however, and in the real world of research some of these steps may run together. Some may even be omitted.

1. Selecting a Topic

The first step is to select a topic. What do you want to know more about? Many sociologists simply follow their curiosity, their drive to learn more about social life. They become interested in a particular topic and they pursue it, as I did in studying the homeless. Some sociologists choose a topic because funding is available for that topic, others because a social problem such as domestic violence is in the news and they want to help people better understand it—and perhaps to help solve it. Let's use spouse abuse as our example.

2. Defining the Problem

The second step is to define the problem, to specify what you want to learn about the topic. My interest in the homeless increased until I wanted to learn about homelessness across the nation. Ordinarily, sociologists' interests are much more focused than

Figure 5.1 The Research Model

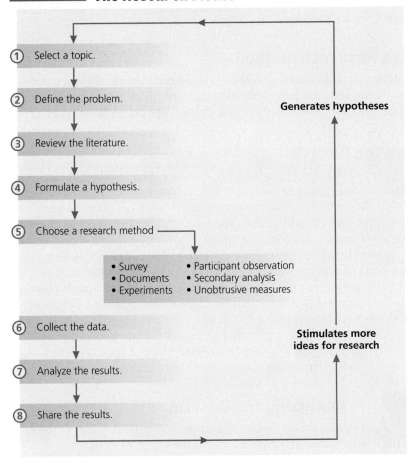

1. Select a topic.
2. Define the problem.
3. Review the literature.
4. Formulate a hypothesis.
5. Choose a research method
   - Survey
   - Documents
   - Experiments
   - Participant observation
   - Secondary analysis
   - Unobtrusive measures
6. Collect the data.
7. Analyze the results.
8. Share the results.

Generates hypotheses

Stimulates more ideas for research

Source: Modification of Figure 2.2 of Schaeffer 1989.

this; they examine some specific aspect of the topic, such as how homeless people survive on the streets. In the case of spouse abuse, sociologists may want to know whether violent and nonviolent husbands have different work experiences. Or they may want to learn what can be done to reduce spouse abuse.

The topics that sociologists study are broad. In fact, sociologists do research on any aspect of social life that interests them. The "problem" can be as earth shattering as trying to figure out why nations would ever contemplate nuclear war, as perplexing as understanding how "good" people can torture and kill (see Chapter 15), or as simple as wanting to find out why Native Americans like Westerns (see the Mass Media in Social Life box on page 56).

3. Reviewing the Literature

You must read what has been published on your topic. This helps you to narrow the problem, identify areas that are already known, and learn what areas need to be researched. Reviewing the literature may also help you to pinpoint the questions that you will want to ask. You might even find out that the problem has been answered already. You don't want to waste your time rediscovering what is already known.

4. Formulating a Hypothesis

The fourth step is to formulate a **hypothesis,** a statement of what you expect to find according to predictions from a theory. A hypothesis predicts a relationship between or among **variables,** factors that change, or vary, from one person or situation to another. For example, the statement "Men who are more socially isolated are more likely to abuse their wives than are men who are more socially integrated" is a hypothesis.

hypothesis a statement of how variables are expected to be related to one another, often according to predictions from a theory

variable a factor thought to be significant for human behavior, which can *vary* (or change) from one case to another

operational definition the way in which a researcher measures a variable

research method (or **research design**) one of six procedures that sociologists use to collect data: surveys, participant observation, secondary analysis, documents, experiments, and unobtrusive measures

validity the extent to which an operational definition measures what it was intended to measure

reliability the extent to which research produces consistent or dependable results

replication repeating a study in order to test its findings

Your hypothesis will need **operational definitions**—that is, precise ways to measure the variables. In this example, you would need operational definitions for three variables: social isolation, social integration, and spouse abuse.

5. Choosing a Research Method

The means by which you collect your data is called a **research method** (or *research design*). Sociologists use six basic research methods, which are outlined in the next section. You will want to choose the method that will best answer your particular questions.

6. Collecting the Data

When you gather your data, you have to take care to assure their **validity;** that is, your operational definitions must measure what they are intended to measure. In this case, you must be certain that you really are measuring social isolation, social integration, and spouse abuse—and not something else. Spouse abuse, for example, seems to be obvious. Yet what some people consider to be abuse is not regarded as abuse by others. Which will you choose? In other words, you must define your operational definitions so precisely that no one has any question about what you are measuring.

You must also be sure that your data are reliable. **Reliability** means that if other researchers use your operational definitions, their findings will be consistent with yours. If your operational definitions are sloppy, husbands who have committed the same act of violence might be included in some research but excluded from other studies. You would end up with erratic results. If you show a 10 percent rate of spouse abuse, for example, but another researcher determines it to be 30 percent, the research is unreliable.

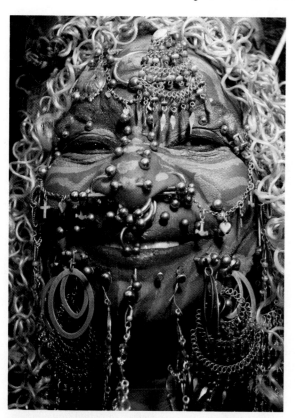

Because sociologists find all human behavior to be valid research topics, their research runs from the unusual to the routines of everyday life. Their studies range from broad scale social change, such as the globalization of capitalism, to such events as exhibitions of tattooing, piercing, and body painting. Shown here is a tattooed and pierced woman at an international tattoo exposition in London, England.

7. Analyzing the Results

You can choose from a variety of techniques to analyze the data you gather. If a hypothesis has been part of your research, it is during this step that you will test it. (Some research, especially that done by participant observation, has no hypothesis. You may know so little about the setting you are going to research that you cannot even specify the variables in advance.)

With today's software, in just seconds you can run tests on your data that used to take days or even weeks to perform. Two basic programs that sociologists and many undergraduates use are Microcase and the Statistical Package for the Social Sciences (SPSS). Some software, such as the Methodologist's Toolchest, provides advice about collecting data and even about ethical issues.

8. Sharing the Results

To wrap up your research, you will write a report to share your findings with the scientific community. You will review how you did your research, including your operational definitions. You will also show how your findings fit in with what has already been published on the topic and how they support or disagree with the theories that apply to your topic.

When research is published, usually in a scientific journal or a book, it "belongs" to the scientific community. Your findings will be available for **replication;** that is, others can repeat your study to see if they come up with similar results. As Table 5.1 illustrates, sociologists often summarize their findings in tables. As finding is added to finding, scientific knowledge builds.

Let's look in greater detail at the fifth step to see what research methods sociologists use.

THE FAR SIDE® By GARY LARSON

© 1984 FarWorks, Inc. All Rights Reserved/Dist. by Creators Syndicate

The Far Side® by Gary Larson © 1984 FarWorks, Inc. All Rights Reserved. The Far Side® and the Larson® signature are registered trademarks of FarWorks, Inc. Used with permission.

"Anthropologists! Anthropologists!"

A major concern of sociologists and other social scientists is that their research methods do not influence their findings. Respondents often change their behavior when they know they are being studied.

Research Methods

As we review the six research methods (or *research designs*) that sociologists use, we will continue our example of spouse abuse. As you will see, the method you choose will depend on the questions you want to answer. So that you can have a yardstick for comparison, you will want to know what "average" is in your study. Table 5.2 on page 133 discusses ways to measure average.

Surveys

Let's suppose that you want to know how many wives are abused each year. Some husbands also are abused, of course, but let's assume that you are going to focus on wives. An appropriate method for this purpose would be the **survey,** in which you would ask individuals a series of questions. Before you begin your research, however, you must deal with practical matters that face all researchers. Let's look at these issues.

Selecting a Sample   Ideally, you might want to learn about all wives in the world. Obviously, your resources will not permit such research, and you will have to narrow your **population,** the target group that you are going to study.

Let's assume that your resources (money, assistants, time) allow you to investigate spouse abuse only on your campus. Let's also assume that your college enrollment is large, so you won't be able to survey all the married women who are enrolled. Now you must select a **sample,** individuals from among your target population. How you choose a sample is crucial, for your choice will affect the results of your research. For example, married women enrolled in introductory sociology and engineering courses might have quite different experiences. If so, surveying just one or the other would produce skewed results.

Because you want to generalize your findings to your entire campus, you need a sample that is representative of the campus. How do you get a representative sample?

survey the collection of data by having people answer a series of questions

population the target group to be studied

sample the individuals intended to represent the population to be studied

Table 5.1 **How to Read a Table**

Tables summarize information. Because sociological findings are often presented in tables, it is important to understand how to read them. Tables contain six elements: title, headnote, headings, columns, rows, and source. When you understand how these elements fit together, you know how to read a table.

(1) The **title** states the topic. It is located at the top of the table. What is the title of this table? Please determine your answer before looking at the correct answer at the bottom of the page.

(2) The **headnote** is not always included in a table. When it is, it is located just below the title. Its purpose is to give more detailed information about how the data were collected or how data are presented in the table. What are the first eight words of the headnote of this table?

(3) The **headings** tell what kind of information is contained in the table. There are three headings in this table. What are they? In the second heading, what does n = 25 mean?

(4) The **columns** present information arranged vertically. What is the fourth number in the second column and the second number in the third column?

(5) The **rows** present information arranged horizontally. In the fourth row, which husbands are more likely to have less education than their wives?

(6) The **source** of a table, usually listed at the bottom, provides information on where the data in the table originated. Often, as in this instance, the information is specific enough for you to consult the original source. What is the source for this table?

Comparing Violent and Nonviolent Husbands

Based on interviews with 150 husbands and wives in a Midwestern city who were getting a divorce.

Husband's Achievement and Job Satisfaction	Violent Husbands $n = 25$	Nonviolent Husbands $n = 125$
He started but failed to complete high school or college.	44%	27%
He is very dissatisfied with his job.	44%	18%
His income is a source of constant conflict.	84%	24%
He has less education than his wife.	56%	14%
His job has less prestige than his father-in-law's.	37%	28%

Source: Modification of Table 1 in O'Brien 1975.

Some tables are much more complicated than this one, but all follow the same basic pattern. To apply these concepts to a table with more information, see page 356.

ANSWERS
1. Comparing Violent and Nonviolent Husbands
2. Based on interviews with 150 husbands and wives
3. Husband's Achievement and Job Satisfaction, Violent Husbands, Nonviolent Husbands. The *n* is an abbreviation for number, and *n* = 25 means that 25 violent husbands were in the sample.
4. 56%, 18%
5. Violent Husbands
6. A 1975 article by O'Brien (listed in the References section of this text).

random sample a sample in which everyone in the target population has the same chance of being included in the study

The best way is to get a **random sample.** This does *not* mean that you stand on some campus corner and ask questions of any woman who happens to walk by. *In a random sample, everyone in your population (the target group) has the same chance of being included in the study.* In this case, because your population is every married woman enrolled in your college, all married women—whether first-year or graduate students, full- or part-time—must have the same chance of being included in your sample.

Table 5.2 Three Ways to Measure "Average"

The Mean	The Median	The Mode
The term average seems clear enough. As you learned in grade school, to find the average you add a group of numbers and then divide the total by the number of cases that you added. Assume that the following numbers represent men convicted of battering their wives:	To compute the second average, the *median*, first arrange the cases in order–either from the highest to the lowest or the lowest to the highest. That arrangement will produce the following distribution.	The third measure of average, the *mode*, is simply the cases that occur the most often. In this instance the mode is 57, which is way off the mark.

The Mean

EXAMPLE

321	
229	
57	
289	
136	
57	
1,795	

The total is 2,884. Divided by 7 (the number of cases), the average is 412. Sociologists call this form of average the *mean*.

The mean can be deceptive because it is strongly influenced by extreme scores, either low or high. Note that six of the seven cases are less than the mean.

Two other ways to compute averages are the median and the mode.

The Median

EXAMPLE

57		1,795
57		321
136		289
229	or	229
289		136
321		57
1,795		57

Then look for the middle case, the one that falls halfway between the top and the bottom. That number is 229, for three numbers are lower and three numbers are higher. When there is an even number of cases, the median is the halfway mark between the two middle cases.

The Mode

EXAMPLE

57
57
136
229
289
321
1,795

Because the mode is often deceptive, and only by chance comes close to either of the other two averages, sociologists seldom use it. In addition, not every distribution of cases has a mode. And if two or more numbers appear with the same frequency, you can have more than one mode.

How can you get a random sample? First, you need a list of all the married women enrolled in your college. Then you assign a number to each name on the list. Using a table of random numbers, you then determine which of these women become part of your sample. (Tables of random numbers are available in statistics books, or they can be generated by a computer.)

A random sample represents your study's population fairly—in this case, married women enrolled at your college. This means that you can generalize your findings to *all* the married women students on your campus, even if they were not included in your sample.

What if you want to know only about certain subgroups, such as freshmen and seniors? You could use a **stratified random sample.** You would need a list of the freshmen and senior married women. Then, using random numbers, you would select a sample from each group. This would allow you to generalize to all the freshmen and senior married women at your college, but you would not be able to draw any conclusions about the sophomores or juniors.

Asking Neutral Questions   After you have decided on your population and sample, your next task is to make certain that your questions are neutral. Your questions must allow **respondents,** the people who answer your questions, to express their own opinions. Otherwise, you will end up with biased answers—which are worthless. For example, if you were to ask, "Don't you think that men who beat their wives should go to prison?" you would be tilting the answer toward agreement with a prison sentence. The *Doonesbury* cartoon on page 135 illustrates a more blatant example of biased questions. For examples of flawed research, see the Down-to-Earth Sociology box on the next page.

stratified random sample a sample from selected subgroups of the target population in which everyone in those subgroups has an equal chance of being included in the research

respondents people who respond to a survey, either in interviews or by self-administered questionnaires

Down-to-Earth Sociology

Loading the Dice: How *Not* to Do Research

THE METHODS OF SCIENCE LEND themselves to distortion, misrepresentation, and downright fraud. Consider these findings from surveys:

> Americans overwhelmingly prefer Toyotas to Chryslers.
> Americans overwhelmingly prefer Chryslers to Toyotas.

> Americans think that cloth diapers are better for the environment than disposable diapers.
> Americans think that disposable diapers are better for the environment than cloth diapers.

Obviously, these opposite conclusions cannot both be true. In fact, both sets of findings are misrepresentations, even though the responses came from surveys conducted by so-called independent researchers. These researchers, however, are biased, not independent and objective.

It turns out that some consumer researchers load the dice. Hired by firms that have a vested interest in the outcome of the research, they deliver the results their clients are looking for. Here are six ways to load the dice.

1. **Choose a biased sample.** If you want to "prove" that Americans prefer Chryslers over Toyotas, interview unemployed union workers who trace their job loss to Japanese imports. The answer is predictable. You'll get what you're looking for.

2. **Ask biased questions.** Even if you choose an unbiased sample, you can phrase questions in such a way that most people see only one logical choice. The diaper study just cited is a case in point. When the disposable diaper companies paid for the survey, the researchers used an excellent sample, but they worded the question this way:

"It is estimated that disposable diapers account for less than 2 percent of the trash in today's landfills. In contrast, beverage containers, third-class mail, and yard waste are estimated to account for about 21 percent. Given this, in your opinion, would it be fair to ban disposable diapers?"

Is it surprising, then, that 84 percent of the respondents said that disposable diapers are better for the environment than cloth diapers? Similarly, when the cloth diaper companies funded their survey, they worded the questions to load the dice in their favor.

Although some biases are difficult to spot, others are obvious. Consider this question on a national survey conducted by Republicans:

• Is President Bush right in trying to rein in the size and scope of the federal government against the wishes of the big government Democrats?

This question is obviously designed to channel people's thinking toward a predetermined answer—quite contrary to the standards of scientific research. Democrats, by the way, do the same thing.

3. **List biased choices.** Another way to load the dice is to use closed-ended questions that push people into the answers you want. Consider this finding:

• U.S. college students overwhelmingly prefer Levis 501 to the jeans of any competitor.

Sound good? Before you rush out to buy Levis, note what these researchers did: In asking students which jeans would be the most popular in the coming year, their list of choices included no other jeans but Levis 501!

4. **Discard undesirable results**. Researchers can keep silent about results they find embarrassing, or they can continue to survey samples until they find one that matches what they are looking for.

As has been stressed in this chapter, research must be objective if it is to be scientific. Obviously, none of the preceding results qualifies. The underlying problem with the research cited here—and with so many surveys bandied about in the media as fact—is that survey research has become big business. Simply put, the money offered by corporations has corrupted some researchers.

The beginning of the corruption is subtle. Paul Light, dean at the University of Minnesota, put it this way: "A funder will never come to an academic and say, 'I want you to produce finding X, and here's a million dollars to do it.' Rather, the subtext is that if the researchers produce the right finding, more work—and funding—will come their way."

The first four sources of bias are inexcusable, intentional fraud. The next two sources of bias reflect sloppiness, which is also inexcusable in science.

5. **Misunderstand the subjects' world.** This route can lead to errors every bit as great as those just cited. Even researchers who use an adequate sample and word their questions properly can end up with skewed results. They may, for example, fail to anticipate that people may be embarrassed to express an opinion that isn't "politically correct." For example, surveys show that 80 percent of Americans are environmentalists. Most Americans, however, are probably embarrassed to tell a stranger otherwise. Today, that would be like going against the flag, motherhood, and apple pie.

6. **Analyze the data incorrectly.** Even when researchers strive for objectivity, the sample is good, the wording is neutral, and the respondents answer the questions honestly, the results can still be skewed. The researchers may make a mistake in their calculations, such as entering incorrect data into computers. This, too, of course, is inexcusable in science.

Sources: Based on Crossen 1991; Goleman 1993; Barnes 1995; Resnik 2000; "Ask America" 2004; Armstrong 2007.

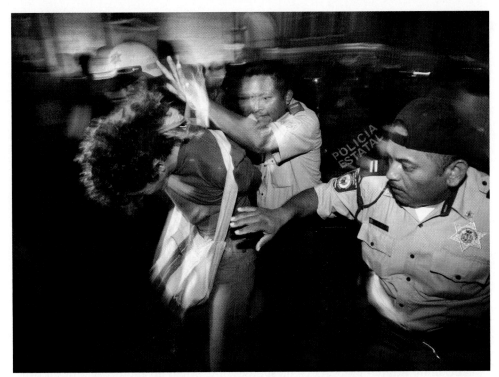

Sociologists usually cannot interview or observe every member of a group or participant in an event that they want to study. As explained in the text, to be able to generalize their findings, they select samples. Sociologists would have several ways to study this protest in Merida, Mexico. The demonstrators were protesting U.S. policies.

Questionnaires and Interviews Even if you have a representative sample and ask neutral questions, you can still end up with biased findings. **Questionnaires,** the list of questions to be asked, can be administered in ways that are flawed. There are two basic techniques for administering questionnaires. The first is to ask the respondents to fill them out. These **self-administered questionnaires** allow a larger number of people to be sampled at a lower cost, but the researchers lose control of the data collection. They don't know the conditions under which people answered the questions. For example, others could have influenced their answers.

The second technique is the **interview.** Researchers ask people questions, often face to face, but sometimes by telephone or e-mail. The advantage of this method is that the researchers can ask each question in the same way. The main disadvantage is that interviews are time-consuming, so researchers end up with fewer respondents. Interviews can also create **interviewer bias;** that is, the presence of interviewers can affect what people say. For example, instead of saying what they really feel, respondents might give "socially acceptable" answers. Although they may be willing to write their true opinions on an anonymous questionnaire, they won't tell them to another person. Some respondents even shape their answers to match what they think an interviewer wants to hear.

questionnaires a list of questions to be asked of respondents

self-administered questionnaires questionnaires that respondents fill out

interview direct questioning of respondents

interviewer bias effects that interviewers have on respondents that lead to biased answers

Improperly worded questions can steer respondents toward answers that are not their own, which produces invalid results.

Table 5.3 Closed and Open-Ended Questions	
A. Closed-Ended Question	**B. Open-Ended Question**
Which of the following best fits your idea of what should be done to someone who has been convicted of spouse abuse?	What do you think should be done to someone who has been convicted of spouse abuse?
1. probation 2. jail time 3. community service 4. counseling 5. divorce 6. nothing—it's a family matter	

In some cases, **structured interviews** work best. This type of interview uses **closed-ended questions**—each question is followed by a list of possible answers. Structured interviews are faster to administer, and they make it easier to *code* (categorize) answers so they can be fed into a computer for analysis. As you can see from Table 5.3, the answers listed on a questionnaire might fail to include the respondent's opinions. Consequently, some researchers prefer **unstructured interviews.** Here the interviewer asks **open-ended questions,** which allow people to answer in their own words. Although open-ended questions allow you to tap the full range of people's opinions, they make it difficult to compare answers. For example, how would you compare the following answers to the question "What do you think causes men to abuse their wives?"

"They're sick."

"I think they must have had problems with their mother."

"We oughta string 'em up!"

Establishing Rapport   Research on spouse abuse brings up another significant issue. You may have been wondering if your survey would be worth anything even if you rigorously followed scientific procedures. Will women who have been abused really give honest answers to strangers?

If your method of interviewing consisted of walking up to women on the street and asking if their husbands had ever beaten them, there would be little basis for taking your findings seriously. Researchers have to establish **rapport** ("ruh-POUR"), a feeling of trust, with their respondents, especially when it comes to sensitive topics—those that elicit feelings of embarrassment, shame, or other deep emotions.

We know that once rapport is gained (often by first asking nonsensitive questions), victims will talk about personal, sensitive issues. A good example is rape. To go beyond police statistics, each year researchers interview a random sample of 100,000 Americans. They ask them whether they have been victims of burglary, robbery, and other crimes. After establishing rapport, the researchers ask about rape. They find that rape victims will talk about their experiences. The national crime victimization survey shows that the actual incidence of rape is three times higher than the official statistics (*Statistical Abstract* 2007: page 188).

Participant Observation (Fieldwork)

In the second method, **participant observation (or fieldwork),** the researcher *participates* in a research setting while *observing* what is happening in that setting. But how is it possible to study spouse abuse by participant observation? Obviously, this method does not mean that you would sit around and watch someone being abused. Spouse abuse, however, is a broad topic, and many questions about abuse cannot be answered adequately by any method other than participant observation.

Let's suppose that you are interested in learning how spouse abuse affects wives. You might want to know how the abuse has changed the wives' relationship with their husbands. How has it changed their hopes and dreams? Or their ideas about men? Certainly it has affected their self-concept as well. But how? Participant observation could provide insight into such questions.

For example, if your campus has a crisis intervention center, you might be able to observe victims of spouse abuse from the time they report the attack through their participation in counseling. With good rapport, you might even be able to spend time with them in other settings, observing further aspects of their lives. What they say and how they in-

structured interviews interviews that use closed-ended questions

closed-ended questions questions that are followed by a list of possible answers to be selected by the respondent

unstructured interviews interviews that use open-ended questions

open-ended questions questions that respondents answer in their own words

rapport (ruh-POUR) a feeling of trust between researchers and the people they are studying

participant observation (or **fieldwork**) research in which the researcher participates in a research setting while observing what is happening in that setting teract with others might help you to understand how the abuse has affected them. This, in turn, could give you insight into how to improve college counseling services.

Participant observers face a problem with **generalizability,** applying their findings to larger populations. Most of these studies are exploratory, documenting in detail the experiences of people in a particular setting. Although such research suggests that other people who face similar situations react in comparable ways, we don't know how far the findings apply beyond their original setting. Participant observation, however, can stimulate hypotheses and theories that can be tested in other settings, using other research techniques.

Secondary Analysis

In **secondary analysis,** a third research method, researchers analyze data that have already been collected by others. For example, if you were to examine the original data from a study of women who had been abused by their husbands, you would be doing secondary analysis. Ordinarily, researchers prefer to gather their own data, but lack of resources, especially money, may make this impossible. In addition, existing data could contain a wealth of information that wasn't pertinent to the goals of the original researchers, which you can then analyze for your own purposes.

Like the other methods, secondary analysis also poses its own problems. How can a researcher who did not carry out the initial study be sure that the data were gathered systematically and recorded accurately, and that biases were avoided? This problem plagues researchers who do secondary analysis, especially if the original data have been gathered by a team of researchers, not all of whom were equally qualified.

Documents

The fourth method that sociologists use is the study of **documents,** recorded sources. To investigate social life, sociologists examine such diverse documents as books, newspapers, diaries, bank records, police reports, immigration files, and records kept by organizations. The term documents is broad, and it also includes video and audio recordings.

To study spouse abuse, you might examine police reports and court records. These could reveal what proportion of complaints result in arrest and what proportion of the men arrested are charged, convicted, or put on probation. If these were your questions, police statistics would be valuable.

But for other questions, those records would be useless. If you want to learn about the victims' social and emotional adjustment, for example, those records would tell you little. Other documents, however, might provide answers. For example, diaries kept by victims could yield insight into their reactions to abuse, showing how their attitudes and relationships change. If no diaries were available, you might ask victims to keep diaries. Perhaps the director of a crisis intervention center might ask clients to keep diaries for you—or get the victims' permission for you to examine records of their counseling sessions. To my knowledge, no sociologist has yet studied spouse abuse in this way.

Sociologists who enter a research setting to discover information are using a research method known as *participant observation*. As discussed in the text, sociologists sometimes conduct research in controversial settings, such as this dog fight in Kandahar, Afghanistan.

Of course, I am presenting an ideal situation, a crisis intervention center that opens its arms to you. In actuality, the center might not cooperate at all. It might refuse to ask victims to keep diaries—or it might not even let you near its records. *Access,* then, is another problem that researchers face. Simply put, you can't study a topic unless you can gain access to it.

Sociologists use different methods of research to answer different questions. One method that can be used to study spouse abuse is to examine the documents kept by shelters for battered women, which log the number of calls and visits made by victims. This woman is answering calls at the Rape and Sexual Assault Hotline in New York City.

Experiments

A lot of people say that abusers need therapy. But no one knows if therapy really works. Let's suppose that you want to find out. Frankly, no one knows how to change a wife abuser into a loving husband—it might be impossible—but knowing if therapy works would certainly

experimental group the group of subjects who are exposed to the independent variable

control group the group of subjects who are not exposed to the independent variable

independent variable a factor that causes a change in another variable, called the dependent variable

dependent variable a factor that is changed by an independent variable

be a step in the right direction. To find out, you may want to conduct an **experiment,** for experiments are useful for determining cause and effect. Causation has three necessary conditions, which are discussed in Table 5.4 on the next page.

Let's suppose that you propose such an experiment to a judge, she likes your idea, and she gives you access to men who have been arrested for spouse abuse. You would randomly divide the men into two groups. (See Figure 5.2 below.) This helps to ensure that their individual characteristics (attitudes, number of arrests, severity of crimes, education, race-ethnicity, age, and so on) are distributed evenly between the groups. You then would arrange for the men in the **experimental group** to receive some form of therapy. The men in the **control group** would not get therapy.

Your **independent variable,** something that causes a change in another variable, would be therapy. Your **dependent variable,** the variable that might change, would be the men's behavior: whether they abuse women after they get out of jail. To make that determination, you would need to rely on a sloppy operational definition: either reports from the wives or records indicating which men were rearrested for abuse. This is sloppy because some of the women will not report the abuse, and some of the men who abuse their wives will not be arrested. Yet it may be the best you can do.

Figure 5.2 **The Experiment**

Source: By the author.

Table 5.4   Cause, Effect, and Spurious Correlations

Causation means that a change in one variable is caused by another variable. Three conditions are necessary for causation: correlation, temporal priority, and no spurious correlation. Let's apply each of these conditions to spouse abuse and alcohol abuse.

1 The first necessary condition is *correlation*.

If two variables exist together, they are said to be correlated. If batterers get drunk, battering and alcohol abuse are correlated.

Spouse Abuse + Alcohol Abuse

People sometimes assume that correlation is causation. In this instance, they conclude that alcohol abuse causes spouse abuse.

Alcohol Abuse ⟶ Spouse Abuse

But *correlation never proves causation. Either* variable could be the cause of the other. Perhaps battering upsets men and they then get drunk.

Spouse Abuse ⟶ Alcohol Abuse

2 The second necessary condition is *temporal priority*.

Temporal priority means that one thing happens before something else does. For a variable to be a cause (*the independent variable*), it must *precede* that which is changed (*the dependent variable*).

               precedes
Alcohol Abuse ⟶ Spouse Abuse

If the men had not drunk alcohol until after they beat their wives, obviously alcohol abuse could not be the cause of the spouse abuse. Although the necessity of temporal priority is obvious, in many studies this is not easy to determine.

3 The third necessary condition is *no spurious correlation*.

This is the necessary condition that really makes things difficult. Even if we identify the correlation of getting drunk and spouse abuse and can determine temporal priority, we still don't know that alcohol abuse is the cause. We could have a *spurious correlation;* that is, the cause may be some underlying third variable. These are usually not easy to identify. Some sociologists think that male culture is that underlying third variable.

Male Culture ⟶ Spouse Abuse

Socialized into dominance, some men learn to view women as objects on which to take out their frustration. In fact, this underlying third variable could be a cause of both spouse abuse and alcohol abuse.

Male Culture ⟶ Spouse Abuse / Alcohol Abuse

But since only some men beat their wives, while all males are exposed to male culture, other variables must also be involved. Perhaps specific subcultures that promote violence and denigrate women lead to both spouse abuse and alcohol abuse.

Male Subculture ⟶ Spouse Abuse / Alcohol Abuse

If so, this does *not* mean that it is the only causal variable, for spouse abuse probably has many causes. Unlike the movement of amoebas or the action of heat on some object, human behavior is infinitely complicated. What is especially important is people's *definitions of the situation*, including their views of right and wrong. To explain spouse abuse, then, we need to add such variables as men's views of violence and their definitions of the relative rights of women and men. It is precisely to help unravel such complicating factors in human behavior that we need the experimental method.

MORE ON CORRELATIONS

Correlation simply means that two or more variables are present together. The more often that these variables are found together, the stronger their relationship. To indicate their strength, sociologists use a number called a *correlation coefficient*. If two variables are always related, that is, they are always present together, they have what is called a *perfect positive correlation*. The number 1.0 represents this correlation coefficient. Nature has some 1.0's, such as the lack of water and the death of trees. 1.0's also apply to the human physical state, such as the absence of nutrients and the absence of life. But social life is much more complicated than physical conditions, and there are no 1.0's in human behavior.

Two variables can also have a *perfect negative correlation*. This means that when one variable is present, the other is always absent. The number −1.0 represents this correlation coefficient.

Positive correlations of 0.1, 0.2, and 0.3 mean that one variable is associated with another only 1 time out of 10, 2 times out of 10, and 3 times out of 10. In other words, in most instances the first variable is *not* associated with the second, indicating a weak relationship. A strong relationship may indicate causation, but not necessarily. Testing the relationship between variables is the goal of some sociological research.

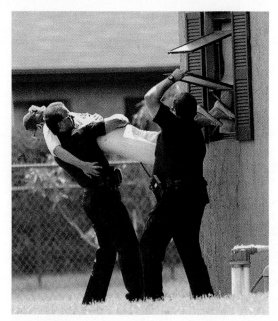

Spouse abuse is one of the most common forms of violence. Shown here are police pulling a woman from her bathroom window, where she had fled from her husband, who was threatening to shoot her.

Let's assume that you choose rearrest as your operational definition. If you find that the men who received therapy are *less* likely to be rearrested for abuse, you can attribute the difference to the therapy. If you find *no difference* in rearrest rates, you can conclude that the therapy was ineffective. If you find that the men who received the therapy have a *higher* rearrest rate, you can conclude that the therapy backfired.

Ideally, you would test different types of therapy. Perhaps only some types work. You might even want to test self-therapy by assigning articles, books, and videos.

As described in the Down-to-Earth Sociology box below, some experiments are not conducted this rigorously. This increases the likelihood that cause and effect will be confused.

Unobtrusive Measures

Researchers sometimes use **unobtrusive measures,** observing the behavior of people who are not aware that they are being studied. For example, social researchers studied the level of whisky consumption in a town that was legally "dry" by counting empty bottles in trashcans. (Lee 2000). Researchers have also gone high-tech in their unobtrusive measures. To trace customers' paths through stores, they have attached infrared surveillance devices to shopping carts. Grocery chains use these findings to place higher-profit items in more

Down-to-Earth Sociology

The Hawthorne Experiments

RESEARCH FROM THE 1920S, KNOWN AS the Hawthorne experiments, has become a classic in sociology. This research drives home how necessary it is to accurately identify independent and dependent variables.

The managers of the Hawthorne plant of the Western Electric Company near Chicago wanted to know if different levels of lighting would affect productivity. Several groups of women participated in what are known as the Relay Room Experiments. In the control room, the level of lighting was held constant, while in the experimental room, the lighting was varied. To everyone's surprise, output increased at *both* locations. In the experimental room, productivity remained high even when the lights were dimmed to about the level of moonlight—so low that workers could barely see what they were doing!

To solve this mystery, management called in a team of researchers headed by Elton Mayo of the University of Chicago. This team tested thirteen different work conditions. When they changed the women's' pay from hourly wages to piecework (paying them at a set rate for each unit they produced), productivity increased. When they served refreshments, output again went up. When they added two 5-minute rest periods, productivity jumped. When they changed the rest periods to two 10-minute periods, again

output increased. When they let the workers go home early, they found the same result. Confused, the researchers restored the original conditions, offering none of these added benefits. The result? Even higher productivity.

The situation grew even more confusing when the researchers turned their focus on men. In what is known as the Bank Wiring Room Study, the researchers didn't change the work conditions at all. They simply observed the men while they worked and interviewed them after work. They expected no change in productivity. Instead, productivity *dropped.*

None of this made sense. Finally, Mayo concluded that the changes in productivity were due to the research itself. The women, pleased at the attention being paid to them, responded by increasing their efforts. The men, in contrast, became suspicious about why the researchers were observing them. They feared that if they increased their productivity, they would be expected to produce more each day, or that higher productivity might even cost some of them their jobs. Consequently, they decreased their output.

The Hawthorne research is important—not for its findings on worker productivity, but for what it revealed about the research process. Today, researchers carefully monitor the *Hawthorne effect,* the change in behavior that occurs when people know they are being studied.

Sources: Based on Roethlisberger and Dickson 1939; Mayo 1966; Baron and Greenberg 1990; Rowe et al. 2006.

strategic locations (McCarthy 1993). Casino operators use chips that transmit radio frequencies, allowing them to track how much their high rollers are betting at every hand of poker or blackjack (Sanders 2005). Billboards are being developed that can read information embedded on a chip in your car key. As you drive by, the billboard will display *your* name with a personal message (Feder 2007). The same device can *collect* information as you drive by.

It would be considered unethical to use most unobtrusive measures to research spouse abuse. You could, however, analyze 911 calls. If there were a *public* forum held by abused or abusing spouses on the Internet, you also could record and analyze the online conversations.

Deciding Which Method to Use

How do sociologists choose among these methods? Four primary factors affect their decision. First, *resources* are crucial. Sociologists must match methods with available resources. For example, they may want to conduct a survey, but they may find that finances won't permit it. Instead, they turn to the study of documents. The second significant factor is *access to subjects.* If the people who comprise a sample live far away, researchers may have to mail them questionnaires or conduct a survey by telephone or e-mail even if they would prefer face-to-face interviews. The third factor concerns the *purpose of the research,* the questions that the sociologist wants to investigate and answer. Each method is better for answering certain types of questions. Participant observation, for example, is good for uncovering people's attitudes, while experiments are better at resolving questions of cause and effect. Fourth, *the researcher's background or training* comes into play. In graduate school, sociologists study many methods, but they are able to practice only some of them. Consequently, after graduate school, they generally use the methods in which they have had the most training.

Thus, sociologists who have been trained in **quantitative research methods,** which emphasize measurement, numbers, and statistics, are likely to use surveys. Sociologists who have been trained in **qualitative research methods,** which emphasize observing and interpreting people's behavior, lean toward participant observation. In the Down-to-Earth Sociology box on the next page, you can see how applied sociologists use a combination of quantitative and qualitative methods.

unobtrusive measures ways of observing people who do not know they are being studied

quantitative research methods research in which the emphasis is placed on measurement, the use of statistics, and numbers

qualitative research methods research in which the emphasis is placed on observing, describing, and interpreting people's behavior

Controversy in Sociological Research

Sociologists sometimes find themselves in the hot seat because of their research. Some poke into private areas of life, which upsets people. Others investigate political matters, and their findings threaten those who have a stake in the situation. When researchers in Palestine asked refugees if they would be willing to accept compensation and not return to Israel if there were a peace settlement, most said they would take the buyout. When the head researcher released these findings, an enraged mob beat him and trashed his office (Bennet 2003). In the following Thinking Critically section, you can see how even such a straightforward task as counting the homeless can land sociologists in the midst of controversy.

Thinking Critically

Doing Controversial Research—Counting the Homeless

What could be less offensive than counting the homeless? As sometimes occurs, however, even basic research lands sociologists in the midst of controversy. This is what happened to sociologist Peter Rossi and his associates.

There was a dispute between advocates for the homeless and the federal government. The advocates claimed that 3 to 7 million Americans were homeless; the government claimed that the

(continued p. 143)

Applied Sociology: Marketing Research as a Blend of Quantitative and Qualitative Methods

IF A COMPANY IS going to survive in the highly competitive business world, it must figure out what consumers need and want, and then supply it—or else convince people that what they need or want is what the company is already producing.

What Marketing Research Is

To increase sales, manufacturers try to improve the position of their products. "Position" is marketing jargon for how customers think about a product.

This is where marketing researchers come into play. They find out what customers want, how they select products, how they use them, and the impressions they have of a product or service. They also assess how the public will react to either a new product or a change in an established product.

Marketing researchers use both qualitative and quantitative methods. An example of a qualitative method is *focus groups*. Groups of about ten people are invited to discuss a product. A moderator leads a discussion while other team members observe or videotape the session from behind a one-way mirror. To control for regional variations, the researchers may hold other focus groups at the same time in other cities. Sociologist Roger Straus points out that his training in symbolic interactionism has been especially useful for interpreting these results.

Marketing researchers also use quantitative techniques. For example, they may conduct surveys to determine what the public thinks of a new product. They also use the "bar codes" found on products to gather sales

Before they launch a product, companies research the public's interest. They continue to stimulate that interest.

data. They use statistics to analyze the data, and they prepare tables and graphics to summarize the findings for their clients.

A Sociological Controversy

Marketing research occupies a controversial position in sociology. Most of the results of marketing research are proprietary (owned by the client) and are therefore confidential. This means that the findings do not appear in sociology journals and are not used to create social theory. In addition, clients are usually interested in specific marketing problems, and they seldom commission research on important social issues. For such reasons, many sociologists do not consider marketing research a "legitimate" sociological activity. Some even scorn marketing researchers as wasting their sociological talents. They chide them for having "sold out"—for using sociological methods to help corporations exploit the public by convincing them to purchase unneeded goods and services.

Marketing researchers, of course, do not see things this way. They argue that marketing research is a neutral activity, that there is no reason to be against it on principle. They add that they do more than just help sell beer and soft drinks. They point out that they have helped colleges attract students and communities assess public needs. They argue that the decision to do research on any topic involves the researcher's own values. This applies to studying how to reduce juvenile delinquency as well as how to sell facial scrubs for acne. It is presumptuous, they say, for anyone to pass judgment on marketing research—as though other research were morally superior.

Sources: Based on Straus 1991 and communication with Straus 1993; Hays 2004; Cherrier and Murray 2006.

actual number was only one-twelfth to one-twenty-eighth that amount—about a quarter of a million people. Each side accused the other of gross distortion—the one to place pressure on Congress, the other to keep the public from knowing how bad the situation really was.

Only an accurate count could clear up the picture, for both sides were only guessing at the numbers. Peter Rossi and the National Opinion Research Center decided to make an accurate count. They had no vested interest in supporting one side or the other, only in answering this question honestly.

The challenge was immense. The *population* was evident—the U.S. homeless. A *survey* would be appropriate, but how do you survey a *sample* of the homeless? No one has a list of the homeless, and only some of the homeless stay at shelters. As for *validity,* to make certain that they were counting only people who were really homeless, the researchers needed a good *operational definition* of homelessness. To include people who weren't really homeless would destroy the study's *reliability*. The researchers wanted results that would be consistent if others were to *replicate,* or repeat, the study.

As an operational definition, the researchers used "literally homeless," people "who do not have access to a conventional dwelling and who would be homeless by any conceivable definition of the term." Because a national count would cost about $6 million, far beyond their resources, the researchers decided to count just the homeless in Chicago. The cost was still high, however—about $600,000.

By using a *stratified random sample,* the researchers were able to *generalize* to the entire city. How could they do this since there is no list of the homeless? For the homeless who sleep in shelters, they used a stratified random sample of the city's shelters. For the homeless who sleep in the streets, vacant buildings, and so forth, they used a stratified random sample of the city's blocks. To make doubly certain that their count was accurate, the researchers conducted two surveys. At night, trained teams visited the shelters and searched the alleys, bridges, and vacant houses.

They found that on an average night, Chicago has 2,722 homeless people. Because people move in and out of homelessness, between 5,000 and 7,000 are homeless at some point during the year. On warm nights, only two out of five sleep in the shelters, and even in winter only three out of four do so. The median age is 40; 75 percent are men, and 60 percent are African Americans. One in four is a former mental patient, one in five a former prisoner. A homeless person's income from all sources is less than $6 a day. Projecting these findings to the United States resulted in a national total of about 350,000 homeless people, a figure that was much closer to the government's estimate of 250,000 than to the advocates' estimate of 3 to 7 million.

The reactions were predictable. Government officials were elated. The stunned homeless advocates denied the findings and began a sniping campaign at the researchers.

Remember that Rossi and his associates had no interest in proving which side in the debate was right, only in getting reliable figures. Using impeccable methods, this is what they did.

The researchers had no intention of minimizing the problem of homelessness. They stressed that 350,000 Americans are so poor that they sleep in city streets, live in shelters, eat out of garbage cans, and suffer from severe health problems. In short, these people live hopeless, desperate lives.

Research sometimes lands sociologists in the midst of controversy. As described here, the results of a study to determine how many homeless people there are in the United States displeased homeless advocates. Homelessness is a global problem. Shown here is a doctor talking to a homeless man in Moscow, Russia.

It is good to *know* how many Americans are homeless. Guesses aren't worth much. Even though the number is far less than what the homeless advocates had estimated, this information can still serve their cause: Having fewer homeless people makes the problem more manageable. It means that if we choose to do so, we can put our resources to work with greater certainty of success.

Those whose positions are not supported by research, however, are never pleased, and they tend to take potshots at the researchers. This is one of the risks of doing sociological research, for sociologists never know whose toes they will step on.

Sources: Based on Anderson 1986; Rossi et al. 1986; Rossi et al. 1987; Coughlin 1988; Rossi 1989; Rossi 1991; De Parle 1994; Rossi 1999; Bialik 2006.

Gender in Sociological Research

You know how significant gender is in your own life, how it affects your orientations and your attitudes. You also may be aware that gender opens and closes doors to you, a topic that we will explore in Chapter 11. Because gender is also a factor in social research, researchers must take steps to prevent it from biasing their findings. For example, sociologists Diana Scully and Joseph Marolla (1984, 2007) interviewed convicted rapists in prison. They were concerned that their gender might lead to *interviewer bias*—that the prisoners might shift their answers, sharing certain experiences or opinions with Marolla, but saying something else to Scully. To prevent gender bias, each researcher interviewed half the sample. Later in this chapter, we'll look at what they found out.

Gender certainly can be an impediment in research. In our imagined research on spouse abuse, for example, could a man even do participant observation of women who have been beaten by their husbands? Technically, the answer is yes. But because the women have been victimized by men, they might be less likely to share their experiences and feelings with men. If so, women would be better suited to conduct this research, more likely to achieve valid results. The supposition that these victims will be more open with women than with men, however, is just that—a supposition. Research alone will verify or refute this assumption.

Gender is significant in other ways, too. As feminist sociologists point out, it is a mistake to assume that what applies to one sex is also relevant to the other (Bird and Rieker 1999; Neuman 2006). Women's and men's lives differ significantly, and if we do research on just half of humanity, our research will be vastly incomplete. Today's huge numbers of women sociologists guarantee that women will not be ignored in social research. In the past, however, when almost all sociologists were men, women's experiences were neglected.

Gender issues can pop up in unexpected ways in sociological research. I vividly recall an incident in San Francisco.

The streets were getting dark, and I was still looking for homeless people. When I saw someone lying down, curled up in a doorway, I approached the individual. As I got close, I began my opening research line, "Hi, I'm Dr. Henslin from . . . ." The individual began to scream and started to thrash wildly. Startled by this sudden, high-pitched scream and by the rapid movements, I quickly backed away. When I later analyzed what had happened, I concluded that I had intruded into a woman's bedroom.

Of course, one can draw another lesson from this incident. Researchers do their best, but they make mistakes. Sometimes these mistakes are minor, and even humorous. The woman sleeping in the doorway wasn't frightened. It was only just getting dark, and there were many people on the street. She was just assertively marking her territory and letting me know in no uncertain terms that I was an intruder. If we make a mistake in research, we pick up and go on. As we do so, we take ethical considerations into account, which is the topic of our next section.

Ethics in Sociological Research

In addition to choosing an appropriate research method, we must also follow the ethics of sociology, which center on assumptions of science and morality (American Sociological Association 1999). Research ethics require openness (sharing findings with the scientific community), honesty, and truth. Ethics clearly forbid the falsification of results. They also condemn plagiarism—that is, stealing someone else's work. Another ethical guideline is that research subjects should generally be informed that they are being studied and never be harmed by the research. Ethics also require that sociologists protect the anonymity of those who provide information. Sometimes people reveal things that are intimate, potentially embarrassing, or otherwise harmful to themselves. Finally, although not all sociologists agree, it generally is considered unethical for researchers to misrepresent themselves.

Sociologists take these ethical standards seriously. To illustrate the extent to which they will go to protect their respondents, consider the research conducted by Mario Brajuha.

Protecting the Subjects: The Brajuha Research

Mario Brajuha, a graduate student at the State University of New York at Stony Brook, was doing participant observation of restaurant workers. He lost his job as a waiter when the restaurant where he was working burned down—a fire of "suspicious origin," as the police said. When detectives learned that Brajuha had taken field notes (Brajuha and Hallowell 1986), they asked to see them. Because he had promised to keep the information confidential, Brajuha refused to hand them over. When the district attorney subpoenaed the notes, Brajuha still refused. The district attorney then threatened to put Brajuha in jail. By this time, Brajuha's notes had become rather famous, and unsavory characters—perhaps those who had set the fire—also wanted to know what was in them. They, too, demanded to see them, accompanying their demands with threats of a different nature. Brajuha found himself between a rock and a hard place.

For two years, Brajuha refused to hand over his notes, even though he grew anxious and had to appear at several court hearings. Finally, the district attorney dropped the subpoena. When the two men under investigation for setting the fire died, the threats to Brajuha, his wife, and their children ended.

Misleading the Subjects: The Humphreys Research

Sociologists agree on the necessity to protect respondents, and they applaud the professional manner in which Brajuha handled himself. Although there is less agreement about whether researchers should be allowed to misrepresent themselves, sociologists who violate this norm

Ethics in social research are of vital concern to sociologists. As discussed in the text, sociologists may disagree on some of the issue's finer points, but none would approve of slipping LSD to unsuspecting subjects like these Marine recruits in basic training at Parris Island, South Carolina. This was done to U.S. servicemen in the 1960s under the guise of legitimate testing—just "to see what would happen."

can become embroiled in ethical controversy. Let's look at the case of Laud Humphreys, whose research forced sociologists to rethink and refine their ethical stance.

Laud Humphreys, a classmate of mine at Washington University in St. Louis, was an Episcopal priest who decided to become a sociologist. For his Ph.D. dissertation, Humphreys (1970, 1971, 1975) studied social interaction in "tearooms," public restrooms where some men go for quick, anonymous oral sex with other men.

Humphreys found that some restrooms in Forest Park, just across from our campus, were tearooms. He began a participant observation study by hanging around these restrooms. He found that in addition to the two men having sex, a third man—called a "watchqueen"—served as a lookout for police and other unwelcome strangers. Humphreys took on the role of watchqueen, not only watching for strangers but also observing what the men did. He wrote field notes after the encounters.

Humphreys decided that he wanted to learn about the regular lives of these men. For example, what was the significance of the wedding rings that many of the men wore? He came up with an ingenious technique: Many of the men parked their cars near the tearooms, and Humphreys recorded their license plate numbers. A friend in the St. Louis police department gave Humphreys each man's address. About a year later, Humphreys arranged for these men to be included in a medical survey conducted by some of the sociologists on our faculty.

Disguising himself with a different hairstyle and clothing, Humphreys visited the men's homes. He interviewed the men, supposedly for the medical study. He found that they led conventional lives. They voted, mowed their lawns, and took their kids to Little League games. Many reported that their wives were not aroused sexually or were afraid of getting pregnant because their religion did not allow them to use birth control. Humphreys concluded that heterosexual men were also using the tearooms for a form of quick sex.

This study stirred controversy among sociologists and nonsociologists alike. Many sociologists criticized Humphreys, and a national columnist even wrote a scathing denunciation of "sociological snoopers" (Von Hoffman 1970). As the controversy heated up and a court case loomed, Humphreys feared that his list of respondents might be subpoenaed. He gave me the list to take from Missouri to Illinois, where I had begun teaching. When he called and asked me to destroy it, I burned the list in my backyard.

Was this research ethical (Galliher et al. 2004)? This question is not decided easily. Although many sociologists sided with Humphreys—and his book reporting the research won a highly acclaimed award—the criticisms continued. At first, Humphreys defended his position vigorously, but five years later, in a second edition of his book (1975), he stated that he should have identified himself as a researcher.

How Research and Theory Work Together

Research cannot stand alone. Nor can theory. As sociologist C. Wright Mills (1959) argued so forcefully, research without theory is simply a collection of unrelated "facts." But theory without research, Mills added, is abstract and empty—it can't represent the way life really is.

Research and theory, then, are both essential for sociology. Every theory must be tested, which requires research. And as sociologists do research, they often come up with surprising findings. Those findings must be explained, and for that we need theory. As sociologists study social life, then, they combine research and theory.

The Real World: When the Ideal Meets the Real

Although we can list the ideals of research, real-life situations often force sociologists to settle for something that falls short of the ideal. In the following Thinking Critically section, let's look at how two sociologists confronted the ideal and the real.

Thinking Critically

Are Rapists Sick? A Close-Up View of Research

Two sociologists, Diana Scully and Joseph Marolla, whose research was mentioned earlier, were not satisfied with the typical explanation that rapists are "sick," psychologically disturbed, or different from other men. They developed the hypothesis that rape is like most human behavior—it is learned through interaction with others. That is, some men learn to think of rape as appropriate behavior.

To test this hypothesis, it would be best to interview a random sample of rapists. But this is impossible. There is no list of all rapists, so there is no way to give them all the same chance of being included in a sample. You can't even use prison populations to select a random sample, for many rapists have never been caught, some who were caught were found not guilty, and some who were found guilty were given probation. In addition, some who were convicted of rape are innocent. Consequently, Scully and Marolla confronted the classic dilemma of sociologists—either to not do the study or to do it under less than ideal conditions.

They chose to do the study. When they had the opportunity to interview convicted rapists in prison, they jumped at it. They knew that whatever they learned would be more than we already knew. They sent out 3,500 letters to men serving time in seven prisons in Virginia, the state where they were teaching. About 25 percent of the prisoners agreed to be interviewed. They matched these men on the basis of age, education, race, severity of offense, and previous criminal record. This resulted in a sample of 98 prisoners who were convicted of rape and a control sample of 75 men convicted of other offenses.

As noted earlier, because the sex of the interviewer can bias research results, Scully and Marolla each interviewed half the sample. It took them 600 hours to gather information on the prisoners, including their psychological, criminal, and sexual history. To guard against lies, they checked what the individuals told them against their institutional records. They used twelve scales to measure the men's attitudes about women, rape, and themselves. In order to find out what circumstances the men defined as rape or when they viewed the victim as responsible, they also gave the men nine vignettes of forced sexual encounters and asked them to determine responsibility in each one.

Scully and Marolla discovered something that goes against common sense—that most rapists are not sick, and that they are not overwhelmed by uncontrollable urges. The psychological histories of the rapists and the nonrapists were similar. Rapists, they concluded, are emotionally average men who have learned to view rape as appropriate in certain situations. Some rape spontaneously, while others plan their rapes. Some use rape as a form of revenge, to get even with someone, not necessarily their victim. For some, rape is even a form of recreation, and they rape with friends on weekends.

Scully and Marolla also found support for what feminists had been pointing out for years, that power is a major element in rape. Here is what one man said:

> Rape gave me the power to do what I wanted to do without feeling I had to please a partner or respond to a partner. I felt in control, dominant. Rape was the ability to have sex without caring about the woman's response. I was totally dominant.

To discover that most rape is calculated behavior—that rapists are not "sick"; that the motivating force is power, not passion; that the behavior stems from the criminal pursuit of pleasure, not from mental illness—is significant. It makes the sociological quest worthwhile.

In comparing their sample of rapists with their control group of nonrapists, Scully and Marolla also made another significant finding: The rapists are more likely to believe "rape myths." They are more likely to believe that women cause their own rape by the way they act and the clothes they wear, that a woman who charges rape has simply changed her mind after participating in consensual sex, and that most men accused of rape are innocent.

Connecting Research and Theory

Such findings go far beyond simply adding to our storehouse of "facts." As indicated in Figure 5.1 on page 129, research stimulates both the development of theory and the need for more research.

Scully and Marolla suggest that rape myths act as neutralizers, that they allow "potential rapists to turn off social prohibitions against injuring others."

This hypothesis, in turn, pinpoints the need to determine how such myths are transmitted. Which male subcultures perpetuate them? Do the mass media contribute to these myths? Do family, religion, and education create respect for females and help keep males from learning such myths? Or do they somehow contribute to these myths? If so, how?

Sociologists have begun to build on this path-breaking research, which was done, as usual, under less than ideal conditions. The resulting theorizing and research may provide the basis for making changes that reduce the incidence of rape in our society.

Sources: Marolla and Scully 1986; Scully 1990; Hale 2003; Scully and Marolla 1984, 2007.

Sociology needs more of this type of research—imaginative and sometimes daring investigations conducted in an imperfect world under less than ideal conditions. This is really what sociology is all about. Sociologists study what people do—whether their behaviors are conforming or deviant, whether they please others or disgust them and arouse intense anger. No matter what behavior is studied, systematic research methods and the application of social theory take us beyond common sense. They allow us to penetrate surface realities so we can better understand human behavior—and, in the ideal case, make changes to help improve social life.

Summary *and* Review

What Is a Valid Sociological Topic?

Any human behavior is a valid sociological topic, even disreputable behavior. Spouse abuse is an example. Sociological research is based on the sociologist's interests, access to subjects, appropriate methods, and ethical considerations. P. 128.

Common Sense and the Need for Sociological Research

Why isn't common sense adequate?

Common sense doesn't provide reliable information. When subjected to scientific research, commonsense ideas often are found to be limited or false. P. 128.

A Research Model

What are the eight basic steps of scientific research?

1. Selecting a topic, 2. Defining the problem, 3. Reviewing the literature, 4. Formulating a **hypothesis,** 5. Choosing a research method, 6. Collecting the data, 7. Analyzing the results, 8. Sharing the results. These steps are explained in detail on Pp. 128–131.

Research Methods

How do sociologists gather data?

To gather data, sociologists use six **research methods** (or research designs): **surveys, participant observation** (fieldwork), **secondary analysis, documents, experiments,** and **unobtrusive measures.** Pp. 131–142.

How do sociologists choose a research method?

Sociologists choose their research method based on questions to be answered, their access to potential subjects, the resources available, their training, and ethical considerations. P. 142.

Controversy in Sociological Research

Why is sociological research often controversial?

Some people get upset because sociologists do research on disreputable or illegal activities or on personal or intimate areas of life. Other people get upset when research findings go against their interest or biases. Pp. 142–145.

Gender in Sociological Research

What is the relationship between gender and research?

There are two aspects. First, findings based on samples of men do not necessarily apply to women and findings based on samples of women do not necessarily apply to men. Second, in some kinds of research, such as studying abused spouses, rape victims, and rapists, the gender of the researcher could affect findings. Pp. 145–146.

Ethics in Sociological Research

How important are ethics in sociological research?

Ethics are of fundamental concern to sociologists, who are committed to openness, honesty, truth, and protecting their subjects from harm. The Brajuha research on restaurant workers and the Humphreys research on "tearooms" were cited to illustrate ethical issues of concern to sociologists. Pp. 146–148.

How Research and Theory Work Together

What is the relationship between theory and research?

Theory and research depend on one another. Sociologists use theory to interpret the data they gather. Theory also generates questions that need to be answered by research. Research, in turn, helps to generate theory: Findings that don't match what is expected can indicate a need to modify theory. Pp. 148–149.

Thinking Critically
about Chapter 5

1. Why do we need sociological research?
2. Should sociologists be allowed to do research on disreputable or disapproved behavior? On illegal behavior? Why or why not?
3. What factors make for *bad* sociological research? How can these be avoided?
4. What ethics govern sociological research?
5. Is it right for sociologists to not identity themselves when they do research? To misrepresent themselves? What if identifying themselves as researchers will destroy their access to the research setting or to informants?

Additional Resources

What can you use MySocLab for? www.mysoclab.com

- **Study and Review:** Pre- and Post-Tests, Practice Tests, Flash Cards, Individualized Study Plans.
- **Current Events:** *Sociology in the News,* the daily *New York Times,* and more.

- **Research and Writing:** *Research Navigator, Writing About Sociology,* and more.

Where Can I Read More on This Topic?

Suggested readings for this chapter are listed at the back of this book.

Societies to Social Networks

Bharati Chaudhuri, *Unity*

When Kody Scott joined the L.A. Crips, his initiation had two parts. Here's the first:

"How old is you now anyway?"

"Eleven, but I'll be twelve in November."

I never saw the blow to my head come from Huck. Bam! And I was on all fours . . . Kicked in the stomach, I was on my back counting stars in the blackness. Grabbed by the collar, I was made to stand again. A solid blow to my chest exploded pain on the blank screen that had now become my mind. Bam! Another, then another. Blows rained on me from every direction . . .

Up until this point not a word had been spoken. . . . Then I just started swinging, with no style or finesse, just anger and the instinct to survive. . . . (This) reflected my ability to represent the set [gang] in hand-to-hand combat. The blows stopped abruptly . . . My ear was bleeding, and my neck and face were deep red . . .

Scott's beating was followed immediately by the second part of his initiation. For this, he received the name *Monster*, which he carried proudly:

"Give Kody the pump" [12-gauge pump action shotgun] . . . Tray Ball spoke with the calm of a football coach. "Tonight we gonna rock they world." . . .

Kody, you got eight shots, you don't come back to the car unless they all are gone.

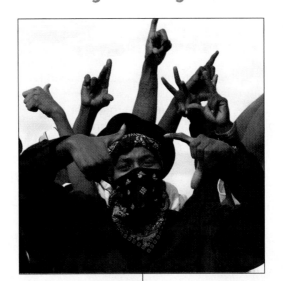

Hand slaps were passed around the room . . . "Kody, you got eight shots, you don't come back to the car unless they all are gone."

"Righteous," I said, eager to show my worth. . . .

Hanging close to buildings, houses, and bushes, we made our way, one after the other, to within spitting distance of the Bloods. . . . Huck and Fly stepped from the shadows simultaneously and were never noticed until it was too late. Boom! Boom! Heavy bodies hitting the ground, confusion, yells of dismay, running, . . . By my sixth shot I had advanced past the first fallen bodies and into the street in pursuit of those who had sought refuge behind cars and trees. . . .

Back in the shack we smoked more pot and drank more beer. I was the center of attention for my acts of aggression. . . .

Tray Ball said. "You got potential, 'cause you eager to learn. Bangin' [being a gang member] ain't no part-time thang, it's full-time, it's a career. It's bein' down when ain't nobody else down with you. It's gettin' caught and not tellin'. Killin' and not caring, and dyin' without fear. It's love for your set and hate for the enemy. You hear what I'm sayin'?"

Kody adds this insightful remark:

Though never verbally stated, death was looked upon as a sort of reward, a badge of honor, especially

(continued)

if one died in some heroic capacity for the hood . . . The supreme sacrifice was to "take a bullet for a homie" [fellow gang member]. The set functioned as a religion. Nothing held a light to the power of the set. If you died on the trigger you surely were smiled upon by the Crip God.

Excerpts from Scott 1994:8–13, 103.

Groups are the essence of life in society. We become who we are because of our membership in human groups. As we saw in Chapter 3, even our minds are a product of society, or, more specifically phrased, of the groups to which we belong.

In this chapter, we'll consider how groups influence our lives—and examine the power that groups wield over us. Although none of us wants to think that we could participate in killings such as those recounted in our opening vignette, don't bet on it. You are going to read some surprising things about groups in this chapter.

Societies and Their Transformation

To better understand **groups**—people who interact with one another and who think of themselves as belonging together—let's first look at the big picture. The largest and most complex group that sociologists study is **society,** which consists of people who share a culture and a territory. Society, which surrounds us, sets the stage for our life experiences. Not only does it lay the broad framework for our behavior but also it influences the ways we think and feel. Its effect is so significant that if you had grown up in a different society, you would be a different type of person.

group people who have something in common and who believe that what they have in common is significant; also called a social group

society people who share a culture and a territory

As society—the largest and most complex type of group—changes, so, too, do the groups, activities, and, ultimately, the type of people who form that society. This photo of Russian and Austrian wrestlers in the Olympics at Greece captures some of the changes occurring in Western societies. What social changes can you identify from this photo?

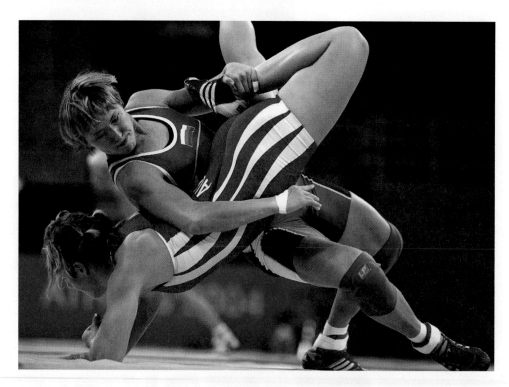

To see how our society developed, look at Figure 6.1. You can see that technology is the key to understanding the broad, sweeping changes that produced our society. As we summarize these changes, picture yourself as a member of each society. Consider how your life—even your thoughts and values—would be different in each society.

Hunting and Gathering Societies

Societies with the fewest social divisions are called **hunting and gathering societies.** As the name implies, in order to survive, these groups depend on hunting animals and gathering plants. In some groups, the men do the hunting, and the women the gathering. In others, both men and women (and children) gather plants, the men hunt large animals, and both men and women hunt small animals. Beyond this basic division of labor by sex, there are few social divisions. The groups usually have a **shaman,** an individual thought to be able to influence spiritual forces, but shamans, too, must help obtain food. Although these groups give greater prestige to the men hunters, the women gatherers contribute more food to the group, perhaps even four-fifths of their total food supply (Bernard 1992).

Because a region cannot support a large number of people who hunt animals and gather plants (group members do not plant—they only gather what is already there), hunting and gathering societies are small. They usually consist of only twenty-five to forty people. These groups are nomadic. As their food supply dwindles in one area, they move to another location. They place high value on sharing food, which is essential to their survival. Because of disease, drought, and pestilence, children have only about a fifty-fifty chance of surviving to adulthood (Lenski and Lenski 1987).

Of all societies, hunters and gatherers are the most egalitarian. Because what they hunt and gather is perishable, the people accumulate few personal possessions. Consequently, no one becomes wealthier than anyone else. There are no rulers, and most decisions are

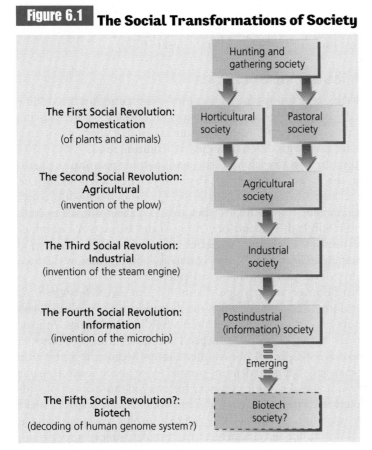

Figure 6.1 **The Social Transformations of Society**

Source: By the author.

The simplest forms of societies are called hunting and gathering societies. Members of these societies have adapted well to their environments, and they have more leisure than the members of other societies, Shown here are tribal members in the rainforest of Paraguay. What cultural diffusion do you see?

arrived at through discussion. Because their needs are basic and they do not work to store up material possessions, hunters and gatherers have the most leisure of all human groups (Sahlins 1972; Lorber 1994; Volti 1995).

All human groups were once hunters and gatherers, and until several hundred years ago such societies were common. Their demise came when other groups took over the regions in which they moved about in their search for food. Today, fewer than 300 hunter-gatherer groups remain; they include the pygmies of central Africa, the aborigines of Australia, and groups in South America represented by the photo above (Stiles 2003). These groups seem doomed to a similar fate, and it is likely that their way of life will soon disappear from the human scene (Lenski and Lenski 1987).

Pastoral and Horticultural Societies

About ten thousand years ago, some groups found that they could tame and breed some of the animals they hunted—primarily goats, sheep, cattle, and camels. Others discovered that they could cultivate plants. As a result, hunting and gathering societies branched into two directions, each with different means of acquiring food.

The key to understanding the first branching is the word *pasture;* **pastoral** (or herding) **societies** are based on the *pasturing of animals.* Pastoral societies developed in arid regions, where low rainfall made it impractical to build life around growing crops. Groups that took this turn remained nomadic, for they followed their animals to fresh pasture. The key to understanding the second branching is the word *horticulture,* or plant cultivation. **Horticultural** (or gardening) **societies** are based on the *cultivation of plants by the use of hand tools.* Because they no longer had to abandon an area as the food supply gave out, these groups developed permanent settlements.

We can call the domestication of animals and plants the *first social revolution.* As shown in Figure 6.2, it transformed society. Although the **domestication revolution** was gradual, occurring over thousands of years, it represented a fundamental break with the past and it changed human history. The more dependable food supply ushered in changes that touched almost every aspect of human life. Groups became larger because the more dependable food supply supported more people. With more food available than was needed for survival, no longer was it necessary for everyone to work at providing food. This allowed groups to develop a *division of labor.* Some people began to make jewelry, others tools, others weapons, and so on. This led to a surplus of objects, which, in turn, stimulated trade. With trading, groups began to accumulate objects they prized, such as gold, jewelry, and utensils.

pastoral society a society based on the pasturing of animals

horticultural society a society based on cultivating plants by the use of hand tools

domestication revolution the first social revolution, based on the domestication of plants and animals, which led to pastoral and horticultural societies

agricultural revolution the second social revolution, based on the invention of the plow, which led to agricultural societies

agricultural society a society based on large-scale agriculture; plows drawn by animals are the source of food production

Industrial Revolution the third social revolution, occurring when machines powered by fuels replaced most animal and human power

Figure 6.2 illustrates how these changes set the stage for *social inequality*. Some families (or clans) acquired more goods than others. This led to feuds and war, for groups now possessed animals, pastures, croplands, jewelry, and other material goods to fight about. War, in turn, opened the door to slavery, for people found it convenient to let captives do their drudge work. Social inequality remained limited, however, for the surplus itself was limited. As individuals passed their possessions on to their descendants, wealth grew more concentrated. So did power, and for the first time, some individuals became chiefs.

Note the primary pattern that runs through this transformation of group life: the change *from fewer to more possessions and from greater to lesser equality*. Where people were located *within* the hierarchy of a society became vital for determining what happened to them in life. Again, Figure 6.2 summarizes how these changes led to social inequality.

Agricultural Societies

When the plow was invented about five or six thousand years ago, social life was once again changed forever. Compared with hoes and digging sticks, the use of animals to pull plows was immensely efficient. As the earth was plowed, more nutrients were returned to the soil, making the land more productive. The food surplus of the **agricultural revolution** was unlike anything ever seen in human history. It allowed even more people to engage in activities other than farming. In this new **agricultural society,** people developed cities and what is popularly known as "culture," such as philosophy, art, music, literature, and architecture. Accompanied by the inventions of the wheel, writing, and numbers, the changes were so profound that this period is sometimes referred to as "the dawn of civilization."

The tendency toward social inequality of previous societies was only a forerunner of what was to come. *Inequality became a fundamental feature of life in society.* Some people managed to gain control of the growing surplus of resources. To protect their expanding privileges and power, this elite surrounded itself with armed men. They even levied taxes on others, who now had become their "subjects." As conflict theorists point out, this concentration of resources and power—along with the oppression of people not in power—was the forerunner of the state.

No one knows exactly how it happened, but during this period females also became subject to males. Sociologist Elise Boulding (1976) theorizes that this change occurred because men were in charge of plowing and the cows. She suggests that when metals were developed, men took on the new job of attaching the metal as tips to the wooden plows and doing the plowing. As a result,

the shift of the status of the woman farmer may have happened quite rapidly, once there were two male specializations relating to agriculture: plowing and the care of cattle. This situation left women with all the subsidiary tasks, including weeding and carrying water to the fields. The new fields were larger, so women had to work just as many hours as they did before, but now they worked at more secondary tasks. . . . This would contribute further to the erosion of the status of women.

This explanation, however, creates more questions than it answers. Why, for example, did men take over metal work and plowing? Why didn't women? It also does not account for why men control societies in which women are in charge of the cattle. In short, we are left in the dark as to why and how men became dominant, a reason likely to remain lost in human history.

Industrial Societies

The *third* social invention also turned society upside down. The **Industrial Revolution** began in Great Britain in 1765 when the steam engine was first used to run machinery. Before this, a few machines (such as windmills and water wheels) had been used to harness nature, but most machines depended on human and animal power.

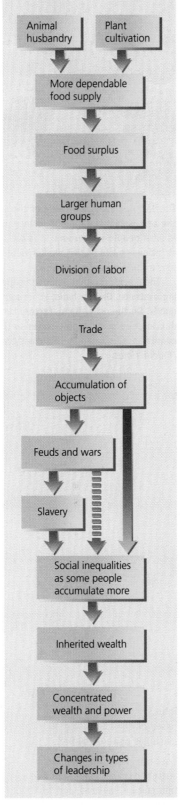

Figure 6.2 Consequences of Animal Domestication and Plant Cultivation

Source: By the author.

The sociological significance of the social revolutions discussed in the text is that the type of society in which we live determines the kind of people we become. It is obvious, for example, that the orientations to life of this worker would differ markedly from the people in the photo on page 154.

The machinery that ushered in industrial society was met with ambivalence. On one hand, it brought a multitude of welcomed goods. On the other hand, factory time clocks and the incessant production line made people slaves to the very machines they built, a condition illustrated by this classic scene of Charlie Chaplin's in *Modern Times*.

The resulting **industrial society** is defined by sociologist Herbert Blumer (1990) as one in which goods are produced by machines powered by fuels, instead of by the brute force of humans or animals.

The steam engine was followed by another leap in social inequality. This new technology was far more efficient than anything that preceded it. Just as its surplus was greater, so also were its effects on social life. Those who first used the steam engine accumulated such wealth that in some instances their riches outran the imagination of royalty. Gaining an early position in the markets, the early industrialists were able not only to control the means of production (factories, machinery, tools) but also to dictate people's working conditions. The breakdown of feudal society also helped them to control the workers. Masses of people were thrown off the lands that their ancestors had farmed as tenants for centuries. Having become homeless, these landless peasants moved to the cities. There they faced the choice of stealing, starving, or working for wages barely sufficient to sustain life (the equivalent of a loaf of bread for a day's work).

Workers had no legal right to safe working conditions, nor the right to unionize. Employment was a private contract between the employer and the individual worker. If workers banded together to protest or to ask for higher wages, they were fired. If they returned to the factory, they were arrested for trespassing on private property. Strikes were illegal, and strikers were beaten savagely by the employer's private security force. On some occasions during the early 1900s, U.S. strikers were shot by private police, and even by the National Guard. Against these odds, workers gradually won their fight for better working conditions.

As industrialization continued, more goods were produced and more money circulated. As a result, the earlier pattern of growing inequality was reversed. Home ownership became common, as did the ownership of automobiles and an incredible variety of consumer goods. Today's typical worker enjoys a high standard of living in terms of health care, longevity, material possessions, and access to libraries and education. On an even broader level are the abolition of slavery, the shift from monarchies to more representative political systems, greater rights for women and minorities, the rights to a jury trial, to cross-examine witnesses, to vote, and to travel. A recent extension of these equalities is the right to set up your own Internet blog where you can bemoan life in your school or criticize the President.

It is difficult to overstate the sociological principle that the type of society we live in is the fundamental reason for why we become who we are. To see how industrial society affects your life, note that you would not be taking this course if it were not for industrialization. Clearly you would not have a computer, car, cell phone, television, iPod, or your type of clothing or home. You wouldn't even have electric lights. And on a much deeper level, you would not feel the same about life, or have your particular aspirations for the future. Actually, no aspect of your life would be the same; you would be locked into the attitudes and views that come with an agricultural or horticultural way of life.

Postindustrial (Information) Societies

If you were to choose one word that characterizes our society, what would it be? Of the many candidates, the word *change* would have to rank high among them. The primary source of the sweeping changes that are transforming our lives is the technology centering around the microchip. The change is so vast that sociologists say that a new type of society has emerged. They call it the **postindustrial** (or **information**) **society**.

industrial society a society based on the harnessing of machines powered by fuels

postindustrial (information) society a society based on information, services, and high technology, rather than on raw materials and manufacturing

What are the main characteristics of this new society? Unlike the industrial society, its hallmark is not raw materials and manufacturing. Rather, its basic component is *information*. Teachers pass on knowledge to students, while lawyers, physicians, bankers, pilots, and interior decorators sell their specialized knowledge of law, the body, money, aerodynamics, and color schemes to clients. Unlike the factory workers of an industrial society, these individuals don't *produce* anything. Rather, they transmit or use information to provide services that others are willing to pay for.

The United States was the first country to have more than 50 percent of its workforce in service industries such as education, health, research, the government, counseling, banking, investments, insurance, sales, law, and the mass media. Australia, New Zealand, western Europe, and Japan soon followed. This trend away from manufacturing and toward selling information and services shows no sign of letting up.

The changes have been so profound that they have led to a *fourth social revolution*. The microchip is transforming established ways of life, uprooting old perspectives and replacing them with new ones. This new technology allows us to work at home, even while we ride in cars, trucks, and airplanes, to talk to others in distant cities and to people on the other side of the globe. This tiny device lets us examine the surface of Mars and to probe other remote regions of space. It is changing our shopping patterns as we spend billions of dollars on Internet purchases. And because of it, millions of children spend countless hours battling virtual video villains. For a review of other changes, see the section on the computer in Chapter 22 (pages 664–667).

Biotech Societies: Is a New Type of Society Emerging?

- Tobacco that fights cancer. ("Yes, smoke your way to health!")
- Corn that fights herpes and is a contraceptive. ("Corn flakes in the morning—and safe sex all day!")
- Goats whose milk contains spider silk (to make fishing lines and body armor) ("Got milk? The best bulletproofing.")
- Animals that are part human: Human genes have been inserted into animal genes, so they produce medicines for humans—-and creamier mozzarella cheese. (You can write your own jingle for this one.)
- No-Sneeze kitties—hypoallergenic cats at $4,000 each.

I know that this sounds like science fiction, but we *already* have the goats that make spider silk and the part-human animals that produce medicine (Elias 2001; Kristoff 2002; Osborne 2002). The no-sneeze cats are for sale—and there is a waiting list (Rosenthal 2006). Some suggest that the changes in which we are immersed are revolutionary, that we are entering another new type of society. In this new **biotech society,** the economy will center on applying and altering genetic structures—both plant and animal—to produce food, medicine, and materials.

If there is a new society, then when did it begin? There are no firm edges to new societies, for each new one overlaps the one it is replacing. The opening to the biotech society could have been 1953, when Francis Crick and James Watson identified the double-helix structure of DNA. Or perhaps historians will trace the date to the decoding of the human genome in 2001.

Whether the changes that are swirling around us are part of a new type of society is not the main point. *The sociological significance of these changes is that just as the larger group called society always profoundly affects people's thinking and behavior, so, too, these recent developments will do the same for us.* As society is transformed, we will be swept along with it. The transformation will change even the ways we think about the self and life.

Projecting a new type of society so soon after the arrival of the information society is risky. The wedding of genetics and economics could turn out to be simply another aspect of our information society—or we really may have just stepped into a new type of society. In either case, we can anticipate revolutionary changes in health care (more emphasis on prevention, instead of just treating disease) and, with cloning and bioengineering, perhaps even changes in the human species. The Sociology and the New Technology box on the next page examines implications of cloning.

biotech society a society whose economy increasingly centers around the application of genetics—human genetics for medicine, and plant and animal genetics for the production of food and materials

> SOCIOLOGY *and the* NEW TECHNOLOGY

"So, You Want to Be Yourself?" Cloning in the Coming Biotech Society

NO TYPE OF SOCIETY ENDS ABRUPTLY. The edges are fuzzy, and the new one overlaps the old. As the information society matures, it looks as though it is being overtaken by a biotech society. Let's try to peer over the edge of our current society to glimpse the one that may be arriving. What will life be like? There are many issues we could examine, but since space is limited, let's consider just one: cloning.

Consider this scenario:

Your four-year-old daughter has drowned, and you can't get over your sorrow. You go to the regional cloning clinic, where you have stored DNA from all members of your family. You pay the standard fee, and the director hires a surrogate mother to bring your daughter back as a newborn.

Will cloning humans become a reality? Since human embryos already have been cloned, it seems inevitable that some group somewhere will complete the process. If cloning humans becomes routine—well, consider these scenarios:

Suppose that a couple can't have children. Testing shows that the husband is sterile. The couple talk about their dilemma, and the wife agrees to have her husband's genetic material implanted into one of her eggs. Would this woman, in effect, be rearing her husband as a little boy?

Or suppose that you love your mother dearly, and she is dying. With her permission, you decide to clone her. Who is the clone? Would you be rearing your own mother?

What if a woman gave birth to her own clone? Would the clone be her daughter or her sister?

When genetic duplicates appear, the questions of what humans are, what their relationship is to their "parents," and indeed what "parents" and children" are, will be brought up at every kitchen table.

for your Consideration

As these scenarios show, the issue of cloning provokes profound questions. Perhaps the most weighty concerns the future of society. Let's suppose that mass cloning becomes possible.

Many people object that cloning is immoral, but some will argue the opposite. They will ask why we should leave human reproduction to people who have inferior traits—genetic diseases, low IQs, perhaps even the propensity for crime and violence. They will suggest that we select people with the finer characteristics—high creative ability, high intelligence, compassion, and a propensity for peace.

Let's assume that geneticists have traced the characteristics just mentioned to specific genes—along with the ability to appreciate and create beautiful poetry, music, and architecture; to excel in mathematics, science, and other intellectual pursuits; and to be successful in love. Do you think that it should be our moral obligation to populate society with people like this? To try to build a society that is better for all—one without terrorism, war, violence, and greed? Could this perhaps even be our evolutionary destiny?

Source: Based on Kaebnick 2000; McGee 2000; Bjerklie et al. 2001; Davis 2001; Weiss 2004; Regalado 2005.

IN SUM Our society sets boundaries around our lives. By laying out a framework of statuses, roles, groups, and social institutions, society establishes the values and beliefs that prevail. It also determines the type and extent of social inequality. These factors, in turn, set the stage for relationships between men and women, the young and the elderly, racial–ethnic groups, the rich and the poor, and so on.

It is difficult to overstate the sociological principle that the type of society in which we live is the fundamental reason why we become who we are—why we feel about things the way we do, and even why we think our particular thoughts. On the obvious level, if you lived in a hunting and gathering society you would not be listening to your favorite music, watching TV programs, or playing video games. On a deeper level, you would not feel the same about life or hold your particular aspirations for the future.

Finally, we should note that not all the world's societies will go through the transformations shown in Figure 6.1 (page 153). Whether any hunting and gathering societies will survive, however, remains to be seen. Perhaps a few will, maybe kept on "small reserves" that will be off limits to developers—but open to guided ecotours at a hefty fee.

Now that we have reviewed the major historical shifts in societies, let's turn to groups within society. Just how do they affect our lives?

Groups Within Society

Our society is huge, dominating, sometimes even threatening and oppressive. This can create a bewildering sense of not belonging. Sociologist Emile Durkheim (1893/1933) called this condition *anomie* (AN-uh-mee). He said that small groups help prevent anomie by standing as a buffer between the individual and the larger society. By providing intimate relationships, small groups give us a sense of belonging, something that we all need.

Small groups, then, are vital for our well-being, but before we examine them in detail, we should distinguish some terms. Two terms sometimes confused with "group" are *aggregate* and *category.* An **aggregate** consists of individuals who temporarily share the same physical space but who do not see themselves as belonging together. People standing in a checkout line or drivers waiting at a red light are an aggregate. A **category** is a statistic. It consists of people who share similar characteristics, such as all college women who wear glasses or all men over 6 feet tall. Unlike groups, the individuals who make up a category neither interact with one another nor take one another into account. The members of a *group,* in contrast, think of themselves as belonging together, and they interact with one another. These concepts are illustrated in the photos on the next page.

Primary Groups

Our first group, the family, gives us our basic orientations to life. Later, among friends, we find more intimacy and an expanded sense of belonging. These groups are what sociologist Charles Cooley called **primary groups.** By providing intimate, face-to-face interaction, they give us an identity, a feeling of who we are. As Cooley (1909) put it,

> By primary groups I mean those characterized by intimate face-to-face association and cooperation. They are primary in several senses, but chiefly in that they are fundamental in forming the social nature and ideals of the individual.

Producing a Mirror Within Cooley called primary groups the "springs of life." By this, he means that primary groups, such as family and friends, are essential to our emotional well-being. As humans, we have an intense need for face-to-face interaction that generates feelings of self-esteem. By offering a sense of belonging and a feeling of being appreciated—and sometimes even loved—primary groups are uniquely equipped to meet this basic need. From our opening vignette, you can see that gangs are also primary groups.

Primary groups are also significant because their values and attitudes become fused into our identity. We internalize their views, which then become the lenses through which we view life. Even as adults—no matter how far we move away from our childhood roots—early primary groups remain "inside" us. There, they continue to form part of the perspective from which we look out onto the world. Ultimately, then, it is difficult, if not impossible, for us to separate the self from our primary groups, for the self and our groups merge into a "we."

Secondary Groups

Compared with primary groups, **secondary groups** are larger, more anonymous, more formal, and more impersonal. Secondary groups are based on some common interest or activity, and their members are likely to interact on the basis of specific statuses, such as president, manager, worker, or student. Examples are a college class, the American Sociological Association, and the Democratic Party. Contemporary society could not function without secondary groups. They are part of the way we get our education, make our living, spend our money, and use our leisure time.

As necessary as secondary groups are for contemporary life, they often fail to satisfy our deep needs for intimate association. Consequently, *secondary groups tend to break down into primary groups.* At school and work, we form friendships. Our interaction with our friends is so important that we sometimes feel that if it weren't for them, school or work "would drive us crazy." The primary groups that we form within secondary groups, then, serve as a buffer between ourselves and the demands that secondary groups place on us.

aggregate individuals who temporarily share the same physical space but who do not see themselves as belonging together

category people who have similar characteristics

primary group a group characterized by intimate, long-term, face-to-face association and cooperation

secondary group compared with a primary group, a larger, relatively temporary, more anonymous, formal, and impersonal group based on some interest or activity. Its members are likely to interact on the basis of specific statuses

Categories, Aggregates, Primary and Secondary Groups

Groups have a deep impact on our views and attitudes, even what we feel and think about life. Yet, as illustrated by these photos, not everything that appears to be a group is actually a group in the sociological sense.

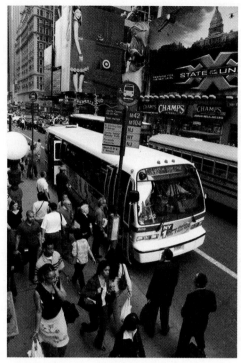

Secondary groups are larger and more anonymous, formal, and impersonal than primary groups. Why is this photo of a political convention an example of a secondary group?

Aggregates are simply people who happen to be in the same place at the same time.

Primary groups such as the family play a key role in the development of the self. As a small group, the family also servers as a buffer from the often-threatening larger group known as society. The family has been of primary significance in forming the basic orientations of this couple, as it will be for their daughter.

The outstanding trait that these three people have in common does not make them a group, but a **category.**

In-Groups and Out-Groups

Groups toward which we feel loyalty are called **in-groups;** those toward which we feel antagonism are called **out-groups.** For Monster Kody in our opening vignette, the Crips were an in-group, while the Bloods were an out-group. That the Crips—and we—make such a fundamental division of the world has far-reaching consequences for our lives.

Producing Loyalty, a Sense of Superiority, and Rivalries Identification with a group can generate not only a sense of belonging, but also loyalty and feelings of superiority. These, in turn, often produce rivalries. Usually the rivalries are mild, such as sports rivalries among neighboring towns, in which the most extreme act is likely to be the furtive invasion of the out-group's territory to steal a mascot, paint a rock, or uproot a goal post. The consequences of in-group membership can also be discrimination, hatred, and, as we saw in our opening vignette, even participation in murder.

Implications for a Socially Diverse Society Our strong identifications with in-groups are the basis of many gender and racial-ethnic divisions. As sociologist Robert Merton (1968) observed, our favoritism leads to biased perception. Following a fascinating double standard, we tend to view the traits of our in-group as virtues, while we see those *same* traits as vices in out-groups. Men may perceive an aggressive man as assertive but an aggressive woman as pushy. They may think that a male employee who doesn't speak up "knows when to keep his mouth shut," while they consider a quiet woman as too timid to make it in the business world.

To divide the world into "we" and "they" poses a danger for a pluralistic society. For the Nazis, the Jews were an out-group that came to symbolize evil. One consequence of biased perception is that harming others can come to be viewed as justifiable. The Nazis weren't alone in their views; many ordinary, "good" Germans defended the Holocaust as "dirty work" that someone had to do (Hughes 1962/2005). This principle might seem to pertain only to the past, but it continues today—and likely always will. Consider what happened following the terrorist attacks of 9/11. Viewing Arabs as sinister, bloodthirsty villains, top U.S. officials approved "cruel, inhuman, and degrading" treatment of prisoners—as long as they didn't call it torture (Gonzales 2002). Alan M. Dershowitz, a prominent civil libertarian at Harvard Law School, went further, suggesting that judges should be able to issue "torture warrants" (Schulz 2002). This would give torture a legal standing, making it a tidy matter. Cruel interrogation and torture—for the sake of the lives they might save—quickly became "dirty work" that someone had to do.

Economic downturns are especially perilous in this regard. The Nazis took power during a depression so severe that it was wiping out the middle classes. If such a depression were to occur in the United States, immigrants would be transformed from "nice people who do jobs that Americans think are beneath them" to "sneaky people who steal jobs from friends and family." A national anti-immigration policy would follow, accompanied by a resurgence of hate groups such as the neo-Nazis, the Ku Klux Klan, and skinheads.

In short, to divide the world into in-groups and out-groups is a natural part of social life. But in addition to bringing functional consequences, it can also bring dysfunctional ones.

"So long, Bill. This is my club. You can't come in."

How our participation in social groups shapes our self-concept is a focus of symbolic interactionists. In this process, knowing who we are *not* is as significant as knowing who we are.

Reference Groups

Suppose you have just been offered a good job. It pays double what you hope to make even after you graduate from college. You have only two days to make up your mind. If you accept it, you will have to drop out of college. As you consider the matter, thoughts like this may go through your mind: "My friends will say I'm a fool if I don't take the job . . . but Dad and Mom will practically go crazy. They've made sacrifices for me, and they'll be crushed if I don't finish college. They've always said I've got to get my education first, that good jobs will always be there. . . . But, then, I'd like to see the look on the faces of those neighbors who said I'd never amount to much!"

Evaluating Ourselves This is an example of how people use **reference groups,** the groups we use as standards to evaluate ourselves. Your reference groups may include your family, neighbors, teachers, classmates, co-workers, and the Scouts or the members of a church, synagogue, or mosque. If you were like Monster Kody in our opening vignette, the "set" would be your main reference group. Even a group you don't belong to can be a reference group. For example, if you are thinking about going to graduate school, graduate students or members of the profession you want to join may form a reference group. You would consider their standards as you evaluate your grades or writing skills.

Reference groups exert tremendous influence over our lives. For example, if you want to become a corporate executive, you might start to dress more formally, try to improve your vocabulary, read the *Wall Street Journal,* and change your major to business or law. In contrast, if you want to become a rock musician, you might wear jewelry in several places where you have pierced your body, get elaborate tattoos, dress in ways your parents and many of your peers consider extreme, read *Rolling Stone,* drop out of college, and hang around clubs and rock groups.

Exposure to Contradictory Standards in a Socially Diverse Society From these examples, you can see how we use reference groups to evaluate our behavior. When we see ourselves as measuring up to a reference group's standards, we feel no conflict. If our behavior—or even aspirations—does not match the group's standards, however, the mismatch can lead to inner turmoil. For example, to want to become a corporate executive would create no inner turmoil for most of us. It would, however, if you had grown up in an Amish home, for the Amish strongly disapprove of such aspirations for their children. They ban high school and college education, three-piece suits, and corporate employment. Similarly, if you wanted to join the military and your parents were dedicated pacifists, you likely would feel deep conflict, as your parents would hold quite different aspirations for you.

Given the social diversity of our society and our social mobility, as we grow up many of us are exposed to contradictory ideas and standards from the groups that become significant to us. The "internal recordings" that play contradictory messages from these reference groups, then, are one price we pay for our social mobility.

Social Networks

Although we live in a huge and diverse society, we don't experience social life as a sea of nameless, strange faces. Instead, we interact within social networks. The term **social network** refers to people who are linked to one another. Your social network includes your family, friends, acquaintances, people at work and school, and even your "friends of friends." Think of your social network as lines that extend outward from yourself, gradually encompassing more and more people.

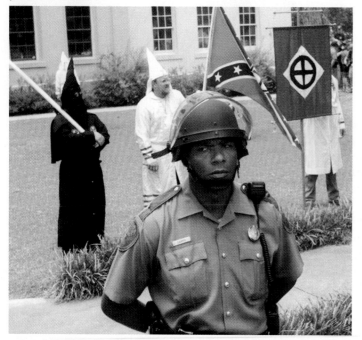

All of us have *reference groups*—the groups we use as standards to evaluate ourselves. How do you think the reference groups of these members of the KKK who are demonstrating in Jaspar, Texas, differ from those of the police officer who is protecting their right of free speech? Although the KKK and this police officer use different groups to evaluate their attitudes and behaviors, the process is the same.

We all use *reference groups* to evaluate our accomplishments, failures, values, and attitudes. We compare what we see in ourselves with what we perceive as normative in our reference groups. As is evident in these two photos, the reference groups these youths are using are not likely to lead them to the same social destination.

If you are a member of a large group, you probably associate regularly with a few people within that group. In a sociology class I was teaching at a commuter campus, six women who didn't know one another ended up working together on a project. They got along well, and they began to sit together. Eventually they planned a Christmas party at one of their homes. This type of social network, the clusters within a group, or its internal factions, is called a **clique** (cleek).

The analysis of social networks has moved from theory and laboratory study to the practical world. As you may recall from Chapter 1 (page 23), analyzing social networks was the way that U.S. forces located Saddam Hussein. On a more personal level, a fascinating development in social networks is *facebooking*, the topic of the Sociology and the New Technology box on the next page.

The Small World Phenomenon Social scientists have wondered just how extensive the connections are between social networks. If you list everyone you know, each of those individuals lists everyone he or she knows, and you keep doing this, would almost everyone in the United States eventually be included on those lists?

It would be too cumbersome to test this hypothesis by drawing up such lists, but psychologist Stanley Milgram (1933–1984) came up with an interesting idea. In a classic study known as "the small world phenomenon," Milgram (1967) addressed a letter to "targets": the wife of a divinity student in Cambridge and a stockbroker in Boston. He sent the letter to "starters," who did not know these people. He asked them to send the letter to someone they knew on a first-name basis, someone they thought might know the "target." The recipients, in turn, were asked to mail the letter to someone they knew who might know the "target," and so on. The question was: Would the letters ever reach the "target"? If so, how long would the chain be?

Think of yourself as part of this study. What would you do if you were a "starter," but the "target" lived in a state in which you knew no one? You would send the letter to someone you know who might know someone in that state. This, Milgram reported, is just what happened. Although none of the senders knew the targets, the letters reached the designated individual in an average of just six jumps.

Milgram's study caught the public's fancy, leading to the phrase, "six degrees of separation." This expression means that, on average, everyone in the United States is

clique a cluster of people within a larger group who choose to interact with one another; an internal faction

Facebooking: Social Networks Online

MAKING NEW FRIENDS AND MAINTAINING friendships can take effort. You have to clean up, put on clothes, leave your room, and engage in conversations. The talk can turn in directions that don't interest you, and people that you don't particularly care for can drop into your group. Situations can arise that make you feel awkward or embarrassed. Maybe you would like to disengage for a few minutes—to take a little power nap or to read a book. You can't do this without offending someone.

Not so with facebooking. You are in charge. Talk with people when you want. Stop when you want.

This is part of the allure of facebooking. The facebook is like an ever-changing, online yearbook. To find people with similar interests, just type in that interest. Your favorite book is Kerouac's *On The Road? The DaVinci Code? Pride and Prejudice?* Your favorite movie is *Fight Club? Barbarella? Reefer Madness?* You enjoy *J. Crew* or *Wheezer?* Your favorite activity is making out? Fiddling with guns? Looking at pink shoes? And you want to find people who share your interest? Just a mouse-click away.

You can even form your own group—and invite others to join it. The group can be as esoteric as you prefer. Some actual groups: "Ann Coulter Fan Club." "Republican Princesses." "Preppy Since Conception." "Cancer Corner" (for students who love to smoke). "I Want to Be a Trophy Wife and You Can't Stop Me." There is even an "anti-group" group.

You see a cute guy or girl in class. Back in your room, with one click you learn not only their e-mail address but also the other classes they are taking and their interests. This will give you good pick-up info. That person won't even know they've been cyberstalked.

One woman who contacted a man after reading his profile said, "We had all the same interests. Books. Movies. Everything. It was a little weird, though—like dating a website."

Facebooking is free. Just answer a few questions, post your picture—and start making friends. You can do a search of your own campus or even locate old friends who might be attending college somewhere else.

A photo blinks onto your computer screen, and someone asks to be listed as part of your social network. You consider it for a couple of seconds, faintly recalling the individual from high school, and you click yes. You have just "friended" him.

You have control. You can set the privacy settings to determine who can view which parts of your profile: the contact information, personal information, courses you are taking, and a list of your friends.

Many students find the allure of facebooking irresistible, a new form of creative procrastination. And in college, there is so much to procrastinate from.

"The Wall" is a favorite facebooking site. On this virtual "wall" friends scrawl messages, some fanciful ("Meathead was here") and some private ("My love for you grows with each passing minute. I can hardly wait until I'm in your arms again.") In our new online world, private messages are proudly made public.

Change your mind about someone? Just click the "defriend" button. But this is risky. It's a slap in the face.

Not only do you see a list of your friends but also you can track your social network—the friends of friends, the people you can reach in three or fewer steps. In just three steps, your network could balloon to several thousand.

Facebooking has a touch of whimsy. The poke option lets you "poke" others. No one knows what the "poke" really means, but it seems to be, "Hey! How ya doin'?" The poke can be a conversation starter, like "'zup" ("What's up?"), a tap on the shoulder as it were.

The usual popularity contest has reared its head, of course. Who has the most friends listed? Some students even contact members they've never met just to ask to be "friended." Larger numbers give them bragging rights. Pathetic, but true.

There is something strange about groups that exist only in cyberspace, profiles that might be faked, and friends you may not even know. But life itself is strange.

Facebooking's implications extend beyond dates and popularity. Employers have used facebooking to check out some well-dressed, serious job applicants. There they discovered their prospective employees bragging about getting drunk, getting laid, and smoking substances other than tobacco.

Source: Based on Copeland 2004; Sales 2004; Schackner 2004; Coughlan 2006.

---

separated by just six individuals. Milgram's conclusions have become so popular that a game, "Six Degrees of Kevin Bacon," was built around it.

Is the Small World Phenomenon an Academic Myth? Unfortunately, things are not this simple. There is a problem with Milgram's research, as psychologist Judith

Kleinfeld (2002a, 2002b) discovered when she decided to replicate Milgram's study. When she went to the archives at Yale University Library to get more details, she found that Milgram had stacked the deck in favor of finding a small world. The "starters" came from mailing lists of people who were likely to have higher incomes and therefore were not representative of average people. In addition, one of the "targets" was a stockbroker, and that person's "starters" were investors in blue-chip stocks. Kleinfeld also found another discrepancy: On average, only 30 percent of the letters reached their "target." In one of Milgram's studies, the success rate was just 5 percent.

Since most letters did *not* reach their targets, even with the deck stacked in favor of success, we can draw the *opposite* conclusion from the one that Milgram reported: People who don't know one another are dramatically separated by social barriers. How great the barriers are is illustrated by another attempt to replicate Milgram's study, this one using e-mail. Only 384 of 24,000 chains reached their targets (Dodds et al. 2003).

As Kleinfeld says, "Rather than living in a small world, we may live in a world that looks a lot like a bowl of lumpy oatmeal, with many small worlds loosely connected and perhaps some small worlds not connected at all." Somehow, I don't think that the phrase, "lumpy oatmeal phenomenon," will become standard, but the criticism of Milgram's research is valid.

Implications for a Socially Diverse Society Besides geography, the barriers that separate us into many small worlds are primarily those of social class, gender, and race-ethnicity. Overcoming these social barriers is difficult because even our own social networks contribute to social inequality, a topic that we explore in the Cultural Diversity box on the next page.

Implications for Science Kleinfeld's revelations of Milgram's research reinforce the need of replication, a topic discussed in the previous chapter. For our knowledge of social life, we cannot depend on single studies—there may be problems of generalizability on the one hand, or those of negligence or even fraud on the other. Replication by objective researchers is essential to build and advance solid social knowledge.

A New Group: Electronic Communities

In the 1990s, a new type of human group, the **electronic community,** made its appearance. People "meet" online in chat rooms to talk about almost any conceivable topic, from donkey racing and bird-watching to sociology and quantum physics. Most news groups are simply a way of communicating. Some, however, meet our definition of *group,* people who interact with one another and who think of themselves as belonging together. They pride themselves on the distinctive nature of their interests and knowledge—factors that give them a common identity and bind them together.

Group Dynamics

As you know from personal experience, the lively interaction *within* groups—who does what with whom—has profound consequences for how you adjust to life. Sociologists use the term **group dynamics** to refer to how groups influence us and how we affect groups. Let's consider how the size of a group makes a difference, and then examine leadership, conformity, and decision making.

Before doing this, we should see how sociologists define the term *small group.* In a **small group,** there are few enough members that each one can interact directly with all the other members. Small groups can be either primary or secondary. A wife, husband, and children make up a primary small group, as do workers who take their breaks together, while bidders at an auction and students in an introductory sociology class are secondary small groups.

Effects of Group Size on Stability and Intimacy

Writing in the early 1900s, sociologist Georg Simmel (1858–1918) noted the significance of group size. He used the term **dyad** for the smallest possible group, which consists of two people. Dyads, which include marriages, love affairs, and close friendships, show two distinct qualities. First, they are the most intense or intimate of human groups. Because only two people are involved, the interaction is focused on them. Second, because dyads require

electronic community individuals who regularly interact with one another on the Internet and who think of themselves as belonging together

group dynamics the ways in which individuals affect groups and the ways in which groups influence individuals

small group a group small enough for everyone to interact directly with all the other members

networking using one's social networks for some gain

dyad the smallest possible group, consisting of two persons

How Our Own Social Networks Perpetuate Social Inequality

CONSIDER SOME OF THE PRINCIPLES we have reviewed. People tend to form in-groups with which they identify; they use reference groups to evaluate their attitudes and behavior; and they interact in social networks. Our in-groups, reference groups, and social networks are likely to consist of people whose backgrounds are similar to our own. This means that, for most of us, just as social inequality is built into society, so it is built into our own relationships. One consequence is that we tend to perpetuate social inequality.

To see why, suppose that an outstanding job—great pay, interesting work, opportunity for advancement—has just opened up where you work. Who are you going to tell? Most likely it will be someone you know, a friend or at least someone to whom you owe a favor. And most likely your social network is made up of people who look much like yourself—especially their race-ethnicity, age, social class, and probably also, gender. This tends to keep good jobs moving in the direction of people whose characteristics are similar to those of the people already in an organization. You can see how our social networks both reflect the inequality that characterizes our society and help to perpetuate it.

Consider a network of white men who are established in an organization. As they learn of opportunities (jobs, investments, real estate, and so on), they share this information with their networks. Opportunities and good jobs flow to people who have characteristics similar to their own. Those who benefit from this information, in turn, reciprocate with similar information when they learn of it. This bypasses people who have different characteristics, in this ex-

Social networks, which open and close doors of opportunity, are important for careers. Despite the official program of sociology conventions, much of the "real" business centers around renewing and extending social networks.

ample women and minorities, while it perpetuates the "good old boy'" network. No intentional discrimination need be involved.

To overcome this barrier, women and minorities do **networking.** They try to meet people who can help advance their careers. Like the "good old boys," they go to parties and join clubs, churches, synagogues, mosques, and political parties. African American leaders, for example, cultivate a network of African American leaders. As a result, the network of African American leaders is so tight that one-fifth of the entire national African American leadership are personal acquaintances. Add some "friends of a friend," and *three-fourths* of the entire leadership belong to the same network (Taylor 1992).

Similarly, women cultivate a network of women. As a result, some women who reach top positions end up in a circle so tight that the term "new girl" network is being used, especially in the field of law. Remembering those who helped them and sympathetic to those who are trying to get ahead, these women tend to steer business to other women. Like the "good old boys" who preceded them, the new insiders have a ready set of reasons to justify their exclusionary practice (Jacobs 1997).

for your **Consideration**

The perpetuation of social inequality does not require intentional discrimination. Just as social inequality is built into society, so is it built into our personal relationships. How do you think your own social network helps to perpetuate social inequality? How do you think we can break this cycle? (The key must center on creating diversity in social networks.)

---

that both members participate and be committed, it takes just one member to lose interest for the dyad to collapse. In larger groups, by contrast, even if one member withdraws, the group can continue, for its existence does not depend on any single member (Simmel 1950).

A **triad** is a group of three people. As Simmel noted, the addition of a third person fundamentally changes the group. With three people, interaction between the first two decreases. This can create strain. For example, with the birth of a child, hardly any aspect of a couple's relationship goes untouched. Attention focuses on the baby, and interaction between the husband and wife diminishes. Despite this, the marriage usually becomes stronger. Although the intensity of interaction is less in triads, they are inherently stronger and give greater stability to a relationship.

Yet, as Simmel noted, triads, too, are inherently unstable. They tend to form **coalitions**—some group members aligning themselves against others. In a triad, it is not

triad a group of three people

coalition the alignment of some members of a group against others uncommon for two members to feel a strong bond and to prefer one another. This leaves the third person feeling hurt and excluded. Another characteristic of triads is that they often produce an arbitrator or mediator, someone who tries to settle disagreements between the other two. In one-child families, you can often observe both of these characteristics of triads—coalitions and arbitration.

The general principle is this: *As a small group grows larger, it becomes more stable, but its intensity, or intimacy, decreases.* To see why, look at Figure 6.3. As each new person comes into a group, the connections among people multiply. In a dyad, there is only 1 relationship; in a triad, there are 3; in a group of four, 6; in a group of five, 10. If we expand the group to six,

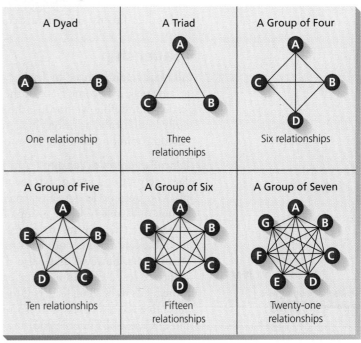

Japanese who work for the same firm think of themselves more as a group or team, Americans perceive themselves more as individuals. Japanese corporations use many techniques to encourage group identity, such as making group exercise a part of the work day. Similarity of appearance and activity helps to fuse group identity and company loyalty.

we have 15 relationships, while a group of seven yields 21 relationships. If we continue adding members, we soon are unable to follow the connections: A group of eight has 28 possible relationships; a group of nine, 36 relationships; a group of ten, 45; and so on.

It is not only the number of relationships that makes larger groups more stable. As groups grow, they also tend to develop a more formal structure to accomplish their goals. For example, leaders emerge and more specialized roles come into play. This often results in such familiar offices as president, secretary, and treasurer. This structure provides a framework that helps the group survive over time.

Effects of Group Size on Attitudes and Behavior

Imagine that your social psychology professors have asked you to join a few students to discuss your adjustment to college life. When you arrive, they tell you that to make the discussion anonymous they want you to sit unseen in a booth. You will participate in the discussion over an intercom, talking when your microphone comes on. The professors say that they will not listen to the conversation, and they leave.

You find the format somewhat strange, to say the least, but you go along with it. You have not seen the other students in their booths, but when they talk about their experiences, you find yourself becoming wrapped up in the problems that they begin to share. One student even mentions how frightening he has found college because of his history of epileptic seizures. Later, you hear this individual breathe heavily into the microphone. Then he stammers and cries for help. A crashing noise follows, and you imagine him lying helpless on the floor.

Nothing but an eerie silence follows. What do you do?

Figure 6.3 **The Effects of Group Size on Relationships**

A Dyad	A Triad	A Group of Four
One relationship	Three relationships	Six relationships
A Group of Five	A Group of Six	A Group of Seven
Ten relationships	Fifteen relationships	Twenty-one relationships

Group size has a significant influence on how people interact. When a group changes from a dyad (two people) to a triad (three people), the relationships among the participants undergo a shift. How do you think the birth of this child affected the relationship between the mother and father?

Your professors, John Darley and Bibb Latané (1968), staged the whole thing, but you don't know this. No one had a seizure. In fact, no one was even in the other booths. Everything, except your comments, was on tape.

Some participants were told that they would be discussing the topic with just one other student, others with two, others with three, four, and five. Darley and Latané found that all students who thought they were part of a dyad rushed out to help. If they thought they were part of a triad, only 80 percent went to help—and they were slower in leaving the booth. In six-person groups, only 60 percent went to see what was wrong—and they were even slower.

This experiment demonstrates how deeply group size influences our attitudes and behavior: It even affects our willingness to help one another. Students in the dyad knew that it was up to them to help the other student. The professor was gone, and if they didn't help there was no one else. In the larger groups, including the triad, students felt *a diffusion of responsibility:* Giving help was no more their responsibility than anyone else's.

You probably have observed the second consequence of group size firsthand. When a group is small, its members act informally, but as the group grows, the members lose their sense of intimacy and become more formal with one another. No longer can the members assume that the others are "insiders" in sympathy with what they say. Now they must take a "larger audience" into consideration, and instead of merely "talking," they begin to "address" the group. As their speech becomes more formal, their body language stiffens.

You probably have observed a third aspect of group dynamics, too. In the early stages of a party, when only a few people are present, almost everyone talks with everyone else. But as others arrive, the guests break into smaller groups. Some hosts, who want their guests to mix together, make a nuisance of themselves trying to achieve *their* idea of what a group should be like. The division into small groups is inevitable, however, for it follows the basic sociological principles that we have just reviewed. Because the addition of each person rapidly increases connections (in this case, "talk lines"), conversation becomes more difficult. The guests break into smaller groups in which they can look at each other directly and interact comfortably with one another.

Leadership

All of us are influenced by leaders, so it is important to understand leadership. Let's look at how people become leaders, the types of leaders there are, and their different styles of leadership. Before we do this, though, it is important to clarify that leaders don't necessarily hold formal positions in a group. **Leaders** are simply people who influence the behaviors, opinions, or attitudes of others. Even a group of friends has leaders.

Who Becomes a Leader? Are leaders born with characteristics that propel them to the forefront of a group? No sociologist would agree with such an idea. In general, people who become leaders are perceived by group members as strongly representing their values, or as able to lead a group out of a crisis (Trice and Beyer 1991). Leaders also tend to be more talkative and to express determination and self-confidence.

These findings may not be surprising, as such traits appear to be related to leadership. Researchers, however, have also discovered traits that seem to have no bearing on the ability to lead. For example, taller people and those who are judged better looking are more likely to become leaders (Stodgill 1974; Judge and Cable 2004). The taller and more attractive are also likely to earn more, but that is another story (Deck 1968; Feldman 1972; Case and Paxson 2006).

leader someone who influences other people

Many other factors underlie people's choice of leaders, most of which are quite subtle. A simple experiment performed by social psychologists Lloyd Howells and Selwyn Becker (1962) uncovered one of these factors. They formed groups of five people who did not know one another, seating them at a rectangular table, three on one side and two on the other. After discussing a topic for a set period of time, each group chose a leader. The findings are startling: Although only 40 percent of the people sat on the two-person side, 70 percent of the leaders emerged from that side. The explanation is that we tend to direct more interactions to people facing us than to people to the side of us.

Types of Leaders Groups have two types of leaders (Bales 1950, 1953; Cartwright and Zander 1968). The first is easy to recognize. This person, called an **instrumental leader** (or *task-oriented leader*), tries to keep the group moving toward its goals. These leaders try to keep group members from getting sidetracked, reminding them of what they are trying to accomplish. The **expressive leader** (or *socioemotional leader*), in contrast, usually is not recognized as a leader, but he or she certainly is one. This person is likely to crack jokes, to offer sympathy, or to do other things that help to lift the group's morale. Both types of leadership are essential: the one to keep the group on track, the other to increase harmony and minimize conflicts.

It is difficult for the same person to be both an instrumental and an expressive leader, for these roles contradict one another. Because instrumental leaders are task oriented, they sometimes create friction as they prod the group to get on with the job. Their actions often cost them popularity. Expressive leaders, in contrast, who stimulate personal bonds and reduce friction, are usually more popular (Olmsted and Hare 1978).

Leadership Styles Let's suppose that the president of your college has asked you to head a task force to determine how the college can improve race relations on campus. Although this position requires you to be an instrumental leader, you can adopt a number of **leadership styles,** or ways of expressing yourself as a leader. The three basic styles are those of **authoritarian leader,** one who gives orders; **democratic leader,** one who tries to gain a consensus; and **laissez-faire leader,** one who is highly permissive. Which style should you choose?

Social psychologists Ronald Lippitt and Ralph White (1958) carried out a classic study of these leadership styles. Boys who were matched for IQ, popularity, physical energy, and leadership were assigned to "craft clubs" made up of five boys each. The experimenters trained adult men in the three leadership styles. As the researchers peered through

Adolf Hitler, shown here in Nuremberg in 1933, was one of the most influential—and evil—persons of the twentieth century. Why did so many people follow Hitler? This question stimulated the research by Stanley Milgram (discussed on pages 171–173).

peepholes, taking notes and making movies, each adult rotated among the clubs, playing all three styles to control possible influences of their individual personalities.

The *authoritarian* leaders assigned tasks to the boys and told them exactly what to do. They also praised or condemned the boys' work arbitrarily, giving no explanation for why they judged it good or bad. The *democratic* leaders held discussions with the boys, outlining the steps that would help them reach their goals. They also suggested alternative approaches and let the boys work at their own pace. When they evaluated the projects, they gave "facts" as the bases for their decisions. The *laissez-faire* leaders were passive. They gave the boys almost total freedom to do as they wished. They offered help when asked, but made few suggestions. They did not evaluate the boys' projects, either positively or negatively.

The results? The boys who had authoritarian leaders grew dependent on their leader and showed a high degree of internal solidarity. They also became either aggressive or apathetic, with the aggressive boys growing hostile toward their leader. In contrast, the boys who had democratic leaders were friendlier, and looked to one another for mutual approval. They did less scapegoating, and when the leader left the room they continued to work at a steadier pace. The boys with laissez-faire leaders asked more questions, but they made fewer decisions. They were notable for their lack of achievement. The researchers concluded that the democratic style of leadership works best. Their conclusion, however, may have been biased, as the researchers favored a democratic style of leadership in the first place (Olmsted and Hare 1978). Apparently, this same bias in studies of leadership continues (Cassel 1999).

You may have noticed that only boys and men were involved in this experiment. It is interesting to speculate how the results might differ if we were to repeat the experiment with all-girl groups and with mixed groups of girls and boys—and if we used both men and women as leaders. Perhaps you will become the sociologist to study such variations of this classic experiment.

Leadership Styles in Changing Situations Different situations require different styles of leadership. Suppose, for example, that you are leading a dozen backpackers in the Sierra Madre mountains north of Los Angeles, and it is time to make dinner. A laissez-faire style would be appropriate if the backpackers had brought their own food, or perhaps a democratic style if everyone were supposed to pitch in. Authoritarian leadership—you telling the hikers how to prepare their meals—would create resentment. This, in turn, would likely interfere with meeting the primary goal of the group, which in this case is to have a good time while enjoying nature.

Now assume the same group but a different situation: One of your party is lost, and a blizzard is on its way. This situation calls for you to exercise authority. To simply shrug your shoulders and say, "You figure it out," would invite disaster—and probably a lawsuit.

The Power of Peer Pressure: The Asch Experiment

How influential are groups in our lives? To answer this, let's look first at *conformity* in the sense of going along with our peers. Our peers have no authority over us, only the influence that we allow.

Imagine that you are taking a course in social psychology with Dr. Solomon Asch and you have agreed to participate in an experiment. As you enter his laboratory, you see seven chairs, five of them already filled by other students. You are given the sixth. Soon the seventh person arrives. Dr. Asch stands at the front of the room next to a covered easel. He explains that he will first show a large card with a vertical line on it, then another card with three vertical lines. Each of you is to tell him which of the three lines matches the line on the first card (see Figure 6.4).

Dr. Asch then uncovers the first card with the single line and the comparison card with the three lines. The correct answer is easy, for two of the lines are obviously wrong, and one is exactly right. Each person, in order, states his or her answer aloud. You all answer correctly. The second trial is just as easy, and you begin to wonder why you are there.

Then on the third trial, something unexpected happens. Just as before, it is easy to tell which lines match. The first student, however, gives a wrong answer. The second gives the same incorrect answer. So do the third and the fourth. By now, you are wondering what is wrong. How will the person next to you answer? You can hardly believe it when he, too, gives the same wrong answer. Then it is your turn, and you give what you know is the right answer. The seventh person also gives the same wrong answer.

On the next trial, the same thing happens. You know that the choice of the other six is wrong. They are giving what to you are obviously wrong answers. You don't know what to think. Why aren't they seeing things the same way you are? Sometimes they do, but in twelve trials they don't. Something is seriously wrong, and you are no longer sure what to do.

When the eighteenth trial is finished, you heave a sigh of relief. The experiment is finally over, and you are ready to bolt for the door. Dr. Asch walks over to you with a big smile on his face, and thanks you for participating in the experiment. He explains that you were the only real subject in the experiment! "The other six were stooges. I paid them to give those answers," he says. Now you feel real relief. Your eyes weren't playing tricks on you after all.

What were the results? Asch (1952) tested fifty people. One-third (33 percent) gave in to the group half the time, giving what they knew to be wrong answers. Another two out of five (40 percent) gave wrong answers, but not as often. One out of four (25 percent) stuck to their guns and always gave the right answer. I don't know how I would do on this test (if I knew nothing about it in advance), but I like to think that I would be part of the 25 percent. You probably feel the same way about yourself. But why should we feel that we wouldn't be like *most* people?

The results are disturbing, and more researchers have replicated Asch's experiment than any other study (Levine 1999). The replications continue (Bond 2005). In our "land of individualism," the group is so powerful that most people are willing to say things that they know are not true. And this was a group of strangers! How much more conformity can we expect when our group consists of friends, people we value highly and depend on for getting along in life? Again, maybe you will become the sociologist to run that variation of Asch's experiment, perhaps using female subjects.

The Power of Authority: The Milgram Experiment

Even more disturbing are the results of the experiment described in the following Thinking Critically section.

Figure 6.4 **Asch's Cards**

Card 1

Card 2

The cards used by Solomon Asch in his classic experiment on group conformity

Source: Asch 1952:452–453.

Thinking Critically

If Hitler Asked You to Execute a Stranger, Would You? The Milgram Experiment

Imagine that you are taking a course with Dr. Stanley Milgram (1963, 1965), a former student of Dr. Asch. Assume that you do not know about the Asch experiment and have no reason to be wary. You arrive at the laboratory to participate in a study on punishment and learning. You and a second student draw lots for the roles of "teacher" and "learner." You are to be the teacher. When you see that the learner's chair has protruding electrodes, you are glad that you are the teacher. Dr. Milgram shows you the machine you will run. You see that one side of the control panel is marked "Mild Shock, 15 volts," while the center says "Intense Shock, 350 Volts," and the far right side reads "DANGER: SEVERE SHOCK."

"As the teacher, you will read aloud a pair of words," explains Dr. Milgram. "Then you will repeat the first word, and the learner will reply with the second word. If the learner can't remember the word, you press this lever on the shock generator. The shock will serve as punishment, and we can then determine if punishment improves memory." You nod, now very relieved that you haven't been designated the learner.

"Every time the learner makes an error, increase the punishment by 15 volts," instructs Dr. Milgram. Then, seeing the look on your face, he adds, "The shocks can be extremely painful, but they won't cause any permanent tissue damage." He pauses, and then says, "I want you to see."

In the 1960s, U.S. social psychologists ran a series of creative but controversial experiments. Among these were Stanley Milgram's experiments. From this photo of the "learner" being prepared for the experiment, you can get an idea of how convincing the situation would be for the "teacher."

You then follow him to the "electric chair," and Dr. Milgram gives you a shock of 45 volts. "There. That wasn't too bad, was it?" "No," you mumble.

The experiment begins. You hope for the learner's sake that he is bright, but unfortunately he turns out to be rather dull. He gets some answers right, but you have to keep turning up the dial. Each turn makes you more and more uncomfortable. You find yourself hoping that the learner won't miss another answer. But he does. When he received the first shocks, he let out some moans and groans, but now he is screaming in agony. He even protests that he suffers from a heart condition.

How far do you turn that dial?

By now, you probably have guessed that there was no electricity attached to the electrodes and that the "learner" was a stooge who only pretended to feel pain. The purpose of the experiment was to find out at what point people refuse to participate. Does anyone actually turn the lever all the way to "DANGER: SEVERE SHOCK"?

Milgram wanted the answer because millions of ordinary people did nothing to stop the Nazi slaughter of Jews, gypsies, Slavs, homosexuals, people with disabilities, and others whom the Nazis designated as "inferior." The cooperation of so many ordinary people in the face of all this killing seemed bizarre, and Milgram wanted to see how ordinary, intelligent Americans might react in an analogous situation.

Milgram was upset by what he found. Many "teachers" broke into a sweat and protested that the experiment was inhuman and should be stopped. But when the experimenter calmly replied that the experiment must go on, this assurance from an "authority" ("scientist, white coat, university laboratory") was enough for most "teachers" to continue, even though the "learner" screamed in agony. Even "teachers" who were "reduced to twitching, stuttering wrecks" continued to follow orders.

Milgram varied the experiments (Nestar and Gregory 2005). He used both men and women. In some experiments, he put the "teachers" and "learners" in the same room, so the "teacher" could clearly see the suffering. In others, he put the "learners" in a separate room, and had them pound and kick the wall during the first shocks and then go silent. The results varied. When there was no verbal feedback from the "learner," 65 percent of the "teachers" pushed the lever all the way to 450 volts. Of those who could see the "learner," 40 percent turned the lever all the way. When Milgram added a second "teacher," a stooge who refused to go along with the experiment, only 5 percent of the "teachers" turned the lever all the way, a result that bears out some of Asch's findings.

A stormy discussion about research ethics erupted. Not only were researchers surprised and disturbed by what Milgram found but also they were alarmed at his methods. Universities began to require that subjects be informed of the nature and purpose of social research. Researchers agreed that to reduce subjects to "twitching, stuttering wrecks" was unethical, and almost all deception was banned.

for your Consideration

What connections do you see between Milgram's experiment and the actions of Monster Kody in our opening vignette? Taking into account how significant these findings are, do you think that the scientific community overreacted to Milgram's experiments? Should we allow such research? Consider both the Asch and Milgram experiments, and use symbolic interactionism, functionalism, and conflict theory to explain why groups have such influence over us.

Global Consequences of Group Dynamics: Groupthink

Suppose you are a member of the President's inner circle. It is midnight, and the President has just called an emergency meeting to deal with a terrorist attack. At first, several options are presented. Eventually, these are narrowed to only a couple of choices, and at some point, everyone seems to agree on what now appears to be "the only possible course of action." To express doubts at that juncture will bring you into conflict with all the other important people in the room. To criticize will mark you as not being a "team player." So you keep your mouth shut, with the result that each step commits you—and them—more and more to the "only" course of action.

From the Milgram and Asch experiments, we can see the power of authority and the influence of peers. Under some circumstances, as in this example, this can lead to **groupthink.** Sociologist Irving Janis (1972, 1982) coined this term to refer to the collective tunnel vision that group members sometimes develop. As they begin to think alike, they become convinced that there is only one "right" viewpoint and a single course of action to follow. They take any suggestion of alternatives as a sign of disloyalty. With their perspective narrowed and fully convinced that they are right, they may even put aside moral judgments and disregard risk (Hart 1991; Flippen 1999).

Groupthink can bring serious consequences. Consider the *Columbia* space shuttle disaster of 2003.

Foam broke loose during launch, and engineers were concerned that it might have damaged tiles on the nose cone. Because this would make reentry dangerous, they sent e-mails to NASA officials, warning them about the risk. One engineer even suggested that the crew do a "space walk" to examine the tiles (Vartabedian and Gold 2003). The team in charge of the Columbia shuttle, however, disregarded the warnings. Convinced that a piece of foam weighing less than two pounds could not seriously harm the shuttle, they refused to even consider the possibility (Wald and Schwartz 2003). The fiery results of their mental closure were transmitted around the globe.

The consequences of groupthink can be even greater than this. In 1941, President Franklin D. Roosevelt and his chiefs of staff had evidence that the Japanese were preparing to attack Pearl Harbor. They simply refused to believe it and decided to continue naval operations as usual. The destruction of the U.S. naval fleet ushered the United States into World War II. In the war with Vietnam, U.S. officials had evidence of the strength and determination of the North Vietnamese military. They arrogantly threw such evidence aside, refusing to believe that "little, uneducated, barefoot people in pajamas" could defeat the U.S. military.

In each of these cases, options closed as officials committed themselves to a single course of action. Questioning the decisions would have indicated disloyalty and disregard for "team playing." Those in power plunged ahead, unable to see alternative perspectives.

groupthink a narrowing of thought by a group of people, leading to the perception that there is only one correct answer; to even suggest alternatives becomes a sign of disloyalty

No longer did they try to objectively weigh evidence as it came in; instead, they interpreted everything as supporting their one "correct" decision.

Groupthink knows few bounds. Consider the aftermath of 9/11, when government officials defended torture as moral, "the lesser of two evils." Groupthink narrowed thought to the point that the U.S. Justice Department ruled that the United States was not bound by the Geneva Convention that prohibits torture. Facing protests, the Justice Department backed down (Lewis 2005).

The U.S. military involvement in Iraq appears to be a similar example. Top leaders, convinced that they made the right decision to go to war and that they were being successful in building a new Iraqi society, continuously interpreted even disconfirming evidence as favorable. Opinions and debate that contradicted their mindset were written off as signs of ignorance and disloyalty. Despite mounting casualties and growing negative public sentiment and political opposition to the war, the President and his advisors seem to have been blinded by groupthink.

Preventing Groupthink Groupthink is a danger that faces government leaders, who tend to surround themselves with an inner circle that closely reflects their own views. In "briefings," written summaries, and "talking points," this inner circle spoon feeds the leaders the information it has selected. The result is that top leaders, such as the President, become cut off from information that does not support their own opinions.

Perhaps the key to preventing the mental captivity and intellectual paralysis known as groupthink is the widest possible circulation—especially among a nation's top government officials—of research that has been conducted by social scientists independent of the government and information that has been gathered freely by media reporters. If this conclusion comes across as an unabashed plug for sociological research and the free exchange of ideas, it is. Giving free rein to diverse opinions can curb groupthink, which—if not prevented—can lead to the destruction of a society and, in today's world of nuclear, chemical, and biological weapons, the obliteration of Earth's inhabitants.

Summary *and* Review

Societies and Their Transformation

What is a group?

Sociologists use many definitions of groups, but, in general, **groups** consist of people who interact with one another and think of themselves as belonging together. **Societies** are the largest and most complex group that sociologists study. P. 152.

How is technology linked to the change from one type of society to another?

On their way to postindustrial society, humans passed through four types of societies. Each emerged from a social revolution that was linked to new technology. The **domestication revolution,** which brought the pasturing of animals and the cultivation of plants, transformed **hunting and gathering societies** into **pastoral** and **horticultural societies.** Then the invention of the plow ushered in the **agricultural society,** while the **Industrial Revolution,** brought about by machines that were powered by fuels, led to **industrial society.** The computer chip ushered in a new type of society called

postindustrial (or **information**) **society.** Another new type of society, the **bioetech society,** may be emerging. Pp. 152–158.

How is social inequality linked to the transformation of societies?

Social equality was greatest in hunting and gathering societies, but over time social inequality grew. The root of the transition to social inequality was the accumulation of a food surplus, made possible through the domestication revolution. This surplus stimulated the division of labor, trade, accumulation of material goods, the subordination of females by males, the emergence of leaders, and the development of the state. Pp. 152–158.

Groups Within Society

How do sociologists classify groups?

Sociologists divide groups into primary groups, secondary groups, in-groups, out-groups, reference groups, and networks. The cooperative, intimate, long-term, face-to-face relationships provided by **primary groups** are fundamental to our sense of self. **Secondary groups** are larger, relatively temporary, and more anonymous, formal, and impersonal than primary groups. **In-groups** provide members with a strong sense of identity and belonging. **Out-groups** also foster identity by showing in-group members what they are *not*. **Reference groups** are groups whose standards we refer to as we evaluate ourselves. **Social networks** consist of social ties that link people together. Developments in communications technology have given birth to a new type of group, the **electronic community.** Pp. 159–165.

Group Dynamics

How does a group's size affect its dynamics?

The term **group dynamics** refers to how individuals affect groups and how groups influence individuals. In a **small group,** everyone can interact directly with everyone else. As a group grows larger, its intensity decreases but its stability increases. A **dyad,** consisting of two people, is the most unstable of human groups, but it provides the most intense or intimate relationships. The addition of a third person, forming a **triad,** fundamentally alters relationships. Triads are unstable, as **coalitions** (the alignment of some members of a group against others) tend to form. Pp. 165–168.

What characterizes a leader?

A **leader** is someone who influences others. **Instrumental leaders** try to keep a group moving toward its goals, even though this causes friction and they lose popularity. **Expressive leaders** focus on creating harmony and raising group morale. Both types are essential to the functioning of groups. Pp. 168–169.

What are the three main leadership styles?

Authoritarian leaders give orders, **democratic leaders** try to lead by consensus, and **laissez-faire leaders** are highly permissive. An authoritarian style appears to be more effective in emergency situations, a democratic style works best for most situations, and a laissez-faire style is usually ineffective. Pp. 169–170.

How do groups encourage conformity?

The Asch experiment was cited to illustrate the power of peer pressure, the Milgram experiment to illustrate the influence of authority. Both experiments demonstrate how easily we can succumb to **groupthink,** a kind of collective tunnel vision. Preventing groupthink requires the free circulation of contrasting ideas. Pp. 170–174.

Thinking Critically

about Chapter 6

1. How would your orientations to life (your ideas, attitudes, values, goals) be different if you had been reared in a hunting and gather society? In an agricultural society?

2. Identify your in-groups and your out-groups. How have your in-groups influenced the way you see the world? And what influence have your out-groups had on you?

3. Asch's experiments illustrate the power of peer pressure. How has peer pressure operated in your life? Think about something that you did not want to do but did anyway because of peer pressure.

Additional Resources

What can you use MySocLab for? www.mysoclab.com

- **Study and Review:** Pre- and Post-Tests, Practice Tests, Flash Cards, Individualized Study Plans.

- **Current Events:** *Sociology in the News,* the daily *New York Times,* and more.

- **Research and Writing:** *Research Navigator, Writing About Sociology,* and more.

Where Can I Read More on This Topic?

Suggested readings for this chapter are listed at the back of this book.

Bureaucracy and Formal Organizations

David Tillinghast, *Human Pyramid of Businesspeople*, 1998

Imagine for a moment that you are a high school senior and you have applied to Cornell University. It's a long shot, you know, since you aren't in the top of your class—but what the heck? It's worth the extra hour it takes to fill out the application—since you have everything together for the other applications you've already sent to your state universities and regional colleges.

Now imagine the unthinkable. Like betting on the 125-to-1 long shot at the racetrack, your horse comes in! You open the letter from Cornell, expecting to see a polite rejection. Instead, with hands shaking and tears of joy welling up within you, you stare at the first words, scarcely grasping what your eyes are seeing: "Greetings from Cornell, your future alma mater!" and, below this, "Cornell is pleased to welcome you to its incoming freshman class."

You don't know whether to laugh, scream, cry, or what. You shout to your parents, who come running

in to see what the problem is. They, too, are flabbergasted. While your Dad and Mom are proudly saying that they knew you could do it, you are already rushing to the phone to call your friends.

The next day, you are the talk of your class at school. Hardly anyone can believe it, for you are just an average student. "They must be trying for diversity of ability," jealously mumbles someone (who just took a sociology course), whom you *used* to count as a friend.

"This is just too good to be true," you keep telling yourself, as you imagine yourself on the ivy-covered campus.

And it is.

The call from the solemn Cornell admissions counselor explains that they had sent the wrong letter to 550 students. "We apologize for any confusion and distress this has caused," she says.

Confusion? How about shattered dreams?

—Based on Arenson 2003

"Just too good to be true," you keep telling yourself, as you imagine yourself on the ivy-covered campus.

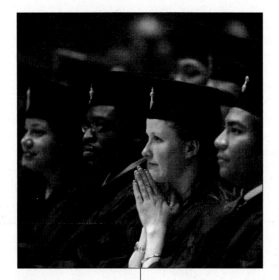

Some colleges admit thousands of students. To make the job manageable, they have broken the admissions process into several separate steps. Each step is an integrated part of the entire procedure. Computer programs have facilitated this process, but, as this event indicates, things don't always go as planned. In this case, a low-level bureaucrat at Cornell had mixed up the codes, releasing the wrong letter.

Despite their flaws, we need bureaucracies, and in this chapter we'll look at how society is organized to "get its job done." As you read this analysis, you may be able to trace the source of some of your frustrations to this social organization—as well as understand how your welfare depends on it.

The Rationalization of Society

In the previous chapter, we discussed how societies have undergone transformations so extensive that whole new types of societies have emerged. We also saw that we are now in the midst of one of those earth-shattering transformations. Underlying our information society (which may be merging into a biotech society) is an emphasis on **rationality,** the idea that efficiency and practical results should dominate human affairs. Let's examine how this approach to life—which today we take for granted—came about.

Why Did Society Make a Deep Shift in Human Relationships?

Until recently, people were immersed in a **traditional orientation** to life—the idea that the past is the best guide for making decisions today. In this view, what exists is good because it has passed the test of time. Customs—and relationships based on them—have served people well, and they should not be abandoned lightly. A central orientation of a traditional society is to protect the status quo. Change is viewed with suspicion and comes about slowly, if at all.

The traditional orientation to life stands in the way of industrialization. As Table 7.1 shows, the traditional orientation is based on personal relationships. Deep obligation and responsibility, which are often lifelong, permeate society. What counts in production is not who is best at doing something, but the relationships that people have with one another. Based on origins that are lost in history, everyone—even children—has an established role to play. The past is prized, and it rules the present.

To understand the sociological significance of this photo from Portugal, compare what you see here with the list of characteristics of traditional societies in Table 7.1.

Table 7.1　A Model of Production in Traditional and Nontraditional Societies

Traditional Societies (Horticultural, Agricultural)	Nontraditional Societies (Industrial, Postindustrial)
PRODUCTION	
1. Production is done by family members and same-sex groups (men's and women's groups).	1. Production is done by workers hired for the job.
2. Production takes place in the home, or in fields and other areas adjacent to the home.	2. Production takes place in a centralized location. (Some decentralization is occurring in the information society.)
3. Tasks are assigned according to personal relationships (men, women, and children do specific tasks based on custom).	3. Tasks are assigned according to agreements and training.
4. The "how" of production is not evaluated; the attitude is, "We want to keep doing it the way we've always done it."	4. The "how" of production is evaluated; the attitude is, "How can we make this more efficient?"
RELATIONSHIPS	
5. Relationships are based on history ("the way it's always been").	5. Relationships are based on contracts, which change as the situation changes.
6. Relationships are diffuse (vague, covering many areas of life).	6. Relationships are specific; contracts (even if not written) specify conditions.
7. Relationships are long-term, often lifelong.	7. Relationships are short-term, for the length of the contract.
EVALUATIONS	
8. It is assumed that arrangements will continue indefinitely.	8. Arrangements are evaluated periodically, to decide whether to continue or to change them.
9. People are evaluated according to how they fulfill their traditional roles.	9. People are evaluated according to the "bottom line" (the organization's goals).

Note: This model is an ideal type. Rationality is never totally absent from any society, and no society (or organization) is based entirely on rationality. Even the most rational organizations (those that most carefully and even ruthlessly compute the "bottom line") have traditional components. To properly understand this table, consider these nine characteristics as being "more" or "less" present.

Capitalism requires an entirely different way of looking at life. If a society is to industrialize, a deep shift must occur in people's thinking and relationships. Tradition ("This is the way we've always done it") must be replaced with *rationality* ("Let's find the most efficient way to do it"). As Table 7.1 shows, personal relationships are replaced by impersonal, short-term contracts. The "bottom line" (results) becomes the primary concern, and rule-of-thumb methods give way to explicit ways of measuring results.

This change to *rationality*—judging things according to the bottom line instead of by personal relationships—is a fundamental divergence from all of human history. Yet today we take rationality so much for granted that it is difficult for us to grasp how different it really is. The following illustration may help.

> Let's suppose that family relationships change from personal to rational. This would be like a wife saying to her husband, "Each year, I'm going to evaluate how much you've contributed to the family budget and how much time you've put in on household tasks—and I'll keep or replace you on that basis."

I'm sure you'll agree that this would be a fundamental change in human relationships, that it would mean a new type of marriage and family. Organizations went through this kind of severe change when they moved from tradition to rationality. What brought about this fundamental change, called the **rationalization of society**—the widespread acceptance of rationality and the construction of social organizations built largely around this idea?

[the] rationalization of society a widespread acceptance of rationality and social organizations that are built largely around this idea

Marx: Capitalism Broke Tradition

An early sociologist, Karl Marx (1818–1883), was one of the first to note how tradition was giving way to rationality. As he thought about why this change was taking place, he concluded that capitalism was breaking the bonds of tradition. As people who had money experimented with capitalism, they saw that it was more efficient. They were impressed that capitalism produced things they wanted in greater abundance and yielded high profits. This encouraged them to invest capital in manufacturing. As capitalism spread, traditional thinking receded. Gradually, the rationality of capitalism replaced the traditional approach to life. Marx's conclusion: The change to capitalism changed the way people thought about life.

Weber: Religion Broke Tradition

To sociologist Max Weber (1864–1920), this problem was as intriguing as an unsolved murder is to a detective. Weber wasn't satisfied with Marx's answer, and he kept searching for another solution. He found a clue when he noted that capitalism thrived only in certain parts of Europe. "There has to be a reason for this," he mused. As Weber pursued the matter, he noted that capitalism flourished in Protestant countries, while Roman Catholic countries held on to tradition and were relatively untouched by capitalism. "Somehow, then, religion holds the key," he thought.

But why did Roman Catholics cling to the past, while Protestants embraced change? Weber's solution to this puzzle has been the source of controversy ever since he first proposed it in his influential book, *The Protestant Ethic and the Spirit of Capitalism* (1904–1905). Weber concluded that Roman Catholic doctrine emphasized the acceptance of present arrangements: "God wants you where you are. You owe allegiance to the Church, to your family, and to your king. Accept your lot in life and remain rooted." Weber argued that Protestant theology, in contrast, opened its followers to change. Weber was intimately familiar with Calvinism, his mother's religion. Calvinists (followers of the teachings of John Calvin, 1509–1564) believed that before birth, people are destined for either heaven or hell—and they do not know their destiny until after they die. Weber said that this teaching filled Calvinists with anxiety. Salvation became their chief concern—they wanted to know *now* where they were going after death.

To resolve their spiritual dilemma, Calvinists arrived at an ingenious solution: God surely did not want those chosen for heaven to be ignorant of their destiny. Therefore, those who were in God's favor would know it—they would receive a sign from God. But what sign? The answer, claimed Calvinists, would be found not in mystical, spiritual experiences, but in things that people could see and measure. The sign of God's approval was success: Those whom God had predestined for heaven would be blessed with visible success in this life.

This idea transformed the lives of Calvinists. It motivated them to work hard, and because Calvinists also believed that thrift is a virtue, their dedication to work led to an accumulation of money. They could not spend this money on themselves, however, for to purchase items beyond the basic necessities was considered sinful. **Capitalism,** the investment of capital in the hope of making profits, became an outlet for their excess money. The success of those investments, in turn, became another sign of God's approval. In this way, Calvinists transformed worldly success into a spiritual virtue. Other branches of Protestantism, although not in agreement with the notion of predestination, also adopted the creed of thrift and hard work. Consequently, said Weber, Protestant countries embraced capitalism.

But what has this to do with rationalization? Simply put, capitalism demands rationalization, that investors carefully calculate results. If profits are your goal, you must keep track of your income and expenses. You must calculate inventories and wages, the cost of producing goods and how much income they bring. You must determine "the bottom line." Rationality, then, not tradition, becomes the drumbeat to which you march. If traditional ways of doing things are inefficient, they are replaced, for what counts are the results. Weber's equation: A changed way of thinking (God will give a sign to the elect) produced capitalism.

capitalism an economic system characterized by the private ownership of the means of production, the pursuit of profit, and market competition

The Two Views Today Who is correct? Weber, who concluded that Protestantism produced rationality, which then paved the way for capitalism? Or Marx, who concluded that capitalism produced rationality? No analyst has yet reconciled these two opposing answers to the satisfaction of sociologists: The two views still remain side by side.

Formal Organizations and Bureaucracies

formal organization a secondary group designed to achieve explicit objectives

bureaucracy a formal organization with a hierarchy of authority, a clear division of labor, an impersonality of positions, and an emphasis on written rules, communications, and records

Regardless of whether Marx or Weber was right about its cause, rationality was a totally different way of approaching life. As this new orientation began to permeate society, it led to new types of organizations. Let's look at these organizations and how they affect our lives.

Formal Organizations

A major consequence of rationality was the development of **formal organizations,** secondary groups designed to achieve explicit objectives. Although they are fairly new to the human scene, formal organizations have become a central feature of our society. Today, most of us are born within them, we are educated in them, we spend our working lives in them, and we are buried by them.

Prior to industrialization, there were few formal organizations. The guilds of western Europe during the twelfth century are a rare example of a formal organization. People who performed the same type of work organized to control their craft in a local area. They set prices and standards of workmanship (Bridgwater 1953; "Guilds" 2005). Much like modern unions, guilds also prevented outsiders (nonmembers of the guild) from working at their particular craft. Another example of an early formal organization is the army, with its hierarchical structure of senior officers, junior officers, and ranks. Armies with commanders and subleaders, of course, existed far back in history.

With industrialization, secondary groups became common. Today we take their existence for granted and, beginning with grade school, all of us spend a good deal of time in them. Formal organizations tend to develop into bureaucracies, and in general, the larger the formal organization, the more likely it is to be bureaucratic. Because they are so important to our lives, let's look at bureaucracies in detail.

The Characteristics of Bureaucracies

What do the Russian army and the U.S. postal service have in common? Or the government of Mexico and your college? The sociological answer is that all are *bureaucracies.* As Weber (1913/1947) pointed out, **bureaucracies** have

1. *Clear levels, with assignments flowing downward and accountability flowing upward.* Each level assigns responsibilities to the level beneath it, while each lower level is accountable to the level above it for fulfilling those assignments. Figure 7.1 on the next page shows the bureaucratic structure of a typical university.

Today's armies, no matter what country they are from, are bureaucracies. They have a strict hierarchy of rank, division of labor, impersonality and replaceability (an emphasis on the office, not the person holding it), and they stress written records, rules, and communications—essential characteristics identified by Max Weber. Though its outward appearance may differ from Western standards, this army in India is no exception to this principle.

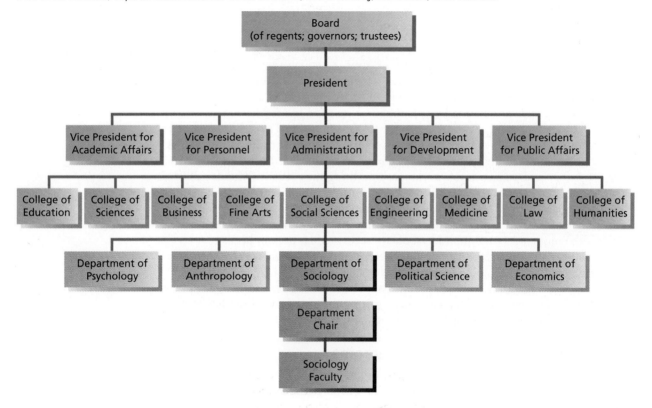

Figure 7.1 **The Typical Bureaucratic Structure of a Medium-Sized University**

This is a scaled-down version of a university's bureaucratic structure. The actual lines of a university are likely to be much more complicated than those depicted here. A large university may have a chancellor and several presidents under the chancellor, each president being responsible for a particular campus. Although in this figure extensions of authority are shown only for the Vice President for Administration and the College of Social Sciences, each of the other vice presidents and colleges has similar positions. If the figure were to be extended, departmental secretaries would be shown, and eventually, somewhere, even students.

Board
(of regents; governors; trustees)

President

Vice President for Academic Affairs | Vice President for Personnel | Vice President for Administration | Vice President for Development | Vice President for Public Affairs

College of Education | College of Sciences | College of Business | College of Fine Arts | College of Social Sciences | College of Engineering | College of Medicine | College of Law | College of Humanities

Department of Psychology | Department of Anthropology | Department of Sociology | Department of Political Science | Department of Economics

Department Chair

Sociology Faculty

2. *A division of labor.* Each worker has a specific task to fulfill, and all the tasks are coordinated to accomplish the purpose of the organization. In a college, for example, a teacher does not fix the heating system, the president does not teach, and a secretary does not evaluate textbooks. These tasks are distributed among people who have been trained to do them.

3. *Written rules.* In their attempt to become efficient, bureaucracies stress written procedures. In general, the longer a bureaucracy exists and the larger it grows, the more written rules it has. The rules of some bureaucracies cover just about every imaginable situation. In my university, for example, the rules are published in

When society began to be rationalized, production of items was broken into its various components, with individuals assigned only specific tasks. This painting of a pottery shop in England in the late 1800s is by Alfred Morgan (1862–1904).

handbooks: separate ones for faculty, students, administrators, civil service workers, and perhaps others that I don't even know about.

4. *Written communications and records.* Records are kept of much of what occurs in a bureaucracy ("Be sure to CC all immediate supervisors."). In some organizations, workers spend a fair amount of time sending memos and e-mail back and forth. Sometimes, workers must detail their activities in written reports. My university, for example, requires that each semester, faculty members compile a summary of the number of hours they spent performing specified activities. They must also submit an annual report listing what they accomplished in teaching, research, and service—all accompanied by copies of publications, evidence of service, and written teaching evaluations from each course. These materials go to committees that evaluate the performance of each faculty member.

5. *Impersonality and replaceability.* It is the office that is important, not the individual who holds the office. You work for the organization, not for the replaceable person who heads some post in the organization. Each worker is a replaceable unit, for many others are available to fulfill each particular function. For example, when a professor retires, someone else is appointed to take his or her place. This makes you a small cog in a large machine.

These five characteristics help bureaucracies reach their goals. They also allow them to grow and endure. One bureaucracy in the United States, the postal service, has become so large that one out of every 175 employed Americans works for it (*Statistical Abstract* 2007:587, 1105). If the head of a bureaucracy resigns, retires, or dies, the organization continues without skipping a beat, for unlike a "mom and pop" operation, its functioning does not depend on the individual who heads it. The expansion (some would say domination) of bureaucracies in contemporary society is illustrated by the Down-to-Earth Sociology box on the next page.

"Ideal" Versus "Real" Bureaucracy

Just as people often act differently from the way the norms say they should, so it is with bureaucracies. The characteristics of bureaucracies that Weber identified are *ideal types*; that is, they are a composite of characteristics based on many specific examples. Think of the judges at a dog show. They have a mental image of how each particular breed of dog should look and behave, and they judge each individual dog according to that mental image. Each dog will rank high on some of these characteristics, and lower on others. In the same way, a particular organization will rank higher or lower on the traits of a bureaucracy, yet still qualify as a bureaucracy. Instead of labeling a particular organization

Technology has changed our lives fundamentally. As you can see from this 1904 photo, telephone operators used to make connections by hand. Labor was so intensive and problems so numerous that it required about one supervisor for every four workers. Long distance calls, with their numerous hand-made connections, not only were slower, but also more expensive—perhaps 100 times higher than what they now cost. You can also see that this was "women's" work.

Down-to-Earth Sociology

The McDonaldization of Society

THE MCDONALD'S RESTAURANTS THAT seem to be all over the United States—and, increasingly, the world—have a significance that goes far beyond the convenience of quick hamburgers and milk shakes. As sociologist George Ritzer (1993, 1998, 2001) says, our everyday lives are being "McDonaldized." Let's see what he means by this.

McDonald's in Beijing, China

The McDonaldization of society—the standardization of everyday life—does not refer just to the robot-like assembly of food. As Ritzer points out, this process is occurring throughout society—and it is transforming our lives. Want to do some shopping? Shopping malls offer one-stop shopping in controlled environments. Planning a trip? Travel agencies offer "package" tours. They will transport middle-class Americans to ten European capitals in fourteen days. All visitors experience the same hotels, restaurants, and other scheduled sites—and no one need fear meeting a "real" native. Want to keep up with events? *USA Today* spews out McNews—short, bland, unanalytical pieces that can be digested between gulps of the McShake or the McBurger.

Efficiency brings dependability. You can expect your burger and fries to taste the same whether you buy them in Los Angeles or Beijing. Although efficiency also lowers prices, it does come at a cost. Predictability washes away spontaneity, changing the quality of our lives. It produces a sameness, a bland version of what used to be unique experiences. In my own travels, for example, had I taken packaged tours I never would have had the enjoyable, eye-opening experiences that have added so much to my appreciation of human diversity.

For good or bad, our lives are being McDonaldized, and the predictability of packaged settings seems to be our social destiny. When education is rationalized, no longer will our children have to put up with real professors, who insist on discussing ideas endlessly, who never come to decisive answers, and who come saddled with idiosyncrasies. At some point, such an approach to education is going to be a bit of quaint history.

Our programmed education will eliminate the need for discussion of social issues—we will have packaged solutions to social problems, definitive answers that satisfy our need for closure. Computerized courses will teach the same answers to everyone—the approved, "politically correct" ways to think about social issues. Mass testing will ensure that students regurgitate the programmed responses.

Our coming prepackaged society will be efficient, of course. But it also means that we will be trapped in the "iron cage" of bureaucracy—just as Weber warned would happen.

---

as a "bureaucracy" or "not a bureaucracy," it probably makes more sense to think in terms of the *extent* to which it is bureaucratized (Udy 1959; Hall 1963).

As with culture, then, a bureaucracy often differs from its ideal image. The actual lines of authority ("going through channels"), for example, may be different from those portrayed on organizational charts such as the one shown in Figure 7.1 on page 182. For example, suppose that before being promoted, the university president taught in the history department. As a result, friends from that department may have direct access to him or her. If they wish to provide "input" (ranging from opinions about how to solve problems to personal grievances or even gossip), these individuals might be able to skip their chairperson or even the dean of their college, and go directly to the president.

Dysfunctions of Bureaucracies

Although in the long run no other form of social organization is more efficient, as Weber recognized, bureaucracies also have a dark side. Let's look at some of their dysfunctions.

Red Tape: A Rule Is a Rule   Bureaucracies can be so bound by procedures that their rules impede the purpose of the organization. Some rules ("red tape" in common speech and "correct procedures" in bureaucratic jargon) are enough to try the patience of a saint.

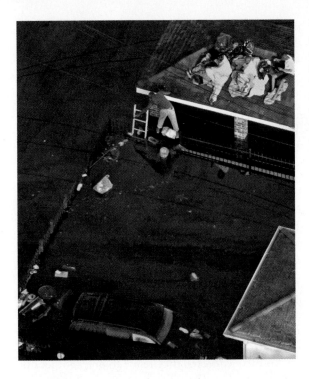

When dealing with the routine, bureaucracies usually function quite efficiently. In emergencies, however, they sometimes fail miserably. This dysfunction was evident during Hurricane Katrina, which hit the U.S. Gulf Coast in 2005. Due to bureaucratic bungling, the pleas of thousands of people in flooded New Orleans went unanswered.

In the Bronx, Mother Teresa spotted a structurally sound abandoned building and wanted to turn it into a homeless shelter. But she ran head on into a rule: The building must have an elevator for people with disabilities. Not having the funds for the elevator, Mother Teresa struggled to get permission to bypass this rule. Two frustrating years later, she gave up. The abandoned building was left to rot away. (Tobias 1995)

Obviously this rule about elevators was not intended to stop Mother Teresa from ministering to the down and out. But, hey, rules is rules!

Lack of Communication Between Units   Each unit within a bureaucracy performs specialized tasks, which are designed to contribute to the organization's goals. At times, units fail to communicate with one another and end up working at cross purposes. In Granada, Spain, for example, the local government was concerned about the run-down appearance of buildings along one of its main streets. Consequently, one unit of the government fixed the fronts of these buildings, repairing concrete and restoring decorations

This is the way that some people view bureaucracies: stilted, slow-moving, and destructive to the individual. Bureaucracies can be like this, but not all bureaucracies are alike. Some are innovative and unleash creative energy.

alienation Marx's term for workers' lack of connection to the product of their labor (being assigned repetitive tasks on a small part of a product leads to a sense of powerlessness and normlessness); others use the term in the general sense of not feeling a part of something

of iron and stone. The results were impressive, and the unit was proud of what it had accomplished. The only problem was that another unit of the government had slated these same buildings for demolition (Arías 1993). Because neither unit of this bureaucracy knew what the other was doing, one beautified the buildings while the other planned to turn them into a heap of rubble.

Bureaucratic Alienation Perceived in terms of roles, rules, and functions rather than as individuals, many workers begin to feel more like objects than people. Marx termed these reactions **alienation,** a result, he said, of workers being cut off from the finished product of their labor. He pointed out that before industrialization, workers used their own tools to produce an entire product, such as a chair or table. Now the capitalists own the tools (machinery, desks, computers), and assign each worker only a single step or two in the entire production process. Relegated to performing repetitive tasks that seem remote from the final product, workers no longer identify with what they produce. They come to feel estranged not only from the results of their labor but also from their work environment.

Resisting Alienation Because workers need to feel valued and want to have a sense of control over their work, they resist alienation. Forming primary groups at work is a major form of that resistance. Workers band together in informal settings—at lunch, around desks, or for a drink after work. There, they give one another approval for jobs well done and express sympathy for the shared need to put up with cantankerous bosses, meaningless routines, and endless rules. In these contexts, they relate to one another not just as workers, but as people who value one another. They flirt, laugh and tell jokes, and talk about their families and goals. Adding this multidimensionality to their work relationships maintains their sense of being individuals rather than mere cogs in a machine.

As in the photo below, workers often decorate their work areas with personal items. The sociological implication is that of workers who are striving to resist alienation. By staking a claim to individuality, the workers are rejecting an identity as machines that exist simply to perform functions.

The Alienated Bureaucrat Not all workers succeed in resisting alienation. Some become alienated and leave. Others became alienated but remain in the organization because they see no viable alternative, or they wait it out because they have "only so many years until retirement." They hate every minute of work, and it shows—in their attitudes toward clients, toward fellow workers, and toward authority in the organization.

Workers develop many ways to avoid becoming a depersonalized unit in a bureaucratic-economic machine. In this photo, which I took at a major publisher, you can see how Rebecca, by personalizing her work setting, is claiming an identity that transcends that of worker. What "personalized messages" do you see in this photo?

The alienated bureaucrat does not take initiative, will not do anything for the organization beyond what is absolutely required, and uses company rules to justify doing as little as possible.

Despite poor attitude and performance, alienated workers often retain their jobs. Some keep their jobs because of seniority, while others threaten expensive, time-consuming, and embarrassing legal action if anyone tries to fire them. Some alienated workers are shunted off into small bureaucratic corners, where they spend the day doing trivial tasks and have little chance of coming in contact with the public. This treatment, of course, only alienates them further.

Bureaucratic Incompetence   In a tongue-in-cheek analysis of bureaucracies, Laurence Peter proposed what has become known as the **Peter principle:** Each employee of a bureaucracy is promoted to his or her *level of incompetence* (Peter and Hull 1969). People who perform well in a bureaucracy come to the attention of those higher up the chain of command and are promoted. If they continue to perform well, they are promoted again. This process continues *until* they are promoted to a level at which they can no longer handle the responsibilities well—their level of incompetence. There they hide behind the work of others, taking credit for the accomplishments of employees under their direction. In our opening vignette, the employee who sent the wrong mail has already reached his or her level of incompetence.

Although the Peter principle contains a grain of truth, if it were generally true, bureaucracies would be staffed by incompetents, and these organizations would fail. In reality, bureaucracies are remarkably successful. Sociologists Peter Evans and James Rauch (1999) examined the government bureaucracies of 35 developing countries. They found that prosperity comes to the countries that have central bureaucracies that hire workers on the basis of merit and offer them rewarding careers.

Goal Displacement and the Perpetuation of Bureaucracies

Bureaucracies have become a standard feature of our lives because they are a powerful form of social organization. They harness people's energies to reach specific goals. Once in existence, however, bureaucracies tend to take on a life of their own. In a process called **goal displacement,** even after the organization achieves its goal and no longer has a reason to continue, continue it does.

A classic example is the National Foundation for the March of Dimes, organized in the 1930s to fight polio (Sills 1957). At that time, the origin of polio was a mystery. The public was alarmed and fearful, for overnight a healthy child could be stricken with this crippling disease. To raise money to find a cure, the March of Dimes placed posters of children on crutches near cash registers in almost every store in the United States. (See the photo on the next page.) They raised money beyond the organization's wildest dreams. When Dr. Jonas Salk developed a vaccine for polio in the 1950s, the threat was wiped out almost overnight.

The staff that ran the March of Dimes did not quietly fold up their tents and slip away. Instead, they found a way to keep their jobs by targeting a new enemy—birth defects. But then in 2001, researchers finished mapping the human genome system. Perceiving that some day this information could help to eliminate birth defects—and their jobs—officials of the March of Dimes came up with a new slogan, "Breakthroughs for Babies." This latest goal should ensure the organization's existence forever: It is so vague that we are not likely to ever run out of the need for "breakthroughs."

Then there is NATO (North Atlantic Treaty Organization), founded during the Cold War to prevent Russia from invading western Europe. When the Cold War ended, removing the organization's purpose, the Western powers tried to find a reason to continue their organization. I mean, why waste a perfectly good bureaucracy? They appear to have found one: to create "rapid response forces" to combat terrorism and "rogue nations" (Tyler 2002). To keep this bureaucracy going, they even allowed Russia to become a junior partner.

Peter principle a tongue-in-cheek observation that the members of an organization are promoted for their accomplishments until they reach their level of incompetence; there they cease to be promoted, remaining at the level at which they can no longer do good work

goal displacement the adoption of new goals by an organization; also known as *goal replacement*

The March of Dimes was founded by President Franklin Roosevelt in the 1930s to fight polio. When a vaccine for polio was discovered in the 1950s, the organization did not declare victory and disband. Instead, its leaders kept the organization intact by creating new goals, such as combatting premature births. Sociologists use the term *goal displacement* to refer to this process of adopting new goals.

The Sociological Significance of Bureaucracies

The sociological significance of bureaucracies and the rationalization of society in general go far beyond what is readily visible. Bureaucracies require a fundamental change in the traditional ways that people relate to one another (see Table 7.1 on page 179). When work is rooted in personal relationships, much more is at stake than performing tasks efficiently and keeping an eye on the bottom line. Seeing that all relatives and friends have jobs, for example, was once a major factor in making business decisions. Bureaucracies, or the rationalization of society, changed this fundamental aspect of social life, which had been a factor that cemented human relationships.

Voluntary Associations

Although bureaucracies have become the dominant form of organization for large, task-oriented groups, even more common are voluntary associations. Let's examine their characteristics.

Back in the 1830s, Alexis de Tocqueville, a Frenchman, traveled across the United States, observing the customs of this new nation. His report, *Democracy in America* (1835), was popular both in Europe and in the United States. It is still quoted for its insights into the American character. One of de Tocqueville's observations was that Americans joined a lot of **voluntary associations,** groups made up of volunteers who organize on the basis of some mutual interest.

Over the years, Americans have maintained this pattern and are quite proud of it. A visitor entering one of the thousands of small towns that dot the U.S. landscape is often greeted by a highway sign proclaiming some of the town's voluntary associations: Girl Scouts, Boy Scouts, Kiwanis, Lions, Elks, Eagles, Knights of Columbus, Chamber of Commerce, American Legion, Veterans of Foreign Wars, and perhaps a host of others. One type of voluntary association is so prevalent that a separate sign sometimes indicates which varieties are present in the town: Roman Catholic, Baptist, Lutheran, Methodist, Episcopalian, and so on. Not listed on these signs are many other voluntary associations, such as political parties, unions, health clubs, the National Right to Life, the National Organization for Women, Alcoholics Anonymous, Gamblers Anonymous, Association of Pinto Racers, and Citizens United For or Against This and That.

Americans love voluntary associations, and use them to express a wide variety of interests. Some groups are local, consisting of only a few volunteers; others are national, with a paid professional staff. Some are temporary, organized to accomplish some

voluntary association a group made up of people who voluntarily organize on the basis of some mutual interest; also known as *voluntary memberships* and *voluntary organizations* specific task, such as arranging for Fourth of July fireworks. Others, such as the Scouts and political parties, are permanent—large, secondary organizations with clear lines of command—and they are also bureaucracies.

Functions of Voluntary Associations

Whatever their form, voluntary associations are numerous because they meet people's needs. People do not *have* to belong to these organizations. They join because they obtain benefits from their participation. Functionalists have identified seven functions of voluntary associations.

1. Voluntary organizations advance particular interests. For example, adults who are concerned about children's welfare volunteer for the Scouts because they think kids are better off joining this group than hanging out on the street. In short, voluntary associations get things done, whether that means organizing a neighborhood crime watch or informing people about the latest legislation on abortion.
2. Voluntary groups offer people an identity. Some even provide a sense of purpose in life. As in-groups, they give their members a feeling of belonging, and, in many cases, a sense of doing something worthwhile. This function is so important for some individuals that their participation in voluntary associations becomes the center of their lives.
3. Voluntary associations help govern the nation and maintain social order. Groups that help "get out the vote" or assist the Red Cross in coping with disasters are obvious examples.

The first two functions apply to all voluntary associations. In a general sense, so does the third. Even though an organization does not focus on politics, it helps to incorporate individuals into society, which helps to maintain social order.

Sociologist David Sills (1968) identified four other functions, which apply only to some voluntary associations.

4. Some voluntary groups mediate between the government and the individual. For example, some groups provide a way for people to join forces to put pressure on lawmakers.
5. By providing training in organizational skills, some groups help individuals climb the occupational ladder.
6. Other groups help bring people into the political mainstream. The National Association for the Advancement of Colored People (NAACP) is an example of such a group.
7. Finally, some voluntary associations pave the way to social change. As they challenge established ways of doing social life, boundaries start to give way. The actions of groups such as Greenpeace, for example, are reshaping taken-for-granted definitions of "normal" when it comes to the environment.

Shared Interests

Voluntary associations, then, represent no single interest or purpose. They can be reactionary, resisting new ways of doing things, or they can be visionary, standing at the vanguard of social change. Despite their diversity, however, a common thread runs through voluntary associations. That thread is mutual interest. Although the particular interest varies from group to group, shared interest in some point of view or activity is the tie that binds group members together.

Motivations for joining these groups differ. Some people join because they hold strong convictions concerning the stated purpose of the organization, others simply because membership helps them politically or professionally—or looks good on a college or job application. Some may even join because they have romantic interests in a group member.

With so many motivations for joining, and because the commitment of some members is fleeting, voluntary associations often have high turnover. Some people move in and out of groups almost as fast as they change clothes. Within each organization, however, is an *inner circle*—individuals who actively promote the group, who stand firmly behind the group's goals, and who are committed to maintaining the organization itself. If this inner circle loses its commitment, the group is likely to fold.

The "Iron Law" of Oligarchy

A significant aspect of voluntary associations is that its key members, its inner circle, often grow distant from the regular members. They become convinced that only they can be trusted to make the group's important decisions. To see this principle at work, let's look at the Veterans of Foreign Wars (VFW).

Sociologists Elaine Fox and George Arquitt (1985) studied three local posts of the VFW, a national organization of former U.S. soldiers who have served in foreign wars. They found that although the leaders conceal their attitudes from the other members, the inner circle views the rank and file as a bunch of ignorant boozers. Because the leaders can't stand the thought that such people might represent them in the community and at national meetings, a curious situation arises. Although the VFW constitution makes rank-and-file members eligible for top leadership positions, they never become leaders. In fact, the inner circle is so effective in controlling these top positions that even before an election they can tell you who is going to win. "You need to meet Jim," the sociologists were told. "He's the next post commander after Sam does his time."

At first, the researchers found this puzzling. The election hadn't been held yet. As they investigated further, they found that leadership is actually determined behind the scenes. The elected leaders appoint their favored people to chair the key committees, which highlights the names and accomplishments of these individuals. This publicity then propels the members to elect these favored ones as their leaders. By appointing its own members to highly visible positions, then, the inner circle maintains control over the entire organization.

Like the VFW, most organizations are run by only a few of their members. Building on the term *oligarchy*, a system in which many are ruled by a few, sociologist Robert Michels (1876–1936) coined the term **the iron law of oligarchy** to refer to how organizations come to be dominated by a small, self-perpetuating elite (Michels 1911). Most members are passive, and an elite inner circle keeps itself in power by passing the leadership positions to one another.

What many find disturbing about the iron law of oligarchy is that people are excluded from leadership because they don't represent the inner circle's values—or, in some instances, their background. This is true even of organizations that are committed to democratic principles. For example, U.S. political parties—supposedly the backbone

In a process called *the iron law of oligarchy*, a small, self-perpetuating elite tends to take control of formal organizations. Veterans' organizations are no exception to this principle, as sociological studies have shown.

of the nation's representative government are run by an inner circle that passes leadership positions from one elite member to another. This principle also applies to the U.S. Senate. With their statewide control of political machinery and access to free mailing, about 90 percent of U.S. senators who choose to run are reelected (*Statistical Abstract* 2006:Table 394).

The iron law of oligarchy is not without its limitations, of course. Members of the inner circle must remain attuned to the opinions of the other members, regardless of their personal feelings. If the oligarchy gets too far out of line, it runs the risk of a grassroots rebellion that would throw the elite out of office. This threat often softens the iron law of oligarchy by making the leadership responsive to the membership. In addition, because not all organizations become captive to an elite, this is a tendency, not an inevitability.

Working for the Corporation

Since you are likely to end up working in a bureaucracy, let's look at how its characteristics may affect your career.

Self-Fulfilling Stereotypes in the "Hidden" Corporate Culture

As you might recall from Chapter 4, stereotypes can be self-fulfilling. That is, stereotypes can produce the very characteristics that they are built around. The example used in Chapter 4 was that of stereotypes of appearance and people's personality. You might want to review the Down-to-Earth Sociology box on page 111.

Stereotypes also operate in corporate life—and are so powerful that they can affect *your* career. Here's how they work.

Self-Fulfilling Stereotypes and Promotions Corporate and department heads have ideas of "what it takes" to get ahead. Not surprisingly, since they themselves got ahead, they look for people who have characteristics similar to their own. They feed better information to workers with these characteristics, bring them into stronger networks, and put them on "fast track" positions. With such advantages, these workers perform better and become more committed to the company. This, of course, confirms the boss's initial expectation or stereotype. But for workers who don't look or act like the corporate leaders, the opposite happens. Thinking of them as less capable, the bosses give them fewer opportunities and challenges. When these workers see others get ahead, and realize that they are working beneath their own abilities, they lose morale, become less committed to the company, and don't perform as well. This, of course, confirms the stereotypes the bosses had of them.

In her studies of U.S. corporations, sociologist Rosabeth Moss Kanter (1977, 1983) found such self-fulfilling stereotypes to be part of a "hidden" corporate culture. That is, these stereotypes and their powerful effects on workers remain hidden to everyone, even the bosses. What bosses and workers see is the surface: Workers who have superior performance and greater commitment to the company get promoted. To everyone, this seems to be just the way it should be. Hidden below this surface, however, as Kanter found, are these higher and lower expectations and the open and closed opportunities that produce the attitudes and accomplishments—or the lack of them.

Stereotypes and the Iron Law of Oligarchy You can see how the self-fulfilling prophecy contributes to the *iron law of oligarchy* we just reviewed. Often without intending to do so, the inner circle reproduces itself by favoring people who "look" like its own members, generally white and male. Women and minorities, who don't match the stereotype, are often "showcased"—placed in highly visible but powerless positions in order to avoid charges of discrimination or to demonstrate how progressive the company is. The accomplishments of those in these "slow-track" positions seldom come to the attention of top management.

IN SUM Significant aspects of organizations often lie below the surface. The "hidden" corporate culture, though difficult to perceive, is so significant that it can have a profound effect on your own career. Because workers tend to see only what is readily visible, they usually ascribe differences in people's behaviors and attitudes to their personalities. When sociologists probe beneath the surface, however, they examine how corporate culture shapes people's attitudes, and, by extension, the quality of their work.

As corporations grapple with growing diversity, the stereotypes in the hidden corporate culture are likely to give way, although slowly and grudgingly. In the following Thinking Critically section, we'll consider other aspects of diversity in the workplace.

Thinking Critically

Managing Diversity in the Workplace

Times have changed. The San Jose, California, electronic phone book lists *ten* times more *Nguyens* than *Joneses* (Albanese 2007). More than half of U.S. workers are minorities, immigrants, and women. Diversity in the workplace is much more than skin color. Diversity includes ethnicity, gender, age, religion, social class, and sexual orientation.

In our growing global context of life, diversity is increasing. In the past, the idea was for people to join the "melting pot," to give up their distinctive traits and become like the dominant group. Today, with the successes of the civil rights and women's movements, people are more likely to prize their distinctive traits. Realizing that assimilation (being absorbed into the dominant culture) is probably not the wave of the future, most large companies have "diversity training" (Johnson 2004). They hold lectures and workshops so that employees can learn to work with colleagues of diverse cultures and racial-ethnic backgrounds.

Coors Brewery is a prime example of this change. Coors went into a financial tailspin after one of the Coors brothers gave a racially charged speech in the 1980s. Today, Coors offers diversity workshops, has sponsored a gay dance, and has paid for a corporate-wide mammography program. In 2004, Coors opposed an amendment to the Colorado constitution that would ban the marriage of homosexuals. The company has even had rabbis certify its suds as kosher. Its proud new slogan: "Coors cares" (Cloud 1998). Now, that's quite a change.

What Coors cares about, of course, is the bottom line. It's the same with other corporations. Blatant racism and sexism once made no difference to profitability. Today, they do. To promote profitability, companies must promote diversity—or at least pretend to. The sincerity of corporate leaders is not what's important; diversity in the workplace is.

The cultural and racial-ethnic diversity of today's work force has led to the need for diversity training, the topic of this Thinking Critically section.

Diversity training has the potential to build bridges, but it can backfire. Managers who are chosen to participate can resent it, thinking that it is punishment for some unmentioned insensitivity on their part (Sanchez and Medkik 2004). Some directors of these programs are so incompetent that they create antagonisms and reinforce stereotypes. For example, the leaders of a diversity training session at the U.S. Department of Transportation had women grope men as the men ran by. They encouraged blacks and whites to insult one another and to call each other names (Reibstein 1996). The intention may have been good (understanding the other through role reversal and getting hostilities "out in the open"), but the approach was moronic. Instead of healing, such behaviors wound and leave scars.

Pepsi provides a positive example of diversity training. Managers at Pepsi are given the assignment of sponsoring a group of employees who are unlike themselves. Men sponsor women, African Americans sponsor whites, and so on. The executives are expected to try to understand work from the perspective of the people they sponsor, to identify key talent, and to personally mentor at least three people in their group. Accountability is built in—the sponsors have to give updates to executives even higher up (Terhune 2005).

for your Consideration

Do you think that corporations and government agencies should offer diversity training? If so, how can we develop diversity training that fosters mutual respect? Can you suggest practical ways to develop workplaces that are not divided by gender and race-ethnicity?

Humanizing the Corporate Culture

Bureaucracies have transformed society by harnessing people's energies to reach goals and monitoring their progress to achieve those goals. Weber (1946) predicted that because bureaucracies were so efficient and had the capacity to replace themselves, they would come to dominate social life. More than any prediction in sociology, this one has withstood the test of time (Rothschild and Whitt 1986; Perrow 1991).

Attempts to Humanize the Work Setting

Bureaucracies appear likely to remain our dominant form of social organization, and like it or not, most of us are destined to spend our working lives in bureaucracies. Many people have become concerned about the negative side of bureaucracies, and would like to make them more humane. **Humanizing a work setting** means to organize work in such a way that it develops rather than impedes human potential. Humanized work settings have more flexible rules, are more open in decision making, distribute power more equally, and offer more uniform access to opportunities.

Can bureaucracies adapt to such a model? Contrary to some images, not all bureaucracies are unyielding, unwieldy monoliths. There is nothing in the nature of bureaucracies that makes them *inherently* insensitive to people's needs or that prevents them from fostering a corporate culture that maximizes human potential.

But what about the cost of such changes? The United States faces formidable economic competitors—Japan, Europe, South America, and now China and India. Humanizing corporate culture, however, does not require huge expense. Kanter (1983) compared forty-seven companies that were rigidly bureaucratic with competitors of the same size that were more flexible. Kanter found that the more flexible companies were more profitable—probably because their greater flexibility encouraged greater creativity, productivity, and company loyalty.

In light of such findings, many corporations have experimented with humanizing their work settings. As we look at them, keep in mind that they are not motivated by some altruistic urge to make life better for workers, but by the same motivation as always—the bottom line. It is in management's self-interest to make their company more competitive.

humanizing a work setting organizing a workplace in such a way that it develops rather than impedes human potential

Humanizing the work setting means to make the work site a more pleasant place in order to better meet the needs of workers. In this photo, workers are being instructed in yoga. In some instances, as sociologist Arlie Hochschild discovered, work places have become so rewarding that workers prefer work to the tensions of family life.

Work Teams Work teams are small groups of workers who analyze their work situation to develop creative ideas and solutions to problems. These self-managed teams instill a high sense of loyalty to the company. Employees who belong to work teams work harder, are absent less, and are more productive. Workers in these groups also react more quickly to threats posed by technological change and competitors' advances. Corporations around the world are finding that people work more effectively in small groups than in a centralized command structure (Drucker 1992).

The concepts we discussed in the last chapter help to explain these results. In small work groups, people form primary relationships, and their identities become intertwined with their group. This reduces alienation, for rather than being lost in a bureaucratic maze, their individuality is appreciated and their contributions are more readily recognized. The group's successes become the individual's successes—as do its failures. As a consequence of their accountability within a system of personal ties, workers make more of an effort. The results have been so good that, in what is known as *worker empowerment*, some self-managed teams have even replaced bosses as the ones who control everything from schedules to hiring and firing (Lublin 1991; Vanderburg 2004).

Corporate Child Care Some companies help to humanize the work setting by offering on-site child care facilities. This eases the strain on parents. While they are at work, they can keep in touch with a baby or toddler, and observe the care their child is receiving. They are able to spend time with their children during breaks and lunch hours. Mothers can even nurse their children at the child care center or express milk in the "lactation room" (Kantor 2006).

Most U.S. companies, however, offer no child care at all. In the face of global competition, especially cheap labor in the Least Industrialized Nations, can U.S. firms afford child care? Surprisingly, providing child care can reduce labor costs. When the Union Bank of Monterey, California, decided to measure the cost of its day care center, they found that the annual turnover of employees who used the center was just one-fourth that of employees who did not use it. Users of the center were also absent from work less, and they took shorter maternity leaves. The net cost? After subtracting the center's costs from these savings, the bank saved more than $200,000 (Solomon 1988).

Providing back-up child care falls somewhere in between offering on-site child care and no child care at all. With this approach, parents use their own babysitter, but if the sitter can't make it, parents can use the center's back-up services; this allows them to be at work—and to do their job without worry.

As the number of women in management increases, it is likely that more U.S. firms will offer child care services as part of a benefits package designed to attract and hold capable workers.

Employee Stock Ownership Plans If workers are shareholders, it is thought that their loyalty and productivity will increase. Consequently, many companies let their employees buy the firm's stock either at a discount or as part of their salary. About 10 million U.S. workers own part of 11,000 companies. What are the results? Some studies show that these companies are more profitable than other firms (White 1991; Logue and Yates 2000). Other studies, in contrast, report that their profits are about the same, although their productivity may be higher (Blassi and Conte 1996). We need more definitive research on this matter.

If the employees own *all* or most of the company stock, it should eliminate problems between workers and management. This should be obvious—after all, the workers and owners are the same people. But this is not the case. United Airline pilots, for example, who own the largest stake in their airline, staged a work slowdown during their 2001 contract negotiations, forcing the cancellation of thousands of flights. The machinists, who are also owners, followed suit. The machinists' union even threatened to strike. As passengers fled the airline, United racked up huge losses, and its stock plummeted (Zuckerman 2001). The irony is that the company's losses were the worker-owners' losses.

Profitability, not ownership, appears to be the key to reducing worker-management conflict. Unprofitable firms put more pressure on their employee-owners, while profitable companies are quicker to resolve problems.

The Conflict Perspective

Conflict theorists point out that the term humanizing the work setting is camouflage for what is really going on. The basic relationship between workers and owners is always confrontational. Workers and owners walk different paths in life, with owners exploiting workers to extract greater profits and workers trying to resist that exploitation. Because their basic interests are fundamentally opposed, what employers call humanizing the work setting (or managing diversity) is an attempt to manipulate workers into cooperating in their own exploitation. The term humanizing is intended to conceal the capitalists' goal of exploiting workers.

Fads in Corporate Culture

Business practices go through fads, and something that is hot one day may be cold the next. Twenty years ago, the rage was *quality circles,* workers and a manager or two who met regularly to try to improve the quality of both working conditions and the company's products. Because quality circles were used in Japan, U.S. managers embraced them, thinking they had discovered the secret of Japanese success. At its height of popularity in 1983, tens of thousands of U.S. firms were using quality circles, and 60 consultants specialized in teaching them (Strang and Macy 2001). Plummeting in popularity, quality circle has become a term relegated to dictionaries.

As corporations continue to seek ways to get their employees to solve problems as a team, they hop from one fad to another. "Cook offs" are one of the latest. Going cleaver to cleaver, corporate teams slice, chop, and sauté against the clock (Hafner 2007). Professional chefs lend an aura of credibility by overseeing the cook offs and judging the teams' culinary efforts. It seems safe to predict that, like rope-climbing, these team-building exercises will soon pass—and be replaced by still another fad.

Technology and the Control of Workers

The microchip has brought us higher quality manufactured goods and has reduced drudgery. Records are much easier to keep, and we can type just one letter and let the computer print it out and address it to ten individuals—or to ten thousand. Working on my computer, I can modify this sentence, this paragraph, or any section of this book with ease. The other side of the computer is its potential for abuse. Computers make it easier for governments to operate a police state by monitoring our every move. The Big Brother in Orwell's classic novel, *1984,* may turn out to be a computer.

DILBERT: © Scott Adams/Dist. by United Feature Syndicate, Inc.

Despite the rationality that is essential to them, bureaucracies are also marked by non-rational elements. Fads that sweep businesses and universities are an example.

Perhaps, as Orwell suggests, our destiny is to become servants to a master computer. We'll know shortly. In the meantime, we can see that the computer has allowed managers to increase surveillance without face-to-face supervision. For example, sitting in their office, managers know the exact number of keystrokes workers make each minute. They know precisely how long each worker takes for each telephone call. Workers who fall below the average are singled out for discipline. It doesn't matter that the slower workers may be more polite or more helpful, only that the computer reports slower performance.

Then there are the surveillance cameras mounted in the workplace. These cameras, called "little brothers" (as compared with Orwell's "Big Brother"), let bosses in remote locations peer over the shoulders of workers. As sociologist Gary Marx (1995) says, we may be moving to a *maximum-security workplace*. Computers are able to measure motion, air currents, vibrations, odors, pressure changes, and voice stress. To prevent employees from punching in someone else's time card, some companies are using a device to scan their workers' eyes. It compares retinal images with computerized data on file. Because these scans are so precise, I anticipate that soon we will all have to undergo them to even get a driver's license—and, eventually, to use a credit or debit card.

The maximum-security workplace seems an apt term, but with computers and surveillance cameras, the workplace may be just one aspect of a coming "maximum-security society" (Marx 1995). The Sociology and the New Technology box on the next page discusses how computers are being used to monitor workers who think that their actions have gone unnoticed.

U.S. and Japanese Corporations

How were the Japanese able to recover from the defeat of World War II—including the nuclear devastation of two of their major cities—to become a giant in today's global economy? Some analysts trace part of the answer to the way their corporations are organized. Let's compare Japanese and U.S. corporations.

How the Corporations Differ

One analyst, William Ouchi (1981), pinpointed five ways in which Japanese corporations differ from those of the United States. But are these differences myth or reality?

Hiring and Promoting Teams   In *Japan,* teamwork is central. College graduates who join a corporation are all paid about the same starting salary. They also get raises as a team. To learn about the company, they are rotated as a team through the various levels of the organization. They develop intense loyalty to one another and to their company, for the welfare of one represents the welfare of all. Only in later years are individuals singled out for recognition. When there is an opening in the firm, outsiders are not even considered.

In the *United States,* personal achievement is central. A worker is hired on the basis of what the firm thinks that individual can contribute. Employees try to outperform each other, and they strive for raises and promotions as signs of personal success. The individual's loyalty is to himself or herself, not to the company. Outsiders are considered for openings in the firm.

Lifetime Security   In *Japan,* lifetime security is taken for granted. Employees can expect to work for the same firm for the rest of their lives. In return for not being laid off or fired, the firm expects employees to be loyal to the company, to stick with it through good and bad times. Workers do not go job shopping, for their careers—and many aspects of their lives—are wrapped up in this one firm.

In the *United States,* lifetime security is unusual. It is limited primarily to teachers and some judges, who receive what is called *tenure.* Companies lay off workers in slow times. To remain competitive, they even reorganize and eliminate entire divisions. Workers, too, "look out for number one." They seek better pay and opportunities elsewhere. Job shopping and job hopping are common.

Almost Total Involvement   In *Japan,* work is like a marriage: The worker and the company are committed to each other. The employee supports the company with loyalty and long hours at work, while the company supports its workers with lifetime security, health services, recreation, sports and social events, even a home mortgage. Involvement with the company does not stop when the workers leave the building. They join company study and exercise groups, and are likely to spend evenings with co-workers in bars and restaurants.

> SOCIOLOGY and the NEW TECHNOLOGY

Cyberloafers and Cybersleuths: Surfing at Work

FEW PEOPLE WORK CONSTANTLY at their jobs. Most of us take breaks and, at least once in a while, goof off. We meet fellow workers at the coffee machine, and we talk in the hallway. Much of this interaction is good for the company, for it bonds us to fellow workers and ties us to our jobs.

Our personal lives may even cross over into our workday. Some of us make personal calls from the office. Bosses know that we need to check in with our child's preschool or make arrangements for a babysitter. They expect such calls. Some even wink as we make a date or nod as we arrange to have our car worked on. And most bosses make personal calls of their own from time to time. It's the abuse that bothers bosses, and it's not surprising that they fire anyone who talks on the phone all day for personal reasons.

Using computers at work for personal purposes is called *cyberslacking.* Many workers fritter away some of their workday online. They trade stocks, download music, gamble, and play games. They read books, shop, exchange jokes, send personal e-mail, post messages in chat rooms, and visit online red-light districts. Some cyberslackers even operate their own businesses online—when they're not battling virtual enemies during "work."

To take a day off without the boss knowing it, some use remote devices to make their computer switch screens and their printer spew out documents (Spencer 2003). It looks as though they just stepped away from their desk. Some equip their cell phones with audio recordings: Although they may be sitting on the beach when they call the office, their boss hears background sounds of a dentist's drill or of honking horns (Richtel 2004).

Some workers defend their cyberloafing. They argue, reasonably enough, that since their work invades their homes—forcing them to work evenings and weekends—employers should accommodate their personal lives. Some Web sites protect cyberloafers: They feature a panic button in case the boss pokes her head in your office. Click the button and a phony spreadsheet pops onto your screen while typing sounds emerge from your speakers.

Cyberslacking has given birth to the *cybersleuth.* With specialized software, cybersleuths can recover every note employees have written and every Web site they have visited (Nusbaum 2003). They can bring up every file that employees have deleted, even every word they've erased. What some workers don't know (and what some of us forget) is that "delete" does not mean erase. Hitting the delete button simply pushes the text into the background of our hard drive. With a few clicks, the cybersleuth, like magic ink, exposes our "deleted" information, opening our hidden diary for anyone to read.

for your Consideration

Do you think that cybersleuthing is an abuse of power? An invasion of privacy? Or do employers have a right to check on what their employees are doing with company computers on company time? Can you think of a less invasive solution to cyberloafing?

In the *United States,* work is a specific, often temporary contract. Workers are hired to do a certain job. When they have done that job, they have fulfilled their obligation to the company. Their after-work hours are their own. They go home to their private lives, which usually are separate from the firm.

Broad Training   In *Japan,* workers move from one job to another within the company. Not only are they not stuck doing the same thing for years on end but also they gain a bigger picture of the corporation and how the specific jobs they are assigned fit into that bigger picture.

In the *United States,* workers are expected to perform one job, do it well, and then be promoted upward to a job with more responsibility. Their understanding of the company is largely tied to the particular corner they occupy, often making it difficult for them to see how their job fits into the overall picture.

Decision Making by Consensus   In *Japan,* decision making is a lengthy process. Each person who will be affected by a decision is consulted. After extensive deliberations, a consensus emerges, and everyone agrees on which suggestion is superior. This makes workers feel that they are an essential part of the organization, not simply cogs in a giant machine.

In the *United States,* the person in charge of the unit to be affected does as much consulting with others as he or she thinks is necessary and then makes the decision.

The Myth Versus Reality

If we peer beneath the surface, we see that a distorting myth clouds the reality of the Japanese corporation. Most Japanese workers never find lifetime job security, for example—only 20 to 30 percent do (Tokoro 2005). Management by consensus is also a myth. This was not how decisions were made at Sony, one of Japan's most successful companies (Nathan 1999). Akio Morita, Sony's founder, was a take-charge entrepreneur, who relied on his gut feeling about products. Before investing company resources in a risky new product called the Walkman, he didn't send memos throughout the company to get consensus–he simply ordered Sony to manufacture it. One day over lunch, without checking with anyone, Morita decided to spend $2 billion to buy CBS Records.

In the Cultural Diversity box with which we close this chapter, we look at the major changes that are transforming Japanese corporations.

For a time, Americans stood in awe of the Japanese corporate model. The passage of time, however, has revealed serious flaws. Lifetime job security, for example, is a myth. These homeless men are living in the Shinjuko train station in Tokyo. Note how they have followed the Japanese custom of placing their shoes outside before entering their "home."

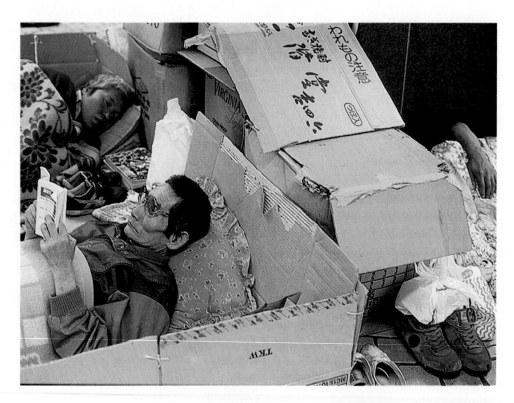

Cultural Diversity *around the* World

Japanese and U.S. Corporations in an Age of Greed

DO YOU KNOW WHICH OF THESE statements is false?

> The Japanese are more productive than Americans.
> The living standard of Americans has fallen behind that of the Japanese.
> Japanese workers enjoy lifetime job security.
> The Japanese are paid less than Americans.

From what you just read, you know that the third one is false. So are the other three.

A while back, Japanese corporations seemed invincible. There was even talk that the United States had won World War II, but had lost the economic war. Impressed with Japan's success, Western corporations, including those from the United States, sent executives to Japan to study their companies. U.S. corporations then copied parts of that model.

Cracks in the facade soon appeared. Small at first, they grew, destroying some of Japan's major corporations. These companies had been built on personal relationships, on mutual obligations that transcend contracts. This had been a key to creating fierce loyalty, a corporate strength that turned out to be an Achilles heel. When Japan's economy went into a nose dive, companies did not lay off workers; layoffs were not part of their corporate culture. Costs mounted while profits disappeared and debts piled up, sinking companies in a sea of red ink.

In a surprising move, Japan turned to U.S. corporations to see why they were more efficient. Flying in the face of their traditions, Japanese corporations have begun to lay off workers and to use merit pay. Although this is standard U.S. practice, it had been unthinkable in Japan (Tokoro 2005).

One of the biggest surprises was Ford's takeover of Mazda. With Mazda teetering on the edge of bankruptcy, its creditors decided that Ford knew more about building and marketing cars than Mazda and invited Ford to manage the company. In true U.S. fashion, Ford laid off workers and renegotiated contracts with suppliers. With its work force slashed from 46,000 to 36,000, Mazda again became profitable. Similarly, when Sony's profits plummeted, an American who couldn't even speak Japanese was made its CEO (Kane and Dvorak 2007).

A much leaner, meaner Japanese production machine is emerging.

for your Consideration

The real bottom line is that we live in a global marketplace—of ideas as well as products. Companies from different countries learn from one another. Do you think that it will become common for Japanese corporations—with their cultural background of relationships and cooperation–to lay off workers in order to compete more effectively in global competition?

In another twist, Ford, which had led the successful turnaround of Mazda in Japan, found itself unable to compete successfully with Toyota. Like General Motors, Ford lost market share and billions of dollars, putting itself on the brink of financial disaster. Do you think Toyota will become the poster child of the corporate car world, and, perhaps, in a double twist, be brought back to Japan to apply its U.S. lessons?

Summary *and* Review

The Rationalization of Society

How did the rationalization of society come about?

The term **rationalization of society** refers to a transformation in people's thinking and behaviors—one that shifts the focus from following time-honored ways to being efficient in producing results. Max Weber, who developed this term, traced this change to Protestant theology, which he said brought about capitalism. Karl Marx attributed rationalization to capitalism itself. Pp. 178–180.

Formal Organizations and Bureaucracies

What are formal organizations?

Formal organizations are secondary groups designed to achieve specific objectives. Their dominant form is the **bureaucracy,** which Weber said consists of a hierarchy, a division of labor, written rules and communications, and impersonality and replaceability of positions—characteristics that make bureaucracies efficient and enduring. Pp. 181–184.

What dysfunctions are associated with bureaucracies?

The dysfunctions of bureaucracies include alienation, red tape, lack of communication between units, **goal displacement,** and incompetence (as seen in the **Peter principle**). In Weber's view, the impersonality of bureaucracies tends to produce **alienation** among workers—the feeling that no one cares about them and that they do not really fit in. Marx's view of alienation is somewhat different—workers do not identify with the product of their labor because they participate in only a small part of the production process. Pp. 184–188.

Voluntary Associations

What are the functions of voluntary associations?

Voluntary **associations** are groups made up of volunteers who organize on the basis of common interests. These associations promote mutual interests, provide a sense of identity and purpose, help to govern and maintain order, mediate between the government and the individual, give training in organizational skills, help provide access to political power, and pave the way for social change. Pp. 188–190.

What is "the iron law of oligarchy"?

Sociologist Robert Michels noted that formal organizations have a tendency to become controlled by an inner circle that limits leadership to its own members. The dominance of a formal organization by an elite that keeps itself in power is called **the iron law of oligarchy.** Pp. 190–191.

Working for the Corporation

How does the corporate culture affect workers?

The term **corporate culture** refers to an organization's traditions, values, and unwritten norms. Much of corporate culture, such as its hidden values and stereotypes, is not readily visible. Often, a **self-fulfilling prophecy** is at work: People who match a corporation's hidden values tend to be put on career tracks that enhance their chance of success, while those who do not match those values are set on a course that minimizes their performance. Pp. 191–193.

Humanizing the Corporate Culture

What does it mean to humanize the work setting?

Humanizing a work setting means to organize it in a way that develops rather than impedes human potential. Among the attempts to make bureaucracies more humane are work teams and corporate day care. Employee stock ownership plans give workers a greater stake in the outcomes of their work organizations, but they do not prevent worker-management conflict. Conflict theorists see attempts to humanize work as a way of manipulating workers. Pp. 193–195.

Technology and the Control of Workers

What is the maximum security workplace?

It is the use of computers and surveillance devices to monitor almost all the actions of workers. Pp. 193–195.

U.S. and Japanese Corporations

How do Japanese and U.S. corporations differ?

The Japanese corporate model contrasts sharply with the U.S. model in terms of hiring and promotion, lifetime security, interaction of workers after work, broad training of workers, and collective decision making. Much of this model is a myth, an idealization of reality, and does not reflect Japanese corporate life today. Pp. 196–199.

Thinking Critically
about Chapter 7

1. You are likely to work for a bureaucracy. How do you think that it will affect your orientations to life? How can you make the "hidden culture" work to your advantage?

2. Do you think the Peter principle is right? Why or why not?

3. Do you think U.S. corporations should have diversity training? Why or why not? If so, how should they go about it?

Additional Resources

What can you use MySocLab for? www.mysoclab.com

- **Study and Review:** Pre- and Post-Tests, Practice Tests, Flash Cards, Individualized Study Plans.

- **Current Events:** *Sociology in the News*, the daily *New York Times*, and more.

- **Research and Writing:** *Research Navigator, Writing About Sociology*, and more.

Where Can I Read More on This Topic?

Suggested readings for this chapter are listed at the back of this book.

Deviance and Social Control

Vincent Van Gogh, *Prisoners Exercising*, 1890

In just a few moments I was to meet my first Yanomamö, my first primitive man. What would it be like? . . . I looked up (from my canoe) and gasped when I saw a dozen burly, naked, filthy, hideous men staring at us down the shafts of their drawn arrows. Immense wads of green tobacco were stuck between their lower teeth and lips, making them look even more hideous, and strands of dark-green slime dripped or hung from their noses. We arrived at the village while the men were blowing a hallucinogenic drug up their noses. One of the side effects of the drug is a runny nose. The mucus is always saturated with the green powder, and the Indians usually let it run freely from their nostrils. . . . I just sat there holding my notebook, helpless and pathetic . . .

The whole situation was depressing, and I wondered why I ever decided to switch from civil engineering to anthropology in the first place. . . . (Soon) I was covered with red pigment, the result of a dozen or so

They would "clean" their hands by spitting slimy tobacco juice into them.

complete examinations. . . . These examinations capped an otherwise grim day. The Indians would blow their noses into their hands, flick as much of the mucus off that would separate in a snap of the wrist, wipe the residue into their hair, and then carefully examine my face, arms, legs, hair, and the contents of my pockets. I said (in their language), "Your hands are dirty"; my comments were met by the Indians in the following way: they would "clean" their hands by spitting a quantity of slimy tobacco juice into them, rub them together, and then proceed with the examination.

This is how Napoleon Chagnon describes the cultural shock he felt when he met the Yanomamö tribe of the rain forests of Brazil. His ensuing months of fieldwork continued to bring surprise after surprise, and often Chagnon (1977) could hardly believe his eyes—or his nose.

deviance the violation of rules or norms

crime the violation of norms written into law

stigma "blemishes" that discredit a person's claim to a "normal" identity

If you were to list the deviant behaviors of the Yanomamö, what would you include? The way they appear naked in public? Use hallucinogenic drugs? Let mucus hang from their noses? Or the way they rub hands filled with mucus, spittle, and tobacco juice over a frightened stranger who doesn't dare to protest? Perhaps. But it isn't this simple, for as we shall see, deviance is relative.

What Is Deviance?

Sociologists use the term **deviance** to refer to any violation of norms, whether the infraction is as minor as driving over the speed limit, as serious as murder, or as humorous as Chagnon's encounter with the Yanomamö. This deceptively simple definition takes us to the heart of the sociological perspective on deviance, which sociologist Howard S. Becker (1966) described this way: *It is not the act itself, but the reactions to the act, that make something deviant.* What Chagnon saw disturbed him, but to the Yanomamö those same behaviors represented normal, everyday life. What was deviant to Chagnon was *conformist* to the Yanomamö. From their viewpoint, you *should* check out strangers the way they did, and nakedness is good, as are hallucinogenic drugs and letting mucus be "natural."

Chagnon's abrupt introduction to the Yanomamö allows us to see the *relativity of deviance*, a major point made by symbolic interactionists. Because different groups have different norms, *what is deviant to some is not deviant to others.* (See the photo on this page.) This principle holds both *within* a society as well as across cultures. Thus, acts that are acceptable in one culture—or in one group within a society—may be considered deviant in another culture, or by another group within the same society. This idea is explored in the Cultural Diversity box on the next page.

This principle also applies to a specific form of deviance known as **crime,** the violation of rules that have been written into law. In the extreme, an act that is applauded by one group may be so despised by another group that it is punishable by death. Making a huge profit on business deals is one example. Americans who do this are admired. Like Donald Trump, Jack Welch, and Warren Buffet, they may even write books about their exploits. In China, however, until recently this same act was considered a crime called *profiteering.* Anyone who was found guilty was hanged in a public square as a lesson to all.

Unlike the general public, sociologists use the term *deviance* nonjudgmentally, to refer to any act to which people respond negatively. When sociologists use this term, it does not mean that they agree that an act is bad, just that people judge it negatively. To sociologists, then, *all* of us are deviants of one sort or another, for we all violate norms from time to time.

To be considered deviant, a person does not even have to *do* anything. Sociologist Erving Goffman (1963) used the term **stigma** to refer to characteristics that discredit people. These include violations of norms of ability (blindness, deafness, mental handicaps) and norms of appearance (a facial birthmark, obesity). They also include involuntary memberships, such as being a victim of AIDS or the brother of a rapist. The stigma can become a person's master status, defining him or her as deviant. Recall from Chapter 4 that a master status cuts across all other statuses that a person occupies.

I took this photo on the outskirts of Hyderabad, India. Is this man deviant? If this were a U.S. street, he would be. But here? No houses have running water in his neighborhood, and the men, women, and children bathe at the neighborhood water pump. This man, then, would not be deviant in his culture. And yet, he is actually mugging for my camera, making the three bystanders laugh. Does this additional factor make this a scene of deviance?

How Norms Make Social Life Possible

No human group can exist without norms, for *norms make social life possible by making behavior predictable.* What would life be like if you could not predict what others would do? Imagine for a moment that you have gone to a store to purchase milk:

> Suppose the clerk says, "I won't sell you any milk. We're overstocked with soda, and I'm not going to sell anyone milk until our soda inventory is reduced."

Human Sexuality in Cross-Cultural Perspective

HUMAN SEXUALITY ILLUSTRATES how a group's *definition* of an act, not the act itself, determines whether it will be considered deviant. Let's look at some examples reported by anthropologist Robert Edgerton (1976).

Norms of sexual behavior vary so widely around the world that what is considered normal in one society may be considered deviant in another. In Kenya, a group called the Pokot place high emphasis on sexual pleasure, and they expect that both a husband and wife will reach orgasm. If a husband does not satisfy his wife, he is in trouble—especially if she thinks that his failure is because of adultery. If this is so, the wife and her female friends will sneak up on her husband when he is asleep. The women will tie him up, shout obscenities at him, beat him, and then urinate on him. As a final gesture of their contempt, before releasing him, they will slaughter and eat his favorite ox. The husband's hours of painful humiliation are intended to make him more dutiful concerning his wife's conjugal rights.

Pokot married man, northern Kenya

that sexual relations should take place exclusively between husband and wife. Yet the *only* person in one Zapotec community who had not had any extramarital affairs was considered deviant. Evidently, these people have an unspoken understanding that married couples will engage in affairs, but be discreet about them. When a wife learns that her husband is having an affair, she usually has one, too.

One Zapotec wife did not follow this covert norm. Instead, she would praise her own virtue to her husband—and then voice the familiar "headache" excuse. She also told other wives the names of the women their husbands were sleeping with. As a result, this virtuous woman was condemned by everyone in the village. Clearly, real norms can conflict with ideal norms—another illustration of the gap between ideal and real culture.

for your Consideration

How do the behaviors of the Pokot wife and husband look from the perspective of U.S. norms? Are there U.S. norms in the first place? How about the Zapotec woman? The rest of the Zapotec community? How does cultural relativity apply? (We discussed this concept in Chapter 2, pages 41–42.)

People can also become deviants for failing to understand that the group's ideal norms may not be its real norms. As with many groups, the Zapotec Indians of Mexico profess

---

You don't like it, but you decide to buy a case of soda. At the checkout, the clerk says, "I hope you don't mind, but there's a $5 service charge on every fifteenth customer." You, of course, are the fifteenth.

Just as you start to leave, another clerk stops you and says, "We're not working any more. We decided to have a party." Suddenly a CD player begins to blast, and everyone in the store begins to dance. "Oh, good, you've brought the soda," says a different clerk, who takes your package and passes sodas all around.

Life is not like this, of course. You can depend on grocery clerks to sell you milk. You can also depend on paying the same price as everyone else, and not being forced to attend a party in the store. Why can you depend on this? Because we are socialized to follow norms, to play the basic roles that society assigns to us.

Without norms, we would have social chaos. Norms lay out the basic guidelines for how we should play our roles and interact with others. In short, norms bring about **social order,** a group's customary social arrangements. Our lives are based on these arrangements, which is why deviance often is perceived as threatening: Deviance undermines predictability, the foundation of social life. Consequently, human groups develop a system of **social control**—formal and informal means of enforcing norms.

social order a group's usual and customary social arrangements, on which its members depend and on which they base their lives

social control a group's formal and informal means of enforcing its norms

There is no norm that says, "Do not hang in the air, suspended by flesh hooks," as this woman is doing at a tattoo festival in Woodstock, New York. What sanctions might come into play if she did this at work during her lunch hour? Why the difference?

Sanctions

As we discussed in Chapter 2, people do not enforce folkways strictly, but they become upset when people break mores (MORE-rays). Expressions of disapproval of deviance, called **negative sanctions,** range from frowns and gossip for breaking folkways to imprisonment and capital punishment for breaking mores. In general, the more seriously the group takes a norm, the harsher the penalty for violating it. In contrast, **positive sanctions**—from smiles to formal awards—are used to reward people for conforming to norms. Getting a raise is a positive sanction; being fired is a negative sanction. Getting an *A* in intro to sociology is a positive sanction; getting an *F* is a negative one.

Most negative sanctions are informal. You might stare if you observe someone dressed in what you consider to be inappropriate clothing, or you might gossip if a married person you know spends the night with someone other than his or her spouse. Whether you consider the breaking of a norm merely an amusing matter that warrants no severe sanction or a serious infraction that does, however, depends on your perspective. If a woman appears at your college graduation ceremonies in a bikini, you may stare and laugh, but if this is *your* mother, you are likely to feel that different sanctions are appropriate. Similarly, if it is *your* father who spends the night with an 18-year-old college freshman, you are likely to do more than gossip.

Shaming and Degradation Ceremonies

Shaming is another sanction. Shaming is especially effective when members of a primary group use it. For this reason, parents sometimes use it to keep children in line. Shaming is also effective in small communities, where the individual's reputation is at stake. As our society grew large and urban, its sense of community diminished, and shaming lost its effectiveness. Shaming seems to be making a comeback. One Arizona sheriff makes the men in his jail wear pink underwear (Boxer 2001). Digital cameras and camera cell phones have encouraged online shaming sites. They feature bad drivers, older men who leer at teenaged girls, and dog walkers who don't pick up their dog's poop (Saranow 2007). Some sites include photos of the offenders, as well as their addresses and phone numbers.

In small communities, shaming can be the centerpiece of the enforcement of norms, with the violator marked as a deviant and held up for all the world to see. In Nathaniel Hawthorne's *The Scarlet Letter*, town officials forced Hester Prynne to wear a scarlet A sewn on her dress. The A stood for *adulteress.* Wherever she went, Prynne had to wear this badge of shame, and the community expected her to wear it every day for the rest of her life.

Sociologist Harold Garfinkel (1956) gave the name **degradation ceremony** to formal attempts to brand someone as an outsider. The individual is called to account before the group, witnesses denounce him or her, the offender is pronounced guilty, and steps are taken to strip the individual of his or her identity as a group member. In some court martials, officers who are found guilty stand at attention before their peers while the insignia of rank are ripped from their uniforms. This procedure dramatizes that the individual is no longer a member of the group. Although Hester Prynne was not banished from the group physically, she was banished morally; her degradation ceremony proclaimed her a *moral* outcast from the community. The scarlet A marked her as "not one" of them.

Although we don't use scarlet A's today, informal degradation ceremonies still occur. Consider what happened to Joseph Gray (Chivers 2001):

Joseph Gray, a fifteen-year veteran of the New York City police force, was involved in a fatal accident. The *New York Times* and New York television stations reported that Gray had spent the afternoon drinking in a topless bar before plowing his car into a vehicle carrying a pregnant woman, her son, and her sister. All three died. Gray was accused of manslaughter and drunk driving. (He was later convicted on both counts.)

The news media kept hammering this story to the public. Three weeks later, as Gray left police headquarters after resigning from his job, an angry crowd gathered around him. Gray hung his head in public disgrace as Victor Manuel Herrera, whose wife and son were killed in the crash, followed him, shouting, "You're a murderer!"

IN SUM In sociology, the term *deviance* refers to all violations of social rules, regardless of their seriousness. The term is not a judgment about the behavior. Deviance is relative, for what is deviant in one group may be conformist in another. Consequently, we must consider deviance from *within* a group's own framework, for it is *their* meanings that underlie their behavior. The following Thinking Critically section focuses on this issue.

Degradation ceremonies are intended to humiliate norm violators and mark them as "not members" of the group. This photo was taken by the U.S. army in 1945 after U.S. troops liberated Cherbourg, France. Members of the French resistance shaved the heads of these women, who had "collaborated" (had sex with) the occupying Nazis. They then marched the shamed women down the streets of the city, while the public shouted insults and spat on them.

Thinking Critically

Is It Rape, Or Is It Marriage? A Study in Culture Clash

Surrounded by cornfields, Lincoln, Nebraska, is about as provincial as a state capital gets. Most of its residents have little experience dealing with people who come from different ways of life. Their baptism into cultural diversity came as a shock.

The wedding was traditional and followed millennia-old Islamic practices (Annin and Hamilton 1996). A 39-year-old immigrant from Iraq had arranged for his two eldest daughters, ages 13 and 14, to marry two fellow Iraqi immigrants, ages 28 and 34. A Muslim cleric flew in from Ohio to perform the ceremony.

Nebraska went into shock. So did the immigrants. What is marriage in Iraq is rape in Nebraska. The husbands were charged with rape, the girls' father with child abuse, and their mother with contributing to the delinquency of minors.

The event made front page news in Saudi Arabia, where people shook their heads in amazement at Americans. Nebraskans shook their heads in amazement, too.

In Fresno, California, a young Hmong immigrant took a group of friends to a local college campus. There, they picked up the Hmong girl whom he had selected to be his wife (Sherman 1988; Lacayo 1993b). The young men brought her to his house, where he had sex with her. The young woman, however, was not in agreement with this plan.

The Hmong call this *zij poj niam*, "marriage by capture." For them, this is an acceptable form of mate selection, one that mirrors Hmong courtship ideals of strong men and virtuous, resistant women. The Fresno District Attorney, however, called it kidnapping and rape.

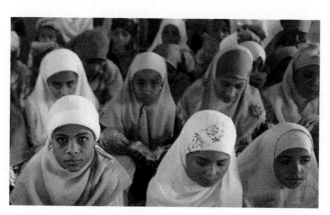

Culture conflict centered around parents giving girls like this in marriage to men 15 to 20 years older.

As migration intensifies, other countries are experiencing similar culture shock. Germans awoke one morning to the news that a 28-year-old Turkish man had taken his 11-year-old wife to the registry office in Dusseldorf to get her an ID card. The shocked officials detained the girl and shipped her back to Turkey (Stephens 2006).

In Bishkek, Kyrgystan, a former republic of the Soviet Union, one father said that he wouldn't mind if a man kidnapped his daugher to marry her. "After all," he said, "that's how I got my wife" (Smith 2005).

for your Consideration

To apply *symbolic interactionism* to these real-life dramas, ask how the perspectives of the people involved explain why they did what they did. To apply *functionalism*, ask how the U.S. laws that were violated are "functional" (that is, what are their benefits, and to whom?). To apply *conflict theory*, ask what groups are in conflict in these examples. (Do not focus on the individuals involved, but on the groups to which they belong.)

Understanding events in terms of different theoretical perspectives does not tell us which reaction is "right" when cultures clash. Science can analyze causes and consequences, but it cannot answer questions of what is "right" or moral. Any "ought" that you feel about these cases comes from your values, which brings us, once again, to the initial issue: the relativity of deviance.

Competing Explanations of Deviance: Sociology, Sociobiology, and Psychology

If social life is to exist, norms are essential. So why do people violate them? To better understand the reasons, it is useful to know how sociological explanations differ from biological and psychological ones.

Sociobiologists explain deviance by looking for answers *within* individuals. They assume that **genetic predispositions** lead people to such deviances as juvenile delinquency and crime (Lombroso 1911; Wilson and Herrnstein 1985; Goozen et al. 2007). Among their explanations are the following three theories: (1) intelligence—low intelligence leads to crime; (2) the "XYY" theory—an extra Y chromosome in males leads to crime; and (3) body type—people with "squarish, muscular" bodies are more likely to commit **street crime**—acts such as mugging, rape, and burglary.

How have these theories held up? We should first note that most people who have these supposedly "causal" characteristics do not become criminals. Regarding intelligence, you already know that some criminals are very intelligent, and that most people of low intelligence do not commit crimes. Regarding the extra Y chromosome, most men who commit crimes have the normal XY chromosome combination, and most men with the XYY combination do not become criminals. No women have this combination of genes, so this explanation can't even be applied to female criminals. Regarding body type, criminals exhibit the full range of body types, and most people with "squarish, muscular" bodies do not become street criminals.

Psychologists also focus on abnormalities *within* the individual. They examine what are called **personality disorders.** Their supposition is that deviating individuals have deviating personalities (Barnes 2001; Mayer 2007), and that subconscious motives drive people to deviance. No specific childhood experience, however, is invariably linked with deviance. For example, children who had "bad toilet training," "suffocating mothers," or "emotionally aloof fathers" may become embezzling bookkeepers—or good accountants. Just as college students, teachers, and police officers represent a variety of bad—and good—childhood experiences, so do deviants. Similarly, people with "suppressed anger" can become freeway snipers or military heroes—or anything else. In short, there is no inevitable outcome of any childhood experience. Deviance is not associated with any particular personality.

In contrast with both sociobiologists and psychologists, *sociologists* search for factors *outside* the individual. They look for social influences that "recruit" people to break norms. To account for why people commit crimes, for example, sociologists examine such external influences as socialization, membership in subcultures, and social class.

genetic predisposition inborn tendencies; in this context, to commit deviant acts

street crime crimes such as mugging, rape, and burglary

personality disorders the view that a personality disturbance of some sort causes an individual to violate social norms

Social class, a concept that we will discuss in depth in Chapter 10, refers to people's relative standing in terms of education, occupation, and especially income and wealth.

The point stressed earlier, that deviance is relative, leads sociologists to ask a crucial question: Why should we expect to find something constant within people to account for a behavior that is conforming in one society and deviant in another?

To see how sociologists explain deviance, let's contrast the three sociological perspectives—symbolic interactionism, functionalism, and conflict theory.

The Symbolic Interactionist Perspective

As we examine symbolic interactionism, it will become more evident why sociologists are not satisfied with explanations that are rooted in biology or personality. A basic principle of symbolic interactionism is this: We act according to our interpretations of situations, not according to blind predisposition. Let's consider how our membership in groups influences our views of life and thus affects our behavior.

Differential Association Theory

The Theory Contrary to theories built around biology and personality, sociologists stress that people *learn* deviance. Edwin Sutherland coined the term **differential association** to indicate that we learn to deviate from or conform to society's norms primarily from the *different* groups we *associate* with (Sutherland 1924, 1947; Sutherland et al. 1992). On the most obvious level, some boys and girls join street gangs, while others join the Scouts. As sociologists have repeatedly demonstrated, what we learn influences us toward or away from deviance (Deflem 2006; Chambliss 1973/2007).

Sutherland's theory is actually more complicated than this, but he basically said that deviance is learned. This goes directly against the view that deviance is due to biology or personality. Sutherland stressed that the different groups with which we associate (our "*different*ial association") give us messages about conformity and deviance. We may receive mixed messages, but we end up with more of one than the other (an "excess of definitions," as Sutherland put it). The end result is an imbalance—attitudes that tilt us more toward one direction than another. Consequently, either we conform or we deviate.

Families Since our family is so important for teaching us attitudes, it probably is obvious to you that the family makes a big difference in whether we learn deviance or conformity. Researchers have confirmed this informal observation. They have found that delinquents are more likely to come from families that get in trouble with the law. Of the many studies that show this, one stands out: Of all jail inmates across the United States, almost *half* have a father, mother, brother, sister, or spouse who has served time in prison (*Sourcebook of Criminal Justice Statistics* 2003:Table 6.0011). In short, families that are involved in crime tend to set their children on a lawbreaking path.

Friends, Neighborhoods, and Subcultures Most people don't know the term *differential association,* but they do know how it works. Most parents want to move out of "bad" neighborhoods because they know that if their kids have delinquent friends, they are likely to become delinquent, too. Sociological research supports this common observation (Miller 1958; Chung and Steinberg 2006; Yonas et al. 2006). Some neighborhoods even develop a subculture of violence. In these places, even a teasing remark can mean instant death. If the neighbors feel that a victim deserved to be killed, they refuse to testify because "he got what was coming to him" (Kubrin and Weitzer 2003).

differential association Edwin Sutherland's term to indicate that associating with some groups results in learning an "excess of definitions" of deviance, and, by extension, in a greater likelihood that one will become deviant

To experience a sense of belonging is a basic human need. Membership in groups, especially peer groups, is a primary way that people meet this need. Regardless of the orientation of the group— whether to conformity or to deviance—the process is the same. These members of a street gang in Cali, Colombia, are showing off their home-made guns.

Some neighborhoods even develop subcultures in which killing is considered an honorable act:

Sociologist Ruth Horowitz (1983, 2005), who did participant observation in a lower-class Chicano neighborhood in Chicago, discovered how associating with people who have a certain concept of "honor" propels young men to deviance. The formula is simple. "A real man has honor. An insult is a threat to one's honor. Therefore, not to stand up to someone is to be less than a real man."

Now suppose you are a young man growing up in this neighborhood. You likely would do a fair amount of fighting, for you would interpret many things as attacks on your honor. You might even carry a knife or a gun, for words and fists wouldn't always be sufficient. Along with members of your group, you would define fighting, knifing, and shooting quite differently from the way most people do.

Members of the Mafia also intertwine ideas of manliness with violence. For them, *to kill is a measure of their manhood.* Not all killings are accorded the same respect, however, for "the more awesome and potent the victim, the more worthy and meritorious the killer" (Arlacchi 1980). Some killings are done to enforce norms. A member of the Mafia who gives information to the police, for example, has violated *omertá* (the Mafia's vow of secrecy). This offense can never be tolerated, for it threatens the very existence of the group. Mafia killings further illustrate just how relative deviance is. Although killing is deviant to mainstream society, for members of the Mafia, *not* to kill after certain rules are broken—such as when someone "squeals" to the cops—is the deviant act.

Prison or Freedom?   As was mentioned in Chapter 3, an issue that comes up over and over again in sociology is whether we are prisoners of socialization. Symbolic interactionists stress that we are not mere pawns in the hands of others. We are not destined to think and act as our group memberships dictate. Rather, we *help to produce our own orientations to life.* By joining one group rather than another (differential association), for example, we help to shape the self. For instance, one college student may join a feminist group that is trying to change the treatment of women in college; another may associate with a group of women who shoplift on weekends. Their choice of groups points them in different directions. The one who associates with shoplifters may become even more oriented toward criminal activities, while the one who joins the feminist group may develop an even greater interest in producing social change.

Control Theory

Inside most of us, it seems, are desires to do things that would get us in trouble—inner drives, temptations, urges, hostilities, and so on. Yet most of the time we stifle these desires. Why?

The Theory   Sociologist Walter Reckless (1973), who developed **control theory,** stresses that two control systems work against our motivations to deviate. Our *inner controls* include our internalized morality—conscience, religious principles, ideas of right and wrong. Inner controls also include fears of punishment, feelings of integrity, and the desire to be a "good" person (Hirschi 1969; Rogers 1977; McShane and Williams 2007). Our *outer controls* consist of people—such as family, friends, and the police—who influence us not to deviate.

The stronger our bonds are with society, the more effective our inner controls are (Hirschi 1969). Bonds are based on *attachments* (feeling affection and respect for people who

The social control of deviance takes many forms, some rather subtle. With its mayhem, "cage fighting" might look like the opposite of social control, but it is a way to channel aggressive impulses in a way that leaves no vendetta, feud, or "score to settle."

conform to mainstream norms), *commitments* (having a stake in society that you don't want to risk, such as a respected place in your family, a good standing at college, a good job), *involvements* (putting time and energy into approved activities), and *beliefs* (believing that certain actions are morally wrong).

This theory can be summarized as *self*-control, says sociologist Travis Hirschi. The key to learning high self-control is socialization, especially in childhood. Parents help their children to develop self-control by supervising them and punishing their deviant acts (Gottfredson and Hirschi 1990).

Applying the Theory

Suppose that some friends have invited you to a night club. When you get there, you notice that everyone seems unusually happy—almost giddy would be a better word. They seem to be euphoric in their animated conversations and dancing. Your friends tell you that almost everyone here has taken the drug Ecstasy, and they invite you to take some with them.

What do you do? Let's not explore the question of whether taking Ecstasy in this setting is a deviant or a conforming act. That is a separate issue. Instead, concentrate on the pushes and pulls you would feel. The pushes toward taking the drug: your friends, the setting, and your curiosity. Then there are the inner controls: the inner voices of your conscience and your parents, perhaps of your teachers, as well as your fears of arrest and of the dangers of illegal drugs. There are also the outer controls—perhaps the uniformed security guard looking in your direction.

So, what *did* you decide? Which was stronger: your inner and outer controls or the pushes and pulls toward taking the drug? It is you who can best weigh these forces, for they differ with each of us.

Labeling Theory

Symbolic interactionists have developed **labeling theory,** which focuses on the significance of the labels (names, reputations) that we are given. Labels tend to become a part of our self-concept, and help to set us on paths that either propel us into or divert us from deviance. Let's look at how people react to society's labels—from "whore" and "pervert" to "cheat" and "slob."

Rejecting Labels: How People Neutralize Deviance   Most people resist the negative labels that others try to pin on them. Some are so successful that even though they persist in deviance, they still consider themselves conformists. For example, even though they beat up people and vandalize property, some delinquents consider themselves to be conforming members of society. How do they do it?

Sociologists Gresham Sykes and David Matza (1957/1988) studied boys like this. They found that the boys used five **techniques of neutralization** to deflect society's norms.

Denial of Responsibility Some boys said, "I'm not responsible for what happened because . . ." and then they were quite creative about the "becauses." Some said that what happened was an "accident." Other boys saw themselves as "victims" of society. What else could you expect? They were like billiard balls shot around the pool table of life.

Denial of Injury Another favorite explanation of the boys was "What I did wasn't wrong because no one got hurt." They would define vandalism as "mischief," gang fights as a "private quarrel," and stealing cars as "borrowing." They might acknowledge that what they did was illegal, but claim that they were "just having a little fun."

Denial of a Victim Some boys thought of themselves as avengers. Vandalizing a teacher's car was done to get revenge

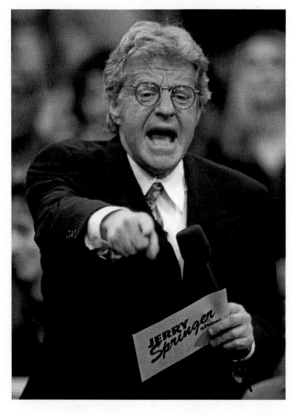

Jerry Springer guides people to publicly reveal their deviances. As Springer parades deviants before the public, the shock and surprise wear off, making the deviance seem "more" normal. What is occurring is the *mainstreaming of deviance*—disapproved behaviors moving into the mainstream, or becoming more socially acceptable.

labeling theory the view that the labels people are given affect their own and others' perceptions of them, thus channeling their behavior either into deviance or into conformity

techniques of neutralization ways of thinking or rationalizing that help people deflect (or neutralize) society's norms for an unfair grade, while shoplifting was a way to even the score with "crooked" store owners. In short, even if the boys did accept responsibility and admit that someone had gotten hurt, they protected their self-concept by claiming that the people "deserved what they got."

Condemnation of the Condemners Another technique the boys used was to deny that others had the right to judge them. They might accuse people who pointed their fingers at them of being "a bunch of hypocrites": The police were "on the take," teachers had "pets," and parents cheated on their taxes. In short, they said, "Who are *they* to accuse *me* of something?"

Appeal to Higher Loyalties A final technique the boys used to justify antisocial activities was to consider loyalty to the gang more important than following the norms of society. They might say, "I had to help my friends. That's why I got in the fight." Not incidentally, the boy may have shot two members of a rival group, as well as a bystander!

In sum: These five techniques of neutralization have implications far beyond this group of boys, for it is not only delinquents who try to neutralize the norms of mainstream society. Look again at these five techniques—don't they sound familiar? (1) "I couldn't help myself"; (2) "Who really got hurt?"; (3) "Don't you think she deserved that, after what *she* did?"; (4) "Who are *you* to talk?"; and (5) "I had to help my friends—wouldn't you have done the same thing?" All of us attempt to neutralize the moral demands of society, for neutralization helps us to sleep at night.

Embracing Labels: The Example of Outlaw Bikers Although most of us resist attempts to label us as deviant, some people revel in a deviant identity. Some teenagers, for example, make certain by their clothing, choice of music, hairstyles, and "body art" that no one misses their rejection of adult norms. Their status among fellow members of a subculture—within which they are almost obsessive conformists—is vastly more important than any status outside it.

One of the best examples of a group that embraces deviance is motorcycle gangs. Sociologist Mark Watson (1980/2006) did participant observation with outlaw bikers. He rebuilt Harleys with them, hung around their bars and homes, and went on "runs" (trips) with them. He concluded that outlaw bikers see the world as "hostile, weak, and effeminate." They pride themselves on looking "dirty, mean, and generally undesirable" and take pleasure in provoking shocked reactions to their appearance and behavior. Holding the conventional world in contempt, they also pride themselves on getting into trouble, laughing at death, and treating women as lesser beings whose primary value is to provide them with services—especially sex. Outlaw bikers also regard themselves as losers, a factor that becomes woven into their unusual embrace of deviance.

The Power of Labels: The Saints and the Roughnecks We can see how powerful labeling is by referring back to the study of the "Saints" and the "Roughnecks" that was cited in Chapter 4 (page 121). As you recall, both groups of high school boys were "constantly occupied with truancy, drinking, wild parties, petty theft, and vandalism." Yet their teachers looked on the Saints as "headed for success" and the Roughnecks as "headed for trouble." By the time they finished high school, not one Saint had been arrested, while the Roughnecks had been in constant trouble with the police.

Why did the members of the community perceive these boys so differently? Chambliss (1973/2007) concluded that this split vision was due to *social class*. As symbolic interactionists emphasize, social class vitally affects our perceptions and behavior. The Saints came from respectable, middle-class families, while the Roughnecks were from less respectable, working-class families. These backgrounds led teachers and the authorities to expect good behavior from the Saints but trouble from the Roughnecks. And, like the rest of us, teachers and police saw what they expected to see.

The boys' social class also affected their visibility. The Saints had automobiles, and they did their drinking and vandalism outside of town. Without cars, the Roughnecks hung around their own street corners, where their drinking and boisterous behavior drew the attention of police and confirmed the negative impressions that the community already had of them.

The boys' social class also equipped them with distinct *styles of interaction*. When police or teachers questioned them, the Saints were apologetic. Their show of respect for authority elicited a positive reaction from teachers and police, allowing the Saints to escape school and legal problems. The Roughnecks, said Chambliss, were "almost the polar opposite." When questioned, they were hostile. Even when they tried to assume a respectful attitude, everyone could see through it. Consequently, while teachers and police let the Saints off with warnings, they came down hard on the Roughnecks.

Although what happens in life is not determined by labels alone, the Saints and the Roughnecks did live up to the labels that the community gave them. As you may recall, all but one of the Saints went on to college. One earned a Ph.D., one became a lawyer, one a doctor, and the others business managers. In contrast, only two of the Roughnecks went to college. They earned athletic scholarships and became coaches. The other Roughnecks did not fare so well. Two of them dropped out of high school, later became involved in separate killings, and were sent to prison. One became a local bookie, and no one knows the whereabouts of the other.

How do labels work? Although the matter is complex, because it involves the self-concept and reactions that vary from one individual to another, we can note that labels open and close doors of opportunity. Unlike its meaning in sociology, the term *deviant* in everyday usage is emotionally charged with a judgment of some sort. This label can lock people out of conforming groups and push them into almost exclusive contact with people who have been similarly labeled.

IN SUM Symbolic interactionists examine how people's definitions of the situation underlie their deviating from or conforming to social norms. They focus on group membership (differential association), how people balance pressures to conform and to deviate (control theory), and the significance of the labels that are given to people (labeling theory).

The label *deviant* involves competing definitions and reactions to the same behavior. This central point of symbolic interactionism is explored in the Mass Media box on the next page.

The Functionalist Perspective

When we think of deviance, its dysfunctions are likely to come to mind. Functionalists, in contrast, are as likely to stress the functions of deviance as they are to emphasize its dysfunctions.

Can Deviance Really Be Functional for Society?

Most of us are upset by deviance, especially crime, and assume that society would be better off without it. The classic functionalist theorist Emile Durkheim (1893/1933, 1895/1964), however, came to a surprising conclusion. Deviance, he said—including crime—is functional for society, for it contributes to the social order. Its three main functions are:

1. *Deviance clarifies moral boundaries and affirms norms.* A group's ideas about how people should think and act mark its *moral boundaries*. Deviant acts challenge those boundaries. To call a member into account is to say, in effect, "You broke an important rule, and we cannot tolerate that." Punishing deviants affirms the group's norms and clarifies what it means to be a member of the group.
2. *Deviance promotes social unity.* To affirm the group's moral boundaries by punishing deviants fosters a "we" feeling among the group's members. In saying, "You can't get away with that," the group collectively affirms the rightness of its own ways.

mass Media in social life

Pornography on the Internet: Freedom Versus Censorship

Pornography vividly illustrates one of the sociological principles discussed in this chapter: the relativity of deviance. It is not the act, but reactions to the act, that make something deviant. Consider one of today's major issues, pornography on the Internet.

Web surfers have such a wide choice of pornography that some sites are indexed by race-ethnicity, hair color, body type, heterosexual or gay, single or group, teenagers, cheerleaders, and older women who "still think they have it." Some offer only photographs, others video. There also are live sites. After signing in and agreeing to the hefty per-minute charges, you can command your "model" to do anything your heart desires. The Internet sex industry even has an annual trade show, Internext. Predictions at Internext are that hotels will soon offer not just sex videos on demand but also live images of people having sex (Johnston 2007).

What is the problem? Why can't people exchange nude photos electronically if they want to? Or watch others having sex online, if someone offers that service?

Although some people object to any kind of sex site, what disturbs many are the sites that feature bondage, torture, rape, bestiality (humans having sex with animals), and sex with children.

The Internet abounds with chat rooms, where people "meet" online to discuss some topic. No one is bothered by the chat rooms where the topic is Roman architecture or rap music or sports. But those whose focus is how to torture women are another matter. So are those that offer lessons on how to seduce grade school children—or that extol the delights of having sex with three-year-olds.

The state and federal governments have passed laws against child pornography, and the police seize computers and search them for illegal pictures. The penalties can be severe. When photos of children in sex acts were found on an Arizona man's computer, he was sentenced to 200 years in prison (Greenhouse 2007). When he appealed his sentence as unconstitutional, his sentence was upheld. To exchange pictures of tortured and sexually abused women, however, remains legal.

for your Consideration

Some people feel that no matter how much they may disagree with a point of view or find it repugnant, communications about it (including photos and videos) must be allowed. They believe that if we let the government censor the Internet in any way, it will censor other communications. Do you think it should be legal to exchange photos of women being sexually abused or tortured? Should it be legal to discuss ways to seduce children? If not, on what basis should they be banned? If we make these activities illegal, then what other communications should we prohibit? On what basis?

Finally, can you disprove the central point of the symbolic interactionists—that an activity is deviant only because people decide that it is deviant? You may use examples cited in this box, or any others that you wish. You cannot invoke God or moral absolutes in your argument, however, as they are outside the field of sociology. Sociology cannot decide moral issues, even in extreme cases.

---

3. *Deviance promotes social change.* Groups do not always agree on what to do with people who push beyond their accepted ways of doing things. Some group members may even approve of the rule-breaking behavior. Boundary violations that gain enough support become new, acceptable behaviors. Thus, deviance may force a group to rethink and redefine its moral boundaries, helping groups—and whole societies—to change their customary ways.

Strain Theory: How Social Values Produce Deviance

Functionalists argue that crime is a *natural* part of society, not an aberration or some alien element in our midst. Indeed, they say, some mainstream values actually generate crime. To understand what they mean, consider what sociologists Richard Cloward and Lloyd Ohlin (1960) identified as the crucial problem of the industrialized world: the need to locate and train the most talented people of every generation—whether they were born into wealth or into poverty—so that they can take over the key technical jobs of society. When children are born, no one knows which ones will have the ability to become dentists, nuclear physicists, or engineers. To get the most talented people to compete with one another, society tries to motivate *everyone* to strive for success. It does this by arousing discontent—making people feel dissatisfied with what they have so that they will try to "better" themselves.

Most people, then, end up with strong desires to reach **cultural goals** such as wealth or high status, or to achieve whatever other objectives society holds out for them. However, not everyone has equal access to society's **institutionalized means,** the legitimate ways of achieving success. Some people find their path to education and good jobs blocked. These people experience *strain* or frustration, which may motivate them to take a deviant path.

This perspective, known as **strain theory,** was developed by sociologist Robert Merton (1956, 1968). People who experience strain, he said, are likely to feel *anomie*, a sense of normlessness. Because mainstream norms (such as working hard or pursuing higher education) don't seem to be getting them anywhere, people who experience strain find it difficult to identify with these norms. They may even feel wronged by the system, and its rules may seem illegitimate.

Table 8.1 compares people's reactions to cultural goals and institutionalized means. The first reaction, which Merton said is the most common, is *conformity,* using socially acceptable means to try to reach cultural goals. In industrialized societies most people try to get good jobs, a good education, and so on. If well-paid jobs are unavailable, they take less desirable jobs. If they are denied access to Harvard or Stanford, they go to a state university. Others take night classes and go to vocational schools. In short, most people take the socially acceptable road.

Four Deviant Paths   The remaining four responses, which are deviant, represent reactions to strain. Let's look at each. *Innovators* are people who accept the goals of society but use illegitimate means to try to reach them. Crack dealers, for instance, accept the goal of achieving wealth, but they reject the legitimate avenues for doing so. Other examples are embezzlers, robbers, and con artists.

The second deviant path is taken by people who become discouraged and give up on achieving cultural goals. Yet they still cling to conventional rules of conduct. Merton called this response *ritualism.* Although ritualists have given up on getting ahead at work, they survive by following the rules of their job. Teachers whose idealism is shattered (who are said to suffer from "burnout"), for example, remain in the classroom, where they teach without enthusiasm. Their response is considered deviant because they cling to the job even though they have abandoned the goal, which may have been to stimulate young minds or to make the world a better place.

People who choose the third deviant path, *retreatism*, reject both the cultural goals and the institutionalized means of achieving them. Those who drop out of the pursuit of success by way of alcohol or drugs are retreatists. Although their withdrawal takes them on a different path, women who enter a convent or men a monastery are also retreatists.

cultural goals the legitimate objectives held out to the members of a society

institutionalized means approved ways of reaching cultural goals

strain theory Robert Merton's term for the strain engendered when a society socializes large numbers of people to desire a cultural goal (such as success), but withholds from many the approved means of reaching that goal; one adaptation to the strain is crime, the choice of an innovative means (one outside the approved system) to attain the cultural goal

Table 8.1   How People Match Their Goals to Their Means

Do They Feel the Strain That Leads to Anomie?	Mode of Adaptation	Cultural Goals	Institutionalized Means
No	Conformity	Accept	Accept
	Deviant Paths:		
	1. Innovation	Accept	Reject
Yes	2. Ritualism	Reject	Accept
	3. Retreatism	Reject	Reject
	4. Rebellion	Reject/Replace	Reject/Replace

Source: Based on Merton 1968.

illegitimate opportunity structure opportunities for crimes that are woven into the texture of life

white-collar crime Edwin Sutherland's term for crimes committed by people of respectable and high social status in the course of their occupations; for example, bribery of public officials, securities violations, embezzlement, false advertising, and price fixing

corporate crime crimes committed by executives in order to benefit their corporation

The final type of deviant response is *rebellion.* Convinced that their society is corrupt, rebels, like retreatists, reject both society's goals and its institutionalized means. Unlike retreatists, however, rebels seek to give society new goals. Revolutionaries are the most committed type of rebels.

In sum: Strain theory underscores the sociological principle that deviants are the product of society. Mainstream social values (cultural goals and institutionalized means to reach those goals) can produce strain (frustration, dissatisfaction). People who feel this strain are more likely than others to take the deviant (nonconforming) paths summarized in Table 8.1.

Illegitimate Opportunity Structures: Social Class and Crime

One of the more interesting sociological findings in the study of deviance is that the social classes have distinct styles of crime. Let's see how unequal access to the institutionalized means to success helps to explain this.

Street Crime Functionalists point out that industrialized societies have no trouble socializing the poor into wanting to own things. Like others, the poor are bombarded with messages urging them to buy everything from X boxes and iPods to designer jeans and new cars. Television and movies show images of middle-class people enjoying luxurious lives. These images reinforce the myth that all full-fledged Americans can afford society's many goods and services.

In contrast, the school system, the most common route to success, often fails the poor. The middle class runs it, and there the children of the poor confront a bewildering world, one that is at odds with their background. Their speech, with its nonstandard grammar, is often sprinkled with what the middle class considers obscenities. Their ideas of punctuality, as well as their poor preparation in paper-and-pencil skills, are also a mismatch with their new environment. Facing such barriers, the poor are more likely than their more privileged counterparts to drop out of school. Educational failure, in turn, closes the door on many legitimate avenues to financial success.

Not infrequently, however, a different door opens to the poor, one that Cloward and Ohlin (1960) called **illegitimate opportunity structures.** Woven into the texture of life in urban slums, for example, are robbery, burglary, drug dealing, prostitution, pimping, gambling, and other crimes, commonly called "hustles" (Liebow 1967/1999; Sanchez-Jankowski 2003; Anderson 1978, 1990/2006). For many of the poor, the "hustler" is a role model—glamorous, in control, the image of "easy money," one of the few people in the area who comes close to attaining the cultural goal of success. For such reasons, then, these activities attract disproportionate numbers of the poor. As is discussed in the Down-to-Earth Sociology box on the next page, gangs are one way that the illegitimate opportunity structure beckons disadvantaged youth.

Social class divides people into such distinct ways of life that even crimes differ by social class. Jeffrey Skilling, former CEO of Enron Corporation, was convicted of 19 counts of fraud, conspiracy, and insider trading. The poor have neither the opportunity to commit these types of crimes nor the chance to make the huge profits they offer. In addition to his sentence of 24 years in prison, Skilling also had to pay back $45 million to victims of his crimes.

White-Collar Crime The more privileged social classes are not crime-free, of course, but for them different illegitimate opportunities beckon. They find *other forms* of crime to be functional. Physicians, for example, don't hold up cabbies, but many do cheat Medicare. You've heard about bookkeepers who embezzle from their employers and corporate officers who manipulate stock prices. In other words, rather than mugging, pimping, and committing burglary, the more privileged encounter "opportunities" for evading income tax, bribing public officials, embezzling, and so on. Sociologist Edwin Sutherland (1949) coined the term **white-collar crime** to refer to crimes that people of respectable and high social status commit in the course of their occupations.

A special form of white-collar crime is **corporate crime,** crimes committed by executives in order to benefit their corporation. For example, to increase corporate profits, Sears executives defrauded the poor of over $100 million. Their victims were so poor that they had filed for bankruptcy. To avoid a

Down-to-Earth Sociology

Islands in the Street: Urban Gangs in the United States

FOR MORE THAN TEN YEARS, sociologist Martín Sánchez Jankowski (1991) did participant observation of thirty-seven African American, Chicano, Dominican, Irish, Jamaican, and Puerto Rican gangs in Boston, Los Angeles, and New York City. The gangs earned money through gambling, arson, mugging, armed robbery, and selling moonshine, drugs, guns, stolen car parts, and protection. Jankowski ate, slept, and sometimes fought with the gangs, but by mutual agreement he did not participate in drug dealing or other illegal activities. He was seriously injured twice during the study.

Contrary to stereotypes, Jankowski did not find that the motive for joining was to escape a broken home (there were as many members from intact families as from broken homes) or to seek a substitute family (the same number of boys said they were close to their families as those that said they were not). Rather, the boys joined to gain access to money, to have recreation (including girls and drugs), to maintain anonymity in committing crimes, to get protection, and to help the community. This last reason may seem surprising, but in some neighborhoods, gangs protect residents from outsiders and spearhead political change (Kontos et al. 2003). The boys also saw the gang as an alternative to the dead-end—and deadening—jobs held by their parents.

Neighborhood residents are ambivalent about gangs. On the one hand, they fear the violence. On the other hand, many of the adults once belonged to gangs, some gangs provide better protection than the police, and gang members are the children of people who live in the neighborhood.

Particular gangs will come and go, but gangs will likely always remain part of the city. As functionalists point out, gangs fulfill needs of poor youth who live on the margins of society.

for your Consideration

What are the functions that gangs fulfill (the needs they meet)? Suppose that you have been hired as an urban planner by the City of Los Angeles. How could you arrange to meet the needs that gangs fulfill in ways that minimize violence and encourage youth to follow mainstream norms?

---

criminal trial, Sears pleaded guilty. This frightened the parent companies of Macy's and Bloomingdales, which had similar deceptive practices, and they settled with their debtors out of court (McCormick 1999). Similarly, Citigroup had to pay $70 million for preying on the poor (O'Brien 2004). None of the corporate thieves at Sears, Macy's, Bloomingdales, or Citigroup spent a day in jail.

Seldom is corporate crime taken seriously, even when it results in death. One of the most notorious corporate crimes involved the decision by Firestone executives to allow faulty tires to remain on U.S. vehicles—even though they were recalling the tires in Saudi Arabia and Venezuela. These tires cost the lives of about 200 Americans (White et al. 2001). No Firestone executive went to jail.

Consider this: Under federal law, causing the death of a worker by willfully violating safety rules is a misdemeanor punishable by up to six months in prison. Yet harassing a wild burro on federal lands is punishable by a year in prison (Barstow and Bergman 2003).

At $400 billion a year (Reiman 2004), "crime in the suites" actually costs more than "crime in the streets." This refers only to dollar costs. No one has yet figured out a way to compare, for example, the suffering experienced by a rape victim with the pain felt by an elderly couple who have lost their life savings to white-collar fraud.

The greatest concern of Americans, however, is street crime. They fear the violent stranger who will change their life forever. As the Social Map on the next page shows, the chances of such an encounter depend on where you live. From this map, you can see that entire regions are safer or more dangerous than others. In general, the northern states are the safest, and the southern states the most dangerous.

Figure 8.1 Some States Are Safer: Violent Crime in the United States

Violent crimes are murder, rape, robbery, and aggravated assault. As this figure illustrates, violent crime varies widely among the states. The chances of becoming a victim of these crimes are ten times higher in South Carolina, the most dangerous state, than in North Dakota, the safest state. Washington, D.C., not a state, is in a class by itself. Its rate of 1,371 is three times the national average and over 17 times North Dakota's rate.

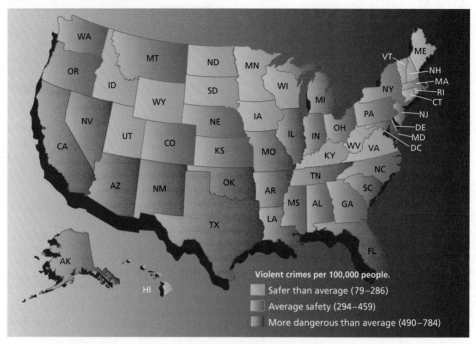

Violent crimes per 100,000 people.
- Safer than average (79–286)
- Average safety (294–459)
- More dangerous than average (490–784)

Source: By the author. Based on *Statistical Abstract of the United States* 2007:Table 297.

Gender and Crime A major change in the nature of crime is the growing number of female offenders. As Table 8.2 shows, women are committing a larger proportion of crime—from car theft to possession of illegal weapons. The basic reason for this increase is women's changed social location. As more women work in factories, corporations, and

Table 8.2 Women and Crime: What a Difference a Dozen Years Make

Of all those arrested, what percentage are women?

Crime	1992	2004	Change
Car Theft	10.8%	17.1%	+58%
Burglary	9.2%	14.2%	+54%
Stolen Property	12.5%	18.6%	+49%
Aggravated Assault	14.8%	20.6%	+39%
Drunken Driving	13.8%	18.6%	+35%
Robbery	8.5%	11.0%	+29%
Arson	13.4%	16.2%	+21%
Larceny/Theft	32.1%	38.2%	+19%
Illegal Drugs	16.4%	18.9%	+15%
Forgery and Counterfeiting	34.7%	39.7%	+14%
Illegal Weapons	7.5%	8.2%	+9%
Fraud	42.1%	45.0%	+7%

Source: By the author. Based on *Statistical Abstract of the United States* 2007:Table 317.

the professions, their opportunities for crime increase. Like men, women are also enticed by illegitimate opportunities.

IN SUM | Functionalists conclude that much street crime is the consequence of socializing everyone into equating success with owning material possessions, while denying many in the lower social classes the legitimate means to attain that success. People from higher social classes encounter different opportunities to commit crimes. The growing crime rates of women illustrate how changing gender roles are giving more women access to illegitimate opportunities.

Most white-collar crime is a harmless nuisance, but some brings horrible costs. Shown here is Alisha Parker, who, with three siblings, was burned when the gas tank of her 1979 Chevrolet Malibu exploded after a rear-end collision. Although General Motors executives knew about the problem with the Malibu gas tanks, they had ignored it. Outraged at the callousness of GM's conduct, the jury awarded these victims the staggering sum of $4.9 billion.

The Conflict Perspective

Class, Crime, and the Criminal Justice System

Two leading U.S. aerospace companies, Hughes Electronics and Boeing Satellite Systems, were accused of illegally exporting missile technology to China. The technology places the United States at risk, for it allowed China to improve its delivery system for nuclear weapons. The two companies pleaded guilty and paid fines. No executives went to jail. (Gerth 2003)

Contrast this corporate crime—which places you in danger—with stories in newspapers about people who are sentenced to several years in prison for stealing cars. How can a legal system that is supposed to provide "justice for all" be so inconsistent? According to conflict theorists, this question is central to the analysis of crime and the **criminal justice system**—the police, courts, and prisons that deal with people who are accused of having committed crimes. Let's see what conflict theorists have to say about this.

This 1871 wood engraving depicts children as they are being paid for their day's work in a London brickyard. In early capitalism, most street criminals came from the *marginal working class*, as did these children. It is the same today.

criminal justice system the system of police, courts, and prisons set up to deal with people who are accused of having committed a crime

"If you want justice, it's two hundred dollars an hour. Obstruction of justice runs a bit more."

The cartoonist's hyperbole makes an excellent commentary on the social class disparity of our criminal justic system. Not only are the crimes of the wealthy not as likely to come to the attention of authorities as are the crimes of the poor, but when they do, the wealthy can afford legal expertise that the poor cannot.

Power and Inequality

Conflict theorists regard power and social inequality as the main characteristics of society. They stress that the power elite that runs society also controls the criminal justice system. This group makes certain that laws are passed that will protect its position in society. Other norms, such as those that govern informal behavior (chewing with a closed mouth, appearing in public with combed hair, and so on), may come from other sources, but they are not as important. Such norms influence our everyday behavior, but they do not determine who has power or who gets sent to prison.

Conflict theorists see the most fundamental division in capitalist society as that between the few who own the means of production and the many who sell their labor. Those who buy labor, and thereby control workers, make up the **capitalist class;** those who sell their labor form the **working class.** Toward the most depressed end of the working class is the **marginal working class:** people who have few skills, who are subject to layoffs, and whose jobs are low paying, part time, or seasonal. This class is marked by unemployment and poverty. From its ranks come most of the prison inmates in the United States. Desperate, these people commit street crimes, and because their crimes threaten the social order that keeps the elite in power, they are punished severely.

The Law as an Instrument of Oppression

According to conflict theorists, the idea that the law operates impartially and administers a code that is shared by all is a cultural myth promoted by the capitalist class. These theorists see the law as an instrument of oppression, a tool designed by the powerful to maintain their privileged position (Spitzer 1975; Reiman 2004; Chambliss 2000, 2007). Because the working class has the potential to rebel and overthrow the current social order, when its members get out of line, the law comes down hard on them.

For this reason, the criminal justice system does not focus on the owners of corporations and the harm they do through manufacturing unsafe products, creating pollution, and manipulating prices—or the crimes of Hughes and Boeing mentioned on the previous page. Instead, it directs its energies against violations by the working class. The violations of the capitalist class cannot be ignored totally, however, for if they become too outrageous or oppressive, the working class might rise up and revolt. To prevent this, a flagrant violation by a member of the capitalist class is occasionally prosecuted. The publicity given to the case helps to stabilize the social system by providing evidence of the "fairness" of the criminal justice system.

Usually, however, the powerful are able to bypass the courts altogether, appearing instead before an agency that has no power to imprison (such as the Federal Trade Commission). People from wealthy backgrounds who sympathize with the intricacies of the corporate world direct these agencies. It is they who oversee most cases of manipulating the price of stocks, insider trading, violating fiduciary duty, and so on. Is it surprising, then, that the typical sanction for corporate crime is a token fine?

When groups that have been denied access to power gain that access, we can expect to see changes in the legal system. This is precisely what is occurring now. Racial-ethnic minorities and homosexuals, for example, have more political power today than ever before. In line with conflict theory, a new category called *hate crime* has been formulated. We analyze this change in a different context on pages 228–229.

capitalist class the wealthy who own the means of production and buy the labor of the working class

working class those people who sell their labor to the capitalist class

marginal working class the most desperate members of the working class, who have few skills, little job security, and are often unemployed

IN SUM From the perspective of conflict theory, the small penalties that are imposed for crimes committed by the powerful are typical of a legal system that has been designed by the elite (capitalists) to keep themselves in power, to control workers, and, ultimately, to stabilize the social order. From this perspective, law enforcement is a cultural device through which the capitalist class carries out self-protective and repressive policies.

Reactions to Deviance

Whether it involves cheating on a sociology quiz or holding up a liquor store, any violation of norms invites reaction. Reactions, though, vary with culture. Before we examine reactions in the United States, let's take a little side trip to Greenland, an island nation three times the size of Texas located between Canada and Denmark. I think you'll enjoy this little excursion in cultural diversity.

Cultural Diversity *around the* World

"What Kind of Prison Is This?"

THE PRISON IN NUUK, the capital of Greenland, has no wall around it. It has no fence. It doesn't even have bars.

The other day, Meeraq Lendenhann, a convicted rapist, walked out of prison. He didn't run or hide. He just walked out. Meeraq went to a store he likes to shop at, bought a CD of his favorite group, U2, and then walked back to the prison.

If Meeraq tires of listening to music, he can send e-mail and play games on a computer. Like other prisoners, he also has a personal TV with satellite hookup.

The prison holds 60 prisoners—the country's killers, rapists, and a few thieves. The prisoners leave the prison to work at regular jobs, where they average $28,000 or so a year. But they have to return to the prison after work. And they are locked into their rooms at 9:30.

The prisoners have to work, because the prison charges them $150 a week for room and board. The extra money goes into their savings accounts, or to help support their families.

And, of course, the prisoners can have guns. At least during the summer. A major summer sport for Greenlanders is hunting reindeer and seals. Prisoners don't want to miss out on the fun, so if they ask, they are given shotguns.

But gun use isn't as easy as it sounds. Judges have set a severe requirement: The prisoners have to be accompanied by armed guards. If that isn't bad enough, the judges have added another requirement—that the prisoners not get drunk while they hunt.

One woman prisoner who said she was going to a beauty salon got sidetracked and went to a bar instead. When it got late and she was quite drunk, she called the prison and asked somone to come and get her.

If someone from another culture asks about the prisoners running away, the head of the prison says, "Where would they run? It's warm inside, and cold outside."

Then, of course, the prisoners probably wouldn't want to miss breakfast—a buffet of five kinds of imported cheese, various breads, marmalade, honey, coffee, and tea.

—Based on Naik 2004.

for your Consideration

Greenland's unique approach arose out of its history of hunting and fishing for a living. If men were locked up, they wouldn't be able to hunt or fish, and their families would suffer. From this history has come the main goal of Greenland's prison—to integrate offenders into society. This treatment helps prisoners slip back into village life after they have served their sentence. The incorrigibles, those who remain dangerous, about 20 men—are sent to a prison in Copenhagen, Denmark. Meeraq, the rapist, is given injections of androcur, a testosterone-reducing drug that lowers his sex drive. Alcoholics are given antabuse, a drug that triggers nasty reactions if someone drinks alcohol.

How do you think we could apply Greenland's approach to the United States?

Street Crime and Prisons

Let's turn back to the United States. Figure 8.2 illustrates the remarkable growth in the U.S. prison population. The number of prisoners is actually higher than the total shown in this figure. If we add jail inmates, the total comes to over two million people—one out of every 143 citizens. Not only does the United States have more prisoners than any other nation, but it also has a larger percentage of its population in prison as well. The number of prisoners has grown so fast that the states have had to hire private companies to operate jails for them. About 110,000 prisoners are in these "private" jails (*Sourcebook of Criminal Justice Statistics* 2006:Table 6.32).

To better understand U.S. prisoners, let's compare them with the U.S. population. As you look at Table 8.3 on the next page, several things may strike you. Almost all prisoners (87 percent) are ages 18 to 44, and almost all of them are men. Then there is this remarkable statistic: Although African Americans make up just 12.8 percent of the U.S. population, close to half of all prisoners are African Americans. On any given day, about

| Figure 8.2 | **How Much Is Enough? The Explosion in the Number of U.S. Prisoners** |

To better understand how remarkable this change is, compare the increase in U.S. prisoners with the increase in the U.S. population. Between 1970 and 2004, the U.S. population increased 43 percent, while the number of prisoners increased 764 percent, *18 times greater*. If the number of prisoners had grown at the same rate as the U.S. population, there would be about 280,000 prisoners, only 13 percent of today's total. (Or, if the U.S. population had increased at the same rate as that of U.S. prisoners, the U.S. population would be 3,650,000,000—more than the population of China, India, Canada, Mexico, and all of Europe combined.)

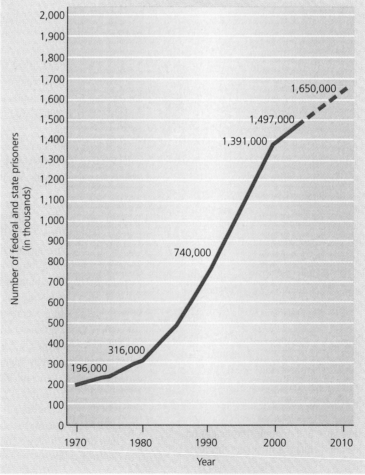

Sources: By the author. Based on *Statistical Abstract of the United States* 1995:Table 349; 2007:Table 334. The broken line is the author's estimate.

Table 8.3 Inmates in U.S. State Prisons

Characteristics	Percentage of Prisoners with These Characteristics	Percentage of U.S. Population with These Characteristics
Age		
18–24	26.4%	9.9%
25–34	35.4%	13.5%
35–44	25.2%	14.8%
45–54	10.4%	14.3%
55 and older	1.0%	22.7%
Race-Ethnicity		
African American	47.3%	12.8%
White	36.9%	66.9%
Latino	14.2%	14.4%
Asian Americans	0.6%	4.3%
Native Americans	0.9%	1.0%
Sex		
Male	93.4%	49.3%
Female	6.3%	50.7%
Marital Status		
Never Married	59.8%	28.2%
Divorced	15.5%	10.2%
Married	17.3%	58.6%
Widowed	1.1%	6.4%
Education		
Less than high school	39.7%	14.8%
High school graduate	49.0%	32.2%
Some college	9.0%	25.4%
College graduate (BA or higher)	2.4%	27.6%

Source: By the author. Based on *Sourcebook of Criminal Justice Statisitcs* 2003:Tables 6.000b, 6.28; 2006:Tables 6.34, 6.45; *Statistical Abstract of the United States* 2007:Tables 12, 14, 23, 55, 216.

one out of eight African American men ages 20 to 34 is in jail or prison (Butterfield 2003). Finally, note how marriage and education—two of the major techniques society has of "anchoring" us—provide protection from prison.

As I mentioned earlier, social class funnels some people into the criminal justice system and diverts others away from it. This table illuminates the power of education, a major component of social class. You can see how people who drop out of high school have a high chance of ending up in prison—and how unlikely it is for a college graduate to have this unwelcome destination in life.

For about the past 20 years or so, the United States has followed a "get tough" policy. "Three strikes and you're out" laws upon conviction for a third felony have become common. When someone is convicted of a third felony, judges are required to give a mandatory sentence, sometimes life imprisonment. While few of us would feel sympathy if a man convicted of a third brutal rape or a third murder were sent to prison for life, these laws have had unanticipated consequences, as you will see in the following Thinking Critically section.

Thinking Critically

"Three Strikes and You're Out!" Unintended Consequences of Well-Intended Laws

In the 1980s, the violent crime rate soared. Americans grew fearful, and they demanded that their lawmakers do something. Politicians heard the message, and they responded by passing the recidivism rate the proportion of released convicts who are rearrested

"three strikes" law. Anyone who is convicted of a third felony receives an automatic mandatory sentence. Judges are not allowed to consider the circumstances. Some mandatory sentences carry life imprisonment.

In their haste to appease the public, the politicians did not limit the three-strike laws to *violent* crimes. And they did not consider that some minor crimes are considered felonies. As the functionalists would say, this has led to unanticipated consequences.

Here are some actual cases:

- In Los Angeles, a 27-year-old man was sentenced to 25 years for stealing a pizza (Cloud 1998).
- In New York City, a man who was about to be sentenced for selling crack said to the judge, "I'm only 19. This is terrible." He then hurled himself out of a courtroom window, plunging to his death sixteen stories below (Cloud 1998).
- In Sacramento, a man who passed himself off as Tiger Woods to go on a $17,000 shopping spree was sentenced to 200 years in prison (Reuters 2001).
- In California, a man who stole 9 videotapes from Kmart was sentenced to 50 years in prison without parole. He appealed to the U.S. Supreme Court, which upheld his sentence (Greenhouse 2003).
- In Utah, a 25-year-old was sentenced to 55 years in prison for selling small bags of marijuana to a police informant. The judge who sentenced the man said the sentence was unjust (Madigan 2004).

for your Consideration

Apply the symbolic interactionist, functionalist, and conflict perspectives to mandatory sentencing. For *symbolic interactionism*, what do these laws represent to the public? How does your answer differ depending on what part of "the public" you are referring to? For *functionalism*, who benefits from these laws? What are some of their dysfunctions? For the *conflict perspective*, what groups are in conflict? Who has the power to enforce their will on others?

The Decline in Violent Crime

As you saw in Figure 8.2, judges have put more and more people in prison. In addition, legislators passed the three-strikes laws and reduced early releases of prisoners. As these changes occurred, the crime rate dropped sharply, which has led to a controversy in sociology. Some sociologists conclude that getting tough on criminals was the main reason for the drop in violent crime (Conklin 2003). Others point to higher employment, a drop in drug use, and even abortion (Rosenfeld 2002; Reiman 2004; Blumstein and Wallman 2006). This matter is not yet settled, but both tough sentencing and the economy seem to be important factors.

Recidivism

A major problem with prisons is that they fail to teach their clients to stay away from crime. Our **recidivism rate**—the percentage of former prisoners who are rearrested—is high. For those who are sentenced to prison for crimes of violence, within just three

Beneath the humor of this cartoon lies a serious point about the high recidivism of U.S. prisoners.

Figure 8.3   Recidivism of U.S. Prisoners

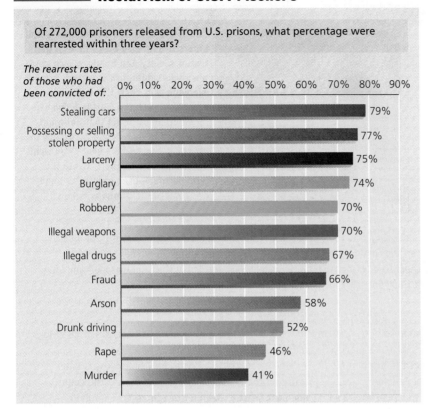

Of 272,000 prisoners released from U.S. prisons, what percentage were rearrested within three years?

The rearrest rates of those who had been convicted of:

- Stealing cars — 79%
- Possessing or selling stolen property — 77%
- Larceny — 75%
- Burglary — 74%
- Robbery — 70%
- Illegal weapons — 70%
- Illegal drugs — 67%
- Fraud — 66%
- Arson — 58%
- Drunk driving — 52%
- Rape — 46%
- Murder — 41%

Note: The individuals were not necessarily rearrested for the same crime for which they had originally been imprisoned.
Source: By the author. Based on *Sourcebook of Criminal Justice Statistics* 2003:Table 6.50.

years of their release, two out of three (62 percent) are rearrested, and half (52 percent) are back in prison (*Sourcebook of Criminal Justice Statistics* 2003:Table 6.52). Figure 8.3 shows recidivism by type of crime. It is safe to conclude that if—and this is a big if—the purpose of prisons is to teach people that crime doesn't pay, they are colossal failures.

The Death Penalty and Bias

Capital punishment, the death penalty, is the most extreme measure the state takes. The death penalty is mired in controversy, arousing impassioned opposition and support on both moral and philosophical grounds. Advances in DNA testing have given opponents of the death penalty a strong argument: Innocent people have been sent to death row, and some have been executed. Others are passionate about retaining the death penalty, pointing to such crimes as those of the serial killers discussed in the Down-to-Earth Sociology box on the next page.

Apart from anyone's personal position on the death penalty, it certainly is clear that the death penalty is not administered evenly. Consider geography: The Social Map on page 227 shows that where people commit murder greatly affects their chances of being put to death.

The death penalty also shows social class bias. As you know from news reports on murder and sentencing, it is rare for a rich person to be sentenced to death. Although the government does not collect statistics on social class and the death penalty, this common observation is borne out by the average education of the prisoners on death row. *Most* prisoners on death row (51 percent) have not finished high school (*Sourcebook of Criminal Justice Statistics* 2006:Table 6.81).

Figure 8.5 on page 228 shows gender bias in the death penalty. It is almost unheard of for a woman to be sentenced to death. Although women commit 9.6 percent of the

capital punishment the death penalty

Down-to-Earth Sociology

The Killer Next Door: Serial Murderers in Our Midst

I WAS STUNNED BY THE IMAGES. Television cameras showed the Houston police digging up dozens of bodies from under a boat storage shed. Fascinated, I waited impatiently for spring break. A few days later, I drove from Illinois to Houston, where 33-year-old Dean Corll had befriended Elmer Wayne Henley and David Brooks, two teenagers from broken homes. Together, they had killed 27 boys. Elmer and David would pick up young hitchhikers and deliver them to Corll to rape and kill. Sometimes they even brought him their high school classmates.

I talked to one of Elmer's neighbors, as he was painting his front porch. His 15-year-old son had gone to get a haircut one Saturday morning; it was the last time he had seen his son alive. The police insisted that the boy had run away, and they refused to investigate. On a city map, I plotted the locations of the homes of the local murder victims. Many clustered around the homes of the teenage killers.

I was going to spend my coming sabbatical writing a novel on this case, but, to be frank, I became frightened and didn't write the book. I didn't know if I could recover psychologically if I were to immerse myself in grisly details day after day for months on end. One of these details was a piece of plywood, with a hole in each of its four corners. Corll and the boys would spreadeagle their victims handcuffed to the plywood. There, they would torture the boys (no girl victims) for hours. Sometimes, they would even pause to order pizza.

My interviews confirmed what has since become common knowledge about serial killers: They lead double lives so successfully that their friends and family are unaware of their criminal activities. Henley's mother swore to me that her son was a good boy and couldn't possibly be guilty. Some of his high school friends told me the same thing. They stressed that Elmer couldn't be involved in homosexual rape and murder because he was interested only in girls. I conducted my interviews in Henley's bedroom, and for proof of what they told me, his friends pointed to a pair of girls' panties that were draped across a lamp shade.

Serial murder is the killing of several victims in three or more separate events. The murders may occur over several days, weeks, or years. The elapsed time between murders distinguishes serial killers from *mass murderers*, who do their killing all at once. Here are some infamous examples:

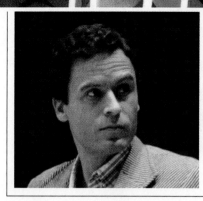

One of the striking traits of most serial killers is how they blend in with the rest of society. Ted Bundy, shown here, was remarkable in this respect. Almost everyone who knew this law student liked him. Even the Florida judge who found him guilty said that he would have liked to have him practice law in his court, but, as he added, "You went the wrong way, partner." (Note the term partner—used even after Bundy was convicted of heinous crimes.)

- Between 1962 and 1964, Albert De Salvo ("the Boston Strangler") raped and killed 13 women.
- During the 1960s and 1970s, Ted Bundy raped and killed dozens of women in four states.
- In the 1970s, John Wayne Gacy raped and killed 33 young men in Chicago.
- Between 1979 and 1981, Wayne Williams killed 28 boys and young men in Atlanta.
- During the 1980s and 1990s, the "Green River" killer scattered the bodies of prostitutes around the countryside near Seattle, Washington. In 2003, Gary Ridgway was convicted of the crimes and given 48 consecutive life sentences for killing 48 women.
- In 2005, in Wichita, Kansas, Dennis Rader pleaded guilty as the BTK (Bind, Torture, and Kill) strangler, a name he had proudly given himself. His 10 killings spanned 1974 to 1991.
- The serial killer with the most victims appears to be Harold Shipman of Manchester, England. From 1977 to 2000, this quiet, unassuming physician killed 230 to 275 of his elderly women patients. While making housecalls, he gave the women lethal injections.
- One of the most bizarre serial killers was Jeffrey Dahmer of Milwaukee. Dahmer fried and ate parts of his victims. When he did, he felt a "unity" with the victim.

Almost all serial killers are men, but an occasional woman joins this list of infamy:

- In North Carolina, Blanche Taylor Moore used arsenic to kill her father, her first husband, and a boyfriend. She was tripped up in 1986 when she tried to poison her current husband.
- In 1987 and 1988, Dorothea Montalvo Puente, who operated a boarding house in Sacramento, killed 7 of her boarders. Her motive was to collect their Social Security checks.
- In Missouri, from 1986 to 1989, Faye Copeland and her husband killed 5 transient men.
- In the late 1980s and early 1990s, Aileen Wuornos, hitchhiking along Florida's freeways, killed 7 men after having sex with them.

Many serial killers are motivated by lust and are sexually aroused by killing, so the FBI sometimes uses the term "lust murder." As with Ted Bundy and Jeffrey Dahmer, some have sex with their dead victims. Bundy returned day after day to the countryside to copulate with the corpses of his victims. Other serial killers, however, are more "garden variety," motivated by greed, like Dorothea Puente, who killed for money.

Is serial murder more common now than it used to be? Not likely. In the past, police departments had little communication with one another. When killings occurred in different jurisdictions, seldom did anyone connect them.

Today's more efficient communications, investigative techniques, and DNA matching make it easier for the police to conclude that a serial killer is operating in an area. Part of the perception that there are more serial killers today is also due to ignorance of our history: In our frontier past, serial killers went from ranch to ranch. Some would say that mass murderers wiped out entire villages of Native Americans.

for your Consideration

Do you think that serial killers should be given the death penalty? Why or why not? How do your social locations influence your opinion?

murders, they make up only 1.6 percent of death row inmates (*Sourcebook of Criminal Justice Statistics* 2006:Table 3.129). It is possible that this statistic reflects not only gender bias but also the relative brutality of the women's murders. We need research to determine this.

Bias used to be so flagrant that it once put a stop to the death penalty. Donald Partington (1965), a lawyer in Virginia, was shocked by the bias he saw in the courtroom, and he decided to document it. He found that 2,798 men had been convicted for rape and attempted rape in Virginia between 1908 and 1963—56 percent whites and 44 percent blacks. For attempted rape, 13 had been executed. For rape, 41 men had been executed. *All those executed were black.* Not one of the whites was executed.

After listening to evidence like this, in 1972 the Supreme Court ruled in *Furman* v. *Georgia* that the death penalty, as applied, was unconstitutional. The execution of prisoners stopped—but not for long. The states wrote new laws, and in 1977 they again began to execute prisoners. Since then, 67 percent of those put to death have been white and 33 percent African American (*Statistical Abstract* 2007:Table 340). (Latinos are evidently counted as whites in this statistic.) Table 8.4 on the next page shows the race-ethnicity of the prisoners who are on death row.

serial murder the killing of several victims in three or more separate events

Figure 8.4 **Executions in the United States**

Executions since 1977, when the death penalty was reinstated.

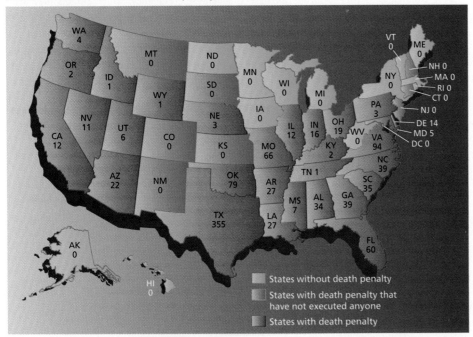

Source: By the author. Based on *Statistical Abstract of the United States* 2007:Table 341.

Figure 8.5 Women and Men on Death Row

98.4%

Men | Women

1.6%

Source: By the author. Based on
Sourcebook of Criminal Justice Statistics
2006:Table 6.81.

Table 8.4 The Racial-Ethnicity of the 3,486 Prisoners on Death Row

	Percentage	
	on Death Row	in U.S. Population
Whites	45%	68%
African Americans	42%	12%
Latinos	11%	14%
Asian Americans	1%	4%
Native Americans	1%	1%

Source: By the author. Based on Sourcebook of Criminal Justice Statistics 2007:Table 6.80 and Figure 12.5 of this text.

Legal Change

Did you know that it is a crime in Saudi Arabia for a woman to drive a car (Fattah 2007)? A crime in Florida to sell alcohol before 1 p.m. on Sundays? Or illegal in Wells, Maine, to advertise on tombstones? As has been stressed in this chapter, deviance, including the form called *crime*, is relative. It varies from one society to another, and from group to group within a society. Crime also varies from one time period to another, as opinions change or as different groups gain access to power.

Hate crimes are an example of legal change, the topic of the next Thinking Critically Section.

Thinking Critically

Changing Views: Making Hate a Crime

Because crime consists of whatever acts authorities decide to assign that label, new crimes emerge from time to time. A prime example is juvenile delinquency, which Illinois lawmakers designated a separate type of crime in 1899. Juveniles committed crimes before this time, of course, but youths were not considered to be a separate type of lawbreaker. They were just young people who committed crimes, and they were treated the same as adults who committed the same crime. Sometimes new technology leads to new crimes. Motor vehicle theft, a separate crime in the United States, obviously did not exist before the automobile was invented.

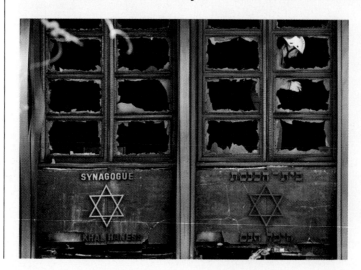

Hate crimes, which range from murder and injury to defacing property with symbols of hatred, include arson, the suspected cause of the fire at this synagogue.

In the 1980s, another new crime was born when state governments developed the classification **hate crime.** This is a crime that is motivated by *bias* (dislike, hatred) against someone's race-ethnicity, religion, sexual orientation, disability, or national origin. Before this, of course, people attacked others or destroyed their property out of these same motivations, but in those cases the motivation was not the issue. If someone injured or killed another person because of that person's race-ethnicity, religion, sexual orientation, national origin, or disability, he or she was charged with assault or murder. Today, motivation has become a central issue, and hate crimes carry more severe sentences than do the same acts that do not have hatred as their motive. Table 8.5 summarizes the victims of hate crimes.

We can be certain that the "evolution" of crime is not yet complete. As society changes and as different groups gain access to power, we can expect the definitions of crime to change accordingly.

Table 8.5 Hate Crimes	
Directed Against	**Number of Victims**
Race-Ethnicity	
African Americans	3,494
Whites	1,027
Latinos	646
Asian Americans	272
Native Americans	102
Religion	
Jews	1,086
Muslims	202
Catholics	68
Protestants	48
Sexual Orientation	
Male Homosexual	902
Homosexual (general)	314
Female Homosexual	213
Heterosexual	32
Bisexual	18
Disabilities	
Mental	49
Physical	24

Source: *Statistical Abstract of the United States* 2007:Table 308.

for your Consideration

Why should we have a separate classification called hate crime? Why aren't the crimes of assault, robbery, and murder adequate? As one analyst (Sullivan 1999) said: "Was the brutal murder of gay college student Matthew Shepard [a hate crime] in Laramie, Wyoming, in 1998 worse than the abduction, rape, and murder of an eight-year-old Laramie girl [not a hate crime] by a pedophile that same year?"

How do you think your social location (race-ethnicity, gender, social class, sexual orientation, or physical ability) affects your opinion?

The Trouble with Official Statistics

Both the findings of symbolic interactionists (that stereotypes operate when authorities deal with groups such as the Saints and the Roughnecks) and the conclusion of conflict theorists (that the criminal justice system exists to serve the ruling elite) demonstrate the need for caution in interpreting official statistics. Crime statistics do not have an objective, independent existence. They are not like oranges that you pick out in a grocery store. Rather, crime statistics are a human creation. One major element in producing them is the particular laws that exist. Another is how those laws are enforced. Still another is how officials report their statistics. Change these factors, and the statistics also change.

Consider this: According to official statistics, working-class boys are clearly more delinquent than middle-class boys. Yet, as we have seen, who actually gets arrested for what is influenced by social class, a point that has far-reaching implications. As symbolic interactionists point out, the police follow a symbolic system as they enforce the law. Their ideas of "typical criminals" and "typical good citizens," for example, permeate their work. The more a suspect matches their stereotypes (which they call "criminal profiles"), the more likely that person is to be arrested. **Police discretion,** the decision of whether to arrest someone or even to ignore a matter, is a routine part of police work. Consequently, official crime statistics always reflect these and many other biases.

hate crime crimes to which more severe penalties are attached because they are motivated by hatred (dislike, animosity) of someone's race-ethnicity, religion, sexual orientation, disability, or national origin

police discretion the practice of the police, in the normal course of their duties, to either arrest or ticket someone for an offense or to overlook the matter

Reactions to deviants vary from such mild sanctions as frowns and stares to such severe responses as imprisonment and death. Some sanctions are formal—court hearings, for example—but most are informal, as when friends refuse to talk to each other. One sanction is to label someone a deviant, which can have powerful consequences for the person's life, especially if the label closes off conforming activities and opens deviant ones. The degradation ceremony, in which someone is publicly labeled "not one of us," is a powerful sanction. So is imprisonment. Official statistics must be viewed with caution, for they reflect biases.

The Medicalization of Deviance: Mental Illness

Another way in which society deals with deviance is to "medicalize" it. Let's look at what this entails.

Neither Mental Nor Illness?   To *medicalize* something is to make it a medical matter, to classify it as a form of illness that properly belongs in the care of physicians. For the past hundred years or so, especially since the time of Sigmund Freud (1856–1939), the Viennese physician who founded psychoanalysis, there has been a growing tendency toward the **medicalization of deviance.** In this view, deviance, including crime, is a sign of mental sickness. Rape, murder, stealing, cheating, and so on are external symptoms of internal disorders, consequences of a confused or tortured mind.

Thomas Szasz (1986, 1996, 1998), a renegade in his profession of psychiatry, argues that *mental illnesses are neither mental nor illnesses. They are simply problem behaviors.* Some forms of so-called mental illnesses have organic causes; that is, they are *physical* illnesses that result in unusual perceptions or behavior. Some depression, for example, is caused by a chemical imbalance in the brain, which can be treated by drugs. The depression, however, may appear in the forms of crying, long-term sadness, and lack of interest in family, work, school, or one's appearance. When someone becomes deviant in ways that disturb others, *and* when these others cannot find a satisfying explanation for why the person is "like that," a "sickness in the head" is often taken as the cause of the unacceptable behavior.

Attention deficit disorder (ADD) is an excellent example. As Szasz says, "No one explains where this disease came from, why it didn't exist 50 years ago. No one is able to diagnose it with objective tests." It is diagnosed by a teacher or a parent complaining about a child misbehaving. Misbehaving children have been a problem throughout history, but now their problem behavior has become a sign of mental illness.

All of us have troubles. Some of us face a constant barrage of problems as we go through life. Most of us continue the struggle, perhaps encouraged by relatives and friends and motivated by job, family responsibilities, religious faith, and life goals. Even when the odds seem hopeless, we carry on, not perfectly, but as best we can.

Some people, however, fail to cope well with life's challenges. Overwhelmed, they become depressed, uncooperative, or hostile. Some strike out at others, while some, in Merton's terms, become retreatists and withdraw into their apartments or homes, not wanting to come out. These are *behaviors, not mental illnesses*, stresses Szasz. They may be inappropriate coping devices, but they are coping devices nevertheless, not mental illnesses. Thus, Szasz concludes that "mental illness" is a myth foisted on a naive public by a medical profession that uses pseudoscientific jargon in order to expand its area of control and force nonconforming people to accept society's definitions of "normal."

Szasz's extreme claim forces us to look anew at the forms of deviance that we usually refer to as mental illness. To explain behavior that people find bizarre, he directs our attention not to causes hidden deep within the "subconscious," but, instead, to how people learn such behaviors. To ask, "What is the origin of someone's inappropriate or bizarre behavior?" then becomes similar to asking "Why do some women steal?" "Why do some men rape?" "Why do some teenagers cuss their parents and stalk out of

medicalization of deviance to make deviance a medical matter, a symptom of some underlying illness that needs to be treated by physicians

People whose behaviors violate norms often are called mentally ill. "Why else would they do such things?" is a common response to deviant behaviors that we don't understand. Mental illness is a label that contains the assumption that there is something wrong "within" people that "causes" their disapproved behavior. The surprise with this man, who changed his legal name to "Scary Guy," is that he speaks at schools across the country, where he promotes acceptance, awareness, love, and understanding.

the room, slamming the door?" *The answers depend on those people's particular experiences in life, not on an illness in their mind.* In short, some sociologists find Szasz's renegade analysis refreshing because it indicates that *social experiences*, not some illness of the mind, underlie bizarre behaviors—as well as deviance in general.

The Homeless Mentally Ill

Jamie was sitting on a low wall surrounding the landscaped courtyard of an exclusive restaurant. She appeared unaware of the stares that were elicited by her layers of mismatched clothing, her matted hair and dirty face, and the shopping cart that overflowed with her meager possessions.

When I saw Jamie point to the street and concentrate, slowly moving her finger horizontally. I asked her what she was doing.

"I'm directing traffic," she replied. "I control where the cars go. Look, that one turned right there," she said, now withdrawing her finger.

"Really?" I said.

After a while she confided that her cart talked to her.

"Really?" I said again.

"Yes," she replied. "You can hear it, too." At that, she pushed the shopping cart a bit.

"Did you hear that?" she asked.

When I shook my head, she demonstrated again. Then it hit me. She was referring to the squeaking wheels!

I nodded.

When I left, Jamie was pointing to the sky, for, as she told me, she also controlled the flight of airplanes.

To most of us, Jamie's behavior and thinking are bizarre. They simply do not match any reality we know. Could you or I become like Jamie?

Suppose for a bitter moment that you are homeless and have to live on the streets. You have no money, no place to sleep, no bathroom. You do not know *if* you are going to eat, much less where. You have no friends or anyone you can trust, and you live in constant fear of rape and other violence. Do you think this might be enough to drive you over the edge?

Consider just the problems involved in not having a place to bathe. (Shelters are often so dangerous that many homeless people prefer to sleep in public settings.) At first, you try to wash in the rest rooms of gas stations, bars, the bus station, or a shopping center. But you are dirty, and people stare when you enter and call the management when they see you wash your feet in the sink. You are thrown out and told in no uncertain terms never to come back. So you get dirtier and dirtier. Eventually, you come to think of being dirty as a fact of life. Soon, maybe, you don't even care. The stares no longer bother you—at least not as much.

No one will talk to you, and you withdraw more and more into yourself. You begin to build a fantasy life. You talk openly to yourself. People stare, but so what? They stare anyway. Besides, they are no longer important to you.

Jamie might be mentally ill. Some organic problem, such as a chemical imbalance in her brain, might underlie her behavior. But perhaps not. How long would it take you to exhibit bizarre behaviors if you were homeless—and hopeless? The point is that *just being on the streets can cause mental illness*—or whatever we want to label socially inappropriate behaviors that we find difficult to classify. *Homelessness and mental illness are reciprocal:* Just as "mental illness" can cause homelessness, so the trials of being homeless, of living on cold, hostile streets, can lead to unusual thinking and behaviors.

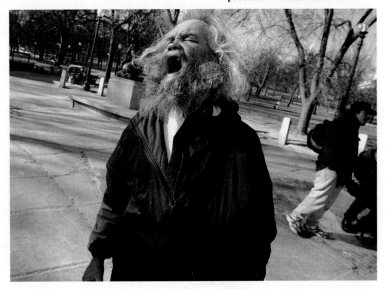

Mental illness is common among the homeless. This man, who hangs out near Boston Commons in Boston, Massachusetts, has been homeless for 44 years. This gives you an idea of the depth of the problem of rehabilitation.

The Need for a More Humane Approach

As Durkheim (1895/1964:68) pointed out, deviance is inevitable—even in a group of saints.

> Imagine a society of saints, a perfect cloister of exemplary individuals. Crimes, properly so called, will there be unknown; but faults which appear [invisible] to the layman will create there the same scandal that the ordinary offense does in ordinary [society].

With deviance inevitable, one measure of a society is how it treats its deviants. Our prisons certainly don't say much good about U.S. society. Filled with the poor, they are warehouses of the unwanted. They reflect patterns of broad discrimination in our larger society. White-collar criminals continue to get by with a slap on the wrist while street criminals are punished severely. Some deviants, who fail to meet current standards of admission to either prison or mental hospital, take refuge in shelters, as well as in cardboard boxes tucked away in urban recesses. Although no one has *the* answer, it does not take much reflection to see that there are more humane approaches than these.

Because deviance is inevitable, the larger issues are to find ways to protect people from deviant behaviors that are harmful to themselves or others, to tolerate those behaviors that are not harmful, and to develop systems of fairer treatment for deviants. In the absence of fundamental changes that would bring about a truly equitable social system, most efforts are, unfortunately, like putting a Band Aid on a gunshot wound. What we need is a more humane social system, one that would prevent the social inequalities that are the focus of the next four chapters.

Summary *and* Review

What Is Deviance?

From a sociological perspective, **deviance** (the violation of norms) is relative. What people consider deviant varies from one culture to another and from group to group within the same society. As symbolic interactionists stress, it is not the act, but the reactions to the act, that make something deviant. All groups develop systems of **social control** to punish **deviants**—those who violate their norms. Pp. 204–208.

How do sociological and individualistic explanations of deviance differ?

To explain why people deviate, sociobiologists and psychologists look for reasons *within* the individual, such as **genetic predispositions** or **personality disorders.** Sociologists, in contrast, look for explanations *outside* the individual, in social experiences. Pp. 208–209.

The Symbolic Interactionist Perspective

How do symbolic interactionists explain deviance?

Symbolic interactionists have developed several theories to explain deviance such as **crime** (the violation of norms that are written into law). According to **differential association theory,** people learn to deviate by associating with others. According to **control theory,** each of us is propelled toward deviance, but most of us conform because of an effecti ve system of inner and outer controls. People who have less effective controls deviate. Pp. 209–211.

Labeling theory focuses on how labels (names, reputations) help to funnel people into or divert them away from deviance. People who commit deviant acts often use **techniques of neutralization** to continue to think of themselves as conformists. Pp. 211–213.

The Functionalist Perspective

How do functionalists explain deviance?

Functionalists point out that deviance, including criminal acts, is functional for society. Functions include affirming norms and promoting social unity and social change. According to **strain theory,** societies socialize their members into desiring **cultural goals.** Many people are unable to achieve these goals in socially acceptable ways—that is, by **institutionalized means.** *Deviants,* then, are people who either give up on the goals or use deviant means to attain them. Merton identified five types of responses to cultural goals and institutionalized means: conformity, innovation, ritualism, retreatism, and rebellion. **Illegitimate opportunity theory** stresses that some people have easier access to illegal means of achieving goals. Pp. 213–219.

The Conflict Perspective

How do conflict theorists explain deviance?

Conflict theorists take the position that the group in power (the **capitalist class**) imposes its definitions of deviance on other groups (the **working class** and the **marginal working class**). From the conflict perspective, the law is an instrument of oppression used to maintain the power and privilege of the few over the many. The marginal working class has little income, is desperate, and commits highly visible property crimes. The ruling class directs the **criminal justice system,** using it to punish the crimes of the poor while diverting its own criminal activities away from this punitive system. Pp. 219–221.

Reactions to Deviance

What are common reactions to deviance in the United States?

In following a "get-tough" policy, the United States has imprisoned millions of people. African Americans and Latinos make up a disproportionate percentage of U.S. prisoners. The death penalty shows biases by geography, social class, race–ethnicity, and gender. In line with conflict theory, as groups gain political power, their views are reflected in the criminal code. **Hate crime** legislation was considered in this context. Pp. 221–229.

Are official statistics on crime reliable?

The conclusions of both symbolic interactionists (that the police operate with a large measure of discretion) and conflict theorists (that the capitalist class controls the legal system) indicate that we must be cautious when using crime statistics. P. 229.

What is the medicalization of deviance?

The medical profession has attempted to **medicalize** many forms of **deviance,** claiming that they represent mental illnesses. Thomas Szasz disagrees, asserting that they are problem behaviors, not mental illnesses. Research on homeless people illustrates how problems in living can lead to bizarre behavior and thinking. Pp. 230–231.

What is a more humane approach?

Deviance is inevitable, so the larger issues are to find ways to protect people from deviance that harms themselves and others, to tolerate deviance that is not harmful, and to develop systems of fairer treatment for deviants. P. 231.

Thinking Critically
about Chapter 8

1. Select some deviance with which you are personally familiar. (It does not have to be your own—it can be something that someone you know did.) Choose one of the three theoretical perspectives to explain what happened.

2. As is explained in the text, deviance can be mild. Recall some instance in which you broke a social rule in dress, etiquette, or speech. What was the reaction? Why do you think people reacted like that? What was your response to their reactions?

3. What do you think should be done about the U.S. crime problem? What sociological theories support your view?

Additional Resources

What can you use MySocLab for? www.mysoclab.com

- **Study and Review:** Pre- and Post-Tests, Practice Tests, Flash Cards, Individualized Study Plans.
- **Current Events:** *Sociology in the News,* the daily *New York Times,* and more.

- **Research and Writing:** *Research Navigator, Writing About Sociology,* and more.

Where Can I Read More on This Topic?

Suggested readings for this chapter are listed at the back of this book.

Global Stratification

Franklin McMahon, *Farmers Work in Rice Paddies in Taiwan*

Let's contrast three "average" families from around the world:

For Getu Mulleta, 33, and his wife, Zenebu, 28, of rural Ethiopia, life is a constant struggle to keep themselves and their seven children from starving. They live in a 320-square-foot manure-plastered hut with no electricity, gas, or running water. They have a radio, but the battery is dead. The family farms teff, a grain, and survives on $130 a year.

The Mulletas' poverty is not due to a lack of hard work. Getu works about 80 hours a week, while Zenebu puts in even more hours. "Housework" for Zenebu includes fetching water, cleaning animal stables, and making fuel pellets out of cow dung for the open fire over which she cooks the family's food. Like other Ethiopian women, she eats after the men.

In Ethiopia, the average male can expect to live to age 48, the average female to 50.

The Mulletas' most valuable possession is their oxen. Their wishes for the future: more animals, better seed, and a second set of clothing.

* * *

They live in a 320-square-foot manure-plastered hut with no electricity, gas, or running water.

In Guadalajara, Mexico, Ambrosio and Carmen Castillo Balderas and their five children, ages 2 to 10, live in a four-room house. They also have a walled courtyard, where the family spends a good deal of time. They even have a washing machine, which is hooked up to a garden hose that runs to a public water main several hundred yards away. Like most Mexicans, they do not have a telephone, nor do they own a car.

Unlike many, however, they own a refrigerator, a stereo, and a recent purchase that makes them the envy of their neighbors: a television.

Ambrosio, 29, works full time as a wholesale distributor of produce. He also does welding on the side. The family's total annual income is $3,600. They spend 57 percent of their income on food. Carmen works about 60 hours a week taking care of their children and keeping their home spotless. The neatness of their home stands in stark contrast to the squalor of their neighborhood, whose dirt roads are covered in litter. As in many other Mexican neighborhoods, public utilities and roadwork do not keep pace with people's needs.

(continued)

The average life expectancy for males in Mexico is 70. For females, it is 76.

The Castillo Balderas' most valued possessions are their refrigerator and television. Their wish for the future: a truck.

* * *

Springfield, Illinois, is home to the Kellys—Rick, 36, Patti, 34, Julie, 10, and Michael, 7. The Kellys live in a four-bedroom, 2½ bath, 2,434-square-foot, carpeted ranch-style house, with a fireplace, central heating and air conditioning, a basement, and a two-car garage. Their home is equipped with a refrigerator, washing machine, clothes dryer, dishwasher, garbage disposal, vacuum cleaner, food processor, microwave, and convection oven. They also own six telephones (three cellular), four color televisions (two high definition), two CD players, two digital cameras, digital camcorder, two DVD players, iPod, X-box, and a computer, printer, scanner, and fax machine, not to mention two blow dryers, an answering machine, a juicer, and an espresso coffee machine. This count doesn't include such items as electric can openers, battery-powered tooth brushes, or the stereo-radio-CD/DVD players in their pickup truck and SUV.

Rick works 40 hours a week as a cable splicer for a telephone company. Patti teaches school part time. Together they make $54,061, plus benefits. The Kellys can choose from among dozens of superstocked supermarkets. They spend $4,809 for food they eat at home, and another $3,362 eating out, a total of 15 percent of their annual income.

In the United States, the average life expectancy is 75 for males, 80 for females.

On the Kellys' wish list are a new hybrid car with satellite radio, a 160-gigabyte laptop with Bluetooth wi-fi, a 50-inch plasma TV with surround sound, a DVD camcorder, a boat, a motor home, an ATV, and, oh, yes, farther down the road, an in-ground heated swimming pool. They also have an eye on a cabin at a nearby lake.

Sources: Menzel 1994; *Statistical Abstract* 2007:Tables 99, 668, 676, 937.

"Worlds Apart" could be the title for these photos, which illustrate how life chances depend on global stratification. On the left is the Mulleta family of Ethiopia, featured in the opening vignette, standing in front of their home with all their material possessions. On the right is the Skeen family of Texas, surrounded by their possessions.

Systems of Social Stratification

Some of the world's nations are wealthy, others poor, and some in between. This division of nations, as well as the layering of groups of people within a nation, is called *social stratification*. Social stratification is one of the most significant topics we shall discuss in this book, for, as you saw in the opening vignette, it affects our life chances—from our access to material possessions to the age at which we die.

Social stratification also affects the way we think about life. If you had been born into the Ethiopian family in our opening vignette, for example, you would be illiterate and would assume that your children would be as well. You also would expect hunger to be a part of life and would not expect all of your children to survive. To be born into either of the other two families, however, would give you quite a different picture of the world.

Social stratification is a system in which groups of people are divided into layers according to their relative property, prestige, and power. It is important to emphasize that social stratification does not refer to individuals. It is a way of ranking large groups of people into a hierarchy according to their relative privileges.

It is also important to note that *every society stratifies its members*. Some societies have greater inequality than others, but social stratification is universal. In addition, in every society of the world, *gender* is a basis for stratifying people. On the basis of their gender, people are either allowed or denied access to the good things offered by their society.

Let's consider four major systems of social stratification: slavery, caste, estate, and class.

Slavery

Slavery, whose essential characteristic is that *some individuals own other people*, has been common throughout world history. The Old Testament even lays out rules for how owners should treat their slaves. So does the Koran. The Romans also had slaves, as did the Africans and Greeks. In classical Greece and Rome, slaves did the work, freeing citizens to engage in politics and the arts. Slavery was most widespread in agricultural societies and least common among nomads, especially hunters and gatherers (Landtman 1938/1968). As we examine the major causes and conditions of slavery, you will see how remarkably slavery has varied around the world.

Causes of Slavery   Contrary to popular assumption, slavery was usually based not on racism but on one of three other factors. The first was *debt*. In some societies, creditors would enslave people who could not pay their debts. The second was *crime*. Instead of being killed, a murderer or thief might be enslaved by the victim's family as compensation for their loss. The third was *war*. When one group of people conquered another, they often enslaved some of the vanquished. Historian Gerda Lerner (1986) notes that women were the first people enslaved through warfare. When tribal men raided another group, they killed the men, raped the women, and then brought the women back as slaves. The women were valued for sexual purposes, for reproduction, and for their labor.

Roughly twenty-five hundred years ago, when Greece was but a collection of city-states, slavery was common. A city that became powerful and conquered another city would enslave some of the vanquished. Both slaves and slaveholders were Greek. Similarly, when Rome became the supreme power of the Mediterranean area about two thousand years ago, following the custom of the time, the Romans enslaved some of the Greeks they had conquered. More educated than their conquerors, some of these slaves served as tutors in Roman homes. Slavery, then, was a sign of debt, of crime, or of defeat in battle. It was not a sign that the slave was inherently inferior.

Conditions of Slavery   The conditions of slavery have varied widely around the world. *In some places, slavery was temporary.* Slaves of the Israelites were set free in the year of jubilee, which occurred every fifty years. Roman slaves ordinarily had the right to buy themselves out of slavery. They knew what their purchase price was, and some were able to meet this price by striking a bargain with their owner and selling their services to others. In most instances, however, slavery was a lifelong condition. Some criminals, for example, became slaves when they were given life sentences as oarsmen on Roman war ships. There they served until death, which often came quickly to those in this exhausting service.

social stratification the division of large numbers of people into layers according to their relative power, property, and prestige; applies to both nations and to people within a nation, society, or other group

slavery a form of social stratification in which some people own other people

Slavery was not necessarily inheritable. In most places, the children of slaves were automatically slaves themselves. But in some instances, the child of a slave who served a rich family might even be adopted by that family, becoming an heir who bore the family name along with the other sons or daughters of the household. In ancient Mexico, the children of slaves were always free (Landtman 1938/1968:271).

Slaves were not necessarily powerless and poor. In almost all instances, slaves owned no property and had no power. Among some groups, however, slaves could accumulate property and even rise to high positions in the community. Occasionally, a slave might even become wealthy, loan money to the master, and, while still a slave, own slaves himself or herself (Landtman 1938/1968). This, however, was rare.

Slavery in the New World　A gray area between a contract and slavery is **bonded labor,** also called **indentured service.** Many people who wanted to start a new life in the American colonies were unable to pay their passage across the ocean. Ship captains would transport them on credit, and colonists would "buy their paper" when they arrived. This arrangement provided passage for the penniless, payment for the ship's captain, and, for wealthier colonists, servants for a set number of years. During that specified period, the servants were required by law to serve their master. If they ran away, they became outlaws who were hunted down and forcibly returned. At the end of the period of indenture, they became full citizens, able to live where they chose and free to sell their labor (Main 1965; Elkins 1968).

Negroes for Sale.

A Cargo of very fine stout Men and Women, in good order and fit for immediate service, just imported from the Windward Coast of Africa, in the Ship Two Brothers.——

Conditions are one half Cash or Produce, the other half payable the first of January next, giving Bond and Security if required.

The Sale to be opened at 10 o'Clock each Day, in Mr. Bourdeaux's Yard, at No. 48, on the Bay.

May 19, 1784.　JOHN MITCHELL.

Under slavery, humans are sold like a commodity. This 1784 announcement reveals that slaves could be bought for cash or exchanged for produce (crops).

When there were not enough indentured servants to meet their growing need for labor, some colonists tried to enslave Native Americans. This attempt failed miserably. One reason was that when Indians escaped, they knew how to survive in the wilderness and were able to make their way back to their tribe. The colonists then turned to Africans, who were being brought to North and South America by the Dutch, English, Portuguese, and Spanish.

Because slavery has a broad range of causes, some analysts conclude that racism didn't lead to slavery, but, rather, slavery led to racism. Finding it profitable to make people slaves for life, U.S. slave owners developed an **ideology,** beliefs that justify social arrangements. Ideology leads to a perception of the world that makes current social arrangements seem inevitable, necessary, and fair. The colonists developed the view that their slaves were inferior. Some even said that they were not fully human. In short, the colonists wove elaborate justifications for slavery, built on the presumed superiority of their own group.

To make slavery even more profitable, slave states passed laws that made slavery *inheritable;* that is, the babies born to slaves became the property of the slave owners (Stampp 1956). These children could be sold, bartered, or traded. To strengthen their control, slave states passed laws making it illegal for slaves to hold meetings or to be away from the master's premises without carrying a pass (Lerner 1972). As sociologist W. E. B. Du Bois (1935/1992:12) noted, "gradually the entire white South became an armed camp to keep Negroes in slavery and to kill the black rebel."

The Civil War did not end legal discrimination. For example, until 1954 the states operated two separate school systems. Even until the 1950s, in order to keep the races from "mixing," it was illegal in Mississippi for a white and an African American to sit together on the same seat of a car! The reason there was no outright ban on blacks and whites being in the same car was to allow whites to employ African American chauffeurs.

Slavery Today　Slavery has again reared its ugly head in several parts of the world. The Ivory Coast, Mauritania, Niger, and Sudan have a long history of slavery, and not until the 1980s was slavery made illegal in Mauritania and Sudan (Ayittey 1998). It took until 2004 for slavery to be banned in Niger (Andersson 2005). Although officially abolished, slavery in this region continues, the topic of the Mass Media box on the next page.

bonded labor, or **indentured service** a contractual system in which someone sells his or her body (services) for a specified period of time in an arrangement very close to slavery, except that it is voluntarily entered into

ideology beliefs about the way things ought to be that justify social arrangements

What Price Freedom? Slavery Today

Children of the Dinka tribe in rural Sudan don't go to school. They work. Their families depend on them to tend the cattle that are essential to their way of life.

> On the morning of the raid, ten-year-old Adhieu had been watching the cattle. "We were very happy because we would soon leave the cattle camps and return home to our parents. But in the morning, there was shooting. There was yelling and crying everywhere. My uncle grabbed me by the hand, and we ran. We swam across the river. I saw some children drowning. We hid behind a rock."

By morning's end, 500 children were either dead or enslaved. Their attackers were their fellow countrymen—Arabs from northern Sudan. The children who were captured were forced to march hundreds of miles north. Some escaped on the way. Others tried to—and were shot (Akol 1998).

Tens of thousands of Dinkas were killed or enslaved after civil war broke out in Sudan in the 1980s. Yet the Arab-led government—the National Islamic Front—insisted that slavery did not exist. It claimed that foreign politicians and Christian humanitarians who didn't like the Sudanese government invented the slavery. Then the hostile foreign media publicized the nonexistent slavery (Akol 1998).

That was quite a creative defense. But the slavery did exist. There were too many witnesses and too much documentation by human rights groups. Journalists also provided devastating accounts: In the United States, public television (PBS) ran film footage of captive children in chains. And escaped slaves recounted their ordeal in horrifying detail (Salopek 2003; Mende and Lewis 2005).

The United States bombed Kosovo (in Serbia) into submission for its crimes against humanity, yet it remained largely silent in the face of the outrage in Sudan. A cynic might say that Kosovo was located at a politically strategic spot in Europe, whereas Sudan occupies an area of Africa in which the U.S. and European powers have had little interest. A cynic might add that these powers fear Arab retaliation, which might take the form of oil embargoes and terrorism. A cynic might also suggest that outrages against black Africans are not as significant to these powers as those against white Europeans. Finally, a cynic might add that this will change as Sudan's oil reserves become more strategic to Western interests.

When the world's most powerful governments didn't act on behalf of the slaves, private groups stepped in. One was Christian Solidarity International (CSI), based in Zurich, Switzerland. CSI sent Arab "retrievers" to northern Sudan, where they either bought or abducted slaves. Walking by night and hiding by day, the retrievers eluded security forces and brought the slaves south. There, CSI paid the retrievers $50 per slave (Mabry 1999).

> As CBS news cameras rolled, the rescuer paid the slave trader $50,000 in Sudanese pounds. At $50 per person, the bundle of bills was enough to free 1,000 slaves. The liberated slaves, mostly women and children, were then free to return to their villages. (Jacobs 1999)

These payments brought harsh criticism from those who claimed that buying slaves, even to free them, encourages slavery. Critics said that the money provides motivation to enslave people in order to turn around and sell them. Certainly $50 is a lot of money in Sudan, where people are lucky to make $50 a month (*Statistical Abstract* 2007:Table 1324).

CSI said that this was a bogus argument. What is intolerable, they said, is to leave women and children in slavery where they are deprived of their freedom and families, and beaten and raped by brutal masters.

for your Consideration

What do you think about buying the freedom of slaves? Can you suggest a workable alternative in such a situation? Why do you think the U.S. government remained largely silent about this issue, when it invaded other countries such as Serbia and Haiti for human rights abuses? Do you think that, perhaps, political motivations outweigh human rights motivations? If not, why the silence in the face of slavery?

The media coverage of this issue motivated many Americans to become active in freeing slaves. Some high schools—and even grade schools—raised money to participate in slave buyback programs. If you were a school principal, would you encourage this practice? Why or why not?

In this photo, a representative of the Liason Agency Network (on the left) is buying the freedom of the Sudanese slaves (in the background).

During my research in India, I interviewed this 8-year-old girl. Mahashury is a *bonded laborer* who was exchanged by her parents for a 2,000 rupee loan (about $14). To repay the loan, Mahashury must do construction work for one year. She will receive one meal a day and one set of clothing for the year. Because this centuries-old practice is now illegal, the master bribes Indian officials, who inform him when they are going to inspect the construction site. He then hides his bonded laborers. I was able to interview and photograph Mahashury because her master was absent the day I visited the construction site.

The enslavement of children for work and sex is a problem in Africa, Asia, and South America (LaFraniere 2006). A unique form of child slavery occurs in Kuwait, Qatar, and the United Arab Emirates. There, little boys are held in captivity because they are prized as jockeys in camel races (Brinkley 2005). It is thought that their screams make the camels run faster.

Caste

The second system of social stratification is caste. In a **caste system,** status is determined by birth and is lifelong. Someone who is born into a low-status group will always have low status, no matter how much that person may accomplish in life. In sociological terms, a caste system is built on ascribed status (discussed on page 101). Achieved status cannot change an individual's place in this system.

Societies with this form of stratification try to make certain that the boundaries between castes remain firm. They practice **endogamy,** marriage within their own group, and prohibit intermarriage. To reduce contact between castes, they even develop elaborate rules about *ritual pollution,* teaching that contact with inferior castes contaminates the superior caste.

caste system a form of social stratification in which one's status is determined by birth and is lifelong

endogamy the practice of marrying within one's own group

India's Religious Castes   India provides the best example of a caste system. Based not on race but on religion, India's caste system has existed for almost three thousand years (Chandra 1993a; Jaffrelot 2006). India's four main castes are depicted in Table 9.1. These four castes are subdivided into about three thousand subcastes, or *jati.* Each *jati* specializes in a particular occupation. For example, one subcaste washes clothes, another sharpens knives, and yet another repairs shoes.

The lowest group listed in Table 9.1, the Dalit, make up India's "untouchables." If a Dalit touches someone of a higher caste, that person becomes unclean. Even the shadow of an untouchable can contaminate. Early morning and late afternoons are especially risky, for the long shadows of these periods pose a danger to everyone higher up the caste system. Consequently, Dalits are not allowed in some villages during these times. Anyone who becomes contaminated must follow *ablution,* or washing rituals, to restore purity.

Although the Indian government formally abolished the caste system in 1949, centuries-old practices cannot be eliminated so easily, and the caste system remains part of everyday life in India. The ceremonies people follow at births, marriages, and deaths, for example, are dictated by caste (Chandra 1993a). The upper castes dread the upward mobility of the untouchables, sometimes resisting it even with violence and ritual suicide (Crossette 1996; Deliege 2001; Jaffrelot 2006). From personal observations in India, I can add that in some villages Dalit children are not allowed in the government schools. If they try to enroll, they are beaten.

Table 9.1	India's Caste System
Caste	**Occupation**
Brahman	Priests and teachers
Kshatriya	Rulers and soldiers
Vaishya	Merchants and traders
Shudra	Peasants and laborers
Dalit (untouchables)	The outcastes; degrading or polluting labor

An untouchable summed up his situation in life this way:

> At the tea stalls, we have separate cups to drink from, chipped and caked with dirt. We have to walk for 15 minutes to carry water to our homes, because we're not allowed to use the taps in the village that the upper castes use. We're not allowed into temples. When I attended school, my friends and I were forced to sit outside the classroom. The upper caste children would not allow us even to touch the football they played with. We played with stones instead. (Guru and Sidhva 2001)

South Africa Until recently, South Africa provided another example of social stratification based on caste. Europeans of Dutch descent, a numerical minority called Afrikaners, controlled the government, the police, and the military. They used these sources of power to enforce a system called **apartheid** (ah-PAR-tate), the separation of the races. Everyone was classified by law into one of four groups: Europeans (whites), Africans (blacks), Coloureds (mixed races), and Asians. These classifications determined where people could live, work, and go to school. It also established where they could swim or see movies—for by law whites were not allowed to mix socially with the others.

After years of trade sanctions and sports boycotts, Afrikaners reluctantly dismantled their caste system. Black Africans no longer carry special passes, public facilities are integrated, and all racial-ethnic groups have the right to vote and to hold office. Although apartheid has been dismantled, its legacy haunts South Africa. Whites still dominate the country's social institutions, and most blacks remain uneducated and poor. Many new rights—such as the right to higher education, to eat in restaurants, even to see a doctor—are of little use to people who can't afford them. Political violence has been replaced by old-fashioned crime. Even though the U.S. murder rate is so high it intimidates foreigners, South Africa's murder rate is *seven* times higher (Van Marsh 2006; *Statistical Abstract* 2007:Table 303). Apartheid's legacy of prejudice, bitterness, and hatred appears destined to fuel racial tensions for generations to come.

A U.S. Racial Caste System Before leaving the subject of caste, we should note that when slavery ended in the United States, it was replaced by a *racial caste system*. From the moment of birth, everyone was marked for life (Berger 1963/2007). In this system, *all* whites, even if they were poor and uneducated, considered themselves to have a higher status than *all* African Americans. As in India and South Africa, the upper caste, fearing pollution from the lower caste, prohibited intermarriage, and insisted on separate schools, hotels, restaurants, and even toilets and drinking fountains

apartheid the separation of racial-ethnic groups as was practiced in South Africa in public facilities. When any white met any African American on a Southern sidewalk, the African American had to move aside—which the untouchables of India still must do when they meet someone of a higher caste (Deliege 2001).

Estate

During the middle ages, Europe developed the **estate stratification system.** There were three groups, or estates. The *first estate* was made up of the nobility, the wealthy families who ruled the country. This group owned the land, which was the source of wealth at that time. The nobility did no farming themselves, or any "work" for that matter. Work was considered beneath their dignity, something to be done by servants. The nobility's responsibility was to administer their lands, and to live "genteel" lives worthy of their high position.

The *second estate* consisted of the clergy. The Roman Catholic Church was a political power at this time. It also owned vast amounts of land and collected taxes from everyone who lived within the boundaries of a parish. The church's power was so great that in order to be crowned, kings had to obtain the pope's permission.

To prevent their vast land holdings from being carved into smaller chunks, members of the nobility practiced *primogeniture,* allowing only firstborn sons to inherit land. The other sons had to find some way to support themselves, and joining the clergy was a favored way. (Other ways included becoming an officer in the military or practicing law.) The church was appealing because priests held lifetime positions and were guaranteed a comfortable living. At that time, the church sold offices, and, for example, a wealthy man could buy the position of bishop, which guaranteed a high income.

The *third estate* consisted of the commoners. Known as *serfs,* they belonged to the land. If someone bought or inherited land, the serfs came with it. Serfs were born into the third estate, and they died within it, too. The rare person who made it out of the third estate was a man who was knighted for extraordinary bravery in battle or someone "called" into a religious vocation.

Women in the Estate System

Women belonged to the estate of their husbands. Women in the first estate had no occupation, for, as in the case of their husbands, work was considered beneath their dignity. Their responsibility was to administer the household, overseeing the servants. The women in the second estate, nuns, were the exception to the rule that women belonged to the estate of their husbands, as the Roman Catholic clergy did not marry. Women of the third estate shared the hard life of their husbands, including physical labor and food shortages. In addition, they faced the peril of rape by men of the first estate. A few commoners who caught the eye of men of the first estate did marry and join them in the first estate. This, however, was rare.

Class

estate stratification system the stratification system of medieval Europe, consisting of three groups or estates: the nobility, clergy, and commoners

class system a form of social stratification based primarily on the possession of money or material possessions

social mobility movement up or down the social class ladder

As we have seen, stratification systems based on slavery, caste, and estate are rigid. The lines drawn between people are firm, and there is little or no movement from one group to another. A **class system,** in contrast, is much more open, for it is based primarily on money or material possessions, which can be acquired. This system, too, is in place at birth, when children are ascribed the status of their parents, but, unlike the other systems, individuals can change their social class by what they achieve (or fail to achieve) in life. In addition, no laws specify people's occupations on the basis of birth or prohibit marriage between the classes.

A major characteristic of the class system, then, is its relatively fluid boundaries. A class system allows **social mobility,** movement up or down the class ladder. The potential for improving one's life—or for falling down the class ladder—is a major force that drives people to go far in school and to work hard. In the extreme, the family background that a child inherits at birth may present such obstacles that he or she has little chance of climbing very far—or it may provide such privileges that it makes it almost impossible to fall down the class ladder.

How the children of the poor were treated in earlier periods comes as a shock to our generation. This cartoon from the late 1880s is part of a campaign of that time to arouse outrage to reform the law and the treatment of children. The children are working in an English coal mine.

Global Stratification and the Status of Females

In *every* society of the world, gender is a basis for social stratification. In no society is gender the sole basis for stratifying people, but gender cuts across *all* systems of social stratification—whether slavery, caste, estate, or class (Huber 1990). In all these systems, on the basis of their gender, people are sorted into categories and given different access to the good things available in their society.

Apparently these distinctions always favor males. It is remarkable, for example, that in *every* society of the world men's earnings are higher than women's. Men's dominance is even more evident when we consider female circumcision (see the box on page 313). That most of the world's illiterate are females also drives home women's relative position in society. Of the several hundred million adults who cannot read, about two-thirds are women (UNESCO 2006). Because gender is such a significant factor in what happens to us in life, we shall focus on it more closely in Chapter 11.

What Determines Social Class?

In the early days of sociology, a disagreement arose about the meaning of social class. Let's compare how Marx and Weber analyzed the issue.

Karl Marx: The Means of Production

As was discussed in Chapter 1, the breakup of the feudal system displaced masses of peasants from their traditional lands and occupations. Fleeing to cities, they competed for the few available jobs. Paid only a pittance for their labor, they wore rags, went hungry, and slept under bridges and in shacks. In contrast, the factory owners built mansions, hired servants, and lived in the lap of luxury. Seeing this great disparity between owners and workers, Karl Marx (1818–1883) concluded that social class depends on a single factor: people's relationship to the **means of production**—the tools, factories, land, and investment capital used to produce wealth (Marx 1844/1964; Marx and Engels 1848/1967).

Marx argued that the distinctions people often make among themselves—such as clothing, speech, education, paycheck, the neighborhood they live in, even the car they drive—are superficial matters. These things camouflage the only dividing line that counts. There are just two classes of people, said Marx: the **bourgeoisie** (*capitalists*), those who own the means of production, and the **proletariat** (*workers*), those who work for the owners. In short, people's relationship to the means of production determines their social class.

means of production the tools, factories, land, and investment capital used to produce wealth

bourgeoisie Marx's term for capitalists, those who own the means of production

proletariat Marx's term for the exploited class, the mass of workers who do not own the means of production

Taken at the end of the 1800s, these photos illustrate the contrasting worlds of *social classes* produced by capitalism. The sleeping boys shown in this classic 1890 photo by Jacob Riis sold newspapers in London. They did not go to school, and they had no home. The children on the right, Cornelius and Gladys Vanderbilt, are shown in front of their parents' estate. They went to school and did not work. You can see how the social locations illustrated in these photos would have produced different orientations to life and, therefore, politics, ideas about marriage, values, and so on—the stuff of which life is made.

Marx did recognize other groups: farmers and peasants; a *lumpenproletariat* (people living on the margin of society, such as beggars, vagrants, and criminals); and a middle group of self-employed professionals. Marx did not consider these groups social classes, however, for they lack **class consciousness**—a shared identity based on their position in the means of production. In other words, they did not perceive themselves as exploited workers whose plight could be solved by collective action. Consequently, Marx thought of these groups as insignificant in the future he foresaw—a workers' revolution that was destined to overthrow capitalism.

The capitalists will grow even wealthier, Marx said, and the hostilities will increase. When workers come to realize that capitalists are the source of their oppression, they will unite and throw off the chains of their oppressors. In a bloody revolution, they will seize the means of production and usher in a classless society, in which no longer will the few grow rich at the expense of the many. What holds back the workers' unity and their revolution is **false class consciousness,** workers mistakenly thinking of themselves as capitalists. For example, workers with a few dollars in the bank may forget that they are workers and instead see themselves as investors, or as capitalists who are about to launch a successful business.

The only distinction worth mentioning, then, is whether a person is an owner or a worker. This decides everything else, Marx stressed, for property determines people's lifestyles, establishes their relationships with one another, and even shapes their ideas.

Max Weber: Property, Prestige, and Power

Max Weber (1864–1920) was an outspoken critic of Marx. Weber argued that property is only part of the picture. *Social class,* he said, has three components: property, prestige, and power (Gerth and Mills 1958; Weber 1922/1968). Some call these the three P's of social class. (Although Weber used the terms *class, status,* and *power,* some sociologists find *property, prestige,* and *power* to be clearer terms. To make them even clearer, you may wish to substitute *wealth* for *property.*)

Property (or wealth), said Weber, is certainly significant in determining a person's standing in society. On that point he agreed with Marx. But, added Weber, ownership is not the only significant aspect of property. For example, some powerful people, such as managers of corporations, *control* the means of production even though they do not *own* them. If managers can control property for their own benefit—awarding themselves huge bonuses and magnificent perks—it makes no practical difference that they do not own the property that they use so generously for their own benefit.

class consciousness Marx's term for awareness of a common identity based on one's position in the means of production

false class consciousness Marx's term to refer to workers identifying with the interests of capitalists

Prestige, the second element in Weber's analysis, is often derived from property, for people tend to admire the wealthy. Prestige, however, can be based on other factors. Olympic gold medalists, for example, might not own property, yet they have high prestige. Some are even able to exchange their prestige for property—such as those who are paid a small fortune for endorsing a certain brand of sportswear or for claiming that they start their day with "the breakfast of champions." In other words, property and prestige are not one-way streets: Although property can bring prestige, prestige can also bring property.

Power, the third element of social class, is the ability to control others, even over their objections. Weber agreed with Marx that property is a major source of power, but he added that it is not the only source. For example, prestige can be turned into power. Two well-known examples are actors Arnold Schwarzeneggar, who became governor of California, and Ronald Reagan, who became president of the United States. Figure 9.1 shows how property, prestige, and power are interrelated.

IN SUM For Marx, social class was based solely on a person's relationship to the means of production. One is a member of either the bourgeoisie or the proletariat. Weber argued that social class is a combination of property, prestige, and power.

Why Is Social Stratification Universal?

What is it about social life that makes all societies stratified? We shall first consider the explanation proposed by functionalists, which has aroused much controversy in sociology, and then explanations proposed by conflict theorists.

The Functionalist View: Motivating Qualified People

Functionalists take the position that the patterns of behavior that characterize a society exist because they are functional for that society. Because social inequality is universal, inequality must help societies survive. But how?

Davis and Moore's Explanation Two functionalists, Kingsley Davis and Wilbert Moore (1945, 1953), wrestled with this question. They concluded that stratification of society is inevitable because:

1. Society must make certain that its positions are filled.
2. Some positions are more important than others.
3. The more important positions must be filled by the more qualified people.
4. To motivate the more qualified people to fill these positions, society must offer them greater rewards.

To flesh out this functionalist argument, consider college presidents and military generals. The position of college president is more important than that of student because the president's decisions affect a large number of people, including many students. College presidents are also accountable for their performance to boards of trustees. It is the same with generals. Their decisions affect many people, and can determine life and death. Generals are accountable to superior generals and to the country's leader.

Why do people accept such high-pressure positions? Why don't they just take less demanding jobs? The answer, said Davis and Moore, is that society offers greater rewards—prestige, pay, and benefits—for its more demanding and accountable positions. To get highly qualified people to compete with one another, some positions offer a salary of $2 million a year, country club membership, a private jet and pilot, and a chauffeured limousine. For less demanding positions, a $30,000 salary without fringe benefits is enough to get hundreds of people to compete. If a job requires rigorous training, it, too, must offer more salary and benefits. If you can get the same pay with a high school diploma, why suffer through the many tests and term papers that college requires?

Figure 9.1 **Weber's Three Components of Social Class**

Property → Power (Bill Gates; the wealthy men who become presidents)

Property → Prestige (the wealthy in general)

Prestige → Power (Ronald Reagan; Arnold Schwarzenegger)

Prestige → Property (Olympic gold medalists who endorse products)

Power → Property (crooked politicians)

Power → Prestige (Abe Lincoln; Colin Powell*)

*Colin Powell illustrates the circularity of these components. Powell's power as Chairman of the Joint Chiefs of Staff led to prestige. Powell's prestige, in turn, led to power when he was called from retirement to serve as Secretary of State in George W. Bush's first administration.

The text describes the many relationships among Weber's three components of *social class:* property, prestige, and power. Colin Powell is an example of power that was converted into prestige—which was then converted back into power. Power of course, can be lost, as it was when Powell resigned after disagreeing with the Bush administration.

Sisters Venus and Serena Williams have dominated the women's tennis world for over a decade. To determine the social class of athletes as highly successful as the Williams sisters presents a sociological puzzle. With their fame and growing wealth, what do you think their social class is? Why?

Tumin's Critique of Davis and Moore   Davis and Moore tried to explain *why* social stratification is universal, not justify social inequality. Nevertheless, their view makes many sociologists uncomfortable, for they see it as coming close to justifying the inequalities in society. Its bottom line seems to be: The people who contribute more to society are paid more, while those who contribute less are paid less.

Melvin Tumin (1953) was the first sociologist to point out what he saw as major flaws in the functionalist position. Here are three of his arguments.

First, how do we know that the positions that offer the higher rewards are more important? A heart surgeon, for example, saves lives and earns much more than a garbage collector, but this doesn't mean that garbage collectors are less important to society. By helping to prevent contagious diseases, garbage collectors save thousands of lives. We need independent methods of measuring importance, and we don't have them.

Second, if stratification worked as Davis and Moore described it, society would be a **meritocracy;** that is, positions would be awarded on the basis of merit. But is this what we have? The best predictor of who goes to college, for example, is not ability but income: The more a family earns, the more likely their children are to go to college (Carnevale and Rose 2003). This has nothing to do with merit. It is simply another form of the inequality that is built into society. In short, people's positions in society are based on many reasons other than merit.

Third, if social stratification is so functional, it ought to benefit almost everyone. Yet social stratification is *dysfunctional* for many. Think of the people who could have made valuable contributions to society had they not been born in slums, dropped out of school, and taken menial jobs to help support their families. Then there are the many who, born female, are assigned "women's work," thus ensuring that they do not maximize their mental abilities.

meritocracy a form of social stratification in which all positions are awarded on the basis of merit

IN SUM   Functionalists argue that society works better if its most qualified people hold its most important positions. Therefore, those positions offer higher rewards. For example, to get highly talented people to become surgeons—to undergo years of rigorous training and then cope with life-and-death situations, as well as malpractice suits—society must provide a high payoff.

The Conflict Perspective: Class Conflict and Scarce Resources

Conflict theorists don't just criticize details of the functionalist argument. Rather, they go for the throat and attack its basic premise. Conflict, not function, they stress, is the reason that we have social stratification. Let's look at the major arguments.

Mosca's Argument Italian sociologist Gaetano Mosca argued that every society will be stratified by power. This is inevitable, he said in an 1896 book titled *The Ruling Class*, because:

1. No society can exist unless it is organized. This requires leadership of some sort in order to coordinate people's actions and get society's work done.
2. Leadership (or political organization) requires inequalities of power. By definition, some people take leadership positions, while others follow.
3. Human nature is self-centered. Therefore, people in power will use their positions to seize greater rewards for themselves.

There is no way around these facts of life, added Mosca. They make social stratification inevitable, and every society will stratify itself along lines of power.

Marx's Argument If he were alive to hear the functionalist argument, Karl Marx would be enraged. From his point of view, the people in power are not there because of superior traits, as the functionalists would have us believe. This view is simply an ideology that members of the elite use to justify their being at the top—and to seduce the oppressed into believing that their welfare depends on keeping society stable. Human history is the chronicle of class struggle, of those in power using society's resources to benefit themselves and to oppress those beneath them—and of oppressed groups trying to overcome domination.

Marx predicted that the workers would revolt. The day will come, he said, when class consciousness will overcome the ideology that now blinds workers. When they realize their common oppression, workers will rebel against the capitalists. The struggle to control the means of production may be covert at first, taking the form of work slowdowns or industrial sabotage. Ultimately, however, resistance will break out into the open. The revolution will not be easy, for the bourgeoisie control the police, the military, and even the educational system, where they implant false class consciousness in the minds of the workers' children.

Current Applications of Conflict Theory Just as Marx focused on overarching historic events—the accumulation of capital and power and the struggle between workers and capitalists—some of today's conflict sociologists are doing the same. Their focus is on the current capitalist triumph on a global level (Sklair 2001). They analyze both the use of armed forces to keep capitalist nations dominant and the exploitation of workers as capital is moved from the Most Industrialized Nations to the Least Industrialized Nations.

Some conflict sociologists, in contrast, examine conflict wherever it is found, not just as it relates to capitalists and workers. They examine how groups *within the same class* compete with one another for a larger slice of the pie (Schellenberg 1996; Collins 1988, 1999). Even within the same industry, for example, union will fight against union for higher salaries, shorter hours, and more power. A special focus has been conflict between racial–ethnic groups as they compete for education, housing, and even prestige—whatever benefits society has to offer. Another focus has been relations between women and men, which conflict theorists say are best understood as a conflict over power—over who controls society's resources. Unlike functionalists, conflict theorists say that just beneath the surface of what may appear to be a tranquil society lies conflict that is barely held in check.

Lenski's Synthesis

As you can see, functionalist and conflict theorists disagree sharply. Is it possible to reconcile their views? Sociologist Gerhard Lenski (1966) thought so. He suggested that surplus is the key. He said that the functionalists are right when it comes to groups that don't accumulate a surplus, such as hunting and gathering societies. These societies give a greater share of their resources to those who take on important tasks, such as warriors who risk their lives in battle. It is a different story, said Lenski, with societies that accumulate surpluses. In them, groups fight over the surplus, and the group that wins becomes an elite. This dominant group rules from the top, controlling the groups below it. In the resulting system of social stratification, where you are born in that society, not personal merit, becomes important.

IN SUM Conflict theorists stress that in every society groups struggle with one another to gain a larger share of their society's resources. Whenever a group gains power, it uses that power to extract what it can from the groups beneath it. This elite group also uses the social institutions to keep itself in power.

How Do Elites Maintain Stratification?

Suppose that you are part of the ruling elite of your society. What can you do to make sure you don't lose your privileged position? The key lies in controlling people's ideas, the information they receive, and the threat and use of force.

Ideology Versus Force

Medieval Europe provides a good example of the power of ideology. In the estate system that we reviewed, land was the primary source of wealth—and only the nobility and the church could own it. Almost everyone was a peasant (or serf) who worked for these powerful landowners. The peasants farmed the land, took care of the livestock, and built the roads and bridges. Each year, they had to turn over a designated portion of their crops to their feudal lord. Year after year, for centuries, they did so. Why?

Ideas Controlling the Masses Why didn't the peasants rebel and take over the land themselves? There were many reasons, not the least of which was that the nobility and church controlled the army. Coercion, however, only goes so far, for it breeds hostility and nourishes rebellion. How much more effective it is to get the masses to *want* to do what the ruling elite desires. This is where *ideology* (beliefs that justify the way things are) comes into play, and the nobility and clergy used it to great effect. They developed an ideology known as the **divine right of kings**—the idea that the king's authority comes directly from God. The king delegates authority to nobles, who, as God's representatives, must be obeyed. To disobey is a sin against God; to rebel is to merit physical punishment on earth and eternal suffering in hell.

Controlling people's ideas can be remarkably more effective than using brute force. Although this particular ideology governs few peoples' minds today, the elite in *every* society develops ideologies to justify its position at the top. For example, around the world, schools teach that their country's form of government— *no matter what form of government that is*—is good. Religious leaders teach that we owe obedience to authority, that laws are to be obeyed. To the degree that their ideologies are accepted by the masses, the elite remains securely in power.

Ideas Controlling the Elite Contemporary events illustrate how the prevailing ideology also sets limits on the elite. Although leaders use ideas to control the people, the people can also insist that their leaders conform to those ideas. Pakistan is an outstanding example. If Pakistani leaders depart from fundamentalist Islamic ideology, their position is in jeopardy. Regardless of their personal views, Pakistani leaders cannot support Western ideas of morality,

The *divine right of kings* was an ideology that made the king God's direct representative on earth—to administer justice and punish evildoers. This theological-political concept was supported by the Roman Catholic Church, whose representatives crowned the king. Shown here is Pope Clement IV crowning Charles Anjou as king of Sicily in 1226.

such as it being okay for a woman to appear in public alone or while wearing a short skirt. To take this position would threaten not only their position of leadership but also their lives. To protect their position within a system of stratification, leaders, regardless of their personal opinion, must conform at least outwardly to the controlling ideas.

Controlling Information and Using Technology   To maintain their positions of power, elites try to control information. Fear is a favorite tactic of dictators. To muffle criticism, they imprison, torture, and kill reporters who dare to criticize their regime. (Under Saddam Hussein, the penalty for telling a joke about Hussein was having your tongue cut out [Nordland 2003].) Lacking such power, the ruling elites of democracies rely on more covert means. They manipulate the media by selectively releasing information—and by withholding information "in the interest of national security."

The new technology is another tool for the elite. Telephones can be turned into microphones even when they are off the hook. Machines can read the entire contents of a computer in a second, without leaving evidence that they have done so. Security cameras—"Tiny Brothers"—have sprouted almost everywhere. Face-recognition systems can scan a crowd of thousands, instantly matching the scans with digitized files of individuals. With these devices, the elite can monitor citizens' activities without anyone knowing that they are being observed. Dictatorships have few checks on how they employ such technology, but in democracies, checks and balances, such as requiring court orders for search and seizure, at least partially curb their abuse. The threat of bypassing such restraints on power are always present, as with the Homeland Security laws discussed in Chapter 15 (page 453).

The new technology is a two-edged sword. Just as it gives the elite powerful tools for monitoring citizens, it also makes it more difficult for them to control information. Satellite communications, e-mail, and the Internet pay no respect to international borders. Information (both true and fabricated) flies around the globe in seconds. Internet users also have free access to PGP (Pretty Good Privacy), a code that no government has been able to break. Then, too, there is zFone, voice encryption for telephone calls, that prevents wiretappers from understanding what people are saying.

Feeling threatened that their citizens will criticize them, Chinese leaders have put tight controls on Internet cafes and search engines (French 2005; Hutton 2007). U.S. officials, unable to wield the sword, have distributed fake news reports to be broadcast to the nation (Barstow and Stein 2005). We are still in the early stages of the new technology, so we will see how this cat and mouse game plays out.

IN SUM   To maintain stratification within a society, the elite tries to dominate its society's institutions. In a dictatorship, the elite makes the laws. In a democracy, the elite influences the laws. In both, the elite controls the police and military and can give orders to crush a rebellion—or to run the post office or air traffic control if workers strike. Force has its limits, and a nation's elite prefers to maintain its stratification system by peaceful means, especially by influencing the thinking of its people.

Comparative Social Stratification

Now that we have examined systems of social stratification, considered why stratification is universal, and looked at how elites keep themselves in power, let's compare social stratification in Great Britain and in the former Soviet Union. In the next chapter, we'll look at social stratification in the United States.

Social Stratification in Great Britain

Great Britain is often called England by Americans, but England is only one of the countries that make up the island of Great Britain. The others are Scotland and Wales. In addition, Northern Ireland is part of the United Kingdom of Great Britain and Northern Ireland.

Like other industrialized countries, Great Britain has a class system that can be divided into a lower, a middle, and an upper class. Great Britain's population is about evenly divided between the middle class and the lower (or working) class. A tiny upper class, perhaps 1 percent of the population, is wealthy, powerful, and highly educated.

Compared with Americans, the British are very class conscious. Like Americans, they recognize class distinctions on the basis of the type of car a person drives or the stores someone patronizes. But the most striking characteristics of the British class system are language and education. This often shows up in distinctive speech, which has a powerful impact on British life. Accent almost always betrays class. As soon as someone speaks, the listener is aware of that person's social class—and treats him or her accordingly (Sullivan 1998).

Education is the primary way by which the British perpetuate their class system from one generation to the next. Almost all children go to neighborhood schools. Great Britain's richest 5 percent, however—who own *half* the nation's wealth—send their children to exclusive private boarding schools (which, strangely, they call "public" schools). There the children of the elite are trained in subjects that are considered "proper" for members of the ruling class. An astounding 50 percent of the students at Oxford and Cambridge, the country's most prestigious universities, come from this 5 percent of the population. To illustrate how powerfully this system of stratified education affects the national life of Great Britain, sociologist Ian Robertson (1987) said,

> [E]ighteen former pupils of the most exclusive of [England's high schools], Eton, have become prime minister. Imagine the chances of a single American high school producing eighteen presidents!

The contrast between wealth and poverty is a characteristic of all contemporary societies. This photo was taken in the Ginza shopping district of Tokyo, Japan.

Social Stratification in the Former Soviet Union

Heeding Karl Marx's call for a classless society, Vladimir Ilyich Lenin (1870–1924) and Leon Trotsky (1879–1940) led a revolution in Russia in 1917. They, and the nations that followed their banner, never claimed to have achieved the ideal of communism, in which all contribute their labor to the common good and receive according to their needs. Instead, they used the term *socialism* to describe the intermediate step between capitalism and communism, in which social classes are abolished but some inequality remains.

To tweak the nose of Uncle Sam, the socialist countries would trumpet their equality and point a finger at glaring inequalities in the United States. These countries, however, also were marked by huge disparities in privilege. Their major basis of stratification was membership in the Communist Party. Party members decided who would gain admission to the better schools or obtain the more desirable jobs and housing. The equally qualified son or daughter of a nonmember would be turned down, for such privileges came with demonstrated loyalty to the Party.

The Communist Party, too, was highly stratified. Most members occupied a low level, where they fulfilled such tasks as spying on fellow workers. For this, they might get easier jobs in the factory or occasional access to special stores to purchase hard-to-find goods. The middle level consisted of bureaucrats who were given better than average access to resources and privileges. At the top level was a small elite: Party members who enjoyed not only power but also limousines, imported delicacies, vacation homes, and even servants and hunting lodges. As with other stratification systems around the world, women held lower positions in the Party. This was evident at each year's May Day, when the top members of the Party reviewed the latest weapons paraded in Moscow's Red Square. Photos of these events showed only men.

The leaders of the USSR became frustrated as they saw the West thrive. They struggled with a bloated bureaucracy, the inefficiencies of central planning, workers who did the minimum because they could not be fired, and a military so costly that it spent one of every eight of the nation's rubles (*Statistical Abstract* 1993:1432, table dropped in later editions). Socialist ideology did not call for their citizens to be deprived, and in an attempt to turn things around, the Soviet leadership initiated reforms. They allowed elections to be held in which more than one candidate ran for an office. (Before this, voters had a choice of only one candidate per office.) They also sold huge chunks of state-owned businesses to the public. Overnight, making investments to try to turn a profit changed from being a crime into a respectable goal.

Russia's transition to capitalism took a bizarre twist. As authority broke down, a powerful Mafia has emerged (Varese 2005; Chazman 2006). These criminal groups are headed by gangsters, corrupt government officials (including the former KGB, now FSB), and crooked businessmen. In some towns, they buy the entire judicial system—the police force, prosecutors, and judges. They assassinate business leaders, reporters, and politicians who refuse to cooperate. They amass wealth, launder money through banks they control, and buy luxury properties in popular tourist areas in South America, Asia, and Europe. A favorite is Marbella, a watering and wintering spot on Spain's Costa del Sol.

As Moscow reestablishes its authority, Mafia ties are bringing wealth to some of the members of this central government. This group of organized criminals is destined to take its place as part of Russia's new capitalist class.

Global Stratification: Three Worlds

As was noted at the beginning of this chapter, just as the people within a nation are stratified by property, prestige, and power, so are the world's nations. Until recently, a simple model consisting of First, Second, and Third Worlds was used to depict global stratification. *First World* referred to the industrialized capitalist nations, *Second World* to the communist (or socialist) countries, and *Third World* to any nation that did not fit into the first two categories. The breakup of the Soviet Union in 1989 made these terms outdated. In addition, although *first, second,* and *third* did not mean "best," "better," and "worst," they implied it. An alternative classification that some now use—developed, developing, and undeveloped nations—has the same drawback. By calling ourselves "developed," it sounds as though we are mature and the "undeveloped" nations are somehow retarded.

To try to solve this problem, I use more neutral, descriptive terms: *Most Industrialized, Industrializing,* and *Least Industrialized* nations. We can measure industrialization with no judgment implied as to whether a nation's industrialization represents "development," ranks it "first," or is even desirable at all. The intention is to depict on a global level the three primary dimensions of social stratification: property, power, and prestige. The Most Industrialized Nations have much greater property (wealth), prestige (they are looked up to as world leaders), and power (they usually get their way in international relations). The three families sketched in the opening vignette illustrate the far-reaching effects of global stratification.

The Most Industrialized Nations

The Most Industrialized Nations are the United States and Canada in North America; Great Britain, France, Germany, Switzerland, and the other industrialized countries of western Europe; Japan in Asia; and Australia and New Zealand in the area of the world known as Oceania. Although there are variations in their economic systems, these nations are capitalistic. As Table 9.2 on page 254 shows, although these nations have only 16 percent of the world's people, they possess 31 percent of the earth's land. Their wealth is so enormous that even their poor live better and longer lives than do the average citizens of the Least Industrialized Nations. The Social Map on pages 252–253 shows the tremendous disparities in income among the world's nations.

Figure 9.2 Global Stratification: Income[1] of the World's Nations

The Most Industrialized Nations

	Nation	Income per Person
1	Luxembourg	$58,900
2	United States	$39,820
3	Norway	$38,680
4	Switzerland	$35,660
5	Ireland	$32,930
6	Iceland	$31,900
7	Austria	$31,800
8	Denmark	$31,770
9	Hong Kong (a part of China)	$31,560
10	Belgium	$31,530
11	United Kingdom	$31,430
12	Netherlands	$31,360
13	Canada	$30,760
14	Sweden	$29,880
15	Japan	$29,810
16	Finland	$29,800
17	France	$29,460
18	Australia	$29,340
19	Germany	$28,170
20	Italy	$28,020
21	Singapore	$27,370
22	Taiwan	$25,300
23	Israel	$23,770
24	New Zealand	$22,260

The Industrializing Nations

	Nation	Income per Person
25	Spain	$24,750
26	Greece	$22,230
27	Slovenia	$20,830
28	Korea, South	$20,530
29	Portugal	$19,240
30	Czech Republic	$18,420
31	Hungary	$15,800
32	Slovakia	$14,480
33	Saudi Arabia	$13,810
34	Estonia	$13,630
35	Poland	$12,730
36	Lithuania	$12,690
37	Argentina	$12,530
38	Croatia	$11,920
39	Latvia	$11,820
40	South Africa	$10,960
41	Chile	$10,610
42	Malaysia	$9,720
43	Russia	$9,680
44	Mexico	$9,640
45	Costa Rica	$9,220
46	Uruguay	$9,030
47	Romania	$8,330
48	Brazil	$7,940
49	Bulgaria	$7,940
50	Thailand	$7,930
51	Bosnia	$7,230
52	Colombia	$6,940
53	Venezuela	$5,830

The Least Industrialized Nations

	Nation	Income per Person		Nation	Income per Person
54	Botswana[3]	$9,580	70	Lebanon	$5,550
55	Turkey	$7,720	71	Peru	$5,400
56	Namibia	$7,520	72	Albania	$5,070
57	Tunisia	$7,430	73	Philippines	$4,950
58	Belarus	$6,970	74	El Salvador	$4,890
59	Kazakhstan	$6,930	75	Paraguay	$4,820
60	Dominican Republic	$6,860	76	Jordan	$4,770
61	Panama	$6,730	77	Suriname	$4,300
62	Macedonia	$6,560	78	Guatemala	$4,260
63	Belize	$6,500	79	Morocco	$4,250
64	Ukraine	$6,330	80	Sri Lanka	$4,210
65	Algeria	$6,320	81	Egypt	$4,200
66	China	$5,890	82	Armenia	$4,160
67	Gabon	$5,700	83	Jamaica	$3,950
68	Turkmenistan	$5,700	84	Azerbaijan	$3,810
69	Swaziland	$5,650	85	Guyana	$3,800
			86	Ecuador	$3,770

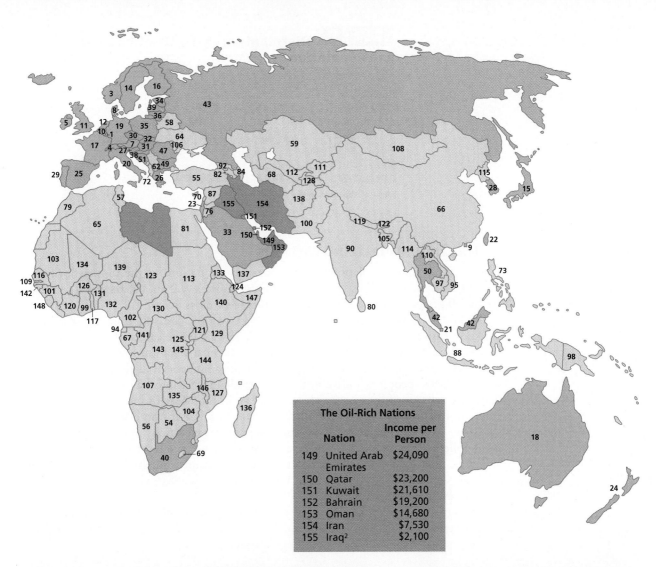

The Oil-Rich Nations		
	Nation	Income per Person
149	United Arab Emirates	$24,090
150	Qatar	$23,200
151	Kuwait	$21,610
152	Bahrain	$19,200
153	Oman	$14,680
154	Iran	$7,530
155	Iraq[2]	$2,100

The Least Industrialized Nations

	Nation	Income per Person		Nation	Income per Person		Nation	Income per Person		Nation	Income per Person
87	Syria	$3,500	102	Cameroon	$2,120	119	Nepal	$1,480	135	Zambia	$890
88	Indonesia	$3,480	103	Mauritania	$2,050	120	Cote d'Ivoire	$1,470	136	Madagascar	$840
89	Nicaragua	$3,480	104	Zimbabwe	$2,040	121	Uganda	$1,450	137	Yemen	$810
90	India	$3,120	105	Bangladesh	$1,970	122	Bhutan	$1,400	138	Afghanistan	$800
91	Cuba	$3,000	106	Moldova	$1,950	123	Chad	$1,340	139	Niger	$780
92	Georgia	$2,900	107	Angola	$1,930	124	Djibouti	$1,300	140	Ethiopia	$750
93	Honduras	$2,760	108	Mongolia	$1,900	125	Rwanda	$1,240	141	Congo	$740
94	Equatorial Guinea	$2,700	109	Gambia	$1,890	126	Burkina Faso	$1,170	142	Guinea-Bissau	$690
95	Vietnam	$2,700	110	Laos	$1,880	127	Mozambique	$1,170	143	Congo, Democratic Republic	$680
96	Bolivia	$2,600	111	Krygyzstan	$1,860	128	Tajikistan	$1,160			
97	Cambodia	$2,310	112	Uzbekistan	$1,860	129	Kenya	$1,130	144	Tanzania	$670
98	Papua-New Guinea	$2,280	113	Sudan	$1,810	130	Central African Republic	$1,100	145	Burundi	$660
			114	Burma	$1,700				146	Malawi	$630
99	Ghana	$2,220	115	Korea, North	$1,700	131	Benin	$1,090	147	Somalia	$600
100	Pakistan	$2,170	116	Senegal	$1,660	132	Nigeria	$970	148	Sierra Leone	$550
101	Guinea	$2,160	117	Togo	$1,510	133	Eritrea	$960			
			118	Haiti	$1,500	134	Mali	$950			

[1]Income is a country's purchasing power parity based on its per capita gross domestic product measured in U.S. dollars. Since some totals vary widely from year to year, they must be taken as approximate. [2]Iraq's oil has been disrupted by war. [3]Botswana's relative wealth is based on its diamond mines.

Sources: By the author. Based on *Statistical Abstract of the United States* 2007:Table 1324, with a few missing countries taken from the CIA's latest *World Factbook*.

Table 9.2 **Distribution of the World's Land and Population**

	Land	Population
Most Industrialized Nations	31%	16%
Industrializing Nations	20%	16%
Least Industrialized Nations	49%	68%

Sources: Computed from Kurian 1990, 1991, 1992.

The Industrializing Nations

The Industrializing Nations include most of the nations of the former Soviet Union and its former satellites in eastern Europe. As Table 9.2 shows, these nations account for 20 percent of the earth's land and 16 percent of its people.

The dividing points between the three "worlds" are soft, making it difficult to know how to classify some nations. This is especially the case with the Industrializing Nations. Exactly how much industrialization must a nation have to be in this category? Although soft, these categories do pinpoint essential differences among nations. Most people who live in the Industrializing Nations have much lower incomes and standards of living than those who live in the Most Industrialized Nations. The majority, however, are better off than those who live in the Least Industrialized Nations. For example, on such measures as access to electricity, indoor plumbing, automobiles, telephones, and even food, most citizens of the Industrializing Nations rank lower than those in the Most Industrialized Nations, but higher than those in the Least Industrialized Nations. As you saw in the opening vignette, stratification affects even life expectancy.

The benefits of industrialization are uneven. Large numbers of people in the Industrializing Nations remain illiterate and desperately poor. Conditions can be gruesome, as we explore in the following Thinking Critically section.

Thinking Critically

Open Season: Children As Prey

What is childhood like in the Industrializing Nations? The answer depends on who your parents are. If you are the son or daughter of rich parents, childhood can be pleasant—a world filled with luxuries, and even servants. If you are born into poverty, but living in a rural area where there is plenty to eat, life can still be good—although there may be no books, television, and little education. If you live in a slum, however, life can be horrible—worse even than in the slums of the Most Industrialized Nations. Let's take a glance at a notorious slum of Brazil.

There is not enough food—this you can take for granted—and wife abuse, broken homes, alcoholism, and drug abuse, along with a lot of crime. From your knowledge of slums in the Most Industrialized Nations, you would expect these things. What you may not expect, however, are the brutal conditions in which Brazilian slum (*favela*) children live.

Sociologist Martha Huggins (Huggins et al. 2002) reports that poverty is so deep that children and adults swarm over garbage dumps to try to find enough decaying food to keep them alive. You might also be surprised to discover that the owners of some of these dumps hire armed guards to keep the poor out—so that they can sell the garbage for pig food. And you might be shocked to learn that the Brazilian police and death squads murder some of these children. Some shop owners even hire hit men and auction designated victims off to the lowest bidder! The going rate is half a month's salary—figured at the low Brazilian minimum wage.

Life is cheap in the poor nations—but death squads for children? To understand this, we must first note that Brazil has a long history of violence. Brazil also has a high rate of poverty, has only a tiny middle class, and is controlled by a small group of families who, under a veneer of democracy, make the country's major decisions. Hordes of homeless children, with no schools or jobs, roam the streets. To survive, they wash windshields, shine shoes, beg, and steal (Huggins and Rodrigues 2004).

The "respectable" classes see these children as nothing but trouble. They hurt business, for customers feel intimidated when they see begging children—especially teenaged males—clustered in front of stores. Some shoplift; others dare to sell items that place them in competition with the stores. With no effective social institutions to care for these children, one solution is to kill them. As Huggins notes, murder sends a clear message—especially if it is accompanied by ritual torture: gouging out the eyes, ripping open the chest, cutting off the genitals, raping the girls, and burning the victim's body.

Not all life is bad in the Industrializing Nations, but this is about as bad as it gets.

for your Consideration

Do you think there is anything the Most Industrialized Nations can do about this situation? Or is it any of their business? Is it, though unfortunate, just an "internal" affair that is up to the Brazilians to handle as they wish?

The Least Industrialized Nations

In the Least Industrialized Nations, most people live on small farms or in villages, have large families, and barely survive. These nations account for 68 percent of the world's people but only 49 percent of the Earth's land.

Poverty plagues these nations to such an extent that some families actually *live* in city dumps. This is hard to believe, but look at the photos on pages 256–257, which I took in Phnom Penh, the capital of Cambodia. Although wealthy nations have their pockets of poverty, *most* people in the Least Industrialized nations are poor. *Most* of them have no running water, indoor plumbing, or access to trained teachers or physicians. As we will review in Chapter 20, most of the world's population growth occurs in these nations, placing even greater burdens on their limited resources and causing them to fall farther behind each year.

Modifying the Model

To classify countries into Most Industrialized, Industrializing, and Least Industrialized is helpful in that it pinpoints gross differences among them. But then there are the oil-rich nations of the Middle East, the ones that provide the oil and gasoline that fuel the machinery of the Most Industrialized Nations. Although these nations are not industrialized, some have become immensely wealthy. To classify them simply as Least Industrialized would gloss over significant distinctions, such as their modern hospitals, extensive prenatal care, desalinization

Homeless people sleeping on the streets is a common sight in India's cities. I took this photo in Chennai (formerly Madrás).

plants, abundant food and shelter, high literacy, and computerized banking. On the Social Map on pages 252–253, I classify them separately. Table 9.3 on page 258 reflects this significant distinction.

The Dump People:

Working and Living and Playing in the City Dump of Phnom Penh, Cambodia

went to Cambodia to inspect orphanages, to see how well the children were being cared for. While in Phnom Penh, Cambodia's capital, I was told about people who live in the city dump. *Live* there? I could hardly believe my ears. I knew that people made their living by picking scraps from the city dump, but I didn't know they actually lived among the garbage. This I had to see for myself.

I did. And there I found a highly developed social organization—an intricate support system. Because words are inadequate to depict the abject poverty of the Least Industrialized Nations, these photos can provide more insight into these people's lives than anything I could say.

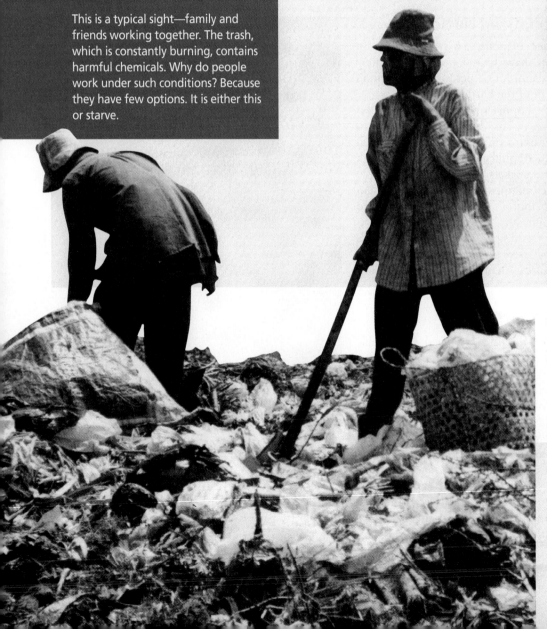

This is a typical sight—family and friends working together. The trash, which is constantly burning, contains harmful chemicals. Why do people work under such conditions? Because they have few options. It is either this or starve.

The people live at the edge of the dump, in homemade huts (visible in the background). This woman, who was on her way home after a day's work, put down her sack of salvaged items to let me take her picture.

After the garbage arrives by truck, people stream around it, struggling to be the first to discover something of value. To sift through the trash, the workers use metal picks, like the one this child is holding. Note that children work alongside the adults.

The children who live in the dump also play there. These children are riding bicycles on a "road," a packed, leveled area of garbage that leads to their huts. The huge stacks in the background are piled trash. Note the ubiquitous Nike.

One of my many surprises was to find food stands in the dump. Although this one primarily offers drinks and snacks, others serve more substantial food. One even has chairs for its customers.

I was surprised to learn that ice is delivered to the dump. This woman is using a hand grinder to crush ice for drinks for her customers. The customers, of course, are other people who also live in the dump.

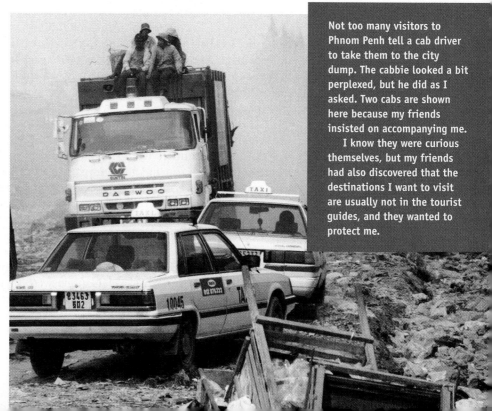

At the day's end, the workers wash at the community pump. This hand pump serves all their water needs—drinking, washing, and cooking. There is no indoor plumbing. The weeds in the background serve that purpose.

© James M. Henslin, all photos

Not too many visitors to Phnom Penh tell a cab driver to take them to the city dump. The cabbie looked a bit perplexed, but he did as I asked. Two cabs are shown here because my friends insisted on accompanying me.

I know they were curious themselves, but my friends had also discovered that the destinations I want to visit are usually not in the tourist guides, and they wanted to protect me.

Table 9.3 An Alternative Model of Global Stratification

Four Worlds of Development
1. Most Industrialized Nations
2. Industrializing Nations
3. Least Industrializing Nations
4. Oil-rich, nonindustrialized nations

Kuwait, on whose formal behalf the United States and other Most Industrialized Nations fought Iraq in the first Gulf War, is an excellent example of this distinction. Kuwait is so wealthy that almost none of its citizens works for a living. The government simply pays them an annual salary just for being citizens. Everyday life in Kuwait still has its share of onerous chores, of course, but migrant workers from the poor nations do most of them. To run the specialized systems that keep Kuwait's economy going, Kuwait imports trained workers from the Most Industrialized Nations, who, as with the first Gulf War, apparently fight its wars for it as well.

How Did the World's Nations Become Stratified?

How did the globe become stratified into such distinct worlds? The commonsense answer is that the poorer nations have fewer resources than the richer nations. As with many commonsense answers, however, this one, too, falls short. Many of the Industrializing and Least Industrialized Nations are rich in natural resources, while one Most Industrialized Nation, Japan, has few. Three theories explain how global stratification came about.

Colonialism

The first theory, **colonialism,** stresses that the countries that industrialized first got the jump on the rest of the world. Beginning in Great Britain about 1750, industrialization spread throughout western Europe. Plowing some of their immense profits into powerful armaments and fast ships, these countries invaded weaker nations, making colonies out of them (Harrison 1993). After subduing these weaker nations, the more powerful countries left behind a controlling force in order to exploit the nations' labor and natural resources. At one point, there was even a free-for-all among the industrialized European countries as they rushed to divide up an entire continent. As they sliced Africa into pieces, even tiny Belgium got into the act and acquired the Congo, which was *seventy-five* times larger than itself.

The purpose of colonialism was to establish *economic colonies*—to exploit the nation's people and resources for the benefit of the "mother" country. The more powerful European countries would plant their national flags in a colony and send their representatives to run the government, but the United States usually chose to plant corporate flags in a colony and let these corporations dominate the territory's government. Central and South America are prime examples. There were exceptions, such as the conquest of the Philippines, which President McKinley said was motivated by the desire "to educate the Filipinos, and uplift and civilize and Christianize them" (Krugman 2002).

Colonialism, then, shaped many of the Least Industrialized Nations. In some instances, the Most Industrialized Nations were so powerful that when dividing their spoils, they drew lines across a map, creating new states without regard for tribal or cultural considerations (Kifner 1999). Britain and France did just this as they divided up

colonialism the process by which one nation takes over another nation, usually for the purpose of exploiting its labor and natural resources

North Africa and parts of the Middle East—which is why the national boundaries of Libya, Saudi Arabia, Kuwait, and other countries are so straight. This legacy of European conquests is a background factor in much of today's racial-ethnic and tribal violence: Groups with no history of national identity were incorporated arbitrarily into the same political boundaries.

World System Theory

The second explanation of how global stratification came about was proposed by Immanuel Wallerstein (1974, 1979, 1990). According to **world system theory,** industrialization led to four groups of nations. The first group is the *core nations*, the countries that industrialized first (Britain, France, Holland, and later Germany), which grew rich and powerful. The second group is the *semiperiphery.* The economies of these nations, located around the Mediterranean, stagnated because they grew dependent on trade with the core nations. The economies of the third group, the *periphery*, or fringe nations, developed even less. These are the eastern European countries, which sold cash crops to the core nations. The fourth group of nations includes most of Africa and Asia. Called the *external area,* these nations were left out of the development of capitalism altogether. The current expansion of capitalism has changed the relationships among these groups. Most notably, Asia is no longer left out of capitalism.

The **globalization of capitalism**—the adoption of capitalism around the world—has created extensive ties among the world's nations. Production and trade are now so interconnected that events around the globe affect us all. Sometimes this is immediate, as happens when a civil war disrupts the flow of oil, or—perish the thought—as would be the case if terrorists managed to get their hands on nuclear or biological weapons. At other times, the effects are like a slow ripple, as when a government adopts some policy that gradually impedes its ability to compete in world markets. All of today's societies, then, no matter where they are located, are part of a *world system.*

The interconnections are most evident among nations that do extensive trading with one another. The following Thinking Critically section explores implications of Mexico's *maquiladoras.*

Thinking Critically

When Globalization Comes Home: *Maquiladoras* South of the Border

When Humberto drives his truck among Ciudad Juarez's shanties—patched together from packing crates, discarded tires, and cardboard—women and children flock around him. Humberto is the water man, and his truckload of water means life.

Two hundred thousand Mexicans rush to Juarez each year, fleeing the hopelessness of the rural areas in pursuit of a better life. They didn't have running water or plumbing in the country anyway, and here they have the possibility of a job, a weekly check to buy food for the kids.

The pay is $10 a day.

This may not sound like much, but it is more than twice the minimum daily wage in Mexico.

Assembly-for-export plants, known as *maquiladoras,* dot the Mexican border (Wise and Cypher 2007). The North American Free Trade Agreement (NAFTA) allows U.S. companies to import materials to Mexico without paying tax and to then export the finished products into the United States, again without tax. It's a sweet deal: few taxes and $10 a day for workers starved for jobs. Some companies get an even sweeter deal. They pay their workers Mexico's minimum wage of $4—for 10-hour days with a 30-minute break (Darweesh 2000).

That these workers live in shacks, with no running water or sewage disposal is not the employers' concern.

world system theory economic and political connections that tie the world's countries together

globalization of capitalism capitalism (investing to make profits within a rational system) becoming the globe's dominant economic system

A photo taken inside a *maquiladora* in Matamoros, Mexico. The steering wheels are for U.S. auto makers.

Nor is the pollution. The stinking air doesn't stay on the Mexican side of the border. Neither does the garbage. Heavy rains wash torrents of untreated sewage and industrial wastes into the Rio Grande (Lacey 2007).

There is also the loss of jobs for U.S. workers. Six of the fifteen poorest cities in the United States are located along the sewage-infested Rio Grande. NAFTA didn't bring poverty to these cities. They were poor before this treaty, but residents resent the jobs they've seen move across the border (Thompson 2001).

What if the *maquiladora* workers organize and demand better pay? Farther south, even cheaper labor beckons. Guatemala and Honduras will gladly take the *maquiladoras*. So will China, where workers make $1 a day. Mexico has already lost many of its *maquiladora* jobs to places where people even more desperate will work for even less (Luhnow 2004).

Many Mexican politicians would say that this presentation is one-sided. "Sure there are problems," they would say, "but that is always how it is when a country industrializes. Don't you realize that the *maquiladoras* bring jobs to people who have no work? They also bring roads, telephone lines, and electricity to undeveloped areas." "In fact," said Vicente Fox, when he was the president of Mexico, "workers at the *maquiladoras* make more than the average salary in Mexico—and that's what we call fair wages" (Fraser 2001).

This is where the workers live.

Let's apply our three theoretical perspectives to see where reality lies. Conflict theorists say that capitalists try to weaken the bargaining power of workers by exploiting divisions among them. In what is known as the *split labor market*, capitalists pit one group of workers against another to lower the cost of labor. How do you think that *maquiladoras* fit this conflict perspective?

When functionalists analyze a situation, they identify its functions and dysfunctions. What functions and dysfunctions of *maquiladoras* do you see?

Do *maquiladoras* represent exploitation or opportunity? As symbolic interactionists point out, reality is a perspective based on one's experience. What multiple realities do you see here?

Culture of Poverty

The third explanation of global stratification is quite unlike the other two. Economist John Kenneth Galbraith (1979) claimed that the cultures of the Least Industrialized Nations hold them back. Building on the ideas of anthropologist Oscar Lewis (1966a, 1966b), Galbraith argued that some nations are crippled by a **culture of poverty,** a way of life that perpetuates poverty from one generation to the next. He explained it this way: Most of the world's poor people are farmers who live on little plots of land. They barely produce enough food to survive. Living so close to the edge of starvation, they have little room for risk—so they stick closely to tried-and-true, traditional ways. To experiment with new farming techniques could bring disaster, for failure would lead to hunger and death.

Their religion also encourages them to accept their situation, for it teaches fatalism: the belief that an individual's position in life is God's will. For example, in India, the Dalits are taught that they must have done very bad things in a previous life to suffer so. They are supposed to submit to their situation—and in the next life maybe they'll come back in a more desirable state.

Evaluating the Theories

Most sociologists prefer colonialism and world system theory. To them, an explanation based on a culture of poverty places blame on the victim—the poor nations themselves. It points to characteristics of the poor nations, rather than to international political arrangements that benefit the Most Industrialized Nations at the expense of the poor nations. But even taken together, these theories yield only part of the picture. None of these theories, for example, would have led anyone to expect that after World War II, Japan would become an economic powerhouse: Japan had a religion that stressed fatalism, two of its major cities had been destroyed by atomic bombs, and it been stripped of its colonies.

Each theory, then, yields but a partial explanation, and the grand theorist who will put the many pieces of this puzzle together has yet to appear.

Maintaining Global Stratification

Regardless of how the world's nations became stratified, why do the same countries remain rich year after year, while the rest stay poor? Let's look at two explanations of how global stratification is maintained.

Neocolonialism

Sociologist Michael Harrington (1977) argued that when colonialism fell out of style it was replaced by **neocolonialism.** When World War II changed public sentiment about sending soldiers and colonists to exploit weaker countries, the Most Industrialized Nations turned to the international markets as a way of controlling the Least Industrialized Nations. By selling them goods on credit—especially weapons that their elite desire so they can keep themselves in power—the Most Industrialized Nations entrap the poor nations with a circle of debt.

culture of poverty the assumption that the values and behaviors of the poor are different from other people, that these factors are largely responsible for their poverty, and that parents perpetuate poverty across generations by passing these characteristics to their children

neocolonialism the economic and political dominance of the Least Industrialized Nations by the Most Industrialized Nations

As many of us learn the hard way, owing a large debt and falling behind on payments puts us at the mercy of our creditors. So it is with neocolonialism. The *policy* of selling weapons and other manufactured goods to the Least Industrialized Nations on credit turns those countries into eternal debtors. The capital they need to develop their own industries goes instead as payments toward the debt, which becomes bloated with mounting interest. Keeping these nations in debt forces them to submit to trading terms dictated by the neocolonialists (Carrington 1993; S. Smith 2001).

The oil-rich Middle Eastern nations provide an example of neocolonialism that has become highly significant for our own lives. Because of the two Gulf Wars and the terrorism that emanates from this region, it is worth focusing on Saudi Arabia (*Strategic Energy Policy* 2001; Mouawad 2007). Great Britain founded Saudi Arabia, drawing its boundaries and naming the country after the man (Ibn Saud) that Great Britain picked to lead it. The Most Industrialized Nations need low-priced oil to keep their factories running at a profit—and the Saudis have been providing it. When other nations pumped less—no matter the cause, whether revolution or an attempt to raise prices—the Saudis made up the shortfall. For decades, this arrangement brought us low oil prices. In return, the United States overlooked the human rights violations of the Saudi royal family and propped them up by selling them the latest weapons. Oil shortages have short-circuited this arrangement, at least temporarily, and have brought higher gasoline prices at the pump.

Multinational Corporations

Multinational corporations, companies that operate across many national boundaries, also help to maintain the global dominance of the Most Industrialized Nations. In some cases, multinational corporations exploit the Least Industrialized Nations directly. A prime example is the United Fruit Company, which used to control national and local politics in Central America. This U.S. corporation ran these nations as fiefdoms for the company's own profit while the U.S. Marines waited in the wings. An occasional invasion to put down dissidents reminded regional politicians of the military power that supported U.S. financial interests.

Most commonly, however, it is simply by doing business that multinational corporations help to maintain international stratification. A single multinational corporation may manage mining operations in several countries, do manufacturing in others, and run marketing networks around the globe. No matter where the profits are made, or where they are reinvested, the primary beneficiaries are the Most Industrialized Nations, especially the one in which the multinational corporation has its world headquarters.

In this game of profits, the elites of the Least Industrialized Nations are essential players (Sklair 2001; Wise and Cypher 2007). The multinational corporations funnel money to these elites, who, in return, create what is known as a "favorable business climate"—that is, low taxes and cheap labor. The money paid to the elites is politely called "subsidies" and "offsets," not bribes. Although most people in the Least Industrialized Nations live in remote villages where they eke out a meager living on small plots of land, the elites of these countries favor urban projects, such as building laboratories and computer centers in the capital city. The elites live a sophisticated upper-class life in the major cities of their home country, with many sending their children to prestigious Western universities, such as Oxford, the Sorbonne, and Harvard.

The money given to the elites (whether by direct payment or by letting the elites share in the investments) helps to maintain stratification. Not only do these payoffs allow the elites to maintain a genteel lifestyle but also they give them the ability to purchase hi-tech weapons. This allows them to continue to oppress their people and to preserve their positions of dominance. The result is a political stability that keeps alive the diabolical partnership between the multinational corporations and the national elites.

This, however, is not the full story. Multinational corporations also play a role in changing international stratification. This is an unintentional byproduct of their

multinational corporations
companies that operate across national boundaries; also called *transnational corporations*

worldwide search for cheap resources and labor. When these corporations move manufacturing from the Most Industrialized Nations to the Least Industrialized Nations, not only do they exploit cheap labor but also they bring jobs and money to these nations. Although workers in the Least Industrialized Nations are paid a pittance, it is more than they can earn elsewhere. With new factories come opportunities to develop skills and a capital base.

This does not occur in all nations, but it did in the Pacific Rim nations, nicknamed the "Asian tigers" (Hong Kong, Singapore, South Korea, and Taiwan, with some "emerging tigers" now appearing in this region). In return for providing the "favorable business climate" just mentioned, the multinational corporations invested billions of dollars in this region. These nations now have such a strong capital base that they have begun to rival the older capitalist countries. Subject to capitalism's "boom and bust" cycles, many workers and investors in these nations, including those in the *maquiladoras* that you just read about, will have their dreams smashed as capitalism moves into its next downturn.

Technology and Global Domination

The race between the Most and Least Industrialized Nations to develop and apply the new technologies is like a race between a marathon runner and someone with a broken leg. Can the outcome be in doubt? As the multinational corporations amass profits, they are able to invest huge sums in the latest technology. Gillette, for example, spent $100 million simply so that it could adjust its production "on an hourly basis" (Zachary 1995). These millions came from just one U.S. company. Many Least Industrialized Nations would love to have $100 million to invest in their entire economy, much less to use for fine-tuning the production of razor blades.

The race is not this simple, however. Although the Most Industrialized Nations have a seemingly insurmountable head start, in a surprise move, some of the Least Industrialized Nations are shortening the distance between themselves and the front runners. India and China are adopting high technology at a furious pace. With cheap telecommunications and the outsourcing of labor by many Western multinational corporations, workers in India and China are able to compete with their Western counterparts (Friedman 2005). Although the maintenance of global domination is not in doubt at this point, it could be on the verge of a major shift from West to East.

Unintended Public Relations   Bono and others have used the media well in a campaign to get G-8 to forgive the debts of some of the poorest of the world's nations. Their efforts have made a good story, which the mass media have loved to promote. G-8, however, knows how to milk the media, too. To cancel the debts of poor nations amidst television reporters and global drum rolls projects an image of good-hearted capitalists having mercy on the poor. Although G-8 had written these debts off as uncollectible in the first place, the publicity that accompanied their pronouncements helps to soften opposition to the global dominance of capitalism.

A Concluding Note

The term *global stratification* is such a remote-sounding term, but let's return to the three families featured in our opening vignette. These families represent distinct worlds of privilege and power, that is, unique locations in global stratification. By comparing these families, we can see how global stratification profoundly affects our life chances—from access to material possessions to our opportunity for education and even the likely age at which we will die. The division of the globe into interconnected units of nations with more or less wealth and more or less power and prestige, then, is much more than a matter of theoretical interest. In fact, it is *your* life we are talking about.

Summary *and* Review

Systems of Social Stratification

What is social stratification?

Social stratification refers to a hierarchy of relative privilege based on power, property, and prestige. Every society stratifies its members, and in every society men as a group are placed above women as a group. P. 237.

What are four major systems of social stratification?

Four major stratification systems are slavery, caste, estate, and class. The essential characteristic of **slavery** is that some people own other people. Initially, slavery was based not on race but on debt, punishment, or defeat in battle. Slavery could be temporary or permanent, and was not necessarily passed on to one's children. North American slaves had no legal rights, and the system was gradually buttressed by a racist **ideology.** In a **caste system,** status is determined by birth and is lifelong. The **estate system** of feudal Europe consisted of the nobility, clergy, and peasants (serfs). A **class system** is much more open than these other systems, for it is based primarily on money or material possessions. Industrialization encourages the formation of class systems. Gender cuts across all forms of social stratification. Pp. 237–243.

What Determines Social Class?

Karl Marx argued that a single factor determines social class: If you own the means of production, you belong to the **bourgeoisie;** if you do not, you are one of the **proletariat.** Max Weber argued that three elements determine social class: *property, prestige,* and *power.* Pp. 243–245.

Why Is Social Stratification Universal?

To explain why stratification is universal, functionalists Kingsley Davis and Wilbert Moore argued that to attract the most capable people to fill its important positions, society must offer them greater rewards. Melvin Tumin said that if this view were correct, society would be a **meritocracy,** with all positions awarded on the basis of merit. Gaetano Mosca argued that stratification is inevitable because every society must have leadership, which by definition means inequality. Conflict theorists argue that stratification came about because resources are limited, and an elite emerges as groups struggle for them. Gerhard Lenski suggested a synthesis between the functionalist and conflict perspectives. Pp. 245–248.

How Do Elites Maintain Stratification?

To maintain social stratification within a nation, the ruling class adopts an ideology that justifies its current arrangements. It also controls information and uses technology. When all else fails, it turns to brute force. Pp. 248–249.

Comparative Social Stratification

What are key characteristics of stratification systems in other nations?

The most striking features of the British class system are speech and education. In Britain, accent reveals social class, and almost all of the elite attend "public" schools (the equivalent of our private schools). In the former Soviet Union, communism was supposed to abolish class distinctions. Instead, it merely ushered in a different set of classes. Pp. 248–251.

Global Stratification: Three Worlds

How are the world's nations stratified?

The model presented here divides the world's nations into three groups: the Most Industrialized, the Industrializing, and the Least Industrialized. This layering represents relative property, prestige, and power. The oil-rich nations are an exception. Pp. 251–258.

How Did the World's Nations Become Stratified?

Why are some nations rich and others poor?

The main theories that seek to account for global stratification are **colonialism, world system theory,** and the **culture of poverty.** Pp. 258–261.

Maintaining Global Stratification

How do elites maintain global stratification?

There are two basic explanations for why the world's countries remain stratified. **Neocolonialism** is the ongoing dominance of the Least Industrialized Nations by the Most Industrialized Nations. The second explanation points to the influence of **multinational corporations.** The new technology gives further advantage to the Most Industrialized Nations. Pp. 261–263.

Thinking Critically

about Chapter 9

1. How do slavery, caste, estate, and class systems of social stratification differ?
2. Why is social stratification universal?
3. Do you think that the low-wage factories of the multinational corporations, located in such countries as Mexico, represent exploitation or opportunity? Why?

Additional Resources

What can you use MySocLab for? www.mysoclab.com

- **Study and Review:** Pre- and Post-Tests, Practice Tests, Flash Cards, Individualized Study Plans.

- **Current Events:** *Sociology in the News*, the daily *New York Times*, and more.

- **Research and Writing:** *Research Navigator, Writing About Sociology*, and more.

Where Can I Read More on This Topic?

Suggested readings for this chapter are listed at the back of this book.

CHAPTER 4

Social Class in the United States

Frank Freed, *Have and Have Not,* 1970

Ah, New Orleans, that fabled city on the Mississippi Delta. Images from its rich past floated through my head—pirates, treasure, intrigue. Memories from a pleasant vacation stirred my thoughts—the exotic French Quarter with its enticing aroma of Creole food and sounds of earthy jazz drifting through the air.

The shelter for the homeless, however, forced me back to an unwelcome reality. The shelter was the same as those I had visited in the North, West, and East—only dirtier. The dirt, in fact, was the worst that I had encountered during my research, and this shelter was the only one to insist on payment in exchange for sleeping in one of its filthy beds.

The men looked the same—disheveled and haggard, wearing that unmistakable expression of despair—just like the homeless anywhere in the country. Except for the accent, you wouldn't know what region you were in. Poverty wears the same tired face wherever you are, I realized. The accent may differ, but the look remains the same.

I had grown used to the sights and smells of abject poverty. Those no longer surprised me. But after my fitful sleep with the homeless, I saw something that did.

> **I was startled by a sight so out of step with the misery and despair that I stopped in midtrack.**

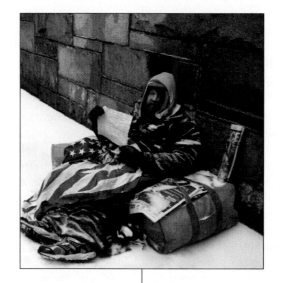

Just a block or so from the shelter, I was startled by a sight so out of step with the misery and despair I had just experienced that I stopped in midtrack.

Indignation swelled within me. Confronting me were life-size, full-color photos mounted on the transparent plexiglass shelter of a bus stop. Staring back at me were images of finely dressed men and women proudly strutting about as they modeled elegant suits, dresses, diamonds, and furs.

A wave of disgust swept over me. "Something is cockeyed in this society," I thought, my mind refusing to stop juxtaposing these images of extravagance with the suffering I had just witnessed. Occasionally, the reality of social class hits home with brute force. This was one of those moments.

The disjunction that I felt in New Orleans was triggered by the ads, but it was not the first time that I had experienced this sensation. Whenever my research abruptly transported me from the world of the homeless to one of another social class, I experienced a sense of disjointed unreality. Each social class has its own way of being, and because these fundamental orientations to the world contrast so sharply, the classes do not mix well.

What Is Social Class?

If you ask most Americans about their country's social class system, you are likely to get a blank look. If you press the matter, you are likely to get an answer like this: "There are the poor and the rich—and then there are you and I, neither poor nor rich." This is just about as far as most Americans' consciousness of social class goes. Let's try to flesh out this idea.

Our task is made somewhat difficult because sociologists have no clear-cut, agreed-on definition of social class. As was noted in the last chapter, conflict sociologists (of the Marxist orientation) see only two social classes: those who own the means of production and those who do not. The problem with this view, say most sociologists, is that it lumps too many people together. Teenage "order takers" at McDonald's who work for $15,000 a year are lumped together with that company's executives who make $500,000 a year—because they both are workers at McDonald's, not owners.

Most sociologists agree with Weber that there is more to social class than just a person's relationship to the means of production. Consequently, most sociologists use the components Weber identified and define **social class** as a large group of people who rank closely to one another in property, prestige, and power. These three elements separate people into different lifestyles, give them different chances in life, and provide them with distinct ways of looking at the self and the world.

Let's look at how sociologists measure these three components of social class.

Property

Property comes in many forms, such as buildings, land, animals, machinery, cars, stocks, bonds, businesses, furniture, and bank accounts. When you add up the value of someone's property and subtract that person's debts, you have what sociologists call **wealth.** This term can be misleading, as some of us have little wealth—especially most college students. Nevertheless, if your net total comes to $10, then that is your wealth. (Obviously, wealth as a sociological term does not equal wealthy.)

Distinguishing Between Wealth and Income   Wealth and income are sometimes confused, but they are not the same. Where *wealth* is a person's net worth, **income** is a flow of money. Income can come from a number of sources: usually a business or wages, but also from rent, interest, or royalties, even from alimony, an allowance, or gambling. Some people have much wealth and little income. For example, a farmer may own much land (a form of wealth), but bad weather, combined with the high cost of fertilizers and machinery, can cause the income to dry up. Others have much income and little wealth. An executive with a $250,000 annual income may be debt-ridden. Below the surface prosperity—the exotic vacations, country club membership, private schools for the children, sports cars, and an elegant home—the credit cards may be maxed out, the sports cars in danger of being repossessed, and the mortgage payments "past due." Typically, however, wealth and income go together.

Distribution of Property   Who owns the property in the United States? One answer, of course, is "everyone." Although this statement has some merit, it overlooks how the nation's property is divided among "everyone."

Overall, Americans are worth a hefty sum, about $38 trillion (*Statistical Abstract* 2007:Table 704). This includes all real estate, stocks, bonds, and business assets in the entire country. Figure 10.1 shows how highly concentrated this wealth is. Most wealth, 70 percent, is owned by only *10 percent* of the nation's families. As you can also see from this figure, 1 percent of Americans own one third of all the U.S. assets.

Distribution of Income   How is income distributed in the United States? Economist Paul Samuelson (Samuelson and Nordhaus 2005) put it this way: "If we made an income pyramid out of a child's blocks, with each layer portraying $500 of income, the peak would be far higher than Mount Everest, but most people would be within a few feet of the ground."

Actually, if each block were 1-½ inches tall, the typical American would be just 9 *feet off the ground,* for the average per capita income in the United States is about $35,000

social class according to Weber, a large group of people who rank close to one another in property, prestige, and power; according to Marx, one of two groups: capitalists who own the means of production or workers who sell their labor

property material possessions

wealth the total value of everything someone owns, minus the debts

income money received, usually from a job, business, or assets per year. (This average income includes every American, even children.) The typical family climbs a little higher, for most families have more than one worker, and together they average about $54,000 a year. Compared with the few families who are on the mountain's peak, the average U.S. family would find itself only 14 feet off the ground (*Statistical Abstract* 2007:Tables 660, 677). Figure 10.2 portrays these differences.

Figure 10.1 Distribution of the Property of Americans

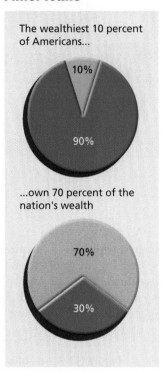

The wealthiest 10 percent of Americans...

10%
90%

...own 70 percent of the nation's wealth

70%
30%

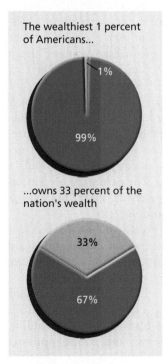

The wealthiest 1 percent of Americans...

1%
99%

...owns 33 percent of the nation's wealth

33%
67%

Source: By the author. Based on Beeghley 2008.

Figure 10.2 Distribution of the Income of Americans

Some U.S. families have incomes that exceed the height of Mt. Everest, 29,028 feet

Average U.S. family income $54,000 or 14 feet

Average U.S. individual income $35,000 or 9 feet

If a 1 1/2 inch child's block equals $500 of income, the average individual's annual income of $35,000 would represent a height of 9 feet, and the average family's annual income of $54,000 would represent a height of 14 feet. The income of some families, in contrast, would represent a height greater than that of Mt. Everest.

MONEY

Source: By the author.

The More Things Change, the More They Stay the Same: The Percentage of the Nation's Income Received by Each Fifth of U.S. Families

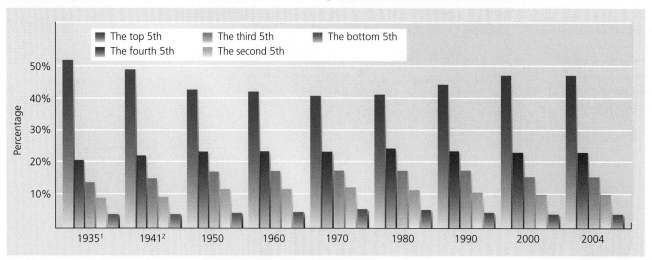

¹Earliest year available.
²No data for 1940.

Source: By the author. Based on *Statistical Abstract* 1960:Table 417; 1970:Table 489; 2007:Table 678.

The fact that some Americans enjoy the peaks of Mount Everest while most—despite their efforts—make it only 9 to 14 feet up the slope presents a striking image of income inequality in the United States. Another picture emerges if we divide the U.S. population into five equal groups and rank them from highest to lowest income. As Figure 10.3 shows, the top 20 percent of the population receive *almost half* (47.9 percent) of all income in the United States. In contrast, the bottom 20 percent of Americans receive only 4.0 percent of the nation's income.

A mere one-half of 1 percent of Americans owns over a quarter of the entire nation's wealth. Very few minorities are numbered among this 0.5 percent. An exception is Oprah Winfrey, who has had an ultra-successful career in entertainment and investing. Worth $1.3 billion, she is the 215th richest person in the United States. Winfrey, who has given millions of dollars to help minority children, is shown here as she is interviewed by David Letterman.

Two features of Figure 10.3 are outstanding. First, notice how little change there has been in the distribution of income through the years. Second, look at how income inequality decreased from 1935 to 1970. *Since 1970, the richest 20 percent of U.S. families have grown richer, while the poorest 20 percent have grown poorer.* Despite numerous government antipoverty programs, the poorest 20 percent of Americans receive *less* of the nation's income today than they did a generation ago. The richest 20 percent, in contrast, are receiving more, but not as much as they did in 1935.

The chief executive officers (CEOs) of the nation's largest corporations are especially affluent. The *Wall Street Journal* surveyed the 350 largest U.S. companies to find out what they paid their CEOs ("The Boss's Pay" 2007). Their median compensation (including salaries, bonuses, and stock options) came to $6,549,000 a year. (Median means that half received more than this amount, and half less.)

The CEOs' income—which does *not* include their income from interest, dividends, or rents, or the value of company-paid limousines and chauffeurs, airplanes and pilots, and private boxes at the symphony and sporting events—is *166 times* higher than the average pay of U.S. workers (*Statistical Abstract* 2007:Table 629). To really see the disparity consider this: The average U.S. worker would have to work *1,475 years* to earn the amount received by the highest-paid executive listed in Table 10.1.

Imagine how you could live with an income like this. And this is precisely the point. Beyond cold numbers lies a dynamic reality that profoundly affects people's lives. The difference in wealth between those at the top and those at the bottom of the U.S. class structure means that these individuals experience vastly different lifestyles. For example, a colleague of mine who was teaching at an exclusive Eastern university piqued his students' curiosity when he lectured on poverty in Latin America. That weekend, one of the students borrowed his parents' corporate jet and pilot, and in class on Monday, he and his friends related their personal observations on poverty in Latin America. Americans who are at the low end of the income ladder, in contrast, lack the funds to travel even to a neighboring town for the weekend. For young parents, choices may revolve around whether to spend the little they have at the laundromat or on milk for the baby. The elderly might have to choose between purchasing the medicines they need or buying food. In short, divisions of wealth represent not "mere" numbers, but choices that make vital differences in people's lives, a topic that we explore in the Down-to-Earth Sociology box on the next page.

Table 10.1	The 5 Highest-Paid CEOs	
Executive	**Company**	**Compensation**
1. Lloyd Blankfein	Goldman Sachs Group	$55 million
2. Stanley O'Neal	Merrill Lynch	$50 million
3. Ray Irani	Occidental Petroleum	$48 million
4. John Mack	Morgan Stanley	$40 million
5. Lawrence Ellison	Oracle	$39 million

Note: Compensation includes salary, bonuses, and stock options.
Source: "The Boss's Pay" 2007.

Power

Like many people, you may have said to yourself, "Sure, I can vote, but somehow the big decisions are always made despite what I might think. Certainly *I* don't make the decision to send soldiers to Afghanistan or Iraq. *I* don't launch missiles against Kosovo or Baghdad. *I* don't decide to raise taxes or lower interest rates. It isn't *I* who decides to change Social Security or Medicare benefits."

And then another part of you may say, "But I do participate in these decisions through my representatives in Congress, and by voting for president." True enough—as far as it goes. The trouble is, it just doesn't go far enough. Such views of being a participant in the nation's "big" decisions are a playback of the ideology we learn at an early age—an ideology that Marx said is promoted by the elites to both legitimate and perpetuate their power. Sociologists Daniel Hellinger and Dennis Judd (1991) call this the "democratic facade" that conceals the real source of power in the United States.

Back in the 1950s, sociologist C. Wright Mills (1956) was criticized for insisting that **power**—the ability to carry out your will despite resistance—was concentrated in the hands of a few, for his analysis contradicted the dominant ideology of equality. As was discussed in earlier chapters, Mills coined the term **power elite** to refer to those who make the big decisions in U.S. society.

Mills and others have stressed how wealth and power coalesce in a group of like-minded individuals who share ideologies and values. These individuals belong to the same private clubs, vacation at the same exclusive resorts, and even hire the same bands for their daughters' debutante balls. Their shared backgrounds and vested interests reinforce their view of both the world and their special place in it (Domhoff 1999a, 2006). This elite wields extraordinary power in U.S. society, so much so that *most* U.S. presidents have come from this group—millionaire white men from families with "old money" (Baltzell and Schneiderman 1988).

Continuing in the tradition of Mills, sociologist William Domhoff (1990, 2006) argues that this group is so powerful that no major decision of the U.S. government is

power the ability to carry out your will, even over the resistance of others

power elite C. Wright Mills' term for the top people in U.S. corporations, military, and politics who make the nation's major decisions made without its approval. He analyzed how this group works behind the scenes with elected officials to determine both the nation's foreign and domestic policy—from setting Social Security taxes to imposing trade tariffs. Although Domhoff's conclusions are controversial—and alarming—they certainly follow logically from the principle that wealth brings power, and extreme wealth brings extreme power.

Prestige

Occupations and Prestige What are you thinking about doing after college? Chances are, you don't have the option of lolling under palm trees at the beach. Almost all of us have to choose an occupation and go to work. Look at Table 10.2 to see how the career you are considering stacks up in terms of **prestige** (respect or regard). Because we are moving toward a global society, this table also shows how the rankings given by Americans compare with those of the residents of sixty other countries.

Down-to-Earth Sociology

How the Super-Rich Live

IT'S GOOD TO SEE how other people live. It gives us a different perspective on life. Let's take a glimpse at the life of John Castle (his real name). After earning a degree in physics at MIT and an MBA at Harvard, John went into banking and securities, where he made more than $100 million (Lublin 1999).

Wanting to be connected to someone famous, John bought President John F. Kennedy's "Winter White House," an ocean-front estate in Palm Beach, Florida. John spent $11 million to remodel the 13,000-square-foot house so that it would be more to his liking. Among those changes: adding bathrooms numbers 14 and 15. He likes to show off John F. Kennedy's bed and also the dresser that has the drawer labeled "black underwear," carefully hand-lettered by Rose Kennedy.

At his beachfront estate, John gives what he calls "refined feasts" to the glitterati ("On History . . . " 1999). If he gets tired of such activities—or weary of swimming in the Olympic-size pool where JFK swam the weekend before his assassination—he entertains himself by riding one of his thoroughbred horses at his nearby 10-acre ranch. If this fails to ease his boredom, he can relax aboard his custom-built 42-foot Hinckley yacht.

The yacht is a real source of diversion. John once boarded it for an around-the-world trip. He didn't stay on board, though—just joined the cruise from time to time. A captain and crew kept the vessel on course, and whenever

How do the super-rich live? This photo helps give you an idea of how different their lifestyles are from most of us. Shown here is Wayne Huizenga, who is featured in this box, with one of his vintage automobiles.

John felt like it he would fly in and stay a few days. Then he would fly back to the States to direct his business. He did this about a dozen times, flying perhaps 150,000 miles. An interesting way to go around the world.

How much does a custom-built Hinckley yacht cost? John can't tell you. As he says, "I don't want to know what anything costs. When you've got enough money, price doesn't make a difference. That's part of the freedom of being rich."

Right. And for John, being rich also means paying $1,000,000 to charter a private jet to fly Spot, his Appaloosa horse, back and forth to the vet. John didn't want Spot to have to endure a long trailer ride. Oh, and of course, there was the cost of Spot's medical treatment, another $500,000.

Other wealthy people put John to shame. Wayne Huizenga, the founder of Blockbuster, wanted more elbow room for his estate at Nantucket, so he added the house next door for $2.5 million (Fabrikant 2005). He also bought a 2,000-acre country club, complete with an 18-hole golf course, a 55,000-square-foot-clubhouse, and 68 slips for visiting vessels. The club is so exclusive that its only members are Wayne and his wife.

Why do people give more prestige to some jobs than to others? If you look at Table 10.2, you will notice that the jobs at the top share four features:

1. They pay more.
2. They require more education.
3. They entail more abstract thought.
4. They offer greater autonomy (independence, or self-direction).

If you look at the bottom of the list, you can see that people give less prestige to jobs with the opposite characteristics: These jobs are low-paying, require less preparation or education, involve more physical labor, and are closely supervised. In short, the professions and the white-collar jobs are at the top of the list, the blue-collar jobs at the bottom.

One of the more interesting aspects of these rankings is how consistent they are across countries and over time. For example, people in every country rank college professors higher than nurses, nurses higher than social workers, and social workers higher than janitors. Similarly, the occupations that were ranked high 25 years ago still rank high today—and likely will rank high in the years to come.

Displaying Prestige People want others to acknowledge their prestige. In times past, in some countries only the emperor and his family could wear purple—for it was the royal color. In France, only the nobility could wear lace. In England, no one could sit while the king was on his throne. Some kings and queens required that subjects walk backward as they left the room—so no one would "turn their back" on the "royal presence."

Concern with displaying prestige has not let up. For some, it is almost an obsession. Military manuals specify precisely who must salute whom. The U.S. president enters a room only after everyone else attending the function is present (to show that *he* isn't the one waiting for *them*). They also must be standing when he enters. In the courtroom, bailiffs, sometimes armed, make certain that everyone stands when the judge enters.

The display of prestige permeates society. In parts of Los Angeles, some people list their address as the prestigious Beverly Hills and then add their own correct ZIP code. When East Detroit changed its name to East Pointe to play off its proximity to swank Grosse Pointe, property values shot up (Fletcher 1997). Many pay more for clothing that bears a "designer" label. Prestige is often a primary factor in deciding which college to attend. Everyone knows how the prestige of a generic sheepskin from Regional State College compares with a degree from Harvard, Princeton, Yale, or Stanford.

Status symbols vary with social class. Clearly, only the wealthy can afford certain items, such as

Table 10.2 Occupational Prestige: How the United States Compares with 60 Countries

Occupation	United States	Average of 60 Countries
Physician	86	78
Supreme court judge	85	82
College president	81	86
Astronaut	80	80
Lawyer	75	73
College professor	74	78
Airline pilot	73	66
Architect	73	72
Biologist	73	69
Dentist	72	70
Civil engineer	69	70
Clergy	69	60
Psychologist	69	66
Pharmacist	68	64
High school teacher	66	64
Registered nurse	66	54
Professional athlete	65	48
Electrical engineer	64	65
Author	63	62
Banker	63	67
Veterinarian	62	61
Police officer	61	40
Sociologist	61	67
Journalist	60	55
Classical musician	59	56
Actor or actress	58	52
Chiropractor	57	62
Athletic coach	53	50
Social worker	52	56
Electrician	51	44
Undertaker	49	34
Jazz musician	48	38
Real estate agent	48	49
Mail carrier	47	33
Secretary	46	53
Plumber	45	34
Carpenter	43	37
Farmer	40	47
Barber	36	30
Store sales clerk	36	34
Truck driver	30	33
Cab driver	28	28
Garbage collector	28	13
Waiter or waitress	28	23
Bartender	25	23
Lives on public aid	25	16
Bill collector	24	27
Factory worker	24	29
Janitor	22	21
Shoe shiner	17	12
Street sweeper	11	13

Note: For five occupations not located in the 1994 source, the 1991 ratings were used: Supreme Court judge, astronaut, athletic coach, lives on public aid, and street sweeper.

Sources: Treiman 1977, Appendices A and D; Nakao and Treas 1991; 1994: Appendix D.

Display of prestige and social position varies over time and from one culture to another. Shown here is Elizabeth I, Queen of England and Ireland. Elizabeth became queen in 1558 at the age of 25 and ruled for 45 years, until 1603. This painting hangs in the National Portrait Gallery.

yachts and huge estates. But beyond affordability lies a class-based preference in status symbols. For example, people who are striving to be upwardly mobile are quick to flaunt labels, Hummers, Land Rovers, and other material symbols to show that they have "arrived," while the rich, more secure in their status, often downplay such images. The wealthy regard the designer labels of the "common" classes as cheap and showy. They, of course, flaunt their own status symbols, such as $50,000 Rolex watches. Like the other classes, they, too, try to outdo one another; they boast about who has the longest yacht or that they have a helicopter fly them to their meetings or their golf games (Fabrikant 2005).

Status Inconsistency

Ordinarily, a person has a similar rank on all three dimensions of social class—property, power, and prestige. The homeless men in the opening vignette are an example. Such people are **status consistent.** Sometimes that match is not there, however, and someone has a mixture of high and low ranks, a condition called **status inconsistency.** This leads to some interesting situations.

Sociologist Gerhard Lenski (1954, 1966) analyzed how people try to maximize their **status,** their position in a social group. Individuals who rank high on one dimension of social class but lower on others want people to judge them on the basis of their highest status. Others, however, who are trying to maximize their own position, may respond to status inconsistent individuals according to their lowest ranking.

A classic study of status inconsistency was done by sociologist Ray Gold (1952). He found that after apartment-house janitors unionized, they made more money than some of the tenants whose garbage they carried out. Tenants became upset when they saw their janitors driving more expensive cars than they did. Some attempted to "put the janitor in his place" by making "snotty" remarks to him. For their part, the janitors took delight in knowing "dirty" secrets about the tenants, gleaned from their garbage.

Individuals with status inconsistency, then, are likely to confront one frustrating situation after another (Heames et al. 2006). They claim the higher status, but are handed the lower one. The significance of this condition, said Lenski (1954), is that such people tend to be more politically radical. An example is college professors. Their prestige is very high, as we saw in Table 10.2, but their incomes are relatively low. Hardly anyone in U.S. society is more educated, and yet college professors don't even come close to the top of the income pyramid. In line with Lenski's prediction, the politics of most college professors are left of center. This hypothesis may also hold true among academic departments; that is, the higher a department's average pay, the less radical are the members' politics. Teachers in departments of business and medicine, for example, are among the most highly paid in the university—and they also are the most politically conservative.

Instant wealth, the topic of the Down-to-Earth Sociology box on the next page, provides an interesting case of status inconsistency.

Sociological Models of Social Class

The question of how many social classes there are is a matter of debate. Sociologists have proposed several models, but no single model has gained universal support. There are two main models: one that builds on Marx, the other on Weber.

Updating Marx

Marx argued that there are just two classes—capitalists and workers—with membership based solely on a person's relationship to the means of production (see Figure 10.4 on page 276). Sociologists have criticized this view, saying that these categories are too broad. For example, because executives, managers, and supervisors don't own the means

status consistency ranking high or low on all three dimensions of social class

status inconsistency ranking high on some dimensions of social class and low on others, also called *status discrepancy*

status the position that someone occupies in society or a social group

anomie Durkheim's term for a condition in which people become detached from the norms that usually guide their behavior

The Big Win: Life After the Lottery

"IF I JUST WIN THE LOTTERY, life will be good. These problems I've got, they'll be gone. I can just see myself now."

So goes the dream. And many Americans shell out megabucks every week, with the glimmering hope that "Maybe this week, I'll hit it big."

Most are lucky to get $20, or maybe just win another scratch-off ticket.

But there are the big hits. What happens to these winners? Are their lives all wine, roses, and chocolate afterward?

Unfortunately, we don't yet have any systematic studies of the big winners, so I can't tell you what life is like for the average winner. But several themes are apparent from reporters' interviews.

The most common consequence of hitting it big is that life becomes topsy-turvy (Ross 2004). All of us are rooted somewhere. We have connections with others that provide the basis for our orientations to life and how we feel about the world. Sudden wealth can rip these moorings apart, and the resulting *status inconsistency* can lead to a condition sociologists call **anomie.**

First comes the shock. As Mary Sanderson, a telephone operator in Dover, New Hampshire, who won $66 million, said, "I was afraid to believe it was real, and afraid to believe it wasn't." Mary says that she never slept worse than her first night as a multimillionaire. "I spent the whole time crying—and throwing up" (Tresniowski 1999).

Reporters and TV camera operators appear on your doorstep. "What are you going to do with all that money?" they demand. You haven't the slightest idea, but in a daze you mumble something.

Then come the calls. Some are welcome. Your Mom and Dad call to congratulate you. But long-forgotten friends and distant relatives suddenly remember how close they really are to you—and strangely enough, they all have emergencies that your money can solve. You even get calls from strangers who have ailing mothers, terminally ill kids, sick dogs . . .

You have to unplug the phone and get an unlisted number.

Some lottery winners are flooded with marriage proposals. These individuals certainly didn't become more attractive or sexy overnight—or did they? Maybe money makes people sexy.

You can no longer trust people. You don't know what their real motives are. Before, no one could be after your money because you didn't have any. You may even fear kidnappers. Before, this wasn't a problem—unless some kidnapper wanted the ransom of a seven-year-old car.

The normal becomes abnormal. Even picking out a wedding gift is a problem. If you give the usual toaster, everyone will think you're stingy. But should you write a check for $25,000? If you do, you'll be invited to every wedding in town—and everyone will expect the same.

Status inconsistency is common for lottery winners, whose new wealth is vastly greater than their education and occupational status. Shown here are John and Sandy Jarrell of Chicago, after they learned that they were one of 13 families to share a $295 million jackpot. How do you think their $22 million will affect their lives?

Here is what happened to some lottery winners:

As a tip, a customer gave a lottery ticket to Tonda Dickerson, a waitress at the Waffle House in Grand Bay, Alabama. She won $10 million. (Yes, just like the Nicholas Cage movie, *It Could Happen to You*.) Her coworkers sued her, saying that they had always agreed to split such winnings ("House Divided" 1999).

Then there is Michael Klinebiel of Rahway, New Jersey. When he won $2 million, his mother, Phyllis, said that they had pooled $20 a month for years to play the lottery. He said that was true, but his winning ticket wasn't from their pool. He had bought this one on his own. Phyllis sued her son ("Sticky Ticket" 1998).

Frank Capaci, a retired electrician in Streamwood, Illinois, who won $195 million, is no longer welcome at his old neighborhood bar. Two bartenders had collected $5 from customers and driven an hour to Wisconsin to buy tickets. When Frank won, he gave $10,000 to each of them. They said that he promised them more. Also, his former friends say that Capaci started to act "like a big shot," buying rounds of drinks but saying, "Except him," while pointing to someone he didn't like (Annin 1999).

Mack Metcalf of Corbin, Kentucky, wasn't as fortunate as Frank Capaci. After Mack hit the jackpot for $34 million, he built a beautiful home—but his former wife sued him, his current wife divorced him, his new girlfriend got $500,000 while he was drunk, and within three years of his good fortune he had drunk himself to death (Dao 2005).

Winners who avoid *anomie* seem to be people who don't make sudden changes in their lifestyle or their behavior. They hold onto their old friends, routines, and other anchors in life that give them identity and a sense of belonging. Some even keep their old jobs—not for the money, of course, but because working anchors them to an identity with which they are familiar and comfortable.

Sudden wealth, in other words, poses a threat that has to be guarded against.

And I can just hear you say, "I'll take the risk!"

Figure 10.4 Marx's Model of the Social Classes

> **Capitalists**
> (*Bourgeoisie*, those who own the means of production)

> **Workers**
> (*Proletariat*, those who work for the capitalists)

> **Inconsequential Others**
> (beggars, etc.)

Table 10.3 Wright's Modification of Marx's Model of the Social Classes

1. Capitalists
2. Petty bourgeoisie
3. Managers
4. Workers

contradictory class locations Erik Wright's term for a position in the class structure that generates contradictory interests

of production, they would be classified as workers. But what do these people have in common with assembly-line workers? The category of "capitalist" is also too broad. Some people, for example, employ a thousand workers, and their decisions directly affect a thousand families. Compare these people with a man I know in Godfrey, Illinois, who used to fix cars in his backyard. As Frank gained a following, he quit his regular job, and in a few years he put up a building with five bays and an office. Frank is now a capitalist, for he employs five or six mechanics and owns the tools and the building (the "means of production"). But what does he have in common with a factory owner who controls the lives of one thousand workers? Not only is Frank's work different but so are his lifestyle and the way he looks at the world.

To resolve this problem, sociologist Erik Wright (1985) suggests that some people are members of more than one class at the same time. They occupy what he calls **contradictory class locations.** By this, Wright means that a person's position in the class structure can generate contradictory interests. For example, the automobile mechanic-turned-business owner may want his mechanics to have higher wages because he, too, has experienced their working conditions. At the same time, his current interests—making profits and remaining competitive with other repair shops—lead him to resist pressures to raise their wages.

Because of such contradictory class locations, Wright modified Marx's model. As summarized in Table 10.3, Wright identifies four classes: (1) *capitalists,* business owners who employ many workers; (2) *petty bourgeoisie,* small business owners; (3) *managers,* who sell their own labor but also exercise authority over other employees; and (4) *workers,* who simply sell their labor to others. As you can see, this model allows finer divisions than the one Marx proposed, yet it maintains the primary distinction between employer and employee.

Problems persist, however. For example, in which category would we place college professors? And as you know, there are huge differences in the power of managers. An executive at Toyota, for example, may manage a thousand workers, while a shift manager at McDonald's may be responsible for only a handful. They, too, have little in common.

Updating Weber

Sociologists Joseph Kahl and Dennis Gilbert (Gilbert and Kahl 1998; Gilbert 2003) developed a six-tier model to portray the class structure of the United States and other capitalist countries. Think of this model, illustrated in Figure 10.5 on the next page, as a ladder. Our discussion starts with the highest rung and moves downward. In line with Weber, on each lower rung you find less property (wealth), less power, and less prestige. Note that in this model education is also a primary measure of class.

The Capitalist Class Sitting on the top rung of the class ladder is a powerful elite that consists of just 1 percent of the U.S. population. As you saw in Figure 10.1 on page 269, this capitalist class is so wealthy that it owns one–third of all U.S. assets. *This tiny 1 percent is worth more than the entire bottom 90 percent of the country* (Beeghley 2008).

Power and influence cling to this small elite. They have direct access to top politicians, and their decisions open or close job opportunities for millions of people. They even help to shape the consciousness of the nation: They own our major media and entertainment outlets—newspapers, magazines, radio and television stations, and sports franchises. They also control the boards of directors of our most influential colleges and universities. The super-rich perpetuate themselves in privilege by passing on their assets and social networks to their children.

The capitalist class can be divided into "old" and "new" money. The longer that wealth has been in a family, the more it adds to the family's prestige. The children of "old" money seldom mingle with "common" folk. Instead, they attend exclusive private schools where they learn views of life that support their privileged position. They don't work for wages; instead, many study business or enter the field of law so that they can manage the family fortune. These old-money capitalists (also called "blue-bloods") wield vast power as they use their extensive political connections to protect their economic empires (Sklair 2001; Domhoff 1990, 1999b, 2006).

Figure 10.5 The U.S. Social Class Ladder

Social Class	Education	Occupation	Income	Percentage of Population
Capitalist	Prestigious university	Investors and heirs, a few top executives	$1,000,000+	1%
Upper Middle	College or university, often with postgraduate study	Professionals and upper managers	$125,000+	15%
Lower Middle	High school or college; often apprenticeship	Semiprofessionals and lower managers, craftspeople, foremen	About $60,000	34%
Working	High school	Factory workers, clerical workers, low-paid retail sales, and craftspeople	About $35,000	30%
Working Poor	Some high school	Laborers, service workers, low-paid salespeople	About $17,000	16%
Underclass	Some high school	Unemployed and part-time, on welfare	Under $10,000	4%

Source: Based on Gilbert and Kahl 1998 and Gilbert 2003; income estimates are modified from Duff 1995.

At the lower end of the capitalist class are the *nouveau riche,* those who have "new money." Although they have made fortunes in business, the stock market, inventions, entertainment, or sports, they are outsiders to the upper class. They have not attended the "right" schools, and they don't share the social networks that come with old money. Not blue-bloods, they aren't trusted to have the right orientations to life (Burris 2000). Even their "taste" in clothing and status symbols is suspect (Fabricant 2005). Donald Trump, whose money is "new," is not listed in the *Social Register,* the "White Pages" of the blue-bloods that lists the most prestigious and wealthy one-tenth of 1 percent of the U.S. population. Trump says he "doesn't care," but he reveals his true feelings by adding that his heirs will be in it

With a fortune of $48 billion, Bill Gates, a cofounder of Microsoft Corporation, is the second wealthiest person in the world. His 40,000-square-foot home (sometimes called a "technopalace") in Seattle, Washington, was appraised at $110 million.

Gates has given more money to the poor and minorities than any individual in history. His foundation is now focusing on fighting infectious diseases, developing vaccines, and improving schools.

(Kaufman 1996). He is probably right, for the children of the new-moneyed can ascend into the top part of the capitalist class—if they go to the right schools *and* marry old money.

Many in the capitalist class are philanthropic. They establish foundations and give huge sums to "causes." Their motivations vary. Some feel guilty because they have so much while others have so little. Others seek prestige, acclaim, or fame. Still others feel a responsibility—even a sense of fate or purpose—to use their money for doing good. Bill Gates, who has given more money to the poor and to medical research than anyone else has, seems to fall into this latter category.

The Upper Middle Class   Of all the classes, the upper middle class is the one most shaped by education. Almost all members of this class have at least a bachelor's degree, and many have postgraduate degrees in business, management, law, or medicine. These people manage the corporations owned by the capitalist class or else operate their own business or profession. As Gilbert and Kahl (1998) say, these positions

> may not grant prestige equivalent to a title of nobility in the Germany of Max Weber, but they certainly represent the sign of having "made it" in contemporary America. . . . Their income is sufficient to purchase houses and cars and travel that become public symbols for all to see and for advertisers to portray with words and pictures that connote success, glamour, and high style.

Consequently, parents and teachers push children to prepare for upper-middle-class jobs. About 15 percent of the population belong to this class.

Sociologists use income, education, and occupational prestige to measure social class. For most people, this classification works well, but not for everyone. Entertainers sometimes are difficult to fit in. To what social class do Depp, Cruz, Oh, and James belong? Johnny Depp makes $10 million a year, Penelope Cruz $1 to 2 million, and Sandra Oh around $300,000. When Lebron James got out of high school, he signed more than $100 million in endorsement contracts, as well as a $4 million contract to play basketball for the Cleveland Cavaliers.

Johnny Depp

LeBron James

Penelope Cruz

Sandra Oh

The Lower Middle Class About 34 percent of the population belong to the lower middle class. Members of this class have jobs that call for them to follow orders given by those who have upper-middle-class credentials. With their technical and lower-level management positions, they can afford a mainstream lifestyle, and many anticipate being able to move up the social class ladder. Feelings of insecurity are common, however, with the threat of inflation, recession, and job insecurity bringing a nagging sense that they might fall down the class ladder (Kefalas 2007).

The distinctions between the lower middle class and the working class on the next rung below are more blurred than those between other classes. In general, however, members of the lower middle class work at jobs that have slightly more prestige, and their incomes are generally higher.

The Working Class About 30 percent of the U.S. population belong to this class of relatively unskilled blue-collar and white-collar workers. Compared with the lower middle class, they have less education and lower incomes. Their jobs are also less secure, more routine, and more closely supervised. One of their greatest fears is that of being laid off during a recession. With only a high school diploma, the average member of the working class has little hope of climbing up the class ladder. Job changes usually bring "more of the same," so most concentrate on getting ahead by achieving seniority on the job rather than by changing their type of work. They tend to think of themselves as having "real jobs," and regard the "suits" above them as paper pushers who have no practical experience (Morris and Grimes 2005).

The Working Poor Members of this class, about 16 percent of the population, work at unskilled, low-paying, temporary and seasonal jobs, such as sharecropping, migrant farm work, housecleaning, and day labor. Most are high school dropouts. Many are functionally illiterate, finding it difficult to read even the want ads. They are not likely to vote (Gilbert and Kahl 1998; Beeghley 2008), for they believe that no matter what party is elected to office, their situation won't change.

Although they work full time, millions of the working poor depend on help such as food stamps and donations from local food pantries to survive on their meager incomes (O'Hare 1996b). It is easy to see how you can work full time and still be poor. Suppose that you are married and have a baby 3 months old and another child 3 years old. Your spouse stays home to care for them, so earning the income is up to you. But as a high-school dropout, all you can get is a minimum wage job. At $7.25 an hour, you earn $290 for 40 hours. In a year, this comes to $15,080—before deductions. Your nagging fear—and daily nightmare—is of ending up "on the streets."

The Underclass On the lowest rung, and with next to no chance of climbing anywhere, is the **underclass.** Concentrated in the inner city, this group has little or no connection with the job market. Those who are employed—and some are—do menial, low-paying, temporary work. Welfare, if it is available, along with food stamps and food pantries, is their main support. Most members of other classes consider these people the "ne'er-do-wells" of society. Life is the toughest in this class, and it is filled with despair. About 4 percent of the population fall into this class.

The homeless men described in the opening vignette of this chapter, and the women and children like them, are part of the underclass. These are the people whom most Americans wish would just go away. Their presence on our city streets bothers passersby from the more privileged social classes—which includes just about everyone. "What are those obnoxious, dirty, foul-smelling people doing here, cluttering up my city?" appears to be a common response. Some people react with sympathy and a desire to do something. But what? Almost all of us just shrug our shoulders and look the other way, despairing of a solution and somewhat intimidated by their presence.

"There are plenty of jobs around. People just don't want to work."

A primary sociological principle is that people's views are shaped by their social location. Many people from the middle and upper classes cannot understand how anyone can work and still be poor.

underclass a group of people for whom poverty persists year after year and across generations

The homeless are the "fallout" of our postindustrial economy. In another era, they would have had plenty of work. They would have tended horses, worked on farms, dug ditches, shoveled coal, and run the factory looms. Some would have explored and settled the West. Others would have been lured to California, Alaska, and Australia by the prospect of gold. Today, however, with no frontiers to settle, factory jobs scarce, and farms that are becoming technological marvels, we have little need for unskilled labor.

Social Class in the Automobile Industry

Let's use the automobile industry to illustrate the social class ladder. The Fords, for example, own and control a manufacturing and financial empire whose net worth is truly staggering. Their power matches their wealth, for through their multinational corporation, their decisions affect production and employment in many countries. The family's vast fortune and its accrued power are now several generations old. Consequently, Ford children go to the "right" schools, know how to spend money in the "right" way, and can be trusted to make family and class interests paramount in life. They are without question at the top level of the *capitalist* class.

Next in line come top Ford executives. Although they may have an income of several hundred thousand dollars a year (and some, with stock options and bonuses, earn several million dollars annually), most are new to wealth and power. Consequently, they would be classified at the lower end of the capitalist class.

A husband and wife who own a Ford agency are members of the *upper middle class.* Their income clearly sets them apart from the majority of Americans, and their reputation in the community is enviable. More than likely, they also exert greater-than-average influence in their community, but their capacity to wield power is limited.

A Ford salesperson, as well as people who work in the dealership office, belongs to the *lower middle class.* Although there are some exceptional salespeople–even a few who make handsome incomes selling prestigious, expensive cars to the capitalist class—those at a run-of-the-mill Ford agency are lower middle class. Compared with the owners of the agency, their income is less, their education is likely to be less, and their work is less prestigious.

Mechanics who repair customers' cars are members of the *working class.* A mechanic who is promoted to supervise the repair shop joins the lower middle class. Those who "detail" used cars (making them appear newer by washing and polishing the car, painting the tires, spraying "new car scent" into the interior, and so on) belong to the *working poor.* Their income and education are low, and the prestige accorded to their work minimal. They are laid off when selling slows down.

Ordinarily, the *underclass* is not represented in the automobile industry. It is conceivable, however, that the agency might hire a member of the underclass to do a specific job such as mowing the grass or cleaning up the used car lot. In general, however, personnel at the agency do not trust members of the underclass and do not want to associate with them—even for a few hours. They prefer to hire someone from the working poor for such jobs.

Consequences of Social Class

Each social class can be thought of as a broad subculture with distinct approaches to life. Social class affects people's health, family life, and education. It also influences their religion and politics, and even their experiences with crime and the criminal justice system. Let's look at these consequences of social class, as well as how the new technology is related to social class.

Physical Health

If you want to get a sense of how social class affects health, take a ride on Washington's Metro system. Start in the blighted Southeast section of downtown D.C. For every mile you travel to where the wealthy live in Montgomery County in Maryland, life expectancy rises about a year and a half. By the time you get off, you will find a twenty-year gap between the poor blacks where you started your trip and the rich whites where you ended it. (Cohen 2004). (The foldout at the front of the book illustrates these effects of social class.)

The effects of social class on physical health are startling. The principle is simple: The lower a person's social class, the more likely that individual is to die before the expected age. This principle holds true at all ages. Infants born to the poor are more likely than other infants to die before their first birthday. In old age—whether 75 or 95—a larger proportion of the poor die each year than do the wealthy.

How can social class have such dramatic effects? While there is some controversy over the reasons, there seem to be three basic explanations. First, social class opens and closes doors to medical care. Consider this example:

> Terry Takewell (his real name), a 21-year-old diabetic, lived in a trailer park in Somerville, Tennessee. When Zettie Mae Hill, Takewell's neighbor, found the unemployed carpenter drenched with sweat from a fever, she called an ambulance. Takewell was rushed to nearby Methodist Hospital, where, it turned out, he had an outstanding bill of $9,400. A notice posted in the emergency room told staff members to alert supervisors if Takewell ever returned.
>
> When the hospital administrator was informed of the admission, Takewell was already in a hospital bed. The administrator went to Takewell's room, helped him to his feet, and escorted him to the parking lot. There, neighbors found him under a tree and took him home.
>
> Takewell died about twelve hours later.
>
> Zettie Mae Hill wonders whether Takewell would be alive today if she had directed his ambulance to a different hospital. She said, "I didn't think a hospital would just let a person die like that for lack of money." (Based on Ansberry 1988)

Why was Terry Takewell denied medical treatment and his life cut short? The fundamental reason is that health care in the United States is not a citizens' right but a commodity for sale. This gives us a two-tier system of medical care: superior care for those who can afford the cost and inferior care for those who cannot (Budrys 2003). Unlike the middle and upper classes, few poor people have a personal physician, and they often spend hours waiting in crowded public health clinics. After waiting most of a day, some don't even get to see a doctor. Instead, they are told to come back the next day. And when the poor are hospitalized, they are likely to find themselves in understaffed and underfunded public hospitals, treated by rotating interns who do not know them and cannot follow up on their progress.

A second reason is lifestyles, which are shaped by social class. People in the lower social classes are more likely to smoke, eat a lot of fats, be overweight, abuse drugs and alcohol, get little or no exercise, and practice unsafe sex (Chin et al. 2000; Navarro 2002; Liu 2007). This, to understate the matter, does not improve people's health.

There is a third reason, too. Life is hard on the poor. The persistent stresses they face cause their bodies to wear out faster (Spector 2007). The rich find life better. They have fewer problems and more resources to deal with the ones they have. This gives them a sense of control over their lives, a source of both physical and mental health.

Mental Health

From the 1930s until now, sociologists have found that the mental health of the lower classes is worse than that of the higher classes (Faris and Dunham 1939; Srole et al. 1978; Pratt et al. 2007). Greater mental problems are part of the higher stress that accompanies poverty. Compared with middle- and upper-class Americans, the poor have less job security and lower wages. They are more likely to divorce, to be the victims of crime, and to have more physical illnesses. Couple these conditions with bill collectors and the threat of eviction, and you can see how they can deal severe blows to people's emotional well-being.

People higher up the social class ladder experience stress in daily life, of course, but their stress is generally less, and their coping resources are greater. Not only can they afford vacations, psychiatrists, and counselors but also *their class position gives them greater control over their lives, a key to good mental health.*

Family Life

Social class also plays a significant role in family life. It even affects our choice of spouse, our chances of getting divorced, and how we rear our children.

Choice of Husband or Wife   Members of the capitalist class place strong emphasis on family tradition. They stress the family's ancestors, history, and even a sense of purpose or destiny in life (Baltzell 1979; Aldrich 1989). Children of this class learn that their choice of husband or wife affects not just themselves but also the entire family, that their spouse will have an impact on the "family line." Because of these background expectations, the field of "eligible" marriage partners is much narrower than it is for the children of any other social class. As a result, parents in this class play a strong role in their children's mate selection.

Divorce   The more difficult life of the lower social classes, especially the many tensions that come from insecure jobs and inadequate incomes, leads to higher marital friction and a greater likelihood of divorce. Consequently, children of the poor are more likely to grow up in broken homes.

Child Rearing   As discussed on page 83, sociologists have found significant class differences in child rearing. Lower-class parents focus on getting their children to follow rules and obey authority, while middle-class parents focus on developing their children's creative and leadership skills. The reason for this difference appears to be the parents' occupation (Kohn 1977). Lower-class parents are closely supervised at work, and they anticipate that their children will have similar jobs. Consequently, they try to teach their children to defer to authority. Middle-class parents, in contrast, enjoy

How much difference does social class make in our lives? Shown here are actress Jillian Barberie in the walk-in closet of her home in Los Angeles, California, and Paulina Rodriguez in the living room of her home in Rio Grande Valley, Texas. Can you see why these women are likely to see the world in highly distinctive ways, and why even their politics and aspirations in life are likely to differ?

greater independence at work. Anticipating similar jobs for their children, they encourage them to be more creative. Out of these contrasting orientations arise different ways of disciplining children; lower-class parents are more likely to use physical punishment, while the middle classes rely more on verbal persuasion.

Working-class and middle-class parents also have different ideas about child development and children's play (Lareau 2002). Working-class parents think that children develop naturally, a sort of unfolding from within. If parents provide comfort, food, shelter, and other basic support, the child's development will take care of itself. Consequently, they set limits and let their children play as they wish. Middle-class parents, however, think that children need a lot of guidance to develop correctly, and they encourage play and extracurricular activities that they think will help develop their children's mental and social skills.

Education

As we saw in Figure 10.5 on page 277, education increases as one goes up the social class ladder. It is not just the amount of education that changes, but also the type of education. Children of the capitalist class bypass public schools. They attend exclusive private schools where they are trained to take a commanding role in society. Prep schools such as Phillips Exeter Academy, Groton School, and Woodberry Forest School teach upper-class values and prepare their students for prestigious universities (Cookson and Persell 2005; Beeghley 2008).

Keenly aware that private schools can be a key to social mobility, some upper middle class parents do their best to get their children into the prestigious preschools that feed into these exclusive prep schools. Although some preschools cost $23,000 a year, they have a waiting list (Rohwedder 2007). Parents even elicit letters of recommendation for their 2- and 3-year-olds. Such parental expectations and resources are major reasons why children from the more privileged classes are more likely to go to college—and to graduate.

Religion

One area of social life that we might think would not be affected by social class is religion. ("People are just religious, or they are not. What does social class have to do with it?") As we shall see in Chapter 18, however, the classes tend to cluster in different denominations. Episcopalians, for example, are more likely to attract the middle and upper classes, while Baptists draw heavily from the lower classes. Patterns of worship also follow class lines: The lower classes are attracted to more expressive worship services and louder music, while the middle and upper classes prefer more "subdued" worship.

Politics

As has been stressed throughout this text, symbolic interactionists emphasize that people perceive events from their own corner in life. Political views are no exception to this principle, and the rich and the poor walk different political paths. The higher that people are on the social class ladder, the more likely they are to vote for Republicans (Burris 2005). In contrast, most members of the working class believe that the government should intervene in the economy to provide jobs and to make citizens financially secure. They are more likely to vote for Democrats. Although the working class is more liberal on *economic* issues (policies that increase government spending), it is more conservative on *social* issues (such as opposing abortion and the Equal Rights Amendment) (Lipset 1959; Houtman 1995). People toward the bottom of the class structure are also less likely to be politically active—to campaign for candidates or even to vote (Soss 1999; Gilbert 2003; Beeghley 2008).

Crime and Criminal Justice

If justice is supposed to be blind, it certainly is not when it comes to one's chances of being arrested (Henslin 2008). In Chapter 8 (pages 216–221), we discussed how the upper and lower social classes have different styles of crime. The white-collar crimes of the more privileged classes are more likely to be dealt with outside the criminal justice system, while the police and courts deal with the street crimes of the lower classes. One consequence of this class standard is that members of the lower classes are more likely to be in prison, on probation, or on parole. In addition, since people tend to commit crimes in or near their own neighborhoods, the lower classes are more likely to be robbed, burglarized, or murdered.

The Changing Economy

Two major forces in today's world are the globalization of capitalism and rapidly changing technology. If the United States does not remain competitive by producing low-cost, high-quality, state-of-the-art goods, its economic position will decline. The result will be dwindling opportunities—fewer jobs, shrinking paychecks, and vast downward social mobility.

The upheaval in the economy does not affect all social classes in the same way. For the *capitalist class,* globalization is a dream come true: Although the competition is keen, by minimizing the obstacles of national borders, capitalists are able to move factories to countries that provide cheaper labor. They produce components in one country, assemble them in another, and market the product throughout the world. Members of the *upper middle class* are well prepared for this change. Their higher education enables them to take a leading role in managing this global system for the capitalist class, or for using the new technology to advance in their professions.

Below these two most privileged classes, however, changes in capitalism and technology add to the insecurities to life. As job markets shift, the skills of many in the *lower middle class* become outdated. Those who work at specialized crafts are especially at risk, for changing markets and technology can reduce or even eliminate the need for their skills. People in lower management are more secure, for they can transfer their skills from one job to another.

From this middle point on the ladder down, these changes in capitalism and technology hit people the hardest. The threat of plant closings haunts the *working class,* for they have few alternatives. The *working poor* are even more vulnerable, for they have even less to offer in the new job market. As unskilled jobs dry up, many workers are tossed into the industrial garbage bin.

The *underclass* has been bypassed altogether. This point was driven home to me when I saw the homeless sitting dejected in the shelters. There were our high school dropouts, our technological know-nothings. Of what value are they to this new technological society competing on a global level? They simply have no productive place in it. Their base of social belonging and self-esteem—tied into work and paychecks—has been pulled out from under them.

Social Mobility

■■ ▰▰ ■■   No aspect of life, then—from marriage to politics—goes untouched by social class. Because life is so much more satisfying in the more privileged classes, people strive to climb the social class ladder. What affects their chances?

Three Types of Social Mobility

There are three basic types of social mobility: intergenerational, structural, and exchange. **Intergenerational mobility** refers to a change that occurs between generations—when grown-up children end up on a different rung of the social class ladder from the one occupied by their parents. If the child of someone who sells used cars graduates from college and buys a Saturn dealership, that person experiences **upward social mobility.** Conversely, if a child of the dealership's owner parties too much, drops out of college, and ends up selling cars, he or she experiences **downward social mobility.**

We like to think that individual efforts are the reason people move up the class ladder—and their faults the reason they move down. In these examples, we can identify hard work,

intergenerational mobility the change that family members make in social class from one generation to the next

upward social mobility movement up the social class ladder

downward social mobility movement down the social class ladder sacrifice, and ambition on the one hand, versus indolence and substance abuse on the other. Although individual factors such as these do underlie social mobility, sociologists consider **structural mobility** to be the crucial factor. This second basic type of mobility refers to changes in society that cause large numbers of people to move up or down the class ladder.

To better understand structural mobility, think of how opportunities opened when computers were invented. New types of jobs appeared overnight. Huge numbers of people attended workshops and took crash courses, switching from blue-collar to white-collar work. Although individual effort certainly was involved—for some seized the opportunity while others did not—the underlying cause was a change in the *structure* of work. Consider the opposite—how opportunities disappear during a depression, which forces millions of people downward on the class ladder. In this instance, too, their changed status is due less to individual behavior than to *structural* changes in society.

The term *structural mobility* refers to changes in society that push large numbers of people either up or down the social class ladder. A remarkable example was the stock market crash of 1929, when tens of thousands of people suddenly lost immense amounts of wealth. People who once "had it made" found themselves standing on street corners selling apples or, as depicted here, selling their possessions at fire-sale prices.

The third type of social mobility, **exchange mobility,** occurs when large numbers of people move up and down the social class ladder, but, on balance, the proportions of the social classes remain about the same. Suppose that a million or so working-class people are trained in some new technology, and they move up the class ladder. Suppose also that because of a surge in imports, about a million skilled workers have to take lower-status jobs. Although millions of people change their social class, there is, in effect, an *exchange* among them. The net result more or less balances out, and the class system remains basically untouched.

Women in Studies of Social Mobility

In classic studies, sociologists concluded that about half of sons passed their fathers on the social class ladder; about one-third stayed at the same level, and about one-sixth moved down (Blau and Duncan 1967; Featherman and Hauser 1978; Featherman 1979).

Feminists objected that it wasn't good science to focus on sons and ignore daughters (Davis and Robinson 1988). They also pointed out that it was wrong to assume that women had no social class position of their own, that wives should not simply be assigned the class of their husbands. The defense made by male sociologists of the time was that too few women were in the labor force to make a difference.

With huge numbers of women now working for pay, more recent studies include women (Gofen 2007; Beeghley 2008). Sociologists Elizabeth Higginbotham and Lynn Weber (1992), for example, studied 200 women from working-class backgrounds who became professionals, managers, and administrators in Memphis. They found that almost without exception, the women's parents had encouraged them while they were still little girls to postpone marriage and get an education. This study confirms how important the family is in the socialization process. It also supports the observation that the primary entry to the upper middle class is a college education. At the same time, if there had not been a *structural* change in society, the millions of new positions that women occupy would not exist.

Interpreting Statistics on Social Mobility

The United States is famous worldwide for its intergenerational mobility. That children can pass up their parents on the social class ladder is one of the attractions of this country. How much mobility is there? It turns out that most apples don't fall far from the tree. Of children who are born to the poorest 10 percent of Americans, about a third are

structural mobility movement up or down the social class ladder because of changes in the structure of society, not to individual efforts

exchange mobility about the same numbers of people moving up and down the social class ladder, such that, on balance, the social class system shows little change still there when they are grown up—half end up in the poorest 20 percent. Similarly, of children who are born to the richest 10 percent of families, about a third stay there—two of five end up among the richest 20 percent (Krueger 2002). In short, the benefits that high-income parents enjoy tend to keep their children afloat, while the obstacles that low-income parents confront tend to weigh their children down.

But is the glass half empty or half full? We could also stress the other end of these findings: Two-thirds of the very poorest kids move upward, and two-thirds of the very richest kids drop down. Remember that statistics don't lie, but liars use statistics. In this case, you can stress either part of these findings, depending on what you are trying to prove.

The Pain of Social Mobility

You know that to be knocked down the social class ladder is painful, but were you aware that climbing it also brings pain? Sociologist Steph Lawler (1999) interviewed British women who had moved from the working class to the middle class. The women were caught between two worlds—their working-class background and their current middle-class life. As the women's mothers criticized their new middle-class ways—their tastes in furniture and food, their speech, and even the way they reared their children—the relationship between daughters and mothers grew strained. Sociologists Richard Sennett and Jonathan Cobb (1972/1988), who studied working-class parents in Boston, found something similar. The parents had made deep sacrifices so their children could go to college, and they expected their children to appreciate their sacrifice. Because the children's educated world was so distant from that of their parents, however, the children grew aloof, and the family members had difficulty talking to one another. Not surprisingly, the parents felt betrayed and bitter.

In short, social class separates people into worlds so distinct that communication and mutual understanding become difficult. Sociologists also have studied fellow sociologists: Those who make the jump from the working class to college and university positions also feel a tearing away of their roots. Some never become comfortable with their new social class (Morris and Grimes 2005). The Cultural Diversity box on the next page discusses other costs that come with the climb up the social class ladder.

Poverty

Many Americans find that the "limitless possibilities" on which the American dream is based are really quite elusive. As is illustrated in Figure 10.5 on page 277, the working poor and underclass together form about one-fifth of the U.S. population. This translates into a huge number, about 60 million people. Who are these people?

Drawing the Poverty Line

To determine who is poor, the U.S. government draws a **poverty line.** This measure was set in the 1960s, when poor people were thought to spend about one-third of their incomes on food. On the basis of this assumption, each year the government computes a low-cost food budget and multiplies it by 3. Families whose incomes are less than this amount are classified as poor; those whose incomes are higher—even by a dollar—are determined to be "not poor."

This official measure of poverty is grossly inadequate. Poor people actually spend only about 20 percent of their incomes on food, so to determine a poverty line, we ought to multiply their food budget by 5 instead of 3 (Uchitelle 2001). No political party in power wants to do this, as redrawing the line in this way would make it appear that poverty increased under their watch. Another problem with the poverty line is that some mothers work outside the home and have to pay for child care, but they are treated the same as mothers who don't have this expense. The poverty line is also the same for everyone across the nation, even though the cost of living is much higher in New York than in Alabama. In addition, the government does not count food stamps as income.

poverty line the official measure of poverty; calculated to include incomes that are less than three times a low-cost food budget

Social Class and the Upward Social Mobility of African Americans

THE OVERVIEW OF SOCIAL CLASS presented in this chapter doesn't apply equally to all the groups that make up U.S. society. Consider geography: What constitutes the upper class of a town of 5,000 people will be quite different from that of a city of a million. The extremes of wealth and the diversity and prestige of occupations will be less in the small town, where family background is likely to play a more significant role.

So, too, there are differences within racial-ethnic groups. While all racial-ethnic groups are marked by divisions of social class, what constitutes a particular social class can differ from one group to another—as well as from one historical period to another. Consider social class among African Americans (Cole and Omari 2003).

The earliest class divisions can be traced to slavery—to slaves who worked in the fields and those who worked in the "big house." Those who worked in the plantation home were exposed to more "genteel" manners and forms of speech. Their more privileged position—which brought with it better food, clothing, and lighter work—was often based on skin color. Mulattos, lighter-skinned slaves, were often chosen for this more desirable work. One result was the development of a "mulatto elite," a segment of the slave population that, proud of its distinctiveness, distanced itself from the other slaves. At this time, there also were free blacks. Not only were they able to own property but some of them even owned black slaves.

After the War Between the States (as the Civil War is known in the South), these two groups, the mulatto elite and the free blacks, became the basis of an upper class. Proud of their earlier status, they distanced themselves from other blacks. From these groups came most of the black professionals.

After World War II, just as with whites, the expansion of the black middle class opened access to a wider range of

occupations and residential neighborhoods. Beginning about 1960, the numbers of African Americans who were middle class surged. Today, more than half of all African American adults work at white-collar jobs, with twenty-two percent working at the professional or managerial level (Beeghley 2008). As with members of other racial-ethnic groups, African Americans who move up the social class ladder experience a hidden cost: They feel an uncomfortable distancing from their roots, a separation from significant others—parents, siblings, and childhood friends (hooks 2000). The upwardly mobile individual has entered a world unknown to those left behind.

The cost of upward mobility that comes with trying to straddle two worlds is common to individuals from all groups. What appears to be different for African Americans, however, is a sense of leaving one's racial-ethnic group, of the necessity—if one is to succeed in the new world—of conforming to a dominant culture. This includes appearance and speech, but also something much deeper—values, aspirations, and ways of evaluating the self. In addition, the increased contact with whites that comes with social mobility often brings a greater sense of deprivation. Whites become a primary reference group, yet racism, mostly subtle and beneath the surface, continues. Awareness that they are not fully accepted in their new world engenders frustration, dissatisfaction, and cynicism.

for your Consideration

If you review the box on upward social mobility on page 85, you will find that Latinos face a similar situation. Why do you think this is? What connections do you see among upward mobility, frustration, and strong racial-ethnic identity? How do you think that the upward mobility of whites is different? Why?

That a change in the poverty line would instantly make millions of people poor—or take away their poverty—would be a laughable matter, if it weren't so serious. (The absurdity has not been lost on Parker and Hart, as you can see from their sarcastic cartoon on page 289.) Although this line is arbitrary, it is the official measure of poverty, and the government uses it to decide who will receive help and who will not. On the basis of this line, let's see who in the United States is poor. Before we do this, though, compare your ideas of the poor with the myths explored in the Down-to-Earth Sociology box on the next page.

Down-to-Earth Sociology

Exploring Myths About the Poor

Myth 1 Most poor people are lazy. They are poor because they do not want to work. Half of the poor are either too old or too young to work: About 40 percent are under age 18, and another 10 percent are age 65 or older. About 30 percent of the working-age poor work at least half the year.

Myth 2 Poor people are trapped in a cycle of poverty that few escape. Long-term poverty is rare. Most poverty lasts less than a year (Lichter and Crowley 2002). Only 12 percent remain in poverty for five or more consecutive years (O'Hare 1996a). Most children who are born in poverty are *not* poor as adults (Ruggles 1989; Corcoron 2001).

Myth 3 Most of the poor are African Americans and Latinos. As shown in Figure 10.6, the poverty rates of African Americans and Latinos are much higher than that of whites. Because there are so many more whites in the U.S. population, however, *most*

of the poor are white. Of the 37 million U.S. poor, about 57 percent are white, 20 percent African American, 20 percent Latino, and 3 percent Asian American (*Statistical Abstract* 2007:Table 694).

Myth 4 Most of the poor are single mothers and their children. Although about 38 percent of the poor match this stereotype, 34 percent of the poor live in married-couple families, 22 percent live alone or with nonrelatives, and 6 percent live in other settings.

Myth 5 Most of the poor live in the inner city. This one is close to fact, as about 42 percent do live in the inner city. But 36 percent live in the suburbs, and 22 percent live in small towns and rural areas.

Myth 6 The poor live on welfare. This stereotype is far from reality. Only about 25 percent of the income of poor adults comes from welfare. About half comes from wages and pensions, and about 22 percent from Social Security.

Sources: Primarily O'Hare 1996a, 1996b, with other sources as indicated.

Figure 10.6 **Poverty in the United States, by Age and Race-Ethnicity**

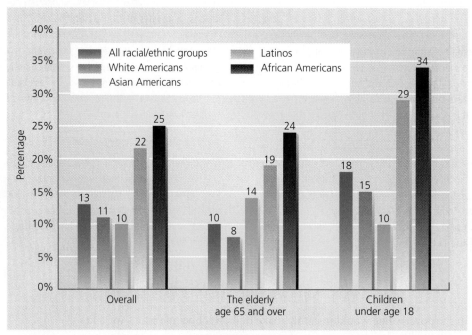

Note: Only these groups are listed in the source. The poverty line on which this figure is based is $19,307 for a family of four.

Source: By the author. Based on *Statistical Abstract* 2007:Table 694.

This cartoon pinpoints the arbitrary nature of the poverty line. This makes me almost think that the creators of the Wizard of Id have been studying sociology.

Who Are the Poor?

Geography   As you can see from the Social Map below, the poor are not evenly distributed among the states. This map shows a clustering of poverty in the South, a pattern that has prevailed for more than 150 years.

A second aspect of geography is also significant. About 59 million Americans live in rural areas. Of these, 9 million are poor. At 16 percent, the rate of poverty of rural Americans is higher than the national average of 13 percent. The rural poor are less likely to be single parents, and more likely to be married and to have jobs. Compared with urban Americans, the rural poor are less educated, and the jobs available to them pay less than similar jobs in urban areas (Lichter and Crowley 2002; Arseneault 2006).

Geography, however, is not the main factor in poverty. The greatest predictors of poverty are race-ethnicity, education, and the sex of the person who heads the family. Let's look at these factors.

Race-Ethnicity   One of the strongest factors in poverty is race-ethnicity. As Figure 10.6 on the previous page shows, only 10 percent of Asian Americans and 11 percent of whites are poor, but 22 percent of Latinos and 25 percent of African Americans live in

Figure 10.7   Patterns of Poverty

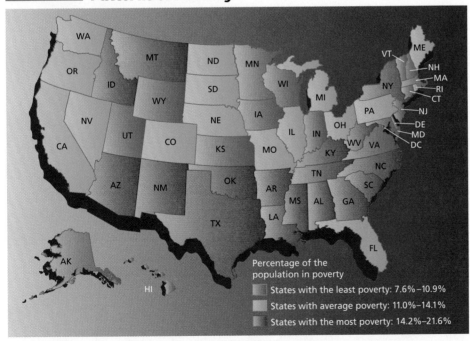

Percentage of the population in poverty
- States with the least poverty: 7.6%–10.9%
- States with average poverty: 11.0%–14.1%
- States with the most poverty: 14.2%–21.6%

Note: Poverty varies tremendously from one state to another. In the extreme, poverty is about three times greater in Mississippi (21.6%) than in Connecticut and New Hampshire (7.6% each).

Source: By the author. Based on *Statistical Abstract of the United States* 2007:Table 690.

Beyond the awareness of most Americans are the rural poor, such as this family in Kentucky. This family is typical of the rural poor: white and headed by a woman. What do you think the future holds for these children?

poverty. The stereotype that most poor people are African Americans and Latinos is untrue. Because there are so many more whites in U.S. society, their much lower rate of poverty translates into larger numbers. As a result, most poor people are white.

Education   You are aware that education is a vital factor in poverty, but you may not know just how powerful it is. Figure 10.8 below shows that 3 of 100 people who finish college end up in poverty, but one of every four people who drop out of high school is poor. As you can see, the chances that someone will be poor become less with each higher level of education. Although this principle applies regardless of race-ethnicity, this figure shows that at every level of education race-ethnicity makes an impact.

The Feminization of Poverty   One of the best indicators of whether or not a family is poor is family structure. Those least likely to be poor are families that are headed by both the mother and the father. Families headed by only a father or a mother are more likely to be poor, with poverty the most common among mother-headed families. The reason for this can be summed up in this one statistic: On average, women who head families earn only 70 percent of the income of men who head families (*Statistical Abstract* 2007:Table 679). With our high rate of divorce combined with our high number of births to single women, mother-headed families have become more common. This association of poverty with women has come to be known by sociologists as the **feminization of poverty.**

(the) feminization of poverty a trend in U.S. poverty whereby most poor families are headed by women

Old Age   As Figure 10.6 on page 288 shows, the elderly are *less* likely than the general population to be poor. This is quite a change. It used to be that growing old increased people's chances of being poor, but government policies to redistribute income—Social Security and subsidized housing, food, and medical care—slashed the rate of poverty among the elderly. This figure also shows how the prevailing racial-ethnic patterns carry over into old age. You can see how much more likely an elderly African American or Latino is to be poor than an elderly white or Asian American.

Figure 10.8   **Who Ends Up Poor? Poverty by Education and Race-Ethnicity**

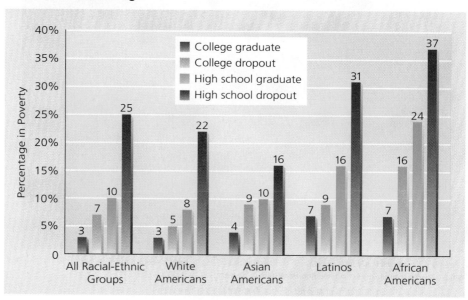

Source: By the author. Based on *Statistical Abstract of the United States* 2007:Table 697.

Children of Poverty

Children are more likely to live in poverty than are adults or the elderly. This holds true regardless of race-ethnicity, but from Figure 10.6 on page 288, you can see how much greater poverty is among Latino and African American children. That millions of U.S. children are reared in poverty is shocking when one considers the wealth of this country and the supposed concern for the well-being of children. This tragic aspect of poverty is the topic of the following Thinking Critically section.

Thinking Critically

The Nation's Shame: Children in Poverty

One of the most startling statistics in sociology is shown in Figure 10.6 on page 288. Look at the rate of childhood poverty: For Asian Americans, one of ten children is poor; for whites, one of seven; for Latinos, one of three or four; and for African Americans, an astounding one of three. These percentages translate into incredible numbers—approximately *16 million* children live in poverty: 8 million white children, 4 million Latino children, 4 million African American children, and 300,000 Asian American children.

Why do so many U.S. children live in poverty? The main reason, said sociologist and former U.S. Senator Daniel Moynihan (1991), is an increase in births outside marriage. In 1960, one of twenty U.S. children was born to a single woman. Today that total is about *seven times higher,* and single women now account for one of three (36 percent) of all U.S. births (*Statistical Abstract* 2007:Table 84). Sociologists Lee Rainwater and Timothy Smeeding (2003), who note that *the poverty rate of U.S. children is the highest in the industrialized world,* point to another cause: the lack of government support to children.

Births to single women follow patterns that are significant for their children's welfare. The less education a woman has, the more likely she is to bear children when she is not married. As you can see from Figure 10.9, births to single women drop with each gain in education. Because people with lower education earn less, this means that the single women who can least afford children are those most likely to give birth. Their children are likely to live in poverty and to face the suffering and obstacles to a satisfying life that poverty entails. They are more likely to die in infancy, to go hungry, to be malnourished, to develop more slowly, and to have more health problems. They also are more likely to drop out of school, to become

Figure 10.9 **Births to Single Mothers**

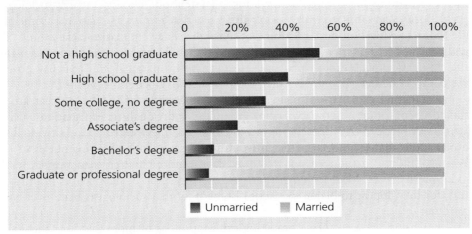

Note: Based on a national U.S. sample of all births in the preceding 12 months.

Source: Dye 2005.

involved in criminal activities, and to have children while still in their teens—thus perpetuating the cycle of poverty.

for your Consideration

With education so important to obtain jobs that pay better, in light of Figure 10.9, what programs would you suggest for helping women attain more education? Be specific and practical.

The Dynamics of Poverty

Some have suggested that the poor tend to get trapped in a **culture of poverty** (Harrington 1962; Lewis 1966a). They assume that the values and behaviors of the poor "make them fundamentally different from other Americans, and that these factors are largely responsible for their continued long-term poverty" (Ruggles 1989:7).

Lurking behind this concept is the idea that the poor are lazy people who bring poverty on themselves. Certainly, some individuals and families match this stereotype—many of us have known them. But is a self-perpetuating culture—one that is transmitted across generations and that locks people in poverty—the basic reason for U.S. poverty?

Researchers who began following 5,000 U.S. families in 1968 uncovered some surprising findings. Contrary to common stereotypes, most poverty is short-lived, lasting only a year or less. The researchers found that most poverty comes about because of a dramatic life change such as divorce, the loss of a job, or even the birth of a child (O'Hare 1996a). As Figure 10.10 shows, only 12 percent of poverty lasts five years or longer. Contrary to the stereotype of lazy people content to live off the government, few poor people enjoy poverty—and they do what they can to avoid being poor.

Yet from one year to the next, the number of poor people remains about the same. This means that the people who move out of poverty are replaced by people who move *into* poverty. Most of these newly poor will also move out of poverty within a year. Some people even bounce back and forth, never quite making it securely out of poverty. Poverty, then, is dynamic, touching a lot more people than the official totals indicate. Although 12 percent of Americans may be poor at any one time, twice that number—about one-fourth of the U.S. population—is or has been poor for at least a year.

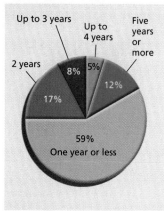

Figure 10.10 How Long Does Poverty Last?

Up to 3 years

Up to 4 years

Five years or more

2 years

8%

5%

12%

17%

59% One year or less

Source: Gottschalk et al. 1994:89.

Why Are People Poor?

Two explanations for poverty compete for our attention. The first, which sociologists prefer, focuses on *social structure.* Sociologists stress that *features of society* deny some people access to education or the learning of job skills. They emphasize racial-ethnic, age, and gender discrimination, as well as changes in the job market—the closing of plants, the elimination of unskilled jobs, and the increase in marginal jobs that pay poverty wages. In short, some people find their escape routes to a better life blocked.

A competing explanation focuses on the *characteristics of individuals* that are assumed to contribute to poverty. Sociologists reject individualistic explanations such as laziness and lack of intelligence, viewing these as worthless stereotypes. Individualistic explanations that sociologists reluctantly acknowledge include dropping out of school, bearing children in the teen years, and averaging more children than women in the other social classes. Most sociologists are reluctant to speak of such factors in this context, for they appear to blame the victim, something that sociologists bend over backward not to do.

The tension between these competing explanations is of more than just theoretical interest. Each explanation affects our perception and has practical consequences, as is illustrated in the following Thinking Critically section.

culture of poverty the assumption that the values and behaviors of the poor make them fundamentally different from other people, that these factors are largely responsible for their poverty, and that parents perpetuate poverty across generations by passing these characteristics to their children

The Welfare Debate: The Deserving and the Undeserving Poor

Throughout U.S. history, Americans have divided the poor into two types: the deserving and the undeserving. The deserving poor are people who, in the public mind, are poor through no fault of their own. Most of the working poor, such as the Lewises, are considered deserving:

> Nancy and Ted Lewis are in their early 30s and have two children. Ted works three part-time jobs, earning $13,000 a year; Nancy takes care of the children and house and is not employed. To make ends meet, the Lewises rely on food stamps, Medicaid, and housing subsidies.

The undeserving poor, in contrast, are viewed as people who brought on their own poverty. They are freeloaders who waste their lives in laziness, alcohol and drug abuse, and promiscuous sex. They don't deserve help, and, if given anything, will waste it on their dissolute lifestyles. Some would see Joan as an example:

> Joan, her mother, and her three brothers and two sisters lived on welfare. Joan started having sex at 13, bore her first child at 15, and, now, at 23, is expecting her fourth child. Her first two children have the same father, the third a different father, and Joan isn't sure who fathered her coming child. Joan parties most nights, using both alcohol and whatever drugs are available. Her house is filthy, the refrigerator usually empty, and social workers have threatened to take away her children.

This division of the poor into deserving and undeserving underlies the heated debate about welfare. "Why should we use *our* hard-earned money to help *them*? They are just going to waste it. Of course, there are others who want to get back on their feet, and helping them is okay."

for your Consideration

Why do people make a distinction between deserving and undeserving poor? Should we let some people starve because they "brought poverty upon themselves"? Should we let children go hungry because their parents are drug abusers? Does "unworthy" mean that we should not offer assistance to people who "squander" the help they are given?

In contrast to thinking of poor people as deserving or undeserving, use the sociological perspective to explain poverty without blaming the victim. What *social* conditions (conditions of society) create poverty? Are there *social* conditions that produce the lifestyles that the middle class so despises?

Welfare Reform

After decades of criticism, the U.S. welfare system was restructured in 1996. A federal law—the Personal Responsibility and Work Opportunity Reconciliation Act—requires states to place a lifetime cap on welfare assistance and compels welfare recipients to look for work and to take available jobs. The maximum length of time that someone can collect welfare is five years. In some states, it is less. Unmarried teen parents must attend school and live at home or in some other adult-supervised setting.

This law set off a storm of criticism. Some called it an attack on the poor. Defenders replied that the new rules would rescue people from poverty. They would transform welfare recipients into self-supporting and hard-working citizens—and reduce welfare costs. National welfare rolls plummeted, dropping by about 60 percent (Urban Institute 2006). Two out of five who left welfare also moved out of poverty (Hofferth 2002).

This is only the rosy part of the picture, however. Three of five are still in poverty or are back on welfare. A third of those who were forced off welfare have no jobs (Hage 2004; Urban Institute 2006). Some can't work because they have health problems. Others lack transportation. Some are addicted to drugs and alcohol. Still others are trapped in economically depressed communities where there are no jobs. Then there are those who have jobs, but earn so little that they remain in poverty. Consider one of the "success stories":

> JoAnne Sims, 37, lives in Erie, New York, with her 7-year-old daughter Jamine. JoAnne left welfare, and now earns $6.75 an hour as a cook for Head Start. Her 37-hour week brings $239.75 before deductions. With the help of medical benefits and a mother who provides child care, JoAnne "gets by." She says, "From what I hear, a lot of us who went off welfare are still poor . . . let me tell you, it's not easy." (Peterson 2000)

Conflict theorists have an interesting interpretation of welfare. They say that welfare's purpose is not to help people, but, rather, to maintain a *reserve labor force*. It is designed to keep the unemployed alive during economic downturns until they are needed during the next economic boom. Reducing the welfare rolls through the 1996 law fits this model, as it occurred during the longest economic boom in U.S. history. Recessions are inevitable, however, and just as inevitable is surging unemployment. In line with conflict theory, we can predict that during the coming recession, welfare rules will be softened—in order to keep the reserve labor force ready for the next time they are needed.

Deferred Gratification

One consequence of a life of deprivation punctuated by emergencies—*and of viewing the future as promising more of the same*—is a lack of **deferred gratification**, giving up things in the present for the sake of greater gains in the future. It is difficult to practice this middle-class virtue if one does not have a middle-class surplus—or middle-class hope.

Back in 1967, sociologist Elliot Liebow noted that black streetcorner men did not defer gratification. Their jobs were low-paying and insecure, their lives pitted with emergencies. With the future looking exactly like the present, and any savings they did manage gobbled up by emergencies, it seemed pointless to save for the future. The only thing that made sense from their perspective was to enjoy what they could at that moment. Immediate gratification, then, was not the cause of their poverty, but, rather, its consequence. Cause and consequence loop together, however, for their immediate gratification helped perpetuate their poverty. For another look at this "looping," see the Down-to-Earth Sociology box on the next page, in which I share my personal experiences with poverty.

If both causes are at work, why do sociologists emphasize the structural explanation? Reverse the situation for a moment. Suppose that members of the middle class drove old cars that broke down, faced threats from the utility company to shut off the electricity and heat, and had to make a choice between paying the rent or buying medicine and food and diapers. How long would they practice deferred gratification? Their orientations to life would likely make a sharp U-turn.

Sociologists, then, do not view the behaviors of the poor as the cause of their poverty, but, rather, as the result of their poverty. Poor people would welcome the middle-class opportunities that would allow them the chance to practice the middle-class virtue of deferred gratification. Without those opportunities, though, they just can't afford it.

Where Is Horatio Alger? The Social Functions of a Myth

In the late 1800s, Horatio Alger was one of the country's most talked-about authors. The rags-to-riches exploits of his fictional boy heroes and their amazing successes in overcoming severe odds motivated thousands of boys of that period. Although Alger's characters have disappeared from U.S. literature, they remain alive and well in the psyche of Americans. From real-life examples of people of humble origin who climbed the social class ladder, Americans know that anyone can get ahead if they really try. In fact, they believe that most Americans, including minorities and the working poor, have an average or better-than-average chance of getting ahead—obviously a statistical impossibility (Kluegel and Smith 1986).

A society's dominant ideologies are reinforced throughout the society, including its literature. Horatio Alger provided inspirational heroes for thousands of boys. The central theme of these many novels, immensely popular in their time, was rags to riches. Through rugged determination and self-sacrifice, a boy could overcome seemingly insurmountable obstacles to reach the pinnacle of success. (Girls did not strive for financial success, but were dependent on fathers and husbands.)

Poverty: A Personal Journey

I WAS BORN IN POVERTY. MY PARENTS, who could not afford to rent a house or apartment, rented the tiny office in their minister's house. That is where I was born.

My father began to slowly climb the social class ladder. His fitful odyssey took him from laborer to truck driver to the owner of a series of small businesses (tire repair shop, bar, hotel), then to vacuum cleaner salesman, and back to bar owner. He converted a garage into a house. Although it had no indoor plumbing or insulation (in northern Minnesota!), it was a start. Later, he bought a house, and then he built a new home. After that we moved into a trailer, and then back to a house. My father's seventh grade education was always an obstacle. Although he never became wealthy, poverty eventually become a distant memory for him.

My social class took a leap—from working class to upper middle class—when, after attending college and graduate school, I became a university professor. I entered a world that was unknown to my parents, one that was much more pampered and privileged. I had opportunities to do research, to publish, and to travel to exotic places. My reading centered on sociological research, and I read books in Spanish as well as in English. My father, in contrast, never read a book in his life, and my mother read only detective stories and romance paperbacks. One set of experiences isn't "better" than the other, just significantly different in determining what windows of perception it opens onto the world.

My interest in poverty, which was rooted in my own childhood experiences, stayed with me. I traveled to a dozen or so skid rows across the United States and Canada, talking to homeless people and staying in their shelters. In my own town, I spent considerable time with people on welfare, observing how they lived. I constantly marveled at the connections between *structural* causes of poverty (low education and skills, undependable transportation, the lack of unskilled jobs) and *personal* causes (the *culture of poverty*—alcohol and drug abuse, multiple out-of-wedlock births, frivolous spending, all-night partying, and a seeming incapacity to keep appointments—except to pick up the welfare check).

Sociologists haven't unraveled this connection, and as much as we might *like* for only structural causes to apply, clearly *both* are at work (Duneier 1999:122). The situation can be illustrated by looking at the perennial health problems I observed among the poor—the constant colds, runny noses, backaches, and injuries. The health problems stem from the *social structure* (less access to medical care, less trained or less capable physicians, drafty houses, lack of education regarding nutrition, and more dangerous jobs). At the same time, *personal* characteristics—hygiene, eating habits, and overdrinking—cause health problems. Which is the cause and which the effect? Both, of course, for one feeds into the other. The medical problems (which are based on both personal and structural causes) feed into the poverty these people experience, making them less able to perform their jobs successfully—or even to show up at work regularly. What an intricate puzzle for sociologists!

The accuracy of the **Horatio Alger myth** is less important than the belief that limitless possibilities exist for everyone. Functionalists would stress that this belief is functional for society. On the one hand, it encourages people to compete for higher positions, or, as the song says, "to reach for the highest star." On the other hand, it places blame for failure squarely on the individual. If you don't make it—in the face of ample opportunities to get ahead—the fault must be your own. The Horatio Alger myth helps to stabilize society: Since the fault is viewed as the individual's, not society's, current social arrangements can be regarded as satisfactory. This reduces pressures to change the system.

As Marx and Weber pointed out, social class penetrates our consciousness, shaping our ideas of life and our "proper" place in society. When the rich look at the world around them, they sense superiority and anticipate control over their own destiny. When the poor look around them, they are more likely to sense defeat, and to anticipate that unpredictable forces will batter their lives. Both rich and poor know the dominant ideology, that their particular niche in life is due to their own efforts, that the reasons for success—or failure—lie solely with the self. Like fish that don't notice the water, people tend not to perceive the effects of social class on their own lives.

Horatio Alger myth the belief that due to limitless possibilities anyone can get ahead if he or she tries hard enough

Summary *and* Review

What Is Social Class?

What is meant by the term social class?

Most sociologists have adopted Weber's definition of **social class:** a large group of people who rank closely to one another in terms of property (wealth), power, and prestige. **Wealth**—consisting of the value of property and income—is concentrated in the upper classes. From the 1930s to the 1970s, the trend in the distribution of wealth in the United States was toward greater equality. Since that time, it has been toward greater inequality. Pp. 268–271.

Power is the ability to get one's way even though others resist. C. Wright Mills coined the term **power elite** to refer to the small group that holds the reins of power in business, government, and the military. **Prestige** is linked to occupational status. People's rankings of occupational prestige have changed little over the decades and are similar from country to country. Globally, the occupations that bring greater prestige are those that pay more, require more education and abstract thought, and offer greater independence. Pp. 271–274.

What is meant by the term status inconsistency?

Status is social position. Most people are **status consistent;** that is, they rank high or low on all three dimensions of social class. People who rank higher on some dimensions than on others are status inconsistent. The frustrations of **status inconsistency** tend to produce political radicalism. P. 274.

Sociological Models of Social Class

What models are used to portray the social classes?

Erik Wright developed a four-class model based on Marx: (1) capitalists (owners of large businesses), (2) petty bourgeoisie (small business owners), (3) managers, and (4) workers. Kahl and Gilbert developed a six-class model based on Weber. At the top is the capitalist class. In descending order are the upper middle class, the lower middle class, the working class, the working poor, and the **underclass.** Pp. 274–280.

Consequences of Social Class

How does social class affect people's lives?

Social class leaves no aspect of life untouched. It affects our chances of benefiting from the new technology, dying early, becoming ill, receiving good health care, and getting divorced. Social class membership also affects child rearing, educational attainment, religious affiliation, political participation, the crimes people commit, and contact with the criminal justice system. Pp. 280–284.

Social Mobility

What are three types of social mobility?

The term **intergenerational mobility** refers to changes in social class from one generation to the next. **Structural mobility** refers to changes in society that lead large numbers of people to change their social class. **Exchange mobility** is the movement of large numbers of people from one class to another, with the net result that the relative proportions of the population in the classes remain about the same. Pp. 284–286.

Poverty

Who are the poor?

Poverty is unequally distributed in the United States. Racial–ethnic minorities (except Asian Americans), children, women-headed households, and rural Americans are more likely than others to be poor. The poverty rate of the elderly is less than that of the general population. Pp. 286–292.

Why are people poor?

Some social analysts believe that characteristics of *individuals* cause poverty. Sociologists, in contrast, examine *structural* features of society, such as employment opportunities, to find the causes of poverty. Sociologists generally conclude that life orientations are a consequence, not the cause, of people's position in the social class structure. Pp. 292–294.

How is the Horatio Alger myth functional for society?

The **Horatio Alger myth**—the belief that anyone can get ahead if only he or she tries hard enough—encourages people to strive to get ahead. It also deflects blame for failure from society to the individual. Pp. 294–295.

Thinking Critically

about Chapter 10

1. The belief that the United States is the land of opportunity draws millions of legal and illegal immigrants to the United States each year. How do the materials in this chapter support or undermine this belief?

2. How does social class affect people's lives?

3. What social mobility has your own family experienced? In what ways has this affected your life?

Additional Resources

What can you use MySocLab for? mysoclab ALLYN & BACON www.mysoclab.com

- **Study and Review:** Pre- and Post-Tests, Practice Tests, Flash Cards, Individualized Study Plans.

- **Current Events:** *Sociology in the News,* the daily *New York Times,* and more.

- **Research and Writing:** *Research Navigator, Writing About Sociology,* and more.

Where Can I Read More on This Topic?

Suggested readings for this chapter are listed at the back of this book.

CHAPTER 11

OUTLINE

Sex and Gender

Pacita Abad, *Women in Burkah* 1979

In Tunis, the capital of Tunisia, on Africa's northern coast, I met some U.S. college students, and spent a couple of days with them. They wanted to see the city's red light district, but I wondered whether it would be worth the trip. I already had seen other red light districts, including the unusual one in Amsterdam where the state licenses the women, requires that they have medical checkups (certificates must be posted so that customers can check them), sets their prices, and pays them social security benefits upon retirement. The prostitutes sit behind lighted picture windows while customers stroll along the canal side streets and browse from the outside.

I decided to go with them. We ended up on a wharf that extended into the Mediterranean. Each side was lined with a row of one-room wooden shacks, crowded one against the next. In front of each open door stood a young woman. Peering from outside into the dark interiors, I could see that each door led to a tiny room with a well-worn bed.

The wharf was crowded with men who were eyeing the women. Many of the men wore sailor uniforms from countries that I couldn't identify.

As I looked more closely, I could see that some of the women had runny sores on their legs. Incredibly, with such visible evidence of their disease, customers still sought them out. Evidently, the $2 price was too low to resist.

With a sick feeling in my stomach and the desire to vomit, I kept a good distance between the beckoning women and myself. One tour of the two-block area was more than sufficient.

Somewhere nearby, out of sight, I knew that there were men whose wealth derived from exploiting these women who were condemned to live short lives punctuated by fear and misery.

In front of each open door stood a young woman. I could see . . . a well-worn bed.

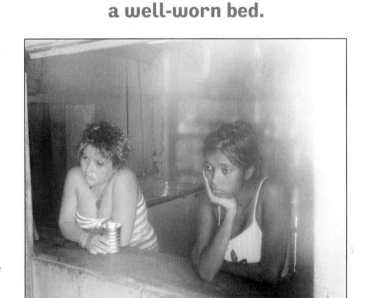

In this chapter, we examine **gender stratification**—males' and females' unequal access to property, power, and prestige. Gender is especially significant because it is a *master status;* that is, it cuts across *all* aspects of social life. No matter what we attain in life, we carry the label *male* or *female.* These labels convey images and expectations about how we should act. They not only guide our behavior but also serve as a basis of power and privilege.

In this chapter's fascinating journey, we shall look at inequality between the sexes both around the world and in the United States. We shall explore whether it is biology or culture that makes us the way we are, and review sexual harassment, unequal pay, and violence against women. This excursion will provide a good context for understanding the power differences between men and women that lead to situations such as the one described in our opening vignette. It should also give you insight into your own experiences with gender.

Issues of Sex and Gender

When we consider how females and males differ, the first thing that usually comes to mind is **sex,** the *biological characteristics* that distinguish males and females. *Primary sex characteristics* consist of a vagina or a penis and other organs related to reproduction. *Secondary sex characteristics* are the physical distinctions between males and females that are not directly connected with reproduction. These characteristics become clearly evident at puberty when males develop more muscles and a lower voice, and gain more body hair and height, while females develop breasts and form more fatty tissue and broader hips.

Gender, in contrast, is a *social,* not a biological characteristic. **Gender** consists of whatever behaviors and attitudes a group considers proper for its males and females. Consequently, gender varies from one society to another. Whereas *sex* refers to male or female, *gender* refers to masculinity or femininity. In short, you inherit your sex, but you learn your gender as you are socialized into the behaviors and attitudes your culture asserts are appropriate for your sex.

As the photo montage illustrates, these expectations differ around the world. They vary so greatly that some sociologists suggest that we replace the terms *masculinity* and *femininity* with *masculinities* and *femininities.*

The sociological significance of gender is that it is a device by which society controls its members. Gender sorts us, on the basis of sex, into different life experiences. It opens and closes doors to property, power, and even prestige. Like social class, gender is a structural feature of society.

Before examining inequalities of gender, let's consider why the behaviors of men and women differ.

Gender Differences in Behavior: Biology or Culture?

Why are most males more aggressive than most females? Why do women enter "nurturing" occupations such as teaching young children and nursing in far greater numbers than men? To answer such questions, many people respond with some variation of "They're just born that way."

Is this the correct answer? Certainly biology plays a significant role in our lives. Each of us begins as a fertilized egg. The egg, or ovum, is contributed by our mother, the sperm that fertilizes the egg by our father. At the very moment the egg is fertilized, our sex is determined. Each of us receives twenty-three chromosomes from the ovum and twenty-three from the sperm. The egg has an X chromosome. If the sperm that fertilizes the egg also has an X chromosome, we become a girl (XX). If the sperm has a Y chromosome, we become a boy (XY).

That's the biology. Now, the sociological question is: Does this biological difference control our behavior? Does it, for example, make females more nurturing and submissive and males more aggressive and domineering? Almost all sociologists take the side of "nurture" in this "nature versus nurture" controversy, but a few do not, as you can see from the following Thinking Critically section.

gender stratification males' and females' unequal access to power, prestige, and property on the basis of their sex

sex biological characteristics that distinguish females and males, consisting of primary and secondary sex characteristics

gender the behaviors and attitudes that a society considers proper for its males and females; masculinity or femininity

Merida, Mexico

Madaba, Jordan

Standards of Gender

Each human group determines its ideas of "maleness" and "femaleness." As you can see from these photos of four women and four men, standards of gender are arbitrary and vary from one culture to another. Yet, in its ethnocentrism, each group thinks that its preferences reflect what gender "really" is. As indicated here, around the world men and women try to make themselves appealing by aspiring to their group's standards of gender.

Altamira, Brazil

India

Moran, Kenya

Sichuan Province, Tibet

Chile

Turmi, Ethiopia

Cynthia Fuchs Epstein, whose position in the ongoing "nature versus nurture" debate is summarized here.

Biology Versus Culture—Culture Is the Answer

Sociologist Cynthia Fuchs Epstein (1988, 1999, 2007) stresses that differences between the behavior of males and females are solely the result of social factors—specifically, socialization and social control. Her argument is as follows:

1. The anthropological record shows greater equality between the sexes in the past than we had thought. In earlier societies, women, as well as men, hunted small game, made tools, and gathered food. In hunting and gathering societies, the roles of both women and men are less rigid than those created by stereotypes. For example, the Agta and Mbuti are egalitarian. This proves that hunting and gathering societies exist in which women are not subordinate to men. Anthropologists claim that in these societies women have a separate but equal status.

2. The types of work that men and women do in each society are determined not by biology but by social arrangements. Few people can escape these arrangements, and almost everyone works within his or her assigned narrow range. This gender division of work serves the interests of men, and both informal customs and formal laws enforce it. When these socially constructed barriers are removed, women's work habits are similar to those of men.

3. Biology "causes" some human behaviors, but they are related to reproduction or differences in body structure. These differences are relevant for only a few activities, such as playing basketball or "crawling through a small space."

4. Female crime rates are rising in many parts of the world. This indicates that aggression, which is often considered a biologically dictated male behavior, is related instead to social factors. When social conditions permit, such as when women become lawyers, they, too, become "adversarial, assertive, and dominant." Not incidentally, another form of this "dominant behavior" is the challenges that women make in scholarly journals to the biased views about human nature proposed by men.

In short, rather than "women's incompetence or inability to read a legal brief, perform brain surgery, [or] to predict a bull market," social factors—socialization, gender discrimination, and other forms of social control—create gender differences in behavior. Arguments that assign "an evolutionary and genetic basis" to explain differences in the behaviors of women and men are simplistic. They "rest on a dubious structure of inappropriate, highly selective, and poor data, oversimplification in logic and in inappropriate inferences by use of analogy."

The Dominant Position in Sociology

The dominant sociological position is that social factors, not biology, are the reasons we behave the way we do. Our visible differences of sex do not come with meanings built into them. Rather, each human group makes its own interpretation of these physical differences and on this basis assigns males and females to separate groups. In these groups, people learn what is expected of them and are given different access to property, power, prestige, and other privileges available in their society.

Most sociologists find compelling the argument that if biology were the principal factor in human behavior, all around the world we would find women behaving in one way and men in another. In fact, however, ideas of gender vary greatly from one culture to another—and, as a result, so do male–female behaviors.

Opening the Door to Biology

The matter of "nature" versus "nurture" is not so easily settled, however, and some sociologists acknowledge that biological factors are involved in some human behavior other than reproduction and childbearing (Udry 2000). Alice Rossi, a feminist sociologist and former president of the American Sociological Association, has suggested that women are better prepared biologically for "mothering" than are men. Rossi (1977, 1984) says

Thinking Critically

Biology Versus Culture—Biology Is the Answer

Sociologist Steven Goldberg (1974, 1986, 1993, 2003) finds it astonishing that anyone should doubt "the presence of core-deep differences in males and females, differences of temperament and emotion we call masculinity and femininity." Goldberg's argument—that it is not environment but inborn differences that "give masculine and feminine direction to the emotions and behaviors of men and women"—is as follows:

1. The anthropological record shows that all societies for which evidence exists are (or were) **patriarchies** (societies in which men dominate women). Stories about long-lost **matriarchies** (societies in which women dominate men) are myths.
2. In all societies, past and present, the highest statuses are associated with men. In every society, politics is ruled by "hierarchies overwhelmingly dominated by men."
3. Men dominate societies because they "have a lower threshold for the elicitation of dominance behavior . . . a greater tendency to exhibit whatever behavior is necessary in any environment to attain dominance in hierarchies and male-female encounters and relationships." Men are more willing "to sacrifice the rewards of other motivations—the desire for affection, health, family life, safety, relaxation, vacation and the like—in order to attain dominance and status."
4. Just as a 6-foot woman does not prove the social basis of height, so exceptional individuals, such as highly achieving and dominant women, do not refute "the physiological roots of behavior."

In short, there is only one valid interpretation of why every society from that of the Pygmy to that of the Swede associates dominance and attainment with men. Male dominance of society is "an inevitable resolution of the psychophysiological reality." Socialization and social institutions merely *reflect*—and sometimes exaggerate—inborn tendencies. Any interpretation other than inborn differences is "wrongheaded, ignorant, tendentious, internally illogical, discordant with the evidence, and implausible in the extreme." The argument that males are more aggressive because they have been socialized that way is equivalent to the claim that men can grow moustaches because boys have been socialized that way.

To acknowledge this reality is *not* to defend discrimination against women. Approval or disapproval of what societies have done with these basic biological differences is not the issue. The point is that biology leads males and females to different behaviors and attitudes—regardless of how we feel about this or whether we wish it were different.

Steven Goldberg, whose position in the ongoing "nature versus nurture" debate is summarized here.

---

that women are more sensitive to the infant's soft skin and to their nonverbal communications. She stresses that the issue is not either biology or society. Instead, nature provides biological predispositions, which are then overlaid with culture.

To see why the door to biology is opening just slightly in sociology, let's consider a medical accident and a study of Vietnam veterans.

A Medical Accident　The drama began in 1963, when 7-month-old identical twin boys were taken to a doctor for a routine circumcision (Money and Ehrhardt 1972). The inept physician, who was using a heated needle, turned the electric current too high and accidentally burned off the penis of one of the boys. You can imagine the parents' disbelief—and then their horror—as the truth sank in.

What can be done in a situation like this? The damage was irreversible. The parents were told that their boy could never have sexual relations. After months of soul-searching and tearful consultations with experts, the parents decided that their son should have a sex change operation. When he was 22 months old, surgeons castrated the boy, using the skin to construct a vagina. The parents then gave the child a new name, Brenda, dressed him in frilly clothing, let his hair grow long, and began to treat him as a girl. Later, physicians gave Brenda female steroids to promote female pubertal growth (Colapinto 2001).

patriarchy a society in which men as a group dominate women as a group; authority is vested in males

matriarchy a society in which women as a group dominate men as a group; authority is vested in females

At first, the results were promising. When the twins were 4 years old, the mother said (remember that the children are biologically identical):

> One thing that really amazes me is that she is so feminine. I've never seen a little girl so neat and tidy. . . . She likes for me to wipe her face. She doesn't like to be dirty, and yet my son is quite different. I can't wash his face for anything. . . . She is very proud of herself, when she puts on a new dress, or I set her hair. . . . She seems to be daintier. (Money and Ehrhardt 1972)

About a year later, the mother described how their daughter imitated her while their son copied his father:

> I found that my son, he chose very masculine things like a fireman or a policeman. . . . He wanted to do what daddy does, work where daddy does, and carry a lunch kit. . . . [My daughter] didn't want any of those things. She wants to be a doctor or a teacher. . . . But none of the things that she ever wanted to be were like a policeman or a fireman, and that sort of thing never appealed to her. (Money and Ehrhardt 1972)

If the matter were this clear-cut, we could use this case to conclude that gender is entirely up to nurture. Seldom are things in life so simple, however, and a twist occurs in this story. Despite this promising start and her parents' coaching, Brenda did not adapt well to femininity. She preferred to mimic her father shaving, rather than her mother putting on makeup. She rejected dolls, favoring guns and her brother's toys. She liked rough and tumble games and insisted on urinating standing up. Classmates teased her and called her a "cavewoman" because she walked like a boy. At age 14, she was expelled from school for beating up a girl who teased her. Despite estrogen treatment, she was not attracted to boys, and at age 14, in despair over her inner turmoil, she was thinking of suicide. In a tearful confrontation, her father told her about the accident and her sex change.

"All of a sudden everything clicked. For the first time, things made sense, and I understood who and what I was," the twin said of this revelation. David (his new name) then had testosterone shots and, later, surgery to partially reconstruct a penis. At age 25, he married a woman and adopted her children (Diamond and Sigmundson 1997; Colapinto 2001). There is an unfortunate end to this story, however. In 2004, David committed suicide.

The Vietnam Veterans Study   Time after time, researchers have found that boys and men who have higher levels of testosterone tend to be more aggressive. In one study, researchers compared the testosterone levels of college men in a "rowdy" fraternity with those of men in a fraternity that had a reputation for academic achievement and social responsibility. Men in the "rowdy" fraternity had higher levels of testosterone (Dabbs et al. 1996). In another study, researchers found that prisoners who had committed sex crimes and acts of violence against people had higher levels of testosterone than those who had committed property crimes (Dabbs et al. 1995). The samples that the researchers used were small, however, leaving the nagging uncertainty that these findings might be due to chance.

Then in 1985, the U.S. government began a health study of Vietnam veterans. To be certain that the study was representative, the researchers chose a random sample of 4,462 men. Among the data they collected was a measurement of testosterone. This gave sociologists a large random sample to analyze, one that is still providing surprising clues about human behavior.

This sample supports earlier studies showing that men who have higher levels of testosterone tend to be more aggressive and to have more problems as a consequence. When the veterans with higher testosterone levels were boys, they were more likely to get in trouble with parents and teachers and to become delinquents. As adults, they were more likely to use hard drugs, to get into fights, to end up in lower-status jobs, and to have more sexual partners. Knowing this, you probably won't be surprised to learn that they also were less likely to marry—certainly their low-paying jobs and trouble with the police made them less appealing candidates for marriage. Those who did marry were

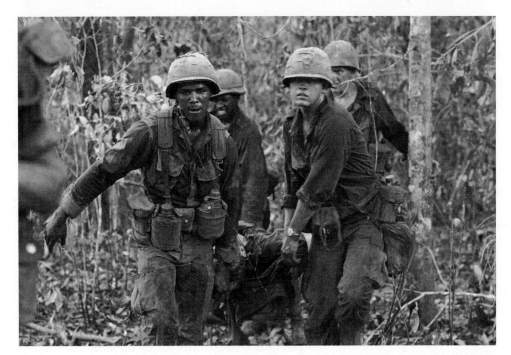

Sociologists stress the social factors that underlie human behavior, the experiences that mold us, funneling us into different directions in life. The study of Vietnam veterans discussed in the text is one indication of how the sociological door is opening slowly to also consider biological factors in human behavior. Using a shirt as a stretcher, these soldiers are carrying a wounded buddy from the jungle after heavy fighting near the Cambodian border in Tay Ninh, South Vietnam, on April 6, 1967.

more likely to have affairs, to hit their wives, and, it follows, to get divorced (Dabbs and Morris 1990; Booth and Dabbs 1993).

Fortunately, the Vietnam veterans study does not leave us sociologists with biology as the sole basis for behavior. Not all men with high testosterone get in trouble with the law, do poorly in school, or mistreat their wives. A chief difference, in fact, is social class. High-testosterone men from higher social classes are less likely to be involved in antisocial behaviors than are high-testosterone men from lower social classes (Dabbs and Morris 1990). *Social* factors such as socialization, life goals, and self-definitions, then, also play a part. The matter becomes even more complicated, for in some instances men with higher testosterone have better marriages (Booth, Johnson, and Granger 2004). Discovering how social factors work in combination with testosterone level is of great interest to sociologists.

IN SUM The findings are preliminary, but significant and provocative. They indicate that human behavior is not a matter of either nature or nurture, but of the two working together. Some behavior that we sociologists usually assume to be due entirely to socialization is apparently influenced by biology. In the years to come, this should prove to be an exciting—and controversial—area of sociological research. One level of research will be to determine if any behaviors are due only to biology. The second level will be to discover the ways that social factors modify biology. The third level will be, in sociologist Janet Chafetz's (1990:30) phrase, to determine how "different" becomes translated into "unequal."

"Nature or nurture?" The matter continues to be controversial. In the Down-to-Earth Sociology box on the next page, we see that gender differences have even become the focus of national attention.

Gender Inequality in Global Perspective

Around the world, gender is *the* primary division between people. Every society sets up barriers to provide unequal access to property, power, and prestige on the basis of sex. The barriers *always* favor men-as-a-group. After reviewing the historical record, historian and feminist Gerda Lerner (1986) concluded that "there is not a single society known where women-as-a-group have decision-making power over men (as a group)." Consequently, sociologists classify females as a *minority group*. Because females

The Gender Gap in Math and Science: A National Debate

OVERWHELMINGLY, ENGINEERS AND SCIENTISTS are men. Why? A national debate erupted in 2005 when Larry Summers, president of Harvard University at that time, suggested that the reason might be innate differences between men and women. In essence, he was suggesting that women's inborn characteristics might make them less qualified to succeed in these endeavors.

Summers' statement landed him squarely on editorial pages throughout the nation. Harvard's Arts and Sciences faculty, which was already upset over what they called his authoritarian manner, took his statement as a "last straw." The faculty met and gave Summers a "no confidence" vote, the equivalent of saying that he should resign. This was the first such repudiation of a president since Harvard was founded in 1636 (Finer 2005). In the face of such opposition, Summers resigned from the presidency of Harvard.

Summers' suggestion that biology *might* be the reason why men dominate science and engineering indicated that he had touched a sore spot in academia. Among the many who weighed in with replies to Summers was the Council of

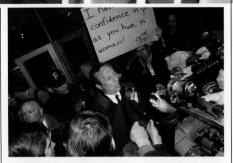

Larry Summers, president of Harvard University, after the faculty gave him a vote of no confidence.

the American Sociological Association ("ASA Council . . ." 2005). The council replied that research gives us clear and compelling evidence that social factors, not genetics, are the reason that women have not done as well as men in science and engineering. To support its position, the council made this compelling argument:

Gender differences in test results in math and science abilities have changed over time. There are now hardly any differences in test scores among male and female U.S. students. In Great Britain, girls now outperform boys on these tests. Biology didn't change—but social factors did: more access to courses in school, changed attitudes of school counselors, and more role models for women.

The council added that women's interests change as opportunities open to them. This, too, is social, not biological. As a result, we can expect many more women to enter the fields of science and engineering. These women, unfortunately, will have to struggle against negative stereotypes about their abilities, as their predecessors have.

Anthropologist George Murdock surveyed 324 traditional societies worldwide. In all of them, some work was considered "men's work," while other tasks were considered "women's work." He found that hunting is almost universally considered "men's work." These men, who live on the steppes of Mongolia, ride reindeer when they go hunting.

outnumber males, you may find this strange. The term *minority group* applies, however, because it refers to people who are discriminated against on the basis of physical or cultural characteristics, regardless of their numbers (Hacker 1951). For an overview of gender discrimination in a changing society, see the Cultural Diversity box on the next page.

How Females Became a Minority Group

Have females always been a minority group? Some analysts speculate that in hunting and gathering societies, women and men were social equals (Leacock 1981; Hendrix 1994) and that horticultural societies also had less gender discrimination than is common today (Collins et al. 1993). In these societies, women may have contributed about 60 percent of the group's total food. Yet, around the world, gender is the basis for discrimination. How, then, did it happen that women became a minority group? Let's consider the primary theory that has been proposed.

"Pssst. You Wanna Buy a Bride?" China in Transition

NGUYEN THI HOAN, AGE 22, thanked her lucky stars. A Vietnamese country girl, she had just arrived in Hanoi to look for work, and while she was still at the bus station a woman offered her a job in a candy factory.

It was a trap. After Nguyen had loaded a few sacks of sugar, the woman took her into the country to "get supplies." There some men took her to China, which was only 100 miles away. Nguyen was put up for auction, along with a 16-year-old Vietnamese girl. Each brought $350. Nguyen was traded from one bride dealer to another until she was taken to a Chinese village. There she was introduced to her new husband, who had paid $700 for her (Marshall 1999).

Why are tens of thousands of women kidnapped and sold as brides in China each year (Rosenthal 2001b)? First, parts of China have a centuries-old tradition of bride selling. Second, China has a shortage of women. The government enforces a "one couple–one child" policy. Since sons are preferred, female infanticide has become common. One result is a shortage of women of marriageable age. In some provinces, for every 100 women there are over 120 men. Yet all the men are expected to marry and produce heirs (Rosenthal 2001b).

Actually, Nguyen was lucky. Some kidnapped women are sold as prostitutes.

Bride selling and forced prostitution are ancient practices. But China is also entering a new era, which is bringing with it new pressures for Chinese women. Ideas of beauty are changing, and blonde, blue-eyed women are becoming a fetish. As a consequence, Chinese women feel a pressure to "Westernize" their bodies. Surgeons promise to give them bigger breasts and Western-looking eyes. A Western style of advertising is gaining ground, too: Ads now show scantily clad women perched on top of sports cars (Chen 1995; Johansson 1999; Yat-ming Sin and Hon-ming Yau 2001).

China in transition . . . It is continuing the old—bride selling—while moving toward the new, Western ideas of beauty and advertising. In both the old and new, women are commodities for the consumption of men.

The Origins of Patriarchy

The major theory of the origin of *patriarchy*—men dominating society—points to social consequences of human reproduction (Lerner 1986; Friedl 1990). In early human history, life was short. To balance the high death rate and maintain the population, women had to give birth to many children. This brought severe consequences for women. Because only females get pregnant, carry a child for nine months, give birth, and nurse, women were limited in their activities for a considerable part of their lives. To survive, an infant needed a nursing mother. With a child at her breast or in her uterus, or one carried on her hip or on her back, women were physically encumbered. Consequently, around the world women assumed tasks that were associated with the home and child care, while men took over the hunting of large animals and other tasks that required both greater speed and longer absences from the base camp (Huber 1990).

As a result, men became dominant. It was the men who left camp to hunt animals, who made contact with other tribes, who traded with these other groups, and who quarreled and waged war with them. It was also the men who made and controlled the instruments of death, the weapons that were used for hunting and warfare. It was

Throughout history, women have been denied the right to pursue various occupations on the basis of presumed biological characteristics. As society—and sex roles—have changed, women have increasingly entered occupations traditionally reserved for men. This woman is "hot tarring" a roof.

A theory of how *patriarchy* originated centers on childbirth. Because only women give birth, they assumed tasks associated with home and child care, while men hunted and performed other survival tasks that required greater strength, speed, and absence from home. This woman farmer in Burma, Myanmar, also takes care of her child—just as her female ancestors have done for centuries.

they who accumulated possessions in trade and gained prestige by returning to the camp triumphantly, leading captured prisoners or bringing large animals they had killed to feed the tribe. In contrast, little prestige was given to the routine, taken-for-granted activities of women—who were not perceived as risking their lives for the group. Eventually, men took over society. Their sources of power were their weapons, items of trade, and knowledge gained from contact with other groups. Women became second-class citizens, subject to men's decisions.

Is this theory correct? Remember that the answer lies buried in human history, and there is no way of testing it. Male dominance may be the result of some entirely different cause. For example, anthropologist Marvin Harris (1977) proposed that because most men are stronger than most women and hand-to-hand combat was necessary in tribal groups, men became the warriors, and women became the reward that enticed men to risk their lives in battle. Frederick Engels proposed that patriarchy came with the development of private property (Lerner 1986; Mezentseva 2001). He could not explain why private property should have produced male dominance, however. Gerda Lerner (1986) suggests that patriarchy may even have had different origins in different places.

Whatever its origins, a circular system of thought evolved. Men came to think of themselves as inherently superior—based on the evidence that they dominated society. They shrouded many of their activities with secrecy, and constructed elaborate rules and rituals to avoid "contamination" by females, whom they openly deemed inferior by that time. Even today, patriarchy is always accompanied by cultural supports designed to justify male dominance—such as designating certain activities as "not appropriate" for women.

As tribal societies developed into larger groups, men, who enjoyed their power and privileges, maintained their dominance. Long after hunting and hand-to-hand combat ceased to be routine, and even after large numbers of children were no longer needed to maintain the population, men held to their power. Male dominance in contemporary societies, then, is a continuation of a millennia-old pattern whose origin is lost in history.

Sex Typing of Work

Anthropologist George Murdock (1937) analyzed data that researchers had reported on 324 societies around the world. He found that in all of them, activities are *sex typed*. In other words, every society associates certain activities with one sex or the other. He also found that activities that are considered "female" in one society may be considered "male" in another. In some groups, for example, taking care of cattle is women's work, while other groups assign this task to men.

The exception was metalworking, which was considered men's work in all of the societies that Murdock examined. Three other pursuits—making weapons, pursuing sea mammals, and hunting—also were almost universally the domain of men. In a few societies, however, women participated in these activities. Although Murdock found no specific work that was universally assigned only to women, he did find that making clothing, cooking, carrying water, and grinding grain were almost always female tasks. In a few societies, however, such activities were regarded as men's work.

From Murdock's cross-cultural survey, we can conclude that nothing about biology requires men and women to be assigned different work. Anatomy does not have to equal destiny when it comes to occupations, for as we have seen, pursuits that are considered feminine in one society may be deemed masculine in another, and vice versa. On pages 310–311 is a photo essay on women at work in India that underscores this point.

Gender and the Prestige of Work

You might ask whether this division of labor really illustrates social inequality. Does it perhaps simply represent arbitrary ways of dividing up labor, not gender discrimination?

This could be the case, except for this finding: *Universally, greater prestige is given to male activities—regardless of what those activities are* (Linton 1936; Rosaldo 1974). If taking care of goats is men's work, then the care of goats is considered important and carries high prestige, but if it is women's work, it is considered less important and given less prestige. Or, to take an example closer to home, when delivering babies was "women's work" and was done by midwives, it was given low prestige. But when men took over this task, they became "baby doctors" with high prestige (Ehrenreich and English 1973). In short, it is not the work that provides the prestige, but the sex with which the work is associated.

Other Areas of Global Discrimination

Let's briefly consider four additional aspects of global gender discrimination. Later, when we focus on the United States, we shall examine these topics in greater detail.

The Global Gap in Education   Almost 1 billion adults around the world cannot read; two-thirds are women (UNESCO 2006). Table 11.1 lists the countries in which less than half the women can read and write, illustrating this point further. In *every* one of these countries, a higher percentage of men are literate. This table also shows how illiteracy is clustered, for 22 of these 32 countries are in Africa.

The Global Gap in Politics   Around the world, women lack equal access to national decision making. Except for Rwanda (at 49 percent), no national legislature of any country has as many women as men. In some countries, such as Kuwait and Papua New Guinea, the total is only 1 percent. In the United Arab Emirates, women still can't vote, but, then, neither can men. In most nations, women hold about 15 percent of the seats in parliaments and congress ("Women in Politics" 2006).

The Global Gap in Pay   In every nation, women average less pay than men. In the United States, full-time working women average only 70 percent of what men make (see Figure 11.8 on page 322). In some countries, women make much less than this.

Violence Against Women   A global human rights issue is violence against women. Historical examples are foot binding in China, witch burning in Europe, and *suttee* (burning the living widow with the body of her

Foot binding was practiced in China until about 1900. Tiny feet were a status symbol. Making it difficult for a woman to walk, small feet indicated that a woman's husband did not need his wife's labor. To make the feet even smaller, sometimes the baby's feet were broken and wrapped tightly. Some baby's toes were cut off. This photo was taken in Hubei Province, China. The woman getting the pedicure is reportedly 105 years old.

Table 11.1   Countries Where Half or More Men and Women Cannot Read and Write

Country	CANNOT READ	
	Women	Men
Niger	92%	76%
Burkina Faso	86%	66%
Guinea-Bissau	81%	40%
Pakistan	79%	40%
Afghanistan	78%	48%
Sierra Leone	77%	49%
Nepal	76%	41%
Benin	75%	43%
Yemen	75%	32%
Senegal	72%	53%
Mozambique	71%	40%
Bangladesh	70%	48%
Mauritania	68%	47%
Ethiopia	67%	56%
Laos	67%	36%
Mali	66%	51%
Chad	66%	48%
Bhutan	66%	39%
Libya	64%	38%
Morocco	64%	38%
Liberia	62%	30%
Cote d'Ivoire	61%	45%
Burundi	59%	43%
Togo	59%	25%
Egypt	56%	33%
Central African Republic	55%	40%
Eritrea	55%	33%
India	55%	32%
Iraq	54%	34%
Sudan	54%	30%
Malawi	53%	25%
Haiti	52%	48%

Source: "Women of Our World" 2002.

Work and Gender:
Women at Work in India

traveling through India was both a pleasant and an eye-opening experience. The country is incredibly diverse, the people friendly, and the land culturally rich. For this photo essay, wherever I went—whether city, village, or countryside—I took photos of women at work.

From these photos, you can see that Indian women work in a wide variety of occupations. Some of their jobs match traditional Western expectations, and some diverge sharply from our gender stereotypes. Although women in India remain subservient to men—with the women's movement hardly able to break the cultural surface—women's occupations are hardly limited to the home. I was surprised at some of the hard, heavy labor that Indian women do.

Indian women are highly visible in public places. A storekeeper is as likely to be a woman as a man. This woman is selling glasses of water at a beach on the Bay of Bengal. The structure on which her glasses rest is built of sand.

The villages of India have no indoor plumbing. Instead, each village has a well with a hand pump, and it is the women's job to fetch the water. This is backbreaking work, for, after pumping the water, the women wrestle the heavy buckets onto their heads and carry them home. This was one of the few occupations I saw that was limited to women.

Women also take care of livestock. It looks as though this woman dressed up and posed for her photo, but this is what she was wearing and doing when I saw her in the field and stopped to talk to her. While the sheep are feeding, her job is primarily to "be" there, to make certain the sheep don't wander off or that no one steals them.

Sweeping the house is traditional work for Western women. So it is in India, but the sweeping has been extended to areas outside the home. These women are sweeping a major intersection in Chennai. When the traffic light changes here, the women will continue sweeping, with the drivers swerving around them. This was one of the few occupations that seems to be limited to women.

As in the West, food preparation in India is traditional women's work. Here, however, food preparation takes an unexpected twist. Having poured rice from the 60-pound sack onto the floor, these women in Chittoor search for pebbles or other foreign objects that might be in the rice.

When I saw this unusual sight, I had to stop and talk to the workers. From historical pictures, I knew that belt-driven machines were common on U.S. farms 100 years ago. This one in Tamil Nadu processes sugar cane. The woman feeds sugar cane into the machine, which disgorges the stalks on one side and sugar cane juice on the other.

I visited quarries in different parts of India, where I found men, women, and children hard at work in the tropical sun. This woman works 8 1/2 hours a day, six days a week. She earns 40 rupees a day (about ninety cents). Men make 60 rupees a day (about $1.35). Like many quarry workers, this woman is a bonded laborer. She must give half of her wages to her master.

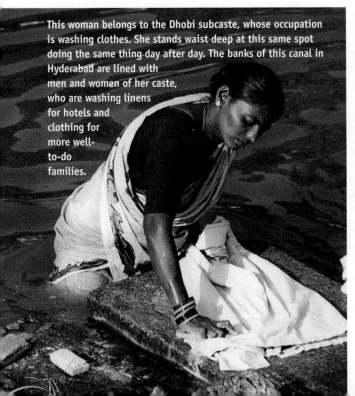

This woman belongs to the Dhobi subcaste, whose occupation is washing clothes. She stands waist deep at this same spot doing the same thing day after day. The banks of this canal in Hyderabad are lined with men and women of her caste, who are washing linens for hotels and clothing for more well-to-do families.

A common sight in India is women working on construction crews. As they work on buildings and on highways, they mix cement, unload trucks, carry rubble, and, following Indian culture, carry loads of bricks atop their heads. This photo was taken in Raipur, Chhattisgarh.

dead husband) in India. Today we have rape, wife beating, female infanticide, and forced prostitution, which was probably the case in our opening vignette. One of today's most notorious examples is female circumcision, the topic of the Cultural Diversity box on the next page.

"Honor killings" are another form of violence against women (Werbner 2007). In some societies, such as Pakistan, Jordan, and Kurdistan, a woman who is thought to have brought disgrace on her family is killed by a male relative—usually a brother or husband, but sometimes her father or uncles. What threat to the family's honor can be so severe that the men kill a daughter, wife, or sister? The usual reason is sex outside of marriage. In Iraq, even a woman who has been raped is in danger of becoming the victim of an honor killing (Banerjee 2003). Killing the girl or woman removes the "stain" she has brought to the family, and restores their honor in the community. Sharing this perspective, the police in these countries generally ignore honor killings, viewing them as private family matters.

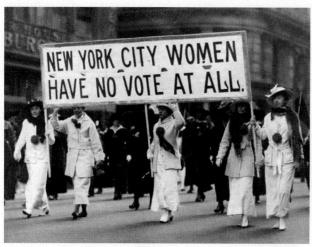

The women's struggle for equal rights has been long and hard. Shown here is a 1919 photo from the first wave of the U.S. women's movement. Only against enormous opposition from men did U.S. women win the right to vote. Women first voted in national elections in 1920.

Gender Inequality in the United States

Gender inequality is not some accidental, hit-or-miss affair. Rather, the institutions of each society work together to maintain the group's particular forms of inequality. Customs, often venerated throughout history, both justify and maintain these arrangements. Let's take a brief look at how change in this vital area of social life came about in the United States.

Fighting Back: The Rise of Feminism

To see how far we have come, it is useful to see where we used to be. In early U.S. society, the second-class status of women was taken for granted. A husband and wife were legally one person—him (Chafetz and Dworkin 1986). Women could not vote, buy property in their own name, make legal contracts, or serve on juries. How could things have changed so much in the last century that these examples sound like fiction?

A central lesson of conflict theory is that power yields privilege; like a magnet, power draws society's best resources to the elite. Because men tenaciously held onto their privileges and used social institutions to maintain their position, basic rights for women came only through prolonged and bitter struggle.

Feminism—the view that biology is not destiny and that stratification by gender is wrong and should be resisted—met with strong opposition, both by men who had privilege to lose and by women who accepted their status as morally correct. In 1894, for example, Jeannette Gilder said that women should not have the right to vote because "Politics is too public, too wearing, and too unfitted to the nature of women" (Crossen 2003).

Feminists, then known as suffragists, struggled against such views. In 1916, they founded the National Women's Party, and in 1917 they began to picket the White House. After picketing for six months, the women were arrested. Hundreds were sent to prison, including Lucy Burns, a leader of the National Women's Party. The extent to which these women had threatened male privilege is demonstrated by how they were treated in prison.

feminism the philosophy that men and women should be politically, economically, and socially equal; organized activities on behalf of this principle

Two men brought in Dorothy Day [the editor of a periodical that promoted women's rights], twisting her arms above her head. Suddenly they lifted her and brought her body down twice over the back of an iron bench. . . . They had been there a few minutes when Mrs. Lewis, all doubled over like a sack of flour, was thrown in. Her head struck the iron bed and she fell to the floor senseless. As for

Cultural Diversity *around the* World

Female Circumcision

"LIE DOWN THERE," the excisor suddenly said to me [when I was 12], pointing to a mat on the ground. No sooner had I laid down than I felt my frail, thin legs grasped by heavy hands and pulled wide apart. . . . Two women on each side of me pinned me to the ground . . . I underwent the ablation of the labia minor and then of the clitoris. The operation seemed to go on forever. I was in the throes of agony, torn apart both physically and psychologically. It was the rule that girls of my age did not weep in this situation. I broke the rule. I cried and screamed with pain. . . !

Afterwards they forced me, not only to walk back to join the other girls who had already been excised, but to dance with them. I was doing my best, but then I fainted. . . . It was a month before I was completely healed. When I was better, everyone mocked me, as I hadn't been brave, they said. (Walker and Parmar 1993:107–108)

Female circumcision is common in parts of Muslim Africa and in some parts of Malaysia and Indonesia. Often called female genital cutting by Westerners, this practice is also known as clitoral excision, clitoridectomy, infibulation, and labiadectomy, depending on how much of the tissue is removed. Worldwide, between 100 million and 200 million females have been circumcised. In Egypt, 97 percent of the women have been circumcised (Boyle et al. 2001; Douglas 2005).

In some cultures, only the girl's clitoris is cut off; in others, more is removed. In Sudan, the Nubia cut away most of the girl's genitalia, then sew together the remaining outer edges. They bind the girl's legs from her ankles to her waist for several weeks while scar tissue closes up the vagina. They leave a small opening the diameter of a pencil for the passage of urine and menstrual fluids.

Among most groups, the surgery takes place between the ages of 4 and 8. In some cultures, it occurs seven to ten days after birth. In others, it is not performed until girls reach adolescence. Because the surgery is usually done without anesthesia, the pain is so excruciating that adults must hold the girl down. In urban areas, physicians sometimes perform the operation; in rural areas, a neighborhood woman usually does it.

Shock, bleeding, infection, infertility, and death are among the risks. Common side-effects are vaginal spasms, painful intercourse, and lack of orgasms. Urinary tract infec-

This poster is used in Sudan to try to get parents to stop circumcising their daughters.

tions also occur as urine and menstrual flow build up behind the tiny opening.

When a woman marries, the opening is cut wider to permit sexual intercourse. In some groups, this is the husband's responsibility. Before a woman gives birth, the opening is enlarged further. After birth, the vagina is again sutured shut; this cycle of surgically closing and opening begins anew with each birth.

What are the reasons for this custom? Some groups believe that it reduces female sexual desire, making it more likely that a woman will be a virgin at marriage, and, afterward, remain faithful to her husband. Others think that women can't bear children if they aren't circumcised.

Feminists call female circumcision a form of ritual torture to control female sexuality. They point out that men dominate the societies that practice it. Mothers cooperate with the surgery because in these societies an uncircumcised woman is considered impure and is not allowed to marry. Grandmothers insist that the custom continue out of concern that their granddaughters marry well.

The growing opposition to female circumcision has created intense controversy in Africa, perhaps nowhere demonstrated more forcefully than this contrast: On the one hand, fourteen African countries have banned female circumcision (the laws, however, are seldom enforced). On the other hand, to drum up votes for her husband, the wife of the president of Sierra Leone personally sponsored the circumcision of 1,500 girls (Douglas 2005; "Sierra Leone" 2005).

for your Consideration

Do you think that the United States should try to make other nations stop this custom? Or would this be ethnocentric, the imposition of Western values on other cultures? As one Somali woman said, "The Somali woman doesn't need an alien woman telling her how to treat her private parts." Do you think that it is ever legitimate for members of one culture to interfere with another?

How would you respond to those who oppose male circumcision, also a growing movement? How would you respond to those who point out that female circumcision was a custom of Victorian England (Silverman 2004)?

Sources: As cited, and Lightfoot-Klein 1989; Merwine 1993; Chalkley 1997; Collymore 2000; "Ethiopia" 2005; Tuhus-Dubrow 2007.

Lucy Burns, they handcuffed her wrists and fastened the handcuffs over [her] head to the cell door. (Cowley 1969)

This *first wave* of the women's movement had a radical branch that wanted to reform all the institutions of society and a conservative branch whose concern was to win the vote for women (Freedman 2001). The conservative branch dominated, and after the right to vote was won in 1920, the movement basically dissolved.

The *second wave* began in the 1960s. Sociologist Janet Chafetz (1990) points out that up to this time most women thought of work as a temporary activity intended to fill the time between completing school and getting married. To see how children's books reinforced such thinking, see Figure 11.1. As more women took jobs and began to regard them as careers, however, they began to compare their working conditions with those of men. This shift in their reference group changed the way women viewed their conditions at work. The result was a second wave of protest against gender inequalities. The goals of this second wave (which continues today) are broad, ranging from raising women's pay to changing policies on violence against women.

A *third wave* of feminism is emerging. Three main aspects are apparent. The first is a greater focus on the problems of women in the Least Industrialized Nations (Spivak 2000; Hamid 2006). The second is a criticism of the values that dominate work and society. Some feminists argue that competition, toughness, calloused emotions, and independence represent "male" qualities and need to be replaced with cooperation, connection, openness, and interdependence (England 2000). A third aspect is the removal of impediments to women's love and sexual pleasure (Gilligan 2002). As this third wave develops, we can assume that it, too, will have its liberal and conservative branches.

Figure 11.1 Teaching Gender

By looking at the past, we get an idea of how far we have come. This illustration from a 1970s children's book shows the mind-set of the day. You can see how children who grew up during this period were taught to view gender and work.

Boys are pilots.

Girls are stewardesses.

Boys are presidents.

Girls are First Ladies.

Boys are doctors.

Girls are nurses.

Boys build houses.

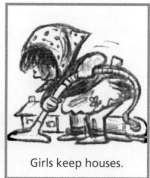

Girls keep houses.

Source: From a 1970's children's book.

Although women enjoy fundamental rights today, gender inequality continues to play a central role in social life. Let's look at gender relations in health care, education, and everyday life, and then, in greater detail, at discrimination in the world of work.

Gender Inequality in Health Care

Medical researchers were perplexed. Reports were coming in from all over the country: Women were twice as likely as men to die after coronary bypass surgery. Researchers at Cedars-Sinai Medical Center in Los Angeles checked their own records. They found that of 2,300 coronary bypass patients, 4.6 percent of the women died as a result of the surgery, compared with 2.6 percent of the men.

These findings presented a sociological puzzle. To solve it, researchers first turned to biology (Bishop 1990). In coronary bypass surgery, a blood vessel is taken from one part of the body and stitched to an artery on the surface of the heart. Perhaps this operation was more difficult to perform on women because they have smaller arteries. To find out, researchers measured the amount of time that surgeons kept patients on the heart-lung machine while they operated. They were surprised to learn that women spent *less* time on the machine than men. This indicated that the operation was not more difficult to perform on women.

As the researchers probed, a surprising answer unfolded: unintended sexual discrimination. Physicians had not taken the chest pains of their women patients as seriously as they took the complaints of their men patients. The physicians were *ten* times more likely to give men exercise stress tests and radioactive heart scans. They also sent men to surgery on the basis of abnormal stress tests but waited until women showed clear-cut symptoms of heart disease before sending them to surgery. Patients who have surgery after the disease is more advanced are less likely to survive.

As more women become physicians, perhaps such subconscious discrimination will change. Women doctors are more likely to order Pap smears and mammograms (Lurie et al. 1993). They also offer more encouragement to patients and engage them more in making decisions about their care, so it is likely that they will be more responsive to the health problems of women (Levinson and Lurie 2004).

In the Down-to-Earth Sociology box on the next page, we look at a more blatant form of sexism in medicine.

Gender Inequality in Education

In education, too, a glimpse of the past sheds light on the present. Until 1832, women were not allowed to attend college with men. When women were admitted—first at Oberlin College in Ohio—they had to remain silent at public assemblies, do the men students' laundry, clean their rooms, and serve them their meals (Flexner 1971/1999). Educators thought that women were less qualified for higher education because their female organs dominated their minds. Referring to menstruation, Dr. Edward Clarke, of Harvard University, expressed the dominant sentiment this way:

> **A girl upon whom Nature, for a limited period and for a definite purpose, imposes so great a physiological task, will not have as much power left for the tasks of school, as the boy of whom Nature requires less at the corresponding epoch. (Andersen 1988)**

Because women were so much weaker, Clarke urged them to study only one-third as much as young men—and not to study at all during menstruation.

Like out-of-fashion clothing, such ideas were discarded, and women entered college in growing numbers. As Figure 11.2 on the next page shows, by 1900, one third of college students were women. The change has been so extensive that 57 percent of today's college students are women. Women also earn 57 percent of all bachelor's degrees and 59 percent of all master's degrees (*Statistical Abstract* 2007:Table 288). Because men are now lagging behind, some have begun to call for *affirmative action for men* (Kleinfeld 2002a). To see why, look at Figure 11.3 on page 317.

Down-to-Earth Sociology

Cold-Hearted Surgeons and Their Women Victims

SOCIOLOGIST SUE FISHER (1986), who did participant observation in a hospital, was surprised to hear surgeons recommend total hysterectomy (removal of both the uterus and the ovaries) *when no cancer was present.* When she asked why, the men doctors explained that the uterus and ovaries are "potentially disease producing." They also said that these organs are unnecessary after the childbearing years, so why not remove them? Doctors who reviewed hysterectomies confirmed this bias: They found that three out of four of these surgeries were, in their term, inappropriate (Broder et al. 2000).

Greed is a powerful motivator in life, and it certainly shows up in surgical sexism. Surgeons perform hysterectomies to make money, but they have to "sell" this operation, since women, to understate the matter, are reluctant to part with these organs. Here is how one resident explained the "hard sell" to sociologist Diana Scully (1994):

> You have to look for your surgical procedures; you have to go after patients. Because no one is crazy enough to come and say, "Hey, here I am. I want you to operate on me." You have to sometimes convince the patient that she

is really sick—if she is, of course [laughs], and that she is better off with a surgical procedure.

To "convince" a woman to have this surgery, the doctor puts on a serious face and tells her that the examination has turned up fibroids in her uterus—and they *might* turn into cancer. This statement is often sufficient, for it frightens women, who picture themselves dying from cancer. To clinch the sale, the surgeon withholds the rest of the truth—that fibroids are common, that they most likely will *not* turn into cancer, and that the patient has several nonsurgical alternatives.

I wonder how men would feel if surgeons systematically suggested to them that they be castrated when they get older—since "that organ is no longer necessary, and it might cause disease."

for your Consideration

Hysterectomies have become so common that one of three U.S. women eventually has her uterus surgically removed (Elson 2004). Why do you think that surgeons are so quick to operate? How can women find nonsurgical alternatives?

Figure 11.2 Changes in College Enrollment, by Sex

What percentages of U.S. college students are female and male?

Note: This sharp drop in female enrollment is probably due to the large numbers of male soldiers returning from World War II who attended college under the new GI Bill of Rights.

Source: By the author. Based on *Statistical Abstract* 1938:Table 114; 1959:Table 158; 1991:Table 261; 2007:Table 268.

Figure 11.3 **College Students, by Sex and Race-Ethnicity**

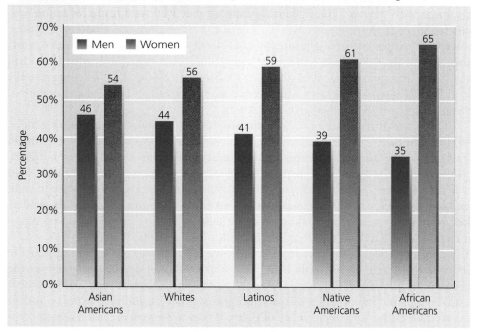

Note: This figure can be confusing. To read it, ask: What percentage of the group in college are men or women? (For example, what percentage of Asian American college students are men or women?)

Source: By the author. Based on *Statistical Abstract* 2007:Table 268.

Figure 11.4 illustrates another major change. From this figure, you can see how women have increased their share of professional degrees. The greatest change is in dentistry: In 1970, across the entire United States, only 34 women earned degrees in dentistry. Today, about 1,800 women become dentists each year. The change is so extensive that about as many women as men now graduate from U.S. law schools.

Figure 11.4 **Gender Changes in Professional Degrees**

Source: By the author. Based on *Statistical Abstract* 2007:Table 293.

From grade school through college, male sports have been emphasized, and women's sports underfunded. Due to federal laws (*Title IX*), the funding gap has closed considerably, and there is an increasing emphasis on women's accomplishments in sports. Shown here is Mia Hamm, who played forward on the U.S. Women's National Soccer team.

That men have fallen behind women in college enrollment and need to catch up with them in bachelor's and master's degrees is a new situation. This is certainly a major break with the past, and in coming years we may well see affirmative action programs for men. If we probe beneath the surface, however, we still find old practices. Women's sports, for example, are usually considered less important than men's sports (Fisher 2002). And whenever I attend a high school or college football or basketball game, I still see a group of slender girls in short, brightly colored skirts jumping into the air and wildly cheering the boys—but there is no such group of boys leading organized cheers for the girls when they play *their* sports.

Then there is the matter of *gender tracking;* that is, degrees tend to follow gender, which reinforces male–female distinctions. Here are two extremes: Men earn 94 percent of the associate degrees in the "masculine" field of construction trades, while women are awarded 89 percent of the associate degrees in the "feminine" field of library science (*Statistical Abstract* 2007:Table 290). Because gender socialization gives men and women different orientations to life, they enter college with gender-linked aspirations. It is their socialization—not some presumed innate characteristics—that channels men and women into different educational paths.

If we follow students into graduate school, we see that with each passing year the proportion of women drops. Table 11.2 gives us a snapshot of doctoral programs in the sciences. Note how aspirations (enrollment) and accomplishments (doctorates earned) are sex linked. In five of these doctoral programs, men outnumber women, and in three, women outnumber men. In *all* of them, however, women are less likely to complete the doctorate.

If we follow those who earn doctoral degrees to their teaching careers at colleges and universities, we find gender stratification in rank and pay. Throughout the United States, women are less likely to become full professors, the highest-paying and most prestigious rank. In both private and public colleges, professors average more than twice the salary of instructors (*Statistical Abstract* 2007:Table 284). Even when women do become full professors, their average pay is less than that of men who are full professors (AAUP 2007:Table 5).

Beyond the pay gap lies more subtle and invasive discrimination. Women professors are not taken as seriously as men (Epstein 2007). As Barbara Grosz, a professor at Harvard, put it (Zernike 2001):

The first time you're mistaken for a secretary is funny. The 99th time is not. The first time the guys [men professors] don't include you in the conversation at a meeting, you

Table 11.2 Doctorates in Science, By Sex

Field	STUDENTS ENROLLED		DOCTORATES CONFERRED		COMPLETION RATIO* (HIGHER OR LOWER THAN EXPECTED)	
	Women	Men	Women	Men	Women	Men
Mathematics	36%	64%	28%	72%	−22	+13
Computer sciences	27%	73%	21%	79%	−22	+8
Social sciences	53%	47%	44%	56%	−17	+19
Biological sciences	55%	45%	46%	54%	−16	+20
Agriculture	45%	55%	38%	62%	−16	+13
Physical sciences	31%	69%	26%	74%	−16	+7
Engineering	21%	79%	18%	82%	−14	+4
Psychology	74%	26%	67%	33%	−9	+27

*The formula for the completion ratio is X minus Y divided by Y, where X is the doctorates conferred and Y is the proportion enrolled in a program.

Source: By the author. Based on *Statistical Abstract* 2007:Tables 785, 789.

think, "I'm not interested anyway." But a whole year of these conversations—there's this kind of constant erosion.

Gender Inequality in Everyday Life

Of the many aspects of gender discrimination in everyday life that we could examine, we have space to look only at two: the general devaluation of femininity in U.S. society, and male dominance of conversation.

General Devaluation of Things Feminine

Leaning against the water cooler, two men—both minor executives—are nursing their cups of coffee, discussing last Sunday's Giants game, postponing for as long as possible the moment when work must finally be faced.

A [male] vice president walks by and hears them talking about sports. Does he stop and send them back to their desks? Does he frown? Probably not. Being a man, he is far more likely to pause and join in the conversation, anxious to prove that he, too, is "one of the boys," feigning an interest in football that he may very well not share at all. These men—all the men in the office—are his troops, his comrades-in-arms.

Now, let's assume that two women are standing by the water cooler discussing whatever you please: women's liberation, clothes, work, any subject—except football, of course. The vice president walks by, sees them, and moves down the hall in a fury, cursing and wondering whether it is worth the trouble to complain—but to whom?— about all those bitches standing around gabbing when they should be working. "Don't they know," he will ask, in the words of a million men, "that this is an office?" (Korda 1973: 20–21)

As indicated in this scenario, women often have a difficult time being taken seriously by men. In general, a higher value is placed on things considered masculine, for masculinity symbolizes strength and success. In contrast, femininity is devalued, for it is perceived as representing weakness and lack of accomplishment.

Sociologist Samuel Stouffer headed a research team that produced *The American Soldier* (1949), a classic study of World War II combat soldiers. To motivate their men, officers used feminine terms as insults. If a man showed less-than-expected courage or endurance, an officer might say, "Whatsa matter, Bud—got lace on your drawers?" A generation later, as they trained soldiers to fight in Vietnam, officers still used accusations of femininity to motivate their men. Drill sergeants would mock their troops by saying, "Can't hack it, little girls?" (Eisenhart 1975). The practice continues. Male soldiers who show hesitation during maneuvers are mocked by others, who call them girls (Miller 1997/2007).

In sports, we see the same thing. Anthropologist Douglas Foley (1990/2006) notes that football coaches insult boys who don't play well by saying that they are "wearing skirts." In her research, sociologist Donna Eder (1995) heard junior high boys call one another "girl" when they didn't hit hard enough in football. When they play basketball, boys of this age also call one another a "woman" when they miss a basket (Stockard and Johnson 1980). In professional hockey, if players are not rough enough on the ice, their teammates call them "girls" (Gallmeier 1988:227).

These insults roll so easily off the tongues of men in sports and war that it is easy to lose sight of their significance: They represent a devaluation of females. As Stockard and Johnson (1980:12) point out, "There is no comparable phenomenon among women, for young girls do not insult each other by calling each other 'man.'"

Gender and Conversation

You may have noticed that men are more likely than women to interrupt conversations. Some sociologists note that talk between a man and a woman is often more like talk between a boss and an employee than between social equals (West and Garcia 1988; Smith-Lovin and Brody 1989; Tannen 1990, 2007). A tally of who makes topic switches in conversations, however, indicates that men and women are about equally as likely to do so (Okamoto and Smith-Lovin 2001). Perhaps more significant than gender is the relative status of the speakers, with higher status people exerting greater control over conversations. As sociologists do more research, we should be able to resolve this question.

The inequality of gender in everyday life is related to a structural inequality that runs throughout society. Let's look at this structural feature in the workplace.

Gender Inequality in the Workplace

To examine the work setting is to make visible basic relations between men and women. Let's begin with one of the most remarkable areas of gender inequality at work, the pay gap.

The Pay Gap

One of the chief characteristics of the U.S. workforce is a steady growth in the numbers of women who work for wages outside the home. Figure 11.5 shows that in 1890 about one of every five paid workers was a woman. By 1940, this ratio had grown to one of four; by 1960 to one of three; and today it is almost one of two. As shown on this figure, the projections are that the ratio will remain 55 percent men and 45 percent women for the next few years.

Women who work for wages are not evenly distributed throughout the United States. From the Social Map on the next page, you can see that where a woman lives makes a difference in how likely she is to work outside the home. Why is there such a clustering among the states? The geographical patterns evident in this map reflect regional-subcultural differences about which we currently have little understanding.

After college, you might like to take a few years off, travel around Europe, sail the oceans, or maybe sit on a beach in some South American paradise and drink piña coladas. But chances are, you are going to go to work instead. Since you have to work, how would you like to earn an extra $1,100,000 on your job? If this sounds appealing, read on. I'm going to reveal how you can make an extra $2,300 a month between the ages of 25 and 65.

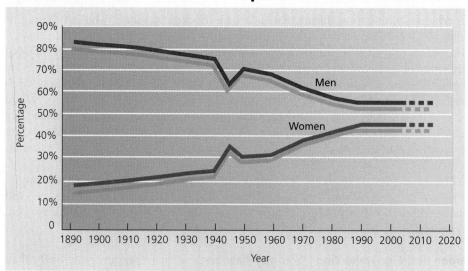

Figure 11.5 **Women's and Men's Proportion of the U.S. Labor Force**

Note: Pre-1940 totals include women 14 and over: totals for 1940 and after are for women 16 and over. Broken lines are the author's projections.

Sources: By the author. Based on 1969 *Handbook on Women Workers,* 1969:10; *Manpower Report to the President,* 1971:203, 205; Mills and Palumbo, 1980:6, 45; *Statistical Abstract* 2007:Table 574.

Figure 11.6 Women in the Workforce

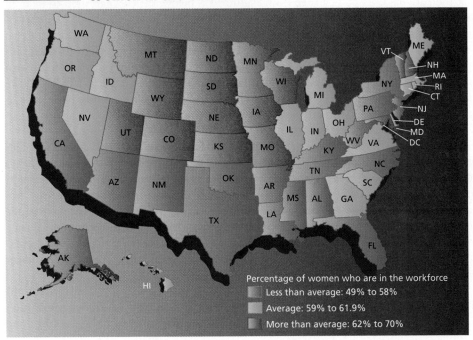

Percentage of women who are in the workforce
- Less than average: 49% to 58%
- Average: 59% to 61.9%
- More than average: 62% to 70%

Note: At 49.1%, West Virginia has the lowest rate of women in the workforce, while South Dakota, at 69.4%, has the highest.

Source: By the author. Based on *Statistical Abstract* 2007:Table 579.

Is this hard to do? Actually, it is simple for some, but impossible for others. As Figure 11.7 shows, all you have to do is be born a male and graduate from college. If we compare full-time workers, based on current differences in earnings this is how much more money the *average male* college graduate can expect to earn over the course of his career. Hardly any single factor pinpoints gender discrimination better than this total. As you can see, the pay gap shows up at *all* levels of education.

Figure 11.7 The Gender Pay Gap, by Education[1]

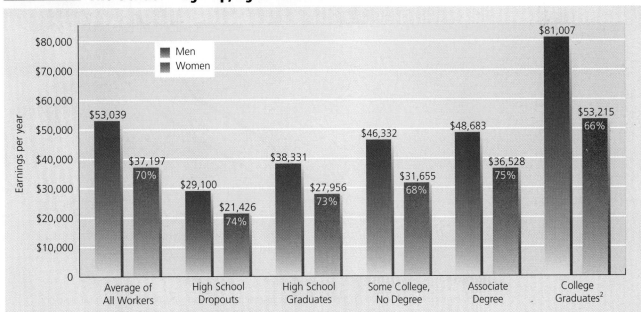

[1]Full-time workers in all fields.
[2]Bachelor's and all higher degrees, including professional degrees.

Source: By the author. Based on *Statistical Abstract* 2007:Table 684.

The pay gap is so great that U.S. women who work full time average *only 70 percent* of what men are paid. As you can see from Figure 11.8 below, the pay gap used to be even worse. The gender gap in pay occurs not only in the United States but also in *all* industrialized nations.

If $1,100,000 additional earnings aren't enough, how would you like to make another $166,000 extra at work? If so, just make sure that you are not only a man but also a *tall* man. Over their lifetimes, men who are over 6 feet tall average $166,000 more than men who are 5 feet 5 inches or less (Judge and Cable 2004). Taller women also make more than shorter women. But even when it comes to height, the gender pay gap persists, and tall men make more than tall women.

What logic can underlie the gender pay gap? Earlier we saw that college degrees are gender linked, so perhaps this gap is due to career choices. Maybe women are more likely to choose lower-paying jobs, such as teaching grade school, while men are more likely to go into better-paying fields, such as business and engineering. Actually, this is true, and researchers have found that about *half* of the gender pay gap is due to such factors. And the balance? It consists of a combination of gender discrimination (Jacobs 2003; Roth 2003) and what is called the "child penalty"—women missing out on work experience and opportunities while they care for children (Hundley 2001; Chaker and Stout 2004).

For college students, the gender gap in pay begins with the first job after graduation. You might know of a particular woman who was offered a higher salary than most men in her class, but she would be an exception. On average, men enjoy a "testosterone

Figure 11.8 **The Gender Pay Gap Over Time: What Percentage of Men's Income Do Women Earn?**

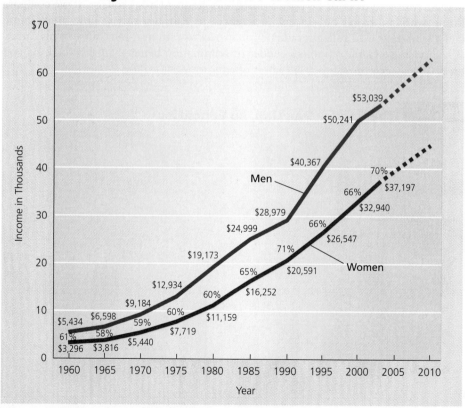

Note: The income jump from 1990 to 1995 could be due to a statistical procedure. The 1995 source (for 1990 income) uses "median income," while the 1997 source (for 1995 income) merely says "average earnings." How the "average" is computed is not stated. For a review of this distinction, see Table 5.2 of this text (page 133). The last year for which the source has data is 2003. Broken lines indicate the author's estimates.

Source: By the author. Based on *Statistical Abstract* 1995:Table 739; 2002:Table 666; 2007:Table 684, and earlier years.

bonus," and employers start them out at higher salaries than women (Fuller and Schoenberger 1991; Harris et al. 2005). Depending on your sex, then, you will either benefit from the pay gap or be victimized by it.

As a final indication of the extent of the U.S. gender pay gap, consider this. Of the nation's top 500 corporations (the so-called "Fortune 500"), only 10 are headed by women (Fuhrmans and Hymowitz 2007). And 10 is a record-breaking number! I examined the names of the CEOs of the 350 largest U.S. corporations, and I found that your best chance to reach the top is to be named (in this order) John, Robert, James, William, or Charles. Edward, Lawrence, and Richard are also advantageous names. Amber, Katherine, Leticia, and Maria, however, apparently draw a severe penalty. Naming your baby girl John or Robert might seem a little severe, but it could help her reach the top. (I say this only slightly tongue-in-cheek. One of the few women to head a Fortune 500 company—before she was fired and given $21 million severance pay—had a man's first name: Carleton Fiorina of Hewlett-Packard.)

The Cracking Glass Ceiling

What keeps women from breaking through the **glass ceiling,** the mostly invisible barrier that prevents women from reaching the executive suite? Researchers have identified a "pipeline" that leads to the top: the marketing, sales, and production positions that directly affect the corporate bottom line (Hymowitz 2004; DeCrow 2005). Men, who dominate the executive suite, stereotype women as being less capable of leadership than they are (Heilman 2001). Viewing women as good at "support," they steer women into human resources or public relations. There, successful projects are not appreciated in the same way as those that bring corporate profits—and bonuses for their managers.

Another reason the glass ceiling is so powerful is that women lack mentors—successful executives who take an interest in them and teach them the ropes. Lack of a mentor is no trivial matter, for mentors can provide opportunities to develop leadership skills that open the door to the executive suite (Heilman 2001; Hymowitz 2007).

The glass ceiling is cracking, however (Solomon 2000; Hymowitz 2004). A look at women who have broken through reveals highly motivated individuals with a fierce competitive spirit who are willing to give up sleep and recreation for the sake of career advancement. They also learn to play by "men's rules," developing a style that makes men comfortable. Most of these women also have supportive husbands who share household duties and adapt their careers to accommodate the needs of their executive wives (Lublin 1996). In addition, women who began their careers 20 to 30 years ago are running many major divisions within the largest companies (Hymowitz 2004). With this background, some of these women have begun to emerge as the new top CEOs.

Then there is the *glass escalator*. Sociologist Christine Williams (1995) interviewed men and women who worked in traditionally female jobs—as nurses, elementary school teachers, librarians, and social workers. Instead of bumping their heads against a glass ceiling, the men

glass ceiling the mostly invisible barrier that keeps women from advancing to the top levels at work

Dilbert

One of the frustrations felt by many women in the labor force is that no matter what they do, they hit a glass ceiling. Another is that to succeed they feel forced to abandon characteristics they feel are essential to their self.

in these occupations found themselves aboard a **glass escalator.** They were given higher-level positions, more desirable work assignments, and higher salaries. The motor that drives the glass escalator is gender—the stereotype that because someone is male he is more capable.

Gender and the Control of Workers

Conflict theorists analyze how capitalists exploit gender divisions among workers in order to control them. This does not come in an overt form, such as "Men, if you don't agree to what we are proposing, we'll hire women to take your place." Rather, owners and managers divide workers in subtle ways. For example, a Silicon Valley manufacturing firm specifies the color of the smocks that it requires its workers to wear. The color of the men's smocks depends on the particular job they do, but all the women wear the same color, regardless of their jobs.

Why should management have such a policy? According to sociologist Karen Hossfeld (2000), who studied these workers, the underlying message is: No matter what your job is, you are primarily a woman. Encouraging the women to think of themselves not as workers, but as *women* workers, makes them easier to control. For example, Hossfeld found that when their bosses flirted with them, the women were less inclined to file grievances.

This same company has a "Ladies' Corner" in its newsletter, but it has no "Men's Corner." The subtle message: It is the men's newsletter, with a little corner devoted to women. In other words, men are the *real* workers, but women are there, too.

Sexual Harassment—and Worse

Sexual harassment—unwelcome sexual attention at work or at school, which may affect a person's job or school performance or create a hostile environment—was not recognized as a problem until the 1970s. Before this, women considered unwanted sexual comments, touches, looks, and pressure to have sex to be a personal matter.

With the prodding of feminists, women began to perceive unwanted sexual advances at work and school as part of a *structural* problem. That is, they began to realize that the issue was more than a man here or there doing obnoxious things because he was attracted to a woman; rather, it was men abusing their positions of authority in order to force unwanted sexual activities on women. Now that women have moved into positions of authority, they, too, have become sexual harassers (Wayne et al. 2001). With most authority vested in men, however, the majority of sexual harassers are men.

As symbolic interactionists stress, labels affect our perception. Because we have the term *sexual harassment,* we perceive actions in a different light than did our predecessors. The meaning of sexual harassment is vague and shifting, however, and court cases constantly change what this term does and does not include. Originally sexual desire was an element of sexual harassment, but it no longer is. This changed when the U.S. Supreme Court considered the lawsuit of a homosexual who had been tormented by his supervisors and fellow workers. The Court ruled that sexual desire is not necessary—that sexual harassment laws also apply to homosexuals who are harassed by heterosexuals while on the job (Felsenthal 1998). By extension, the law applies to heterosexuals who are sexually harassed by homosexuals.

Central to sexual harassment is the abuse of power, a topic that is explored in the following Thinking Critically section.

glass escalator the mostly invisible accelerators that push men into higher-level positions, more desirable work assignments, and higher salaries

sexual harassment the abuse of one's position of authority to force unwanted sexual demands on someone

Thinking Critically

Sexual Harassment and Rape of Women in the Military

Women raped at West Point! Other women raped at the U.S. Air Force Academy!

So shrieked the headlines and the TV news teasers. For once, the facts turned out to be just as startling. Women cadets, who were studying to become officers in the U.S. military, had been sexually assaulted by their fellow cadets.

And when the women reported the attacks, *they* were the ones who were punished. The women found themselves charged with drinking alcohol and socializing with upperclassmen. For the most part, the women's charges against the men were ignored. The one man who faced a court martial was acquitted (Schemo 2003a).

This got the attention of Congress. Hearings were held, and the commander of the Air Force Academy was replaced.

A few years earlier, several male Army sergeants at Aberdeen Proving Ground in Maryland had been accused of forcing sex on unwilling female recruits (McIntyre 1997). The drill sergeants, who claimed that the sex was consensual, were found guilty of rape. One married sergeant, who had pleaded guilty to having consensual sex with 11 trainees (adultery is a crime in the Army), was convicted of raping another 6 trainees a total of 18 times and was sentenced to 25 years in prison.

The Army appointed a blue-ribbon panel to investigate sexual harassment in its ranks. When Sgt. Major Gene McKinney, the highest-ranking of the Army's 410,000 noncommissioned officers, was appointed to this committee, former subordinates accused him of sexual harassment (Shenon 1997). McKinney was relieved of his duties and court-martialed. Found not guilty of sexual harassment, but guilty of obstruction of justice, McKinney was reprimanded and demoted. His embittered accusers claimed the Army had sacrificed them for McKinney.

Rape in the military is not an isolated event. Researchers who interviewed a random sample of women veterans found that 4 of 5 had experienced sexual harassment during their military service, and 30 percent had been victims of attempted or completed rape. Three-fourths of the women who had been raped did not report their assault (Sadler et al. 2003). A study of women graduates of the Air Force Academy showed that 12 percent had been victims of rape or attempted rape (Schemo 2003b). In light of such findings, the military appointed a coordinator of sexual assault at every military base (Stout 2005), and apparently, more sexual assaults are being reported (Associated Press 2007; Gleason 2007).

After the U.S. military was sent to Iraq and Afghanistan, the headlines again screamed rape, this time in the Persian Gulf. Again, the headlines were right. And once again, Congress held hearings (Schmitt 2004). We'll have to see how long this cycle of rape followed by hearings repeats itself before adequate reforms are put in place.

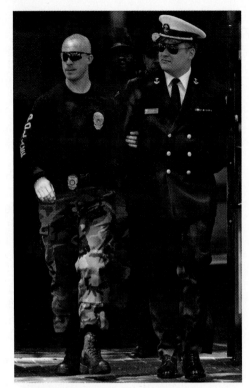

With the publicity about rape scarring our military schools, accusations are being taken more seriously. Shown here is a Navy Midshipman being escorted from his court martial after being sentenced to two years for sexual assault.

for your Consideration

How can we set up a structure to minimize sexual harassment and rape in the military? Can we do this and still train men and women together? Can we do this and still have men and women sleep in the same barracks and on the same ships? Be specific about the structure you would establish.

Gender and Violence

One of the consistent characteristics of violence in the United States—and the world—is its gender inequality. That is, females are much more likely to be the victims of males, not the other way around. Let's briefly review this almost one-way street in gender violence as it applies to the United States.

Violence Against Women

In the Thinking Critically section above, we considered rape in the military; on pages 309 and 312, we examined violence against women in other cultures; on page 316, we reviewed a form of surgical violence; and in Chapter 16 we shall review violence in the home. Here, due to space limitations, we can review only briefly some primary features of violence.

Forcible Rape   Being raped is a common fear of U.S. women, a fear that is far from groundless. According to FBI statistics, each year 8 of every 10,000 females age 12 and older are raped. From the National Crime Victimization Survey, however, we know that only one third of rape victims report this crime to the police (*Statistical Abstract* 2007:Table 311). A more accurate total, then, is *three* times the official rate, or about 24 victims per 10,000 rather than 8. Despite these high numbers, women are safer now than they were 10 and 20 years ago, as the rape rate has been declining.

Although any woman can be a victim of sexual assault—and victims included babies and elderly women—the typical victim is 12 to 34 years old. As you can see from Table 11.3, sexual assault drops sharply for women older than 34 and continues to decline with age.

Women's most common fear seems to be that of strangers—who appear as if from nowhere, catch them unprepared, and abduct and rape them. Contrary to the stereotypes that underlie these fears, however, most victims know their attacker. As you can see from Table 11.4, about one of three rapes is committed by strangers.

An aspect of rape that is usually overlooked is the rape of men in prison. With prison officials reluctant to let the public know about the horrible conditions behind bars, our studies are far from perfect. Those we have, however, indicate that about 15 to 20 percent of men in prison are raped. From court cases, we know that some guards even punish prisoners by placing them in cells with sexual predators (Donaldson 1993; Lewin 2001b).

Date (Acquaintance) Rape   What has shocked so many about date rape (also known as *acquaintance rape*) are studies showing that it does not consist of a few isolated events (Collymore 2000; Goode 2001). Some researchers even report that most women students experience unwanted, forced, or coerced sex (Kalof 2000). Others report much smaller numbers. Researchers who used a representative sample of courses to survey the students at Marietta College, a private school in Ohio, found that 2.5 percent of the women had been physically forced to have sex (Felton et al. 2001). About as many men (23 percent) as women (24 percent) had given in to pressure to have sex when they didn't want to, but—and this is no surprise—none of the men had been physically forced to have sex.

Most date rapes go unreported. A primary reason is that the victim feels partially responsible because she knows the person and was with him voluntarily. However, as a physician who treats victims of date rape said, "Would you feel responsible if someone hit you over the head with a shovel—just because you knew the person?" (Carpenito 1999).

Murder   All over the world, men are more likely than women to be killers. Figure 11.9 illustrates this gender pattern in U.S. murders. Note that although females make up about 51 percent of the U.S. population, they don't even come close to making up 51 percent of the nation's killers. As you can see from this figure, when women are murdered, about eight or nine times out of ten the killer is a man.

Table 11.3   Rape Victims

Age	Rate per 1,000 Females
12–15	1.2
16–19	1.3
20–24	1.7
25–34	1.6
35–49	0.6
50–64	0.4
65 and Older	0.1

Source: By the author. Based on *Statistical Abstract* 2007:Table 311.

Table 11.4   Relationship of Rapists to Victims

Relationship	Percentage
Relative	3.6%
Known Well	27.1%
Casual Acquaintance	26.1%
Stranger	33.5%
Not Reported	9.7%

Source: By the Author. Based on *Statistical Abstract* 2007:Table 315.

Figure 11.9 Killers and Their Victims

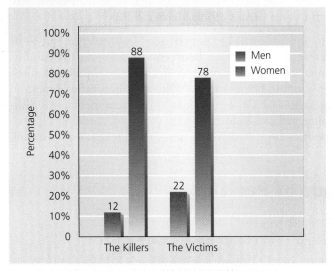

Source: By the author. Based on *Statistical Abstract* 2007:Tables 300, 317.

Violence in the Home Women are also the typical victims of family violence. Spouse battering, marital rape, and incest are discussed in Chapter 16, pages 491–493. A particular form of violence against women, genital circumcision, is the focus of the Cultural Diversity box on page 313.

Women in the Criminal Justice System There is another side to gender and violence. Although women are much less likely to kill, when they do kill, judges tend to be more lenient with them. As Table 11.5 shows, women are more likely to be given probation for murder (as well as for robbery, burglary, and all crimes listed on this table). Sexual stereotypes probably underlie these decisions—such as the idea that women are less of a menace than men and should be given another chance. It is also possible that women defendants have less of a criminal history ("rap sheet") when they are charged with crimes. We need research on this topic.

Feminism and Gendered Violence Feminist sociologists have been especially effective in bringing violence against women to the public's attention. Some use symbolic interactionism, pointing out that to associate strength and virility with violence—as is

Table 11.5 Going Easier on Women

When Men and Women Are Convicted of the Same Crime, Who Gets Off Easier?*

	PRISON		PROBATION	
Crime	**Men**	**Women**	**Men**	**Women**
Murder	97%	89%	1%	5%
Robbery	78%	67%	9%	13%
Burglary	55%	43%	19%	23%
Aggravated Assault	54%	30%	18%	26%
Drug Dealing	50%	37%	20%	26%
Weapons	49%	28%	22%	30%
Larceny	42%	28%	24%	34%
Fraud	39%	31%	28%	41%

*This table examines the extremes of sentencing; totals do not add to 100 percent because of jail sentences and the source's unspecified "other" dispositions.

Source: Sourcebook of Criminal Justice Statistics 1997:Table 5.50. (Table dropped in later editions.)

done in many cultures—is to promote violence. Others use conflict theory. They argue that men are losing power, and that some men turn violently against women as a way to reassert their declining power and status (Reiser 1999; Meltzer 2002).

Solutions There is no magic bullet for this problem of gendered violence, but to be effective, any solution must break the connection between violence and masculinity. This would require an educational program that encompasses schools, churches, homes, and the media. Given the gun-slinging heroes of the Wild West and other American icons, as well as the violent messages that are so prevalent in the mass media, it is difficult to be optimistic that a change will come any time soon.

Our next topic, women in politics, however, gives us much more reason for optimism.

The Changing Face of Politics

What do these nations have in common?

Africa: Liberia and Rwanda

Asia: Indonesia and the Philippines

Europe: Great Britain, Finland, France, Germany, Ireland, Latvia, Portugal, Poland, Switzerland, and Turkey

Middle East: Israel

North America: Canada and Haiti

South and Central America: Argentina, Bolivia, Chile, Ecuador, Guyana, Nicaragua, and Panama

The Subcontinent: Bangladesh, India, Pakistan, and Sri Lanka

The answer is that all have had a woman president or prime minister ("Women in Politics" 2006).

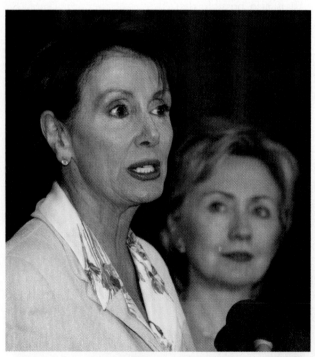

Although women are underrepresented severely in U.S. politics, the situation is changing, at least gradually. The two highest profile women as this edition was being written are Nancy Pelosi, the first woman minority and majority leader, and Hillary Clinton, U.S. Senator and contender for the U.S. presidency.

Then why not the United States? Why don't women, who outnumber men, take political control of the nation? Eight million more women than men are of voting age, and more women than men vote in U.S. national elections. As Table 11.6 shows, however, men greatly outnumber women in political office. Despite the gains women have made in recent elections, since 1789 over 1,800 men have served in the U.S. Senate, but only 35 women have served, including 16 current senators. Not until 1992 was the first African American woman (Carol Moseley-Braun) elected to the U.S. Senate. No Latina or Asian American woman has yet been elected to the Senate (National Women's Political Caucus 1998; *Statistical Abstract* 2007:Table 395).

Why are women underrepresented in U.S. politics? First, women are still underrepresented in law and business, the careers from which most politicians emerge. Most women also find that the irregular hours kept by those who run for office are incompatible with their role as mother. Fathers, in contrast, whose traditional roles are more likely to take them away from home, are less likely to feel this conflict. Women are also not as likely to have a supportive spouse who is willing to play an unassuming background role while providing solace, encouragement, child care, and voter appeal. Finally, preferring to hold on to their positions of power, men have been reluctant to incorporate women into centers of decision making or to present them as viable candidates.

These conditions are changing. Watershed events occurred when Nancy Pelosi was elected by her colleagues in

Table 11.6 U.S. Women in Political Office

	Percentage of Offices Held by Women	Number of Offices Held by Women
National Office		
U.S. Senate	16%	16
U.S. House of Representatives	16%	71
State Office		
Governors	18%	9
Lt. Governors	22%	11
Attorneys General	8%	4
Secretaries of State	24%	12
Treasurers	22%	11
State Auditors	12%	6
State Legislators	24%	1,734

Source: Center for American Women and Politics 2007.

2002 as the first woman minority leader, and then in 2007 as the first woman Speaker of the House. These posts made her the most powerful woman ever in the House of Representatives. We can also note that more women are becoming corporate executives, and, as indicated in Figure 11.4 (on page 317), more women are also becoming lawyers. In these positions, women are doing more traveling and making statewide and national contacts. Another change is that child care is increasingly seen as a responsibility of both mother and father. This generation, then, is likely to mark a fundamental change in women's political participation, and it appears to be only a matter of time until a woman occupies the Oval Office.

Glimpsing the Future—with Hope

Women's fuller participation in the decision-making processes of our social institutions has shattered stereotypes that tended to limit females to "feminine" activities and push males into "masculine" ones. As structural barriers continue to fall and more activities are degendered, both males and females will have greater freedom to pursue activities that are more compatible with their abilities and desires as individuals.

In the midst of this change, what may be developing are new ideas of what males and females are. As stereotypes continue to be broken, new role models develop, and socialization of children changes, males and females will gain new perceptions of themselves and of one another. As sociologists Janet Chafetz (1974), Janet Giele (1978), Judith Lorber (1994), and others have pointed out, this will allow men and women to express needs and emotions that traditional social arrangements denied them. Women and girls will likely perceive themselves as more in control of their environment, become more assertive, and strive more for positions of leadership. Men and boys will likely feel and express more emotional sensitivity—becoming warmer, more affectionate and tender, and giving greater expression to anxieties and stresses that their gender has forced them to suppress.

As females and males develop a new consciousness both of their capacities and of their potential, relationships will change. Distinctions between the sexes will not disappear, but there is no reason for biological differences to be translated into social inequalities. If current trends continue, we may see a growing appreciation of sexual differences coupled with greater equality of opportunity—which has the potential of transforming society (Gilman 1911/1971; Offen 1990). If this happens, as sociologist Alison Jaggar (1990) observed, gender equality can become less a goal than a background condition for living in society.

Summary *and* Review

Issues of Sex and Gender

What is gender stratification?

The term **gender stratification** refers to unequal access to property, power, and prestige on the basis of sex. Each society establishes a structure that, on the basis of sex and gender, opens and closes doors to its privileges. P. 300.

How do sex and gender differ?

Sex refers to biological distinctions between males and females. It consists of both primary and secondary sex characteristics. **Gender,** in contrast, is what a society considers proper behaviors and attitudes for its male and female members. Sex physically distinguishes males from females; gender defines what is "masculine" and "feminine." P. 300.

Why do the behaviors of males and females differ?

The "nature versus nurture" debate refers to whether differences in the behaviors of males and females are caused by inherited (biological) or learned (cultural) characteristics. Almost all sociologists take the side of nurture. In recent years, however, sociologists have begun to cautiously open the door to biology. Pp. 300–305.

Gender Inequality in Global Perspective

Is gender stratification universal?

George Murdock surveyed information on tribal societies and found that all of them have sex-linked activities and give greater prestige to male activities. **Patriarchy,** or male dominance, appears to be universal. Besides work, other areas of discrimination include education, politics, and violence. Pp. 305–312.

How did females become a minority group?

The origin of discrimination against females is lost in history, but the primary theory of how females became a minority group in their own societies focuses on the physical limitations imposed by childbirth. Pp. 306–308.

Gender Inequality in the United States

Is the feminist movement new?

In what is called the "first wave," feminists made political demands for change in the early 1900s—and were met with hostility, and even violence. The "second wave" began in the 1960s and continues today. A "third wave" is emerging. P. 314.

What forms do gender discrimination in health care and gender stratification in education take?

Physicians don't take women's health complaints as seriously as those of men. Hysterectomies are a special case of discrimination. In education, more women than men attend college, but each tends to select fields that are categorized as "feminine" or "masculine." Women are less likely to complete the doctoral programs in science. Fundamental change is indicated by the growing numbers of women in law and medicine. Pp. 315–319.

Is there gender inequality in everyday life?

An indication of gender inequality in everyday life is the devaluation of femininity. The question of male dominance of conversation needs more research. Pp. 319–320.

Gender Inequality in the Workplace

How does gender inequality show up in the workplace?

All occupations show a gender gap in pay. For college graduates, the lifetime pay gap runs over a million dollars in favor of men. **Sexual harassment** also continues to be a reality of the workplace. Pp. 320–325.

Gender and Violence

What is the relationship between gender and violence?

Overwhelmingly, the victims of rape and murder are females. Female circumcision is a special case of violence against females. Conflict theorists point out that men use violence to maintain their power and privilege. Pp. 325–329.

The Changing Face of Politics

What is the trend in gender inequality in politics?

A traditional division of gender roles—women as child care providers and homemakers, men as workers outside the home—used to keep women out of politics. Women continue to be underrepresented in politics, but the trend toward greater political equality is firmly in place. Pp. 328–329.

Glimpsing the Future—with Hope

How might changes in gender roles and stereotypes affect our lives?

In the United States, women are more involved in the decision-making processes of our social institutions. Men, too, are reexamining their traditional roles. New gender expectations may be developing, ones that allow both males and females to pursue more individual, less stereotypical interests. P. 329.

Thinking Critically
about Chapter 11

1. What is your position on the "nature versus nurture" (biology or culture) debate? What materials in this chapter support your position?

2. Why do you think that the gender gap in pay exists all over the world?

3. What do you think can be done to reduce gender inequality?

Additional Resources

What can you use MySocLab for? www.mysoclab.com

- **Study and Review:** Pre- and Post-Tests, Practice Tests, Flash Cards, Individualized Study Plans.

- **Current Events:** *Sociology in the News,* the daily *New York Times,* and more.

- **Research and Writing:** *Research Navigator, Writing About Sociology,* and more.

Where Can I Read More on This Topic?

Suggested readings for this chapter are listed at the back of this book.

CHAPTER 12

Race
and Ethnicity

Ron Waddams, *All Human Beings Are Born Free and Equal in Dignity and Human Rights*, 1998

Imagine that you are an African American man living in Macon County, Alabama, during the Great Depression of the 1930s. Your home is a little country shack with a dirt floor. You have no electricity or running water. You never finished grade school, and you make a living, such as it is, by doing odd jobs. You haven't been feeling too good lately, but you can't afford a doctor.

Then you hear the fantastic news. You rub your eyes in disbelief. It is just like winning the lottery! If you join *Miss Rivers' Lodge* (and it is free to join), you will get free physical examinations at Tuskegee University. You will even get free rides to and from the clinic, hot meals on examination days, and free treatment for minor ailments.

You eagerly join *Miss Rivers' Lodge*.

After your first physical examination, the doctor gives you the bad news. "You've got bad blood," he says. "That's why you've been feeling bad. Miss Rivers will give you some medicine and schedule you for your next exam. I've got to warn you, though. If you

go to another doctor, there's no more free exams or medicine."

You can't afford another doctor anyway. You take your medicine and look forward to the next trip to the university.

What has really happened? You have just become part of what is surely slated to go down in history as one of the most callous experiments of all time, outside of the infamous World War II Nazi and Japanese experiments. With heartless disregard for human life, the U.S. Public Health Service told 399 African American men that they had joined a social club and burial society called "Miss Rivers' Lodge." What the men were *not* told was that they had syphilis. For forty years, the "Public Health Service" allowed these men to go without treatment for their syphilis—just "to see what would happen." There was even a control group of 201 men who were free of the disease (Jones 1993).

By the way, you do get one further benefit: a free autopsy to determine the ravages of syphilis on your body.

You have just become part of one of the most callous experiments of all time.

Laying the Sociological Foundation

 As unlikely as it seems, this is a true story. It really did happen. Seldom do race and ethnic relations degenerate to this point, but troubled race relations are no stranger to us. Today's newspapers and TV news shows regularly report on racial problems. Sociology can contribute greatly to our understanding of this aspect of social life—and this chapter may be an eye-opener for you. To begin, let's consider to what extent race itself is a myth.

Race: Myth and Reality

With its more than 6.5 billion people, the world offers a fascinating variety of human shapes and colors. People see one another as black, white, red, yellow, and brown. Eyes come in shades of blue, brown, and green. Lips are thick and thin. Hair is straight, curly, kinky, black, blonde, and red—and, of course, all shades of brown.

As humans spread throughout the world, their adaptations to diverse climates and other living conditions resulted in this profusion of complexions, hair textures and colors, eye hues, and other physical variations. Genetic mutations added distinct characteristics to the peoples of the globe. In this sense, the concept of **race**—a group of people with inherited physical characteristics that distinguish it from another group—is a reality. Humans do, indeed, come in a variety of colors and shapes.

In two senses, however, race is a myth, a fabrication of the human mind. The *first* myth is the idea that any race is superior to others. All races have their geniuses—and their idiots. As with language, no race is superior to another.

Ideas of racial superiority abound, however. They are not only false but also dangerous. Adolf Hitler, for example, believed that the Aryans were a superior race, responsible for the cultural achievements of Europe. The Aryans, he said, were destined to establish a superior culture and usher in a new world order. This destiny required them to avoid the "racial contamination" that would come from breeding with inferior races; therefore, it was necessary to isolate or destroy races that threatened Aryan purity and culture.

Put into practice, Hitler's views left an appalling legacy—the Nazi slaughter of those they deemed inferior: Jews, Slavs, gypsies, homosexuals, and people with mental and physical disabilities. Horrific images of gas ovens and emaciated bodies stacked like cordwood haunted the world's nations. At Nuremberg, the Allies, flush with victory, put the top Nazis on trial, exposing their heinous deeds to a shocked world. Their public executions, everyone assumed, marked the end of such grisly acts.

Obviously, they didn't. In the summer of 1994 in Rwanda, Hutus slaughtered about 800,000 Tutsis—mostly with machetes (Cowell 2006). A few years later, the Serbs in Bosnia massacred Muslims, giving us the new term "ethnic cleansing." As these events sadly attest, **genocide,** the attempt to destroy a group of people because of their presumed race or ethnicity, remains alive and well. Although more recent killings are not accompanied by swastikas and gas ovens, the perpetrators' goal is the same.

The *second* myth is that "pure" races exist. Humans show such a mixture of physical characteristics—in skin color, hair texture, nose shape, head shape, eye color, and so on—that there are no "pure" races. Instead of falling into distinct types that are clearly separate from one another, human characteristics flow endlessly together. The mapping of the human genome system shows that humans are strikingly homogenous, that so-called racial groups differ from one another only once in a thousand subunits of the genome (Angler 2000). Humans, then, vary from one another in only

Humans show such remarkable diversity that, as the text explains, there are no pure races. Shown here are Verne Troyer, who weighs about 45 pounds and is 2 feet 8 inches short, and Yao Ming, who weighs 296 pounds and is 7 feet 5 inches tall.

race physical characteristics that distinguish one group from another

genocide the systematic annihilation or attempted annihilation of a people because of their presumed race or ethnic group

The reason I selected these photos is to illustrate how seriously we must take all preaching of hatred and of racial supremacy, even though it seems to come from harmless or even humorous sources. The strange-looking person on the left, who is wearing lederhosen, traditional clothing of Bavaria, Germany, is Adolf Hitler. He caused the horrific scene on the right, which greeted the British army when it liberated the concentration camp in Buchenwald, Germany: Thousands of people were dying of starvation and diseases amidst piles of rotting corpses awaiting mass burial.

very slight ways. As you can see from the example of Tiger Woods, discussed in the Cultural Diversity box on the next page, these minute gradations make any attempt to draw lines of race purely arbitrary.

Although large groupings of people can be classified by blood type and gene frequencies, even these classifications do not uncover "race." Rather, race is so arbitrary that biologists and anthropologists cannot even agree on how many "races" there are. They have drawn up many lists, each containing a different number. Ashley Montagu (1964, 1999), a physical anthropologist, pointed out that some scientists have classified humans into only two "races," while others have found as many as two thousand. Montagu (1960) himself classified humans into forty "racial" groups. As the Down-to-Earth Sociology box on page 337 illustrates, even a plane ride can change someone's race!

The *idea* of race, of course, is far from a myth. Firmly embedded in our culture, it is a powerful force in our everyday lives. That no race is superior and that even biologists cannot decide how people should be classified into races is not what counts. "I know what I see, and you can't tell me any different" seems to be the common attitude. As was noted in Chapter 4, sociologists W. I. and D. S. Thomas (1928) observed that "If people define situations as real, they are real in their consequences." In other words, people act on beliefs, not facts. As a result, we will always have people like Hitler and, as illustrated in our opening vignette, officials like those in the U.S. Public Health Service who thought that it was fine to experiment with people whom they deemed inferior. While few people hold such extreme views, most people appear to be ethnocentric enough to believe that their own race is—at least just a little—superior to others.

IN SUM Race, then, lies in the eye of the beholder. Humans show such a mixture of physical characteristics—in skin color, hair texture, nose shape, head shape, eye color, and so on—that there is no inevitable, much less universal, way to classify our many biological differences. Instead of falling into distinct types clearly separate from one another, human characteristics flow endlessly together. Because racial classifications are arbitrary, the categories people use differ from one society to another, and the categories are fluid, changing over time. In this sense, then, the concept of race and its accompanying notions of racial superiority are myths.

Ethnic Groups

Whereas people use the term *race* to refer to supposed biological characteristics that distinguish one group of people from another, **ethnicity** and **ethnic** apply to cultural

ethnicity (and **ethnic**) having distinctive cultural characteristics

Tiger Woods and the Emerging Multiracial Identity: Mapping New Ethnic Terrain

TIGER WOODS, PERHAPS THE TOP golfer of all time, calls himself Cablinasian. Woods invented this term as a boy to try to explain to himself just who he was—a combination of Caucasian, Black, Indian, and Asian (Leland and Beals 1997; Hall 2001). Woods wants to embrace all sides of his family. To be known by a racial-ethnic identity that applies to just one of his parents is to deny the other parent.

Like many of us, Tiger Woods' heritage is difficult to specify. Analysts who like to quantify ethnic heritage put Woods at one-quarter Thai, one-quarter Chinese, one-quarter white, an eighth Native American, and an eighth African American. From this chapter, you know how ridiculous such computations are, but the sociological question is why many people consider Tiger Woods an African American. The U.S. racial scene is indeed complex, but a good part of the reason is simply that this is the label the media placed on him. "Everyone has to fit somewhere" seems to be our attitude. If they don't, we grow uncomfortable. And for Tiger Woods, the media chose African American.

Tiger Woods as he answers questions at a news conference.

The United States once had a firm "color line"—barriers between racial-ethnic groups that you didn't dare cross, especially in dating or marriage. This invisible barrier has broken down, and today such marriages are common (*Statistical Abstract* 2007:Table 58). Several campuses have interracial student organizations. Harvard has two, one just for students who have one African American parent (Leland and Beals 1997).

As we march into unfamiliar ethnic terrain, our classifications are bursting at the seams. Consider how Kwame Anthony Appiah, of Harvard's Philosophy and Afro-American Studies Departments, described his situation:

"My mother is English; my father is Ghanaian. My sisters are married to a Nigerian and a Norwegian. I have nephews who range from blond-haired kids to very black kids. They are all first cousins. Now according to the American scheme of things, they're all black—even the guy with blond hair who skis in Oslo" (Wright 1994).

I marvel at what racial experts the U.S. census takers once were. When they took the census, which is done every ten years, they looked at people and assigned them a race. At various points, the census contained these categories: mulatto, quadroon, octoroon, Negro, black, Mexican, white, Indian, Filipino, Japanese, Chinese, and Hindu. Quadroon (one-fourth black and three-fourths white) and octoroon (one-eighth black and seven-eighths white) proved too difficult to "measure," and these categories were used only in 1890. Mulatto appeared in the 1850 census, but disappeared in 1930. The Mexican government complained about Mexicans being treated as a race, and this category was used only in 1930. I don't know whose strange idea it was to make Hindu a race, but it lasted for three censuses, from 1920 to 1940 (Bean et al. 2004; Tafoya, Johnson, and Hill 2005).

Today people are able to choose their own categories—and they have a lot of choices. In the 2000 census, everyone first declared that they were or were not "Spanish/Hispanic/Latino." Then they marked "one or more races" that they "consider themselves to be." They could choose from White; Black, African American, or Negro; American Indian or Alaska Native; Asian Indian, Chinese, Filipino, Japanese, Korean, Vietnamese, Native Hawaiian, Guamanian or Chamorro, Samoan, and other Pacific Islander. If these didn't do it, they could check a box called "Some Other Race" and then write whatever they wanted.

Perhaps the census should list Cablinasian, after all. There should also be ANGEL for African-Norwegian-German-English-Latino Americans, DEVIL for those of Danish-English-Vietnamese-Italian-Lebanese descent, and STUDY for the Swedish-Turkish-Uruguayan-Djibouti-Yugoslavian Americans. As you read farther in this chapter, you will see why these terms make as much sense as the categories we currently use.

for your Consideration

Just why do we count people by "race" anyway? Why not eliminate race from the U.S. census? (Race became a factor in 1790 during the first census when, for purposes of taxation and determining the number of representatives from each state, slaves were counted as three-fifths of whites!) Why is race so important to some people? Perhaps you can use the materials in this chapter to answer these questions.

Down-to-Earth Sociology

Can a Plane Ride Change Your Race?

AT THE BEGINNING OF this text (pages 8–9), I mentioned that common sense and sociology often differ. This is especially so when it comes to race. According to common sense, our racial classifications represent biological differences between people. Sociologists, in contrast, stress that what we call races are *social* classifications, not biological categories.

Sociologists point out that *our "race" depends more on the society in which we live than on our biological characteristics.* For example, the racial categories common in the United States are merely one of *numerous* ways by which people around the world classify physical appearances. Although various groups use different categories, each group assumes that its categories are natural, merely a response to visible biology.

To better understand this essential sociological point—that race is more social than it

What "race" are these two Brazilians? Is the child of a different "race" than the mother? The text explains why "race" is such an unreliable concept that it changes even with geography.

is biological—consider this: In the United States, children born to the same parents are all of the same race. "What could be more natural?" Americans assume. But in Brazil, children born to the same parents may be of different races—if their appearances differ. "What could be more natural?" assume Brazilians.

Consider how Americans usually classify a child born to a "black" mother and a "white" father. Why do they usually say that the child is "black"? Wouldn't it be equally as logical to classify the child as "white"? Similarly, if a child has one grandmother who is "black," but all her other ancestors are "white," the child is often considered "black." Yet she has much more "white blood" than "black blood." Why, then, is she considered "black"? Certainly not because of biology. Rather, such thinking is a legacy of slavery. In an attempt to preserve the "purity" of their "race" in the face of numerous children whose fathers were white slave masters and mothers were black slaves, whites classified anyone

with even a "drop of black blood" as black. This was actually known as the "one-drop" rule.

Even a plane trip can change a person's race. In the city of Salvador in Brazil, people classify one another by color of skin and eyes, breadth of nose and lips, and color and curliness of hair. They use at least seven terms for what we call white and black. Consider again a U.S. child who has "white" and "black" parents. If she flies to Brazil, she is no longer "black"; she now belongs to one of their several "whiter" categories (Fish 1995).

If the girl makes such a flight, would her "race" actually change? Our common sense revolts at this, I know, but it actually would. We want to argue that because her biological characteristics remain unchanged, her race remains unchanged. This is because we think of race as biological, when *race is actually a label we use to describe perceived biological characteristics.* Simply put, the race we "are" depends on our social location—on who is doing the classifying.

"Racial" classifications are also fluid, not fixed. You can see change occurring even now in the classifications that are used in the United States. The category "multiracial," for example, indicates changing thought and perception.

for your Consideration

How would you explain to "Joe and Suzie Six-Pack" that race is more a social classification than a biological one? Can you come up with any arguments to refute it? How do you think our racial-ethnic categories will change in the future?

---

characteristics. Derived from the word *ethnos* (a Greek word meaning "people" or "nation"), ethnicity and ethnic refer to people who identify with one another on the basis of common ancestry and cultural heritage. Their sense of belonging may center on their nation of origin, distinctive foods, clothing, language, music, religion, or family names and relationships.

People often confuse the terms *race* and *ethnic group*. For example, many people, including many Jews, consider Jews a race. Jews, however, are more properly considered an ethnic group, for it is their cultural characteristics, especially their religion, that bind them together. Wherever Jews have lived in the world, they have intermarried. Consequently,

Because ideas of *race and ethnicity* are such a significant part of society, all of us are classified according to those ideas. This photo illustrates the difficulty such assumptions posed for Israel. The Ethiopians, shown here as they arrived in Israel, although claiming to be Jews, looked so different from other Jews that it took several years for Israeli authorities to acknowledge this group's "true Jewishness."

Jews in China may have Chinese features, while some Swedish Jews are blue-eyed blonds. This matter is strikingly illustrated in the photo on this page. Ethiopian Jews look so different from European Jews that when they immigrated to Israel many European Jews felt that the Ethiopians could not be *real* Jews.

Minority Groups and Dominant Groups

Sociologist Louis Wirth (1945) defined a **minority group** as people who are singled out for unequal treatment and who regard themselves as objects of collective discrimination. Worldwide, minorities share several conditions: Their physical or cultural traits are held in low esteem by the dominant group, which treats them unfairly, and they tend to marry within their own group (Wagley and Harris 1958). These conditions tend to create a sense of identity among minorities (a feeling of "we-ness"). In many instances, a sense of common destiny emerges (Chandra 1993b).

Surprisingly, a minority group is not necessarily a *numerical* minority. For example, before India's independence in 1947, a handful of British colonial rulers discriminated against tens of millions of Indians. Similarly, when South Africa practiced apartheid, a smaller group of Dutch discriminated against a much larger number of blacks. And all over the world, females are a minority group. Accordingly, sociologists usually refer to those who do the discriminating not as the *majority*, but, rather, as the **dominant group,** for they have the greater power, privileges, and social status.

Possessing political power and unified by shared physical and cultural traits, the dominant group uses its position to discriminate against those with different—and supposedly inferior—traits. The dominant group considers its privileged position to be the result of its own innate superiority.

Emergence of Minority Groups   A group becomes a minority in one of two ways. The *first* is through the expansion of political boundaries. With the exception of females, tribal societies contain no minority groups. Everyone shares the same culture, including the same language, and belongs to the same group. When a group expands its political boundaries, however, it produces minority groups if it incorporates people with different customs, languages, values, and physical characteristics into the same political

minority group people who are singled out for unequal treatment and who regard themselves as objects of collective discrimination

dominant group the group with most power, greatest privileges, and highest social status entity and discriminates against them. For example, after defeating Mexico in war in 1848, the United States took over the Southwest. The Mexicans living there, who had been the dominant group prior to the war, were transformed into a minority group, a master status that has influenced their lives ever since. Referring to his ancestors, one Latino said, "We didn't move across the border—the border moved across us."

A *second* way in which a group becomes a minority is by migration. This can be voluntary, as with the millions of people who have chosen to move from Mexico to the United States, or involuntary, as with the millions of Africans who were brought in chains to the United States. (The way females became a minority group represents a third way, but, as discussed in the previous chapter, no one knows just how this occurred.)

How People Construct Their Racial-Ethnic Identity

Some of us have a greater sense of ethnicity than others. Some of us feel firm boundaries between "us" and "them." Others have assimilated so extensively into the mainstream culture that they are only vaguely aware of their ethnic origins. With interethnic marrying common, some do not even know the countries from which their families originated— nor do they care. If asked to identify themselves ethnically, they respond with something like "I'm Heinz 57—German and Irish, with a little Italian and French thrown in—and I think someone said something about being one-sixteenth Indian, too."

Why do some people feel an intense sense of ethnic identity, while others feel hardly any? Figure 12.1 portrays four factors, identified by sociologist Ashley Doane, that heighten or reduce our sense of ethnic identity. From this figure, you can see that the keys are relative size, power, appearance, and discrimination. If your group is relatively small, has little power, looks different from most people in society, and is an object of discrimination, you will have a heightened sense of ethnic identity. In contrast, if you belong to the dominant group that holds most of the power, look like most people in the society, and feel no discrimination, you are likely to experience a sense of "belonging"—and to wonder why ethnic identity is such a big deal.

We can use the term **ethnic work** to refer to the way people construct their ethnicity. For people who have a strong ethnic identity, this term refers to how they enhance and maintain their group's distinctions—from clothing, food, and language to religious practices and holidays. For people whose ethnic identity is not as firm, it refers to attempts to recover their ethnic heritage, such as trying to trace family lines or visiting the country or region of their family's origin. Millions of Americans are engaged in ethnic work, which has confounded the experts who thought that the United States would be a **melting pot,** with most of its groups blending into a sort of ethnic stew. Because so many Americans have become fascinated with their "roots," some analysts have suggested that "tossed salad" is a more appropriate term than "melting pot."

Figure 12.1 **A Sense of Ethnicity**

Source: By the author. Based on Doane 1997.

ethnic work activities designed to discover, enhance, or maintain ethnic and racial identification

melting pot the view that Americans of various backgrounds would blend into a sort of ethnic stew

Prejudice and Discrimination

With prejudice and discrimination so significant in social life, let's consider the origin of prejudice and the extent of discrimination.

Learning Prejudice

Distinguishing Between Prejudice and Discrimination   Prejudice and discrimination are common throughout the world. In Mexico, Hispanic Mexicans discriminate against Native American Mexicans; in Israel, Ashkenazi Jews, primarily of European descent, discriminate against Sephardi Jews from the Muslim world. In some places, the elderly discriminate against the young; in others, the young discriminate against the elderly. And all around the world, men discriminate against women.

Discrimination is an *action*—unfair treatment directed against someone. Discrimination can be based on many characteristics: age, sex, height, weight, clothing, income, education, marital status, sexual orientation, disease, disability, religion, and politics. When the basis of discrimination is someone's perception of race, it is known as **racism.** Discrimination is often the result of an *attitude* called **prejudice**—a prejudging of some sort, usually in a negative way. There is also *positive prejudice*, which exaggerates the virtues of a group, as when people think that some group (usually their own) is more capable than others. Most prejudice, however, is negative and involves prejudging a group as inferior.

Learning from Association   As with our other attitudes, we are not born with prejudice. Rather, we learn prejudice from the people around us. In a fascinating study, sociologist Kathleen Blee (2005) interviewed women who were members of the KKK and Aryan Nations. Her first finding is of the "ho hum" variety: Most women were recruited by someone who already belonged to the group. Blee's second finding, however, holds a surprise: Some women learned to be racists *after* they joined the group. They were attracted to the group not because it matched their racist beliefs but because someone they liked belonged to it. Blee found that their racism was not the *cause* of their joining but, rather, the *result* of their membership.

The Far-Reaching Nature of Prejudice   It is amazing how much prejudice people can learn. In a classic article, psychologist Eugene Hartley (1946) asked people how they felt about several racial and ethnic groups. Besides blacks, Jews, and so on, he included the Wallonians, Pireneans, and Danireans—names he had made up. Most people who expressed dislike for Jews and blacks also expressed dislike for these three fictitious groups.

Hartley's study shows that prejudice does not depend on negative experiences with others. It also reveals that people who are prejudiced against one racial or ethnic group also tend to be prejudiced against other groups. People can be, and are, prejudiced against people they have never met—and even against groups that do not exist!

The neo-Nazis and the Ku Klux Klan base their existence on prejudice. These groups believe that race is real, that white is best, and that society's surface conceals underlying conspiracies (Ezekiel 2002). What would happen if a Jew attended their meetings? Would he or she survive? In the Down-to-Earth Sociology box on the next page, sociologist Raphael Ezekiel reveals some of the insights he gained during his remarkable study of these groups.

Internalizing Dominant Norms   People can even learn to be prejudiced against their *own* group. A national survey of black Americans conducted by black interviewers found that African Americans think that lighter-skinned African American women are more attractive than those with darker skin (Hill 2002). Sociologists call this *the internalization of the norms of the dominant group.*

To study the internalization of dominant norms, psychologists Mahzarin Banaji and Anthony Greenwald created the "Implicit Association Test." In one version of this test,

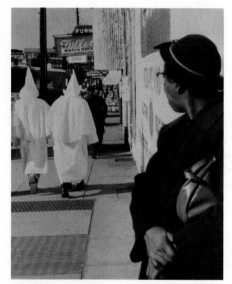

In the early 1900s, the Ku Klux Klan was a powerful political force. By the 1950s when this photo was taken in Montgomery, Alabama, the Klan possessed only a shadow of its former power. Today's Klan gets a headline here and there, but few are listening to its message. The group continues to have followers, however.

discrimination an act of unfair treatment directed against an individual or a group

racism prejudice and discrimination on the basis of race

prejudice an attitude or prejudging, usually in a negative way

Down-to-Earth Sociology

The Racist Mind

SOCIOLOGIST RAPHAEL EZEKIEL WANTED to get a close look at the racist mind. The best way to study racism from the inside is to do participant observation (see page 136). But Ezekiel is a Jew. Could he study these groups by participant observation? To find out, Ezekiel told Ku Klux Klan and neo-Nazi leaders that he wanted to interview them and attend their meetings. He also told them that he was a Jew. Surprisingly, they agreed. Ezekiel published his path-breaking research in a book, *The Racist Mind* (1995). Here are some of the insights he gained during his fascinating sociological adventure:

> [The leader] builds on mass anxiety about economic insecurity and on popular tendencies to see an Establishment as the cause of economic threat; he hopes to teach people to identify that Establishment as the puppets of a conspiracy of Jews. [He has a] belief in exclusive categories. For the white racist leader, it is profoundly true . . . that the socially defined collections we call races represent fundamental categories. A man is black or a man is white; there are no in-betweens. Every human belongs to a racial category, and all the members of one category are radically different from all the members of other categories. Moreover, race represents the essence of the person. A truck is a truck, a car is a car, a cat is a cat, a dog is a dog, a black is a black, a white is a white. . . . These axioms have a rock-hard quality in the leaders' minds; the world is made up of racial groups. That is what exists for them.
>
> Two further beliefs play a major role in the minds of leaders. First, life is war. The world is made of distinct racial groups; life is about the war between these groups. Second, events have secret causes, are never what they seem superficially. . . . Any myth is plausible, as long as it involves intricate plotting. . . . It does not matter to him what others say. . . . He lives in his ideas and in the little world he has created where they are

taken seriously. . . . Gold can be made from the tongues of frogs; Yahweh's call can be heard in the flapping swastika banner. (pp. 66–67)

Who is attracted to the neo-Nazis and Ku Klux Klan? Here is what Ezekiel discovered:

> [There is a] ready pool of whites who will respond to the racist signal. . . . This population [is] always hungry for activity—or for the talk of activity—that promises dignity and meaning to lives that are working poorly in a highly competitive world. . . . Much as I don't want to believe it, [this] movement brings a sense of meaning—at least for a while—to some of the discontented. To struggle in a cause that transcends the individual lends meaning to life, no matter how ill-founded or narrowing the cause. For the young men in the neo-Nazi group . . . membership was an alternative to atomization and drift; within the group they worked for a cause and took direct risks in the company of comrades. . . .
>
> When interviewing the young neo-Nazis in Detroit, I often found myself driving with them past the closed factories, the idled plants of our shrinking manufacturing base. The fewer and fewer plants that remain can demand better educated and more highly skilled workers. These fatherless Nazi youths, these high-school dropouts, will find little place in the emerging economy . . . a permanently underemployed white underclass is taking its place alongside the permanent black underclass. The struggle over race merely diverts youth from confronting the real issues of their lives. Not many seats are left on the train, and the train is leaving the station. (pp. 32–33)

for your Consideration

Use functionalism, conflict theory, and symbolic interaction to explain how the leaders and followers of these hate groups view the world. Use these same perspectives to explain why some people are attracted to the message of hate.

---

good and bad words are flashed on a screen along with photos of African Americans and whites. Most subjects are quicker to associate positive words (such as "love," "peace," and "baby") with whites and negative words (such as "cancer," "bomb," and "devil") with blacks. Here's the clincher: This is true for *both* white and black subjects (Dasgupta et al. 2000; Greenwald and Krieger 2006). Apparently, we all learn the *ethnic maps* of our culture, and, along with them, their route to biased perception.

Individual and Institutional Discrimination

Sociologists stress that we need to move beyond thinking in terms of **individual discrimination,** the negative treatment of one person by another. Although such behavior creates problems, it is primarily an issue between individuals. With their focus on the broader picture, sociologists encourage us to examine **institutional discrimination,** that is, to see how discrimination is woven into the fabric of society. Let's look at two examples.

individual discrimination
the negative treatment of one person by another on the basis of that person's perceived characteristics

institutional discrimination
the negative treatment of a minority group that is built into a society's institutions; also called *systemic discrimination*

Home Mortgages and Car Loans   Bank lending provides an excellent illustration of institutional discrimination. As shown in Figure 12.2, race-ethnicity is a significant factor in getting a mortgage. When bankers looked at the statistics shown in this figure, they cried foul. It might *look* like discrimination, they said, but the truth is that whites have better credit histories. To see if this were true, researchers went over the data again, comparing the credit histories of the applicants. The lending gap did narrow a bit, but the bottom line was that even when applicants were identical in all these areas, African Americans and Latinos were *60 percent* more likely than whites to be rejected (Thomas 1992; Passell 1996). African Americans are also likely to be charged more than whites for their mortgages (Avery et al. 2005) and for car loans ("Judge Rules . . ." 2005; Peters and Hakim 2005). In short, it is not a matter of a banker here or there discriminating according to personal prejudices; rather, discrimination is built into the country's financial institutions.

Health Care   Discrimination does not have to be deliberate. It can occur without the awareness of both those doing the discriminating and those being discriminated against. White patients, for example, are more likely than either Latino or African American patients to receive knee replacements (Skinner et al. 2003) and coronary bypass surgery (Smedley et al. 2003). Treatment after a heart attack follows a similar pattern. A study of 40,000 patients shows that whites are more likely than blacks to be given cardiac catheterization, a test to detect blockage of blood vessels. This study holds a surprise: Both black *and* white doctors are more likely to give this preventive care to whites (Stolberg 2001).

Researchers do not know why race-ethnicity is a factor in medical decisions. With both white and black doctors involved, we can be certain that physicians *do not intend* to discriminate. In ways we do not yet understand—but which could be related to the implicit bias that apparently comes with the internalization of dominant norms—discrimination is built into the medical delivery system. Race seems to work like gender: Just as women's higher death rates in coronary bypass surgery can be traced to implicit attitudes about gender (see page 316), so also race-ethnicity becomes a subconscious motivation for giving or denying access to advanced medical procedures.

Figure 12.2   Race-Ethnicity and Mortgages: An Example of Institutional Discrimination

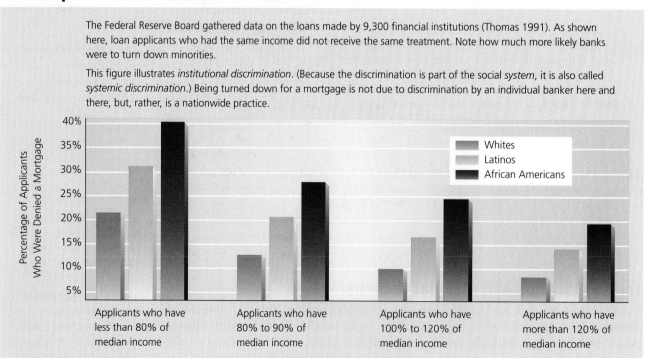

The Federal Reserve Board gathered data on the loans made by 9,300 financial institutions (Thomas 1991). As shown here, loan applicants who had the same income did not receive the same treatment. Note how much more likely banks were to turn down minorities.

This figure illustrates *institutional discrimination*. (Because the discrimination is part of the social *system*, it is also called *systemic discrimination*.) Being turned down for a mortgage is not due to discrimination by an individual banker here and there, but, rather, is a nationwide practice.

Source: By the author. Based on Thomas 1991.

Theories of Prejudice

Social scientists have developed several theories to explain prejudice. Let's first look at psychological explanations, then sociological ones.

Psychological Perspectives

Frustration and Scapegoats   In 1939, psychologist John Dollard suggested that prejudice is the result of frustration. People who are unable to strike out at the real source of their frustration (such as unemployment) look for someone to blame. They unfairly attribute their troubles to a **scapegoat**—often a racial, ethnic, or religious minority—and this person or group becomes a target on which they vent their frustrations. Gender and age also provide common bases for scapegoating.

Even mild frustration can increase prejudice. A team of psychologists led by Emory Cowen (1959) measured the prejudice of a sample of students. They then gave the students two puzzles to solve, making sure the students did not have enough time to solve them. After the students had worked furiously on the puzzles, the experimenters shook their heads in disgust and said that they couldn't believe the students hadn't finished such a simple task. They then retested the students and found that their scores on prejudice had increased. The students had directed their frustrations outward, transferring them to people who had nothing to do with the contempt that the experimenters had directed toward them.

The Authoritarian Personality   Have you ever wondered whether personality is a cause of prejudice? Maybe some people are more inclined to be prejudiced, and others more fair-minded. For psychologist Theodor Adorno, who had fled from the Nazis, this was no idle speculation. With the horrors he had observed still fresh in his mind, Adorno wondered whether there might be a certain type of person who is more likely to fall for the racist spewings of people like Hitler, Mussolini, and those in the Ku Klux Klan.

To find out, Adorno (1950) tested about two thousand people, ranging from college professors to prison inmates. To measure their ethnocentrism, anti-Semitism (bias against Jews), and support for strong, authoritarian leaders, he gave them three tests. Adorno found that people who scored high on one test also scored high on the other two. For example, people who agreed with anti-Semitic statements also said that governments should be authoritarian and that foreign ways of life pose a threat to the "American" way.

Adorno concluded that highly prejudiced people are insecure conformists. They have deep respect for authority and are submissive to superiors. He termed this the **authoritarian personality.** These people believe that things are either right or wrong. Ambiguity disturbs them, especially in matters of religion or sex. They become anxious when they confront norms and values that vary from their own. To view people who differ from themselves as inferior assures them that their own positions are right.

Adorno's research stirred the scientific community, stimulating more than a thousand research studies. In general, the researchers found that people who are older, less educated, less intelligent, and from a lower social class are more likely to be authoritarian. Critics say that this doesn't indicate a particular personality, just that the less educated are more prejudiced—which we already knew (Yinger 1965; Ray 1991). Nevertheless, researchers continue to study this concept (Stenner 2005).

Sociological Perspectives

Sociologists find psychological explanations inadequate. They stress that the key to understanding prejudice cannot be found by looking *inside* people, but rather by examining conditions *outside* them. Therefore, sociologists focus on how social environments influence prejudice. With this background, let's compare functionalist, conflict, and symbolic interactionist perspectives on prejudice.

Functionalism   In a telling scene from a television documentary, journalist Bill Moyers interviewed Fritz Hipler, a Nazi intellectual who at age 29 was put in charge of the entire German film industry. Hipler said that when Hitler came to power the Germans were

scapegoat an individual or group unfairly blamed for someone else's troubles

authoritarian personality Theodor Adorno's term for people who are prejudiced and rank high on scales of conformity, intolerance, insecurity, respect for authority, and submissiveness to superiors no more anti-Semitic than the French, and probably less so. He was told to create anti-Semitism. Obediently, Hipler produced movies that contained vivid scenes comparing Jews to rats—with their breeding threatening to infest the population.

Why was Hipler told to create hatred? Prejudice and discrimination were functional for the Nazis. Germany was on its knees at this time. It had been defeated in World War I and was being economically devastated by war reparations. The middle class was being destroyed by runaway inflation. The Jews provided a scapegoat, a common enemy against which the Nazis could unite Germany. In addition, the Jews owned businesses, bank accounts, fine art, and other property that the Nazis could confiscate. Jews also held key positions (as university professors, reporters, judges, and so on), into which the Nazis could place their own flunkies. In the end, hatred also showed its dysfunctional side, as the Nazi officials who were hanged at Nuremberg discovered.

Prejudice becomes practically irresistible when state machinery is harnessed to advance the cause of hatred. To produce prejudice, the Nazis exploited government agencies, the schools, police, courts, and mass media. The results were devastating. Recall the identical twins featured in the Down-to-Earth Sociology box on page 66. Oskar and Jack had been separated as babies. Jack was brought up as a Jew in Trinidad, while Oskar was reared as a Catholic in Czechoslovakia. Under the Nazi regime, Oskar learned to hate Jews, unaware that he himself was a Jew.

That prejudice is functional and is shaped by the social environment was demonstrated by psychologists Muzafer and Carolyn Sherif (1953). In a boys' summer camp, they assigned friends to different cabins and then had the cabin groups compete in sports. In just a few days, strong in-groups had formed, and even former lifelong friends were calling one another "crybaby" and "sissy," and showing intense dislike for one another.

The Sherif study teaches us several important lessons about social life. Note how it is possible to arrange the social environment to generate either positive or negative feelings about people, and how prejudice arises if we pit groups against one another in an "I win, you lose" situation. You can also see that prejudice is functional, how it creates in-group solidarity. And, of course, it is obvious how dysfunctional prejudice is, when you observe the way it destroys human relationships.

Conflict Theory   Conflict theorists also analyze how groups are pitted against one another, but they focus on how this arrangement benefits those with power. They begin by noting that workers want better food, health care, housing, and education. To attain these goals, workers need good jobs. If workers are united, they can demand higher wages and better working conditions, but if capitalists can keep workers divided, they can hold wages down. To do this, capitalists use two main tactics.

The first tactic is to keep workers insecure. Fear of unemployment works especially well. The unemployed serve as a **reserve labor force** for capitalists. The capitalists draw on the unemployed to expand production during economic booms, and when the economy contracts, they release these workers to rejoin the ranks of the unemployed. The lesson is not lost on workers who have jobs. They fear eviction and worry about having their cars and furniture repossessed. Many know they are just one paycheck away from ending up "on the streets." This helps to keep workers docile.

The second tactic is encouraging and exploiting racial-ethnic divisions (Patterson 2007). Pitting worker against worker weakens labor's bargaining power. When white workers went on strike in California in the 1800s, owners of factories replaced them with Chinese workers. To break strikes by Japanese workers on plantations in Hawaii, owners used to hire Koreans (Xie and Goyette 2004). This division of workers along racial-ethnic and gender lines is known as a **split labor market** (Du Bois 1935/1992; Roediger 2002). Although today's exploitation is more subtle, fear and suspicion continue to split workers. Whites are aware that other groups are ready to take their jobs, African Americans often perceive Latinos as competitors, and men know that women are eager to get promoted. All of this helps to make workers more docile.

The consequences are devastating, say conflict theorists. It is just like the boys in the Sherif experiment. African Americans, Latinos, whites, and others see themselves as able to make gains only at the expense of members of the other groups. This rivalry shows up

reserve labor force the unemployed; unemployed workers are thought of as being "in reserve"—capitalists take them "out of reserve" (put them back to work) during times of high production and then lay them off (put them back in reserve) when they are no longer needed

split labor market workers split along racial, ethnic, gender, age, or any other lines; this split is exploited by owners to weaken the bargaining power of workers along even finer racial-ethnic lines, such as that in Miami between Haitians and African Americans, who distrust each other as competitors. Divisions among workers deflect anger and hostility away from the power elite and direct these powerful emotions toward other racial and ethnic groups. Instead of recognizing their common class interests and working for their mutual welfare, workers learn to fear and distrust one another.

Symbolic Interactionism While conflict theorists focus on the role of the capitalist class in exploiting racial and ethnic divisions, symbolic interactionists examine how labels affect perception and create prejudice.

How Labels Create Prejudice Symbolic interactionists stress that *the labels we learn affect the way we see people.* Labels cause **selective perception;** that is, they lead us to see certain things while they blind us to others. If we apply a label to a group, we tend to perceive its members as all alike. We shake off evidence that doesn't fit (Simpson and Yinger 1972). Racial and ethnic labels are especially powerful. They are shorthand for emotionally charged stereotypes. The term *nigger,* for example, is not neutral. Nor are *honky, cracker, spic, mick, kike, limey, kraut, dago, guinea,* or any of the other scornful words people use to belittle ethnic groups. Such words overpower us with emotions, blocking out rational thought about the people to whom they refer (Allport 1954).

Labels and the Self-Fulfilling Prophecy Some stereotypes not only justify prejudice and discrimination but even produce the behavior depicted in the stereotype. Let's consider Group X. Negative stereotypes characterize the members of Group X as lazy, so they don't deserve good jobs. ("They are lazy and undependable and wouldn't do well.") This attitude creates a *self-fulfilling prophecy.* Because they are denied jobs that require high dedication and energy, most members of Group X are limited to doing "dirty work," the kind of employment thought appropriate for "that kind" of people. Since much "dirty work" is sporadic, members of Group X are often seen "on the streets." The sight of their idleness reinforces the original stereotype of laziness. The discrimination that created the "laziness" in the first place passes unnoticed.

To apply these three theoretical perspectives and catch a glimpse of how amazingly different things were in the past, read the Down-to-Earth Sociology box on the next page.

Global Patterns of Intergroup Relations

Sociologists have studied racial-ethnic relations around the world. They have found six basic patterns that characterize the relationship of dominant groups and minorities. These patterns are shown in Figure 12.3. Let's look at each.

Figure 12.3 **Global Patterns of Intergroup Relations: A Continuum**

Inhumanity ← → Humanity

Rejection ← → Acceptance

Genocide	Population Transfer	Internal Colonialism	Segregation	Assimilation	Multiculturalism (Pluralism)
The dominant group tries to destroy the minority group (e.g., Germany and Rwanda)	The dominant group expels the minority group (e.g., Native Americans moved to reservations)	The dominant group exploits the minority group (e.g., low-paid, menial work)	The dominant group structures the social institutions to maintain minimal contact with the minority group (e.g., the U.S. South before the 1960s)	The dominant group absorbs the minority group (e.g., American Czechoslovakians)	The dominant group encourages racial and ethnic variation; when successful, there is no longer a dominant group (e.g., Switzerland)

The Man in the Zoo

YOU ARE GOING TO THINK I'm kidding, but listen to this:

The Bronx Zoo in New York City used to keep a 22-year-old pygmy in the Monkey House. The man—and the orangutan he lived with—became the most popular exhibit at the zoo. Thousands of visitors would arrive daily, and head straight for the Monkey House. Eyewitnesses to what they thought was a lower form of human in the long chain of evolution, the visitors were fascinated by the pygmy, especially by his sharpened teeth.

To make the exhibit even more alluring, the zoo director ordered that animal bones be scattered in front of the man.

Ota Benga, 1906, on exhibit in the Bronx Zoo.

© Wildlife Conservation Society.

I know it sounds as though I must have made this up. Could this really have happened? Actually, this is a true story, and here's the background on it.

The World's Fair was going to be held in St. Louis in 1904, and the Department of Anthropology wanted to show genuine villages from different cultures. They asked Samuel Verner, an explorer familiar with Africa, if he could get some pygmies to come to St. Louis to serve as live exhibits for a few months. Verner agreed, and on his next trip to Africa, in the Belgian Congo he came across Ota Benga (or Otabenga), a pygmy who had been enslaved by another tribe. Benga, then about age 20, said he was willing to go to St. Louis. After Verner bought Benga's freedom for a few yards of cloth, Benga recruited another half dozen pygmies to go with them.

As promised, after the World's Fair, Verner took the pygmies back to Africa. In his absence, however, a hostile tribe had wiped out Benga's village and killed his family. With few alternatives before him, Benga asked Verner if he could return with him to the United States. Verner agreed.

Unfortunately, after they arrived in New York, Verner ran into financial troubles. He cashed a few bad checks, and creditors confiscated his collection of African artifacts. Unable to care for Benga, Verner asked friends at the American Museum of Natural History to help out. After a few weeks, they grew tired of some of Benga's antics, and turned him over to the Bronx Zoo. There, on exhibit in the Monkey House, living with an orangutan as a roommate, Benga became a sensation.

In their official bulletin, the New York Zoological Society described Benga as "an acquisition" of the Bronx Zoo.

An article in the *New York Times* said that it was fortunate that Benga couldn't think very deeply, or else he might be bothered by living with monkeys.

When African American ministers protested, saying that the zoo's exhibit was degrading, zoo officials defended themselves. They said that they were "taking excellent care of the little fellow." To further make their case, they added that "he has one of the best rooms at the primate house."

As the protest of members of the Colored Baptist Ministers' Conference grew louder and more insistent, zoo officials finally gave in. They decided to let Benga out of his cage. They put a white shirt on him and let him walk around the zoo wherever he wanted. Benga returned at night to sleep in the monkey house.

This limited freedom made life even more miserable for Benga. Now zoo visitors followed him around, howling, jeering, laughing, and poking at him. One day, Benga found a knife in the feeding room of the Monkey House and flourished it at the visitors. Zoo officials took the knife away.

Benga then made a little bow and some arrows and began shooting at the obnoxious visitors. At that point, all the fun was over for the zoo officials. Not liking this turn of events, they decided that Benga had to leave.

After living in several orphanages for African American children, Benga ended up working as a laborer in a tobacco factory in Lynchburg, Virginia.

Benga remained desperately lonely, never fitting in, always being treated as a freak, and in despair that he had no home or family to return to in Africa. In 1916, at the age of 26, Benga ended his misery, shooting himself in the heart.

—Based on Bradford and Blume 1992; Crossen 2006; Richman 2006.

for your Consideration

1. See what different views emerge as you apply the three theoretical perspectives (functionalism, symbolic interactionism, and conflict theory) to exhibiting Benga at the Bronx Zoo.
2. How does the concept of ethnocentrism apply to this event?
3. Explain how the concepts of prejudice and discrimination apply to what happened to Benga.

Genocide

Last century's two most notorious examples of genocide occurred in Europe and Africa. In Germany during the 1930s and 1940s, Hitler and the Nazis attempted to destroy all Jews. In the 1990s, in Rwanda, the Hutus tried to destroy all Tutsis. One of the horrifying aspects of these slaughters was that those who participated did not crawl out from under a rock someplace. Rather, they were ordinary citizens whose participation was facilitated by labels that singled out the victims as enemies who deserved to die (Huttenbach 1991; Browning 1993; Gross 2001).

To better understand how ordinary people can participate in genocide, let's look at an example from the United States. To call the Native Americans "savages," as U.S. officials and white settlers did, was to label them as inferior, as somehow less than human. This identification made it easier to justify killing the Native Americans in order to take over their resources.

> When gold was discovered in northern California in 1849, the fabled "Forty-Niners" rushed in. With the region already inhabited by 150,000 Native Americans, the white government put a bounty on the heads of Native Americans. It even reimbursed the whites for their bullets. The result was the slaughter of 120,000 Native American men, women, and children. (Schaefer 2004)

Most Native Americans, however, died not from bullets but from diseases that the whites brought with them. The Native Americans had no immunity against diseases such as measles, smallpox, and the flu (Dobyns 1983; Schaefer 2004). The settlers also ruthlessly destroyed the Native Americans' food supply (buffalos, crops). As a result, about *95 percent* of Native Americans died (Thornton 1987; Churchill 1997).

The same thing was happening in other places. In South Africa, the Boers, or Dutch settlers, viewed the native Hottentots as jungle animals and totally wiped them out. In Tasmania, the British settlers stalked the local aboriginal population, hunting them for sport and sometimes even for dog food.

Labels are powerful forces in human life. Labels that dehumanize others help people to **compartmentalize**—to separate their acts from their sense of being good and moral people. To regard members of a particular group as inferior or even less than human means that it is okay to treat them inhumanely. Thus people can kill—and still retain a good self-concept (Bernard et al. 1971). In short, *labeling the targeted group as inferior or even less than fully human facilitates genocide.*

Population Transfer

There are two types of **population transfer:** indirect and direct. *Indirect transfer* is achieved by making life so unbearable for members of a minority that they leave "voluntarily." Under the bitter conditions of czarist Russia, for example, millions of Jews made this "choice." *Direct transfer* occurs when a dominant group expels a minority. Examples include the U.S. government relocating Native Americans to reservations and transferring Americans of Japanese descent to internment camps during World War II.

In the 1990s, a combination of genocide and population transfer occurred in Bosnia and Kosovo, parts of the former Yugoslavia. A hatred nurtured for centuries had been kept under wraps by Tito's iron-fisted rule

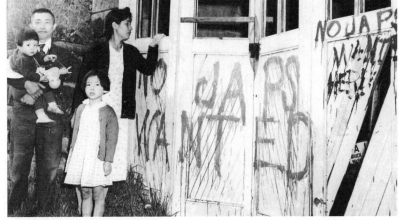

Amid fears that Japanese Americans were "enemies within" who would sabotage industrial and military installations on the West Coast, in the early days of World War II Japanese Americans were transferred to "relocation camps." Many returned home after the war to find that their property had been confiscated or vandalized.

from 1944 to 1980. After Tito's death, these suppressed, smoldering hostilities soared to the surface, and Yugoslavia split into warring factions. When the Serbs gained power, Muslims rebelled and began guerilla warfare. The Serbs vented their hatred by what they termed **ethnic cleansing:** They terrorized villages with killing and rape, forcing survivors to flee in fear.

Internal Colonialism

In Chapter 9, the term *colonialism* was used to refer to one way that the Most Industrialized Nations exploit the Least Industrialized Nations (p. 258). Conflict theorists use the term **internal colonialism** to describe the way in which a country's dominant group exploits minority groups for its economic advantage. The dominant group manipulates the social institutions to suppress minorities and deny them full access to their society's benefits. Slavery, reviewed in Chapter 9, is an extreme example of internal colonialism, as was the South African system of *apartheid.* Although the dominant Afrikaners despised the minority, they found its presence necessary. As Simpson and Yinger (1972) put it, who else would do the hard work?

Segregation

Internal colonialism is often accompanied by **segregation**—the separation of racial or ethnic groups. Segregation allows the dominant group to maintain social distance from the minority and yet to exploit their labor as cooks, cleaners, chauffeurs, housekeepers, nannies, factory workers, and so on. In the U.S. South until the 1960s, by law, African Americans and whites had to use separate public facilities such as hotels, schools, swimming pools, bathrooms, and even drinking fountains. In thirty-eight states, laws prohibited marriage between blacks and whites. Violators could be sent to prison (Mahoney and Kooistra 1995; Crossen 2004). The last law of this type was repealed in 1967 (Spickard 1989). In the villages of India, an ethnic group, the Dalits (untouchables), is forbidden to use the village pump. Dalit women must walk long distances to streams or pumps outside of the village to fetch their water (author's notes).

Racial-ethnic segregation in housing is still a fact of life for most Americans. In the Cultural Diversity box on the next page, you can see how residential segregation is related to internal colonialism.

Assimilation

Assimilation is the process by which a minority group is absorbed into the mainstream culture. There are two types. In *forced assimilation,* the dominant group refuses to allow the minority to practice its religion, to speak its language, or to follow its customs. Before the fall of the Soviet Union, for example, the dominant group, the Russians, required that Armenian children attend schools where they were taught in Russian. Armenians could celebrate only Russian holidays, not Armenian ones. *Permissible assimilation,* in contrast, allows the minority to adopt the dominant group's patterns in its own way and at its own speed.

Multiculturalism (Pluralism)

A policy of **multiculturalism,** also called **pluralism,** permits or even encourages racial and ethnic variation. The minority groups are able to maintain their separate identities, yet participate freely in the country's social institutions, from education to politics. Switzerland provides an outstanding example of multiculturalism. The Swiss population includes four ethnic groups: French, Italians, Germans, and Romansh. These groups have kept their own languages, and they live peacefully in political and economic unity. Multiculturalism has been so successful that none of these groups can properly be called a minority.

ethnic cleansing a policy of population elimination, including forcible expulsion and genocide

internal colonialism the policy of economically exploiting minority groups

segregation the policy of keeping racial-ethnic groups apart

assimilation the process of being absorbed into the mainstream culture

multiculturalism (also called **pluralism**) a philosophy or political policy that permits or encourages ethnic difference

Cultural Diversity *in the* United States

"You Can Work for Us, But You Can't Live Near Us"

NEVER BEFORE HAD SO MANY people crowded into the city hall in Glen Cove, Long Island. What drew them was nothing less than the future of their community, which had become an ethnic and social class crucible. At the front sat the well-groomed Long Islanders in their designer clothing. At the back were men in soiled jeans and work boots whose calloused hands bespoke their occupations as landscape laborers and construction workers. Most of them had fled the civil war in El Salvador, seeking safety and jobs in the United States.

The meeting was called to order by the town mayor, the son of Italian immigrants, who had launched a campaign to rid the town of a day labor shape-up area. He had asked the Immigration and Naturalization Service to raid the area where men gathered on the sidewalks in the early mornings to look for day jobs. This evening he proposed an ordinance making it illegal for groups of five or more to assemble on city streets for the purpose of seeking

Day laborers soliciting work in Farmingville, New York.

work. City residents testified that the men made cat calls at women and urinated in public. They called the shape-up area an eyesore. Representatives of the immigrants countered by affirming the immigrants' constitutional right to freedom of assembly and argued that they were not loitering in the streets but waiting peacefully on the sidewalks.

The larger issue that haunted the Long Islanders, one that they were reluctant to acknowledge publicly but that a few individuals admitted to me privately, was the fear that the immigrants gave the impression that the town was in decline. Such a perception in suburbia jeopardizes real estate values—the bedrock of U.S. middle-class security. Even

the hint of racial or ethnic turnover frightens homeowners and potential buyers. In Glen Cove, this fear led to the campaign to get rid of the "shape-up," the single most vivid image of the ethnically distinct people residing in the community.

In the town meeting the point was made that the immigrants had been attracted to the area precisely because the suburbanites desired their inexpensive labor. Almost all the landscapers on Long Island are now Salvadoran, and many families depend on immigrant women to clean their houses and take care of their children and elderly. Immigrants, especially from El Salvador and other Latin American countries, toil in the island's restaurants, factories, and laundries, and, at night, in office buildings. They do the jobs that U.S. workers do not want to do or cannot afford to do because the jobs pay too little to support their families.

When the Salvadorans and other immigrants arrived on Long Island, seeking their futures, they first lived in communities with high minority populations. But as the immigrants moved closer to their jobs, their numbers swelled in more traditional bedroom communities like Glen Cove. These other towns also began to adopt "not in my backyard" policies by passing new ordinances or enforcing old ones, even refusing to let undocumented immigrant children attend their public schools. Old-timers felt that such measures could stem the decline in their way of life. What they overlooked was how the immigrant labor is preserving their standard of living.

Source: Sarah Maher, University of Vermont, *Salvadorans in Suburbia.*

Race and Ethnic Relations in the United States

To write on race-ethnicity is like stepping onto a minefield: One never knows where to expect the next explosion. Even basic terms are controversial. The term African American, for example, is rejected by those who ask why this term doesn't include white immigrants from South Africa. Some people classified as African Americans also reject this term because they identify themselves as blacks. Similarly, some Latinos prefer the term *Hispanic American,* but others reject it, saying that it ignores the Indian side of their heritage. Some would limit the term *Chicanos*—commonly used to

Figure 12.4 Race-Ethnicity
of the U.S. Population

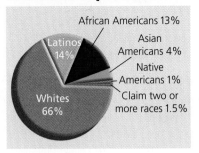

Source: By the author. See Figure 12.5.

refer to Americans from Mexico—to those who have a sense of oppression and ethnic unity; they say that it does not apply to those who have assimilated.

No term that I use here, then, will satisfy everyone. Racial-ethnic identity is fluid, constantly changing, and all terms carry a risk as they take on politically charged meanings. Nevertheless, as part of everyday life, we classify ourselves and one another as belonging to distinct racial-ethnic groups. As Figures 12.4 and 12.5 show, on the basis of these self-identities, whites make up 66 percent of the U.S. population, minorities (African Americans, Asian Americans, Latinos, and Native Americans) 32 percent. Between 1 and 2 percent claim membership in two or more racial-ethnic groups.

As you can see from the Social Map on the next page, the distribution of dominant and minority groups among the states seldom comes close to the national average. This is because minority groups tend to be clustered in regions. The extreme distributions are represented by Maine and Vermont, each of which has only 4 percent minority, and by Hawaii, where minorities outnumber whites 77 percent to 23 percent. With this as background, let's review the major groups in the United States, going from the largest to the smallest.

Figure 12.5 **U.S. Racial-Ethnic Groups**

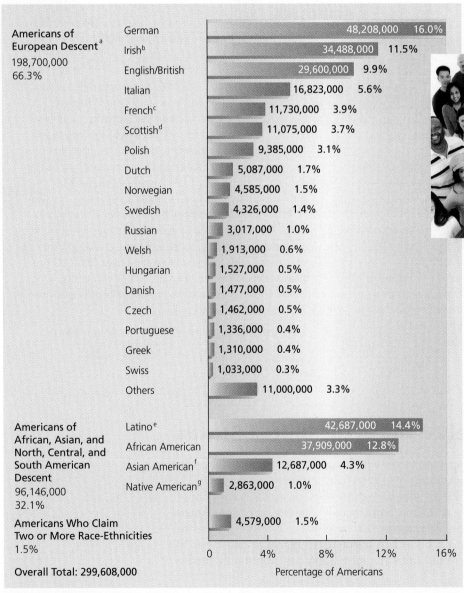

Americans of European Descent[a] 198,700,000 66.3%		
German	48,208,000	16.0%
Irish[b]	34,488,000	11.5%
English/British	29,600,000	9.9%
Italian	16,823,000	5.6%
French[c]	11,730,000	3.9%
Scottish[d]	11,075,000	3.7%
Polish	9,385,000	3.1%
Dutch	5,087,000	1.7%
Norwegian	4,585,000	1.5%
Swedish	4,326,000	1.4%
Russian	3,017,000	1.0%
Welsh	1,913,000	0.6%
Hungarian	1,527,000	0.5%
Danish	1,477,000	0.5%
Czech	1,462,000	0.5%
Portuguese	1,336,000	0.4%
Greek	1,310,000	0.4%
Swiss	1,033,000	0.3%
Others	11,000,000	3.3%

Americans of African, Asian, and North, Central, and South American Descent 96,146,000 32.1%		
Latino[e]	42,687,000	14.4%
African American	37,909,000	12.8%
Asian American[f]	12,687,000	4.3%
Native American[g]	2,863,000	1.0%

Americans Who Claim Two or More Race-Ethnicities 1.5%		
	4,579,000	1.5%

Overall Total: 299,608,000

0   4%   8%   12%   16%

Percentage of Americans

USA—the land of diversity

Notes:

[a]The totals in this figure should be taken as broadly accurate only. The totals for groups and even for the U.S. population vary from table to table in the source. Because the total of the individual white ethnic groups listed in the source is 10 percent above the total of whites, I arbitrarily reduced each white ethnic group by 10 percent.

[b]Interestingly, this total is *six* times higher than all the Irish who live in Ireland.

[c]Includes French Canadian.

[d]Includes "Scottish-Irish."

[e]Most Latinos trace at least part of their ancestry to Europe.

[f]In descending order, the largest groups of Asian Americans are from China, the Philippines, India, Korea, Vietnam, and Japan. See Figure 12.10 on page 361. Also includes those who identify themselves as Native Hawaiian or Pacific Islander.

[g]Includes Native American, Inuit, and Aleut.

Source: By the author. Based on *Statistical Abstract* 2007:Table 50.

Figure 12.6 **The Distribution of Dominant and Minority Groups**

This social map indicates how unevenly distributed U.S. minority groups are. The extremes are Hawaii with 77 percent minority and Maine and Vermont with 4 percent minority.

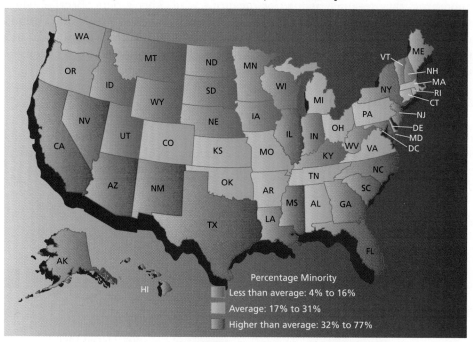

Source: By the author. Based on *Statistical Abstract* 2007:Table 23.

European Americans

Perhaps the event that best crystallizes the racial view of the nation's founders occurred at the first Continental Congress of the United States. There they passed the Naturalization Act of 1790, declaring that only white immigrants could apply for citizenship. The sense of superiority and privilege of **WASPs** (white Anglo-Saxon Protestants) was not limited to their views of race. They also viewed as inferior white Europeans from countries other than England. They greeted **white ethnics**—immigrants from Europe whose language and other customs differed from theirs—with disdain and negative stereotypes. They especially despised the Irish, viewing them as dirty, lazy drunkards, but they also painted Germans, Poles, Jews, Italians, and others with similarly broad disparaging brush strokes.

To get an idea of how intense these feelings were, consider this statement by Benjamin Franklin regarding immigrants from Germany:

> Why should the Palatine boors be suffered to swarm into our settlements and by herding together establish their language and manners to the exclusion of ours? Why should Pennsylvania, founded by the English, become a colony of aliens, who will shortly be so numerous as to germanize us instead of our anglifying them? (In Alba and Nee 2003:17)

The cultural and political dominance of the WASPs placed pressure on immigrants to assimilate into the mainstream culture. The children of most immigrants embraced the new way of life and quickly came to think of themselves as Americans rather than as Germans, French, Hungarians, and so on. They dropped their distinctive customs, especially their language, often viewing them as symbols of shame. This second generation of immigrants was sandwiched between two worlds: "the old country" of their parents and their new home. Their children, the third generation, had an easier adjustment, for they had fewer customs to discard. As immigrants from other parts of Europe assimilated into this Anglo culture, the meaning of WASP expanded to include people of this descent.

WASP White Anglo-Saxon Protestant; narrowly, an American

white ethnics white immigrants to the United States whose cultures differ from that of WASPs

IN SUM Because Protestant English immigrants settled the colonies, they established the culture—from the dominant language to the dominant religion. Highly ethnocentric, they regarded as inferior the customs of other groups. Because white Europeans took power, they determined the national agenda to which other ethnic groups had to react and conform. Their institutional and cultural dominance still sets the stage for current ethnic relations, a topic that is explored in the Down-to-Earth Sociology box below.

Latinos (Hispanics)

A Note on Terms. Before reviewing major characteristics of Latinos, it is important to stress that *Latino* and *Hispanic* refer not to a race but to ethnic groups. Latinos may identify themselves racially as black, white, or Native American. With changing self-identifications, some Latinos who have an African heritage refer to themselves as Afro-Latinos (Navarro 2003).

Down-to-Earth Sociology

Unpacking the Invisible Knapsack: Exploring Cultural Privilege

OVERT RACISM IN THE United States has dropped sharply, but doors still open and close on the basis of the color of our skin. Whites have a difficult time grasping the idea that good things come their way because they are white. They usually fail to perceive how "whiteness" operates in their own lives.

Peggy McIntosh, of Irish descent, began to wonder why she was so seldom aware of her race-ethnicity, while her African American friends were so conscious of theirs. She realized that people are not highly aware of things that they take for granted—and that "whiteness" is a "taken-for-granted" background assumption of U.S. society. To explore this, she drew up a list of things that she can take for granted because of her "whiteness," what she calls her "invisible knapsack."

What is in this "knapsack"? That is, what taken-for-granted privileges can most white people in U.S. society assume? Because she is white, McIntosh (1988) says:

1. If I don't do well as a leader, I can be sure people won't say that it is because of my race.
2. When I go shopping, store detectives won't follow me.
3. When I watch television or look at the front page of the paper, I see people of my race positively presented.
4. When I study our national heritage, I see people of my color and am taught that they made our country great.

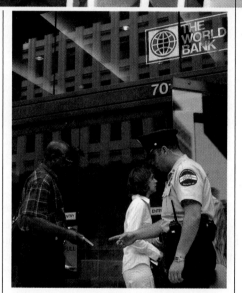

One of the cultural privileges of being white in the United States is less suspicion of wrongdoing.

5. When I cash a check or use a credit card, my skin color does not make the clerk think that I may be financially irresponsible.
6. To protect my children, I do not have to teach them to be aware of racism.
7. I can talk with my mouth full and not have people put this down to my color.
8. I can speak at a public meeting without putting my race on trial.
9. I can achieve at something and not be "a credit to my race."
10. I am never asked to speak for all the people of my race.
11. If a traffic cop pulls me over, I can be sure that it isn't because I'm white.
12. I can be late to a meeting without people thinking I was late because "That's how *they* are."

for your Consideration

Can you think of other "unearned privileges" of everyday life that come to whites because of their skin color? (McIntosh's list contains 46 items.) Why are whites seldom aware that they carry this invisible knapsack?

Numbers, Origins, and Location. When birds still nested in the trees that would be used to build the *Mayflower,* Latinos had already established settlements in Florida and New Mexico (Bretos 1994). Today, Latinos are the largest minority group in the United States. As shown in Figure 12.7, about 28 million people trace their origin to Mexico, 3 to 4 million to Puerto Rico, 1 to 2 million to Cuba, and about 7 million to Central or South America.

Although Latinos are officially tallied at 42 million, another 7 million Latinos are living here illegally, 5 million from Mexico and 2 million from Central and South America (*Statistical Abstract* 2006:Table 7). Most Latinos are legal residents, but each year more than *1 million* Mexicans are apprehended at the border or at points inland and are returned to Mexico (*Statistical Abstract* 2007:Table 518). Several hundred thousand others manage to enter the United States each year. With this vast migration, there are millions more Latinos in the United States than there are Canadians in Canada (33 million). As Figure 12.8 shows, two-thirds live in just four states: California, Texas, Florida, and New York.

The migration of Mexicans across the U.S. border became a major social issue. As public concern grew, it led to an emotionally charged debate in the U.S. Congress. One response was to tighten the border, and, despite protests from the Mexican government, U.S. officials built a wall at various points on the U.S. side of the border. Helping to shape the international debate was the arrival of volunteers, calling themselves Minutemen, organized through the Internet to patrol the border. Their arrival in Arizona spread fear among Mexicans and upset U.S. officials, who worried that there would be bloody clashes between the volunteers and the "coyotes" who were smuggling migrants (Peña 2005; Ramos 2005; Rotstein 2005). The violence didn't happen, and the unwelcome unofficial patrolling of the border continued. So did the migration. Despite walls, patrols, and attempts at political compromises in immigration bills, as long as there is a need for unskilled labor and so many Mexicans live in poverty, this flow of undocumented workers will continue. To gain insight into why, see the Cultural Diversity box on the next page.

Figure 12.7 **Geographical Origin of U.S. Latinos**

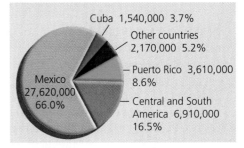

Source: By the author. Based on *Statistical Abstract* 2007:Table 44.

Figure 12.8 **Where U.S. Latinos Live**

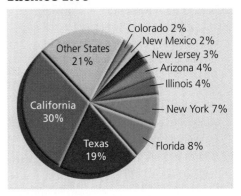

Source: By the author. Based on *Statistical Abstract* 2007:Table 23.

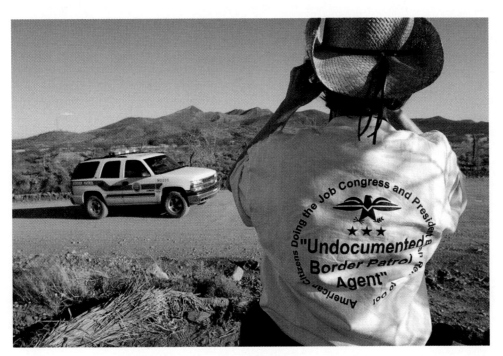

The illegal migration of Mexicans into the United States has become a major social issue. For political reasons, especially that of relations with Mexico, U.S. officials have hesitated to close the border. The appearance of citizen patrols proved an embarrassment to the official U.S. Border Patrol, as well as a threat to international relations.

Cultural Diversity *in the* United States

The Illegal Travel Guide

MANUEL WAS A DRINKING BUDDY of Jose, a man I had met in Colima, Mexico. At 45, Manuel was friendly, outgoing, and enterprising.

Manuel, who had lived in the United States for seven years, spoke fluent English. Preferring to live in his home town in Colima, where he palled around with his childhood friends, Manuel always seemed to have money and free time.

When Manuel invited me to go on a business trip with him, I accepted. I never could figure out what he did for a living or how he could afford a car, a luxury that none of his friends had. As we traveled from one remote village to another, Manuel would sell used clothing that he had heaped in the back of his older-model Ford station wagon.

At one stop, Manuel took me into a dirt-floored, thatched-roof hut. While chickens ran in and out, Manuel whispered to a slender man who was about 23 years old. The poverty was overwhelming. Juan, as his name turned out to be, had a partial grade school education. He also had a wife, four hungry children under the age of 5, and two pigs—his main food supply. Although eager to work, Juan had no job, for there was simply no work available in this remote village.

As we were drinking a Coke, which seems to be the national beverage of Mexico's poor, Manuel explained to me that he was not only selling clothing—he was also lining up migrants to the United States. For $200 he would take a man to the border and introduce him to a "wolf," who would help him make a night crossing into the promised land.

Mexicans crossing the Rio Grande. Photo taken from the Mexican side of the border, near Nuevo Laredo.

When I saw the hope in Juan's face, I knew nothing would stop him. He was borrowing every cent he could from every friend and relative to scrape the money together. Although he risked losing everything if apprehended and he would be facing unknown risks, Juan would make the trip, for wealth beckoned on the other side. He knew people who had been to the United States and spoke glowingly of its opportunities. Manuel, of course, stoked the fires of hope.

Looking up from the children playing on the dirt floor with the chickens pecking about them, I saw a man who loved his family. In order to make the desperate bid for a better life, he would suffer an enforced absence, as well as the uncertainties of a foreign culture whose language he did not know.

Juan opened his billfold, took something out, and slowly handed it to me. I looked at it curiously. I felt tears as I saw the tenderness with which he handled this piece of paper. It was his passport to the land of opportunity: a Social Security card made out in his name, sent by a friend who had already made the trip and who was waiting for Juan on the other side of the border.

It was then that I realized that the thousands of Manuels scurrying about Mexico and the millions of Juans they were transporting could never be stopped, for only the United States could fulfill their dream of a better life.

for your Consideration

The vast stream of immigrants crossing illegally across the Mexican-U.S. border has become a national issue. What do you think is the best way to deal with this issue? Why?

Spanish Language   The Spanish language distinguishes most Latinos from other U.S. ethnic groups. With 31 million people speaking Spanish at home, the United States has become one of the largest Spanish-speaking nations in the world (*Statistical Abstract* 2007:Table 51). Because about half of Latinos are unable to speak English, or can do so only with difficulty, many millions face a major obstacle to getting good jobs.

The growing use of Spanish has become a matter of controversy. Perceiving the prevalence of Spanish as a threat, Senator S. I. Hayakawa of California initiated an "English-only" movement in 1981. The constitutional amendment that he sponsored never got off the ground, but 26 states have passed laws that declare English their official language (Schaefer 2004).

Diversity For Latinos, country of origin is highly significant. Those from Puerto Rico, for example, feel that they have little in common with people from Mexico, Venezuela, or El Salvador—just as earlier immigrants from Germany, Sweden, and England felt they had little in common with one another. A sign of these divisions is that many refer to themselves in terms of their country of origin, such as puertorriqueños or cubanos, rather than as Latino or Hispanic.

As with other ethnic groups, Latinos are separated by social class. The half-million Cubans who fled Castro's rise to power in 1959, for example, were mostly well-educated, well-to-do professionals or businesspeople. In contrast, the "boat people" who fled later were mostly lower-class refugees, people with whom the earlier arrivals would not have associated in Cuba. The earlier arrivals, who are firmly established in Florida and who control many businesses and financial institutions, distance themselves from the more recent immigrants.

These divisions of national origin and social class are a major obstacle to political unity. One consequence is a severe underrepresentation in politics. Because Latinos make up 14.4 percent of the U.S. population, we might expect 14 or 15 U.S. Senators to be Latino. How many are there? *Two.* In addition, Latinos hold only 5 percent of the seats in the U.S. House of Representatives (*Statistical Abstract* 2007:Table 395).

The potential political power of Latinos, however, is remarkable, and in coming years we will see more of this potential realized. As Latinos have become more visible in U.S. society and more vocal in their demands for equality, they have come face to face with African Americans who fear that Latino gains in employment and at the ballot box will come at their expense (Cose 2006). Together, Latinos and African Americans make up more than one-fourth of the U.S. population. If these two groups were to join together, their unity would produce an unstoppable political force.

When the U.S. government took control of what is now the southwestern United States, Mexicans living there were transformed from the dominant group into a minority group. To try to maintain their culture, *Chicanos,* Americans of Mexican origin, do *ethnic work,* such as this dance by Danza Teocalt at a Cinco de Mayo celebration in Los Angeles. (The Cinco de Mayo—Fifth of May—holiday marks the Mexican army's 1862 defeat of French troops at the city of Puebla.)

Comparative Conditions To see how Latinos are doing on some major indicators of well-being, look at Table 12.1 on the next page. As you can see, compared with white Americans and Asian Americans, Latinos have less income, higher unemployment, and more poverty. They are also less likely to own their homes. Now look at how closely Latinos rank with African Americans and Native Americans. From this table, you can see how significant country of origin is. People from Cuba score higher on all these indicators of well-being, while those from Puerto Rico score lower.

The significance of country or region of origin is also underscored by Table 12.2. You can see that people from Cuba attain considerably more education than do those who come from other areas. You can also see that two of every five Latinos do not complete high school, and only 12 percent graduate from college. In a postindustrial society that increasingly requires advanced skills, these totals indicate that huge numbers of Latinos will be left behind.

African Americans

After slavery was abolished, the Southern states passed legislation (*Jim Crow* laws) to segregate blacks and whites. In 1896, the U.S. Supreme Court ruled in *Plessy v. Ferguson* that state laws requiring "separate but equal" accommodations for blacks were a reasonable use of state power. Whites used this ruling to strip blacks of the political power they had gained after the Civil War. One way they did this was to prohibit blacks from voting in "white" primaries. It was not until 1944 that the Supreme Court ruled that African Americans could vote in Southern primaries, and not until 1954 that they had the legal

Table 12.1 Race-Ethnicity and Comparative Well-Being[1]

Racial-Ethnic Group	INCOME		UNEMPLOYMENT		POVERTY		HOME OWNERSHIP	
	Median Family Income	Compared to Whites	Percentage Unemployed	Compared to Whites	Percentage Below Poverty Line	Compared to Whites	Percentage Who Own Their Homes	Compared to Whites
Whites	$59,907	—	3.5%	—	7.7%	—	76.3%	—
Latinos	$36,820	39% lower	4.8%	37% higher	21.9%	184% higher	49.4%	35% lower
Country or Area of Origin								
Cuba	NA[2]	NA	2.0%	57% lower	14.5%	88% higher	61.3%	20% lower
Central and South America	NA	NA	NA	NA	17.8%	131% higher	39.2%	49% lower
Mexico	NA	NA	4.2%	20% higher	23.8%	209% higher	51.4%	33% lower
Puerto Rico	NA	NA	4.7%	34% higher	22.9%	197% higher	39.7%	48% lower
African Americans	$34,851	42% lower	7.5%	114% higher	24.5%	218% higher	49.5%	35% lower
Asian Americans[3]	$65,132	9% higher	3.5%	The same	11.7%	52% higher	57.6%	25% lower
Native Americans	$35,981	40% lower	NA	NA	24.6%	219% higher	55.5%	27% lower

[1]Data are from 2004 and 2005.
[2]Not Available
[3]Includes Pacific Islanders

Source: By the author. Based on *Statistical Abstract* 2007:Tables 40, 41, 44, 613, 677.

Table 12.2 Race-Ethnicity and Education

Racial-Ethnic Group	EDUCATION COMPLETED				DOCTORATES		Percentage of U.S. Population
	Less than High School	High School	Some College	College (BA or Higher)	Number Awarded	Percentage of all U.S. Doctorates[1]	
Whites	9.7%	33.4%	28.0%	28.9%	28,214	81.0%	66.3%
Latinos	41.1%	27.3%	19.6%	12.1%	1,662	4.7%	14.4%
Country or Area of Origin							
Cuba	26.5%	30.4%	18.4%	24.7%	NA	NA	
Puerto Rico	27.8%	33.7%	24.7%	13.8%	NA	NA	
Central and South America	37.6%	25.6%	18.3%	18.5%	NA	NA	
Mexico	47.7%	26.6%	17.4%	8.3%	NA	NA	
African Americans	19.4%	36.0%	27.0%	17.6%	2,900	8.1%	12.8%
Asian Americans	15.1%	17.2%	19.3%	48.2%	2,632	7.4%	4.3%
Native Americans	23.3%	31.3%	31.1%	14.1%	217	0.6%	1.0%

[1]Percentage after the doctorates awarded to nonresidents are deducted from the total.

Source: By the author. Based on *Statistical Abstract* 2007:Tables 41, 44, 289 and Figure 12.5 of this text.

right to attend the same public schools as whites (Schaefer 2004). Well into the 1960s, the South was still openly—and legally—practicing segregation.

The Struggle for Civil Rights

It was 1955, in Montgomery, Alabama. As specified by law, whites took the front seats of the bus, and blacks went to the back. As the bus filled up, blacks had to give up their seats to whites.

When Rosa Parks, a 42-year-old African American woman and secretary of the Montgomery NAACP, was told that she would have to stand so that white folks could sit, she refused (Bray 1995). She stubbornly sat there while the bus driver raged and whites felt insulted. Her arrest touched off mass demonstrations, led 50,000 blacks to boycott the city's buses for a year, and thrust an otherwise unknown preacher into a historic role.

Reverend Martin Luther King, Jr., who had majored in sociology at Morehouse College in Atlanta, Georgia, took control. He organized car pools and preached nonviolence. Incensed at this radical organizer and at the stirrings in the normally compliant black community, segregationists also put their beliefs into practice—by bombing the homes of blacks and dynamiting their churches.

Rising Expectations and Civil Strife   The barriers came down, but they came down slowly. Not until 1964 did Congress pass the Civil Rights Act, making it illegal to discriminate on the basis of race. African Americans were finally allowed in "white" restaurants, hotels, theaters, and other public places. Then in 1965, Congress passed the Voting Rights Act, banning the fraudulent literacy tests that the Southern states had used to keep African Americans from voting.

Encouraged by these gains, African Americans experienced what sociologists call **rising expectations;** that is, they believed that better conditions would soon follow. The lives of the poor among them, however, changed little, if at all. Frustrations built, finally exploding in Watts in 1965, when people living in that African American ghetto of central Los Angeles took to the streets in the first of what were termed "urban revolts." When King was assassinated by a white supremacist on April 4, 1968, inner cities across the nation erupted in fiery violence. Under threat of the destruction of U.S. cities, Congress passed the sweeping Civil Rights Act of 1968.

Until the 1960s, the South's public facilities were segregated. Some were reserved for whites only, others for blacks only. This *apartheid* was broken by blacks and whites who worked together and risked their lives to bring about a fairer society. Shown here is a 1963 sit-in at a Woolworth's lunch counter in Jackson, Mississippi. Sugar, ketchup, and mustard are being poured over the heads of the demonstrators.

Continued Gains   Since then, African Americans have made remarkable gains in politics, education, and jobs. At 10 percent, the number of African Americans in the U.S. House of Representatives is almost *three times* what it was a generation ago (*Statistical Abstract* 1989:Table 423; 2007:Table 395). As college enrollments increased, the middle class expanded, and today half of all African American families make more than $35,000 a year. One in three makes more than $50,000 a year, and one in six earns more than $75,000 (*Statistical Abstract* 2007:Table 675). Contrary to stereotypes, the average African American family is *not* poor.

The extent of African American political prominence was highlighted when Jesse Jackson (another sociology major) competed for the Democratic presidential nomination in 1984 and 1988. Political progress was further confirmed in 1989 when L. Douglas Wilder was elected governor of Virginia and again in 2006 when Deval Patrick became governor of Massachusetts. The most publicized African American political candidate has been Barack Obama, who was elected Senator from Illinois in 2004 and ran for the Democratic nomination for president in 2007.

Current Losses   Despite these gains, African Americans continue to lag behind in politics, economics, and education. Only *one* U.S. Senator is African American, but on the basis of the percentage of African Americans in the U.S. population we would expect about 13. As Tables 12.1 and 12.2 on page 356 show, African Americans average only 58 percent of white income, have much more unemployment and poverty, and are less likely to own their home or to have a college education. That half of African American families have incomes over $35,000 is only part of the story. Table 12.3 shows the other part—how much more likely white and Asian American families are to have the higher incomes and that one of every five families makes less than $15,000 a year.

These changes have created two worlds of African American experience—one educated and affluent, the other uneducated and poor. Concentrated among the poor are those with the least hope, the highest despair, and the violence that so often dominates the evening news. Although homicide rates have dropped to their lowest point in 30 years, African Americans are *six* times as likely to be murdered as are whites (*Statistical Abstract* 2007:Table 302). Compared with whites,

Table 12.3   **Race-Ethnicity and Income Extremes**

	Less than $15,000	Over $75,000
Asian Americans	6.3%	53.2%
Whites	6.7%	38.6%
African Americans	21.1%	17.7%
Latinos	15.8%	16.6%

Note: These are family incomes. Only these groups are listed in the source.

Source: By the author: Based on *Statistical Abstract* 2007:Table 675.

African Americans are severely underrepresented in Congress. In 2004, Barack Obama became the first African American man to be elected to the U.S. Senate since the period immediately following the Civil War. This photo was taken of Obama working a crowd in Austin, Texas, after he announced that he was running for president.

African Americans are also *eleven* times more likely to die from AIDS (*Statistical Abstract* 2007:Table 117).

Race or Social Class? A Sociological Debate   This division of African Americans into "haves" and "have-nots" has fueled a sociological controversy. Sociologist William Julius Wilson (1978, 1987, 2000) argues that social class has become more important than race in determining the life chances of African Americans. Before civil rights legislation, he says, the African American experience was dominated by race. Throughout the United States, African Americans were excluded from avenues of economic advancement: good schools and good jobs. When civil rights legislation opened new opportunities, African Americans seized them. Just as legislation began to open doors to African Americans, however, manufacturing jobs dried up, and many blue-collar jobs were moved to the suburbs. As better-educated African Americans obtained middle-class, white-collar jobs and moved out of the inner city, they left behind the African Americans with poor education and few skills.

Sociologists disagree about the relative significance of race and social class in determining social and economic conditions of African Americans. William Julius Wilson, shown here, is an avid proponent of the social class side of this debate.

Wilson stresses the significance of these two worlds of African American experience. The group that is stuck in the inner city lives in poverty, attends poor schools, and faces dead-end jobs or welfare. This group is filled with hopelessness and despair, combined with apathy or hostility. In contrast, those who have moved up the social class ladder live in comfortable homes in secure neighborhoods. They work at jobs that provide decent incomes, and they send their children to good schools. Their middle-class experiences and lifestyle have changed their views on life, and their aspirations and values have little in common with those of African Americans who remain poor. According to Wilson, then, social class—not race—has become the most significant factor in the lives of African Americans.

Some sociologists reply that this analysis overlooks the discrimination that continues to underlie the African American experience. They note that even when African Americans do the same work as whites they average less pay (Willie 1991; Herring 2002). This, they argue, points to racial discrimination, not to social class.

What is the answer to this debate? Wilson would reply that it is not an either-or question. My book is titled *The **Declining** Significance of Race,* he would say, not *The **Absence** of Race.* Certainly racism is still alive, he would add, but today social class is more central to the African American experience than is racial discrimination. He stresses that for the poor in the inner city, we need to provide jobs—for work provides an anchor to a responsible life (Wilson 1996, 2000).

Racism as an Everyday Burden   Today, racism is more subtle than it used to be, but it still walks among us (Feagin and McKinney 2003; Perry 2006). To study discrimination in the job market, researchers sent out 5,000 resumes in response to help wanted ads in the Boston and Chicago Sunday papers (Bertrand and Mullainathan 2002). The resumes were identical, except for the names of the job applicants. Some applicants had white-sounding names, such as Emily and Brandon, while others had black-sounding names, such as Lakisha and Jamal. Although the qualifications of the supposed job applicants were identical, the white-sounding names elicited *50 percent* more callbacks than the black-sounding names. The Down-to-Earth Sociology box on the next page presents another study of subtle racism.

African Americans who occupy higher statuses enjoy greater opportunities, and they also face less discrimination. The discrimination that they encounter, however, is no less painful. Unlike whites of the same social class, they feel discrimination constantly hovering over them. Here is how an African American professor described it:

> [One problem with] being black in America is that you have to spend so much time thinking about stuff that most white people just don't even have to think about. I worry when I get pulled over by a cop. . . . I worry what some white cop is going to think when he walks over to our car, because he's holding on to a gun. And I'm very aware of how many black folks accidentally get shot by cops. I worry when I walk into a store, that someone's going to think I'm in there shoplifting. . . . And I get resentful that I have to think about things that a lot of people, even my very close white friends whose politics are similar to mine, simply don't have to worry about. (Feagin 1999:398)

Down-to-Earth Sociology

Stealth Racism in the Rental Market: What You Reveal by Your Voice

BLATANT DISCRIMINATION HAS BECOME a thing of the past. There was a time when whites could burn crosses with impunity at the homes of blacks. Some whites even lynched African Americans and Asian Americans without fear of the law. Today, cross burning and lynching will make the national news and the perpetrators will be investigated and prosecuted. If local officials don't make an arrest, the FBI will step in. Similarly, discrimination in public accommodations was once standard—and legal. With today's changed laws and the vigilance of groups such as the NAACP, no hotel, restaurant, or gas station would refuse service on the basis of race-ethnicity.

Racism, however, is not a thing of the past. Although overt racism has been relegated to the back shelves of social life, stealth racism is alive and well, as sociologists have demonstrated (Pager 2003; Farley and Squires 2005). At the University of Pennsylvania, for example, Douglas Massey and the students in his undergraduate course in research methods discussed how Americans often identify one another racially by their speech. In Massey's class were whites who spoke what is called White Middle Class English, African Americans who spoke a dialect known as Black English Vernacular, and other African Americans who spoke middle-class English with a black accent.

The discussion stimulated Massey and his students to investigate how voice is used to discriminate in the housing market. They designed standard identities for the class members who spoke these variants of English, assigning them similar incomes, jobs, and education. They also developed a standard script and translated it into Black English Vernacular. The students called on 79 apartments that were advertised for rent in newspapers. The study was done blindly, with the white and black students not knowing how the others were being treated.

What did they find? Compared with whites, African Americans were less likely to get to talk to rental agents, who often used answering machines to screen calls. When they did get through, they were less likely to be told that an apartment was available, more likely to have to pay an application fee, and more likely to be asked about their credit history. Students who posed as lower-class blacks (speakers of Black English Vernacular) had the least access to apartments. Figure 12.9 summarizes the percentages of callers who were told an apartment was available.

As you can see from this figure, although both men and women were discriminated against, the discrimination was worse for the women. Sociologists refer to this as the *double bind* that African American women experience: being discriminated against both because they are African American and because they are women.

Figure 12.9 **Cloaked Discrimination in Apartment Rentals**

Callers who were told an apartment was available

Source: Massey and Lundy 2001.

Asian Americans

I have stressed in this chapter that our racial-ethnic categories are based more on social considerations than on biological ones. This point is again obvious when we examine the category Asian American. As Figure 12.10 shows, those who are called Asian Americans came to the United States from many nations. With no unifying culture or "race," why should they ever be clustered together in a single category—except that others perceive them as a unit? Think about it. What culture or race-ethnicity do Samoans and Vietnamese have in common? Or Laotians and Pakistanis? Or Native Hawaiians and Chinese? Or people from India and those from Guam? Yet all these groups—and more—are lumped together and called Asian Americans. Apparently, the U.S. government is not satisfied until it is able to pigeonhole everyone into a racial-ethnic category.

Since *Asian American* is a standard term, however, let's look at the characteristics of the 13 million people who are lumped together and assigned this label.

A Background of Discrimination From their first arrival in the United States, Asian Americans confronted discrimination. Lured by gold strikes in the West and an urgent need for unskilled workers to build the railroads, 200,000 Chinese immigrated between 1850 and 1880. When the famous golden spike was driven at Promontory, Utah, in 1869 to mark the completion of the railroad to the West Coast, white workers prevented Chinese workers from being in the photo—even though Chinese made up 90 percent of Central Pacific Railroad's labor force (Hsu 1971).

After the railroad was complete, the Chinese took other jobs. Feeling threatened by their cheap labor, Anglos formed vigilante groups to intimidate them. They also used the law. California's 1850 Foreign Miner's Act required Chinese (and Latinos) to pay a fee of $20 a month in order to work—when wages were a dollar a day. The California Supreme Court ruled that Chinese could not testify against whites (Carlson and Colburn 1972). In 1882, Congress passed the Chinese Exclusion Act, suspending all Chinese immigration for ten years. Four years later, the Statue of Liberty was dedicated. The tired, the poor, and the huddled masses it was intended to welcome were obviously not Chinese.

When immigrants from Japan arrived, they encountered *spillover bigotry*, a stereotype that lumped Asians together, depicting them as sneaky, lazy, and untrustworthy. After Japan attacked Pearl Harbor in 1941, conditions grew worse for the 110,000 Japanese Americans who called the United States their home. U.S. authorities feared that Japan would invade the United States and that the Japanese Americans would fight on Japan's side. They also feared that Japanese Americans would sabotage military installations on the West Coast. Although no Japanese American had been involved in even a single act of sabotage, on February 19, 1942, President Franklin D. Roosevelt ordered that everyone who was *one-eighth Japanese or more* be confined in detention centers (called "internment camps"). These people were charged with no crime, and they had no trials. Japanese ancestry was sufficient cause for being imprisoned.

Diversity As you can see from Table 12.1 on page 356, the annual income of Asian Americans has outstripped that of whites. This has led to an assumption that all Asian Americans are successful, a stereotype that masks huge differences. With a poverty rate that is actually 50 percent higher than that of whites, between one and two million Asian Americans live in poverty. Like Latinos, country of origin is significant: Poverty is unusual among Chinese and Japanese Americans, but it clusters among Americans from Southeast Asia.

Reasons for Success As you can see from Table 12.1, the average income of Asian Americans is high. This can be traced to three major factors: family life, educational achievement, and assimilation into mainstream culture.

Of all ethnic groups, including whites, Asian American children are the most likely to grow up with two parents and the least likely to be born to a single mother (*Statistical Abstract* 2007:Tables 53, 64). Most grow up in close-knit families that stress self-discipline, thrift, and

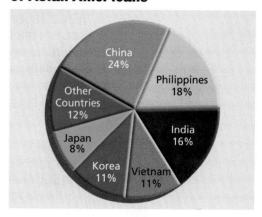

Figure 12.10 The Country of Origin of Asian Americans

Source: By the author. Based on *Statistical Abstract* 2006: Table 24.

Of the racial-ethnic groups in the United States, Asian Americans have the highest rate of intermarriage.

hard work (Suzuki 1985; Bell 1991). This early socialization provides strong impetus for the other two factors.

The second factor is their high rate of college graduation. As Table 12.2 on page 356 shows, 48 percent of Asian Americans complete college. To realize how stunning this is, compare this with the other groups shown on this table. This educational achievement, in turn, opens doors to economic success.

Assimilation, the third factor, is indicated by housing and marriage. Asian Americans are more likely than other racial-ethnic groups to live in integrated neighborhoods (Lee 1998). Those who trace their descent from Japan and China—who are the most successful financially—are also the most assimilated. The intermarriage rate of Japanese Americans is so high that two of every three children born to a Japanese American have one parent who is not of Japanese descent (Schaefer 2004). The Chinese are close behind (Alba and Nee 2003).

Asian Americans are becoming more prominent in politics. With more than half of its citizens being Asian American, Hawaii has elected Asian American governors and sent several Asian American senators to Washington, including the two now serving there (Lee 1998, *Statistical Abstract* 2007:Table 395). The first Asian American governor outside of Hawaii is Gary Locke, who in 1996 was elected governor of Washington, a state in which Asian Americans make up less than 6 percent of the population.

Native Americans

"I don't go so far as to think that the only good Indians are dead Indians, but I believe nine out of ten are—and I shouldn't inquire too closely in the case of the tenth. The most vicious cowboy has more moral principle than the average Indian."

—Teddy Roosevelt, 1886 President of the United States, 1901–1909

Diversity of Groups   This quote from Teddy Roosevelt provides insight into the rampant racism of earlier generations. Yet, even today, thanks to countless grade B Westerns, some Americans view the original inhabitants of what became the United States as wild, uncivilized savages, a single group of people subdivided into separate tribes. The European immigrants to the colonies, however, encountered diverse groups of people with a variety of cultures—from nomadic hunters and gatherers to people who lived in wooden houses in settled agricultural communities. Altogether, they spoke over 700 languages (Schaefer 2004). Each group had its own norms and values—and the usual ethnocentric pride in its own culture. Consider what happened in 1744 when the colonists of Virginia offered college scholarships for "savage lads." The Iroquois replied:

"Several of our young people were formerly brought up at the colleges of Northern Provinces. They were instructed in all your sciences. But when they came back to us, they were bad runners, ignorant of every means of living in the woods, unable to bear either cold or hunger, knew neither how to build a cabin, take a deer, or kill an enemy. . . . They were totally good for nothing."
    They added, "If the English gentlemen would send a dozen or two of their children to Onondaga, the great Council would take care of their education, bring them up in really what was the best manner and make men of them." (Nash 1974; in McLemore 1994)

Native Americans, who numbered about 10 million, had no immunity to the diseases the Europeans brought with them. With deaths due to disease—and warfare, a much lesser cause—their population plummeted. The low point came in 1890, when the census reported only 250,000 Native Americans. If the census and the estimate of the original population are accurate, Native Americans had been reduced to about *one-fortieth* their original size. The population has never recovered, but Native Americans now number almost 3 million (see Figure 12.5 on page 350). Native Americans, who today speak 150 different languages, do not think of themselves as a single people who fit neatly within a single label (McLemore 1994).

From Treaties to Genocide and Population Transfer   At first, the Native Americans tried to accommodate the strangers, as there was plenty of land for both the few newcomers and themselves. Soon, however, the settlers began to raid Indian villages and pillage their food supplies (Horn 2006). As wave after wave of settlers arrived, Pontiac, an Ottawa chief, saw the future—and didn't like it. He convinced several tribes to unite in an effort to push the Europeans into the sea. He almost succeeded, but failed when the English were reinforced by fresh troops (McLemore 1994).

A pattern of deception evolved. The U.S. government would make treaties to buy some of a tribe's land, with the promise to honor forever the tribe's right to what it had not sold. European immigrants, who continued to pour into the United States, would then disregard these boundaries. The tribes would resist, with death tolls on both sides. The U.S. government would then intervene—not to enforce the treaty, but to force the tribe off its lands. In its relentless drive westward, the U.S. government embarked on a policy of genocide. It assigned the U.S. cavalry the task of "pacification," which translated into slaughtering Native Americans who "stood in the way" of this territorial expansion.

The acts of cruelty perpetrated by the Europeans against Native Americans appear endless, but two are especially notable. The first is the Trail of Tears. In the winter of 1838–1839, the U.S. Army rounded up 15,000 Cherokees and forced them to walk a thousand miles from the Carolinas and Georgia to Oklahoma. Coming from the South, many of the Cherokees wore only light clothing. Conditions were so inhumane that about 4,000 of those who were forced on this midwinter march died before they reached Oklahoma. About 50 years later came the symbolic end to Native American resistance to the European expansion. In 1890, at Wounded Knee, South Dakota, the U.S. cavalry gunned down 300 men, women, and children. After the massacre, the soldiers threw the bodies of the Dakota Sioux into a mass grave (Thornton 1987; Lind 1995; DiSilvestro 2006). These acts took place after the U.S. government had begun a policy called *Indian Removal*, forcefully confining Native Americans to specified areas called *reservations*.

The Native Americans stood in the way of the U.S. government's westward expansion. To seize their lands, the government followed a policy of *genocide*, later replaced by *population transfer*. This depiction of Apache shepherds being attacked by the U.S. Cavalry is by Rufus Zogbaum, a popular U.S. illustrator of the 1880s.

The Invisible Minority and Self-Determination   Native Americans can truly be called the invisible minority. Because about half live in rural areas and one-third in just three states—Oklahoma, California, and Arizona—most other Americans are hardly aware of a Native American presence in the United States. The isolation of about half of Native Americans on reservations further reduces their visibility (Schaefer 2004).

The systematic attempts of European Americans to destroy the Native Americans' way of life and their forced resettlement onto reservations continue to have deleterious effects. The rate of suicide of Native Americans is the highest of any racial-ethnic group, and their life expectancy is lower than that of the nation as a whole (Murray et al. 2006; Centers for Disease Control 2007b). Table 12.2 on page 356 shows that their education also lags behind most groups: Only 14 percent graduate from college.

Native Americans are experiencing major changes. In the 1800s, U.S. courts ruled that Native Americans did not own the land on which they had been settled and determined that they had no right to develop its resources. Native Americans were made wards of the state and treated like children by the Bureau of Indian Affairs (Mohawk 1991; Schaefer 2004). Then, in the 1960s, Native Americans won a series of legal victories that gave them control over reservation lands. As a result, many Native American tribes have opened businesses—ranging from industrial parks serving metropolitan areas to fish canneries. The Skywalk, opened by the Hualapai, which offers breathtaking views of the Grand Canyon, gives an idea of the varieties of businesses to come.

It is the casinos, though, that have attracted the most attention. In 1988, the federal government passed a law that allowed Native Americans to operate gambling establishments on reservations. Now over 200 tribes operate casinos. *They bring in about $25 billion a year, twice as much as all the casinos in Las Vegas* (Werner 2007). The Oneida tribe of New York, which has only 1,000 members, runs a casino that nets $232,000 a year for each man, woman, and child (Peterson 2003). This huge amount, however, pales in comparison with that of the Pequot of Connecticut. With only 310 members, they bring in more than $2 million a day (Zielbauer 2000). Incredibly, one tribe has only *one* member: She has her own casino (Barlett and Steele 2002).

A highly controversial issue is *separatism*. Because Native Americans were independent peoples when the Europeans arrived and they never willingly joined the United States, many tribes maintain the right to remain separate from the U.S. government and U.S. society. The chief of the Onondaga tribe in New York, a member of the Iroquois Federation, summarized the issue this way:

> For the whole history of the Iroquois, we have maintained that we are a separate nation. We have never lost a war. Our government still operates. We have refused the U.S. government's reorganization plans for us. We have kept our language and our traditions, and when we fly to Geneva to UN meetings, we carry Hau de no sau nee passports. We made some treaties that lost some land, but that also confirmed our separate-nation status. That the U.S. denies all this doesn't make it any less the case. (Mander 1992)

One of the most significant changes is **pan-Indianism.** This emphasis on common elements that run through Native American cultures is an attempt to develop an identity that goes beyond the tribe. Pan-Indianism ("We are all Indians") is a remarkable example of the plasticity of ethnicity. The label "Indian"—originally imposed by whites—is embraced and substituted for individual tribal identities. As sociologist Irwin Deutscher (2002:61) puts it, "The peoples who have accepted the larger definition of who they are, have, in fact, little else in common with each other than the stereotypes of the dominant group which labels them."

Native Americans say that they must be the ones to determine whether they want to establish a common identity and work together as in pan-Indianism or to stress separatism and identify solely with their own tribe; to assimilate into the dominant culture or to remain apart from it; to move to cities or to remain on reservations; or to operate casinos or to engage only in traditional activities. "Such decisions must be ours," say the Native Americans. "We are sovereign, and we will not take orders from the victors of past wars."

Looking Toward the Future

Back in 1903, sociologist W. E. B. Du Bois said, "The problem of the twentieth century is the problem of the color line—the relation of the darker to the lighter races." Incredibly, over a hundred years later, the color line remains one of the most volatile topics facing the nation. From time to time, the color line takes on a different complexion, as with the war on terrorism and the corresponding discrimination directed against people of Middle Eastern descent.

In another hundred years, will yet another sociologist lament that the color of people's skin still affects human relationships? Given our past, it seems that although racial-ethnic walls will diminish, even crumble at some points, the color line is not likely to disappear. Let's close this chapter by looking at two issues we are currently grappling with, immigration and affirmative action.

pan-Indianism a movement that focuses on common elements in the cultures of Native Americans in order to develop a cross-tribal self-identity and to work toward the welfare of all Native Americans

The Immigration Debate

Throughout its history, the United States has both welcomed immigration and feared its consequences. The gates opened wide (numerically, if not in attitude) for waves of immigrants in the 1800s and early 1900s. During the past 20 years, a new wave of immigration has brought close to a million new residents to the United States each year. Today, more immigrants (34 million) live in the United States than at any time in the country's history (*Statistical Abstract* 2007:Tables 5, 45).

In contrast to earlier waves, in which immigrants came almost exclusively from Western Europe, the composition of this current wave is more diverse. In fact, it is changing the U.S. racial-ethnic mix. If current trends in immigration (and birth) persist, in about 50 years the "average" American will trace his or her ancestry to Africa, Asia, South America, the Pacific Islands, the Middle East—almost anywhere but white Europe. This change is discussed in the Cultural Diversity box on the next page.

In some states, the future is arriving much sooner than this. In California, racial-ethnic minorities constitute a large majority. California has 20 million minorities and 16 million whites (*Statistical Abstract* 2007:Table 23). Californians who request new telephone service from Pacific Bell can speak to customer service representatives in Spanish, Korean, Vietnamese, Mandarin, Cantonese—or in English.

As in the past, there is concern that "too many" immigrants will change the character of the United States. "Throughout the history of U.S. immigration," write sociologists Alejandro Portés and Ruben Rumbaut (1990), "a consistent thread has been the fear that the 'alien element' would somehow undermine the institutions of the country and would lead it down the path of disintegration and decay." A hundred years ago, the widespread fear was that the immigrants from southern Europe would bring communism with them. Today, some fear that Spanish-speaking immigrants threaten the primacy of the English language. In addition, the age-old fear that immigrants will take jobs away from native-born Americans remains strong. Finally, minority groups that struggled for political representation fear that newer groups will gain political power at their expense.

Affirmative Action

The role of affirmative action in our multicultural society lies at the center of a national debate about race and ethnic relations. In this policy, initiated by President Kennedy in 1961, goals based on race (and sex) are used in hiring, promotion, and college admission. Sociologist Barbara Reskin (1998) examined the results of affirmative action. She concluded that although it is difficult to separate the results of affirmative action from economic booms and busts and the greater numbers of women in the work force, affirmative action has had a modest impact.

The results may have been modest, but the reactions to this program have been anything but modest. Affirmative action has been at the center of controversy for almost two generations. Liberals, both white and minority, say that this program is the most direct way to level the playing field of economic opportunity. If whites are passed over, this is an unfortunate cost that we must pay if we are to make up for past discrimination. In contrast, conservatives, both white and minority, agree that opportunity should be open to all, but claim that putting race (or sex) ahead of an individual's training and ability to perform a job is reverse discrimination. Because of their race (or sex), qualified people who had nothing to do with past inequity are discriminated against. They add that affirmative action stigmatizes the people who benefit

Cultural Diversity *in the* United States

Glimpsing the Future: The Shifting U.S. Racial-Ethnic Mix

DURING THE NEXT TWENTY-FIVE years, the population of the United States is expected to grow by about 22 percent. To see what the U.S. population will look like at the end of that time, can we simply multiply the current racial-ethnic mix by 22 percent? The answer is a resounding no. As you can see from Figure 12.11, some groups will grow much more than others, giving us a different-looking United States. Some of the changes in the U.S. racial-ethnic mix will be dramatic. In twenty-five years, one of every nineteen Americans is expected to have an Asian background, and one of every four or five a Latino background.

Two basic causes underlie this fundamental shift: immigration and birth rates. Immigration is by far the more important. The racial-ethnic groups have different rates of immigration and birth, and these will change their proportions of the U.S. population. From Figure 12.11, you can see how the proportion of non-Hispanic whites is expected to shrink, that of Native Americans to remain the same, and that of African Americans to increase slightly. With both vast immigration and higher-than-average birth rates, in fifty years almost one of four Americans is expected to be of Latino ancestry.

for your Consideration

This shifting racial-ethnic mix is one of the most significant events occurring in the United States. To better understand its implications, apply the three theoretical perspectives.

Use the *conflict perspective* to identify the groups that are likely to be threatened by this change. Over what resources are struggles likely to develop? What impact do you think this changing mix might have on European Americans? On Latinos? On African Americans? On Asian Americans? On Native Americans? What changes in immigration laws (or their enforcement) can you anticipate?

To apply the *symbolic interactionist perspective*, consider how groups might perceive one another differently as their proportion of the population changes. How do you think that this changed perception will affect people's behavior?

To apply the *functionalist perspective*, try to determine how each racial-ethnic group will benefit from this changing mix. How will other parts of society (such as businesses) benefit? What functions and dysfunctions can you anticipate for politics, economics, education, or religion?

Figure 12.11 Projections of the Racial-Ethnic Makeup of the U.S. Population

Sources: By the author. Based on Bernstein and Bergman 2003; *Statistical Abstract* 2004:Table 16; 2005:Table 16. The projections I modified are the projections based on the new census category of membership in two or more groups and trends in interethnic marriage.

from it, because it suggests that they hold their jobs because of race (or sex), rather than merit.

This national debate crystallized with a series of controversial rulings. One of the most significant was *Proposition 209,* a 1996 amendment to the California state constitution. This amendment banned preferences to minorities and women in hiring, promotion, and college admissions. Despite appeals by a coalition of civil rights groups, the U.S. Supreme Court upheld this California law.

A second significant ruling was made by the Supreme Court of Michigan in 2003. White students who had been denied admission to the University of Michigan claimed that they had been discriminated against because less qualified applicants had been admitted on the basis of their race. The Court ruled that universities can give minorities an edge in admissions, but there must be a meaningful review of individual applicants. Mechanical systems, such as giving extra points because of race, are unconstitutional. This murky message satisfied no one, as no one knew what it really meant.

To remove ambiguity, opponents of affirmative action in Michigan proposed *Proposition 2,* an amendment to the state constitution that would make it illegal for public institutions to even consider race or sex in college admissions, in hiring, or in awarding contracts. Like the proposal in California, *Proposition 2* became law (Lewin 2007).

With opponents and proponents of affirmative action gearing up for similar battles in other states, this issue of the proper role of affirmative action in a multicultural society is likely to remain center stage for quite some time.

Toward a True Multicultural Society

The United States has the potential to become a society in which racial-ethnic groups not only coexist, but also respect one another—and thrive—as they work together for mutually beneficial goals. In a true multicultural society, the minority groups that make up the United States will participate fully in the nation's social institutions while maintaining their cultural integrity. Reaching this goal will require that we understand that "the biological differences that divide one race from another add up to a drop in the genetic ocean." For a long time, we have given racial categories an importance they never merited. Now we need to figure out how to reduce them to the irrelevance they deserve. In short, we need to make real the abstraction called equality that we profess to believe (Cose 2000).

The United States is the most racially-ethnically diverse society in the world. This can be our central strength, with our many groups working together to build a harmonious society, a stellar example for the world. Or it can be our Achilles heel, with us breaking into feuding groups, a Balkanized society that marks an ill-fitting end to a grand social experiment. Our reality will probably fall somewhere between these extremes.

Summary *and* Review

Laying the Sociological Foundation

How is race both a reality and a myth?

In the sense that different groups inherit distinctive physical traits, race is a reality. There is no agreement regarding what constitutes a particular race, however, or even how many races there are. In the sense of one race being superior to another and of there being pure races, race is a myth. The *idea* of race is powerful, shaping basic relationships among people. Pp. 334–335.

How do race and ethnicity differ?

Race refers to inherited biological characteristics; **ethnicity,** to cultural ones. Members of ethnic groups identify with one another on the basis of common ancestry and cultural heritage. Pp. 334–338.

What are minority and dominant groups?

Minority groups are people who are singled out for unequal treatment by members of the **dominant group,** the group with more power, privilege, and social status. Minorities originate with migration or the expansion of political boundaries. Pp. 338–339.

What heightens ethnic identity, and what is "ethnic work"?

A group's relative size, power, physical characteristics, and amount of discrimination heighten or reduce ethnic identity. **Ethnic work** is the process of constructing an ethnic identity. For people with strong ties to their culture of origin, ethnic work involves enhancing and maintaining group distinctions. For those without a firm ethnic identity, ethnic work is an attempt to recover one's ethnic heritage. P. 339.

Prejudice and Discrimination

Why are people prejudiced?

Prejudice is an attitude, and **discrimination** is an action. Like other attitudes, prejudice is learned in association with others. Prejudice is so extensive that people can show prejudice against groups that don't even exist. Minorities also internalize the dominant norms, and some show prejudice against their own group. Pp. 340–341.

How do individual and institutional discrimination differ?

Individual discrimination is the negative treatment of one person by another, while **institutional discrimination** is negative treatment that is built into social institutions. Institutional discrimination can occur without the awareness of either the perpetrator or the object of discrimination. Discrimination in health care is one example. Pp. 341–342.

Theories of Prejudice

How do psychologists explain prejudice?

Psychological theories of prejudice stress the **authoritarian personality** and frustration displaced toward **scapegoats.** P. 343.

How do sociologists explain prejudice?

Sociological theories focus on how different social environments increase or decrease prejudice. *Functionalists* stress the benefits and costs that come from discrimination. *Conflict theorists* look at how the groups in power exploit racial and ethnic divisions in order to control workers and maintain power. *Symbolic interactionists* stress how labels create **selective perception** and self-fulfilling prophecies. Pp. 343–345.

Global Patterns of Intergroup Relations

What are the major patterns of minority and dominant group relations?

Beginning with the least humane, they are **genocide, population transfer, internal colonialism, segregation, assimilation,** and **multiculturalism (pluralism).** Pp. 345–349.

Race and Ethnic Relations in the United States

What are the major ethnic groups in the United States?

From largest to smallest, the major ethnic groups are European Americans, Latinos, African Americans, Asian Americans, and Native Americans. Pp. 349–350.

What are some issues in racial-ethnic relations and characteristics of minority groups?

Latinos are divided by social class and country of origin. African Americans are increasingly divided into middle and lower classes, with two sharply contrasting worlds of experience. On many measures, Asian Americans are better off than white Americans, but their well-being varies with their country of origin. For Native Americans, the primary issues are poverty, nationhood, and settling treaty obligations. The overarching issue for minorities is overcoming discrimination. Pp. 351–364.

Looking Toward the Future

What main issues dominate U.S. racial-ethnic relations?

The main issues are immigration, affirmative action, and how to develop a true multicultural society. The answers affect our future. Pp. 364–367.

Thinking Critically
about Chapter 12

1. How many races do your friends think there are? Do they think that one race is superior to the others? What do you think their reaction would be to the sociological position that racial categories are primarily social?

2. A hundred years ago, sociologist W. E. B. Du Bois said, "The problem of the twentieth century is the problem of the color line—the relation of the darker to the lighter races." Why do you think that the color line remains one of the most volatile topics facing the nation?

3. If you were appointed head of the U.S. Civil Service Commission, what policies would you propose to reduce racial-ethnic strife in the United States? Be ready to explain the sociological principles that might give your proposals a higher chance of success.

Additional Resources

What can you use MySocLab for? mysoclab ALLYN & BACON Where learning & the sociological imagination intersect. www.mysoclab.com

- **Study and Review:** Pre-and Post-Tests, Practice Tests, Flash Cards, Individualized Study Plans.
- **Current Events:** *Sociology in the News*, the daily *New York Times*, and more.
- **Research and Writing:** *Research Navigator*, *Writing About Sociology*, and more.

Where Can I Read More on This Topic?

Suggested readings for this chapter are listed at the back of this book.

CHAPTER 13

The Elderly

Deidre Scherer, *Woman and Cello*, 2003

In 1928, Charles Hart, who was working on his Ph.D. in anthropology, did fieldwork with the Tiwi, residents of an island off the northern coast of Australia. Because every Tiwi belonged to a clan, they assigned Hart to the bird (Jabijabui) clan and told him that a particular woman was his mother. Hart described the woman as "toothless, almost blind, withered." He added that she was "physically quite revolting and mentally rather senile." He then recounted this remarkable event:

> [T]oward the end of my time on the islands an incident occurred that surprised me because it suggested that some of them had been taking my presence in the kinship system much more seriously than I had thought. I was approached by a group of about eight or nine senior men . . . They were the senior members of the Jabijabui clan and they had decided among themselves that the time had come to get rid of the decrepit old woman who had first called me son and whom I now called mother . . . As I knew, they said, it was Tiwi custom, when an old woman became too feeble to look after herself, to "cover her up." This could only be done by her sons and brothers and all of them had to agree beforehand, since once it was done, they did not want any dissension among the brothers or clansmen, as that might lead to a feud. My "mother" was now completely blind, she was constantly falling over logs or into fires, and they, her senior clansmen, were in agreement that she would be better out of the way. Did I agree?
>
> I already knew about "covering up." The Tiwi, like many other hunting and gathering peoples, sometimes got rid of their ancient and decrepit females. The method was to dig a hole in the ground in some lonely place, put the old woman in the hole and fill it in with earth until only her head was showing. Everybody went away for a day or two and then went back to the hole to discover to their great surprise, that the old woman was dead, having been too feeble to raise her arms from the earth. Nobody had "killed" her; her death in Tiwi eyes was a natural one. She had been alive when her relatives last saw her. I had never seen it done, though I knew it was the custom, so I asked my brothers if it was necessary for me to attend the "covering up."
>
> They said no and that they would do it, but only after they had my agreement. Of course I agreed, and a week or two later we heard in our camp that my "mother" was dead, and we all wailed and put on the trimmings of mourning. (C.W.M. Hart in Hart and Pilling 1979:125–126)

[They would] put the old woman in the hole and fill it in with earth until only her head was showing.

Aging in Global Perspective

We won't deal with the question of whether it was moral or ethical for Hart to agree that the old woman should be "covered up." What is of interest for our purposes is how the Tiwi treated their frail elderly—or, more specifically, their frail *female* elderly. You probably noticed that the Tiwi "covered up" only old women. As was noted in Chapter 11, females are discriminated against throughout the world. As this case makes evident, in some places that discrimination extends even to death.

Every society must deal with the problem of people growing old, and of some becoming frail. Although few societies choose to bury old people alive, all societies must decide how to allocate limited resources among their citizens. With the percentage of the population that is old increasing in many nations, these decisions are generating tensions between the generations.

The Social Construction of Aging

The way the Tiwi treated frail elderly women reflects one extreme of how societies cope with aging. Another extreme, one that reflects an entirely different attitude, is illustrated by the Abkhasians, an agricultural people who live in a mountainous region of Georgia, a republic of the former Soviet Union. The Abkhasians pay their elderly high respect and look to them for guidance. They would no more dispense with their elderly by "covering them up" than we would "cover up" a sick child in our culture.

The Abkhasians may be the longest-lived people on earth. Many claim to live past 100—some beyond 120 and even 130 (Benet 1971; Robbins 2006). Although it is difficult to document the accuracy of these claims, government records indicate that an extraordinary number of Abkhasians do live to a very old age.

Three main factors appear to account for their long lives. The first is their diet, which consists of little meat, much fresh fruit, vegetables, garlic, goat cheese, cornmeal, buttermilk, and wine. The second is their lifelong physical activity. They do slow down after age 80, but even after the age of 100 they still work about four hours a day. The third factor—a highly developed sense of community—lies at the very heart of the Abkhasian culture. From childhood, each individual is integrated into a primary group, and remains so throughout life. There is no such thing as a nursing home, nor do the elderly live alone. Because they continue to work and contribute to the group's welfare, the elderly aren't a burden to anyone. They don't vegetate, nor do they feel the need to "fill time" with bingo and shuffleboard. In short, the elderly feel no sudden rupture between what they "were" and what they "are."

The examples of the Tiwi and the Abkhasians reveal an important sociological principle— that, like gender, aging is *socially constructed.* That is, nothing in the nature of aging summons forth any particular viewpoint. Rather, attitudes toward the aged are rooted in society and, therefore, differ from one social group to another. As we shall see, even the age at which people are considered old depends not on biology, but on culture.

The man riding the horse is Temir Tarba, who was 100 years old when the photo was taken. As discussed in the text, the Abkhasians have an extraordinarily large number of elderly, but due to a lack of records, there are questions about their exact age.

Industrialization and the Graying of the Globe

As was noted in previous chapters, industrialization is a worldwide trend. The higher standard of living that industrialization brings includes more food, better public health practices (especially a purer water supply), and more effective ways of fighting the diseases that kill children. Consequently, when a country industrializes, more of its people live longer and reach older ages. The Social Map on the next page illustrates this principle.

From this global map, you can see that the industrialized countries have the highest percentage of elderly. The range among nations is broad, from just 1 of 48 citizens in nonindustrialized Uganda to *ten* times higher than this, to almost 1 of 4.5 in postindustrial Japan (*Statistical Abstract* 2007:Table 1309). In just two decades, *half* the population

Central to a group's culture are ways of viewing reality. Living for centuries in isolation on Bathurst and Melville Islands off the northern coast of Australia, the Tiwi, featured in the vignette on "covering up," developed a unique culture. Shown here is Wurabuti, who has prepared himself to lead his uncle's funeral dance. To be certain that his uncle's ghost will not recognize him, Wurabuti is wearing a "shirt" painted with ocher and clay, a topknot of cockatoo feathers, and a beard of goose feathers.

of Italy and Japan will be older than 50 (Kinsella and Phillips 2005). The graying of the globe is so new that *two-thirds of all people who have ever passed age 50 in the history of the world are alive today* (Zaslow 2003).

As a nation's elderly population increases, so, too, does the bill its younger citizens pay to provide for their needs. This expense has become a major social issue. Although Americans complain that Social Security taxes are too high, the U.S. rate of 15.3 percent is comparatively low. Polish workers are hit the hardest; they pay 37 percent of their wages into social security. Only a percentage or two less is paid by workers in Austria, France, Greece, Holland, and Hungary (*Statistical Abstract* 2007:Tables 531, 1335). Workers in the Least Industrialized Nations pay no social security taxes. There, families are expected to take care of their own elderly, with no help from the government.

As the numbers of elderly continue to grow, analysts have become alarmed about future liabilities for their care. This issue is especially troubling in Western Europe, which has the largest percentage of citizens over the age of 60. The basic issue is: How can nations provide high quality care for their growing numbers of elderly without burdening future generations with impossible taxes? No one has proposed a solution yet, and the number of nations in other parts of the world confronting this issue is growing.

Figure 13.1 The Graying of the Globe

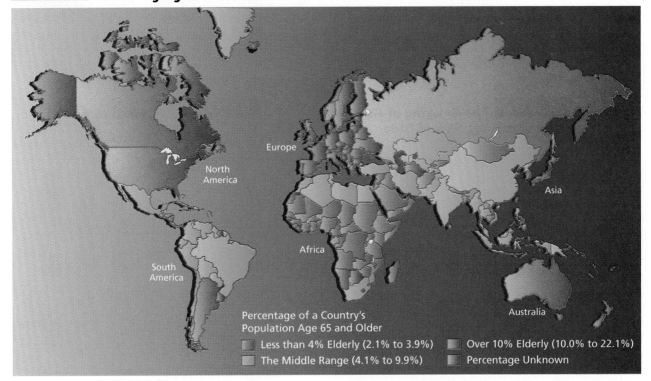

Percentage of a Country's Population Age 65 and Older

- Less than 4% Elderly (2.1% to 3.9%)
- The Middle Range (4.1% to 9.9%)
- Over 10% Elderly (10.0% to 22.1%)
- Percentage Unknown

Source: By the author. Based on *Statistical Abstract* 2007:Table 1309.

Figure 13.2 **U.S. Life Expectancy by Year of Birth**

Sources: By the author. Based on *Historical Statistics of the United States, Colonial Times to 1970,* Bicentennial Edition, Part I, Series B, 107–115; *Statistical Abstract* 2007:Table 98.

The Graying of America

life expectancy the number of years that an average person at any age, including newborns, can expect to live

graying of America refers to the growing percentage of older people in the U.S. population

As Figure 13.2 illustrates, the United States is part of this global trend. This figure shows how U.S. **life expectancy,** the number of years people can expect to live, has increased since 1900. To me, and perhaps to you, it is startling to realize that a hundred years ago the average American could not even expect to see age 50. Since then, we've added about *30* years to our life expectancy, and Americans born today can expect to live into their 70s or 80s.

The term **graying of America** refers to this increasing percentage of older people in the U.S. population. Look at Figure 13.3. In 1900 only 4 percent of Americans were age 65 and older. Today about 13 percent are. The average 65-year-old can expect to live another eighteen years (*Statistical Abstract* 2007:Table 100). U.S. society has become so "gray" that, as Figure 13.4 shows, the median age has almost *doubled* since 1850. Today, there are seven million *more* elderly Americans than there are teenagers (*Statistical Abstract* 2007:Table 11). Despite this vast change, as Figure 13.5 shows, life expectancy in the United States is far from the highest. As you can see, Japan holds this record.

Figure 13.3 **The Graying of America: Americans Age 65 and Older**

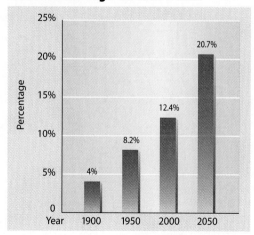

Source: By the author. Based on *Statistical Abstract* 2007:Tables 11 and 12, and earlier years.

Figure 13.4 **The Median Age of the U.S. Population**

Source: By the author. Based on *Statistical Abstract* 2000:Table 14; 2007:Tables 11 and 12, and earlier years.

Figure 13.5 Life Expectancy in Global Perspective

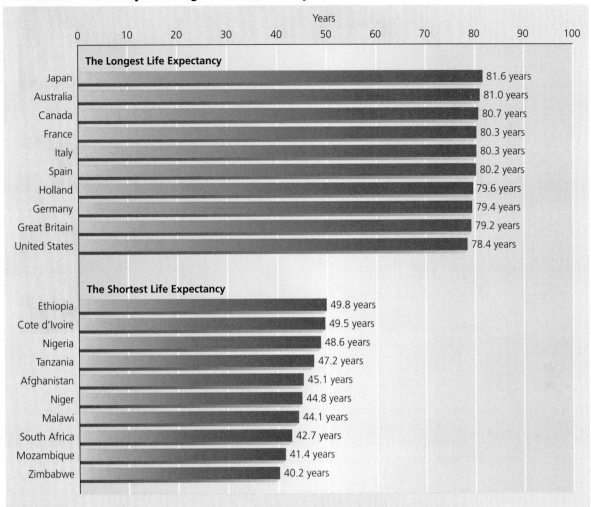

The Longest Life Expectancy

Country	Years
Japan	81.6 years
Australia	81.0 years
Canada	80.7 years
France	80.3 years
Italy	80.3 years
Spain	80.2 years
Holland	79.6 years
Germany	79.4 years
Great Britain	79.2 years
United States	78.4 years

The Shortest Life Expectancy

Country	Years
Ethiopia	49.8 years
Cote d'Ivoire	49.5 years
Nigeria	48.6 years
Tanzania	47.2 years
Afghanistan	45.1 years
Niger	44.8 years
Malawi	44.1 years
South Africa	42.7 years
Mozambique	41.4 years
Zimbabwe	40.2 years

Note: The countries listed in the source with a life expectancy higher than the United States and those with a life expectancy less than 50 years. The totals are projections for year 2010. All the countries in the top group are industrialized, and none of those in the bottom group are.

Source: By the author. Based on *Statistical Abstract* 2007:Table 1310.

As anyone who has ever visited Florida has noticed, the elderly population is not evenly distributed around the country. (As Jerry Seinfeld sardonically noted, "There's a law that when you get old, you've got to move to Florida.") The Social Map on the next page shows how uneven this distribution is.

Race-Ethnicity and Aging Just as the states have different percentages of elderly, so do the racial-ethnic groups that make up the United States. As you can see from Table 13.1, whites have the largest percentage of elderly and Latinos the smallest. The difference is so great that the proportion of elderly whites (16 percent) is almost three times that of Latinos (5.9 percent). The percentage of older Latinos is small because so many younger Latinos have

Table 13.1 Race-Ethnicity and Aging

	AGE				Total 65 and Over
	Median	65–74	75–84	85+	
Whites	41.3	8.3%	5.2%	2.6%	16.0%
Asian Americans	36.7	5.9%	2.8%	0.9%	9.6%
African Americans	31.5	4.9%	2.6%	1.2%	8.7%
Native Americans	29.6	4.0%	2.0%	0.7%	6.7%
Latinos	28.1	3.4%	1.8%	0.7%	5.9%
U.S. Average	37.0	6.9%	4.2%	2.0%	13.0%

Note: For year 2010, except Native Americans, which are year 2005.

Source: By the author. Based on *Statistical Abstract* 2007:Tables 15 and 16.

Figure 13.6 As Florida Goes, So Goes the Nation

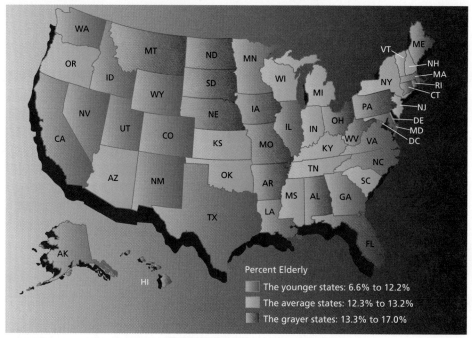

Percent Elderly
- The younger states: 6.6% to 12.2%
- The average states: 12.3% to 13.2%
- The grayer states: 13.3% to 17.0%

Source: By the author. Based on *Statistical Abstract* 2007:Table 21.

migrated to the United States. Differences in cultural attitudes about aging, family relationships, work histories, and health practices will be important areas of sociological investigation in coming years.

Although more people are living to old age, the maximum length of life possible, the **life span,** has not increased. Experts disagree, however, on what that maximum is. It is at least 122, for this was the well-documented age of Jeanne Louise Calment of France at her death in 1997. If the reports on the Abkhasians are correct (and this is a matter of controversy), the human life span may exceed even this number by a comfortable margin. It is also likely that advances in genetics will extend the human life span—perhaps to hundreds of years—a topic we will return to later. For now, let's see the different pictures of aging that emerge when we apply the three theoretical perspectives.

The Symbolic Interactionist Perspective

To better understand how aging is socially constructed, let's look beyond biology to some of the symbols associated with age. How does culture signal to us that we are "old"? How do stereotypes and the mass media influence our perceptions of aging?

When Are You "Old"?

Changing Perceptions as You Age You probably can remember when you thought that a 12-year-old was "old"—and anyone older than that, beyond reckoning. You probably were 5 or 6 at the time. Similarly, to a 12-year-old, someone of 21 seems "old." To someone who is 21, 30 may mark the point at which one is no longer "young," and 40 may seem very old. As people add years, "old" gradually recedes further from the self. To people who turn 40, 50 seems old; at 50, the late 60s look old—not the early 60s, for the passing of years seems to accelerate as we age, and at 50 the 60s don't seem so far away.

In Western culture, most people have difficulty applying the label "old" to themselves. In the typical case, they have become used to what they see in the mirror. The changes have taken place gradually, and each change, if it has not exactly been taken in stride, has been accommodated. Consequently, it comes as a shock to meet a long-lost friend and see how much that person has changed. At class reunions, *each* person can hardly believe how much older *the others* appear!

Four Factors in Our Decision   If there is no fixed age line that people cross, then what makes someone "old"? Sociologists have identified several factors that spur people to apply the label of old to themselves.

The first factor is *biology.* One person may experience "signs" of aging earlier than others: wrinkles, balding, aches, difficulty in doing something that he or she used to take for granted. Consequently, one person will *feel* "old" at an earlier or later age than others.

A second factor is *personal history* or biography. An accident that limits someone's mobility, for example, can make that person feel old sooner than others. Or consider a woman who gave birth at 16 and has a daughter who, in turn, has a child at 18. She has become a biological grandmother at age 34. It is most unlikely, however, that she will play any stereotypical role—spending the day in a rocking chair, for example—but *knowing* that she is a grandmother has an impact on her self-concept. At a minimum, she must *deny* that she is old.

Then there is **gender age,** the relative value that a culture places on men's and women's ages. For example, graying hair on a man, and even a few wrinkles, may be perceived as signs of "maturity," while on a woman, those same features may indicate that she is getting "old." "Mature" and "old," of course, carry different meanings in Western cultures; the first is desired, the second shunned. Similarly, around the world, most men are able to marry younger spouses than women can. Maria might be an exception and marry Bill, who is fourteen years younger than she. But in most marriages in which there is a fourteen-year age gap, the odds greatly favor the wife being the younger of the pair. This is not biology in action; rather, it is the social construction of appearance and gender age.

The fourth factor in deciding when people label themselves as "old" is *timetables,* the signals societies use to inform their members that old age has begun. Since there is no automatic age at which people become "old," these timetables vary around the world. One group may choose a particular birthday, such as the 60th or 65th, to signal the onset of old age. Other groups do not even have birthdays, making such numbers meaningless. In the West, retirement is sometimes a cultural signal of the beginning of old age—which is one reason that some people resist retirement.

Yone Minagawa, the world's oldest living person, who was born in 1893, is shown here as she celebrates her 114th birthday in Fukuoka, Japan. The world's record for age that has been documented by a birth certificate is held by Jeanne Calment of France who died in 1997 at the age of 122.

Changing Perceptions of the Elderly

At first, the audience sat quietly as the developers explained their plans to build a high-rise apartment building. After a while, people began to shift uncomfortably in their seats. Then they began to show open hostility.

"That's too much money to spend on those people," said one.

"You even want them to have a swimming pool?" asked another incredulously.

Finally, one young woman put their attitudes in a nutshell when she asked, "Who wants all those old people around?"

When physician Robert Butler (1975, 1980) heard these complaints about plans to build apartments for senior citizens, he began to realize how deeply antagonistic feelings toward the elderly can run. He coined the term **ageism** to refer to prejudice, discrimination, and hostility directed against people because of their age. Let's see how ageism developed in U.S. society.

gender age the relative value placed on men's and women's ages

ageism prejudice, discrimination, and hostility directed against people because of their age; can be directed against any age group, including youth

When does old age begin? And what activities are appropriate for the elderly? From this photo that I took of Munimah, a 65-year-old bonded laborer in Chennai, India, you can see how culturally relative these questions are. No one in Chennai thinks it is extraordinary that this woman makes her living by carrying heavy rocks all day in the burning, tropical sun. Working next to her in the quarry is her 18-year-old son, who breaks the rocks into the size that his mother carries.

PEANUTS WE'RE BROTHER AND SISTER AND WE LOVE EACH OTHER

YOU'RE HYPOCRITES, THAT'S WHAT YOU ARE! DO YOU REALLY THINK YOU CAN FOOL SANTA CLAUS THIS WAY?

WHY NOT? WE'RE A COUPLE OF SHARP KIDS, AND HE'S JUST AN OLD MAN!

I WEEP FOR OUR GENERATION!

PEANUTS® by Charles M. Schulz

Stereotypes, which play such a profound role in social life, are a basic area of sociological investigation. In contemporary society, the mass media are a major source of stereotypes.

Shifting Meanings As we have seen, there is nothing inherent in old age to summon forth any particular attitude, negative or not. Old age may even have been regarded positively in early U.S. society (Cottin 1979; Kart 1990; Clair et al. 1993). In Colonial times, growing old was seen as an accomplishment because so few people made it to old age. With no pensions, the elderly continued to work at jobs that changed little over time. They were viewed as storehouses of knowledge about work skills and sources of wisdom about how to live a long life.

The coming of industrialization, however, eroded these bases of respect. With better sanitation and medical care, more people reached old age. No longer was being elderly an honorable distinction. The new forms of mass production made young workers as productive as the elderly. Coupled with mass education, this stripped away the elderly's superior knowledge (Cowgill 1974; Hunt 2005). In the Cultural Diversity box on the next page, you can see how a similar process is now occurring in China as it, too, industrializes.

A basic principle of symbolic interactionism is that people perceive both themselves and others according to the symbols of their culture. Following this principle, as the meaning of old age was transformed—when it changed from an asset to a liability—not only did younger people come to view the elderly differently but also the elderly began to perceive themselves in a new light. This shift in meaning is demonstrated in the way people lie about their age: They used to claim that they were older than they were, but now they say that they are younger than they are (Clair et al. 1993).

The meaning of old age is shifting once again. Today, most U.S. elderly can take care of themselves financially, and many are well-off. In addition, members of the baby boom generation have entered their late 50s. With their vast numbers, better health, and financial strength, they also are destined to positively affect our images of the elderly. The next step in this symbolic shift, now in process, is to celebrate old age as a time of renewal—not simply as a period that precedes death, but, rather, as a new stage of growth.

Even in scholarly theories, perceptions of the elderly have become more positive. A theory that goes by the mouthful *gerotranscendence* was developed by Swedish sociologist Lars Tornstam. The thrust of his theory is that the elderly undergo a self-transformation and begin to feel more at one with the universe. Coming to see things as less black and white, they develop more subtle ways of viewing right and wrong, and can tolerate more ambiguity (Manheimer 2005). This theory is not likely to be universal. I have seen some elderly people grow softer and more spiritual, but I have also seen others grow bitter, close up, and become even more judgmental of life. The theory's limitations should become apparent shortly.

The Influence of the Mass Media

In Chapter 3 (pages 80–82), we noted that the mass media help to shape our ideas about both gender and relationships between men and women. As a powerful source of symbols, the media also influence our ideas of the elderly, the topic of the Mass Media box on page 380.

China: Changing Sentiment About the Elderly

AS SHE CONTEMPLATES HER future, Zhao Chunlan, a 71-year-old widow, smiles shyly, with evident satisfaction. She has heard about sons abandoning their aged parents. She has even heard whispering about abuse.

But Zhao has no such fears.

It is not that her son is so devoted that he would never swerve from his traditional duty to his mother. Rather, it is a piece of paper that has eased Zhao's mind. Her 51-year-old son has signed a support agreement: He will cook her special meals, take her to medical checkups, even give her the largest room in his house and put the family's color television in it (Sun 1990).

The high status of the elderly in China is famed around the world: The elderly are considered a source of wisdom, given honored seating at both family and public gatherings—even venerated after death in ancestor worship.

Although this outline may represent more ideal than real culture, it appears to generally hold true—for the past, that is. Today, the authority of elders has eroded, leading to less respect from the adult children (Yan 2003). For some, the cause is the children's success in the new market economy, which places them in a world unknown to their parents (Chen 2005). But other structural reasons are also tearing at the bonds between generations, especially the longer life expectancy that has come with industrialization. The change is startling: In 1950, China's life expectancy was 41 years. It has now jumped to 70 years (Li 2004). With China's policy that allows each married couple only one child, the responsibility for supporting aged parents falls on fewer shoulders: One younger couple must now support four elderly parents (Zhang and Goza 2007). Try putting yourself in that situation, and see how it would interfere with your plans for life and affect your attitude toward your aging parents.

All of this is occurring while the population of China that is over 65 is mushrooming. China's elderly already number 110 million—8 percent of the population. As these numbers continue to grow, at some point the number of China's elderly could become larger than the entire population of the United States (*Statistical Abstract* 2007:Tables 1308, 1309).

Alarmed by signs that parent-child bonds are weakening, some local officials require adult children to sign support agreements for their aged parents. One province has come up with an ingenious device: To get a marriage license, a couple must sign a contract pledging to support their parents after they reach age 60 (Sun 1990). "I'm sure he would do right by me, anyway," says Zhao, "but this way I know he will."

As China industrializes and urbanizes, the structure of village relationships that nurtured the elderly is breaking down.

for your Consideration

Do you think we could solve our Social Security crisis by requiring adult children to sign a parental support agreement in order to get a marriage license? Why or why not? What do you think Chinese officials can do to solve the problem of supporting their huge and growing numbers of elderly?

mass Media in social life

Shaping Our Perceptions of the Elderly

THE MASS MEDIA PROFOUNDLY INFLUENCE our lives. What we hear and see on television and in the movies, the songs we listen to, the books and magazines we read—all become part of our world view. Without our knowing it, the media shape our images of people. They influence how we view minorities and dominant groups; men, women, and children; people with disabilities; people from other cultures—and the elderly.

The shaping of our images and perception of the elderly is subtle, so much so that it usually occurs without our awareness. The elderly, for example, are underrepresented on television and in most popular magazines. This leaves a covert message—that the elderly are of little consequence and can be safely ignored.

Then there is advertising. Ads often depict the elderly as being feeble or foolish. The AARP (formerly, American Association of Retired Persons) claims this happens because younger people dominate advertising firms, and their ads reflect their negative images of older people. They pick out the

"worst traits of the group, making everyone believe that old is something you don't want to be" (Goldman 1993).

Or consider how the media reflect and reinforce stereotypes of *gender age*. Older male news anchors are likely to be retained, while female anchors who turn the same age are more likely to be transferred to less visible positions. Similarly, in movies older men are more likely to play romantic leads—and to play them opposite much younger rising stars.

Although usually subtle, the message is not lost. The more television that people watch, the more they perceive the elderly in negative terms. The elderly, too, internalize these negative images, which, in turn, affects the way they view themselves. These images are so powerful that they affect the elderly's health, even the way they walk (Donlon et al. 2005).

We become fearful of growing old, and we go to great lengths to deny that this is happening to us. Fear and denial play into the hands of advertisers, of course, who exploit our concerns about losing our youth. They help us deny this biological reality by selling us hair dyes, skin creams, and other products that are designed to conceal even the appearance of old age. For these same

Age is more than biology. In some cultures, Demi Moore, 42, would be considered elderly. Moore is shown here with her husband, Ashton Kutcher, 27. Almost inevitably, when there is a large age gap between a husband and wife, it is the husband who is the older one. The marriage of Kutcher and Moore is a reversal of the typical pattern.

reasons, Americans visit plastic surgeons to remove telltale signs of aging.

The elderly's growing numbers and affluence translate into economic clout and political power. It is inevitable, then, that the media's images of the elderly will change. An indication of that change is shown in the photo above.

for your Consideration

What other examples of fear and denial of growing old are you familiar with? What examples of older males playing romantic leads with younger costars can you give? Of older females and younger males? Why do you think we have a gender age?

IN SUM Symbolic interactionists stress that old age has no inherent meaning. There is nothing about old age to automatically summon forth responses of honor and respect, as with the Abkhasians, or any other response. Culture shapes how we perceive the elderly, including the way we view our own aging. In short, the social modifies the biological.

The Functionalist Perspective

Functionalists analyze how the parts of society work together. Among the components of society are **age cohorts**—people who were born at roughly the same time and who pass through the life course together. Although not visible to us, our age cohort has major effects on our lives. For example, if the age cohort nearing retirement is large (a "baby boom" generation), many jobs open up at roughly the same time. In contrast, if it is a small group (a "baby bust" generation), fewer jobs open up. Let's look at theories that focus on how people adjust to retirement.

age cohort people born at roughly the same time who pass through the life course together

Disengagement Theory

Elaine Cumming and William Henry (1961) analyzed how society prevents disruption when the elderly leave their positions of responsibility. In what is called **disengagement theory,** they explained how it would be disruptive if the elderly left their positions only when they died or became incompetent. To avoid this, pensions are offered to entice the elderly to hand over their positions to younger people. Retirement (or disengagement), then, is a mutually beneficial arrangement between two parts of society. It helps to smooth the transition between the generations.

Cumming (1976) also examined disengagement from the individual's perspective. She pointed out that people start to disengage during middle age, long before retirement, when they sense that the end of life is closer than its start. They do not immediately disengage, however, but begin to assign priority to goals and tasks, realizing that time is limited. Disengagement begins in earnest when children leave home, then increases with retirement and eventually widowhood.

Evaluation of the Theory   Disengagement theory came under attack almost immediately after the ink had dried on the theorists' paper. One of the main criticisms is that this theory contains an implicit bias against older people—assumptions that the elderly disengage from productive social roles, and then sort of slink into oblivion (Manheimer 2005). Instead of disengaging, the elderly *exchange* one set of roles for another (Jerrome 1992). The new roles, which often center on friendship, are no less satisfying than the earlier roles. They are less visible to researchers, however, who tend to have a youthful orientation—and who show their bias by assuming that productivity is the measure of self-worth.

The concept of retirement is changing as well. Computers, the Internet, and new types of work have blurred the dividing line between work and retirement. Less and less does retirement mean to abruptly stop working. Many workers just slow down. Some continue at their jobs, but put in fewer hours or work occasionally as consultants. Others switch careers, even though they are in their 60s. Some move to a warmer climate, but take their work with them. Many never "retire"—at least not in the sense of sinking into a recliner or being forever on the golf course. If disengagement theory is ever resurrected, it must come to grips with this fundamental change.

Activity Theory

Are retired people more satisfied with life? Are intimate activities more satisfying than formal ones? Such questions are the focus of **activity theory,** which assumes that the more activities elderly people engage in, the more they find life satisfying. Although we could consider this theory from other perspectives, we are examining it from the functionalist perspective because its focus is how disengagement is functional or dysfunctional.

Evaluation of the Theory   The results are mixed. In general, researchers have found that more active people are more satisfied. But not always. A study of retired people in France found that some people are happier when they are more active, others when they are less involved (Keith 1982). Similarly, most people find informal, intimate activities, such as spending time with friends, to be more satisfying than formal activities. But not everyone does. In one study, 2,000 retired U.S. men reported formal activities to be as important as informal ones. Even solitary activities, such

disengagement theory the view that society prevents disruption by having the elderly vacate (or disengage from) their positions of responsibility so the younger generation can step into their shoes

activity theory the view that satisfaction during old age is related to a person's amount and quality of activity

Researchers are exploring factors that can make old age an enjoyable period of life, those conditions that increase people's mental, social, emotional, and physical wellbeing. As research progresses, do you think we will reach the point where the average old person will be in this woman's physical condition?

as doing home repairs, had about the same impact as intimate activities on these men's life satisfaction (Beck and Page 1988). It is similarly the case with spending time with adult children. The amount of interaction with adult children that increases satisfaction with life differs for each person—when, in their words, they see their children "frequently enough" (Hatch 2000).

Continuity Theory

Another theory of how people adjust to growing old is **continuity theory.** As its name implies, the focus of this theory is how people adjust to old age by continuing ties with their past (Kinsella and Phillips 2005). When they retire, many people take on new roles that are similar to the ones they gave up. For example, a former CEO might serve as a consultant, a retired electrician might do small electrical repairs, or a pensioned banker might volunteer to direct the finances of her church. Researchers have found that people who are active in multiple roles (wife, author, mother, intimate friend, church member, etc.) are better equipped to handle the changes that growing old entails. They have also found that with their greater resources to meet the challenges of old age, people from higher social classes adjust better to aging.

Evaluation of the Theory   The basic criticism of continuity theory is that it is too broad (Hatch 2000). We all have anchor points based on our experiences, and we all rely on them to make adjustments to the changes we encounter in life. This applies to people of all ages beyond infancy. This theory is really a collection of loosely connected ideas, with no specific application to the elderly.

IN SUM | The *broader* perspective of the functionalists is how society's parts work together to keep society running smoothly. Although it is inevitable that younger workers replace the elderly, this transition could be disruptive. To entice the elderly out of their positions so that younger people can take over, the elderly are offered pensions. Functionalists also use a *narrower* perspective, focusing on how individuals adjust to their retirement. The findings of this narrower perspective are too mixed to be of much value—except that people who have better resources and are active in multiple roles adjust better to old age (Crosnoe and Elder 2002).

The theories discussed here were developed when retirement at age 65 was required by law. Today, people can keep their jobs if they want to. Choice, then, needs to be a factor in any theory—especially how people reconstruct their identities and come to terms with the new life they choose.

The Conflict Perspective

From the conflict perspective, the guiding principle of social life is the struggle of social groups for power and resources. How does this apply to society's age groups? Regardless of whether the young and old recognize it, they are opponents in a struggle that threatens to throw society into turmoil. The passage of Social Security legislation is an example of this struggle.

Social Security Legislation

In the 1920s, before Social Security provided an income for the aged, two-thirds of all citizens over 65 had no savings and could not support themselves (Holtzman 1963; Crossen 2004a). The fate of workers sank even deeper during the Great Depression, and in 1930 Francis Townsend, a physician, started a movement to rally older citizens. He soon had one-third of all Americans over age 65 enrolled in his Townsend Clubs. They demanded that the federal government impose a national sales tax of 2 percent to provide $200 a month for every person over 65 ($2,100 a month in today's money). In 1934, the Townsend Plan went before Congress. Because it called for such high payments and many were afraid that it would destroy

continuity theory the focus of this theory is how people adjust to retirement by continuing aspects of their earlier lives people's incentive to save for the future, members of Congress looked for a way to reject the plan without appearing to oppose the elderly. When President Roosevelt announced his own, more modest Social Security plan in 1934, Congress embraced it (Schottland 1963; Amenta 2006).

To provide jobs for younger people, the new Social Security law required that workers retire at age 65. It did not matter how well people did their work, or how much they needed the pay. For decades, the elderly protested. Finally, in 1986, Congress eliminated mandatory retirement. Today, almost 90 percent of Americans retire by age 65, but most do so voluntarily. No longer can they be forced out of their jobs simply because of their age.

Conflict theorists point out that Social Security did not come about because the members of Congress had generous hearts. Rather, Social Security emerged from a struggle between competing interest groups. As conflict theorists stress, when competing groups are in equilibrium, it is only a temporary balancing of oppositional forces, one that can be upset at any time. Perhaps more direct conflict may emerge. Let's consider this possibility.

Intergenerational Conflict

Will the future bring conflict between the elderly and the young? Although violence is not likely, if you listen closely, you can hear ripples of grumbling—complaints that the elderly are getting more than their fair share of society's resources. The huge costs of Social Security and Medicare have become a national concern. These two programs alone account for *one of every three* (31 percent) tax dollars (*Statistical Abstract* 2007:Table 462). As Figure 13.7 shows, Social Security payments were $781 million in 1950; now they run more than *700 times* higher. The Down-to-Earth Sociology box on the next page examines stirrings of resentment that could become widespread.

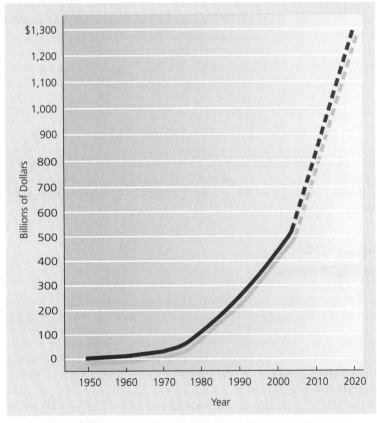

Figure 13.7 Social Security Payments to Beneficiaries

Source: By the author. Based on *Statistical Abstract* 1997:Table 518; 2007:Table 462. Broken line indicates the author's projections.

Down-to-Earth Sociology

Changing Sentiment About the U.S. Elderly

MOST U.S. ELDERLY USED to be poor. Social Security has been so successful that, as we saw in Figure 10.6 on page 288, the poverty rate of today's elderly is *less* than the national average. Many of the elderly who draw Social Security don't need it. Some travel about the country in motor homes and spend huge amounts on recreation. The golf courses are packed with retired Americans. So are the cruise ships wending their way to exotic destinations. Is this changed situation leading to a new sentiment about the elderly?

There are indications that it is. Senator Alan Simpson called the elderly "greedy geezers" who demand government handouts while they "tee off near their second homes in Florida" (Duff 1995). Some younger people feel resentful when they pay more than the elderly for an identical room in the same hotel. Teresa Anderson (1985) said, "My parents work and own several pieces of property. Something is wrong when people are automatically entitled to a 'senior citizen discount' regardless of need."

Some even argue that we should ration medical care for the elderly (Thau 2001). Considering costs, asks Daniel Callahan (1987), why should we perform open-heart surgery on people in their 80s? This only prolongs their life by two or three years. Doesn't it make more sense to use those same resources to give a kidney transplant to a child, whose life might be prolonged by fifty years?

Attitudes toward the elderly have undergone major shifts during the short history of the United States. As the economic circumstances of the elderly improve, attitudes are changing once again.

Robert Samuelson (1988) accuses the elderly's powerful lobby, the American Association of Retired Persons (AARP), of using misleading stereotypes. He says, "In the real world, the stereotypes of the elderly as sedentary, decrepit, and poor have long vanished, but in politics the cliché is promoted and perpetuated." He also accuses the AARP of hypocrisy: "They insist (rightfully) that age alone doesn't rob people of vitality and independence, while also arguing (wrongfully) that age alone entitles them to special treatment." They can't have it both ways, he says.

for your Consideration

Use information in this chapter to analyze why perceptions of the elderly are changing. Note two sides of the coin. On the one side, our current 65-plus generation is enjoying the highest standard of living in U.S. history. One of three golfers is over 65, as are 60 percent of people who take ocean cruises. On the other side are the elderly who live in poverty—24 percent of African Americans, 19 percent of Latinos, 14 percent of Asian Americans, and 8 percent of whites (*Statistical Abstract* 2007:Table 694). Note also the contrasting images—on the one hand, "blood-sucking vultures"; on the other hand, "pathetic creatures saving pennies to buy the best meal they can afford—dog food."

Some form of conflict seems inevitable. The graying of the United States leaves fewer workers to pay for the benefits received by the increasing millions who collect Social Security. This and other problems are discussed in the following Thinking Critically section.

Thinking Critically

The Social Security Trust Fund: There Is No Fund, and You Can't Trust It

Each month the Social Security Administration mails checks to 48 million people. Across the country, 196 million U.S. workers pay into the Social Security system, looking to it to provide for their basic necessities—and even a little more than that—in their old age (*Statistical Abstract* 2007:Tables 531, 533).

How dependable is Social Security? The short answer is "Don't bet your old age on it."

The first problem is well known. Social Security is not a bank account. The money taken from our checks is not deposited into our individual accounts. No money in the Social Security system is attached to anyone's name. At retirement, we don't withdraw the money we paid into Social Security. Instead, the government writes checks on money that it collects from current workers. When these workers retire, they, too, will be paid, not from their own savings, but from money collected from others who are still working.

The Social Security system is like a giant chain letter—it works as long as enough new people join the chain. If you join early enough, you'll collect more than you paid in—but if you join toward the end, you're simply out of luck. And, say some conflict theorists, we are nearing the end of the chain. The shift in the **dependency ratio**—the number of people who collect Social Security compared with the number of workers who contribute to it—is especially troubling. As Figure 13.8 shows, sixteen workers used to support each person who was collecting Social Security. Now the dependency ratio has dropped to four to one. In another generation, it could hit two to one. If this happens, Social Security taxes could become so high that they stifle the country's economy. To prevent this, Congress raised Social Security taxes and established a Social Security trust fund. Supposedly, this fund has trillions of dollars. But does it?

This question takes us to the root of the crisis, or, some would say, the fraud. In 1965, President Lyndon Johnson was bogged down in a war in Vietnam. To conceal the war's costs from the public, he arrived at the diabolical solution of forcing the Social Security Administration to invest only in U.S. Treasury bonds, a form of government IOUs. This put the money collected for Social Security into the general fund, where Johnson could siphon it off to finance the war. Politicians love this easy source of money, and they have continued this practice. They use the term "off budget" to refer to the Social Security money they spend. And *each year, they spend it all.*

Suppose that you buy a $10,000 U.S. Treasury bond. The government takes your $10,000 and hands you a document that says it owes you $10,000 plus interest. This is how Social Security works. The Social Security Administration (SSA) collects the money from workers, pays the retired, disabled, and survivors of deceased workers, and then hands the excess over to the U.S. government. The government, in turn, gives SSA IOUs in the form of U.S. Treasury bonds. The government spends the money on whatever it wants—whether that means building roads and schools, subsidizing tobacco crops, or buying bombs and fighting a war in some far off place.

Think of it this way: Suppose you are spending more money than you make, but you'd still like to spend more. You talk Aunt Mary into letting you take care of her purse, and you deposit some of her money in your bank account. If you don't count what you owe Aunt Mary, you have a surplus. The government simply does not count those huge IOUs that it owes the elderly. Instead, it reports a fake surplus to the public.

This arrangement is a politician's dream. Each month the government wipes the Social Security trust fund clean. Politicians grab the money and hand out the giant IOUs. And then they pretend that they haven't even spent it.

The Gramm-Rudman law, which was designed to limit the amount of federal debt, does *not* count the money that the government "borrows" from Social Security. It is as though the debt owed to Social Security does not exist—and to politicians it doesn't. To them, Social Security is a magical money machine—it produces billions from thin air. To politicians, those are just numbers on paper, not money that has been confiscated from workers.

As one analyst said, the Social Security trust fund isn't a fund and you shouldn't trust it (Sloan 2001).

for your Consideration

Here are two proposals to solve this problem.

1. Raise the retirement age to 70.
2. Keep the retirement age the same, but put what workers pay as Social Security taxes into their own individual retirement accounts. Most political proposals to do this lack controls to

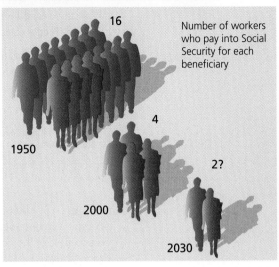

Figure 13.8 **Fewer Workers Supporting a Larger Number of Retirees and Disabled Workers**

Number of workers who pay into Social Security for each beneficiary

16
1950

4
2000

2?
2030

Source: By the author. Based on Social Security Administration; *Statistical Abstract* 2007:Tables 531 and 533.

dependency ratio the number of workers who are required to support one dependent person age 15 and younger or 65 and older make the new system work. Here are controls: A board, independent of the government, would select money managers to invest these accounts in real estate, stocks, and bonds—both foreign and domestic. Annually, the board would review the performance of the money managers, retaining those who do the best job and replacing the others. All investment results would be published, and individuals could select the management team that they prefer. People could not withdraw funds before retirement.

Think in terms of your own Social Security. Do you prefer to retain the current Social Security system? Do you prefer one of these two proposals? Neither is perfect. What problems might each have? Can you think of a better alternative?

Sources: Smith 1986; Smith 1987; Hardy 1991; Genetski 1993; Stevenson 1998, *Statistical Abstract* 2007. Government publications that list Social Security receipts as deficits can be found in *Monthly Treasury Statement of Receipts and Outlays,* the *Winter Treasury Bulletin,* and the *Statement of Liabilities and Other Financial Commitments of the United States Government.*

Figure 13.9 below shows how medical costs for the elderly have soared. This, too, has become a major social controversy, and like gasoline poured on a bonfire, these medical costs will fuel the coming intergenerational battle. The point I want to make here, however, is how greatly the condition of the elderly improved as the government transferred resources to the elderly. On Figure 13.10, you can trace their declining rate of poverty.

As you look at Figure 13.10, trace the path of poverty of U.S. children. Notice how it increased from 1967 until the early 1990s, fell during the 1990s, and is again on the rise.

Figure 13.9 Health Care Costs for the Elderly and Disabled

Medicare is intended for the elderly and disabled, Medicaid for the poor. About 24 percent of Medicaid payments ($55 billion) go to the elderly (*Statistical Abstract* 2007:Table 138).

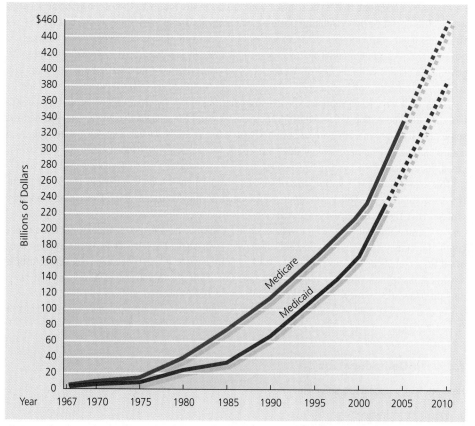

Note: Broken lines indicate the author's projections.

Source: By the author. Based on *Statistical Abstract,* various years, and 2007:Tables 135, 138.

Figure 13.10 **Trends in Poverty**

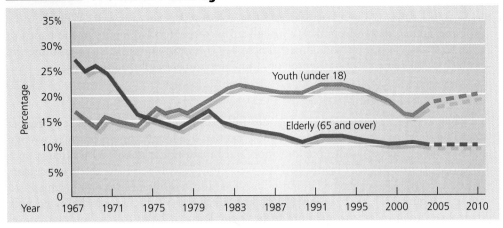

Source: By the author. *Statistical Abstract,* various years, and 2007:Table 694. Broken lines indicate the author's projections.

Some analysts have suggested that the decline in the elderly's rate of poverty came at the expense of the nation's children. Conflict sociologists Meredith Minkler and Ann Robertson (1991) pointed out how misleading this comparison is. Would anyone say that the money the government gives to flood victims comes from the children? Or to build highways? Of course not. Politicians make choices about where to spend taxes, and, if they want to they can increase spending to relieve the poverty of *both* the elderly and children.

As conflict theorists point out, framing the issue as a case of money going to one group at the expense of another group can divide the working class. To get working-class people to think that they must choose between pathetic children and suffering old folks can splinter them into opposing groups, breaking their power to work together to improve society.

Fighting Back

Some organizations work to protect the hard-won gains of the elderly. Let's consider two.

The Gray Panthers   The Gray Panthers, who claim 20,000 members, are aware that the working class can be split along age lines (Gray Panthers n.d.). This organization, founded in 1970 by Margaret Kuhn (1905–1995), encourages people of all ages to work for the welfare of both the old and the young. On the micro level, the goal is to develop positive self-concepts (Kuhn 1990). On the macro level, the goal is to build a base so broad that it can challenge institutions that oppress the poor, whatever their age, and fight attempts to pit people against one another along age lines. One indication of their effectiveness is that Gray Panthers frequently testify before congressional committees concerning pending legislation.

The American Association of Retired Persons   The AARP also combats negative images of the elderly. With 35 million members, this organization is politically powerful. It monitors federal and state legislation and mobilizes its members to act on issues affecting their welfare. A statement of displeasure about some proposed law from the AARP can trigger tens of thousands of telephone calls, telegrams, letters, and e-mails from irate elderly citizens. To protect their chances of reelection, politicians try not to cross swords with the AARP. As you can expect, critics claim that this organization is too powerful, that it muscles its way to claim more than its share of the nation's resources.

All of this helps to prove our point, say conflict theorists. Age groups are just one of society's many groups that are struggling for scarce resources, and conflict is the inevitable result.

Before we close this chapter, let's look at problems of dependency and the sociology of death and dying.

Recurring Problems

"When I get old, will I be able to take care of myself? Will I become frail and unable to get around? Will I end up in some nursing home, in the hands of strangers who don't care about me?" These are common concerns. Let's examine the problems that some elderly face: isolation, nursing homes, abuse, and poverty.

Gender and Old Age

In Chapter 11, we examined how gender influences our lives. The impact of gender doesn't stop when we get old. Because most women live longer than most men, women are more likely to experience the loneliness and isolation that widowhood often brings. This is one implication of Figure 13.11, which shows how much more likely women are to be widowed. This difference in mortality also leads to different living arrangements in old age. Figure 13.12 shows how much more likely elderly men are to be living with their wives than elderly women are to be living with their husbands. Another consequence is that most patients in nursing homes are women.

Before we review nursing homes, I think you will enjoy reading the Down-to-Earth Sociology box on the next page. It will give you a glimpse of some of the variety that exists among the elderly, as well as how people carry gender roles into old age.

Nursing Homes

In one nursing home, the nurses wrote in the patient's chart that she had a foot lesion. She actually had gangrene and maggots in her wounds (Rhone 2001). In another nursing home—supposedly a premier retirement home in Southern California—a woman suffered a stroke in her room. Her "caretakers" didn't discover her condition for 15 hours. She didn't survive. (Morin 2001)

Although most elderly are cared for by their families, a million and a half Americans age 65 and over are in nursing homes. This comes to about 4 percent of the nation's elderly (*Statistical Abstract* 2007:Tables 11, 161). Some patients return home after only a few weeks or a few months. Others die after a short stay. Overall, about one half of elderly women and one-third of elderly men spend at least some time in nursing homes.

Figure 13.11 Of Those Who Have Ever Married, Who Is Widowed?

Source: By the author. Based on *Statistical Abstract* 2007:Table 38.

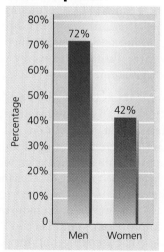

Figure 13.12 The Elderly Who Live with a Spouse

Source: By the author. Based on *Statistical Abstract* 2007:Table 38.

Feisty to the End: Gender Roles Among the Elderly

THIS IMAGE OF MY FATHER makes me laugh— not because he was arrested as an old man, but, rather, because of the events that led to his arrest. My dad had always been a colorful character, ready with endless, ribald jokes and a hearty laugh. He carried these characteristics into his old age.

My dad, in his late 70s, was living in a small apartment in a complex for the elderly in Minnesota. The adjacent building was a nursing home, the next destination for the residents of these apartments. None of them liked to think about this "home," because no one survived it—yet they all knew what was in store for them. Under the watchful eye of these elderly neighbors, care in the nursing home was fairly good. Until they were transferred to this unwelcome last stopping-place, life went on "as usual" in the complex for the elderly.

According to the police report and my dad's account, here is what happened:

> Dad was sitting in the downstairs lounge with other residents, waiting for the mail to arrive, a daily ritual that the residents looked forward to. For some reason known only to my dad, he hooked his cane under the dress of an elderly woman, lifted up her skirt, and laughed. Understandably, this upset her husband, who was standing next to her. Angry, the man moved toward my father, threatening him.
>
> I say "moved," rather than "lunged," because this man was using a walker. My dad started to run away from this threat. Actually, "run" isn't quite the right word. "Hobbled" would be a better term.

During their elderly years, men and women continue to exhibit aspects of the gender roles that they learned and played in their younger years.

My dad fled as fast as he could using his cane, while this other man pursued him as fast as he could using his walker. Wheezing, puffing, and panting as they went from the lounge into the long adjoining hall, the two paused to catch their breath now and then. Tiring the most, the other man gave up the pursuit. He then called the police.

When the police officer arrived, he said, "Uncle Marv, I'm sorry, but I'm going to have to arrest you." (This event occurred in a small town, and the officer assigned this case turned out to be dad's nephew.)

Dad went before a judge, who could hardly keep a straight face. He gave dad a small fine and warned him to behave himself. The apartment manager also gave dad a warning: One more incident, and he would have to move out of the complex.

Dad's wife wasn't too happy about the situation, either.

This event was brought to mind by a newspaper account of a fight that broke out at the food bar of a retirement home ("Melee Breaks" . . . 2004). It seems that one elderly man criticized the way another man was picking through the salad. When a fight broke out between the two, several elderly people were hurt as they tried either to intervene or to flee.

for your Consideration

People carry their personalities, values, and other traits into old age. Part of these characteristics are gender roles. What examples of gender roles do you see in the events related here? Are you familiar with how old people continue to show their femininity or masculinity?

Nursing home residents are *not typical* of the elderly. Most (52 percent) are age 85 or older. Those in nursing homes are likely to be widowed, or never to have married, leaving them without family to take care of them. Most are in such poor health that they need help even to go to the bathroom or to use the telephone. Over 90 percent are in wheelchairs or have to use walkers (*Statistical Abstract* 2005:Table 172).

Understaffing, Dehumanization, and Death It is difficult to say good things about nursing homes. The literature on nursing homes, both popular and scientific, is filled with horror stories of neglected and abused patients. With events like those in the quotation that opens this section, Congress ordered a national study of nursing homes. The researchers found that in nursing homes that are understaffed, patients are more likely to have bedsores and to be malnourished, underweight, and dehydrated. *Ninety percent* of nursing homes are understaffed (Pear 2002).

It is easy to see why nursing homes are understaffed. Who—if he or she has a choice—works for poverty-level wages in a place that smells of urine, where you have to clean up feces, and where you are surrounded by dying people? Forty to 100 percent of nursing home staff quit each year (DeFrancis 2002).

The residents of nursing homes are not typical of the elderly. They are older, their health is worse, and most of them are more isolated.

Even the few nursing homes with adequate staff have a tendency to strip away human dignity. Here is how a paralyzed woman was treated in one of the *better* nursing homes, as reported by her daughter:

> Another highly disconcerting and recurring event in Mama's life took place whenever she had to be transferred. In medical settings, to "transfer" someone is to move an immobilized person from one conveyance to another—from bed to geri-chair or wheelchair, from chair to toilet, etc., and back again. . . . Mama often screamed when she was being transferred, a habit that rattled many of her aides. . . . To . . . limit the possibility of injury, there is an approved procedure for moving dependent residents. Two aides or nurses lift the resident along four points—the two armpits and the backs of the two knees—so that the person's weight is evenly distributed. In Mama's case, she was often transferred, whether by one aide or two, by lifting her up by her armpits only. . . . I tried constantly to get the aides to use their other hand to support Mama beneath her knees. Trying to motivate them, I pointed out that Mama surely wouldn't cry out so much if they used this method, but with each subsequent visit I would see that the aides had reverted to their armpit-only transfer. Considering that Mama was probably transferred between bed and chair an average of 6 times a day, 365 days a year, it was quite an ordeal for her to endure. . . .
>
> Mama's skin had gotten as thin as an old shirt that's been worn and washed so many times it has become transparent and easily torn. Yet, the aides would take a terry washcloth, coarse from heavy bleaching, and scrub her as though she had been digging ditches all day. Although stimulating the skin is beneficial, their methods looked excessive. When I suggested that mama didn't need such vigorous bathing, they humored me and washed her more gently; but I had no doubt that as soon as I wasn't available to monitor them, they returned to doing it their way. (Loucks 2002:183–184)

We can add that this type of callous care doesn't come cheap. Nursing homes are big business. They have over a million employees and bring in $80 billion a year (*Statistical Abstract* 2007:Tables 149, 161).

But all the criticisms of nursing homes pale in comparison with this finding: Compared with the elderly who have similar health conditions but remain home, those who go to nursing homes tend to get sicker and to die sooner (Wolinsky et al. 1997). This is a remarkable finding. Could it be, then, that a function of nursing homes is to dispose of the frail and unwanted elderly? If so, could we consider nursing homes the Western equivalent of the Tiwi's practice of "covering up," which we reviewed in the chapter's opening vignette?

Technology and Nursing Homes   You probably are aware of how important social interaction is for your well-being. The same is true for the elderly. Isolation can lead to their mental and physical deterioration. Researchers have found that an active social life helps to prevent the deterioration of the brain that can lead to Alzheimer's and Parkinson's diseases. Social isolation is not the cause of these brain conditions—which can strike anyone—but people who are socially isolated are more likely to come down with them (Ross 2000).

Social activity comes in many forms. Some residents of nursing homes find that the computer and Internet help them overcome isolation, loneliness, and depression. Sending and receiving e-mail helps them to keep in contact with relatives and friends, who may be dispersed throughout the country, and, in our emerging global society, throughout the world. With our capacity for video e-mail, this will become an even more important element in their mental and social well-being.

A New Model   There is nothing inherently bad about nursing homes that makes them places to be feared. It is their current arrangement that nurtures abuse—the relative isolation of the elderly in these homes and the presence of a harried, overworked staff. With this in mind, a new model is being developed. In what is called the Green House Project, elderly people who are able to take care of themselves at least partially live in a home-like setting. Instead of a sterile hallway lined with rooms, about ten residents live in a carpeted ranch-style house. There, they share meals at a communal dining table. They are even encouraged to cook together in an open kitchen.

Initial results are encouraging, for this setting fosters a sense of community among residents and staff. With a smaller staff, the annual cost is about the same as care in the standard nursing home—about $58,000 per person, paid mostly by Medicaid and Medicare (Hamilton 2005).

Elder Abuse

Stories of elder abuse abound—and so does the abuse itself. In interviews with a random sample of nursing home staff, 17 percent admitted that during the preceding year they had pushed, grabbed, or shoved a resident. Half (51 percent) reported that they had yelled at a resident in anger (Pillemer and Hudson 1993). Other studies report similar results ("National Ombudsman . . ." 2003). Most abuse of the elderly,

however, takes place not in nursing homes but at home. Most abusers are not paid staff, but family members, who hit, verbally and emotionally abuse, or financially exploit their aged relatives (Pillemer and Wolf 1987; Shellenbarger 2003). The most likely abuser is an adult child (Teaster et al. 2006).

Why do adult children, spouses, and other relatives abuse their own elderly? Sociologists Karl Pillemer and Jill Suitor (1992) interviewed more than 200 people who were caring for family members who suffered from Alzheimer's disease. One husband told them,

> Frustration reaches a point where patience gives out. I've never struck her, but sometimes I wonder if I can control myself. . . . This is . . . the part of her care that causes me the frustration and the loss of patience. What I tell her, she doesn't register. Like when I tell her, "You're my wife." "You're crazy," she says.

From this husband's statement, we can glean some insight into the stress that comes with caring for a person who is dependent, demanding, and uncomprehending. Since most people who care for the elderly undergo stress but are not violent toward those they care for, however, we do not have the answer to why some caregivers become violent. For this, we must await future research.

More important than understanding the causes of abuse, however, is preventing the elderly from being abused in the first place. There is little that can be done about abuse at home—except to enforce current laws when abuse comes to the attention of authorities. For nursing home workers, however, we can require background checks to screen out people who have been convicted of robbery, rape, and other violence. This is similar to requiring background checks of preschool workers in order to screen out people who have been convicted of molesting children. Such laws are only a first step to solving this problem. They will not prevent abuse, only avoid the obvious.

In old age, as in all other stages of the life course, people find life more pleasant if they have friends and enough money to meet their needs. How do you think that an elderly man who lives by himself in a rundown camper finds life? How about women who can afford to go to a "beauty shop" once a week and who cycles with friends of many years? While neither welcomes old age, you can see what a difference social factors make in how people experience this time of life.

The Elderly Poor

Many elderly live in nagging fear of poverty. Since they do not know how long they will live, nor how much inflation there will be, they fear that they will outlive their savings. How

Figure 13.13 Gender and Poverty in Old Age

The percentage of Americans aged 65 and older who are poor

Men 7.0%
Women 12.0%

Source: By the author. Based on *Statistical Abstract* 2007:Table 38.

Figure 13.14 Race-Ethnicity and Poverty in Old Age

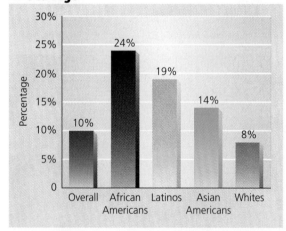

Overall 10%
African Americans 24%
Latinos 19%
Asian Americans 14%
Whites 8%

Source: By the author. Based on *Statistical Abstract* 2007:Table 694.

realistic is this fear? Statistics don't apply to any individual case, but they help us to understand how earlier social patterns carry over to the elderly as a group.

Gender and Poverty   As reviewed in Chapter 11, during their working years most women earn less than men. Figure 13.13 shows that this pattern follows women and men into their old age. As you can see, elderly women are about 70 percent more likely than elderly men to be poor.

Race–Ethnicity and Poverty   As we reviewed earlier, Social Security has successfully lifted most elderly Americans out of poverty, and today's elderly are less likely than the average American to be poor. There is poverty among the elderly, of course, and it follows the racial-ethnic patterns of the general society. From Figure 13.14, you can see how much less likely elderly whites and Asian Americans are to be poor than are African Americans and Latinos.

The Sociology of Death and Dying

How does culture shape the ways that we experience death? It is especially interesting how we use linguistic masks to try to distance ourselves from death. We have constructed an elaborate language of avoidance, ways to refer to death without using the word itself. Instead of dead, we use terms such as "gone," "passed on," "no longer with us," and "at peace now." We don't have space to explore this characteristic of social life, but we can take a brief look at why sociologists emphasize that, like old age, dying is more than a biological event. Let's look at death and dying, a fascinating subfield of sociology.

Industrialization and the New Technology

Before industrialization, death was no stranger. Because life was short, *most* children saw a sibling or parent die (Blauner 1966). The family took care of the sick at home, and the sick died at home. As noted in Chapter 1 (page 28), the family even prepared corpses for burial. Industrialization brought about drastic changes. Now that the process of dying has been placed in the hands of professionals in hospitals, death has become strange and alien to most of us. Dying now takes place behind closed doors—isolated, remote, and managed by strangers.

Not only did new technologies remove the dying from our presence but they also created *technological life*—a form of existence that lies between life and death, but is neither (Cerulo and Ruane 1996). The "brain dead" in our hospitals have no self. Their "person" is gone—dead—yet our technology keeps the body alive. This muddles the boundary between life and death, which used to seem so certain.

For most of us, however, that boundary will remain firm, and we will face a definite death. Some of us will even learn in advance that we will die shortly. If so, how are we likely to cope with this knowledge? Let's look at what researchers have found.

Death as a Process

Psychologist Elisabeth Kübler-Ross (1969/1981) studied how people cope during the *living-dying interval,* that period between discovering they are going to die soon and death itself. After interviewing people who had been informed that they had an incurable disease, she concluded that people who come face to face with their own death go through five stages:

1. *Denial.* At first, people cannot believe that they are going to die. ("The doctor must have made a mistake. Those test results can't be right.") They avoid the topic of death and situations that remind them of it.
2. *Anger.* After a while, they acknowledge that they are going to die, but they view their death as unjust. ("I didn't do anything to deserve this. So-and-so is much worse than I am, and he's in good health. It isn't right that I should die.")
3. *Negotiation.* Next, the individual tries to get around death by making a bargain with God, with fate, or even with the disease itself. ("I need one more Thanksgiving with my family. I never appreciated them as much as I should have. After Thanksgiving, I'll be ready.")
4. *Depression.* During this stage, people become resigned to their death, but they grieve because their life is about to end, and they have no power to change the course of events.
5. *Acceptance.* In this final stage, people come to terms with their impending death. They put their affairs in order—make wills, pay bills, instruct their children to take care of the surviving parent. They also express regret at not having done certain things when they had the chance. Devout Christians are likely to talk about the hope of salvation and their desire to be in heaven with Jesus.

Dying is more individualized than this model indicates. Not everyone, for example, tries to make bargains. What is important sociologically is that *death is a process,* not just an event. People who expect to die soon face a reality quite different from the one experienced by those of us who expect to be alive years from now. Their impending death powerfully affects their thinking and behavior. Let me share an intimate event from my own life.

When my mother was informed that she had inoperable cancer, she immediately went into a vivid stage of denial. If she later went through anger or negotiation, she kept it to herself. After a short depression, she experienced a longer period of questioning why this was happening to her. She then moved quickly into stage 5, which occurred very much as Kübler-Ross described it.

After her funeral, my two brothers and I went to her apartment, as she had instructed us. There, to our surprise, attached to each item in every room—from the bed and the television to the boxes of dishes and knickknacks—was a piece of masking tape with one of our names on it. At first we found this strange. We knew she was an orderly person, but to this extent? As we sorted through her things, reflecting on why she had given certain items to whom, we began to appreciate the "closure" she had given to this aspect of her material life.

Hospices

What a change. In earlier generations, life was short, and people took death at an early age for granted. Today, we take it for granted that most people will see old age. Due to advances in medical technology and better public health practices, *most* deaths in the United States (about 75 percent) occur after age 65. People want to die with dignity, in the comforting presence of friends and relatives, but hospitals, to put the matter bluntly, are awkward places in which to die. There people experience what sociologists call *institutional death*—they die surrounded by strangers in formal garb, in sterile rooms filled with machines, in an organization that puts its routines ahead of patients' needs.

Hospices emerged as a way to reduce the emotional and physical burden of dying—and to lower the costs of death. Hospices are built around the idea that the people who are dying and their families should control the process of dying. The term **hospice** originally referred to a place, but now it generally refers to home care. Services are brought into a dying person's home—from counseling to such basic help as providing babysitters or driving the person to a doctor or lawyer. During the course of a year, about 600,000 people are in hospice care in the United States. The average stay before death is short, and at any one time about 100,000 people are in hospices (*Statistical Abstract* 2006:Table 171).

Whereas hospitals are dedicated to prolonging life, hospices are dedicated to providing dignity in death and making people comfortable during the *living-dying interval.* In the hospital, the focus is on the patient; in the hospice, the focus switches to both the dying

hospice a place (or services brought to someone's home) for the purpose of giving comfort and dignity to a dying person

person and his or her friends and family. In the hospital, the goal is to make the patient well; in the hospice, it is to relieve pain and suffering. In the hospital, the primary concern is the individual's physical welfare; in the hospice, although medical needs are met, the primary concern is the individual's social—and in some instances, spiritual—well-being.

Suicide and Age

We noted in Chapter 1 how Durkheim stressed that suicide has a *social* base. Suicide, he said, is much more than an individual act. Each country, for example, has its own suicide rate, which remains quite stable year after year. In the United States, we can predict that 31,000 people will commit suicide this year. If we are off by more than 1,000, it would be a surprise. As we saw in Figure 1.1 (page 13), we can also predict that Americans will choose firearms as the most common way to kill themselves, and that hanging will come in second. We can also be certain that this year more men than women will kill themselves, and more people in their 60s than in their 20s. It is this way year after year.

Statistics often fly in the face of the impressions we get from the mass media, and here we have such an example. Although the suicides of young people are given much publicity, such deaths are relatively rare. The suicide rate of adolescents is *lower* than that of adults of any age. Because adolescents have such a low death rate, however, suicide does rank as their third leading cause of death—after accidents and homicide. The highest suicide rate is that of people age 85 and over (*Statistical Abstract* 2007:Tables 11, 110, 111).

These findings on suicide are an example of the primary sociological point stressed throughout this text: Recurring patterns of human behavior—whether education, marriage, work, crime, use of the Internet, or even suicide—represent underlying social forces. Consequently, if no basic change takes place in the social conditions under which the groups that make up U.S. society live, you can expect these same patterns of suicide to prevail five to ten years from now.

Adjusting to Death

The feelings that people experience after the death of a loved one often surprise them. Along with grief and loneliness, they may feel guilt, anger, or even relief. During the period of mourning that follows, usually one or two years, the family members come to terms with the death. In addition to sorting out their feelings, they also reorganize their family system to deal with the absence of the person who was so important to it.

In general, when death is expected, family members find it less stressful. They have begun to cope with the coming death by managing a series of smaller losses, including the person's inability to fulfill his or her usual roles or to do specific tasks. They also have been able to say a series of goodbyes to their loved one. In contrast, unexpected deaths—accidents, suicides, and murders—bring greater emotional shock. The family members have had no time to get used to the idea that the individual is going to die. One moment, the person is there; the next, he or she is gone. The sudden death gave them no chance to say goodbye or to bring any form of "closure" to their relationship.

Looking Toward the Future

Let's not lose sight of one of the major changes stressed in this chapter—that for the first time in human history huge numbers of people are becoming elderly. It is inevitable that such a fundamental change will have a powerful impact on society, so much so that it might even transform them. We don't have space to explore such potential transformations, which are only speculative at the moment, so let's try to catch a glimpse of what is happening with the elderly themselves.

A New Model of Aging

As huge numbers of Americans move into old age, the elderly have begun not only to challenge the demeaning stereotypes of the aged but also to develop new models of aging. These new approches build on the idea that old age should not be viewed as

As discussed in the text, the number of elderly people is increasing, and older people are making up a larger proportion of our population. Because of medical advances and better nutrition, millions of the elderly enjoy good health. Rather than being considered a sequel to ill health and death, older age is being redefined as a period of opportunity to pursue interests and develop talents that provide new perspectives and a continued sense of satisfaction with life.

"a-time-next-to-death," but, rather, as a new period of life, one with its specific challenges, to be sure, but also one to be enjoyed, even celebrated. This new time of life provides unique opportunities to develop one's creativity and to enhance the appreciation of one's humanity. Let's look at how this new model is being applied.

Creative Aging   The change began in the 1970s. As larger numbers of people became elderly, many said that having endless amounts of leisure time was not their idea of how to enjoy being old. Pioneering the view that old age is a time to embark on new learning, they promoted free, space-available, non-credit attendance at colleges and universities, group travel to historical sites around the world, and the writing of memoirs about the past.

In the second phase, which we are just entering, emphasis is being placed on mental growth and enhancing people's creative abilities. An example is "The Colony," a retirement home in Hollywood, where the emphasis is on the arts. There, residents write plays and perform them, make sculptures, write and record songs, paint, and write novels (Brown 2006). Some residents, who did none of these things in their preretirement life, have become so good that they perform on radio and television.

This approach to aging is new, so we don't know the directions it will take. But if this emphasis continues, it will change how the younger generations view the elderly—as well as the elderly's image of themselves. The stereotype of despondent, disengaged old people might even be replaced with a stereotype of robust, engaged, thriving older adults (Manheimer 2005). We need to keep in mind that the views and conditions of aging are not universal. Not only will cultural differences remain but so will differences of social class. "The Colony," for example, is directed toward the middle class. It seems certain that the poor, with their fewer resources, will not be affected as directly by creative aging.

The Impact of Technology

Throughout this text, we have examined some of the deep impacts that technology is having on our lives. To close this chapter, I would like you to reflect on how technological breakthroughs might affect your own life as you grow older.

Thinking Critically

How Long Do You Want to Live? Approaching Methuselah

Would you like to live to 200? To 500? To 1,000?

Such a question may strike you as absurd. But with our new and still developing technology, science may stretch the life span to limits unheard of since biblical days.

We are just at the beginning stages of genetic engineering, and ahead of us may lie a brave new world. Predictions are that technicians will be able to snip out our bad DNA and replace it with more compliant bits. The caps at the ends of our chromosomes, the telomeres, shrink as we age, causing the cells to die. An enzyme called telomerase may be able to modify this process, allowing cells to reproduce many more times than they currently are able to (Demidov 2005).

By manipulating genes, scientists have already been able to extend the life span of worms by six times. Humans have these same genes. A human life span six times longer than what we now have would take the longest living people to over 600 (Chase 2003). We are only peering over the edge of the future, glimpsing what might be possible. Some optimistic geneticists predict that some people will live 1,000 years or longer (Gorman 2003; Vincent 2006).

Some geneticists say that we should think of our body as being like a house (Gorman 2003). A house keeps standing, not because it is built to last forever, but because people keep repairing it. This is what science will allow us to do with our bodies. In the future, we will grow spare body parts. From the same stem cells will come livers, hearts, kidneys, fingers. As parts of our body wear out, we'll simply replace them with new ones.

In grade school, many of us heard stories about Ponce de Leon, an explorer from Spain who searched for the fountain of youth. He eventually "discovered" Florida, but the fountain of youth eluded him. In our perpetual search for immortality, could we be discovering what eluded Ponce de Leon?

for your Consideration

Let's assume that biomedical science does stretch the human life span, that living to be 150 or 200 becomes common. If people retire at age 65, how could society afford to support them for 100 years or so? People can't work much past 70, for—and this may be the basic flaw in this brave new world scenario—even with new body parts, the world would not be filled with 200-year-olds who functioned as though they were 25. They would be very old people, subject to the diseases and debilities that come with advanced age. If Medicare costs are bulging at the seams now, what would they be like in such a world?

Finally, how would you answer this question: Is the real issue how we can live longer, or how we can live better? Because of medical advances, public health, and better nutrition, millions of the elderly enjoy good health. Rather than being considered a sequel to ill health and death, older age is being redefined as a period of opportunity to pursue interests and develop talents that provide new perspectives and a continued sense of satisfaction with life.

Summary *and* Review

Aging in Global Perspective

How are the elderly treated around the world?

No single set of attitudes, beliefs, or policies regarding the aged characterizes the world's nations. Rather, they vary from exclusion and killing to integration and honor. The global trend is for more people to live longer. P. 372.

What does the social construction of aging mean?

Nothing in the nature of aging summons forth any particular set of attitudes. Rather, attitudes toward the elderly are rooted in society and differ from one social group to another. Pp. 372–373.

What does the phrase "graying of America" mean?

The phrase **graying of America** refers to the growing percentage of Americans who reach old age. The costs of Social Security and health care for the elderly have become major social issues. Pp. 373–376.

The Symbolic Interactionist Perspective

What factors influence perceptions of aging?

Symbolic interactionists stress that aging is socially constructed. That is, no age has any particular built-in meaning; rather, we use cultural cues to define age. Four factors influence when people label themselves as "old": biological changes, biographical events, **gender age,** and cultural timetables. Cross-cultural comparisons demonstrate how culture shapes the ways that people experience aging. **Ageism,** negative reactions to the elderly, is based on stereotypes. Pp. 376–380.

The Functionalist Perspective

How is retirement functional for society?

Functionalists focus on how the withdrawal of the elderly from positions of responsibility benefits society. **Disengagement theory** examines retirement as a device for ensuring that a society's positions of responsibility will be passed smoothly from one generation to the next. **Activity theory** examines how people adjust when they disengage from productive roles. **Continuity theory** focuses on how people adjust to growing old by continuing their roles and coping techniques. Pp. 380–382.

The Conflict Perspective

Is there conflict among different age groups?

Social Security legislation is an example of one generation making demands on another generation for limited resources. As the number of retired people grows, there are relatively fewer workers to support them. The Social Security Trust Fund may be a gigantic fraud perpetrated by the power elite on the nation. Organizations such as the Gray Panthers and the AARP watch out for the interests of the elderly. Pp. 382–387.

Recurring Problems

What are some of the problems that today's elderly face?

Women are more likely to live alone and to be poor. At any one time, about 4 percent of the elderly live in nursing homes. Nursing homes are understaffed, and patients are sometimes neglected and dehumanized. The most common abusers of the elderly are members of their own family. Poverty in old age, greatly reduced through government programs, reflects the gender and racial-ethnic patterns of poverty in the general society. Pp. 388–392.

The Sociology of Death and Dying

How does culture affect the way we experience death and dying?

Like old age, death is much more than a biological event. Industrialization brought with it modern medicine, hospitals—and dying in a formal setting surrounded by strangers. Kübler-Ross identified five stages in the dying process, which, though insightful, do not characterize all people. **Hospices** are a cultural device designed to overcome the negative aspects of dying in hospitals. Suicide shows distinct patterns by age, sex, and method. Pp. 392–394.

Looking Toward the Future

What technological developments can be a wild card in social planning for the aged?

A major change is to view old age as a time of creativity. If this trend continues, it will transform the image of the elderly. Technological breakthroughs may stretch the human **life span.** If so, it is difficult to see how younger workers would be able to support retired people for 100 years or so. Pp. 394–396.

Thinking Critically
about Chapter 13

1. How does culture influence people's ideas about the elderly and when old age begins? Can you identify cultural changes that are likely to affect our own perceptions of the onset of old age and of the elderly?

2. How do the functionalist and conflict perspectives on the elderly differ?

3. If you were appointed to head the U.S. Department of Health and Human Services, how would you improve the nation's nursing homes?

Additional Resources

What can you use MySocLab for? www.mysoclab.com

- **Study and Review:** Pre- and Post-Tests, Practice Tests, Flash Cards, Individualized Study Plans.

- **Current Events:** *Sociology in the News,* the daily *New York Times,* and more.

- **Research and Writing:** *Research Navigator, Writing About Sociology,* and more.

Where Can I Read More on This Topic?

Suggested readings for this chapter are listed at the back of this book.

The Economy

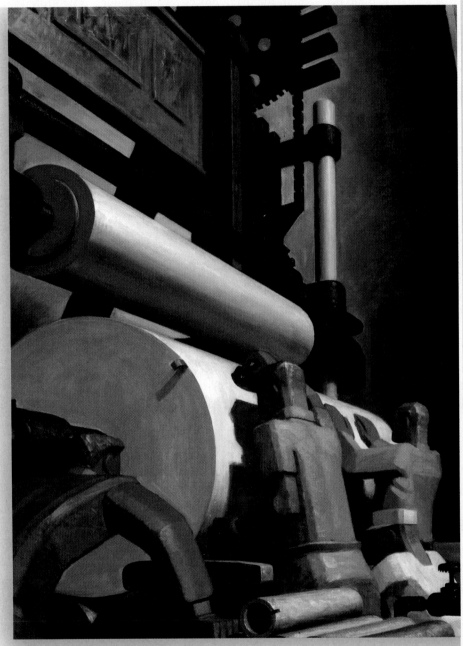

Douglass Crockwell, *Paperworkers*, 1934

If you are like most students, you are wondering how changes in the economy are going to affect your chances of getting a good job. Let's see if we can shed some light on this question. We'll begin with this story:

The sound of her alarm rang in Kim's ears. "Not Monday already," she groaned. "There must be a better way of starting the week." She pressed the snooze button on the clock (from Germany) to sneak another ten minutes' sleep. In what seemed like just thirty seconds, the alarm shrilly insisted that she get up and face the week.

Still bleary-eyed after her shower, Kim peered into her closet and picked out a silk blouse (from China), a plaid wool skirt (from Scotland), and leather shoes (from India). She nodded, satisfied, as she added a pair of simulated pearls (from Taiwan). Running late, she hurriedly ran a brush (from Mexico) through her hair. As Kim wolfed down a bowl of cereal (from the United States) topped with milk (from the United States), bananas (from Costa Rica), and sugar (from the Dominican Republic), she turned on her kitchen television (from Korea) to listen to the weather forecast.

She said to herself, "If people were more like me, this country would be in better shape."

Gulping the last of her coffee (from Brazil), Kim grabbed her briefcase (from Wales), purse (from Spain), and jacket (from Malaysia), left her house, and quickly climbed into her car (from Japan). As she glanced at her watch (from Switzerland), she hoped that the traffic would be in her favor. She muttered to herself as she pulled up at a stoplight (from Great Britain) and eyed her gas gauge. She muttered again when she pulled into a station and paid for gas (from Saudi Arabia), for the price had risen over the weekend. "My paycheck never keeps up with prices," she moaned.

When Kim arrived at work, she found the office abuzz. Six months ago, New York headquarters had put the company up for sale, but there had been no takers. The big news was that both a German company and a Canadian company had put in bids over the weekend. No one got much work done that day, as the whole office speculated about how things might change.

As Kim walked to the parking lot after work, she saw a tattered "Buy American" bumper sticker on the car next to hers. "That's right," she said to herself. "If people were more like me, this country would be in better shape."

The Transformation of Economic Systems

Although this vignette may be slightly exaggerated, many of us are like Kim: We use a multitude of products from around the world, and yet we're concerned about our country's ability to compete in global markets. Today's **economy**—our system of producing and distributing goods and services—differs radically from the economies of all but our most recent past. The products that Kim uses make it apparent that today's economy knows no national boundaries. To better understand how global forces affect the U.S. economy—and your life—let's begin with an overview of sweeping historical changes.

Preindustrial Societies: The Birth of Inequality

The earliest human groups, *hunting and gathering societies,* had a **subsistence economy.** In small groups of about twenty-five to forty, people lived off the land. They gathered plants and hunted animals in one location, and then moved to another place as these sources of food ran low. Because these people had few possessions, they did little trading with one another. With no excess to accumulate, as was mentioned in Chapter 6, everybody owned as much (or, really, as little) as everyone else.

Then people discovered how to breed animals and cultivate plants. The more dependable food supply in what became *pastoral and horticultural societies* allowed humans to settle down in a single place. Human groups grew larger, and for the first time in history, it was no longer necessary for everyone to work at producing food. Some people became leather workers, others weapon makers, and so on. This new division of labor produced a surplus, and groups traded items with one another. The primary sociological significance of surplus and trade is this: They fostered *social inequality,* for some people accumulated more possessions than others. The effects of that change remain with us today.

The plow brought the next major change, ushering in *agricultural societies.* Plowed land was much more productive, allowing even more people to specialize in activities other than producing food. More specialized divisions of labor followed, and trade expanded. Trading centers then developed, which turned into cities. As power passed from the heads of families and clans to a ruling elite, social, political, and economic inequality grew.

The common-sense meaning of market is a place where people exchange or buy and sell goods. Such old-fashioned markets remain common in the Least Industrialized Nations, such as this one in Guatemala. Here people find the social interaction every bit as rewarding as the goods and money that they exchange.

Industrial Societies: The Birth of the Machine

The steam engine, invented in 1765, ushered in *industrial societies*. Based on machines powered by fuels, these societies created a surplus unlike anything the world had seen. This, too, stimulated trade among nations and brought even greater social inequality. A handful of individuals opened factories and exploited the labor of many.

Then came more efficient machines. As the surpluses grew even greater, the emphasis gradually changed—from producing goods to consuming them. In 1912, sociologist Thorstein Veblen coined the term **conspicuous consumption** to describe this fundamental change in people's orientations. By this term, Veblen meant that the Protestant ethic identified by Weber—an emphasis on hard work, savings, and a concern for salvation (discussed on page 180)—was being replaced by an eagerness to show off wealth by the "elaborate consumption of goods."

Postindustrial Societies: The Birth of the Information Age

In 1973, sociologist Daniel Bell noted that *a new type of society was emerging*. This new society, which he called the *postindustrial society*, has six characteristics: (1) a service sector so large that *most* people work in it; (2) a vast surplus of goods; (3) even more extensive trade among nations; (4) a wider variety and quantity of goods available to the average person; (5) an information explosion; and (6) a *global village*—that is, the world's nations are linked by fast communications, transportation, and trade.

Biotech Societies: The Merger of Biology and Economics

As we discussed in Chapter 6, we may be on the verge of yet another new type of society. This one is being ushered in by advances in biology, especially the deciphering of the human genome system. While the specifics of this new society have yet to unfold, the marriage of biology and economics should yield even greater surpluses and more extensive trade. The global village will continue to expand. The technological advances that will emerge in this new society may also allow us to lead longer and healthier lives. As history is our guide, it also may create even greater inequality between the rich and poor nations.

Implications for Your Life

The broad changes in societies that I have just sketched may seem to be abstract matters, but they are far from irrelevant to your life. Whenever society changes, so do our lives. Consider the information explosion. When you graduate from college, you will most likely do some form of "knowledge work." Instead of working in a factory, you will manage information or design, sell, or service products. The type of work you do has profound implications for your life. It produces social networks, nurtures attitudes, and even affects how you view yourself and the world.

Consider how vastly different your perspectives on life would be if you were one of the children discussed in the Cultural Diversity box on the next page.

It is the same with the global village. Think of the globe as being divided into three neighborhoods—the three worlds of industrialization and postindustrialization that we reviewed in Chapter 9 (pages 251–258). Some nations are located in the poor part of the village. Their citizens barely eke out a living from menial work. Some even starve to death. In contrast, their fellow villagers in the rich neighborhood feast on the best that the globe has to offer. It's the same village, but what a difference the neighborhood makes.

Now visualize any one of the three neighborhoods. Again you will see gross inequalities. Not everyone who lives in the poor neighborhood is poor, and some areas of the rich neighborhood are packed with poor people. The United States is the global economic leader, occupying the most luxurious mansion in the best neighborhood and is spearheading the new biotech society.

conspicuous consumption Thorstein Veblen's term for a change from the Protestant ethic to an eagerness to show off wealth by the consumption of goods

The Child Workers

NINE-YEAR-OLD ALONE BANDA works in an abandoned quarry in Zambia. Using a bolt, he breaks rocks into powder. In a week, he makes enough powder to fill half a cement bag. Alone gets $3 for the half bag.

Three dollars doesn't sound like much, but without it he and his grandmother would starve to death.

It is still a slow death for Alone. Robbed of his childhood and breathing rock dust continuously, Alone is likely to come down with what his fellow quarry workers call a "heavy chest," an early sign of silicosis.

As the mothers of children—some as young as 7—who work at the quarry say, "If I feel pity for them, what are they going to eat?" (Wines 2006a)

In Ghana, 6-year-old Mark Kwadwo, who only weighs about 30 pounds, works for a fisherman. For up to 14 hours a day, seven days a week, he paddles a boat, and takes fish out of nets. Exhausted, he falls asleep at night in a little mud hut that he shares with five other boys.

Mark is still too little to dive, but he knows what is coming when he is older. His fear is that he will dive to free a tangled net—and never resurface.

If Mark doesn't paddle hard enough, or pull in the fish from a net fast enough, Takyi will hit him on the head with a paddle.

"I prefer to have older boys work for me," says Takyi, "but I can't afford them. That's why I go for these."

"I prefer to have my boy home with me," says the mother of Kwabena, whom she leased four years ago when Kwabena was 7, "but I need the money to survive." The fisherman has paid as promised. Kwabena's mother has received $66 for the four years' work (LaFraniere 2006).

Around the world, children are forced to work. Like Mark, some work in the fishing industry, and like Alone, some work in quarries. Others work on construction (see the photo on page 240). Still other children work as miners, pesticide sprayers, street vendors, and household servants. Children weave carpet in India, race camels in the Middle East, and, all over the world, children work as prostitutes.

One of the negative consequences of early industrialization in the West was the use of child labor. In the photo on the left, of the U.S. textile industry in the 1800s, you can see spindle boys at work in a Georgia cotton mill. Today's Least Industrialized Nations are experiencing the same negative consequence as they industrialize. The photo on the right shows boys at work in a contemporary textile factory in Varanas, India. About the only improvement is that the child workers in India are able to sit down as they exhaust their childhood.

The underlying cause of children working is poverty so severe that the few dollars the children bring in can make the difference between life and death. In Ghana, where Mark works on the fishing boat, two out of three people live on less than $1 a day (LaFraniere 2006).

Then, too, there is the cultural factor. The view of children in many parts of the world differs significantly from the one common in the West. Many cultures do not have the idea that children have the right to be educated and to be spared from adult burdens.

When prosperity comes, so will this perspective.

In the meantime, people do what they must to survive, even if that requires desperate measures.

for your Consideration

How do you think the Most Industrialized (and postindustrialized) Nations can help alleviate the suffering of child workers? Not all child workers are mistreated. Prior to industrialization, and for a period afterwards, having children work at hard jobs was also common in the West. Just because our economic system has changed, bringing with it different ideas of childhood and of the rights of children, what right do we have to impose our changed ideas on other nations?

in contrast, using an electronic form for the exchange. The value of an electronic gold account goes up or down depending on the price of gold. Because electronic gold is not issued by any national government, it does not represent the transfer of euros or dollars or any other currency. This makes electronic gold a non-national money that can be used by citizens of any government. Governments dislike the development of e-cash, in general, as the transactions bypass banks, making it difficult for governments to monitor the financial activities of their citizens. Electronic gold, however, poses a special threat, for it bypasses government-issued currencies entirely. Consequently, we can expect extensive legislation designed to allow governments to regain control over money.

World Economic Systems

Now that we have sketched the main historical changes in the means of exchange, let's compare capitalism and socialism, the two main economic systems in force today. This will help us to understand where the United States stands in the world economic order.

Capitalism

People who live in a capitalist society may not understand its basic tenets, even though they see them reflected in their local shopping malls and fast-food chains. Table 14.1 distills the many businesses of the United States down to their basic components. As you can see, **capitalism** has three essential features: (1) *private ownership of the means of production* (individuals own the land, machines, and factories); (2) *market competition* (competing with one another, the owners decide what to produce and set the prices for their products); and (3) *the pursuit of profit* (the owners try to sell their products for more than what they cost).

Some people believe that the United States is an example of pure capitalism. Pure capitalism, however, known as **laissez-faire capitalism** (literally "hands off" capitalism), means that the government doesn't interfere in the market. Such is not the case in the United States. The current form of U.S. capitalism is **welfare** or **state capitalism.** Private citizens own the means of production and pursue profits, but they do so within a vast system of laws designed to protect the welfare of the population.

Consider this example:

> Suppose that you discover what you think is a miracle tonic: It will grow hair, erase wrinkles, and dissolve excess fat. If your product works, you will become an overnight sensation—not only a multimillionaire, but also the toast of television talk shows and the darling of Hollywood.
>
> But don't count on your money or fame yet. You still have to reckon with **market restraints,** the laws and regulations of welfare capitalism that limit your capacity to produce and sell. First, you must comply with local and state rules. You must obtain a business license and a state tax number that allows you to buy your ingredients without paying sales taxes. Then come the federal regulations. You cannot simply take your product to local stores and ask them to sell it; you first must seek approval from federal agencies that monitor compliance with the Pure Food and Drug Act. This means that you

Table 14.1 Comparing Capitalism and Socialism

Capitalism	Socialism
1. Individuals own the means of production	1. The public owns the means of production
2. Based on competition, the owners determine production and set prices	2. Central committees plan production and set prices; no competition
3. The pursuit of profit is the reason for distributing goods and services	3. No profit motive in the distribution of goods and services

capitalism an economic system characterized by the private ownership of the means of production, market competition, and the pursuit of profit

laissez-faire capitalism unrestrained manufacture and trade (literally "hands off" capitalism)

welfare (or state) capitalism an economic system in which individuals own the means of production but the state regulates many economic activities for the welfare of the population

market restraints laws and regulations that limit the capacity to manufacture and sell products must prove that your product will not cause harm to the public. In addition, you must be able to substantiate your claims—or else face being shut down by state and federal agencies that monitor the market for fraud. Your manufacturing process is also subject to federal, state, and local laws concerning hygiene and the disposal of hazardous wastes.

Suppose that you overcome these obstacles, and your business prospers. Other federal agencies will monitor your compliance with laws concerning racial, sexual, and disability discrimination; minimum wages; and Social Security taxes. State agencies will examine your records to see whether you have paid unemployment taxes and sales taxes. Finally, the Internal Revenue Service will look over your shoulder and demand a share of your profits (about 35 percent).

To see how welfare or state capitalism developed in the United States, let's go back to an earlier era. Back in the 1800s, when capitalism was in its infancy, you could have made your "magic" potion at home and sold it at any outlet willing to handle it. You could have advertised that it cured baldness, erased wrinkles, and dissolved fat, for no agency existed to monitor your product or your claims. As you can see from the 1885 poster, this is precisely what thousands of individuals did at that time. They made "elixirs" in their basements and gave them whimsical names such as "Granny's Miracle Medicine" and "Elixir of Health and Happiness." They might claim that their product could restore sexual potency, purge the intestines, and make people more intelligent. These tonics often made people feel better, for many elixirs were braced with alcohol—and even cocaine (Ashley 1975). (Coca-Cola was a "pick me up" during this period, for until 1903 it contained cocaine. This is what the *Coca* of Coca-Cola refers to.) To protect the public's health, in 1906 the federal government passed the Pure Food and Drug Act and began to regulate products.

This advertisement from 1885 represents an early stage of capitalism when individuals were free to manufacture and market products with little or no interference from the government. Today, the production and marketing of goods take place under detailed, complicated government laws and regulations.

John D. Rockefeller's remarkable success in unregulated markets helps to explain why the government began to regulate capitalism. After a ruthless drive to eliminate competition, Rockefeller managed to corner the U.S. oil and gasoline market. He slashed prices and then doubled them after driving out the competition. He even sabotaged competitors' pipelines and refineries (Josephson 1949). With his competitors crippled or eliminated, his company, Standard Oil, was able to dictate prices to the entire nation. Rockefeller had achieved the capitalist's dream, a **monopoly,** the control of an entire industry by a single company.

Rockefeller had played the capitalist game too well, however, for he had wiped out one of its essential components: competition. Consequently, to protect this cornerstone of capitalism, the federal government passed antimonopoly legislation and broke up Standard Oil. Today, the top firms in each industry—such as General Electric in household appliances—must obtain federal approval before acquiring another company in the same industry. If the government determines that one firm dominates a market, it can force that company to *divest* (sell off) some of the businesses it owns.

Another characteristic of welfare capitalism is that although the government encourages competition, it establishes its own monopoly over what it calls "common good" items. These are items and services presumed essential for the common good of the citizens, such as armed forces, highways, and sewers.

Socialism

As shown in Table 14.1 on page 405, **socialism** also has three essential components: (1) public ownership of the means of production; (2) central planning; and (3) the distribution of goods without a profit motive.

In socialist economies, the government owns the means of production—not only the factories but also the land, railroads, oil wells, and gold mines. Unlike capitalism, in which **market forces**—supply and demand—determine both what will be produced and the prices that will be charged, a central committee decides that the country needs X number of toothbrushes, Y toilets, and Z shoes. The committee decides how many of each will be produced, which factories will produce them, what price will be charged for the items, and where they will be distributed.

Socialism is designed to eliminate competition, for goods are sold at predetermined prices regardless of the demand for an item or the cost of producing it. The goal is not to make a profit, nor is it to encourage the consumption of goods that are in low demand (by lowering the price) or to limit the consumption of hard-to-get goods (by raising the price). Rather, the goal is to produce goods for the general welfare and to distribute them according to people's needs, not their ability to pay.

In a socialist economy *everyone* in the economic chain works for the government. The members of the central committee who set production goals are government employees, as are the supervisors who implement their plans, the factory workers who produce the merchandise, the truck drivers who move it, and the clerks who sell it. Those who buy the items may work at different jobs—in offices, on farms, or in day care centers—but they, too, are government employees.

Just as capitalism does not exist in a pure form, neither does socialism. Although the ideology of socialism calls for resources to be distributed according to need and not the ability to pay, socialist countries found it necessary to offer higher salaries for some jobs in order to entice people to take on greater responsibilities. For example, in socialist countries factory managers always earned more than factory workers. These differences in pay follow the functionalist argument of social stratification presented in Chapter 9 (pages 245–246). By narrowing the huge pay gaps that characterize capitalist nations, however, socialist nations established considerably greater equality of income.

Dissatisfied with the greed and exploitation of capitalism and the lack of freedom and individuality of socialism, Sweden and Denmark developed **democratic socialism** (also called *welfare socialism*). In this form of socialism, both the state and individuals produce and distribute goods and services. The government owns and runs the steel, mining, forestry, and energy concerns, as well as the country's telephones, television stations, and airlines. Remaining in private hands are the retail stores, farms, factories, and most service industries.

Ideologies of Capitalism and Socialism

Not only do capitalism and socialism have different approaches to producing and distributing goods but also they represent opposing belief systems. *Capitalists* believe that market forces should determine both products and prices. They also believe that profits are good for humanity. If people strive for profits, it stimulates them to produce and distribute goods efficiently, as well as to develop new products. This benefits society, bringing a more abundant supply of goods at cheaper prices. The Mass Media box on the next page examines how capitalists create demand for their products.

Socialists, in contrast, consider profit to be immoral. Karl Marx said that an item's value is based on the work that goes into it. The only way there can be profit, he stressed, is by paying workers less than the value of their labor. Profit, then, is the *excess value* that has been withheld from workers. Socialists believe that the government should protect workers from this exploitation. To do so, the government should own the means of production, using them not to generate profit but to produce items that match people's needs, not their ability to pay.

Adherents to these ideologies paint each other in such stark colors that *each perceives the other system as one of exploitation.* Capitalists believe that socialists violate the basic human rights of freedom of decision and opportunity. Socialists believe that capitalists violate the basic human right of freedom from poverty. With each side claiming moral superiority while viewing the other as a threat to its very existence, the last century witnessed the world split into two main blocs. In what was known as the *Cold War,* the West armed itself to defend and promote capitalism, the East to defend and promote socialism.

Criticisms of Capitalism and Socialism

The primary criticism leveled against capitalism is that it leads to social inequality. Capitalism, say its critics, produces a tiny top layer of wealthy, powerful people who exploit an immense bottom layer of poorly paid workers. Another criticism is that the tiny top layer

Successful capitalists can buy most things in life, including trophy wives. Some trade their entrepreneurial success (money, property, sometimes fame) for younger, beautiful women. Rupert Murdoch, a billionaire publisher, discarded a wife of 31 years to marry Wendi Deng, who is 40 years younger than he is.

democratic socialism a hybrid economic system in which capitalism is mixed with state ownership

mass Media in Social Life

Greed Is Good—Selling the American Dream

ADVERTISING IS SUCH AN INTEGRAL part of our lives that being deluged with ads almost appears to be our human destiny. When we open a newspaper or magazine, we expect to find pages that proclaim the virtues of products and firms. To turn on the television means to be assailed with commercials for ten minutes of every half hour. Some social analysts even claim that the purpose of television is to round up an audience to watch the commercials—that the programs are mere diversions from the medium's real objective of selling advertising!

And advertising is effective. It is so powerful that it can produce the desire to consume products for which we previously felt no need whatsoever. U.S. kitchens, filled with gadgets that slice and dice, attest to this power.

Advertising's power to turn people into gluttons goes far beyond the purchase of unnecessary kitchen gadgets. Many Americans would not think of going out in pub-

lic without first shampooing, rinsing, conditioning, and blow-drying their hair. Many feel the need to apply an underarm deodorant so powerful that it overcomes the body's natural need to sweat. For many women, public appearance also demands the application of foundation, lipstick, eye shadow, mascara, rouge, powder, and perfume. For many men, after-shave lotion is essential. And only after covering the body with clothing that displays designer labels do Americans feel that they are presentable to the public.

Advertising influences not only what we put on our bodies, what we eat, and what we do for recreation, but also how we feel about ourselves. Our perceptions of whether we are too fat, too skinny, too hippy, or too buxom, whether our hair is too oily or too dry, our body too hairy, or our skin too rough are largely a consequence of advertising. As we weigh our self-image against the idealized images that bombard us in our daily fare of commercials, we conclude that we are lacking something. Advertising assures us that there is salvation—some new product that promises to deliver us from what we lack.

Feeling incomplete, plain, ugly, or somehow unpresentable without certain products. What a capitalist's dream.

The approach is ingenious in its simplicity: Create discontent by presenting ideal images that are impossible to attain. And it works. We grow dissatisfied with ourselves. And we snatch the advertisers' solution: We strive to consume more of the never-ending products that the corporations offer us—those they have decided we need.

The American Dream . . . built on greed, discontent, enticing images, and the promise of redemption. Of course, dreams often juxtapose incompatible realities.

---

wields vast political power. Those few who own the means of production reap huge profits, accrue power, and get legislation passed that goes against the public good.

The primary criticism leveled against socialism is that it does not respect individual rights (Berger 1991). Others (in the form of some government body) control people's lives. They decide where people will live, work, and go to school. In China, they even decide how many children women may bear (Mosher 1983, 2006). Critics also argue that central planning is grossly inefficient and that socialism is not capable of producing much wealth. They say that its greater equality really amounts to giving almost everyone an equal chance to be poor.

The Convergence of Capitalism and Socialism

Regardless of the validity of these mutual criticisms, as nations industrialize they come to resemble one another. They urbanize, produce similar divisions of labor (such as professionals and skilled technicians), and encourage higher education. Even similar values emerge (Kerr 1983). By itself, this tendency would make

Throughout most of the twentieth century, capitalism and communism were pitted against one another in a deadly struggle. Each thought of itself as the correct economic form, and each viewed the other as an evil to be eradicated. In support of this view of essential goodness and evil, proponents of each system launched global propaganda campaigns. Shown here is an example from the socialist campaign, a 1930 painting of Vladimir Lenin, leader of the workers' revolution.

capitalist and socialist nations grow more alike, but another factor also brings them closer to one another (Form 1979): Despite their incompatible ideologies, both capitalist and socialist systems have adopted features of each other.

That capitalism and socialism are growing similar is known as **convergence theory.** This view points to a coming hybrid or mixed economy. Fundamental changes in socialist countries give evidence for convergence theory. The people of Russia and China suffered from the production of shoddy goods, they were plagued by shortages, and their standard of living lagged severely behind that of the West. To try to catch up, in the 1980s and 1990s, the governments of Russia and China reinstated market forces. They made the private ownership of property legal, and they auctioned off many of their state-owned industries. Making a profit—which had been a crime—was encouraged. In China, capitalists were even invited to join the Communist Party (Kahn 2002). The Cultural Diversity box on the next page provides a glimpse of the new capitalism in China. Even Vietnam, whose communism the United States was so concerned about, has embraced capitalism (Mydens 2006).

Changes in capitalism also support this theory. The United States has adopted many socialist practices. One of the most obvious is extracting money from some individuals to pay for the benefits it gives to others. Examples include unemployment compensation (taxes paid by workers are distributed to those who no longer produce a profit); subsidized housing (shelter, paid for by the many, is given to the poor and elderly, with no motive of profit); welfare (taxes from the many are distributed to the needy); a minimum wage (the government, not the employer, determines the minimum that workers receive); and Social Security (the retired do not receive what they paid into the system, but, rather, money that the government collects from current workers). Such embracing of socialist principles indicates that the United States has produced its own version of a mixed type of economy.

Perhaps, then, convergence is unfolding before our very eyes. On the one hand, capitalists have assumed, reluctantly, that their system should provide workers with at least minimal support during unemployment, extended illness, and old age. On the other hand, socialist leaders have admitted, reluctantly, that profit and private ownership do motivate people to work harder.

The matter is not this simple, however. That each has adopted features of the other is only part of the picture. The systems remain far from "converged." Although it is muted compared to what it was in the heady days of the Cold War, the struggle between the systems continues. For example, longing for greater stability, Russian and Polish citizens have voted Communists back into top government positions. In the United States, Republicans try to roll back socialistic measures and return to a purer capitalism, while Democrats resist, proposing even more socialistic measures. Meanwhile, the Chinese, longing to transform themselves into the world's number one capitalist nation, await a new leadership that will adopt capitalistic principles at a faster pace.

convergence theory the view that as capitalist and socialist economic systems each adopt features of the other, a hybrid (or mixed) economic system will emerge

In their march toward globalization, multinational companies locate their corporate headquarters in one country, manufacture their components in another country, assemble them in still another, and sell the finished product throughout the world. This factory in Guangzhou, China, fills orders from U.S. corporations.

The Functionalist Perspective on the Globalization of Capitalism

Sun Microsystems uses a single phone number to offer round-the-globe, round-the-clock technical service. The number is staffed by teams in California, England, and Australia. They electronically hand work off as a team when another country comes on line.

When the Turkish economy plunged, Goodyear didn't let its tire plant in Turkey sit idle. Instead, using flexible tire-making technology, Goodyear swiftly regeared its tire models and redirected output to the rest of Europe. (Zachary 1995)

The globalization of capitalism may be the most significant economic change in the past 100 years. Its impact on our lives may rival that of the Industrial Revolution itself. As

The New Capitalism in China

SOCIALISM HAS THE VIRTUE of making people more equal. Socialism's equality, however, is poverty distributed throughout a society. Under socialism, almost everyone becomes equally poor.

Capitalism, in contrast, has the virtue of producing wealth. A lot of people remain poor, however, leaving a sharp contrast in wealth and poverty, one that produces envy and sometimes creates social unrest.

Now that China has embarked on the capitalist road—or at least its version of it—wealth is being produced. The poor who are left behind, however, aren't happy about what they see, especially when their land is taken from them to help make others wealthy. The anger and resentment have kept the Communist Party busy, for its army has had to squelch a lot of riots.

In Beijing, the capital of China, stands a mansion, recently built by Zhang Yuchen. This is no ordinary mansion, like those belonging to China's other newly rich. This imposing building is a twin of the Chateau Maisons-Laffitte, an architectural landmark on the Seine River outside Paris. At a cost of $50 million, the Beijing replica matches the original edifice detail for detail. Built using the original blueprints of the French chateau, it even features the same Chantilly stone.

This Chinese version of the chateau—and the acreage set aside for a coming housing development of luxury homes, also to be developed by Yuchen—made eight hundred farmers landless.

The building built by Zhang Yuchen, featured in this box.

But not to worry. The spiked fence, the moat, and the armed guards—looking sharp in their French-style uniforms complete with capes and kepis—keep the peasants out of the chateau.

In most places, you need connections to become wealthy. In China, this means connections with the Communist Party, for this group holds the power. Yuchen has those connections. As a member of the Party, it was his job to direct Beijing's construction projects. With his deep connections, Yuchen was able to get the wheat fields that had been farmed by the peasants redesignated as a "conservation area." He was also able to divert a river to construct the moat, one of the finishing touches on his architectural wonder.

It isn't as though the peasants have been left with nothing. As part of Yuchen's deal to get the land, he gives $45 a month to each of the elderly. And the younger peasants can work in the vineyards that Yuchen is planting. French wine will top off the project.

—Based on Kahn 2004, 2007b.

for your Consideration

As China makes its gradual transition to capitalism, what do you think the final version will look like (that is, what characteristics do you think it will have)? Where will the top Party leaders fit in the class system that is emerging? Why? (To answer this, consider the connections and resources of the elite.)

Louis Gallambos, a historian of business, says, "This new global business system will change the way everyone lives and works" (Zachary 1995).

The New Global Division of Labor

To apply functionalism to the globalization of capitalism, we must first step back a moment and look at the nature of work itself. Work is functional for society. Only because people work do we have electricity, hospitals, schools, automobiles, and homes. Beyond this obvious point, however, lies a basic sociological principle: *Work binds us together.* As you may recall from Chapter 4, Emile Durkheim noted that in agricultural societies people do similar work and directly share most aspects of life. Because of this, they look at the world in similar ways. Durkheim used the term **mechanical solidarity** to refer to the sense of unity that comes from doing similar activities.

When an agricultural society industrializes, many different types of jobs develop. As the division of labor grows, people come to feel less solidarity with one another. Grape pickers in California, for example, may feel that they have little in common with workers

mechanical solidarity
Durkheim's term for the unity (or shared consciousness) that people feel as a result of performing the same or similar tasks

who make aircraft in Missouri. Yet, each worker is performing a specific function that contributes to the economic system, and, therefore, to the welfare of the others. Because they are *like the separate organs that make up the same body,* Durkheim called this type of unity **organic solidarity.**

Durkheim observed the beginning of what has turned out to be a global process. With our new *global division of labor,* each of us depends on workers around the globe. People who live in California or New York—or even Michigan—depend on workers in Tokyo to produce cars. Tokyo workers, in turn, depend on Saudi Arabian workers for oil and South American workers to operate ships that deliver that oil. We may not feel a sense of unity with one another, but we all are linked in the same global economic web.

We are only in the early stage of a process that is engulfing the world. As this global division of labor continues to develop, corporations face cultural hurdles, a topic of the next Cultural Diversity box.

organic solidarity Durkheim's term for the interdependence that results from the division of labor; people depending on others to fulfill their jobs

Cultural Diversity *around the* World

Doing Business in the Global Village

THE GLOBALIZATION OF CAPITAL-ISM MEANS that businesspeople face cultural hurdles as they sell products in other cultures. At times, even experienced firms fail to break through cultural barriers. Ford, for example, was successful in marketing an automobile, the Pinto, in the United States. When Ford tried to export that success to Brazil, Brazilians snickered. It turns out that *pinto* is Portuguese slang for "little penis." Ford changed the car's name to Corcel, "the horse" (Archbold and Harmon 2001).

Then there is Hershey's new candy bar, *Cajeta Elegancita,* marketed to Spanish-speaking customers. While *cajeta* can mean nougat, its most common meaning is "little box." The literal translation of *cajeta elegancita* is elegant or fancy little box. Some customers are snickering about this one, too, for *cajeta* is also slang for an intimate part of the female anatomy ("Winner . . ." 2006).

Parker Pen used to use this slogan "It won't leak in your pocket and em-barrass you." The Spanish translation, however, came out as "It won't leak in your pocket and make you pregnant." Frank Perdue's cute chicken slogan, "It takes a strong man to make a tender chicken," didn't fare any bet-ter. It came out as "It takes an aroused man to make a chicken affectionate." And when American Airlines launched a "Fly in Leather" campaign to promote its leather seats in first class, the Mexican campaign stumbled just a bit. "Fly in Leather" (*vuela en cuero*), while literally correct, came out as "Fly Naked." I suppose that slogan did appeal to some.

Some businesspeople have managed to avoid such prob-lems. They have seized profit opportunities in cultural differ-

A device that makes the sound of a flushing toilet? Apparently useless in the United States, but popular in Japan, this product illustrates cultural differences in marketing.

ences. For example, Japanese women are embarrassed by the sounds they make in public toilets. To drown out the offensive sounds, they flush the toilet an average of 2.7 times a visit (Iori 1988). This wastes a lot of water, of course. Seeing this cultural trait as an opportunity, a U.S. entrepreneur developed a battery-powered device that is mounted in the toilet stall. When a woman activates the device, it emits a 25-second flushing sound. A toilet-sound duplicator may be useless in our cul-ture, but the Japanese have bought thousands of them.

Let's suppose that you decide to publish a magazine in Japan. Your market research shows that a maga-zine about sports heroes would be popular. It wouldn't surprise you to learn that your readers expect you to present details about their idols' vital statistics and hobbies. But you would miss something essential if you didn't learn that the Japanese also expect to read about their heroes' blood type. They view it as a sort of zodiac birth sign (Ono 1993; Picker 2006). And you might learn that Japanese mothers save their baby's umbilical cord in a wooden box. If you could get hold of a sports hero's umbilical cord, you could make a small fortune.

for your Consideration

1. Why do you think that it is often difficult to do businss across cultures?
2. How can businesspeople avoid cross-cultural mistakes?
3. If a company offends a culture in which it is trying to do business, what should it do?

Ownership and Management of Corporations

Capitalism is driving today's global interdependence. Its triumph as the world's dominant economic force can be traced to a social invention called the corporation. A **corporation** is a business that is treated legally as a person. A corporation can make contracts, incur debts, sue and be sued. Its liabilities and obligations, however, are separate from those of its owners. For example, each shareholder of Ford Motor Company—whether he or she has 1 or 100,000 shares—owns a portion of the company. However, Ford, not its individual owners, is responsible for fulfilling its contracts and paying its debts. To indicate how corporations have come to dominate the economy, sociologists use the term **corporate capitalism.**

One of the most surprising, but functional, aspects of corporations is their *separation of ownership and management.* Unlike most businesses, it is not the owners—those who own the company's stock—who run the day-to-day affairs of the company (Walters 1995; Sklair 2001). Instead, managers run the corporation, and they are able to treat it *as though it were their own.* The result is the "ownership of wealth without appreciable control, and control of wealth without appreciable ownership" (Berle and Means 1932). Sociologist Michael Useem (1984) put it this way:

> When few owners held all or most of a corporation's stock, they readily dominated its board of directors, which in turn selected top management and ran the corporation. Now that a firm's stock [is] dispersed among many unrelated owners, each holding a tiny fraction of the total equity, the resulting power vacuum allow[s] management to select the board of directors; thus management [becomes] self-perpetuating and thereby acquire[s] de facto control over the corporation.
>
> Management determines its own salaries, sets goals and awards itself bonuses for meeting them, authorizes market surveys, hires advertising agencies, determines marketing strategies, and negotiates with unions. The management's primary responsibility to the owners is to produce profits.

Because of this power vacuum, at their annual meetings the stockholders ordinarily rubber-stamp management's recommendations. It is so unusual for this *not* to happen that these rare cases are called a **stockholders' revolt.** The irony of this term is generally lost, but remember that in such cases it is not the workers who are rebelling at the control of the owners but the owners who are rebelling at the control of the workers!

Functions and Dysfunctions on a Global Scale

The globalization of capitalism is leading to a new world structure. Three primary trading blocs are emerging: North and South America, dominated by the United States; Europe, dominated by Germany; and Asia, currently dominated by Japan, but with China hard at its heels. Functionalists stress that this new global division benefits not only the multinational giants but also the citizens of the world.

Consider free trade. Free trade leads to greater competition, which, in turn, drives the search for greater productivity. This lowers prices and brings a higher standard of living. Free trade also has dysfunctions. As production moves to countries where labor costs are lower, millions of U.S., U.K., French, and German workers lose their jobs. Functionalists point out that this is merely a temporary dislocation. As the Most Industrialized Nations lose production jobs, their workers shift into service and high-tech jobs. Meanwhile, some of the poor of the Least Industrialized Nations are given work and the chance for a better life.

The shift to new types of work requires a bitter adjustment for workers. As the U.S. steel industry lost out to global competition, for example, the closings of plants led to the "rust belts" of the northern states. Similarly, the globalization of capitalism has brought special challenges to small towns, which were already suffering long-term losses because of urbanization. Their struggle to survive is the topic of the photo essay on pages 414–415.

corporation the joint ownership of a business enterprise, whose liabilities and obligations are separate from those of its owners

corporate capitalism the domination of the economic system by giant corporations

stockholders' revolt the refusal of a corporation's stockholders to rubber-stamp decisions made by its managers

The Conflict Perspective on the Globalization of Capitalism

Conflict theorists say that to place the focus on global interdependence is to miss the point. What we should look at is how the wealthy benefit at the expense of workers. Let's see what they mean by this.

The Inner Circle of Corporate Capitalism

The **multinational corporations**—corporations that operate across national borders—are headed by a group that Michael Useem (1984) calls the *inner circle*. Members of this inner circle, although in competition with one another, are united by a mutual interest in making capitalism flourish (Mizruchi and Koenig 1991; Sklair 2001). Within their own country, they consult with high-level politicians, promote legislation favorable to big business, and serve on the boards of directors at the nation's most influential foundations and universities. They also promote political candidates who stand firmly for the private ownership of property. On a global level, they move capital from one nation to another as they search for greater profits.

Table 14.2 lists the world's 25 largest corporations. You can see how the United States dominates world trade. It accounts for 11 of these companies. No other country even comes close. The other companies are spread among 5 other nations.

If the giant corporations cannot attain a monopoly, they strive for an **oligopoly,** where several large companies dominate a single industry, such as gasoline, breakfast cereal,

Table 14.2 The World's Largest Corporations

Rank	Company	Country	Profits (in $Billions)	Market Value (in $Billions)
1	Citigroup	United States	21.54	247.42
2	Bank of America	United States	21.13	226.61
3	HSBC Holdings	Great Britain	16.63	202.29
4	General Electric	United States	20.83	358.98
5	JPMorgan Chase	United States	14.44	170.97
6	American Intl Group	United States	14.01	174.47
7	ExxonMobil	United States	39.50	410.65
8	Royal Dutch Shell	Netherlands	25.44	208.25
9	UBS	Switzerland	9.78	116.84
10	ING Group	Netherlands	9.65	93.99
11	BP	Great Britain	22.29	198.14
12	Toyota Motor	Japan	11.68	217.69
13	Royal Bank of Scotland	Great Britain	12.51	124.13
14	BNP Paribas	France	9.64	97.03
15	Allianz	Germany	8.81	87.22
16	Berkshire Hathaway	United States	11.02	163.79
17	Wal-Mart Stores	United States	11.29	201.36
18	Barclays	Great Britain	8.95	94.79
19	Chevron	United States	17.14	149.37
19	Total	France	15.53	152.62
21	HBOS	Great Britain	7.59	79.83
22	ConocoPhillips	United States	15.55	107.39
23	AXA Group	France	6.38	87.64
24	Société Générale Group	France	6.55	77.62
25	Goldman Sachs Group	United States	9.54	83.31

Source: "Global 2000," 2007.
Size is measured by sales, market volume, assets, and profits.

multinational corporations companies that operate across national boundaries; also called *transnational corporations*

oligopoly the control of an entire industry by several large companies

Small Town USA:
Struggling to Survive

all across the nation, small towns are struggling to survive. Parents and town officials are concerned because so few young adults remain in their home town. There is little to keep them there, and when they graduate from high school, most move to the city. With young people leaving and old ones dying, the small towns are shriveling.

How can small towns contend with cutthroat global competition when workers in some countries are paid a couple of dollars a day? Even if you open a store down the road, Wal-Mart sells the same products for about what you pay for them—and offers much greater variety.

There are exceptions: Some small towns are located close to a city, and they receive the city's spillover. A few possess a rare treasure—some unique historical event or a natural attraction— that draws visitors with money to spend. Most of the others, though, are drying up, left in a time warp as history shifts around them. This photo essay tells the story.

I was struck by the grandiosity of people's dreams, at least as reflected in the names that some small-towners give their businesses. Donut Palace has a nice ring to it—inspiring thoughts of wealth and royalty (note the crowns). Unfortunately, like so many others, this business didn't make it.

The small towns are filled with places like this—small businesses, locally owned, that have enough clientele for the owner and family to eke out a living. They have to offer low prices because there is a fast food chain down the road. Fixing the sign? That's one of those "I'll get-to-its."

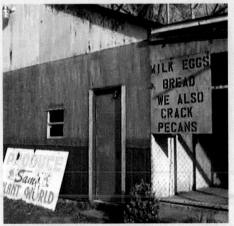

People do whatever they can to survive. This enterprising proprietor uses the building for an unusual combination of purposes: a "plant world," along with the sale of milk, eggs, bread, and, in a quaint southern touch, cracking pecans.

In striking contrast to the grandiosity of some small town business names is the utter simplicity of others. Cafe tells everyone that some type of food and drinks are served here. Everyone in this small town knows the details.

One of the few buildings consistently in good repair in the small towns is the U.S. Post Office. Although its importance has declined in the face of telecommunications, for "small towners" the post office still provides a vital link with the outside world.

With little work available, it is difficult to afford adequate housing. This house, although cobbled together and in disrepair, is a family's residence.

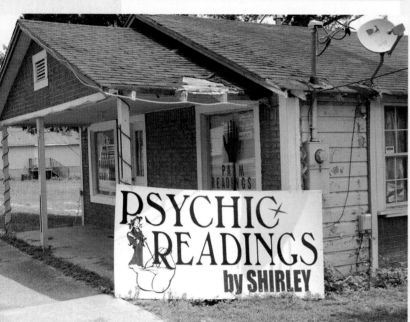

There is no global competition for this home-grown business. Shirley has located her sign on a main highway just outside Niceville, Florida. By the looks of the building, business could be better.

This is a successful business. The store goes back to the early 1900s, and the proprietors have capitalized on the "old timey" atmosphere.

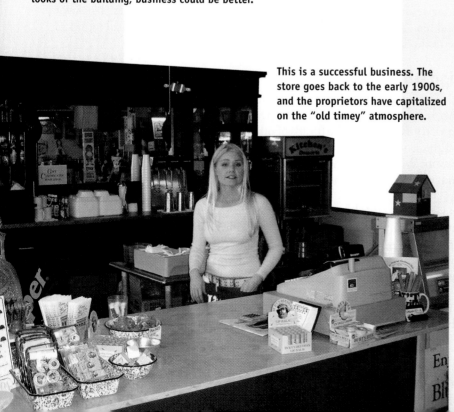

This general store used to be the main business in the area; it even has a walk-in safe. It has been owned by the same family since the 1920s, but is no longer successful. To get into the building, I had to find out where the owner (shown here) lived, knock on her door, and then wait while she called around to find out who had the keys.

or light bulbs. If they achieve this, then they can divide the market among themselves. They are also able to dictate the quality and prices of their products. To get legislation that gives them special tax breaks, oligopolies also cultivate political connections. (Some simply say that they "buy" politicians.)

One of the more significant, and to some, sinister, developments in capitalism is the merger of giant corporations from different nations. Merging, or one company buying another, reduces competition. This also makes it easier to set prices, to control quality, and to trounce smaller competitors. In short, mergers consolidate the power of the multinational corporations and make it easier for them to dominate global markets.

Consolidation of power is one of the primary goals of these corporations. The inner circle looks for cooperative politicians and develops a cozy relationship with them. If they find hostility, some are not above plotting murder and overthrowing governments. In 1973, a U.S. multinational, the International Telephone & Telegraph Company (ITT), joined the CIA in a plot to unseat Chile's elected government. They first attempted to bring about the economic collapse of Chile. When this failed, they plotted a coup d'état, which led to the assassination of the Chilean president, Salvador Allende (Coleman 1995; Rohter 2002).

U.S. economic power is so integrated with politics that the inner circle can even get the U.S. president to pitch their products. If this sounds like an exaggeration, consider this report from the Associated Press (October 29, 1995):

> The White House celebrated Saudi Arabia's $6 billion purchase of U.S.-made airplanes Thursday, calling it a victory for both American manufacturers and the Clinton administration. . . . President Clinton helped broker the sale. . . . Prince Bandar bin Sultan, [Saudi Arabia's] minister of defense and aviation, credited Clinton for closing the purchase. *Clinton personally pitched the quality of the U.S. planes to Saudi King Fahd.* (Italics added.)
>
> . . . (T)he Clinton Administration worked this sale awfully damn hard because of the president's commitment to promoting U.S. business abroad. . . . He has done that routinely, instructed his ambassadors and his diplomats to put the economic interests of Americans forward as they conduct their diplomacy.

Although the president wasn't selling toothpaste, it was the same principle.

In short, the interests of the heads of the multinational corporations and those of the top political leaders converge. Together, they form a *power elite,* with top government leaders dedicated to promoting the interests of the country's economic leaders. To protect their far-flung resources and markets, they provide weapons to regimes that favor their interests and send armed forces against those that threaten them. We shall return to this topic in the next chapter.

Interlocking Directorates

Conflict theorists stress how the wealthy expand their power through **interlocking directorates;** that is, they serve on the board of directors of several companies. Their fellow members on those boards also sit on the boards of other companies, and so on. Like a spider's web that starts at the center and then fans out in all directions, the top companies are interlocked into a network (Mintz and Schwartz 1985; Davis 2003). The chief executive officer of a firm in England, who sits on the board of directors of half a dozen other companies, said:

> If you serve on, say, six outside boards, each of which has, say, ten directors, and let's say out of the ten directors, five are experts in one or another subject, you have a built-in panel of thirty friends who are experts who you meet regularly, automatically each month, and you really have great access to ideas and information. You're joining a club, a very good club. (Useem 1984)

interlocking directorates the same people serving on the board of directors of several companies

This concentration of power reduces competition, for a director is not going to approve a plan that will be harmful to another company in which he or she (mostly he)

has a stake. The top executives of the top U.S. companies are part of the powerful capitalist class described on pages 276–278. They even get together in recreational settings, where they renew their sense of solidarity, purpose, and destiny (Domhoff 1999b; 2002; 2006).

Global Investing

The next two social maps, below and on the next page, illustrate how corporations have outgrown their national boundaries. The world map shows the investments that U.S. corporations have made in other countries. Cross-border investments are not a one-way street, however, as the U.S. map illustrates. About 1 of every 20 U.S. businesses is owned by people in other countries. If you buy a book from New York's Random House, you are making a purchase from Bertelsmann, a German company. If you fill up at a Shell station, you are buying gasoline from a Dutch company. And if you buy a package of Tums, you are buying a product from an old-line U.S. company that is owned by Beecham Group, a British corporation.

Although we take the presence of multinational corporations for granted—as well as their cornucopia of products—their power and presence are new to the world scene. As multinational corporations do business across national borders, they tend to become detached from the interests and values of their country of origin. A U.S. executive made this revealing statement, "The United States does not have an automatic call on our resources. There is no mindset that puts the country first" (Greider 2001). These global giants move investments and production from one part of the globe to another—with no concern for consequences other than profits. How opening or closing factories affects workers is of no concern to them. With profit as their moral guide, the conscience of multinational corporations is written in dollar signs.

This primary allegiance to profits and market share, rather than to their workers or to any country, accompanied by a web of interconnections around the globe, is of high sociological significance. The shift in orientation and organization is so new, however, that we don't yet know its implications. But we can consider two stark contrasts. The first:

Figure 14.2 **The Globalization of Capitalism: U.S. Ownership in Other Countries**

Source: By the author. Based on *Statistical Abstract* 2007:Table 1288.

Figure 14.3 The Globalization of Capitalism: Foreign Ownership of U.S. Business

Businesses in which at least 10 percent of the voting interest is controlled by a non-U.S. owner.

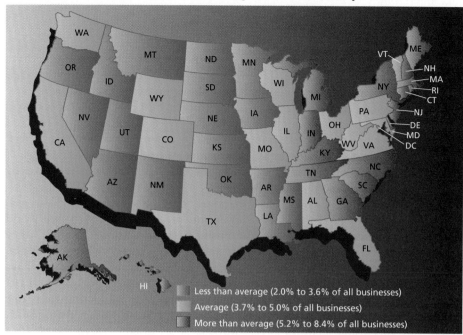

Less than average (2.0% to 3.6% of all businesses)

Average (3.7% to 5.0% of all businesses)

More than average (5.2% to 8.4% of all businesses)

Source: By the author. Based on *Statistical Abstract* 2007:Table 1275.

Figure 14.4 The Revolutionary Change in the U.S. Work Force

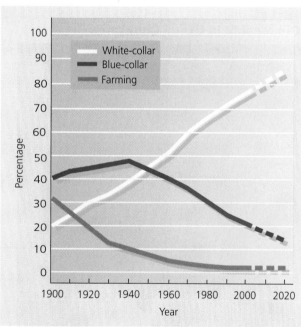

Note: From 1900 to 1940, "workers" refers to people age 14 and over; from 1970 to people age 16 and over. Broken lines are the author's projections. The totals shown here are broadly accurate only, as there is disagreement on how to classify some jobs. Agriculture, for example, includes forestry, fishing, and hunting.
Source: By the author. Based on *Statistical Abstract,* various years, and 2007:Tables 602, 1341.

Removed from tribal loyalties and needing easy access across national boundaries, the global interconnections of the multinational corporations may be a force for global peace. The second: They could create a New World Order dominated by a handful of corporate leaders. If so, we all may find ourselves at the mercy of a global elite in a system of interconnected societies, directed by the heads of the world's corporate giants. We will discuss this possibility in the next chapter.

Work in U.S. Society

With this broad, even global, background, let's turn our focus on work in U.S. society.

The Transition to Postindustrial Society

At various times in this text, I have used the term *postindustrial society* to describe the United States. Figure 14.4 illustrates why this term is appropriate. This figure shows a change that is without parallel in human history. In the 1800s, most U.S. workers were farmers. Today, farmers make up about 2 percent of the work force. With the technology of the 1800s, a typical farmer produced enough food to feed five people. With today's powerful machinery and hybrid seeds, a farmer now feeds about eighty. In 1940, about half of U.S. workers wore a blue collar; then changing technology shrank the market for blue-collar jobs. White-collar work continued its ascent, reaching the dominant position it holds today.

When you look at Figure 14.4, the change in type of work is readily apparent. But this is merely a surface change. The significance of the figure is that it indicates the arrival of a new type of society. To live in a postindustrial society is to live in a different world. Not only is your work different but so are your lifestyle, your relationships, the age at which you marry, the amount of education you attain, the number of children you have, your attitudes and values, and even the way you view the world.

Women and Work

Among these major changes that have transformed our world is the unprecedented increase in the numbers of women who work for wages. In Figure 11.5 of Chapter 11 (page 320), you saw how this number has increased so greatly that today almost half of all U.S. workers are women. Figure 14.5 shows how the United States ranks among the nations that have the highest percentage of women in the work force.

Researchers have found two primary distinctions between women and men in the world of work. First, women seem to be more concerned than men with maintaining a balance between their work and family lives (Statham et al. 1988; Caproni 2004). Second, men and women tend to follow different models for success: Men seem to emphasize individualism, power, and competition, while women seem more likely to stress collaboration, persuasion, and helping (Miller-Loessi 1992; Moore, Grunberg, and Greenberg 2005).

Note the caution with which I have presented these findings—the use of *seem to* and *tend to*. I am not convinced that there are any substantial or essential differences between women's and men's orientations to work. The few studies that we have on this topic

Figure 14.5 **What Percentage of Women Are in the Labor Force?**

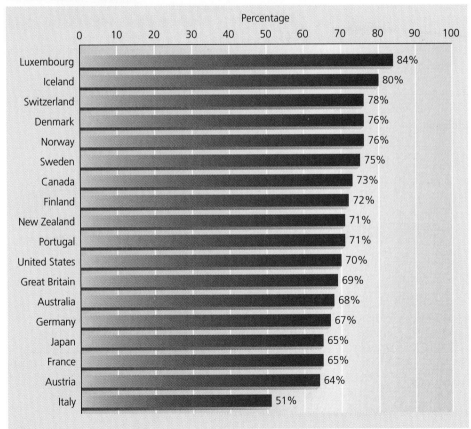

Country	Percentage
Luxembourg	84%
Iceland	80%
Switzerland	78%
Denmark	76%
Norway	76%
Sweden	75%
Canada	73%
Finland	72%
New Zealand	71%
Portugal	71%
United States	70%
Great Britain	69%
Australia	68%
Germany	67%
Japan	65%
France	65%
Austria	64%
Italy	51%

Note: Female labor force participation rates are derived by dividing the female labor force of all ages by the female population ages 15–64. These totals include women who work part time.

Source: By the author. Based on *Statistical Abstract* 2007:Table 1339.

could be tapping core differences—or they could be measuring temporary tendencies owing to women having more recently entered the paid work force. If so, as women's work experiences accumulate, these differences will disappear. It will be interesting to see what happens as more women reach the top levels of their professions and attain the more powerful positions in the business world.

How likely is it that a woman will be in the labor force? Figure 14.6a shows how working for wages increases with each level of education. This is probably because women who have more education find more satisfying work—and get higher pay. Figure 14.6b shows the influence of marital status. You can see that single women are the most likely to work for wages; married women follow closely behind; and divorced, widowed, and separated women are the least likely to be in the work force. From Figure 14.6c, you can see that African American women are the most likely to be in the work force, but that race-ethnicity makes little difference in whether women work for wages. You can also see that the racial-ethnic groups have been following a parallel course.

Figure 14.6 Percentage of Women in the U.S. Labor Force

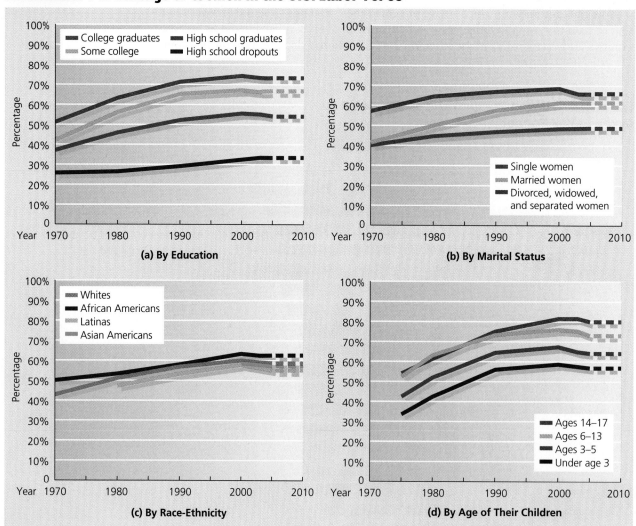

(a) By Education

(b) By Marital Status

(c) By Race-Ethnicity

(d) By Age of Their Children

Note: Earlier years in Part A have been adjusted to match how the source changed computations for later years. Broken lines indicate the author's projections.

Source: By the author. Based on *Statistical Abstract* 1989:Tables 638, 639, 640; 1990:Tables 625, 627, 637; 2001:Table 578; 2007:Tables 574, 578, 583, 585.

The gradual changes shown in Figure 14.6 have profound implications for social life. Because of this, sociologists use the term **quiet revolution** to refer to the consequences of so many women joining the ranks of paid labor. This quiet revolution has transformed self-concepts, spending patterns, and relations at work. It has also changed relationships with boyfriends, husbands, and children. It has even transformed views of life. I'll give just one example. It used to be considered most undesirable—perhaps immoral—for women with preschoolers to work for wages. Believing that they would be neglecting their children and that neighbors would talk, mothers of preschoolers took jobs only as a last resort. Now, as Figure 14.6d shows, *most* mothers of preschoolers have paid jobs—even those who have children under age 3. The neighbors don't gossip, for what was once considered wrong is now considered right—and most of the mothers in the neighborhood are at work.

As discussed in Chapter 11, women face discrimination at work. The Down-to-Earth Sociology box below explores how some women cope with this discrimination.

quiet revolution the fundamental changes in society that follow when vast numbers of women enter the work force

Down-to-Earth Sociology

Women in Business: Maneuvering the Male Culture

I WORK FOR A LARGE insurance company. Of its twenty-five hundred employees, about 75 percent are women. Only 5 percent of the upper management positions, however, are held by women.

I am one of the more fortunate women, for I hold a position in middle management. I am also a member of the twelve-member junior board of directors, of whom nine are men and three are women.

Recently one of the female members of the board suggested that the company become involved in Horizons for Tomorrow, a program designed to provide internships for disadvantaged youth. Two other women and I spent many days developing a proposal for our participation.

The problem was how to sell the proposal to the company president. From past experiences, we knew that if he saw it as a "woman's project" it would be shelved into the second tier of "maybes." He hates what he calls "aggressive bitches."

We three decided, reluctantly, that the proposal had a chance only if it were presented by a man. We decided that Bill was the logical choice. We also knew that we had to "stroke" Bill if we were going to get his cooperation.

We first asked Bill if he would "show us how to present our proposal." (It is ridiculous to have to play the role of the "less capable female," but, unfortunately, the corporate culture sometimes dictates this strategy.) To clinch matters, we puffed up Bill even more by saying, "You're the logical choice for the next chairmanship of the board."

Bill, of course, came to our next planning session, where we "prepped" *him* on what to say.

At our meeting with the president, we had Bill give the basic presentation. We then backed *him* up, providing the background and rationale for why the president should endorse the project. As we answered the president's questions, we carefully deferred to Bill.

The president's response? "An excellent proposal," he concluded, "an appropriate project for our company."

To be successful, we had to maneuver through the treacherous waters of the "hidden culture" (actually not so "hidden" to women who have been in the company for a while). The proposal was not sufficient on its merits, for the "who" behind a proposal is at least as significant as the proposal itself.

"We shouldn't have to play these games," Laura said, summarizing our feelings.

But we all know that we have no choice. To become labeled "pushy" is to commit "corporate suicide"—and we're no fools.

Source: Written by an insurance executive in the author's introductory sociology class who, out of fear of retaliation at work, has chosen to remain anonymous.

The Underground Economy

> The underground economy. The term has a sinister ring—suggestive of dope deals struck in alleys and wads of bills hastily exchanged. The underground economy is this, but it is a lot more—and it is usually a lot more innocent. If you pay the plumber with a check made out to "cash," if you purchase a pair of sunglasses from a street vendor or a kitchen gadget at a yard sale, if you so much as hand a neighbor's kid a $20 bill to mow the lawn or to baby sit, you are participating in the underground economy. (Pennar and Farrell 1993)

Also known as the *informal economy* and the *off-the-books economy,* the **underground economy** consists of economic activities—whether legal or illegal—that people don't report to the government. What interests most of us is not unreported babysitting money, but the illegal activities that people could not report even if they wanted to. As a 20-year-old child care worker in one of my classes who also worked as a prostitute two or three nights a week told me, "Why do I do this? For the money! Where else can I make this kind of money in a few hours? And it's all tax free."

The largest source of illegal income is probably drug dealing. Nineteen million Americans currently use illegal drugs (*Statistical Abstract* 2007:Tables 11, 194). To serve them, billions of dollars flow from users to sellers and to their networks of growers, importers, processors, transporters, dealers, and enforcers. These particular networks are so huge that each year the police arrest more than a million Americans for illegal drug activities (*Statistical Abstract* 2007:Table 317).

The million or so illegal immigrants who enter the United States each year are also part of the underground economy. Often called *undocumented workers* (referred to as *los sin documentos* in Mexico), they work for employers who either ignore their fake Social Security cards or pay them in cash. I asked a housekeeper from Mexico who had entered the United States illegally if she had a "green card" (the card given to immigrants who enter the country legally). She said that she did, adding, "They're sold on the street like candy."

When terrorists struck the World Trade Center, 43 restaurant workers were killed. Of them, 12 were working with fake Social Security cards (Cleeland 2001). Undocumented workers from China work primarily in Chinese restaurants and in New York's garment industry. Many from India and Pakistan work in fast food restaurants (Rosenbaum 1998). Those from Mexico and Central and South America are concentrated in California and Texas, but they disperse throughout the country. They do housework, pick lettuce on farms, sew garments in clandestine sweatshops, clean rooms in hotels, and serve food at restaurants. For the most part, they do the low-paying and dirty jobs that U.S. citizens try to avoid. The rest of us benefit from their labor, for they bring us cheaper goods and services.

Because of its subterranean nature, no one knows the exact size of the underground economy, but it probably runs around 10 percent of the regular economy (McTague 2005). Since the official gross domestic product of the United States is about $12 trillion (*Statistical Abstract* 2007:Table 648), the underground economy probably totals over $1 trillion a year. It is so huge that it distorts the official statistics of the country's gross domestic product. It also costs the IRS billions of dollars a year in lost taxes.

Stagnant Paychecks

With our extensive automation, the productivity of U.S. workers has increased year after year, making them some of the most productive in the world (*Statistical Abstract* 2007:Table 1361). One might think, therefore, that their pay would be increasing. This brings us to a disturbing trend.

Look at Figure 14.7. The gold bars show current dollars. These are the dollars the average worker finds in his or her paycheck. You can see that since 1970 the average pay of U.S. workers has soared from just over $3 an hour to over $16 an hour. Workers today are bringing home *five* times as many dollars as workers used to. But let's strip away the illusion. Look at the green bars, which show the dollars adjusted for

underground economy exchanges of goods and services that are not reported to the government and thereby escape taxation inflation, the *buying power* of those paychecks. You can see how inflation has whittled away the value of the dollars that workers earn. Today's workers, with their $16 an hour, can only buy the same amount of goods as workers in 1970 could with their "measly" $3 an hour. The question is not "How could workers live on just $3 an hour back then?" but, rather, "How can workers get by on a 14-cent-an-hour raise that it took 35 years to get?" Incredibly, despite higher education and technical training of workers, the use of computers, and increased productivity, this is how much the average worker's purchasing power has increased from 1970 to 2005.

Patterns of Work and Leisure

> Suppose that it is 1860 and you work for a textile company in Lowell, Massachusetts. When you arrive at work one day, you find that the boss has posted a new work rule: All workers will have to come in at the same time and remain until quitting time. Like the other workers, you feel outrage. You join them as they shout, "This is slavery!" and march out of the plant, indignant at such a preposterous rule. (Zuboff 1991)

This is a true story. The workers were angry because up until then, they had been able to come and go when they wanted. Let's consider how patterns of work and leisure are related to the transformation of economies.

Effects of Industrialization Hunting and gathering societies provide enormous amounts of **leisure,** time not taken up by work or necessary activities such as eating and sleeping. Assuming they didn't live in a barren place or have to deal with some unusual event, such as drought or pestilence, it did not take long for people to hunt and gather what they needed for the day. In fact, *most of their time was leisure,* and the rhythms of nature were an essential part of their lives. Agricultural economies also allowed much leisure, for, at least in the western hemisphere, work peaked with the spring planting, let up in the summer, and then peaked again with the fall harvest. During the winter work again receded, for by this time the harvest was in, animals had been slaughtered, food had been preserved and stored, and wood had been laid up.

Industrialization, however, broke this harnessing of work to seasonal rhythms. Going against all of human history, bosses and machines began to dictate when work was to be done. Workers resisted, clinging to their traditional patterns. After working for several weeks—or even just a few days—a worker would disappear, only to reappear when money ran out. For most workers, enjoying leisure was considerably more important than amassing money (Weber 1958/1904–1905). Since regular, efficient production brought more profits, bosses began to insist that all workers start work at the same time. To workers of that period, this seemed like slavery. Today, in contrast, work patterns that corporations and bosses impose on us have become part of the taken-for-granted cultural rhythms that coordinate our lives.

Trends in Leisure It is not the activity itself that makes something leisure, but the purpose for which it is done. Consider driving a car. If you do it for pleasure, it is leisure, but if you are an on-duty police officer or if you must commute to the office, it is work. If done for enjoyment, horseback riding and reading a book are leisure—but these activities are work for jockeys and students.

Patterns of leisure change with the life course, following the U-curve shown on Figure 14.8. Young children enjoy the most leisure, but teenagers still have considerably

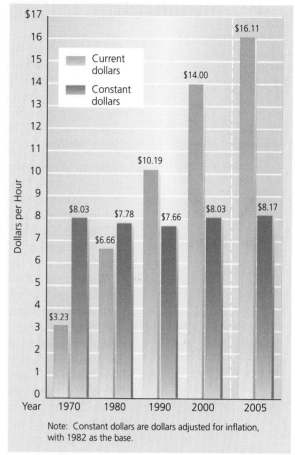

Figure 14.7 **Average Hourly Earnings of U.S. Workers in Current and Constant (1982) Dollars**

Note: Constant dollars are dollars adjusted for inflation, with 1982 as the base.

Source: By the author. Based on *Statistical Abstract* 1992:Table 650; 1999:Table 698; 2007:Table 626.

leisure time not taken up by work or necessary activities

Figure 14.8 Leisure and the Life Course: The "U" Curve of Leisure

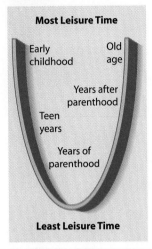

Source: By the author.

more leisure than their parents. Parents with small children have the least leisure, but after the children leave home, leisure picks up again. After the age of 60 or so, the amount of leisure for adults peaks.

Compared with workers during early industrialization, today's workers have far more leisure. A hundred years ago the work week was half again as long as today's, for then workers had to be at their machines 60 hours a week. When workers unionized, they demanded a shorter work week. Over the years, the work week has gradually shrunk. In Germany the work week is 35 hours, with Friday afternoons usually off. Volkswagen was the world's first multinational corporation to adopt a 30-hour work week. In addition, German workers get six weeks of paid vacation a year. A strange thing has happened in the United States, though. This trend toward more leisure has reversed course. U.S. workers now average over 1,800 hours of work a year, as much as workers in Japan (Gornick and Heron 2006).

Teleworking Just as the Industrial Revolution took workers from home to factory and office, so our technological revolution has allowed several million workers to leave the office and work at home ("New Report . . ." 2006). Corporations save office space, and workers avoid traffic jams. Managers often fret about a loss of control over workers, and teleworking does produce mixed results. For some workers, out of sight means that it's time to goof off. Without the structure that forces them to quit at the end of the day, others go on 24/7 work binges (Johnson 2004).

Work is more than just the job a person performs. Although the paycheck is the typical motivation for taking a job, friendships at work become so significant that they affect even the self-concept. It isn't surprising that teleworkers miss the camaraderie of their office mates. Lacking face-to-face communications with coworkers and bosses, they are also deprived of nonverbal cues—the facial expressions and body language—that are so essential for our understanding one another. E-mail helps, but it isn't the same as seeing the look on Bob's and Mary's faces when they tell a joke or repeat the latest office gossip. Some teleworkers power up at coffee houses, just so they can see the faces of others (Cava 2006).

Many teleworkers find work at home to be a soulless experience. Here is what a student who read this text reported:

> My husband is still working as a software engineer. His company "wired" most of their employees for home offices. So he now works from home and has a boss in another state whom he rarely sees in person. He misses his "community" at the office and often, out of the blue, will just go in for a few hours for no good reason. He's usually disappointed, though, because most everyone else works at home, and he finds few people to chat with. His company recognizes this as a big problem. It's hard to keep the team spirit, so they have tried to gently "mandate" once a week togetherness lunches. But it's not the same as everyday contact.

Teleworkers, of course, enjoy not having a boss breathing down their necks, and they revel in the ability to plan their days or even to take an afternoon off to visit the zoo when the kids don't have school. And they don't miss the traffic jams, either.

Facing the Future: Implications of Global Capitalism

We can catch a glimpse of the future by looking at two trends that are firmly in place: global trade and the new technology.

Global Trade: Inequalities and Conflict

The giant multinational corporations are carving up the world into major trading blocs and pushing for the reduction or elimination of tariffs. As a result, we can expect trade among nations to increase beyond anything the world has ever seen. U.S. corporations will continue to support an expansion of global trade, for world markets have become crucial for their success. For example, with the huge costs of making movies (the average movie now runs $50 million in production costs), the U.S. movie industry would go broke if it weren't for global distribution.

Not all nations will benefit equally, of course. The Most Industrialized Nations (even as they transition to their postindustrial phase) will continue to garner the lion's share of the world's wealth. (You may want to look again at Table 14.2 on page 413.) If economic inequality between the richer and the poorer nations increases, it spells trouble. The growing wealth of the nations that control global trade does not sit easily with the Least Industrialized Nations. Their poverty and powerlessness—illuminated and reinforced by televised images of wealth and privilege beamed from the Most Industrialized Nations—breed discontent. So do growing pressures on their limited resources from their mushrooming populations. All this provides fertile ground for the recruitment of terrorists, who, if able, will vent their frustrations against those nations that they perceive as exploiting them.

New Technologies and Downsizing: Utopia or Nightmare?

Computer-driven production will continue to reduce the number of workers who are needed to make the goods we use. As conflict theorists stress, the jobs that the new technology destroys are not located at the top managerial levels of the multinationals, nor are they held by the capitalists who own the company stock. Although investors and managers must modify their strategies to match changing markets, which can be treacherous, the global manufacturing and distribution that the new technology opens are an opportunity for greater profits. The low-level workers who live from paycheck to paycheck, in contrast, suffer the wrenching adjustments that come from being forced from their jobs.

Let's close this chapter, then, with a Thinking Critically section that focuses on the far-reaching implications of this global transformation of our economy.

As capitalism globalizes, it is not just the products but also the cultures of the dominant capitalist nations that are exported around the world. Shown here is an outdoor ad in Tokyo. What aspects of Western culture can you identify in the ad?

Thinking Critically

What Type of New Society? New Technology and the Restructuring of Work

The fear of being automated out of a job plagues many workers. They have seen machines displace people who worked next to them, with the lucky ones getting "early retirement" and a pension, and the others being told to hit the bricks.

The workers' fears of automation are not irrational. Technology causes job after job to become obsolete. The automobile industry makes about as many cars as it did 30 or 40 years ago, but it employs less than half as many production workers. The 120,000 workers at U.S. Steel plummeted to just 20,000—yet production remained the same (Volti 1995). As computers continue to replace workers, millions more jobs will be wiped out—not only unskilled jobs in manufacturing but also skilled work in information technology. If you contact Verizon's call center, for example, you will speak to polite operators who will try to track down the problem by asking intelligent questions. They will also check your telephone line on the spot. If they can't fix the problem, they will schedule and dispatch a technician. You will not be talking to a person, however, but to a Voice Response Unit (VRU) that uses a new generation of intelligent speech recognition. The VRU will "talk" with you in plain English (Landry et al. 2005). It won't be long until we will talk to robotic secretaries and receptionists whose gestures, facial expressions, and conversations will be practically indistiguishable from those of humans ("The Dawn of Artificial Intelligence" 2007).

Then, too, there is another side to the story; technology also creates jobs. The automobile industry is an outstanding example. Although the popularity of cars wiped out the livelihood of stable hands, tens of thousands more people gained jobs in the new steel and gasoline industries. Hundreds of thousands of others began to work as mechanics, salespeople, and advertisers. Many took jobs in the body shops that dot our landscape.

Each new technology, then, both destroys existing jobs and creates new ones. Some of these jobs are highly visible, as with those in the shops that do instant oil changes. Others are less evident. The technology that went into airplanes, for example, not only spawned pilots, mechanics, and reservation clerks but also stimulated global tourism. To put this in a nutshell: *Most of us work at jobs that did not even exist when our grandparents were born.*

With rapidly developing technologies, the overall workforce is likely to shrink (Strangleman 2007). This can be either good or bad. Consider two futures (Rifkin 1995). The *first* is a technoparadise of abundance and leisure. Because fewer workers will produce everything we need, work is spread around. Working just 10 or 15 hours a week, everyone is able to possess goods in abundance. We recover the leisure that humans used to enjoy in their early days as hunters and gatherers. What people do with this leisure will be up to them. Some will simply watch more soap operas or fight limitless virtual enemies in video games. Others, with a beer in one hand and a remote in the other, will sit transfixed by mind-numbing, endless hours of televised sports and reality shows. Still others will spend time in intellectual pursuits. They will study the sciences, philosophy, and languages. They will follow the arts—painting, poetry, the theater. The average person will be able to enjoy global travel. Parents will spend more time with their children.

The *second* future is quite different. It consists of a society that is split into two main groups. The smaller group consists of affluent people who are secure in their jobs. With their skills in high demand, they enjoy the many benefits that society offers. The larger group consists of two main types of people: those who still have jobs, but they pay little, and those who no longer have jobs, for automation has dispossessed them from the work force. In this second future, millions of people survive in hopelessness and despair, receiving meager handouts that are given only grudgingly. With no work available, many of the nation's

This poorly paid worker, who carries sulphur from the I-jen crater in Java, is an expendable part of the profit system that drives the economic machine called capitalism.

youth, displaced from job opportunities, participate in a large, violent criminal subculture. This frightens and confuses those in the affluent group, who retreat from this threat, locking themselves behind gated communities.

We can't turn back the clock. New technology is here to stay, and, as always, the new technology will change the nature of work. The basic issue is not whether we will have new technology, but how we, as a society, will apply it. The transformation of work is inevitable, but the choices that we make regarding that restructuring of work are not.

for your Consideration

Which of these two futures seems more likely? In answering this question, refer to the discussion in this chapter about the effects of the new technologies on work, the globalization of capitalism, and the growing power of multinational corporations.

The growing gap between the "haves" and the "have-nots" of our society reveals an ominous trend. Look at Figure 14.9. Each rectangle on the left represents a fifth of the U.S. population, about 60 million people. The inverted pyramid on the right renders a snapshot of how the nation's income is divided. The rectangles in the inverted pyramid represent the proportion of the nation's income that goes to each fifth of the population. You can see that *48 percent* of the entire country's income goes to the richest fifth of Americans; only *4 percent* goes to the poorest fifth. This gap is now greater than it has been in generations. Rather than bringing equality, then, the postindustrial economy has perpetuated and enlarged the income inequalities of the industrial economy. What implications of this division of the nation's wealth do you see for our future?

Figure 14.9 The Inverted Income Pyramid: The Proportion of Income Received by Each Fifth of the U.S. Population

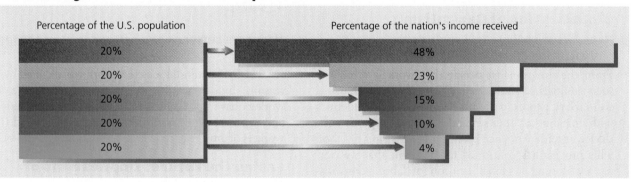

Source: By the author. Based on *Statistical Abstract* 2007:Table 678.

Summary *and* Review

The Transformation of Economic Systems

How are economic systems linked to types of societies?

The earliest societies (hunting and gathering) were **subsistence economies:** Small groups lived off the land and produced little or no surplus. Economic systems grew more complex as people discovered how to do-mesticate animals and grow plants (pastoral and horticultural societies), farm (agricultural societies), and manufacture (industrial societies). As people produced a *surplus,* trade developed. Trade, in turn, brought social inequality as some people accumulated more than others. Service industries dominate the postindustrial societies. If a biotech society is emerging, it is too early to know its consequences. Pp. 400–403.

The Transformation of the Medium of Exchange

How has the medium of exchange evolved?

A **medium of exchange** is any means by which people exchange goods and services. In hunting and gathering and pastoral and horticultural societies, people **bartered** goods and services. In agricultural societies, **money** came into use, and evolved into **currency,** or paper money, representing a specific amount of gold or silver on deposit. Postindustrial societies rely increasingly on electronic transfer of funds in the form of **credit cards, debit cards,** and **e-cash.** Pp. 403–405.

World Economic Systems

How do the major economic systems differ?

The world's two major economic systems are capitalism and socialism. In **capitalism,** private citizens own the means of production and pursue profits. In **socialism,** the state owns the means of production and has no goal of profit. Adherents of each have developed ideologies that defend their own systems and paint the other as harmful or even evil. As expected from **convergence theory,** each system has adopted features of the other. Pp. 405–409.

The Functionalist Perspective on the Globalization of Capitalism

How does functionalism apply to the globalization of capitalism?

From the functionalist perspective, work is a basis of social solidarity. Traditional societies have **mechanical solidarity;** people perform similar tasks and identify with one another. Industrialization brings **organic solidarity,** interdependence based on the division of labor. This process has continued to the point that we now are developing a global division of labor. **Corporations,** with their separation of ownership and management, underlie the success of capitalism. Pp. 409–412.

The Conflict Perspective on the Globalization of Capitalism

How does a conflict perspective apply to the globalization of capitalism?

Conflict theorists, who focus on power, note that global capitalism is a means by which capitalists exploit workers. From the major owners of the **multinational corporations** come an *inner circle*. While workers lose jobs to automation, the inner circle maintains its political power and profits from the new technology. The term **corporate capitalism** indicates that giant corporations dominate capitalism today. Pp. 413–418.

Work in U.S. Society

How has the workforce changed?

In the transition to a postindustrial society, the number of farm workers has plummeted, blue-collar work has shrunk, and most people work at service jobs. Pp. 418–421.

What is the underground economy?

The **underground economy** consists of any economic activity not reported to the government, from babysitting to prostitution. The size of the underground economy runs about 10 percent of the regular economy. Pp. 422–423.

How have patterns of work and leisure changed?

In hunting and gathering societies, most time was **leisure.** In agricultural societies, work was dictated by the seasons. Industrialization reduced workers' leisure, but workers have now gained some leisure back. Americans and Japanese work more hours per week than do the workers of any other industrialized nation. Pp. 423–424.

Facing the Future: Implications of Global Capitalism

What economic trends will affect our future?

Because of expanding global trade and new technologies, the nature of work will continue to be transformed. Choices made now can lead either to a better society or to a nightmare. Pp. 424–427.

Thinking Critically
about Chapter 14

1. What global forces are affecting the U.S. economy? What consequences are they having? How might they affect your own life?

2. What are the major characteristics and ideologies of capitalism and socialism? How are these related to the earlier political and economic competition called the *Cold War*?

3. How can anyone say that the average U.S. worker hasn't gotten ahead in recent years, when the average hourly wage has jumped from $3 to $16 an hour? What implications does this have for your own future?

Additional Resources

Where Can I Read More on This Topic?

Suggested readings for this chapter are listed at the back of this book.

CHAPTER 15

Politics

Fred Otnes, *We The People* 1978

In 1949, George Orwell wrote *1984,* a book about a time in the future in which the government, known as "Big Brother," dominates society, dictating almost every aspect of each individual's life. Even loving someone is considered sinister—a betrayal of the supreme love and total allegiance that all citizens owe Big Brother.

Despite the danger, Winston and Julia fall in love. They delight in each other, but they must meet furtively, always with the threat of discovery hanging over their heads. When informers turn them in, interrogators separate Julia and Winston and try to destroy their affection and restore their loyalty to Big Brother.

Winston's tormentor is O'Brien, who straps Winston into a chair so tightly that he can't even move his head. O'Brien explains that inflicting pain is not always enough to break a person's will, but everyone has a breaking point. There is some worst fear that will push anyone over the edge.

O'Brien tells Winston that he has discovered his worst fear. Then he sets a cage with two giant, starving sewer rats on the table next to Winston. O'Brien picks up a hood connected to the door of the cage and places it over Winston's head. He then explains that when he presses the lever, the door of the cage will slide up, and the rats will shoot out like bullets and bore straight into Winston's face. Winston's eyes, the only part of his body that he can move, dart back and forth, revealing his terror. Speaking so quietly that Winston has to strain to hear him, O'Brien adds that the rats sometimes attack the eyes first, but sometimes they burrow through the cheeks and devour the tongue. When O'Brien places his hand on the lever, Winston realizes that the only way out is for someone else to take his place. But who? Then he hears his own voice screaming, "Do it to Julia! . . . Tear her face off. Strip her to the bones. Not me! Julia! Not me!"

Even loving someone is considered sinister—a betrayal of the supreme love and total allegiance that all citizens owe Big Brother

Orwell does not describe Julia's interrogation, but when Julia and Winston see each other later, they realize that each has betrayed the other. Their love is gone. Big Brother has won.

Winston's and Julia's misplaced loyalty had made them political heretics, a danger to the state, for every citizen had the duty to place the state above all else in life. To preserve the state's dominance over the individual, their allegiance to one another had to be stripped from them. As you see, it was.

The ultimate foundation of any political order is violence. At no time is this more starkly demonstrated than when a government takes a human life. Shown in this 1910 photo from New York's Sing Sing Prison is a man who is about to be executed.

Although seldom this dramatic, politics is always about power and authority. Let's explore this topic that is so significant for our lives.

Micropolitics and Macropolitics

The images that come to mind when we think of *politics* are those of government: kings, queens, coups, dictatorships, people running for office, voting. These are examples of politics, but the term actually has a much broader meaning. **Politics** refers to *power relations wherever they exist,* including those in everyday life. As Weber (1922/1978) said, **power** is the ability to get your way even over the resistance of others. You can see the struggle for power all around you. When workers try to gain the favor of their bosses, they are attempting to maneuver into a stronger position. Students do the same with their teachers. Power struggles are also part of family life, such as when parents try to enforce a curfew over the protests of a reluctant daughter or son. Ever have a struggle over the remote control to the TV? All these examples illustrate attempts to gain power—and, thus, are political actions. *Every group, then, is political, for in every group there is a power struggle of some sort.* Symbolic interactionists use the term **micropolitics** to refer to the exercise of power in everyday life (Schwartz 1990).

In contrast, **macropolitics**—the focus of this chapter—refers to the exercise of power over a large group. Governments—whether dictatorships or democracies—are examples of macropolitics. Because authority is essential to macropolitics, let's begin with this topic.

Power, Authority, and Violence

To exist, every society must have a system of leadership. Some people must have power over others. As Max Weber (1913/1947) pointed out, we perceive power as either legitimate or illegitimate. *Legitimate* power is called **authority.** This is power that people accept as right. In contrast, *illegitimate* power—called **coercion**—is power that people do not accept as just.

> Imagine that you are on your way to buy a digital TV that is on sale for $250. As you approach the store, a man jumps out of an alley and shoves a gun in your face. He demands your money. Frightened for your life, you hand over your $250. After filing a police report, you head back to college to take a sociology exam. You are running late, so you step on the gas. As you hit 85, you see flashing blue and red lights in your rear-view mirror. Your explanation about the robbery doesn't faze the officer—or the judge who hears your case a few weeks later. She first lectures you on safety and then orders you to pay $50 in court costs plus $10 for every mile over 65. You pay the $250.

The mugger, the police officer, and the judge—each has power, and in each case you part with $250. What, then, is the difference? The difference is that the mugger has no authority. His power is *illegitimate*—he has no *right* to do what he did. In contrast, you acknowledge that the officer has the right to stop you and that the judge has the right to fine you. They have authority, or *legitimate* power.

Authority and Legitimate Violence

As sociologist Peter Berger observed, it makes little difference whether you willingly pay the fine that the judge levies against you or refuse to pay it. The court will get its money one way or another.

---

politics the exercise of power and attempts to maintain or to change power relations

power the ability to carry out your will, even over the resistance of others

micropolitics the exercise of power in everyday life, such as deciding who is going to do the housework or use the remote control

macropolitics the exercise of large-scale power, the government being the most common example

authority power that people consider legitimate, as rightly exercised over them; also called *legitimate power*

coercion power that people do not accept as rightly exercised over them; also called *illegitimate power*

There may be innumerable steps before its application [of violence], in the way of warnings and reprimands. But if all the warnings are disregarded, even in so slight a matter as paying a traffic ticket, the last thing that will happen is that a couple of cops show up at the door with handcuffs and a Black Maria [billy club]. Even the moderately courteous cop who hands out the initial traffic ticket is likely to wear a gun—just in case. (Berger 1963)

The *government,* then, also called the **state,** claims a monopoly on legitimate force or violence. This point, made by Max Weber (1946, 1922/1978)—that the state claims both the exclusive right to use violence and the right to punish everyone else who uses violence—is crucial to our understanding of politics. If someone owes you a debt, you cannot take the money by force, much less imprison that person. The state, however, can. The ultimate proof of the state's authority is that you cannot kill someone because he or she has done something that you consider absolutely horrible—but the state can. As Berger (1963) summarized this matter, *"Violence is the ultimate foundation of any political order."*

Before we explore the origins of the modern state, let's first look at a situation in which the state loses legitimacy.

The Collapse of Authority Sometimes the state oppresses its people, and they resist their government just as they do a mugger. The people cooperate reluctantly—with a smile if that is what is required—while they eye the gun in the hand of the government's representatives. But, as they do with a mugger, when they get the chance, they take up arms to free themselves. **Revolution,** armed resistance with the intent to overthrow and replace a government, is not only a people's rejection of a government's claim to rule over them but also their rejection of its monopoly on violence. In a revolution, people assert that right for themselves. If successful, they establish a new state in which they claim the right to monopolize violence.

What some see as coercion, however, others see as authority. Consequently, while some people are ready to take up arms against a government, others remain loyal to it, willingly defend it, and perhaps even die for it. *The more that its power is seen as legitimate, then, the more stable a government is.*

But just why do people accept power as legitimate? Max Weber (1922/1978) identified three sources of authority: traditional, rational-legal, and charismatic. Let's examine each.

Traditional Authority

Throughout history, the most common basis for authority has been tradition. **Traditional authority,** which is based on custom, is the hallmark of tribal groups. In these societies, custom dictates basic relationships. For example, birth into a particular family makes an individual the chief, king, or queen. As far as members of that society are concerned, this is the right way to determine who shall rule because "We've always done it this way."

Gender relations often open a window on traditional authority. For example, as shown in the photo to the right, in the villages of Spain, widows are expected to wear only black until they remarry. This generally means that they wear black for the rest of their lives. By law, a widow is free to wear any color she wishes, but custom dictates otherwise. Tradition has been so strong that if a widow were to violate this dress code by wearing a color other than black, she would be perceived as having profaned the memory of her deceased husband and would be ostracized by the community.

When a traditional society industrializes, its transformation undermines traditional authority. Social change brings with it new experiences. This opens up new perspectives on life, and no longer does traditional authority go unchallenged. In some

For centuries, widows in Mediterranean countries, such as these widows in Spain, were expected to dress in black and to mourn for their husbands the rest of their lives. Their long dresses were matched by black stockings, black shoes, and black head coverings. Widows conformed to this expression of lifetime sorrow for their deceased husband not because of law, but because of custom. As industrialization erodes traditional authority, fewer widows follow this practice.

state a political entity that claims monopoly on the use of violence in some particular territory; commonly known as a country

revolution armed resistance designed to overthrow and replace a government

traditional authority authority based on custom

villages of Spain, for example, you can still see old women dressed in black from head to toe—and you immediately know their marital status. Younger widows, however, are likely to be indistinguishable from other women.

Although traditional authority declines with industrialization, it never dies out. Even though we live in a postindustrial society, parents continue to exercise authority over their children *because* parents always have had such authority. From generations past, we inherit the idea that parents should discipline their children, choose their children's doctors and schools, and teach their children religion and morality.

Rational-Legal Authority

The second type of authority, **rational-legal authority,** is based not on custom but on written rules. *Rational* means reasonable, and *legal* means part of law. Thus *rational-legal* refers to matters that have been agreed to by reasonable people and written into law (or regulations of some sort). The matters that are agreed to may be as broad as a constitution that specifies the rights of all members of a society or as narrow as a contract between two individuals. Because bureaucracies are based on written rules, rational-legal authority is sometimes called *bureaucratic authority.*

Rational-legal authority comes from the *position* that someone holds, not from the person who holds that position. In a democracy, for example, the president's authority comes from the legal power assigned to that office, as specified in a written constitution, not from custom or the individual's personal characteristics. In rational-legal authority, everyone—no matter how high their office—is subject to the organization's written rules. In governments based on traditional authority, the ruler's word may be law, but in those based on rational-legal authority, the ruler's word is subject to the law.

Charismatic Authority

A few centuries back, in 1429, the English controlled large parts of France. When they prevented the coronation of a new French king, a farmer's daughter heard a voice telling her that God had a special assignment for her—that she should put on men's clothing, recruit an army, and go to war against the English. Inspired, Joan of Arc raised an army, conquered cities, and defeated the English. Later that year, her visions were fulfilled as she stood next to Charles VII while he was crowned king of France. (Bridgwater 1953)

Joan of Arc is an example of **charismatic authority,** the third type of authority Weber identified. (*Charisma* is a Greek word that means a gift freely and graciously given [Arndt and Gingrich 1957].) People are drawn to a charismatic individual because they believe that individual has been touched by God or has been endowed by nature with exceptional qualities (Lipset 1993). The armies did not follow Joan of Arc because it was the custom to do so, as in traditional authority. Nor did they risk their lives alongside her because she held a position defined by written rules, as in rational-legal authority. Instead, people followed her because they were attracted by her outstanding traits. They saw her as a messenger of God, fighting on the side of justice, and they accepted her leadership because of these appealing qualities.

One of the best examples of *charismatic authority* is Joan of Arc, shown here at the coronation of Charles VII, whom she was instrumental in making king. Uncomfortable at portraying Joan of Arc wearing only a man's coat of armor, the artist has made certain she is wearing plenty of makeup, and also has added a ludicrous skirt.

The Threat Posed by Charismatic Leaders Kings and queens owe allegiance to tradition, and presidents to written laws. To what, however, do charismatic leaders owe allegiance? Their authority resides in their ability to attract followers, which is often based on their sense of a special mission or calling. Not tied to tradition or the regulation of law, charismatic leaders pose a threat to the established political order. Following their personal inclination, charismatic leaders can inspire followers to disregard—or even to overthrow—traditional and rational-legal authorities.

This threat does not go unnoticed, and traditional and rational-legal authorities often oppose charismatic leaders. If they are not careful, however, their opposition may arouse even more positive sentiment in favor of the charismatic leader, with him or her viewed as an underdog persecuted by the powerful. Occasionally the Roman Catholic Church faces such a threat, as when a priest claims miraculous powers that appear to be accompanied by amazing healings. As people flock to this individual, they bypass parish priests and the formal ecclesiastical structure. This transfer of allegiance from the organization to an individual threatens the church hierarchy. Consequently, church officials may encourage the priest to withdraw from the public eye, perhaps to a monastery, to rethink matters. This defuses the threat, reasserts rational-legal authority, and maintains the stability of the organization.

Charismatic authorities can be of any morality, from the saintly to the most bitterly evil. Like Joan of Arc, Adolf Hitler attracted throngs of people, providing the stuff of dreams and arousing them from disillusionment to hope. This poster from the 1930s, titled *Es Lebe Deutschland* ("Long Live Germany"), illustrates the qualities of leadership that Germans of that period saw in Hitler.

Authority as Ideal Type

Weber's classifications—traditional, rational-legal, and charismatic—represent ideal types of authority. As noted on page 183, *ideal type* does not refer to what is ideal or desirable, but to a composite of characteristics found in many real-life examples. A particular leader, then, may show a combination of characteristics.

An example is John F. Kennedy, who combined rational-legal and charismatic authority. As the elected head of the U.S. government, Kennedy represented rational-legal authority. Yet his mass appeal was so great that his public speeches aroused large numbers of people to action. When in his inaugural address Kennedy said, "Ask not what your country can do for you; ask what you can do for your country," millions of Americans were touched. When Kennedy proposed a Peace Corps to help poorer countries, thousands of idealistic young people volunteered for challenging foreign service.

Charismatic and traditional authority can also overlap. The Ayatollah Khomeini of Iran, for example, was a religious leader, holding the traditional position of ayatollah. His embodiment of the Iranian people's dreams, however, as well as his austere life and devotion to principles of the Koran, gave him such mass appeal that he was also a charismatic leader. Khomeini's followers were convinced that God had chosen him, and his speeches could arouse tens of thousands of followers to action.

In rare instances, then, traditional and rational-legal leaders possess charismatic traits. This is unusual, however, and most authority is clearly one type or another.

The Transfer of Authority

The orderly transfer of authority from one leader to another is crucial for social stability. Under traditional authority, people know who is next in line. Under rational-legal authority, people might not know who the next leader will be, but they do know how that person will be selected. South Africa provides a remarkable example of the orderly transfer of authority under a rational-legal organization. This country had been ripped apart by decades of racial strife, including horrible killings committed by each side. Yet, by maintaining its rational-legal authority, the country was able to transfer power peacefully from the dominant group led by President de Klerk to the minority group led by Nelson Mandela.

Charismatic authority has no such rules of succession, however. This makes it less stable than either traditional or rational-legal authority. Because charismatic authority is built around a single individual, the death or incapacitation of a charismatic leader can mean a bitter struggle for succession. To avoid this, some charismatic leaders make arrangements for an orderly transition of power by appointing a successor. This does not guarantee orderly succession, of course, for the followers may not have the same confidence in the designated heir as did the charismatic leader. A second strategy is for the charismatic leader to build an organization. As the organization develops a system of rules or regulations, it transforms itself into a rational-legal organization. Weber used the term the **routinization of charisma** to refer to the transition of authority from a charismatic leader to either traditional or rational-legal authority.

Types of Government

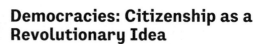 How do the various types of government—monarchies, democracies, dictatorships, and oligarchies—differ? As we compare them, let's also look at how the state arose, and why the concept of citizenship was revolutionary.

Monarchies: The Rise of the State

Early societies were small and needed no extensive political system. They operated more like an extended family. As surpluses developed and societies grew larger, cities evolved—perhaps around 3500 B.C. (Fischer 1976). **City-states** then came into being, with power radiating outward from the city like a spider's web. Although the ruler of each city controlled the immediate surrounding area, the land between cities remained in dispute. Each city-state had its own **monarchy,** a king or queen whose right to rule was passed on to their children. If you drive through Spain, France, or Germany, you can still see evidence of former city-states. In the countryside, you will see only scattered villages. Farther on, your eye will be drawn to the outline of a castle on a faraway hill. As you get closer, you will see that the castle is surrounded by a city. Several miles farther, you will see another city, also dominated by a castle. Each city, with its castle, was once a center of power.

City-states often quarreled, and wars were common. The victors extended their rule, and eventually a single city-state was able to wield power over an entire region. As the size of these regions grew, the people slowly began to identify with the larger region. That is, they began to see distant inhabitants as "we" instead of "they." What we call the **state**—the political entity that claims a monopoly on the use of violence within a territory—came into being.

Democracies: Citizenship as a Revolutionary Idea

The United States had no city-states. Each colony, however, was small and independent like a city-state. After the American Revolution, the colonies united. With the greater strength and resources that came from political unity, they conquered almost all of North America, bringing it under the power of a central government.

The government formed in this new country was called a **democracy.** (Derived from two Greek words—*demos* [common people] and *kratos* [power]—*democracy* literally means "power to the people.") Because of the bitter antagonisms associated with the revolution against the British king, the founders of the new country were distrustful of monarchies. They wanted to put political decisions into the hands of the people.

This was not the first democracy the world had seen, but such a system had been tried before only with smaller groups. Athens, a city-state of Greece, practiced democracy two thousand years ago, with each free male above a certain age having the right to be heard and to vote. Members of some Native American tribes, such as the Iroquois, also elected their chiefs,

"We probably look like fools, but we have to do this" could be what Presidents Bush and Putkin are thinking as they participate in an economic summit in Vietnam. The orderly transfer of power is important for political stability. Unlike its recent past—with political intrigues and murder (called purges)—Russia has developed a democratic system in which the transfer of power occurs through elections. Elected politicians have to do some strange things.

and in some, women were able to vote and to hold the office of chief. (The Incas and Aztecs of Mexico and Central America had monarchies.)

Because of their small size, tribes and cities were able to practice **direct democracy.** That is, they were small enough for the eligible voters to meet together, express their opinions, and then vote publicly—much like a town hall meeting today. As populous and spread out as the United States was, however, direct democracy was impossible, and the founders invented **representative democracy.** Certain citizens (at first only white male landowners) voted for men to represent them in Washington. Later, the vote was extended to men who didn't own property, to African American men, and, finally, to women. Our new communications technologies, which make "electronic town meetings" possible, could even allow a new form of direct democracy to develop. This issue is explored in the Mass Media box on the next page.

Democracy (or "democratization") is a global social movement. People all over the world yearn for the freedoms that are taken for granted in the Western democracies. Shown here is a man in a remote village in Indonesia, where democracy has gained a foothold.

Today we take the concept of citizenship for granted. What is not evident to us is that this idea had to be envisioned in the first place. There is nothing natural about citizenship; it is simply one way in which people choose to define themselves. Throughout most of human history, people were thought to *belong* to a clan, to a tribe, or even to a ruler. The idea of **citizenship**—that by virtue of birth and residence people have basic rights—is quite new to the human scene (Turner 1990; Abowitz and Harnish 2006).

The concept of representative democracy based on citizenship—perhaps the greatest gift the United States has given to the world—was revolutionary. Power was to be vested in the people themselves, and government was to flow from the people. That this concept was revolutionary is generally forgotten, but its implementation meant *the reversal of traditional ideas. It made the government responsive to the people's will, not the people responsive to the government's will.* To keep the government responsive to the needs of its citizens, people were expected to express dissent. In a widely quoted statement, Thomas Jefferson observed that

> A little rebellion now and then is a good thing. . . . It is a medicine necessary for the sound health of government. . . . God forbid that we should ever be twenty years without such a rebellion. . . . The tree of liberty must be refreshed from time to time with the blood of patriots and tyrants. (In Hellinger and Judd 1991)

The idea of **universal citizenship**—of *everyone* having the same basic rights by virtue of being born in a country (or by immigrating and becoming a naturalized citizen)—flowered slowly, and came into practice only through fierce struggle. When the United States was founded, for example, this idea was still in its infancy. Today it seems inconceivable to Americans that gender or race-ethnicity should be the basis to deny anyone the right to vote, hold office, make a contract, testify in court, or own property. For earlier generations of property–owning white American men, however, it seemed just as inconceivable that women, racial-ethnic minorities, and the poor should be *allowed* such rights.

Over the years, then, rights have been extended, and in the United States citizenship and its privileges now apply to all. No longer do property ownership, gender, or race-ethnicity determine the right to vote, testify in court, and so on. These characteristics, however, do influence whether one votes, as we shall see in a later section on voting patterns.

Dictatorships and Oligarchies: The Seizure of Power

If an individual seizes power and then dictates his will onto the people, the government is known as a **dictatorship.** If a small group seizes power, the government is called an

direct democracy a form of democracy in which the eligible voters meet together to discuss issues and make their decisions

representative democracy a form of democracy in which voters elect representatives to meet together to discuss issues and make decisions on their behalf

citizenship the concept that birth (and residence) in a country impart basic rights

universal citizenship the idea that everyone has the same basic rights by virtue of being born in a country (or by immigrating and becoming a naturalized citizen)

dictatorship a form of government in which an individual has seized power

mass Media in Social Life

Politics and Democracy in a Technological Society

"Politics is just like show business."
—Ronald Reagan

The new technology holds tremendous promise for democracy, but does it also pose a threat to democracy?

Certainly the new technology is a powerful tool for politicians. Candidates use the Internet to state their position on issues, to organize supporters, and to raise funds. They also use computers, telephone link-ups, faxes, e-mail, Web sites, and blogs.

Even Chinese leaders listen to the opinions that their people express on Web sites. When officials were deciding whether to award a Japanese company a contract to build a bullet train between Beijing and Shanghai, there was an online outpouring of resentment against the Japanese for not atoning for their war crimes in China. Communist officials dropped Japan from consideration.

The Internet holds the potential for transforming the way we vote and pass laws. If we "televote,"no longer will we have to travel to polling places in rain and snow. More people would probably vote, for they could cast their ballots from the comfort of their own living rooms and offices. When almost everyone owns a computer, televoting could even replace our representational democracy with a form of direct democracy.

The Internet also holds the potential of making politicians more responsive to our will. Voters will be able to circulate petitions online, sign them with digital signatures, and force politicians to respond. On many matters, voters might be able to bypass politicians entirely, Online, they would be able to decide issues that politicians now resolve for them. They could even pass laws online.

With all these potential benefits, how could the new technology pose a threat to democracy?

Some fear that the Internet isn't safe for voting. With no poll watchers, how would threats, promises, or gifts in return for votes be detected? There is also the threat of hackers, so proficient that they even find ways to break into "secure" financial and government sites. Proponents counter with a litany of the shortcomings of other voting methods—that ballot boxes have been stuffed, and that electronic voting machines can be rigged with chips to redistribute votes already cast (Duffy 2006).

Others raise a more fundamental issue: Direct democracy might be a detour around the U.S. Constitution's system of checks and balances, which was designed to safeguard us from the "tyranny of the majority." To determine from a poll that 51 percent of adults hold a certain opinion on an issue is one thing—that information can guide our leaders. But to have 51 percent of televoters determine a law is not the same as having elected representatives argue the merits of a proposal in public and then try to balance the interests of the many groups that make up their constituency.

Others counter that before people televote, the merits of a proposal would be debated vigorously in newspapers, on radio

Under its constitutional system, the United States is remarkably stable: Power is transferred peacefully—even when someone of an unusual background wins an election. Arnold Schwarzenegger, shown here in his role in *Predator*, was elected governor of California in 2003 and reelected in 2006.

and television, and on the Internet itself. Voters would certainly be no less informed than they now are. As far as balancing interest groups is concerned, that would take care of itself, for people from all interest groups would participate in televoting.

for your Consideration

Do you think that direct democracy would be superior to representative democracy? How about the issue of the "tyranny of the majority"? (This means that the interests of smaller groups—whether racial-ethnic, regional, or any other group—are overwhelmed by the voting power of the majority.) How can we use the mass media and the Internet to improve government?

Sources: Diamond and Silverman 1995; Seib 2000; Hutzler 2004; Duffy 2006.

---

oligarchy a form of government in which a small group of individuals holds power; the rule of the many by the few

totalitarianism a form of government that exerts almost total control over people

oligarchy. The occasional coups in Central and South America and Africa, in which military leaders seize control of a country, are examples of oligarchies. Although one individual may be named president, often it is military officers, working behind the scenes, who make the decisions. If their designated president becomes uncooperative, they remove him from office and appoint another.

Monarchies, dictatorships, and oligarchies vary in the amount of control they wield over their citizens. **Totalitarianism** is almost *total* control of a people by the government. In Nazi Germany, Hitler organized a ruthless secret police force, the Gestapo, which searched for any sign of dissent. Spies even watched how moviegoers reacted to newsreels, reporting those who did not respond "appropriately" (Hipler 1987). Saddam Hussein acted just as ruthlessly toward Iraqis. The lucky ones who opposed Hussein were shot; the unlucky ones had their eyes gouged out, were bled to death, or were buried alive (Amnesty International 2005). The punishment for telling a joke about Hussein was to have your tongue cut out.

People around the world find great appeal in the freedom that is inherent in citizenship and representative democracy. Those who have no say in their government's decisions, or who face prison or even death for expressing dissent, find in these ideas the hope for a brighter future. With today's electronic communications, people no longer remain ignorant of whether they are more or less politically privileged than others. This knowledge produces pressure for greater citizen participation in government. As electronic communications develop further, this pressure will increase.

The U.S. Political System

 With this global background, let's examine the U.S. political system. We shall consider the two major political parties, compare the U.S. political system with other democratic systems, and examine voting patterns and the role of lobbyists and PACs.

Political Parties and Elections

After the founding of the United States, numerous political parties emerged. By the time of the Civil War, however, two parties dominated U.S. politics: the Democrats, who in the public mind are associated with the working class, and the Republicans, who are associated with wealthier people (Burnham 1983). Each party nominates candidates, and in pre-elections, called *primaries,* the voters decide which candidates will represent their party. Each candidate then campaigns, trying to appeal to the most voters. The Social Map below shows how Americans align themselves with political parties.

Figure 15.1 **Which Political Party Dominates?**

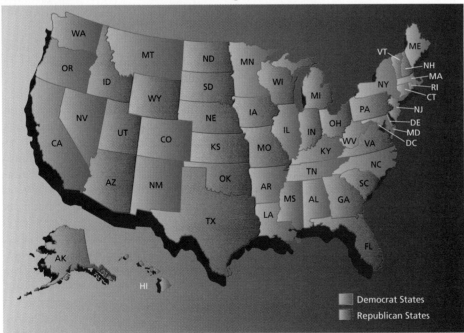

Note: Domination by a political party does *not* refer to votes for President or Congress. This social map is based on the composition of the states' upper and lower houses. When different parties dominate a state's houses, the total number of legislators was used. In case of ties (or, as with Nebraska, which has no party designation), the percentage vote for President was used.

Source: By the author. Based on *Statistical Abstract* 2007:Tables 389,400.

As Latinos have grown in numbers, so has their political prominence. Shown here is Antonio Villaraigosa, the mayor of Los Angeles, California. People have many reasons for voting the way they do, including the ethnicity of the candidate. When political parties select candidates, their race-ethnicity is always a consideration.

Although the Democrats and Republicans represent somewhat different philosophical principles, each party appeals to a broad membership, and it is difficult to distinguish a conservative Democrat from a liberal Republican. The extremes are easy to discern, however. Deeply committed Democrats support legislation that transfers income from those who are richer to those who are poorer or that controls wages, working conditions, and competition. Deeply committed Republicans, in contrast, oppose such legislation.

Those who are elected to Congress may cross party lines. That is, some Democrats vote for legislation proposed by Republicans, and vice versa. This happens because office-holders support their party's philosophy, but not necessarily its specific proposals. When it comes to a particular bill, such as raising the minimum wage, some conservative Democrats may view the measure as unfair to small employers and vote with the Republicans against the bill. At the same time, liberal Republicans—feeling that the proposal is just, or sensing a dominant sentiment in voters back home—may side with its Democratic backers.

Regardless of their differences and their public quarrels, the Democrats and Republicans represent *different slices of the center.* Although each party may ridicule the opposing party and promote different legislation, they both firmly support such fundamentals of U.S. political philosophy as free public education; a strong military; freedom of religion, speech, and assembly; and, of course, capitalism—especially the private ownership of property.

Third parties also play a role in U.S. politics, but to gain power, they must also support these centrist themes. Any party that advocates radical change is doomed to a short life. Because most Americans consider a vote for a third party a waste, third parties do notoriously poorly at the polls. Two exceptions are the Bull Moose party, whose candidate, Theodore Roosevelt, won more votes in 1912 than Robert Taft, the Republican presidential candidate, and the United We Stand (Reform) party, founded by billionaire Ross Perot, which won 19 percent of the vote in 1992. Amidst internal bickering, the Reform Party declined rapidly, dropping to 8 percent of the presidential vote in 1996, less than 1 percent in 2000, and then off the political map (Bridgwater 1953; *Statistical Abstract* 1995:Table 437; 2007:Table 386).

Contrast with Democratic Systems in Europe

We tend to take our political system for granted and to assume that any other democracy looks like ours—even down to having two major parties. Such is not the case. To gain a comparative understanding, let's look at the European system.

Although both their system and ours are democracies, there are fundamental distinctions between the two (Lind 1995). First, elections in most of Europe are not winner-take-all. In the United States, a simple majority determines an election. For example, if a Democrat wins 51 percent of the votes cast in an electoral district, he or she takes office. The Republican candidate, who may have won 49 percent, loses everything. Most European countries, in contrast, base their elections on a system of **proportional representation;** that is, the seats in the legislature are divided according to the proportion of votes that each party receives. If one party wins 51 percent of the vote, for example, that party is awarded 51 percent of the seats; while a party with 49 percent of the votes receives 49 percent of the seats.

Second, proportional representation encourages minority parties, while the winner-take-all system discourages them. In a proportional representation system, if a party can get 10 percent of the voters to support its candidate, it will get 10 percent of the seats. This system encourages the formation of **noncentrist parties,** those that propose less popular ideas, such as the shutting down of nuclear power reactors. In the United States, in contrast, 10 percent of the votes means 0 seats. So does 49 percent of the votes. This pushes parties to the center: If a party is to have any chance of "taking it all," it must strive to obtain broad support. For this reason, the United States has **centrist parties.**

The proportional representation system bestows publicity and power on noncentrist parties. Winning a few seats in the national legislature allows even a tiny party to gain

proportional representation an electoral system in which seats in a legislature are divided according to the proportion of votes that each political party receives

noncentrist party a political party that represents less central (or popular) ideas

centrist party a political party that represents the center of political opinion access to the media throughout the year, which helps keep its issues alive. Small parties also gain power beyond their numbers. Because votes are fragmented among the many parties that compete in elections, seldom does a single party gain a majority of the seats in the legislature. To muster the required votes, the party with the most seats must form a **coalition government** by aligning itself with one or more of the smaller parties. A party with only 10 or 15 percent of the seats, then, may be able to trade its vote on some issues for the larger party's support on others. Because coalitions often fall apart, these governments tend to be less stable than that of the United States. Italy, for example, has had 60 different governments since World War II (some lasting as little as two weeks, none longer than four years) (Fisher 2007). During this same period, the United States has had eleven presidents. Seeing the greater stability of the U.S. government, the Italians have voted that three-fourths of their Senate seats will be decided on the winner-take-all system (Katz 2006).

coalition government a government in which a country's largest party aligns itself with one or more smaller parties

voter apathy indifference and inaction on the part of individuals or groups with respect to the political process

Voting Patterns

Year after year, Americans show consistent voting patterns. From Table 15.1 on page 443, you can see that the percentage of people who vote increases with age. This table also shows how significant race-ethnicity is. Non-Hispanic whites are more likely to vote than are African Americans, while Latinos and Asian Americans are the least likely to vote. The significance of race-ethnicity is so great that Latinos are only half as likely to vote as are African Americans and non-Hispanic whites. A crucial aspect of the socialization of newcomers to the United States is to learn the U.S. political system, the topic of the Cultural Diversity box on the next page.

From Table 15.1, you can see how voting increases with education—that college graduates are almost twice as likely to vote as are high school graduates. You can also see how much more likely the employed are to vote. And look at how powerful income is in determining voting. At each higher income level, people are more likely to vote. Finally, note that women are slightly more likely than men to vote.

Social Integration   How can we explain the voting patterns shown in Table 15.1? Look at the extremes. Those who are most likely to vote are whites who are older, more educated, affluent, and employed. Those who are least likely to vote are Latinos who are younger, less educated, poor, and unemployed. From these extremes, we can draw this principle: *The more that people feel they have a stake in the political system, the more likely they are to vote.* They have more to protect, and they feel that voting can make a difference. In effect, people who have been rewarded more by the political and economic system feel more socially integrated. They vote because they perceive that elections make a difference in their lives, including the type of society in which they and their children live.

Alienation and Apathy   In contrast, those who gain less from the system—in terms of education, income, and jobs—are more likely to feel alienated from politics. Perceiving themselves as outsiders, many feel hostile toward the government. Some feel betrayed, believing that politicians have sold out to special-interest groups. They are convinced that all politicians are liars. Minorities who feel that the U.S. political system is a "white" system are less likely to vote.

From Table 15.1, we see that many highly educated people with good incomes also stay away from the polls. Many people do not vote because of **voter apathy,** or indifference. Their view is that "next year will just bring more of the same, regardless of who is in office." A common attitude of those who are apathetic is "What difference will my one vote make when there are millions of voters?" Many also see little difference between the two major political parties.

Alienation and apathy are so widespread that only *half* of the nation's eligible voters cast ballots in presidential elections, and even fewer vote for candidates for Congress (*Statistical Abstract* 2007: Table 408).

The Politics of Immigrants: Power, Ethnicity, and Social Class

THAT THE UNITED STATES IS THE land of immigrants is a truism. Every schoolchild knows that since the English Pilgrims landed on Plymouth Rock, group after group has sought relief from hardship by reaching U.S. shores. Some, such as the Irish immigrants in the late 1800s and early 1900s, left to escape brutal poverty and famine. Others, such as the Jews of czarist Russia, fled religious persecution. Some sought refuge from lands ravaged by war. Others, called entrepreneurial immigrants, came primarily for better economic opportunities. Still others were sojourners who planned to return home after a temporary stay. Some, not usually called immigrants, came in chains, held in bondage by early immigrants.

Today, the United States is in the midst of its second largest wave of immigration. In the first wave, immigrants accounted for 15 percent of the U.S. population. Almost all of those immigrants in the early 1900s came from Europe. During our current second wave, immigrants make up about 12 percent of the U.S. population, with a mix that is far more diverse: Immigration from Europe has slowed to a trickle, with twice as many of our most recent immigrants coming from Asia as from Europe (*Statistical Abstract* 2007:Table 47). In the past 25 years, about 20 million immigrants have settled legally in the United States (*Statistical Abstract* 2007:Table 5). Millions more—estimated at 8 to 15 million—are here illegally. Counting them, immigrants make up 15 or 16 percent of the U.S. population, as much as the great wave of immigration 100 years ago.

In the last century, U.S.-born Americans feared that immigrants would bring socialism or communism with them. Today's fear is that the millions of immigrants from Spanish-speaking countries threaten the primacy of the English language. Last century brought a fear that immigrants would take jobs away from U.S.-born Americans. This fear has returned. In addition, African Americans fear

This photo from 1920 shows immigrants arriving at Ellis Island, New York. They are being inspected for obvious signs of disease. If any disease is detected, they will be refused entry. Sociologists have studied the process by which immigrants are assimilated.

a loss of political power as immigrants from Mexico and Central and South America swell the Latino population.

After they are in the country, what path to political activity do immigrants take? In general, they first organize as a group on the basis of *ethnicity* rather than *class*. They respond to common problems, especially discrimination and issues associated with adapting to a new way of life. This first step in political activity is to reaffirm their cultural identity. As sociologists Alejandro Portés and Ruben Rumbaut (1990) note, "By mobilizing the collective vote and by electing their own to office, immigrant minorities have learned the rules of the democratic game and absorbed its values in the process."

As Portés and Rumbaut observe, immigrants don't become "American" overnight. Instead, they begin by fighting for their own interests as a group—as Irish, Italians, and so on. Only after the group attains enough political power to overcome discrimination do they become "like everyone else"—that is, like those who have power. As a group gains representation somewhat proportionate to its numbers, a major change occurs: At that point, social class becomes more significant than race-ethnicity.

Irish immigrants to Boston illustrate this pattern. Banding together on the basis of ethnicity, they built a power base that put the Irish in political control of Boston. As the significance of ethnicity faded, social class became prominent. Ultimately, they saw John F. Kennedy, one of their own, from the upper class, sworn in as president of the United States.

for your Consideration

Try to project the path to political participation of the many millions of new U.S. immigrants. What obstacles will they have to overcome? Why do you think their path will or will not be similar to that of the earlier U.S. immigrants?

Table 15.1 Who Votes for President?

	1980	1984	1988	1992	1996	2000	2004
Overall							
Americans Who Vote	59%	60%	57%	61%	54%	55%	58%
Age							
18–20	36%	37%	33%	39%	31%	28%	41%
21–24	43%	44%	46%	46%	33%	35%	43%
25–34	55%	58%	48%	53%	43%	44%	47%
35–44	64%	64%	61%	64%	55%	55%	57%
45–64	69%	70%	68%	70%	64%	64%	67%
65 and older	65%	68%	69%	70%	67%	68%	69%
Sex							
Male	59%	59%	56%	60%	53%	53%	56%
Female	59%	61%	58%	62%	56%	56%	60%
Race/Ethnicity							
Whites	61%	61%	59%	64%	56%	56%	60%
African Americans	51%	56%	52%	54%	51%	54%	56%
Asians	NA	NA	NA	NA	NA	25%	30%
Latinos	30%	33%	29%	29%	27%	28%	28%
Education							
High school dropouts	46%	44%	41%	41%	34%	34%	40%
High school graduates	59%	59%	55%	58%	49%	49%	56%
College dropouts	67%	68%	65%	69%	61%	60%	69%
College graduates	80%	79%	78%	81%	73%	72%	74%
Marital Status							
Married	NA	NA	NA	NA	66%	67%	71%
Divorced	NA	NA	NA	NA	50%	53%	58%
Labor Force							
Employed	62%	62%	58%	64%	55%	56%	60%
Unemployed	41%	44%	39%	46%	37%	35%	46%
Income[a]							
Under $20,000	NA	NA	NA	NA	NA	NA	48%
$20,000 to $30,000	NA	NA	NA	NA	NA	NA	58%
$30,000 to $40,000	NA	NA	NA	NA	NA	NA	62%
$40,000 to $50,000	NA	NA	NA	NA	NA	NA	69%
$50,000 to $75,000	NA	NA	NA	NA	NA	NA	72%
$75,000 to $100,000	NA	NA	NA	NA	NA	NA	78%
Over $100,000	NA	NA	NA	NA	NA	NA	81%

[a]The primary source used different income categories for 2004, making the data from earlier presidential election years incompatible.

Sources: By the author. Data on marital status are from Casper and Bass 1998, Jamieson et al. 2002, and Holder 2006. Data on income are from Holder 2006. The other data are from *Statistical Abstract* 1991:Table 450; 1997:Table 462; 2007:Table 405.

The Gender and Racial-Ethnic Gap in Voting   Historically, men and women voted the same way, but now we have a *political gender gap.* That is, when they go to the polls, men and women are somewhat more likely to vote for different presidential candidates. As you can see from Table 15.2 on the next page, men are more likely to favor the Republican candidate, while women are more likely to vote for the Democratic candidate. This table also illustrates the much larger racial-ethnic gap in politics. Note how few African Americans vote for a Republican presidential candidate.

Table 15.2   How the Two-Party Presidential Vote Is Split

	1988	1992	1996	2000	2004
Women					
Democrat	50%	61%	65%	56%	53%
Republican	50%	39%	35%	44%	47%
Men					
Democrat	44%	55%	51%	47%	46%
Republican	56%	45%	49%	53%	54%
African Americans					
Democrat	92%	94%	99%	92%	90%
Republican	8%	6%	1%	8%	10%
Whites					
Democrat	41%	53%	54%	46%	42%
Republican	59%	47%	46%	54%	58%
Latinos					
Democrat	NA	NA	NA	61%	58%
Republican	NA	NA	NA	39%	42%
Asian Americans					
Democrat	NA	NA	NA	62%	77%
Republican	NA	NA	NA	38%	23%

Sources: *Statistical Abstract* 1999:Table 464; 2002:Table 372; 2007:Table 387.

As we saw in Table 15.1, voting patterns reflect life experiences, especially people's economic conditions. On average, women earn less than men, and African Americans earn less than whites. As a result, at this point in history, women and African Americans tend to look more favorably on government programs that redistribute income, and they are more likely to vote for Democrats.

Lobbyists and Special-Interest Groups

Suppose that you are president of the United States, and you want to make milk more affordable for the poor. As you check into the matter, you find that part of the reason that prices are high is because the government is paying farmers billions of dollars a year in price supports. You propose to eliminate these subsidies.

Immediately, large numbers of people leap into action. They contact their senators and representatives and hold news conferences. Your office is flooded with calls, faxes, and e-mail. Reuters and the Associated Press distribute pictures of farm families—their Holsteins grazing contentedly in the background—and inform readers that your harsh proposal will destroy these hard-working, healthy, happy, good Americans who are struggling to make a living. President or not, you have little chance of getting your legislation passed.

special-interest group a group of people who support a particular issue and who can be mobilized for political action

lobbyists people who influence legislation on behalf of their clients

What happened? The dairy industry went to work to protect its special interests. A **special-interest group** consists of people who think alike on a particular issue and who can be mobilized for political action. The dairy industry is just one of thousands of such groups that employ **lobbyists,** people who are paid to influence legislation on behalf of their clients. Special-interest groups and lobbyists have become a major force in U.S. politics. Members of Congress who want to be reelected must pay attention to them, for they represent blocs of voters who share a vital interest in the outcome of specific bills. Well financed and able to contribute huge sums, lobbyists can deliver votes to you—or to your opponent.

Some members of Congress who lose an election have a pot of gold waiting for them. So do people who have served in the White House as assistants to the President. With their influence and contacts opening doors to them that are closed to others, they are sought after as lobbyists (Revkin and Wald 2007). Some can demand $2 million a year (Shane 2004). *Half* of the top one hundred White House officials go to work for or advise the very companies that they regulated while they worked for the President (Ismail 2003).

What about the laws that prohibit office holders and White House officials from lobbying during the first year after they leave their jobs? They skirt these laws by calling themselves "strategic advisors," not lobbyists. Drawing one of Washington's fine moral lines, they direct other lobbyists and—supposedly—do not make direct contacts for a year (Wayne 2000). After that year, they come out into the open and register as lobbyists.

Another law is also easily skirted. To prevent special-interest groups from unduly influencing legislation, Congress passed a law that limits the amount of money that any individual, corporation or special-interest group can donate to a candidate. This law also requires all contributions over $1,000 to be reported. To get around this law, special-interest groups form **political action committees (PACs).** These organizations solicit contributions from many donors—each contribution being within the legal limit—and then use the large total to influence legislation.

PACs are powerful, for they bankroll lobbyists and legislators. To influence politics, about 4,000 PACs shell out hundreds of millions of dollars a year directly to their candidates (*Statistical Abstract* 2007:Tables 409, 410, 414). PACs also contribute millions in indirect ways. Some give "honoraria" (a gift of money) to senators who agree to say a few words at a breakfast. A few PACs represent broad social interests such as environmental protection. Most, however, represent the financial interests of specific groups, such as the dairy, oil, banking, and construction industries.

PACs in U.S. Elections

Suppose that you want to run for the Senate. To have a chance of winning, not only do you have to shake hands around the state, be photographed hugging babies, and eat a lot of chicken dinners at local civic organizations, you also must send out hundreds of thousands of pieces of mail to solicit votes and raise financial support. During the home stretch, your TV ads can cost hundreds of thousands of dollars a week. If you are an *average* candidate for the Senate, you will spend about $5 million on your campaign. To run for the House will cost a paltry $1,000,000 (*Statistical Abstract* 2007:Table 413).

Now suppose that it is only a few weeks from the election. You are exhausted from a seemingly endless campaign, and the polls show you and your opponent neck and neck. Your war chest is empty. The representatives of a couple of PACs pay you a visit. One says that his organization will pay for a mailing, while the other offers to buy TV and radio ads. You feel somewhat favorable toward their positions anyway, and you accept. Once elected, you owe them. When legislation that affects their interests comes up for vote, their representatives call you—on your private cell phone or at your unlisted number at home—and tell you how they want you to vote. It would be political folly to double-cross them.

It is said that the first duty of a politician is to get elected—and the second duty is to get reelected. If you are an average senator, to finance your reelection campaign you must raise over $2,000 *every single day* of your six-year term. It is no wonder that money has been dubbed the "mother's milk of politics."

Criticism of Lobbyists and PACs The major criticism leveled against lobbyists and PACs is that their money, in effect, buys votes. Rather than representing the people who elected them, legislators support the special interests of groups that have the ability to help them stay in power. The PACs that have the most clout in terms of money and votes gain the ear of Congress. To politicians, the sound of money talking apparently sounds like the voice of the people.

political action committee (PAC) an organization formed by one or more special-interest groups to solicit and spend funds for the purpose of influencing legislation

Even if the United States were to outlaw PACs, special-interest groups would not disappear from U.S. politics. Lobbyists walked the corridors of the Senate long before PACs, and since the time of Alexander Graham Bell they have carried the unlisted numbers of members of Congress. For good or for ill, lobbyists play an essential role in the U.S. political system.

Who Rules the United States?

With lobbyists and PACs wielding such influence, just whom do U.S. senators and representatives really represent? This question has led to a lively debate among sociologists.

The Functionalist Perspective: Pluralism

Functionalists view the state as having arisen out of the basic needs of the social group. To protect themselves from oppressors, people formed a government and gave it the monopoly on violence. The risk is that the state can turn that force against its own citizens. To return to the example used earlier, states have a tendency to become muggers. Thus, people must find a balance between having no government—which would lead to **anarchy,** a condition of disorder and violence—and having a government that protects them from violence, but also may turn against them. When functioning well, then, the state is a balanced system that protects its citizens both from one another *and* from government.

What keeps the U.S. government from turning against its citizens? Functionalists say that **pluralism,** a diffusion of power among many special-interest groups, prevents any one group from gaining control of the government and using it to oppress the people (Polsby 1959; Dahl 1961, 1982; Newman 2006). To keep the government from coming under the control of any one group, the founders of the United States set up three branches of government: the executive branch (the president), the judiciary branch (the courts), and the legislative branch (the Senate and House of Representatives). Each is sworn to uphold the Constitution, which guarantees rights to citizens, and each can nullify the actions of the other two. This system, known as **checks and balances,** was designed to ensure that no one branch of government dominates the others.

Our pluralist society has many parts—women, men, racial-ethnic groups, farmers, factory and office workers, religious organizations, bankers, bosses, the unemployed, the retired—as well as such broad categories as the rich, middle class, and poor. No group dominates. Rather, as each group pursues its own interests, it is balanced by other groups that are pursuing theirs. To attain their goals, groups must negotiate with one another and make compromises. This minimizes conflict. Because these groups have political muscle to flex at the polls, politicians try to design policies that please as many groups as they can. This, say functionalists, makes the political system responsive to the people, and no one group rules.

The Conflict Perspective: The Power Elite

If you focus on the lobbyists scurrying around Washington, stress conflict theorists, you get a blurred image of superficial activities. What really counts is the big picture, not its fragments. The important question is who holds the power that determines the country's overarching policies. For example, who determines interest rates—and their impact on the price of our homes? Who sets policies that encourage the transfer of jobs from the United States to countries where labor costs less? And the ultimate question of power: Who is behind the decision to go to war?

Sociologist C. Wright Mills (1956) took the position that the country's most important matters are not decided by lobbyists or even by Congress. Rather, the decisions that have the greatest impact on the lives of Americans—and people across the globe—are made by a **power elite.** As depicted in Figure 15.2, the power elite consists of the top leaders of the largest corporations, the most powerful generals and admirals of the armed forces, and certain elite politicians—the president, his cabinet, and senior members of Congress who

anarchy a condition of lawlessness or political disorder caused by the absence or collapse of governmental authority

pluralism the diffusion of power among many interest groups that prevents any single group from gaining control of the government

checks and balances the separation of powers among the three branches of U.S. government—legislative, executive, and judicial—so that each is able to nullify the actions of the other two, thus preventing the domination of any single branch

power elite C. Wright Mills' term for the top people in U.S. corporations, military, and politics who make the nation's major decisions chair the major committees. It is they who wield power, who make the decisions that direct the country and shake the world.

Are the three groups that make up the power elite—the top business, political, and military leaders—equal in power? Mills said that they were not, but he didn't point to the president and his staff or even to the generals and admirals as the most powerful. The most powerful, he said, are the corporate leaders. Because all three segments of the power elite view capitalism as essential to the welfare of the country, Mills said that business interests take center stage in setting national policy. (Remember the incident mentioned in the previous chapter (page 416) of a U.S. president selling airplanes.)

Sociologist William Domhoff (1990, 2006) uses the term **ruling class** to refer to the power elite. He focuses on the 1 percent of Americans who belong to the super-rich, the powerful capitalist class analyzed in Chapter 10 (pages 276–278). Members of this class control our top corporations and foundations, even the boards that oversee our major universities. It is no accident, says Domhoff, that from this group the president chooses most members of his cabinet and appoints ambassadors to the most powerful countries of the world.

Conflict theorists point out that we should not think of the power elite (or ruling class) as some secret group that meets together to agree on specific matters. Rather, their unity springs from the similarity of their backgrounds and orientations to life. All have attended prestigious private schools, they belong to exclusive clubs, and they are millionaires many times over. Their behavior stems not from some grand conspiracy to control the country but from a mutual interest in solving the problems that face big business (Useem 1984). With their political connections extending to the highest centers of power, this elite determines the economic and political conditions under which the rest of the country operates (Domhoff 1990, 1998).

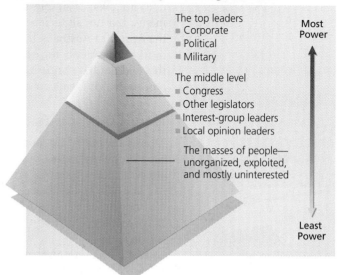

Figure 15.2 **Power in the United States: The Model Proposed by C. Wright Mills**

The top leaders
- Corporate
- Political
- Military

The middle level
- Congress
- Other legislators
- Interest-group leaders
- Local opinion leaders

The masses of people—unorganized, exploited, and mostly uninterested

Most Power

Least Power

Source: Based on Mills 1956.

Which View Is Right?

The functionalist and conflict views of power in U.S. society cannot be reconciled. Either competing interests block any single group from being dominant, as functionalists assert, or a power elite oversees the major decisions of the United States, as conflict theorists maintain. The answer may have to do with the level you look at. Perhaps at the middle level of power depicted in Figure 15.2, the competing groups do keep each other at bay, and none is able to dominate. If so, the functionalist view would apply to this level. But which level holds the key to U.S. power? Perhaps the functionalists have not looked high enough, and activities at the peak remain invisible to them. On that level, does an elite dominate? To protect its mutual interests, does a small group make the major decisions of the United States?

The answer is not yet conclusive. For this, we must await more research.

War and Terrorism: Implementing Political Objectives

As we have noted, an essential characteristic of the state is that it claims a monopoly on violence. At times, a state may direct that violence against other nations. **War,** armed conflict between nations (or politically distinct groups), is often part of national policy. Let's look at this aspect of politics.

ruling class another term for the power elite

war armed conflict between nations or politically distinct groups

Is War Universal?

Although human aggression and individual killing characterize all human groups, war does not. War is simply *one option* that groups may choose for dealing with disagreements, but not all societies choose this option. The Mission Indians of North America, the Arunta of Australia, the Andaman Islanders of the South Pacific, and the Inuit (Eskimos) of the Arctic, for example, had procedures to handle aggression and quarrels, but they did not have organized battles that pitted one tribe or group against another. These groups do not even have a word for war (Lesser 1968).

How Common Is War?

One of the contradictions of humanity is that people long for peace while at the same time they glorify war. The glorification of war can be seen by noting how major battles are central to a country's retelling of its history and how monuments to generals, patriots, and battles are scattered throughout the land. From May Day parades in Moscow's Red Square to the Fourth of July celebrations in the United States and the Cinco de Mayo victory marches in Mexico, war and revolution are interwoven into the fabric of national life.

War is so common that a cynic might say it is the normal state of society. Sociologist Pitirim Sorokin (1937) counted the wars in Europe from 500 B.C. to A.D. 1925. He documented 967 wars, an average of one war every two to three years. Counting years or parts of a year in which a country was at war, at 28 percent Germany had the lowest record of warfare. Spain's 67 percent gave it the dubious distinction of being the most war-prone. Sorokin found that Russia, the land of his birth, had experienced only one peaceful quarter-century during the entire previous thousand years. Since the time of William the Conqueror, who took power in 1066, England had been at war an average of 56 out of each 100 years. It is worth noting the history of the United States in this regard: Since 1850, it has intervened militarily around the world about 160 times, an average of *once a year* (Kohn 1988; current events).

Why Nations Go to War

Why do nations choose war as a means to handle disputes? Sociologists answer this question not by focusing on factors *within* humans, such as aggressive impulses, but by looking for *social* causes—conditions in society that encourage or discourage combat between nations.

Sociologist Nicholas Timasheff (1965) identified three essential conditions of war. The first is an antagonistic situation in which two or more states confront incompatible objectives. For example, each may want the same land or resources. The second is a cultural tradition of war. Because their nation has fought wars in the past, the leaders of a group see war as an option for dealing with serious disputes with other nations. The third is a "fuel" that heats the antagonistic situation to a boiling point, so that politicians cross the line from thinking about war to actually waging it.

Timasheff identified seven such "fuels." He found that war is likely if a country's leaders see the antagonistic situation as an opportunity to achieve one or more of these objectives:

1. *Revenge:* settling "old scores" from earlier conflicts
2. *Power:* dictating their will to a weaker nation
3. *Prestige:* defending the nation's "honor"
4. *Unity:* uniting rival groups within their country
5. *Position:* [the leaders] protecting or exalting their own position
6. *Ethnicity:* bringing under their rule "our people" who are living in another country
7. *Beliefs:* forcibly converting others to religious or political beliefs

Timasheff's analysis is excellent, and you can use these three essential conditions and seven fuels to analyze any war. They will help you understand why politicians at that time chose this political action.

Costs of War

One side effect of the new technologies stressed in this text is a higher capacity to inflict death. During World War I, bombs claimed fewer than 3 of every 100,000 people in England and Germany. With World War II's more powerful airplanes and bombs, these deaths increased a hundredfold, to 300 of every 100,000 civilians (Hart 1957). With today's higher killing capacity, if a war were fought with nuclear bombs, the death rate could run 100 percent. War is also costly in terms of money. As shown in Table 15.3, the United States has spent $6 trillion on ten major wars.

Despite its massive costs in lives and property, warfare remains a common way to pursue political objectives. For about seven years, the United States fought in Vietnam—at a cost of 59,000 American and about 2 million Vietnamese lives (Hellinger and Judd 1991). For nine years, the Soviet Union waged war in Afghanistan—with a death toll of about 1 million Afghans and perhaps 50,000 Soviet soldiers (Armitage 1989; Binyon 2001). An eight-year war between Iran and Iraq cost about 400,000 lives. Cuban mercenaries in Africa and South America brought an unknown number of deaths. Civil wars in Africa, Asia, and South America claimed hundreds of thousands of lives, mostly of civilians. Also unknown is the number of lives lost in fighting the Taliban in Afghanistan and in Gulf Wars I and II, but they, too, run into the hundreds of thousands.

A Special Cost of War: Dehumanization

> Proud of his techniques, the U.S. trainer was demonstrating to the South American soldiers how to torture a prisoner. As the victim screamed in anguish, the trainer was interrupted by a phone call from his wife. His students could hear him say, "A dinner and a movie sound nice. I'll see you right after work." Hanging up the phone, he then continued the lesson. (Stockwell 1989)

War exacts many costs in addition to killing people and destroying property. One of the most remarkable is its effect on morality. Exposure to brutality and killing often causes **dehumanization,** the process of reducing people to objects that do not deserve to be treated as humans. This numbs the conscience, allowing people to participate in acts they would ordinarily condemn. As you can see from the opening quote, even acts of torture become dissociated from one's "normal self."

The Basic Principles Let's review findings on dehumanization to understand the process better and see how it breeds callousness and cruelty. Perhaps we can better understand how "good, ordinary people" can torture prisoners and still feel good about themselves. Consider the four main characteristics of dehumanization (Bernard et al. 1971):

1. *Increased emotional distance from others.* People stop identifying with others, no longer seeing them as having qualities similar to themselves. They perceive them as "the enemy," or as objects of some sort. Sometimes they think of their opponents as less than human, or even not as people at all.
2. *Emphasis on following orders.* The individual clothes acts of brutality in patriotic language: To follow orders is "a soldier's duty." Torture is viewed as a tool that helps soldiers do their duty. People are likely to say, "I don't like doing this, but I have to follow orders—and someone has to do the 'dirty work'" (Hughes 1962/2005).
3. *Inability to resist pressures.* Ideas of morality take a back seat to fears of losing one's job, losing the respect of peers, or having one's integrity and loyalty questioned.
4. *A diminished sense of personal responsibility.* People come to see themselves as only small cogs in a large machine. The higher-ups who give the orders are thought to

Table 15.3 — What U.S. Wars Cost

War	Cost
American Revolution	$3,072,000,000
War of 1812	$967,000,000
Mexican War	$1,707,000,000
Civil War	$69,418,000,000
Spanish-American War	$6,259,000,000
World War I	$569,000,000,000
World War II	$4,644,747,000,000
Korean War	$394,317,000,000
Vietnam War	$846,672,000,000
Gulf War I	$85,600,000,000
Gulf War II	$?
Total	$6,621,759,000,000

Plus $70 billion a year for veterans, for pensions and service-connected disabilities.

Note: These totals are in 2005 dollars. Where a range was listed, I used the mean. The 1967 dollar totals listed in *Statistical Abstract* were multiplied by 5.69, the inflation rate between 1967 and 2005. The cost of Gulf War I from the *New York Times,* given in 2002 dollars, was multiplied by its inflation figure, 1.07.

Not included are veterans' benefits, which run about 40 percent of these totals. Also not included are interest payments on war loans. The ongoing expenditures of the military, currently about $550 billion a year, are also not included. Nor are these costs reduced by the financial benefits to the United States, such as the acquisition during the Mexican War of California, Texas, Arizona, and New Mexico

The military costs for the numerous U.S. involvements in "small" clashes such as the Barbary Coast War of 1801–1805 and more recently in Grenada, Panama, Somalia, Haiti, Kosovo, and Afghanistan are not listed in the sources.

Sources: "In Perspective" 2003; *Statistical Abstract* 1993:Table 553; 2007:Tables 490, 510.

dehumanization the act or process of reducing people to objects that do not deserve the treatment accorded humans

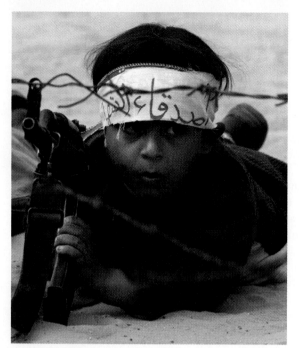

The hatred and vengeance of adults becomes the children's heritage. The headband on this 4-year old Palestinian boy reads: "Friends of Martyrs."

have more complete or even secret information that justifies the torture. The thinking becomes, "Those who make the decisions are responsible, for they are in a position to judge what is right and wrong. In my low place in the system, who am I to question these acts?"

Sociologist Martha Huggins (2004) interviewed Brazilian police who used torture to extract confessions. She found that torturers sometimes use another technique to neutralize guilt: They *blame the victim.* "He was just stupid. If he had confessed in the first place, he wouldn't have been tortured." You can see how this technique removes the blame from the torturer—who is just doing a job—and places it on the victim.

One of my students, a Vietnam veteran, who read this section remarked, "You missed the major one we used. We killed kids. Our dehumanizing technique was this saying, 'The little ones are the soldiers of tomorrow.'" Such sentiments may be more common than we suppose. A good Spanish friend, a mild-mannered man, said that we should kill even the children of terrorists. "It's like weeds," he told me. "You have to pull up the little ones, too, or they'll grow into big weeds."

As sociologist Tamotsu Shibutani (1970) stressed, dehumanization is aided by the tendency for prolonged conflicts to be transformed into a struggle between good and evil. The enemy, of course, represents evil. The thinking becomes: To defeat absolute evil requires the suspension of moral standards—for we are fighting for the precarious survival of good. The Down-to-Earth Sociology box on the next page illustrates how the abuse of prisoners in Iraq fits this analysis.

Success and Failure of Dehumanization Dehumanization can be remarkably effective in protecting people's mental adjustment. During World War II, surgeons, who were highly sensitive to patients' needs in ordinary medical situations, became capable of mentally removing the humanity of Jewish prisoners. By thinking of Jews as "lower people" (*Üntermenschen*), they were able to mutilate them just to study the results.

Dehumanization does not always insulate the self from guilt, however, and its failure to do so can bring severe consequences. During the war, while soldiers are surrounded by buddies who agree that the enemy is less than human and deserves inhuman treatment, it is easier for such definitions to remain intact. After returning home, however, the dehumanizing definitions can break down. Many soldiers find themselves disturbed by what they did during the war. Although most eventually adjust, some cannot, such as this soldier from California who wrote this note before putting a bullet through his brain (Smith 1980):

> I can't sleep anymore. When I was in Vietnam, we came across a North Vietnamese soldier with a man, a woman, and a three- or four-year-old girl. We had to shoot them all. I can't get the little girl's face out of my mind. I hope that God will forgive me . . . I can't.

Terrorism

> Mustafa Jabbar, a young father in Najaf, Iraq, is proud of his first born, a baby boy, but he said, "I will put mines in the baby and blow him up" (Sengupta 2004).

The deep resolve that underlies such an act of terrorism is difficult for many to grasp. But hatred runs deep, and it is promoted by groups that endlessly chronicle the atrocities committed by their archenemy. Nurtured in such a cauldron of bitterness, hatred spans generations, sometimes continuing for centuries. Such bitter antagonisms encourage **terrorism,** the use of violence to create fear in an effort to bring about political objectives. Stronger groups use terrorism "just because they can." They delight to see the suffering of their opponents. Terrorism, however, is most often used by weaker groups, for

terrorism the use of violence or the threat of violence to produce fear in order to attain political objectives

Prisoner Abuse at Abu Ghraib: A Normal Event

DURING GULF WAR II, Americans—and the world—were shocked at revelations that U.S. soldiers had abused prisoners at Abu Ghraib prison in Iraq. (Abuse of prisoners occurred in Afghanistan, too [Tracy 2007], but we'll focus on Abu Ghraib.)

To understand the prisoner abuse in at Abu Ghraib, we need to place it within its social context. When we do, we will see that this abuse was a normal event—so much so that it would have been abnormal for prisoner abuse *not* to occur.

The social context begins before U.S. forces took over the Abu Ghraib prison, even before Gulf War II. The watershed event that precipitated the prisoner abuse is 9/11. U.S. officials thought that 9/11 would be followed by other attacks. The next one, they feared, could be a conventional bomb detonated at a sports event or a mall—or even a weapon of mass destruction unleashed in a major city. Officials needed to find out where and when the next attack would take place. To get the information immediately, they decided that they needed harsh methods to interrogate prisoners. The Geneva Accords that specify humane treatment for prisoners of war stood in the way—but not for long. U.S. officials decided that Al-Qaeda prisoners were not prisoners of war: They had not worn uniforms, and they did not represent a country.

The next obstacle to harsh treatment came from international treaties that ban torture. U.S. officials had to find some way to get around these agreements. But how? The answer lay in the definition of torture: No one had actually defined torture. After long discussions, U.S. officials decided that they could come up with their own definition of torture. The CIA then determined that *water boarding* is not an act of torture (Risen et al. 2004). In water boarding, a prisoner is made to believe that his captors are going to drown him. They strap the prisoner to a board and forcibly push him under water. When they raise the prisoner out of the water, they again ask their questions. If they don't get an answer, they continue to repeat this procedure.

This is not torture? That is quite a definition that U.S. officials used. In fact, water boarding and other forms of treatment of prisoners that were determined to be "not torture" were so severe that the FBI ordered its agents to stay out of these interrogations.

The reconceptualization of acceptable interrogation following 9/11, then, is the first context for what happened at Abu Ghraib. To this, we must add that U.S. soldiers serving in Iraq had been told that they were on the side of good, protecting democracy and freedom. The enemy was evil,

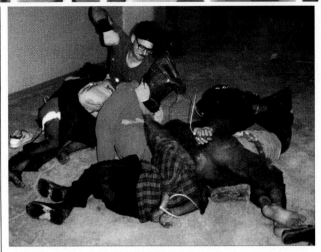

The abuse of Iraqi prisoners at Abu Ghraib prison in Baghdad is not a surprise to sociologists. Set up the right conditions—absolute power over an enemy accompanied by secrecy and lack of accountability—and such events are the logical outcome.

threatening the very foundations of good. In addition, there was an urgent need to get prisoners to talk. U.S. soldiers were dying from roadside bombs and artillery attacks, and the prisoners might have information to protect fellow soldiers. Now combine these factors with utter control over the prisoners, secrecy, and superiors who gave commands to "soften up" the prisoners.

Within this social context, the abuse of prisoners was normal. That is, how could anyone expect a different outcome? If the attention of the world had not been directed to the events at Abu Ghraib, the inevitable result would have been a torture machine. Like the many torture machines that came before it, this one would have been run by "good" people—soldiers and civilians—who were convinced that they had to suspend "normal" standards of right and wrong so they could do the "dirty work" necessary to maintain "goodness."

Something else about Abu Ghraib caught the media's attention: The abusers took trophy photographs, which they proudly shared with one another. These photos, such as the one in this box, shocked the world. They provided clear evidence of abuse, and no longer could convoluted definitions of torture rule the dark.

for your Consideration

1. How can good people do such things as abuse or even torture and kill prisoners?
2. What system would you set up to prevent the abuse of prisoners?
3. Is the abuse of prisoners, or even their torture, justified if it prevents the deaths of others, perhaps even hundreds or thousands of other people?

if a weaker group wants to attack a more powerful group, terrorism is one of its few options. It cannot meet its enemy on the battlefield, but it can use terror as a weapon.

Suicide terrorism is sometimes the weapon of choice, a tactic that captures headlines around the world. Among the groups that have used suicide terrorism effectively are the Palestinians versus the Israelis and the Iraqis against the U.S.-led occupation. The most dramatic example of suicide terrorism, of course, was the attack on the World Trade Center and the Pentagon under the direction of Osama bin Laden. Flowing from this attack is a civil rights issue that is having fundamental effects on our lives, a topic we explore in the Down-to-Earth Sociology box on the next page.

The suicide attacks on New York and Washington were tiny in comparison with the real danger: that of biological, nuclear, and chemical weapons. Unleashed against a civilian population, such weapons could cause millions of deaths. In 2001, Americans caught a glimpse of how easily such weapons can be unleashed when anthrax powder was mailed to a few select victims. When the Soviet empire broke up, its nuclear weapons were no longer secure. The interception of enriched uranium as it was being smuggled out of a former Soviet republic foreshadowed the chilling possibility of terrorism on U.S. soil so great that it could dwarf the 9/11 attacks (Sheets and Broad 2007a, b).

It is sometimes difficult to tell the difference between war and terrorism. This is especially the case in civil wars, when the opposing sides don't wear uniforms, and their attacks are often directed against civilian populations. Africa is embroiled in such wars. One of the unfortunate developments arising from this situation is that of child soldiers, a topic discussed in the Down-to-Earth Sociology box on page 454.

Sowing the Seeds of Future Wars and Terrorism

Selling War Technology   Selling advanced weapons to the Least Industrialized Nations sows the seeds of future wars and terrorism. When a Least Industrialized Nation buys high-tech weapons, its neighbors get nervous, which sparks an arms race among them (Broad and Sanger 2007). Table 15.4 shows that the United States is, by far, the chief merchant of death. Russia and Great Britain place a distant second and third.

This table also shows the major customers in the business of death. Two matters are of interest. First, India, where the average annual income is only $600 and Egypt, where it is only $1,500, are some of the world's biggest spenders. Either their power elites are drastically insecure (and seek to bolster their power through these tremendous expenditures) or else their elites are incredibly secure because of the weapons they have purchased. Second, the huge purchase of arms by Saudi Arabia indicates that U.S. dollars spent on oil tend to return to the United States. There is, in reality, an exchange of arms and oil. As mentioned in Chapter 9 (page 262), Saudi Arabia cooperates with the United States by trying to keep oil prices down and, in return, the United States props up its dictators.

Table 15.4   The Business of Death

The Top Arms Sellers	The Top Arms Buyers
1. $28 billion, United States	1. $19 billion, Saudi Arabia
2. $16 billion, Russia	2. $9 billion, China
3. $12 billion, Great Britain	3. $7 billion, United Arab Emirates
4. $9 billion, France	4. $6 billion, Egypt
5. $3 billion, China	5. $6 billion, India
6. $2 billion, Israel	6. $4 billion, Israel
7. $1 billion, Germany	7. $4 billion, Taiwan
8. $1 billion, Ukraine	8. $3 billion, South Korea

Note: For years 2001-2004.
Source: By the author. Based on Grimmett 2005:Tables 2F, 2I.

The seeds of future wars and terrorism are also sown by nuclear proliferation. Some Least Industrialized Nations, such as India, China, and North Korea, possess nuclear weapons. So does Pakistan, whose head of nuclear development sold blueprints for atomic bombs to North Korea, Libya, and Iran (Perry et al. 2007). As I write this, Iran is furiously following those blueprints, trying to develop its own nuclear arsenal. In the hands of terrorists or a dictator who wants to settle grudges—whether nationalistic or personal—these weapons can mean nuclear blackmail or nuclear destruction, or both.

Making Alignments and Protecting Interests   The current alignments of the powerful nations also sow the seeds of future conflicts. The seven richest, most powerful, and most technologically advanced nations (Canada, France, Germany, Great Britain, Italy, Japan, and the United States) formed a loose alliance which they called G-7 (the

Down-to-Earth Sociology

Is Big Brother Knocking on the Door? Civil Liberties and Homeland Security

SEE IF YOU CAN GUESS which country this is. Government agents can break into your home while you are at work, copy the files on your computer, and leave a "bug" that records every keystroke from then on—all this without a search warrant. Government agents can also check with the local library and make a list of every book, record, or movie that you've ever checked out.

Is this Russia? Albania? Maybe there, too, but this is now how it is in the United States.

We have had fundamental changes since 9/11. There is no question that we must have security. Our nation cannot be at risk, and we cannot live in peril. But does security have to come at the price of our civil liberties?

Balancing security and civil liberties has always been a sensitive issue in U.S. history. In times of war, the U.S. government has curtailed freedoms. During the War Between the States, as the Civil War is called in the South, Abraham Lincoln even banned the right of *habeas corpus* (Neely 1992). This took away people's right to appear in court and ask judges to determine whether they had been unlawfully arrested and imprisoned.

After the terrorist attacks on New York City and Washington, D.C. in 2001, Congress authorized the formation of the Department of Homeland Security. Other than beefed-up security at airports, few citizens noticed a difference. People who were suspected of terrorism, however, felt a major impact. They were imprisoned without charges being lodged against them in a court, and they were denied the right to consult lawyers or to have a hearing in court.

People shrugged this off. "Terrorists deserve whatever they get," they said. What ordinary citizens didn't realize was that behind the scenes, their own liberties were being curtailed. FBI agents placed listening devices on cars, in buildings, and on streets. They used Nightstalkers (aircraft outfitted with electronic surveillance equipment) to listen to conversations (Hentoff 2003). No longer does the FBI need a judge's order to search your e-mails, telephone records, travel records, or credit and bank transactions. The FBI can simply demand that telephone and Internet access companies, colleges, libraries, banks, and credit companies produce them—and be punished as criminals if they reveal that the FBI has demanded these records ("FBI Director . . ." 2007).

Then there is the "no-fly list" of the Transportation Security Agency. Anyone who *might* have some kind of connection with some kind of terrorist is not allowed to board an airplane. This agency has also developed CAPPS II (Computer Assisted Passenger Pre-Screening System). Each traveler is labeled as a "green," "yellow," or "red" security risk. Green means you're fine, and red is reserved for known terrorists.

"Look, you've got to accept some curtailment of your freedom in exchange for increased security."

But what about the yellow code? These people are "suspects." The American Civil Liberties Union points out that anyone can get stamped yellow—with no way to know it or to change it. (For all I know, I could be coded yellow for criticizing Homeland Security in this box.) Agents in "government intelligence"—an oxymoron, if ever there was one—are known for being humorless, suspicious, and almost downright paranoid. You could get stamped yellow simply for reading the wrong books—because agents of the Department of Homeland Security now have the right to track the books we buy or those we check out at libraries. They can even record the Internet sites we visit at libraries. This is all done in secret. When librarians receive orders to reveal who has checked out certain books, they can be arrested if they even tell anyone that they received such an order (Lichtblau 2005).

If such surveillance continues, our government will become like the former police state of East Germany and eventually keep secret files on almost all of us. If you get coded yellow, that information could be shared with other government agencies. This, in turn, could affect your chances of getting a job or even a college scholarship.

Security we must have. But at what cost? Government watchdogs looking over our shoulders, writing down the names of our friends and associates, even the books and magazines we read? Microphones planted to eavesdrop on our conversations? Will they eventually install a computer chip in our right hand or in our forehead?

for your Consideration

What civil liberties do you think we should give up to help our nation be secure from terrorists? Are you willing to have the government keep track of your everyday affairs in the name of homeland security? What is your opinion of the government keeping a list of the books you check out at the library? Listening to your conversations? Keeping track of the people you associate with?

Down-to-Earth Sociology

Child Soldiers

SALIFOU WANKENE WAS JUST 15 when rebels attacked his village in the Ivory Coast. When the men grabbed Salifou and his 13–year-old brother, Abdul, their mother held onto Abdul's arm, trying to pull him away and yelling that he was too young to take. The soldier agreed that Abdul would not be of much use to them as he chopped off Abdul's hand with a machete.

The rebels then threw Salifou in the back of a truck with other boys (Bernstein 2007). He had become a boy soldier.

When rebels entered 12-year-old Ishmael Beah's village in Sierra Leone, they lined up the boys (Beah 2007). One of the rebels said, "We are going to initiate you by killing these people. We will show you blood and make you strong."

Before the rebels could do the killing, however, shots rang out and the rebels took cover. In the confusion, Ishmael escaped into the jungle. When he returned, he found his family dead and his village burned.

With no place to go and rebels roaming the countryside, killing, looting, and raping, Ishmael continued to hide in the jungle. As he peered out at a village one day, he saw a rebel carrying the head of a man, which he held by the hair. With blood dripping from where the neck had been, Ishmael said that the head looked as though it were still feeling its hair being pulled.

Months later, still hiding from the rebels, Ishmael was found by government soldiers. The "rescue" meant that he had to become a soldier—on their side, of course.

Ishmael's indoctrination was short but to the point. Hatred is a strong motivator.

> "You can revenge the death of your family, and make sure that more children do not lose their parents," the lieutenant said. "The rebels cut peoples heads off. They cut open pregnant women's stomachs and take the babies out and kill them. They force sons to have sex with their mothers. Such people do not deserve to live. This is why we must kill every single one of them. Think of it as destroying a great evil. It is the highest service you can perform for your country."

Along with 30 other boys, most of whom were ages 13 to 16, with two just 7 and 11, Ishmael was trained to shoot and clean an AK-47.

Banana trees served for bayonet practice. With thoughts of disemboweling evil rebels, the boys would slash at the leaves.

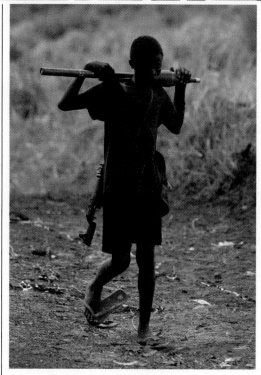

A young teenage soldier in Liberia.

The things that Ishmael had seen, he did.

Killing was difficult at first, but after a while, Ishmael says that "killing became as easy as drinking water."

The corporal wasn't satisfied with the boys' performance with bayonets. To improve their expertise, he held a contest. He chose 5 boys and placed them opposite five prisoners with their hands tied. He told the boys to slice the men's throats on his command. The boy whose prisoner died the quickest would win the contest.

"I stared at my prisoner," said Ishmael. "He was just another rebel who was responsible for the death of my family. The corporal gave the signal with a pistol shot, and I grabbed the man's head and sliced his throat in one fluid motion. His eyes rolled up, and he looked me straight in the eyes before they suddenly stopped in a frightful glance. I dropped him on the ground and wiped my bayonet on him. I reported to the corporal who was holding a timer. I was proclaimed the winner. The other boys clapped at my achievement."

"No longer was I running away from the war," adds Ishmael. "I was in it. I would scout for villages that had food, drugs, ammunition, and the gasoline we needed. I would report my findings to the corporal, and the entire squad would attack the village. We would kill everyone."

In another of his memorable statements which indicates how thoroughly his life and thinking had been transformed, Ishmael says that when he was recovering from a gunshot wound on his foot, he was given six prisoners. The lieutenant said, "These are the men responsible for the bullet holes in your foot. It's time to make sure they never shoot at you or your comrades."

"I am not sure if one of the captives was the shooter, but any captive would do at that time. So they were all lined up, six of them, with their hands tied. I shot them on their feet and watched them suffer for an entire day before finally shooting them in the head so that they would stop

(continued)

crying. Before I shot each man, I looked at him and saw his eyes give up hope before I pulled the trigger. I found their somber eyes irritating."

Ishmael was one of the lucky ones. Of the approximately 300,000 child soldiers worldwide, Ishmael is one of the few who has been rescued and given counseling at a UNICEF rehabilitation center. Ishmael has also had the remarkable turn of fate of graduating from college in the United States and becoming a permanent U.S. resident.

for your **Consideration**

1. Why are there child soldiers?

2. What can be done to prevent the recruitment of child soldiers? Why is passing a law that there must be a minimum age to serve in the military inadequate?

3. How can child soldiers be helped? What agencies can take what action?

Note: Quotations are summaries.

Group of 7). The goal was to coordinate their activities so they could perpetuate their global dominance, divide up the world's markets, and regulate global economic activity. Although Russia did not qualify for membership on the basis of wealth, power, or technology, the other nations feared Russia's nuclear arsenal and invited Russia as an observer at its annual summits. Russia became a full member in 2002, and the organization is now called G-8. Because China has increased both its economic clout and its nuclear arsenal, it has been invited to be an observer—a form of trial membership.

G-8, soon to be G-9, may be a force for peace—if these nations can agree on how to divide up the world's markets and force weaker nations to cooperate. Dissension became apparent in 2003, however, when the United States attacked Iraq, with the support of only Great Britain and Italy from this group. On several occasions, U.S. officials have vowed that the United States will not allow Iran to become a nuclear power. If the United Nations does not act and if a course similar to that which preceded Gulf War II is followed, the United States, with the support of Great Britain, will bomb Iran's nuclear facilities. An alternative course of action is for the United States to quietly give the go-ahead to Israel to do the bombing. One way or the other, the United States will protect its interests in this oil-rich region of the world.

It does not take much imagination to foresee the implications of these current alignments: the propping up of cooperative puppet governments that support the interests of G-8, the threat of violence to those that do not cooperate, and the inevitable resistance—including the use of terrorism—of various ethnic groups to the domination of these more powerful countries. With these conditions in place, the perpetuation of war and terrorism is guaranteed.

A New World Order?

War and terrorism, accompanied as they so often are by torture and dehumanization, are tools that some nations use to dominate other nations. So far, their use to dominate the globe has failed. A New World Order, however, might actually come about, but it is likely to be ushered in, not by war, but by nations cooperating for economic reasons. Perhaps the key political event in our era is the globalization of capitalism. Why the term *political*? Because politics and economics are twins, with each setting the stage for the other.

Major Trends Indicating Our Future Let's look at major trends and try to see what implications they hold for our future. As discussed in the previous chapter, the world's nations are almost frantically embracing capitalism. With nations forming coalitions of trading partners, national borders are becoming increasingly insignificant. The United States, Canada, and Mexico have formed a North American Free-Trade Association (NAFTA). We also have CAFTA, the Central American Free Trade Association. Eventually, all of North and South America may belong to such an organization. Ten Asian countries with a combined population of a half billion people have formed a

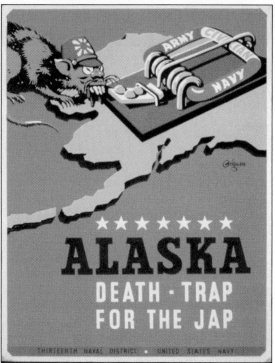

All governments—all the time—use propaganda to influence public opinion. During times of war, the propaganda becomes more obvious and direct. These two World War II posters are from the United States. The anti-Nazi poster indicates that Germany threatens our way of life. The anti-Japanese poster indicates that we will be victorious. (That Japan might attack us by way of Alaska indicates how pervasive our fear was.) Depicting the enemy as ugly, cruel, and inhuman was standard. To motivate their people, Germany and Japan produced anti-U.S. posters similar to these.

regional trading partnership called ASEAN (Association of South East Asian Nations). Struggling for dominance is an even more encompassing group called the *World* Trade Organization.

The European Union (EU) may point to this unifying future. Transcending their national boundaries, twenty-seven European countries (with a combined population of 450 million) formed this economic and political unit. These nations have adopted a single, cross-national currency, the Euro, which has replaced their marks, francs, liras, lats, and pesetas. The EU has also established a military staff in Brussels, Belgium (Mardell 2007).

Could this process continue until there is just one state or empire that envelops the earth? The major trend is heading in this direction. The United Nations is striving to become the legislative body of the world, wanting its decisions to supersede those of any individual nation. The UN operates a World Court (formally titled The International Court of Justice). It also has a rudimentary army and has sent "peace-keeping" troops to several nations.

Obstacles to Unity   Although we can identify the trend toward a single worldwide government—forged through increasingly encompassing trade organizations—we are unlikely to see its conclusion during our lifetimes. National boundaries, national patriotism, and ethnic loyalties die only hard deaths, a topic explored in the Cultural Diversity box on the next page. The EU is not as united as it appears to be on the surface. In 2005, France and Holland rejected the proposed EU constitution, which created an obstacle to EU's unity. The United Nations is continuously frustrated as individual countries clash over competing interests. The United Nations is also haunted by a constitutional inconsistency that hinders unity: Any one of the five nations that are the permanent members of its Security Council (Russian Federation, China, France, Great Britain, and the United States) can veto any action decided by the entire United Nations.

nationalism a strong identification with a nation, accompanied by the desire for that nation to be dominant

Cultural Diversity *around the* World

Roadblocks in the Path to the New World Order: The Globalization of Capitalism Versus the Resurgence of Nationalism

THE WORLD HAS ABOUT FIVE THOU-SAND nations. What makes each one a *nation* is that its people share a language, culture, territory, and political organization. A *state,* in contrast, claims a monopoly on violence over a territory. A state (or country) may contain many nations. The Kayapo Indians are but one nation within the state called Brazil. The Chippewa and Sioux are two nations within the state called the United States. The world's five thousand nations have existed for hundreds, some even for thousands, of years. In contrast, most of the world's states have been around only since World War II.

Most modern states have incorporated nations into their boundaries—usually by conquest. Some states have far better records than others, but overall, no ideology, left or right, religious or sectarian, has proved much better or worse at protecting nations or promoting pluralism. The last century probably saw more genocides and *ethnocides* (the destruction of an ethnic group) than any other.

For nation-peoples (referring not to a country), group identity transcends political affiliation. The Palestinians who live within Israel's borders, for example, do not identify themselves as Israelis. But did you know that the Oromos in Ethiopia have more members than do three-quarters of the states in the United Nations, and that they do not think of themselves as Ethiopians? The 22 million Kurds don't consider themselves first and foremost to be Iranians, Iraqis, Syrians, or Turks. There are about 450 nations in Nigeria, 350 in India, 180 in Brazil, 130 in the former USSR, and 90 in Ethiopia. That nations are squeezed into states with which they don't identify is the nub of the problem.

In most states, control resides in the hands of a power elite that operates by a simple credo: Winner takes all. The power elite controls foreign investment and aid, and uses both to enforce its position. It controls exports, levies taxes—and buys the weapons. It confiscates the resources of the nations under its control, whether those take the form of Native American land in North and South America or oil from the Kurds in Iraq. When nations resist, the result is armed conflict—and sometimes genocide.

A vicious cycle forms. The appropriation of a nation's resources leads to conflict, conflict leads to insecurity and the purchase of weapons, weapons purchases lead to debt, and debt leads to the appropriation of more resources. This self-perpetuating cycle helps to ensure that elites of most of the least industrialized states will cooperate with G-8, which supplies the arms, as it divides the globe's resources among its members.

G-8's march to a New World Order has met a serious obstacle, the resurgence of **nationalism**—identity with and loyalty to a nation. Because nationalism means loyalty to smaller groups instead of to the regional divisions into which G-8 wants to carve the globe, it threatens the evolving New World Order. When nationalism turns into a shooting war, it is fought over issues and animosities that are rooted in history. These are only faintly understood by those who are not a party to them, but they have been kept vividly alive in the folklore and collective memory of these nations.

G-8 will continue to divide the globe into regional trading blocs, and we will continue to witness this oppositional struggle. We will see seemingly contradictory outcomes: the formation of global coalitions matched by the simultaneous outbreak of local shooting wars as nations struggle for independence.

The end result? It is sufficient to note how greatly the scales are tipped in favor of the most industrialized states and the multinational corporations. David is not likely to defeat Goliath this time. Yet where David had five small stones and needed only one, some nations have discovered the powerful weapon of terrorism. It, too, has become part of the balance of political power.

Even within G-8, nationalism sometimes impedes unity, putting G-8's goals and those of individual nations at odds with each other. Especially troublesome to G-8 is the takeover of many prominent positions in Russia by former military and KGB officers. These men perceive many of NATO's and G-8's goals as incompatible with their desire to recover Russia's lost global power (Rivera and Rivera 2006). This could be the ingredient that brings back the Cold War and breaks G-8's monopoly on global power.

The World

Shown here are Russian troops in what remains of downtown Grozny, the capital of Chechnya. Russia bombed the city in order to stop the former colony from gaining independence.

for your Consideration

How can the rights of nations within a country be protected—and yet allow the country to operate as a unit? Should nations, if they possess self-identity and a common history and culture, have the right to secede from a country?

Sources: Clay 1990; Ohmae 1995; Jáuregui 1996; Marcus 1996; Alter 2000, Hechter 2000; Fletcher 2001; Kaplan 2003; Simons 2006.

Domination by the Elite Despite these obstacles, the broad historical trend is toward increasingly broader, cross-national units. We occasionally catch a glimpse of what is going on behind the scenes. When Russia was struggling to join the capitalist club, its communist background made it an object of suspicion. When Russia was finally acknowledged as a true capitalist country by being accepted into NATO, its prime minister made a proud acceptance speech. During this speech, he made this remarkable statement: "We must now together build the New World Order" (Purdum 2002).

It is fascinating to speculate on the type of government that might emerge if global political and economic unity were to come about. Certainly a New World Order holds potential benefits for human welfare. It could bring global peace. And if we had a benevolent government, our lives and participation in politics could be satisfying. But we must be mindful of Hitler. If his conquests had resulted in world domination, not only would we all be speaking German but also we would be living under a single dictator in a global totalitarian regime based on racial identification. If the world's resources and people come under the control of a dictatorship or an oligarchy, then, the future for humanity could be bleak.

Summary *and* Review

Micropolitics and Macropolitics

What is the difference between micropolitics and macropolitics?

The essential nature of **politics** is **power,** and every group is political. The term **micropolitics** refers to the exercise of power in everyday life. **Macropolitics** refers to large-scale power, such as governing a country. P. 432.

Power, Authority, and Violence

How are authority and coercion related to power?

Authority is power that people view as legitimately exercised over them, while **coercion** is power they consider unjust. The **state** is a political entity that claims a monopoly on violence over some territory. If enough people consider a state's power illegitimate, **revolution** is possible. Pp. 432–433.

What kinds of authority are there?

Max Weber identified three types of authority. In **traditional authority,** power is derived from custom—patterns set down in the past serve as rules for the present. In **rational-legal authority** (also called *bureaucratic authority*), power is based on law and written procedures. In **charismatic authority,** power is derived from loyalty to an individual to whom people are attracted. Charismatic authority, which undermines traditional and rational-legal authority, has built-in problems in transferring authority to a new leader. Pp. 433–436.

Types of Government

How are the types of government related to power?

In a **monarchy,** power is based on hereditary rule; in a **democracy,** power is given to the ruler by citizens; and in a **dictatorship,** power is seized by an individual or small group. Pp. 436–439.

The U.S. Political System

What are the main characteristics of the U.S. political system?

The United States has a "winner take all" system, in which a simple majority determines the outcome of elections. Most European democracies, in contrast, have **proportional representation;** legislative seats are allotted according to the percentage of votes each political party receives. Pp. 439–441.

Voter turnout is higher among people who are more socially integrated—those who sense a greater stake in the outcome of elections, such as the more educated and well-to-do. **Lobbyists** and **special-interest groups,** such as **political action committees** (PACs), play a significant role in U.S. politics. Pp. 441–446.

Who Rules the United States?

Is the United States controlled by a ruling class?

In a view known as **pluralism,** functionalists say that no one group holds power, that the country's many competing interest groups balance one another. Conflict theorists, who focus on the top level of power, say that the United States is governed by a **power elite,** a **ruling class** made up of the top corporate, political, and military leaders. At this point, the matter is not settled. Pp. 446–447.

War and Terrorism: Implementing Political Objectives

How are war and terrorism related to politics—and what are their costs?

War and **terrorism** are both means of attempting to accomplish political objectives. Timasheff identified three essential conditions of war and seven fuels that bring about war. His analysis can be appled to terrorism. Because of technological advances in killing, the costs of war in terms of money spent and human lives lost have escalated. Another cost is **dehumanization,** whereby people no longer see others as worthy of human treatment. This paves the way for torture and killing. Pp. 447–455.

A New World Order?

Is humanity headed toward a world political system?

The globalization of capitalism and the trend toward regional economic and political unions may indicate that a world political system is developing. The oppositional trend is a fierce **nationalism.** If a New World Order develops, the possible consequences for human welfare range from excellent to calamitous. Pp. 455–458.

Thinking Critically
about Chapter 15

1. What does biological terrorism have to do with politics? What does the globalization of capitalism have to do with politics?

2. What are the three sources of authority, and how do they differ from one another?

3. Apply the findings on "Why Nations Go to War" (page 448) to a recent war that the United States has been a part of.

Additional Resources

What can you use MySocLab for? www.mysoclab.com

- **Study and Review:** Pre- and Post-Tests, Practice Tests, Flash Cards, Individualized Study Plans.

- **Current Events:** *Sociology in the News,* the daily *New York Times,* and more.

- **Research and Writing:** *Research Navigator, Writing About Sociology,* and more.

Where Can I Read More on This Topic?

Suggested readings for this chapter are listed at the back of this book.

CHAPTER 16

Marriage and Family

Michael Escoffery, *Circle of Love*, 1996

"**H**old still. We're going to be late," said Sharon as she tried to put shoes on 2-year-old Michael, who kept squirming away.

Finally succeeding with the shoes, Sharon turned to 4-year-old Brittany, who was trying to pull a brush through her hair. "It's stuck, Mom," Brittany said.

"Well, no wonder. Just how did you get gum in your hair? I don't have time for this, Brittany. We've got to leave."

Getting to the van fifteen minutes behind schedule, Sharon strapped the kids in, and then herself. Just as she was about to pull away, she remembered that she had not checked the fridge for messages.

"Just a minute, kids. I'll be right back."

Running into the house, she frantically searched for a note from Tom. She vaguely remembered him mumbling something about being held over at work. She grabbed the Post-It and ran back to the van.

"He's picking on me," complained Brittany when her mother climbed back in.

"Oh, shut up, Brittany. He's only 2. He can't pick on you."

"Yes, he did," Brittany said, crossing her arms defiantly as she stretched out her foot to kick her brother's seat.

"Oh, no! How did Mikey get that smudge on his face? Did you do that, Brit?"

Brittany crossed her arms again, pushing out her lips in her classic pouting pose.

"Yes, he did," Brittany said, crossing her arms defiantly as she kicked her brother's seat.

As Sharon drove to the day care center, she tried to calm herself. "Only two more days of work this week, and then the weekend. Then I can catch up on housework and have a little relaxed time with the kids. And Tom can finally cut the grass and buy the groceries," she thought. "And maybe we'll even have time to make love. Boy, that's been a long time."

At a traffic light, Sharon found time to read Tom's note. "Oh, no. That's what he meant. He has to work Saturday. Well, there go those plans."

What Sharon didn't know was that her boss had also made plans for Sharon's Saturday. And that their emergency Saturday babysitter wouldn't be available. And that Michael was coming down with the flu. And that Brittany would follow next. And that . . .

"There just isn't enough time to get everything done!" Most of us have this complaint, but it is especially true for working parents of young children. Unlke the past, today's young partents find themselves without the support systems that parents used to take for granted: stay-at-home moms who provided stability to the neighborhood, husbands whose sole income was enough to support a wife and several children, a safe neighborhood where even small children could play outside, and grandmas who could pitch in during emergencies.

Those days are gone, most likely forever. Today, more and more families are like Sharon and Tom's. They are harried, working more but staying in debt, and seeming to have less time for one another. In this chapter, we shall try to understand what is happening to the U.S. family, and to families worldwide.

Marriage and Family in Global Perspective

To better understand U.S. patterns of marriage and family, let's first look at how customs differ around the world. This will give us a context for interpreting our own experience in this vital social institution.

What Is a Family?

"What is a family, anyway?" asked William Sayres at the beginning of an article on this topic. In posing this question, Sayres (1992) meant that although the family is so significant to humanity that it is universal—every human group in the world organizes its members in families—the world's cultures display so much variety that the term *family* is difficult to define. For example, although the Western world regards a family as a husband, wife, and children, other groups have family forms in which men have more than one wife (**polygyny**) or women more than one husband (**polyandry**). How about the obvious? Can we define the family as the approved group into which children are born? Then we would be overlooking the Banaro of New Guinea. In this group, a young woman must give birth *before* she can marry—and she *cannot* marry the father of her child (Murdock 1949).

What if we were to define the family as the unit in which parents are responsible for disciplining children and providing for their material needs? This, too, is not universal. Among the Trobriand Islanders, it is not the parents but the wife's eldest brother who is responsible for providing the children's discipline and their food (Malinowski 1927).

Such remarkable variety means that we have to settle for a broad definition. A **family** consists of people who consider themselves related by blood, marriage, or adoption. A **household,** in contrast, consists of people who occupy the same housing unit—a house, apartment, or other living quarters.

We can classify families as **nuclear** (husband, wife, and children) and **extended** (including people such as grandparents, aunts, uncles, and cousins in addition to the nuclear unit). Sociologists also refer to the **family of orientation** (the family in which an individual grows up) and the **family of procreation** (the family that is formed when a couple have their first child).

Often one of the strongest family bonds is that of mother–daughter. The young artist, an eleventh grader, wrote: "This painting expresses the way I feel about my future with my child. I want my child to be happy and I want her to love me the same way I love her. In that way we will have a good relationship so that nobody will be able to take us apart. I wanted this picture to be alive; that is why I used a lot of bright colors."

What Is Marriage?

We have the same problem here. For just about every element you might regard as essential to marriage, some group has a different custom.

Consider the sex of the bride and groom. Until recently, this was a taken-for-granted assumption. Then in the 1980s and 1990s, several European countries legalized same-sex marriages. In 2003, so did Canada, followed by the state of Massachusetts in 2004.

These, however, were not the first groups to approve marriage between people of the same sex. When Columbus landed in the Americas, some Native American tribes were already practicing same-sex marriage. A man or woman who wanted to be a member of the opposite sex went through a ceremony (*berdache*) that officially *declared* that their sex was changed. The "new" man or woman then wore the clothing of the opposite sex, performed the tasks associated with his or her new sex, and was allowed to marry.

Even sexual relationships don't universally characterize marriage. The Nayar of Malabar never allow a bride and groom to have sex. After a three-day celebration of the marriage, they send the groom packing—and never allow him to see his bride again (La Barre 1954). (In case you're wondering, the groom comes from another tribe. Nayar women are allowed to have sex, but only with approved lovers—who can never be the husband. This system keeps family property intact—along matrilineal lines.)

At least we can be certain that a man and a woman have to be alive to get married. Or so it would seem. Even here, however, we find an exception. On the Loess Plateau in China, if a man dies without a wife, his parents look for a dead woman to be his bride. After finding one—and there are families who sell their dead unmarried daughters—the dead man and woman are married and then buried together. The parents, who feel that having a bride gives their son comfort and support in the afterlife, celebrate the marriage by inviting friends to a reception (Fremson 2006).

With such cultural variety, we can conclude that, regardless of its form, **marriage** is a group's approved mating arrangements—usually marked by a ritual of some sort (the wedding) to indicate the couple's new public status.

Common Cultural Themes

Despite this diversity, several common themes run through marriage and family. As Table 16.1 illustrates, all societies use marriage and family to establish patterns of mate selection, descent, inheritance, and authority. Let's look at these patterns.

Mate Selection   Each human group establishes norms to govern who marries whom. If a group has norms of **endogamy,** it specifies that its members must marry *within* their group. For example, some groups prohibit interracial marriage. In some societies, these

Table 16.1   **Common Cultural Themes: Marriage in Traditional and Industrialized Societies**

Characteristic	Traditional Societies	Industrial (and Postindustrial) Societies
What is the structure of marriage?	*Extended* (marriage embeds spouses in a large kinship network of explicit obligations)	*Nuclear* (marriage brings fewer obligations toward the spouse's relatives)
What are the functions of marriage?	Encompassing (see the six functions listed on pp. 464 and 466)	More limited (many functions are fulfilled by other social institutions)
Who holds authority?	*Patriarchal* (authority is held by males)	Although some patriarchal features remain, authority is divided more equally
How many spouses at one time?	Most have one spouse (*monogamy*), while some have several (*polygamy*)	One spouse
Who selects the spouse?	Parents, usually the father, select the spouse	Individuals choose their own spouse
Where does the couple live?	Couples usually reside with the groom's family (*patrilocal residence*), less commonly with the bride's family (*matrilocal residence*)	Couples establish a new home (*neolocal residence*)
How is descent figured?	Usually figured from male ancestors (*patrilineal kinship*), less commonly from female ancestors (*matrilineal kinship*)	Figured from male and female ancestors equally (*bilateral kinship*)
How is inheritance figured?	Rigid system of rules; usually patrilineal, but can be matrilineal	Highly individualistic; usually bilateral

norms are written into law, but in most cases they are informal. In the United States most whites marry whites and most African Americans marry African Americans—not because of any laws but because of informal norms. In contrast, norms of **exogamy** specify that people must marry *outside* their group. The best example of exogamy is the **incest taboo,** which prohibits sex and marriage among designated relatives.

As you can see from Table 16.1, how people find mates varies around the world, from the father selecting them, with no choice by the individuals, to the highly individualistic, personal choices of members of Western cultures. Changes in mate selection are the focus of the Sociology and the New Technology box on the next page.

Descent   How are you related to your father's father or to your mother's mother? The answer to this question is not the same all over the world. Each society has a **system of descent,** the way people trace kinship over generations. We use a **bilineal system,** for we think of ourselves as related to *both* our mother's and our father's sides of the family. "Doesn't everyone?" you might ask. Ours, however, is only one logical way to reckon descent. Some groups use a **patrilineal system,** tracing descent only on the father's side; they don't think of children as being related to their mother's relatives. Others follow a **matrilineal system,** tracing descent only on the mother's side, and not considering children to be related to their father's relatives. The Naxi of China, for example, don't even have a word for father (Hong 1999).

Inheritance   Marriage and family—in whatever form is customary in a society—are also used to compute rights of inheritance. In a bilineal system, property is passed to both males and females, in a patrilineal system only to males, and in a matrilineal system (the rarest form), only to females. No system is natural. Rather, each matches a group's ideas of justice and logic.

Authority   Historically, some form of **patriarchy,** a social system in which men dominate women, has formed a thread that runs through all societies. Contrary to what some think, there are no historical records of a true **matriarchy,** a social system in which women as a group dominate men as a group. Our marriage and family customs, then, developed within a framework of patriarchy. Although U.S. family patterns are becoming more **egalitarian,** or equal, some of today's customs still reflect their patriarchal origin. One of the most obvious examples is U.S. naming patterns. Despite some changes, the typical bride still takes the groom's last name, and children usually receive the father's last name.

Marriage and Family in Theoretical Perspective

As we have seen, human groups around the world have chosen numerous forms of mate selection, ways to trace descent, and ways they view the parent's responsibility. Although these patterns are arbitrary, each group perceives its own forms of marriage and family as natural. Now let's see what picture emerges when we view marriage and family theoretically.

The Functionalist Perspective: Functions and Dysfunctions

Functionalists stress that to survive, a society must fulfill basic functions (that is, meet its basic needs). When functionalists look at marriage and family, they examine how they are related to other parts of society, especially the ways they contribute to the well-being of society.

Why the Family Is Universal   Although the form of marriage and family varies from one group to another, the family is universal. The reason for this, say functionalists, is that the family fulfills six needs that are basic to the survival of every society. These needs, or functions, are (1) economic production, (2) socialization of children,

---

exogamy the practice of marrying outside one's group

incest taboo the rule that prohibits sex and marriage among designated relatives

system of descent how kinship is traced over the generations

bilineal (system of descent) a system of reckoning descent that counts both the mother's and the father's side

patrilineal (system of descent) a system of reckoning descent that counts only the father's side

matrilineal (system of descent) a system of reckoning descent that counts only the mother's side

patriarchy a society or group in which men dominate women; authority is vested in males

matriarchy a society in which women as a group dominate men as a group

egalitarian authority more or less equally divided between people or groups, in this instance between husband and wife

Finding a Mate: Not the Same as It Used to Be

THINGS HAVEN'T CHANGED ENTIRELY. Boys and girls still get interested in each other at their neighborhood schools, and men and women still meet at college. Friends still serve as matchmakers and introduce friends, hoping they might click. People still meet at churches and bars, at the mall and at work.

But technology is bringing about some fundamental changes.

Among traditional people—Jews, Arabs, and in the villages of China and India—for centuries matchmakers have brought couples together. They carefully match a prospective couple by background—or by the position of the stars, whatever their tradition dictates—arranging marriages to please the families of the bride and groom, and, hopefully, the couple, too.

In China, this process is being changed by technology. Matchmakers use computerized records—age, sex, education, personal interests, and, increasingly significant, education and earnings—to identify compatibility and predict lifelong happiness.

But parents aren't leaving the process up to technology. They want their input, too. In one park in Beijing, hundreds of mothers and fathers gather twice a week to try to find spouses for their adult children. They bring photos of their children and share them with one another, talking up their kids' virtues while evaluating the sales pitch they get from the other parents. Some of the parents even sit on the grass, next to handwritten ads they've written about their children (Ang 2006).

Closer to home, Americans are turning more and more to the Internet. Numerous sites advertise that they offer thousands of potential companions, lovers, or spouses. For a low monthly fee, you, too, can meet the person of your dreams.

The photos are fascinating in their variety. Some seem to be lovely people, attractive and vivacious, and one wonders why they are posting their photos and personal information online. Do they have some secret flaw that they need to do this? Others seem okay, although perhaps, a bit needy. Then there are the pitiful, and one wonders if they will ever find a mate, or even a hookup, for that matter. Some are desperate, begging for someone—anyone—to make contact with them: women who try for sexy poses, exposing too much flesh, suggesting the promise of at least a good time; and men who try their best to look like hulks, their muscular presence promising the same.

The Internet dating sites are not filled with losers, although there are plenty of them. A lot of regular, ordinary people post their profiles, too. And some do so successfully. More and more, Internet postings are losing their stigma, and couples are finding mates via electronic matchmaking.

A frustrating aspect of these sites is that the "thousands of eligible prospects" that they tout are spread over the nation. You might find that a person who piques your interest lives in another part of the country. You can do a search for your area, but there are likely to be few from it.

Not to worry. Technology to the rescue.

The latest is dating on demand. You sit at home, turn on your TV, and search for your partner. Your local cable company has already done all the hard work. They have hosted singles events at bars and malls and helped singles make three-to-five minute tapes talking about themselves and what they are looking for in a mate (Grant 2005).

You can view the videos free—which is often more interesting than watching reruns of old TV shows. But if you get interested, for a small fee—again—you have the opportunity to contact the individuals who have caught your interest.

Now all you need is to get a private detective service—also available by online contact, for another fee—to see if this engaging person is already married, has a dozen kids, has been sued for paternity or child support, or is a child molester or a rapist.

Hmm, maybe the old village matchmaker wasn't such a bad idea, after all.

for your Consideration

What is your opinion of electronic dating sites? Would you consider using an electronic dating site (if you were single and unattached)?

(3) care of the sick and aged, (4) recreation, (5) sexual control, and (6) reproduction. To make certain that these functions are performed, every human group has adopted some form of the family.

Functions of the Incest Taboo   Functionalists note that the incest taboo helps families to avoid *role confusion*. This, in turn, facilitates the socialization of children. For example, if father-daughter incest were allowed, how should a wife treat her daughter—as a daughter, as a subservient second wife, or even as a rival? Should the daughter consider her mother as a mother, as the first wife, or as a rival? Would her father be a father or a lover? And would the wife be the husband's main wife, a secondary wife—or even the "mother of the other wife" (whatever role that might be)? And if the daughter had a child by her father, what relationships would everyone have? Maternal incest would also lead to complications every bit as confusing as these.

The incest taboo also forces people to look outside the family for marriage partners. Anthropologists theorize that *exogamy* was especially functional in tribal societies, for it forged alliances between tribes that otherwise might have killed each other off. Today, exogamy still extends both the bride's and the groom's social networks by adding and building relationships with their spouse's family and friends.

Isolation and Emotional Overload   As you know, functionalists also analyze dysfunctions. One of those dysfunctions comes from the relative isolation of today's nuclear family. Because extended families are enmeshed in large kinship networks, their members can count on many people for material and emotional support. In nuclear families, in contrast, the stresses that come with crises such as the loss of a job—or even the routine pressures of a harried life, as depicted in our opening vignette—are spread among fewer people. This places greater strain on each family member, creating *emotional overload*. In addition, the relative isolation of the nuclear family makes it vulnerable to a "dark side"— incest and various other forms of abuse, matters that we examine later in this chapter.

The Conflict Perspective: Struggles Between Husbands and Wives

Anyone who has been married or who has seen a marriage from the inside knows that— regardless of a couple's best intentions—conflict is a part of marriage. It is inevitable that conflict will arise between two people who live intimately and who share most everything in life—from their goals and checkbooks to their bedroom and children. At some point, their desires and approaches to life clash, sometimes mildly and sometimes quite harshly. Conflict among married people is so common that it is the grist of soap operas, movies, songs, and novels.

Throughout the generations, power has been a major source of conflict between wives and husbands: Husbands have had more power, and wives have resented it. Power differences show up throughout marriage, from disagreements over responsibilities for doing housework and taking care of children to quarrels about spending money and the lack of attention, respect, and sex.

As you know well, divorce is one way that couples try to end marital conflict. Divorce can mark the end of hostilities, or it can merely indicate a changed legal relationship within which the hostilities persist as the couple continues to quarrel about finances and children. We will return to the topic of divorce later in this chapter.

The Symbolic Interactionist Perspective: Gender, Housework, and Child Care

Throughout the generations, housework has been regarded as "women's work," and men have resisted getting involved. Child care, too, has traditionally been considered women's work. As more women began to work for wages, however, men came to feel pressure to do housework and to be more involved in the care of their children. But no man wanted to be labeled a sissy or be accused of being under the control of a woman. That would conflict with his culturally rooted feelings of manhood and the reputation he wanted to maintain in the community, especially around his friends.

As women put in more hours at paid work, men gradually began to do more housework and to take on more responsibility for the daily care of their children. When men first began to change diapers—at least openly—it was big news. Comedians even told jokes about Mr. Mommy, giving expression to common concerns of what the future would be like if men continued to be feminized.

Ever so slowly, cultural ideas changed. Eventually, doing housework and helping care for children came to be regarded in terms of fairness. No longer was it a sissy thing, but it became the right thing to do for husbands whose wives were in the paid labor force. Husband/fathers who refused to participate in these activities were labeled Neanderthals, and their wives pitied.

Now this is quite a change. This fundamental reorientation does not apply across the board, of course. Not all segments of the population have undergone the same change to the same degree, and we have not reached equality in housework and child care, but this is the general direction of our changing orientations.

One of the best indicators of this change is the research sociologists have done on how husbands and wives divide up housework and child care. If you look at Table 16.2, you can see how husbands have increased the amount of housework they do, and how wives have decreased the amount they do. Look at the changes in child care. Husbands are spending more time taking care of the children, and so are wives. This is fascinating: *Both* husbands and wives are spending more time in child care.

Contrary to popular assumptions, then, children are getting *more* attention from their parents than they used to. This flies in the face of common ideas of the *Leave It to Beaver* and *Ozzie and Harriet* families, part of our mythical past that colors our perception of the present. But if wives are working so many more hours in paid jobs *and* spending more time with their children, just where is the time coming from?

Today's parents have squeezed out more hours for their children by visiting other couples less and by reducing their participation in organizations. But this accounts for only a little bit. Look again at Table 16.2, but this time focus on women's hours at housework. You can see how women have cut down the amount of time they spend doing housework. Although husbands are doing more housework than they used to, the combined hours that husbands and wives spend doing housework have dropped from 38.9 to 29.1 hours a week. One explanation is that today's parents aren't as fussy as their parents were, leaving today's houses dirtier and messier. Another explanation is that the microwaves, more efficent washing machines and clothes dryers, and wrinkle-free clothing have saved hours of drudgery, leaving home hygiene about the same as before (Bianchi et al. 2006).

With the many changes in how married couples divide up family responsibilities, today's husbands and wives put in about the same number of hours per week at supporting the family. Wives spend more of their time in housework and child care but less in paid work. Husbands, in contrast, spend less of their time in housework and child care but more in paid work. Husbands and wives are following what sociologists call a *gendered division of labor;* that is, husbands remain primarily responsible for earning the income and wives primarily responsible for the house and children. If you follow the changes over time, shown in Figure 16.1, you can see something more significant than a growing equality in the time that husbands and wives spend in supporting the family: The trend is for wives to take on more of the responsibility

Table 16.2 Husbands and Wives: Who Does What?

	HOURS PER WEEK				
	1965	1975	1985	1995	2000
Housework					
Husbands	4.4	5.6	10.7	10.9	9.7
Wives	34.5	25.2	22.5	21.6	19.4
Child Care					
Husbands	2.6	2.7	3.0	5.0	6.5
Wives	10.6	8.8	9.3	11.0	12.9
Paid Work					
Husbands	47.8	47.2	42.5	39.8	42.5
Wives	6.0	15.2	19.7	24.9	23.8
Other Services to the Family					
Husbands	5.3	3.7	5.2	5.1	5.3
Wives	7.7	5.8	7.9	7.9	8.8
Total Hours					
Husbands	60.1	59.2	61.4	60.8	64.0
Wives	58.8	55.0	59.4	65.4	64.9

Note: Housework includes cooking, cleaning, and laundry, as well as plant and pet care. Husbands/wives refers to married couples who have children and are living together. Other services includes shopping, paying bills, and running errands.

Source: By the author. Based on Bianchi et al. 2006. Housework hours are from Table 5.1, child care from Table 4.1, and total hours from Table 3.4. Other services is derived by subtracting the hours for housework, child care, and paid work from total hours.

Figure 16.1 In Two Paycheck Marriages, How Do Husbands and Wives Divide Up the Responsibilities?

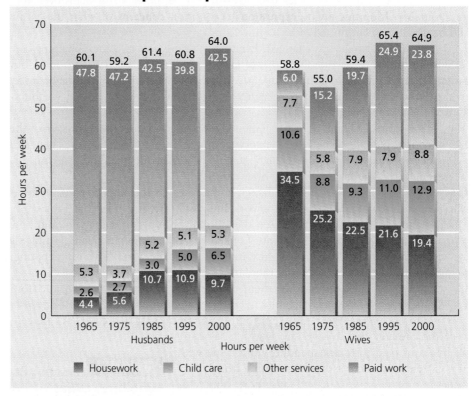

Source: By the author. Based on Bianchi et al. 2006. Housework hours are from Table 5.1, child care from Table 4.1, and work hours and total hours from Table 3.4. Other services is derived by subtracting the hours for housework, child care, and paid work from the total hours.

for earning the income and for husbands to take on more of the responsibilty for household and child care. This trend is firmly in place, and we can anticipate more changes like this in the future.

The Family Life Cycle

We have seen how the forms of marriage and family vary widely, and we have examined marriage and family theoretically. Now let's discuss love, courtship, and the family life cycle.

Love and Courtship in Global Perspective

Until recently, social scientists thought that romantic love originated in western Europe during the medieval period (Mount 1992). When anthropologists William Jankowiak and Edward Fischer (1992) surveyed the data available on 166 societies around the world, however, they found that this was not so. **Romantic love**—people being sexually attracted to one another and idealizing each other—showed up in 88 percent (147) of these groups. The role of love, however, differs from one society to another. As the Cultural Diversity box on the next page details, for example, Indians don't expect love to occur until *after* marriage.

In Hindu marriages, the roles of husband and wife are firmly established. Neither this woman, whom I photographed in Chittoor, India, nor her husband question whether she should carry the family wash to the village pump. Women here have done this task for millennia. As India industrializes, as happened in the West, who does the wash will be questioned—and may eventually become a source of strain in marriage.

East Is East and West Is West: Love and Arranged Marriage in India

AFTER ARUN BHARAT RAM returned to India with a degree from the University of Michigan, his mother announced that she wanted to find him a wife. Arun would be a good catch anywhere: 27 years old, educated, well mannered, intelligent, handsome—and, not incidentally, heir to a huge fortune.

Arun's mother already had someone in mind. Manju came from a middle-class family and was a college graduate. Arun and Manju met in a coffee shop at a luxury hotel—along with both sets of parents. He found her pretty and quiet. He liked that. She was impressed that he didn't boast about his background.

After four more meetings, including one at which the two young people met by themselves, the parents asked their children whether they were willing to marry. Neither had any major objections.

The Prime Minister of India and fifteen hundred other guests came to the wedding.

"I didn't love him," Manju says. "But when we talked, we had a lot in common." She then adds, "But now I couldn't live without him. I've never thought of another man since I met him."

Although India has undergone extensive social change, Indian sociologists estimate that parents still arrange 90 to 95 percent of marriages. Today, however, as with Arun and Manju, couples have veto power over their parents' selection. Another innovation is that the prospective bride and groom are allowed to talk to each other before the wedding—unheard of just a generation ago.

Why do Indians have arranged marriages? And why does this practice persist today, even among the educated and upper classes? We can also ask why the United States has such an individualistic approach to marriage.

The answers to these questions take us to two sociological principles. First, *a group's marriage practices match its values.* Individual mate selection matches U.S. values of individuality and independence, while arranged marriages match the Indian value of children deferring to parental authority.

This billboard in Chennai, India, caught my attention. As the text indicates, even though India is industrializing, most of its people still follow traditional customs. This billboard is a sign of changing times.

To Indians, allowing unrestricted dating would mean entrusting important matters to inexperienced young people.

Second, *a group's marriage practices match its patterns of social stratification.* Arranged marriages in India affirm caste lines by channeling marriage within the same caste. Unchaperoned dating would encourage premarital sex, which, in turn, would break down family lines. Virginity at marriage, in contrast, assures the upper castes that they know the fatherhood of the children. Consequently, Indians socialize their children to think that parents have superior wisdom in these matters. In the United States, where family lines are less important and caste is an alien concept, the practice of young people choosing their own dating partners mirrors the relative openness of our social class system.

These different backgrounds have produced contrasting ideas of love. Americans idealize love as being mysterious, a passion that suddenly seizes an individual. Indians view love as a peaceful feeling that develops when a man and a woman are united in intimacy and share common interests and goals in life. For Americans, love just "happens," while Indians think of love as something that can be created between two people by arranging the right conditions. Marriage is one of those right conditions.

The end result is this startling difference: *For Americans, love produces marriage—while for Indians, marriage produces love.*

for your Consideration

What advantages do you see to the Indian approach to love and marriage? Do you think that the Indian system could work in the United States? Why or why not? Do you think that love can be created? Or does love suddenly "seize" people? What do you think love is?

Sources: Based on Gupta 1979; Bumiller 1992; Sprecher and Chandak 1992; Dugger 1998; Gautham 2002; Derne 2003; Easley 2003, Berger 2004.

Because love plays such a significant role in Western life—and often is regarded as the *only* proper basis for marriage—social scientists have probed this concept with the tools of the trade: experiments, questionnaires, interviews, and observations. In a fascinating experiment, psychologists Donald Dutton and Arthur Aron discovered that fear can produce romantic love (Rubin 1985). Here's what they did.

> About 230 feet above the Capilano River in North Vancouver, British Columbia, a rickety footbridge sways in the wind. It makes you feel like you might fall into the rocky gorge below. A more solid footbridge crosses only ten feet above the shallow stream.
>
> The experimenters had an attractive woman approach men who were crossing these bridges. She told them she was studying "the effects of exposure to scenic attractions on creative expression." She showed them a picture, and they wrote down their associations. The sexual imagery in their stories showed that the men on the unsteady, frightening bridge were more sexually aroused than were the men on the solid bridge. More of these men also called the young woman afterward—supposedly to get information about the study.

You may have noticed that this research was really about sexual attraction, not love. The point, however, is that romantic love usually begins with sexual attraction. Finding ourselves sexually attracted to someone, we spend time with that person. If we discover mutual interests, we may label our feelings "love." Apparently, then, *romantic love has two components.* The first is emotional, a feeling of sexual attraction. The second is cognitive, a label that we attach to our feelings. If we attach this label, we describe ourselves as being "in love."

Marriage

In the typical case, marriage in the United States is preceded by "love," but, contrary to folklore, whatever love is, it certainly is not blind. That is, love does not hit us willy-nilly, as if Cupid had shot darts blindly into a crowd. If it did, marital patterns would be unpredictable. An examination of who marries whom, however, reveals that love is socially channeled.

The Social Channels of Love and Marriage The most highly predictable social channels are age, education, social class, and race-ethnicity. For example, a Latina with a college degree whose parents are both physicians is likely to fall in love with and marry a Latino slightly older than herself who has graduated from college. Similarly, a girl who drops out of high school and whose parents are on welfare is likely to fall in love with and marry a man who comes from a background similar to hers.

Sociologists use the term **homogamy** to refer to the tendency of people who have similar characteristics to marry one another. Homogamy occurs largely as a result of *propinquity,* or spatial nearness. That is, we tend to "fall in love" with and marry people who live near us or whom we meet at school, church, or work. The people with whom we associate are far from a random sample of the population, for social filters produce neighborhoods, schools, and places of worship that follow racial-ethnic and social class lines.

As with all social patterns, there are exceptions. Although 93 percent of Americans who marry choose someone of their same racial-ethnic background, 7 percent do not. Because there are 60 million married couples in the United States, those 7 percent add up, totaling over 4 million couples (*Statistical Abstract* 2007:Table 58).

One of the more dramatic changes in U.S. marriage patterns is a sharp increase in marriages between African Americans and whites. Today it is difficult to realize how norm shattering such marriages are, but in some states they used to be illegal and carry a jail sentence. In Mississippi, the penalty for interracial marriage was life in prison (Crossen 2004b). The last law of this type (called *antimiscegenation* laws) was not repealed until 2000. It had been a part of the Alabama constitution (Lee and Edmonston 2005).

There always have been a few couples who crossed the "color line," but the social upheaval of the 1960s broke this barrier permanently.

Figure 16.2 illustrates this increase. Look at the racial-ethnicity of the husbands and wives in these marriages. You can see that here, too, Cupid's arrows strike far from random. If you look closely, you can see an emerging change. Since 2000, marriages between African American women and white men are increasing faster than those between African American men and white women.

Childbirth

Marital Satisfaction   Sociologists have found that after the birth of a child marital satisfaction usually decreases (Rogers and Amato 2000; Twenge et al. 2003). To understand why, recall from Chapter 6 that a dyad (two persons) provides greater intimacy than a triad (after adding a third person, interaction must be shared). In addition, the birth of a child unbalances the roles that the couple have worked out (Knauth 2000). To move from the abstract to the concrete, think about the implications for marriage of coping with a fragile newborn's 24-hour-a-day needs of being fed, soothed, and diapered—while having less sleep and heavier expenses.

Yet husbands and wives continue to have children, not because they don't know how to avoid conceiving them, but because having their own child brings them so much satisfaction. New parents bubble over with joy, saying things like, "There's no feeling to compare with holding your own child in your arms. Those little hands, those tiny feet, those big eyes, that little nose, that sweet face . . ." and they gush on and on.

This is why there really is no equivalent to parents. It is *their* child, and no one else takes such delight in a baby's first steps, its first word, and so on. Let's turn, then, to child rearing.

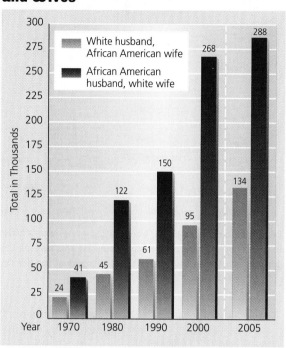

Figure 16.2 **Marriages Between Whites and African Americans: The Race-Ethnicity of the Husbands and Wives**

Source: By the author. Based on *Statistical Abstract* 1990:Table 53; 2007:Table 58.

No adequate substitute has been found for the family. Although its form and functions vary around the world, the family remains the primary socializer of children.

"Your attitude is sucking all the fulfillment out of motherhood."

One of the most demanding, exasperating—and also fulfilling—roles in life is that of parent. To really appreciate this cartoon, however, perhaps one has to have experienced this part of the life course.

Child Rearing

As you saw in Figure 16.1 and Table 16.2, today's parents—both mothers and fathers—are spending more time with their children than parents did in the 1970s and 1980s. Despite this trend, with mothers and fathers spending so many hours away from home at work, we must ask: Who's minding the kids while the parents are at work?

Married Couples and Single Mothers Figure 16.3 on the next page compares the child care arrangements of married couples and single mothers. As you can see, their overall arrangements are similar. A main difference is the role of the child's father while the mother is at work. For married couples, about one of five children is cared for by the father, while for single mothers, care by the father drops to one of ten. As you can see, grandparents help fill the gap left by the absent father. Single mothers also rely more on organized day care.

Day Care Figure 16.3 also shows that about one of four or five children is in day care. The broad conclusions of research on day care were reported in Chapter 3 (page 84). Apparently only a minority of U.S. day care centers offer high-quality care as measured by whether they provide stimulating learning activities, safety, and emotional warmth (Bergmann 1995; Blau 2000). A primary reason for this dismal situation is the low salaries paid to day care workers, who average only about $15,000 a year (*Statistical Abstract* 2007:Table 561, adjusted for inflation).

It is difficult for parents to judge the quality of day care, since they don't know what takes place when they are not there. If you ever look for day care, however, two factors best predict that children will receive quality care: staff who have taken courses in early childhood development and a low ratio of children per staff member (Blau 2000; Belsky et al. 2007). If you have nagging fears that your children might be neglected or even abused, choose a center that streams live Web cam images on the Internet. While at work, you can "visit" each room of the day care center via cyberspace, and monitor your toddler's activities and care.

Nannies For upper-middle-class parents, nannies have become a popular alternative to day care centers. Parents love the one-on-one care. They also like the convenience of in-home care, which eliminates the need to transport the child to an unfamiliar environment, reduces the chances of their child catching illnesses, and eliminates the hardship of parents having to take time off from work when their child becomes ill. A recurring problem, however, is tensions between the parents and the nanny: jealousy that the nanny might see the first step, hear the first word, or—worse yet—be called "mommy." There are also tensions over different discipline styles; disdain on the part of the nanny that the mother isn't staying home with her child; and feelings of guilt or envy as the child cries when the nanny leaves but not when the mother goes to work.

Social Class Social class makes a huge difference in child rearing. If you thought about it, you probably would guess that people's views on how children develop affect their child-rearing practices. Sociologists have found this to be true—and that the working and middle classes hold different views of how children develop (Lareau 2002). Working-class parents think of children as wild flowers that develop naturally, while middle-class parents think of children as garden flowers that need a lot of nurturing if they are to bloom. Consequently, working-class parents are more likely to set limits on their children and then let them choose their own activities. Middle-class parents, in contrast, are more likely to try to involve their children in leisure activities that they think will develop the children's thinking and social skills.

Figure 16.3 **Who Takes Care of Preschooolers While Their Mothers Are at Work?**

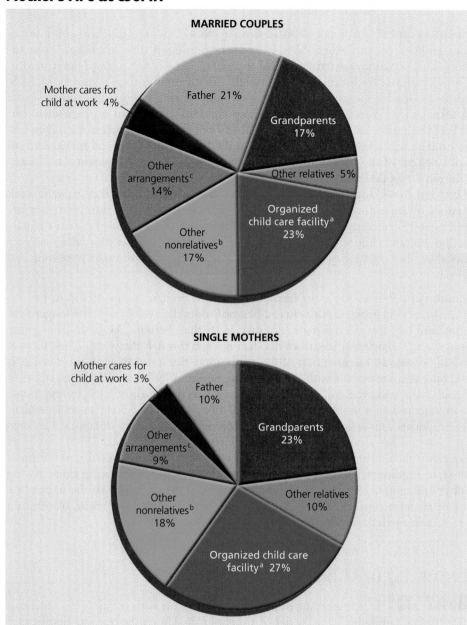

MARRIED COUPLES

Mother cares for child at work 4%

Father 21%

Grandparents 17%

Other arrangements[c] 14%

Other relatives 5%

Other nonrelatives[b] 17%

Organized child care facility[a] 23%

SINGLE MOTHERS

Mother cares for child at work 3%

Father 10%

Grandparents 23%

Other arrangements[c] 9%

Other nonrelatives[b] 18%

Other relatives 10%

Organized child care facility[a] 27%

[a] Includes in-home babysitters and other non-relatives providing care in either the child's or the provider's home.
[b] Includes self-care and no regular arrangements.
[c] Includes daycare center, nursery schools, preschools, and Head Start programs.

Source: America's Children 2005: Table POP8.B.

Sociologist Melvin Kohn (1963, 1977; Kohn and Schooler 1969) also found that the type of work that parents do has an impact on how they rear their children. Because members of the working class are closely supervised on their jobs, where they are expected to follow explicit rules, their concern is less with their children's motivation and more with their outward conformity. These parents are more apt to use physical punishment—which brings about outward conformity without regard for internal attitude. Middle-class workers, in contrast, are expected to take more initiative on the job. Consequently, middle-class parents have more concern that their children develop curiosity and self-expression. They are also more likely to withdraw privileges or affection than to use physical punishment.

Family Transitions

The later stages of family life bring their own pleasures to be savored and problems to be solved. Let's look at two transitions.

"Adultolescents" and the Not-So-Empty Nest When the last child leaves home, the husband and wife are left, as at the beginning of their marriage, "alone together." This situation, sometimes called the *empty nest*—is not as empty as it used to be. With prolonged education and the high cost of establishing a household, U.S. children are leaving home later. Many stay home during college, and others move back after college. Some (called "boomerang children") strike out on their own, but then find the cost or responsibility too great and return home. Much to their own disappointment, some even leave and return to the parent's home several times. As a result, 42 percent of all U.S. 25- to 29-year-olds are living with their parents (U.S. Census Bureau 2006:Table A2).

Although these "adultolescents" enjoy the protection of home, they have to work out issues of remaining dependent on their parents at the same time that they are grappling with concerns and fears about establishing independent lives. For the parents, "boomerang children" mean not only a disruption of routines but also disagreements about turf, authority, and responsibilities—items they thought were long ago resolved.

Widowhood Women are more likely than men to become widowed and to have to face the wrenching problems this entails. Not only does the average wife live longer than her husband but also she has married a man older than herself. The death of a spouse tears at the self, clawing at identities that had merged through the years. When the one who had become an essential part of the self is gone, the survivor, as in adolescence, is forced once again to wrestle with the perplexing question "Who am I?"

Most of the widowed adjust well within a year of the death of their spouse. Some even experience a gain in self-esteem, especially those who had been the most dependent on their spouse. This is apparently a consequence of learning to do things on their own (Carr 2004). When death is expected, the adjustment is easier (Hiltz 1989). Survivors who know that death is impending make preparations that smooth the transition—from arranging finances to preparing themselves psychologically for being alone. Saying goodbye and cultivating treasured last memories help people adjust to the impending death of an intimate companion. Sudden death rips the loved one away, offering no chance at this predeath healing process.

Diversity in U.S. Families

It is important to note that there is no such thing as *the* American family. Rather, family life varies widely throughout the United States. The significance of social class, noted earlier, will continue to be evident as we examine diversity in U.S. families.

African American Families

Note that the heading reads African American *families,* not *the* African American family. There is no such thing as *the* African American family any more than there is *the* white family or *the* Latino family. The primary distinction is not between African Americans and other groups, but between social classes (Willie and Reddick 2003). Because African Americans who are members of the upper class follow the class interests reviewed in Chapter 10—preservation of privilege and family fortune—they are especially concerned about the family background of those whom their children marry (Gatewood 1990). To them, marriage is viewed as a merger of family lines. Children of this class marry later than children of other classes.

Middle-class African American families focus on achievement and respectability. Both husband and wife are likely to work outside the home. A central concern is that

There is no such thing as *the* African American family, any more than there is *the* Native American, Asian American, Latino, or Irish American family. Rather, each racial-ethnic group has different types of families, with the primary determinant being social class.

their children go to college, get good jobs, and marry well—that is, marry people like themselves, respectable and hardworking, who want to get ahead in school and pursue a successful career.

African American families in poverty face all the problems that cluster around poverty (Wilson 1987, 1996; Anderson 1990/2006; Venkatesh 2006). Because the men are likely to have few skills and to be unemployed, it is difficult for them to fulfill the cultural roles of husband and father. Consequently, these families are likely to be headed by a woman and to have a high rate of births to single women. Divorce and desertion are also more common than among other classes. Sharing scarce resources and "stretching kinship" are primary survival mechanisms. People who have helped out in hard times are considered brothers, sisters, or cousins to whom one owes obligations as though they were blood relatives; and men who are not the biological fathers of their children are given fatherhood status (Stack 1974; Fischer et al. 2005). Sociologists use the term *fictive kin* to refer to this stretching of kinship.

From Figure 16.4 you can see that, compared with other groups, African American families are the least likely to be headed by married couples and the most likely to be headed by women. Because African American women tend to go farther in school than African American men, they are more

Figure 16.4 **Family Structure: The Percentage of U.S. Families Headed by Men, Women, and Married Couples**

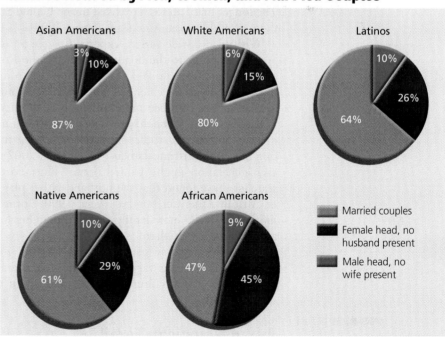

Sources: By the author. For Native Americans, "American Community . . ." 2004. For other groups, *Statistical Abstract* 2007:Tables 41, 44, 62. Data for Asian Americans are for families with children under 18, while the other groups don't have this limitation. Totals may not equal 100 percent due to rounding.

As with other groups, there is no such thing as *the* Latino family. Some Latino families have assimilated into U.S. culture to such an extent that they no longer speak Spanish. Others maintain Mexican customs, such as this family, which is celebrating *quincianera*, the "coming of age" of girls at age 15 (traditionally, an announcement to the community that a girl is eligible for courtship).

likely than women in other racial-ethnic groups to marry men who are less educated than themselves (South 1991; Eshleman 2000).

Latino Families

As Figure 16.4 shows, the proportion of Latino families headed by married couples and women falls in between that of whites and African Americans. The effects of social class on families, which I just sketched, also apply to Latinos. In addition, families differ by country of origin. Families from Mexico, for example, are more likely to be headed by a married couple than are families from Puerto Rico (*Statistical Abstract* 2007:Table 44). The longer that Latinos have lived in the United States, the more their families resemble those of middle-class Americans (Saenz 2004).

With such a wide variety, experts disagree on what is distinctive about Latino families. Some point to the Spanish language, the Roman Catholic religion, and a strong family orientation coupled with a disapproval of divorce. Others add that Latinos emphasize loyalty to the extended family, with an obligation to support the extended family in times of need (Cauce and Domenech-Rodriguez 2002). Descriptions of Latino families used to include **machismo**—an emphasis on male strength, sexual vigor, and dominance—but current studies show that *machismo* now characterizes only a small proportion of Latino husband-fathers (Torres et al. 2002). *Machismo* apparently decreases with each generation in the United States (Hurtado et al. 1992; Wood 2001). Some researchers have found that the husband-father plays a stronger role than in either white or African American families (Vega 1990; Torres et al. 2002). Apparently, the wife-mother is usually more family-centered than her husband, displaying more warmth and affection for her children.

It is difficult to draw generalizations because, as with other racial–ethnic groups, individual Latino families vary considerably (Contreras et al. 2002). Some Latino families, for example, have acculturated so such an extent that they are Protestants who do not speak Spanish.

machismo an emphasis on male strength and dominance

Asian American Families

As you can see from Figure 16.4 on the previous page, Asian American children are more likely than children in any other racial-ethnic group to grow up with both parents.

As with the other groups, family life also reflects social class. In addition, because Asian Americans emigrated from many different countries, their family life reflects those many cultures (Xie and Goyette 2004). As with Latino families, the more recent their immigration, the more closely their family life reflects the patterns in their country of origin (Kibria 1993; Glenn 1994).

Despite such differences, sociologist Bob Suzuki (1985), who studied Chinese American and Japanese American families, identified several distinctive characteristics of Asian American families. Although Asian Americans have adopted the nuclear family structure, they have retained Confucian values that provide a framework for family life: humanism, collectivity, self-discipline, hierarchy, respect for the elderly, moderation, and obligation. Obligation means that each member of a family owes respect to other family members and is responsible never to bring shame on the family. Conversely, a child's success brings honor to the family (Zamiska 2004). To control their children, Asian American parents are more likely to use shame and guilt rather than physical punishment.

The ideal does not always translate into the real, however, and so it is here. The children born to Asian immigrants confront a bewildering world of incompatible expectations—those of the new culture and those of their parents. As a result, they experience more family conflict and mental problems than do children of Asian Americans who are not immigrants (Meyers 2006).

Native American Families

Perhaps the single most significant issue that Native American families face is whether to follow traditional values or to assimilate into the dominant culture (Garrett 1999). This primary distinction creates vast differences among families. The traditionals speak native languages and emphasize distinctive Native American values and beliefs. Those who have assimilated into the broader culture do not.

Figure 16.4 on page 475 depicts the structure of Native American families. You can see how close it is to that of Latinos. In general, Native American parents are permissive with their children and avoid physical punishment. Elders play a much more active role in their children's families than they do in most U.S. families: Elders, especially grandparents, not only provide child care but also teach and discipline children. Like others, Native American families differ by social class.

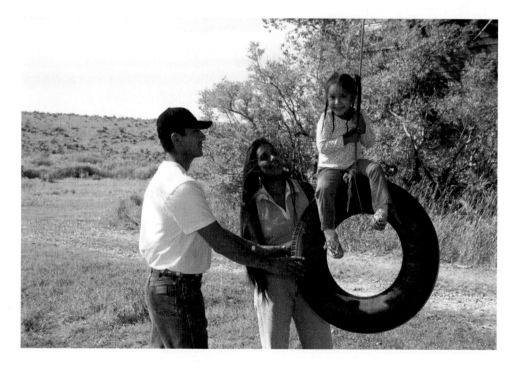

To search for *the* Native American family would be fruitless. There are rural, urban, single-parent, extended, nuclear, rich, poor, traditional, and assimilated Native American families, to name just a few. Shown here is a Shoshone family in Fort Hall, Idaho.

IN SUM From this brief review, you can see that race-ethnicity signifies little for understanding family life. Rather, social class and culture hold the keys. The more resources a family has, the more it assumes the characteristics of a middle-class nuclear family. Compared with the poor, middle-class families have fewer children and fewer unmarried mothers. They also place greater emphasis on educational achievement and deferred gratification.

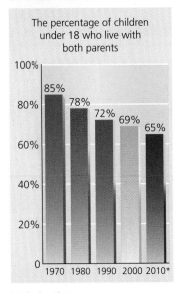

Figure 16.5 The Decline of Two-Parent Families

The percentage of children under 18 who live with both parents

*Author's estimate

Source: By the author. Based on *Statistical Abstract* 1995:Table 79; 2007:Table 62.

One-Parent Families

Another indication of how extensively U.S. families are changing is the increase in one-parent families. From Figure 16.5, you can see that the percentage of U.S. children who live with two parents (not necessarily their biological parents) has dropped sharply. The concerns that are often expressed about one-parent families may have more to do with their poverty than with children being reared by one parent. Because women head most one-parent families, these families tend to be poor. Most divorced women earn less than their former husbands, yet about 85 percent of children of divorce live with their mothers ("Child Support" 1995; Aulette 2002).

To understand the typical one-parent family, then, we need to view it through the lens of poverty, for that is its primary source of strain. The results are serious, not just for these parents and their children but also for society as a whole. Children from one-parent families are more likely to drop out of school, to get arrested, to have emotional problems, and to get divorced (McLanahan and Sandefur 1994; Menaghan et al. 1997; McLanahan and Schwartz 2002; Amato and Cheadle 2005). If female, they are more likely to become sexually active at a younger age and to bear children while still unmarried teenagers.

Families Without Children

While most married women give birth, about one of five (19 percent) do not (DeOilos and Kapinus 2003). The number of childless couples has *doubled* from what it was 20 years ago. As you can see from Figure 16.6, this percentage varies by racial-ethnic group, with whites and Latinas representing the extremes. Some couples are infertile, but most childless couples have made a *choice* to not have children. Why do they make this choice? Some women believe they would be stuck at home—bored, lonely, with dwindling career opportunities. Some couples perceive their marriage as too fragile to withstand the strains that a child would bring (Gerson 1985). A common reason is to attain a sense of freedom—to pursue a career, to be able to change jobs, to travel, and to have less stress (Lunneborg 1999; Letherby 2002).

Figure 16.6 What Percentage of U.S. Married Women Never Give Birth?

Source: By the author. Based on Bachu and O'Connell 2000:Table A.

With trends firmly in place—more education and careers for women, advances in contraception, legal abortion, the high cost of rearing children, and an emphasis on possessing more material things—the proportion of women who never bear children is likely to increase. Consider this statement in a newsletter:

> We are DINKS (Dual Incomes, No Kids). We are happily married. I am 43; my wife is 42. We have been married for almost twenty years. . . . Our investment strategy has a lot to do with our personal philosophy: "You can have kids—or you can have everything else!"

Many childless couples, in contrast, are not childless by choice. Desperately wanting to have children, they keep trying to do so. Coming to the soul-searching conclusion that they can never bear children, the most common solution is adoption. As featured in the Sociology and the New Technology box on the next page, some turn to solutions not available to previous generations.

The Brave New World of High-Tech Reproduction: Where Technology Outpaces Law and Sometimes Common Sense

JAYCEE HAS FIVE PARENTS—or none, depending on how you look at it. The story goes like this. Luanne and John Buzzanca were infertile. Although they spent more than $100,000 on treatments, nothing worked. Then a fertility clinic mixed a man's sperm with a woman's egg. Both the man and the woman remained anonymous. Pamela Snell agreed to be a surrogate mother, and a surgeon implanted the fertilized egg in Pamela, who gave birth to Jaycee (Davis 1998a; Foote 1998).

At Jaycee's birth, Pamela handed Jaycee over to Luanne, who was waiting at her bedside. Luanne's husband, John, decided not to be there. He had filed for divorce just a month before.

Luanne asked John for child support. John refused, and Luanne sued. The judge ruled that John didn't have to pay. He said that because Jaycee had been conceived in a petri dish with an egg and sperm from anonymous donors, John wasn't the baby's father. The judge added that Luanne wasn't the baby's mother either.

Five parents—or none? Welcome to the brave—and very real—new world of high-tech reproduction. Reproductive technologies have laid a trap for the unsuspecting, calling into question even what a mother is. Although Pamela Snell gave birth to Jaycee, she is not a mother. How about the donor of the egg? Biologically, yes, but legally, no. Is Luanne a mother? Fortunately, for Jaycee's sake, a higher court ruled that she is.

What is a father? Consider this case. Elizabeth Higgins of Jacksonville, Indiana, had difficulty conceiving. She gave eggs to Memorial Hospital. Her husband gave sperm. A hospital technician mistakenly mixed someone else's sperm with Mrs. Higgins' eggs. The fertilized eggs were implanted in Mrs. Higgins, who gave birth to twin girls. Mrs. Higgins is white, her husband black. Mr. Higgins was bothered because the girls had only Caucasian features, and he couldn't bond with them. Mr. and Mrs. Higgins separated. They sued the hospital for child support, arguing that the hospital, not Mr. Higgins, is the father (Davis 1998b).

If a hospital can be a father in this brave new world, then what's a grandparent? A man in New Orleans donated sperm to a fertility clinic. He died, and his girlfriend decided to be artificially inseminated with his sperm. The grieved parents of the man were upset that their son, although dead, could still father children. They also feared that those children, who would be their grandchildren, would have a legal claim to their estate (Davis 1998b).

How would you apply common sense to these situations?

for your Consideration

With artificial insemination becoming more common, many children are aware of their conception and want to meet the other children from the same sperm donor. To help locate their (half) brothers and sisters, they can consult a Web site, the Donor Sibling Registry. If your biological father were a sperm donor, would you want to meet him? How about your biological siblings? Why or why not?

The Gosselin family of Pennsylvania: Cara, Madelyn (twins), Alexis, Hannah, Aaden, Collin, Leah, and Joel (sextuplets).

blended family a family whose members were once part of other families

Blended Families

The **blended family,** one whose members were once part of other families, is an increasingly significant type of family in the United States. Two divorced people who marry and each bring their children into a new family unit become a blended family. With divorce common, millions of children spend some of their childhood in blended families. One result is more complicated family relationships. Consider this description written by one of my students:

I live with my dad. I should say that I live with my dad, my brother (whose mother and father are also my mother and father), my half sister (whose father is my dad, but whose mother is my father's last wife), and two stepbrothers and stepsisters (children of my father's current wife). My father's wife (my current stepmother, not to be confused with his second wife who, I guess, is no longer my stepmother) is pregnant, and soon we all will have a new brother or sister. Or will it be a half brother or half sister?

If you can't figure this out, I don't blame you. I have trouble myself. It gets very complicated around Christmas. Should we all stay together? Split up and go to several other homes? Who do we buy gifts for, anyway?

Gay and Lesbian Families

In 1989, Denmark became the first country to legalize marriage between people of the same sex. Since then, several European countries have passed such laws. In 2004, Massachusetts became the first of the U.S. states to legalize same-sex marriages. Walking a fine conceptual tightrope, other states have passed laws that give legal rights to "registered domestic partnerships." This is an attempt to give legal status to same-sex unions and yet sidestep controversy by not calling them marriages.

At this point, most gay and lesbian couples lack both legal marriage and the legal protection of registered "partnerships." Although these couples live throughout the United States, about half are concentrated in just twenty cities. The greatest concentrations are in San Francisco, Los Angeles, Atlanta, New York City, and Washington, D.C. About one-fifth of gay and lesbian couples were previously married to heterosexuals. Twenty-two percent of female couples and 5 percent of male couples have children from their earlier heterosexual marriages (Bianchi and Casper 2000).

What are same-sex relationships like? Like everything else in life, these couples cannot be painted with a single brush stroke. As with opposite-sex couples, social class is significant, and orientations to life differ according to education, occupation, and income. Sociologists Philip Blumstein and Pepper Schwartz (1985) interviewed same-sex couples and found their main struggles to be housework, money, careers, problems with relatives, and sexual adjustment—the same problems that face heterosexual couples. Some also confront discrimination at work, which can add stress to their relationship (Todosijevic et al. 2005). Same-sex couples are more likely to break up, and one argument for legalizing gay marriages is that the marriage contract will make these relationships more stable. If they were surrounded by laws, same-sex marriages would be like opposite-sex marriages—to break them would require negotiating around legal obstacles.

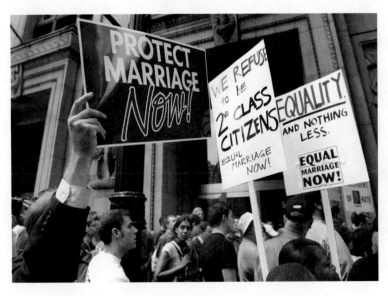

A major issue that has caught the public's attention is whether same-sex couples should have the right of legal marriage. This issue will be decided not by public protest but by legislation and the courts.

Trends in U.S. Families

cohabitation unmarried couples living together in a sexual relationship

As is apparent from this discussion, marriage and family life in the United States is undergoing a fundamental shift. Let's examine other indicators of this change.

Postponing Marriage and Childbirth

Figure 16.7 below illustrates one of the most significant changes in U.S. marriages. As you can see, the average age of first-time brides and grooms declined from 1890 to about 1950. In 1890, the typical first-time bride was 22, but by 1950, she had just left her teens. For about twenty years, there was little change. Then in 1970, the average age started to increase sharply. *Today's average first-time bride and groom are older than at any other time in U.S. history.*

Since postponing marriage is today's norm, it may come as a surprise to many readers to learn that *most* U.S. women used to be married by the time they reached age 24. To see this remarkable change, look at Figure 16.8 on the next page. Postponing marriage has become so extensive that the percentage of women of this age who are unmarried is now more than *double* what it was in 1970. Another consequence of postponing marriage is that the average age at which U.S. women have their first child is also the highest in U.S. history (Mathews and Hamilton 2002).

Why have these changes occurred? The primary reason is cohabitation (Michael et al. 2004). Although Americans have postponed the age at which they first marry, they have *not* postponed the age at which they first set up housekeeping with someone of the opposite sex. Let's look at this trend.

Cohabitation

Figure 16.9 on the next page shows the increase in **cohabitation,** adults living together in a sexual relationship without being married. This figure is one of the most remarkable

---

Figure 16.7 **The Median Age at Which Americans Marry for the First Time**

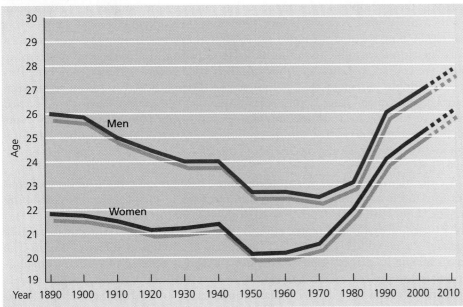

Note: The broken lines indicate the author's estimate.

Source: By the author. Based on *Statistical Abstract* 1999:Table 158 (table dropped in later editions); U.S. Bureau of the Census 2003; Fields 2004.

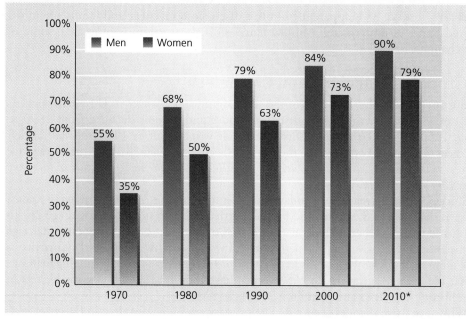

Figure 16.8 **Americans Ages 20–24 Who Have Never Married**

*Author's estimate.

Source: By the author. Based on *Statistical Abstract* 1993:Table 60; 2002:Table 48; 2007:Table 55.

Figure 16.9

Cohabitation in the United States

Note: Broken line indicates author's estimate.

Source: By the author. Based on *Statistical Abstract* 1995:Table 60; 2007:Table 61.

in sociology. Hardly ever do we have totals that rise this steeply and consistently. Cohabitation is *almost ten times* more common today than it was 30 years ago. Today, 60 percent of the couples who marry for the first time have lived together before marriage. A generation ago, it was just 8 percent (Bianchi and Casper 2000; Batalova and Cohen 2002). Cohabitation has become so common that about 40 percent of U.S. children will spend some time in a cohabiting family (Scommegna 2002).

Commitment is the essential difference between cohabitation and marriage. In marriage, the assumption is permanence; in cohabitation, couples agree to remain together for "as long as it works out." For marriage, individuals make public vows that legally bind them as a couple; for cohabitation, they simply move in together. Marriage requires a judge to authorize its termination; if a cohabiting relationship sours, the couple separates and they tell their friends that it didn't work out. Perhaps the single statement that pinpoints the difference in commitment between marriage and cohabitation is this: Cohabiting couples are less likely than married couples to have a joint bank account (Brines and Joyner 1999). As you know, some cohabiting couples do marry. But do you know how this is related to what cohabitation means to them? This is the subject of our Down-to-Earth Sociology box on the next page.

Are the marriages of couples who cohabited stronger than the marriages of couples who did not live together before they married? It would seem that cohabiting couples might have worked out a lot of problems prior to marriage. To find out, sociologists compared their divorce rates. It turns out that couples who cohabit before marriage are *more* likely to divorce. This presented another sociological puzzle. The key to solving it, suggest some sociologists, is the greater ease of ending a cohabiting relationship than a marriage (Dush et al. 2003). As a result, people are less picky about whom they live with than whom they marry. After they cohabit, however, they experience a push toward marriage—from having common possessions, pets, and children to pressures from friends and family. Many end up marrying a partner that they would not otherwise have chosen.

"You Want Us to Live Together? What Do You Mean By That?"

WHAT HAS LED TO the surge of cohabitation in the United States? Let's consider two fundamental changes in U.S. culture.

The first is changed ideas of sexual morality. It is difficult for today's college students to grasp the sexual morality that prevailed before the 1960s sexual revolution. Almost everyone used to consider sex before marriage to be immoral. Premarital sex existed, to be sure, but it took place furtively and often with guilt. To live together before marriage was called "shacking up," and the couple was said to be "living in sin." A double standard prevailed. It was the woman's responsibility to say no to sex before marriage. Consequently, she was considered to be the especially sinful one in cohabitation.

The second cultural change is the high U.S. divorce rate. Although the rate has declined since 1980, today's young adults have seen more divorce than any prior generation. This makes marriage seem fragile, as if it is something that is not likely to last regardless of how much you devote yourself to it. This is scary. Cohabitation reduces the threat by offering a relationship of intimacy in which divorce is impossible. You can break up, but you can't get divorced.

From the outside, all cohabitation may look the same, but not to the people who are living together. As you can see from Table 16.3, for about 10 percent of couples, cohabitation is a substitute for marriage. These couples consider themselves married but for some reason don't want a marriage certificate. Some object to marriage on philosophical grounds ("What difference does a piece of paper make?"); others do not yet have a legal divorce from a spouse. Almost half of cohabitants (46 percent) view cohabitation as a step on the path to marriage. For them, cohabitation is more than "going steady" but less than engagement. Another 15 percent of couples are simply "giving it a try." They want to see what marriage to one another might be like. For the least committed, about 29 percent, cohabitation is a form of dating. It provides a dependable source of sex and emotional support.

Do these distinctions make a difference in whether couples marry? Let's look at these couples a half dozen years after they began to live together. As you can see from Table 16.3, couples who view cohabitation as a substitute for marriage are the least likely to marry and the most likely to continue to cohabit. For couples who see cohabitation as a step toward marriage, the outcome is just the opposite: They are the most likely to marry and the least likely to still be cohabiting. Couples who are the most likely to break up are those who "tried" cohabitation and those for whom cohabitation was a form of dating.

for your Consideration

Can you explain why the meaning of cohabitation makes a difference in whether couples marry? Can you classify cohabiting couples you know into these four types? Do you think there are other types? If so, what would they be?

Table 16.3 **Commitment in Cohabitation: Does It Make a Difference?**

Level of Commitment	Percent of Couples	Split Up	Still Together	After 5 to 7 years — Of those still together	
				Married	Cohabitating
Substitute for Marriage	10%	35%	65%	37%	63%
Step toward Marriage	46%	31%	69%	73%	27%
Trial Marriage	15%	51%	49%	66%	34%
Coresidential Dating	29%	46%	54%	61%	39%

Source: Recomputed from Bianchi and Casper 2000.

Unmarried Mothers

Births to single women in the United States have increased steadily during the past decades, going from 10 percent in 1970 to 36 percent today (*Statistical Abstract* 1995:Table 94; 2007:Table 84). Let's place these births in global perspective. As Figure 16.10 shows, the

Figure 16.10 Births to Unmarried Women in Ten Industrialized Nations

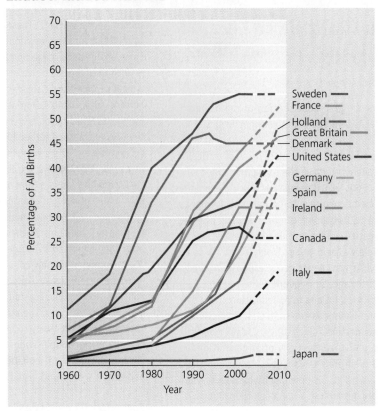

Note: The broken lines indicate the author's estimates.

Source: By the author. Based on *Statistical Abstract* 1993:Table 1380; 2001:Table 1331; 2007:Table 1311.

United States is not alone in its increase. Of the twelve nations for which we have data, all except Japan have experienced sharp increases in births to unmarried mothers. As you can see, the U.S. rate falls higher than average but not at the extreme.

From this figure, it would seem fair to conclude that industrialization sets in motion social forces that encourage out-of-wedlock births. There are several problems with this conclusion, however. Why was the rate so much lower in 1960? Industrialization had been in process for many decades before that time. Why are the rates of Japan and Italy so much lower than the other nations? Why does Japan's rate remain low? Why is Sweden's rate so high? Why have the rates of some nations leveled off—and all at about the same time? Industrialization is too simple an answer. A fuller explanation must focus on customs and values embedded within these cultures. For those answers, we will have to await further research.

Grandparents as Parents

It is becoming more common for grandparents to rear their grandchildren. About 4 percent of white children, 7 percent of Latino children, and 14 percent of African American children are being reared by their grandparents (Waldrop and Weber 2001). The main reason for these *skipped-generation families* is that the parents are incapable of caring for their children (Goldberg-Glen et al. 1998). Some of the parents have died, but the most common reasons are that the parents are ill, homeless, addicted to drugs, or in prison. In other instances, the grandparents stepped in when the parents neglected or abused their children.

Caring for grandchildren can bring great satisfaction. The grandparents know that their grandchildren are in loving hands, they build strong emotional bonds with them, and they are able to transmit their family values. But taking over as parents also brings stress: the unexpected responsibilities of parenthood, the squeezed finances, the need to continue working when they were anticipating retirement, and conflict with the parents of the children (Waldrop and Weber 2001). This added wear and tear takes its toll, and these grandmothers are 55 percent more likely to have heart disease (Lee et al. 2003). (We don't have these data for the grandfathers.)

The "Sandwich Generation" and Elder Care

The *"sandwich generation"* refers to people who find themselves sandwiched between two generations, responsible for both their children and their own aging parents. Typically between the ages of 40 and 55, these people find themselves pulled in two compelling directions. Overwhelmed by two sets of competing responsibilities, they are plagued with guilt and anger because they can be only in one place at a time and have little time to pursue personal interests.

Concerns about elder care have gained the attention of the corporate world, and half of the 1,000 largest U.S. companies offer elder care assistance to their employees (Hewitt Associates 2004). This assistance includes seminars, referral services, and flexible work schedules to help employees meet their responsibilities without missing so much work. Why are companies responding more positively to the issue of elder care than to child care? Most CEOs are older men whose wives stayed home to take care of their children, so they don't understand the stresses of balancing work and child care. In contrast, nearly all have aging parents, and many have faced the turmoil of trying to cope with both their parents' needs and those of work and their own family.

With people living longer, this issue is likely to become increasingly urgent.

Divorce and Remarriage

The topic of family life would not be complete without considering divorce. Let's first try to determine how much divorce there really is.

Problems in Measuring Divorce

You probably have heard that the U.S. divorce rate is 50 percent, a figure that is popular with reporters. The statistic is true in the sense that each year about half as many divorces are granted as there are marriages performed. The totals are 2.2 million marriages and about 1.1 million divorces (*Statistical Abstract* 2007:Tables 17, 76, 119).

What is wrong, then, with saying that the divorce rate is about 50 percent? Think about it for a moment. Why should we compare the number of divorces and marriages that take place during the same year? The couples who divorced do not—with rare exceptions—come from the group that married that year. The one number has *nothing* to do with the other, so these statistics in no way establish the divorce rate.

What figures should we compare, then? Couples who divorce are drawn from the entire group of married people in the country. Since the United States has 60,000,000 married couples, and only about 1 million of them obtain divorces in a year, the divorce rate for any given year is less than 2 percent. A couple's chances of still being married at the end of a year are over 98 percent—not bad odds—and certainly much better odds than the mass media would have us believe. As the Social Map on the next page shows, the "odds"—if we want to call them that—depend on where you live.

Over time, of course, each year's small percentage adds up. A third way of measuring divorce, then, is to ask, "Of all U.S. adults, what percentage are divorced?" Figure 16.12 on the next page answers this question. You can see how divorce has increased

Figure 16.11 The "Where" of U.S. Divorce

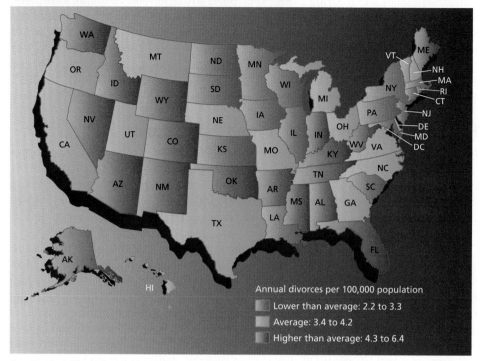

Annual divorces per 100,000 population

Lower than average: 2.2 to 3.3
Average: 3.4 to 4.2
Higher than average: 4.3 to 6.4

Note: Data for California, Georgia, Hawaii, Indiana, and Louisiana, based on the earlier editions in the source, have been decreased by the average decrease in U.S. divorce.

Source: By the author. Based on *Statistical Abstract* 1995:Table 149; 2002:Table 111; 2007:Table 119.

over the years and how race-ethnicity makes a difference for the likelihood that couples will divorce. If you look closely, you can also see that the rate of divorce has slowed down.

Figure 16.12 shows us the percentage of Americans who are currently divorced, but we get yet another answer if we ask the question, "What percentage of Americans have *ever* been divorced?" This percentage increases with each age group, peaking when people reach their 50s. Forty percent of women in their 50s have been divorced at some point in their lives; for men, the total is 43 percent ("Marital History . . ." 2004).

Figure 16.12 What Percentage of Americans Are Divorced?

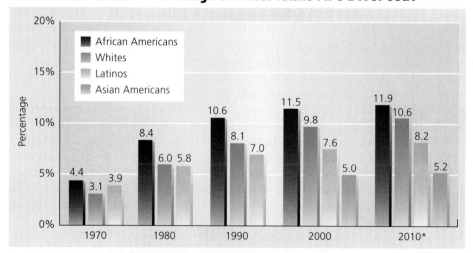

Note: This figure shows the percentage who are divorced and have not remarried, not the percentage who have *ever* divorced. Only these racial-ethnic groups are listed in the source. The source only recently added data on Asian Americans. *Author's estimate

Source: By the author. Based on *Statistical Abstract* 1995:Table 58; 2007:Table 54.

What most of us want to know is what *our* chances of divorce are. It is one thing to know that a certain percentage of Americans are divorced, but have sociologists found out anything that will tell me about *my* chances of divorce? This is the topic of the Down-to-Earth Sociology box below.

Children of Divorce

Each year, more than 1 million U.S. children learn that their parents are divorcing. Numbers like this are cold. They don't tell us what divorce feels like, what the children experience. In the Down-to-Earth Sociology box on the next page, we try to catch a glimpse of this.

Down-to-Earth Sociology

"What Are Your Chances of Getting Divorced?"

IT IS PROBABLY TRUE that over a lifetime about half of all marriages fail (Whitehead and Popenoe 2004). If you have that 50 percent figure dancing in your head, you might as well make sure that you have an escape door open even while you're saying "I do."

Not every group carries the same risk of divorce. Some have a much higher risk, and some much lower. Let's look at some factors that reduce people's risk. As Table 16.4 shows, sociologists have worked out percentages that you might find useful (Whitehead and Popenoe 2004).

As you can see, people who go to college, participate in a religion, wait to get married before having children and earn more, have a much better chance that their marriage will last. You can also see that having parents who did not divorce is significant. If you reverse these factors, you will see how the likelihood of divorce increases for people who have a baby before they marry, who marry in their teens, and so on. It is important to note, however, that these factors reduce the risk of divorce for groups of people, not for any certain individual.

Here are two other factors that increase the risk for divorce (Aberg 2003). For these, sociologists have not computed percentages. Having co-workers who are of the opposite sex (I'm sure you can figure out why) and working with people who are recently divorced increase the risk of divorce. Apparently, divorce is "contagious," following a pattern like measles. Perhaps being around divorced people makes divorce more acceptable. This would increase the likelihood that married people will act on their inevitable dissatisfactions and attractions. Or it could be that divorced people are more likely to "hit" on their fellow workers—and human nature being what it is . . .

for your Consideration

Why do you think that people who go to college have a lower risk of divorce? How would you explain the other factors

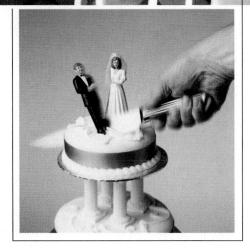

shown in Table 16.4? What other factors discussed in this chapter indicate a greater or lesser risk of divorce?

Why can't you figure your own chances of divorce by starting with some percentage (say 30 percent likelihood of divorce for the first 10 years of marriage) and then reducing it according to this table (subtracting 13 percent of the 30 percent for going to college, and so on)? To better understand this, you might want to read the section on the misuse of statistics on page 494.

Table 16.4 What Reduces the Risk of Divorce?

Factors that Reduce People's Chances of Divorce	How Much Does This Decrease the Risk of Divorce?
Some college (vs. high-school dropout)	−13%
Affiliated with a religion (vs. none)	−14%
Parents not divorced	−14%
Age 25 or over at marriage (vs. under 18)	−24%
Having a baby 7 months or longer after marriage (vs. before marriage)	−24%
Annual income over $50,000 (vs. under $25,000)	−30%

Note: These percentages apply to the first ten years of marriage.

Caught Between Two Worlds: The Children of Divorce

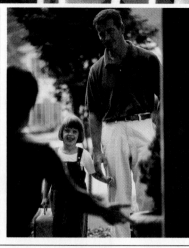

THE STATISTICS CAN TELL you how many couples divorce, how many children these couples have, and other interesting information. But the numbers can't tell what divorce is like—how children feel that their world is falling apart when they learn their parents are going to get a divorce. Or how torn apart they feel when they shuffle from one house to another.

Elizabeth Marquardt, a child of divorce herself, did a national study of children of divorce. In her book, *Between Two Worlds* (2005), she skillfully weaves her own experiences with those of the people she interviewed, taking us into the thought world of children who are being pulled apart by their parents.

It's the many little things that the statistics don't touch. The children feel like they are growing up in two families, not one. This creates painful complications that make the children feel like insiders *and* outsiders in their parents' worlds. They are outsiders when they look or act like one of the parents. This used to be a mark of an insider, a part of the family to which the child and the two parents belonged. But now it reminds one parent of their former spouse, the one they want to forget. And those children who end up with different last names than one of their parents—what a dramatic symbol of *outsider* that is. And when children learn something about one parent that they can't tell the other parent—which happens often—how uncomfortable they feel at being unable to share this information. Outsider-insider again.

What information do you share, anyway—or what do you *not* dare to share—as you travel from one world to the other? What do you say when dad asks if mom has a boyfriend? Is this supposed to be a secret? Will dad get mad if you tell him? Will he feel hurt? You don't want him to get angry or to feel hurt. Yet you don't want to keep secrets. And will mom get mad if you tell dad? It's all so complicated for a kid.

Marquardt says that as a child of divorce she tried to keep her two worlds apart, but they sometimes collided forcefully. At her mom's house, she could say that things were "screwed up." But if she used "screwed up" at her dad's house, he would correct her, saying, "*Messed up*." He meant the best for her, teaching her better language, but this left her feeling silly and ashamed. Things like this, little to most people, are significant to kids who feel pinched between their parents' differing values, beliefs, and ways of living.

To shuttle between two homes is to enter and leave different worlds—feeling things in common with each, but also sensing differences from each. And then come the strangely evolving relationships—their parent's girlfriends or boyfriends. Eventually, come the new blended families, which may not blend so easily, those that bring the new stepmom or stepdad, and perhaps their children. And then there are the new break-ups, with a recurring cycle of supposedly permanent relationships. What a complicated world for a child to traverse.

Marquardt pinpoints the dilemma for the child of divorce when she says: Being with one parent always means *not* being with the other.

for your Consideration

If you are a child of divorce, did you have two worlds of experience? Were your experiences like those mentioned here? If you lived with both parents, how do you think your life has been different because your parents didn't divorce?

Children whose parents divorce are more likely than children reared by both parents to experience emotional problems, both during childhood and after they grow up (Amato and Sobolewski 2001; Weitoft et al. 2003). They are also more likely to become juvenile delinquents (Wallerstein et al. 2001), and less likely to complete high school, to attend college, and to graduate from college (McLanahan and Schwartz 2002). Finally, the children of divorce are themselves more likely to divorce (Wolfinger 2003), perpetuating a marriage-divorce cycle.

Is the greater maladjustment of the children of divorce a serious problem? This question initiated a lively debate between two researchers, both psychologists. Judith Wallerstein claims that divorce scars children, making them depressed and leaving them with insecurities that follow them into adulthood (Wallerstein et al. 2001). Mavis Hetherington

It is difficult to capture the anguish of the children of divorce, but when I read these lines by the fourth-grader who drew these two pictures, my heart was touched:

Me alone in the park . . .
All alone in the park.
My Dad and Mom are divorced
that's why I'm all alone.

This is me in the picture with my son.
We are taking a walk in the park.
I will never be like my father.
I will never divorce my wife and kid.

replies that 75 to 80 percent of children of divorce function as well as children who are reared by both of their parents (Hetherington and Kelly 2003).

Without meaning to weigh in on either side of this debate, it doesn't seem to be a simple case of the glass being half empty or half full. If 75 to 80 percent of children of divorce don't suffer long-term harm, this leaves one-fourth to one-fifth who do. Any way you look at it, one-fourth or one-fifth of a million children each year is a lot of kids who are having a lot of problems.

What helps children adjust to divorce? Children of divorce who feel close to both parents make the best adjustment, and those who don't feel close to either parent make the worst adjustment (Richardson and McCabe 2001). Other studies show that children adjust well if they experience little conflict, feel loved, live with a parent who is making a good adjustment, and have consistent routines. It also helps if their family has adequate money to meet its needs. Children also adjust better if a second adult can be counted on for support (Hayashi and Strickland 1998). Urie Bronfenbrenner (1992) says this person is like the third leg of a stool, giving stability to the smaller family unit. Any adult can be the third leg, he says—a relative, friend, or even a former mother-in-law—but the most powerful stabilizing third leg is the father, the ex-husband.

As mentioned, when the children of divorce grow up and marry, they are more likely to divorce than are adults who grew up in intact families. Have researchers found any factors that increase the chances that the children of divorce will have successful marriages? Actually, they have. They are more likely to have a lasting marriage if they marry someone whose parents did not divorce. In these marriages, the level of trust is higher and the amount of conflict is less. If both husband and wife come from broken families, however, it is not good news. Those marriages are likely to be marked by high distrust and conflict, leading to a higher chance of divorce (Wolfinger 2003).

Grandchildren of Divorce

Paul Amato and Jacob Cheadle (2005), the first sociologists to study the grandchildren of divorced parents, found that the effects of divorce continue across generations. Using a national sample, they compared children whose grandparents divorced with those whose grandparents did not divorce. Their findings are astounding. The grandchildren of divorce have weaker ties to their parents, they don't go as far in school, and they don't get along as well with their spouses. As these researchers put it, when parents divorce, the consequences ripple through the lives of children who are not yet born.

The Absent Father and Serial Fatherhood

serial fatherhood a pattern of parenting in which a father, after divorce, reduces contact with his own children, acts as a father to the children of the woman he marries or lives with, then ignores these children, too, after moving in with or marrying another woman

With divorce common and mothers usually granted custody of the children, a new fathering pattern has emerged. In this pattern, known as **serial fatherhood,** a divorced father maintains high contact with his children during the first year or two after the divorce. As the man develops a relationship with another woman, he begins to play a fathering role with the woman's children and reduces contact with his own children. With another breakup, this pattern may repeat. Only about one-sixth of children who live apart from their fathers see their dad as often as every week. Actually, *most* divorced fathers stop seeing their children altogether (Ahlburg and De Vita 1992; Furstenberg and Harris 1992; Seltzer 1994). Apparently, for many men, fatherhood has become a short-term commitment.

The Ex-Spouses

Anger, depression, and anxiety are common feelings at divorce. But so is relief. Women are more likely than men to feel that divorce is giving them a "new chance" in life. A few couples manage to remain friends through it all—but they are the exception. The spouse who initiates the divorce usually gets over it sooner (Kelly 1992; Wang and Amato 2000). This spouse also usually remarries sooner (Sweeney 2002).

Divorce does not necessarily mean the end of a couple's relationship. Many divorced couples maintain contact because of their children (Fischer et al. 2005). For others, the "continuities," as sociologists call them, represent lingering attachments (Vaughan 1985; Masheter 1991; author's file 2005). The former husband may help his former wife hang a picture, paint a room, or move furniture; she may invite him over for a meal or to watch television. They might even go to dinner or to see a movie together. Some couples even continue to make love after their divorce.

After divorce, the ex-spouses' cost of living increases—two homes, two utility bills, and so forth. But the financial impact hits women the hardest. For them, divorce often spells economic hardship. This is especially true for mothers of small children, whose standard of living drops about a third (Seltzer 1994). Finally, as you would expect, women with more education cope better financially.

Remarriage

Despite the number of people who emerge from divorce court swearing "Never again!" many do remarry. The rate at which they remarry, however, has slowed, and today only half of women who divorce remarry (Bramlett and Mosher 2002). Figure 16.13 shows how significant race-ethnicity is in determining whether women remarry. Comparable data are not available for men.

As Figure 16.14 shows, most divorced people marry other divorced people. You may be surprised that the women who are most likely to remarry are young mothers and those with less education (Glick and Lin 1986; Schmiege et al. 2001). Apparently women who are more educated and more independent (no children) can afford to be more selective. Men are more likely than women to remarry, perhaps because they have a larger pool of potential mates.

How do remarriages work out? The divorce rate of remarried people *without* children is the same as that of first marriages. Those who bring children into a new marriage, however, are more likely to divorce again (MacDonald and DeMaris 1995). Certainly these relationships are more complicated and stressful. A lack of clear norms to follow may also play a role (Coleman

" I NOW PRONOUNCE YOU SECOND HUSBAND AND FOURTH WIFE."

This fanciful depiction of marital trends may not be too far off the mark.

Reprinted with special permission of King Features Syndicate et al. 2000). As sociologist Andrew Cherlin (1989) noted, we lack satisfactory names for stepmothers, stepfathers, stepbrothers, stepsisters, stepaunts, stepuncles, stepcousins, and stepgrandparents. At the very least, these are awkward terms to use, but they also represent ill-defined relationships.

Two Sides of Family Life

Let's first look at situations in which marriage and family have gone seriously wrong and then try to answer the question of what makes marriage work.

The Dark Side of Family Life: Battering, Child Abuse, Marital Rape, and Incest

The dark side of family life involves events that people would rather keep in the dark. We shall look at spouse battering, child abuse, rape, and incest.

Spouse Battering To study spouse abuse, some sociologists have studied just a few victims in depth (Goetting 2001), while others have interviewed nationally representative samples of U.S. couples (Straus and Gelles 1988; Straus 1992). Although not all sociologists agree (Dobash et al. 1992, 1993; Pagelow 1992), Murray Straus concludes that husbands and wives are about equally likely to attack one another. If gender equality exists here, however, it certainly vanishes when it comes to the effects of violence—85 percent of the injured are women (Rennison 2003). A good part of the reason, of course, is that most husbands are bigger and stronger than their wives, putting women at a physical disadvantage in this literal battle of the sexes. The Down-to-Earth Sociology box on the next page discusses why some women remain with their abusive husbands.

Violence against women is related to the sexist structure of society, which we reviewed in Chapter 11, and to the socialization that we analyzed in Chapter 3. Because they grew up with norms that encourage aggression and the use of violence, some men feel that it is their right to control women. When frustrated in a relationship—or even by events outside it—some men become violent. The basic sociological question is how to socialize males to handle frustration and disagreements without resorting to violence (Rieker et al. 1997). We do not yet have this answer.

Child Abuse

I answered an ad about a lakeside house in a middle-class neighborhood that was for sale by owner. As the woman showed me through her immaculate house, I was surprised to see a plywood box in the youngest child's bedroom. About 3 feet high, 3 feet wide, and 6 feet long, the box was perforated with holes and had a little door with a padlock. Curious, I asked what it was. The woman replied matter-of-factly that her son had a behavior problem, and this was where they locked him for "time out." She added that other times they would tie him to a float, attach a line to the dock, and put him in the lake.

I left as soon as I could. With thoughts of a terrorized child filling my head, I called the state child abuse hotline.

As you can tell, what I saw upset me. Most of us are bothered by child abuse—helpless children being victimized by their parents and other adults who are supposed to love, protect, and nurture them. The most gruesome of these cases make the evening news:

Figure 16.13 The Probability that Divorced Women Will Remarry in Five Years

Note: Only these groups are listed in the source.

Source: By the author. Based on Bramlett and Mosher 2002.

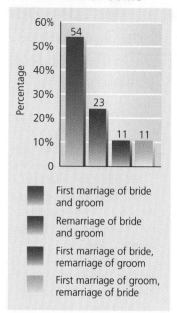

Figure 16.14 The Marital History of U.S. Brides and Grooms

- First marriage of bride and groom
- Remarriage of bride and groom
- First marriage of bride, remarriage of groom
- First marriage of groom, remarriage of bride

Source: By the author. Based on *Statistical Abstract* 2000:Table 145. Table dropped in later editions.

"Why Doesn't She Just Leave?" The Dilemma of Abused Women

"WHY WOULD SHE EVER put up with violence?" is a question on everyone's mind. From the outside, it looks so easy. Just pack up and leave. "I know I wouldn't put up with anything like that."

Yet this is not what typically happens. Women tend to stay with their men after they are abused. Some stay only a short while, to be sure, but others remain in abusive situations for years. Why?

Sociologist Ann Goetting (2001) asked this question, too. To learn the answer, she interviewed women who had made the break. She wanted to find out what it was that set them apart. How were they able to leave, when so many women couldn't seem to? She found that

1. They had a positive self-concept.
   Simply put, they believed that they deserved better.
2. They broke with traditional values.
   They did not believe that a wife had to stay with her husband no matter what.
3. They found adequate finances.
   For some, this was easy. But to move out, others had to save for years, putting away just a dollar or two a week.
4. They had supportive family and friends.
   A support network served as a source of encouragement to help them rescue themselves.

If you take the opposite of these four characteristics, you can understand why some women put up with abuse: They don't think they deserve anything better, they believe it is their duty to stay, they don't think they can make it financially, and they lack a supportive network. These four factors are not of equal importance to all women, of course. For some, the

Why do women stay with husbands who abuse them? This question has been a topic of sociological research.

lack of finances is the most important, while for others, it is their low self-concept. The lack of a supportive network is also significant.

There are two additional factors: The woman must define that what her husband is doing is abuse that warrants her leaving, and she must decide that he is not going to change. If she defines her husband's acts as normal, or perhaps as deserved in some way, she does not have a motive to leave. If she defines his acts as temporary, thinking that her husband will change, she is likely to stick around to try to change her husband.

Sociologist Kathleen Ferraro (2006) reports that when she was a graduate student, her husband "monitored my movements, eating, clothing, friends, money, make-up, and language. If I challenged his commands, he slapped or kicked me or pushed me down." Ferraro was able to leave only after she defined her husband's acts as intolerable abuse—not simply that she was caught up in an unappealing situation that she had to put up with—and after she decided that her husband was not going to change. Fellow students formed the supportive network that Ferraro needed to act on her new definition. Her graduate mentor even hid her from her husband after she left him.

for your Consideration

On the basis of these findings, what would you say to a woman whose husband is abusing her? How do you think battered women's shelters fit into this explanation? What other parts of this puzzle can you think of—such as the role of love?

The 4-year-old girl who was beaten and raped by her mother's boyfriend, who passed into a coma and then three days later passed out of this life; the 6- to 10-year-old children whose stepfather videotaped them engaging in sex acts. Unlike these cases, which made headlines in my area, most child abuse is never brought to our attention: the children who live in filth, who are neglected—left alone for hours or even days at a time—or who are beaten with extension cords—cases like the little boy I learned about when I went house hunting.

Child abuse is extensive. Each year, about 3 million U.S. children are reported to the authorities as victims of abuse or neglect. About 900,000 of these cases are substantiated (*Statistical Abstract* 2007:Table 333). The excuses that parents make are incredible. Of those I have read, one I can only describe as fantastic is this statement, made by a mother to a Manhattan judge, "I slipped in a moment of anger, and my hands accidentally wrapped around my daughter's windpipe" (LeDuff 2003).

Marital or Intimacy Rape Sociologists have found that marital rape is more common than is usually supposed. For example, between one-third and one-half of women who seek help at shelters for battered women are victims of marital rape (Bergen 1996). Women at shelters, however, are not representative of U.S. women. To get a better answer of how common marital rape is, sociologist Diana Russell (1990) used a sampling technique that allows generalization. She found that 14 percent of married women report that their husbands have raped them. Similarly, 10 percent of a representative sample of Boston women interviewed by sociologists David Finkelhor and Kersti Yllo (1985, 1989) reported that their husbands had used physical force to compel them to have sex. Compared with victims of rape by strangers or acquaintances, victims of marital rape are less likely to report the rape (Mahoney 1999).

With the huge numbers of couples who are cohabiting, the term marital rape needs to include sexual assault in these relationships. Perhaps, then, we should use the term *intimacy rape.* And intimacy rape is not limited to men who sexually assault women. In pathbreaking research, sociologist Lori Girshick (2002) interviewed lesbians who had been sexually assaulted by their partners. In these cases, both the victim and the offender were women. Girshick points out that if the pronoun "he" were substituted for "she" in her interviews, a reader would believe that the events were being told by women who had been battered and raped by their husbands (Bergen 2003). Like wives who have been raped by their husbands, these victims, too, suffered from shock, depression, and self-blame.

Incest Sexual relations between certain relatives (for example, between brothers and sisters or between parents and children) constitute **incest.** Incest is most likely to occur in families that are socially isolated (Smith 1992). Sociologist Diana Russell (n.d.) found that incest victims who experience the greatest trauma are those who were victimized the most often, whose assaults occurred over longer periods of time, and whose incest was "more intrusive," for example, sexual intercourse as opposed to sexual touching.

Who are the offenders? The most common incest is apparently between brothers and sisters, with the sex initiated by the brother (Canavan et al. 1992; Carlson et al. 2006). With no random samples, however, we do not know how common incest is, and researchers report different results. Russell found that uncles are the most common offenders, followed by first cousins, fathers (stepfathers especially), brothers, and, finally, other relatives ranging from brothers-in-law to stepgrandfathers. From the studies we have, we can conclude that incest between mothers and their children is rare, more so than between fathers and their children.

The Bright Side of Family Life: Successful Marriages

Successful Marriages After examining divorce and family abuse, one could easily conclude that marriages seldom work out. This would be far from the truth, however, for about three of every five married Americans report that they are "very happy" with their marriages (Whitehead and Popenoe 2004). (Keep in mind that each year divorce removes the most unhappy marriages from this population.) To find out what makes marriage successful, sociologists Jeanette and Robert Lauer (1992) interviewed 351 couples who had been married fifteen years or longer. Fifty-one of these marriages were unhappy, but the couples stayed together for religious reasons, because of family tradition, or "for the sake of the children."

Of the others, the 300 happy couples, all:

1. Think of their spouse as their best friend
2. Like their spouse as a person
3. Think of marriage as a long-term commitment
4. Believe that marriage is sacred
5. Agree with their spouse on aims and goals

incest sexual relations between specified relatives, such as brothers and sisters or parents and children

6. Believe that their spouse has grown more interesting over the years

7. Strongly want the relationship to succeed

8. Laugh together

Sociologist Nicholas Stinnett (1992) used interviews and questionnaires to study 660 families from all regions of the United States and parts of South America. He found that happy families:

1. Spend a lot of time together

2. Are quick to express appreciation

3. Are committed to promoting one another's welfare

4. Do a lot of talking and listening to one another

5. Are religious

6. Deal with crises in a positive manner

Sociologists have uncovered two other factors: Marriages are happier when couples get along with their in-laws (Bryant et al. 2001) and when they do leisure activities that they both enjoy (Crawford et al. 2002).

Symbolic Interactionism and the Misuse of Statistics   Many students express concerns about their own marital future, a wariness born out of the divorce of their parents, friends, neighbors, relatives—even their pastors and rabbis. They wonder about their chances of having a successful marriage. Because sociology is not just about abstract ideas, but is really about our lives, it is important to stress that you are an individual, not a statistic. That is, if the divorce rate were 33 percent or 50 percent, this would *not* mean that if you marry, your chances of getting divorced are 33 percent or 50 percent. That is a misuse of statistics—and a common one at that. Divorce statistics represent all marriages and have absolutely *nothing* to do with any individual marriage. Our own chances depend on our own situations—especially the way we approach marriage.

To make this point clearer, let's apply symbolic interactionism. From a symbolic interactionist perspective, we create our own worlds. That is, because our experiences don't come with built-in meanings, we interpret our experiences, and act accordingly. As we do so, we can create a self-fulfilling prophecy. For example, if we think that our marriage might fail, we are more likely to run when things become difficult. If we think that our marriage is going to work out, we are more likely to stick around and to do things to make the marriage successful. The folk saying "There are no guarantees in life" is certainly true, but it does help to have a vision that a good marriage is possible and that it is worth the effort to achieve.

The Future of Marriage and Family

What can we expect of marriage and family in the future? Despite its many problems, marriage is in no danger of becoming a relic of the past. Marriage is so functional that it exists in every society. Consequently, the vast majority of Americans will continue to find marriage vital to their welfare.

Certain trends are firmly in place. Cohabitation, births to single women, age at first marriage, and parenting by grandparents will increase. As more married women join the work force, wives will continue to gain marital power. The number of elderly will increase, and more couples will find themselves sandwiched between caring for their parents and rearing their own children.

Our culture will continue to be haunted by distorted images of marriage and family: the bleak ones portrayed in the mass media and the rosy ones perpetuated by cultural myths. Sociological research can help to correct these distortions and allow us to see how our own family experiences fit into the patterns of our culture. Sociological research can also help to answer the big question: How can we help formulate social policy that will support and enhance family life?

To conclude this chapter, in the Down-to-Earth Sociology box on the next page we look at a subtle but fundamental change that may have begun to impact the family.

When Work Becomes Home and Home Becomes Work

WORKERS CAN'T STAND THEIR bosses, and almost everyone would quit work and stay home if they had the chance, right? Don't be too sure.

As sociologist Arlie Hochschild (1997, 2006) did participant observation at a company she calls Amerco, she found that both work and family are changing. The family has become harried, with two working parents juggling their schedules around their work and personal lives as well as their children's school and after-school activities. As with Sharon and Tom in this chapter's opening vignette, parents can feel overwhelmed by responsibilities that come flying at them from several directions at once. Hochschild puts it this way:

> [A]t home . . . the emotional demands have become more baffling and complex. In addition to teething, tantrums and the normal developments of growing children, the needs of elderly parents are creating more tasks for the modern family—as are the blending, unblending, reblending of new stepparents, stepchildren, exes and former in-laws.

At the same time that pressures at home have increased, work for many has become less demanding and more rewarding. As Hochschild says,

> [N]ew management techniques so pervasive in corporate life have helped transform the workplace into a more appreciative, personal sort of social world . . . many companies now train workers to make their own work decisions, and . . . [many workers] feel recognized for job accomplishments. Amerco regularly strengthens the family-like ties of co-workers by holding "recognition ceremonies" . . . Amerco employees speak of "belonging to the Amerco family". . . . The education-and-training division offers free courses (on company time) in "Dealing with Anger," "How to Give and Accept Criticism," and "How to Cope with Difficult People."

What sort of "recognition ceremonies" do family members have? Or free courses on "How to Cope with Mom" or "How to Understand Your Two-Year-Old—or Unruly Teenager"? With pressures increasing at home and decreasing at work, Hochschild found that some workers volunteer for overtime "just to get away from the house." As Linda, one of the women Hochschild talked to, said,

> When I get home, and the minute I turn the key, my daughter is right there. Granted she needs somebody to talk to about her day. . . . The baby is still up. He should have been in bed two hours ago, and that upsets me. The dishes are piled in the sink. My daughter comes right up to the door and complains about anything her stepfather said or did, and she wants to talk about her job. My husband is in the other room hollering to my daughter, "Tracy, I don't ever get any time to talk to your mother, because you're always monopolizing her time before I even get a chance!" They all come at me at once.

Reflecting on what she observed, Hochschild says that for many people, the worlds of home and work have begun to reverse places. Home is becoming more like work, and work is becoming more like home. The key phrase, of course, is "for many people"—because many workplaces are not supportive, and workers still find them disagreeable places (Ducharme et al. 2004).

for your Consideration

It is difficult to pinpoint changes as they first occur, although some sociologists have been able to do so. As mentioned in Chapter 1, sociologist William Ogburn noted in 1933 that personality was becoming more important in mate selection, and in 1945 sociologists Ernest Burgess and Harvey Locke observed that mutual affection and compatibility were becoming more important in marriage. The change has been so complete that today it is difficult to conceive of getting married apart from affection and compatibility.

Could Hochschild have also put her finger on a historical shift just as it has begun to occur? Are the ways we view home and work in the process of reversing? In 50 years or so, will this be the taken-for-granted life for most of us? What do you think?

The cartoonist has aptly picked up the findings of sociologist Arlie Hochschild on the reversal of home and work.

King Features, James Cavett; 800-708-7311 x 246; Orlando, FL

Summary *and* Review

Marriage and Family in Global Perspective

What is a family—and what themes are universal?

Family is difficult to define. There are exceptions to every element that one might consider essential. Consequently, **family** is defined broadly—as people who consider themselves related by blood, marriage, or adoption. Universally, **marriage** and family are mechanisms for governing mate selection, reckoning descent, and establishing inheritance and authority. Pp. 462–464.

Marriage and Family in Theoretical Perspective

What is a functionalist perspective on marriage and family?

Functionalists examine the functions and dysfunctions of family life. Examples include the **incest taboo** and how weakened family functions increase divorce. Pp. 464–466.

What is a conflict perspective on marriage and family?

Conflict theorists focus on inequality in marriage, especially unequal power between husbands and wives. P. 466.

What is a symbolic interactionist perspective on marriage and family?

Symbolic interactionists examine the contrasting experiences and perspectives of men and women in marriage. They stress that only by grasping the perspectives of wives and husbands can we understand their behavior. Pp. 466–468.

The Family Life Cycle

What are the major elements of the family life cycle?

The major elements are love and courtship, marriage, childbirth, child rearing, and the family in later life. Most mate selection follows predictable patterns of age, social class, race-ethnicity, and religion. Childbirth and child-rearing patterns also vary by social class. Pp. 468–474.

Diversity in U.S. Families

How significant is race-ethnicity in family life?

The primary distinction is social class, not race-ethnicity. Families of the same social class are likely to be similar, regardless of their race-ethnicity. Pp. 474–478.

What other diversity in U.S. families is there?

Also discussed are one-parent, childless, **blended,** and gay and lesbian families. Each has its unique characteristics, but social class is significant in determining their primary characteristics. Poverty is especially significant for single-parent families, most of which are headed by women. Pp. 478–480.

Trends in U.S. Families

What major changes characterize U.S. families?

Three changes are postponement of first marriage, an increase in **cohabitation,** and more grandparents serving as parents to their grandchildren. With more people living longer, many middle-aged couples find themselves sandwiched between rearing their children and taking care of their aging parents. Pp. 481–485.

Divorce and Remarriage

What is the current divorce rate?

Depending on what numbers you choose to compare, you can produce almost any rate you wish, from 50 percent to less than 2 percent. Pp. 485–487.

How do children and their parents adjust to divorce?

Divorce is difficult for children, whose adjustment problems often continue into adulthood. Most divorced fathers do not maintain ongoing relationships with their children. Financial problems are usually greater for the former wives. Although most divorced people remarry, their rate of remarriage has slowed. Pp. 487–491.

Two Sides of Family Life

What are the two sides of family life?

The dark side is abuse—spouse battering, child abuse, marital rape, and **incest.** All these are acts that revolve around the misuse of family power. The bright side is that most people find marriage and family to be rewarding. Pp. 491–494.

The Future of Marriage and Family

What is the likely future of marriage and family?

We can expect cohabitation, births to unmarried women, age at first marriage, and parenting by grandparents to increase. The growing numbers of women in the work force are likely to continue to shift the balance of marital power. Pp. 494–495.

Thinking Critically
about Chapter 16

1. Functionalists stress that the family is universal because it provides basic functions for individuals and society. What functions does your family provide? Hint: In addition to the section "The Functionalist Perspective," also consider the section "Common Cultural Themes."

2. Explain why social class is more important than race-ethnicity in determining a family's characteristics.

3. Apply this chapter's contents to your own experience with marriage and family. What social factors affect your family life? In what ways is your family life different from that of your grandparents when they were your age?

Additional Resources

What can you use MySocLab for? mysoclab www.mysoclab.com

ALLYN & BACON

Where learning & the sociological imagination intersect.

- **Study and Review:** Pre- and Post-Tests, Practice Tests, Flash Cards, Individualized Study Plans.

- **Current Events:** *Sociology in the News,* the daily *New York Times,* and more.

- **Research and Writing:** *Research Navigator, Writing About Sociology,* and more.

Where Can I Read More on This Topic?

Suggested readings for this chapter are listed at the back of this book.

CHAPTER 17

Education

Stephen Schildbach, *Students*, 1999

Kathy Spiegel was upset. Horace Mann, the school principal in her hometown in Oregon, had asked her to come to his office. He explained that Kathy's 11-year-old twins had been acting up in class. They were disturbing other children and the teacher—and what was Kathy going to do about this?

Kathy didn't want to tell Mr. Mann what he could do with the situation. *That* would have gotten her kicked out of the office. Instead, she bit her tongue and said she would talk to her daughters.

. . . .

On the other side of the country, Jim and Julia Attaway were pondering their own problem. When they visited their son's school in the Bronx, they didn't like what they saw. The boys looked like they were gang members, and the girls dressed and acted as though they were sexually active. Their own 13-year-old son had started using street language at home, and it was becoming increasingly difficult to communicate with him.

. . . .

Kathy's 11-year-old twins were disturbing other children and the teacher—and what was Kathy going to do about this?

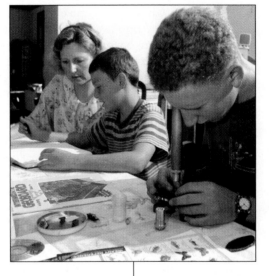

In Minneapolis, Denzil and Tamika Jefferson were facing a much quieter crisis. They found life frantic as they hurried from one school activity to another. Their 13-year-old son attended a private school, and the demands were so intense that it felt like the junior year in high school. They no longer seemed to have any relaxed family time together.

. . . .

In Atlanta, Jaime and Maria Morelos were upset at the ideas that their 8-year-old daughter had begun to express at home. As devout first-generation Protestants, Jaime and Maria felt moral issues were a top priority, and they didn't like what they were hearing.

. . . .

Kathy talked the matter over with her husband, Bob. Jim and Julia discussed their problem, as did Denzil and Tamika and Jaime and Maria. They all came to the same conclusion: The problem was not their children. The problem was the school their children attended. All four sets of parents also came to the same solution: home schooling for their children.

Home schooling might seem to be a radical solution to today's education problems, but it is one that the parents of over a million U.S. children have chosen. We'll come back to this topic, but, first, let's take a broad look at education.

The Development of Modern Education

To provide a background for understanding our own educational system, let's look first at education in earlier societies, then trace the development of universal education.

Education in Earlier Societies

Earlier societies had no separate social institution called education. They had no special buildings called schools, and no people who earned their living as teachers. Rather, as an integral part of growing up, children learned what was necessary to get along in life. If hunting or cooking were the essential skills, then people who already possessed those skills taught them to the next generation. *Education was synonymous with acculturation,* learning a culture. It still is in today's tribal groups.

In some societies—such as China, Greece, and North Africa—when a sufficient surplus developed, a separate institution for education appeared. Some people then devoted themselves to teaching, while those who had the leisure—the children of the wealthy—became their students. In ancient China, for example, Confucius taught a few select pupils, while in Greece, Aristotle, Plato, and Socrates taught science and philosophy to upper-class boys. Education, then, came to be something distinct from informal acculturation. **Education** is a group's *formal* system of teaching knowledge, values, and skills. Such instruction stood in marked contrast to the learning of traditional skills such as farming or hunting, for it was intended to develop the mind. Education flourished during the period roughly marked by the birth of Christ, then slowly died out. During the Dark Ages of Europe, monks kept the candle of enlightenment burning. Except for a handful of the wealthy and some members of the nobility, only the monks could read and write. Although the monks delved into philosophy, they focused on learning Greek, Latin, and Hebrew so that they could study the Bible and writings of early church leaders. The Jews also kept formal learning alive as they studied the Torah.

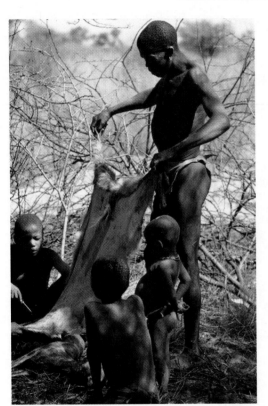

In hunting and gathering societies, there is no separate social institution called *education*. Instead, children learn from their parents and elders. These boys in the Kalahari desert of Botswana are learning survival skills as they watch their father skin a duiker.

Formal education remained limited to those who had the leisure to pursue it. (The word *school* comes from the Greek word *schole* meaning "leisure.") Industrialization transformed education, for some of the machinery and new types of jobs required workers to read, write, and work accurately with numbers—the classic three R's of the nineteenth century (Reading, 'Riting, and 'Rithmetic).

Industrialization and Universal Education

After the American Revolution, the founders of the new republic were concerned that the many religious and ethnic groups (nationalities) would make the nation unstable. To help create a uniform national culture, Thomas Jefferson and Noah Webster proposed universal schooling. Standardized texts would instill patriotism and teach the principles of representative government (Hellinger and Judd 1991). If this new political experiment were to succeed, they reasoned, it would need educated citizens who were capable of making sound decisions and voting wisely. A national culture remained elusive, however, and the country remained politically fragmented into the 1800s. Many states even considered themselves to be near-sovereign nations.

Education reflected this disunity. There was no comprehensive school system, just a hodgepodge of independent schools. Public schools even charged tuition. Lutherans,

Presbyterians, and Roman Catholics operated their own schools (Hellinger and Judd 1991). Children of the rich attended private schools. Children of the poor received no formal education—nor did slaves. High school was considered higher education (hence the name *high* school), and only the wealthy could afford it. College, too, was beyond the reach of almost everyone.

Horace Mann, an educator from Massachusetts, found it deplorable that parents with an average income could not afford to send their children to grade school. In 1837 he proposed that "common schools," supported through taxes, be established throughout his state. Mann's idea spread, and state after state began to provide free public education. It is no coincidence that universal education and industrialization occurred at the same time. As they observed the transformation of the economy, political and civic leaders recognized the need for an educated work force. They also feared the influx of "foreign" values and, like the founders of the country, looked on public education as a way to "Americanize" immigrants (Hellinger and Judd 1991).

By 1918, all U.S. states had **mandatory education laws** requiring children to attend school, usually until they completed the eighth grade or turned 16, whichever came first. In the early 1900s, graduation from the eighth grade marked the end of education for most people. "Dropouts" at that time were students who did not complete grade school.

As industrialization progressed and fewer people made their living from farming, formal education came to be regarded as essential to the well-being of society. With the distance to the nearest college too far and the cost of tuition and lodging too great, many high school graduates were unable to attend college. As is discussed in the Down-to-Earth Sociology box on the next page, this predicament gave birth to community colleges. As you can see from Figure 17.1, receiving a bachelor's degree in the United States

In this 1900 photo taken in Washington, D.C., girls are learning the survival skills they need for their society. Previously, mothers had taught these skills to their daughters, but by this point schools had begun to take over this responsibility. What survival skills have schools taught you?

Figure 17.1 Educational Achievement in the United States

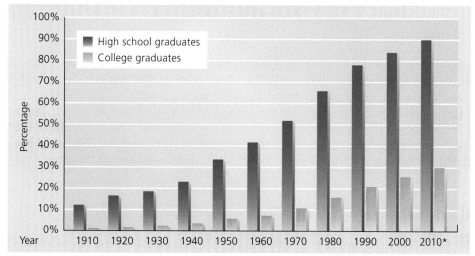

- ■ High school graduates
- ■ College graduates

Note: Americans 25 years and over. Asterisk indicates author's estimate.

Sources: By the author. Based on National Center for Education Statistics 1991:Table 8; *Statistical Abstract* 2007:Table 214.

mandatory education laws laws that require all children to attend school until a specified age or until they complete a minimum grade in school

Community Colleges: Challenges Old and New

I ATTENDED A JUNIOR COLLEGE in Oakland, California. From there, with fresh diploma in hand, I transferred to a senior college— a college in Ft. Wayne, Indiana, that had no freshmen or sophomores.

I didn't realize that my experimental college matched the vision of some of the founders of the community college movement. In the early 1900s, they foresaw a system of local colleges that would be accessible to the average high school graduate—a system so extensive that it would be unnecessary for universities to offer courses at the freshman and sophomore levels (Manzo 2001).

A group with an equally strong opinion questioned whether preparing high school graduates for entry to four-year colleges and universities should be the goal of junior colleges. They insisted that the purpose of junior colleges should be vocational preparation, to equip people for the job market as electricians and other technicians. In some regions, where the proponents of transfer dominated, the admissions requirements for junior colleges were higher than those of Yale (Pedersen 2001). This debate was never won by either side, and you can still hear its echoes today.

The name *junior* college also became a problem. Some felt that the word *junior* made their institution sound as though it weren't quite a real college. A struggle to change the name ensued, and several decades ago *community* college won out.

The name change didn't settle the debate about whether the purpose was preparing students to transfer to universities or training them for jobs, however. Community colleges continue to serve this dual purpose.

Community colleges have opened higher education to millions of students who would not otherwise have access to college because of cost or distance.

Community colleges have become such an essential part of the U.S. educational system that about two of every five of all undergraduates in the United States are enrolled in them (*Statistical Abstract* 2007:Table 268). Most students are *nontraditional* students: Many are age 25 or older, are from the working class, have jobs, and attend college part time (Bryant 2001).

To help their students transfer to four-year colleges and universities, many community colleges work closely with top-tier public and private universities (Chaker 2003b). Some provide admissions guidance on how to enter flagship state schools. Others coordinate courses, making sure that they match the university's title and numbering system, as well as its rigor of instruction and grading. More than a third offer honors programs that prepare talented students to transfer with ease into these schools (Padgett 2005).

The challenges that community colleges face are the usual ones of securing adequate budgets in the face of declining resources, continuing an open-door policy, meeting changing job markets, and maintaining quality instruction. New challenges include meeting the shifting needs of students, such as the growing need to teach students for whom English is a second language and to provide on-campus day care for parents.

for your Consideration

Do you think the primary goal of community colleges should be to prepare students for jobs or prepare them to transfer to 4-year colleges and universities? Why?

is now *twice* as common as completing high school used to be. Two-thirds (67 percent) of all high school graduates enter college (*Statistical Abstract* 2007:Table 265).

One of seven Americans has not made it through high school, however, which leads to economic problems for most of them for the rest of their lives (*Statistical Abstract* 2007:Table 214). The Social Map on the next page shows how unevenly distributed high school graduation is among the states. You may want to compare this Social Map with the one on page 289 that shows how poverty is distributed among the states.

Education in Global Perspective

To further place our own educational system in perspective, let's look at education in three countries at different levels of industrialization. This will help us see how education is directly related to a nation's culture and its economy.

Figure 17.2 Not Making It: Dropping Out of High School

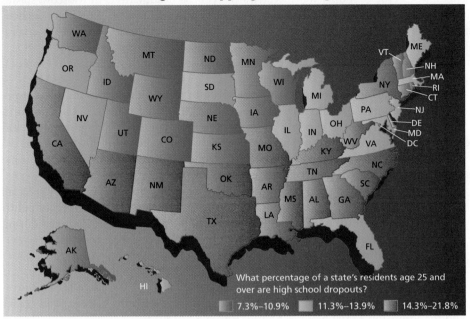

What percentage of a state's residents age 25 and over are high school dropouts?

■ 7.3%–10.9%　■ 11.3%–13.9%　■ 14.3%–21.8%

Note: The states vary widely. The extremes range from 7.3 percent in Minnesota to 21.8 percent in Texas.

Source: By the author. Based on *Statistical Abstract* 2007:Table 218.

Education in the Most Industrialized Nations: Japan

A central sociological principle of education is that a nation's education reflects its culture. Because a core Japanese value is solidarity with the group, the Japanese discourage competition among individuals. In the work force, people who are hired together work as a team. They are not expected to compete with one another for promotions; instead, they are promoted as a group (Ouchi 1993). Japanese education reflects this group-centered approach to life. Children in grade school work as a group, all mastering the same skills and materials. On any one day, children all over Japan study the same page from the same textbook ("Less Rote . . ." 2000).

In a fascinating cultural contradiction, college admissions in Japan are highly competitive. The Scholastic Assessment Test (SAT) that U.S. college-bound high school juniors and seniors take is voluntary, but Japanese seniors who want to attend college must take a national test. U.S. high school graduates who perform poorly on their tests can usually find some college to attend—as long as their parents can pay the tuition. In Japan, however, only the top scorers—rich and poor alike—are admitted to college. Japanese sociologists have found that even though the tests are open to all, children from the richer families are more likely to be admitted to college. The reason is not favoritism on the part of college officials, but, rather, that the children of richer parents score higher on these tests. One reason is that their parents spend more for tutors and intensive training classes to prepare their children for the college entrance exams (Ono 2001).

Education in the Industrializing Nations: Russia

After the Russian Revolution of 1917, the Soviet Communist party changed the nation's educational system. At that time, as in most countries, education was limited to children of the elite. The communists expanded the educational system until eventually it encompassed all children. Following the sociological principle that education reflects culture, the new government made certain that socialist values dominated its schools, for it saw education as a means to undergird the new political system. As a result, schoolchildren were taught that capitalism was evil and that communism was the salvation of the world. Every classroom was required to prominently display photographs of Lenin and Stalin.

Education, including college, was free. Schools stressed mathematics and the natural sciences. Just as the economy was directed from central headquarters in Moscow, so was education. Schools throughout the country followed the same state-prescribed curriculum, and all students in the same grade used the same textbooks. To prevent critical thinking, which might lead to criticisms of communism, few courses in the social sciences were taught, and students memorized course materials, repeating lectures on oral exams (Deaver 2001).

Russia's switch from communism to capitalism brought a change in culture—especially new ideas about profit, private property, and personal freedom. This, in turn, meant that the educational system had to adjust to the country's changing values and views of the world. Not only did the photos of Lenin and Stalin come down, but, for the first time, private, religious, and even foreign-run schools were allowed. For the first time also, teachers were able to encourage students to think for themselves.

The problems that Russia confronted in "reinventing" its educational system are mind-boggling. Tens of thousands of teachers who were used to teaching rote political answers had to learn new methods of instruction. As the economy faltered during Russia's early transition to capitalism, school budgets dwindled. Some teachers went unpaid for months; instead of money, at one school teachers were given toilet paper and vodka (Deaver 2001). Teachers are now paid regularly (and in money), but the salaries are low. University professors are paid between $470 and $980 a month. Abysmal salaries have encouraged corruption, and some students pay for good grades and for admission to the better schools ("Russia Sets Out to . . ." 2007).

Because it is true of education everywhere, we can confidently predict that Russia's educational system will continue to reflect its culture. Its educational system will glorify Russia's historical exploits and reinforce its values and world views—no matter how they might change.

Education in the Least Industrialized Nations: Egypt

Education in the Least Industrialized Nations stands in sharp contrast to that in the industrialized world. Because most of the citizens of these nations work the land or take care of families, there is little emphasis on formal schooling. Even if a Least Industrialized Nation has mandatory attendance laws, they are not enforced. Formal education is expensive, and most of these nations cannot afford it. As we saw in Figure 9.2 (pages 252–253), many people in the Least Industrialized Nations live on less than $1,000 a year. Consequently, in some of these nations few children go to school beyond the first couple of grades. Figure 17.3 contrasts education in China with that of the United States. As was once common around the globe, it is primarily the wealthy in the Least Industrialized Nations who have the means and the leisure for formal education—especially anything beyond the basics. As an example, let's look at education in Egypt.

Several centuries before the birth of Christ, Egypt's world-renowned centers of learning produced such acclaimed scientists as Archimedes and Euclid. The primary areas of study during this classic period were physics, astronomy, geometry, geography, mathematics, philosophy, and medicine. The largest library in the world was at Alexandria. Fragments from the papyrus manuscripts of this library, which burned to the ground, have been invaluable in deciphering ancient manuscripts. After Rome defeated Egypt, however, education declined, and has never regained its former prominence.

Although the Egyptian constitution guarantees five years of free grade school for all children, many poor children receive no education at all. For those who do attend school, qualified teachers are few and classrooms are crowded (Cook 2001). As a result, one-third of Egyptian men and over half of Egyptian women are illiterate (UNESCO 2005). Those who go beyond the five years of grade school attend a preparatory school for three years. High school also lasts for three years. During the first two years, all students take the same courses, but during the third year they specialize in arts, science, or mathematics. The emphasis has been on memorizing facts to pass national tests. Reflecting growing concerns that this approach leaves minds less capable of evaluating life and opens the door to religious extremism, critical thinking is being added to the curriculum (Gauch 2006).

Figure 17.3 Education in a Most Industrialized (Postindustrial) Nation and a Least Industrialized Nation

Who Goes to These Schools? Comparing China and the United States

China / United States

Grade School: 97% / 100%

Junior High School: 40% / 99%

High School: 12% / 90%

College: 1% / 40%

Note: These are initial attendance rates, not completion rates. The U.S. junior high school total is the author's estimate.

Sources: Brauchli 1994; Kahn 2004; Zeng and Wang 2007; *Statistical Abstract* 2007:Tables 208, 210, 262.

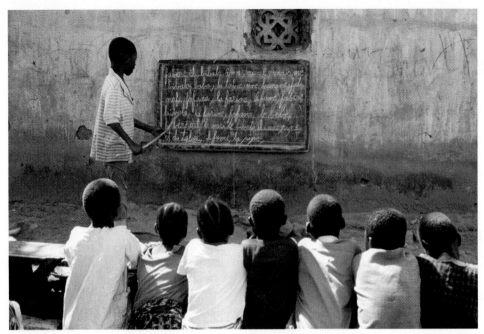

The poverty of some of the Least Industrialized Nations defies the imagination of most people who have been reared in the industrialized world. Their educational systems are similarly marked by poverty. This photo shows a street school in Bobo Dioulasso, Burkina Faso.

Within the Least Industrialized Nations are pockets of high quality schools taught by and for Westerners. This bicycle-school bus in Nepal transports children to the English Boarding School.

The Functionalist Perspective: Providing Social Benefits

A central position of functionalism is that when the parts of society are working properly, each contributes to the well-being or stability of that society. The positive things that people intend their actions to accomplish are known as **manifest functions.** The positive consequences they did not intend are called **latent functions.** Let's look at the functions of education.

"Hey, how come no diplomas?" "Oh, I'm self-taught."

The cartoonist captures a primary reason that we have become a credential society.

Teaching Knowledge and Skills

Education's most obvious manifest function is to teach knowledge and skills—whether the traditional three R's or their more contemporary counterparts, such as computer literacy. Each generation must train the next to fulfill the group's significant positions. Because our postindustrial society needs highly educated people, the schools supply them.

Sociologist Randall Collins (1979) observed that industrialized nations have become **credential societies.** By this, he means that employers use diplomas and degrees as *sorting devices* to determine who is eligible for a job. Because employers don't know potential workers, they depend on schools to weed out the capable from the incapable. For example, when you graduate from college, potential employers will presume that you are a responsible person—that you have shown up on time for numerous classes, have turned in scores of assignments, and have demonstrated basic writing and thinking skills. They will then graft their particular job skills onto this foundation, which has been certified by your college.

In some cases, job skills must be mastered before an individual is allowed to do certain work. On-the-job training was once adequate for physicians, engineers, and airline pilots, but with changes in information and technology it is no longer sufficient. This is precisely why doctors display their credentials so prominently. Their framed degrees declare that they have been certified by an institution of higher learning to work on your body.

Cultural Transmission of Values

Another manifest function of education is the **cultural transmission of values,** a process by which schools pass on a society's core values from one generation to the next. Consequently, schools in a socialist society stress values of socialism, while schools in a capitalist society teach values that support capitalism. U.S. schools, for example, stress respect for private property, individualism, and competition.

Regardless of a country's economic system, loyalty to the state is a cultural value, and schools around the world teach patriotism. U.S. schools teach that the United States is the best country in the world; Russians learn that no country is better than Russia; and French, Japanese, and Afghani students all learn the virtues of their respective countries. Teachers extol the society's founders, their struggle for freedom from oppression, and the goodness of the country's basic social institutions. Seldom is this function as explicit as it is in Japan, where the law requires that schools "cultivate a respect for tradition and culture, and love for the nation and homeland that have fostered them" (Nakamura 2006).

To visualize this point of the functionalists, consider how differently a course in current events or U.S. history would be taught in France, Iran, and Kokomo, Indiana.

Social Integration

Schools also bring about *social integration.* They promote a sense of national identity by having students salute the flag and sing the national anthem, as in the photo on the next page. One of the best examples of how schools promote political integration is how they have taught mainstream ideas and values to tens of millions of immigrants. Coming to regard themselves as Americans, the immigrants gave up their earlier national and cultural identities (Rodriguez 1995; Carper 2000).

This integrative function of education goes far beyond making people similar in their appearance, speech or even ways of thinking. *To forge a national identity is to stabilize the political system.* If people identify with a society's institutions and *perceive them as the basis of their own welfare,* they have no reason to rebel. This function is especially significant when it comes to the lower social classes, from which most social revolutionaries emerge.

credential society the use of diplomas and degrees to determine who is eligible for jobs, even though the diploma or degree may be irrelevant to the actual work

cultural transmission of values in reference to education, the ways in which schools transmit a society's culture, especially its core values

The wealthy already have a vested interest in maintaining the status quo, but getting the lower classes to identify with a social system *as it is* goes a long way toward preserving the system in its current state.

People with disabilities often have found themselves left out of the mainstream of society. To overcome this, U.S. schools have added a manifest function, **mainstreaming,** or inclusion. This means that educators try to incorporate students with disabilities into regular school activities. As a matter of routine policy, students with disabilities used to be placed in special classes or schools. There, however, they learned to adjust to a specialized situation, leaving them ill prepared to cope with the dominant world. Educational philosophy then shifted to encourage or even to require students with disabilities to attend regular schools. For people who cannot walk, wheelchair ramps are provided; for those who cannot hear, interpreters who use sign language may attend classes with them. Most students who are blind attend special schools, as do people with severe learning disabilities. Overall, one half of students with disabilities now attend school in regular classrooms (U.S. Department of Education 2007).

These students are learning that the identity of "American" overrides family, gender, and racial-ethnic identities. They are also learning patriotism and civic duties.

Gatekeeping

Gatekeeping, or determining which people will enter what occupations, is another function of education. One type of gatekeeping is *credentialing*—using diplomas and degrees to determine who is eligible for a job—which opens the door of opportunity for some and closes it to others. Gatekeeping is often accomplished by **tracking,** sorting students into different educational programs on the basis of their perceived abilities. Some U.S. high schools funnel students into one of three tracks: general, college prep, or honors. Students on the lowest track are likely to go to work after high school, or to take vocational courses. Those on the highest track usually attend prestigious colleges. Those in between usually attend a local college or regional state university. The impact is lifelong, affecting opportunities for jobs, income, and lifestyle. Schools have retreated from formal tracking, but placing students in "ability groups" and "advanced" classes serves the same purpose (Lucas 1999; Tach and Farkas 2003).

Gatekeeping sorts people on the basis of merit, said functionalists Talcott Parsons (1940), Kingsley Davis, and Wilbert Moore (1945). They pioneered a view known as **social placement,** arguing that some jobs require few skills and can be performed by people of lesser intelligence. Other jobs, however, such as that of physician, require high intelligence and advanced education. To motivate capable people to postpone gratification and to put up with years of rigorous education, rewards of high income and prestige are offered. Thus, functionalists look at education as a system that, to benefit society, sorts people according to their abilities and ambitions.

Replacing Family Functions

Over the years, the functions of U.S. schools have expanded, and they now rival some family functions. Child care is an example. Grade schools do double duty as babysitters for families in which both parents work, or for single working mothers. Child care has always been a latent function of formal education, for it was an unintended consequence. Now, however, with two wage earners in most families, child care has become a manifest

mainstreaming helping people to become part of the mainstream of society

gatekeeping the process by which education opens and closes doors of opportunity; another term for the social placement function of education

tracking the sorting of students into different educational programs on the basis of real or perceived abilities

social placement a function of education—funneling people into a society's various positions function, and some schools offer child care both before and after the school day. Some high schools even provide nurseries for the children of their teenaged students (Bosman 2007). Another function is providing sex education and birth control advice. This has stirred controversy, for some families resent schools taking this function away from them. Disagreement over values has fueled the social movement for home schooling, featured in our opening vignette and in the Down-to-Earth Sociology box on the next page.

Other Functions

Education also fulfills other functions. One is *matchmaking*. Because most students are unmarried, it is at high school and college that many people meet their future spouses. The sociological significance is that schools funnel people into marriage with mates of similar background, interests, and education. Schools are also a source of *social networks;* some students make lifetime friendships, while others make contacts that benefit their careers. Schools also help to *reduce the unemployment rate.* To keep millions of young people in the classroom is to keep them out of the labor market. Schools also *stabilize society* by keeping these millions off the streets, where they might be committing crimes or holding demonstrations to protest their unemployment and the exporting of millions of jobs to other nations.

Another function of schools is to provide employment. With 56 million students in grade and high schools, and another 19 million enrolled in college, U.S. education is big business. Elementary and secondary schools provide jobs for almost 4 million teachers, while another million teach in colleges and universities (*Statistical Abstract* 2007:Tables 206, 267). Millions more work as support personnel—aides, administrators, bus drivers, janitors, and secretaries. Another several million earn their living in industries that service schools—from writing textbooks to building schools and manufacturing pencils, paper, desks, and computers.

A Surprising Latent Function   Researchers have found that people who go farther in school live longer. For each additional year of education, people average at least a year longer life than people with the same characteristics who don't attain that education (Lleras-Muney 2005). The most likely reason for this effect on life expectancy is that additional education gives access to better jobs, higher pay, and superior medical services.

Conflict theorists stress that education reproduces a country's social class system. As part of the evidence to support this position, they point out that the U.S. social classes attend separate schools, where they learn perspectives of the world that match their place in it. Shown here is a student at The Andrews School in Willoughby, Ohio. What do you think the *hidden curriculum* is at this school?

The Conflict Perspective: Perpetuating Social Inequality

Unlike functionalists, who look at the benefits of education, conflict theorists examine how *the educational system reproduces the social class structure.* By this, they mean that schools perpetuate the social divisions of society and help members of the elite to maintain their dominance.

Let's look, then, at how education is related to social classes, how it is a factor in people inheriting the life opportunities that were laid down before they were born.

The Hidden Curriculum

The term **hidden curriculum** refers to the attitudes and the unwritten rules of behavior that schools teach in addition to the formal curriculum. Examples are obedience to authority and conformity to mainstream norms. Conflict theorists stress that the hidden curriculum helps to perpetuate social inequalities.

To understand this central point, consider the way English is taught. Middle-class schools—whose teachers know

Home Schooling: The Search for Quality and Values

"YOU'RE DOING WHAT? You're going to teach your kids at home?" is the typical, incredulous response to parents who decide to home school their children. The unspoken questions are, "How can you teach? You're not trained. And taking your kids out of the public schools—Do you want your kids to be dumb and social misfits?"

The home schooling movement was small at first, just a trickle of parents who were dissatisfied with the rigidity of the school bureaucracy, lax discipline, incompetent teachers, low standards, lack of focus on individual needs, and, in some instances, hostility to their religion.

The trickle has grown. While not yet a raging river, the number of children who are being taught at home is more than twice the size of the public school system of Chicago. More than one million children are being home schooled (Princiotta, Bielick, and Chapman 2004; *Statistical Abstract* 2007:Table 227).

Home schooling is far from new. In the colonial era, home schooling was the *typical* form of education (Carper 2000). Today's home schooling movement is restoring this earlier pattern, but it also reflects a fascinating shift in U.S. politics. Political and religious *liberals* began the contemporary home schooling movement in the 1950s and 1960s. Their objection was that the schools were too conservative. Then the schools changed, and in the 1970s and 1980s, political and religious *conservatives* embraced home schooling (Lines 2000; Stevens 2001). Their objection was that the schools were too liberal. Other parents have no political motivation. They are homeschooling their children because of concerns about safety at school and the lack of individual attention (Shellenbarger 2006).

Does home schooling work? Can parents who are not trained as teachers actually teach? The early results of testing home schoolers were promising, but they were limited to small groups or to single states. Then in 1990, a national sample of 2,000 home schoolers showed that these students did better than students who were in public schools. Could this really be true?

To find out, researchers tested 21,000 home schoolers across the nation (Rudner 1999). The results are astounding. The median scores for every test at every grade were in the 70th to 80th percentiles. The home schoolers outscored students in both public and Catholic schools.

The basic reason for the stunning success of home schooling appears to be the parents' involvement in their

As the home schooling social movement has grown, it has become increasingly institutionalized. Home schoolers now have their own class rings.

children's education. Home schoolers receive an intense, one-on-one education. Their curriculum—although it includes the subjects that are required by the state—is designed around the student's interests and needs. Ninety percent of students are taught by their mothers, ten percent by their fathers (Lines 2000). Ninety-eight percent of the fathers of home schoolers are in the labor force, but only twenty-two percent of the mothers. The parents' income is also above average.

What we do not know is what these home schoolers' test scores would have been if they had been taught in public schools. With their parents' involvement in their education, they likely would have done very well there, too. In addition, although the Rudner study was large, it was not a random sample, and we cannot say how the *average* home schooler is doing. But, then, we have no random sample of all public school students, either.

What about the children's social skills? Since they don't attend school with dozens and even hundreds of other students, do they become social misfits? The studies show that they do just fine on this level, too. They actually have fewer behavior problems than children who attend conventional schools (Lines 2000). Contrary to stereotypes, homeschooled children are not isolated. As part of their educational experience, their parents take them to libraries, museums, factories, and nursing homes (Medlin 2000). Some home schoolers participate in the physical education and sports programs of the public schools. For social activities, many of the children meet with other homeschooled children and go on field trips together. There are even homeschooling associations, which run conferences for parents and children and hold sporting events. As the photo shows, the same companies that sell class rings to public high schools also sell class rings to home schoolers (McGinn and McLure 2003).

for your Consideration

Two of every one hundred students across the country are being taught at home. Why do you think that home schooling has become so popular? Do you think this social movement could eventually become a threat to U.S. public schools? Would you consider home schooling your children? Why or why not?

where their students are headed—stress "proper" English and "good" manners. In contrast, the teachers in inner-city schools—who also know where *their* students are headed—allow ethnic and street language in the classroom. Each type of school is helping to reproduce the social class structure. That is, each is preparing students to work in positions similar to those of their parents. The social class of some children destines them for higher positions. For these jobs, they need "refined" speech and manners. The social destiny of others is low-status jobs. For this type of work, they need only to obey rules (Bowles and Gintis 1976; 2002). Teaching these students "refined" speech and manners would be a wasted effort. In other words, even the teaching of English and manners helps keep the social classes intact across generations.

From the conflict perspective, even kindergarten has a hidden curriculum, as the Down-to-Earth Sociology box below illustrates.

Tilting the Tests: Discrimination by IQ

Even intelligence tests play a part in keeping the social class system intact. For example, how would you answer the following question?

A symphony is to a composer as a book is to a(n) ____

____ paper ____ sculptor ____ musician ____ author ____ man

You probably had no difficulty coming up with "author" as your choice. Wouldn't any intelligent person have done so?

In point of fact, this question raises a central issue in intelligence testing. Not all intelligent people would know the answer. This question contains *cultural biases.*

Down-to-Earth Sociology

Kindergarten as Boot Camp

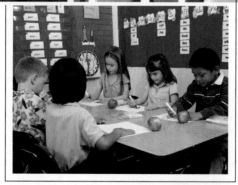

AFTER HE DID PARTICIPANT observation in a kindergarten, sociologist Harry Gracey (2007) concluded that kindergarten is a sort of boot camp for education. Here, tender students from diverse backgrounds are molded into a compliant group that will, on command, follow classroom routines. "Show and tell," for example, does more than allow children to be expressive. It also teaches them to talk only when they are asked to speak. ("It's your turn, Jarmay.") The format instructs children to request permission to talk ("Who knows what Adela has?") by raising a hand and being acknowledged. This ritual also teaches children to acknowledge the teacher's ideas as superior. She alone has the capacity to evaluate what students say and do.

Gracey also found a *hidden curriculum* in other activities he observed. Whether students were drawing pictures, listening to music, eating snacks, or resting, the teachers would scold talkative students and give approval to those who conformed. In short, the children received the message that the teacher—and, by inference, the entire school system—is the authority.

This, Gracey concluded, is not a side issue—it is *the* purpose of kindergarten. The kindergarten teacher's job is to teach children to "follow orders with unquestioning obedience." It is to "create and enforce a rigid social structure in the classroom through which they effectively control the behavior of most of the children for most of the school day."

This produces three kinds of students: (1) "good" students, those who submit to school-imposed discipline and come to identify with it; (2) "adequate" students, those who submit to the school's discipline but do not identify with it; and (3) "bad" students, those who refuse to submit to school routines. Children in the third category are called "problem children." To bring them into line, tougher drill sergeants—the principal and the school psychologist—are called in. If that doesn't work, the problem children are drugged into docility with Ritalin.

These early lessons extend beyond the classroom. As Gracey notes, school serves as a boot camp to prepare students for the routines of the work world, both on the assembly line and at the office. School helps turn children into docile workers who follow the routines imposed by "the company."

Children from some backgrounds are more familiar with the concepts of symphonies, composers, and sculptors than are other children. Consequently, the test is tilted in their favor.

Perhaps asking a different question will make the bias clearer. How would you answer this question?

If you throw dice and "7" is showing on the top, what is facing down?

___ *seven* ___ *snake eyes* ___ *box cars* ___ *little Joes* ___ *eleven*

This question, suggested by Adrian Dove (n.d.), a social worker in Watts, a poor area of Los Angeles, is slanted toward a lower-class experience. It surely is obvious that this *particular* cultural bias tilts the test so that children from certain social backgrounds will perform better than others.

It is no different with IQ (intelligence quotient) tests that use such words as *composer* and *symphony*. A lower-class child may have heard about rap, rock, hip hop, or jazz, but not about symphonies. In other words, IQ tests measure not only intelligence but also acquired knowledge. Whatever else we can say, the cultural bias that is built into the standard IQ tests is clearly *not* tilted in favor of the lower classes. One consequence is that the children of the poor, who score lower on these tests, are assigned to less demanding courses to match their supposedly inferior intelligence. This destines them for lower-paying jobs in adult life. As conflict theorists view them, IQ tests are another weapon in an arsenal designed to maintain the social class structure across the generations.

correspondence principle the sociological principle that schools correspond to (or reflect) the social structure of their society

Stacking the Deck: Unequal Funding

As you can see from the Social Map below, the amount spent on educating children varies widely among the states. Although there is no one-for-one match, in general, the states that spend more on education have higher quality schools. A main reason is that they attract more highly qualified teachers. Conflict theorists go beyond this, however, and stress the significance of *how* U.S. schools are funded. Because public schools are supported largely by local property taxes, the richer communities (where property values are higher) have more to spend on their children, and the poorer communities have less to spend on theirs. Consequently, the richer communities can offer higher salaries and take their pick of the most highly qualified and motivated teachers. They can also afford to buy the latest textbooks, computers, and software, as well as offer courses in foreign languages, music, and the arts. This, stress conflict theorists, means that in *all* states the deck is stacked against the poor.

The Correspondence Principle

In a classic analysis, conflict sociologists Samuel Bowles and Herbert Gintis (1976; 2002) used the term **correspondence principle** to refer to how

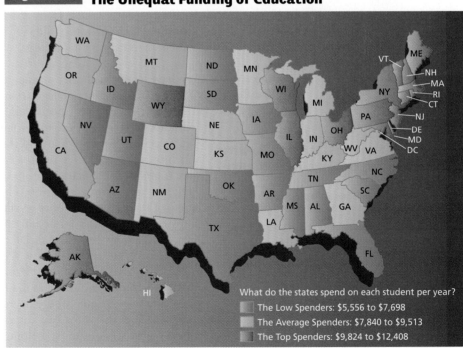

Figure 17.4 **The Unequal Funding of Education**

What do the states spend on each student per year?
- The Low Spenders: $5,556 to $7,698
- The Average Spenders: $7,840 to $9,513
- The Top Spenders: $9,824 to $12,408

Note: Some states spend more than twice as much to educate their students. The range is from $5,556 in Utah to $12,408 in New York. At $14,621, the District of Columbia is in a class by itself.

Source: By the author. Based on *Statistical Abstract* 2007:Table 245.

schools reflect society. This term means that what is taught in a nation's schools *corresponds* to the characteristics of that society. Here are some examples.

Characteristics of Society	Characteristics of Schools
1. Capitalism	1. Encourage competition
2. Social inequality	2. Unequal funding of schools
3. Social class bias	3. Funnel children of the poor into job training programs that demand little intellect
4. Bureaucratic structure of corporations	4. Provide a model of authority in the classroom
5. Need for submissive workers	5. Make students submissive, as in the kindergarten boot camp
6. Need for dependable workers	6. Enforce punctuality in attendance and homework
7. Need to maintain armed forces	7. Promote patriotism (to fight for capitalism)

Conflict theorists conclude that the correspondence principle demonstrates that the U.S. educational system is designed to turn students into dependable workers who will not question their bosses. It also is intended to produce some who are innovators in thought and action, but who can still be counted on to be loyal to the social system as it exists (Olneck and Bills 1980).

The Bottom Line: Family Background

The end result of unequal funding, IQ tests, and the other factors we have discussed is this: Family background is more important than test scores in predicting who attends college. In a classic study, sociologist Samuel Bowles (1977) compared the college attendance of the brightest 25 percent of high school students with that of the intellectually weakest 25 percent. Figure 17.5 shows the results. Of the *brightest* 25 percent of high school students, 90 percent of those from affluent homes went to college, while only half of those from low-income homes did. Of the *intellectually weakest* students, 26 percent from affluent homes went to college, while only 6 percent from poorer homes did so.

Other sociologists have confirmed this classic research. Anthony Carnevale and Stephen Rose (2003) compared students' college attendance with their intellectual abilities and their parents' social class. Regardless of personal abilities—children from more well-to-do families not only are more likely to go to college but also to attend the nation's most elite schools. This, in turn, piles advantage upon advantage. Students at these colleges are more likely to graduate from college, and they enter higher paying positions upon graduation. The elite colleges are the icing on the cake of these students' more privileged birth.

Conflict theorists point out that the educational system reproduces not only the U.S. social class structure but also its racial-ethnic divisions. From Figure 17.6 on the next page, you can see that, compared with whites, African Americans and Latinos are less likely to complete high school and less likely to go to college. Because adults without college degrees are likely to end up with low-paying, dead-end jobs, you can see how this supports the conflict view—how education is helping to reproduce the racial-ethnic structure for the next generation.

Table 17.1 on the next page gives us another snapshot of the significance of race-ethnicity and college attendance. From this table,

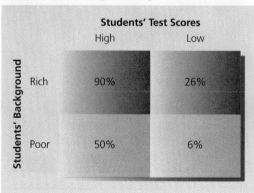

Figure 17.5 **Who Goes to College? Comparing Social Class and Ability in Determining College Attendance**

Students' Test Scores

Students' Background	High	Low
Rich	90%	26%
Poor	50%	6%

Source: Bowles 1977.

Table 17.1 Types of College and Race-Ethnicity

	Public	Private	2-Year	4-Year
Whites	75%	25%	36%	64%
African Americans	73%	27%	42%	58%
Asian Americans	78%	22%	39%	61%
Latinos	82%	18%	54%	46%
Native Americans	82%	18%	47%	53%

Source: By the author. Based on *Statistical Abstract* 2007:Table 268.

you can see that whites are the most likely to attend four-year colleges, and that African Americans are the most likely to attend private colleges. These totals do not support the conflict view. There isn't much difference in the percentage of whites, African Americans, and Asian Americans who go to private colleges. But look at how much less likely Latinos and Native Americans are to attend these colleges. Coupled with Latinos and Native Americans being less likely to attend college in the first place, you can see how this helps to perpetuate some of society's racial-ethnic divisions.

IN SUM U.S. schools closely reflect the U.S. social class system. They equip the children of the elite with the tools they need to maintain their dominance, while they prepare the children of the poor for lower-status positions. Because education's doors of opportunity swing wide open for some but have to be pried open by others, conflict theorists say that the educational system perpetuates social inequality across generations (or, as they often phrase it, helps to reproduce the social class structure). In fact, they add, this is one of its primary purposes.

The Symbolic Interactionist Perspective: Teacher Expectations

Functionalists look at how education benefits society, and conflict theorists examine how education perpetuates social inequality. Symbolic interactionists, in contrast, study face-to-face interaction in the classroom. They have found that the expectations of teachers have profound consequences for their students.

The Rist Research

Why do some people get tracked into college prep courses and others into vocational ones? There is no single answer, but in what has become a classic study, sociologist Ray Rist came up with some intriguing findings. Rist (1970) did participant observation in an African American grade school with an African American faculty. He found that after only eight days in the classroom, the kindergarten teacher felt that she knew the children's abilities well enough to assign them to three separate worktables. To Table 1, Mrs. Caplow assigned those she considered to be "fast learners." They sat at the front of the room, closest to her. Those whom she saw as "slow learners," she assigned to Table 3, located at the back of the classroom. She placed "average" students at Table 2, in between the other tables.

This seemed strange to Rist. He knew that the children had not been tested for ability, yet their teacher was certain that she could identify the bright and slow children. Investigating further, Rist found that social class was the underlying basis for assigning the children to the different tables. Middle-class students were separated out for Table 1, and children from poorer homes were assigned to Tables 2 and 3. The teacher paid the most attention to the children at Table 1, who were closest to her, less to Table 2, and the least to Table 3. As the year went on, children from Table 1 perceived that they were treated better and came to see themselves as smarter. They became the leaders in class

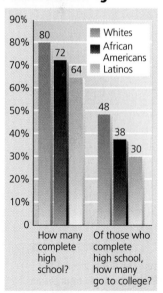

Figure 17.6 The Funneling Effects of Education: Race-Ethnicity

Note: The source gives totals only for these three groups.

Source: By the author. Based on *Statistical Abstract* 2007:Table 262.

Education can be a dangerous thing. Socrates, who taught in Greece about 400 years before the birth of Christ, was forced to take poison because his views challenged those of the establishment. Usually, however, educators reinforce the perspectives of the elite, teaching students to take their place within the social structure. This fresco is from Rome, about 50 B.C.

activities and even ridiculed children at the other tables, calling them "dumb." Eventually, the children at Table 3 disengaged themselves from many classroom activities. At the end of the year, only the children at Table 1 had completed the lessons that prepared them for reading.

This early tracking stuck. Their first-grade teacher looked at the work these students had done, and she placed students from Table 1 at her Table 1. She treated her tables much as the kindergarten teacher had, and the children at Table 1 again led the class.

The children's reputations continued to follow them. The second-grade teacher reviewed their scores and also divided her class into three groups. The first she named the "Tigers" and, befitting their name, gave them challenging readers. Not surprisingly, the Tigers came from the original Table 1 in kindergarten. The second group she called the "Cardinals." They came from the original Tables 2 and 3. Her third group consisted of children she had failed the previous year, whom she called the "Clowns." The Cardinals and Clowns were given less advanced readers.

Rist concluded that *each child's journey through school was determined by the eighth day of kindergarten!* This research, confirmed by others (Espinosa and Laffey 2003) and like that done on the Saints and Roughnecks (reported in Chapter 4), demonstrates the power of labels: They can set people on courses of action that affect the rest of their lives.

What occurred was a **self-fulfilling prophecy.** This term, coined by sociologist Robert Merton (1949/1968), refers to a false assumption of something that is going to happen but which then comes true simply because it was predicted. For example, if people believe an unfounded rumor that a credit union is going to fail because its officers have embezzled their money, they all rush to the credit union to demand their money. The prediction—although originally false—is now likely to come true.

The Rosenthal-Jacobson Experiment

All of us know about teacher expectations—that some teachers have higher standards and expect work of a higher quality. Teacher expectations, however, also work at a subtle level. In what has become a classic experiment, social psychologists Robert Rosenthal and Lenore Jacobson (1968) tried out a new test in a San Francisco grade school. They tested the children's abilities and then told the teachers which students would probably "spurt" ahead during the year. They instructed the teachers to watch these students' progress, but not to let the students or their parents know about the test results. At the end of the year, they tested the students again and found that the IQs of the predicted "spurters" had jumped ten to fifteen points higher than those of the other children.

You might think that Rosenthal and Jacobson became famous for developing such a powerful scholastic aptitude test. Actually, their "test" was another of those covert experiments. Rosenthal and Jacobson had simply given routine IQ tests to the children and had then *randomly* chosen 20 percent of the students as "spurters." These students were *no* different from the others in the classroom. A self-fulfilling prophecy had taken place: The teachers expected more from those particular students, and the students responded. In short, expect dumb and you get dumb. Expect smart, and you get smart.

Although attempts to replicate this experiment have had mixed results (Pilling and Pringle 1978), a good deal of research confirms that, *regardless of their ability,* students who are expected to do better generally do better, and those who are expected to do poorly do poorly (Snyder 1993; McKown and Weinstein 2002).

How Do Teacher Expectations Work?

Sociologist George Farkas (1990a, 1990b, 1996) became interested in how teacher expectations affect grades. Using a stratified sample of students in a large school district in Texas, he found that teacher expectations produced gender and racial-ethnic biases. *On the gender level:* Even though boys and girls had the same test scores, girls on average were given higher

self-fulfilling prophecy
Robert Merton's term for an originally false assertion that becomes true simply because it was predicted

course grades. *On the racial-ethnic level:* Asian Americans who had the same test scores as the other groups averaged higher grades than did African Americans, Latinos, and whites.

At first, this may sound like more of the same old news—another case of discrimination. But this explanation doesn't fit, which is what makes the finding fascinating. Look at who the victims are. It is most unlikely that the teachers would be prejudiced against boys and whites. To interpret these unexpected results, Farkas used symbolic interactionism. He observed that some students "signal" to their teachers that they are "good students." They show an eagerness to cooperate, and they quickly agree with what the teacher says. They also show that they are "trying hard." The teachers pick up these signals and reward these "good students" with better grades. Girls and Asian Americans, the researcher concluded, are better at displaying these characteristics so coveted by teachers.

We do not have enough information on how teachers communicate their expectations to students. Nor do we know much about how students "signal" messages to teachers. Perhaps you will become the educational sociologist who will shed more light on this significant area of human behavior.

The Sociology and New Technology box on the next page discusses how technology is producing new forms of "signaling" and of student-teacher interaction.

Problems in U.S. Education— and Their Solutions

To conclude this chapter, let's examine two problems facing U.S. education—and consider their potential solutions.

Problems: Mediocrity and Violence

The Rising Tide of Mediocrity   This will sound like a joke, but it isn't. Sociologist Robert Benford (2007) got his hands on a copy of a 20-question final examination given to basketball players who took a credit course on coaching principles at the University of Georgia. Here are some of the questions:

1. How many goals are on a basketball court?   a. 1   b. 2   c. 3   d. 4
2. How many players are allowed to play at one time on any one team in a regulation game?   a. 2   b. 3   c. 4   d. 5
3. How many halves are in a college basketball game?   a. 1   b. 2   c. 3   d. 4
4. How many points does a three-point field goal account for in a basketball game?   a. 1   b. 2   c. 3   d. 4

It is usually difficult to refer to athletes, sports, and academics in the same breath, but this is about as mediocre as mediocrity can get.

How about academic mediocrity in other areas? Let's look at much broader examples that reveal severe problems in our educational system:

- All Arizona high school sophomores took a math test. It covered the math that sophomores should know. *One of ten passed.*
- To enable its students to graduate, New York state had to drop its passing grade to 55 out of 100 (Steinberg 2000). Some New York City schools are so bad that officials have given up and turned them over to private, for-profit companies (Wyatt 2000).
- Michigan school officials didn't like it when test results showed that 1,500 of the state's high schools "needed improvement." Their solution was simple. They lowered the percentage needed to pass, and overnight, 1,300 schools "improved," leaving only 200 that still needed "improvement" (Dillon 2003). (One wonders why the officials didn't lower the passing score to the point that no schools "needed improvement." Then all of Michigan's schools would have been "good.")
- Tennessee state officials, in contrast, were so pleased at their test results that they called a news conference. They boasted that 87 percent of their students were proficient at math—and they had the test results to prove it. When the

Internet University: No Walls, No Ivy, No All Night Parties

DISTANCE LEARNING, COURSES TAUGHT TO students who are not physically present with their instructor, is not new. For decades, we have had correspondence courses. Today, however, telecommunications have transformed distance learning. Satellites, computers, and video cameras are making cyber colleges part of mainstream education. Using video links, students are able to watch the professor on their screen. Clicking an icon, they can "raise their hands" to ask questions. Spider-web diagrams let the instructor know who is e-mailing others—and who is holding back. Tucked deeper in the software is a program to allow deans (supervisors) to scrutinize the instructors. The deans get reports, for example, that let them know how long it takes instructors to answer e-mail from students.

Broadening the experience of both students and instructors through cultural diversity is one of the interesting potentials of distance learning. Students can enjoy stimulating international experiences without ever leaving the country. For example, sociology professors at the State University of New York and the State University of Belarus (Minsk, Russia) jointly taught an online course on Social Control. Coming from such different political experiences, the American and Russian students found that the course opened their eyes to different perspectives (Beaman 2003).

Why should formal education be limited to walled classrooms? Think of the possibilities the Net opens to us. We could study human culture and compare notes on eating, dating, or burial customs with fellow students in Thailand, Iceland, South Africa, Germany, Egypt, China, and Australia. We could write a joint paper in which we compare our experiences with one another, within the context of theories taught in the text, and then submit our paper to our mutual instructor.

This student is at home, but is taking a credit course in economic crime investigation.

Then there are students who don't fit in. They might not look like the "cool" students, and they certainly don't think like them. Some find school boring. Others find it a threatening place. For still others, an inability to focus, a tendency to drift off, puts them out of sync with both teachers and classmates. For outsiders like these, virtual classes have become a viable alternative. The students can even enter an online classroom without their classmates noticing by clicking a "make yourself invisible" icon (White 2003).

Some teachers are using a format that combines classroom and distance learning. Instructors upload to a university Web site the lectures they give to a classroom of students, and students who missed class or who don't want to attend class sessions download them to their iPods. Some professors have their students listen to their recorded lectures, and then use the classroom to involve their students in interactive discussion groups (Tyre 2005).

Of course, there are limitations. You couldn't give gym classes over the Net. Or could you? This, too is being done. In some schools, students can do any vigorous exercises they want for 30 minutes, four times a week. They report their activity and heart rate to gym instructors, with their parents certifying their accuracy (Dillon 2005a).

As distance learning expands, will we eventually go from kindergarten to grad school with classmates from around the world? While this may sound intriguing, no walls also means no joking in the hallway or dorm, no flirting after class, no getting together over a cup of coffee. . . .

A different view of distance learning is presented in the Sociology and the New Technology box on the next page.

---

federal government retested the students, the results dropped just a bit—to 21 percent (Dillon 2005b).

As appalling as these conditions are, the situation is actually even worse. I would like you to go back and look at Figure 17.1 on page 501, which shows how our rate of high school graduation has increased through the years. It turns out that smoke and mirrors underlie some of these totals. Some school officials have been hiding their low graduation rates by asking students who quit high school if they plan to get a GED. If students say yes, they count them as graduates. On top of this, states have reduced their standards so greatly that only 34 percent of high school graduates are ready for college (Greene and Winters 2005).

Conditions aren't all bad, of course. Figure 17.7 on page 518 illustrates the sharp decline of student SAT scores from the 1960s to 1980. At that point, educators—and even Congress—expressed concern and demanded greater accountability. Schools raised their standards, and the scores started to climb. The recovery in math has been encouraging.

Capitalism and Distance Learning: Selling Education in Cyberspace

ALWAYS EAGER FOR PROFITS and seeking new areas for investment, capitalists looked for ways to apply advanced technology to education. For them, distance learning was a perfect answer. The potential for profits is huge, as distance learning requires little infrastructure—no classrooms, desks, blackboards, or parking lots. In addition, once developed, the course can be repackaged and sold over and over. Capitalists also want expanding markets, and with the demand for education increasing around the world, distance learning supplies this, too. In many ways, distance learning is a capitalist's dream.

Distance learning has become part of the globalization of capitalism that is transforming our world. Since the United States is the world's leading capitalist country, it was only natural that U.S. universities would lead the charge. They have cobbled together degrees in cyberspace, and are selling them around the globe.

But to attract the best-paying customers, marketers need to sell name brands. University of Phoenix—what is that? The name of a bird? A town in Arizona? Is a degree from this virtual school worth anything? The name Cardean University has the same problem. It sounds like a sweater.

How, then, could marketers of virtual schools manufacture brand names? The promoters of Cardean University, which exists only in cyberspace, arrived at an ingenious solution. To sell a master's degree in business, they would publicize such brand names as Stanford, Columbia, Carnegie Mellon, the University of Chicago, and the London School of Economics (Pohl 2003). How impressive that professors from such prestigious universities would partner with Cardean. But it turns out that they don't teach courses for Cardean at all. It is just marketing jargon on Cardean's website. Probe a little and you find only that these professors'

"input is extensive and their imprint on the course deep." Yeah, sure, whatever that means.

Seeing the money flowing, Oxford, Stanford, and Yale decided to get in the game and offer online degrees, too. This was shortlived, however. These prestigious universities found it too expensive to maintain quality (Foster 2006). Yes, they actually tried to maintain quality—or so they said.

Virtual education opens such a global market that the new educational capitalists envision a student body of *millions*. Vast numbers of people in Asia and Africa don't have access to universities. Of course, most of them don't have access to money either—but the children of the elite do. So do the children of the *nouveau riche*. Admittedly, the $24,000 for the Cardean M.B.A. (Pohl 2003) is a bit steep for most of the market, but theirs is a "world class" degree. Yes, that's what Cardean officials call it. But it is a bargain. Duke University charges $100,000 for its online M.B.A. (Forelle 2003).

for your Consideration

Do you think online teaching might replace traditional in-class instruction? Why or why not? What do you think are the advantages of an online degree? The disadvantages?

Its cyperspace identity apparently bothers the University of Phoenix. This organization paid $154 million to get its name on a stadium—but still no football team.

As you can see, today's high school seniors score the same in math as seniors did in the 1960s. Administrators are requiring more of teachers, and teachers are requiring more of students. Following the basic principle we discussed, each is performing according to these higher expectations. The improvement—which only takes us back to the level we had in the past—leaves U.S. students ill prepared. Compared with students from 40 other nations, U.S. students rank 25th in math performance (Chaddock 2004).

As you can see from Figure 17.7, the verbal score has refused to budge. Today's students perform so poorly that the makers of the SAT eliminated the analogy part of the

Figure 17.7 National Results of the Scholastic Assessment Test (SAT)

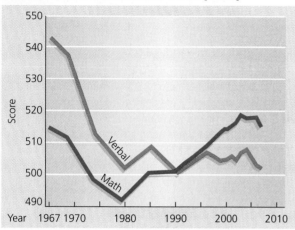

Source: By the author. Based on Chaker 2007; *Statistical Abstract* 2007:Table 254.

verbal test. Analogies demand penetrating thinking, and, unfortunately, today's students just couldn't handle it. No one knows exactly why, although the culprits are often identified as television watching, "dummied down" textbooks, less rigorous teaching, and less reading.

How to Cheat on the SATs If you receive poor grades this semester, wouldn't you like to use a magic marker—to—presto!—change them into higher grades? I suppose every student would. Now imagine that you had that power. Would you use it?

Some people in authority apparently have found such a magic marker, and they have used it to raise our low national SAT scores. Table 274 of the 1996 edition of the *Statistical Abstract of the United States* reports that in 1995 only 8.3 percent of students earned 600 or more on the verbal portion of the SAT test. The very next edition, in 1997, however, holds a pleasant surprise. Table 276 tells us that it was really 21.9 percent of students who scored 600 or higher in 1995. Later editions of this source retain the higher figure. What a magic marker!

In the twinkle of an eye, we get another bonus. Somehow, between 1996 and 1997 the scores of *everyone* who took the test in previous years improved. Now that's the kind of power we all would like to have. Students, grab your report cards. Workers, change those numbers on your paycheck.

It certainly is easier to give simpler tests than to teach more effectively. And this is what has happened to the SAT. The results were so embarrassing to U.S. educators that the SAT was made easier. Not only was testing on antonyms and analogies dropped, but also the test was shortened and students were given more time to answer the fewer questions. The test makers then "rescored" the totals of previous years to match the easier test. This "dummying down" of the SAT is yet another form of grade inflation, the topic to which we shall now turn.

Grade Inflation, Social Promotion, and Functional Illiteracy High school teachers used to give about twice as many *C*'s as *A*'s, but now they give more *A*'s than *C*'s. Grades are so inflated that some of today's *A*'s are the *C*'s of years past. **Grade inflation** is so pervasive that *47 percent* of all college freshmen have an overall high school grade point average of *A*. This is more than *twice* what it was in 1970 (*Statistical Abstract* 2007:Table 274). Grade inflation has also hit the Ivy League. At Harvard University, *half* of the course grades are *A*'s and *A*−'s. *Ninety* percent of Harvard students graduate with honors. To rein in the "honor inflation," the Harvard faculty voted to limit the number of students who graduate with honors to 60 percent of a class (Hartocollis 2002; Douthat 2005).

Grade inflation in the face of declining standards has been accompanied by **social promotion,** the practice of passing students from one grade to the next even though they have not mastered the basic materials. One result is **functional illiteracy,** high school graduates having difficulty with reading and writing. Some high school graduates cannot fill out job applications; others can't even figure out whether they get the right change at the grocery store.

The Influence of Peer Groups What do you think is the most important factor in how teenagers do in school? Two psychologists and a sociologist, who studied 20,000 high school students in California and Wisconsin, found that it is the student's peer group (Steinberg et al. 1996). Simply put: Teens who hang out with good students tend to do well, and those who hang out with friends who do poorly in school do poorly. Student subcultures include informal norms about grades. Some groups have norms of classroom excellence, while others sneer at good grades. The applied question that arises from this research, of course, is how to build educational achievement into student culture.

Violence in Schools Some U.S. schools have deteriorated to the point that safety is an issue. In these schools, uniformed guards and metal detectors have become a permanent fixture. Some grade schools even supplement their traditional fire drills with "drive-by

grade inflation higher grades given for the same work; a general rise in student grades without a corresponding increase in learning

social promotion passing students on to the next level even though they have not mastered basic materials

functional illiterate a high school graduate who has difficulty with basic reading and math shooting drills." Because they might be targeted by terrorists, other schools hold "Code Blue" drills: The classrooms—each equipped with a phone—are locked, the windows are locked, and the shades are drawn. Whether these measures create feelings of security or produce fear is yet to be studied by sociolgists.

School shootings are another concern. For a surprising analysis of deaths at school, read the Mass Media box on the next page.

Solutions: Safety, Standards, and Other Reforms

It is one thing to identify problems, quite another to find solutions for them. Let's consider solutions to the problems we just reviewed.

A Secure Learning Environment   The first step in offering a good education is to keep students safe and free from fear. With the high rate of violence in U.S. society, we can expect some violence to spill over into the schools. To minimize this spillover, school administrators can expel all students who threaten the welfare of others. They also can refuse to tolerate threats, violence, and weapons. The zero tolerance policy for guns and other weapons on school property that school boards and administrators have adopted helps to make schools safer.

Higher Standards for Students   To offer a quality education, we need quality teachers. Don't we already have them? Most teachers are qualified, and if motivated, can do an excellent job. But a large number of teachers are not qualified. Consider just a couple of items. California requires that its teachers pass an educational skills test. California's teachers did so poorly that to get enough teachers to fill their classrooms, officials had to drop the passing grade to the 10th grade level. These are college graduates who are teachers—and they are expected to perform at the 10th grade level! It gets even worse. For fifteen of our states, teachers need to be able to read only at the lowest quarter of the national average (Schemo 2002). I don't know about you, but I think this situation is a national disgrace. If we want to improve teaching, we need to insist that teachers meet high standards.

Our schools compete with private industry for the same pool of college graduates. If the starting salary in other fields is higher than it is in education, those fields will attract brighter, more energetic graduates. Figure 17.8 highlights the abysmal job we are doing in this competition for talent.

Figure 17.8   **Starting Salaries of U.S. College Graduates: Public School Teachers Compared with Private Industry**

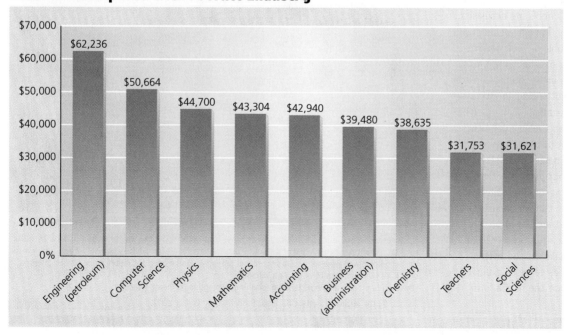

Sources: By the author. Based on American Federation of Teachers 2007; *Statistical Abstract* 2007:Table 287.

School Shootings: Exploring a Myth

The media sprinkle their reports of school shootings with such dramatic phrases as "alarming proportions," "outbreak of violence," and "out of control." They give us the impression that schools all over the nation are set to erupt in gunfire. The public views the shootings as convincing evidence that something is seriously wrong with society. Parents used to consider schools safe havens, but no longer. Those naïve thoughts have been shattered by the bullets that have sprayed our schools—or at least by the media's portrayal of growing danger and violence in our schools.

Have our schools really become war zones, as the mass media would have us believe? Certainly events such as those at Columbine High School are disturbing, but we need to probe deeper than newspaper headlines and televised images.

When we do, we find that the media's sensationalist reporting has created a myth. Contrary to "what everyone knows," *there is no trend toward greater school violence*. In fact, the situation is just the opposite—*the trend is toward greater safety*. Despite the dramatic school shootings that make headlines, as Table 17.2 shows, shooting deaths at schools are decreasing.

This is not to say that school shootings are not a serious problem. Even one student being wounded or killed is too many. But, contrary to the impression fostered by the media, we are not seeing an increase of school shooting deaths.

This is one reason that we need sociology: to quietly, dispassionately search for facts so we can better understand the events that shape our lives. The first requirement for solving any problem is accurate data, for how can we create rational solutions that are based on hysteria? The information presented in this box may not make for sensational headlines, but it does serve to explode one of the myths that the media have created.

This frame from a home video shows Eric Harris (on the left) and Dylan Klebold (on the right) as they pretend that they are searching for victims. They put their desires into practice in the infamous Columbine High School shootings.

Table 17.2 — Exploding a Myth: Deaths at U.S. Schools[a]

School Year	Shooting Deaths	Other Deaths[b]	VICTIMS Boys	Girls	Total
1992–1993	45	11	49	7	56
1993–1994	41	12	41	12	53
1994–1995	16	5	18	3	21
1995–1996	29	7	26	10	36
1996–1997	15	11	18	8	26
1997–1998	36	8	27	17	44
1998–1999	25	6	24	7	31
1999–2000	16	16	26	6	32
2000–2001	19	5	20	4	24
2001–2002	4	1	5	0	5
2002–2003	14	8	16	6	22
2003–2004	29	13	37	5	42
2004–2005	20	8	20	8	28
2005–2006	5	0	4	1	5
2006–2007	16	3	12	7	19
Total 1992–2007	330	114	343	101	444
Mean 1992–2007	22.0	7.6	22.9	6.7	29.6

[a]Includes all school-related homicides, even those that occurred on the way to or from school. Includes suicides, school personnel killed at school by other adults, and even adults who had nothing to do with the school but who were found dead on school property. Source does not report on deaths at colleges, only K-12 (kindergarten through high school).
[b]Beating, hanging, jumping, stabbing, slashing, strangling, or heart attack.

Source: By the author. Based on National School Safety Center 2007.

What else can we do to improve the quality of education? An older study by sociologists James Coleman and Thomas Hoffer (1987) provides helpful guidelines. They wanted to see why the test scores of students in Roman Catholic schools average 15 to 20 percent higher than those of students in public schools. Is it because Catholic schools attract better students, while public schools have to put up with everyone? To find out, they tested 15,000 students in public and Catholic high schools.

Their findings? From the sophomore through the senior years, students at Catholic schools pull ahead of public school students by a full grade in verbal and math skills. The superior test performance of students in Catholic schools, they concluded, is due not to better students, but to higher standards. Catholic schools have not watered down their curricula as have public schools. The researchers also underscored the importance of parental involvement. Parents and teachers in Catholic schools reinforce each other's commitment to learning.

On average, students in Roman Catholic schools score higher on national tests than students in public schools. Is it because Roman Catholic schools have better students, or because they do better teaching? The text reports the sociological findings.

These findings support the basic principle reviewed earlier about teacher expectations: Students perform better when they are expected to meet higher standards. To this, you might want to reply, "Of course. I knew that. Who wouldn't?" Somehow, however, this basic principle is lost on many teachers, who end up teaching at a low level because they expect little of their students and have supervisors who accept low student performance. The reason, actually, is probably not their lack of awareness of such basics, but, rather, the organization that entraps them, a bureaucracy in which ritual replaces performance. To understand this point better, you may want to review Chapter 7.

If we raise standards, we can expect protest. It is less upsetting to use low standards and to tell students that they are doing well than it is to do rigorous teaching and use high standards to measure student performance. When Florida decided that its high school seniors needed to pass an assessment test in order to receive a diploma, 13,000 students failed the test. Parents of failed students banded together—not to demand better teaching but to pressure the state to drop the new test. They asked people to boycott Disney World and to not buy Florida orange juice (Canedy 2003). Those actions would certainly improve their children's learning!

Higher Standards for Teachers We must expect (and require) more not only of students, but also of teachers and administrators. They, too, must be held accountable to higher standards. One way to do this is to peg their raises, or at least bonuses, to the performance of their students. In one form that seems exemplary, students are first evaluated. Then the teacher is given specific goals, such as bringing the reading or math levels of underachieving students to the average for their age (Schemo 2004). "Pay for performance," however, is controversial and resisted by teachers and their unions—who seem to be more interested in preserving jobs than in implementing quality teaching.

Reform in anything needs a guiding principle. I suggest that this serve as the guiding principle in reforming education: The problem is *not* the ability of the students, but, rather, the nature of the educational system. This principle is illustrated by the following Thinking Critically section, with which we close this chapter.

Thinking Critically

Breaking Through the Barriers: Restructuring The Classroom

Jaime Escalante taught in an East Los Angeles inner-city school that was plagued with poverty, crime, drugs, and gangs. In this self-defeating environment, he taught calculus. His students scored so highly on national tests that officials suspected cheating. They asked his students to retake the test. They did. This time, they earned even higher scores.

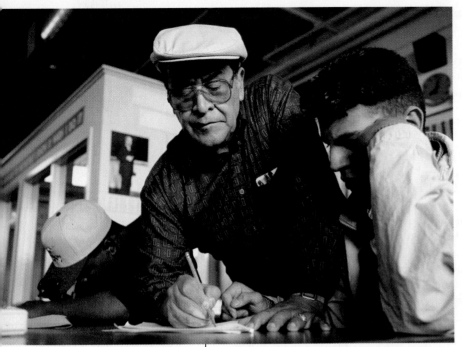

How did Escalante do it?

First, Escalante had to open his students' minds to the possibility of success: They had to believe that they *could* excel. Most Latino students were being tracked into craft classes where they made jewelry and birdhouses. "Our kids are just as talented as anyone else. They just need the opportunity to show it," Escalante said. "They just don't think about becoming scientists or engineers."

Students also need to see learning as a way out of the inner city, as the path to good jobs. Escalante arranged for foundations to provide money for students to attend the colleges of their choice. Students learned that if they did well, their poverty wouldn't stop them.

Escalante also changed the system of instruction. He had his students think of themselves as a team, of him as the coach, and of the national math exams as a sort of

To say that today's schoolchildren can't learn as well as previous schoolchildren is to blame the victim. As discussed in the text, Jaime Escalante (shown here) demonstrated that teachers can motivate even highly deprived students to study hard and to excel in learning. His experience challenges us to rethink our approach to education.

Olympics for which they were preparing. To foster team identity, students wore team jackets, caps, and T-shirts with logos that identified them as part of the math team. Before class, his students did "warm-ups" (hand clapping and foot stomping to a rock song).

Escalante's team had practice schedules as rigorous as those of a championship football team. Students had to sign a contract that bound them to participate in a summer math program, to complete the daily homework, and to attend Saturday morning and after-school study sessions. To remind students that self-discipline pays off, Escalante covered his walls with posters of sports figures.

The sociological point is this: The problem was not the ability of the students. Their failure to do well in school was not due to something *within* them. The problem was the *system*, the way classroom instruction was designed. When Escalante changed the system of instruction—and brought in hope—both attitudes and performance changed.

for your Consideration

What principles discussed in this or earlier chapters did Escalante apply? What changes do you think we can make in education to bring about similar results all over the country?

Sources: Based on Barry 1989; Meek 1989; Escalante and Dirmann 1990; Hilliard 1991.

Summary *and* Review

The Development of Modern Education

How did modern education develop?

In most of human history, **education** consisted of informal learning, equivalent to *acculturation.* In some earlier societies, centers of formal education did develop, such as among the Arabs, Chinese, Greeks, and Egyptians. Because modern education came about in response to industrialization, formal education is much less common in the Least Industrialized Nations. Pp. 500–502.

Education in Global Perspective

How does education compare among the Most Industrialized, Industrializing, and Least Industrialized Nations?

In general, formal education reflects a nation's economy. Consequently, education is extensive in the Most Industrialized Nations, undergoing vast change in the Industrializing Nations, and spotty in the Least Industrialized Nations. Japan, Russia, and Egypt provide examples of education in countries at three levels of industrialization. Pp. 502–504.

The Functionalist Perspective: Providing Social Benefits

What is the functionalist perspective on education?

Among the functions of education are the teaching of knowledge and skills, providing credentials, **cultural transmission of values,** social integration, **gatekeeping,** and **mainstreaming.** Functionalists also note that education has replaced some traditional family functions. Pp. 505–508.

The Conflict Perspective: Perpetuating Social Inequality

What is the conflict perspective on education?

The basic view of conflict theorists is that *education reproduces the social class structure;* that is, through such mechanisms as unequal funding and operating different schools for the elite and for the masses, education perpetuates a society's basic social inequalities from one generation to the next. Pp. 508–513.

The Symbolic Interactionist Perspective: Teacher Expectations

What is the symbolic interactionist perspective on education?

Symbolic interactionists focus on face-to-face interaction. In examining what occurs in the classroom, they have found that student performance tends to conform to teacher expectations, whether they are high or low. Pp. 513–515.

Problems in U.S. Education—and Their Solutions

What are the chief problems that face U.S. education?

In addition to violence, the major problems are low achievement as shown by SAT scores and international comparisons, **grade inflation, social promotion,** and **functional illiteracy.** Pp. 515–519.

What are the potential solutions to these problems?

The primary solution is to restore high educational standards, which can be done only after providing basic security for students. Any solution for improving quality must be based on expecting more of *both* students and teachers. Pp. 519–522.

Thinking Critically
about Chapter 17

1. How does education in the United States compare with education in Japan, Russia, and Egypt?
2. How have your experiences in education (including teachers and assignments) influenced your goals, attitudes, and values? How have your classmates influenced you? Be specific.
3. How do you think that U.S. schools can be improved?

Additional Resources

What can you use MySocLab for?

 www.mysoclab.com

- **Study and Review:** Pre- and Post-Tests, Practice Tests, Flash Cards, Individualized Study Plans.
- **Current Events:** *Sociology in the News,* the daily *New York Times,* and more.
- **Research and Writing:** *Research Navigator, Writing About Sociology,* and more.

Where Can I Read More on This Topic?

Suggested readings for this chapter are listed at the back of this book.

CHAPTER 18

Religion

Mural on South Street, Philadelphia, PA

The first report was stunning. About a hundred armed agents of the Bureau of Alcohol, Tobacco, and Firearms (ATF) had attacked the compound of the Branch Davidians, an obscure religious group in Waco, Texas. Four of the agents were shot to death. So were six men who tried to defend the compound. Then came a fifty-one-day standoff, televised to the U.S. public, in which the ATF and FBI did such strange things as bombarding the compound with loud music day and night.

At 6 A.M. on the fifty-first day of the siege, following on-again, off-again negotiations with David Koresh, the 33-year-old leader of the group, tanks appeared. One rammed the compound's main building, pumping in gas consisting of chemicals

The government removed the bodies, sealed off the area, and bulldozed the charred remains of the building.

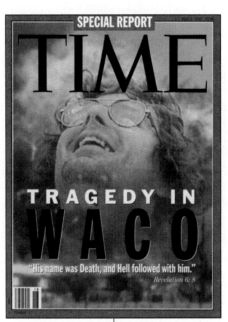

that, according to international law, the U.S. military was forbidden to use against Iraqi soldiers. As a second tank punched holes in the walls, the women and children fled to the second floor. The men shot futilely at the tanks. An explosion rocked the compound, and the buildings burst into flames. Eighty men, women, and children were burned to death. Some of the charred bodies of the twenty-five children were found huddled next to their mothers.

The government removed the bodies, sealed off the area, and bulldozed the charred remains of the buildings. Survivors claimed that the government had set the fire. The government said the Branch Davidians had set it, that they had committed suicide by fire.

sacred Durkheim's term for things set apart or forbidden, that inspire fear, awe, reverence, or deep respect

profane Durkheim's term for common elements of everyday life

religion according to Durkheim, beliefs and practices that separate the profane from the sacred and unite its adherents into a moral community

church according to Durkheim, one of the three essential elements of religion—a moral community of believers; also refers to a type of religious organization, to a large, highly organized group with formal, sedate worship services and little emphasis on personal conversion

Seldom do governments turn this viciously against a religious group, but it does happen. One of the topics we shall consider in this chapter is the relationship of the dominant culture to new religions. Let's begin by asking what religion is.

What Is Religion?

All human societies are organized by some form of the family, as well as by some kind of economic system and political order. As we have seen, these key social institutions touch on aspects of life that are essential to human welfare. This chapter examines religion, another universal social institution.

Sociologists who do research on religion analyze the relationship between society and religion, and study the role that religion plays in people's lives. They do not try to prove that one religion is better than another. Nor is it their goal to verify or disprove anyone's faith. As was mentioned in Chapter 1, sociologists have no tools for deciding that one course of action is more moral than another, much less for determining that one religion is "the" correct one. Religion is a matter of faith—and sociologists deal with empirical matters, things they can observe or measure. When it comes to religion, then, sociologists study the effects of religious beliefs and practices on people's lives. They also analyze how religion is related to stratification systems. Unlike theologians, however, sociologists cannot evaluate the truth of a religion's teachings.

In 1912 Emile Durkheim published an influential book, *The Elementary Forms of the Religious Life,* in which he tried to identify the elements that are common to all religions. After surveying religions around the world, Durkheim could find no specific belief or practice that all religions share. He did find, however, that all religions develop a community around their practices and beliefs. All religions also separate the sacred from the profane. By **sacred,** Durkheim referred to aspects of life having to do with the supernatural that inspire awe, reverence, deep respect, even fear. By **profane,** he meant aspects of life that are not concerned with religion or religious purposes but, instead, are part of ordinary, everyday life. Durkheim (1912/1965) summarized his conclusions by saying:

> A religion is a unified system of beliefs and practices relative to sacred things, that is to say, things set apart and forbidden—beliefs and practices which unite into one single moral community called a Church, all those who adhere to them.

Religion, then, has three elements:

1. *Beliefs* that some things are sacred (forbidden, set apart from the profane)
2. *Practices* (rituals) centering on the things considered sacred
3. *A moral community* (a church) resulting from a group's beliefs and practices

Durkheim used the word **church** in an unusual sense, to refer to any "moral community" centered on beliefs and practices regarding the sacred. In Durkheim's sense, *church* refers to Buddhists bowing before a shrine, Hindus dipping in the Ganges River, and Confucians offering food to their ancestors. Similarly, the term *moral community* does not imply morality in the sense familiar to most of us—of ethical conduct. Rather, a moral community is simply a group of people who are united by their religious practices—and that would include sixteenth-century Aztec priests who each day gathered around an altar to pluck out the beating heart of a virgin.

To better understand the sociological approach to religion, let's see what pictures emerge when we apply the three theoretical perspectives.

When I visited a Hindu temple in Chattisgargh, India, I was impressed by the colorful and expressive statues on its roof. Here is a close-up of some of those figures, which represent some of the millions of gods that Hindus worship.

The Functionalist Perspective

Functionalists stress that religion is universal because it meets basic human needs. Let's look at some of the functions—and dysfunctions—of religion.

Functions of Religion

Questions about Ultimate Meaning Around the world, religions provide answers to perplexing questions about ultimate meaning—such as the purpose of life, why people suffer, and the existence of an afterlife. Those answers give followers a sense of purpose, a framework in which to live. Instead of seeing themselves buffeted by random events in an aimless existence, believers see their lives as fitting into a divine plan.

Emotional Comfort The answers that religion provides about ultimate meaning also comfort people by assuring them that there is a purpose to life, even to suffering. Similarly, religious rituals that enshroud crucial events such as illness and death provide emotional comfort at times of crisis. The individual knows that others care and can find consolation in following familiar rituals.

Social Solidarity Religious teachings and practices unite believers into a community that shares values and perspectives ("we Jews," "we Christians," "we Muslims"). The religious rituals that surround marriage, for example, link the bride and groom with a broader community that wishes them well. So do other religious rituals, such as those that celebrate birth and mourn death.

Guidelines for Everyday Life The teachings of religion are not all abstractions. They also provide practical instructions. For example, four of the Ten Commandments delivered by Moses to the Israelites concern God, but the other six contain instructions on how to live everyday life, from how to get along with parents and neighbors to warnings about lying, stealing, and having affairs.

The consequences for people who follow these guidelines can be measured. People who attend church are less likely to abuse alcohol, nicotine, and illegal drugs than are people who don't go to church (Gillum 2005; Wallace et al 2007). This holds true for both adults and teens. In general, churchgoers follow a healthier lifestyle, and they live longer than those who don't go to church. How religion affects health is discussed in the Down-to-Earth Sociology box on the next page.

One of the many functions of religion is social solidarity. Can you see instances of this function in this photo of a Hindu service in Baltimore, Maryland.

Down-to-Earth Sociology

Religion and Health: What We Know and Don't Know

This boy is being prayed for at a Pentecostal church in Harlem, New York.

DOES RELIGION MAKE A DIFFERENCE in people's health? Although scientists cannot determine the truth of any religion, they can study the effects of religion on people's lives—and health is one of those areas that can be measured.

"After seeing the data, I think I should go to church," said Lynda Powell, an epidemiologist at Rush University Medical Center in Chicago (Helliker 2005). What could prompt such a response?

Powell, along with two colleagues, evaluated the research articles that had been published on the effects of religion on health. They evaluated only research that met solid scientific criteria. For example, they threw out studies that didn't control for age, gender, or race-ethnicity, which are significant variables in health (Powell et al. 2003). Their most outstanding finding is this: People who attend religious services at least once a week have 25 percent fewer deaths than people who don't go to church. Think about it: For every hundred deaths of non-churchgoers, there are only 75 deaths of people who attend church weekly.

How could this possibly be? Perhaps the churchgoers were already healthier. This wasn't the reason, though, for the researchers compared people who were at the same levels of health or illness.

How about healthier lifestyles? Churchgoers are less likely to smoke, to get drunk, and so on. Not this either. The researchers also controlled for lifestyle. Actually, the weekly churchgoers had 30 percent less mortality. When the researchers adjusted for lifestyle and social class, the difference in mortality dropped to 25 percent (Powell et al. 2003).

What explanation could there be, then? Remember that the researchers are scientists, so they aren't going to say: "God." Here are three mechanisms that they suggest might account for the lower mortality of churchgoers: involvement in social statuses that produce a sense of self-worth and purpose in life; experiencing positive emotions; and learning from compassionate role models calming ways of coping with crises. (The first two sound similar to the sense of community that I suggested might be a reason for the possible longer life of the Abkhasians. You might want to review page 372.)

The explanations suggested by the researchers could be correct, but we need further research to find out.

Is there anything about religion itself that could account for this remarkable reduction in mortality? Some researchers think they've put their finger on it: prayer. Apparently, prayer (or meditation) changes people's brain activity and improves their immune response. Scientists are investigating this hypothesis (Kalb 2003).

One researcher points to something else about religion—the practice of forgiveness. It turns out that people who forgive easily are more likely to be in good psychological health. They are especially less likely to be depressed (Krause and Ellison 2003). To forgive someone who has done you wrong apparently brings release from feelings of resentment, bitterness, and hatred—but holding on to grudges rips you apart inside.

What have researchers found about praying for people who are sick? Does this help them get better? So far, most researchers haven't found any difference between people who are prayed for and those who are not (Benson et al. 2006). But researchers have encountered a problem. How do they find a control group of people who are not being prayed for? There is so much prayer—from parents, siblings, aunts and uncles, friends and neighbors—that some people don't even know they are being prayed for. I'm sure that the researchers will solve this.

We are just at the initial stages of research on religion and health. At this point, we have hardly any answers, but we do have this remarkable statistic about mortality and weekly attendance at religious services.

So, if you want to live longer . . .

Social Control Religion not only provides guidelines for everyday life but also sets limits on people's behaviors. Most norms of a religious group apply only to its members, but nonmembers also feel a spillover. Religious teachings, for example, are incorporated into criminal law. In the United States, blasphemy and adultery were once crimes for which people could be arrested, tried, and sentenced. Some states still have laws that prohibit the sale of alcohol before noon on Sunday, laws whose purpose was to get people out of the saloons and into the churches.

Adaptation Religion can help people adapt to new environments. For example, it isn't easy for immigrants to adjust to the customs of a new land. By keeping their native language alive within a community of people who are going through similar experiences, religion serves as a bridge between the old and new: It provides both continuity with the immigrants' cultural past and encouragement to adapt to the new culture. This was the case for earlier immigrants from Europe, and it remains true today for immigrants from all over the globe. The thousands of Spanish-speaking churches around the United States are an outstanding example.

Support for the Government Most religions provide support for the government. An obvious example is the way some churches so prominently display the U.S. flag. Some fly it in front of the church building, and many display both the U.S. flag and a church flag on stands at the front of their worship center. Regions that become hostile to the government run into trouble, as in the example of our opening vignette.

For their part, governments reciprocate by supporting God. In the extreme, some governments sponsor a particular religion, ban all others, provide financial support for building churches and seminaries, and even pay salaries to the clergy. These religions are known as **state religions.** During the sixteenth and seventeenth centuries in Sweden, the government sponsored Lutheranism; in Switzerland, Calvinism; and in Italy, Roman Catholicism.

In some instances, even though the government sponsors no particular religion, religious beliefs are embedded in a nation's life. This is called **civil religion** (Bellah 1970). For

example, U.S. presidents—regardless of whether they are believers—invariably ask God to bless the nation in their inaugural speeches. U.S. officials take office by swearing that they will, in the name of God, fulfill their duty. Similarly, Congress opens each session with a prayer led by its own chaplain. The pledge of allegiance includes the phrase "one nation under God," and coins bear the inscription "In God We Trust."

Social Change Although religion is often so bound up with the prevailing social order that it resists social change, religion occasionally spearheads change. In the 1960s, for example, the civil rights movement, whose goal was to desegregate public facilities and abolish racial discrimination at southern polls, was led by religious leaders, especially leaders of African American churches such as Martin Luther King, Jr. Churches also served as centers at which demonstrators were trained and rallies were organized.

Religion can promote social change, as was evident in the U.S. civil rights movement. Dr. Martin Luther King, Jr., a Baptist minister, shown here in his famous "I have a dream" speech, was the foremost leader of this movement.

state religion a government-sponsored religion; also called *ecclesia*

civil religion Robert Bellah's term for religion that is such an established feature of a country's life that its history and social institutions are intertwined with the group's teachings about God

functional equivalent in this context, a substitute that serves the same functions (or meets the same needs) as religion; examples are psychotherapy and deep participation in "causes" or social movements

Functional Equivalents of Religion

If some component of society other than religion answers questions about ultimate meaning and provides emotional comfort and guidelines for daily life, sociologists call it a **functional equivalent** of religion. For some people, Alcoholics Anonymous is a functional equivalent of religion (Chalfant 1992). For others, psychotherapy, humanism, transcendental meditation, or even a political party perform similar functions.

Some functional equivalents are difficult to distinguish from a religion (Brinton 1965; Luke 1985). For example, communism had its prophets (Marx and Lenin), sacred writings (everything written by Marx, Engels, and Lenin, but especially the *Communist Manifesto*), high priests (the heads of the Communist party), sacred buildings (the Kremlin), shrines (Lenin's body on display in Red Square), rituals (the annual May Day parade in Red Square), and even martyrs (Cuba's Ché Guevara). Soviet communism was avowedly atheistic and tried to wipe out all traces of Christianity, Judaism, and Islam from its midst. It even replaced baptisms and circumcisions with state-sponsored rituals that dedicated the child to the state. The Communist party also devised its own rituals for weddings and funerals.

As sociologist Ian Robertson (1987) pointed out, however, there is a fundamental distinction between a religion and its functional equivalent. Although the substitute may perform similar functions, its activities are not directed toward God, gods, or the supernatural.

Dysfunctions of Religion

Functionalists also examine ways in which religion is *dysfunctional*, that is, how it can bring harmful results. Two dysfunctions are religious persecution and war and terrorism.

Religion as Justification for Persecution Beginning in the 1200s and continuing into the 1800s, in what has become known as the Inquisition, special commissions of the Roman Catholic Church tortured women to make them confess that they were witches, and then burned them at the stake. In 1692, Protestant leaders in Salem, Massachusetts, executed 21 women and men who were accused of being witches. In 2001, in the Democratic Republic of the Congo, about 1,000 alleged witches were hacked to death (Jenkins 2002). Similarly, it seems fair to say that the Aztec religion had its dysfunctions—at least for the virgins who were offered to appease angry gods. In short, religion has been used to justify oppression and any number of brutal acts.

War and Terrorism History is filled with wars based on religion—commingled with politics. Between the eleventh and fourteenth centuries, for example, Christian monarchs conducted nine bloody Crusades in an attempt to wrest control of the region they called the Holy Land from the Muslims. Terrorist acts, too, are sometimes committed in the name of religion, as discussed in the Down-to-Earth Sociology box on the next page.

The Symbolic Interactionist Perspective

Symbolic interactionists focus on the meanings that people give their experiences, especially how they use symbols. Let's apply this perspective to religious symbols, rituals, and beliefs to see how they help to forge a community of like-minded people.

Religious Symbols

Symbolic interactionists stress that a basic characteristic of humans is that they attach meaning to objects and events and then use representations of those objects or events to communicate with one another. Michaelangelo's *Pietà*, depicting Mary tenderly holding her son, Jesus, after his crucifixion, is one of the most acclaimed symbols in the Western world. It is admired for its beauty by believers and nonbelievers alike.

Suppose that it is about two thousand years ago and you have just joined a new religion. You have come to believe that a recently crucified Jew named Jesus is the Messiah, the Lamb of God offered for your sins. The Roman leaders are persecuting the followers of Jesus. They hate your religion because you and your fellow believers will not acknowledge Caesar as God.

Christians are few in number, and you are eager to have fellowship with other believers. But how can you tell who is a believer? Spies are everywhere. The government has sworn to destroy this new religion, and you do not relish the thought of being fed to lions in the Coliseum.

You use a simple technique. While talking with a stranger, as though doodling absentmindedly in the sand or dust, you casually trace the outline of a fish. Only fellow believers know the meaning—that, taken together, the first letter of each word in the Greek sentence "Jesus (is) Christ the Son of God" spell the Greek word for fish. If the other person gives no response, you rub out the outline and continue the interaction as usual. If there is a response, you eagerly talk about your new faith.

All religions use symbols to provide identity and social solidarity for their members. For Muslims, the primary symbol is the crescent moon and star; for Jews, the Star of David; for Christians, the cross. For members, these are not ordinary

Down-to-Earth Sociology

Terrorism and the Mind of God

WARNING: The "equal time" contents of this box are likely to offend just about everyone.

AFTER 9/11, THE QUESTION on many people's minds was some form of, "How can people do such evil in the name of God?"

To answer this question, we need to broaden the context. The question is fine, but it cannot be directed solely at Islamic terrorists. If it is, it misses the point.

We need to consider other religions, too. For Christians, we don't have to go back centuries to the Inquisition or to the Children's Crusades. We only have to look at Ireland, and the bombings in Belfast. There, Protestants and Catholics slaughtered each other in the name of God.

In the United States, we can consider the killing of abortion doctors. Paul Hill, a minister who was executed for killing a doctor in Florida, was convinced that his act was good, that he had saved the lives of unborn babies. Before his execution, he said that he was looking forward to heaven. His friend, Reverend Michael Bray, took no lives; instead, he burned abortion clinics.

Since I want to give equal time to the major religions, we can't forget the Jews. Dr. Baruch Goldstein was convinced that Yahweh wanted him to take a Galil assault rifle, go to the Tomb of the Patriarchs, and shoot into a crowd of praying Palestinian men and boys. His admirers built a monument on his grave (Juergensmeyer 2000).

Finally, for the sake of equality, let's not let the Hindus, Buddhists, and Sikhs off the hook. In India, they continue to slaughter one another. In the name of their gods, they attack the houses of worship of the others and blow one another up. (The Hindus are actually equal opportunists—they kill Christians, too. I visited a state in India where Hindus had doused a jeep with gasoline and burned alive an Australian missionary and his two sons.)

None of these terrorists—Islamic, Christian, Jew, Sikh, Buddhist, or Hindu—represent the mainstream of their religion, but they do commit violence for religious reasons. How can they do so? Here are five elements that religious terrorists seem to have in common. (I have extrapolated these principles from the acts of individuals and small groups. Terrorism by the state is another matter.)

First, the individuals believe that they are under attack. Evil forces are bent on destroying the good of their world—whether that be their religion, their way of life, or unborn babies.

Second, they become convinced that God wants the evil destroyed.

Violence and killing are a dysfunction of religion. The execution of John Rogers took place at Smithfield, England, in 1555, during the reign of Mary I.

Third, they conclude that only violence will resolve the situation, and that violence in this case is good.

Fourth, they become convinced that God has chosen them for this task. They don't necessarily want to kill or to die, but they reluctantly accept their fate. Dying for God's cause is greater than living as a coward who won't stand up for what is right.

Fifth, these perspectives are nurtured by a community, a group in which the individuals find identity. This group may realize that most members of their faith do not support their views, but that is because the others are uninformed, even brainwashed by the enemy or by the liberal, secularized media. The smaller community holds the truth.

For those groups that have scriptures, there are enough references to violence that they are able to interpret selective passages as "God's mandated" solution to the threat they feel.

If these orientations are accompanied by the view that we are in a final confrontation between good and evil, they become even more powerful. If we are in the end times and this is the final battle, there is no retreat. Some Christians, Jews, Muslims, and Sikhs hold such a view (Juergensmeyer 2000).

Under these conditions, morality is turned upside down. Killing becomes a moral act, a good done for a greater cause. This greater good may require self-sacrifice—the most notable example being a suicide bombing.

There is just enough truth in these points of view to keep the delusion alive. After all, wouldn't it have been better for the millions of Jews and the millions of other victims if someone had had the nerve and foresight to kill Hitler? Wouldn't his death and one's own self-sacrifice have been a greater good? Today, there are those bad Protestants, those bad Catholics, those bad Jews, those bad Palestinians, those bad abortionists, those bad Americans—an endless list. And the violence is for the Greater Good: what God wants.

Once people buy into this closed system of thought, discussion in which contrasting views are shared and considered flies out the window. The individuals become convinced that they have access to the mind of God.

This analysis would not be complete without stressing that religious terrorism is often a political instrument. There are those who exploit the conditions analyzed here to enforce their political agenda. Religious riots in India, for example, are usually not spontaneous, but, rather, are "produced" by leaders who benefit from them (Brass 2003).

This photo of people having a religious experience is from Billy Graham's last crusade, held in New York City in 2005, when Graham was 86 years old. Here is the caption from the *New York Times* where this photo first appeared: "The altar call is the moment at the end of an evangelical Protestant church service when the minister urges audience members to step forward, make a public decision to accept Jesus Christ as their savior and be born anew."

symbols, but sacred emblems that evoke feelings of awe and reverence. In Durkheim's terms, religions use symbols to represent what the group considers sacred and to separate the sacred from the profane.

A symbol is a condensed way of communicating. Worn by a fundamentalist Christian, for example, the cross says, "I am a follower of Jesus Christ. I believe that He is the Messiah, the promised Son of God, that He loves me, that He died to take away my sins, that He rose from the dead and is going to return to earth, and that through Him I will receive eternal life."

That is a lot to pack into one symbol—and it is only part of what the symbol means to a fundamentalist believer. To people in other traditions of Christianity, the cross conveys somewhat different meanings—but to all Christians, the cross is a shorthand way of expressing many meanings. So it is with the Star of David, the crescent moon and star, the cow (expressing to Hindus the unity of all living things), and the various symbols of the world's many other religions.

Rituals

Rituals, ceremonies or repetitive practices, are also symbols that help to unite people into a moral community. Some rituals, such as the bar mitzvah of Jewish boys and the Holy Communion of Christians, are designed to create in devout believers a feeling of closeness with God and unity with one another. Rituals include kneeling and praying at set times; bowing; crossing oneself; singing; lighting candles and incense; reading scripture; and following prescribed traditions at processions, baptisms, weddings, and funerals.

Beliefs

Symbols, including rituals, develop from beliefs. The belief may be vague ("God is") or highly specific ("God wants us to prostrate ourselves and face Mecca five times each day"). Religious beliefs include not only *values* (what is considered good and desirable in life—how we ought to live) but also a **cosmology,** a unified picture of the world. For example, the Jewish, Christian, and Muslim belief that there is only one God, the Creator of the universe, who is concerned about the actions of humans and who will hold us accountable for what we do, is a cosmology. It presents a unifying picture of the universe.

Religious Experience

The term **religious experience** refers to a sudden awareness of the supernatural or a feeling of coming into contact with God. Some people undergo a mild version, such as feeling closer to God when they look at a mountain or listen to a certain piece of music. Others report a life-transforming experience. St. Francis of Assisi, for example, said that he became aware of God's presence in every living thing.

Some Protestants use the term **born again** to describe people who have undergone such a life-transforming religious experience. These people say that they came to the realization that they had sinned, that Jesus had died for their sins, and that God wants them to live a new life. Their worlds become transformed. They look forward to the Resurrection and to a new life in heaven, and they see relationships with spouses, parents, children, and even bosses in a new light. They also report a need to make changes in how they interact with others so that their lives reflect their new, personal commitment to Jesus as their "Savior and Lord." They describe a feeling of beginning life anew; hence the term *born again*.

Community

Finally, the shared meanings that come through symbols, rituals, and beliefs (and for some, a religious experience) unite people into a moral community. People in a moral community feel a bond with one another, for their beliefs and rituals bind them together—and at the same time separate them from those who do not share their unique symbolic world. Mormons, for example, feel

One of the functions of religion is to create community—a sense of being connected with one another and, in this case, also a sense of being connected with God. To help accomplish this, religions often use rituals. Shown here are Javanese Muslim women in Surinam as they celebrate Id al Fatr at the end of Rammadan.

a "kindred spirit" (as it is often known) with other Mormons. Baptists, Jews, Jehovah's Witnesses, and Muslims feel similar bonds with members of their respective faiths.

As a symbol of their unity, members of some religious groups address one another as "brother" or "sister." "Sister Luby, we are going to meet at Brother and Sister Maher's on Wednesday" is a common way of expressing a message. The terms *brother* and *sister* are intended to symbolize a relationship so close that the individuals consider themselves members of the same family.

Community is powerful. Not only does it provide the basis for mutual identity but also it establishes norms that govern the behavior of its members. Members either conform or they lose their membership. In Christian churches, for example, an individual whose adultery becomes known, and who refuses to admit wrongdoing and ask forgiveness, may be banned from the church. He or she may be formally excommunicated, as in the Catholic tradition, or more informally "stricken from the rolls," as is the usual Protestant practice.

Removal from the community is a serious matter for people whose identity is bound up in that community. Sociologists John Hostetler (1980), William Kephart, and William Zellner (2001) describe the Amish practice of *shunning*—ignoring an offender in all situations. Persons who are shunned are treated as though they do not exist (for if they do not repent by expressing sorrow for their act, they have ceased to exist as members of the community). The shunning is so thorough that even family members, who themselves remain in good standing in the congregation, are not allowed to talk to the person being shunned. This obviously makes for some interesting times at the dinner table.

The Conflict Perspective

 The conflict perspective has an entirely different focus. Conflict theorists examine how religion supports the status quo and helps to maintain social inequalities.

Opium of the People

In general, conflict theorists are highly critical of religion. Karl Marx, an avowed atheist who believed that the existence of God was impossible, set the tone for conflict theorists with his most famous statement on this subject: "Religion is the sigh of the oppressed creature, the sentiment of a heartless world. . . . It is the opium of the people" (Marx 1844/1964). By this statement, Marx meant that oppressed workers find escape in religion. For them, religion is like a drug that helps them to forget their misery. By diverting their thoughts toward future happiness in an afterlife, religion takes their eyes off their suffering in this world, thereby greatly reducing the possibility that they will rebel against their oppressors.

A Legitimation of Social Inequalities

Conflict theorists say that religion legitimates the social inequalities of the larger society. By this, they mean that religion teaches that the existing social arrangements of a society represent what God desires. For example, during the Middle Ages, Christian theologians decreed the *divine right of kings*. This doctrine meant that God determined who would become king, and set him on the throne. The king ruled in God's place, and it was the duty of a king's subjects to be loyal to him (and to pay their taxes). To disobey the king was to disobey God.

In what was perhaps the supreme technique of legitimating the social order (and one that went even a step farther than the divine right of kings), the religion of ancient Egypt held that the Pharaoh himself was a god. The Emperor of Japan was similarly declared divine. If this were so, who could ever question his decisions? Today's politicians would give their right arm for such a religious teaching.

Conflict theorists point to many other examples of how religion legitimates the social order. In India, Hinduism supports the caste system by teaching that an individual who tries to change caste will come back in the next life as a member of a lower caste—or even as an animal. In the decades before the American Civil War, Southern ministers used scripture to defend slavery, saying that it was God's will—while Northern ministers legitimated *their* region's social structure by using scripture to denounce slavery as evil (Ernst 1988; Nauta 1993; White 1995).

This engraving is of a Quaker meeting in the 1700s when women sat on one side of the church, and men on the other. Some Jewish and Muslim groups continue this practice today. Do you think that sex-segregated seating supports the conflict perspective that religion reflects and legitimates social inequalities? Why or why not?

QUAKERS MEETING.

Religion and the Spirit of Capitalism

Max Weber disagreed strongly with the conflict perspective that religion merely reflects and legitimates the social order, and that it impedes social change by encouraging people to focus on the afterlife. In contrast, Weber said that religion's focus on the afterlife is a source of profound social change.

Like Marx, Weber observed the early industrialization of European countries. Weber became intrigued with the question of why some societies embraced capitalism while others clung to their traditional ways. Tradition is strong and tends to hold people in check; yet some societies had been transformed by capitalism, while others remained untouched. As he explored this puzzle, Weber concluded that religion held the key to **modernization**—the transformation of traditional societies to industrial societies.

To explain his conclusions, Weber wrote *The Protestant Ethic and the Spirit of Capitalism* (1904–1905/1958). Because Weber's argument was presented in Chapter 7 (page 180), it is only summarized here.

(page 180)

1. Capitalism is not just a superficial change. Rather, capitalism represents a fundamentally different way of thinking about work and money. *Traditionally, people worked just enough to meet their basic needs, not so that they could have a surplus to invest.* To accumulate money (capital) as an end in itself, not just to spend it, was a radical departure from traditional thinking. People even came to consider it a duty to invest money in order to make profits, which, in turn, they reinvested to make more profits. Weber called this new approach to work and money the **spirit of capitalism.**

2. Why did the spirit of capitalism develop in Europe, and not, for example, in China or India, where the people had similar material resources and education? According to Weber, *religion was the key.* The religions of China and India, and indeed Roman Catholicism in Europe, encouraged a traditional approach to life, not thrift and investment. Capitalism appeared when Protestantism came on the scene.

3. What was different about Protestantism, especially Calvinism? John Calvin taught that God had predestined some people to go to heaven, and others to hell. Neither church membership nor feelings about your relationship with God could assure you that you were saved. You wouldn't know your fate until after you died.

4. This doctrine created intense anxiety among Calvin's followers: "Am I predestined to hell or to heaven?" they wondered. As Calvinists wrestled with this question, they concluded that church members have a duty to prove that they are one of God's elect, and to live as though they are predestined to heaven—for good works are a demonstration of salvation.

5. This conclusion motivated Calvinists to lead moral lives *and* to work hard, to not waste time, and to be frugal—for idleness and needless spending were signs of worldliness. Weber called this self-denying approach to life the **Protestant ethic.**

6. As people worked hard and spent money only on necessities (a pair of earrings or a second pair of dress shoes would have been defined as sinful luxuries), they had money left over. Because it couldn't be spent, this capital was invested, which led to a surge in production.

7. Weber's analysis can be summed up this way: The change in religion (from Catholicism to Protestantism, especially Calvinism) led to a fundamental change in thought and behavior (the *Protestant ethic*). The result was the *spirit of capitalism.* For this reason, capitalism originated in Europe and not in places where religion did not encourage capitalism's essential elements: the accumulation of capital and its investment and reinvestment.

Although Weber's analysis has been influential, it has not lacked critics (Kalberg 2002). Hundreds of scholars have attacked it, some for overlooking the lack of capitalism in Scotland (a Calvinist country), others for failing to explain why the Industrial Revolution was born in England (not a Calvinist country). Hundreds of other scholars

modernization the transformation of traditional societies into industrial societies

spirit of capitalism Weber's term for the desire to accumulate capital as a duty—not to spend the money, but as an end in itself—and to constantly reinvest it

Protestant ethic Weber's term to describe the ideal of a self-denying, highly moral life accompanied by hard work and frugality

"We're thinking maybe it's time you started getting some religious instruction. There's Catholic, Protestant, and Jewish—any of those sound good to you?"

For some Americans, religion is an "easy-going, makes-little-difference" matter, as expressed in this cartoon. For others, religious matters are firmly held, and followers find even slight differences of faith to be significant.

have defended Weber's argument. There is currently no historical evidence that can definitively prove or disprove Weber's thesis.

At this point in history, the Protestant ethic and the spirit of capitalism are not confined to any specific religion or even to any one part of the world. Rather, they have become cultural traits that have spread to societies around the globe (Greeley 1964; Yinger 1970). U.S. Catholics have about the same approach to life as do U.S. Protestants. In addition, Hong Kong, Japan, Malaysia, Singapore, South Korea, and Taiwan—not exactly Protestant countries—have embraced capitalism (Levy 1992). China is in the midst of doing so.

The World's Major Religions

The largest of the thousands of religions in the world are listed in Figure 18.1. Let's briefly review six of them.

Judaism

The origin of Judaism is traced to Abraham, who lived about four thousand years ago in Mesopotamia. Jews believe that God (Jahweh) made a covenant with Abraham, selecting his descendants as a chosen people—promising to make them "as numerous as the sands of the seashore" and to give them a special land that would be theirs forever. The sign of this covenant was the circumcision of males, which was to be performed when a boy was eight days old. Descent is traced through Abraham and his wife, Sarah, their son Isaac, and their grandson Jacob (also called Israel).

Religion, which provides community and identity, is often passed from the older to the younger. Shown here are Hasidic Jews in Brooklyn. Differences among religious groups are often incomprehensible to outsiders. The man on the left is carrying a pouch under his left arm, considered by the men on the right to be a violation of the Sabbath.

Joseph, a son of Jacob, was sold by his brothers into slavery and taken to Egypt. Following a series of hair-raising adventures, Joseph became Pharaoh's right-hand man. When a severe famine hit Canaan, where Jacob's family was living, Jacob and his eleven other sons fled to Egypt. Under Joseph's leadership, they were welcome. A subsequent Pharaoh, however, enslaved the Israelites. After about four hundred years, Moses, an Israelite who had been adopted by Pharaoh's daughter, confronted Pharaoh. He persuaded Pharaoh to release the slaves, who at that time numbered about 2 million. Moses led them out of Egypt, but before they reached their Promised Land, the Israelites spent forty years wandering in the desert. Sometime during those years, Moses delivered the Ten Commandments from Mount Sinai. Abraham, Isaac, Jacob, and Moses hold revered positions in Judaism. The events of their lives and the recounting of the early history of the Israelites are contained in the first five books of the Bible, called the Torah.

The founding of Judaism marked a fundamental change in religion, for it was the first religion based on **monotheism,** the belief that there is only one God. Prior to Judaism, religions were based on **polytheism,** the belief that there are many gods. In Greek religion, for example, Zeus was the god of heaven and earth, Poseidon the god of the sea, and Athena the goddess of wisdom. Other groups followed **animism,** believing that all objects in the world have spirits, some of which are dangerous and must be outwitted.

Contemporary Judaism in the United States comprises three main branches: Orthodox, Reform, and Conservative. Orthodox Jews adhere to the laws espoused by Moses. They eat only foods prepared in a designated manner (kosher), observe the Sabbath in a traditional way, and segregate males and females in their religious services. During the 1800s, a group that wanted to make their practices more compatible with U.S. culture broke from this tradition. This liberal group, known as Reform Judaism, mostly uses English in its religious ceremonies and has reduced much of the use of ritual. The third branch, Conservative Judaism, falls somewhere between the other two. No branch has continued polygyny (allowing a man to have more than one wife), the original marriage custom of the Jews, which was outlawed by rabbinic decree about a thousand years ago.

The history of Judaism is marked by conflict and persecution. The Israelites were conquered by the Babylonians, and were again made slaves. After returning to Israel and rebuilding the temple, they were later conquered by the Romans, and, after their rebellion at Masada in A.D. 70 failed, they were exiled for almost two thousand years into other nations. During those centuries, they faced prejudice, discrimination, and persecution (called **anti-Semitism**) by many peoples and rulers. The most horrendous example was the Nazi Holocaust of World War II, when Hitler attempted to eliminate the Jews as a people. Under the Nazi occupation of Europe and North Africa, about 6 million Jews were slaughtered. Many died in gas ovens that were constructed for just this purpose.

Central to Jewish teaching is the requirement to love God and do good deeds. Good deeds begin in the family, where each member has an obligation toward the others. Sin is a conscious choice to do evil, and must be atoned for by prayers and good works. Jews consider Jerusalem a holy city and believe that the Messiah will one day appear there, bringing redemption for them all.

Christianity

Christianity, which developed out of Judaism, is also monotheistic. Christians believe that Jesus Christ is the Messiah whom God promised the Jews.

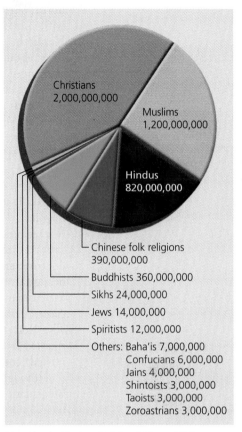

Figure 18.1 **The World's Largest Religions**[a]

- Christians 2,000,000,000
- Muslims 1,200,000,000
- Hindus 820,000,000
- Chinese folk religions 390,000,000
- Buddhists 360,000,000
- Sikhs 24,000,000
- Jews 14,000,000
- Spiritists 12,000,000
- Others: Baha'is 7,000,000
  Confucians 6,000,000
  Jains 4,000,000
  Shintoists 3,000,000
  Taoists 3,000,000
  Zoroastrians 3,000,000

[a]*Note:* The classification of religions is often confusing. Animists, for example, although numerous, are not listed as a separate group in the source. It is sometimes difficult to tell what groups are included in what categories.

Sources: "Adherents of . . ." 2003.

monotheism the belief that there is only one God

polytheism the belief that there are many gods

animism the belief that all objects in the world have spirits, some of which are dangerous and must be outwitted

anti-Semitism prejudice, discrimination, and persecution directed against Jews

Jesus was born in poverty, and traditional Christians believe his mother was a virgin. Within two years of his birth, Herod—named king of Palestine by Caesar, who had conquered Israel—was informed that people were saying a new king had been born. When they realized Herod had sent soldiers to kill the baby, Jesus' parents fled with him to Egypt. After Herod died, they returned, settling in the small town of Nazareth.

At about the age of 30, Jesus began a preaching and healing ministry. His teachings challenged the contemporary religious establishment, and as his popularity grew, the religious leaders plotted to have him killed by the Romans. Christians interpret the death of Jesus as a blood sacrifice made to atone for their sins. They believe that through his death they have peace with God and will inherit eternal life.

The twelve main followers of Jesus, called *apostles*, believed that Jesus rose from the dead. They preached the need to be "born again," that is, to accept Jesus as Savior, give up selfish ways, and live a devout life. The new religion spread rapidly, and after an initial period of hostility on the part of imperial Rome—during which time believers were fed to the lions in the Coliseum—in A.D. 317 Christianity became the empire's official religion.

During the first thousand years of Christianity, there was only one church organization, directed from Rome. During the eleventh century, after disagreement over doctrine and politics, Greek Orthodoxy was declared independent of Rome. It was headquartered in Constantinople (now Istanbul, Turkey). During the Middle Ages, the Roman Catholic Church, which was aligned with the political establishment, became corrupt. Some Church offices, such as that of bishop, were sold for a set price. The Reformation, which was led by Martin Luther in the sixteenth century, was sparked by Luther's outrage that the forgiveness of sins (including those not yet committed) could be purchased by buying an "indulgence."

Although Martin Luther's original goal was to reform the Church, not divide it, the Reformation began a splintering of Christianity. The Reformation coincided with the breakup of feudalism, and as the ancient political structure came apart, people clamored for independence in both political and religious thought. Today, Christianity is the most popular religion in the world, with about 2 billion adherents. Christians are divided into hundreds of groups, some with doctrinal differences so slight that only members of the group can appreciate the extremely fine distinctions that they feel significantly separate them from others. The Social Map on the next page shows how some of these groups are distributed in the United States.

Islam

Islam, whose followers are known as Muslims, began in the same part of the world as Judaism and Christianity. Islam, the world's third monotheistic religion, has over a billion followers. It was founded by Muhammad, who was born in Mecca (now in Saudi Arabia) in about A.D. 570. Muhammad married Khadija, a wealthy widow. About the age of 40, he reported that he had had visions from God. These, and his teachings, were later written down in a book called the Qur'an (Koran). Few paid attention to Muhammad, although Ali, his son-in-law, believed him. When he found out that there was a plot to murder him, Muhammad fled to Medina, where he found a more receptive audience. There he established a *theocracy* (a government based on the principle that God is king, God's laws are the statutes of the land, and priests are the earthly administrators of God). In A.D. 630 he returned to Mecca, this time as a conqueror (Bridgwater 1953).

After Muhammad's death, a struggle for control over the empire he had founded split Islam into two branches that remain today, the Sunni and the Shi'ite. The Shi'ites believe that the *imam* (the religious leader) is inspired as he interprets the Qur'an. They are generally more conservative and are inclined to **fundamentalism,** the belief that modern ways of life threaten religion and that the faith as it was originally practiced should

Figure 18.2 Church Membership: Dominant Religion, by County

When no religious group has 25 percent of the total membership in a county, that county is left blank. When two or more religious groups have 25–49 percent of the membership in a county, the largest is shown.

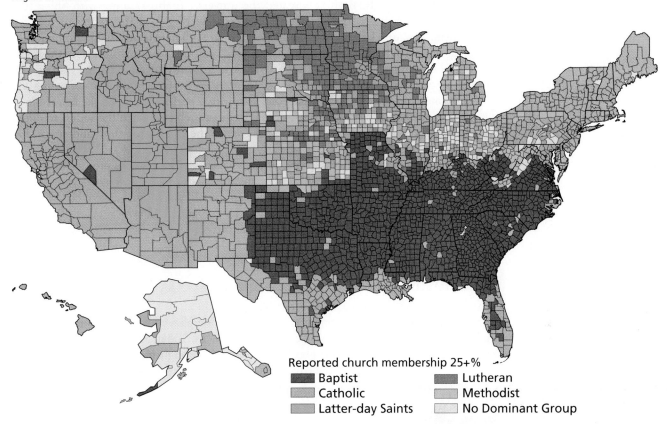

Reported church membership 25+%

- Baptist
- Catholic
- Latter-day Saints
- Lutheran
- Methodist
- No Dominant Group

be restored. The Sunnis, who do not share this belief, are generally more liberal, more accepting of social change.

Like the Jews, Muslims trace their ancestry to Abraham. Abraham fathered a son, Ishmael, by Hagar, his wife Sarah's Egyptian maid (Genesis 25:12). Ishmael had twelve sons, from whom a good portion of today's Arab world is descended. For them also, Jerusalem is a holy city. The Muslims consider the Bibles of the Jews and the Christians to be sacred, but they take the Qur'an as the final word. They believe that the followers of Abraham and Moses (Jews) and Jesus (Christians) changed the original teachings and that Muhammad restored these teachings to their initial purity. It is the duty of each Muslim to make a pilgrimage to Mecca during his or her lifetime. Unlike the Jews, the Muslims continue to practice polygyny. They limit a man to four wives, however.

Hinduism

Unlike the other religions just described, Hinduism has no specific founder. Going back about four thousand years, Hinduism was the chief religion of India. The term *Hinduism,* however, is Western, and in India the closest term is *dharma* (law). Unlike Judaism, Christianity, and Islam, Hinduism has no canonical scripture, that is, no texts thought to be inspired by God. Instead, several books, including the *Brahmanas,*

reincarnation in Hinduism and Buddhism, the return of the soul (or self) after death in a different form

Bhagavad-Gita, and *Upanishads,* expound on the moral qualities that people should strive to develop. They also delineate the sacrifices people should make to the gods.

Hindus are *polytheists;* that is, they believe that there are many gods. They believe that one of these gods, Brahma, created the universe. Brahma, along with Shiva (the Destroyer) and Vishnu (the Preserver), form a triad that is at the center of modern Hinduism. A central belief is *karma,* spiritual progress. There is no final judgment, but, instead, **reincarnation,** a cycle of life, death, and rebirth. Death involves only the body. The soul continues its existence, coming back in a form that matches the individual's moral progress in the previous life (which centers on proper conduct in following the rules of one's caste). If an individual reaches spiritual perfection, he or she has attained *nirvana.* This marks the end of the cycle of death and rebirth, when the soul is reunited with the universal soul. When this occurs, *maya,* the illusion of time and space, has been conquered.

Some Hindu practices have been modified as a consequence of social protest—especially child marriage and *suttee,* the practice of cremating a surviving widow along with her deceased husband (Bridgwater 1953). Other ancient rituals remain unchanged, however, and include *kumbh mela,* a purifying washing in the Ganges River, which takes place every twelve years, and in which many millions participate.

Buddhism

In about 600 B.C., Siddhartha Gautama founded Buddhism. (Buddha means the "enlightened one," a term Gautama was given by his disciples.) Gautama was the son of an upper-caste Hindu ruler in an area north of Benares, India. At the age of 29, he renounced his life of luxury and became an ascetic. Through meditation, he discovered the "four noble truths," which emphasize self-denial and compassion.

1. Existence is suffering.
2. The origin of suffering is desire.
3. Suffering ceases when desire ceases.
4. The way to end desire is to follow the "noble eightfold path."

The noble eightfold path consists of

1. Right belief
2. Right resolve (to renounce carnal pleasure and to harm no living creature)
3. Right speech
4. Right conduct
5. Right occupation or living
6. Right effort
7. Right-mindedness (or contemplation)
8. Right ecstasy

The central symbol of Buddhism is the eight-spoked wheel. Each spoke represents one aspect of the path. As with Hinduism, the ultimate goal of Buddhism is the cessation of rebirth and thereby of suffering. Buddhists teach that all things are temporary, even the self. Because all things are destined to pass away, there is no soul (Reat 1994).

Buddhism spread rapidly. In the third century B.C., the ruler of India adopted Buddhism and sent missionaries throughout Asia to spread the new teaching (Bridgwater 1953). By the fifth century A.D., Buddhism reached the height of its popularity in India, after which it died out. Buddhism, however, had spread to Ceylon, Burma, Tibet, Laos, Cambodia, Thailand, China, Korea, and Japan, where it flourishes today. With increased immigration from Asian nations, vigorous communities of Buddhists have also developed in the United States (Cadge and Bender 2004).

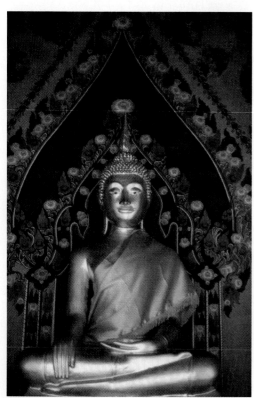

Depictions of Buddha are found throughout the world. Many Buddhists keep small statues in their homes and businesses, at which they make daily offerings of food. This golden Buddha statue is in Bangkok, Thailand.

Confucianism

About the time that Gautama lived, K'ung Fu-tsu (551–479 B.C.) was born in China. Confucius (his name strung together in English), a public official, was distressed by the corruption that he saw in government. Unlike Gautama, who urged withdrawal from social activities, Confucius urged social reform and developed a system of moral principles based on peace, justice, and universal order. His teachings were incorporated into writings called the *Analects*.

The basic moral principle of Confucianism is to maintain *jen*, sympathy or concern for other humans. The key to *jen* is to sustain right relationships—being loyal and placing morality above self-interest. In what is called the "Confucian Golden Rule," Confucius stated a basic principle for *jen:* to treat those who are subordinate to you as you would like to be treated by people superior to yourself. Confucius taught that right relationships within the family (loyalty, respect) should be the model for society. He also taught the "middle way," an avoidance of extremes.

Confucianism was originally atheistic, simply a set of moral teachings without reference to the supernatural. As the centuries passed, however, local gods were added to the teachings, and Confucius himself was declared a god. Confucius' teachings became the basis for the government of China. About A.D. 1000, the emphasis on meditation gave way to a stress on improvement through acquiring knowledge. This emphasis remained dominant until the twentieth century. By this time, the government had become rigid, and respect for the existing order had replaced respect for relationships (Bridgwater 1953). Following the Communist revolution of 1949, political leaders attempted to weaken the people's ties with Confucianism. They succeeded in part, but Confucianism remains embedded in Chinese culture.

Types of Religious Groups

Sociologists have identified four types of religious groups: cult, sect, church, and ecclesia. Why do some of these groups meet with hostility, while others are more accepted? For an explanation, look at Figure 18.3.

Figure 18.3 Religious Groups: From Hostility to Acceptance

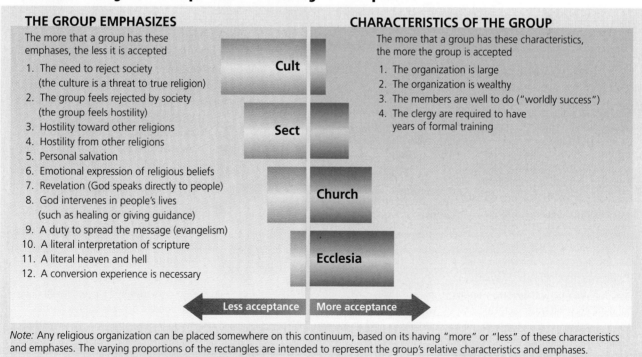

THE GROUP EMPHASIZES

The more that a group has these emphases, the less it is accepted

1. The need to reject society (the culture is a threat to true religion)
2. The group feels rejected by society (the group feels hostility)
3. Hostility toward other religions
4. Hostility from other religions
5. Personal salvation
6. Emotional expression of religious beliefs
7. Revelation (God speaks directly to people)
8. God intervenes in people's lives (such as healing or giving guidance)
9. A duty to spread the message (evangelism)
10. A literal interpretation of scripture
11. A literal heaven and hell
12. A conversion experience is necessary

CHARACTERISTICS OF THE GROUP

The more that a group has these characteristics, the more the group is accepted

1. The organization is large
2. The organization is wealthy
3. The members are well to do ("worldly success")
4. The clergy are required to have years of formal training

Cult

Sect

Church

Ecclesia

← Less acceptance More acceptance →

Note: Any religious organization can be placed somewhere on this continuum, based on its having "more" or "less" of these characteristics and emphases. The varying proportions of the rectangles are intended to represent the group's relative characteristics and emphases.

Sources: By the author. Based on Troeltsch 1931; Pope 1942; and Johnson 1963.

cult a new religion with few followers, whose teachings and practices put it at odds with the dominant culture and religion

charismatic leader literally, someone to whom God has given a gift; more commonly, someone who exerts extraordinary appeal to a group of followers

charisma literally, an extraordinary gift from God; more commonly, an outstanding or "magnetic" personality that draws people to the individual

Let's explore what sociologists have found about these four types of religious groups. The summary that follows is a modification of analyses by sociologists Ernst Troeltsch (1931), Liston Pope (1942), and Benton Johnson (1963).

Cult

The word *cult* conjures up bizarre images—shaven heads, weird music, brainwashing—even ritual suicide may come to mind. Cults, however, are not necessarily weird, and few practice "brainwashing" or bizarre rituals. In fact, *all religions began as cults* (Stark 1989). A **cult** is simply a new or different religion whose teachings and practices put it at odds with the dominant culture and religion. Because the term cult arouses such negative meanings in the public mind, however, some scholars prefer to use the term *new religion* instead. As is evident from the Cultural Diversity box below, "new" can mean that an older, unfamiliar religion from one culture has made its appearance in another culture.

Cults often originate with a **charismatic leader,** an individual who inspires people because he or she seems to have extraordinary qualities. **Charisma** refers to an outstanding gift or to some exceptional quality. People feel drawn to both the person and the message because they find something highly appealing about the individual—in some instances, almost a magnetic charm.

The most popular religion in the world began as a cult. Its handful of followers believed that an unschooled carpenter who preached in remote villages in a backwater

Cultural Diversity *in the* United States

Human Heads and Animal Blood: The Toleration of Religion

AS THE CUSTOMS OFFICIALS LOOKED over the line of people who had just gotten off the plane from Haiti, there was nothing to make this particular woman stand out. She would have passed through without a problem, except for one thing: As the customs agents gave her luggage a routine search, they found something that struck them as somewhat unusual—a human head.

The head had teeth, hair, pieces of skin, and some dirt. It had evidently been dug up from some grave, probably in Haiti.

The 30-year old woman, who lives in Florida, practiced Voodoo. The head was for her religious rituals.

The woman was arrested. She faces up to 15 years in prison for the crime of not filing a report that she was carrying "organic material" ("Mujer con Cabeza . . ." 2006).

• • •

The Santeros from Cuba who live in Florida sacrifice animals. They meet in apartments, where, following a Yoruba religion, they kill goats and chickens. Calling on their gods, they first ask permission to sacrifice the animals. After sacrificing them, they pour out

Human skulls dug up for gajan, a religious ceremony held in Kurmun, India.

the animals' blood, which opens and closes the doors of their destiny. They also cut off the animals' heads and place them at locations in the city that represent the four directions of a compass. This is done to terrorize their enemies and give them safety. The sacrificed heads also protect the city from hurricanes and other destructive forces.

When city officials in Hialeah, Florida, learned that the Santeros were planning to build a church in their city, they passed a law against the sacrifice of animals within the city limits. The Santeros appealed to the U.S. Supreme Court, claiming discrimination, that the law was directed against them. The Court ruled in their favor.

for your Consideration

What do you think the limitations on religious freedom should be? Should people be allowed to sacrifice animals as part of their religious practices?

If the Santeros can sacrifice animals, why shouldn't people who practice voodoo be able to use human heads if they want to? (Assume that the relatives of the dead person have given their permission.)

country was the Son of God, that he was killed and came back to life. Those beliefs made the early Christians a cult, setting them apart from the rest of their society. Persecuted by both religious and political authorities, these early believers clung to one another for support. Many cut off associations with their friends who didn't accept the new message. To others, the early Christians must have seemed deluded and brainwashed.

So it was with Islam. When Muhammad revealed his visions and said that God's name was really Allah, only a few people believed him. To others, he must have seemed crazy, deranged.

Each cult (or new religion) is met with rejection on the part of society. Its message is considered bizarre, its approach to life strange. Its members antagonize the majority, who are convinced that they have a monopoly on the truth. The new religion may claim messages from God, visions, visits from angels—some form of enlightenment or seeing the true way to God. The cult demands intense commitment, and its followers, who are confronting a hostile world, pull together in a tight circle, separating themselves from nonbelievers.

Most cults fail. Not many people believe the new message, and the cult fades into obscurity. Some, however, succeed and make history. Over time, large numbers of people may come to accept the message and become followers of the religion. If this happens, the new religion changes from a cult to a sect.

Sect

A **sect** is larger than a cult, but its members still feel tension between their views and the prevailing beliefs and values of the broader society. A sect may even be hostile to the society in which it is located. At the very least, its members remain uncomfortable with many of the emphases of the dominant culture; in turn, nonmernbers tend to be uncomfortable with members of the sect.

Ordinarily, sects are loosely organized and fairly small. They emphasize personal salvation and an emotional expression of one's relationship with God. Clapping, shouting, dancing, and extemporaneous prayers are hallmarks of sects. Like cults, sects also stress **evangelism,** the active recruitment of new members.

If a sect grows, its members tend to gradually make peace with the rest of society. To appeal to a broader base, the sect shifts some of its doctrines, redefining matters to remove some of the rough edges that create tension between it and the rest of society. As the members become more respectable in the eyes of the society, they feel less hostility and little, if any, isolation. If a sect follows this course, as it grows and becomes more integrated into society, it changes into a church.

Church

At this point, the religious group is highly bureaucratized—probably with national and international headquarters that give direction to the local congregations, enforce rules about who can be ordained, and control finances. The relationship with God has grown less intense. The group is likely to have less emphasis on personal salvation and emotional expression. Worship services are likely to be more sedate, with sermons more formal, and written prayers read before the congregation. Rather than being recruited from the outside by fervent, personal evangelism, most new members now come from within, from children born to existing members. Rather than joining through conversion—seeing the new truth—children may be baptized, circumcised, or dedicated in some other way. At some designated age, children may be asked to affirm the group's beliefs in a confirmation or bar mitzvah ceremony.

Ecclesia

Finally, some groups become so well integrated into a culture, and so strongly allied with their government, that it is difficult to tell where one leaves off and the other takes over. In these *state religions,* also called **ecclesia,** the government and religion work together to try to shape society. There is no recruitment of members, for citizenship makes everyone

sect a religious group larger than a cult that still feels substantial hostility from and toward society

evangelism an attempt to win converts

ecclesia a religious group so integrated into the dominant culture that it is difficult to tell where the one begins and the other leaves off; also called a *state religion*

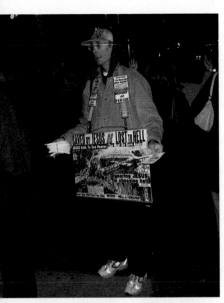

denomination a "brand name" within a major religion, for example, Methodist or Baptist

a member. For most people in the society, the religion provides little meaning: The religion is part of a cultural identity, not an eye-opening experience. Sweden provides a good example of how extensively religion and government intertwine in an ecclesia. In the 1860s, all citizens had to memorize Luther's *Small Catechism* and be tested on it yearly (Anderson 1995). Today, Lutheranism is still the state religion, but most Swedes come to church only for baptisms, marriages, and funerals.

Unlike cults and sects, which perceive God as personally involved with and concerned about an individual's life, ecclesias envision God as more impersonal and remote. Church services reflect this view of the supernatural, for they tend to be highly formal, directed by ministers or priests who, after undergoing rigorous training in approved schools or seminaries, follow prescribed rituals.

Examples of ecclesia include the Church of England (whose very name expresses alignment between church and state), the Lutheran church in Norway and Denmark, Islam in Iran and Iraq, and, during the time of the Holy Roman Empire, the Roman Catholic Church, which was the official religion for the region that is now Europe.

Variations in Patterns

Obviously, not all religious groups go through all these stages—from cult to sect to church to ecclesia. Some die out because they fail to attract enough members. Others, such as the Amish, remain sects. And, as is evident from the few countries that have state religions, very few religions ever become ecclesias.

In addition, these classifications are not perfectly matched in the real world. For example, although the Amish are a sect, they place little or no emphasis on recruiting others. The early Quakers, another sect, shied away from emotional expressions of their beliefs. They would quietly meditate in church, with no one speaking, until God gave someone a message to share with others. Finally, some groups that become churches may retain a few characteristics of sects, such as an emphasis on evangelism or a personal relationship with God.

Although all religions began as cults, not all varieties of a particular religion begin that way. For example, some **denominations**—"brand names" within a major religion, such as Methodism or Reform Judaism—begin as splinter groups. Some members of a church disagree with *particular* aspects of the church's teachings (not its major message), and they break away to form their own organization. An example is the Southern Baptist Convention, which was formed in 1845 to defend the right to own slaves (Ernst 1988; Nauta 1993; White 1995).

When Religion and Culture Conflict

As we have seen, cults and sects represent a break with the past. This division presents a challenge to the social order, and often generates hostility. When religion and the culture in which it is embedded find themselves in conflict, how do they adapt?

First, the members of a religion may reject the dominant culture and have as little as possible to do with nonmembers of their religion. Like the Amish, they may withdraw into closed communities. As noted in the Cultural Diversity box on page 109, the Amish broke away from Swiss-German Mennonites in 1693. They try to preserve the culture of their ancestors, who lived in a simpler time when there were no televisions, movies, automobiles, or even electricity. To do so, they emphasize family life and traditional male and female roles. They continue to wear the style of clothing that their ancestors wore three hundred years ago, to light their homes with oil lamps, and to speak German at home and in church. They also continue to reject radio, television, motorized vehicles, and education beyond the eighth grade. They do mingle with non-Amish when they shop in town—where they are readily distinguishable by their form of transportation (horse-drawn carriages), clothing, and speech.

Like other aspects of culture, religion is filled with background assumptions that usually go unquestioned. In this photo, which I took outside a Boston theater in midwinter, what background assumption of religion is this man violating?

In the *second* pattern, a cult or sect rejects only specific elements of the prevailing culture. For example, religious teachings may dictate that immodest clothing—short skirts, skimpy swimsuits, low-cut dresses, and so on—is immoral, or that wearing makeup or going to the movies is wrong. Most elements of the main culture, however, are accepted. Although specific activities are forbidden, members of the religion are able to participate in most aspects of the broader society. They resolve this mild tension either by adhering to the religion or by "sneaking," doing the forbidden acts on the sly.

In the *third* pattern, the society rejects the religious group. In the extreme, as with the early Christians, political leaders may even try to destroy it. The Roman emperor declared the followers of Jesus to be enemies of Rome and ordered them to be hunted down and destroyed. In the United States, after mobs hounded the new Mormons out of several communities and then killed Joseph Smith, the founder of their religion, the Mormons decided to escape the dominant culture altogether. In 1847, they settled in a wilderness, in what is today Utah's Great Salt Lake Valley (Bridgwater 1953). Our opening vignette focused on another example, the destruction of the Branch Davidians by the U.S. government.

Religion in the United States

With its hundreds of denominations and sects, how can we generalize about religion in the United States? What do these many religious groups have in common? It certainly isn't doctrine (church teaching), but doctrine is not the focus of sociology. Sociologists, rather, are interested in the relationship between society and religion, and the role that religion plays in people's lives. To better understand religion in U.S. society, then, let's first find out who belongs to religious groups, and then look at the groups they belong to.

Characteristics of Members

About 65 percent of Americans belong to a church, synagogue, or mosque. What are the characteristics of people who hold formal membership in a religion?

Social Class Religion in the United States is stratified by social class. As you can see from Figure 18.4 on the next page, some religious groups are "top-heavy," and others are "bottom-heavy." The most top-heavy are Jews and Episcopalians; the most bottom-heavy are Assembly of God, Southern Baptists, and Jehovah's Witnesses. This figure provides further confirmation that churchlike groups tend to appeal to people who are more economically successful, while the more sectlike groups attract the less successful.

From this figure, you can see how *status consistency* (a concept you studied in Chapter 10) applies to religious groups. If a group ranks high (or low) on education, it is also likely to rank high (or low) on income and occupational prestige. Jews, for example, rank the highest on education, income, and occupational prestige, while Jehovah's Witnesses rank the lowest on these three measures of social class. As you can see, the Mormons are status inconsistent. They rank second in income, fourth in education, and tie for sixth in occupational prestige. Even more status inconsistent is the Assembly of God. Their members tie for third in occupational prestige but rank only eighth in income and ninth in education. This inconsistency is so jarring that there could be a problem with the sample.

Americans who change their social class also have a tendency to change their religion. Their new social class experiences create changes in their ideas about the world, molding new preferences for music and styles of speech. Upwardly mobile people are likely to seek a religion that draws more affluent people. An upwardly mobile Baptist, for example, may become a Methodist or a Presbyterian. For Roman Catholics, the situation is somewhat different. Because each parish is a geographical unit, Catholics who move into more affluent neighborhoods are also likely to be moving to a congregation that has a larger proportion of affluent members.

Figure 18.4 **Social Class and Religious Affiliation**

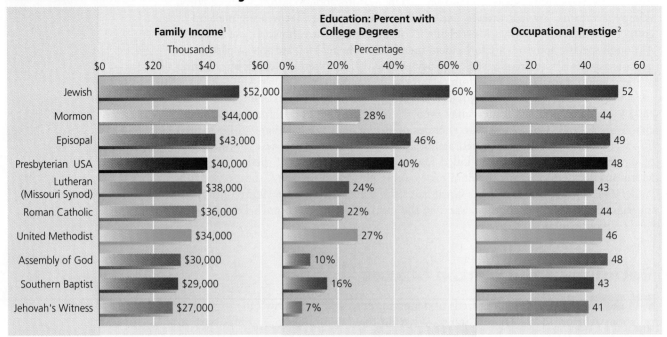

¹Since the income data were reported, inflation has run approximately 24 percent.

²Higher numbers mean that more of the group's members work at occupations that have higher prestige, generally those that require more education and pay more. For more information on occupational prestige, see Table 10.2 on page 273.

Source: By the author. Based on Smith and Faris 2005.

Race-Ethnicity   It is common for religions around the world to be associated with race-ethnicity: Islam with Arabs, Judaism with Jews, Hinduism with Indians, and Confucianism with Chinese. Sometimes, as with Hinduism and Confucianism, a religion and a particular country are almost synonymous. Christianity is not associated with any one country, although it is associated primarily with Western culture.

In the United States, all major religious groups draw from the nation's many racial-ethnic groups. Like social class, however, race-ethnicity tends to cluster. People of Irish descent are likely to be Roman Catholics; those with Greek ancestors are likely to belong to the Greek Orthodox Church. African Americans are likely to be Protestants—more specifically, Baptists—or to belong to fundamentalist sects.

Although many churches are integrated, it is with good reason that Sunday morning between 10 and 11 A.M. has been called "the most segregated hour in the United States." African Americans tend to belong to African American churches, while most whites see only whites in theirs. The segregation of churches is based on custom, not on law.

Characteristics of Religious Groups

Let's examine features of the religious groups in the United States.

Diversity   With its 300,000 congregations and hundreds of denominations, no religious group even comes close to being a dominant religion in the United States (*Statistical Abstract* 2007:Tables 73, 74). Table 18.1 illustrates some of this remarkable diversity.

Pluralism and Freedom   It is the U.S. government's policy not to interfere with religions. The government's position is that its obligation is to ensure an environment in which people can worship as they see fit. Religious freedom is so extensive that anyone can start a church and proclaim himself or herself a minister, revelator, or any other desired term. If officials feel threatened by a religious group, however, the government grossly violates its hands-off policy, as with the Branch Davidians featured in our opening vignette. Since 9/11, the government has infiltrated mosques to monitor the activities of Arab immigrants (Elinson 2004). The Cultural Diversity box on page 542 discusses other limits to this policy.

Competition and Recruitment The many religious groups of the United States compete for clients. They even advertise in the Yellow Pages of the telephone directory and insert appealing advertising—under the guise of news—in the religion section of the Saturday or Sunday edition of the local newspapers. Because of this intense competition, some groups modify their message, making it closer to what their successful competitors are offering (Greeley and Hout 1999).

Commitment Americans are a religious people, and 40 percent report that they attend religious services each week (Gallup Poll 2007). Sociologists have questioned this statistic, suggesting that the high totals are due to an *interviewer effect*. Because people want to please interviewers, they stretch the truth a bit. To find out, sociologists Stanley Presser and Linda Stinson (1998) examined people's written reports (no interviewer present) on how they spent their Sundays. They concluded that about 30 percent or so do attend church each week.

Whether the percentage of weekly church attendance is 30 or 40, Americans are a religious people, and they back up their commitment with generous support for religion and its charities. Each year Americans donate about $88 billion to religious causes (*Statistical Abstract* 2007:Table 567). To appreciate the significance of this huge figure, keep in mind that, unlike a country in which there is an ecclesia, those billions of dollars are not forced taxes, but money that people give away.

Toleration The general religious toleration of Americans can be illustrated by three prevailing attitudes: (1) "All religions have a right to exist—as long as they don't try to brainwash or hurt anyone." (2) "With all the religions to choose from, how can anyone tell which one—if any—is true?" (3) "Each of us may be convinced about the truth of our religion—and that is good—but don't be obnoxious by trying to convince others that you have the exclusive truth."

Fundamentalist Revival The fundamentalist Christian churches are undergoing a revival. They teach that the Bible is literally true and that salvation comes only through a personal relationship with Jesus Christ. They also denounce what they see as the degeneration of U.S. culture: flagrant sex on television, in movies, and in videos; abortion; corruption in public office; premarital sex, cohabitation; and drug abuse. Their answer to these problems is firm, simple, and direct: People whose hearts are changed through religious conversion will change their lives. The mainstream churches, which offer a more remote God and less emotional involvement, fail to meet the basic religious needs of large numbers of Americans. For an example, see the Down-to-Earth Sociology box on the next page.

One result is that mainstream churches are losing members while the fundamentalists are gaining them. Figure 18.5 on page 549 depicts this change. The exception is the Roman Catholic Church, whose growth in North America is due primarily to heavy immigration from Mexico and other Roman Catholic countries.

The Electronic Church What began as a ministry to shut-ins and those who do not belong to a church blossomed into its own type of church. Its preachers, called "televangelists," reach millions of viewers and raise millions of dollars. Some of its most famous ministries are those of Robert Schuller (the "Crystal Cathedral") and Pat Robertson (the 700 Club).

Table 18.1 How U.S. Adults Identify with Religion[a]

Christian	160,000,000
Protestant	108,000,000
Baptist	34,000,000
No denomination	21,300,000
Methodist	14,000,000
Lutheran	9,600,000
Pentecostal	7,600,000
Presbyterian	5,600,000
Churches of Christ	4,000,000
Episcopalian/Anglican	3,500,000
Mormon	2,800,000
United Church of Christ	1,400,000
Jehovah's Witness	1,300,000
Evangelical Church	1,000,000
Seventh Day Adventist	700,000
Church of the Nazarene	550,000
Disciples of Christ	500,000
Reformed Churches	500,000
Church of the Brethren	360,000
Mennonite	350,000
Quakers	200,000
Other	350,000
Roman Catholic	51,000,000
Eastern Orthodox	650,000
Other Religions	8,000,000
Jews	2,800,000
Buddhist	1,100,000
Islamic	1,100,000
Hindu	800,000
Unitarian/Universalist	600,000
Pagan	150,000
Wican	150,000
Native American	100,000
Spiritualist	100,000
Other and unclassified	850,000
No Religion	30,000,000
Refused to answer	11,000,000

[a]All totals must be taken as approximate. Some groups ignore reporting forms. Totals are rounded to the nearest 100,000.

Sources: Niebuhr 2001 (for Muslim total); *Statistical Abstract* 2000:Table 74; 2007:Table 73.

The New Face of Religion: Pentecostals and the Spanish-Speaking Immigrants

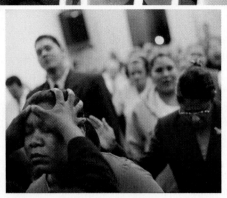

Prayer and blessing at the Ark of Salvation for the New Milennium, a storefront church in New York City.

THAT MILLIONS OF IMMIGRANTS from Spanish-speaking countries have become part of the U.S. social scene is not news. That most of them are poor isn't news, either. Almost all the immigrants who came before them were poor, too.

What is news is that many of these Latinos are abandoning the Roman Catholic religion and are embracing a form of Protestantism called Pentecostalism. Pentecostals, often referred to by the derisive term, holy rollers, believe that the Bible is the inerrant word of God. Taking the Bible literally, they believe there is a real heaven and hell. They lay hands on each other and pray for healings. They expect God to act in their lives in a very personal way. They speak in tongues.

And they are noisily joyful about their faith.

Go into one of their storefront churches, such as those on Amsterdam Avenue in New York City—or in any of the thousands of little churches that are springing up around the country. You'll hear music and clapping—a lot of it and loud. When the preachers preach, they show their enthusiasm to the message. They talk about a real God who is personally concerned about people's lives and the troubles they are going through, about the heaven God has prepared for them. The preachers warn the congregation, too, about the dangers of sins—the adultery that lurks, seductively beckoning them to fall from a righteous way of life; the downfall of drugs and alcohol; the dead end of laziness and extravagance; the value of thrift and hard work. The congregation breaks out into "Amens." "Amen, brother! Bring it on!" will shout one person, while another says, "Yes, sister. Tell it like it is!"

The preachers know what they are talking about. They, too, work at factory jobs during the day. They know what it is to sweat for a living and that J-O-B is really spelled B-R-O-K-E. Cantankerous bosses, unpaid bills, and paychecks that run out before the month does are part of their own lives. They live what they are preaching.

The music is upbeat. The drums and guitars sound like the salsa music you hear on the radio, but this with religious lyrics. The tempo, though, is the same. People clap and sway to the rhythmic sounds.

Some break out into tongues, strange sounds that some pray silently, that others shout out. Some tongues,

they believe, are messages straight from God. But no one can understand them unless someone else is given the interpretation. When this happens, people listen intently for what God has to say to them personally.

This is quite unlike the Roman Catholic religion that most of them have left behind as they adapt to their new land. Here, they say, they find a solidarity that gives them purpose in life, that encourages them to continue to work despite facing one obstacle after another, that strengthens them to resist the drugs and sex that flood their neighborhoods.

It isn't just for an hour on Sunday mornings. These people come night after night, some go every night of the week, for the comfort and encouragement of the message and music—and the opportunity to give expression to their emotions among a like-minded people.

This is the new face of religion. Pentecostalism is not some aberration, some flash in the pan. It is the fastest-growing religion in the United States, and there are perhaps 400 million Pentecostals worldwide. This religion is making such an impact that about 850,000 New Yorkers claim to be Pentecostal. That's one out of every ten (Gonzalez 2007). Not all are Latinos, of course, but about a third of the New York Pentecostals are.

Nor are all Pentecostals poor. This form of Protestantism is also being welcomed by some of the middle class and the educated. But the middle-class arms aren't open as wide. The appeal is primarily to the poor. When the poor make the transition to the middle class—as their religion, with its emphasis on work and thrift will help them do—they are likely to seek new forms of religious expression.

When this happens, we can expect that Pentecostalism will also adapt, that the form will remain recognizable, but the fervor will be lost. For now, though, it is the fervor—the intensity that connects the individuals to God and to one another—that is the driving force of this religion. The Pentecostals would phrase this a little differently. They would say that the fervor is merely the expression of the driving force of their religion, which is the Holy Spirit.

Either way you put it, these people are on fire. And that fire is burning a new imprint on the face of religion.

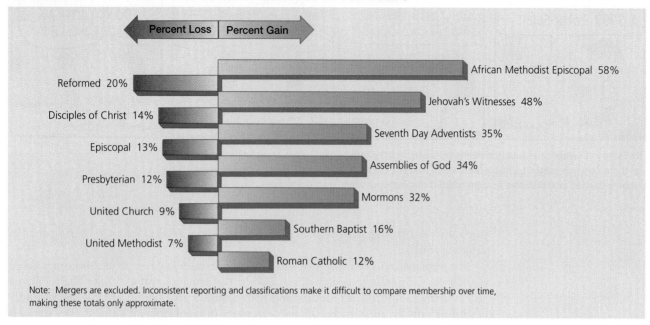

Figure 18.5 **U.S. Churches: Gains and Losses in Ten Years**

Percent Loss | Percent Gain

African Methodist Episcopal 58%
Reformed 20%
Jehovah's Witnesses 48%
Disciples of Christ 14%
Seventh Day Adventists 35%
Episcopal 13%
Assemblies of God 34%
Presbyterian 12%
Mormons 32%
United Church 9%
Southern Baptist 16%
United Methodist 7%
Roman Catholic 12%

Note: Mergers are excluded. Inconsistent reporting and classifications make it difficult to compare membership over time, making these totals only approximate.

Source: By the author. Recomputed from Jones et al. 2002.

Many local ministers view the electronic church as a competitor. They complain that it competes for the attention and dollars of their members. Leaders of the electronic church reply that the money goes to good causes and that through its conversions, the electronic church feeds members into the local churches, strengthening, not weakening them.

The Internet and Religion   As with so many aspects of life, the Internet is having an impact on religion. We will focus on this change in the concluding section. For now, let's look at secularization.

Secularization of Religion and Culture

The term *secularization* refers to the process by which worldly affairs replace spiritual interests. (The term **secular** means "belonging to the world and its affairs.") As we shall see, both religions and cultures can become secularized.

The Secularization of Religion

As the model, fashionably slender, paused before the head table of African American community leaders, her gold necklace glimmering above the low-cut bodice of her emerald-green dress, the hostess, a member of the Church of God in Christ, said, "It's now OK to wear more revealing clothes—as long as it's done in good taste." Then she added, "You couldn't do this when I was a girl, but now it's OK—and you can still worship God." (Author's files)

When I heard these words, I grabbed a napkin and quickly jotted them down, my sociological imagination stirred by their deep implication. As strange as it may seem, this simple event pinpoints the essence of why the Christian churches in the United States have splintered. Let's see how this could possibly be.

The simplest explanation for why Christians don't have just one church, or at most several, instead of the hundreds of sects and denominations that dot the U.S. landscape, is disagreements about doctrine (church teaching). As theologian and sociologist Richard Niebuhr pointed out, however, there are many ways of settling doctrinal disputes besides splintering off and forming other religious organizations.

secular belonging to the world and its affairs

In its technical sense, to evangelize means to "announce the Good News" (that Jesus is the Savior). In its more common usage, to evangelize means to make converts. As *Peanuts* so humorously picks up, evangelization is sometimes accomplished through means other than preaching.

Niebuhr (1929) suggested that the answer lies more in *social* change than it does in *religious* conflict.

The explanation goes like this. As was noted earlier, when a sect becomes more churchlike, tension lessens between it and the mainstream culture. Quite likely, when a sect is first established, its founders and first members are poor, or at least not very successful in worldly pursuits. Feeling like strangers in the dominant culture, they derive a good part of their identity from their religion. In their church services and lifestyle, they stress how different their values are from those of the dominant culture. They are also likely to emphasize the joys of the coming afterlife, when they will be able to escape from their present pain.

As time passes, the group's values—such as frugality and the avoidance of gambling, alcohol, and drugs—help the members become successful. As their children attain more education and become more middle class, members of this group grow more respectable in the eyes of society. They no longer experience the alienation that was felt by the founders of their group. Life's burdens don't seem as heavy, and the need for relief through an afterlife becomes less pressing. Similarly, the pleasures of the world no longer appear as threatening to the "truth." As is illustrated by the woman at the fashion show, people then attempt to harmonize their religious beliefs with their changing ideas about the culture.

This process is called the **secularization of religion**—shifting the focus from spiritual matters to the affairs of this world. Anyone familiar with today's mainstream Methodists would be surprised to know that they once were a sect. Methodists used to ban playing cards, dancing, and going to movies. They even considered circuses to be sinful. As Methodists grew more middle class, however, they began to change their views on sin. They started to dismantle the barriers that they had constructed between themselves and the outside world (Finke and Stark 1992).

Secularization leads to a splintering of the group, for adjusting to the secular culture displeases some of the group's members, especially those who have had less worldly success. These people still feel a gulf between themselves and the broader culture. For them, tension and hostility continue to be real. They see secularization as a desertion of the group's fundamental truths, a "selling out" to the secular world.

After futile attempts by die-hards to bring the group back to its senses, the group splinters. Those who protested the secularization of Methodism, for example, were kicked out—even though *they* represented the values around which the group had organized in the first place. The dissatisfied—who have come to be viewed as complainers—then form a sect that once again stresses its differences from the world; the need for more personal, emotional religious experiences; and salvation from the pain of living in this world. As time passes, the cycle repeats: adjustment to the dominant culture by some, continued dissatisfaction by others, and further splintering.

This process is not limited to sects, but also occurs in churches. When U.S. Episcopalians elected an openly gay bishop in 2003, some pastors and congregations

secularization of religion the replacement of a religion's spiritual or "other worldly" concerns with concerns about "this world" splintered from the U.S. church and affiliated with the more conservative African archbishops. In an ironic twist, this made them mission congregations from Africa. Sociologists have not yet compared the income or wealth of those who stayed with the group that elected the gay bishop and those who joined the splinter groups. If such a study is done and it turns out that there is no difference, we will have to modify the secularization thesis.

The Secularization of Culture Just as religion can secularize, so can culture. Sociologists use the term **secularization of culture** to refer to a culture that was once heavily influenced by religion, but no longer retains much of that influence. The United States provides an example.

secularization of culture the process by which a culture becomes less influenced by religion

Despite attempts to reinterpret history, the Pilgrims and most of the founders of the United States were highly religious people. The Pilgrims were even convinced that God had guided them to found a new religious community whose members would follow the Bible. Similarly, many of the framers of the U.S. Constitution felt that God had guided them to develop a new form of government.

The clause in the Constitution that mandates the separation of church and state was *not* an attempt to keep religion out of government, but a (successful) device to avoid the establishment of a state religion like that in England. Here, people were to have the freedom to worship as they wished. The assumption of the founders was even more specific— that Protestantism represented the true religion.

The phrase in the Declaration of Independence, "All men are *created* equal," refers to a central belief in God as the creator of humanity. A member of the clergy opened Congress with prayer. Many colonial laws were based on principles derived explicitly from the Old and New Testaments. In some colonies, blasphemy was a crime, as was failing to observe the Sabbath. Similarly, sexual affairs were a crime; in some places adultery carried the death penalty. Even public kissing between husband and wife was considered an offense, punishable by placement in the public stocks (Frumkin 1967). In other words, religion permeated U.S. culture. It was part and parcel of how the colonists saw life. Their lives, laws, and other aspects of the culture reflected their religious beliefs.

Today, U.S. culture has secularized; the influence of religion on public affairs has greatly diminished. No longer are laws based on religious principles. It has even become illegal to post the Ten Commandments in civic buildings. Overall, ideas of what is "generally good" have replaced religion as an organizing principle for the culture.

Underlying the secularization of culture is *modernization,* a term that refers to a society industrializing, urbanizing, developing mass education, and adopting science and advanced technology. Science and advanced technology bring with them a secular view of the world that begins to permeate society. They provide explanations for many aspects of life that people traditionally attributed to God. As a consequence, people come to depend much less on religion to explain life. Birth and death—and everything in between, from life's problems to its joys—are attributed to natural causes. When a society has secularized thoroughly, even religious leaders may turn to answers provided by biology, philosophy, psychology, sociology, and so on.

Although the secularization of U.S. culture means that religion has become less important in public life, *personal* religious involvement among Americans has not diminished. Rather, it has increased (Finke and Stark 1992). About 86 percent believe there is a God, and 81 percent believe there is a heaven. Not only do 63 percent claim membership in a church or synagogue, but, as we saw, on any given weekend somewhere between 30 and 40 percent of all Americans attend a worship service (Gallup 1990, 2007).

Table 18.2 underscores the paradox. Look at how religious participation has increased while the culture has secularized. The proportion of Americans who belong to a church or synagogue is now about *four* times higher than it was when the country was founded. Church membership, of course, is only a rough indicator of how significant religion is in people's lives. Some church members are not particularly religious, while many intensely religious people—Lincoln, for one—never join a church.

Table 18.2 **Growth in Religious Membership**

Americans Who Belong To a Church or Synagogue	
Year	Percentage Who Claim Membership
1776	17%
1860	37%
1890	45%
1926	58%
1975	71%
2000	68%
2005	65%

Note: The sources do not contain data on mosque membership.

Sources: Finke and Stark 1992; *Statistical Abstract* 2002:Table 64; Gallup Poll 2005.

The Future of Religion

A group of prominent intellectuals once foresaw an end to religion. As science advanced, they said, it would explain everything. It would transform human thought and replace religion, which was merely superstitious thinking left over from more primitive times. In 1966 Anthony Wallace, one of the world's best-known anthropologists at the time, confidently made the following prediction:

> **The evolutionary future of religion is extinction. Belief in supernatural beings . . . will become only an interesting historical memory. . . . doomed to die out, all over the world, as a result of the increasing adequacy and diffusion of scientific knowledge.**

Wallace and the many other social analysts who took this position were wrong. Religion thrives in the most advanced scientific nations, in capitalist and in socialist countries. It is evident that these analysts did not understand the fundamental significance of religion in people's lives.

Humans are inquiring creatures. They are aware that they have a past, a present, and a future. They reflect on their experiences to try to make sense of them. One of the questions people ponder as they reflect on life concerns the purpose of it all. Why are we born? Is there an afterlife? If so, where are we going, and what will it be like when we get there? Out of these concerns arises this question: If there is a God, what does God want of us in this life? Does God have a preference about how we should live?

Science, including sociology, cannot answer such questions. By its very nature, science cannot tell us about four main concerns that many people have:

1. *The existence of God.* About this, science has nothing to say. No test tube has either isolated God or refuted God's existence.
2. *The purpose of life.* Although science can provide a definition of life and describe the characteristics of living organisms, it has nothing to say about ultimate purpose.
3. *An afterlife.* Science can offer no information on this at all, for it has no tests to prove or disprove a "hereafter."
4. *Morality.* Science can demonstrate the consequences of behavior, but not the moral superiority of one action compared with another. This means that science cannot even prove that loving your family and neighbor is superior to hurting and killing them. Science can describe death and measure consequences, but it cannot determine the moral superiority of any action, even in such an extreme example.

There is no doubt that religion will last as long as humanity lasts, for what could replace it? And if something did, and answered such questions, would it not be religion under a different name?

To glimpse the cutting edge of religious change, we'll close with a look at the online marketing of religion.

A basic principle of symbolic interactionism is that meaning is not inherent in an object or event, but is determined by people as they interpret the object or event. Old bones and fossils are an excellent illustration of this principle. Does this skull of homo erectus "prove" evolution? Does it "disprove" creation? Such "proof" and "disproof" lie in the eye of the beholder, based on the background assumptions by which it is interpreted.

mass **Media in social life**

God on the Net: The Online Marketing of Religion

You want to pray right there at the Holy Land, but you can't leave home? No problem. Buy our special telephone card—now available at your local 7-11. Just record your prayer, and we will broadcast it via the Internet at the site you choose. Press one for the holy site of Jerusalem, press two for the holy site of the Sea of Galilee, press three for the birthplace of Jesus, press four for . . . . (Rhoads 2007)

This service is offered by a company in Israel. No discrimination. Open to Jews and Christians alike. Maybe with expansion plans for Muslims. Maybe to anyone, as long as they can pay $10 for a two-minute card.

Erin Polzin, a 20-year-old college student, listens to a Lutheran worship service on the radio, confesses online, and uses PayPal to tithe. "I don't like getting up early," she says. "This is like going to church without really having to" (Bernstein 2003).

Going to church in your pajamas without even having to comb your hair does have a certain appeal.

And this bothers some religious leaders. They are concerned about what they call the "faithful but lazy." But, then, they always have been. The Internet is just changing the form of the "laziness."

The Internet is doing much more than this. Some say that the Net has put us on the verge of a religious reformation as big as the one set off by Gutenberg's invention of the printing press. This sounds like an exaggeration, but perhaps it is true. We'll see. The Net certainly has become popular for spiritual pursuits (Larsen 2001).

Muslims in France download sermons and join an invisible community of worshippers at virtual mosques. Jews in Sweden type messages that fellow believers in Jerusalem download and insert in the Western Wall. Christians in the United States make digital donations to the Crystal Cathedral. Buddhists in Japan seek enlightenment online. The Internet helps to level the pulpit: On the Net, the leader of a pagan group can compete directly with the Pope.

The Internet is also making religious rebellion easier—and harder for organizations to punish their rebels. Jacques Gaillot is a French Roman Catholic bishop who takes theological positions that upset the church hierarchy. He says that the clergy should marry, women should be ordained, and homosexual partnerships should be blessed. Pope John Paul II exiled him to the Saharan desert of North Africa, a strategy that used to work well to silence dissidents. With our new navigability of space and time, however, in his remote outpost Gaillot logs onto the Internet, where he preaches to a virtual congregation via Real Audio (Huffstutter 1998; Williams 2003).

The Net poses spiritual risks, too. There's always the chance that while you are surfing for religious answers, you'll come across one of those ubiquitous porn sites. But not if you are in the Philippines and using its largest Internet service provider (Sindayen 2001). It is run by the Catholic Bishops' Conference. If someone gives in to temptation and tries to tap into one of the forbidden destinations, up pops this message: "Thank God you're not able to access that bad site."

No one knows the outcome, but the times, they are a-changin'. Because of the Net, we now have:

Churches that exist only in cyber-space

The Internet—and a credit card—can connect believers to holy sites, where prayers can be written out and placed. Shown here is a prayer being inserted in the Western Wall, the last remnant of the Jewish Second Temple, which was destroyed by the Romans in 70 A.D.

Chat rooms directed by rabbis, priests, ministers, imams, and leaders of witchcraft

Online donations by credit card and Internet pay providers

Online counseling for spiritual problems

E-mailing of prayers

A virtual church in which you transform yourself into a computer image. You can direct your computer character to walk around the virtual church, to talk to other computer images if you are bored, or if you are there for religious purposes, to kneel and pray (Feder 2004).

for your Consideration

Do you think that virtual religion can satisfy people's religious needs? How can it replace the warm embrace of fellow believers? Can it bring comfort to someone who is grieving for a loved one?

We are gazing into the future. How do you think this new medium will affect our religious lives? How do you think it might change religion?

Summary *and* Review

What Is Religion?

Durkheim identified three essential characteristics of religion: beliefs that set the **sacred** apart from the **profane, rituals**, and a moral community (a **church**). P. 526.

The Functionalist Perspective

What are the functions and dysfunctions of religion?

Among the functions of religion are answering questions about ultimate meaning, providing emotional comfort, social solidarity, guidelines for everyday life, social control, adaptation, support for the government, and fostering social change. Non-religious groups or activities that provide these functions are called **functional equivalents** of religion. Among the dysfunctions of religion are religious persecution and war and terrorism. Pp. 527–530.

The Symbolic Interactionist Perspective

What aspects of religion do symbolic interactionists study?

Symbolic interactionists focus on the meanings of religion for its followers. They examine religious symbols, rituals, beliefs, **religious experiences,** and the sense of community that religion provides. Pp. 530–533.

The Conflict Perspective

What aspects of religion do conflict theorists study?

Conflict theorists examine the relationship of religion to social inequalities, especially how religion reinforces a society's stratification system. Pp. 533–534.

Religion and the Spirit of Capitalism

What does the spirit of capitalism have to do with religion?

Max Weber saw religion as a primary source of social change. He analyzed how Protestantism gave rise to the **Protestant ethic,** which stimulated what he called the **spirit of capitalism.** The result was capitalism, which transformed society. Pp. 535–536.

The World's Major Religions

What are the world's major religions?

Judaism, Christianity, and Islam, all **monotheistic** religions, can be traced to the same Old Testament roots. Hinduism, the chief religion of India, has no specific founder, but Judaism (Abraham), Christianity (Jesus), Islam (Muhammad), Buddhism (Gautama), and Confucianism (K'ung Fu-tsu) do. Specific teachings and history of these six religions are reviewed in the text. Pp. 536–541.

Types of Religious Groups

What types of religious groups are there?

Sociologists divide religious groups into cults, sects, churches, and ecclesias. All religions began as **cults.** Those that survive tend to develop into **sects** and eventually into **churches.** Sects, often led by **charismatic leaders,** are unstable. Some are perceived as threats and are persecuted by the state. **Ecclesias,** or state religions, are rare. Pp. 541–545.

Religion in the United States

What are the main characteristics of religion in the United States?

Membership varies by social class and race-ethnicity. The major characteristics are diversity, pluralism and freedom, competition, commitment, toleration, a fundamentalist revival, and the electronic church. Pp. 545–549.

What is the connection between secularization of religion and the splintering of churches?

Secularization of religion, a change in a religion's focus from spiritual matters to concerns of "this world," is the key to understanding why churches divide. Basically, as a cult or sect changes to accommodate its members' upward social class mobility, it changes into a church. Left dissatisfied are members who are not upwardly mobile. They tend to splinter off and form a new cult or sect, and the cycle repeats itself. Cultures permeated by religion also secularize. This, too, leaves many people dissatisfied and promotes social change. Pp. 549–551.

The Future of Religion

Although industrialization led to the **secularization of culture,** this did not spell the end of religion, as many social analysts assumed it would. Because science cannot answer questions about ultimate meaning, the existence of God or an afterlife, or provide guidelines for morality, the need for religion will remain. In any foreseeable future, religion will prosper. The Internet is likely to have far-reaching consequences on religion. Pp. 552–553.

Thinking Critically
about Chapter 18

1. Since 9/11, many people have wondered how anyone can use religion to defend or promote terrorism. How does the Down-to-Earth Sociology box on terrorism and the mind of God on page 541 help to answer this question? How do the analyses of groupthink in Chapter 6 (pages 175–176) and dehumanization in Chapter 15 (pages 449–450) fit into your analysis?

2. How has secularization affected religion and culture in the United States (or of your country of birth)?

3. Why is religion likely to remain a strong feature of U.S. life—and remain strong in people's lives around the globe?

Additional Resources

What can you use MySocLab for? www.mysoclab.com

- **Study and Review:** Pre- and Post-Tests, Practice Tests, Flash Cards, Individualized Study Plans.
- **Current Events:** *Sociology in the News,* the daily *New York Times,* and more.

- **Research and Writing:** *Research Navigator, Writing About Sociology,* and more,

Where Can I Read More on This Topic?

Suggested readings for this chapter are listed at the back of this book.

CHAPTER 19

Medicine and Health

Jacob Lawrence, *Harlem Hospital*, 1953

I decided that it was not enough to just study the homeless—I had to help them. I learned that a homeless shelter in St. Louis, just across the river from where I was teaching, was going to help poor people save on utilities by installing free wood stoves in their homes. When their utilities are cut off, the next step is eviction and being forced onto the streets. It wasn't exactly applied sociology, but I volunteered.

I was a little anxious about the coming training session on how to install stoves, as I had never done anything like this. Sociology hadn't trained me to be "handy with my hands," but with the encouragement of a friend, I decided to participate. As I entered the homeless shelter on that Saturday morning, I found the building in semi-darkness. "They must be saving on electricity," I thought. Then I was greeted with an unnerving scene. Two police officers were chasing a naked man, who was running through the halls. They caught him. I watched as the elderly

He was crawling under cars at a traffic light— and they let him out in two days.

man, looking confused, struggled to put on his clothing. From the police, I learned that this man had ripped the wires out of the shelter's main electrical box; that was why there were no lights on.

I asked the officers where they were going to take the man, and they replied, "To Malcolm Bliss" (the state hospital). When I said, "I guess he'll be in there for quite a while," they replied, "Probably just a day or two. We picked him up last week—he was crawling under cars at a traffic light—and they let him out in two days."

The police then explained that one must be a danger to others or to oneself in order to be admitted to the hospital as a long-term patient. Visualizing this old man crawling under stopped cars at an intersection, and considering how he had risked electrocution by ripping out the electrical wires with his bare hands, I marveled at the definition of "danger" that the psychiatrists must be using.

Sociology and the Study of Medicine and Health

▌▌ ▞▞ ▙▙ This incident points to a severe problem in the delivery of medical care in the United States. In this chapter, we will examine why the poor often receive second-rate medical care and, in some instances, abysmal treatment. We'll also look at how skyrocketing costs have created ethical dilemmas such as discharging patients from hospitals before they are well and whether medical care should be rationed.

As we consider these issues, the role of sociology in studying **medicine**—a society's standard ways of dealing with illness and injury—will become apparent. For example, because medicine in the United States is a profession, a bureaucracy, and a big business, sociologists study how it is influenced by self-regulation, the bureaucratic structure, and the profit motive. Sociologists also study how illness and health are much more than biological matters—how, for example, they are related to cultural beliefs, lifestyle, and social class. Because of these emphases, the sociology of medicine is one of the applied fields of sociology. Many medical schools and even hospitals have sociologists on their staffs.

The Symbolic Interactionist Perspective

▌▌ ▞▞ ▙▙ Let's begin, then, by examining how culture influences health and illness. This takes us to the heart of the symbolic interactionist perspective.

The Role of Culture in Defining Health and Illness

Suppose that one morning you look in the mirror and you see strange blotches covering your face and chest. Hoping against hope that it is not serious, you rush to a doctor. If the doctor said that you had "dyschromic spirochetosis," your fears would be confirmed.

Now, wouldn't everyone around the world draw the conclusion that your spots are symptoms of a disease? No, not everybody. In one South American tribe, this skin condition is so common that the few individuals who *aren't* spotted are seen as the unhealthy ones. They are even excluded from marriage because they are "sick" (Ackernecht 1947; Zola 1983).

Consider mental "illness" and mental "health." People aren't automatically "crazy" because they do certain things. Rather, they are defined as "crazy" or "normal" according to cultural guidelines. If an American talks aloud to spirits that no one else can see or hear, he or she is likely to be defined as insane—and, for everyone's good, locked up in a mental hospital. In some tribal societies, in contrast, someone who talks to invisible spirits might be honored for being in close contact with the spiritual world—and, for everyone's good, be declared a **shaman,** or spiritual intermediary. The shaman would then diagnose and treat medical problems.

"Sickness" and "health," then, are not absolutes, as we might suppose. Rather, they are matters of cultural definition. Around the world, each culture provides guidelines that its people use to determine whether they are "healthy" or "sick."

The Components of Health

Back in 1941, international "health experts" identified three components of **health:** physical, mental, and social (World Health Organization 1946). They missed the focus of our previous chapter, however, and I have added a spiritual component to Figure 19.1. Even the dimensions of health, then, are subject to debate. As discussed in the Down-to-Earth Sociology box on the next page, researchers are only now beginning to unravel these interconnections.

Even if we were to agree on the components of health, we would still be left with the question of what makes someone physically, mentally, socially, or spiritually healthy. Again, as symbolic interactionists stress, these are not objective matters. Rather, what is considered "health" or "illness" varies from culture to culture, and, in a pluralistic society, even from group to group.

We define health and illness according to our culture. If almost everyone in a village had this skin disease, the villagers might consider it normal—and those without it the unhealthy ones. I photographed this infant in a jungle village in Orissa, India, so remote that it could be reached only by following a foot path.

medicine one of the social institutions that sociologists study; a society's organized ways of dealing with sickness and injury

shaman the healing specialist of a tribe who attempts to control the spirits thought to cause a disease or injury; commonly called a witch doctor

health a human condition measured by four components: physical, mental, social, and spiritual

"Cry Baby! Cry Baby!": Childhood Social Experiences and Adult Physical Health

In Chapter 3 (pages 70–72), we discussed how our self-concept arises through our interactions with others. But what if those interactions are negative? Then we learn negative views of the self, and we can end up plagued with self-blame and self-doubt. We can also learn to dislike and distrust others. And all of this can affect our physical health.

In our discussion of the self-concept in Chapter 3, we took a brief look at extreme social isolation, such as that experienced by Isabelle and Genie. It is easy to see how extreme cases of isolation can affect people. But most social isolation is much milder than this. I'm sure you are familiar with children who don't seem to fit in. Some children feel rejected by others and spend a lot of time alone in their rooms, trying to find satisfaction in solitary activities. Some kids are teased persistently by their peers—some even ridiculed by their own families.

Some of these children remain loners after they grow up, but most probably shrug off their experiences, fit in okay with other adults who had more fortunate childhoods, and have no negative after-effects on their lives. The surface, at least, often looks like this. Social isolation during childhood, however, has unexpected hidden effects in adulthood.

Childhood events can have surprising consequences for later life. Kids who are picked on a lot and those who are less integrated have more health problems as adults.

Researchers followed a group of about 1,000 children from birth to age 26. (They are still studying them, and this is the latest report.) The researchers took into account (controlled for) factors that are known to lead to health problems, such as being overweight, doing little exercise, smoking, abusing alcohol, and even experiencing stressful life events. After controlling for such health-damaging factors, the researchers found this: The milder types of social isolation in childhood lead to poorer adult health. The adults who had been more socially isolated during childhood had higher blood pressure and higher cholesterol levels (Caspi et al. 2006). As the researchers continue to monitor these adults' health, they are likely to find more heart attacks, strokes, perhaps even somewhat shorter lifespans.

for your Consideration

People are integrated whole units, not isolated components. Mental health is related to physical health, physical health affects mental health, and social experiences affect both mental and physical health. If you were to do research on this topic, what other aspects of social behavior and health would you explore?

As with religion in the previous chapter, then, the concern of sociologists is not to define "true" health or "true" illness. Instead, it is to analyze how people's experiences affect their health, the effects that people's ideas about health and illness have on their lives, and even the ways in which people determine that they are sick.

The Functionalist Perspective

Functionalists begin with an obvious point: If society is to function well, its people need to be healthy enough to perform their normal roles. This means that societies must set up ways to control sickness. One way they do this is to develop a system of medical care. Another way is to make rules that help keep too many people from "being sick." Let's look at how this works.

The Sick Role

Do you remember when your throat began to hurt, and when your mom or dad took your temperature the thermometer registered 102°F? Your parents took you to the doctor, and despite your protests that tomorrow was the first day of summer vacation (or some other important event), you had to spend the next three days in bed taking medicine.

Figure 19.1 **A Continuum of Health and Illness**

Health
Excellent Functioning

PHYSICAL
MENTAL
SOCIAL
SPIRITUAL

Poor Functioning
Illness

Your parents forced you to play what sociologists call the "sick role." What do they mean by this term?

Elements of the Sick Role   Talcott Parsons, the functionalist who first analyzed the **sick role,** pointed out that it has four elements—you are not held responsible for being sick, you are exempt from normal responsibilities, you don't like the role, and you will get competent help so you can return to your routines. People who seek approved help are given sympathy and encouragement; those who do not are given the cold shoulder. People who don't get competent help are considered responsible for being sick, are refused the right to claim sympathy from others, and are denied permission to be excused from their normal routines. They are considered to be wrongfully claiming the sick role.

Ambiguity in the Sick Role   Instead of a fever of 102°F, suppose that the thermometer registers 99.5°F. Do you then "become" sick—or not? That is, do you decide to claim the sick role? Because most instances of illness are not as clear-cut as, say, a limb fracture, decisions to claim the sick role often are based more on social considerations than on physical conditions. Let's also suppose that you are facing a midterm, you are unprepared for it, and you are allowed to make up the test if you are ill. The more you think about the test, the worse you are likely to feel—which makes the need to claim the sick role seem more legitimate. Now assume that the thermometer still shows 99.5, but you have no test and your friends are coming over to take you out to celebrate your twenty-first birthday. You are not likely to play the sick role. Note that in both cases your physical condition is the same.

Gatekeepers to the Sick Role   For children, parents are the primary gatekeepers to the sick role. That is, parents decide whether children's symptoms are sufficient to legitimize their claim that they are sick. Before parents call the school to excuse a child from class, they decide whether the child is faking or has genuine symptoms. If they determine that the symptoms are real, then they decide if the symptoms are serious enough to keep the child home from school, or even severe enough to take the child to a doctor. For adults, the gatekeepers to the sick role are physicians. Adults can bypass the gatekeeper for short periods, but employers will eventually insist on a "doctor's excuse." This can come in such forms as a "doctor's appointment" or insurance forms signed by the doctor. In some instances, company doctors will examine the claims of their workers' private physicians. In sociological terms, these are ways of getting permission to play the sick role.

Gender Differences in the Sick Role   Women are more willing than men to claim the sick role when they don't feel well. They go to doctors more frequently than men, and they are hospitalized more often than men (*Statistical Abstract* 2007:Tables 156, 166). Apparently, the sick role does not match the *macho* image that most boys and men try to project. Most men try to follow the cultural ideal that they should be strong, keep pain to themselves, and "tough it out." The woman's model, in contrast, is more likely to involve sharing feelings and seeking help from others, characteristics that are compatible with the sick role.

The Conflict Perspective

As we stressed in earlier chapters, the primary focus of the conflict perspective is people's struggle over scarce resources. Health care is one of those resources. Let's first take a global perspective on medical care and then, turning our attention to the United States, we will analyze how one group secured a monopoly on U.S. health care.

Effects of Global Stratification on Health Care

In Chapter 9 (pages 258–259), we saw how the first nations to industrialize obtained the economic and military power that brought them riches and allowed them to dominate other nations. This eventually led to the global stratification of medical care, a matter of life and death for people around the world. For example, open heart surgery has become routine in the Most Industrialized Nations. The Least Industrialized Nations, in contrast,

sick role a social role that excuses people from normal obligations because they are sick or injured, while at the same time expecting them to seek competent help and cooperate in getting well cannot afford the technology that open heart surgery requires. The photo on this page goes a long way toward illustrating why. So it is with AIDS. In the United States and other rich nations, costly medicines have extended the lives of those who suffer from AIDS. Most people with AIDS in the Least Industrialized Nations can't afford these medicines. For them, AIDS is a death sentence.

Life expectancy and infant mortality rates also tell the story. Most people in the industrialized world can expect to live to about age 75, but *most* people in Afghanistan, Nigeria, and South Africa don't even make it to 50. Look at Figure 19.2, which shows countries in which fewer than 7 of every 1,000 babies die before they are a year old. Then consider this: Afghanistan's infant mortality rate of 163 is *fifty* times higher than Japan's infant mortality rate (*Statistical Abstract* 2007:Table 1310).

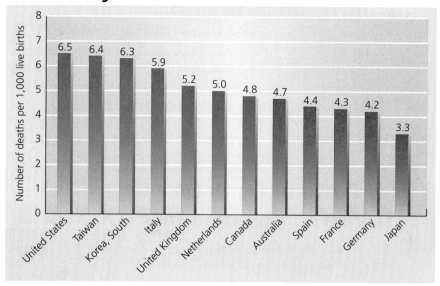

Figure 19.2 How Many Babies Die Before Their First Birthday?

Note: There are other countries that have an infant mortality rate below that of the United States. Belgium, Czech Republic, and Greece likely have rates lower than that of the United States, but they were dropped from this edition of the source. Infant mortality is the number of babies that die before their first birthday, per 1,000 live births.

Source: By the author. Based on *Statistical Abstract* 2007:Table 1310.

Global stratification even helps to determine what diseases we get. Suppose that you had been born in a Least Industrialized Nation located in the tropics. During your much shorter life, you would face four major causes of illness and death: malaria (from mosquitoes), internal parasites (from contaminated water), diarrhea (from food and soil contaminated with human feces), and malnutrition. You would not face heart disease and cancer, for they are "luxury" diseases; that is, they are part of the industrialized world, where people live long enough to get them. As nations industrialize, health care and nutrition improve, and their citizens live longer. The diseases that used to be their primary killers decline, and residents begin to worry about cancer and heart attacks instead.

There is also the matter of social stratification *within* the Least Industrialized Nations. Many diseases that ravage the poor people in these countries could be brought under control if more money were spent on public health. Cheap drugs can prevent malaria, while safer water supplies and higher food production would go a long way toward eliminating the other major killers. The meager funds that these countries have at their disposal are not spent this way, however. Instead, having garnered the lion's share of the country's resources, the elite lavish it on themselves. For their own medical treatment, they even send a few students to top medical schools in the West. This gives them access to advanced technology—from X-rays to life support systems. The poor of these nations, in contrast, go without even basic medical services and continue to die at an early age.

This woman has just given birth in a hospital in Badakshan, Afghanistan, a province that has the highest mortality rate recorded in human history: Sixty-four percent of women of reproductive age have died. If you examine this photo carefully, you probably can pinpoint part of the reasons for these deaths.

Before turning to medical care in the United States, let's consider the international black market in human organs. This stunning example of the inequality that arises from global stratification is the topic of the Down-to-Earth Sociology box below.

Establishing a Monopoly on U.S. Health Care

Let's turn our focus to medicine in the United States. How did medicine become the largest business in the entire country? And how did it become the country's only legal monopoly? To find the answers, we need to understand how medicine became professionalized.

The Professionalization of Medicine   Imagine that you are living in the American colonies in the 1700s and you want to become a physician. Will entrance exams and

Down-to-Earth Sociology

"Where Did You Get That New Liver?" The International Black Market in Human Body Parts

THE ABILITY TO TRANSPLANT LIVERS, lungs, kidneys, and even hearts is one of the marvels of modern medicine. Advanced medical technology and the skills of surgeons have given life to people who just a short time ago were doomed to die.

But where do those organs come from?

You know about organ donors. You might even have checked a box on your driver's license that says it is okay for medical personnel to take your organs if you die in a car accident. Hospitals routinely ask dying patients—or their relatives—for permission to harvest body parts from the deceased.

But do you know about the international black market in human organs?

In Chapter 9, we discussed some of the horrible conditions that people face in the Least Industrialized Nations. It is important to keep these conditions in mind to understand the "donation" of body parts from people in these countries. Jose da Silva, for example, was one of 23 children of a woman in Brazil who sold her flesh to survive. Locked in his memory is the morning when seven children shared a single egg for breakfast.

As an adult, da Silva works for the Brazilian minimum wage, making $80 a month. When he heard that he could sell a kidney for $6,000, it was like a dream come true. This is what he would make in six years of hard work.

Da Silva has the scar to show where a kidney and rib were removed.

The story of how da Silva's kidney became part of an international black market in human organs stretches back to a woman in Brooklyn who had been on dialysis for 15 years. She had also been on two organ recipient waiting lists for 7

A human kidney to be transplanted.

years—along with another 60,000 Americans. The woman's health was deteriorating, and her doctors told her that if she wanted to live she should "get a kidney any way you can."

Selling human organs is illegal in the United States, but the woman's husband heard about a group in Israel that traffics in human organs. He had relatives in Tel Aviv who made contact with them. This group dealt with middlemen in Brazil. After da Silva agreed to sell one of his kidneys, he was flown to South Africa, where he was lodged in a safe house. The U.S. woman also flew to South Africa, where she was put up at a beach house.

Da Silva had to sign a statement that the woman was his cousin.

The transplant took place in a hospital. The South African doctors kept in contact with the woman's U.S. doctors, informing them of the woman's progress.

The woman paid $60,000 for da Silva's kidney. After da Silva was paid $6,000, the rest of the money went to the people who made the arrangements.

When word got out, there was such a rush of Brazil's poor wanting to sell their kidneys—and to get a free trip to South Africa, where they expected to see lions, giraffes, and elephants—that the price dropped to $3,000.

for your Consideration

What is wrong with people selling their body parts, if they want to? Aren't poor people better off with one kidney and six years of extra earnings to buy a home, start a business, get out of debt, or take care of their families than with two kidneys and no such opportunities?

Source: Based on Rohter 2004.

required courses be difficult? Not really. You won't have any. You won't even need *any* formal education, for there is neither licensing nor medical school. You can simply ask a physician to train you. In return for the opportunity to learn, you'll be his assistant and help him with menial tasks. When *you* think that you have learned enough, you'll hang out a shingle and proclaim yourself a doctor. The process was similar to how people become automobile mechanics today. In fact, you can even skip the apprenticeship if you wish, and simply hang out your shingle—just like a mechanic. If you can convince people you are good, you'll make a living. If not, you'll have to turn to something else.

In the 1800s, things began to change. A few medical schools opened, and there was some licensing of physicians. The medical schools of this period were like religions are today: They competed for clients and made different claims to the truth. One medical school would teach a particular idea about what caused illness and how to treat it, while another medical school would teach something else. Training was short, and often not even a high school diploma was required. There was no clinical training, and lectures went unchanged from year to year. The medical school at Harvard University took only two school years to complete—and the school year lasted only four months (Starr 1982; Rosenberg 1987; Riessman 1994).

Then came the 1900s. By 1906, the United States had 160 medical schools. The Carnegie Foundation asked Abraham Flexner, an educator, to evaluate them. Even the most inadequate schools opened their doors to Flexner, for they thought that gifts from the Carnegie Foundation would follow (Rodash 1982). In some schools, the laboratories consisted only of "a few vagrant test tubes squirreled away in a cigar box." Other schools had libraries with no books. Flexner advised that to raise standards, philanthropies should fund the most promising schools. They did, and the schools that were funded upgraded their facilities and were able to attract more capable faculty and students. In the face of higher standards and greater competition, most of the other schools had to close their doors.

The Flexner report (1910) led to the **professionalization of medicine.** When sociologists use the term *profession,* they mean something quite specific. What happened was that physicians began to (1) undergo a rigorous education; (2) claim a theoretical understanding of illness; (3) regulate themselves; (4) assert that they were performing a service for society (rather than just following self-interest); and (5) take authority over clients (Goode 1960; Freidson 2001).

The Monopoly of Medicine When medicine became a profession, it also became a monopoly, and this is the key to understanding our current situation. The group that gained control over U.S. medicine set itself up as *the* medical establishment. This group was able to get laws passed that restricted medical licensing only to graduates of schools they controlled. By controlling the education and licensing of physicians, the medical establishment silenced most competing philosophies of medicine. The men who took charge of medicine also either refused to admit women to medical schools or severely limited their enrollment. It wasn't until 1915 that the American Medical Association (AMA) allowed women members (Campbell and McCammon 2005).

Eliminating the competition paved the way for medicine to become big business. The monopoly was so thorough that by law only an approved group—a sort of priesthood of medicine—was allowed to diagnose and treat medical problems. Only they knew what was right for people's health. Only they could scribble the secret language (Latin) on pieces of parchment (prescription forms) for translators (pharmacists) to decipher (Miner 1956/2007). This group of men became so powerful that it was even able to take childbirth away from midwives—the focus of the Down-to-Earth Sociology box on the next page.

This approach, called **fee-for-service** (payment to a physician in exchange for diagnosis and treatment), usually went unquestioned. Then, as monopolies do, the medical monopoly drove up the price of health care. This led to a public outcry: Because the poor couldn't afford medical treatment, the government should pay for it. The AMA fought against proposals for the government funding of medical care. Physicians were convinced that this would "socialize" medicine—that it would eliminate the fee-for-service system and turn doctors into government employees.

In the 1960s, proponents of government funding won. Medicaid (government-paid medical care for the poor) and Medicare (government-paid medical care for the elderly)

professionalization of medicine the development of medicine into a specialty in which education becomes rigorous, and in which physicians claim a theoretical understanding of illness, regulate themselves, claim to be doing a service to society (rather than just following self-interest), and take authority over clients

fee-for-service payment to a physician to diagnose and treat a patient's medical problems

Down-to-Earth Sociology

To Establish a Monopoly, Eliminate Your Competition: Physicians Versus Midwives

THE HISTORY OF MIDWIFERY helps us to understand the professionalization of medicine and gives us insight into how the U.S. medical establishment came about. In the United States, as in Europe and elsewhere, pregnancy and childbirth were considered natural events. Midwives delivered babies because women were thought best equipped to help other women with childbirth. Some midwives were trained; others were neighborhood women who had experience in childbirth. In many European countries, midwives were licensed by the state—as they still are.

Physicians wanted to expand their business, and taking over the management of childbirth was one way to do it. They encountered two major obstacles, however. The first you can expect, the midwives, who didn't want physicians to cut into their business. The second was ignorance. Almost all physicians were men, and they knew nothing about delivering babies. It was even considered indecent for a man to know much about pregnancy, and unheard of for a man to help a woman give birth.

Some physicians bribed midwives to sneak them into the bedrooms where women were giving birth. To say "sneaked" is no exaggeration, for they crawled on their hands and knees so that the mother-to-be wouldn't know a man that was present. Most physicians, however, weren't fortunate enough to find such cooperative midwives, and they trained with mannequins. Eventually, physicians were allowed to be present at childbirths, but this was still considered indecent, as this meant that a man who was not a woman's husband might see the woman's private parts. To prevent this, the men had to fumble blindly under a sheet in a darkened room, their head decorously turned aside.

As physicians gained political power, they launched a ruthless campaign against their competitors, the midwives. They attacked

This baby was just delivered in a birthing pool. The midwife is about to check the baby's heartbeat.

them as "dirty, ignorant, and incompetent," even calling them a "menace to the health of the community." After physicians formed their union, the American Medical Association, they persuaded many states to pass laws that made it illegal for anyone but physicians to deliver babies. Some states, however, continue to allow nurse-midwives to practice. Even today, this struggle is not over; nurse-midwives and physicians sometimes still clash over who has the right to deliver babies.

Conflict theorists emphasize that this was a gender struggle—men sought to take control over what had been women's work. They stress that the men used their political connections to expand their business. Symbolic interactionists, without denying the political aspect, stress how the physicians manipulated symbols to win this sruggle. They point to the information campaign that physicians launched to eliminate midwives, how they convinced the public that pregnancy and childbirth were not natural processes, but medical conditions that required the assistance of an able man. This new definition—which flew in the face of all human history of women helping women to have babies—turned childbirth into "men's work." When this happened, the prestige of the work went up—and so did the price.

for your Consideration

As mentioned in Chapter 11, a principle of gender is that activities that are associated with women are given lower prestige than the activities that are associated with men. As illustrated here, managing childbirth is an example. As women come to dominate medicine, which seems likely, do you think the prestige of practicing medicine will decline? How about the income of physicians?

Sources: Wertz and Wertz 1981; Rodash 1982; Rothman 1994; Liptak 2006; Phillips 2007.

were established. Physicians' fears proved groundless. Instead of leading to the socialization of medicine, these programs provided millions of new customers. People who previously could not afford medical services now had their medical expenses paid by the government. As Figure 13.9 on page 386 illustrates, these costly programs have put billions of dollars into physicians' pockets.

From its humble origins, medicine has grown into the largest business in the United States. This business consists not only of physicians but also of nurses; physician assistants; hospital personnel; pharmacists; insurance companies; corporations that own hospitals and nursing homes; and the huge research, manufacturing, and sales force that lies behind the drug industry. The medical monopoly is powerful. To protect its interests, it lobbies all state legislatures and the U.S. Congress.

Historical Patterns of Health

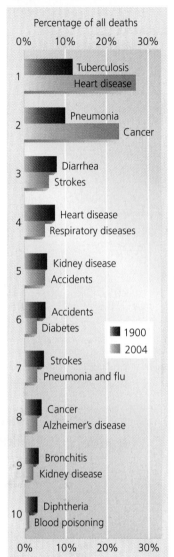

Figure 19.3 The Top Ten Causes of Death in the United States, 1900 and 2004

Let's look at how the patterns of health and illness in the United States have changed. This will take us into the field of **epidemiology,** the study of how medical disorders are distributed throughout a population.

Physical Health

Leading Causes of Death   One way to see how the physical health of Americans has changed is to compare the leading causes of death in two time periods. To get an idea of how dramatic this change is, look at Figure 19.3. Note that four of the leading causes of death in 1900 don't even appear on today's list. Heart disease and cancer, which placed fourth and eighth in 1900, have now jumped to the top of the list, while tuberculosis and diarrhea, which were the number one and number three killers in 1900, don't even show up in today's top ten. Similarly, diabetes and Alzheimer's disease didn't make the top ten in 1900, but they do now. These shifts indicate that extensive changes have occurred in society. Disease and death, then, are not only biological events. They are also *social* indicators, following the contours of social change.

Were Americans Healthier in the Past?   A second way to see how the physical health of Americans has changed is to ask if they are healthier—or sicker—than they used to be. This question brings us face to face with the definitional problem discussed earlier. "Healthy" by whose standards? An additional problem is that many of today's diseases, such as Alzheimer's, went unrecognized in the past. One way around these problems is to look at mortality rates. If Americans used to live longer, we can assume they were healthier. Because most people today live longer than their ancestors, however, we can conclude that contemporary Americans are healthier.

Some may think that this conclusion flies in the face of our polluted air and water—and of our high rates of heart disease and cancer, as shown in Figure 19.3. And it does. Sometimes older people say, "When I was a kid, hardly anyone died from cancer, and now it seems almost everyone does." What they say is true, but what they overlook is that most cancers strike older people, so when life expectancy is shorter, fewer people die from cancer. Also, in the past, most cancer went unrecognized. People were simply said to have died of "old age" or "heart failure."

Mental Health

When it comes to mental health, we have no way to make good comparisons with earlier times. Some people picture an idyllic past: There was little mental illness because almost everyone grew up with two loving parents, married for life, and lived in harmony in close-knit families with everyone helping one another. But do we have any facts? We need solid measures of mental illness or mental health, not stories of how things used to be that make current life look worse than it is (Coontz 2000). Such an idyllic past never existed—except in people's imagination. All groups have their share of mental problems—and beliefs that mental illness is worse today represent a perception, not measured reality. Such perceptions may be true, of course, but the *opposite* could also be true. Since we don't even know how much mental illness there is today (Scheff 1999), we certainly can't judge how much there was in the past.

Issues in Health Care

Let's turn to issues in health care in the United States.

Medical Care: A Right or a Commodity?

A primary controversy in the United States is whether medical care is a right or a commodity—something offered for sale. If medical care is a right, then all citizens should have access to good medical care. If medical care is a commodity, then, as with automobiles and clothing, the rich will have access to one type of care, and the poor to another.

epidemiology the study of disease and disability patterns in a population

Sources: By the author. Based on National Center for Health Statistics; *Statistical Abstract* 2007:Table 109.

Figure 19.4 The Soaring Cost of Medical Care: What the Average American Pays Each Year

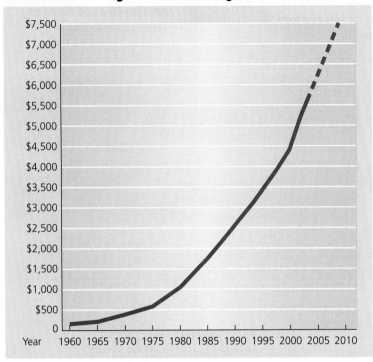

Note: This is the national medical bill divided by the total population. The amount the average American pays out of pocket and by insurance is half this amount.

Source: By the author. Based on *Statistical Abstract* 2007:Table 123, and earlier years.

— STATEMENT —

Grande Ronde Hospital Association

LA GRANDE, OREGON

7-21-62
DATE

Mr.
1902 Washington
La Grande, Ore.

RE: Martha E

DATE ADMITTED 7-18-62 TO 7-21-62 ROOM 220

Balance Due	
General Care 3 days @ $ 18.00	54.00
Operating Room circumcision	10.00
Anesthetic	2.50
Medicines	3.10
Surgical Dressings	2.25
Delivery Room	20.00
Laboratory	3.00
X-Ray	
Oxygen	
Treatments	
Special Drugs	
Nursery	18.00
Bracelet	1.00
total	113.85

Accounts not paid when due are subject to interest charge.

Phrasing the matter this way, I'm sure that you know the answer—that medical care in the United States is *not* the right of citizens. Medical care is a commodity that is sold at the highest price. Those who can afford it can buy better quality health care; those who can't afford it have to settle for less. The many attempts to replace this commodity system with some form of national medical care have been futile.

Related to this issue is the skyrocketing cost of medical care. As shown in Figure 19.4, in 1960, health care cost the average American $150 a year. Today, the total has jumped to $5,900. Consider this: In 1960, a 17-inch black-and-white television cost the same as the average amount people spent on medical care, about $150. If the cost of televisions had risen at the same rate as the cost of health care, a *17-inch black-and-white* television would now cost about $5,900. The reasons for this jump in medical costs include the growing numbers of elderly, our new medical technology, and more expensive malpractice insurance. To try to keep this comparison accurate, since medical care now includes advanced technology, assume that this 17-inch television is color and digital—but it still costs $5,900.

It is difficult to grasp how reasonable medical costs used to be. Look at the hospital bill reproduced on this page. This is the entire amount billed by the private hospital for the delivery of a child. The $118.85 included 3 days stay for the mother and child, the delivery room, the anesthetic, even the circumcision.

Social Inequality

Recall the opening vignette—about the naked man in the homeless shelter who was being taken to the state mental hospital. This event lays bare our **two-tier system of medical care**. A middle-class or rich person who had mental problems would visit a private psychiatrist, not be sent to a state mental hospital—or to jail, where poor people with mental illnesses often end up. Of course, he or she would not have been in that shelter in the first place. Because health care is a commodity—and, today, a costly one—those who can afford it buy superior health care, while, for the most part, the poor get leftovers. In short, medical care is like automobiles—new sports cars for the wealthy and worn out used cars for the poor.

Since 1939, sociologists have found what they call "an inverse correlation between mental problems and social class"; that is, the lower the social class, the more mental problems there are. This finding has been confirmed in numerous studies (Faris and Dunham 1939; Srole et al. 1978; National Center for Health Statistics 2004; Schoenborn 2004). It is not difficult to understand why people in the lower social classes have greater mental problems, for they bear the many stresses that poverty thrusts on them. Compared with middle- and upper-class Americans, the poor have less job security, lower wages, and are hounded by bill collectors. They are also more likely to divorce, to be victims of violent crime, and to abuse alcohol. Such conditions deal severe blows to emotional well-being.

These same stresses are also bad for physical health. Unlike the middle and upper classes, however, few poor people have a personal physician, and some of them spend hours waiting in crowded public health clinics. After waiting most of a day, some don't even get to see a doctor; they are simply told to come back the next day (Fialka 1993). When hospitalized, the poor are likely to find themselves in understaffed and underfunded public hospitals, where they are treated by rotating interns who do not know them and do not follow up on their progress.

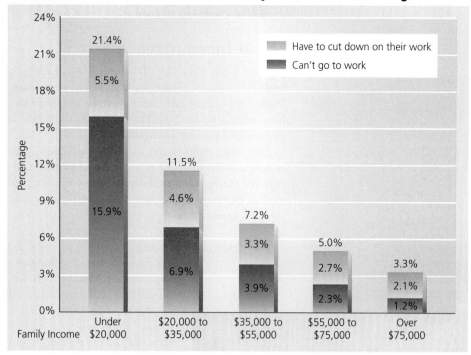

Figure 19.5 Income and Illness: People So Sick That They . . .

Note: These totals refer to families, not to individuals. The first bar means that 15.9 percent of families whose annual incomes are below $20,000 have a family member age 18 or over who is so sick that he or she cannot go to work—not that 15.9 percent of all people whose incomes are below $20,000 are so sick that they cannot go to work. The totals refer to any given day.

Source: By the author. Based on *Vital and Health Statistics,* Series 10, Number 217, December 2003:Table 6.

Figure 19.5 portrays the relationship between income and illness. "Illness" refers to both physical and mental health problems. This is a significant figure, for it illustrates how higher income protects people from illness.

Malpractice Lawsuits and Defensive Medicine

Some analysts have concluded—seriously—that physicians used to kill more patients than they cured. This might be true. Physicians did leave a trail of death behind them. They didn't know about germs, they didn't wash their hands before surgery or childbirth, and their beliefs about the cause of sickness were not exactly helpful. In the 1800s, doctors thought that sickness was caused by "bad fluids." To get rid of these bad fluids, they used four techniques: (1) bleeding (cutting a vein or using leeches to drain out "bad" blood); (2) blistering (applying packs so hot they burned the skin, causing "bad pus" to drain); (3) vomiting (feeding patients liquids that made them vomit up the bad fluids); and (4) purging (giving patients substances that caused diarrhea).

Back then, with such atrocious treatment, there were no medical malpractice suits; but today, with our vastly superior medical care, malpractice suits are common. Why? Previously, the law didn't allow patients to recover damages. The thinking was, "People make mistakes," and that includes doctors. Today, physicians are held to much higher standards—and they are not excused for making mistakes. Malpractice suits are like a sword dangling over their heads, suspended by only a thread. It will fall, but they don't know when. As one anxious physician told me, "I'm looking for something else to do, because medicine is no longer fun. Every time I treat a patient, I wonder if this is the one who is going to turn around and sue me."

To protect themselves, physicians practice **defensive medicine.** They consult with colleagues and order lab tests not because the patient needs them but because the doctors want to leave a paper trail in case they are sued. These consultations and tests—done for the doctor's benefit, not the patient's—are a major reason for the high cost of today's medical bills. To reduce the costs of defensive medicine, the state of Maine created physician

two-tier system of medical care a system of medical care in which the wealthy receive superior medical care and the poor inferior medical care

defensive medicine medical practices done not for the patient's benefit but in order to protect a physician from malpractice suits checklists. If doctors follow them, malpractice suits are dismissed (Felsenthal 1993). Although physicians complain about a "paint-by-numbers" approach to medicine, many prefer this to the threat of lawsuits.

Medical Incompetence

My own father was dying of diabetes. He had a large open sore on his foot that wouldn't heal. Dad lived in Minnesota, and he had been taken to the Mayo Clinic in Rochester. While I was visiting him there—and the last time that I saw him alive—orderlies wheeled him out to X-ray his back. Later, my dad complained that his back hurt because he had to lie for a long time on a hard surface.

Something didn't seem right. Why would they X-ray my Dad's back for either diabetes or a sore on his foot? When I saw the additional pain that my dad was going through, I reported the situation to the head doctor. He examined the records and said that the attending physician had X-rayed the wrong patient. Charts had been bunched together, and my dad's had been pulled instead of the one next to it.

In our era of scientific medicine, the errors made by doctors and nurses are astounding. A surgeon at the University of Washington Medical Center left this stainless steel retractor, resembling a metal ruler, inside a patient.

There are a lot worse cases. A woman entered a hospital because of a problem with her lungs—and her doctor did a hysterectomy. No, I'm not making this up. It happened in New York City (Steinhauer and Fessenden 2001). Another doctor operated on the wrong side of a patient's brain. Yet another removed the wrong kidney—leaving the cancerous one intact. Some physicians operate on the wrong patient altogether (Steinhauer 2001). Although not everyday events, these things do happen.

If a surgeon removes the wrong breast, few would disagree that the patient has the right to sue. But are some malpractice suits unfair? Certainly. Some patients sue doctors for trivial matters, others for matters over which the physician had no control. Despite the rigors of today's medical education, however, medical incompetence is extensive. As the photo on the left shows, doctors even leave tools inside patients.

Consider this stunning statistic: Doctors correctly diagnose their patients' illnesses only 55 percent of the time (McGlynn et al. 2003). In most cases, the misdiagnosis isn't serious, but in many cases it is. The Institute of Medicine reports that mistakes in U.S. hospitals kill 44,000 to 98,000 patients each year. Most medical care takes place in clinics and doctors' offices, not hospitals—so the total is likely to be at least *double* this already huge number (Reisman 2003). *If death from medical errors were an official classification, it would rank as the sixth leading cause of death in the United States* (*Statistical Abstract* 2007:Table 109).

Doctors have developed an interesting term to refer to these needless deaths—and no it isn't "death by incompetence" or "killed by doctors." Instead, they have chosen this innocuous term: "adverse events." (Certainly these deaths and injuries are "adverse events" from the perspective of the patient and family.) The risk of being injured or dying from medical incompetence is so high that some hospitals have taken this unusual step: To prevent surgeons from removing the wrong body part, the doctor makes a mark in ink on the patient's body where the incision is to be made. Then at this point on the patient's body both patient and doctor sign their names in ink.

A leading cause of patient deaths is cross-reactions of prescription drugs. With the many drugs on the market, there is much that doctors don't know about how drugs interact with one another. One solution is to have pharmacists accompany doctors as they make their hospital rounds. When this is done, the number of incidents of incorrectly prescribed medications plummets (Kucukarslan et al. 2003). Some hospitals have doctors enter their prescriptions online. A computer program checks patient records, and a monitor flashes if a doctor tries to prescribe a drug that can interfere with other medications the patient is taking. Even with this safeguard, doctors still blunder. Patients are listed alphabetically in the computer, and some doctors manage to pick the wrong name. Others mistake the number that lists the hospital's inventory of a drug for the dosage that they are supposed to prescribe (Koppel et al. 2005). One wonders how some of these doctors made it through medical school.

The situation is so bad that the Institute of Medicine, which documented the number of patients that die at the hands of doctors each year, made a radical proposal. The Institute recommends that we establish a Federal Center for Patient Safety. All medical deaths and injuries would be reported to the Center. Just as the Federal Aviation Agency investigates each plane crash, the Center would investigate each medical injury and death. Based on the cause it pinpointed, the Center would set up guidelines to reduce similar events. If this proposal were implemented, prospective patients could even check out the hospital they are thinking of using, to see how many people their doctors have injured or killed through incompetence or negligence.

Depersonalization: The Medical Cash Machine

> Mary Duffy, who runs a food service business in San Jose, California, was recovering from surgery. As she was lying in her hospital bed, a group of white-coated strangers came in. Without a word, one of them—a man—leaned over, pulled back her blanket, and stripped her nightgown from her shoulders. He then began to lecture about carcinomas to the group standing around the bed. As the half dozen medical students stared at Mrs. Duffy's naked body, the doctor spoke his first words to Mrs. Duffy, asking, "Have you passed gas yet?" (Carey 2005)

One of the main complaints that patients have about doctors and nurses is **depersonalization.** As was the case with Mrs. Duffy, patients feel as though they are being treated like cases and diseases, not as individuals. Some also get the impression that they are cash machines. The physician who talks to them seems to be impatiently counting minutes and tabulating dollars so that he or she can move on to the next customer and make more money. After all, any extra time spent with a patient is money down the drain.

Some students start medical school with lofty motives, desiring to "treat the whole person." Yet they, too, learn to depersonalize patients. Sociologists Jack Haas and William Shaffir (1993), who did participant observation at McMaster University in Canada, discovered how this happens. As vast amounts of information are thrown at medical students, their feelings for patients become overpowered by the need to be efficient. Consider what this student told the researchers:

> Somebody will say, "Listen to Mrs. Jones's heart. It's just a little thing flubbing on the table." *And you forget about the rest of her* . . . and it helps in learning in the sense that you can go in to a patient, put your stethoscope on the heart, listen to it, and walk out. . . . The advantage is that *you can go in a short time and see a patient, get the important things out of the patient, and leave.* (italics added)

Medical students come to view unconscious patients as opportunities to practice their skills. They view the dying and the newly dead in the same way (Berger et al. 2002). This student's statement to Haas and Shaffir reveals the extent to which patients become objects.

> You don't know the people that are under anesthesia—just practice putting the tube in, and the person wakes up with a sore throat, and well, it's just sort of a part of the procedure. . . . Someone comes in who has croaked (and you say), "Well, come on. Here is a chance to practice your intubation" (inserting a tube in the throat).

Conflict of Interest

> Sandy was surprised when her doctor brought another person with him to her examination. She would have been even more surprised to learn that this other person was a pharmaceutical sales representative who had paid the doctor to be present at the examination. (Petersen 2002)

depersonalization dealing with people as though they were objects; in the case of medical care, as though patients were merely cases and diseases, not people

This representative had paid Sandy's doctor so he could be present and recommend his company's drugs to treat her. Although this representative carried things a little farther than most, drug companies often pay doctors to prescribe their brands of drugs. One doctor received $300,000 for recommending to other doctors that they prescribe a particular drug to their patients (Petersen 2003). Cancer specialists generate *most* of their income by selling drugs. They buy the drugs used for chemotherapy at wholesale prices and charge much higher prices when they administer the drugs to their patients (Abelson 2003). Some surgeons have found another technique to harvest money from patients. They invest in medical supply companies that sell the screws they use in spinal-fusion surgery. The companies charge $1,000 for each screw, a profit of over $900 each (Abelson 2006).

You can see the conflict of interest. Did the doctor use an extra screw in surgery because the patient needed it or because he wanted to get a share of the additional $900 profit? If doctors tell patients to stop chemotherapy when they see that it is not working, their profits stop, but if they continue the treatment, so do their profits. Drug companies give cash and free cruises to exotic resorts to doctors who prescribe their drugs (Harris 2005). How can we know, then, if doctors are selecting drugs based on their patients' best interests—or on the best interest of their own bank accounts?

Medical Fraud

With 2 million Medicare claims filed every day, physicians with Medicare patients are not likely to be audited. Many doctors have not been able to resist the temptation to cheat. The following are not isolated incidents—they are just some of the most outrageous.

> One doctor billed Medicare for multiple services on a patient's eye—the only problem was that the patient was missing that eye (Levy 2003). A dentist charged Medicare for 991 procedures in a single day. In a typical workday, that would come to one every 36 seconds (Levy and Luo 2005). A psychiatrist in California had sex with his patient—and charged Medicaid for the time. (Geis et al. 1995)

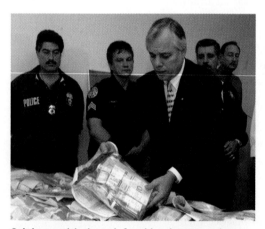

Gaining wealth through fraud has begun to plague the medical profession. In this version, Florida pharmacists gave people cash, instead of medicines, for their prescriptions. They then billed the state for the medications that they never dispensed.

To avoid charges of fraud for billing for surgery that they don't perform, some ingenious doctors pay people to have surgery. They first make sure that the "patients" have good insurance, of course. Then they perform expensive surgery that the patients don't need. One group of doctors paid people to have an operation to stop "sweaty palms." They gave the patients cash or offered them discounts on "tummy tucks" (Pear 2005).

Worse yet is medical fraud that endangers people's lives, like the pharmacist in Kansas City who, although he was worth $10 million, was so driven by greed that he diluted the drugs he sold for patients in chemotherapy (Belluck 2001). Corporations, too, join the infamous. Guidant Corporation, a medical supply manufacturer, had a slight problem: It discovered that its heart devices (defibrillators that are surgically implanted in patients) could short circuit and kill the patient. What do you think the company did? Tell the patients and doctors? No. Instead, they developed a new model that did not have this defect. That makes sense—except that they kept selling the defective model while they developed the new one. Several patients died when their defibrillators short circuited (Meier 2005, 2006).

Then there is Bayer, that household name you trust when you reach for aspirin. Bayer also makes Trasylol, a drug given after heart surgery. Bayer found that its drug had a few slight side affects—it could increase the risk of strokes, kidney damage, heart failure, and death. Did Bayer warn doctors that they might be killing their patients? Not at all. In Bayer's own words, it "mistakenly did not inform" the Federal Drug Administration of the study (Harris 2006). In the same vein that Bayer made its statement, I will assume that the $200 million annual sales of this drug had nothing to do with Bayer making this mistake.

Sexism and Racism in Medicine

In Chapter 11 (page 315), we saw that physicians don't take women's health complaints as seriously as they do those of men. As a result, surgeons operate on women after the women's heart disease has progressed farther, which makes it more likely that the women will die from the disease. This sexism is so subtle that the physicians are not even aware that they are discriminating against women. Some sexism in medicine, in contrast, is blatant. One of the best examples is the bias against women's reproductive organs that we reviewed in Chapter 11 (page 316).

Racism is also an unfortunate part of medical practice. In Chapter 12, we reviewed racism in surgery and in health care after heart attacks. You might want to review these materials on page 342.

The Medicalization of Society

As we have seen, childbirth and women's reproductive organs have come to be defined as medical matters. Sociologists use the term **medicalization** to refer to the process of turning something that was not previously considered a medical issue into a medical matter. "Bad" behavior is an example. If a psychiatric model is followed, crime becomes not willful behavior that should be punished, but a symptom of unresolved mental problems that were created during childhood. These problems need to be treated by doctors. The human body is a favorite target of medicalization. Characteristics that once were taken for granted—such as wrinkles, acne, balding, sagging buttocks and chins, bulging stomachs, and small breasts—have become medical problems, also in need of treatment by physicians.

As usual, the three theoretical perspectives give us contrasting views of the medicalization of such human conditions. Symbolic interactionists would stress that there is nothing inherently medical about wrinkles, acne, balding, sagging chins, and so on. It is a matter of definition: People used to consider such matters as normal problems of life; now they are starting to redefine them as medical problems. Functionalists would stress that the medicalization of such conditions is functional for the medical establishment. It strengthens the medical establishment by broadening its customer base. Conflict sociologists would argue that such medicalization indicates the growing power of the medical establishment: The more conditions of life that physicians can medicalize, the greater their profits and power.

Medically Assisted Suicide

To consider medically assisted suicide takes us face to face with controversial issues that are both disturbing and difficult to resolve. Should doctors be able to write lethal prescriptions for terminally ill patients? Some take the position that this will relieve suffering and help people to die with dignity. Others say that such laws would simply legalize murder. The following Thinking Critically section explores these issues.

Thinking Critically

Should Doctors Be Allowed to Kill Patients?

Except for the name, this is a true story:

> Bill Simpson, in his 70s, had battled leukemia for years. After his spleen was removed, he developed an abdominal abscess. It took another operation to drain it. A week later, the abscess filled, and required more surgery. Again the abscess returned. Simpson began to go in and out of consciousness. His brother-in-law suggested euthanasia. The surgeon injected a lethal dose of morphine into Simpson's intravenous feeding tubes.

At a medical conference in which euthanasia was discussed, a cancer specialist who had treated thousands of patients announced that he had kept count of the patients who had asked

medicalization the transformation of a human condition into a matter to be treated by physicians

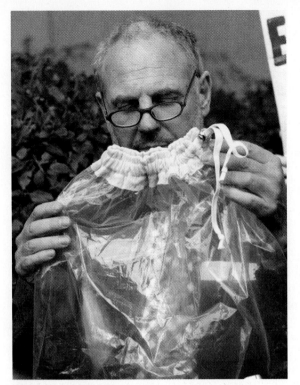

Dr. Philip Nitschke of Brisbane, Australia, a leading proponent of euthanasia, shows the suicide bag he developed. It allows users to suffocate themselves. The bag closes automatically around the neck, typically after the user first takes a sleeping pill.

him to help them die. "There were 127 men and women," he said. Then he added, "And I saw to it that 25 of them got their wish." Thousands of other physicians have done the same (Nuland 1995).

When a doctor ends a patient's life, such as by injecting a lethal drug, it is called *active euthanasia*. To withhold life support (nutrients or liquids) is called *passive euthanasia*. To remove life support, such as disconnecting a patient from oxygen falls somewhere in between. The result, of course, is the same.

Two images seem to dominate the public's ideas of euthanasia: One is of an individual devastated by chronic pain. The doctor mercifully helps to end that pain by performing euthanasia. The second is of a brain-dead individual—a human vegetable—who lies in a hospital bed, kept alive only by machines. How accurate are these images?

We have the example of Holland. There, along with Belgium, euthanasia is legal. Incredibly, in about 1,000 cases a year, physicians kill their patients without the patients' express consent. In one instance a doctor ended the life of a nun because he thought she would have wanted him to do so but was afraid to ask because it was against her religion. In another case, a physician killed a patient with breast cancer who said that she did *not* want euthanasia. In the doctor's words, "It could have taken another week before she died. I needed this bed" (Hendin 1997, 2000).

Some Dutch, concerned that they could be euthanized if they have a medical emergency, carry "passports" that instruct medical personnel that they wish to live. Most Dutch, however, support euthanasia. Many carry another "passport," one that instructs medical personnel to carry out euthanasia (Shapiro 1997).

In Michigan, Dr. Jack Kevorkian, a pathologist (he didn't treat patients—he studied diseased tissues) decided that regardless of laws, he had the right to help people commit suicide. He did, 120 times. Here is how he described one of those times:

I started the intravenous dripper, which released a salt solution through a needle into her vein, and I kept her arm tied down so she wouldn't jerk it. This was difficult as her veins were fragile. And then once she decided she was ready to go, she just hit the switch and the device cut off the saline drip and through the needle released a solution of thiopental that put her to sleep in ten to fifteen seconds. A minute later, through the needle flowed a lethal solution of potassium chloride. (Denzin 1992)

Kevorkian taunted authorities. He sometimes left bodies in vans and dropped them off at hospitals. Although he provided the poison, as well as a "death machine" that he developed to administer the poison, and he watched patients pull the lever that released the drugs, Kevorkian never touched that lever. Frustrated Michigan prosecutors tried Kevorkian for murder four times, but four times juries refused to convict him. Then Kevorkian made a fatal mistake. On national television, he played a videotape showing him giving a lethal injection to a man who was dying from Lou Gehrig's disease. Prosecutors put Kevorkian on trial again. This time, he was convicted of second-degree murder and was sentenced to 10 to 25 years in prison. Kevorkian was released after 8 years. To get out, he had to promise not to kill anyone else (Wanzer 2007).

In 1997, Oregon became the only U.S. state where medically assisted suicide is legal. If Kevorkian had lived in Oregon, and he hadn't begun killing patients until 1997, he would never have been convicted.

for your Consideration

Do you think Michigan or Oregon is right? Why? In the future, do you think we will go the way of Oregon or Michigan?

In addition to what is reported here, Dutch doctors also kill newborn babies who have serious birth defects (Smith 1999; "Piden en Holanda . . ." 2004). Their justification is that these children would not have "quality of life." What do you think? Would you support this?

Curbing Costs: From Health Insurance to Rationing Medical Care

We have seen some of the reasons why the price of medical care in the United States has soared: advanced—and expensive—technology for diagnosis and treatment, a growing elderly population, tests performed as defensive measures rather than for medical reasons, costly malpractice insurance, and health care as a commodity to be sold to the highest bidder. As long as these conditions exist, the price of medical care will continue to outpace inflation. Let's look at some attempts to reduce costs.

Health Maintenance Organizations (HMOs) are medical companies that charge an annual fee in exchange for providing medical care to a company's employees. Prices are lower because HMOs bid against one another. Whatever money is left over at the end of the year is the HMO's profit. While this arrangement eliminates unnecessary medical treatment, it also puts pressure on doctors to save money by reducing *necessary* treatment.

The results are anything but pretty. Over her doctor's strenuous objections, a friend of mine was discharged from the hospital even though she was still bleeding and running a fever. Her HMO representative said he would not authorize another day in the hospital. After suffering a heart attack, a man in Kansas City, Missouri, needed surgery that could be

The cartoonist has captured an unfortunate reality of U.S. medicine.

performed only at Barnes Hospital in St. Louis, Missouri. The HMO said, "Too bad. That hospital is out of our service area." The man died while appealing the HMO decision (Spragins 1996). Some doctors also have HMOs. One doctor, who works for a hospital, noticed a lump in her breast. She went to the X-Ray department to get a mammogram, but her own hospital said she couldn't have one. Her HMO allowed one mammogram every two years, and she had had one 18 months before. After a formal appeal, she was granted an exception. She had breast cancer ("What Scares Doctors?" 2006).

The basic question, of course, is: At what human cost do we reduce spending on medical treatment?

Diagnosis-Related Groups To curb spiraling costs, the federal government has classified all illnesses into diagnosis-related-groups (DRGs) and has set an amount that it will pay for the treatment of each illness. Hospitals make a profit if they move patients through the system quickly—if they discharge patients before the allotted amount is spent. As a consequence, some patients are discharged before they have recovered. Others are refused admittance because they appear to have a "worse than average" case of a particular illness: If they take longer to treat, they will cost the hospital money instead of bringing them a profit.

National Health Insurance

The van from Hollywood Presbyterian Hospital pulled up to the curbside in the center of skid row in Los Angeles, California. The driver got out and walked to the passenger side. As several people watched, she opened the door and helped a paraplegic man out. As she drove away, leaving the befuddled man, people shouted at her, "Where's his wheelchair? Where's his walker?"

Someone called 911. The police found the man crawling in the gutter, wearing a flimsy, soiled hospital gown and trailing a broken colostomy bag,

"I can't think of anything colder than that," said an L.A. detective. "It's the worst area of skid row" (Blankstein and Winton 2007).

This is an example of **dumping,** hospitals discharging unprofitable patients. Seldom is dumping as dramatic as in this instance, but it happens regularly. Dumping is one

dumping the practice of discharging unprofitable patients, or private hospitals, sending unprofitable patients to public hospitals consequence of a system that puts profit ahead of patient care. With 46 million Americans uninsured (*Statistical Abstract* 2007:Table 144), pressure has grown for the government to provide national health insurance. What patterns do you see in the Social Map below, which shows how the uninsured are distributed among the states?

Advocates of national health insurance point out that centralized, large-scale purchases of medical and hospital supplies will reduce costs. They also stress that national health insurance will solve the problem of the poor receiving inferior medical care. Opponents stress that national health insurance will bring expensive red tape. They also ask why anyone would think that federal agencies—such as those that run the post office—should be entrusted with administering something as vital as the nation's health care. Proponents reply that right now no one is in charge of it. This debate is not new, and even if some form of national health insurance is adopted, the arguments will continue.

Maverick Solutions   Some doctors have lowered costs by replacing individual consultations with *group care.* They meet with a group of patients who have similar medical conditions. Eight or ten pregnant women, for example, go in for their obstetrics checkup together. This allows the doctor more time to discuss medical symptoms and treatments, and, at the same time, to charge each patient less. The patients also benefit from the support and encouragement of people who are in their same situation (Bower 2003).

Other doctors refuse to treat patients who want to pay by insurance. The cost of dealing with insurance companies is high: Physicians have to hire people to fill out and submit insurance claims, to follow up to ensure that payments have been made, and to resubmit forms. In what are called *pay-as-you-go* programs, patients pay by cash, credit card, or check. With no billing costs, the doctors can charge less (Rundle 2003).

Rationing Medical Care   The most controversial suggestion for how to reduce medical costs is to ration medical care. The argument is simple: We cannot afford to provide all the available technology to everyone, so we have to ration it. No easy answer has been found for this pressing matter, which is becoming the center of a national debate. This dilemma is the focus of the following Sociology and the New Technology box.

Figure 19.6 **Who Lacks Medical Insurance?**

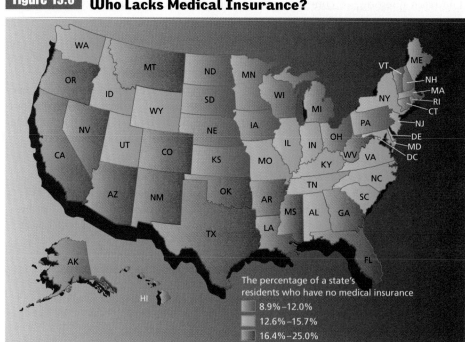

Note: The range is broad, from a low of 8.9 percent who lack medical insurance in Minnesota to a high of 25.0 percent in Texas.

Source: By the author. Based on *Statistical Abstract* 2007:Table 145.

Who Should Live, and Who Should Die? The Dilemma of Rationing Medical Care

VISITING A DOCTOR OR A hospital is not without risk. We have seen that doctors kill somewhere between 50,000 and 100,000 patients a year. But today's risk is small compared to that of earlier times, when physicians bled and gave their patients diarrhea in an effort to cure them. Today's physicians are well trained, and medical care is based on scientific studies. Our new technology allows us to cure medical conditions that just a short time ago doomed people to early deaths. In other instances, the condition can't be cured, but, with treatment, the patient is able to live a longer life.

And therein lies the rub. Even though a particular treatment is essential, there isn't enough of it to go around to everyone who needs it. Other treatments are so costly that they could bankrupt society if they were made available to everyone who had a particular condition. Who, then, should receive the benefits of our new medical technology?

Consider dialysis, the use of machines to cleanse the blood of people who are suffering from kidney disease. Currently, dialysis is available to anyone who needs it, and the cost runs several billion dollars a year. Four percent of all Medicare goes to pay for the dialysis of just one-fourth of 1 percent of Medicare patients (Volti 1995). Great Britain, which faces this same problem, limits dialysis to people under the age of 55 or 60 (Brock 2007).

Open heart surgery is a technological wonder, but its costs are astounding. One percent of all the money the nation spends on its medical bills goes to pay for the bypass surgeries of just four-hundredths of 1 percent of the population. Medical treatment at the end of people's lives also helps us to understand the issue. Of the huge amounts spent on Medicare (see Figure 13.9 on page 386), about one-fourth is used to maintain patients during just the last year of their lives. Almost a third of this amount is spent during just the last month of life (Volti 1995).

The situation will worsen. Medical technology continues to advance—and so do its spiraling costs. In Chapter 13, we saw how rapidly the number of elderly people is increasing. Because the elderly need medical treatment the most, expenses will continue to soar.

The dilemma is harsh: If we ration medical treatment, many sick people will die. If we don't, we could go bankrupt.

for your Consideration

At the heart of this issue lie questions not only of cost but also of fairness—of how to distribute expensive medical care in an equitable manner. Use ideas, concepts, and principles from this and other chapters to develop a proposal for solving this issue. How does this dilemma change if you view it from the contrasting perspectives of conflict theory, functionalism, and symbolic interactionism?

If we ration medical care, what factors do you think should be involved? Should age be a consideration? If so, should the younger get preferred treatment? Or perhaps the older? Why?

Threats to Health

Let's look at major threats to health, both in the United States and worldwide: AIDS, weight, drugs, disabling environments, medical experiments, and the globalization of disease.

HIV/AIDS

In 1981, the first case of AIDS (acquired immune deficiency syndrome) was documented. Since then, about 600,000 Americans have died from AIDS. As you can see from Figure 19.7 on the next page, in the United States this disease has been brought under control. New cases peaked in 1993, and deaths peaked in 1995. This disease is far from conquered, however. Each year about 40,000 Americans are infected with the HIV virus, and about 18,000 die from it. For the 500,000 Americans who receive treatment, HIV/AIDS has become a chronic disease that they live with (Centers for Disease Control 2006b:Table 8).

Globally, in contrast, the AIDS epidemic is exploding. *Every minute* of every hour of every day, about 10 people become infected with HIV. This is about 5 million new HIV

Figure 19.7 **The Path of AIDS in the United States**

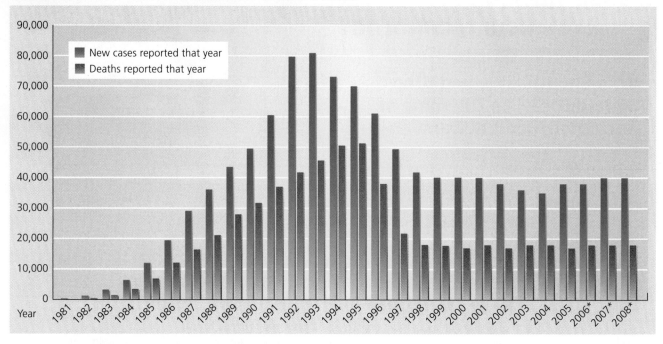

*Indicates the author's Projections.
Sources: By the author. Based on Centers for Disease Control 2003:Table 21; Centers for Disease Control and Prevention 2006b:Tables 1, 7.

infections a year (United Nations 2004). AIDS has killed about 40 million people so far, but the worst is yet to come. The most devastated area is sub-Saharan Africa. Although this region has just 10 percent of the world's population, it has *95 percent* of the world's new HIV infections. In Swaziland, 2 of every 5 adults have HIV/AIDS. The death toll in this region is so high that in several countries life expectancy has dropped below 40 (Lamptey et al 2006). In Lesotho, the average person dies at age 34 (Haub 2006). As Figure 19.8 illustrates, Africa is the hardest hit region of the world.

AIDS is devastating huge areas of Africa. In some countries, one-third or more of the population has AIDS. Millions of children have been orphaned. Governments that first ignored the problem are now trying to battle AIDS. This anti-AIDS billboard is posted in Nairobi, Kenya.

Let's look at some of the major characteristics of this disease.

Origin The question of how AIDS originated baffled scientists for two decades, but it appears to be solved (Kolata 2001). Scientists have traced genetic sequences back to the Congo. Apparently, the virus was present in chimpanzees and was somehow transmitted to humans. How this crossover occurred is not known, but the best guess is that hunters were exposed to the animals' blood as they slaughtered them for meat.

The Transmission of AIDS The only way a person can become infected with AIDS is if bodily fluids pass from one person to another. AIDS is most commonly transmitted through blood, semen, and vaginal secretions, but nursing babies can also get AIDS through the milk of their infected mothers. Since the AIDS virus is present in all bodily fluids (including sweat, tears, spittle, and urine), some people think that AIDS can also be transmitted in these forms. The U.S. Centers for Disease Control, however, stresses that AIDS cannot be transmitted by casual contact in which traces of these fluids would be exchanged. Figure 19.9 compares how U.S. men and women get infected.

Gender, Race-Ethnicity, and AIDS In the United States, AIDS hits men the hardest, but the proportion of women has been growing. In 1982, only 6 percent of AIDS cases were women, but today women account for 26 percent of all new cases (Centers for Disease Control 1997:Tables 3, 10; 2006b:Table 5b). In sub-Saharan Africa, AIDS is more common among women (United Nations 2004).

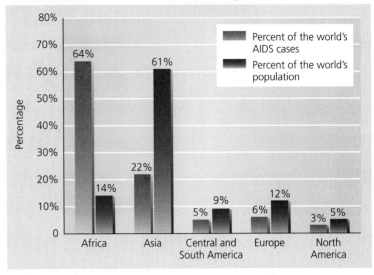

Figure 19.8 AIDS: A Global Glimpse

Source: By the author. Based on Haub 2003; UNAIDS 2006.

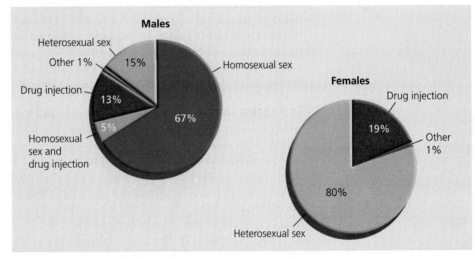

Figure 19.9 How Americans Get AIDS

Note: "Other" includes unknown and blood transfusion.
Source: Centers for Disease Control 2007.

Are HIV infections less common in men who are circumcised? When this idea began to circulate, researchers decided to find out. They divided 3,000 HIV-free men in Kenya into two groups, those who were circumcised and those who were not. As the researchers continued to test the men, they were surprised to find that about twice as many of the uncircumcised men came down with HIV (McNeil 2006).

HIV/AIDS is also related to race-ethnicity. One of the most startling examples is this: African American women are *20 times* more likely to come down with AIDS than are white women (Centers for Disease Control 2006b:Table 5b). Figure 19.10 on the next page summarizes racial-ethnic differences in this disease. The reason for the differences shown on this figure is *not* genetic. No racial-ethnic group is more susceptible to AIDS because of biological factors. Rather, risks differ because of *social* factors, such as the use of condoms and the number of drug users who share needles.

Figure 19.10 People Living with HIV/AIDS by Race-Ethnicity

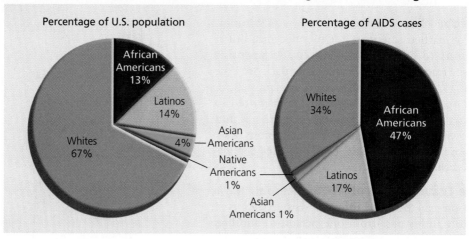

Source: By the author. Based on Figure 12.5 of this text and Centers for Disease Control 2006b:Table 9.

The Stigma of AIDS   One of the most significant sociological aspects of AIDS is its stigma. This provides another example of how social factors are essential to health and illness. Some people refuse even to be tested because they fear the stigma they would bear if they test HIV-positive. One unfortunate consequence is the continuing spread of AIDS by people who "don't want to know." Even some governments put their heads in the sand. Chinese officials, for example, at first refused to admit that they had an AIDS problem, but now they are more open about it. If this disease is to be brought under control, its stigma must be overcome: AIDS must be viewed like any other lethal disease—as the work of a destructive biological organism.

Is There a Cure for AIDS?   As you saw on Figure 19.7 (page 576), the number of AIDS cases in the United States increased dramatically, reached a peak, and then declined. With such a remarkable decline, have we found a cure for AIDS?

With thousands of scientists doing research, the media have heralded each new breakthrough as a possible cure. The most promising treatment to date, the one that lies behind the drop in deaths shown in Figure 19.7, was spearheaded by David Ho, a virologist (virus researcher). If patients in the early stages of the disease take a "cocktail" of drugs (a combination of protease inhibitors, AZT, and 3TC), all signs of the virus can be erased from their bodies. Their immune systems then rebound (Gorman 1997). No one is calling this a cure, however; apparently the virus lingers undetected, ready to flourish if the drugs are withdrawn.

While most praise this new treatment, some researchers have issued a dire warning (Rotello 1996). They suggest that the cocktail may become this decade's penicillin. When penicillin was introduced, everyone was ecstatic about its effectiveness. However, over the years, the microbes that penicillin targets mutated, producing "super germs" against which we have little protection. If this happens with AIDS, a tsunami of a "super-AIDS" virus could hit the world with more fury than the first devastating wave.

Despite the continuing disappointing news, medical researchers remain hopeful that they will develop an effective vaccine. If so, many millions of lives will be saved. If not, this disease will continue its global death march.

Weight: Too Much and Too Little

When a friend from Spain visited, I asked him to comment on the things that struck him as different. He mentioned how surprised he was to see people living in metal houses. It took me a moment to figure out what he meant, but then I understood: He had never seen a mobile home. Then he added, "And there are so many fat Americans."

Is this a valid perception, or just some twisted ethnocentric observation by a foreigner? The statistics bear out his observation. Americans are adding weight—and a lot of it. In 1980, one of four Americans was overweight. By 1990, this percentage had jumped to one of three. Now *two-thirds* (65 percent) of Americans are overweight (*Statistical Abstract* 1998:Table 242; 2007:Table 198). We have become the fattest nation on earth.

Perhaps we should just shrug our shoulders and say, "So what?" Is obesity really anything more than someone's arbitrary idea of how much we should weigh? It turns out that obese people are more likely than thinner people to get a variety of diseases. They are more likely to have strokes (Bonow and Eckel 2003), to suffer heart attacks (Kenchaiah et al. 2002), and to come down with diabetes (Troiano 2002) and cancer (Calle and Kaaks 2004). Overall, obesity's toll is high. It accounts for between 100,000 and 300,000 deaths a year (Saguy 2006).

A surprising side-effect of being overweight is that it helps some people live longer. Evidently, being either seriously overweight (obese) or underweight increases people's chances of dying, but being a little overweight is good. No one yet knows the reason for this, but some suggest that having a few extra pounds reduces bad cholesterol (Centers for Disease Control 2005).

Alcohol and Nicotine

Many drugs, both legal and illegal, harm their users. Let's examine some of the health consequences of alcohol and nicotine, the two most frequently used legal drugs in the United States.

Alcohol Alcohol is *the* standard recreational drug of Americans. The *average* adult American drinks 25 gallons of alcoholic beverages per year—about 22 gallons of beer, 2 gallons of wine, and 1 gallon of whiskey, vodka, or other distilled spirits. Beer is so popular that Americans drink more of it than they do tea and fruit juices combined (*Statistical Abstract* 2007:Table 201).

As you know, despite laws that ban alcohol consumption before the age of 21, underage drinking is common. Table 19.1 shows that two-thirds of all high school students drink alcohol during their senior year. Almost half of them have done so during just the past month. If getting drunk is the abuse of alcohol, then, without doubt, among high school students abusing alcohol is popular. As Table 19.1 also shows, about half of all high school seniors have been drunk during the past year, with 30 percent of all seniors getting drunk during just the past 30 days.

In Table 19.2, we turn to college students. Among them, too, alcohol is the most popular drug, and four out of five of all college students have drunk alcohol during the past year. Six or seven out of ten have done so in the past month. As you can see, men and women are about equally as likely to drink alcohol and to smoke cigarettes, but in general, male college students are slightly more likely to use drugs.

We all know that drunk driving kills, and yet many people continue to drive drunk. This wreck occurred in Hamden, Connecticutt.

Table 19.1 What Drugs Have High School Seniors Used?	In the past month?	In the past year?
Alcohol	45.3%	66.5%
How many have been drunk?	30.0%	47.9%
Nicotine (cigarettes)	21.6%	NA
Marijuana	18.3%	31.5%
Amphetamines	3.7%	8.1%
Barbiturates	3.0%	6.6%
Cocaine	2.5%	5.7%
Hallucinogens*	1.5%	4.9%
MDMA (Ecstasy)	1.3%	4.1%
Steroids	1.1%	1.8%
LSD	0.6%	1.7%
Heroin	0.4%	0.8%
PCP	0.4%	0.7%

* Other than LSD.

Source: By the author. Based on Johnston et al 2007:Tables 2, 3.

Table 19.2 What Drugs Have Full-Time College Students Used?

	IN THE PAST MONTH?		IN THE PAST YEAR?	
	Men	Women	Men	Women
Alcohol	70.5%	66.4%	82.4%	83.4%
Nicotine (cigarettes)	23.7%	23.8%	37.0%	35.4%
Marijuana	20.5%	15.1%	38.0%	30.7%
Amphetamines	4.0%	2.3%	7.4%	6.3%
Cocaine	2.2%	1.5%	6.2%	5.4%
Hallucinogens*	1.8%	0.9%	7.3%	3.8%
Barbiturates	1.5%	1.2%	4.3%	3.8%
MDMA (Ecstasy)	1.3%	0.5%	3.1%	2.8%
LSD	0.2%	0.1%	0.9%	0.6%
Heroin	0.2%	0.1%	0.6%	0.2%

* Other than LSD.

Source: By the author. Based on Johnston et al. 2006:Tables 8-2, 8-3.

disabling environment an environment that is harmful to health

Figure 19.11 Who Is Still Smoking?

The Percentage of Americans Who Smoke Cigarettes

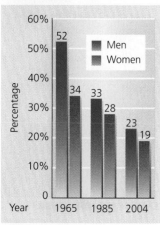

Source: By the author. Based on *Statistical Abstract* 2007:Table 191, and earlier years.

Is alcohol bad for health? This beverage cuts both ways. About two to three drinks a day for men and one to two drinks a day for women help *reduce* the risk of heart attacks and strokes (Hommel and Jaillard 1999; Mukamal 2003). (Women weigh less on average and produce fewer enzymes that metabolize alcohol.) Moderate alcohol consumption also makes the elderly less depressed, helps their mental health, and sharpens their thinking (Lang et al. 2007). Beyond these amounts, however, alcohol consumption *increases* the risk of several diseases, including cancer. It also increases the likelihood of birth defects. One-third of the 43,000 Americans who die each year in vehicle accidents are drunk (*Statistical Abstract* 2007:Table 1089). Each year, 700,000 Americans seek treatment for alcohol problems (*Statistical Abstract* 2007:Table 193).

Nicotine

Let's suppose that you are on your way to the airport to leave for a long-awaited vacation. You are listening to the radio and thinking about the palm trees and ocean waves of sunny Hawaii. Suddenly, an announcer breaks into your reverie with a flash bulletin: Terrorists have hidden bombs aboard five jumbo jets scheduled for takeoff today. The announcer pauses, then adds: "The authorities have not been able to find the bombs. Because they don't know which flights will crash, all flights will depart on schedule."

Five jets are going to crash. On each jet will be 200 passengers and crew. They will plummet from the skies, leaving a trail of agonizing screams as they meet their fiery destiny.

What would you do? My guess is that you would turn your car around and go home. Adios to Hawaii's beaches, and hello to your own backyard.

Nicotine use—with its creeping side-effects of emphysema and several types of cancer—kills about 400,000 Americans each year (Surgeon General 2005). This is the equivalent of five fully loaded, 200-passenger jets with full crews crashing each and every day—leaving no survivors. Who in their right mind would take the risk that *their* plane will not be among those that crash? Yet this is the risk that smokers take.

Nicotine is, by far, the most lethal of all recreational drugs. Smoking causes cancer of the bladder, cervix, esophagus, kidneys, larynx, lungs, and other body organs. Smokers are more likely to have heart attacks and strokes, and even to come down with cataracts and pneumonia (Surgeon General 2005). The list of health problems related to smoking goes on and on.

Then there is second-hand smoke, which is estimated to kill 50,000 nonsmokers a year (Surgeon General 2006). This is the equivalent of another fully loaded jet going down every 2 days.

An antismoking campaign that stresses tobacco's health hazards has been so successful that smoking is banned on public transportation and in most offices, restaurants, and, in some states, even bars. Figure 19.11 shows how this antismoking message has hit home. In four decades, cigarette smoking has been cut by more than *half* among U.S. men, and almost that among U.S. women. As you look at this figure, you might be surprised to see that *most* men used to smoke.

Millions of Americans wouldn't think of flying if they knew that even one jet were going to crash—yet they continue to smoke. Why? The two major reasons are addiction and advertising. Nicotine may be as addictive as heroin (Tolchin 1988). While this may sound far-fetched, consider Buerger's disease:

In this disease, the blood vessels, especially those supplying the legs, become so constricted that circulation is impaired whenever nicotine enters the bloodstream.

If a patient continues to smoke, gangrene may eventually set in. First a toe may have to be amputated, then the foot at the ankle, then the leg at the knee, and ultimately at the hip. . . . Patients are informed that if they will only stop smoking, it is virtually certain that the otherwise inexorable march of gangrene up the legs will be curbed. Yet surgeons report that some patients with Buerger's disease vigorously puff away in their hospital beds following a second or third amputation. (Brecher et al. 1972)

The second reason is advertising. Cigarette ads were banned from television in the 1980s, but cigarettes continue to be advertised in newspapers and magazines and on billboards. Cigarette companies spend huge amounts to encourage Americans to smoke—about $11 billion a year. This comes to $39 for every man, woman, and child in the entire country (Surgeon General 2005). Although the tobacco industry denies it, they target youth, often by associating cigarette smoking with success, high fashion, and independence. Despite these denials, Joe Camel, the industry's most blatant attempt to lure children to smoke, has been banned. (See the photo.) The tobacco industry is relentless in its pursuit of adolescent smokers, however, and in 2004 it introduced cigarettes spiked with candy flavors (O'Connell 2004).

Disabling Environments

A **disabling environment** is one that is harmful to people's health. The health risk of some occupations is evident: Lumberjacking, riding rodeo bulls, and training lions are obvious examples. In many occupations, however, people become aware of the risk only years after they worked at jobs that they thought were safe. For example, during and after World War II, several million people worked with asbestos. The federal government estimates that one-quarter of them will die of cancer from having breathed asbestos particles. It is likely that many other substances also cause slowly developing cancers—including, ironically, some asbestos substitutes (Meier 1987; Hawkes 2001).

Industrialization increased the world's standard of living and brought better health to hundreds of millions of people. Ironically, industrialization also threatens to disable the basic environment of the human race, posing what may be the greatest health hazard of all time. The burning of carbon fuels has led to the *greenhouse effect,* a warming of the earth that may change the globe's climate, melt the polar ice caps, and flood the earth's coastal shores. The pollution of land, air, and water, especially through nuclear waste, pesticides, herbicides, and other chemicals, poses additional risks to life on our planet. We discuss these problems in Chapter 22.

Medical Experiments: Callous and Harmful

At times, physicians and government officials behave so arrogantly that they callously disregard people's health. Harmful medical experiments, though well-intentioned, are an excellent example. We can trace these experiments to 1895, with an attempt to find a way to immunize people against syphilis. In that year, Albert Neisser, a physician in Germany, injected young prostitutes—one was just 10 years old—with syphilis. Many came down with the disease (Proctor 1999). Let's look at two notorious instances in the United States.

The Tuskegee Syphilis Experiment   To review this horrible experiment conducted by the U.S. Public Health Service, read the opening

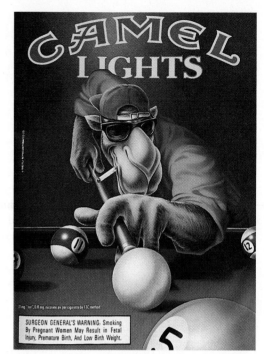

Do you think that this magazine ad is designed to make cigarettes appealing to male youth? Although tobacco industry officials denied that they were trying to entice youth to smoke, evidence such as this ad is overwhelmingly against them. It took pressure from the U.S. Congress to get R.J. Reynolds Tobacco Company to stop its Joe Camel ads.

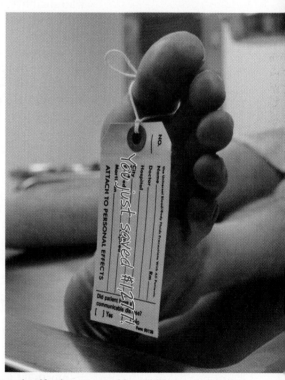

In a mind-boggling attempt to justify cigarette smoking, Philip Morris reported to the Czech government that it saves $1,227 in pensions and health care every time a smoker dies. Following this reasoning, to reduce U.S. government deficits we might want to require smoking classes in kindergarten—for the sooner that people begin to smoke, the sooner they get sick and die—and the more the government saves.

vignette for Chapter 15 (page 431). To summarize here, the U.S. Public Health Service did not tell 399 African American men in Mississippi that they had syphilis. Doctors examined them once a year, recording their symptoms, and letting the disease kill them.

The Cold War Experiments

Assume that you are a soldier stationed in Nevada, and the U.S. Army orders your platoon to march through an area in which an atomic bomb has just been detonated. Because you are a soldier, you obey. Nobody knows much about radiation, and you don't know that the army is using you as a guinea pig: It wants to see if you'll be able to withstand the fallout—without any radiation equipment. Or suppose you are a patient at the University of Rochester in 1946, and your doctor, whom you trust implicitly, says, "I am going to give you something to help you." You are pleased. But the injection, it turns out, is uranium (Noah 1994). He and a team of other doctors are conducting an experiment to find out how much uranium it will take to damage your kidneys. (U.S. Department of Energy 1995)

Like the Tuskegee experiment, radiation experiments like these were conducted on unsuspecting subjects simply because government officials wanted information. There were others, too. Some soldiers were given LSD. And in Palmetto, Florida, officials released whooping cough viruses into the air, killing a dozen children (Conahan 1994). In other tests, deadly chemical and biological agents, such as sarin, were sprayed onto naval ships to see if they were vulnerable. The sailors in these tests wore protective clothing, but were unaware that they had become white mice (Shanker 2002). In 2003, Congress approved a bill to provide health care for 5,842 soldiers harmed by these secret tests.

Playing God   To most of us, it is incredible that government officials and medical personnel would callously disregard human life, but it happens. Those in official positions sometimes reach a point where they think they can play God and determine who shall live and who shall die. And, obviously, the most expendable citizens are the poor and powerless. *It is inconceivable that the doctors who did the syphilis studies would have used wealthy and powerful subjects.* The elite are protected from such callous disregard of human rights and life. The only way the poor can be protected against such gross abuse of professional positions is if we publicize each known instance of abuse and insist on vigorous prosecution of those who plan, direct, and carry out such experiments.

Do such things still happen? You can decide for yourself. Let's look at how medical researchers developed fetal surgery. Surgeons were intrigued with the idea of operating on unborn children. Not only did such surgery hold the possibility of extending medical knowledge but also the pioneers would get their names in prestigious medical journals and be applauded by their peers. But such experimental surgery could cost lives. To reduce the risk, the researchers first experimented on animals. Their next step in refining their skills was to operate on pregnant Puerto Rican women. Now that the procedures are proven, the main patients are the unborn of the white and affluent (Casper 1998). The steps taken in this process expose an underlying assumption about the value of life—from animals to Puerto Rican women to white women. It is almost as though the researchers viewed themselves as climbing an evolutionary ladder.

The Globalization of Disease

The year was 1918. Men and women, seemingly healthy the day before, collapsed and were soon dead. In the morning, men wheeled carts down the streets to pick up corpses that were left on porches like last night's trash. In a matter of months, a half million Americans died. Worldwide, the death toll reached between 20 million and 40 million. (Phillips 1998)

What silent killer had so abruptly hit the United States and most of the world? Incredibly, it was the flu. For some reason, still unknown, a particularly lethal variety of the common flu bug had suddenly appeared.

Medical researchers fear that something like this will happen again. If it does, today's global jet travel, unknown in 1918, may make the outbreak even more deadly. Global travel has destroyed the natural frontiers that used to contain diseases. In a matter of hours, today's airline passengers can spread a disease around the world. The resulting number of deaths could make the 1918 death toll seem puny by comparison.

Such are the fears. New diseases keep appearing on the world scene, and antibiotics are ineffective against many of them. When the Ebola virus made its surprise appearance in 1976, with its particularly hideous form of death, the only way it could be contained was to isolate an entire region of Zaire (Olshansky et al. 1997). When SARS (Severe Acute Respiratory Syndrome) appeared in 2003, the World Health Organization of the United Nations called emergency meetings, as did the Centers for Disease Control in the United States. The fear was that SARS would encircle the globe, killing millions of people in a short time. Each person with SARS was isolated, and cities and regions were declared off limits to visitors. The same thing has happened with outbreaks of Asian bird flu (avian influenza) and the Marburg virus in Angola that causes death from fever, diarrhea, vomiting, and bleeding (LaFraniere 2005). Officials are also fearful of a new form of tuberculosis that appeared in South Africa, where it killed 52 of 53 patients (Wines 2007).

When such deadly diseases—for which there is no cure—break out, world health officials send out emergency medical teams to seal off the area. They have been successful in containing these diseases so far, but they fear that they won't always be so fortunate.

The Search for Alternatives

Let's turn our attention again to the U.S. medical system. What alternatives are there to the way U.S. medicine is usually practiced? One promising alternative is to change the focus from the treatment of disease to the prevention of disease. Another is something called alternative medicine. After considering these approaches to medical care, we will look at the health care systems of other countries. Perhaps these three closing topics will suggest new ideas for you to follow—or to avoid.

Treatment or Prevention?

Effects of Values and Lifestyles   The impact of values and lifestyle on health becomes apparent if we contrast Utah (home of the Mormons, who disapprove of alcohol, caffeine, tobacco, and extramarital sex) with its adjacent state of Nevada (home of a gambling industry that fosters rather different values and lifestyles). Although these two states have similar levels of income, education, urbanization, and medical care, Nevadans are more likely to die from cancer, strokes, heart attacks, and kidney and lung diseases. They also are more likely to die in car wrecks, to be murdered, and to commit suicide (*Statistical Abstract* 2007:Table 112). In short—as mentioned earlier when we discussed nicotine and alcohol—many threats to health are preventable.

Even though it is well known that lifestyle affects health, the message of "wellness" and prevention is not getting through to many millions of Americans. Our schools and the mass media publicize the message that healthy living—exercising regularly, eating nutritious food, maintaining an optimal weight, not smoking, avoiding alcohol abuse, and not having a lot of sexual partners—leads to better health and a longer life. It doesn't take much reading to know that fatty, low-fiber foods bring disease and that a diet rich in fruits, green tea, and leafy, green vegetables stimulates health.

Unfortunately, we are seeing the public divide into those who exercise regularly and watch their diet and weight, and those who gorge on potato chips, cookies, and soft drinks during their mesmerized hours of television watching and wielding mad joy sticks. A shorter life and the misery of sickness are simply not on people's minds while snacks, reruns, and video games beckon. Prevention requires work, while illness requires only a doctor's prescription.

This brings us to a related concern: how to get doctors to turn from writing prescriptions to focusing on preventive medicine and "wellness." To do this, "wellness" will have to be made profitable, for under the "fee for services" system, if doctors and hospitals prevent illness, they lose money. One proposal that seems to have merit is for doctors and hospitals to be paid an annual fee for keeping people well (Cooper 1993). Many companies have started wellness programs. They have found that they can lower medical costs by trying to keep their employees healthy so they don't become patients, (McQueen 2006).

There is also comprehensive prevention: improving disabling environments and decreasing the use of harmful drugs. Stronger legal action can be taken against businesses that spew industrial wastes into the air and use our rivers and oceans as industrial sewers, as well as those that use advertising to seduce youths to use deadly drugs. Finally, since we live in a global village, international controls and cooperation are required to create or maintain a health-producing environment.

Alternative Medicine

Alternative medicine refers to nontraditional medicine, sometimes to medical practices imported from Asian cultures. From the perspective of traditional Western medical theory and practice, most alternative medicine does not make sense. Regarding it as the superstitious practices of ignorant people, Western doctors turned a scornful and hostile eye at alternative medicine. An example is acupuncture. At first, Western doctors ridiculed acupuncture because it violated their understanding of how the body works. But with patients continuing to report results such as pain relief, acupuncture is slowly becoming acceptable in U.S. medical practice.

Many U.S. patients have begun to demand alternatives, and the U.S. medical establishment has started to accommodate those demands. Although the change is slow, in some places the Western and Eastern approaches to medical care are being combined. In two hospitals in Savannah, Georgia, standard and alternative doctors work alongside one another. Patients are given traditional treatment accompanied by yoga, meditation, and Shirodhara, in which warm herbalized sesame oil is slowly dripped onto the patient's forehead. Patients may also choose polarity therapy (to unblock energy), biofeedback, Chinese face-lifting, and aromatherapy (Abelson and Brown 2002). At hospitals affiliated with Stanford University, the University of Maryland School of Medicine, and Harvard Medical School, patients can get a touch of alternative medicine (Keates 2003; Waldholz 2003).

The change is just a trickle at this point, but what is sociologically significant is that alternative medicine has begun to make inroads into the exclusive club run by the U.S. medical establishment.

In auriculotherapy, reflex points of the ear are stimulated to relieve chronic pain and to alleviate substance abuse.

alternative medicine medical treatment other than that of standard Western medicine; often refers to practices that originate in Asia, but may also refer to taking vitamins not prescribed by a doctor

Health Care in Global Perspective

The search for alternatives also points to health care in other nations. We will close this chapter with a comparison of health care in the three worlds of industrialization. This will help us to place both positive and negative aspects of the U.S. health care system in cultural perspective. As with education (see pages 503–505), no one country can adequately illustrate the varieties of medicine that are practiced in nations at a particular stage of industrialization. Nevertheless, the countries highlighted in the following Cultural Diversity box do illustrate major characteristics of health care around the world.

Health Care in Sweden, Russia, and China

Health Care in the Most Industrialized Nations: Sweden

Sweden has the most comprehensive health care system in the world. National health insurance, which is financed by contributions from the state and employers, covers all Swedish citizens and alien residents. The government pays most physicians a salary to treat patients, but 18 percent work in private practice (Glenngard et al. 2005). Except for a small consultation fee, medical and dental treatment by these government-paid doctors is free. Patients pay only minimal fees for prescriptions and hospitalization.

Medical treatment is just one component of Sweden's broad system of social welfare. At the birth of a child, Swedes receive parental leave at 90 percent of their salaries. They also receive this same benefit when they stay home with sick children. The government even reimburses travel expenses for patients and for the parents of a hospitalized child.

Sweden's socialized medicine, however, is inefficient. Swedes have not solved the problem of how to motivate physicians to work hard. Because medical personnel receive the same pay, regardless how many patients they see, they are not productive. When reporters visited Sweden's largest hospital on a weekday morning, when 80 of 120 surgeons were on duty, they found 19 of the hospital's 24 operating rooms idle. When the photos of empty operating rooms appeared in the newspapers—at a time when there was a one- to two-year waiting period for hip replacements and cataract operations—the public became outraged (Bergström 1992). The waiting list for cataract surgery has grown to 30,000 Swedes—in a population of 9 million ("Swedish Health Care . . ." 2002). If the same rate of Americans were waiting for surgery, the U.S. line would be 600,000 people long.

Swedish lawmakers have decided that to to make their medical system more efficient they must abandon the socialized model, and they are gradually turning the health-care system over to the private sector. The government has already sold some hospitals to private companies ("Social Darwinism . . ." 2001). We don't yet know what the Swedish medical system will look like by the time this transition is complete.

Health Care in the Industrializing Nations: Russia

Russia's medical system is in tatters. Under the communists, Russia had established a system that made free health care available to most people. Doctors would even visit patients at their homes (Gaufberg 2004). Like the rest of the nation's production, the health-care system was centralized. The state owned the medical schools and determined how many doctors would be trained in what specialties. The state paid medical salaries, which it set, and determined where doctors would practice. Physicians were poorly trained, had low prestige, and earned less than bus drivers.

Under Russia's fitful transition to capitalism, its health-care system has deteriorated, and the health of the population has declined. The only hospitals comparable to those of the United States are reserved for the elite (Light 1992; Gaufberg 2004). In the rest, conditions are deplorable.

Physicians are paid so little that they walk to work because they cannot afford the equivalent of a dime to take a bus (Goldberg and Kishkovsky 2000). The bright spot is that physicians continue to work despite their low status and miserable pay. Many are motivated by idealism and the desire to help, coupled with the hope that things will get better. A second bright spot is that some doctors are making the transition to private practice, which could be the beginning of a new medical system built on the rubble of the old (Goldberg and Kishkovsky 2000). In the meantime, Russia's medical system remains broken.

The years of environmental degradation under the communists have also taken their toll. Serious birth defects have jumped to four times the U.S. rate. A likely culprit is radiation pollution from decades of nuclear irresponsibility (Specter 1995). Perhaps the single best indicator of the deterioration of health is the drop in life expectancy that began in the 1960s (Cockerham 2007). We can view life expectancy not only as a medical issue but also as a barometer of a society's health. Table 19.3 on the next page compares four nations on major vital statistics.

Health Care in the Least Industrialized Nations: China

Because this nation of 1.3 billion people has a vast shortage of trained physicians, hospitals, and medicine, most Chinese see doctors who have only a rudimentary knowledge of medicine and are paid low wages. Until a few years ago, physicians were employees of the government, and the government owned all the country's medical facilities, but like Russia, China has begun the journey to capitalism. As part of this transition, Chinese authorities decided that profits should be part of the medical system. They withdrew government financing from the local health centers, which are now expected to sell their services (Zhao 2006). Both rural and urban doctors make money by selling prescription drugs. In the major cities, doctors receive bonuses for selling laser surgery and CAT scans (Browne 2007). Most patients who cannot pay for their medical care go untreated. Some physicians are paid so little that, like

(continued)

college students in the United States, they take "after work" part-time jobs.

The crassness of the new capitalism can be astounding. Of all the examples I have read, this one stands out:

> In a hospital in Shantou, a woman who had just given birth was bleeding profusely and needed an emergency blood transfusion. Nurses went to the waiting room and screamed at her husband, "If you don't have any money, we don't operate!" (Browne 2005)

At this point in its transition, China's medical system has deteriorated so greatly that the World Health Organization ranked it 188 of 191 nations. WHO ranked the medical care system of Bangladesh higher (Zhao 2006).

for your Consideration

No nation has discovered the perfect medical system, and every country faces a medical crisis of "too much demand at too great a cost" (Moore and Winslow 1993). In what ways would you say that the U.S. medical system is superior—and inferior—to each of these systems? Would you prefer to be treated within one of these three systems rather than in the U.S. system? Why or why not? Short of socializing medicine, which goes against the values of Americans, how do you think the U.S. medical system can overcome the deficiencies reviewed in this chapter—and maintain its strengths?

Table 19.3 **Indicators of Health**

	Sweden	United States	Russia	China
Life Expectancy	80.0 years	77.7 years	65.8 years	72.3 years
Infant mortality rate	3.7	6.5	11.5	24.2
Birth Rate	11.1	14.1	10.6	13.1
Death Rate	10.5	8.3	15.9	6.9
Health costs as a percentage of Gross Domestic Product	9.2	15.0	2.3	4.8

[1] Deaths of children under one year of age per 1,000 live births.
[2] Number per year per 1,000 population.

Sources: By the author. Based on Liu 2004; Glenngard et al. 2005; Cockerham 2007; *Statistical Abstract* 2007:Table 1310.

Summary *and* Review

Sociology and the Study of Medicine and Health

What is the role of sociology in the study of medicine?

Sociologists study **medicine** as a social institution. As practiced in the United States, three of its primary characteristics are professionalization, bureaucracy, and the profit motive. P. 558.

The Symbolic Interactionist Perspective

What is the symbolic interactionist perspective on health and illness?

Health is not only a biological matter, but it is also intimately related to society. Illness is also far from an objective condition, for illness is always viewed from the framework of culture. The definitions applied to physical and mental conditions vary from one group to another. Pp. 558–559.

The Functionalist Perspective

What is the functionalist perspective on health and illness?

Functionalists stress that in return for being excused from their usual activities, people have to accept the **sick role.** They must assume responsibility for seeking competent medical help and cooperate in getting well so they can quickly resume normal activities. Pp. 559–560.

The Conflict Perspective

What is the conflict perspective on health and illness?

Health care is one of the scarce resources over which groups compete. In 1910, the education of physicians came under the control of a group of men who eliminated most of their competition and turned medicine into a monopoly that has become the largest business in the United States. On a global level, health care follows the stratification that we studied in Chapter 9. The best health care is available in the Most Industrialized Nations, the worst in the Least Industrialized Nations. Pp. 560–564.

Historical Patterns of Health

How have health patterns changed over time?

Patterns of disease in the United States have changed so extensively that of today's top ten killers, four did not even show up on the 1900 top ten list. Because most Americans live longer than their ancestors did, we can conclude that contemporary Americans are healthier. For mental illness, we have no idea how the current rate of mental illness compares with that of the past, for we have no baselines from which to make comparisons. P. 564.

Issues in Health Care

How does treating health care as a commodity lead to social inequalities?

Because health care is a commodity to be sold to the highest bidder, the United States has a **two-tier system of medical care** in which the poor receive inferior health care for both their mental and physical illnesses. Pp. 565–567.

What are some other problems in U.S. health care?

One problem is **defensive medicine,** which refers to medical procedures that are done for the physician's benefit, not for the benefit of the patient. Intended to protect physicians from lawsuits, these tests and consultations add huge amounts to the nation's medical bill. Other problems are incompetence, **depersonalization,** conflict of interest, medical fraud, and racism and sexism. Pp. 567–571.

Why is medically assisted suicide an issue now?

People's bodies can be kept alive by technology even when they have no brain waves. This leads to questions about the meaning of life and when to "pull the plug." Research findings on **euthanasia** in Holland have fueled this controversy. Pp. 571–572.

What attempts have been made to cut medical costs?

Health maintenance organizations (HMOs) and diagnosis-related groups (DRGs) are among the measures that have been taken to reduce medical costs. National health insurance, which has run into immense opposition, has been proposed. The most controversial proposal is to ration medical care. Pp. 573–575.

Threats to Health

What are some threats to the health of Americans?

Discussed here are AIDS, which has stabilized in the United States but is devastating sub-Saharan Africa; obesity and thinness; alcohol and nicotine; **disabling environments;** unethical experiments, of which the Tuskegee syphilis experiments and the Cold War radiation experiments are two examples; and the globalization of disease. Pp. 575–583.

The Search for Alternatives

Are there alternatives to our current health care system?

Two primary alternatives were discussed: a change in focus from treatment to prevention, and alternative medicine. For comparison, we examined the health care systems in Sweden, Russia, and China. Pp. 583–586.

Thinking Critically
about Chapter 19

1. A major issue in this chapter is the tension between medicine as a right and medicine as a commodity. What arguments support each side of this issue?

2. How do values and lifestyle affect health? What does this have to do with sociology?

3. Have you had an experience with alternative medicine? Or do you know someone who has? If so, how did the treatment (and the theory underlying the cause of the medical problem) differ from standard medical practice?

Additional Resources

What can you use MySocLab for?

 www.mysoclab.com

- **Study and Review:** Pre- and Post-Tests, Practice Tests, Flash Cards, Individualized Study Plans.

- **Current Events:** *Sociology in the News,* the daily *New York Times,* and more.

- **Research and Writing:** *Research Navigator, Writing About Sociology,* and more,

Where Can I Read More on This Topic?

Suggested readings for this chapter are listed at the back of this book.

Population and Urbanization

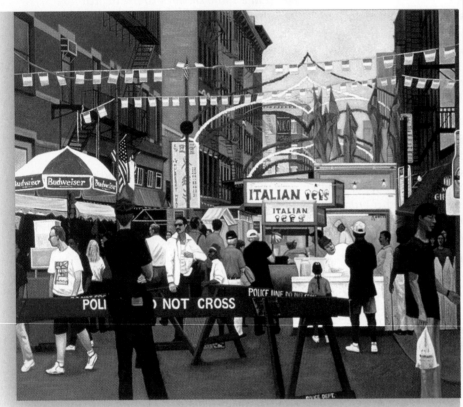

Sharon Florin, *Feast of San Gennaro*, 1998

The image still haunts me. There stood Celia, age 30, her distended stomach visible proof that her thirteenth child was on its way. Her oldest was only 14 years old! A mere boy by our standards, he had already gone as far in school as he ever would. Each morning, he joined the men to work in the fields. Each evening around twilight, I saw him return home, exhausted from hard labor in the subtropical sun.

I was living in Colima, Mexico, and Celia and Angel had invited me for dinner. Their home clearly reflected the family's poverty. A thatched hut consisting of only a single room served as home for all fourteen members of the family. At night, the parents and younger children crowded into a double bed, while the eldest boy slept in a hammock. As in many homes in the village, despite the crawling scorpions, the other children slept on mats spread on the dirt floor.

> **There stood Celia, age 30, her distended stomach visible proof that her thirteenth child was on its way.**

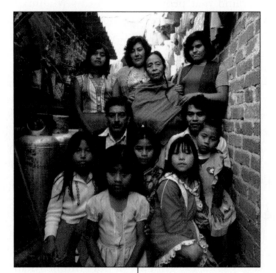

The home was meagerly furnished. It had only a gas stove, a table, and a cabinet where Celia stored her few cooking utensils and clay dishes. There were no closets; clothes were hung on pegs in the walls. There also were no chairs, not even one. I was used to the poverty in this village, but this really startled me. The family was so poor that they could not afford even a single chair.

Celia beamed as she told me how much she looked forward to the birth of her next child. Could she really mean it? It was hard to imagine that any woman would want to be in her situation.

Yet Celia meant every word. She was as full of delighted anticipation as she had been with her first child—and with all the others in between.

How could Celia have wanted so many children—especially when she lived in such poverty? That question bothered me. I couldn't let it go until I understood why.

This chapter helps to provide an answer.

POPULATION IN GLOBAL PERSPECTIVE

Celia's story takes us into the heart of **demography,** the study of the size, composition, growth, and distribution of human populations. It brings us face to face with the question of whether we are doomed to live in a world so filled with people that there will be very little space for anybody. Will our planet be able to support its growing population? Or are chronic famine and mass starvation the sorry fate of most earthlings?

Let's look at how concern about population growth began.

A Planet with No Space for Enjoying Life?

The story begins with the lowly potato. When the Spanish *conquistadores* found that people in the Andes Mountains ate this vegetable, which was unknown in Europe, they brought some home to cultivate. At first, Europeans viewed the potato with suspicion, but gradually it became the main food of the lower classes. With a greater abundance of food, fertility increased, and the death rate dropped. Europe's population soared, almost doubling during the 1700s (McKeown 1977; McNeill 1999).

Thomas Malthus (1766–1834), an English economist, saw this surging growth as a sign of doom. In 1798, he wrote a book that became world famous, *First Essay on Population 1798.* In it, Malthus proposed what became known as the **Malthus theorem.** He argued that although population grows geometrically (from 2 to 4 to 8 to 16 and so forth), the food supply increases only arithmetically (from 1 to 2 to 3 to 4 and so on). This meant, he claimed, that if births go unchecked, the population of a country, or even of the world, will outstrip its food supply.

The New Malthusians

Was Malthus right? This question has become a matter of heated debate among demographers. One group, which can be called the *New Malthusians,* is convinced that today's situation is at least as grim as—if not grimmer than—Malthus ever imagined. For example, *the world's population is growing so fast that in just the time it takes you to read this chapter, another twenty thousand to forty thousand babies will be born!* By this time tomorrow, the earth will have over 200,000 more people to feed. This increase goes on hour after hour, day after day, without letup. For an illustration of this growth, see Figure 20.1.

The New Malthusians point out that the world's population is following an **exponential growth curve.** This means that if growth doubles during approximately equal intervals of time, it suddenly accelerates. To illustrate the far-reaching implications of exponential growth, sociologist William Faunce (1981) retold an old parable about a poor man who saved a rich man's life. The rich man was grateful and said that he wanted to reward the man for his heroic deed.

In earlier generations, large farm families were common. Having many children was functional—there were many hands to help with crops, food production, and food preparation. As the country industrialized and urbanized, this changed to a dysfunction—children became expensive and nonproducing. Consequently, the size of families shrank as we entered Stage 3 of the demographic transition. In 1939, when this photo was taken in McIntosh County, Oklahoma, many farm families had more children than the number shown here.

Figure 20.1 How Fast Is the World's Population Growing?

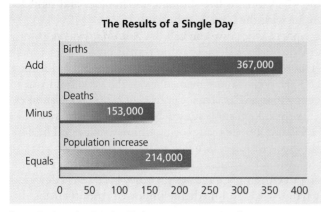

The Results of a Single Day

Add — Births: 367,000
Minus — Deaths: 153,000
Equals — Population increase: 214,000

(0 50 100 150 200 250 300 350 400)

The Accumulating Increase

Each second 2.5
Each minute 150
Each hour 8,900
Each day 214,000

Each week 1,500,000
Each month 6,500,000
Each year 78,000,000

Source: By the author. Based on Haub 2002, 2005, 2006; McFalls 2007.

The man replied that he would like his reward to be spread out over a four-week period, with each day's amount being twice what he received on the preceding day. He also said he would be happy to receive only one penny on the first day. The rich man immediately handed over the penny and congratulated himself on how cheaply he had gotten by.

At the end of the first week, the rich man checked to see how much he owed and was pleased to find that the total was only $1.27. By the end of the second week he owed only $163.83. On the twenty-first day, however, the rich man was surprised to find that the total had grown to $20,971.51. When the twenty-eighth day arrived the rich man was shocked to discover that he owed $1,342,177.28 for that day alone and that the total reward had jumped to $2,684,354.56!

This is precisely what alarms the New Malthusians. They claim that humanity has just entered the "fourth week" of an exponential growth curve. Figure 20.2 shows why they think the day of reckoning is just around the corner. It took from the beginning of time until 1800 for the world's population to reach its first billion. It then took only 130 years (1930) to add the second billion. Just thirty years later (1960), the world population hit 3 billion. The time it took to reach the fourth billion was cut in half, to only fifteen years (1975). Then just twelve years later (in 1987), the total reached 5 billion, and in another twelve years it hit 6 billion (in 1999).

On average, every minute of every day, 150 babies are born. As Figure 20.1 shows, at sunset the world has 214,000 more people than it did the day before. In one year, this amounts to an increase of 78 million people. In just four years, the population of the world increases by an amount larger than the entire U.S. population. You might think of it this way: *In just the next twelve years the world's population will increase as much as it did during the first 1,800 years after the birth of Christ.*

These totals terrify the New Malthusians. They are convinced that we are headed toward a showdown between population and food. In the year 2025, the population of just India, Pakistan, and Bangladesh is expected to be more than the entire world's population was 100 years ago (Haub 2006). It is obvious that we will run out of food if we don't curtail population growth. Soon we are going to see more pitiful, starving Pakistani and Bangladeshi children on television.

Figure 20.2 World Population Growth Over 2,000 Years

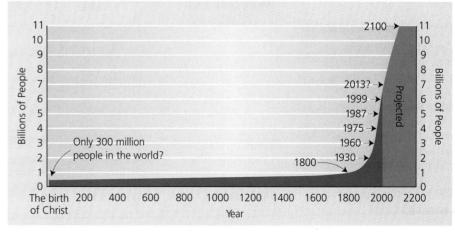

Only 300 million people in the world?

2100
2013?
1999
1987
1975
1960
1930
1800

Sources: Modified from Piotrow 1973; McFalls 2007.

The Anti-Malthusians

All of this seems obvious, and no one wants to live shoulder-to-shoulder and fight for scraps. How, then, can anyone argue with the New Malthusians?

An optimistic group of demographers, whom we can call the *Anti-Malthusians,* paint a far different picture. They believe that Europe's **demographic transition** provides a more accurate glimpse into the future. This transition is diagrammed in Figure 20.3. During most of its history, Europe was in Stage 1. Its population remained about the same from year to year, for high death rates offset the high birth rates. Then came Stage 2, the "population explosion" that so upset Malthus. Europe's population surged because birth rates remained high while death rates went down. Finally, Europe made the transition to Stage 3: The population stabilized as people brought their birth rates into line with their lower death rates.

This, say the Anti-Malthusians, will also happen in the Least Industrialized Nations. Their current surge in population growth simply indicates that they have reached Stage 2 of the demographic transition. Hybrid seeds and medicine imported from the Most Industrialized Nations have cut their death rates, but their birth rates remain high. When they move into Stage 3, as surely they will, we will wonder what all the fuss was about. In fact, their growth is already slowing.

Who Is Correct?

As you can see, both the New Malthusians and the Anti-Malthusians have looked at historical trends and projected them onto the future. The New Malthusians project continued world growth and are alarmed. The Anti-Malthusians project Stage 3 of the demographic transition onto the Least Industrialized Nations and are reassured.

There is no question that the Least Industrialized Nations are in Stage 2 of the demographic transition. The question is: Will these nations enter Stage 3? After World War II, the West exported its hybrid seeds, herbicides, and techniques of public hygiene around the globe. Death rates plummeted in the Least Industrialized Nations as their food supply increased and health improved. Because their birth rates stayed high, their populations mushroomed. Just as Malthus had done 200 years before, demographers predicted worldwide catastrophe if something were not done immediately to halt the population explosion (Ehrlich and Ehrlich 1972, 1978).

We can use the conflict perspective to understand what happened when this message reached the leaders of the industrialized world. They saw the mushrooming populations

demographic transition a three-stage historical process of population growth: first, high birth rates and high death rates; second, high birth rates and low death rates; and third, low birth rates and low death rates; a fourth stage has begun to appear in the Most Industrialized Nations, as depicted in Figure 20.3

Figure 20.3 The Demographic Transition

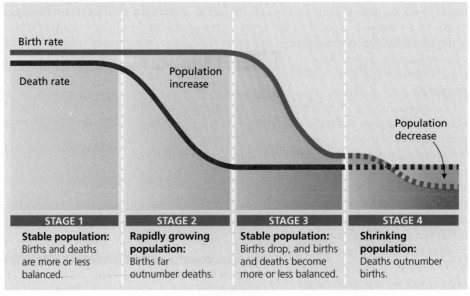

Note: The standard demographic transition is depicted by Stages 1–3. Stage 4 has been suggested by some Anti-Malthusians.

of the Least Industrialized Nations as a threat to the global balance of power they had so carefully worked out. With swollen populations, the poorer countries might demand a larger share of the earth's resources. The leaders found the United Nations to be a willing tool, and they used it to spearhead efforts to reduce world population growth. The results have been remarkable. The annual growth of the Least Industrialized Nations has dropped from an average of 2.1 percent a year in the 1960s to 1.5 percent today (Haub and Yinger 1994; Haub 2006).

The New Malthusians and Anti-Malthusians have greeted this news with significantly different interpretations. For the Anti-Malthusians, this slowing of growth is the signal they had been waiting for: Stage 3 of the demographic transition has begun. First the death rate in the Least Industrialized Nations fell—now, just as they predicted, their birth rates are also falling. Did you notice, they would say, if they looked at Figure 20.2, that it took 12 years to add the fifth billion to the world's population—and also 12 years to add the sixth billion? Population momentum is slowing. The New Malthusians reply that a slower growth rate still spells catastrophe—it just will take longer for it to hit.

The Anti-Malthusians also argue that our future will be the opposite of what the New Malthusians worry about: There are going to be too few children in the world, not too many. The world's problem will not be a population explosion, but **population shrinkage**—populations getting smaller. They point out that births in sixty-five countries have already dropped so low that those countries no longer produce enough children to maintain their populations. Of the forty-two countries of Europe, *all* of them fill more coffins than cradles (Haub 2006).

Some Anti-Malthusians even predict a "demographic free fall" (Mosher 1997). As more nations enter Stage 4 of the demographic transition, the world's population will peak at about 8 or 9 billion, then begin to grow smaller. Two hundred years from now, they say, we will have a lot fewer people on earth.

Who is right? It simply is too early to tell. Like the proverbial pessimists who see the glass of water half empty, the New Malthusians interpret changes in world population growth negatively. And like the eternal optimists who see the same glass half full, the Anti-Malthusians view the figures positively. Sometime during our lifetime we should know the answer.

Why Are People Starving?

Pictures of starving children gnaw at our conscience. We live in such abundance, while these children and their parents starve before our very eyes. Why don't they have enough food? Is it because there are too many of them, or simply that the abundant food produced around the world does not reach them?

The Anti-Malthusians make a point that seems irrefutable. As Figure 20.4 on the next page shows, *there is now more food for each person in the world than there was in 1950.* Although the world's population has more than doubled since 1950, improved seeds and fertilizers have made more food available for *each* person on earth. Even more

Photos of starving people, such as this mother and her child, haunt Americans and other members of the Most Industrialized Nations. Many of us wonder why, when some are starving, we should live in the midst of such abundance, often overeating and even casually scraping excess food into the garbage. We even have eating contests to see who can eat the most food in the least time. The text discusses reasons for such disparities.

Figure 20.4 **How Much Food Does the World Produce Per Person?**

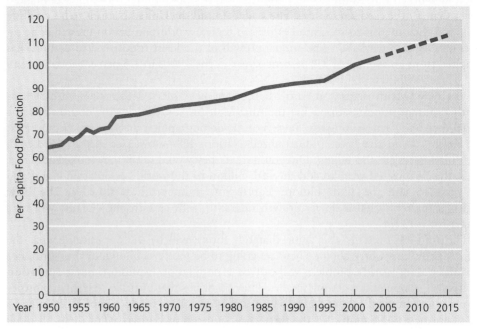

Note: Julian Simon provided the stimulus for producing this figure. I used to reproduce a figure that he had developed, but since his death in 1998 inconsistencies in data have made it difficult to update his work. Based on UN data, this figure overcomes that limitation.

Source: By the author. Based on Simon 1981; Food and Agriculture Organization of the United Nations 2006.

food may be on the way, for bioengineers are making breakthroughs in agriculture. The United Nations estimates that even without agricultural gains through bioengineering, there will be ample food to keep up with the world's growing population for at least the next 30 years (United Nations 2000).

Then why do people die of hunger? From Figure 20.4, we can conclude that starvation occurs not because the earth produces too little food, but because particular places lack food. Droughts and wars are the main reasons. Just as droughts slow or stop food production, so does war. In nations ravaged by civil war, opposing sides either confiscate or burn crops, and farmers flee to the cities (Thurow 2005). While some countries have their food supply disrupted, others are producing more food than their people can consume. At the same time that countries of Africa are hit by drought and civil wars—and people are starving—the U.S. government pays farmers to *reduce* their output of crops. The United States' problem is too much food; West Africa's is too little.

The New Malthusians counter with the argument that the world's population is still growing and that we do not know how long the earth will continue to produce enough food. They remind us of the penny doubling each day. It is only a matter of time, they insist, until the earth no longer produces enough food—not "if," but "when."

Both the New Malthusians and the Anti-Malthusians have contributed significant ideas, but theories will not eliminate famines. Starving children are going to continue to peer out at us from our televisions and magazines, their tiny, shriveled bodies and bloated stomachs nagging at our conscience and imploring us to do something. Regardless of the underlying causes of this human misery, it has a simple solution: Food can be transferred from nations that have a surplus.

These pictures of starving Africans leave the impression that Africa is overpopulated. Why else would all those people be starving? The truth, however, is far different. Africa has 23 percent of the earth's land, but only 14 percent of the earth's population (Haub 2006). Africa even has vast areas of fertile land that have not yet been farmed. The reason for famines in Africa, then, *cannot* be too many people living on too little land.

Population Growth

Even if starvation is the result of a maldistribution of food rather than overpopulation, the fact remains that the Least Industrialized Nations are growing *fifteen times faster* than the Most Industrialized Nations—1.5 percent a year compared with 0.1 percent (Haub 2006). At these rates, it will take 1,000 years for the average Most Industrialized Nation to double its population, but just 48 years for the average Least Industrialized Nation to do so. Figure 20.5 on the next page puts the matter in stark perspective. So does the Down-to-Earth Sociology box below. Why do the nations that can least afford it have so many children?

Down-to-Earth Sociology

How the Tsunami Can Help Us to Understand Population Growth

ON DECEMBER 26, 2004, the world witnessed the worst tsunami in modern history. As the giant waves rolled over the shores of unsuspecting countries, they swept away people from all walks of life—from lowly sellers of fish to wealthy tourists visiting the fleshpots of Sri Lanka. Over the next several days, as the government reports came in, the media kept increasing the death toll. When those reports were tallied two months later, the total stood at 286,000 people.

In terms of lives lost, this was not the worst single disaster the world had seen. Several hundred thousand people had been killed in China's Tangshan earthquake in 1976. And then there was the 1945 firebombing of Dresden, Germany, by U.S. and British forces, where the loss of lives came to between 35,000 and a half million (lower estimates by U.S. sources and higher ones by German sources).

In terms of geography, however, this was the broadest. It involved more countries than any other disaster in modern history. And, unlike its predecessors, this tsunami occurred during a period of instantaneous, global reporting of events.

As news of the tsunami was transmitted around the globe, the world went into shock. The response was almost immediate, and aid poured in—in unprecedented amounts. Governments gave over $3 billion. Citizens pitched in, too, from Little Leaguers and religious groups to the "regulars" at the local bars.

I want to use the tsunami disaster to illustrate the incredible population growth that is taking place in the Least Industrialized Nations. My intention is not to dismiss the tragedy of these deaths, for they were horrible—as were the maiming of so many, the sufferings of families, the lost livelihoods, and the many children who were left without parents.

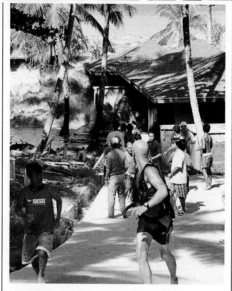

This photo was snapped at Koh Raya in Thailand, just as the tsunami wave of December 26, 2004, landed.

Let's consider Indonesia first. With 233,000 deaths, this country was hit the hardest. Indonesia had an annual growth rate of 1.6 percent (its "rate of natural increase," as demographers call it). With a population of 220 million, Indonesia is growing by 3,300,000 people each year (Haub 2004). This increase, coming to 9,041 people each day, means that it took Indonesia just under four weeks (26 days) to replace the huge number of people it lost to the tsunami.

The next greatest loss of lives took place in Sri Lanka. With its lower rate of natural increase of 1.3 and its smaller population of 19 million, it took Sri Lanka a little longer to replace the 31,000 people it lost: 46 days.

India was the third hardest hit. With India's 1 billion people and its 1.7 rate of natural increase, India is adding 17 million people to its population each year. This comes to 46,575 people each day. At an increase of 1,940 people per hour, India took just 8 or 9 hours to replace the 16,000 people it lost to the tsunami.

The next hardest hit was Thailand. It took Thailand 4 or 5 days to replace the 5,000 people that it lost.

For the other countries, the losses were smaller: 298 for Somalia, 82 for the Maldives; 68 for Malaysia; 61 for Myanmar, 10 for Tanzania, 2 for Bangladesh, and 1 for Kenya ("Tsunami deaths . . ." 2005).

Again, I don't want to detract from the horrifying tragedy of the 2004 tsunami. But by using this event as a comparative backdrop, we can gain a better grasp of the unprecedented population growth that is taking place in the Least Industrialized Nations.

Figure 20.5 World Population Growth, 1750–2150

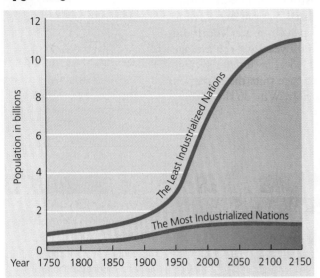

Source: "The World of the Child 6 Billion," 2000; Haub 2006.

Why the Least Industrialized Nations Have So Many Children

Why do people in the countries that can least afford it have so many children? To understand this, let's figure out why Celia is so happy about having her thirteenth child. Here, we need to apply the symbolic interactionist perspective. We must take the role of the other so that we can understand the world of Celia and Angel as *they* see it. As our culture does for us, their culture provides a perspective on life that guides their choices. Celia and Angel's culture tells them that twelve children are *not* enough, that they ought to have a thirteenth—as well as a fourteenth and fifteenth. How can this be? Let's consider three reasons why bearing many children plays a central role in their lives—and in the lives of millions upon millions of poor people around the world.

First is the status of parenthood. In the Least Industrialized Nations, motherhood is the most prized status a woman can achieve. The more children a woman bears, the more she is thought to have achieved the purpose for which she was born. Similarly, a man proves his manhood by fathering children. The more children he fathers, especially sons, the better—for through them his name lives on.

Second, the community supports this view. Celia and those like her live in *Gemeinschaft* communities, where people identify closely with one another and share similar views of life. To them, children are a sign of God's blessing. By producing children, people reflect the values of their community, achieve status, and are assured that they are blessed by God. It is the barren woman, not the woman with a dozen children, who is to be pitied.

These factors certainly provide strong motivations for bearing many children. Yet there is also another powerful incentive: For poor people in the Least Industrialized Nations, children are economic assets. Like Celia and Angel's eldest son, children begin contributing to the family income at a young age. (See Figure 20.6.) But even more than this: Children are also the equivalent of our Social Security. In the Least Industrialized Nations, the government does not provide social security or medical and unemployment insurance. This motivates people to bear *more* children, for when parents become too old to work, or when no work is to be found, their children take care of them. The more children they have, the broader their base of support will be.

To those of us who live in the Most Industrialized Nations, it seems irrational to have many children. And *for us it would be.* Understanding life from the framework of people who are living it, however—the essence of the symbolic interactionist perspective—reveals how it makes perfect sense to have many children. Consider this report by a government worker in India:

> Thaman Singh (a very poor man, a water carrier) . . . welcomed me inside his home, gave me a cup of tea (with milk and "market" sugar, as he proudly pointed out later), and said: "You were trying to convince me that I shouldn't have any more sons. Now, you see, I have six sons and two daughters and I sit at home in leisure. They are grown up and they bring me money. One even works outside the village as a laborer. You told me I was a poor man and couldn't support a large family. Now, you see, because of my large family I am a rich man." (Mamdani 1973)

Conflict theorists offer a different view of why women in the Least Industrialized Nations bear so many children. Feminists argue that women like Celia have internalized values that support male dominance. In Latin America, *machismo*—an emphasis on male virility and dominance—is common. To father many children, especially sons, shows that a man is sexually potent, giving him higher status in the community. From a conflict perspective, then, the reason poor people have so many children is that men control women's reproductive choices.

population pyramid a graphic representation of a population, divided into age and sex

Figure 20.6 Why the Poor Need Children

Children are an economic asset in the Least Industrialized Nations. Based on a survey in Indonesia, this figure shows that boys and girls can be net income earners for their families by the age of 9 or 10.

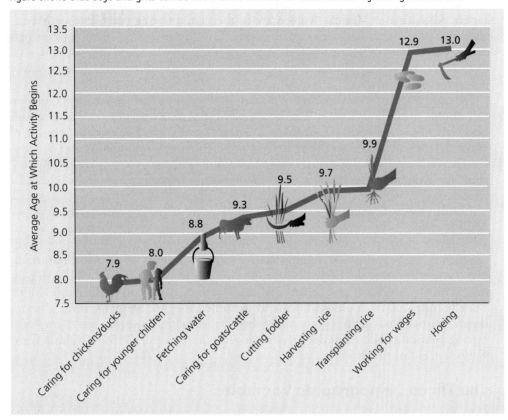

Source: U.N. Fund for Population Activities.

Implications of Different Rates of Growth

The result of Celia and Angel's desire for many children—and of the millions of Celias and Angels like them—is that Mexico's population will double in thirty-five years. In contrast, women in the United States are having so few children that if it weren't for immigration, the U.S. population would begin to shrink. To illustrate population dynamics, demographers use **population pyramids.** These depict a country's population by age and sex. Look at Figure 20.7, which shows the population pyramids of the United States, Mexico, and the world.

To see why population pyramids are important, I would like you to imagine a miracle. Imagine that, overnight, Mexico is transformed into a nation as industrialized as the United States. Imagine also that overnight the average number of children per woman drops to 2.0, the same as in the United States. If this

Figure 20.7 Three Population Pyramids

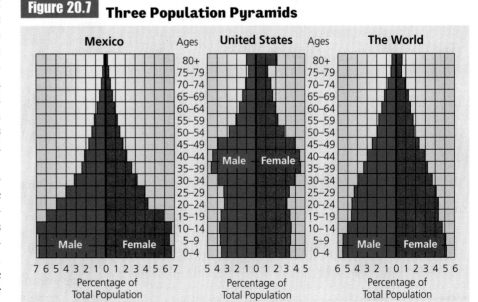

Source: Population Today, 26, 9, September 1998:4, 5.

happened, it would seem that Mexico's population would grow at the same rate as that of the United States, right?

But this isn't at all what would happen. Instead, the population of Mexico would continue to grow much faster. As you can see from these population pyramids, a much higher percentage of Mexican women are in their childbearing years. Even if Mexico and the United States had the same birth rate (2.0 children per woman), a larger percentage of women in Mexico would be giving birth, and Mexico's population would grow faster. As demographers like to phrase this, Mexico's *age structure* gives it greater *population momentum.*

Mexico's population momentum is so strong that, as we saw earlier, its population will double in thirty-five years. The implications of a doubling population are mind-boggling. *Just to stay even,* within thirty-five years Mexico must double the number of available jobs and housing facilities; its food production; its transportation and communication facilities; its water, gas, sewer, and electrical systems; and its schools, hospitals, churches, civic buildings, theaters, stores, and parks. If Mexico fails to double them, its already meager standard of living will drop even further.

Conflict theorists point out that a declining standard of living poses the threat of political instability—protests, riots, even revolution—and, in response, repression by the government. Political instability in one country can spill into others, threatening an entire region's balance of power. Fearing such disruptions, leaders of the Most Industrialized Nations are using the United Nations to direct a campaign of worldwide birth control. With one hand they give agricultural aid, IUDs, and condoms to the masses in the Least Industrialized Nations—while, with the other, they sell weapons to the elites in these countries. Both actions, say conflict theorists, serve the same purpose: that of promoting political stability in order to maintain the dominance of the Most Industrialized Nations in global stratification.

The Three Demographic Variables

How many people will live in the United States fifty years from now? What will the world's population be then? These are important questions. Educators want to know how many schools to build. Manufacturers want to anticipate changes in the market for their products. The government needs to know how many doctors, engineers, and executives to train. Politicians want to know how many people will be paying taxes—and how many young people will be available to fight a war.

To project the future of populations, demographers use three **demographic variables:** fertility, mortality, and migration. Let's look at each.

Fertility The number of children that the average woman bears is called the **fertility rate.** The world's overall fertility rate is 2.7, which means that during her lifetime the average woman in the world bears 2.7 children. At 2.0, the fertility rate of U.S. women is considerably less (Haub 2006). A term that is sometimes confused with fertility is **fecundity,** the number of children that women are *capable* of bearing. This number is rather high, as some women have given birth to 30 children (McFalls 2007).

The region of the world that has the highest fertility rate is Middle Africa, where the average woman gives birth to 6.3 children; the lowest is Eastern Europe, where the average woman bears 1.3 children (Haub 2006). As you can see from Table 20.1, Macao has the world's lowest fertility rate. There, the average woman gives birth to only 0.9 children. Four of the lowest-birth countries are in Asia. The rest are located in Europe. The countries with the highest

Table 20.1 Extremes in Childbirth

WHERE DO WOMEN GIVE BIRTH TO THE FEWEST CHILDREN?		WHERE DO WOMEN GIVE BIRTH TO THE MOST CHILDREN?	
Country	Number of Children	Country	Number of Children
Macau	0.9	Niger	7.9
Hong Kong	1.0	Guinea-Bissau	7.1
South Korea	1.1	Mali	7.1
Taiwan	1.1	Somalia	6.9
Poland	1.2	Uganda	6.9
Slovenia	1.2	Afghanistan	6.8
Ukraine	1.2	Angola	6.8
Germany	1.3	Burundi	6.8
Italy	1.3	Liberia	6.8
Russia	1.3	Chad	6.7

Note: Other countries with 1.2 children per woman are Belarus, Bosnia-Herzegovina, and Moldova; others that average 1.3 children are Bulgaria, Greece, Hungary, and Spain.

Source: Haub 2006.

birth rate are also clustered. With the exception of Afghanistan, all of them are in Africa. Niger in West Africa holds the record for the world's highest birth rate. There, the average woman gives birth to 7.9 children, *nine* times as many children as the average woman in Macao.

To compute the fertility rate of a country, demographers analyze the government's records of births. From these, they figure the country's **crude birth rate,** the annual number of live births per 1,000 population. There may be considerable inaccuracies here, of course. The birth records in many of the Least Industrialized Nations are haphazard, at best.

Mortality The second demographic variable is measured by the **crude death rate,** the annual number of deaths per 1,000 population. It, too, varies widely around the world. The highest death rate is 28, a record held by Botswana and Lesotho in Southern Africa. At 1, the oil-rich country of Kuwait holds the world's record for the lowest death rate (Haub 2006).

Migration The third demographic variable is *migration,* the movement of people from one area to another. There are two types of migration. The first type is people moving from one region to another within the same country. During and after World War II, in what is known as "The Great Migration," millions of African Americans moved from the South to the North. In a historical shift, many are now returning to the South to participate in its growing economy, to enjoy its warmer climate, and to renew ties with family roots (Frey 2001).

The second type of migration is people moving from one country to another. Demographers use the term **net migration rate** to refer to the difference between the number of *immigrants* (people moving into a country) and *emigrants* (people moving out of a country) per 1,000 population. Unlike fertility and mortality, migration does not affect the global population, for people are simply shifting their residence from one country or region to another.

As you know, immigrants are seeking a better life. They are willing to give up the security of their family and friends to move to a country with a strange language and unfamiliar customs. What motivates people to embark on such a venture? To understand migration, we need to look at both push and pull factors. The *push* factors are what people want to escape: poverty or persecution for their religious and political ideas. The *pull* factors are the magnets that draw people to a new land, such as opportunities for education, higher wages, better jobs, the freedom to worship or to discuss political ideas, and a more promising future for their children.

Around the world, the flow of migration is from the Least Industrialized Nations to the industrialized countries. After "migrant paths" are established, immigration often accelerates as networks of kin and friends become additional magnets that attract more people from the same nation—and even from the same villages.

Current U.S. immigration shows greater diversity of origin. These immigrants are Sikhs, members of a religion centered in Punjab, India.

By far, the United States is the world's number one choice of immigrants. The United States admits more immigrants each year than all the other nations of the world combined. Thirty-four million residents—one of every nine Americans—were born in other countries (*Statistical Abstract* 2007:Table 48). Table 20.2 on the next page shows where recent U.S. immigrants were born. To escape grinding poverty, such as that which surrounds Celia and Angel, millions of people also enter the United States illegally, most of them from Mexico and many others from Central and South America.

Experts cannot agree about whether immigrants are a net contributor to the U.S. economy or a drain on it. Some economists claim that immigrants benefit the economy. After subtracting what immigrants collect in welfare and adding what they produce in jobs and taxes, they conclude that immigrants produce more than they cost (Simon 1986, 1993). Other economists conclude that immigrants drain taxpayers of billions of dollars a year (Huddle 1993; Davis and Weinstein 2002). Evidence seems strong that immigrants lower

crude birth rate the annual number of live births per 1,000 population

crude death rate the annual number of deaths per 1,000 population

net migration rate the difference between the number of immigrants and emigrants per 1,000 population

Table 20.2 Country of Birth of U.S. Immigrants

Asia	**400,000**	El Salvador	21,000	Brazil	17,000
India	85,000	Jamaica	18,000	Peru	16,000
China	70,000	Guatemala	17,000	Ecuador	12,000
Philippines	61,000	**Europe**	**177,000**	Venezuela	11,000
Korea	27,000	Ukraine	23,000	Guyana	9,000
Vietnam	33,000	United Kingdom	20,000	Argentina	7,000
Pakistan	15,000	Russia	18,000		
Iran	14,000	Poland	15,000	**Africa**	**85,000**
		Bosnia and Herzegovina	14,000	Ethiopia	11,000
North America	**346,000**	Germany	9,000	Nigeria	11,000
Mexico	161,000	Albania	6,000	Egypt	8,000
Cuba	36,000			Ghana	7,000
Dominican Republic	28,000	**South America**	**103,000**	Somalia	6,000
Canada	22,000	Colombia	26,000	South Africa	5,000

Note: Totals are for the top countries of origin for 2005, the latest year available.

Source: By the author. Based on *Statistical Abstract* 2007:Table 8.

the income of the native-born Americans with whom they compete (Borjas 2004, 2005, 2006). The fairest conclusion seems to be that the more educated immigrants produce more than they cost, while the less educated cost more than they produce.

Problems in Forecasting Population Growth

The total of the three demographic variables—fertility, mortality, and net migration—gives us a country's **growth rate,** the net change after people have been added to and subtracted from a population. What demographers call the **basic demographic equation** is quite simple:

Growth rate = births − deaths + net migration

If population increase depended only on biology, the demographer's job would be easy. But social factors—wars, economic booms and busts, plagues, and famines—push rates of birth and death and migration up or down. As is shown in the Cultural Diversity box on the next page, even infanticide can affect population growth. Politicians also complicate projections. Sometimes governments try to persuade women to bear fewer—or more—children. When Hitler decided that Germany needed more "Aryans," the German government outlawed abortion and offered cash bonuses to women who gave birth. The population increased. Today, European leaders are alarmed that their birth rates have dropped so low that their populations will shrink. With its population dropping by 700,000 people a year, Russia's leaders are offering incentives to women to have children: cash grants for each child and subsidies for day care (Chivers 2006).

In China, we find the opposite situation. Many people know that China tries to limit population growth with its "One couple, one child" policy, but few know how ruthlessly officials enforce this policy. Steven Mosher (2006), an anthropologist who did fieldwork in China, revealed that—whether she wants it or not—after the birth of her first child, each woman is fitted with an IUD (intrauterine device). If a woman has a second child, she is sterilized. If a woman gets pregnant without government permission (yes, you read that right), the fetus is aborted. If she does not consent to an abortion, one is performed on her anyway—even if she is nine months pregnant.

In the face of Western disapproval and in an effort to present a better image to accompany its new role on the world political stage, Chinese leaders have relented somewhat. They have kept their "One couple, one child" policy, but they have begun to make exceptions to it. In rural areas, authorities allow a woman to bear a second child—if the first child is a girl. This improves the couple's chances of getting a son (Baochang et al. 2007). No unmarried women are allowed to give birth; any unmarried woman who gets pregnant is arrested and forced to have an abortion (Mosher 2006).

growth rate the net change in a population after adding births, subtracting deaths, and either adding or subtracting net migration

basic demographic equation growth rate equals births minus deaths plus net migration

Cultural Diversity *around the* World

Killing Little Girls: An Ancient and Thriving Practice

"THE MYSTERIOUS CASE OF THE Missing Girls" could have been the title of this box. Around the globe, for every 100 girls born, about 105 boys are born. In China, however, for every 100 baby girls, there are 120 baby boys. Given China's huge population, this means that China has several million fewer baby girls than it should have. Why?

The answer is *female infanticide,* the killing of baby girls. When a Chinese woman goes into labor, the village midwife sometimes grabs a bucket of water. If the newborn is a girl, she is plunged into the water before she can draw her first breath.

At the root of China's sexist infanticide is economics. The people are poor, and they have no pensions. When parents can no longer work, sons support them. In contrast, a daughter must be married off, at great expense, and at that point, her obligations transfer to her husband and his family.

These women in New Delhi, India, are protesting sex-selection abortion.

In the past few years, the percentage of boy babies has grown. The reason, again, is economics, but this time it has a new twist. As China opened the door to capitalism, travel and trade opened up—but primarily to men, for it is not thought appropriate for women to travel alone. With men finding themselves in a better position to bring profits home to the family, parents have one more reason to want male children.

The gender ratio is so lopsided that for people in their 20s there are six bachelors for every five potential brides. Concerned about this gender imbalance, officials have begun

a campaign to stop the drowning of girl babies. They are also trying to crack down on the abortions of girl fetuses.

In India, female infanticide is also common. Many Indian women use ultrasound to learn the sex of their child and then abort the fetus if it is a girl. Doctors take portable ultrasound machines from village to village, charging $8 for the test and $44 for the abortion. Although the use of ultrasound for this purpose is illegal, this practice accounts for the abortion of about 3 million girls a year.

It is likely that the preference for boys, and the resulting female infanticide, will not disappear until the social structures that perpetuate sexism are dismantled. This is unlikely to take place until women hold as much power as men, a development that, should it ever occur, apparently lies far in the future.

In the meantime, politicians have become concerned about a primary sociological implication of female infanticide—that large numbers of young men who cannot marry pose a political threat. These "bare branches," as they are referred to in China, disgruntled and lacking the stabilizing influences of marriage and children, could become a breeding ground for political dissent. This threat could motivate the national elites to take steps against female infanticide.

Sources: Jordan 2000; Dugger 2001; Eckholm 2002; Raghunathan 2003; French 2004; Hudson and den Boer 2004; Riley 2004; Wonacott 2007; Yardley 2007.

Government actions can change a country's growth rate, but the main factor is not the government, but industrialization. *In every country that industrializes, the birth rate declines.* Not only does industrialization open up economic opportunities but also it makes rearing children more expensive. Children require more education and remain dependent longer. Significantly, the basis for conferring status also changes—from having many children to attaining education and displaying material wealth. People like Celia and Angel begin to see life differently, and their motivation to have many children

The Chinese government uses billboards to remind people of its "one couple, one child" policy. The fat on the child's face on this billboard in Shanghai carries an additional message—that curtailing childbirth brings prosperity, abundant food for all.

drops sharply. Not knowing how rapidly industrialization will progress or how quickly changes in values and reproductive behavior will follow adds to the difficulty of making accurate projections.

Because of these many complications, demographers play it safe by making several projections of population growth. For example, what will the U.S. population be in the year 2050? Between now and then, will we have **zero population growth,** with every 1,000 women giving birth to 2,100 children? (The extra 100 children make up for those who do not survive or reproduce.) Will a larger proportion of women go to college? (The more education women have, the fewer children they bear [Sutton and Matthews 2004].) How will immigration change? Will some devastating disease appear? With such huge variables, it is easy to see why demographers make the three projections of the U.S. population shown in Figure 20.8.

Let's look at a different aspect of population, where people live. Because more and more people around the world are living in cities, we shall concentrate on urban trends and urban life.

Figure 20.8 Population Projections of the United States

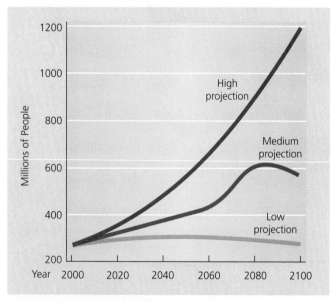

Note: The projections are based on different assumptions of fertility, mortality, and, especially, immigration.

Source: By the author. Based on *Statistical Abstract* 2002:Table 3.

zero population growth a demographic condition in which women bear only enough children to reproduce the population

city a place in which a large number of people are permanently based and do not produce their own food

URBANIZATION

As I was climbing a steep hill in Medellin, Colombia, in a district called El Tiro, my informant, Jaro, said, "This used to be a garbage heap." I stopped to peer through the vegetation alongside the path we were on, and sure enough, I could see bits of refuse still sticking out of the dirt. The "town" had been built on top of garbage.

This was just the first of my many revelations that day. The second was that El Tiro was so dangerous that the Medellin police refused to enter it. I shuddered for a moment, but I had good reason to trust Jaro. He had been a pastor in El Tiro for several years, and he knew the people well. I knew that if I stayed close to him I would be safe.

Actually, El Tiro was safer now than it had been. A group of young men had banded together to make it so, Jaro told me. A sort of frontier justice prevailed. The vigilantes told the prostitutes and drug dealers that there would be no prostitution or drug dealing in El Tiro, and to "take it elsewhere." They killed anyone who robbed or killed someone. And they even made families safer—they would beat up any man who got drunk and beat "his" woman. With the threat of instant justice, the area had become much safer.

Jaro then added that each household had to pay the group a monthly fee, which turned out to be less than a dollar in U.S. money. Each business had to pay a little more. For this, they received security.

As we wandered the streets of El Tiro, it did look safe—but I still stayed close to Jaro. And I wondered about this group of men who had made the area safe. What kept them from turning on the residents? Jaro had no answer. When Jaro pointed to two young men, whom he said were part of the ruling group, I asked if I could take their picture. They refused. I did not try to snap one on the sly.

My final revelation was El Tiro itself. On pages 604–605, you can see some of the things I saw that day.

Early cities were small economic centers surrounded by walls to keep out enemies. These cities had to be fortresses, for they were constantly threatened by armed, roving tribesmen and by leaders of nearby city-states who raised armies to enlarge their domain and enrich their coffers by sacking neighboring cities. Pictured here is Cologne, Germany, as depicted in a 1545 manuscript.

In this second part of the chapter, I will try to lay the context for understanding urban life—and El Tiro. Let's begin by first finding out how the city itself came about.

The Development of Cities

Cities are not new to the world scene. Perhaps as early as seven thousand years ago, people built small cities with massive defensive walls, such as biblically famous Jericho (Homblin 1973). Cities on a larger scale appeared about 3500 B.C., around the time that writing was invented (Chandler and Fox 1974; Hawley 1981). At that time, cities emerged in several parts of the world—first in Mesopotamia (Iran) and later in the Nile, Indus, and Yellow River valleys, in West Africa, along the shores of the Mediterranean, in Central America, and in the Andes (Fischer 1976; Flanagan 1990). In the Americas, the first city was Caral, in what is now Peru (Fountain 2001).

The key to the origin of cities is the development of more efficient agriculture (Lenski and Lenski 1987). Only when farming produces a surplus can some people stop producing food and gather in cities to spend time in other economic pursuits. A **city,** in fact, can be defined as a place in which a large number of people are permanently based and do not produce their own food. The invention of the plow about five thousand years ago created widespread agricultural surpluses, stimulating the development of towns and cities.

In comparison with those of today, most early cities were tiny, merely a collection of a few thousand people in agricultural centers or on major trade routes. The most notable exceptions are two cities that reached 1 million residents for a brief period of time before they declined—Changan in China about A.D. 800 and Baghdad in Persia (Iraq) about A.D. 900 (Chandler and Fox 1974). Even Athens at the peak of its power in the fifth century B.C. had about 250,000 inhabitants. Rome, at its peak, may have had a million people or more, but as it declined, its population fell to just 35,000 (Palen 2005).

Even 200 years ago, the only city in the world that had a population of more than a million was Peking (now Beijing), China (Chandler and Fox 1974). Then in just 100 years, by 1900, the number of such cities jumped to sixteen. The reason was the Industrial Revolution, which drew people to cities by providing work. The Industrial Revolution also stimulated rapid transportation and communication, and allowed people, resources, and products to be moved efficiently—all essential factors (called *infrastructure*) on which large cities depend. Figure 20.9 shows the global growth in the number of cities that have a million or more people (Brockerhoff 2000).

Figure 20.9 The Global Growth of Cities over One Million Residents

Sources: By the author. Based on Chandler and Fox 1974; Brockerhoff 2000.

A Walk Through El Tiro
Medellin, Colombia

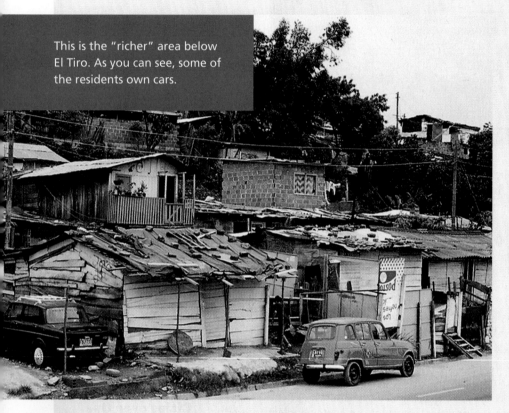

This is the "richer" area below El Tiro. As you can see, some of the residents own cars.

Kids are kids the world over. These children don't know they are poor. They are having a great time playing on a pile of dirt in the street.

This is one of my favorite photos. The woman is happy that she has a home—and proud of what she has done with it. What I find remarkable is the flower garden she so carefully tends, and has taken great effort to protect from children and dogs. I can see the care she would take of a little suburban home.

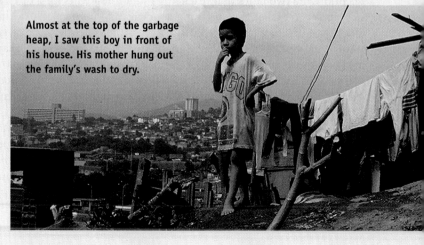

Almost at the top of the garbage heap, I saw this boy in front of his house. His mother hung out the family's wash to dry.

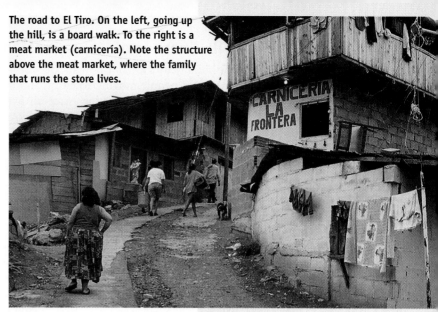

The road to El Tiro. On the left, going up the hill, is a board walk. To the right is a meat market (carnicería). Note the structure above the meat market, where the family that runs the store lives.

It doesn't take much skill to build your own house in El Tiro. A hammer and saw, some nails and used lumber will provide most of what you need. This man is building his house on top of another house.

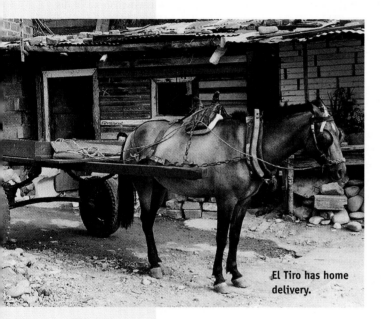

El Tiro has home delivery.

An infrastructure has developed to serve El Tiro. This woman is waiting in line to use the only public telephone.

What do the people do to make a living in El Tiro? Anything they can. This man is sharpening a saw in front of his home.

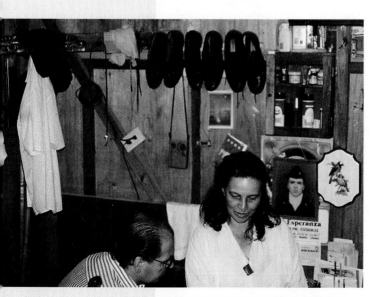

"What does an El Tiro home look like inside?," I kept wondering. Then Jaro, my guide at the left, took me inside the home of one of his parishioners. Amelia keeps a neat house, with everything highly organized.

The Process of Urbanization

Although cities are not new to the world scene, urbanization is. **Urbanization** refers to masses of people moving to cities, and these cities having a growing influence on society. Urbanization is taking place all over the world. In 1800, only 3 percent of the world's population lived in cities (Hauser and Schnore 1965). Then in 2007, for the first time in history, more people lived in cities than in rural areas. Urbanization is uneven across the globe. For the industrialized world, it is 77 percent, and for the Least Industrialized Nations, it is 41 percent (Haub 2006; Robb 2007). Without the Industrial Revolution this remarkable growth could not have taken place, for an extensive infrastructure is needed to support hundreds of thousands and even millions of people in a relatively small area.

To understand the city's attraction, we need to consider the "pulls" of urban life. Because of its exquisite division of labor, the city offers incredible variety—music ranging from rap and salsa to country and classical, shops that feature imported delicacies from around the world and those that sell special foods for vegetarians and diabetics. Cities also offer anonymity, which so many find refreshing in light of the tighter controls of village and small-town life. And, of course, the city offers work.

Some cities have grown so large and have so much influence over a region that the term *city* is no longer adequate to describe them. The term **metropolis** is used instead. This term refers to a central city surrounded by smaller cities and their suburbs. They are linked by transportation and communication and connected economically, and sometimes politically, through county boards and regional governing bodies. St. Louis is an example.

> Although this name, St. Louis, properly refers to a city of 340,000 people in Missouri, it also refers to another 2 million people who live in more than a hundred separate towns in both Missouri and Illinois. Altogether, the region is known as the "St. Louis or Bi-State Area." Although these towns are independent politically, they form an economic unit. They are linked by work (many people in the smaller towns work in St. Louis or are served by industries from St. Louis), by communications (they share the same area newspaper and radio and television stations), and by transportation (they use the same interstate highways, the Bi-State Bus system, and international airport). As symbolic interactionists would note, shared symbols (the Arch, the Mississippi River, Busch Brewery, the Cardinals, the Rams, the Blues—both the hockey team and the music) provide the residents a common identity.
>
> Most of the towns run into one another, and if you were to drive through this metropolis, you would not know that you were leaving one town and entering another—unless you had lived there for some time and were aware of the fierce small town identifications and rivalries that coexist within this overarching identity.

Some metropolises have grown so large and influential that the term **megalopolis** is used to describe them. This term refers to an overlapping area consisting of at least two metropolises and their many suburbs. Of the twenty or so megalopolises in the United States, the three largest are the Eastern seaboard running from Maine to Virginia, the area in Florida between Miami, Orlando, and Tampa, and California's coastal area between San Francisco and San Diego. The California megalopolis extends into Mexico and includes Tijuana and its suburbs.

This process of urban areas turning into a metropolis, and a metropolis developing into a megalopolis, occurs worldwide. When a city's population hits 10 million, it is called a **megacity.** In 1950, New York City was the only megacity in the world. Today there are 19. Figure 20.10 shows the world's ten largest megacities. Note that most megacities are located in the Least Industrialized Nations.

U.S. Urban Patterns

From Country to City   In its early years, the United States was almost exclusively rural. In 1790, only about 5 percent of Americans lived in cities. By 1920, this figure had jumped to 50 percent. Urbanization has continued without letup, and today 79 percent of Americans live in cities.

urbanization the process by which an increasing proportion of a population lives in cities and cities have a growing influence on the culture

metropolis a central city surrounded by smaller cities and their suburbs

megalopolis an urban area consisting of at least two metropolises and their many suburbs

megacity a city of 10 million or more residents

metropolitan statistical area (MSA) a central city and the urbanized counties adjacent to it

New York	
2015	17
2000	17
1975	16

Tokyo	
2015	26
2000	26
1975	19

Los Angeles	
2015	14
2000	13
1975	9

Lagos	
2015	23
2000	13
1975	3

Shanghai	
2015	15
2000	13
1975	11

Mexico City	
2015	19
2000	18
1975	11

Bombay	
2015	26
2000	18
1975	7

Buenos Aires	
2015	14
2000	13
1975	9

Sao Paulo	
2015	20
2000	18
1975	10

Calcutta	
2015	17
2000	13
1975	8

Source: United Nations 2000.

The U.S. Census Bureau divides the country into 274 **metropolitan statistical areas (MSAs).** Each MSA consists of a central city of at least 50,000 people and the urbanized areas linked to it. About three of five Americans live in just fifty or so MSAs. As you can see from the Social Map below, like our other social patterns, urbanization is uneven across the United States.

Figure 20.11 How Urban Is Your State?
The Rural-Urban Makeup of the United States

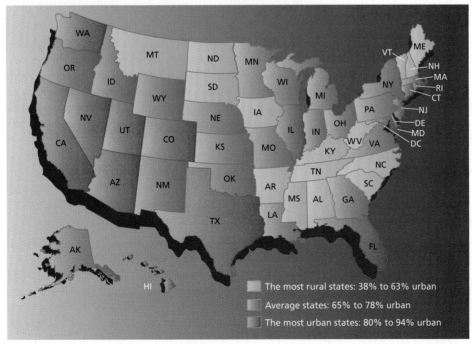

The most rural states: 38% to 63% urban

Average states: 65% to 78% urban

The most urban states: 80% to 94% urban

Note: The most rural state is Vermont (38% urban). The most urban states are California and New Jersey (94% urban).

Source: By the author. Based on *Statistical Abstract* 2007:Table 33.

Table 20.3 The Shrinking and the Fastest-Growing Cities

The Shrinking Cities		The Fastest Growing Cities	
1. −1.9%	Buffalo-Niagara Falls, NY	1. +24.3%	Las Vegas, NV
2. −1.9%	Pittsburgh, PA	2. +23.6%	Cape Coral-Ft. Myers, FL
3. −1.8%	Scranton, PA	3. +22.2%	Naples, FL.
4. −1.6%	Youngstown, Ohio	4. +20.2%	Provo, Utah
5. −1.0%	Cleveland, Ohio	5. +20.1%	Riverside, CA
6. −1.0%	Charleston, WV	6. +19.3%	Port St. Lucie, FL
7. −0.9%	Huntington, WV	7. +19.2%	Raleigh, NC
8. −0.7%	Utica-Rome, NY	8. +19.1%	McAllen, TX
9. −0.5%	Dayton, Ohio	9. +18.9%	Phoenix, AZ
10. −0.4%	Toledo, Ohio	10. +17.8%	Stockton, CA

Note: Population change from 2000 to 2005.

Source: By the author. Based on *Statistical Abstract* 2007:Table 25.

From City to City   As Americans migrate in search of work and better lifestyles, some cities increase in population while others shrink. Table 20.3 compares the fastest-growing U.S. cities with those that are losing people. This table reflects a major shift of people, resources, and power that is occurring between regions of the United States. As you can see, six of the ten fastest-growing cities are in the West, and four are in the South. Of the ten declining cities, eight are in the Northeast and two are in a state that borders the Northeast and the South.

Between Cities   As Americans migrate, **edge cities** have developed to meet their needs. This term refers to clusters of buildings and services near the intersection of major highways. These areas of shopping malls, hotels, office parks, and apartment complexes are not cities in the traditional sense. Rather than being political units with their own mayor or city manager, they overlap political boundaries and include parts of several cities or towns. Yet, edge cities—such as Tysons Corner in Washington and those clustering along the LBJ Freeway in Dallas, Texas—provide a sense of place to those who live or work there.

Within the City   Another U.S. urban pattern is **gentrification,** the movement of middle-class people into rundown areas of a city. They are attracted by the low prices for large houses that, although deteriorated, can be restored. A positive consequence is an improvement in the appearance of some urban neighborhoods—freshly painted buildings, well-groomed lawns, and the absence of boarded-up windows. A negative consequence is that the poor residents are displaced by the more well-to-do newcomers. Tension between the gentrifiers and those being displaced is common (Anderson 1990, 2006).

The usual pattern is for the gentrifiers to be whites and the displaced to be minorities. As is discussed in the Down-to-Earth Sociology box on the next page, in Harlem, New York City, both the gentrifiers and the displaced are African Americans. As middle-class and professional African Americans reclaim this area, an infrastructure—which includes everything from Starbucks coffee shops to dentists—follows. So do soaring real estate prices.

From City to Suburb   Suburbanization refers to people moving from cities to **suburbs,** the communities located just outside a city. Suburbanization is not new. Archaeologists recently found that the Mayan city of Caracol (in what is now Belize) had suburbs, perhaps even with specialized subcenters, the equivalent of today's strip malls (Wilford 2000). The extent to which people have left U.S. cities in search of their dreams is remarkable. Fifty years ago, about 20 percent of Americans lived in the suburbs (Karp et al. 1991). Today, over half of all Americans live in them (Palen 2005).

The automobile was a major impetus for suburbanization. Beginning about one hundred years ago, whites began to move to small towns near the cities where they worked.

edge city a large clustering of service facilities and residential areas near highway intersections that provides a sense of place to people who live, shop, and work there

gentrification middle class people moving into a run-down area of a city, displacing the poor as they buy and restore homes

suburb a community adjacent to a city

Reclaiming Harlem: "It Feeds My Soul"

THE STORY IS WELL KNOWN. The inner city is filled with crack, crime, and corruption. It stinks from foul, festering filth strewn on the streets and piled up around burned-out buildings. Only those who have no choice live in this desolate, despairing environment where danger lurks around every corner.

What is not so well known is that affluent African Americans are reclaiming some of these areas.

West 125th Street in Harlem

Howard Sanders was living the American Dream. After earning a degree from Harvard Business School, he took a position with a Manhattan investment firm. He lived in an exclusive apartment on Central Park West, but he missed Harlem, where he had grown up. He moved back, along with his wife and daughter.

African American lawyers, doctors, professors, and bankers are doing the same.

What's the attraction? The first is nostalgia, a cultural identification with the Harlem of legend and folklore. It was here that black writers and artists lived in the 1920s, here that the blues and jazz attracted young and accomplished musicians.

The second reason is a more practical one. Harlem offers housing value. Five-bedroom homes with 6,000 square feet are available. Some feature Honduran mahogany. Some brownstones are only shells and have to be renovated; others are in perfect condition.

What is happening is the rebuilding of a community. Some people who "made" it want to be role models. They want children in the community to see them going to and returning from work.

When the middle class moved out of Harlem, so did its amenities. Now that young professionals are moving back in, the amenities are returning, too. There were no coffee shops, restaurants, jazz clubs, florists, copy centers, dentist and optometrist offices, or art galleries—the types of things urbanites take for granted. Now there are.

The police have also returned, changing the character of Harlem. Their more visible presence and enforcement of laws have shut down the open-air drug markets. With residents running a high risk of arrest if they carry guns, the shootouts that used to plague this area have become a thing of the past. With the enforcement of laws against public urination and vagrancy, the area has become much safer, further attracting the middle class.

The same thing is happening on Chicago's West Side and in other U.S. cities.

The drive to find community—to connect with others and with one's roots—is strong. As an investment banker who migrated to Harlem said, "It feeds my soul."

"But at what cost?" ask others. This change might be fine for investment bankers and professionals who want to move back and try to rediscover their roots, but what about the people who are displaced? Gentrification always has a cost: residents of an area being pushed out as the area becomes middle class and more expensive. Tenant associations have sprung up to protest the increase in rents and the displacement of residents. And homeowners' associations have emerged to fight to keep renters out of their rehabilitated areas. All are African Americans. The issue is not race, but social class antagonisms.

The "invasion-succession cycle," as sociologists call it, is continuing, but this time with a twist—a flight back in.

Sources: Based on Cose 1999; McCormick 1999; Scott 2001; Taylor 2002; Leland 2003; Hampson 2005; Hyra 2006.

After the racial integration of U.S. schools in the 1950s and 1960s, suburbanization picked up pace as whites fled the cities. Minorities began to move to the suburbs about 1970. In some of today's suburbs, minorities are the majority.

Smaller Centers   The most recent urban trend is the development of *micropolitan areas.* A *micropolis* is a city of 10,000 to 50,000 residents that is not a suburb (McCarthy 2004). Most micropolises are located "next to nowhere." They are fairly self-contained in terms of providing work, housing, and entertainment, and few of their residents commute to urban centers for work. Micropolises are growing, as residents of both rural and urban areas find their cultural attractions and conveniences appealing, especially in the absence of the city's crime and pollution.

The Rural Rebound

The desire to retreat to a safe haven has led to a migration to rural areas that is without precedent in the history of the United States. Some little farming towns are making a comeback, their boarded-up stores and schools once again open for business and learning.

The "push" factors for this fundamental shift are fears of urban crime and violence. The "pull" factors are safety, lower cost of living, and more living space. Interstate highways have made airports—and the city itself—accessible from longer distances. With satellite communications, cell phones, fax machines, and the Internet, people can be "plugged in"—connected with people around the world—even though they live in what just a short time ago were remote areas.

Listen to the wife of one of my former students as she explains why she and her husband moved to a rural area, three hours from the international airport that they fly out of each week:

> I work for a Canadian company. Paul works for a French company, with headquarters in Paris. He flies around the country doing computer consulting. I give motivational seminars to businesses. When we can, we drive to the airport together, but we often leave on different days. I try to go with my husband to Paris once a year.
>
> We almost always are home together on the weekends. We often arrange three- and four-day weekends, because I can plan seminars at home, and Paul does some of his consulting from here.
>
> Sometimes shopping is inconvenient, but we don't have to lock our car doors when we drive, and the new Wal-Mart superstore has most of what we need. E-commerce is a big part of it. I just type in www—whatever, and they ship it right to my door. I get make-up and books online. I even bought a part for my stove.
>
> Why do we live here? Look at the lake. It's beautiful. We enjoy boating and swimming. We love to walk in this park-like setting. We see deer and wild turkeys. We love the sunsets over the lake. (author's files)

She added, "I think we're ahead of the learning curve," referring to the idea that their lifestyle is a wave of the future.

Models of Urban Growth

In the 1920s, Chicago was a vivid mosaic of immigrants, gangsters, prostitutes, the homeless, the rich, and the poor—much as it is today. Sociologists at the University of Chicago studied these contrasting ways of life. One of these sociologists, Robert Park, coined the term **human ecology** to describe how people adapt to their environment (Park and Burgess 1921; Park 1936). (This concept is also known as *urban ecology*.) The process of urban growth is of special interest to sociologists. Let's look at the four main models they developed.

The Concentric Zone Model

To explain how cities expand, sociologist Ernest Burgess (1925) proposed a *concentric-zone model*. As shown in part A of Figure 20.12 on the next page, Burgess noted that a city expands outward from its center. Zone 1 is the central business district. Zone 2, which encircles the downtown area, is in transition. It contains rooming houses and deteriorating housing, which Burgess said breed poverty, disease, and vice. Zone 3 is the area to which thrifty workers have moved in order to escape the zone in transition and yet maintain easy access to their work. Zone 4 contains more expensive apartments, residential hotels, single-family homes, and exclusive areas where the wealthy live. Commuters live in Zone 5, which consists of suburbs or satellite cities that have grown up around transportation routes.

Burgess intended this model to represent "the tendencies of any town or city to expand radially from its central business district." He noted, however, that no "city fits perfectly this ideal scheme." Some cities have physical obstacles such as a lake, river, or railroad that cause their expansion to depart from the model. Burgess also noted that

human ecology Robert Park's term for the relationship between people and their environment (such as land and structures); also known as *urban ecology*

Figure 20.12 **How Cities Develop: Models of Urban Growth**

Concentric zones
(A)

Sectors
(B)

Multiple nuclei
(C)

Districts (for Parts A, B, C)

1. Central business district
2. Wholesale and light manufacturing
3. Low-class residential
4. Medium-class residential
5. High-class residential
6. Heavy manufacturing
7. Outlying business district
8. Residential suburb
9. Industrial suburb
10. Commuters' zone

Peripheral model
(D)

Districts (for Part D)

1. Central city
2. Suburban residential areas
3. Circumferential highway
4. Radial highway
5. Shopping mall
6. Industrial district
7. Office park
8. Service center
9. Airport complex
10. Combined employment and shopping center

Source: Cousins and Nagpaul 1970; Harris 1997.

businesses had begun to deviate from the model by locating in outlying zones (see Zone 10). That was in 1925. Burgess didn't know it, but he was seeing the beginning of a major shift that led businesses away from downtown areas to suburban shopping malls. Today, these malls account for most of the country's retail sales.

The Sector Model

Sociologist Homer Hoyt (1939, 1971) noted that a city's concentric zones do not form a complete circle, and he modified Burgess' model of urban growth. As shown in part B of Figure 20.12, a concentric zone can contain several sectors—one of working-class housing, another of expensive homes, a third of businesses, and so on—all competing for the same land.

An example of this dynamic competition is what sociologists call an **invasion-succession cycle.** Poor immigrants and rural migrants settle in low-rent areas. As their numbers swell, they spill over into adjacent areas. Upset by their presence, the middle class moves out, which expands the sector of low-cost housing. The invasion-succession cycle is never complete, for later another group will replace this earlier one. The cycle, in fact, can go full circle, for as discussed in the Down-to-Earth Sociology box on Harlem on page 609, the "invaders" can be the middle and upper middle classes.

The Multiple-Nuclei Model

Geographers Chauncey Harris and Edward Ullman noted that some cities have several centers or nuclei (Harris and Ullman 1945; Ullman and Harris 1970). As shown in part C of Figure 20.12, each nucleus contains some specialized activity. A familiar example is the

invasion-succession cycle
the process by which a group of people displaces a group whose racial-ethnic or social class characteristics differ from their own

clustering of fast-food restaurants in one area and automobile dealers in another. Sometimes similar activities are grouped together because they profit from cohesion; retail districts, for example, draw more customers if there are more stores. Other clustering occurs because some types of land use, such as factories and expensive homes, are incompatible with one another. One result is that services are not spread evenly throughout the city.

The Peripheral Model

Chauncey Harris (1997) also developed the peripheral model shown in part D of Figure 20.12. This model portrays the impact of radial highways on the movement of people and services away from the central city to the city's periphery, or outskirts. It also shows the development of industrial and office parks.

Critique of the Models

These models tell only part of the story. They are time bound, for medieval cities didn't follow these patterns (see the photo on page 603). In addition, they do not account for urban planning policies. England, for example, has planning laws that preserve green belts (trees and farmlands) around the city. This prevents urban sprawl: Wal-Mart cannot buy land outside the city and put up a store; instead, it must locate in the downtown area with the other stores. Norwich has 250,000 people—yet the city ends abruptly, and on its green belt pheasants skitter across plowed fields while sheep graze in verdant meadows (Milbank 1995).

If you were to depend on these models, you would be surprised if you visited the cities of the Least Industrialized Nations. There, the wealthy often claim the inner city, where fine restaurants and other services are readily accessible. Tucked behind walls and protected from public scrutiny, they enjoy luxurious homes and gardens. The poor, in contrast, especially rural migrants, settle in areas outside the city—or, as in the case of El Tiro, featured in the photo essay on pages 604–605, on top of piles of garbage in what used to be the outskirts of a city. This topic is discussed in the Cultural Diversity box on the next page.

City Life

Life in cities is filled with contrasts. Let's look at two of those contrasts, alienation and community.

Alienation in the City

Impersonality and Self-Interest   If you know urban life, you know that impersonality and self-interest are ordinary characteristics of the city. As you traverse city streets, you can expect people to avoid needless interaction with others and to be absorbed in their own affairs. These are adjustments that people have made to deal with the crowds of strangers with whom they temporarily share the same urban space. Sometimes, however, these characteristics of urban life are carried to extremes. Here is an event that made national headlines when it occurred, upsetting the entire country:

> Twenty-eight-year-old Catherine Genovese, who was known as Kitty in her Queens neighborhood, was returning home from work. After she parked her car, a man grabbed her. Kitty screamed, "Oh my God! He stabbed me! Please help me!"
>
> For more than half an hour, thirty-eight respectable, law-abiding citizens watched the killer stalk and stab Kitty in three separate attacks. Twice the sudden glow from their bedroom lights frightened him off. Each time he returned, sought her out, and stabbed her again. Not one person telephoned the police during the assault.
>
> When interviewed by the police, the witnesses said: "I didn't want to get involved," "We thought it was a lovers' quarrel," "I don't know," and "I was tired. I went back to bed." (Gansberg 1964).

The World

Why City Slums Are Better Than the Country: Urbanization in the Least Industrialized Nations

THOUGHTS OF THE LEAST INDUSTRIALIZED Nations often bring images of people tending animals or harvesting crops, enjoying a peaceful life in the lush, green countryside or along babbling brooks. Such images no longer represent the reality that most people in the Least Industrial Nations face—if ever they did. The rural poor of these countries are flocking to the cities at such a rate that, as we saw in Figure 20.10 on page 607, the Least Industrialized Nations now contain most of the world's largest cities. In the Most Industrialized Nations, industrialization generally preceded urbanization, but in the Least Industrialized Nations *urbanization is preceding industrialization*. These cities cannot support their swelling populations.

The settlement patterns are also different in these cities. When rural migrants and immigrants move to U.S. cities, they usually settle in deteriorating housing near the city's center. The wealthy reside in suburbs and luxurious city enclaves. Migrants to cities of the Least Industrialized Nations, in contrast, establish illegal squatter settlements outside the city. There they build shacks from scrap boards, cardboard, and bits of corrugated metal. Even flattened tin cans are scavenged for building material. The squatters enjoy no city facilities—roads, public transportation, water, sewers, or garbage pickup. After thousands of squatters have settled an area, the city reluctantly acknowledges their right to live there and adds bus service and minimal water lines. Hundreds of people use a single spigot. About *5 million* of Mexico City's residents live in such squalid conditions, with hundreds of thousands more pouring in each year.

Why this rush to live in the city under such miserable conditions? At its core are the "push" factors that arise from a breakdown of traditional rural life. With a safer water supply and the importation of modern medicine, the death rate in rural areas dropped. As a result, rural populations multiplied, and no longer is there enough land for parents to divide up

This photo, taken outside Buenos Aires, Argentina, illustrates the settlement pattern common in the Least Industrialized and Industrializing Nations.

among their children. Without land or jobs, there is hunger. People are deeply dissatisfied with the resulting hardscrabble character of rural life. Then, too, there are the "pull" factors that draw people to the cities—jobs, schools, housing, and even a more stimulating life.

At the bottom of a ravine near Mexico City is a dismal bunch of shacks. Some of the parents have 14 children. "We used to live up there," Señora Gonzalez gestured toward the mountain, "in those caves. Our only hope was one day to have a place to live. And now we do." She smiled with pride at the jerry-built shacks . . . each one had a collection of flowers planted in tin cans. "One day, we hope to extend the water pipes and drainage—perhaps even pave. . . ."

And what was the name of her community? Señora Gonzalez beamed. "Esperanza!" (McDowell 1984:172)

Esperanza is the Spanish word for hope. This is what lies behind the rush to these cities—the hope of a better life. And this is why the rush won't slow down. In 1930, only one Latin American city had over a million people—now fifty do! The world's cities are growing by one million people each week (Brockerhoff 2000).

Will the Least Industrialized Nations adjust to this vast migration? They have no choice. Authorities in Brazil, Guatemala, Venezuela, and other countries have sent in the police and even the army to evict the settlers. It doesn't work. This just leads to violence, and the settlers keep streaming in. The adjustments will be painful. The infrastructure (roads, water, sewers, electricity, and so on) must be built, but these poor countries don't have the resources to build them. As the desperate rural poor flock to the cities, the problems will worsen.

for your Consideration

What solutions do you see to the vast migration to the cities of the Least Industrialized Nations?

It is possible that the report of Kitty's death was exaggerated, that due to darkness, distance, and obstructions people didn't understand that she was being attacked (De May 2005). Regardless, anyone who lives in a large city knows that it is prudent to be alert to danger. You never know who that stranger near you really is. Even traffic accidents hold the danger of angry people whose wrath explodes:

In crowded traffic on a bridge going into Detroit, Deletha Word bumped the car ahead of her. The damage was minor, but the driver, Martell Welch, jumped out. Cursing, he pulled Deletha from her car, pushed her onto the hood, and began beating her. Martell's friends got out to watch. One of them held Deletha down while Martell took a car jack and smashed Deletha's car. Scared for her life, Deletha broke away, fleeing to the bridge's railing. Martell and his friends taunted her, shouting, "Jump, bitch, jump!" Deletha plunged to her death. Whether she jumped or fell is unknown. (*Newsweek*, September 4, 1995)

How Cities Undermine Community   Why should the city be alienating? In a classic essay, sociologist Louis Wirth (1938) said that urban dwellers live anonymous lives marked by segmented and superficial encounters. This undermines kinship and neighborhood, the traditional bases of social control, feelings of solidarity, and identification with others. Urbanites then grow aloof and indifferent to other people's problems—as happened with the neighbors of Kitty Genovese. In short, the price of the personal freedom that the city offers is alienation.

Community in the City

The city, however, is not inevitably alienating. Most drivers who witnessed the tragedy that befell Deletha Word did nothing. But after Deletha went over the railing, two motorists jumped in after her, risking injury and their own lives in a futile attempt to save her. Some urbanites, then, are far from alienated.

The Gans Research   The city also has enclaves of community. Sociologist Herbert Gans, a symbolic interactionist, did participant observation in the West End of Boston. He was so impressed with the sense of community that he titled his book *The Urban Villagers* (1962). In this book, which has become a classic in sociology, Gans said:

> After a few weeks of living in the West End, my observations—and my perceptions of the area—changed drastically. The search for an apartment quickly indicated that the individual units were usually in much better condition than the outside or the hallways of the buildings. Subsequently, in wandering through the West End, and in using it as a resident, I developed a kind of selective perception, in which my eye focused only on those parts of the area that were actually being used by people. Vacant buildings and boarded-up stores were no longer so visible, and the totally deserted alleys or streets were outside the set of paths normally traversed, either by myself or by the West Enders. The dirt and spilled-over garbage remained, but, since they were concentrated in street gutters and empty lots, they were not really harmful to anyone and thus were not as noticeable as during my initial observations.
>
> Since much of the area's life took place on the street, faces became familiar very quickly. I met my neighbors on the stairs and in front of my building. And, once a shopping pattern developed, I saw the same storekeepers frequently, as well as the area's "characters" who wandered through the streets everyday on a fairly regular route and schedule. In short, the exotic quality of the stores and the residents also wore off as I became used to seeing them.

In short, Gans found a *community*, people who identified with the area and with one another. Its residents enjoyed networks of friends and acquaintances. Despite the area's substandard buildings, most West Enders had chosen to live here. *To them, this was a low-rent district, not a slum.*

Most West Enders had low-paying, insecure jobs. Other residents were elderly, living on small pensions. Unlike the middle class, these people didn't care about their "address." The area's inconveniences were something they put up with in exchange for cheap housing. In general, they were content with their neighborhood.

The city dwellers who Gans identified as ethnic villagers find community in the city. Living in tightly knit neighborhoods, they know many other residents. Some first-generation immigrants have even come from the same village in the "old country." This photo was taken in New York City.

Types of Urban Dwellers

As they live in the city, people create a sense of intimacy. They *personalize* their shopping, getting to know clerks as they shop at the same stores week after week. They learn areas of the city that they live in down to the smallest details. In effect, they live in little social worlds within the cities, the little worlds that Wirth called the urban mosaic. Some people fit comfortably in one of these little worlds, within it experiencing emotional security. For them, as Gans noted, they find a village within the city. But not everyone. Some never feel a good fit, or they feel threatened by some "little world" that isn't theirs but with which they have to interact. The city is not a monolith, and people have different urban experiences.

Whether people find alienation or community in the city, then, depends on who you are talking about. Gans (1962, 1968, 1991) identified five types of urban dwellers, who have vastly different experiences in the city. The first three live in the city by choice and are not alienated; the latter two are outcasts of industrial society who live in the city despairingly, without choice or hope.

Where do you think these people fit in Gans' classification of urban dwellers?

The Cosmopolites   These are the intellectuals, professionals, artists, and entertainers who have been attracted to the city. They value its conveniences and cultural benefits.

The Singles   Roughly between the ages of 20 and early 30s, the singles have settled in the city temporarily. For them, urban life is a stage in their life course. Businesses and services, such as singles bars and apartment complexes, cater to their needs and desires. After they marry, many move to the suburbs.

The Ethnic Villagers   Feeling a sense of identity, working-class members of the same ethnic group band together. They form tightly knit neighborhoods that resemble villages and small towns. Family- and peer-oriented, they try to isolate themselves from the dangers and problems of urban life.

The Deprived   Destitute, emotionally disturbed, and having little income, education, or work skills, the deprived live in neighborhoods that are more like urban jungles than urban villages. Some of them stalk those jungles in search of prey. Neither predator nor prey has much hope for anything better in life—for themselves or for their children.

The Trapped   These people don't live in the area by choice, either. Some were trapped when an ethnic group "invaded" their neighborhood and they could not afford to move. Others found themselves trapped in a downward spiral. They started life in a higher social class, but because of personal problems—mental or physical illness or addiction to alcohol or other drugs—they drifted downward. There also are the elderly who are trapped by poverty and not wanted elsewhere. Like the deprived, the trapped suffer from high rates of assault, mugging, and rape.

IN SUM   Gans' typology illustrates the complexity of urban life. With the city a mosaic of social diversity, not all urban dwellers experience the city in the same way. Each group has its own lifestyle, and each has distinct experiences. Some people welcome the city's cultural diversity and mix with several groups. Others find community by retreating into the security of ethnic enclaves. Still others feel trapped and deprived. To them, the city is an urban jungle. It poses threats to their health and safety, and their lives are full of despair.

The Norm of Noninvolvement and the Diffusion of Responsibility

Urban dwellers try to avoid intrusions from strangers. As they go about their everyday lives in the city, they follow a *norm of noninvolvement.*

> To do this, we sometimes use props such as newspapers to shield ourselves from others and to indicate our inaccessibility for interaction. In effect, we learn to "tune others out." In this regard, we might see the Walkman (or iPod) as the quintessential urban prop in

that it allows us to be tuned in and tuned out at the same time. It is a device that allows us to enter our own private world and thereby effectively to close off encounters with others. The use of such devices protects our "personal space," along with our body demeanor and facial expression (the passive "mask" or even scowl that persons adopt on subways). (Karp et al. 1991)

The death of Kitty Genovese, whose story was just recounted, so troubled social psychologists John Darley and Bibb Latané (1968) that they ran the series of experiments featured in Chapter 6, pages 169–170. In their experiments, Darley and Latané uncovered the *diffusion of responsibility*—the more bystanders there are, the less likely people are to help. As a group grows, people's sense of responsibility becomes diffused, with each person assuming that *another* will do the responsible thing. "With these other people here, it is not *my* responsibility," they reason.

The diffusion of responsibility, along with the norm of noninvolvement, helps to explain why people can ignore the plight of others. If there really were witnesses to the death of Kitty Genovese (as I indicated, there is some question about this), the bystanders were *not* uncaring people. They simply were following an urban norm, one that is helpful for getting them through everyday city life but, unfortunately, that is dysfunctional in some crucial situations. This norm, combined with the fears nurtured by urban killings, rapes, and muggings, makes many people want to retreat to a safe haven. This topic is discussed in the Down-to-Earth Sociology box below.

Down-to-Earth Sociology

Urban Fear and the Gated Fortress

GATED NEIGHBORHOODS—WHERE GATES open and close to allow or prevent access to a neighborhood—are not new. They always have been available to the rich. What is new is the rush of the upper middle class to towns where they pay high taxes to keep all of the town's facilities private. Even the city's streets are private.

Towns cannot discriminate on the basis of religion or race-ethnicity, but they can—and do—discriminate on the basis of social class. Klahanie, Washington, is an excellent example. Begun in 1985, it was supposed to take twenty years to develop. With its winding streets, pavilions, gardens, swimming pools, parks, private libraries, infant-toddler playcourt, and 25 miles of hiking-bicycling-running trails on 300 acres of open space, demand for the $300,000 to $500,000 homes nestled by a lake in this private community exceeded supply (Egan 1995; Klahanie Association Web site 2007).

As the upper middle class flees urban areas and tries to build a bucolic dream, we will see many more private towns. A strong sign of the future is Celebration, a town of 20,000 people planned and built by the Walt Disney Company just five minutes from Disney World. Celebration boasts the usual

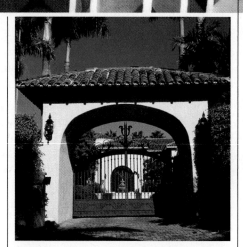

The U.S. economic system has proven highly beneficial to most citizens, but it also has left many in poverty. To protect themselves, primarily from the poor, the upper middle class increasingly seeks sanctuary behind gated communities. Some seek even more safety and privacy by living behind gates within a gated community, as shown here in Miami Beach, Florida.

school, hospital, and restaurants. In addition, Celebration offers a Robert Trent Jones golf course, walking and bicycling paths, a hotel with a lighthouse tower and bird sanctuary, a health and fitness center with a rock-climbing wall, and its own cable TV channel. With fiber-optic technology, the residents of private communities can remain locked within their sanctuaries and still be connected to the outside world.

for your Consideration

Community involves a sense of togetherness, a sense of identity with one another. Can you explain how this concept also contains the idea of separateness from others (not just in the example of gated communities)? What will our future be if we become a nation of gated communities, where middle-class homeowners withdraw into private domains, separating themselves from the rest of the nation?

Urban Problems and Social Policy

To close this chapter, let's look at the primary reasons that U.S. cities have declined, and then consider the potential of urban revitalization.

Suburbanization

The U.S. city has been the loser in the transition to the suburbs. As people moved out of the city, businesses and jobs followed. White-collar corporations, such as insurance companies, first moved their offices to the suburbs, followed by manufacturing firms. This process has continued so relentlessly that today, twice as many manufacturing jobs are located in the suburbs as in the city (Palen 2005). As the city's tax base shrank, it left a budget squeeze that affected not only parks, zoos, libraries, and museums, but also the city's basic services—its schools, streets, sewer and water systems, and police and fire departments.

This shift in population and resources left behind people who had no choice but to stay in the city. As we reviewed in Chapter 12, sociologist William Julius Wilson (1987) says that this exodus transformed the inner city into a ghetto. Left behind were families and individuals who, lacking training and skills, were trapped by poverty, unemployment, and welfare dependency. Also left behind were those who prey on others through street crime. The term *ghetto,* says Wilson, "suggests that a fundamental social transformation has taken place . . . that groups represented by this term are collectively different from and much more socially isolated from those that lived in these communities in earlier years" (quoted in Karp et al. 1991).

City Versus Suburb   Having made the move out of the city—or having been born in a suburb and preferring to stay there—suburbanites want the city to keep its problems to itself. They reject proposals to share suburbia's revenues with the city and oppose measures that would allow urban and suburban governments joint control over what has become a contiguous mass of people and businesses. Suburban leaders generally believe that it is in their best interests to remain politically, economically, and socially separate from their nearby city. They do not mind going to the city to work, or venturing there on weekends for the diversions it offers, but they do not want to help pay the city's expenses.

It is likely that the mounting bill ultimately will come due, however, and that suburbanites will have to pay for their uncaring attitude toward the urban disadvantaged. Karp et al. (1991) put it this way:

> It may be that suburbs can insulate themselves from the problems of central cities, at least for the time being. In the long run, though, there will be a steep price to pay for the failure of those better off to care compassionately for those at the bottom of society.

Our occasional urban riots may be part of that bill—perhaps just the down payment.

Suburban Flight   In some places, the bill is coming due quickly. As they age, some suburbs are becoming mirror images of the city that their residents so despise. Suburban crime, the flight of the middle class, a shrinking tax base, and eroding services create a spiraling sense of insecurity, stimulating more middle-class flight (Herrick 2007). Figure 20.13 on the next page illustrates this process, which is new to the urban-suburban scene.

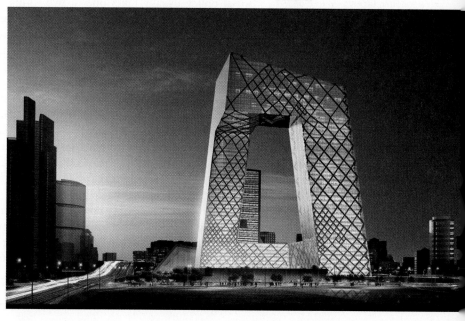

As cities evolve, so does architecture. This is the design of the headquarters for China's flagship television network to be built in Beijing. As a sign of changing times and of China's evolving partnership with the West, the architect is a Westerner, Rem Koolhaas of Holland.

Figure 20.13 Urban Growth and Urban Flight

50 years ago	25 years ago	Now

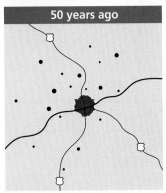

At first, the city and surrounding villages grew independently.

As city dwellers fled urban decay, they created a ring of suburbs.

As middle-class flight continues outward, urban problems are arriving in the outer rings.

Disinvestment and Deindustrialization

As the cities' tax base shrank and their services declined, neighborhoods deteriorated, and banks began **redlining:** Afraid of loans going bad, bankers drew a line on a map around a problem area and refused to make loans for housing or businesses there. This **disinvestment** (withdrawal of investment) pushed these areas into further decline. Youth gangs, muggings, and murders are common in these areas, and good jobs are not—all woven into this process of disinvestment.

The globalization of capitalism has also left a heavy mark on U.S. cities. As we reviewed in Chapter 14, to compete in the global market, many U.S. industries abandoned local communities and moved their factories to countries where labor costs are lower. This process, called **deindustrialization,** made U.S. industries more competitive, but it eliminated millions of U.S. manufacturing jobs. Lacking training in the new information technologies, many poor people are locked out of the benefits of the postindustrial economy that is engulfing the United States. Left behind in the inner cities, many live in despair.

The Potential of Urban Revitalization

Social policy usually takes one of two forms. The first is to tear down and rebuild—something that is fancifully termed **urban renewal.** The result is the renewal of an area—but *not* for the benefit of its inhabitants. Stadiums, high-rise condos, luxury hotels, and boutiques replace run-down, cheap housing. Outpriced, the area's inhabitants are displaced into adjacent areas.

The second is some sort of **enterprise zone,** a designated area of the city that offers economic incentives, such as reduced taxes, to businesses that move into it. Although the intention is good, failure is usually the result. Most businesses refuse to locate in high-crime areas. Those that do relocate pay a high price for security and losses from crime, which can eat up the tax savings. If workers are hired from within the problem area and the jobs pay a decent wage, which most do not, the workers move to better neighborhoods—which doesn't help the area (Lemann 1994). After all, who chooses to live with the fear of violence?

A form of the enterprise zone, called *Federal Empowerment Zones,* has brought some success. In addition to tax breaks, this program offers low-interest loans targeted for redeveloping an area. It is, in effect, the opposite of disinvestment, which devastates areas. The Down-to-Earth Sociology box on page 609 featured the renaissance of Harlem. Stimulating this change was the designation of Harlem as a Federal Empowerment Zone. The economic incentives lured grocery stores, dry cleaners, and video stores, attracting urbanites who expect such services. As middle-class people moved back in, the

urban renewal the rehabilitation of a rundown area, which usually results in the displacement of the poor who are living in that area

enterprise zone the use of economic incentives in a designated area to encourage investment

redlining the officers of a financial institution deciding not to make loans in a particular area

disinvestment the withdrawal of investments by financial institutions, which seals the fate of an urban area

deindustrialization industries moving out of a country or region

U.S. suburbs were once unplanned, rambling affairs that took irregular shapes as people moved away from the city. Today's suburbs tend to be planned to precise details even before the first resident moves in. This photo is of a suburb outside of Venice, CA.

demand for more specialty shops followed. A self-feeding cycle of development has begun, replacing the self-feeding cycle of despair, crime, and drug use that accompanies disinvestment.

U.S. cities can be revitalized and made into safe and decent places to live. There is nothing in the nature of cities that turns them into dangerous slums. Most European cities, for example, are both safe and pleasant. If U.S. cities are to change, they need to become top agenda items of the U.S. government. Adequate resources in terms of money and human talents must be focused on overcoming urban woes. That we have begun to see success in Harlem, Chicago's North Town, and even in formerly riot-torn East Los Angeles indicates that the transformation can be brought about.

Replacing old buildings with new ones, however, is not the answer. Instead, sociological principles of building community need to be followed. Here are guiding principles suggested by sociologist William Flanagan (1990):

> *Scale.* Regional and national planning is necessary. Local jurisdictions, with their many rivalries, competing goals, and limited resources, end up with a hodgepodge of mostly unworkable solutions.
>
> *Livability.* Cities must be appealing and meet human needs, especially the need of community. This will attract the middle classes into the city, which will increase its tax base. In turn, this will help finance the services that make the city more livable.
>
> *Social justice.* In the final analysis, social policy must be evaluated by how it affects people. "Urban renewal" programs that displace the poor for the benefit of the middle class and wealthy do not pass this standard. The same would apply to solutions that create "livability" for select groups but neglect the poor and the homeless.

Finally, unless we address the *root* causes of urban problems—poverty, poor schools, and lack of jobs—any solutions will be only Band-Aids that cover them up. Such fixes will be window dressings for politicians who want to *appear* as though they are doing something constructive about the problems that affect our quality of life.

Urban renewal is occurring in many places across the globe. As the globalization of capitalism makes specific urban spaces more valuable, buildings, still usable for decades, are replaced with other structures. This photo was taken in Shenzhen, China.

Summary *and* Review

A Planet with No Space for Enjoying Life?

What debate did Thomas Malthus initiate?

In 1798, Thomas Malthus analyzed the surge in Europe's population. He concluded that the world's population will outstrip its food supply. The debate between today's New Malthusians and those who disagree, the Anti-Malthusians, continues. Pp. 590–593.

Why are people starving?

Starvation is not due to a lack of food in the world, for there is now *more* food for each person in the entire world than there was fifty years ago. Rather, starvation is the result of a maldistribution of food, which is primarily due to drought and civil war. Pp. 593–594.

Population Growth

Why do people in the poor nations have so many children?

In the Least Industrialized Nations, children often are viewed as gifts from God, they cost little to rear, they contribute to the family income at an early age, and they provide the parents' social security. Consequently, people are motivated to have large families. Pp. 595–598.

What are the three demographic variables?

To compute population growth, demographers use *fertility, mortality,* and *migration.* The **basic demographic equation** is births minus deaths plus net migration equals the growth rate. Pp. 598–600.

Why is forecasting population difficult?

A nation's growth rate is affected by unanticipated variables—from economic cycles, wars, and famines to industrialization and government policies. Pp. 600–602.

The Development of Cities

What is the relationship of cities to farming and the Industrial Revolution?

Cities can develop only if there is a large agricultural surplus, which frees people from food production. The primary impetus to the development of cities was the invention of the plow. After the Industrial Revolution stimulated rapid transportation and communication, cities grew quickly and became much larger. Today **urbanization** is so extensive that some cities have become **metropolises,** dominating the area adjacent to them. The areas of influence of some metropolises have merged, forming a **megalopolis.** Pp. 602–609.

What is the rural rebound?

As people flee cities and suburbs, the population of most U.S. rural counties is growing. This is a fundamental departure from a trend that had been in place for a couple of hundred years. P. 609.

Models of Urban Growth

What models of urban growth have been proposed?

The primary models are concentric zone, sector, multiple-nuclei, and peripheral. These models fail to account for ancient and medieval cities, many European cities, cities in the Least Industrialized Nations, and urban planning. Pp. 610–612.

City Life

Who lives in the city?

Some people experience **alienation** in the city; others find **community** in it. What people find depends largely on their background and urban networks. Five types of people who live in cities are cosmopolites, singles, ethnic villagers, the deprived, and the trapped. Pp. 612–616.

Urban Problems and Social Policy

Why have U.S. cities declined?

Three primary reasons for the decline of U.S. cities are **suburbanization** (as people moved to the suburbs, the tax base of cities eroded and services deteriorated), **disinvestment** (banks withdrawing their financing), and **deindustrialization** (which caused a loss of jobs). Pp. 616–618.

What social policy can salvage U.S. cities?

Three guiding principles for developing urban social policy are scale, livability, and social justice. Pp. 618–619.

Thinking Critically
about Chapter 20

1. Do you think that the world is threatened by a population explosion? Use data from this chapter to support your position.
2. Why do people find alienation or community in the city?
3. What are the causes of urban problems, and what can we do to solve those problems?

Additional Resources

What can you use MySocLab for? www.mysoclab.com

- **Study and Review:** Pre- and Post-Tests, Practice Tests, Flash Cards, Individualized Study Plans.
- **Current Events:** *Sociology in the News,* the daily *New York Times,* and more.

- **Research and Writing:** *Research Navigator, Writing About Sociology,* and more.

Where Can I Read More on This Topic?

Suggested readings for this chapter are listed at the back of this book.

CHAPTER 21

Collective Behavior and Social Movements

Isaak Brodskij, *Demonstration*, 1930

The news spread like wildfire. A police officer had been killed. In just twenty minutes, the white population was armed and heading for the cabin. Men and mere boys, some not more than 12 years old, carried rifles, shotguns, and pistols.

The mob, now swollen to about four hundred, surrounded the log cabin. Tying a rope around the man's neck, they dragged him to the center of town. While the men argued about the best way to kill him, the women and children shouted their advice—some to hang him, others to burn him alive.

Someone pulled a large wooden box out of a store and placed it in the center of the street. Others filled it with straw. Then they lifted the man, the rope still around his neck, and shoved him head first into the box. One of the men poured oil over him. Another lit a match.

One of the men poured oil over him. Another lit a match.

As the flames shot upward, the man managed to lift himself out of the box, his body a mass of flames. Trying to shield his face and eyes from the fire, he ran the length of the rope, about twenty feet, when someone yelled, "Shoot!" In an instant, dozens of shots rang out. Men and boys walked to the lifeless body and emptied their guns into it.

They dragged the man's body back to the burning box, then piled on more boxes from the stores, and poured oil over them. Each time someone threw on more oil and the flames shot upward, the crowd roared shouts of approval.

Standing about seventy-five feet away, I could smell the poor man's burning flesh. No one tried to hide their identity. I could clearly see town officials help in the burning. The inquest, dutifully held by the coroner, concluded that the man met death "at the hands of an enraged mob unknown to the jury." What else could he conclude? Any jury from this town would include men who had participated in the man's death.

They dug a little hole at the edge of the street, and dumped in it the man's ashes and what was left of his body.

The man's name was Sam Pettie, known by everybody to be quiet and inoffensive. I can't mention my name. If I did, I would be committing suicide.

(Based on a May 1914 letter to *The Crisis*)

Race relations in the United States have gone through many stages, some of them very tense. This photo was taken in Birmingham, Alabama, in 1963, at the height of the Civil Rights Movement. The fire department is dispersing demonstrators who are protesting segregation.

COLLECTIVE BEHAVIOR

Why did people in this little town "go mad"? These men—and the women who shouted suggestions about how to kill the captured man—were ordinary, law-abiding citizens. Even some of the "pillars of the community" joined in the vicious killing of Sam Pettie, who may well have been innocent.

Lynching is a form of **collective behavior,** actions by a group of people who bypass the usual norms governing their behavior and do something unusual (Turner and Killian 1987; Harper and Leicht 2002). Collective behavior is a broad term. It includes not only such violent acts as lynchings and riots but also rumors, panics, fads, and fashions. Before examining its specific forms, let's look at theories that seek to explain collective behavior.

Early Explanations: The Transformation of the Individual

When people can't figure something out, they often resort to using "madness" as an explanation. People may say, "She went 'off her rocker'—that's why she drove her car into the river." "He must have 'gone nuts,' or he wouldn't have shot into the crowd." Early explanations of collective behavior were linked to such assumptions. Let's look at how these ideas developed.

How the Crowd Transforms the Individual

The study of collective behavior began when Charles Mackay (1814–1889), a British journalist, noticed that "country folks," who ordinarily are reasonable sorts of people, sometimes "went mad" and did "disgraceful and violent things" when they formed a crowd. The best explanation Mackay (1852) could come up with was that people had a "herd mentality"—they were like a herd of cows that suddenly stampede.

About fifty years later, Gustave LeBon (1841–1931), a French psychologist, built on this initial idea. In an 1895 book, LeBon stressed how people feel anonymous in crowds, less accountable for what they do. Some even develop feelings of invincibility and come to think that they can do virtually anything. A **collective mind** develops, he said, and people are swept up by almost any suggestion. Then contagion, something like mass hypnosis, takes over, releasing the destructive instincts that society so carefully represses.

collective behavior extraordinary activities carried out by groups of people; includes lynchings, rumors, panics, urban legends, and fads and fashions

collective mind Gustave LeBon's term for the tendency of people in a crowd to feel, think, and act in unusual ways

Robert Park (1864–1944), a U.S. sociologist who studied in Germany and wrote a 1904 dissertation on the nature of the crowd, was influenced by LeBon (McPhail 1991). After Park joined the faculty at the University of Chicago, he added the ideas of social unrest and circular reaction. He said,

> Social unrest . . . is transmitted from one individual to another . . . so that the manifestations of discontent in A [are] communicated to B, and from B reflected back to A. (Park and Burgess 1921)

Park used the term **circular reaction** to refer to this back-and-forth communication. Circular reaction, he said, creates a "collective impulse" that comes to "dominate all members of the crowd." If "collective impulse" sounds just like LeBon's "collective mind," that's because it really is. As noted, Park was influenced by LeBon, and his slightly different term did not change the basic idea at all.

circular reaction Robert Park's term for a back-and-forth communication among the members of a crowd whereby a "collective impulse" is transmitted

acting crowd an excited group of people who move toward a goal

The Acting Crowd

Herbert Blumer (1900–1987), who studied under Park, synthesized LeBon's and Park's ideas. As you can see from Figure 21.1, Blumer (1939) identified five stages that precede what he called an **acting crowd,** an excited group that moves toward a goal. This model still dominates today's police manuals on crowd behavior (McPhail 1989). Let's apply it to the killing of Sam Pettie.

1. *A background of tension or unrest.* At the root of collective behavior is a background condition of tension or unrest. Disturbed about some condition of society, people become apprehensive. This makes them vulnerable to rumors and suggestions. Sam Pettie was killed during the early 1900s. At this time, traditional southern life was in upheaval. With the country industrializing, millions of Americans were moving from farm to city in search of jobs, and from South to North. Left behind were many poor, rural southerners, white and black, who faced a bleak future. In addition, African Americans were questioning the legitimacy of their low status and deprivation.
2. *Exciting event.* An exciting event occurs, one so startling that people become preoccupied with it. In this instance, that event was the killing of a police officer.

Figure 21.1 Blumer's Model of How an Acting Crowd Develops

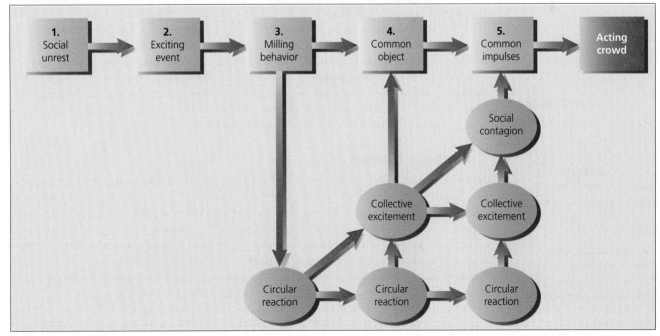

Source: Based on McPhail 1991:11.

3. *Milling.* Next comes **milling,** people standing or walking around, talking about the exciting event. A circular reaction then sets in. Picking up cues about the "right" way to think and feel, people reinforce them in one another. Members of the mob that killed Sam Pettie milled only a short time, but while they did so they became increasingly agitated as they discussed the officer's death.

4. *A common object of attention.* In this stage, people's attention becomes riveted on some aspect of the event. They get caught up in the collective excitement. In this case, people's attention turned to Sam Pettie. Someone may have said that he had been talking to the officer or that they had been arguing.

5. *Common impulses.* People get the feeling that they are in agreement about what should be done. These common impulses are stimulated by *social contagion,* a sense of excitement that is passed from one person to another. In this instance, people concluded that only the killer's immediate, public death would be adequate vengeance—and would serve as a warning for other African Americans who might even think about getting "out of line."

Acting crowds aren't always negative or destructive, as this one was. Some involve spontaneous demonstrations directed against oppression. Nor are they all serious, for students having a food fight in a cafeteria are also acting crowds.

The Contemporary View: The Rationality of the Crowd

If we were to see a lynching—or a screaming mob or a prison riot—most of us might agree with LeBon that some sort of "madness" had swept over the crowd. Sociologists today, however, point out that beneath the chaotic surface, crowds are actually quite rational (Yamaguchi 2000; Horowitz 2001). They point out that crowd participants take deliberate steps to reach some goal. As sociologist Clark McPhail (1991) says, even a lynch mob is cooperative—someone gets the rope while others hold the victim, some tie the knot, and others hoist the body. This is exactly what you saw in Pettie's execution—the men working together: the rope, the boxes, the straw, and the oil.

The Minimax Strategy

A general principle of human behavior is that we try to minimize our costs and maximize our rewards. Sociologist Richard Berk (1974) called this a **minimax strategy.** The fewer costs and the more rewards we anticipate from something, the more likely we are to do it. For example, if we think that others will approve an act, the chances increase that we will do it. Whether someone is yelling for the referee's blood after a bad call in a football game, or shouting for real blood as a member of a lynch mob, this principle applies. In short, whether people are playing a video game with a few friends or are part of a mob, the principles of human behavior remain the same.

Emergent Norms

Since collective behavior is unusual behavior, however, could it also involve unusual norms? Sociologists Ralph Turner and Lewis Killian (1987) use the term **emergent norms** to express this idea. They point out that life typically proceeds pretty much as we expect it to, making our usual norms adequate for dealing with everyday events. If something disrupts our customary ways of doing things, however, our ordinary norms may not cover the new situation. To deal with this new situation, new norms may emerge. People may even develop novel definitions of right and wrong, feeling that the new circumstances justify actions that they otherwise would consider wrong.

To understand how new norms emerge, we need to keep in mind that not everyone in a crowd shares the same point of view (Rodríguez 1994; Surowiecki 2005). As Turner and Killian (1987) point out, crowds have at least five kinds of participants:

milling a crowd standing or walking around as they talk excitedly about some event

minimax strategy Richard Berk's term for the efforts people make to minimize their costs and maximize their rewards

emergent norms Ralph Turner's and Lewis Killian's term for people developing new norms to cope with a new situation; used to explain crowd behavior

1. The *ego-involved* feel a personal stake in the unusual event.
2. The *concerned* also have a personal interest in the event, but less so than the ego-involved.
3. The *insecure* care little about the matter; they join the crowd because it gives them a sense of power, security, or belonging.
4. The *curious spectators* also care little about the issue; they are simply inquisitive about what is going on.
5. The *exploiters* don't care about the event; they use it for their own purposes, such as hawking food or T-shirts. For them, a rock concert would serve just as well.

Most important for setting the crowd on a particular course of action are the "ego-involved." Some of them make suggestions about what should be done; others simply start doing something. As the "concerned" join in, they, too, influence the crowd. If things get heated up, the "insecure" and the "curious spectators" may also join in. Although the "exploiters" are unlikely to participate, they do lend passive support to the crowd. A common mood completes the stage for new norms to emerge: Activities that are "not OK" in everyday life now may seem "OK"—whether they involve throwing bottles at the cops or shouting obscenities at the college president.

This analysis of emergent norms helps us to see that collective behavior is *rational*. The crowd, for example, does not consider all suggestions made by the ego-involved to be equal: To be acceptable, suggestions must match predispositions that the crowd already has. This current view, then, is a far cry from earlier interpretations that people were so transformed by a crowd that they went out of their minds.

Forms of Collective Behavior

Sociologists analyze collective behavior the same way they do other forms of behavior. They ask their usual questions about interaction, such as: How do people influence one another? What is the significance of the participants' age, gender, race-ethnicity, and social class? What were their preexisting attitudes? How did they perceive the situation? How did their perceptions get translated into action? In other words, sociologists view collective behavior as the actions of ordinary people who are responding to extraordinary situations.

In addition to lynchings, collective behavior includes riots, rumors, panics, mass hysteria, moral panics, fads, fashions, and urban legends. Let's look at each.

Riots

The nation watched in horror. White Los Angeles police officers had been caught on videotape beating an African American traffic violator with their nightsticks. The videotape showed the officers savagely bringing their nightsticks down on a man prostrate at their feet. Television stations around the United States—and the world—broadcast the pictures to stunned audiences.

When the officers went on trial for beating the man identified as Rodney King, how could the verdict be anything but guilty? Yet a jury consisting of eleven whites and one Asian American found the officers innocent of using excessive force. The result was a **riot**—violent crowd behavior directed at people and property. Within minutes of the verdict, angry crowds began to gather in Los Angeles. That night, mobs set fire to businesses, and looting and arson began in earnest. The rioting spread to other cities, including Atlanta, Tampa, Las Vegas, and even Madison, Wisconsin. Whites and Koreans were favorite targets of violence.

Americans sat transfixed before their television sets as they saw parts of Los Angeles go up in flames and looters carrying television sets and lugging sofas in full view of the Los Angeles Police Department, which took no steps to stop them. Seared into the public's collective consciousness was the sight of Reginald Denny, a 36-year-old white truck driver who had been yanked from his truck. As Denny sat dazed in the street, Damian Williams, laughing, broke the truck driver's skull with a piece of concrete.

riot violent crowd behavior directed at people and property

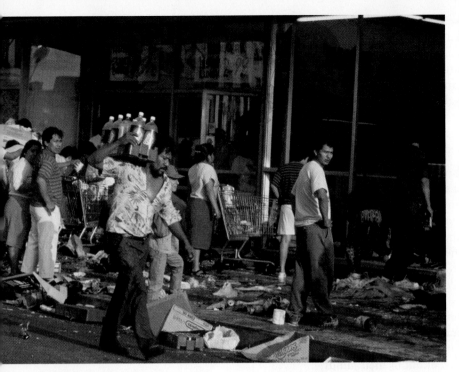

In this photo from the Los Angeles riot of 1992, can you identify emergent norms?

On the third night, after 4,000 fires had been set and more than 30 people killed, President George Bush announced on national television that the U.S. Justice Department had appointed prosecutors to pursue federal charges against the police officers. The president stated that he had ordered the Seventh Infantry, SWAT teams, and the FBI into Los Angeles. He also federalized the California National Guard and placed it under the command of Gen. Colin Powell, the chairman of the Joint Chiefs of Staff. Rodney King went on television and tearfully pleaded for peace.

The Los Angeles riot was the bloodiest since the Civil War. Before it was over, 54 people lost their lives, 2,328 people were treated in hospital emergency rooms, thousands of businesses were burned, and about $1 billion of property was destroyed. Two of the police officers were later sentenced to 2 years in prison on federal charges, and King was awarded $3.8 million in damages. (Rose 1992; Stevens and Lubman 1992; Cannon 1998; "Rodney King" 2007)

The *background conditions* of urban riots are frustration and anger brought on by feelings of deprivation. Frustration and anger simmer in people who feel that they have been denied jobs and justice and are being singled out by the police. If a *precipitating event* brings these pent-up feelings to a boiling point, they can erupt in collective violence. All these conditions existed in the Los Angeles riot, with the jury's verdict being the precipitating event.

Sociologists have found that it is not only the deprived who participate in riots. The first outbursts over the Rodney King verdict didn't come from the poorest neighborhoods, but, rather, from stable neighborhoods. Similarly, after the assassination of Dr. Martin Luther King, Jr., in 1968, when many U.S. cities erupted in riots, even people with good jobs participated (McPhail 1991). Why would middle-class people participate in riots? The answer, says sociologist Victor Rodríguez (1994), is the same: frustration and anger. Even though minorities have good jobs and are living middle-class lives, they can face situations in which they are treated as second-class citizens. They, too, can have simmering resentments that a precipitating event brings to the surface.

Also participating in riots are opportunists—people who feel neither rage at their situation in life nor outrage at the precipitating event. For them, a riot is a handy event. Not only do they get to participate in something exciting, but they also get an opportunity to loot stores.

IN SUM *The event that precipitates a riot is important, but so is the riot's general context.* Both must be present. The precipitating event is the match that lights the fuel, but the fuel is the background of resentment, tension, and unrest. Beneath what may appear to be a placid surface can lie seething rage. To be set ablaze, it takes but a match, such as the Rodney King verdict.

Rumors

In *The Lion King,* Simba, the cuddly lion star, stirs up a cloud of dust that, floating off the screen, spells S-E-X. In *The Little Mermaid,* the bishop who is presiding over a wedding, becomes noticeably aroused. And in *Aladdin,* the handsome young title character murmurs, "All good children, take off your clothes."

Ann Runge, a mother of eight who owned stacks of Disney animated videos, said she felt betrayed when she heard that the Magic Kingdom was sending obscene, subliminal messages. "I felt as though I had entrusted my kids to pedophiles," she said. (Bannon 1995)

A **rumor** is unverified information about some topic of interest that is passed from one person to another. Thriving on conditions of ambiguity, rumors fill in missing information (Turner 1964; Shibutani 1966; Fine and Turner 2001). In response to this particular rumor, Disney reported that Aladdin really says "Scat, good tiger, take off and go." The line is hard to understand, however, leaving enough ambiguity for others to hear what they want to hear, and even to insist that the line is an invitation to a teenage orgy. Similar ambiguity remains with Simba's dust and the aroused bishop.

Most rumors are short-lived. They arise in a situation of ambiguity, only to dissipate when they are replaced by factual information—or by another rumor. Occasionally, however, a rumor has a long life.

Rumors have swirled around the Magic Kingdom's supposed plots to undermine the morality of youth. Could Mickey Mouse be a dark force, and this child his victim? As humorous as this may be, some have taken these rumors seriously.

In the eighteenth and nineteenth centuries, for no known reason, healthy people would grow weak and slowly waste away. No one understood the cause, and people said they had consumption (now called tuberculosis). People were terrified as they saw their loved ones wither into shells of their former selves. With no one knowing when the disease would strike, or who its next victim would be, the rumor began that some of the dead had turned into vampire-like beings. At night, they were coming back from the grave and draining the life out of the living. The evidence was irrefutable—loved ones who wasted away before people's very eyes.

To kill these ghoulish "undead," people began to sneak into graveyards. They would dig up a grave, remove the leg bones and place them on the skeleton's chest, then lay the skull at the feet, forming a skull and crossbones. Having thus killed the "undead," they would rebury the remains. These rumors and the resulting mutilations of the dead continued off and on in New England until the 1890s. (Associated Press, November 30, 1993)

Why do people believe rumors? Three main factors have been identified. Rumors deal with a subject that is important to an individual; they replace ambiguity with some form of certainty; and they are attributed to a credible source. An office rumor may be preceded by "Jane has it on good authority that . . ." or "Bill overheard the boss say that . . ."

Rumors thrive on ambiguity or uncertainty, for where people know the facts about a situation a rumor can have no life. Surrounded by unexplained illnesses and deaths, however, the New Englanders speculated about why people wasted away. Their conclusions seem bizarre to us, but they provided answers to bewildering events. The uncertainty that sparked the Disney rumor may have arisen from fears that the moral fabric of modern society is decaying.

Not only are most rumors short-lived, but most are also of little consequence. As discussed in the Down-to-Earth Sociology box on the next page, however, some rumors not only disrupt people's lives but also lead to the destruction of entire communities.

Rumors usually pass directly from one person to another, although, as you saw with the Tulsa riot, they can originate from the mass media. As the Down-to-Earth Sociology box on page 631 illustrates, the Internet, too, has become a source of rumors.

Panics and Mass Hysteria

The Classic Panic

In 1938, on the night before Halloween, a radio program of dance music was interrupted by a report that explosions had been observed on the surface of Mars. The announcer added that a cylinder of unknown origin had been discovered embedded in the ground on a farm in New Jersey. The radio station then switched to the farm, where a breathless reporter gave details of horrible-looking Martians coming out of the cylinder. Their death-ray weapons had destructive powers unknown to humans. An astronomer then confirmed that Martians had invaded the Earth.

rumor unfounded information spread among people

Down-to-Earth Sociology

Rumors and Riots: An Eyewitness Account to the Tulsa Riot

IN 1921, TULSA, OKLAHOMA, was ripped apart by a race riot. And it all began with a rumor (Gates 2004). Up to this time, Tulsa's black community had been vibrant and prosperous. Many blacks owned their own businesses, and competed successfully with whites. Then on May 31, everything changed after a black man was accused of assaulting a white girl.

Buck Colbert Franklin (Franklin and Franklin 1997), a black attorney in Tulsa at the time, was there. Here is what he says:

Hundreds of men with drawn guns were approaching from every direction, as far I could see as I stood at the steps of my office, and I was immediately arrested and taken to one of the many detention camps. Even then, airplanes were circling overhead dropping explosives upon the buildings that had been looted, and big trucks were hauling all sorts of furniture and household goods away.

Unlike later riots, these were white looters who were breaking in and burning the homes and businesses of blacks. Franklin continues:

Soon I was back upon the streets, but the building where I had my office was a smoldering ruin, and all my lawbooks and office fixtures had been consumed by flames. I went to where my roominghouse had stood a few short hours before, but it was in ashes, with all my clothes and the money to be used in moving my family. As far as one could see, not a Negro dwellinghouse or place of business stood. . . . Negroes who yesterday were wealthy, living in beauti-

Family moving after the riot in Tulsa. Note that the man on the passenger side is holding a rifle.

ful homes in ease and comfort, were now beggars, public charges, living off alms.

The rioters burned all black churches, including the imposing Zion Baptist church, which had just been completed. When they finished destroying homes and businesses, block after block lay in ruins, as though a tornado had swept through the area.

And what about the young man who had been accused of assault, the event that precipitated the riot? Franklin says that the police investigated, and found that there had been no assault. All the man had done was accidentally step on a lady's foot in a crowded elevator, and, as Franklin says, "She became angry and slapped him, and a fresh, cub newspaper reporter, without any experience and no doubt anxious for a byline, gave out an erroneous report through his paper that a Negro had assaulted a white girl."

for your Consideration

It is difficult to place ourselves in such an historical mindset to imagine that stepping on someone's foot could lead to such destruction, but it did. Can you apply the sociological findings on both rumors and riots to explain the riot at Tulsa? Why do you think that so many whites believed this rumor, and why were some of them were so intent on destroying this thriving black community? If "seething rage" underlies riots, it should apply to this one, too. What "seething rage" (or resentments or feelings of injustice) do you think were involved?

Perhaps six million Americans heard this broadcast. About one million were frightened by it. Thousands panicked, grabbed their weapons, and hid in their basements or ran into the streets. Hundreds bundled up their families and jumped into their cars, jamming the roads as they headed to who knows where.

Of course, there was no invasion. This was simply a dramatization of H. G. Wells' *War of the Worlds,* starring Orson Welles. There had been an announcement at the beginning of the program and somewhere in the middle that the account was fictional, but apparently many people missed it. Although the panic reactions to this radio program may appear humorous to us, the situation is far from humorous to anyone who is in a panic. **Panic** occurs when people become so fearful that they cannot function normally, and may even flee the situation they perceive as threatening.

Why did people panic in this instance? Psychologist Hadley Cantril (1941) attributed the reaction to widespread anxiety about world conditions. The Nazis were marching in Europe, and millions of Americans (correctly, as it turned out) were afraid that the

panic the condition of being so fearful that one cannot function normally, and may even flee

Down-to-Earth Sociology

Rumors and Lurking Danger: The Internet and the Uncertainty of Life

LIFE IN OUR MASS SOCIETY is filled with uncertainty. That new neighbor who just moved in across the street could be a child molester, the guy next door a rapist. Evil lurks everywhere, and, who knows, maybe you or some little kid will be the next victim.

Or so it seems. And within this sea of uncertainty comes the Net to feed our gnawing suspicions. Here is an e-mail that I received (reproduced exactly as the original):

> Please, read this very carefully. . . . then send it out to all the people online that you know. Something like this is nothing to take casually; this is something that you do want to pay attention to.

If a guy with a screen-name of SlaveMaster contacts you, do not answer. DO NOT TALK TO THIS PERSON. DO NOT ANSWER ANY OF HIS/HER INSTANT MESSAGES/E-MAIL.

He has killed 56 women (so far) that he has talked to on the Internet.

PLEASE SEND OUT TO ALL THE WOMEN ON YOUR BUDDY LIST. ALSO ASK THEM TO PASS THIS ON.

He has been on Yahoo and AOL and Excite so far. This is no joke!!!

PLEASE SEND THIS TO MEN TOO . . . JUST IN CASE!!!

for your Consideration

How do the three main factors associated with rumors—importance, ambiguity, and source—apply to this note? In what ways do they not apply?

United States would get involved in this conflict. War jitters, he said, created fertile ground for the broadcast to touch off a panic.

Contemporary analysts, however, question whether there even was a panic. Sociologist William Bainbridge (1989) acknowledges that some people did become frightened, and that a few actually did get in their cars and drive like maniacs. But he says that most of this famous panic was an invention of the news media. Reporters found a good story, and they milked it, exaggerating as they went along.

Bainbridge points to a 1973 event in Sweden. To dramatize the dangers of atomic power, Swedish Radio broadcast a play about an accident at a nuclear power plant. Knowing about the 1938 broadcast in the United States, Swedish sociologists were waiting to see what would happen. Might some people fail to realize that it was a dramatization and panic at the threat of ruptured reactors spewing out radioactive gasses? The sociologists found no panic. A few people did become frightened. Some telephoned family members and the police; others shut windows to keep out the radioactivity—reasonable responses, considering what they thought had occurred.

The Swedish media, however, reported a panic! Apparently, a reporter had telephoned two police departments and learned that each had received calls from concerned citizens. With a deadline hanging over his head, the reporter decided to gamble. He reported that police and fire stations were jammed with citizens, people were flocking to the shelters, and others were fleeing south (Bainbridge 1989).

The Occurrence of Panics Panics do occur, of course, and they can be set off by rumors. Here are two real ones.

> On May 17, 2005, Indonesians on Sumatra island fled for the hills. The panic was fed by a rumor—spread by telephone calls and mobile phone text messages—that a tsunami was on its way ("Krakatoa Rumor . . ." 2005).

> On September 1, 2005, hundreds of thousands of Iraqis were walking to the tomb of a Shiite martyr. When someone spotted what he thought was a suicide bomber, the rumor spread quickly through the crowd. Thousands of pilgrims who were crossing a bridge made a mad scramble for safety, crushing and trampling to death about 1,000 people.

Mass Hysteria

LET'S LOOK AT FIVE EVENTS.

Several hundred years ago, a strange thing happened near Naples, Italy. When people were bitten by tarantulas, not only did they feel breathless and have fast-beating hearts but also they felt unusual sexual urges. As though that weren't enough, they also felt an irresistible urge to dance—and to keep dancing to the point of exhaustion.

The disease was contagious. Even people who hadn't been bitten came down with the same symptoms. The situation got so bad that instead of gathering the summer harvest, whole villages would dance in a frenzy.

A lot of remedies were tried, but nothing seemed to work except music. Bands of musicians traveled from village to village, providing relief to the victims of *tarantism* by playing special "tarantula" music (Bynum 2001).

• • •

This 1938 photo was taken in Grover's Mill, New Jersey, after the broadcast of H. G. Wells' *War of the Worlds*. The man is guarding against an attack of Martians.

In the year 2001, in New Delhi, the capital of India, a "monkey-man" stalked people who were sleeping on rooftops during the blistering summer heat. He clawed and bit a hundred victims. Fear struck the capital. People would wake up screaming that the monkey-man was after them. To escape this phantom, some people jumped off two-story buildings. One man was killed when he jumped off the roof of his house during one of the monkey-man's many attacks ("'Monkey' . . ." 2001).

There was no ape-like killer.

• • •

At the United Arab Emirates University in Al-Ain, twenty-three female students rushed to the hospital emergency room after escaping from a fire in their dormitory. As you might expect from people who barely escaped burning to death, they were screaming, weeping, shaking, and fainting (Amin et al. 1997).

But there was no fire. A student had been burning incense in her room. The fumes of the burning incense had been mistaken for the smell of a fire.

• • •

People across France and Belgium became sick after drinking Coca-Cola. After a quick investigation, "experts" diagnosed the problem as "bad carbon dioxide and a fungicide." Coke recalled 15 *million* cases of its soft drink ("Coke . . ." 1999).

Later investigations revealed that there was nothing wrong with the drink.

• • •

In McMinville, Tennessee, a teacher smelled a "funny odor." Students and teachers began complaining of headaches, nausea, and a shortness of breath. The school was evacu-

ated, and doctors treated more than 100 people at the local hospital. Authorities found nothing.

A few days later, a second wave of illness struck. This time, the Tennessee Department of Health shut the high school down for two weeks. They dug holes in the foundation and walls and ran snake cameras through the ventilation and heating ducts. They even tested the victims' blood (Adams 2000).

Nothing unusual was found.

• • •

"It's all in their heads," we might say. In one sense, we would be right. There was no external, objective cause of the illnesses from tarantism or Coca-Cola. There was no "monkey-man," no fire, nor any chemical contaminant at the school.

In another sense, however, we would be wrong to say that it is "all in their heads." The symptoms that these people experienced were real. They had real headaches and stomach aches. They did vomit and faint. And they did experience unusual sexual urges and the desire to dance until they could no longer stand.

There is no explanation for **mass hysteria**—an imagined threat that causes physical symptoms among a large group of people—except suggestibility. Experts might use fancy words to try to explain mass hysteria, but once you cut through their terms, you find that they are really simply saying, "It happens."

Perhaps one day we will know more about the causes of mass hysteria, but for now we have to be content with not knowing the specifics. We do know that such events occur in many cultures. This would indicate that mass hysteria follows basic principles of human behavior. Someday, we will understand these principles.

It is not difficult to understand why these people panicked. After the tsunami had wiped out their homes and killed their friends and families, the Indonesians were living in a state of uncertainty. The rumor of another tsunami stoked their deep fears. The Iraqis, too, lived with fear and uncertainty. At the time suicide bombers did appear out of nowhere, bringing havoc, destruction, and death. To run was a logical response.

Panics can also be caused by real events. If people fear fire in a public place, they will lunge toward the nearest exit in a frantic effort to escape. Such a panic occurred on Memorial Day weekend in 1977 at the Beverly Hills Supper Club in Southgate, Kentucky.

> About half of the Club's 2,500 patrons were crowded into the Cabaret Room. A fire, which began in a small banquet room near the front of the building, burned undetected until it was beyond control. When employees discovered the fire, they warned patrons. People began to exit in orderly fashion, but when flames rushed in, they trampled one another in a furious attempt to reach the exits. The exits were blocked by masses of screaming people trying to push their way through all at once. The writhing bodies at the exits created further panic among the remainder, who pushed even harder to force their way through the bottlenecks. One hundred sixty-five people died. All but two were within thirty feet of two exits in the Cabaret Room.

Table 21.1 Employees' First Action After Learning of the Fire

Action	Percentage
Left the building	29%
Helped others to leave	41%
Fought or reported the fire	17%
Continued routine activities	7%
Other (e.g., looked for a friend or relative)	5%

Note: These figures are based on interviews with 95 of the 160 employees present at the time of the fire: 48 males and 47 females, ranging in age from 15 to 59.

Source: Based on Johnston and Johnson 1989.

Sociologists who studied this panic found what other researchers have discovered in analyzing other disasters. *Not everyone panics.* In disturbances, many people continue to act responsibly (Clarke 2002). Especially important are primary bonds. Parents help their children, for example (Morrow 1995). Gender roles also persist, and more men help women than women help men (Johnson 1993). Even work roles continue to guide some behavior. Sociologists Drue Johnston and Norris Johnson (1989) found that only 29 percent of the employees of the Beverly Hills Supper Club left when they learned of the fire. As noted in Table 21.1, most of the workers helped customers, fought the fire, or searched for friends and relatives.

Sociologists use the term **role extension** to describe the actions of most of these employees. By this term, they mean that the workers extended their occupational role so that it included other activities. Servers, for example, extended their role to include helping people to safety. How do we know that giving help was an extension of their occupational role, and not simply a general act of helping? Johnston and Johnson found that servers who were away from their assigned stations returned to them in order to help *their* customers. For a fascinating and related type of collective behavior, see the Down-to-Earth Sociology box on page 632.

In some life-threatening situations in which we might expect panic, we find that a sense of order prevails instead. This seems to have been the case during the attack on the World Trade Center when, at peril to their own lives, people helped injured friends and even strangers escape down many flights of stairs. These people, it would seem, were highly socialized into the collective good, and had a highly developed sense of empathy.

Moral Panics

"They touched me down there. Then they killed a horse. They said if I told they would kill my sister."

"They took off my clothes. Then they got in a space ship and flew away."

"It was awful when they killed the baby. There was blood all over."

What would you think if you heard little children saying things like this? You probably would shake your head and wonder what kind of TV shows they had been watching.

But not if you were an investigator in the 1980s in the United States. At that time, rumors swept the country that day care centers were run by monsters who were sexually molesting the little kids.

Prosecutors believed the children who told these stories. They knew their statements about space ships and aliens weren't true, but maybe little pets had been killed and families

role extension the incorporation of additional activities into a role

mass hysteria an imagined threat that causes physical symptoms among a large number of people

There was panic when the World Trade Center was attacked, especially among those who jumped to their deaths when their escape was blocked by flames. Among others, there was a sense of order. Shown here are people evacuating the World Trade Center.

threatened. There was no evidence, but interrogators kept hammering away at the children. Kids who kept saying that nothing had happened were said to be "in denial."

Prosecutors took their cases to court, and juries believed the kids. That there was no evidence bothered some people, but those little children—tied up, stripped naked, subjected to ritual sexual assaults, pets killed—it was all too much. The ghoulish child care workers were sent to prison. To say anything in ther defense was to defend child molesters from hell.

Moral panics occur when large numbers of people become concerned, even fearful, about some behavior that they believe threatens morality, and when the fear is out of proportion to any actual danger (Cauthen and Jasper 1994; Bandes 2007). The threat is perceived as enormous, and hostility builds toward those deemed responsible.

The media fed this moral panic, for each new revelation about day care centers sold more papers and brought more viewers to their TVs. The situation grew so bad that almost every day care worker became suspect in someone's eyes. Only fearfully did parents leave their children in day care centers. Although sexual abuse at day care centers has occurred, intensive investigations never substantiated the stories of children supposedly subjected to bizarre sexual rituals.

Like other panics, moral panics center on a sense of danger. In the 1980s and 1990s, strangers were supposedly snatching thousands of U.S. children from playgrounds, city streets, and their own backyards. Parents became fearful, perplexed at how U.S. society could have gone to hell in a hand basket. The actual number of stranger kidnappings in the United States per year is between 64 and 300 (Bromley 1991; Simons and Willie 2000).

Moral panics are often fueled by rumor. In the 1990s, a rumor swept the country that some of these missing children were being sold to Satanists. After sexually abusing the children, the Satanists ritually murdered them. People who said they were eyewitnesses to these sacrifices appeared, telling their stories to horrified audiences. Even though this rumor and the eyewitness reports were outlandish, many believed them because the stories filled in missing information: who was abducting and doing what to those many missing children. The police investigated, but they found no evidence to substantiate the reports.

Moral panics thrive on uncertainty and anxiety. Changes in the family can give rise to anxiety—to concerns that children are receiving inadequate care because so many mothers have joined the work force. These concerns become linked with fears, producing a perspective that pedophiles and killers of children are lurking almost everywhere.

Fads and Fashions

A **fad** is a novel form of behavior that briefly catches people's attention. The new behavior appears suddenly and spreads by imitation and identification with people who are already involved in the fad. Reports by the mass media help to spread the fad. After a short life, the fad fades into oblivion, although it may reappear from time to time (Aguirre et al. 1993; Best 2006).

Fads come in many forms. Very short, intense fads are called *crazes*. They appear suddenly, and are gone almost as quickly. "Tickle Me Elmo" dolls and Beanie Babies were object crazes. There also are behavior crazes, such as streaking, which lasted only a couple of months in 1974; as a joke, an individual or a group would run nude in some public place. "Flash mobs" was a behavior craze of 2003; alerted by e-mail messages, individuals would gather at a specified time, do something, such as point toward the ceiling of a mall, and then, without a word, disperse.

Even administrators of businesses, colleges, and universities can get caught up in fads. For about ten years, quality circles were a fad; these were supposedly an effective way of getting workers and management to cooperate and develop innovative techniques to

moral panic a fear that grips a large number of people that some evil threatens the well-being of society, followed by hostility, sometimes violence, toward those thought responsible

fad a temporary pattern of behavior that catches people's attention increase production. This administrative fad peaked in 1983, then quickly dropped from sight (Strang and Macy 2001). There are also fads in child rearing—permissive versus directive, spanking versus non-spanking. Our food is subject to fads as well; recent fads include tofu, power drinks, herbal supplements, and organically grown foods. Fads in dieting also come and go, with many seeking the perfect diet, and practically all leaving the fad diet disillusioned.

Some fads involve millions of people but still die out quickly. In the 1950s, the hula hoop was so popular that stores couldn't keep them in stock. Children cried and pleaded for these brightly colored plastic hoops. Across the nation, children—and even adults—held contests to see who could keep the hoops up the longest or who could rotate the most hoops at one time. Then, in a matter of months it was over, and parents wondered what to do with these items, which seemed useless for any other purpose. Hula hoops can again be found in toy stores, but now they are just another toy.

When a fad lasts, it is called a **fashion.** Some fashions, as with clothing and furniture, are the result of a coordinated international marketing system that includes designers, manufacturers, advertisers, and retailers. By manipulating the tastes of the public, they sell billions of dollars of products. Fashion, however, also refers to hairstyles, to the design and colors of buildings, and even to the names that parents give their children (Lieberson 2000). Sociologist John Lofland (1985) pointed out that fashion also applies to common expressions, as demonstrated by these roughly comparable terms: "Neat!" in the 1950s, "Right on!" in the 1960s, "Really!" in the 1970s, "Awesome!" in the 1980s, "Bad!" in the 1990s, "Sweet" and "Tight" in the early 2000s, "Hot" in the middle 2000s, and, recurringly, "Cool."

Fads are one of the fascinating aspects of social life that sociologists study. Body scarification, whose origins reach back into antiquity, has begun to appear in the Western world. If body scarification enters the mainstream culture, its extremes won't.

Urban Legends

Did you hear about Kristi and Paul? They were parked at Bluewater Bay, listening to the radio, when the music was interrupted by an announcement that a rapist-killer had escaped from prison. Instead of a right hand, he had a hook. Kristi said they should leave, but Paul laughed and said there wasn't any reason to go. When they heard a strange noise and Kristi screamed, Paul agreed to take her home. When Kristi opened the door, she heard something clink. It was a hook hanging on the door handle!

For decades, some version of "The Hook" has circulated among Americans. It has appeared as a "genuine" letter in "Dear Abby," and some of my students heard it in grade school. **Urban legends** are stories with an ironic twist that sound realistic but are false. Although untrue, they usually are told by people who believe that they happened.

Here is another one:

A horrible thing happened. This girl in St. Louis kept smelling something bad. The smell wouldn't leave even when she took showers. She finally went to the doctor, and it turned out that her insides were rotting. She had gone to the tanning salon too many times, and her insides were cooked.

Folklorist Jan Brunvand (1981, 1984, 2004) reports that urban legends are passed on by people who often think that the event happened just one or two people down the line of transmission, sometimes to a "friend of a friend." These stories have strong appeal and gain their credibility by naming specific people or citing particular events. Note the details of where Kristi and Paul were. Brunvand views urban legends as "modern morality stories"; each one teaches a moral lesson about life.

If we apply Brunvand's analysis to these two urban legends, three principles emerge. First, these stories serve as warnings. "The Hook" warns young people that they should be careful about where they go, with whom they go, and what they do when they get

fashion a pattern of behavior that catches people's attention and lasts longer than a fad

urban legend a story with an ironic twist that sounds realistic but is false there. The tanning salon story warns people about the dangers of new technology. Second, these stories are related to social change: "The Hook" to changing sexual morality, the tanning salon to changing technology. Third, each is calculated to instill fear: We should all be afraid, for dangers abound. They lurk in the dark countryside, or even at our neighborhood tanning salon.

These principles can be applied to an urban legend that made the rounds in the late 1980s. I heard several versions of this one; each narrator swore that it had just happened to a friend of a friend.

Jerry (or whoever) went to a nightclub last weekend. He met a good-looking woman, and they hit it off. They spent the night in a motel. When he got up the next morning, the woman was gone. When he went into the bathroom, he saw a message scrawled on the mirror in lipstick: "Welcome to the wonderful world of AIDS."

SOCIAL MOVEMENTS

When the Nazis, a small group of malcontents in Bavaria, first appeared on the scene in the 1920s, the world found their ideas laughable. This small group believed that the Germans were a race of supermen (*Übermenschen*) and that they would launch a Third Reich (reign or nation) that would control the world for a thousand years. Their race destined them for greatness; lesser races would serve them.

The Nazis started as a little band of comic characters who looked as though they had stepped out of a grade B movie (see the photo on page 335). From this inauspicious start, the Nazis gained such power that they threatened to overthrow Western civilization. How could a little man with a grotesque moustache, surrounded by a few sycophants in brown shirts, ever come to threaten the world? Such things don't happen in real life—only in novels or movies. They are the deranged nightmare of some author with an overactive imagination. Only this was real life. The Nazis' appearance on the human scene caused the deaths of millions of people and changed the course of world history.

Social movements, the second major topic of this chapter, hold the answer to Hitler's rise to power. **Social movements** consist of large numbers of people who organize either to promote or to resist social change. Members of social movements hold strong ideas about what is wrong with the world—or some part of it—and how to make things right.

Examples include the civil rights movement, the white supremacist movement, the women's movement, the animal rights movement, and the environmental movement.

At the heart of social movements lies a sense of injustice (Klandermans 1997). Some find a particular condition of society intolerable, and their goal is to promote social change. Theirs is called a **proactive social movement.** Others, in contrast, feel threatened because some condition of society is changing, and they *react* to resist that change. Theirs is a **reactive social movement.**

To further their goals, people develop **social movement organizations.** Those who want to promote social change develop organizations such as the National Association for the Advancement of Colored People (NAACP). In contrast, those who are trying to resist these particular changes form organizations such as the Ku Klux Klan or Aryan Nations. To recruit followers and publicize their grievances, leaders of social movements use attention-getting devices, from marches and protest rallies to sit-ins and boycotts. Some stage "media events," sometimes quite effectively.

Social movements are like a rolling sea, observed sociologist Mayer Zald (1992). During one period, few social movements may appear, but shortly afterward, a wave of them rolls in, each competing for the public's attention. Zald suggests that a *cultural crisis* can give birth to a wave of social movements. By this, he means that there are times when a society's institutions fail to keep up with social change. During these times many people's needs go unfulfilled, massive unrest follows, and social movements spring into action to bridge this gap.

Social movements involve large numbers of people who, upset about some condition in society, organize to do something about it. Shown here is Carrie Nation, a temperance (anti-alcohol) leader who in 1900 began to break up saloons with a hatchet. Her social movement eventually became so popular and powerful that it resulted in Prohibition.

Types and Tactics of Social Movements

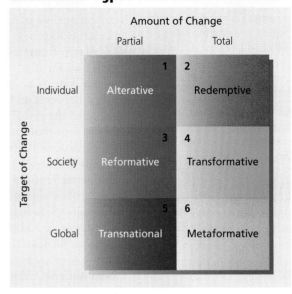

Figure 21.2 Types of Social Movements

	Amount of Change	
Target of Change	Partial	Total
Individual	1 Alterative	2 Redemptive
Society	3 Reformative	4 Transformative
Global	5 Transnational	6 Metaformative

Sources: The first four types are from Aberle 1966; the last two are by the author.

Let's see what types of social movements there are and then examine their tactics.

Types of Social Movements

Since social change is their goal, we can classify social movements according to their *target* and the *amount of change* they seek. Look at Figure 21.2. If you read across, you will see that the target of the first two types of social movements is *individuals*. **Alterative social movements** seek only to *alter* some specific behavior. An example is the Women's Christian Temperance Union, a powerful social movement of the early 1900s. Its goal was to get people to stop drinking alcohol. Its members were convinced that if they could shut down the saloons such problems as poverty and wife abuse would go away. **Redemptive social movements** also target individuals, but their goal is *total* change. An example is a religious social movement that stresses conversion. In fundamentalist Christianity, for example, when someone converts to Christ, the entire person is supposed to change, not just some specific behavior. Self-centered acts are to be replaced by loving behaviors toward others as the convert becomes, in their terms, a "new creation."

The target of the next two types of social movements is *society*. **Reformative social movements** seek to *reform* some specific aspect of society. The animal rights movement, for example, seeks to reform the ways in which society views and treats animals. **Transformative social movements,** in contrast, seek to *transform* the social order itself. Its members want to replace the current social order with their vision of the good society. Revolutions, such as those in the American colonies, France, Russia, and Cuba, are examples.

One of the more interesting examples of transformative social movements is **millenarian social movements,** which are based on prophecies of impending calamity. Of particular interest is a type of millenarian movement called a **cargo cult** (Worsley 1957). About one hundred years ago, Europeans colonized the Melanesian Islands of the South Pacific. Ships from the home countries of the colonizers arrived one after another, each loaded with items the Melanesians had never seen. As the Melanesians watched the cargo being unloaded, they expected that some of it would go to them. Instead, it all went to the Europeans. Melanesian prophets then revealed the secret of this exotic merchandise. Their own ancestors were manufacturing and sending the cargo to them, but the colonists were intercepting the merchandise. Since the colonists were too strong to fight and too selfish to share the cargo, there was little the Melanesians could do.

Then came a remarkable self-fulfilling prophecy. Melanesian prophets revealed that if the people would destroy their crops and food and build harbors, their ancestors would see their sincerity and send the cargo directly to them. The Melanesians did so. When the colonial administrators of the island saw that the natives had destroyed their crops and were just sitting in the hills waiting for the cargo ships to arrive, they informed the home government. The prospect of thousands of islanders patiently starving to death was too horrifying to allow. The British government fulfilled the prophecy by sending ships to the islands loaded with cargo earmarked for the Melanesians.

As Figure 21.2 indicates, some social movements have a global orientation. As with many aspects of life in our new global economy, numerous issues that concern people transcend national boundaries. Participants of **transnational social movements** (also called *new social movements*) want to change some condition that exists not just in their society but also throughout the world. (See Cell 5 of Figure 21.2.) These social movements often center on improving the quality of life (Melucci 1989). Examples are the

alterative social movement a social movement that seeks to alter only some specific aspects of people

redemptive social movement a social movement that seeks to change people totally, to redeem them

reformative social movement a social movement that seeks to reform some specific aspects of society

transformative social movement a social movement that seeks to change society totally, to transform it

millenarian social movement a social movement based on the prophecy of coming social upheaval

cargo cult a social movement in which South Pacific islanders destroyed their possessions in the anticipation that their ancestors would ship them new goods

transnational social movement a social movement whose emphasis is on some condition around the world, instead of on a condition in a specific country; also known as *new social movements*

metaformative social movement a social movement that has the goal to change the social order not just of a country or two, but of a civilization, or even of the entire world

public in this context, a dispersed group of people relevant to a social movement; the sympathetic and hostile publics have an interest in the issues on which a social movement focuses; there is also an unaware or indifferent public

women's movement, labor movement, and the environmental movement (McAdam et al. 1988; Smith et al. 1997; Walter 2001; Tilly 2004). As you can see from these examples, transnational social movements still focus on some specific condition, but that condition cuts across societies.

Cell 6 in Figure 21.2 represents a rare type of social movement. The goal of **metaformative social movements** is to change the social order itself—not just of a specific country, but of an entire civilization, or even the whole world. Their objective is to change concepts and practices of race-ethnicity, class, gender, family, religion, government, and the global stratification of nations. These were the aims of the communist social movement of the early to middle twentieth century and the fascist social movement of the 1920s to 1940s. (The fascists consisted of the Nazis in Germany, the Black Shirts of Italy, and other groups throughout Europe and the United States.) Because these metaformative social movements posed a threat to the existing social order of the time, capitalist and communist nations disregarded their opposing ideologies long enough to band together to fight them.

Today, we are witnessing another metaformative social movement, that of Islamic fundamentalism. Like other social movements before it, this movement is not united, but consists of many separate groups with differing goals and tactics. Al-Qaeda, for example, would not only cleanse Islamic societies of Western influences—which they contend are demonic and degrading to men, women, and morality—but also replace Western civilization with an extremist form of Islam. This frightens both Muslims and non-Muslims, who hold sharply differing views of what constitutes quality of life. If the Islamic fundamentalists—or the communists or fascists before them—have their way, they will usher in a New World Order fashioned after their particular views of the good life.

Tactics of Social Movements

The leaders of a social movement can choose from a variety of tactics. Should they boycott peacefully, stage a march, or hold an all-night candlelight vigil? Or should they bomb a building, burn down a research lab, or assassinate a politician? To understand why the leaders of social movements choose their tactics, let's examine a group's levels of membership, the publics it addresses, and its relationship to authorities.

Levels of Membership   Figure 21.3 shows the composition of social movements. Beginning at the center and moving outward are three levels of membership. At the center is the inner core, those most committed to the movement. The inner core sets the group's goals, timetables, and strategies. People at the second level are also committed to the movement, but somewhat less so than the inner core. They can be counted on to show up for demonstrations and to do the grunt work—help with mailings, pass out petitions and leaflets, make telephone calls. The third level consists of a wider circle of people who are less committed and less dependable. Their participation depends on convenience—if an activity doesn't interfere with something else they want to do, they participate.

The tactics that a group uses depend largely on the backgrounds and predispositions of the inner core. Because of their differing backgrounds, some members of the inner core may be predisposed to engaging in peaceful, quiet demonstrations, or even placing informational ads in newspapers. Others may prefer heated, verbal confrontations. Still others may tend toward violence. Tactics also depend on the number of committed members. Different tactics are called for if the inner core can count on seven hundred—or only seven—committed members to show up.

The Publics   Outside the group's membership is the **public,** a dispersed group of people who may have an interest in the issue. As you can see from Figure 21.3, there are three types of publics. Just outside the third circle of members, and blending into it, is

Figure 21.3 **The Membership and Publics of Social Movements**

Source: By the author.

the *sympathetic* public. Although their sympathies lie with the movement, these people have no commitment to it. Their sympathies with the movement's goals, however, make them prime candidates for recruitment. The second public is *hostile.* The movement's values go against its own, and it wants to stop the social movement. The third public consists of *disinterested* people. They are either unaware of the social movement or, if they are aware, are indifferent to it.

In selecting tactics, the leadership pays attention to these publics. The sympathetic public is especially significant, because it is the source of new members and support at the ballot box. Leaders avoid tactics that they think might alienate the sympathetic public and seek strategies that will bring even more sympathy from this group. To make themselves appear to be victims— people whose rights are being trampled on— leaders may even force a confrontation with the hostile public. Tactics directed toward the indifferent or unaware public are designed to neutralize their indifference and increase their awareness.

As the text explains, people have many reasons for joining social movements. One reason that some people participate in the animal rights movement is illustrated by this photo, which evokes in many an identity with animals.

Relationship to Authorities In determining tactics, the movement's relationship to authorities is also significant. This is especially true when it comes to choosing between peaceful and violent actions. If a social movement is *institutionalized*—accepted by authorities—violence will not be directed toward the authorities, for they are on the movement's side. This, however, does not rule out using violence against the opposition. In contrast, if authorities are hostile to a social movement, they may become the object of aggression or violence. For example, because the goal of a transformative (revolutionary) social movement is to replace the government, the movement and the government are clearly on a collision course.

Other Factors Sociologist Ellen Scott (1993), who studied the movement to stop rape, discovered that friendship, race-ethnicity, and even size of town are important in determining tactics. Women in Santa Cruz, California, chose to directly confront accused rapists—to publicly humiliate them. In a town of 41,000, the tactic worked. In Washington, D.C., women rejected confrontation as ineffective because of the anonymity that comes with a city of 640,000. Another factor was race-ethnicity. Both groups of women were white, but in Santa Cruz, it was white women confronting white men, while in Washington, D.C., it would have been white women confronting black men. Friendships were also important. Public confrontations require a team of people who will back each other up. In Santa Cruz, the women had lived together for years, while the group in Washington, D.C., was a more formal organization and didn't have these ties of friendship.

No matter how careful leaders are, their tactics can backfire. All around Santa Cruz, women from the center hung pictures of a man accused of rape. He sued the center. The long litigation that followed sapped the women's energy, and the Santa Cruz center folded.

Propaganda and the Mass Media

The leaders of social movements try to manipulate the mass media to influence **public opinion,** how people think about some issue. The right kind of publicity enables the leaders to arouse sympathy and to lay the groundwork for recruiting more members. Pictures of bloodied, dead baby seals, for example, go a long way toward getting a group's message across. The photo essay on the next two pages reports on the demonstrations that accompanied the execution of Timothy McVeigh. The significance of this photo essay is not the execution, which occurred in 2001, but, rather, the use of propaganda by both the demonstrators who wanted McVeigh killed and those who wanted his life spared.

public opinion how people think about some issue

Social Movements and Propaganda
The Execution of Timothy McVeigh

t here is so much sociology to do, and so little time to do it! Some events seem irresistible, however.

The execution of Timothy McVeigh, the Oklahoma City bomber who claimed more victims than any single individual in U.S. history, was one such event. The media highlighted the possibility of protests and riots at this first federal execution in 38 years. I knew that I could never get inside the prison to do research. Yet, there would be all those public activities, so readily accessible.

When I arrived in Terre Haute, Indiana, I found that the city had been turned into an armed camp. The federal, state, and local authorities had pre-

pared for an attack on the prison. The local police had been trained in riot control. The state had sent in its Emergency Management Agency. And the federal government had been active, too. Military sharpshooters were present, ready to act in case any group tried to prevent the execution.

To prevent confrontation, the police separated demonstrators on the basis of their sentiment (pro- and anti-execution) and sent them to parks on opposite sides of town. The anti-execution people showed up in full force. So few pro-execution protesters appeared that I was able to interview them all.

Sequestered on one side of town, in a small park, were the pro-execution demonstrators. As is evident from this photo, they were not a large, organized group. These demonstrators had simply used a marking pen to print messages on cardboard.

The pro-execution demonstrators placed their focus on the victims. Some told me that a lethal injection was too good for McVeigh, that he should be made to suffer before he died. The demonstrators in this photo are expressing their view that McVeigh's death is not adequate payment for 168 victims.

The anti-execution demonstrators expressed mixed motives for their position. These two, isolated from the organized anti-execution crowd—both physically and in their point of view—were not against the death penalty. They felt that McVeigh should not be executed because he had been railroaded by the government in an unfair trial. For them, McVeigh had become a folk hero.

The anti-execution demonstrators displayed professionally made signs that they take from one protest site to another. They were hosted by a local Roman Catholic church. After a rally there, they marched as a group to the prison where the execution took place.

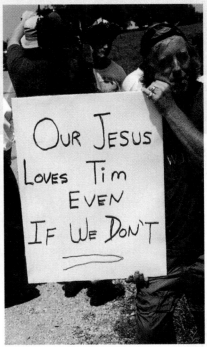

The attempt to stop executions is part of a social movement that, for some demonstrators, extends to the pro-life movement. Leaders of this highly organized movement sent busloads of people to protest McVeigh's execution.

Demonstrators also gathered outside the prison where McVeigh was to be executed. They were kept on the opposite side of the road, where they were constantly scrutinized by armed personnel on the prison side of the road. I was told that inside the prison were hundreds of armed troops—in case anyone tried to rescue McVeigh.

Demonstrators often use attention-getting devices. This individual carried a cross to the federal prison. He said that he was convinced that God wanted him to be at the scene. His attention-getting device was effective, as you can see from the individual who is interviewing him.

The huge puppets of the anti-execution demonstrators were an effective attention-getting device. If you look closely, you can see a reporter interviewing the demonstrators.

© James M. Henslin, all photos

The use of *propaganda* is popular among those committed to the goals of a social movement. They can see only one side to the social issue about which they are so upset. What attention-getting devices is this demonstrator using? Are they effective? Why is this an example of propaganda?

A key to understanding social movements, then, is **propaganda.** Although this word often evokes negative images, it actually is a neutral term. Propaganda is simply the presentation of information in an attempt to influence people. Its original meaning was positive. *Propaganda* referred to a committee of cardinals of the Roman Catholic Church whose assignment was the care of foreign missions. (They were to *propagate*—multiply or spread—the faith.) The term has traveled a long way since then, however, and today it usually refers to a presentation of information so one-sided that it distorts reality.

Propaganda, in the sense of organized attempts to influence public opinion, is a part of everyday life. Our news is filled with propaganda, as various interest groups—from retailers to the government—try to manipulate our perceptions of the world. Our movies, too, although seemingly intended as simply entertainment devices, are actually propaganda vehicles. The basic techniques that underlie propaganda are discussed in the Down-to-Earth Sociology box on the next page.

The mass media play such a crucial role that we can say they are the gatekeepers to social movements. If those who control and work in the mass media—from owners to reporters—are sympathetic to some particular "cause," you can be sure that it will receive sympathetic treatment. If the social movement goes against their views, however, it likely will be ignored or receive unfavorable treatment. If you ever get the impression that the media are trying to manipulate your opinions and attitudes—even your feelings—on some particular issue or social movement, you probably are right. Far from doing unbiased reporting, the media are under the control and influence of people who have an agenda to get across. To the materials in the Down-to-Earth Sociology box on propaganda, then, we need to add the biases of the media establishment—the topics it chooses to publicize, those it chooses to ignore, and its favorable and unfavorable treatment of issues and movements.

Sociology can be a liberating discipline (Berger 1963/2007). Sociology sensitizes us to *multiple realities;* that is, for any single point of view on some topic, there are competing points of view. Each represents reality as people see it, their distinct experiences having led them to different perceptions. Consequently, different people find each point of view equally compelling. Although the committed members of a social movement are sincere—and perhaps even make sacrifices for "the cause"—theirs is but one view of the world. If other sides were presented, the issue would look quite different.

Why People Join Social Movements

As we have seen, social movements are fed by a sense of injustice. They stem from widespread, deeply felt discontent—the conviction that some condition of society is no longer tolerable. However, not everyone who feels dissatisfied with an issue joins a social movement. Why do some join, but not others? Sociologists have found that recruitment generally follows channels of social networks. That is, people most commonly join a social movement because they have friends and acquaintances already in it (McCarthy and Wolfson 1992; Snow et al. 1993a).

Let's look at three explanations for why people join social movements.

Mass Society Theory

To explain why people are attracted to social movements, sociologist William Kornhauser (1959) proposed **mass society theory.** Kornhauser argued that many people feel isolated because they live in a **mass society**—an impersonal, industrialized, highly bureaucratized society. Social movements fill this void by offering a sense of belonging.

This theory has been criticized severely (Thompson 2005). When sociologist Doug McAdam and his colleagues (McAdam et al. 1988) interviewed people who had risked

propaganda in its broad sense, the presentation of information in the attempt to influence people; in its narrow sense, one-sided information used to try to influence people

mass society theory an explanation for why people participate in a social movement based on the assumption that the movement offers them a sense of belonging

mass society industrialized, highly bureaucratized, impersonal society

"Tricks of the Trade"—Deception and Persuasion in Propaganda

SOCIOLOGISTS ALFRED and Elizabeth Lee (1939) found that propaganda relies on seven basic techniques, which they termed "tricks of the trade." To be effective, the techniques should be subtle, with the audience unaware that their minds and emotions are being manipulated. If propaganda is effective, people will not know why they support something, but they'll fervently defend it. Becoming familiar with these techniques can help you keep your mind and emotions from being manipulated.

Why is this recruitment poster for Arnold Schwarzenegger for governor of California an example of propaganda?

Name calling. This technique aims to arouse opposition to the competing product, candidate, or policy by associating it with a negative image. By comparison, one's own product, candidate, or policy is attractive. Republicans who call Democrats "soft on crime" and Democrats who call Republicans "insensitive to the poor" are using this technique.

Glittering generality. Essentially the opposite of the first technique, this one surrounds the product, candidate, or policy with images that arouse positive feelings. "She's a real Democrat" has little meaning, but it makes the audience feel that something substantive has been said. "This Republican stands for individual rights" is so general that it is meaningless; yet the audience thinks that it has heard a specific message about the candidate.

Transfer. In its positive form, this technique associates the product, candidate, or policy with something the public approves of or respects. You might not be able to get by with saying "Coors is patriotic," but surround a beer with images of the country's flag, and beer drinkers will get the idea that it is more patriotic to drink this brand of beer than some other kind. In its negative form, this technique associates the product, candidate, or policy with something generally disapproved of by the public.

Testimonials. Famous individuals endorse a product, candidate, or policy. Michelle Wie lends her name to Nike products, and Tiger Woods tells you that Buicks make fine SUVs. Candidates for political office solicit the endorsement of movie stars who may

know next to nothing about the candidate or even about politics. In the negative form of this technique, a despised person is associated with the competing product. If propagandists (called "spin doctors" in politics) could get away with it, they would show Osama bin Laden announcing support for an opposing candidate.

Plain folks. Sometimes it pays to associate the product, candidate, or policy with "just plain folks." "If Mary or John Q. Public likes it, you will, too." A political candidate who kisses babies, puts on a hard hat, and has lunch at McDonald's while photographers "catch him (or her) in the act" is using the "plain folks" strategy. "I'm just a regular person" is the message of the presidential candidate who poses for photographers in jeans and work shirt—while making certain that the chauffeur-driven Mercedes does not show up in the background.

Card stacking. The aim of this technique is to present only positive information about what you support, and only negative information about what you oppose. The intent is to make it sound as though there is only one conclusion a rational person can draw. Falsehoods, distortions, and illogical statements are often used.

Bandwagon. "Everyone is doing it" is the idea behind this technique. Emphasizing how many other people buy the product or support the candidate or policy conveys the message that anyone who doesn't join in is on the wrong track.

The Lees (1939) added, "Once we know that a speaker or writer is using one of these propaganda devices in an attempt to convince us of an idea, we can separate the device from the idea and see what the idea amounts to on its own merits."

for your Consideration

What propaganda techniques have you seen or heard recently? Recall TV ads, political ads, movies, and newspaper reports. Explain why it was not simply information, but a technique of propaganda.

their lives in the civil rights movement, they found that these people were firmly rooted in families and communities. Their strong desire to right wrongs and to overcome injustices—not their isolation—had motivated their participation. Even the Nazis attracted many people who were firmly rooted in their communities (Oberschall 1973). Finally, the most isolated of all, the homeless, generally do not join anything—except food lines.

Deprivation Theory

A second explanation to account for why people join social movements is *deprivation theory.* According to this theory, people who feel deprived—whether it be of money, justice, status, or privilege—join social movements with the hope of redressing their grievances. This theory may seem so obvious as to need no evidence. Don't the thousands of African Americans who participated in the civil rights movement of the 1950s and 1960s and the World War I soldiers who marched on Washington after Congress refused to pay their promised bonuses provide ample evidence that the theory is true?

Deprivation theory does provide a starting point. But there is more to the matter than this. About 150 years ago, Alexis de Tocqueville (1856/1955) made a telling observation. Both the peasants of Germany and the peasants of France were living under deprived conditions. According to deprivation theory, if revolution were to occur we would expect it to take place in both countries. Only the French peasants rebelled and overthrew their king, however. The reason, said de Tocqueville, is *relative* deprivation. The living conditions of the French peasants had been improving, and they could foresee even better circumstances ahead. German peasants, in contrast, had never experienced anything but depressed conditions, and they had no comparative basis for feeling deprived.

According to **relative deprivation theory,** then, it is not people's actual deprivation that matters. The key to participation in social movements is *relative* deprivation—what people *think* they should have relative to what others have, or relative to their own past or even their perceived future. Relative deprivation theory, which has provided insight into revolutions, holds a surprise. Because improving conditions fuel human desire for even better conditions, *improving* conditions can spark revolutions. As Figure 21.4 shows, this occurs when people's expectations outstrip the actual change they experience. It is likely that we can also apply this to riots.

Relative deprivation also explains an interesting aspect of the civil rights movement. Relatively well-off African Americans—college students and church leaders—were at the center of the sit-ins, marches, and boycotts in the South during the 1950s and 1960s. They went to restaurants and lunch counters that were reserved for whites. When refused service, they sat peacefully while curses and food were heaped on them (Morris 1993). You might want to review the photo on page 357. Why did they subject themselves to such treatment? Remember that according to relative deprivation theory, what is significant is not what we have or don't have, but with whom we compare ourselves. The African American demonstrators compared themselves with whites of similar status, and they perceived themselves as deprived.

How about the white, middle-class college students and the white church leaders from the North? They, too, risked their lives when they joined the Southern protesters. They weren't comparing themselves with people whose situation was better than their own. Nor was their own personal welfare at stake. Relative deprivation theory doesn't help us here. We need to look at the *moral* reasons for their involvement (McAdam et al. 1988; Fendrich and Lovoy 1993). Let's consider that motivation in social movements.

Moral Issues and Ideological Commitment

As sociologists James Jasper and Dorothy Nelkin (1993) point out, we will miss the *basic* reason for many people's involvement in social movements if we overlook the moral issue—people getting upset about the injustice that others experience and wanting to do something about it. Some people join because of *moral shock*—a sense of outrage at finding out what is "really" going on (Jasper and Poulsen 1995). For people who view a social movement in moral terms, great issues hang in the balance. They feel they must choose sides and do what they can to help right wrongs. As sociologists

Figure 21.4 **Relative Deprivation and Revolution**

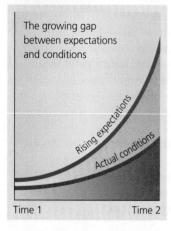

The growing gap between expectations and conditions

Rising expectations

Actual conditions

Time 1 — Time 2

relative deprivation theory in this context, the belief that people join social movements based on their evaluations of what they think they should have compared with what others have put it, they join because of *ideological commitment* to the movement.

Many members on *both* sides of the abortion issue, for example, perceive their involvement in such terms. Similarly, activists in the animal rights movement are convinced that there can be no justification for making animals suffer in order to make safer products for humans. Activists in the peace and environmental movements and those who protest against global capitalism view nuclear weapons, pollution, and global power in similar moral terms. It is for moral reasons that they risk arrest and ridicule for their demonstrations. For them, to *not* act would be an inexcusable betrayal of future generations. The *moral* component of a social movement, then, is a primary reason for many people's involvement.

A Special Case: The Agent Provocateur

Agent provocateurs are a unique type of participant in social movements. These are agents of the government or even of the opposing sides of a social movement whose job is to spy on the leaders and perhaps to sabotage their activities. Some are recruited from the membership itself—people who are willing to betray their friends in the organization for a few Judas dollars. Others are police or members of a rival group who infiltrate the movement.

The radical social change advocated by some social movements poses a threat to the power elite. In such cases, the use of agent provocateurs is not surprising. What may be surprising, however, is that some agents convert to the social movement on which they are spying. Sociologist Gary Marx (1993) explains that to be credible, agents must share at least some of the class, age, gender, racial-ethnic, or religious characteristics of the group. This background makes the agents more likely to be sympathetic to the movement's goals and to become disenchanted with trying to harm the group. To be effective, agents must also work their way into the center of the group. This requires that they spend time with the group's committed members. A basic sociological principle is that the more we interact with people, the more we tend to like them. In addition, as these agents build trust, they often are cut off from their own group. The point of view they represent can start to recede in their minds, and be replaced with concerns about betraying and deceiving people who now trust them as friends.

What also may be surprising is how far some agents are willing to go. During the 1960s, when a wave of militant social movements streamed across the United States, the FBI recruited agent provocateurs to sabotage some of these groups. These agents provoked illegal activities that otherwise would not have occurred: They set the leadership up for arrest and, in some instances, set them up for death. Two examples will let us see how agent provocateurs operate (Marx 1993). In a plot by a group called the Black Liberation Front to blow up the Statue of Liberty, one of the four men involved was an undercover agent. It was he who drew up the plans and even provided funds to pay for the dynamite and rent the car. In another instance, the FBI paid $36,500 to two members of the White Knights of the Ku Klux Klan to arrange for the Klan to bomb a Jewish businessman's home. A trap was set in which one Klansman was killed and another was arrested in the unsuccessful attempt.

The Michigan militia is not run by the federal or state governments or any government agency. It is a private organization, made up of individuals who fear increasing government control over individual freedoms (and, I assume, some state and federal agents).

agent provocateur someone who joins a group in order to spy on it and to sabotage it by provoking its members to commit extreme acts

IN SUM There is no single reason that people join social movements. Most people join because they have friends and acquaintances already in the movement. Some join because of moral convictions, others to further their own careers. Still others join because they find a valued identity, or even because it is fun. Some even participate although they *don't* *want to.* The Cuban government, for example, compels people to turn out for mass demonstrations to show support of the Communist regime (Aguirre 1993). As we just saw, police agents may join social movements in order to spy on them and sabotage their activities. As in all other activities in life, people remain a complex bundle of motivations—a challenge for sociologists to unravel.

On the Success and Failure of Social Movements

Social movements have brought about extensive social change. The women's movement, for example, has led not only to new laws but also to a different way of thinking about relations between women and men. Most social movements, however, are not successful. Let's look at the reasons for their success or failure.

The Stages of Social Movements

Sociologists have identified five stages in the growth and maturity of social movements (Lang and Lang 1961; Mauss 1975; Spector and Kitsuse 1977; Jasper 1991; Tilly 2004):

1. *Initial unrest and agitation.* During this first stage, people are upset about some condition in society and want to change it. Leaders emerge who verbalize people's feelings and crystallize issues. Most social movements fail at this stage. Unable to gain enough support, after a brief flurry of activity, they quietly die.
2. *Resource mobilization.* A crucial factor that enables social movements to make it past the first stage is **resource mobilization.** By this term, sociologists mean the gathering and organizing of resources such as time, money, information, people's skills, and the ability to get the attention of the mass media. Those resources may also include access to churches to organize protests (Mirola 2003). A key resource is communications technology such as cell phones, Internet sites, and blogs. Also important is access to mailing lists for direct mailing, faxing, and e-mailing.

    In some cases, an indigenous leadership arises to mobilize resources. Other groups, lacking capable leadership, turn to "guns for hire," outside specialists who sell their services. As sociologists John McCarthy and Mayer Zald (1977; Zald and McCarthy 1987) point out, even though large numbers of people may be upset over some condition of society, without resource mobilization they are only upset people, perhaps even agitators, but they do not constitute a social movement.
3. *Organization.* A division of labor is set up. The leadership makes policy decisions, and the rank and file carry out the daily tasks necessary to keep the movement going. There is still much collective excitement about the issue, the movement's focal point of concern.
4. *Institutionalization.* At this stage, the movement has developed a bureaucracy, the type of formal hierarchy that was described in Chapter 7. Control lies in the hands of career officers, who may care more about their own position in the organization than the movement for which the organization's initial leaders made sacrifices. The collective excitement diminishes.
5. *Organizational decline and possible resurgence.* During this phase, managing the day-to-day affairs of the organization dominates the leadership. A change in public sentiment may even have occurred, and there may no longer be a group of committed people who share a common cause. The movement is likely to wither away. Decline is not inevitable, however, as we shall see.

resource mobilization a theory that social movements succeed or fail based on their ability to mobilize resources such as time, money, and people's skills

The Rocky Road to Success

These stages, especially resource mobilization and institutionalization, help us to understand why social movements seldom solve social problems. To mobilize adequate resources, a movement must appeal to a broad constituency. This means that the group must focus on things that a lot of people are concerned about. For example, if workers at one particular plant are upset about their safety, their concerns are not sufficient to mobilize the broad support necessary for a social movement. At best, it will result in local agitation. Unsafe working conditions of millions of workers, in contrast, have a chance of becoming the focal point of a social movement.

Broad problems, however, are embedded deeply in society. This, of course, means that minor tinkering will not be adequate. Just as the problem touches many interrelated components of society, so the solutions must be broad. With no quick fix available, the social movement must stay around. But longevity brings its own danger of failure. When social movements become institutionalized, they tend to turn inward and focus their energies on running the organization (see stage 4 on the previous page).

Many social movements vitally affect society, however. Some, such as the civil rights and the women's movements, become powerful forces for social change. They draw the public's attention to problems and turn the society on a path that leads toward solutions. Others become powerful forces for resisting the social change that their members consider undesirable. In either case, social movements are significant for contemporary society, and we can anticipate that new ones will be a regular feature of our social landscape.

As we saw, the fifth and final stage of social movement is decline. However, decline is not inevitable. More idealistic and committed leaders can emerge who reinvigorate the movement. Or, as in the case of abortion, conflict between groups on opposing sides of the issue can invigorate both sides and prevent the movement's decline. Let's close this chapter by focusing on abortion activists.

Thinking Critically

Which Side of the Barricades? Prochoice and Prolife as a Social Movement

No issue so divides Americans as abortion. Although most Americans take a more moderate view, on one side are some who believe that abortion should be permitted under any circumstance, even during the last month of pregnancy. They are matched by individuals on the other side who are convinced that abortion should never be allowed under any circumstances, not even in the case of rape, incest, or during the first month of pregnancy. This polarization constantly breathes new life into the movement.

When the U.S. Supreme Court made its 1973 decision, *Roe* v. *Wade,* that states could not prohibit abortion, the prochoice side relaxed. Victory was theirs, and they thought their opponents would quietly disappear. Instead, large numbers of Americans were disturbed by what they saw as the legal right to murder unborn children.

The views of the two sides could not be more incompatible. Those who favor choice view the 1.3 million abortions that are performed annually in the United States as examples of women exercising their basic reproductive rights. Those who gather under the prolife banner see these abortions as legalized murder. To the prochoice side, those who oppose abortion are blocking women's rights—they would force women to continue pregnancies they want to terminate. To the prolife side, those who advocate choice are perceived as condoning murder—they would sacrifice their unborn children for the sake of school, career, or convenience.

There is no way to reconcile these contrary views. Each sees the other as unreasonable and extremist. And each uses propaganda by focusing on worst-case scenarios: prochoice images of young women raped at gunpoint, forced to bear the children of rapists; prolife images of women who are eight months pregnant killing their babies instead of nurturing them.

With no middle ground, these views remain in perpetual conflict. As each side fights for what it considers to be basic rights, it reinvigorates the other. When in 1989 the U.S. Supreme Court decided in *Webster* v. *Reproductive Services* that states could

With sincere people on both sides of the issue—equally committed and equally convinced that their side is right—abortion is destined to remain a controversial force in U.S. life.

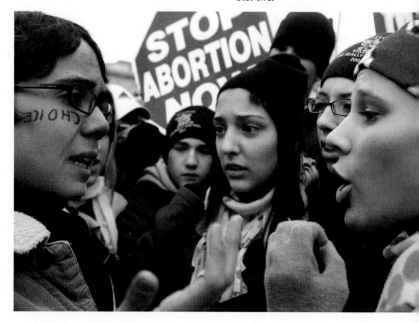

restrict abortion, one side mourned it as a defeat and the other hailed it as a victory. Seeing the political battle going against them, the prochoice side regrouped for a determined struggle. The prolife side, sensing judicial victory within its grasp, gathered forces for a push to complete the overthrow of *Roe* v. *Wade*.

This goal of the prolife side almost became reality in *Casey* v. *Planned Parenthood*. On June 30, 1992, in a 6-to-3 decision the Supreme Court upheld the right of states to require women to wait 24 hours between the confirmation of pregnancy and getting an abortion; to require girls under 18 to obtain the consent of one parent; and to require that women be informed about alternatives to abortion and that they be given materials that describe the fetus In the same case, however, in a 5-to-4 decision, the Court ruled that a wife does not have to inform her husband if she intends to have an abortion. In 2007, in another 5-to-4 decision, the Court ruled a certain type of abortion prodedure illegal. The name given this late-term procedure is significant: One side calls it an "intact dilation and evacuation," while the other side terms it a "partial-birth abortion."

This legal part of the battle comes to the forefront each time the Senate is asked to confirm the President's nominee to the U.S. Supreme Court. Watching these hearings is to view a skirmish between the opposing sides of this issue.

Because the two sides do not share the same reality, this social movement cannot end unless the vast majority of Americans commit to one side or the other. Every legislative and judicial outcome—including the extremes of a constitutional amendment that declares abortion to be either murder or a woman's right—is a victory to one and a defeat to the other. To committed activists, then, no battle is ever complete. Rather, each action is only one small part of a long, hard-fought, moral struggle.

for your Consideration

Typically, the last stage of a social movement is decline. Why hasn't this social movement declined? Under what conditions will it decline?

The longer the duration of the pregnancy, the fewer the number of Americans who approve of abortion. How do you feel about abortion during the second month versus the eighth month? Or late-term abortion (also known as partial-birth abortion)? What do you think about abortion in cases of rape and incest? Can you identify some of the social reasons that underlie your opinions?

Sources: Neikirk and Elsasser 1992; McKenna 1995; Williams 1995; *Statistical Abstract* 2007:Table 96; Henslin 2008.

Summary *and* Review

Early Explanations: The Transformation of the Individual

How did early theorists explain the ways that crowds affect people?

Early theorists of **collective behavior** argued that crowds transform people. Charles Mackay used the term *herd mentality* to explain why people did wild things when they were in crowds. Gustave LeBon said that a **collective mind** develops, and people are swept away by suggestions. Robert Park said that collective unrest develops, which, fed by a **circular reaction**, leads to collective impulses. Pp. 624–625.

What are the five stages of crowd behavior?

Herbert Blumer identified five stages that crowds go through before they become an **acting crowd:** social unrest, an exciting event, **milling,** a common object of attention, and common impulses. Pp. 625–626.

The Contemporary View: The Rationality of the Crowd

What is the current view of crowd behavior?

Current theorists view crowds as rational. Richard Berk suggested a **minimax strategy;** that is, people try to minimize their costs and maximize their rewards, regardless of whether they are alone, with friends, or in crowds. In **emergent norm theory,** Ralph Turner and Lewis Killian suggest that new norms emerge that allow people to do things in crowds that they otherwise would not do. Pp. 626–627.

Forms of Collective Behavior

What forms of collective behavior are there?

Forms of **collective behavior** include lynchings, **riots, rumors, panics, moral panics, mass hysteria, fads, fashions,** and **urban legends.** Conditions of discontent or uncertainty provide fertile ground for collective behavior. Each form of collective behavior provides a way of dealing with these conditions. Pp. 627–636.

Types and Tactics of Social Movements
What types of social movements are there?
Social movements consist of large numbers of people who organize to promote or resist social change. Depending on their target (individuals or society) and the amount of social change that is desired (partial or complete), social movements can be classified as **alterative, redemptive, reformative, transformative, transnational,** and **metaformative.** Pp. 636–638.

How do social movement leaders select their tactics?
Leaders choose tactics on the basis of a group's levels of membership, its **publics,** and its relationship to authorities. The three levels of membership are *the inner core, the committed,* and *the less committed.* The predispositions of the inner core are crucial in choosing tactics, but so is the public they wish to address. If relationships with authorities are bad, the chances of aggressive or violent tactics increase. Friendship, size of city, and the race-ethnicity of movement participants and their targets can also be significant factors. Pp. 638–639.

How are the mass media related to social movements?
The mass media are gatekeepers for social movements. Because the media's favorable or unfavorable coverage affects **public opinion,** leaders choose tactics with the media in mind. Leaders also use **propaganda** to further their causes. Pp. 639–642.

Why People Join Social Movements
Why do people join social movements?
A primary reason people join social movements is they know others in the movement. According to **mass society theory,** social movements relieve feelings of isolation created by an impersonal, bureaucratized society. According to **relative deprivation theory,** people join movements to redress their grievances. A sense of justice, morality, values, and ideological commitment also motivates people to join social movements. **Agent provocateurs** illustrate that even people who oppose a cause may participate in it. Pp. 642–646.

On the Success and Failure of Social Movements
Why do social movements succeed or fail?
Sociologists have identified five stages of social movements: initial unrest and agitation, mobilization, organization, institutionalization, and, finally, decline. Resurgence is also possible, if, as in the case of abortion, opposing sides revitalize one another. Groups that appeal to few people cannot succeed. To appeal broadly in order to attain **resource mobilization,** the movement must focus on broad concerns. These concerns are embedded deeply in society, which makes success difficult. Pp. 646–648.

Thinking Critically
about Chapter 21

1. Describe the different forms of collective behavior, and explain why people participate in collective behavior.
2. Use sociological findings to analyze a rumor or an urban legend you have heard or a fad you've participated in.
3. Pick a social movement and analyze it according to the sociological principles and findings reviewed in this chapter.

Additional Resources

What can you use MySocLab for? www.mysoclab.com

- **Study and Review:** Pre- and Post-Tests, Practice Tests, Flash Cards, Individualized Study Plans.
- **Current Events:** *Sociology in the News,* the daily *New York Times,* and more.

- **Research and Writing:** *Research Navigator, Writing About Sociology,* and more,

Where Can I Read More on This Topic?

Suggested readings for this chapter are listed at the back of this book.

CHAPTER 22

Social Change and the Environment

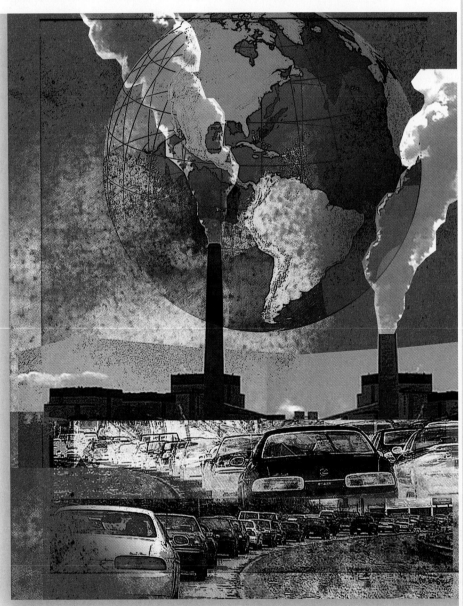

Roy Scott, *Exhaustive Fumes from Cars and Factories Contribute to Global Warming*

The morning of January 28, 1986, dawned clear but near freezing—strange weather for subtropical Florida. At the Kennedy Space Center, icicles 6 to 12 inches long hung like stalactites from launch pad 39B. Shortly after 8 A.M., the crew entered the crew module. By 8:36 A.M., the seven members of the crew were strapped in their seats. They were understandably disappointed when liftoff, scheduled for 9:38 A.M., was delayed because of the ice.

Public interest in the flight ran high. Attention focused on Christa McAuliffe, a 37-year-old high school teacher from Concord, New Hampshire, the first private citizen to fly aboard a space shuttle. Mrs. McAuliffe had been selected from thousands of applicants (including the author of this text). She was to give a televised lesson during the flight about life aboard a spacecraft, and across the nation, schoolchildren watched with anticipation.

Eagerly awaiting the launch at the viewing site were the families and friends of the crew, as well as thousands of spectators. After two hours of delays, they were delighted to see *Challenger*'s two solid-fuel boosters ignite, and they broke into cheers as this product of technological innovation thundered majestically into space. The time was 11:38 A.M.

Seventy-three seconds later, the *Challenger* was 7 miles from the launch site, racing skyward at 2,900 feet per second. Suddenly a brilliant glow appeared on one side of the external tank. In seconds, the glow blossomed into a gigantic fireball. Screams of horror arose from the crowd as the *Challenger,* now 19 miles away, exploded, and bits of debris began to fall from the sky.

In classrooms across the country, children burst into tears. Adults stared at their televisions in stunned disbelief.

Screams of horror arose from the crowd . . . and bits of debris began to fall from the sky

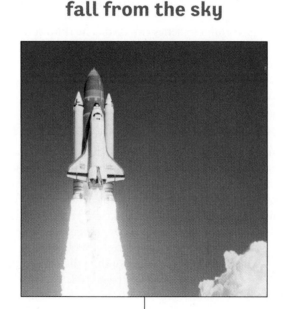

Sources: Based on Broad 1986; Magnuson 1986; Lewis 1988; Maier 1993.

If any characteristic describes social life today, it is rapid social change. As we shall see in this chapter, technology, such as that which made the *Challenger* both a reality and a disaster, is a driving force behind this change. To understand social change is to better understand today's society—and our own lives.

How Social Change Transforms Social Life

Social change, a shift in the characteristics of culture and society, is such a vital part of social life that it has been a recurring theme throughout this book. To make this theme more explicit, let's review the main points about social change that were made in the preceding chapters.

The Four Social Revolutions

The rapid social change that the world is currently experiencing did not "just happen." Rather, today's social change is the result of forces that were set in motion thousands of years ago, beginning with the domestication of plants and animals. This first social revolution allowed hunting and gathering societies to develop into horticultural and pastoral societies (see pages 155–157). The plow brought about the second social revolution, from which agricultural societies emerged. The third social revolution, prompted by the invention of the steam engine, ushered in the Industrial Revolution. Now we are in the midst of the fourth social revolution, stimulated by the invention of the microchip. The process of change has accelerated so greatly that the mapping of the human genome system could be pushing us into yet another new type of society, one based on biotechnology.

From *Gemeinschaft* to *Gesellschaft*

Although so many aspects of our lives have already changed, we have seen only the tip of the iceberg. By the time this fourth—and perhaps fifth—social revolution is full-blown, little of our current way of life will remain. We can assume this because that is how it was with the earlier social revolutions. For example, the change from agricultural to industrial society meant not only that people moved from villages to cities but also that many intimate, life-long relationships were replaced by impersonal, short-term associations. Paid work, contracts, and money replaced the reciprocal obligations (such as exchanging favors) that were essential to relationships based on kinship, social status, and friendship. As reviewed on page 108, sociologists use the terms *Gemeinschaft* and *Gesellschaft* to indicate this fundamental shift in society.

Traditional, or *Gemeinschaft,* societies are small, rural, and slow-changing. They are dominated by men, and they have firm divisions of labor between men and women. People look to the past for guidelines on how to deal with the present. They live in extended families, have little formal education, and treat most illnesses at home. People tend to see life and morals in absolute terms. Modern, or *Gesellschaft,* societies, in contrast, are large, more urbanized, and fast-changing. Divisions of labor between the sexes are more fluid. People stress formal education and are more future-oriented. In the third stage of the demographic transition, they have smaller families and low rates of infant mortality. They live longer lives, have higher incomes, and enjoy vastly more material possessions.

Capitalism, Modernization, and Industrialization

Just why did societies change from *Gemeinschaft* to *Gesellschaft?* Karl Marx pointed to a social invention called *capitalism.* He analyzed how the breakup of feudal society threw people off the land, creating a surplus of labor. These masses moved to cities, where they were exploited by the owners of the means of production (factories, machinery, tools). This set in motion antagonistic relationships between capitalists and workers that remain today.

Social change comes in many forms. Shown here is a Chinese peasant in 1911, whose pigtail is being cut off by the revolutionary army. To retain the custom of never cutting one's hair was considered a sign of allegiance to warlords and of resistance to the new regime.

Max Weber, in contrast, traced capitalism to the Protestant Reformation (see page 180). He noted that the Reformation stripped Protestants of the assurance that church membership saved them. As they agonized over heaven and hell, they concluded that God did not want the elect to live in uncertainty. Surely God would give a sign to assure them that they were predestined to heaven. That sign, they decided, was prosperity. An unexpected consequence of the Reformation, then, was to make Protestants work hard and be thrifty. This created an economic surplus, which stimulated capitalism. In this way, Protestantism laid the groundwork for the Industrial Revolution that transformed the world.

The sweeping changes ushered in by the Industrial Revolution are called **modernization.** Table 22.1 on the next page summarizes these changes. The traits listed on this table are *ideal types* in Weber's sense of the term, for no society exemplifies all of them to the maximum degree. Our new technology has also brought about a remarkable unevenness in the characteristics of nations. For example, in Uganda, a traditional society, the elite have computers. Thus the characteristics shown in Table 22.1 should be interpreted as "more" or "less" rather than "either-or."

When technology changes, societies change. Consider how technology from the industrialized world is transforming traditional societies. When the West exported medicine to the Least Industrialized Nations, for example, death rates dropped while birth rates remained high. As a result, the population exploded. This second stage of the demographic transition upset traditional balances of family and property. It brought hunger and led to mass migration to cities that have little industrialization to support the throngs of people moving into them. The photo essay on pages 604–605 and the Cultural Diversity box on page 613 discuss some of these problems.

modernization the transformation of traditional societies into industrial societies

Table 22.1 Comparing Traditional and Modern Societies

Characteristics	Traditional Societies	Modern Societies
General Characteristics		
Social change	Slow	Rapid
Size of group	Small	Large
Religious orientation	More	Less
Formal education	No	Yes
Place of residence	Rural	Urban
Family size	Larger	Smaller
Infant mortality	High	Low
Life expectancy	Short	Long
Health care	Home	Hospital
Temporal orientation	Past	Future
Demographic transition	First stage	Third stage (or Fourth)
Material Relations		
Industrialized	No	Yes
Technology	Simple	Complex
Division of labor	Simple	Complex
Income	Low	High
Material possessions	Few	Many
Social Relationships		
Basic organization	*Gemeinschaft*	*Gesellschaft*
Families	Extended	Nuclear
Respect for elders	More	Less
Social stratification	Rigid	More open
Statuses	More ascribed	More achieved
Gender equality	Less	More
Norms		
View of life and morals	Absolute	Relativistic
Social control	Informal	Formal
Tolerance of differences	Less	More

Source: By the author.

Social Movements

Social movements reveal the cutting edge of change in society. People band together to express their feelings about something that upsets them. They organize to demand change, or to resist some change they don't like. Because social movements form around issues that bother large numbers of people, they indicate areas of society in which there is great pressure for change. With globalization, these issues increasingly cut across international boundaries, indicating areas of discontent and sweeping change that affect many millions of people in different cultures (see pages 636–648).

Conflict, Power, and Global Politics

In our fast-paced world, our attention goes to the changes that have an immediate impact on our own lives. Often unnoticed is one of the most significant changes of all, the shifting arrangement of power among nations. By the sixteenth century, global divisions had begun to emerge. Those nations that had the most advanced technology (at that time, the swiftest ships and the most powerful cannons) became wealthy by conquering other nations and taking control of their resources. Then, as capitalism emerged, some nations industrialized. The newly industrialized nations then exploited the resources of those countries that had not yet industrialized. According to *world system theory*, this made the nonindustrialized nations dependent and unable to develop their own resources (see page 259).

From G-7 to (Almost) G-9 Since World War II, a realignment of the world's powers (called *geopolitics*) has resulted in a triadic division of the globe: a Japan-centered East (soon to be dominated by China), a Germany-centered Europe, and a United States-centered western hemisphere. These three powers, along with five lesser ones—Canada, France, Great Britain, Italy, and Russia—dominate the globe today. They first called themselves G-7, meaning the "Group of 7." Fear of Russia's nuclear arsenal and an attempt to gain Russia's cooperation in global affairs prompted the G-7 nations to let Russia join its elite club. It is now known as G-8.

Each year, the leaders of the world's eight most powerful nations meet in a secluded place to make world-controlling decisions. And each year, protesters demonstrate near the site. This photo was taken at G-8's 2007 meeting at Heiligendamm, Germany. The 9th member is the President of the European Commission.

Soon it will be G-9. No longer can G-8 ignore the growing wealth and power of China. Wanting to recapture its glory of centuries past, China is expanding its domain of influence. Bowing to the inevitable and attempting to reduce the likelihood of conflict as China steps on turf claimed by others, G-8 has allowed China to become an observer at its annual summits. As mentioned in Chapter 15, if China follows G-8's rules, the next step will be to incorporate China into this exclusive club.

Dividing Up the World   These world powers hold annual meetings at which they decide how to divide up the world's markets and set policies to guide global economic matters such as interest rates, tariffs, and currency exchanges. Their goal is to perpetuate their global dominance, which includes trying to maintain low prices on the raw materials they buy from the Least Industrialized Nations. Access to abundant oil is essential for this goal, which requires that they dominate the Middle East, not letting it become an independent power. If the Middle Eastern countries were to set prices and policies according to their own interests, it would undermine the world order being orchestrated by G-8.

Two Threats to G-8   There are two major threats to the global divisions that G-8 has worked out. The first issue is division from within. Currently, Russia is at the center of the intra-familial feuding that threatens this coalition of powers, even though, for the most part, it has been cooperative. However, because it is still stinging after losing its empire and it wants a more powerful presence on the world stage, Russia is quick to see insult and to threaten retaliation. In 2006, amidst a dispute with the Ukraine over the price of gas, Russia turned off its oil supply that ran through the nation to Western Europe. This was in the dead of winter, and threatened several countries (Crossland 2006). Then in 2007, after fuming for months about a U.S. plan to put missiles in Poland as part of a missile-defense shield, just days before the annual G-8 meeting Russia threatened to aim its missiles at cities in Europe if the U.S. didn't back away from its plan (Blomfield 2007). Disputes are inevitable as these formerly hostile powers work out the shifting details of their newly realigned structure of power. Despite occasional snarling back and forth, it is likely that such disagreements will be resolved peacefully.

The second threat to G-8 is the resurgence of ethnic conflicts. The breakup of the Soviet empire unleashed centuries-old hatreds and frustrated nationalistic ambitions of many ethnic groups. With the Soviet military and the KGB in disarray, these groups turned violently against one another. Ethnic violence in the former Yugoslavia was so severe that this country split into five separate nations. The situation in Africa is similar. When European powers controlled Africa with armed forces, they drew arbitrary political boundaries that lumped ethnic groups and tribal territories together. Every now and then, ethnic rivalries in these African countries turn violent. Ethnic conflicts also threaten to erupt in many other parts of the world—from the United States and Mexico in North America to Germany and France in Europe, China and Vietnam in Asia, and many countries in South America. We do not know how long the lid can be kept on these seemingly bottomless resentments and hatreds, or if they will ever play themselves out.

For global control, G-8 must be able to depend on political and economic stability, both in its own back yard and in those countries that provide the raw materials essential for G-8's industrial machine. This explains why the Most Industrialized Nations have cared little when African nations self-destruct in ethnic slaughter but have refused to tolerate interethnic warfare in their own neighborhoods. For example, to let interethnic warfare in Bosnia or Kosovo go unchecked would be to tolerate conflict that could spread and engulf Europe. In contrast, the deaths of hundreds of thousands of Tutsis in Rwanda had little or no political significance for G-8.

Africa Connections   The Most Industrialized Nations have begun to perceive connections between Africa and their own interests, however, and their attitudes and actions have begun to change. They are realizing that African poverty, and the discontent it breeds, can provide fertile ground for political unrest and for recruiting terrorists. In addition, as the world's last largely untapped market, Africa could provide a huge outlet for their underutilized economic machinery. Then, too, there are Africa's oil reserves, which could counterbalance those of the unstable Middle East. As a result, the United States has raised funds for African AIDS victims and, as in the case of armed conflict in Liberia, Somalia, and Darfur, has begun to intervene in African politics.

Information Technology Just as the development of armaments in the fourteenth and fifteenth centuries had an impact on global stratification, so, too, today's information revolution is destined to have similar far-reaching consequences. Those nations that make the most significant advances in information technology will dominate in the coming generation. Which nations will this be? The forecast points to an inevitable conclusion—a continuation of the dominance of the Most Industrialized Nations and those nations that join this group.

Theories and Processes of Social Change

Social change has always fascinated theorists. Of the many attempts to explain why societies change, we shall consider just four: cultural evolution, natural cycles, conflict and power, and the pioneering views of sociologist William Ogburn.

Cultural Evolution

Evolutionary theories of how societies change are of two types, unilinear and multilinear. *Unilinear* theories assume that all societies follow the same path: Each evolves from simpler to more complex forms. This journey takes each society through uniform sequences (Barnes 1935). Of the many versions of this theory, the one proposed by Lewis Morgan (1877) once dominated Western thought. Morgan said that all societies go through three stages: savagery, barbarism, and civilization. In Morgan's eyes, England, his own society, was the epitome of civilization. All other societies were destined to follow the same path.

Multilinear views of evolution replaced unilinear theories. Instead of assuming that all societies follow the same sequence, multilinear theorists proposed that different routes lead to the same stage of development. Although the paths all lead to industrialization, societies need not pass through the same sequence of stages on their journey (Sahlins and Service 1960; Lenski and Lenski 1987).

Central to all evolutionary theories, whether unilinear or multilinear, is the assumption of *cultural progress.* Tribal societies are assumed to have a primitive form of human culture. As these societies evolve, they will reach a higher state—the supposedly advanced and superior form that characterizes the Western world. Growing appreciation of the rich diversity—and complexity—of tribal cultures discredited this idea. In addition, Western culture is now in crisis (poverty, racism, war, terrorism, sexual assaults, unsafe streets) and is no longer regarded as the apex of human civilization. Consequently, the idea of cultural progress has been cast aside, and evolutionary theories have been rejected (Eder 1990; Smart 1990).

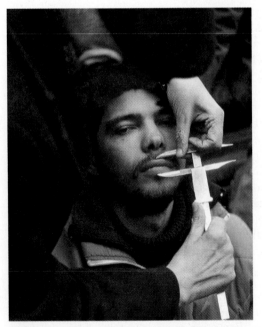

Despite the globe's vast social change, people all over the world continue to make race a fundamental distinction. Shown here is a Ukrainian being measured to see if he is really "full lipped" enough to be called a Tartar.

Natural Cycles

Cyclical theories attempt to account for the rise of entire civilizations. Why, for example, did Egypt, Greece, and Rome wield such power and influence, only to crest and fall into a decline? Cyclical theories assume that civilizations are like organisms: They are born, see an exuberant youth, come to maturity, then decline as they reach old age, and finally die (Hughes 1962).

Why do civilizations go through this cycle? Historian Arnold Toynbee (1946) said that each civilization faces challenges to its existence. Solutions to these challenges are worked out, but they are not satisfactory to all, and oppositional forces remain. The ruling elite manages to keep these forces under control, but at a civilization's peak, when it has become an empire, the ruling elite loses its capacity to keep the masses in line "by charm rather than by force." The fabric of society eventually rips apart. Force may hold the empire together for hundreds of years, but the civilization is doomed.

In a book that provoked widespread controversy, *The Decline of the West* (1926–1928), Oswald Spengler, a high school teacher in Germany, proposed that Western civilization had passed its peak and was in decline. Although the West succeeded in overcoming the crises provoked by Hitler and Mussolini, as Toynbee noted, civilizations don't end in sudden collapse. Because the decline can last hundreds of years, perhaps the crisis in Western civilization mentioned earlier (poverty, rape, murder, and so on) indicates that Spengler was right, and we are now in decline. If so, it appears that China is waiting on the horizon to be the next global power and to forge a new civilization.

Conflict Over Power

Long before Toynbee, Karl Marx identified a recurring process of social change. He said that each *thesis* (a current arrangement of power) contains its own *antithesis* (contradiction or opposition). A struggle develops between the thesis and its antithesis, leading to a *synthesis* (a new arrangement of power). This new social order, in turn, becomes a thesis that will be challenged by its own antithesis, and so on. Figure 22.1 gives a visual summary of this process.

According to Marx's view (called a **dialectical process** of history), each ruling group sows the seeds of its own destruction. Consider capitalism. Marx said that capitalism (the thesis) is built on the exploitation of workers (an antithesis, or built-in opposition). With workers and owners on a collision course, the dialectical process will not stop until workers establish a classless state (the synthesis).

The analysis of G-8 in the previous section follows conflict theory. G-8's current division of the globe's resources and markets is a thesis. Resentment on the part of have-not nations is an antithesis. If one of the Least Industrialized Nations gains in military power, that nation will press for a redistribution of resources. China, India, Pakistan, and soon, North Korea and Iran, with their nuclear weapons, fit this scenario. So do the efforts of al-Qaeda to change the balance of power between the Middle East and the industrialized West. Any new arrangement, a new synthesis, will contain its own antitheses. These may be ethnic hostilities, or leaders feeling that their country has been denied its fair share of resources. These antitheses will haunt the arrangement of power and must at some point be resolved into a synthesis. The process repeats itself.

Ogburn's Theory

Sociologist William Ogburn (1922/1938, 1961, 1964) proposed a theory of social change that is based largely on technology. As you can see from Table 22.2, technology, he said, changes society by three processes: invention, discovery, and diffusion. Let's consider each.

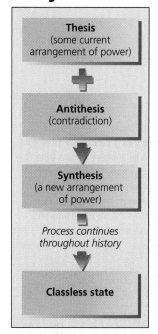

Figure 22.1 Marx's Model of Historical Change

Source: By the author.

dialectical process (of history) each arrangement, or thesis, contains contradictions, or antitheses, which must be resolved; the new arrangement, or synthesis, contains its own contradictions, and so on

---

Table 22.2 Ogburn's Processes of Social Change

Process of Change	What It Is	Examples	Social Changes
Invention	Combination of existing elements to form new ones	1. Cars 2. Computers 3. Plastics	1. Urban sprawl and long commutes to work 2. Telework and Global Positioning System 3. New types of furniture and construction
Discovery	New way of seeing some aspect of the world	1. Columbus—N. America 2. Gold in California 3. DNA	1. Realignment of global power 2. Westward expansion of United States 3. Positive identification of criminals
Diffusion	Spread of an invention or discovery	1. Airplanes 2. Money 3. Condom	1. Global tourism 2. Global trade 3. Smaller families

Note: For each example, there are many changes. For changes ushered in by the automobile and computer, see pages 661–667. You can also see that any particular change, such as global trade, depends not just on one item, but on several preceding changes.

Source: By the author.

Invention   Ogburn defined **invention** as a combining of existing elements and materials to form new ones. We usually think of inventions as being only material items, such as computers, but there also are *social inventions.* We have considered many social inventions in this text including democracy and citizenship (437), capitalism (pages 179–180, 405–406), socialism (pages 406–408), bureaucracy (pages 181–189), the corporation (pages 191, 412), and in Chapter 11, gender equality. As we saw in these instances, social inventions can have far-reaching consequences on society and people's relationships to one another. So can material inventions, and in this chapter we will examine how the automobile and the computer have transformed society.

Discovery   Ogburn identified **discovery,** a new way of seeing reality, as a second process of change. The reality is already present, but people see it for the first time. An example is Columbus' "discovery" of North America, which had consequences so huge that they altered the course of human history. This example also illustrates another principle: A discovery brings extensive change only when it comes at the right time. Other groups, such as the Vikings, had already "discovered" North America in the sense of learning that a new land existed—obviously no discovery to the Native Americans already living in it. Viking settlements disappeared into history, however, and Norse culture was untouched by the discovery.

Culture contact is the source of diffusion, the spread of an invention or discovery from one area to another. Shown here is an aboriginal elder in West Australia following a desert ceremony. How do you think modern communications will affect the aboriginal way of life?

Diffusion   Ogburn stressed how **diffusion,** the spread of an invention or discovery from one area to another, can have extensive effects on people's lives. Consider an object as simple as the axe. When missionaries introduced steel axes to the Aborigines of Australia, it upset their whole society. Before this, the men controlled axe-making. They used a special stone that was available only in a remote region, and fathers passed axe-making skills on to their sons. Women had to request permission to use the axe. When steel axes became common, women also possessed them, and the men lost both status and power (Sharp 1995).

Diffusion also includes the spread of ideas. As we saw in Chapter 15, the idea of citizenship changed political structure around the world. It removed monarchs as an unquestioned source of authority. The concept of gender equality is now circling the globe. Although taken for granted in a few parts of the world, the idea that it is wrong to withhold rights on the basis of someone's sex is revolutionary. Like citizenship, this idea is destined to transform basic human relationships and entire societies.

invention the combination of existing elements and materials to form new ones; identified by William Ogburn as one of three processes of social change

discovery a new way of seeing reality; identified by William Ogburn as one of three processes of social change

diffusion the spread of an invention or a discovery from one area to another; identified by William Ogburn as one of three processes of social change

cultural lag Ogburn's term for human behavior lagging behind technological innovations

Cultural Lag   Ogburn coined the term **cultural lag** to refer to how some elements of a culture lag behind the changes that come from invention, discovery, and diffusion. Technology, he suggested, usually changes first, with culture lagging behind. In other words, we play catch-up with changing technology, adapting our customs and ways of life to meet its needs.

Evaluation of Ogburn's Theory   Some find Ogburn's analysis too one-directional, saying that it makes technology the cause of almost all social change. They point out that the way people adapt to technology is only one part of the story. The other part consists of the way people take control over technology. People develop the technology they need, and they selectively use it. Some groups, such as the Amish (see page 109), reject technologies they perceive as threatening to their culture. Other resistance to technology is discussed in the Sociology and the New Technology box on the next page.

Technology and social change actually form a two-way street: Just as technology stimulates social change, so social change stimulates technology. For example, a major social change is the growing number of elderly in our society. Their needs have spurred new medical technologies, such as those used to treat Alzheimer's disease. Another example is our changing perspectives about people with disabilities—that they should not be shunted aside but should participate in society's mainstream. This changed view has triggered the development of new types of wheelchairs and prosthetic devices that allow

> SOCIOLOGY *and the* NEW TECHNOLOGY

From the Luddites to the Unabomber: Opposition to Technology

IN THE EARLY 1800s in Great Britain, a machine was invented that could make stockings. The owners—those who bought the machines—were delighted: They could foresee greater profits and more control over workers. The workers, in contrast, were not pleased: Perceiving the machines as a threat that put their way of life in jeopardy, they picked up axes and hammers and smashed the machines (Fox 2004). The workers' rebellion spread, and the local police couldn't handle the uprising. It took twelve thousand army troops to restore order. The threat was so great that the government executed some of the rebels and shipped others off to Australia.

One of the apprentice stocking makers who destroyed his machine was Ned Ludlum. Since this time, people who oppose new technology have been called *Luddites* (Volti 1995).

Every new technology replaces some existing technology, so each new technology is a threat to someone. Antagonism is usually directed toward some particular new technology, but there is also concern and protest against technology in general.

Jacques Ellul (1912–1994), a French sociologist, perceived correctly that technology was changing traditional values. This bothered him, because he feared that technology would produce a monolithic world culture in which, as he put it, "variety is mere appearance." Ellul (1965) even said that humans were becoming "a single tightly integrated and articulated component" of technology. Only a few intellectuals paid attention to Ellul and to similar analyses by others, such as Neil Postman (1992). Academics discussed these ideas in faculty seminars and expressed them in obscure papers.

In the 1980s, a new protestor appeared on the scene, with a message that was unlike that of the academics. His messages came thundering into the public's consciousness, not in the form of lectures and articles, but as mailed explosives that maimed and killed their unsuspecting recipients. For seventeen years, the man, who came to be known as the Unabomber, sent explosives to addresses in Michigan, Utah, and California.

Ted Kaczynski after his arrest in Helena, Montana.

The Unabomber, however, didn't leave verbal messages in his seemingly random attacks. No one knew why he was sending the bombs, and they wrote the attacks off as something coming from a mad man. Then unexpectedly, in 1995, the Unabomber delivered a verbal message. He promised to stop his terror if newspapers published his 35,000-word essay against technology. The *New York Times* and the *Washington Post* duly printed it. His message was similar to Ellul's: Technology is destroying us.

When the Unabomber's brother read the essay, he was reminded of things his brother had said. Alerting the authorities, the FBI tracked down Ted Kaczynski, a recluse from technology who was living in a simple cabin in the mountains of Montana. Kaczynski, who had an undergraduate degree from Harvard and a Ph.D. from the University of Michigan, was convicted of the bombings. In an ironic twist of fate, Kaczynski is now surrounded by new technology, as it is used to control the prison that houses him.

for your Consideration

1. What do the Luddites, Jacques Ellul, and the Unabomber have in common?
2. Use concepts presented in this and earlier chapters to analyze the effects of technology on society. Specifically, how do you think that technology is changing our way of life?
3. Given your conclusions, should we fear new technologies?

---

people who cannot move their legs to play basketball, participate in the Special Olympics, and even compete in rigorous downhill wheelchair races. In turn, the greater visibility and participation of people with disabilities has changed attitudes.

In fairness to Ogburn, we must note that he never said that technology is the only force for social change. He did not assert that people are passive pawns in the face of overwhelming technological forces. He did stress, though, that the material culture (technology) usually changes first, and the symbolic culture (people's ideas and ways of life) follows. This direction still holds, as you can see with the many changes that are following on the heels of the development of computers.

Let's consider, then, how technology changes society.

How Technology Changes Society

As you may recall from Chapter 2, *technology* has a double meaning. It refers to both the *tools,* the items used to accomplish tasks, and the skills or procedures needed to make and use those tools. Technology refers to tools as simple as a comb and as complicated as a computer. Technology's second meaning—the skills or procedures needed to make and use tools—refers in this case not only to the procedures used to manufacture combs and computers but also to those that are required to "produce" an acceptable hairdo or to go online. Apart from its particulars, technology always refers to *artificial means of extending human abilities.*

All human groups make and use technology, but the chief characteristic of technology in postindustrial societies (also called **postmodern societies**) is that it greatly extends our abilities to communicate, to travel, and to analyze information. These *new technologies,* as they are called, allow us to do what had never been done before: to communicate almost instantaneously anywhere on the globe; to probe space; to travel greater distances faster; and to store, retrieve, and analyze vast amounts of information.

Change is rapid. Desktop computers are giving way to laptops—and some laptops are being replaced by handheld devices that contain keyboards and cameras. And this is just the beginning. In our coming biotech society, we may even "wear" computers, storing data on holograms located in our own proteins (bacteriorhodopsin) (Guessous et al. 2004). Our journey to the future is going to have many twists and turns, so no one knows what our life will be like. It is enjoyable, however, to try to peer over the edge of the present to catch a glimpse of that future.

The Sociological Signficance of Technology

The sociological significance of technology is how it changes our way of life. When a technology is introduced into a society, it forces other parts of society to give way. In fact, *new technologies can reshape society.* Let's look at four ways that technology changes social life.

Changes in Social Organization   Technology changes how people organize themselves. In Chapter 6, we discussed how prior to machine technology, most workers worked alongside their families at home, but the new power-driven machinery required them to leave their families and go to a place called a factory. In the first factories, each worker still made an entire item. Then it was discovered that production would increase if each worker performed only a specific task. One worker would hammer on a single part, or turn a certain number of bolts, and then someone else would take the item and do some other repetitive task before a third person took over, and so on. Henry Ford built on this innovation by developing the assembly line: Instead of workers moving to the parts, machines moved the parts to the workers. In addition, the parts were made interchangeable and easy to attach (Womack et al. 1991).

Changes in Ideology   Technology also spurs ideology. Karl Marx noted that when workers did repetitive tasks on just a small part of a product, they did not feel connected to the finished product. No longer did they think of the product as "theirs." As Marx put it, workers had become *alienated* from the product of their labor, an **alienation** that breeds dissatisfaction and unrest.

Marx stressed that before factories came on the scene, workers owned their tools. This made them independent. If workers didn't like something, they would pack up their hammers and saws and leave. They would build a wagon or make a table for someone else. The factory was a great contrast, for there the capitalists owned the tools and machinery. This ownership transferred power to the capitalists, who used it to extract every ounce of sweat and blood they could. The workers had to submit, for desperate unemployed workers were lined up, eager to take the place of anyone who left. This exploitation, Marx believed, would lead to a workers' revolution: One day, workers would decide that they had had enough. They would unite, violently take over the means of production, and establish a workers' state.

The new technology that led to this situation also led to a change in ideology. As capitalists made huge profits from their factories, they developed the ideology that maximizing

postmodern society another term for postindustrial society; a chief characteristic is the use of tools that extend human abilities to gather and analyze information, to communicate, and to travel

alienation Marx's term for workers' lack of connection to the product of their labor; caused by their being assigned repetitive tasks on a small part of a product—this leads to a sense of powerlessness and normlessness; others use the term in the general sense of not feeling a part of something profits was a moral, even spiritual endeavor. Profits benefited society—and pleased God as well. Followers of Marx, in turn, built ideologies of socialism to attack capitalism. In their view, profit comes only by exploiting workers, for workers are the true owners of society's resources. As we shall see shortly, just as changes in technology stimulated the development of communism, changes in technology also helped to bring about its downfall.

Changes in Conspicuous Consumption Just as ideology follows technology, so does ostentatious consumption. If technology is limited to clubbing animals, then animal skins are valued. No doubt primitive men and women who wore the skins of some especially unusual or dangerous animal walked with their heads held high—while their neighbors, wearing the same old sheepskins, looked on in envy. With technological change, Americans make certain that their clothing and accessories (sunglasses, handbags, and watches) have trendy labels prominently displayed. They also proudly display their cars, boats, and second homes. In short, while envy and pride may be basic to human nature, the particular material display depends on the state of technology.

It might seem strange to see a family staring at a radio (yes, that big piece of furniture is a radio), but in the 1950s, before television became dominant, this was common. Middle-class families would eat at the dining room table. After dinner, they sometimes would gather in the living room to listen to their favorite programs: Jack Benny, Amos and Andy, Hopalong Cassidy, and so on. Can you see how technology is related to values and social relationships?

Changes in Social Relationships Technology also changes how people relate to one another. When men left home to work in factories, they became isolated from much of the everyday lives of their families. One consequence of becoming relative strangers to their wives and children was more divorce. As more women were drawn from the home to offices and factories, there were similar consequences—greater isolation from husbands and children and even more fragile marriages. A counter-trend is now in force, as the newer technology allows millions of workers to work at home. One consequence may be a strengthening of families.

To get a better idea of how technology shapes our way of life, let's consider the changes ushered in by the automobile and the computer.

When Old Technology Was New: The Impact of the Automobile

If we were to pick out the new technology of 100 years ago that had the greatest impact on social life—and that continues to influence our lives today—it would be the automobile. Let's look at some of the ways in which this invention has shaped U.S. society.

Displacement of Existing Technology In a process that began in earnest when Henry Ford began to mass-produce the Model T in 1908, the automobile gradually pushed aside the old technology. People found automobiles to be cleaner, safer, more reliable, and more economical than horses. People even thought that cars would lower their taxes, for no longer would the public have to pay to clean up the tons of horse manure that accumulated on city streets each day (Flink 1990). Humorous as it sounds now, they also thought that automobiles would eliminate the cities' parking problems, for an automobile took up only half as much space as a horse and buggy.

The automobile also replaced a second technology. The United States had developed a vast system of urban transit, with electric streetcar lines radiating outward from the center of the city. As automobile prices decreased and more Americans bought them, they found cars to be more convenient than public transportation. No longer did they have to wait, sometimes in the rain or freezing weather, for a streetcar to arrive. Instead, they could leave directly from home and determine their own schedules.

In the photo on the left, Henry Ford proudly displays his 1905 car, the latest in automobile technology. As is apparent, especially from the spokes on the car's wheels, new technology builds on existing technology. At the time this photo was taken, who could have imagined that this vehicle would transform society? Mazda's Nagare is a precursor of future Mazda designs. This concept car is said to embody the word "flow".

Effects on Cities   The decline in the use of streetcars changed the *shape* of U.S. cities. U.S. cities had been web-shaped, for residences and businesses had located along the streetcar lines. When automobiles freed people from having to live so close to the tracks, they filled in the areas between the "webs."

The automobile also stimulated suburbanization. By the 1920s, Americans had begun to leave the city. They found that they could commute to jobs in the city from outlying areas where they enjoyed more space and lower taxes (Preston 1979). Eventually, this exodus to the suburbs produced urban sprawl and reduced the cities' tax base, contributing, as discussed in Chapter 20, to many of the problems that U.S. cities experience today.

Effects on Farm Life and Villages   The automobile had a profound impact on farm life and villages. Before the 1920s, most farmers were isolated from the city. Because using horses for a trip to town was slow and cumbersome, they made such trips infrequently. By the 1920s, however, the popularity and low price of the Model T made the "Saturday trip to town" a weekly event. There, farmers would market produce, shop, and visit with friends. This changed farm life. Mail-order catalogs stopped being their primary source of shopping, and farmers gained access to better medical care and education (Flink 1990). Farmers also began to travel to bigger towns, where they found a greater variety of goods. As farmers began to use the nearby villages only for immediate needs, these flourishing centers of social and commercial life dried up.

Changes in Architecture   The automobile's effects on commercial architecture are easy to see—from the huge parking lots that surround shopping malls to the drive-up windows at banks and fast food restaurants. Not so apparent is how the automobile altered the architecture of U.S. homes (Flink 1990). Before cars came on the scene, each home had a stable in the back where the family kept its horse and buggy. As first, people parked their cars there, as it required no change in architecture. Then, in three steps, home architecture changed. First, new homes were built with a detached garage. It was located, like the stable, at the back of the home. As the automobile became more essential to the U.S. family, the garage was incorporated into the home. It was moved from the back yard to the side of the house, and was connected by a breezeway. In the final step, the breezeway was removed, and the garage was integrated into the home. This allowed people to enter their automobiles without going outside.

Changed Courtship Customs and Sexual Norms   By the 1920s, the automobile was used extensively for dating. This removed children from the watchful eye of parents and undermined parental authority. The police began to receive complaints about "night riders" who parked their cars along country lanes, "doused their lights, and indulged in orgies" (Brilliant 1964). Automobiles became so popular for courtship that by the 1960s about 40 percent of marriage proposals took place in them (Flink 1990).

In 1925 Jewett introduced cars with a foldout bed, as did Nash in 1937. The Nash version became known as "the young man's model" (Flink 1990). Mobile lovemaking has declined since the 1970s, primarily because changed sexual norms made bedrooms more accessible.

Effects on Women's Roles   The automobile may also lie at the heart of the changed role of women in U.S. society. To see how, we first need to see what a woman's life was like before the automobile. Historian James Flink (1990) described it this way:

> Until the automobile revolution, in upper-middle-class households groceries were either ordered by phone and delivered to the door or picked up by domestic servants or the husband on his way home from work. Iceboxes provided only very limited space for the storage of perishable foods, so shopping at markets within walking distance of the home was a daily chore. The garden provided vegetables and fruits in season, which were home-canned for winter consumption. Bread, cakes, cookies, and pies were home-baked. Wardrobes contained many home-sewn garments.
>
> Mother supervised the household help and worked alongside them preparing meals, washing and ironing, and housecleaning. In her spare time she mended clothes, did decorative needlework, puttered in her flower garden, and pampered a brood of children. Generally, she made few family decisions and few forays alone outside the yard. She had little knowledge of family finances and the family budget. The role of the lower-middle-class housewife differed primarily in that far less of the household work was done by hired help, so that she was less a manager of other people's work, more herself a maid-of-all-work around the house.

Because automobiles required skill to operate rather than strength, women were able to drive as well as men. This new mobility freed women physically from the narrow confines of the home. As Flink (1990) observed, the automobile changed women "from producers of food and clothing into consumers of national-brand canned goods, prepared foods, and ready-made clothes. The automobile permitted shopping at self-serve supermarkets outside the neighborhood and in combination with the electric refrigerator made buying food a weekly rather than a daily activity." When women began to do the shopping, they gained greater control over the family budget, and as their horizons extended beyond the confines of the home, they also gained different views of life.

In short, the automobile changed women's roles at home, including their relationship with their husbands. It altered their attitudes, transformed their opportunities, and stimulated them to participate in areas of social life not connected with the home.

IN SUM   With changes this extensive, it would not be inaccurate to say that the automobile also shifted basic values and changed the way we look at life. Because they were no longer isolated, women, teenagers, and farmers began to see the world differently. So did husbands and wives, whose marital relationship had also been altered. The automobile even transformed views of courtship, sexuality, and gender relations.

No one attributes such fundamental changes solely to the automobile, of course, for many historical events, as well as many other technological changes, occurred during this same period, and each made its own contribution to social change. Even this brief overview of the social effects of the automobile, however, illustrates that technology is much more than just a tool—that it exerts a profound influence on social life.

The second candidate for bringing about the greatest social change is that technological marvel, the computer. Let's consider its impact on society.

The Cutting Edge of Change

The ominous wail seemed too close for comfort. Angela looked in her rear-view mirror and realized that the flashing lights and screaming siren might be for her. She felt confused. "I'm just on my way to Soc," she thought. "I'm not speeding or anything." After she pulled over, an angry voice over a loudspeaker ordered her out of the car.

As she got out, someone barked the command, "Back up with your hands in the air!" Bewildered, Angela stood frozen for a moment. "Put 'em up now! Right now!" She did as she was told.

The officer crouched behind his open door, his gun drawn. When Angela reached the police car—still backing up—the officer grabbed her, threw her to the ground, and handcuffed her hands behind her back. She heard words she would never forget, "You are under arrest for murder. You have the right to remain silent. Anything you say can and will be used against you in a court of law. You have the right to an attorney. If you cannot afford one, one will be provided for you."

Traces of alarm still flicker across Angela's face when she recalls her arrest. She had never even had a traffic ticket, much less been arrested for anything. Angela's nightmare was due to a "computer error." With the inversion of two numbers, her car's license number had been entered into the police database instead of the number belonging to a woman suspected of killing a child.

None of us is untouched by the computer, but it is unlikely that many of us have felt its power as directly and dramatically as Angela did. For most of us, the computer's control lies quietly in the background. Although the computer has intruded into our daily lives, most of us never think about it. Our grades are computerized, as are our paychecks. When we buy groceries, a computer scans our purchases and presents a printout of the name, price, and quantity of each item.

Many of us are pleased with the computer's capacity to improve our quality of life. We welcome the higher quality of manufactured goods and the reduction of drudgery. With e-mail, we can type just one letter, and with the press of a button that letter will be delivered in seconds to everyone in our address book.

Some people, however, have deep reservations about our computerized society. They worry about errors that can creep into computerized records, fearing that something similar to Angela's misfortune could happen to them. For others, identity theft and privacy are the issues. Then there is the matter of political control. The Federal Drug Administration has approved an identity chip the size of a grain of rice that can be injected under the skin (Stein 2004). The chip is designed to store a patient's medical records, including blood type. This can certainly be helpful for medical treatment, especially for treating unconscious patients brought into an emergency room. Besides name, address, age, weight, height, hair and skin color, and race-ethnicity, the chip can also store our school grades, our work history, the names and addresses of our friends and associates, even any suspected acts of disloyalty. With the chip activated by a scanner, none of us would even know that our activities were under surveillance. This chip could help usher in Orwell's Big Brother society.

At this point, let's consider how the computer is changing education, the workplace, business, and the waging of war. We'll then consider its likely effects on social inequality.

Most of us take computers for granted, but they are new to the world scene—as are their effects on our lives. This photo captures a significant change in the evolution of computers. The laptop held by the super-imposed model has more power than the room-size ENIAC of 1946.

Computers in Education   Computers are having a major impact on education. Students who attend schools that have no teachers who can speak a foreign language are able to take courses in Russian, German, and Spanish. Even though they have no sociology instructors, they can take courses in the sociology of gender, race, social class, or even sex, and sports. (The comma is important. It isn't sex and sports. That course isn't offered—yet.).

We've barely begun to harness the power of computers, but I imagine that the day will come when you will be able to key in the terms *social interaction* and *gender,* select your preference of historical period, geographical area, age, and ethnic group—and the computer will spew out text, maps, moving images, and sounds. You will be able to compare sexual discrimination in the military in 1985 and today or compare the prices of marijuana and cocaine in Los Angeles and New Orleans. If you wish, the computer will give you a test—geared to the level of difficulty you choose—so that you can check your mastery of the material.

Distance learning, courses taught to students who are not physically present with their instructor, will become such a part of mainstream education that most students will take at least some of their high school, college, and graduate courses through this arrangement. Web cameras on their computers allow everyone in the "class" to see everyone else simultaneously, even though the students live in different countries. Imagine this—and likely it soon will be a reality for you: Your fellow students in a course on diversity in human culture will be living in Thailand, Latvia, South Africa, Egypt, China, and Australia. With zero-cost conference calls and e-mail and file exchanges, you will be able to compare your countries' customs on eating, dating, marriage, family, or burial—whatever is of interest to you. You can then write a team paper in which you compare your experiences with one another, applying the theories taught in the text, and then e-mail your paper to your mutual instructor.

Computers in the Workplace   The computer is also transforming the workplace. At the simplest level, it affects how we do our work. For example, I wrote the first two editions of this book on a computer, and a printer produced a copy of the manuscript. A series of archaic, precomputer processes followed: I sent the printed copy via the postal service to an editor, who physically handled the manuscript and sent it to others who did the same. The manuscript, marked up in red pencil, was then returned to me, and I mailed back a revised copy. The process was primitive, much the same as would have occurred during Benjamin Franklin's day—only without the quill and pony.

Practice finally caught up with potential. My editors and I now zap text back and forth electronically. I may be in the United States or Spain or Latvia, while they are in Oregon and Massachusetts. It makes no difference. I print nothing, and until the final step in the process, send no papers. Even then, I have the option of skipping the paper copy, but I like to be able to handle the actual pages. Although the distances are greater, the time lapse has shrunk. For me, the process is marvelous testimony of our changing world—and, perhaps, unsettling confirmation of our steady steps into a brave new world.

The computer is also bringing changes on a deeper level, for it alters social relationships. I used to take my manuscript to a university secretary, wait several days for her to type it, and then retrieve it. With electronic manuscripts, I bypassed the secretary entirely. This enhanced social relationships, for I made fewer demands on the department secretary. It also reduced

Technology, which drives much social change, is at the forefront of our information revolution. This revolution, based on the computer chip, allows reality to cross with fantasy, a merging that sometimes makes it difficult to tell where one ends and the other begins. A computer projects an image onto the front of the coat, making its wearer "invisible."

tensions, for it eliminated the necessity of the secretary making excuses when she didn't have the manuscript ready on time.

For some, including myself, the computer has also reversed the change in work location that industrialization ushered in. As discussed earlier, industrialization shifted much work from home to factory and office. Now several million workers remain at home while satellite communications connect them with their bosses and fellow workers at locations around the country—or even on the other side of the globe. This could be the beginning of another historical shift, one that brings families closer together.

On the negative side are increased surveillance of workers and depersonalization. As a telephone information operator said,

> The computer knows everything. It records the minute I punch in, it knows how long I take for each call. . . . I am supposed to average under eighteen seconds per call. . . . Everything I do is reported to my supervisor on his computer, and if I've missed my numbers I get a written warning. I rarely see the guy. . . . It's intense. It's me and the computer all day. I'm telling you, at the end of the day I'm wiped out. (Mander 1992:57)

Computers in Business and Finance   Not long ago, the advanced technology of businesses consisted of cash registers and adding machines. Connection to the outside world was managed by telephone. Today, those same businesses are electronically "wired" to suppliers, salespeople, and clients around the country—and around the world. Computers track sales of items, tabulate inventory, and set in motion the process of reordering and restocking. Their detailed reports of sales alert managers to changes in their customers' tastes or preferences.

National borders have become meaningless as computers instantaneously transfer billions of dollars from one country to another. No "cash" changes hands in these transactions. The money consists of digits in computer memory banks. In the same day, this digitized money can be transferred from the United States to Switzerland, from there to the Grand Cayman Islands, and then to the Isle of Mann. Its zigzag, instantaneous path around the globe leaves few traces for sleuths to follow. "Where's my share?" governments around the world are grumbling, as they consider how to control—and tax—this new technology.

Computers are also having a major impact on the way war is fought, the topic of the Down-to-Earth Sociology box on the next page.

Cyberspace and Social Inequality

We've already stepped into our future. The Net gives us access to libraries of electronic information. We can utilize software that sifts, sorts, and transmits images, sound, and video. We use e-mail to zap messages and images to people on the other side of the globe—or even in our own homes, dorm, or office. Our world has become linked by almost instantaneous communications, with information readily accessible around the globe. Few places can still be called "remote."

This new technology carries severe implications for national and global stratification. On the national level, this technology could perpetuate present inequalities: We could end up with information have-nots, primarily inner-city residents cut off from the flow of information on which prosperity depends. Or this technology could provide an opportunity to break out of the inner city and the rural centers of poverty. On the global level, the question is similar, but on a grander scale, taking us to one of the more profound issues of this century: Will unequal access to advanced technology destine the Least Industrialized Nations to a perpetual pauper status? Or will access to this new technology be their passport to affluence?

IN SUM   Technology wraps itself around us, changing our society, our culture, and our everyday lives. Apart from the disruptions that technology brings, there are three primary issues: What type of future will technlogy lead us into? Will the new technology perpetuate or alleviate social inequalities on both national and global levels? And will the technology that is transforming the face of war come back to haunt us?

The Coming Star Wars

STAR WARS IS ON its way.

We already have the Predator, an unmanned plane that flies thousands of feet above enemy lines and beams streaming video back to the base. Sensors from the Global Positioning System report the Predator's precise location. When operators at the base identify a target, they press a button; the Predator beams a laser onto the target, and the operators launch guided bombs (Barry and Thomas 2001).

The enemy doesn't know what hit them. They see neither the Predator nor the laser. Perhaps, however, just before they are blown to bits, they do hear the sound of an incoming bomb (Barry 2001).

On its way is Warfighter I, a camera that uses hyperspectral imaging, a way of identifying objects by detecting their "light signatures." This camera is so precise that it can report from space whether a field of grain contains natural or genetically altered grain—and whether the grain has adequate nitrogen. The military use of this camera? It can also locate tanks that are camouflaged or even hiding under trees (Hitt 2001).

Robot soldiers are on their way, too. In a project called Future Combat Systems, the Pentagon is developing robots that will see and react like humans. They might not look like humans. In fact, they might look like hummingbirds—or tractors, or cockroaches. They will gather intelligence, search buildings, and fire weapons (Weiner 2005).

The first robots are already being used in Iraq. These are primitive versions, however, simply remote-controlled devices that dispose of bombs. The next ones are likely to have the capacity to drive vehicles.

The Pentagon is also building its own Internet called the Global Information Grid (GIG). The goal of GIG, encircling the globe, is grandiose: to give the Pentagon a "God's eye view" of every enemy everywhere (Weiner 2004).

All this is but a prelude. The U.S. Defense Department is planning to "weaponize" space. Concerned that other nations will also launch intelligence-gathering devices and space weapons, the United States is set to launch microsatellites the size of a suitcase. These satellites will be able to pull alongside an enemy satellite and, using a microwave gun, fry its electronic system.

Coming also is a laser whose beam will bounce off a mirror in space, making the night battlefield visible to ground soldiers who are wearing special goggles. Also on its way is a series of Star Wars weapons: space-based lasers, pyrotechnic electromagnetic pulsers, holographic decoys, suppression clouds, oxygen suckers, robo-bugs—and whatever else the feverish imaginations of military planners can devise.

The Air Force has nicknamed one of it space programs "Rods from God." Tungsten cylinders would be hurled from space at targets on the ground. Striking at speeds of 7,000 miles an hour, the rods would have the force of a small nuclear weapon. In another program, radio waves would be directed to targets on the earth. As the Air Force explains it, the power of the radio waves could be "just a tap on the shoulder—or they could turn you into toast" (Weiner 2005).

We are on the edge of a surrealistic world. Politicians and the military assume that it is normal both to dominate the world and to weaponize space. The chilling reality is reflected in a report by a congressional commission: "Every medium—air, land and sea—has seen conflict. Reality indicates that space will be no different" (Hitt 2001).

for your Consideration

Do you think we should militarize space? What if other countries do the same? In 2006, China launched a missle to shoot down one of its own orbiting satellites, which could indicate that it is ready to play this deadly space game. What do you think of this comment, made to Congress by the head of the U.S. Air Force Space Command? "We must establish and maintain space superiority. It's the American way of fighting." (Weiner 2005)

The Growth Machine Versus the Earth

Of all the changes swirling around us, those that affect the natural environment seem to hold the most serious implications for human life.

Underlying today's environmental decay is the globalization of capitalism, which I have stressed throughout this text. To maintain their dominance and increase their wealth, the Most Industrialized Nations, spurred by multinational corporations, continue to push for economic growth. At the same time, the Industrializing Nations, playing

Sumatran Tiger
Fewer than 400, Indonesia

Texas Ocelot
Fewer than 250, southern United States, northern Mexico

Gaur
About 36,000, Southeast Asia

Mountain Bongo
About 50, Kenya

catch-up, are striving to develop their economies. Meanwhile, the Least Industrialized Nations are anxious to enter the race: Because they start from even farther behind, they have to strive for even faster growth.

Many people are convinced that the earth cannot withstand such an onslaught. Global economic production creates extensive pollution, and faster-paced production means faster-paced destruction of our environment. The photos on this page illustrate just the tip of the iceberg. In this relentless pursuit of economic development, many animal species are endangered or on the verge of extinction. If the goal is a **sustainable environment,** a world system in which we use our physical environment to meet our needs without destroying humanity's future, we cannot continue to trash the earth. In short, the ecological message is incompatible with an economic message that implies it is OK to rape the earth for the sake of profits.

Before looking at the social movement that has emerged about this issue, let's examine major environmental problems. We'll begin with pollution in the Most Industrialized Nations.

Environmental Problems in the Most Industrialized Nations

Although even tribal groups produced pollution, the frontal assault on the natural environment did not begin in earnest until nations industrialized. Industrialization was equated with progress and prosperity. For the Most Industrialized Nations, the slogan has been "Growth at any cost."

Industrial growth did come, but at a high cost to the natural environment. Today, for example, formerly pristine streams are polluted sewers, and the water supply of some cities is unfit to drink. When Los Angeles announces "smog days," schoolchildren are kept inside during recess and everyone is warned to stay indoors. Nuclear wastes, which we knew would remain lethal for thousand of years, have been stored in rusting containers (Madslien 2006). We simply don't know what to do with this deadly garbage. Hazardous wastes are a special problem. Despite the danger to people and the environment, much toxic waste has simply been dumped. The Social Map on page 670 shows the locations of the worst hazardous waste sites in the United States. These sites represent corporate garbage, some of it subsidized by corporate welfare, the topic of the Down-to-Earth Sociology box on the next page.

The major polluters are the Most Industrialized Nations. Our follies include harming the ozone layer in order to have the convenience of aerosol spray bottles, refrigerators, and air conditioners. With limited space to address this issue, I would like to focus on an overarching aspect of the pollution of our environment, the burning of fossil fuels.

Fossil Fuels and the Environment Burning fossil fuels to run factories, motorized vehicles, and power plants has been especially harmful. Fish can no longer survive in some lakes in Canada and the northeastern United States because of **acid rain.** As Figure 22.3 on page 670 illustrates, the burning of fossil fuels releases sulfur dioxide and nitrogen oxide, which react with moisture in the air to become sulfuric and nitric acids.

An invisible but infinitely more serious consequence is the **greenhouse effect.** Burning fossil fuels releases gases that, like the glass of a greenhouse, allow sunlight to enter the earth's atmosphere freely but inhibit the release of heat. It is as though the gases have smudged the windows of our earth's greenhouse, and our planet can no longer breathe the way it should.

sustainable environment a world system that takes into account the limits of the environment, produces enough material goods for everyone's needs, and leaves a heritage of a sound environment for the next generation

acid rain rain containing sulfuric and nitric acids (burning fossil fuels release sulfur dioxide and nitrogen oxide that become sulfuric and nitric acids when they react with moisture in the air)

greenhouse effect the buildup of carbon dioxide in the earth's atmosphere that allows light to enter but inhibits the release of heat; believed to cause global warming

Corporations and Big Welfare Bucks: How to Get Paid to Pollute

WELFARE IS ONE OF THE MOST controversial topics in the United States. It arouses the ire of many wealthy and middle-class Americans, who view the poor who collect welfare as parasites. But have you heard about *corporate welfare*?

Corporate welfare refers to handouts that are given to corporations. Some states will reduce a company's taxes if it locates within the state, or remains if it has threatened to leave. Some states provide land and buildings at bargain prices. The reason: jobs.

Corporate welfare even goes to companies that foul the land, water, and air. Borden Chemicals in Louisiana has buried hazardous wastes without a permit and released clouds of hazardous chemicals so thick that to protect drivers, the police have sometimes had to shut down the highway that runs near the plant. Borden even contaminated the groundwater beneath its plant, threatening the aquifer that provides drinking water for residents of Louisiana and Texas.

Borden's pollution has cost the company dearly: $3.6 million in fines, $3 million to clean up the groundwater, and $400,000 for local emergency response units. That's a hefty $7 million. But if we add corporate welfare, the company didn't make out so badly. With $15 million in reduced and cancelled property taxes, Borden has enjoyed a net gain of $8 million (Bartlett and Steele 1998). And that's

Local residents call this area of Louisiana Cancer Alley. State officials deny that there is a relationship between the area's factory pollutants and cancer.

not counting the savings the company racked up by not having to properly dispose of its toxic wastes in the first place.

Louisiana has added a novel twist to corporate welfare. It offers an incentive to help start-up companies. This itself isn't novel; the owners of that little "mom and pop" grocery store on your corner may have received some benefits when they first opened. Louisiana's twist is what it counts as a start-up company. One of these little start-ups is called Exxon Corp. Although Exxon opened for business about 130 years ago, it had $213 million in property taxes canceled under this start-up program. Another little company that the state figured could use a nudge to help it get started was Shell Oil Co., which had $140 million slashed from its taxes (Bartlett and Steele 1998). Then there were Interational Paper, Dow Chemical, Union Carbide, Boise Cascade, Georgia Pacific, and another tiny one called Procter & Gamble.

for your Consideration

Apply the functionalist, symbolic interactionist, and conflict perspectives to corporate welfare. Which do you think provides the best explanation of corporate welfare? Why?

The buildup of heat is causing **global warming**: Glaciers are melting and the seas are rising, threatening to flood the world's shorelines. Some island nations will disappear, washed away into the ocean (Kanter and Revkin 2007). As the climate boundaries move north several hundred miles, many animal and plant species will become extinct.

For decades, scientists argued about global warming. Many said that it was part of a natural cycle that the earth goes through. Some even said that it did not exist. As evidence accumulated, more and more scientists concluded that global warming certainly did exist and that human activity—primarily the burning of coal and oil—was its cause. Today, the world's leading climate scientists, forming the United Nations' Intergovernmental Panel on Climate change, have concluded that global warming is "unequivocal" and that human activity is its main driver (Rosenthal and Revkin 2007). The consequences, they predict, are likely to be catastrophic, and we should immediately reduce the burning of fossil fuels.

The Energy Shortage and Multinational Corporations   If you ever read about an energy shortage, you can be sure that what you read is false. There is no energy shortage, nor can there ever be. We can produce unlimited low-cost power, which can help to raise the living standards of humans across the globe. The sun, for example, produces more energy than humanity could ever use. Boundless energy is also available from the

corporate welfare the financial incentives (tax breaks, subsidies, and even land and stadiums) given to corporations in order to attract them to an area or induce them to remain

global warming an increase in the earth's temperature due to the greenhouse effect

Figure 22.2 **The Worst Hazardous Waste Sites**

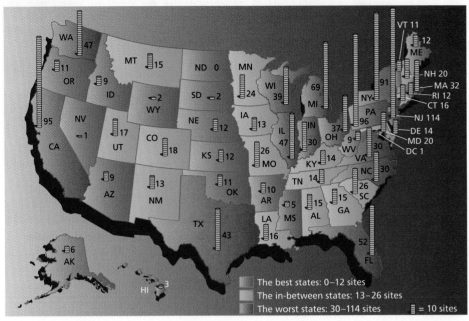

Note: These are the waste sites so outstandingly threatening to public health that they made the national priority list. New Jersey is in a class by itself. This small state has 18 more hazardous waste sites than its nearest competition Pennsylvania, with 96.

Source: By the author. Based on Statistical Abstract of the United States 2007:Table 368.

Figure 22.3 **Acid Rain**

tides and the winds. In some cases, we need better technology to harness these sources of energy; in others, we need only to apply the technology we already have.

Burning fossil fuels in internal combustion engines is the main source of pollution in the Most Industrialized Nations. Of the technologies being developed to use alternative sources of energy in vehicles, the most prominent is the gas-electric hybrid. Some of these cars are expected to eventually get several hundred miles per gallon of gasoline. The hybrid, however, is simply a bridge until vehicles powered by fuel cells become practical. Fuel cells convert hydrogen into electricity; water, instead of carbon monoxide, will come out of a car's exhaust pipe.

Environmental Injustice Unequal power has led to **environmental injustice**— minorities and the poor being the ones who suffer the most from the effects of pollution (Mohal and Saha 2007). Industries locate where land is cheaper, which is *not* where the wealthy live. Nor will the rich allow factories to spew pollution near their homes. As a result, low-income communities, which are often inhabited by minorities, are more likely to be exposed to pollution. Sociologists have studied, formed, and joined *environmental justice* groups that fight to close polluting plants and block construction of polluting industries.

Environmental Problems in the Industrializing and Least Industrialized Nations

Pollution and the destruction of the environment cannot be laid solely at the feet of the Most Industrialized Nations. With their rush to industrialize, along with nonexistent or unenforced environmental laws, the Industrializing Nations have become major polluters (Bradsher 2007).

The lack of environmental protection laws in many of these countries has not gone unnoticed by opportunists in the Most Industrialized Nations. Some dump poisonous wastes in these countries (Polgreen and Simons 2006). Others produce chemicals there

environmental injustice
refers to the pollution of our environment affecting minorities and the poor the most

that have been outlawed in their own countries (Smith 1995; Mol 2001). Alarmed at the growing environmental destruction, the World Bank, the monetary arm of G-8, has pressured the Least Industrialized Nations to reduce pollution. When New Delhi officials tried to comply, workers blocked traffic and set fires, closing down the city for several days (Freund 2001). Understandably, the basic concern of workers is to provide food for their families first, and to worry about the environment later.

The former Soviet Union is a special case. Until this empire broke up, pollution had been treated as a state secret. Scientists and journalists were forbidden to mention pollution in public. Even peaceful demonstrations to call attention to pollution could net participants two years in prison (Feshbach 1992). With protest stifled and no environmental protection laws, pollution was rampant: Almost half of Russia's arable land has been made unsuitable for farming, about a third of Russians live in cities where air pollution is *ten* times greater than levels permitted in the United States, and half of Russia's tap water is unfit to drink. Pollution is so severe that it may be partially responsible for the drop in the life expectancy of Russians. If so, it is a lesson that should not be lost on the rest of us as we make decisions about how to treat our environment.

A special concern is the rainforests. Although they cover just 7 percent of the earth's land area, the rainforests are home to *one-third to one-half* of all the earth's plant and animal species. Despite our knowledge that the rainforests are essential for humanity's welfare, we seem bent on destroying them for the sake of timber and farms. In the process, we extinguish plant and animal species, perhaps thousands a year (Wolfensohn and Fuller 1998). As biologists remind us, once a species is lost, it is gone forever.

As the rainforests disappear, so do the Indian tribes who live in them. With their extinction goes their knowledge of the environment, the topic of the Cultural Diversity box on page 673. Like Esau who traded his birthright for a bowl of porridge, we are exchanging our future for some lumber, farms, and pastures.

The Environmental Movement

Concern about environmental problems has produced a worldwide social movement. One result is *green parties,* political parties whose central issue is the environment. In some European countries, these parties have made a political impact. In Germany, for example, the Green Party has won seats in the national legislature. Green parties have had little success in the United States, but in the 2000 election, a green party headed by Ralph Nader arguably tipped the balance and gave the presidential election to George W. Bush.

Activists in the environmental movement generally seek solutions in politics, education, and legislation. Despairing that pollution continues, that the rainforests are still being cleared, and that species are becoming extinct, some activists are convinced that the planet is doomed unless urgent steps are taken. Choosing a more radical course, they use extreme tactics to try to arouse indignation among the public and to force the government to act. Convinced that they stand for true morality, many are willing to break the law and go to jail for their actions. Such activists are featured in the following Thinking Critically section.

Thinking Critically

Ecosabotage

Chaining oneself to a giant Douglas fir that is slated for cutting, tearing down power lines and ripping up survey stakes, driving spikes into redwood trees, sinking whaling vessels, and torching SUVs and Hummers—are these the acts of dangerous punks who are intent on vandalizing and who have little understanding of the needs of modern society? Or are they the acts of brave men and women who are willing to put their freedom, and even their lives, on the line on behalf of the earth itself?

To understand why **ecosabotage**—actions taken to sabotage the efforts of people who are thought to be legally harming the environment—is taking place, consider the Medicine Tree, a 3,000-year-old redwood in the Sally Bell Grove near the northern California coast. Georgia Pacific,

ecosabotage actions taken to sabotage the efforts of people who are thought to be legally harming the environment

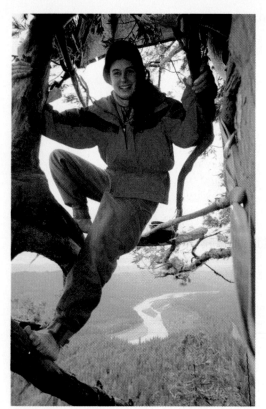

Julia "Butterfly" Hill lived for two years in this 1,000-year-old redwood tree, which she named Luna. The Pacific Lumber Company finally agreed to save the tree and a 200-foot buffer zone.

a lumber company, was determined to cut down the Medicine Tree, the oldest and largest of the region's redwoods, which rests on a sacred site of the Sinkyone Indians. Members of Earth First! chained themselves to the tree. After they were arrested, the sawing began. Other protesters jumped over the police-lined barricade and stood defiantly in the path of men wielding axes and chain saws. A logger swung an axe and barely missed a demonstrator. At that moment, the sheriff radioed a restraining order, and the cutting stopped.

Twenty-four-year-old David Chain's dedication cost him his life. The federal government and the state of California were trying to purchase 10,000 acres of pristine redwoods for half a billion dollars. As last-minute negotiations dragged on, loggers from the Pacific Lumber Company kept felling trees, and Earth First! activists kept trying to stop them. David Chain died of a crushed skull when a felled tree struck him.

How many 3,000-year-old trees remain on this planet? Does our desire for fences and picnic tables for backyard barbecues justify cutting them down? Issues like these—as well as the slaughter of seals, the destruction of the rainforests, and the drowning of dolphins in mile-long drift nets—spawned Earth First! and other organizations devoted to preserving the environment, such as Greenpeace, Rainforest Action Network, the Ruckus Society, and the Sea Shepherds.

"We feel like there are insane people who are consciously destroying our environment, and we are compelled to fight back," explains a member of one of the militant groups. "No compromise in defense of Mother Earth!" says another. "With famine and death approaching, we're in the early stages of World War III," adds another.

Radical environmentalists represent a broad range of activities and purposes. They are united neither on tactics nor on goals. Most espouse a simpler lifestyle that will consume less energy and reduce pressure on the earth's resources. Some want to stop a specific action, such as the killing of whales. Others want to destroy all nuclear weapons and dismantle nuclear power plants. Some want everyone to become a vegetarian. Still others want the earth's population to drop to one billion, roughly what it was in 1800. Some even want humans to return to hunting and gathering societies. These groups are so splintered that the founder of Earth First!, Dave Foreman, quit his own organization when it became too confrontational for his taste.

Radical groups have had some successes. They have brought a halt to the killing of dolphins off Japan's Iki Island, achieved a ban on whaling, established trash recycling programs, and saved hundreds of thousands of acres of trees, including, of course, the Medicine Tree.

for your Consideration

Should we applaud ecosaboteurs or jail them? As symbolic interactionists stress, it all depends on how you view their actions. And as conflict theorists emphasize, your view likely depends on your location in the economy. That is, if you own a lumber company, you will see ecosaboteurs differently from the way a camping enthusiast will. How does your own view of ecosaboteurs depend on your life situation? What effective alternatives to ecosabotage are there for people who are convinced that we are destroying the very life support system of our planet?

Sources: Carpenter 1990; Eder 1990; Foote 1990; Parfit 1990; Reed and Benet 1990; Knickerbocker 2003; Gunther 2004.

Environmental Sociology

About 1970, **environmental sociology** emerged. The focus of this subdiscipline of sociology is the relationship between human societies and the environment (Dunlap and Catton 1979, 1983; Casper 2003). Its main assumptions are:

1. The physical environment should be a significant variable in sociological investigation.
2. Human beings are but one species among many that depend on the natural environment.

environmental sociology a specialty within sociology where the focus is the relationship between human societies and the environment

The Rainforests: Lost Tribes, Lost Knowledge

SINCE 1900, 90 OF BRAZIL'S 270 Indian tribes have disappeared. Other tribes have moved to villages as settlers have taken over their lands. The tribal knowledge is lost as group members adapt to village life.

Tribal groups are not just "wild" people who barely survive despite their ignorance. On the contrary, they have intricate forms of social organization and possess knowledge that has accumulated over thousands of years. The 2,500 Kayapo Indians, for example, belong to one of the Amazon's endangered tribes. The Kayapo use 250 types of wild fruit and hundreds of nut and tuber species. They cultivate thirteen types of bananas, eleven kinds of manioc (cassava), sixteen strains of sweet potato, and seventeen kinds of yams. Many of these varieties are unknown to non-Indians. The Kayapo also use thousands of medicinal plants, one of which contains a drug that is effective against intestinal parasites.

Until recently, Western scientists dismissed tribal knowledge as superstitious and worthless. Now, however, some have come to realize that to lose tribes is to lose valuable knowledge. In the Central African Republic, a man whose chest was being eaten away by an amoeboid infection lay dying because his infection did not respond to drugs. Out of desperation, the Roman Catholic nuns who were treating him sought the advice of a native doctor. He applied crushed termites to the open wounds. To the amazement of the nuns, the man made a remarkable recovery.

A Tari Huli dancer in the New Guinea highlands. The way of life of the world's few remaining rain forest tribes is threatened.

The disappearance of the rainforests means the destruction of plant species that may have healing properties. Some of the discoveries from the rainforests have been astounding. The needles from a Himalayan tree in India contain taxol, a drug that is effective against ovarian and breast cancer. A flower from Madagascar is used in the treatment of leukemia; a frog in Peru produces a painkiller that is more powerful, but less addictive, than morphine (Wolfensohn and Fuller 1998).

On average, one tribe of Amazonian Indians has been lost each year for the past century—because of violence, greed for their lands, and exposure to infectious diseases against which they have little resistance. Ethnocentrism underlies much of this assault. Perhaps the extreme is represented by the cattle ranchers in Colombia who killed eighteen Cueva Indians. The cattle ranchers were perplexed when they were put on trial for murder. They asked why they should be charged with a crime, since everyone knew that the Cuevas were animals, not people. They pointed out that there was even a verb in Colombian Spanish, *cuevar,* which means "to hunt Cueva Indians." So what was their crime, they asked? The jury found them not guilty because of "cultural ignorance."

for your Consideration

What do you think we can do to stop the destruction of the rainforests?

Sources: Durning 1990; Gorman 1991; Linden 1991; Stipp 1992; Nabhan 1998; Simons 2006.

---

3. Because of feedback to nature, human actions have many unintended consequences.
4. The world is finite, so there are physical limits to economic growth.
5. Economic expansion requires increased extraction of resources from the environment.
6. Increased extraction of resources leads to ecological problems.
7. These ecological problems place limits on economic expansion.
8. Governments create environmental problems by encouraging the accumulation of capital.

The goal of environmental sociology is not to stop pollution or nuclear power but, rather, to study how humans (their cultures, values, and behavior) affect the physical environment and how the physical environment affects human activities. Environmental sociologists, however, generally are also environmental activists, and the Section on Environment and Technology of the American Sociological Association tries to influence governmental policies (American Sociological Association n.d.).

Technology and the Environment: The Goal of Harmony It is inevitable that humans will continue to develop new technologies. But the abuse of our environment by those technologies is not inevitable. To understate the matter, the destruction of our planet is an unwise choice.

If we are to live in a world that is worth passing on to coming generations, we must seek harmony between technology and the natural environment. This will not be easy. At one extreme are people who claim that to protect the environment we must eliminate industrialization and go back to a tribal way of life. At the other extreme are people who are blind to the harm being done to the natural environment, who want the entire world to industrialize at full speed. Somewhere, there must be a middle ground, one that recognizes not only that industrialization is here to stay but also that we *can* control it, for it is our creation. Controlled, industrialization can enhance our quality of life; uncontrolled, it will destroy us.

It is essential, then, that we develop ways to reduce or eliminate the harm that technology does to the environment. This includes mechanisms to monitor the production, use, and disposal of technology. The question, of course, is whether we have the resolve to take the steps necessary to preserve the environment for future generations. What is at stake is nothing less than the welfare of planet Earth. Surely that is enough to motivate us to make wise choices.

The social movement that centers on the environment has become global. In all nations, people are concerned about the destruction of the earth's resources. This photo is a sign of changing times. Instead of jumping on this beached whale and carving it into pieces, these Brazilians are doing their best to save its life.

Summary *and* Review

How Social Change Transforms Social Life

What major trends have transformed the course of human history?

The primary changes in human history are the four social revolutions (domestication, agriculture, industrialization, and information); the change from *Gemeinschaft* to *Gesellschaft* societies; capitalism and industrialization; modernization; and global stratification. Social movements indicate cutting edges of social change. Ethnic conflicts and power rivalries threaten the global divisions G-8 is working out. We may also be on the cutting edge of a new biotech society. Pp. 652–656.

Theories and Processes of Social Change

Besides technology, capitalism, modernization, and so on, what other theories of social change are there?

Evolutionary theories presuppose that societies move from the same starting point to some similar ending point. *Unilinear* theories, which assume the same evolutionary path for every society, were replaced by *multilinear* theories, which assume that different paths lead to the same stage of development. *Cyclical* theories view civilizations as going through a process of birth, youth, maturity, decline, and death. Conflict theorists view social change as inevitable, for each *thesis* (basically an arrangement of power) contains *antithesis* (contradictions). A new *synthesis* develops to resolve these contradictions, but it, too, contains contradictions that must be resolved, and so on. This is called a **dialectical** process. Pp. 656–657.

What is Ogburn's theory of social change?

William Ogburn identified technology as the basic cause of social change, which comes through three processes: **invention, discovery,** and **diffusion.** The term **cultural lag** refers to symbolic culture lagging behind changes in technology. Pp. 657–659.

How Technology Changes Society

How does new technology affect society?

Because **technology** is an organizing force of social life, changes in technology can have profound effects. The automobile and the computer were used as extended examples. The computer is changing the way we learn, work, do business, and fight wars. We don't yet know whether information technologies will help to perpetuate or to reduce social inequalities on both a national and a global level. Pp. 660–667.

The Growth Machine Versus the Earth

What are the environmental problems of the Most Industrialized Nations?

The environmental problems of the Most Industrialized Nations range from smog and acid rain to the **greenhouse effect.** Most scientists agree that **global warming** will have consequences that can fundamen-

tally affect our lives. Burning fossil fuels in internal combustion engines lies at the root of many environmental problems. The location of factories and hazardous waste sites creates **environmental injustice,** with environmental problems having a greater impact on minorities and the poor. Pp. 667–668.

What are the environmental problems of the Industrializing and Least Industrialized Nations?

The worst environmental problems are found in the former Soviet Union, a legacy of the unrestrained exploitation of resources by the Communist party. The rush of the Least Industrialized Nations to industrialize is adding to our environmental decay. The world is facing a basic conflict between the lust for profits through the exploitation of the earth's resources and the need to establish a **sustainable environment.** Pp. 668–671.

What is the environmental movement?

The environmental movement is an attempt to restore a healthy environment for the world's people. This global social movement takes many forms, from peaceful attempts to influence the political process to **ecosabotage.** Pp. 671–672.

What is environmental sociology?

Environmental sociology is not an attempt to change the environment, but, rather, is a study of the relationship between humans and the environment. Environmental sociologists are generally also environmental activists. Pp. 672–674.

Thinking Critically

about Chapter 22

1. How has social change affected your life? Be specific—what changes, how? Does Ogburn's theory help to explain your experiences? Why or why not?

2. In what ways does technology change society?

3. Do you think that a sustainable environment should be a goal of the world's societies? Why or why not? If so, what practical steps do you think we can take to produce a sustainable environment?

Additional Resources

What can you use MySocLab for?

 www.mysoclab.com

- **Study and Review:** Pre- and Post-Tests, Practice Tests, Flash Cards, Individualized Study Plans.

- **Current Events:** *Sociology in the News,* the daily *New York Times,* and more.

- **Research and Writing:** *Research Navigator, Writing About Sociology,* and more.

Where Can I Read More on This Topic?

Suggested readings for this chapter are listed at the back of this book.

EPILOGUE:
WHY MAJOR IN SOCIOLOGY?

As you explored social life in this textbook, I hope that you found yourself thinking along with me. If so, you should have gained a greater understanding of why people think, feel, and act as they do—as well as insights into why *you* view life the way you do. Developing your sociological imagination was my intention in writing this book. I have sincerely wanted to make sociology come alive for you.

Majoring in Sociology

If you feel a passion for peering beneath the surface—for seeking out the social influences in people's lives, and for seeing these influences in your own life—this is the best reason to major in sociology. As you take more courses in sociology, you will continue this enlightening process of social discovery. As your sociological imagination grows, you will become increasingly aware of how social factors underlie human behavior.

In addition to people who have a strong desire to continue this fascinating process of social discovery, there is a second type of person whom I also urge to major in sociology. Let's suppose that you have a strong, almost unbridled sense of wanting to explore many aspects of life. Let's also assume that because you have so many interests, you can't make up your mind about what you want to do with your life. You can think of so many things you'd like to try, but for each one there are other possibilities that you find equally as compelling. Let me share what one student who read this text wrote me:

> I'd love to say what my current major is—if only I truly knew. I know that the major you choose to study in college isn't necessarily the field of work you'll be going into. I've heard enough stories of grads who get jobs in fields that are not even related to their majors to believe it to a certain extent. My only problem is that I'm not even sure what it is I want to study, or what I truly want to be in the future for that matter.
>
> The variety of choices I have left open for myself are very wide, which creates a big problem, because I know I have to narrow it down to just one, which isn't something easy at all for me. It's like I want to be the best and do the best (medical doctor), yet I also wanna do other things (such as being a paramedic, or a cop, or firefighter, or a pilot), but I also realize I've only got one life to live. So the big question is: What's it gonna be?

This note reminded me of myself. In my reply, I said:

> You sound so much like myself when I was in college. In my senior year, I was plagued with uncertainty about what would be the right course for my life. I went to a counselor and took a vocational aptitude test. I still remember the day when I went in for the test results. I expected my future to be laid out for me, and I hung on every word. But then I heard the counselor say, "Your tests show that mortician should be one of your vocational choices."
>
> Mortician! I almost fell off my chair. That choice was so far removed from anything that I wanted that I immediately gave up on such tests.
>
> I like your list of possibilities: physician, cop, firefighter, and paramedic. In addition to these, mine included cowboy, hobo, and beach bum. One day, I was at the dry cleaners (end of my sophomore year in college), and the guy standing next to me was a cop. We talked about his job, and when I left the dry cleaners, I immediately went to the police station to get an application. I found out that I had to be 21, and I was just 20. I went back to college.
>
> I'm very happy with my choice. As a sociologist, I am able to follow my interests. I was able to become a hobo (or at least a traveler and able to experience different cultural settings). As far as being a cop, I developed and taught a course in the sociology of law.
>
> One of the many things I always wanted to be was an author. I almost skipped graduate school to move to Greenwich Village and become a novelist. The problem was that I was too timid, too scared of the unknown—and I had no support at all—to give it a try. My ultimate choice of sociologist has allowed me to fulfill this early dream.

It is sociology's breadth that is so satisfying to those of us who can't seem to find the limit to our interests, who can't pin ourselves down to just one thing in life. Sociology covers *all* of social life. Anything and everything that people do is part of sociology. For those of us who feel such broad, and perhaps changing interests, sociology is a perfect major.

But what if you already have a major picked out, yet you really like thinking sociologically? You can *minor* in sociology. Take sociology courses that continue to pique your sociological imagination. Then after college, continue to stimulate your sociological interests through your reading, including novels. This ongoing development of your sociological imagination will serve you well as you go through life.

But What Can You Do With a Sociology Major?

I can just hear someone say: "That's fine for you, since you became a sociologist. I don't want to go to graduate school, though. I just want to get my bachelor's degree and get out of college and get on with life. So, how can a bachelor's in sociology help me?"

This is a fair question. Just what can you do with a bachelor's degree in sociology?

A few years ago, in my sociology department we began to develop a concentration in applied sociology. At that time, since this would be a bachelor's degree, I explored this very question. I was surprised at the answer: *Almost anything!*

It turns out that most employers don't care what you major in. (Exceptions are some highly specialized fields such as nursing, computers, and engineering.) *Most* employers just want to make certain that you have completed college, and for most of them one degree is the same as another. *College provides the base on which the employer builds.*

Because you have your bachelor's degree—no matter what it is in—employers assume that you are a responsible person. This credential implies that you have proven yourself: You were able to stick with a four-year course, you showed up for classes, listened to lectures, took notes, passed tests, and carried out whatever assignments you were given. On top of this base of presumed responsibility, employers add the specifics necessary for you to perform their particular work, whether that be in sales or service, in insurance, banking, retailing, marketing, product development, or whatever.

If you major in sociology, then, you don't have to look for a job as a sociologist. If you ever decide to go on for an advanced degree, that's fine. But such plans are not necessary. The bachelor's in sociology can be your passport to most types of work in society.

Final Note

I want to conclude by stressing the reason to major in sociology that goes far beyond how you are going to make a living. It is the sociological perspective itself, the way of thinking and understanding that sociology provides. Wherever your path in life may lead, the sociological perspective will accompany you.

You are going to live in a fast-paced, rapidly-changing society that, with all its conflicting crosscurrents, is going to be in turmoil. The sociological perspective will cast a different light on life's events, allowing you to perceive them in more insightful ways. As you watch television, attend a concert, converse with a friend, listen to a boss or co-worker—you will be more aware of the contexts that underlie such behavior. The sociological perspective that you develop as you major in sociology will equip you to view what happens to you in life differently from someone who does not have your sociological background. Even events in the news will look different to you.

The final question that I want to leave you with, then, is, "If you enjoy sociology, why not major in it?"

With my best wishes for your success in life,

Jim Henslin

achieved statuses positions that are earned, accomplished, or involve at least some effort or activity on the individual's part

acid rain rain containing sulfuric and nitric acids (burning fossil fuels release sulfur dioxide and nitrogen oxide that become sulfuric and nitric acids when they react with moisture in the air)

acting crowd an excited group of people who move toward a goal

activity theory the view that satisfaction during old age is related to a person's amount and quality of activity

age cohort people born at roughly the same time who pass through the life course together

ageism prejudice, discrimination, and hostility directed against people because of their age; can be directed against any age group, including youth

agent provocateur someone who joins a group in order to spy on it and to sabotage it by provoking its members to commit extreme acts

agents of socialization people or groups that affect our self-concept, attitudes, behaviors, or other orientations toward life

aggregate individuals who temporarily share the same physical space but who do not see themselves as belonging together

agricultural revolution the second social revolution, based on the invention of the plow, which led to agricultural societies

agricultural society a society based on large-scale agriculture; plows drawn by animals are the source of food production

alienation Marx's term for workers' lack of connection to the product of their labor; caused by their being assigned repetitive tasks on a small part of a product—this leads to a sense of powerlessness and normlessness; others use the term in the general sense of not feeling a part of something

alterative social movement a social movement that seeks to alter only some specific aspects of people

alternative medicine medical treatment other than that of standard Western medicine; often refers to practices that originate in Asia, but may also refer to taking vitamins not prescribed by a doctor

anarchy a condition of lawlessness or political disorder caused by the absence or collapse of governmental authority

animism the belief that all objects in the world have spirits, some of which are dangerous and must be outwitted

anomie Durkheim's term for a condition of society in which people become detached from the norms that usually guide their behavior

anti-Semitism prejudice, discrimination, and persecution directed against Jews

anticipatory socialization because one anticipates a future role, one learns parts of it now

apartheid the separation of racial-ethnic groups as was practiced in South Africa

applied sociology the use of sociology to solve problems—from the micro level of family relationships to the macro level of crime and pollution

ascribed statuses positions an individual either inherits at birth or receives involuntarily later in life

assimilation the process of being absorbed into the mainstream culture

authoritarian leader an individual who leads by giving orders

authoritarian personality Theodor Adorno's term for people who are prejudiced and rank high on scales of conformity, intolerance, insecurity, respect for authority, and submissiveness to superiors

authority power that people consider legitimate, as rightly exercised over them; also called *legitimate power*

back stage where people rest from their performances, discuss their presentations, and plan future performances

background assumptions deeply embedded common understandings of how the world operates and of how people ought to act

barter the direct exchange of one item for another

basic demographic equation growth rate equals births minus deaths plus net migration

basic or pure sociology sociological research whose purpose is to make discoveries about life in human groups, not to make changes in those groups

bilineal (system of descent) a system of reckoning descent that counts both the mother's and the father's side

biotech society a society whose economy increasingly centers around the application of genetics—human genetics for medicine, and plant and animal genetics for the production of food and materials

blended family a family whose members were once part of other families

body language the ways in which people use their bodies to give messages to others

bonded labor, (indentured service) a contractual system in which someone sells his or her body (services) for a specified period of time in an arrangement very close to slavery, except that it is voluntarily entered into

born again a term describing Christians who have undergone a life-transforming religious experience so radical that they feel they have become new persons

bourgeoisie Marx's term for capitalists, those who own the means of production

bureaucracy a formal organization with a hierarchy of authority and a clear division of labor; emphasis on written rules, communications, and records; and impersonality of positions

capital punishment the death penalty

capitalism an economic system characterized by the private ownership of the means of production, the pursuit of profit, and market competition

capitalist class the wealthy who own the means of production and buy the labor of the working class

cargo cult a social movement in which South Pacific islanders destroyed their possessions in the anticipation that their ancestors would ship them new goods

caste system a form of social stratification in which one's status is determined by birth and is lifelong

category people who have similar characteristics

centrist party a political party that represents the center of political opinion

charisma literally, an extraordinary gift from God; more commonly, an outstanding, "magnetic" personality

charismatic authority authority based on an individual's outstanding traits, which attract followers

charismatic leader literally, someone to whom God has given a gift; more commonly, someone who exerts extraordinary appeal to a group of followers

checks and balances the separation of powers among the three branches of U.S. government—legislative, executive, and judicial—so that each is able to nullify the actions of the other two, thus preventing the domination of any single branch

church according to Durkheim, one of the three essential elements of religion—a moral community of believers; also refers to a type of religious organization, to a large, highly organized group with formal, sedate worship services and little emphasis on personal conversion

circular reaction Robert Park's term for a back-and-forth communication among the members of a crowd whereby a "collective impulse" is transmitted

citizenship the concept that birth (and residence) in a country impart basic rights

city a place in which a large number of people are permanently based and do not produce their own food

city-state an independent city whose power radiates outward, bringing the adjacent area under its rule

civil religion Robert Bellah's term for religion that is such an established feature of a country's life that its history and social institutions become sanctified by being associated with God

class conflict Marx's term for the struggle between capitalists and workers

class consciousness Marx's term for awareness of a common identity based on one's position in the means of production

class system a form of social stratification based primarily on the possession of money or material possessions

clique a cluster of people within a larger group who choose to interact with one another; an internal faction

closed-ended questions questions that are followed by a list of possible answers to be selected by the respondent

coalition the alignment of some members of a group against others

coalition government a government in which a country's largest party aligns itself with one or more smaller parties

coercion power that people do not accept as rightly exercised over them; also called *illegitimate power*

cohabitation unmarried couples living together in a sexual relationship

collective behavior extraordinary activities carried out by groups of people; includes lynchings, rumors, panics, urban legends, and fads and fashions

collective mind Gustave LeBon's term for the tendency of people in a crowd to feel, think, and act in extraordinary ways

colonialism the process by which one nation takes over another nation, usually for the purpose of exploiting its labor and natural resources

common sense those things that "everyone knows" are true

community a place people identify with, where they sense that they belong and that others care about what happens to them

compartmentalize to separate acts from feelings or attitudes

conflict theory a theoretical framework in which society is viewed as composed of groups that are competing for scarce resources

conspicuous consumption Thorstein Veblen's term for a change from the Protestant ethic to an eagerness to show off wealth by the consumption of goods

continuity theory the focus of this theory is how people adjust to retirement by continuing aspects of their earlier lives

contradictory class locations Erik Wright's term for a position in the class structure that generates contradictory interests

control group the group of subjects who are not exposed to the independent variable

control theory the idea that two control systems—inner controls and outer controls—work against our tendencies to deviate

convergence theory the view that as capitalist and socialist economic systems each adopt features of the other, a hybrid (or mixed) economic system will emerge

corporate capitalism the domination of the economic system by giant corporations

corporate crime crimes committed by executives in order to benefit their corporation

corporate welfare the financial incentives (tax breaks, subsidies, and even land and stadiums) given to corporations in order to attract them to an area or induce them to remain

corporation the joint ownership of a business enterprise, whose liabilities and obligations are separate from those of its owners

correspondence principle the sociological principle that schools correspond to (or reflect) the social structure of their society

cosmology teachings or ideas that provide a unified picture of the world

credential society the use of diplomas and degrees to determine who is eligible for jobs, even though the diploma or degree may be irrelevant to the actual work

credit card a device that allows its owner to purchase goods and to be billed later

crime the violation of norms written into law

criminal justice system the system of police, courts, and prisons set up to deal with people who are accused of having committed a crime

crude birth rate the annual number of live births per 1,000 population

crude death rate the annual number of deaths per 1,000 population

cult a new religion with few followers, whose teachings and practices put it at odds with the dominant culture and religion

cultural goals the legitimate objectives held out to the members of a society

cultural lag Ogburn's term for human behavior lagging behind technological innovations

cultural transmission of values in reference to education, the ways in which schools transmit a society's culture, especially its core values

cultural universal a value, norm, or other cultural trait that is found in every group

culture the language, beliefs, values, norms, behaviors, and even material objects that are passed from one generation to the next

culture of poverty the assumption that the values and behaviors of the poor make them fundamentally different from other people, that these factors are largely responsible for their poverty, and that parents perpetuate poverty across generations by passing these characteristics to their children

currency paper money

debit card a device that allows its owner to charge purchases against his or her bank account

defensive medicine medical practices done not for the patient's benefit but in order to protect a physician from malpractice suits

deferred gratification for going something in the present in the hope of achieving greater gains in the future

degradation ceremony a term coined by Harold Garfinkel to describe an attempt to remake the self by stripping away an individual's self-identity and stamping a new identity in its place

dehumanization the act or process of reducing people to objects that do not deserve the treatment accorded humans

deindustrialization industries moving out of a country or region

democracy a system of government in which authority derives from the people; the term comes from two Greek words that translate literally as "power to the people"

democratic leader an individual who leads by trying to reach a consensus

democratic socialism a hybrid economic system in which capitalism is mixed with state ownership

demographic transition a three-stage historical process of population growth: first, high birth rates and high death rates; second, high birth rates and low death rates; and third, low birth rates and low death rates; a fourth stage has begun to appear in the Most Industrialized Nations, as depicted in Figure 41.3

demographic variables the three factors that influence population growth: fertility, mortality, and net migration

demography the study of the size, composition, growth, and distribution of human populations

denomination a "brand name" within a major religion, for example, Methodist or Baptist

dependency ratio the number of workers who are required to support each dependent person—those 65 and older and those 15 and under

dependent variable a factor that is changed by an independent variable

depersonalization dealing with people as though they were objects; in the case of medical care, as though patients were merely cases and diseases, not people

deposit receipt a receipt stating that a certain amount of goods is on deposit in a warehouse or bank; the receipt is used as a form of money

deviance the violation of rules or norms

dialectical process (of history) each arrangement, or thesis, contains contradictions, or antitheses, which must be resolved; the new arrangement, or synthesis, contains its own contradictions, and so on

dictatorship a form of government in which an individual has seized power

differential association Edwin Sutherland's term to indicate that associating with some groups results in learning an "excess of definitions" of deviance, and, by extension, in a greater likelihood that one will become deviant

diffusion the spread of an invention or a discovery from one area to another; identified by William Ogburn as one of three processes of social change

direct democracy a form of democracy in which the eligible voters meet together to discuss issues and make their decisions

disabling environment an environment that is harmful to health

discovery a new way of seeing reality; identified by William Ogburn as one of three processes of social change

discrimination an act of unfair treatment directed against an individual or a group

disengagement theory the view that society prevents disruption by having the elderly vacate (or disengage from) their positions of responsibility so the younger generation can step into their shoes

disinvestment the withdrawal of investments by financial institutions, which seals the fate of an urban area

divine right of kings the idea that the king's authority comes directly from God

division of labor the splitting of a group's or a society's tasks into specialties

documents in its narrow sense, written sources that provide data; in its extended sense, archival material of any sort, including photographs, movies, CDs, DVDs, and so on

domestication revolution the first social revolution, based on the domestication of plants and animals, which led to pastoral and horticultural societies

dominant group the group with the most power, greatest privileges, and highest social status

downward social mobility movement down the social class ladder

dramaturgy an approach, pioneered by Erving Goffman, in which social life is analyzed in terms of drama or the stage; also called *dramaturgical analysis*

dumping the practice of sending unprofitable patients to public hospitals

dyad the smallest possible group, consisting of two persons

e–cash digital money that is stored on computers

ecclesia a religious group so integrated into the dominant culture that it is difficult to tell where the one begins and the other leaves off; also called a *state religion*

economy a system of producing and distributing goods and services

ecosabotage actions taken to sabotage the efforts of people who are thought to be legally harming the environment

edge city a large clustering of service facilities and residential areas near highway intersections that provides a sense of place to people who live, shop, and work there

education a formal system of teaching knowledge, values, and skills

egalitarian authority more or less equally divided between people or groups, in this instance between husband and wife

ego Freud's term for a balancing force between the id and the demands of society

electronic community individuals who regularly interact with one another on the Internet and who think of themselves as belonging together

emergent norms Ralph Turner and Lewis Killian's term for the idea that people develop new norms to cope with a new situation; used to explain crowd behavior

empty nest a married couple's domestic situation after the last child has left home

endogamy the practice of marrying within one's own group

enterprise zone the use of economic incentives in a designated area to encourage investment

environmental injustice refers to the pollution of our environment affecting minorities and the poor the most

environmental sociology a specialty within sociology where the focus is the relationship between human societies and the environment

epidemiology the study of disease and disability patterns in a population

estate stratification system the stratification system of medieval Europe, consisting of three groups or estates: the nobility, clergy, and commoners

ethnic cleansing a policy of population elimination, including forcible expulsion and genocide

ethnic work activities designed to discover, enhance, or maintain ethnic and racial identification

ethnicity (and **ethnic**) having distinctive cultural characteristics

euthanasia mercy killing

evangelism an attempt to win converts

exchange mobility about the same numbers of people moving up and down the social class ladder, such that, on balance, the social class system shows little change

exogamy the practice of marrying outside one's group

experiment the use of control and experimental groups and dependent and independent variables to test causation

experimental group the group of subjects who are exposed to the independent variable

exponential growth curve a pattern of growth in which numbers double during approximately equal intervals, thus accelerating in the latter stages

expressive leader an individual who increases harmony and minimizes conflict in a group; also known as a *socioemotional leader*

extended family a nuclear family plus other relatives, such as grandparents, uncles, and aunts

face-saving behavior techniques used to salvage a performance that is going sour

fad a temporary pattern of behavior that catches people's attention

false class consciousness Marx's term to refer to workers identifying with the interests of capitalists

family two or more people who consider themselves related by blood, marriage, or adoption

family of orientation the family in which a person grows up

family of procreation the family formed when a couple's first child is born

fashion a pattern of behavior that catches people's attention and lasts longer than a fad

fecundity the number of children that women are capable of bearing

fee-for-service payment to a physician to diagnose and treat a patient's medical problems

feminism the philosophy that men and women should be politically, economically, and socially equal; organized activities on behalf of this principle

(the) **feminization of poverty** a trend in U.S. poverty whereby most poor families are headed by women

feral children children assumed to have been raised by animals, in the wilderness, isolated from other humans

fertility rate the number of children that the average woman bears

fiat money currency issued by a government that is not backed by stored value

formal organization a secondary group designed to achieve explicit objectives

front stage where performances are given

functional analysis a theoretical framework in which society is viewed as composed of various parts, each with a function that, when fulfilled, contributes to society's equilibrium; also known as *functionalism* and *structural functionalism*

functional equivalent in this context, a substitute that serves the same functions (or meets the same needs) as religion, for example, psychotherapy

functional illiterate a high school graduate who has difficulty with basic reading and math

functional requisites the major tasks that a society must fulfill if it is to survive

fundamentalism the belief that true religion is threatened by modernism and its values and that the faith as it was originally practiced should be restored

gatekeeping the process by which education opens and closes doors of opportunity; another term for the *social placement* function of education

Gemeinschaft a type of society in which life is intimate; a community in which everyone knows everyone else and people share a sense of togetherness

gender the behaviors and attitudes that a society considers proper for its males and females; masculinity or femininity

gender age the relative value placed on men's and women's ages

gender role the behaviors and attitudes considered appropriate because one is a female or a male

gender socialization the ways in which society sets children onto different courses in life *because* they are male or female

gender stratification males' and females' unequal access to power, prestige, and property on the basis of their sex

generalizability the extent to which the findings from one group (or sample) can be generalized or applied to other groups (or populations)

generalization a statement that goes beyond the individual case and is applied to a broader group or situation

generalized other the norms, values, attitudes, and expectations of people "in general"; the child's ability to take the role of the generalized other is a significant step in the development of a self

genetic predisposition inborn tendencies; in this context, to commit deviant acts

genocide the systematic annihilation or attempted annihilation of a people because of their presumed race or ethnic group

gentrification middle class people moving into a rundown area of a city, displacing the poor as they buy and restore homes

gerontocracy a society (or some other group) run by the elderly

Gesellschaft a type of society that is dominated by impersonal relationships, individual accomplishments, and self-interest

glass ceiling the mostly invisible barrier that keeps women from advancing to the top levels at work

global warming an increase in the earth's temperature due to the greenhouse effect

globalization the extensive interconnections among nations due to the expansion of capitalism

globalization of capitalism capitalism (investing to make profits within a rational system) becoming the globe's dominant economic system

goal displacement the adoption of new goals by an organization; also known as *goal replacement*

gold standard paper money backed by gold

grade inflation higher grades given for the same work; a general rise in student grades without a corresponding increase in learning

graying of America refers to the growing percentage of older people in the U.S. population

greenhouse effect the buildup of carbon dioxide in the earth's atmosphere that allows light to enter but inhibits the release of heat; believed to cause global warming

gross domestic product (GDP) the amount of goods and services produced by a nation

group people who have something in common and who believe that what they have in common is significant; also called a *social group*

group dynamics the ways in which individuals affect groups and the ways in which groups influence individuals

groupthink a narrowing of thought by a group of people, leading to the perception that there is only one correct answer, in which to even suggest alternatives becomes a sign of disloyalty

growth rate the net change in a population after adding births, subtracting deaths, and either adding or subtracting net migration

hate crime crimes to which more severe penalties are attached because they are motivated by hatred (dislike, animosity) of someone's race-ethnicity, religion, sexual orientation, disability, or national origin

health a human condition measured by four components: physical, mental, social, and spiritual

health maintenance organization (HMO) a health care organization that provides medical treatment to its members for a fixed annual cost

hidden curriculum the unwritten goals of schools, such as teaching obedience to authority and conformity to cultural norms

homogamy the tendency of people with similar characteristics to marry one another

Horatio Alger myth the belief that due to limitless possibilities anyone can get ahead if he or she tries hard enough

horticultural society a society based on cultivating plants by the use of hand tools

hospice a place (or services brought to someone's home) for the purpose of giving comfort and dignity to a dying person

household people who occupy the same housing unit

human ecology Robert Park's term for the relationship between people and their environment (such as land and structures); also known as *urban ecology*

humanizing a work setting organizing a workplace in such a way that it develops rather than impedes human potential

hunting and gathering society a human group that depends on hunting and gathering for its survival

hypothesis a statement of how variables are expected to be related to one another, often according to predictions from a theory

id Freud's term for our inborn basic drives

ideology beliefs about the way things ought to be that justify social arrangements

illegitimate opportunity structure opportunities for crimes that are woven into the texture of life

impression management people's efforts to control the impressions that others receive of them

incest sexual relations between specified relatives, such as brothers and sisters or parents and children

incest taboo the rule that prohibits sex and marriage among designated relatives

income money received, usually from a job, business, or assets

independent variable a factor that causes a change in another variable, called the dependent variable

individual discrimination the negative treatment of one person by another on the basis of that person's perceived characteristics

Industrial Revolution the third social revolution, occurring when machines powered by fuels replaced most animal and human power

industrial society a society based on the harnessing of machines powered by fuels

in-groups groups toward which one feels loyalty

inflation an increase in prices

institutional discrimination negative treatment of a minority group that is built into a society's institutions; also called *systemic discrimination*

institutionalized means approved ways of reaching cultural goals

instrumental leader an individual who tries to keep the group moving toward its goals; also known as a *task-oriented leader*

intergenerational mobility the change that family members make in social class from one generation to the next

interlocking directorates the same people serving on the board of directors of several companies

internal colonialism the policy of economically exploiting minority groups

interview direct questioning of respondents

interviewer bias effects that interviewers have on respondents that lead to biased answers

invasion-succession cycle the process of one group of people displacing a group whose racial-ethnic or social class characteristics differ from their own

invention the combination of existing elements and materials to form new ones; identified by William Ogburn as one of three processes of social change

[the] iron law of oligarchy Robert Michels' term for the tendency of formal organizations to be dominated by a small, self-perpetuating elite

labeling theory the view that the labels people are given affect their own and others' perceptions of them, thus channeling their behavior either into deviance or into conformity

laissez-faire capitalism unrestrained manufacture and trade (literally "hands off" capitalism)

laissez-faire leader an individual who leads by being highly permissive

language a system of symbols that can be combined in an infinite number of ways and can represent not only objects but also abstract thought

latent functions unintended beneficial consequences of people's actions

leader someone who influences other people

leadership styles ways in which people express their leadership

leisure time not taken up by work or necessary activities

life course the stages of our life as we go from birth to death

life expectancy the number of years that an average person at any age, including newborns, can expect to live

life span the maximum length of life of a species; for humans, the longest that a human has lived

lobbyists people who influence legislation on behalf of their clients

machismo an emphasis on male strength and dominance

macro-level analysis an examination of large-scale patterns of society

macropolitics the exercise of large-scale power, the government being the most common example

macrosociology analysis of social life that focuses on broad features of society, such as social class and the relationships of groups to one another; usually used by functionalists and conflict theorists

mainstreaming helping people to become part of the mainstream of society

Malthus theorem an observation by Thomas Malthus that although the food supply increases arithmetically (from 1 to 2 to 3 to 4 and so on), population grows geometrically (from 2 to 4 to 8 to 16 and so forth)

mandatory education laws laws that require all children to attend school until a specified age or until they complete a minimum grade in school

manifest functions the intended beneficial consequences of people's actions

marginal working class the most desperate members of the working class, who have few skills, little job security, and are often unemployed

market forces the law of supply and demand

market restraints laws and regulations that limit the capacity to manufacture and sell products

marriage a group's approved mating arrangements, usually marked by a ritual of some sort

mass hysteria an imagined threat that causes physical symptoms among a large number of people

mass media forms of communication, such as radio, newspapers, and television that are directed to mass audiences

mass society industrialized, highly bureaucratized, impersonal society

mass society theory an explanation for why people participate in a social movement based on the assumption that the movement offers them a sense of belonging

master status a status that cuts across the other statuses that an individual occupies

matriarchy a society in which women as a group dominate men as a group

matrilineal (system of descent) a system of reckoning descent that counts only the mother's side

[the] McDonaldization of society the process by which ordinary aspects of life become rationalized and efficiency comes to rule them, including such things as food preparation

means of production the tools, factories, land, and investment capital used to produce wealth

mechanical solidarity Durkheim's term for the unity (a shared consciousness) that people feel as a result of performing the same or similar tasks

medicalization the transformation of a human condition into a matter to be treated by physicians

medicalization of deviance to make deviance a medical matter, a symptom of some underlying illness that needs to be treated by physicians

medicine one of the social institutions that sociologists study; a society's organized ways of dealing with sickness and injury

medium of exchange the means by which people place a value on goods and services in order to make an exchange, for example, currency, gold, and silver

megacity a city of 10 million or more residents

megalopolis an urban area consisting of at least two metropolises and their many suburbs

melting pot the view that Americans of various backgrounds would blend into a sort of ethnic stew

meritocracy a form of social stratification in which all positions are awarded on the basis of merit

metaformative social movement a social movement that has the goal to change the social order not just of a country or two, but of a civilization, or even of the entire world

metropolis a central city surrounded by smaller cities and their suburbs

metropolitan statistical area (MSA) a central city and the urbanized counties adjacent to it

micro-level analysis an examination of small-scale patterns of society

micropolitics the exercise of power in everyday life, such as deciding who is going to do the housework or use the remote control

microsociology analysis of social life that focuses on social interaction; typically used by symbolic interactionists

millenarian social movement a social movement based on the prophecy of coming social upheaval

milling a crowd standing or walking around as they talk excitedly about some event

minimax strategy Richard Berk's term for the efforts people make to minimize their costs and maximize their rewards

minority group people who are singled out for unequal treatment and who regard themselves as objects of collective discrimination

modernization the transformation of traditional societies into industrial societies

monarchy a form of government headed by a king or queen

money any item (from sea shells to gold) that serves as a medium of exchange; today, currency is the most common form

monopoly the control of an entire industry by a single company

monotheism the belief that there is only one God

moral panic a fear that grips a large number of people that some evil threatens the well-being of society, followed by hostility, sometimes violence, toward those thought responsible

mores norms that are strictly enforced because they are thought essential to core values or the well-being of the group

multiculturalism (also called *pluralism*) a philosophy or political policy that permits or encourages ethnic difference

multinational corporations companies that operate across national boundaries; also called *transnational corporations*

nationalism a strong identification with a nation, accompanied by the desire for that nation to be dominant

natural sciences the intellectual and academic disciplines designed to comprehend, explain, and predict events in our natural environments

negative sanction an expression of disapproval for breaking a norm, ranging from a mild, informal reaction such as a frown to a formal reaction such as a prison sentence or an execution

neocolonialism the economic and political dominance of the Least Industrialized Nations by the Most Industrialized Nations

net migration rate the difference between the number of immigrants and emigrants per 1,000 population

networking using one's social networks for some gain

noncentrist party a political party that represents less popular ideas

nonverbal interaction communication without words through gestures, use of space, silence, and so on

nuclear family a family consisting of a husband, wife, and child(ren)

objectivity total neutrality

oligarchy a form of government in which a small group of individuals holds power; the rule of the many by the few

oligopoly the control of an entire industry by several large companies

open-ended questions questions that respondents answer in their own words

operational definition the way in which a researcher measures a variable

organic solidarity Durkheim's term for the interdependence that results from the division of labor; people depending on others to fulfill their jobs

out-groups groups toward which one feels antagonism

pan-Indianism a movement that focuses on common elements in the cultures of Native Americans in order to develop a cross-tribal self-identity and to work toward the welfare of all Native Americans

panic the condition of being so fearful that one cannot function normally, and may even flee

participant observation (or **fieldwork**) research in which the researcher participates in a research setting while observing what is happening in that setting

pastoral society a society based on the pasturing of animals

patriarchy a society or group in which men dominate women; authority is vested in males

patrilineal (system of descent) a system of reckoning descent that counts only the father's side

patterns recurring characteristics or events

peer group a group of individuals of roughly the same age who are linked by common interests

personality disorders the view that a personality disturbance of some sort causes an individual to violate social norms

Peter principle a tongue-in-cheek observation that the members of an organization are promoted for their accomplishments until they reach their level of incompetence; there they cease to be promoted, remaining at the level at which they can no longer do good work

pluralism the diffusion of power among many interest groups that prevents any single group from gaining control of the government

pluralistic society a society made up of many different groups

police discretion the practice of the police, in the normal course of their duties, to either arrest or ticket someone for an offense or to overlook the matter

political action committee (PAC) an organization formed by one or more special-interest groups to solicit and spend funds for the purpose of influencing legislation

politics the exercise of power and attempts to maintain or to change power relations

polyandry a form of marriage in which women have more than one husband

polygyny a form of marriage in which men have more than one wife

polytheism the belief that there are many gods

population the target group to be studied

population pyramid a graphic representation of a population, divided into age and sex

population shrinkage the process by which a country's population becomes smaller because its birth rate and immigration are too low to replace those who die and emigrate

population transfer forcing a minority group to move

positive sanction a reward or positive reaction for following norms, ranging from a smile to a prize

positivism the application of the scientific approach to the social world

postindustrial (information) society a society based on information, services, and high technology, rather than on raw materials and manufacturing

postmodern society another term for postindustrial society; a chief characteristic is the use of tools that extend human abilities to gather and analyze information, to communicate, and to travel

poverty line the official measure of poverty; calculated to include incomes that are less than three times a low-cost food budget

power the ability to carry out your will, even over the resistance of others

power elite C. Wright Mills' term for the top people in U.S. corporations, military, and politics who make the nation's major decisions

prejudice an attitude or prejudging, usually in a negative way

prestige respect or regard

primary group a group characterized by intimate, long-term, face-to-face association and cooperation

proactive social movement a social movement that promotes some social change

profane Durkheim's term for common elements of everyday life

professionalization of medicine the development of medicine into a specialty in which education becomes rigorous, and in which physicians claim a theoretical understanding of illness, regulate themselves, claim to be doing a service to society (rather than just following self-interest), and take authority over clients

proletariat Marx's term for the exploited class, the mass of workers who do not own the means of production

propaganda in its broad sense, the presentation of information in the attempt to influence people; in its narrow sense, one-sided information used to try to influence people

property material possessions; animals, bank accounts, bonds, buildings, businesses, cars, furniture, land, and stocks.

proportional representation an electoral system in which seats in a legislature are divided according to the proportion of votes that each political party receives

Protestant ethic Weber's term to describe the ideal of a self-denying, highly moral life accompanied by hard work and frugality

public in this context, a dispersed group of people relevant to a social movement; the sympathetic and hostile publics have an interest in the issues on which a social movement focuses; there is also an unaware or indifferent public

public opinion how people think about some issue

qualitative research methods research in which the emphasis is placed on observing, describing, and interpreting people's behavior

quantitative research methods research in which the emphasis is placed on measurement, the use of statistics, and numbers

questionnaires a list of questions to be asked of respondents

quiet revolution the fundamental changes in society that follow when vast numbers of women enter the work force

race physical characteristics that distinguish one group from another

racism prejudice and discrimination on the basis of race

random sample a sample in which everyone in the target population has the same chance of being included in the study

rapport (ruh-POUR) a feeling of trust between researchers and the people they are studying

rational-legal authority authority based on law or written rules and regulations; also called *bureaucratic authority*

rationality using rules, efficiency, and practical results to determine human affairs

[the] rationalization of society a widespread acceptance of rationality and social organizations that are built largely around this idea

reactive social movement a social movement that resists some social change

real culture the norms and values that people actually follow

recidivism rate the proportion of released convicts who are rearrested

redemptive social movement a social movement that seeks to change people totally, to redeem them

redlining the officers of a financial institution deciding not to make loans in a particular area

reference group a group that we use as a standard to evaluate ourselves

reformative social movement a social movement that seeks to reform some specific aspects of society

reincarnation in Hinduism and Buddhism, the return of the soul (or self) after death in a different form

relative deprivation theory in this context, the belief that people join social movements based on their evaluations of what they think they should have compared with what others have

reliability the extent to which research produces consistent or dependable results

religion according to Durkheim, beliefs and practices that separate the profane from the sacred and unite its adherents into a moral community

religious experience a sudden awareness of the supernatural or a feeling of coming in contact with God

replication repeating a study in order to test its findings

representative democracy a form of democracy in which voters elect representatives to meet together to discuss issues and make decisions on their behalf

research method (or **research design**) one of six procedures that sociologists use to collect data: surveys, participant observation, secondary analysis, documents, experiments, and unobtrusive measures

reserve labor force the unemployed; unemployed workers are thought of as being "in reserve"—capitalists take them "out of reserve" (put them back to work) during times of high production and then lay them off (put them back in reserve) when they are no longer needed

resocialization the process of learning new norms, values, attitudes, and behaviors

resource mobilization a theory that social movements succeed or fail based on their ability to mobilize resources such as time, money, and people's skills

respondents people who respond to a survey, either in interviews or by self-administered questionnaires

revolution armed resistance designed to overthrow and replace a government

riot violent crowd behavior directed at people and property

rising expectations the sense that better conditions are soon to follow, which, if unfulfilled, increases frustration

rituals ceremonies or repetitive practices; in this context, religious observances or rites, often intended to evoke a sense of awe of the sacred

role the behaviors, obligations, and privileges attached to a status

role conflict conflicts that someone feels *between* roles because the expectations attached to one role are incompatible with the expectations of another role

role extension the incorporation of additional activities into a role

role performance the ways in which someone performs a role within the limits that the role provides; showing a particular "style" or "personality"

role strain conflicts that someone feels within a role

romantic love feelings of erotic attraction accompanied by an idealization of the other

routinization of charisma the transfer of authority from a charismatic figure to either a traditional or a rational-legal form of authority

ruling class another term for the power elite

rumor unfounded information spread among people

sacred Durkheim's term for things set apart or forbidden, that inspire fear, awe, reverence, or deep respect

sample the individuals intended to represent the population to be studied

scapegoat an individual or group unfairly blamed for someone else's troubles

science the application of systematic methods to obtain knowledge and the knowledge obtained by those methods

(the) scientific method using objective, systematic observations to test theories

secondary analysis the analysis of data that have been collected by other researchers

secondary group compared with a primary group, a larger, relatively temporary, more anonymous, formal, and impersonal group based on some interest or activity. Its members are likely to interact on the basis of specific statuses

sect a religious group larger than a cult that still feels substantial hostility from and toward society

secular belonging to the world and its affairs

secularization of culture the process by which a culture becomes less influenced by religion

secularization of religion the replacement of a religion's spiritual or "other worldly" concerns with concerns about "this world"

segregation the policy of keeping racial–ethnic groups apart

selective perception seeing certain features of an object or situation, but remaining blind to others

self the unique human capacity of being able to see ourselves "from the outside"; the views we internalize of how others see us

self-administered questionnaires questionnaires that respondents fill out

self-fulfilling prophecy Robert Merton's term for an originally false assertion that becomes true simply because it was predicted

serial murder the killing of several victims in three or more separate events

sex biological characteristics that distinguish females and males, consisting of primary and secondary sex characteristics

sexual harassment the abuse of one's position of authority to force unwanted sexual demands on someone

shaman the healing specialist of a tribe who attempts to control the spirits thought to cause a disease or injury; commonly called a witch doctor

sick role a social role that excuses people from normal obligations because they are sick or injured, while at the same time expecting them to seek competent help and cooperate in getting well

sign-vehicles the term used by Goffman to refer to how people use social setting, appearance, and manner to communicate information about the self

significant other an individual who significantly influences someone else's life

slavery a form of social stratification in which some people own other people

small group a group small enough for everyone to interact directly with all the other members

social change the alteration of culture and societies over time

social class according to Weber, a large group of people who rank close to one another in wealth, prestige, and power; according to Marx, one of two groups: capitalists who own the means of production or workers who sell their labor

social construction of reality the use of background assumptions and life experiences to define what is real

social control a group's formal and informal means of enforcing its norms

social environment the entire human environment, including direct contact with others

social facts Durkheim's term for a group's patterns of behavior

social inequality a social condition in which privileges and obligations are given to some but denied to others

social institution the organized, usual, or standard ways by which society meets its basic needs

social integration the degree to which members of a group or a society feel united by shared values and other social bonds; also known as social cohesion

social interaction what people do when they are in one another's presence

social location the group memberships that people have because of their location in history and society

social mobility movement up or down the social class ladder

social movement a large group of people who are organized to promote or resist some social change

social movement organization an organization to promote the goals of a social movement

social network the social ties radiating outward from the self that link people together

social placement a function of education—funneling people into a society's various positions

social promotion passing students on to the next level even though they have not mastered basic materials

social sciences the intellectual and academic disciplines designed to understand the social world objectively by means of controlled and repeated observations

social stratification the division of large numbers of people into layers according to their relative power, property, and prestige; applies to both nations and to people within a nation, society, or other group

social structure the framework that surrounds us, consisting of the relationships of people and groups to one another, which gives direction to and sets limits on behavior

socialism an economic system characterized by the public ownership of the means of production, central planning, and the distribution of goods without a profit motive

socialization the process by which people learn the characteristics of their group—the knowledge, skills, attitudes, values, and actions thought appropriate for them

society people who share a culture and a territory

sociobiology a framework of thought that views human behavior as the result of natural selection and considers biological factors to be the fundamental cause of human behavior

sociological perspective understanding human behavior by placing it within its broader social context

sociology the scientific study of society and human behavior

special-interest group a group of people who support a particular issue and who can be mobilized for political action

spirit of capitalism Weber's term for the desire to accumulate capital as a duty—not to spend it, but as an end in itself—and to constantly reinvest it

split labor market workers split along racial, ethnic, gender, age, or any other lines; this split is exploited by owners to weaken the bargaining power of workers

state a political entity that claims monopoly on the use of violence in some particular territory; commonly known as a country

state religion a government-sponsored religion; also called *ecclesia*

status the position that someone occupies in society or in a social group

status consistency ranking high or low on all three dimensions of social class

status inconsistency ranking high on some dimensions of social class and low on others, also called *status discrepancy*

status set all the statuses or positions that an individual occupies

status symbols items used to identify a status

stereotype assumptions of what people are like, whether true or false

stigma "blemishes" that discredit a person's claim to a "normal" identity

stockholders' revolt the refusal of a corporation's stockholders to rubber-stamp decisions made by its managers

stored value the goods that are stored and held in reserve that back up (or provide the value for) a currency

strain theory Robert Merton's term for the strain engendered when a society socializes large numbers of people to desire a cultural goal (such as success), but withholds from many the approved means of reaching that goal; one adaptation to the strain is crime, the choice of an innovative means (one outside the approved system) to attain the cultural goal

stratified random sample a sample from selected subgroups of the target population in which everyone in those subgroups has an equal chance of being included in the research

street crime crimes such as mugging, rape, and burglary

structural mobility movement up or down the social class ladder that is due to changes in the structure of society, not to individual efforts

structured interviews interviews that use closed-ended questions

subjective meanings the meanings that people give their own behavior

subsistence economy a type of economy in which human groups live off the land and have little or no surplus

suburb a community adjacent to a city

suburbanization the movement from the city to the suburbs

superego Freud's term for the conscience, the internalized norms and values of our social groups

survey the collection of data by having people answer a series of questions

sustainable environment a world system that takes into account the limits of the environment, produces enough material goods for everyone's needs, and leaves a heritage of a sound environment for the next generation

symbolic culture another term for nonmaterial culture

symbolic interactionism a theoretical perspective in which society is viewed as composed of symbols that people use to establish meaning, develop their views of the world, and communicate with one another

system of descent how kinship is traced over the generations

taboo a norm so strong that it often brings revulsion if violated

taking the role of the other putting oneself in someone else's shoes; understanding how someone else feels and thinks and thus anticipating how that person will act

teamwork the collaboration of two or more people to manage impressions jointly

techniques of neutralization ways of thinking or rationalizing that help people deflect (or neutralize) society's norms

terrorism the use of violence or the threat of violence to produce fear in order to attain political objectives

theory a general statement about how some parts of the world fit together and how they work; an explanation of how two or more facts are related to one another

Thomas theorem William I. and Dorothy S. Thomas' classic formulation of the definition of the situation: "If people define situations as real, they are real in their consequences."

total institution a place in which people are cut off from the rest of society and are almost totally controlled by the officials who run the place

totalitarianism a form of government that exerts almost total control over people

traditional authority authority based on custom

traditional orientation the idea that the past is the best guide for the present; characterizes tribal, peasant, and feudal societies

transformative social movement a social movement that seeks to change society totally, to transform it

transitional adulthood a term that refers to a period following high school when young adults have not yet taken on the responsibilities ordinarily associated with adulthood; also called *adultolescence*

transnational social movement a social movement whose emphasis is on some condition around the world, instead of on a condition in a specific country; also known as *new social movements*

triad a group of three people

two-tier system of medical care a system of medical care in which the wealthy receive superior medical care and the poor inferior medical care

underclass a group of people for whom poverty persists year after year and across generations

underground economy exchanges of goods and services that are not reported to the government and thereby escape taxation

universal citizenship the idea that everyone has the same basic rights by virtue of being born in a country (or by immigrating and becoming a naturalized citizen)

unobtrusive measures ways of observing people who do not know they are being studied

unstructured interviews interviews that use open-ended questions

upward social mobility movement up the social class ladder

urban legend a story with an ironic twist that sounds realistic but is false

urban renewal the rehabilitation of a rundown area, which usually results in the displacement of the poor who are living in that area

urbanization the process by which an increasing proportion of a population lives in cities and has a growing influence on the culture

validity the extent to which an operational definition measures what it was intended to measure

value free the view that a sociologist's personal values or biases should not influence social research

values the standards by which people define what is desirable or undesirable, good or bad, beautiful or ugly

variable a factor thought to be significant for human behavior, which can vary (or change) from one case to another

Verstehen a German word used by Weber that is perhaps best understood as "to have insight into someone's situation"

voluntary association a group made up of people who voluntarily organize on the basis of some mutual interest; also known as *voluntary memberships* and *voluntary organizations*

voter apathy indifference and inaction on the part of individuals or groups with respect to the political process

war armed conflict between nations or politically distinct groups

WASP White Anglo-Saxon Protestant; narrowly, an American of English descent; broadly, an American of western European ancestry

wealth the total value of everything someone owns, minus the debts

welfare (or state) capitalism an economic system in which individuals own the means of production but the state regulates many economic activities for the welfare of the population

white ethnics white immigrants to the United States whose cultures differ from that of WASPs

white-collar crime Edwin Sutherland's term for crimes committed by people of respectable and high social status in the course of their occupations; for example, bribery of public officials, securities violations, embezzlement, false advertising, and price fixing

working class those people who sell their labor to the capitalist class

world system theory economic and political connections that tie the world's countries together

zero population growth a demographic condition in which women bear only enough children to reproduce the population

Suggested Readings

CHAPTER 1 The Sociological Perspective

Allan, Kenneth D. *Explorations in Classical Sociological Theory: Seeing the Social World.* Thousand Oaks, Calif.: Pine Forge Press, 2006. The author's emphasis is that sociological theory can be a guide for selecting research projects and for interpreting the results.

Bartos, Otomar J., and Paul Wehr. *Using Conflict Theory.* New York: Cambridge University Press, 2003. In this application of the conflict perspective, the author's primary concerns are the causes of social conflicts and how to manage or resolve conflict.

Berger, Peter L. *Invitation to Sociology: A Humanistic Perspective.* New York: Doubleday, 1972. This analysis of how sociology applies to everyday life has become a classic in the field.

Best, Joel. *More Damned Lies and Statistics: How Numbers Confuse Public Issues.* Berkeley: University of California Press, 2004. The author shows how special-interest groups manipulate and misrepresent statistics in order to promote their agendas.

Charon, Joel M. *Symbolic Interactionism: An Introduction, an Interpretation, an Integration,* 9th ed. Upper Saddle River, N.J.: Prentice Hall, 2007. The author lays out the main points of symbolic interactionism, providing an understanding of why this perspective is important in sociology.

Hedstrom, Peter. *Dissecting the Social: On the Principles of Analytical Sociology.* New York: Cambridge University Press, 2005. By examining the personal perspective of each theorist, the author shows how theoretical and historical perspectives apply to our understanding of the world.

Henslin, James M., ed. *Down to Earth Sociology: Introductory Readings,* 14th ed. New York: Free Press, 2007. This collection of readings about everyday life and social structure is designed to broaden the reader's understanding of society, and of the individual's place within it.

Mills, C. Wright. *The Sociological Imagination.* New York: Oxford University Press, 2000. First published in 1960, this classic analysis provides an overview of sociology from the framework of the conflict perspective.

Ritzer, George. *Classic Sociological Theory,* 5th ed. New York: McGraw-Hill, 2008. To help understand the personal and historical context of how theory develops, the author includes biographical sketches of the theorists.

Journals

Applied Behavioral Science Review, Clinical Sociology Review, International Clinical Sociology, Journal of Applied Sociology, The Practicing Sociologist, Sociological Practice: A Journal of Clinical and Applied Sociology, and *Sociological Practice Review* report the experiences of sociologists who work in applied settings, from peer group counseling and suicide prevention to recommending changes to school boards.

Contexts, published by the American Sociological Association, uses a magazine format to present sociological research in a down-to-earth fashion.

Humanity & Society, the official journal of the Association for Humanist Sociology, publishes articles intended "to advance the quality of life of the world's people."

Electronic Journals

Electronic Journal of Sociology (http://www. sociology. org) and *Sociological Research Online* (http://www. socresonline. org. uk) publish articles on various sociological topics. Access is free.

About Majoring in Sociology

You like sociology and perhaps are thinking about majoring in it, but what can you do with a sociology major? Be sure to check the epilogue of this book (pages 676–677). Also check out the resources that are available from the American Sociological Association. Go to www. asanet. org. This will bring you to the ASA's home page. Here, you can click around and get familiar with what this professional association offers students.

On the menu at the top of ASA's home page, click Students. This will bring you to a page that has links to resources for students. You may be interested in *The Student Sociologist,* a newsletter for students. The link, *Careers,* will take you to several free online publications, including those that feature information on careers in both basic and applied sociology. You will also see such links as the student forum, student involvement, and funding.

If you want to contact the ASA by snail mail or by telephone or fax, here is that information: American Sociological Association, 1307 New York Avenue NW, Suite 700, Washington, D.C. 20005-4701. Tel. (202) 383-9005. Fax (202) 638-0882. E-mail: Executive.Office@asanet.org

You might also be interested in this book. If your library doesn't have it, I'm sure they'll order it if you request it.

Stephens, W. Richard, Jr. *Careers in Sociology,* 4th ed. Boston: Pearson Education, 2004. How can you make a living with a major in sociology? The author explores careers in sociology, from business and government to health care and the law.

CHAPTER 2 Culture

Berger, Peter L., and Samuel P. Huntington, eds. *Many Globalizations: Cultural Diversity in the Contemporary World.* New York: Oxford University Press, 2002. One of the recurring themes of this book is how globalization is changing cultures.

Borofsky, Robert, and Bruce Albert. *Yanomani: The Fierce Controversy and What We Can Learn from It.* Berkeley: University of California Press, 2006. The authors criticize the research on the Yanomani, including that by Chagnon in the next book, with an emphasis on anthropologists' inconsideration of human rights.

Chagnon, Napoleon A. *Yanomamö: The Fierce People,* 5th ed. New York: Harcourt, Brace, Jovanovich, 1997. This account of a tribal people whose customs are extraordinarily different from ours will help you to see how arbitrary the choices are that underlie human culture.

Edgerton, Robert B. *Sick Societies: Challenging the Myth of Primitive Harmony.* New York: Free Press, 1993. The author's thesis is that cultural relativism is misinformed, that we have the obligation to judge cultures that harm their members as inferior to those that do not.

Hull, John R., Mary Jo Neitz, and Marshall Battani. *Sociology on Culture.* New York: Routledge, 2003. The authors present an overview of sociological approaches to culture.

Inglis, David. *Culture and Everyday Life.* Oxford, UK: Routledge, 2006. An overview of how culture shapes, influences, and structures our everyday lives.

Jacobs, Mark D., and Nancy Weiss Hanrahan, eds. *The Blackwell Companion to the Sociology of Culture.* Malden, Mass.: Blackwell Publishing, 2005. The authors of these articles explore cultural systems, everyday life, identity, collective memory, and citizenship in a global economy.

Phillips, Anne. *Multiculturalism without Culture.* Princeton, N.J.: Princeton University Press, 2007. Examines the issue of individual choice within cultural constraints and the arguments of multiculturalism versus cultural differences.

Sullivan, Nikki. *Tattooed Bodies: Subjectivity, Textuality, Ethics, and Pleasure.* Westport, Conn.: Praeger, 2001. A sociological analysis of this very old and very new custom.

Wolf, Mark J. P., and Bernard Perron, eds. *The Video Game: Theory Reader.* New York: Routledge, 2003. The authors of these articles on gamers and games examine sociological and economic issues that surround gaming.

Zellner, William W. *Countercultures: A Sociological Analysis.* New York: St. Martin's Press, 1995. The author's analysis of skinheads, the Ku Klux Klan, survivalists, satanists, the Church of Scientology, and the Unification Church (Moonies) helps us understand why people join countercultures.

Journal

Cultural Sociology and *Space for Difference* focus on sociological analyses of culture, with crossovers into art history, gender studies, human geography, racism, literary studies, and social activism.

CHAPTER 3 Socialization

Ariès, Philippe. *Centuries of Childhood: A Social History of Family Life.* New York: Vintage Books, 1972. The author analyzes how childhood in Europe during the Middle Ages differs from childhood today.

Blumer, Herbert. *George Herbert Mead and Human Conduct.* Lanham, Md.: AltaMira Press, 2004. An overview of symbolic interactionism by a sociologist who studied and taught Mead's thought all of his life.

Corsaro, William, A. *The Sociology of Childhood,* 2nd ed. Thousand Oaks, Calif.: Pine Forge Press, 2004. This sociological analysis of childhood includes social indicators of children in the United States and the world.

Handel, Gerald, Spencer Cahill, and Frederick Elkin. *Children and Society: The Sociology of Children and Childhood Socialization.* New York: Oxford University Press, 2007. A symbolic interactionist perspective of childhood from birth to adolescence with an emphasis on the development of the self.

Hunt, Stephen J. *The Life Course: A Sociological Introduction.* New York: Palgrave McMillan, 2006. Gives an overview of the life course while considering what is distinct about a sociological approach to this topic.

Lareau, Annette. *Unequal Childhoods: Class, Race, and Family Life.* Berkeley: University of California Press, 2003. The author documents differences in child rearing in poor, working-class, and middle-class U.S. families.

Rymer, Russ. *Genie: A Scientific Tragedy.* New York: Harper Perennial Library, 1994. This account of Genie includes the battles to oversee Genie among linguists, psychologists, and social workers, all of whom claimed to have Genie's best interests at heart.

Settersten, Richard A., Jr., and Timothy J. Owens, eds. *New Frontiers in Socialization.* Greenwich, Conn.: JAI Press, 2003. The authors of these articles focus on the adult years in the life course, examining the influence of families, neighborhoods, communities, friendship, education, work, volunteer associations, medical institutions, and the media.

Sociological Studies of Child Development: A Research Annual. Greenwich, Conn.: JAI Press, published annually. Along with theoretical articles, this publication reports on sociological research on the socialization of children.

Walters, Glenn D. *Criminal Belief Systems: An Integrated-Interactive Theory of Lifestyles.* Westport, Conn.: Greenwood Publishing Group, 2003. The author analyzes how five belief systems (self-view, world-view, past-view, present-view, future-view) explain crime initiation and maintenance.

CHAPTER 4 Social Structure and Social Interaction

Goffman, Erving. *The Presentation of Self in Everyday Life.* New York: Peter Smith, Publisher, 1999. First published in 1959. This classic statement of dramaturgical analysis provides a different way of looking at everyday life. As a student, this was one of the best books I read.

Johnson, Kim K. P., and Sharron J. Lennon, eds. *Appearance and Power.* Oxford, England: Berg Publishers, 2000. The authors of these articles analyze how significant appearance, especially clothing, is for what happens to us in social life.

LeBesco, Kathleen. *Revolting Bodies: The Struggle to Redefine Fat Identity.* Amherst: University of Massachusetts Press, 2004. This analysis of the political struggle over the cultural meaning of fatness examines oppression and negative stereotypes.

Schauer, Frederick. *Profiles, Probabilities, and Stereotypes.* Cambridge, Mass.: Belknap Press, 2004. The focus of this book is the question of whether we can generalize about members of a group on the basis of the statistical tendencies of that group.

Schmidt, Kimberly D., Diane Zimmerman Umble, and Steven D. Reschly, eds. *Strangers at Home: Amish and Mennonite Women in History.* Baltimore: Johns Hopkins University Press, 2002. These accounts of the experiences of Amish and Mennonite women provide a window onto history, as well as insight into how social structure influences social interaction.

Seidman, Steven. *The Social Construction of Sexuality.* New York: W.W. Norton, 2004. The author explores how society influences our sexual choices, our beliefs about sexuality, and our sexual standards.

Tönnies, Ferdinand. *Community and Society (Gemeinschaft und Gesellschaft).* New York: Dover Publications, 2003. Originally published in 1887, this classic work, focusing on social change, provides insight into how society influences personality. Rather challenging reading.

Waskul, Dennis, and Phillip Vannini, eds. *Body/embodiment: Symbolic Interaction and the Sociology of the Body.* London: Ashgate, 2006. Using a symbolic interactionist perspective, the authors explore the interrelationship of the body, the self, and social interaction.

Whyte, William Foote. *Street Corner Society: The Social Structure of an Italian Slum,* 4th ed. Chicago: University of Chicago Press, 1993. Originally published in 1943. The author's analysis of interaction in a U.S. Italian slum demonstrates how social structure affects personal relationships.

Journals

Qualitative Sociology, Symbolic Interaction, and *Urban Life* feature articles on symbolic interactionism and analyses of everyday life.

CHAPTER 5 How Sociologists Do Research

Bryman, Alan. *Social Research Methods,* 2nd ed. Oxford: Oxford University Press, 2005. An overview of the research methods used by sociologists, with an emphasis on the logic that underlies these methods.

Creswell, John W., and Vicki L. Plano Clark. *Designing and Conducting Mixed Methods Research.* Thousand Oaks, Calif.: Sage Publications., 2006. The authors explain how to do research that combines research methods.

Drew, Paul, Geoffrey Raymond, and Darin Weinberg. *Talk and Interaction in Social Research Methods.* Thousand Oaks, Calif.: Sage Publications, 2006. The authors stress the importance of talk in a variety of social research methods.

Gosselin, Denise Kindschi. *Heavy Hands: An Introduction to the Crimes of Family Violence,* 3rd ed. Upper Saddle River, N.J.: Prentice Hall, 2005. Explores causes, consequences, and prevalence of domestic violence; also has an emphasis on law enforcement.

Lee, Raymond M. *Unobtrusive Methods in Social Research.* Philadelphia: Open University Press, 2000. This overview of unobtrusive ways of doing social research summarizes many interesting studies.

Lomand, Turner C. *Social Science Research: A Cross Section of Journal Articles for Discussion and Evaluation,* 4th ed. Los Angeles: Pyrczak Publishing, 2005. This overview of the methods of research used by sociologists includes articles on current topics.

Neuman, W. Lawrence. *Social Research Methods: Qualitative and Quantitative Approaches,* 6th ed. Boston: Allyn and Bacon, 2006. This "how-to" book of sociological research describes how sociologists gather data and the logic that underlies each method.

Scully, Diana. *Understanding Sexual Violence: A Study of Convicted Rapists.* New York: Routledge, 1994. This analysis of how rapists rationalize their acts helps us to understand why some men rape.

Whyte, William Foote. *Creative Problem Solving in the Field: Reflections on a Career.* Lanham, Md.: AltaMira Press, 1997. Focusing on his extensive field experiences, the author provides insight into the researcher's role in participant observation.

Wysocki, Diane Kholos, ed. *Readings in Social Research Methods,* 3rd ed. Belmont, Calif.: Wadsworth, 2008. The authors of these articles provide an overview of research methods.

Writing Papers for Sociology

Cuba, Lee J. *A Short Guide to Writing about Social Science,* 4th ed. Boston: Pearson Longman, 2002. The author summarizes the types of social science literature, presents guidelines on how to organize and write a research paper, and explains how to prepare an oral presentation.

Richlin-Klonsky, Judith, and Ellen Strenski, eds. The Sociology Writing Group. *A Guide to Writing Sociology Papers,* 5th ed. New York: St. Martin's Press, 2001. The guide walks students through the steps in writing a sociology paper, from choosing the initial assignment to doing the research and turning in a finished paper. Also explains how to manage time and correctly cite sources.

CHAPTER 6 Societies to Social Networks

Cross, Robert, and Andrew Parker. *The Hidden Power of Social Networks: Understanding How Work Really Gets Done in Organizations.* Cambridge, Mass: Harvard Business School Press, 2004. Based on their research and experience in organizations, the authors explain how understanding networks can improve communication and productivity.

Homans, George C. *The Human Group.* New Brunswick, N.J.: Transaction Publishers, 2001. First published in 1950. In this classic work, the author develops the idea that all human groups share common activities, interactions, and sentiments.

Hughes, Richard L., Robert C. Ginnett, and Gordon J. Curphy. *Leadership: Enhancing the Lessons of Experience,* 5th ed. New York: McGraw-Hill, 2006. Supplementing empirical studies with illustrative anecdotes, the authors focus on what makes effective leaders.

Janis, Irving L. *Groupthink: Psychological Studies of Policy Decisions and Fiascoes,* 2nd ed. New York: Houghton Mifflin, 1982. Janis analyzes how groups can become cut off from alternatives, interpret evidence in light of their preconceptions, and embark on courses of action that they should have seen as obviously incorrect.

Newman, Mark, Albert-Laszlo Barabasi, and Duncan J. Watts, eds. *The Structure and Dynamics of Networks,* 6th ed. Princeton, N.J.: Princeton University Press, 2007. The authors of these papers analyze the significance of social networks for individuals and the functioning of society.

Purcell, Patrick, ed. *Networked Neighborhoods: The Connected Community in Context.* New York: Springer, 2007. The authors of these papers analyze the impact of the Internet on our social relationships, community, work patterns, and lifestyles.

Putnam, Robert D., and Lewis M. Feldstein. *Better Together.* New York: Simon and Schuster, 2003. The authors' premise is that Americans' sense of community has deteriorated over the past two generations; provides case studies on what some communities have done to develop networks of mutual support.

Wilson, Gerald L. *Groups in Context: Leadership and Participation in Small Groups,* 7th ed. New York: McGraw-Hill, 2005. An overview of principles and processes of interaction in small groups, with an emphasis on how to exercise leadership.

CHAPTER 7 Bureaucracy and Formal Organizations

Ackoff, Russell L., and Sheldon Rovin. *Beating the System: Using Creativity to Outsmart Bureaucracies.* San Francisco: Berrett-Koehler, Publishers, 2005. This analysis can be applied to everyday situations, such as avoiding getting lost in a maze as you try to solve a problem with the phone company or some other bureaucracy.

Bakan, Joel. *The Corporation: The Pathological Pursuit of Profit and Power.* New York: The Free Press, 2004. The author's thesis is that the corporation's lust for power undermines democracy, social justice, equality, and compassion.

Cyr, Donald. *The Art of Global Thinking: Integrating Organizational Philosophies of East and West.* West Lafayette, Ind.: Ichor Business Books, 2002. The author compares Western and Eastern organizations and their underlying philosophies and suggests ways of extracting and applying the best of both worlds.

Eberly, Don, and Ryan Streeter. *The Soul of Civil Society: Voluntary Associations and the Public Value of Moral Habits.* Lanham, Md.: Lexington Books, 2002. The authors' thesis is that citizens' involvement in voluntary organizations strengthens society.

Fineman, Stephen, Gabriel Yiannis, and David P. Sims. *Organizing and Organizations,* 3rd ed. Thousand Oaks, Calif.: Sage Publications, 2006. The authors draw on many first-hand accounts to help enliven the study of formal organizations.

Freidson, Eliot. *Professionalism: The 3rd Logic.* Chicago: University of Chicago Press, 2001. The author distinguishes between professions, technical occupations, and crafts, analyzing how they differ by knowledge base, educational requirements, career paths, organization, and ideology.

Hall, Richard H., and Pamela S. Tolbert. *Organizations: Structures, Processes, and Outcomes,* 9th ed. Upper Saddle River, N. J.: Prentice Hall, 2005. The focus of this review of the literature on social organizations is on the impacts that organizations have upon individuals and society.

Parkinson, C. Northcote. *Parkinson's Law.* Boston: Buccaneer Books, 1997. Although this exposé of the inner workings of bureaucracies is delightfully satirical, if what Parkinson analyzes were generally true, bureaucracies would always fail.

Ritzer, George. *The McDonaldization of Society: An Investigation into the Changing Character of Contemporary Life,* 4th ed. Thousand Oaks, Calif.: Pine Forge Press, 2004. The author examines how Durkheim's predictions about the rationalization of society are coming true in everyday life.

Want, Jerome. *Corporate Culture: Illuminating the Black Hole.* New York: St. Martin's Press, 2007. The author uses real-life examples to show how culture determines the success of an organization.

CHAPTER 8 Deviance and Social Control

Conklin, John E. *Why Crime Rates Fell.* Boston: Allyn and Bacon, 2003. The author analyzes the reasons that experts have suggested for why crime rates have fallen: changes in policing, imprisonment, drugs and gun usage, age, and social institutions.

Fox, James Alan, and Jack Levin. *Extreme Killing: Understanding Serial and Mass Murder.* Thousand Oaks, Calif.: Sage, 2005. As the authors analyze the various types of serial and mass murders, they examine the characteristics of both killers and their victims.

Goffman, Erving. *Stigma: Notes on the Management of Spoiled Identity.* New York: Simon & Schuster, 1986. First published in 1968. The author outlines the social and personal reactions to "spoiled identity," appearances that—due to disability, weight, ethnicity, birth marks, and so on—do not match dominant expectations.

Heiner, Robert, ed. *Deviance Across Cultures.* Oxford: Oxford University Press, 2007. Cross-cultural norms and behavior are the focus of this collection of classic and contemporary articles on deviance.

Lintner, Bert. *Blood Brothers: The Criminal Underworld of Asia.* New York: Palgrave MacMillan, 2004. Maps out the topography of organized crime in East Asia.

Lombroso, Cesare, Guglielmo Ferrero, Nicole Hahn Rafter, and Mary Gibson. *Criminal Woman, the Prostitute, and the Normal Woman.* Durham, N.C.: Duke University Press, 2005. This translation of a classic work from the 1800s on women and crime is put in current social context by two researchers on female criminals.

Paul, Pamela. *Pornified: How Pornography Is Transforming Our Lives, Our Relationships, and Our Families.* New York: Henry Holt, 2005. Based on interviews, the author's thesis is that for many people pornography is replacing intimacy and creating emotional isolation.

Rathbone, Cristina. *A World Apart: Women, Prison, and Life Behind Bars.* New York: Random House, 2006. A journalist's account of the four years she spent investigating MCI Framingham, the oldest women's prison in the United States.

Reiman, Jeffrey. *The Rich Get Richer and the Poor Get Prison: Ideology, Class, and Criminal Justice,* 8th ed. Boston: Allyn and Bacon, 2007. An analysis of how social class works to produce different types of criminals and different types of justice.

Rodriguez, Luis J. *The Republic of East L. A.: Stories.* Los Angeles: Rayo, 2003. These hard-hitting vignettes let the reader know what life is like in this poverty-plagued section of Los Angeles.

Silberman, Matthew, ed. *Violence and Society: A Reader.* Upper Saddle River, N.J.: Prentice Hall, 2003. As the authors of these articles analyze the social factors that underlie violence, they focus on social inequality, culture, and family, sexual, and criminal violence.

Journals

Criminal Justice Review: Issues in Criminal, Social, and Restorative Justice and *Journal of Law and Society* examine the social forces that shape law and justice.

CHAPTER 9 Global Stratification

Deliege, Robert. *The Untouchables of India.* Oxford, U.K.: Berg, 2001. An overview of India's caste system, with an emphasis on the *Dalits,* or untouchables.

Friedman, Thomas L. *The World Is Flat.* New York: Farrar, Straus, and Giroux, 2005. The author envisions a global economy where, in addition to powerful transnational corporations, individuals use inexpensive technology to compete for international business.

Held, David, and Anthony McGrew, eds. *Global Transformations Reader: An Introduction to the Globalization Debate.* Cambridge, U.K.: Polity Press, 2003. The authors of these articles analyze how globalization is transforming state power, national cultures, the world economy, global inequality, and environmental challenges.

Huggins, Martha K., Mika Haritos-Fatouros, and Philip G. Zimbardo. *Violence Workers: Police Torturers and Murderers Reconstruct Brazilian Atrocities.* Berkeley: University of California Press, 2002. If you want an insider's perspective in order to understand how ordinary people can rape, torture, and kill, this book will provide it.

Ritzer, George. *The Globalization of Nothing.* Thousand Oaks, Calif.: Pine Forge Press, 2004. The author expresses concerns about the short- and long-term effects of globalization.

Sachs, Jeffrey D. *The End of Poverty: Economic Possibilities for Our Time.* East Rutherford, N.J.: Penguin Press, 2005. After visiting 100 countries, representing 90 percent of the world's population, the author suggests ways that we can end global poverty.

Sernau, Scott. *Worlds Apart: Social Inequalities in a Global Economy,* 2nd ed. Thousand Oaks, Calif.: Pine Forge Press, 2005. The author's thesis is that the market-driven global economy contributes to rather than reduces social inequality.

Sklair, Leslie. *Globalization: Capitalism and Its Alternatives,* 3rd ed. Oxford: Oxford University Press, 2003. The author identifies positive aspects of globalization, along with limitations of capitalism.

Wilkins, David E., and K. Tsianina Lomawaima. *Uneven Ground: American Indian Sovereignty and Federal Law.* Norman: University of Oklahoma Press, 2002. The author traces the relationship of Native Americans and the U.S. government.

Zakaria, Fareed. *The Future of Freedom: Illiberal Democracy at Home and Abroad.* New York: W.W. Norton, 2004. The author considers whether democracy is the best alternative in different parts of the world, and suggests that democracy requires strong limits to function properly.

CHAPTER 10 Social Class in the United States

Beeghley, Leonard. *The Structure of Social Stratification in the United States,* 5th ed. Boston: Pearson, 2008. The author presents a concise overview of the U.S. social classes.

Bowles, Samuel, Herbert Gintis, and Melissa Osborne Groves, eds. *Unequal Chances: Family Background and Economic Success.* Princeton, N.J.: Princeton University Press., 2005. The authors of these articles focus on how our economic origins affect our social destination as adults.

Florida, Richard. *The Rise of the Creative Class: And How It's Transforming Work, Leisure, Community and Everyday Life.* New York: Basic Books, 2004. The author's thesis is that a new social class has evolved, consisting of scientists, engineers, architects, educators, writers, artists, and entertainers, and that this class needs to become cohesive and work for the common good.

Gatewood, Willard B. *Aristocrats of Color: The Black Elite, 1880–1920.* Fayetteville: University of Arkansas Press, 2000. Analyzing the rise and decline of the African American upper class that developed after the Civil War, the author focuses on marriage, occupations, education, religion, clubs, and relationships with whites and with African Americans of lower classes.

Hartmann, Heidi I., ed. *Women, Work, and Poverty: Women Centered Research for Policy Change.* Binghamton, N.Y.: Haworth Press, 2006. The authors present research on women living at or below the poverty line. Major themes are work, marriage, motherhood, and welfare reform.

Iceland, John. *Poverty in America, A Handbook,* 2nd ed. Berkeley, Calif.: University of California Press, 2006. This picture of poverty in the United States shows how both poverty and its related public policies have changed over time.

Neckerman, Kathryn. *Social Inequality.* New York: Russell Sage, 2004. The author examines implications of the increasing economic inequality analyzed in this chapter for the quality of family and neighborhood life, access to education and health care, job satisfaction, and political participation.

Perucci, Robert, and Earl Wyson. *The New Class Society,* 3rd ed. Lanham, Md.: Rowman and Littlefield, 2007. An overview of the U.S. social class structure, with the suggestion that no longer is there a middle class.

Sherman, Rachel. *Class Acts: Service and Inequality in Luxury Hotels.* Berkeley, Calif.: University of California Press, 2007. Based on participant observation, the author explores the relationship between workers and guests at a luxury hotel.

Wilson, William Julius, and Richard P. Taub. *There Goes the Neighborhood: Racial, Ethnic, and Class Tensions in Four Chicago Neighborhoods and Their Meaning for America.* New York: Alfred A. Knopf, 2007. This study of four working- and lower-middle class neighborhoods in Chicago is enlivened with personal narratives that provide insight into how race, class, and ethnicity influence our lives.

Journals

Journal of Children and Poverty and *Journal of Poverty* analyze issues that affect the quality of life of people who live in poverty.

Race, Gender, and Class publishes interdisciplinary articles on the topics listed in its title.

CHAPTER 11 Sex and Gender

Anderson, Margaret L. *Thinking about Women: Sociological Perspectives on Sex and Gender,* 7th ed. New York: Allyn and Bacon, 2006. An overview of the main issues of sex and gender in contemporary society, ranging from sexism and socialization to work and health.

Brettell, Caroline B., and Carolyn F. Sargent, eds. *Gender in Cross-Cultural Perspective,* 4th ed. Upper Saddle River, N.J.: Prentice Hall, 2005. The net is spread wide as the authors examine gender and biology, in prehistory,

at home, and the division of labor, and the body, property, kinship, religion, politics, and the global economy.

Colapinto, John. *As Nature Made Him: The Boy Who Was Raised as a Girl, P.S.* New York: Harper Perennial, 2006. A detailed account of the event summarized in this chapter of the boy whose penis was accidentally burned off.

Edwards, Tim. *Cultures of Masculinities.* London: Routledge, 2006. An analysis of the variations of masculinity as it is shaped by culture.

Gilbert, Paula Ruth, and Kimberly K. Eby, eds. *Violence and Gender: An Interdisciplinary Reader.* Upper Saddle River, N.J.: Prentice Hall, 2004.The authors of these articles examine violence and youth, the human body, war, intimacy, sports, the media, and how to prevent violence.

Gilman, Charlotte Perkins. *The Man-Made World or, Our Androcentric Culture.* New York: Charlton, 1911. Reprinted in 1971 by Johnson Reprint. This early book on women's liberation provides an excellent view of female-male relations at the beginning of the last century.

Goldberg, Steven. *Why Men Rule: A Theory of Male Dominance.* Chicago: Open Court, 1994. A detailed explanation of the author's theory of male dominance featured in this chapter.

Johnson, Allan G. *Privilege, Power, and Difference,* 2nd ed. New York: McGraw-Hill, 2006. The author helps us see the nature and consequences of privilege and our connection to it.

Kimmel, Michael S., ed. *The Gendered Society Reader,* 2nd ed. New York: Oxford University Press, 2004. The authors of these articles examine the relationship of gender and violence in the contexts of culture, family, classroom, workplace, and intimacy.

Kimmel, Michael S., and Michael A. Messner, eds. *Men's Lives,* 7th ed. Boston: Allyn and Bacon, 2007. The authors of these articles examine issues of sex and gender as they affect men. Often provides different views from those presented in the Anderson book.

Lorber, Judith, and Lisa Jean Moore. *Gender and the Social Construction of Illness,* 2nd ed. Lanham, Md.: Rowman and Littlefield, 2003. Taking the position that both gender and medicine are social institutions, the author examines their interrelationships.

Renzetti, Claire, and Daniel J. Curran. *Women, Men, and Society,* 5th ed. Boston: Allyn and Bacon, 2003. A basic text that summarizes major issues in the sociology of gender.

Wharton, Amy S. *The Sociology of Gender: An Introduction to Theory and Research.* Medford, Mass.: Blackwell Publishers, 2005. Research on gender is viewed through three frameworks: the individual, the interactional, and the institutional.

Wolf, Naomi. *The Beauty Myth: How Images of Beauty Are Used Against Women.* New York: Harper Perennial, 2003. The author analyzes the unrealistic images of female beauty portrayed in the media.

Journals

These journals focus on the role of gender in social life: *Feminist Studies; Gender and Behavior; Gender and Society; Forum in Women's and Gender Studies; Gender and History; Gender, Place and Culture: A Journal of Feminist Geography; Journal of Gender, Culture, and Health; Journal of Interdisciplinary Gender Studies; Journal of Men's Health and Gender; Sex Roles;* and *Signs: Journal of Women in Culture and Society.*

CHAPTER 12 Race and Ethnicity

Acosta, Teresa Palomo, and Ruthe Winegarten. *Los Tejanas: 300 Years of History.* Austin: University of Texas Press, 2003. An account of how Tejanas in the colonial period and from the Republic of Texas up to 1900 overcame obstacles to their success.

Blee, Kathleen M. *Inside Organized Racism: Women in the Hate Movement.* Berkeley: University of California Press, 2002. Why and how do people join hate groups? The author's research provides answers to this troubling question.

Deutscher, Irwin, and Linda Lindsey. *Preventing Ethnic Conflict: Successful Cross-National Strategies.* Lanham, Md.: Lexington Books, 2005. Instead of focusing on what doesn't work, the authors examine positive ethnic relationships around the world.

Dray, Phillip. *At the Hands of Persons Unknown: The Lynching of Black America.* New York: The Modern Library, 2004. Examines the history of the lynching of African Americans and the social background behind these acts.

Du Bois, W. E. B. *Black Reconstruction in America: An Essay Toward a History of the Part Which Black Folk Played in the Attempt to Reconstruct Democracy in America, 1860–1880.* New York: Harcourt, Brace 1935; New

York: The Free Press, 2000. This analysis of the role of African Americans in the Civil War and during the years immediately following provides a glimpse into a neglected part of U.S. history.

Hallett, Michael A. *Private Prisons in America: A Critical Race Perspective.* Champaign, Ill.: University of Illinois Press, 2006. The author's thesis is that the growth of private prisons in the United States is due more to racial discrimination than to increasing crime rates.

Hilberg, Raul. *The Destruction of the European Jews,* 3rd ed. New Haven: Yale University Press, 2003. The focus of this book is the machinery of death that the Nazis put together to annihilate the Jewish community of Europe.

Mander, Jerry. *In the Absence of the Sacred: The Failure of Technology and the Survival of the Indian Nations.* New York: Pete Smith, Publisher, 1999. With a focus on the impact of technology, the author analyzes past and present relations of Native Americans and the U.S. government.

Mueller, Timothy, and Sarah Sue Goldsmith. *Nations Within: The Four Sovereign Tribes of Louisiana.* Baton Rouge: Louisiana State University Press, 2004. Analyzes the relationship of four sovereign nations to the dominant, colonizing governmental power.

Parrillo, Vincent N. *Strangers to These Shores: Race and Ethnic Relations in the United States,* 8th ed. Boston: Allyn and Bacon, 2006. This text reviews the experiences of more than 50 racial-ethnic groups.

Ryan, Nick. *Into a World of Hate.* New York: Routledge, 2005. The author spent six years exploring the underworld of hatred in Europe and the United States.

Sowell, Thomas. *Black Rednecks and White Liberals.* San Francisco: Encounter Books, 2005. In this provocative and controversial analysis, the author places ghetto culture, slavery, the education of African Americans, and the exportation of democracy in sociohistorical context.

Walker, Samuel, Cassia Spohn, and Miriam Delone. *The Color of Justice: Race, Ethnicity, and Crime in America,* 4th ed. Belmont, Calif.: Wadsworth, 2007. The authors analyze racial, ethnic, and gender discrimination in the criminal justice system.

Wilson, William Julius. *The Bridge over the Racial Divide: Rising Inequality and Coalition Politics.* Berkeley: University of California Press, 2000. The author analyzes how monetary, trade, and tax policies increase social inequality; includes recommendations to increase multiracial political cooperation.

CHAPTER 13 The Elderly

Dychtwald, Ken. *Age Power: How the 21st Century Will Be Ruled by the New Old.* Los Angeles: J. P. Tarcher, 2001. Speculates on how the growing numbers of elderly will affect society, and suggests how we should prepare for the coming change.

Gass, Thomas Edward, and Bruce C. Vladeck. *Nobody's Home: Candid Reflections of a Nursing Home Aide.* Ithaca, N.Y.: ILR Press, 2004. A firsthand account of the reality of life in a nursing home.

Gubrium, Jaber F., and James A. Holstein, eds. *Ways of Aging.* Malden, Mass.: Blackwell Publishers, 2003. The authors of these articles examine how people construct their self definitions as they adjust to the realities of aging bodies.

Hatch, Laurie Russell. *Beyond Gender Differences: Adaptation to Aging in Life Course Perspective.* Amityville, N.Y.: Baywood Publishing Company, 2000. The author reviews the research on how men and women adapt to growing old.

Hooyman, Nancy, and H. Asuman Kiyak. *Social Gerontology: A Multidisciplinary Perspective,* 8th ed. Boston: Allyn and Bacon, 2008. As the authors consider factors that influence how people experience old age, they cover differences by age and cohort, gender, race-ethnicity, sexual orientation, and socioeconomic status.

Quadagno, Jill S. *Aging and the Life Course: An Introduction to Social Gerontology,* 4th ed. New York: McGraw-Hill, 2008. In this review of major issues in gerontology, the author examines how the quality of life that people experience in old age is the result of earlier choices, opportunities, and constraints.

Roszak, Theodore. *The Longevity Revolution: As Boomers Become Elders.* Berkeley, Calif.: Berkeley Hills Books, 2001. The author's thesis is that the elderly are not a burden to society, but a great resource.

Rubin, Lillian B. *Tangled Lives: Daughters, Mothers, and the Crucible of Aging.* Boston: Beacon Press, 2002. The author reflects on her own experiences with illness and death to try to come to grips with the meaning of growing old—and of life.

Stoller, Eleanor Palo, and Rose Campbell Gibson. *Worlds of Difference: Inequality in the Aging Experience,* 3rd ed. Thousand Oaks, Calif.: Pine Forge Press, 2002. The authors document inequalities borne by the U.S. elderly and explain the social conditions that create those inequalities.

Vincent, John A., Chris R. Phillipson, and Murna Downs. *The Futures of Old Age.* Thousand Oaks, Calif.: Sage Publications, Inc., 2006. Considers how families, services, and economies might adapt to a growing older population.

Journals

Elderly Latinos; The Gerontologist, Journal of Aging and Identity, Journal of Aging and Social Policy, Journal of Aging Studies, Journal of Cross-Cultural Gerontology, Journal of Elder Abuse and Neglect, Journal of Gerontology, Journal of Long Term Home Health Care, and *Journal of Women and Aging* focus on issues of aging, while *Youth and Society* and *Journal of Youth Studies* examine adolescent culture.

CHAPTER 14 The Economy

Amott, Teresa. *Caught in the Crisis: Women and the U.S. Economy Today,* 2nd ed. New York: Monthly Review Press, 2004. An analysis of how the transformation of the economy is affecting women.

Bales, Kevin. *Disposable People: New Slavery in the Global Economy,* revised edition. Berkeley: University of California Press, 2005. The author documents the relationship between the globalization of capitalism and current slavery in Brazil, India, Mauritania, Pakistan, and Thailand.

Bergsten, C. Fred. *The United States and the World Economy.* Washington, D.C.: Institute for International Economics, 2005. This analysis of the globalization of capitalism focuses on how the prosperity of the United States is related to the world economy.

Chua, Amy. *World on Fire: How Exporting Free Market Democracy Breeds Ethnic Hatred and Global Instability.* New York: Doubleday, 2003. The author's thesis is that the globalization of capitalism has brought economic devastation, ethnic hatreds, and genocidal violence throughout the Least Industrialized Nations.

Konecny, Peter. *Gogol's Ghost: Life in St. Petersburg Between Communism and Capitalism.* Lincoln, Neb.: Writer's Club Press, 2003. Examines life in St. Petersburg in the early years of Russia's transformation from communism to capitalism.

Lenin, Vladimir Ilyrich. *The Development of Capitalism in Russia.* Honolulu: University Press of the Pacific, 2004. An English translation of Lenin's 1899 book.

Lucarelli, Bill. *Monopoly Capitalism in Crisis.* New York: Palgrave Macmillan, 2005. Is U.S. prosperity about to end? The author argues the global economy is about to deflate owing to excess global production capacity.

Noland, Marcus, and Howard Pack. *The Arab Economies in a Changing World.* Washington, D.C.: Institute for International Economies, 2007. Places the economies of the Middle East in global context, comparing them with other transition economies.

Stiglitz, Joseph E. *Globalization and Its Discontents.* New York: W.W. Norton, 2003. The thesis of the author, who served as Chair of the President's Council of Economic Advisors, is that politicians put the interests of Wall Street ahead of the needs of the Least Industrialized Nations.

Venkatesh, Sudhir Alladi. *Off the Books: The Underground Economy of the Urban Poor.* Cambridge, Mass.: Harvard University Press, 2006. In this study of Chicago's poor, the author focuses on the significant role the underground economy plays in their struggle to get by.

CHAPTER 15 Politics

Amnesty International. *Amnesty International Report.* London: Amnesty International Publications, published annually. Summarizes human rights violations around the world, country by country, listing specific instances and names.

Andreas, Peter, and Ethan Nadelmenn. *Policing the Globe: Crime Control in International Relations.* New York: Oxford University Press, 2006. The authors' thesis in this bridge between criminal justice and international relations is that Western countries gain political benefits by exporting their definitions of crime.

Beah, Ishmael. *A Long Way Gone: Memoirs of a Boy Soldier.* New York: Farrar, Straus, and Giroux, 2007. This first-person account of a boy who was forced into being a soldier in Sierra Leone provides an understanding of the social dynamics that transform young teenagers into rapists, torturers, and killers.

Byman, Daniel. *Deadly Connections: States that Sponsor Terrorism.* Cambridge, U.K.: Cambridge University Press, 2005. The author examines the different types of support that states provide terrorists, their motivations for doing so, and the impact of their sponsorship.

Domhoff, G. William. *Who Rules America?: Power and Politics,* 5th ed. New York: McGraw-Hill, 2006. An analysis of how the multinational corporations dominate the U.S. government.

Ferguson, Charles D., and William C. Potter. *The Four Faces of Nuclear Terrorism.* New York: Routledge, 2005. The authors examine the motivations and capabilities of terrorist organizations to acquire and use nuclear weapons and recommend ways to prevent nuclear terrorism and to reduce the consequences of the most likely nuclear terror attacks.

Ginzburg, Eugenia Semyonovna. *Journey into the Whirlwind.* New York: Harvest Books, 2003. The autobiographical and moving account of a woman who spent 18 years in Stalin's prison camps.

McFaul, Michael, Nikolai Petrov, and Andrei Ryabov. *Between Dictatorship and Democracy: Russian Post-Communist Political Reform.* Washington D.C.: Carnegie Endowment for International Peace, 2004. An account of Russia's transition to capitalism, including the modification of its social institutions.

Mills, C. Wright. *The Power Elite,* 2nd ed. New York: Textbook Publishers, 2003. First published in 1956. This classic analysis elaborates the conflict thesis summarized in this chapter—that U.S. society is ruled by the nation's top corporate leaders, together with an elite from the military and political institutions.

Research in Political Sociology: A Research Annual. Greenwich, Conn.: JAI Press, published annually. Analyzes political topics of vital concern to our well-being, but not recommended for beginners, as the findings and theories can be difficult and abstract.

Zweigenhaft, Richard L., and G. William Domhoff. *Diversity in the Power Elite: Have Women and Minorities Reached the Top?* Lanham, Md.: Rowman & Littlefield, 2006. The authors explore the extent to which Jews, women, African Americans, Latinos, Asian Americans, and homosexuals have joined the power elite.

Journals

Many sociology journals publish articles on politics. Four that focus on this area of social life are *American Political Science Review, Journal of Political and Military Sociology, Social Policy,* and *Social Politics.*

CHAPTER 16 Marriage and Family

Agger, Ben, and Beth Anne Shelton. *Fast Families, Virtual Children: A Critical Sociology of Families and Schooling.* Boulder, Colo.: Paradigm Publishers, 2007. The authors analyze how technology has changed the way families conduct their lives, raise their children, and try to maintain a boundary between work and home.

Bianchi, Suzanne M., John P. Robinson, and Melissa A. Milkie. *Changing Rhythms of American Family Life.* New York: Russell Sage, 2006. Based on time-diaries, the authors conclude that despite their greater participation in the paid labor force U.S. mothers spend just as much time with their children as the previous generation of women did.

Contreras, Josefina M., Kathryn A. Kerns, and Angela M. Neal-Barnett. *Latino Children and Families in the United States: Current Research and Future Directions.* New York: Praeger, 2003. The authors consider how parenting beliefs and practices of Latinos differ by socioeconomic and cultural backgrounds and try to identify family values that can be considered "Latino."

Coontz, Stephanie. *Marriage, a History: From Obedience to Intimacy or How Love Conquered Marriage.* New York: Viking, 2005. This analysis of how the fundamental orientations to marriage have changed contains enlightening excerpts from the past.

Edin, Kathryn, and Maria Kefalas. *Promises I Can Keep: Why Poor Women Put Motherhood Before Marriage.* Berkeley: University of California Press, 2005. The author's interviews provide insight into how low-income single mothers think about marriage and family.

Epstein, Cynthia Fuchs, and Arne L. Kalleberg, eds. *Fighting for Time: Shifting Boundaries of Work and Social Life.* New York: Russell Sage, 2005. Explores changes in the time people spend at work and the consequences of those changes for individuals and families.

Johnson, Leonor Boulin, and Robert Staples. *Black Families at the Crossroads: Challenges and Prospects.* New York: Jossey-Bass, 2005. After placing today's black families in historical context, the authors analyze the impact of economic policies and social change.

Marquardt, Elizabeth. *Between Two Worlds: The Inner Lives of Children of Divorce.* New York: Crown, 2005. The author deftly weaves her own experiences as a child of divorce into her summary of interviews with children who have had this experience.

Romano, Renee Christine. *Race Mixing: Black-White Marriage in Postwar America.* Cambridge, Mass.: Harvard University Press, 2003. Provides the legislative background on these marriages, plus social trends, accompanied by first-person accounts.

Wallace, Harvey. *Family Violence,* 4th ed. Boston: Allyn and Bacon, 2005. This overview examines family violence through three perspectives: legal, medical, and social.

Journals

Family Relations, The History of the Family, International Journal of Sociology of the Family, Journal of Comparative Family Studies, Journal of Divorce, Journal of Divorce and Remarriage, Journal of Family and Economic Issues, Journal of Family Issues, Journal of Family Violence, Journal of Marriage and the Family, and *Marriage and Family Review* publish articles on almost every aspect of marriage and family life.

CHAPTER 17 Education

Attewell, Paul, David Lavin, Thurston Domina, and Tana Levey. *Passing the Torch: Does Higher Education for the Disadvantaged Pay Off Across the Generations?* New York: Russell Sage, 2007. This study of women from poor families who attended college under open admission programs shows that their children are more likely to succeed in school and to earn college degrees themselves.

Graham, Patricia Albjerg. *Schooling America: How the Public Schools Meet the Nation's Changing Needs.* New York: Oxford University Press, 2007. Examines the relationship between changes in society since 1900 and the educational response to these changing needs.

Hess, Frederick M. *Common Sense School Reform.* New York: Palgrave Macmillan, 2005. Critical of current efforts to reform U.S. education, the author makes the case that reform needs to be based around accountability, competition, and leadership.

Kozol, Jonathan. *Ordinary Resurrections: Children in the Years of Hope.* New York: Crown Publishers, 2001. To listen as these children from a dismal neighborhood in South Bronx talk about life is to become aware of the potential that schools have to transform the lives of children in poverty.

Lee, Valerie E., and David T. Burkam. *Inequality at the Starting Gate: Social Background Differences in Achievement as Children Begin School.* Washington, D.C.: Economic Policy Institute, 2002. A short book and crisp analysis that document social class and racial-ethnic advantage and disadvantage at kindergarten.

Lopez, Nancy. *Hopeful Girls, Troubled Boys: Race and Gender Disparity in Urban Education.* New York: Rutledge, 2003. Building on her thesis that education is failing boys of color, the author suggests ways to improve education.

Patterson, James T. *Brown v. Board of Education: A Civil Rights Milestone and Its Troubled Legacy.* New York: Oxford University Press, 2001. A detailed analysis of the U.S. Supreme Court's 1954 epoch-making decision.

Rothstein, Richard. *Class and Schools: Using Social, Economic, and Educational Reform to Close the Black-White Achievement Gap.* Washington, D.C.: Economic Policy Institute, 2004. The author's thesis is that because social class influences learning in school, public policy must address the social and economic conditions of children's lives.

Spring, Joel H. *Deculturalization and the Struggle for Equality: A Brief History of the Education of Dominated Cultures in the United States.* New York: McGraw-Hill 2004. The author examines how Anglos have used their control of schools to strip away the cultures of minorities and replace them with Anglo culture.

Stevens, Michael L. *Kingdom of Children: Culture and Controversy in the Homeschooling Movement.* Princeton: Princeton University Press, 2003. This analysis of the homeschooling movement, based on interviews and participant observation, contains numerous quotations that provide insight into why parents homeschool their children.

Journals

The following journals contain articles that examine almost every aspect of education: *Education and Urban Society, Harvard Educational Review, Sociology and Education,* and *Sociology of Education.*

CHAPTER 18 Religion

Ault, James M. *Spirit and Flesh: Life in a Fundamentalist Baptist Church.* New York: Alfred A. Knopf, 2004. This participant observation study of an independent Baptist congregation provides insight into the initiation and maintenance of faith and relationships.

Cateura, Linda Brandi, and Omid Safi. *Voices of American Muslims.* New York: Hippocrene Books, 2006. U.S. Muslims describe their religion, experiences with suspicion and misunderstandings, and, in this heated period of terrorist attacks by Muslims, their devotion to the United States.

Gilman, Sander. *Jewish Frontiers: Essays on Bodies, Histories, and Identities.* New York: Macmillan, 2003. Analyzes Jewish identity from the framework of living on a frontier, and the representation of this identity in the mass media.

Juergensmeyer, Mark. *Terror in the Mind of God: The Global Rise of Religious Violence,* 3rd ed. Berkeley: University of California Press, 2003. The author's summaries of religious violence provide a rich background for understanding this behavior.

McRoberts, Omar M. *Streets of Glory: Church and Community in a Black Urban Neighborhood.* Chicago: University of Chicago Press, 2003. Four Corners, one of the toughest areas of Boston, contains twenty-nine mostly storefront churches. The author finds most of them are attended and run by people who do not live in the neighborhood and who have little or no attachment to the surrounding area.

Smith, Christian, and Melinda Denton. *Soul Searching: The Religious and Spiritual Life of American Teenagers.* Oxford: Oxford University Press, 2006. In this survey the spiritual life of U.S. teenagers, the authors let youth express the meaning of their spiritual life in gtheir own words.

Thibodeau, David, and Leon Whiteson. *A Place Called Waco: A Survivor's Story.* New York: Public Affairs, 2000. A first-person account of life inside the Branch Davidian compound, written by one of only four survivors of the fire who were not sentenced to prison.

Wolfe, Alan. *The Transformation of American Religion: How We Actually Live Our Faith.* New York: The Free Press, 2004. The author's thesis is that individualism is changing the shape and substance of religion in the United States, minimizing doctrine and maximizing feelings and personal satisfactions.

Zellner, William W., and William M. Kephart. *Extraordinary Groups: An Examination of Unconventional Lifestyles,* 7th ed. New York: Worth, 2001. This sketch of the history and characteristics of eight groups (the Old Order Amish, Oneida Community, Gypsies, Church of Christ Scientist, Hasidim, Father Divine Movement, Mormons, and Jehovah's Witnesses) illustrates how groups can maintain unconventional beliefs and practices.

Journals

These journals publish articles that focus on the sociology of religion: *Journal for the Scientific Study of Religion, Review of Religious Research,* and *Sociological Analysis: A Journal in the Sociology of Religion.*

CHAPTER 19 Medicine and Health

Aday, Lu Ann, ed. *Reinventing Public Health: Policies and Practices for a Healthy Nation.* Hoboken, New Jersey: Jossey-Bass, 2005. The authors analyze how public policy must respond to changing societal characteristics that influence a population's health.

Fox, Renee C., and Judith P. Swazey. *The Courage to Fail: A Social View of Organ Transplants and Dialysis.* New Brunswick, N.J.: Transaction Publishers, 2002. The authors examine moral and ethical aspects of organ replacement, a social issue destined to grow in importance as medical technology continues to advance.

Grob, Gerald N. *The Deadly Truth: A History of Disease in America.* Cambridge, Mass.: Harvard University Press, 2003. In this history of disease in the United States, the author stresses relationships among society, environment, and human health.

Henderson, Gail E., and Sue E. Estroff, eds. *The Social Medicine Reader, Volume Two: Social and Cultural Contributions to Health, Difference, and Inequality,* 2nd ed. Durham, N.C.: Duke University Press, 2005. The authors combine first-person accounts with empirical studies, drawing on findings in sociology, anthropology, and the history of medicine.

Hilts, Philip J. *Rx for Survival: Why We Must Rise to the Global Health Challenge.* New York: Penguin, 2005. The author makes the case that we must take bold steps now in order to avoid a world crisis in disease that will make terrorism pale by comparison.

Reverby, Susan M., ed. *Tuskegee's Truths: Rethinking the Tuskegee Syphilis Study.* Chapel Hill: University of North Carolina Press, 2000. Analyses of the syphilis experiments conducted by the U.S. Public Health Service at Tuskegee Institute, which were carried out on unwitting African Americans.

Smedley, Brian D., Adrienne Y. Stith, and Alan R. Nelson, eds. *Unequal Treatment: Confronting Racial and Ethnic Disparities in Health Care.* Washington, D.C.: National Academies Press, 2003. The authors of these articles examine how stereotyping and biases on the part of healthcare providers, accompanied by barriers of language, geography, and culture, contribute to inequality in healthcare.

Weitz, Rose. *The Sociology of Health, Illness, and Health Care,* 3rd ed. Belmont, Calif.: Wadsworth, 2004. With an emphasis on how gender, race-ethnicity, and social class affect people's experiences of health and illness, the author examines the health care system, alternative health care, and the experiences of those who live with illness or disability.

Journals

Health: An Interdisciplinary Journal for the Social Study of Health, Illness and Medicine, Journal of Health and Social Behavior, Research in the Sociology of Health Care, Social Science and Medicine, and *Sociological Practice: A Journal of Clinical and Applied Sociology* publish research articles and essays in the field of medical sociology.

CHAPTER 20 Population and Urbanization

Department of Agriculture. *Yearbook of Agriculture.* Washington, D.C.: Department of Agriculture, published annually. This yearbook focuses on specific aspects of U.S. agribusiness, especially international economies and trade.

Duneier, Mitchell. *Sidewalk.* New York: Farrar, Straus, and Giroux, 2000. This analysis of city streets provides insight into how the urban mosaic works.

Jacobs, Jane. *Dark Age Ahead.* New York: Random House, 2004. The author's thesis is that there are severe indications that the West is headed for another Dark Age, unless we take steps to prevent it.

Lang, Robert E., and Jennifer LeFurgy. *Boomburgs: The Rise of America's Accidental Cities.* Washington, D.C.: Brookings Institution Press, 2007. Contending that many fast-growing "cities" are really overgrown suburbs ("boomburgs"), the authors look at what attracts people to them and how they are governed.

Lin, Jan, and Christopher Mele, eds. *The Urban Sociology Reader.* New York: Routledge, 2006. The authors of these articles review the major issues in urban change and development.

Low, Setha. *Behind the Gates: Life, Security, and the Pursuit of Happiness in Fortress America.* New York: Routledge, 2004. An account of what life is like inside gated communities.

Orfield, Myron. *American Metropolitics: The New Suburban Reality.* Washington, D.C.: Brookings Institution Press, 2002. Explains why regionalism is needed in order to meet the needs of urban areas.

Palen, John J. *The Urban World,* 7th ed. New York: McGraw-Hill, 2005. A short, basic text that summarizes major issues in urban sociology.

Ross, Andrew. *The Celebration Chronicles: Life, Liberty and the Pursuit of Property Values in Disney's New Town.* New York: Ballantine Books, 2000. An analysis of Disney's planned utopian community in Florida, written by a social scientist who lived in Celebration for a year.

Taylor, Monique M. *Harlem: Between Heaven and Hell.* Minneapolis: University of Minnesota Press, 2002. A history and analysis of contemporary Harlem, with many quotes from current residents.

Yaukey, David, and Douglas L. Anderton. *Demography: The Study of Human Population,* 3rd ed. Bellevue, Wash.: Waveland Press, 2007. Focusing on both the United States and the world, the authors analyze major issues in population.

Journals

City and Community, Journal of Rural Studies, Journal of Urban Affairs, Review of Regional and Urban Development Studies, Rural Sociology, and *Urban Studies* publish articles whose focus is the city, community, immigration, migration, rural life, and suburbs.

CHAPTER 21 Collective Behavior and Social Movements

Best, Joel. *Flavor of the Month: Why Smart People Fall for Fads.* Berkeley, Ca.: University of California Press, 2006. If you want to smile, perhaps even laugh, as you read a sociological account, this little book is for you.

Brunvand, Jan Harold. *Too Good to Be True: The Colossal Book of Urban Legends.* New York: W. W. Norton, 2002. In this collection of over 200 urban legends, you'll probably find some that you heard and thought were true.

Cohen, Stanley. *Folk Devils and Moral Panics: Thirtieth Anniversary Edition,* 3rd ed. New York: Rutledge, 2003. The author's thesis is that the mass media create moral panics and stifle rational discussion about social problems.

Gupta, Dipak K. *Path to Collective Madness: A Study in Social Order and Political Pathology.* New York: Praeger, 2002. The author analyzes the process by which people participate in "collective madness"—such events as parents poisoning their children in Jonestown and the genocide of Rwanda.

Meyer, David S., Nancy Whittier, and Belinda Robnett, eds. *Social Movements: Identity, Culture, and the State.* New York: Oxford University Press, 2002. Examining wide-ranging social movements, the authors analyze mobilization, organization, strategies, identities, and the culture of social movements.

Schnapp, Jeffrey T., and Matthew Tiews, eds. *Crowds.* Stanford, Calif.: Stanford University Press, 2006. The role of crowds in modern life, based on Stanford University's "Big Humanities" project.

Surowiecki, James. *The Wisdom of Crowds.* New York: Anchor, 2005. The author proposes that the collective knowledge of the people who make up crowds is greater than that of the individuals within them.

Tilly, Charles. *The Politics of Collective Violence.* New York: Cambridge University Press, 2003. The author analyzes causes, combinations, and settings that underlie collective violence and tries to identify ways to reduce violence.

Tilly, Charles. *Social Movements: 1768–2004.* Boulder, Colo.: Paradigm Publishers, 2004. The author presents an overview of the history of social movements, with conjecture concerning their future.

Tobin, Kathleen A. *Politics and Population Control: A Documentary History.* Westport, Conn.: Greenwood Press, 2005. From the past to the present, the author analyzes how population issues have concerned authorities for centuries.

Journal

Social Movement Studies examines the origins, development, organization, context, and impact of social movements.

CHAPTER 22 Social Change and the Environment

Brown, Lester R., ed. *State of the World.* New York: Norton, published annually. Experts on environmental issues analyze environmental problems throughout the world; a New Malthusian perspective.

Council on Environmental Quality. *Environmental Quality.* Washington, D.C.: U.S. Government Printing Office, published annually. Each report evaluates the condition of some aspect of the environment.

DuPuis, E. Melanie, ed. *Smoke and Mirrors: The Politics and Culture of Air Pollution.* New York: New York University Press, 2004. The 15 articles in this book review the emergence of air pollution as a social problem and the status of air pollution today.

Fox, Nicols. *Against the Machine: The Hidden Luddite Tradition in Literature, Art, and Individual Lives.* Washington, D.C.: Island Press, 2004. The author covers broad historical ground as he analyzes reactions against modernization in the West.

Homer-Dixon, Thomas F. *Environment, Scarcity, and Violence.* Princeton: Princeton University Press, 2002. The author argues that the growth in population and production will create environmental scarcities, which, in turn, will lead to insurrections, ethnic clashes, urban unrest, and other forms of violence.

Howard, Russell D., and Reid L. Sawyer, eds. *Terrorism and Counterterrorism: Understanding the New Security Environment, Readings and Interpretations,* revised ed.. New York: McGraw-Hill, 2004. These analysts stress causes of terrorism and suggest steps to take to combat terrorism; a militaristic emphasis runs through the articles.

Inglehart, Ronald L., ed. *Human Values and Social Change: Findings from the World Values Surveys.* Boston: Brill Academic Publishers, 2003. An overview of how values are changing around the world.

Irwin, Allen. *Sociology and the Environment: A Critical Introduction to Society, Nature and Knowledge.* Malden, Mass.: Blackwell Publishers, 2001. Presents competing sociological perspectives on the construction of a sustainable environment.

Kleinman, Daniel, and Daniel Lee Kleinman. *Science and Technology in Society: From Biotechnology to the Internet.* Malden, Mass.: Blackwell Publishing, 2005. Analyzes how power shapes the development of technoscience and how the impact of technology depends on class, race, gender, and location.

Markell, David L. *Greening NAFTA: The North American Commission for Environmental Cooperation.* Stanford, Calif: Stanford University Press, 2003. As this book makes evident, without winning elections, green politics is having tremendous influence in international affairs and on our lives.

Naco, Brigitte Lebens. *Terrorism and Counterterrorism: Understanding Threats and Responses in the Post 9/11 World.* New York: Longman, 2006. This overview of terrorism includes both new terror in the post-Cold War world and historical acts of terror.

Rogers, Everett M. *Diffusion of Innovations,* 5th ed. New York: The Free Press, 2003. The author will take you on a tour of the world, examining the acceptance and rejection of innovations, and the success and failure of each.

Journals

Earth First! Journal and *Sierra,* magazines published by Earth First! and the Sierra Club respectively, are excellent sources for keeping informed of major developments in the environmental movement.

References

All new references are printed in blue.

AAUP (American Association of University Professors). "2006–07 Report on the Economic Status of the Profession," April 2007.

Abelson, Reed. "The Spine as Profit Center." *New York Times,* December 30, 2006.

Abelson, Reed. "Drug Sales Bring Huge Profits, and Scrutiny, to Cancer Doctors." *New York Times,* January 26, 2003.

Abelson, Reed, and Patricia Leigh Brown. "Alternative Medicine Is Finding Its Niche in Nation's Hospitals." *New York Times,* April 14, 2002.

Aberg, Yvonne. *Social Interactions: Studies of Contextual Effects and Endogenous Processes.* Doctoral Dissertation, Department of Sociology, Stockholm University, 2003.

Aberle, David. *The Peyote Religion Among the Navaho.* Chicago: Aldine, 1966.

Aberle, David F., A. K. Cohen, A. K. David, M. J. Leng, Jr., and F. N. Sutton. "The Functional Prerequisites of a Society." *Ethics, 60,* January 1950:100–111.

Abowitz, Kathleen Knight, and Jason Harnish. "Contemporary Discourses of Citizenship." *Review of Educational Research, 76,* 4, Winter 2006:653–690.

Ackernecht, Erwin H. "The Role of Medical History in Medical Education." *Bulletin of the History of Medicine, 21,* 1947:135–145.

Adams, Noah. "All Things Considered." *New England Journal of Medicine* report. January 12, 2000.

Addams, Jane. *Twenty Years at Hull-House.* New York: Signet, 1981. First published in 1910.

"Adherents of All Religions, By Six Continental Areas." *World Almanac and Book of Facts,* 2003.

Adler, Patricia A., and Peter Adler. *Peer Power: Preadolescent Culture and Identity.* New Brunswick, N.J.: Rutgers University Press, 1998.

Adorno, Theodor W., Else Frenkel-Brunswick, D. J. Levinson, and R. N. Sanford. *The Authoritarian Personality.* New York: Harper & Row, 1950.

Aeppel, Timothy. "More Amish Women Are Tending to Business." *Wall Street Journal,* February 8, 1996:B1, B2.

Aguirre, Benigno E. "The Conventionalization of Collective Behavior in Cuba." In *Collective Behavior and Social Movements,* Russell I. Curtis, Jr., and Benigno E. Aquirre, eds. Boston: Allyn and Bacon, 1993: 413–428.

Aguirre, Benigno E., E. L. Quarantelli, and Jorge L. Mendoza. "The Collective Behavior of Fads: The Characteristics, Effects, and Career of Streaking." In *Collective Behavior and Social Movements,* Russell L. Curtis, Jr., and Benigno E. Aguirre, eds. Boston: Allyn and Bacon, 1993:168–182.

Ahlburg, Dennis A., and Carol J. De Vita. "New Realities of the American Family." *Population Bulletin, 47,* 2, August 1992:1–44.

Akol, Jacob. "Slavery in Sudan." *New African,* September 1998.

Alarid, Leanne Fiftal, Velmer S. Burton, Jr., and Francis T. Cullen. "Gender and Crime among Felony Offenders: Assessing the Generality of Social Control and Differential Association Theories." *Journal of Research in Crime and Delinquency, 37,* 2, May 2000:171–199.

Alba, Richard, and Victor Nee. *Remaking the American Mainstream: Assimilation and Contemporary Immigration.* Cambridge, Mass.: Harvard University Press, 2003.

Albanese, Jennifer. Personal research for the author. March 2007.

Albert, Ethel M. "Women of Burundi: A Study of Social Values." In *Women of Tropical Africa,* Denise Paulme, ed. Berkeley: University of California Press, 1963:179–215.

Aldrich, Nelson W., Jr. *Old Money: The Mythology of America's Upper Class.* New York: Vintage Books, 1989.

Alexander, Gerianne M., and Melissa Hines. "Sex Differences in Response to Children's Toys in Nonhuman Primates." *Evolution and Human Behavior, 23,* 2002:467–479.

Allport, Floyd. *Social Psychology.* Boston: Houghton Mifflin, 1954.

Alter, Jonathan. "From the Prison of the 'Isms.' " *Newsweek,* January 1, 2000:31.

Amato, Paul R., and Jacob Cheadle. "The Long Reach of Divorce: Divorce and Child Well-Being Across Three Generations." *Journal of Marriage and Family, 67,* February 2005:191–206.

Amato, Paul R., and Juliana M. Sobolewski. "The Effects of Divorce and Marital Discord on Adult Children's Psychological Well-Being." *American Sociological Review, 66,* 6, December 2001:900–921.

Amenta, Edwin. "The Social Security Debate, Now, and Then." *Contexts, 5,* 3, Summer 2006.

America's Children: Key National Indicators of Well-Being 2005. Washington, D.C.: Federal Interagency Forum on Child and Family Statistics, 2005.

"American Community Survey 2003." Washington, D.C.: U.S. Census Bureau, 2004.

American Federation of Teachers. "Survey and Analysis of Teacher Salary Trends, 2005." Washington, D.C.: AFT Research and Information Services Department, 2007.

American Sociological Association. "An Invitation to Public Sociology." 2004.

American Sociological Association. "Code of Ethics and Policies and Procedures of the ASA Committee on Professional Ethics." Washington, D.C.: American Sociological Association, 1999.

American Sociological Association, "Section on Environment and Technology." Pamphlet, no date.

"Americans Work More." Associated Press, September 1, 2001.

Amin, Yousreya, Emad Hamdi, et. al. "Mass Hysteria in an Arab Culture." *International Journal of Social Psychiatry, 43,* 4, Winter 1997:303–306.

Amnesty International. "Decades of Human Rights Abuse in Iraq." Online, 2005.

Andersen, Margaret L. *Thinking About Women: Sociological Perspectives on Sex and Gender.* New York: Macmillan, 1988.

Anderson, Chris. "NORC Study Describes Homeless." *Chronicle,* 1986:5, 9.

Anderson, Elijah. "Streetwise." In *Exploring Social Life: Readings to Accompany Essentials of Sociology, Sixth Edition,* 2nd ed., James M. Henslin, ed. Boston: Allyn and Bacon, 2006:147–156.

Anderson, Elijah. *Streetwise: Race, Class, and Change in an Urban Community.* Chicago: University of Chicago Press, 1990.

Anderson, Elijah. *A Place on the Corner.* Chicago: University of Chicago Press, 1978.

Anderson, Nels. *Desert Saints: The Mormon Frontier in Utah.* Chicago: University of Chicago Press, 1966. First published in 1942.

Anderson, Philip. "God and the Swedish Immigrants." *Sweden and America,* Autumn 1995:17–20.

Anderson, Teresa A. "The Best Years of Their Lives." *Newsweek,* January 7, 1985:6.

Andersson, Hilary. "Born to Be a Slave in Niger." BBC News, World Edition, February 11, 2005.

Ang, Audra. "In China, High-Tech Mixes With Tradition to Make Matches." *Houston Chronicle,* February 13, 2006.

Angler, Natalie. "Do Races Differ? Not Really, DNA Shows." *New York Times,* August 22, 2000.

Annin, Peter. "Big Money, Big Trouble." *Newsweek,* April 19, 1999:59.

Annin, Peter, and Kendall Hamilton. "Marriage or Rape?" *Newsweek,* December 16, 1996:78.

Ansberry, Clare. "Despite Federal Law, Hospitals Still Reject Sick Who Can't Pay." *Wall Street Journal,* November 29, 1988:A1, A4.

Aptheker, Herbert. "W. E. B. Du Bois: Struggle Not Despair." *Clinical Sociology Review, 8,* 1990:58–68.

Archbold, Ronna, and Mary Harmon. "International Success: Acceptance." Online: The Five O'clock Club, 2001.

Arenson, Karen W. "Scores on Reading and Math Portions of the SAT Show a Significant Decline." *New York Times,* August 30, 2006.

Arenson, Karen W. "(Big) Red Faces at Cornell Over E-Mail Error." *New York Times,* February 28, 2003.

Arías, Jesús. "La Junta rehabilita en Grenada casas que deberá tirar por ruina." *El Pais,* January 2, 1993:1.

Ariès, Philippe. *Centuries of Childhood.* R. Baldick, trans. New York: Vintage Books, 1965.

Arlacchi, P. *Peasants and Great Estates: Society in Traditional Calabria.* Cambridge, England: Cambridge University Press, 1980.

Armitage, Richard L. "Red Army Retreat Doesn't Signal End of U.S. Obligation." *Wall Street Journal,* February 7, 1989:A20.

Armstrong, David. "Hard Case: When Academics Double as Expert Witnesses." *Wall Street Journal,* June 22, 2007.

Arndt, William F., and F. Wilbur Gingrich. *A Greek-English Lexicon of the New Testament and Other Early Christian Literature.* Chicago: University of Chicago Press, 1957.

Arsneault, Shelly. "Implementing Welfare Reform in Rural and Urban Communities: Why Place Matters." *American Review of Public Administration, 36,* 2, June 2006:173–188.

"ASA Council Statement on the Causes of Gender Differences in Science and Math Career Achievement." *Footnotes,* March 2005:10.

Asch, Solomon. "Effects of Group Pressure Upon the Modification and Distortion of Judgments." In *Readings in Social Psychology,* Guy Swanson, Theodore M. Newcomb, and Eugene L. Hartley, eds. New York: Holt, Rinehart and Winston, 1952.

Ashley, Richard. *Cocaine: Its History, Uses, and Effects.* New York: St. Martin's, 1975.

"Ask America: 2004 Nationwide Policy Survey." National Republican Congressional Committee, 2004.

Associated Press. "Military Sex Assault Reports Rose by 24 Percent." March 21, 2007.

Association of Statisticians of American Religious Bodies. *Religious Congregations and Membership in the United States: 2000.* Nashville: Glenmary Research Center, 2002.

Aulette, Judy Root. *Changing American Families.* Boston: Allyn and Bacon, 2002.

Avery, Robert B., Glenn B. Canner, and Robert E. Cook. "New Information Reported Under FMDA and Its Application in Fair Lending Enforcement." *Federal Reserve Bulletin,* Summer 2005:344–394.

Ayittey, George B. N. "Black Africans Are Enraged at Arabs." *Wall Street Journal,* interactive edition, September 4, 1998.

Bachu, Amara, and Martin O'Connell. "Fertility of American Women: Population Characteristics." *Current Population Reports.* Washington, D.C.: U.S. Bureau of the Census, September 2000.

Bainbridge, William Sims. "Collective Behavior and Social Movements." In *Sociology,* Rodney Stark. Belmont, Calif.: Wadsworth, 1989:608–640.

Bales, Robert F. "The Equilibrium Problem in Small Groups." In *Working Papers in the Theory of Action,* Talcott Parsons et al., eds. New York: Free Press, 1953:111–115.

Bales, Robert F. *Interaction Process Analysis.* Reading, Mass.: Addison-Wesley, 1950.

Baltzell, E. Digby. *Puritan Boston and Quaker Philadelphia.* New York: Free Press, 1979.

Baltzell, E. Digby, and Howard G. Schneiderman. "Social Class in the Oval Office." *Society, 25,* Sept/Oct, 1988:42–49.

Bandes, Susan. "The Lessons of Capturing the Friedmans: Moral Panic, Institutional Denial and Due Process." *Law, Culture and the Humanities, 3,* 2007:293–319.

Banerjee, Neela. "Rape (and Silence About It) Haunts Baghdad." *New York Times,* July 16, 2003.

Bannon, Lisa. "How a Rumor Spread About Subliminal Sex in Disney's 'Aladdin'." *Wall Street Journal,* October 24, 1995:A1, A6.

Baochang, Gu, Wang Feng, Guo Zhigang, and Zhang Erli. "China's Local and National Fertility Policies at the End of the Twentieth Century." *Population and Development Review, 33,* 1, March 2007:129–147.

Barlett, Donald L., and James B. Steele. "Wheel of Misfortune." *Time,* December 16, 2002:44–58.

Barnes, Fred. "How to Rig a Poll." *Wall Street Journal,* June 14, 1995:A14.

Barnes, Harry Elmer. *The History of Western Civilization,* Vol. 1. New York: Harcourt, Brace, 1935.

Barnes, Helen. "A Comment on Stroud and Pritchard: Child Homicide, Psychiatric Disorder and Dangerousness." *British Journal of Social Work, 31,* 3, June 2001.

Barnes, Julian E. "A Bicycling Mystery: Head Injuries Piling Up." *New York Times,* July 29, 2001.

Baron, Robert, and Gerald Greenberg. *Behavior in Organizations.* Boston: Allyn and Bacon, 1990.

Barrett, Paul M. "One Imam Traces the Path of Islam in Black America." *New York Times,* October 24, 2003.

Barry, John. "A New Breed of Soldier." *Newsweek,* December 10, 2001: 24–31.

Barry, John, and Evan Thomas. "Dropping the Bomb." *Newsweek,* June 25, 2001.

Barry, Paul. "Strong Medicine: A Talk with Former Principal Henry Gradillas." *College Board Review,* Fall 1989:2–13.

Barstow, David, and Lowell Bergman. "Death on the Job, Slaps on the Wrist." *Wall Street Journal,* January 10, 2003.

Barstow, David, and Robin Stein. "Between News and P. R., More Blurred Lines Found." *New York Times,* March 13, 2005.

Bartlett, Donald L., and James B. Steele. "Paying a Price for Polluters." *Time,* November 23, 1998:72–80.

Bartos, Otomar J., and Paul Wehr. *Using Conflict Theory.* New York: Cambridge University Press, 2002.

Batalova, Jeanne A., and Philip N. Cohen. "Premarital Cohabitation and Housework: Couples in Cross-National Perspectives." *Journal of Marriage and the Family, 64,* 3, August 2002: 743–755.

Bates, Marston. *Gluttons and Libertines: Human Problems of Being Natural.* New York: Vintage Books, 1967. Quoted in Crapo, Richley H. *Cultural Anthropology: Understanding Ourselves and Others,* 5th ed. Boston: McGraw Hill, 2002.

Beah, Ishmael. *A Long Way Gone: Memoirs of a Boy Soldier.* New York: Farrar, Straus and Giroux, 2007.

Beals, Ralph L., and Harry Hoijer. *An Introduction to Anthropology,* 3rd ed. New York: Macmillan, 1965.

Beaman, Jean. "New York to Belarus: Sociology in International Distance-learning." *Footnotes,* February 2003:7.

Bean, Frank D., Jennifer Lee, Jeanne Batalova, and Mark Leach. "Immigration and Fading Color Lines in America." Washington, D.C.: Population Reference Bureau, 2004.

Bearman, Peter S., and Hannah Bruckner. "Opposite-Sex Twins and Adolescent Same-Sex Attraction." *American Journal of Sociology, 107,* March 2002:1179–1205.

Beck, Scott H., and Joe W. Page. "Involvement in Activities and the Psychological Well-Being of Retired Men." *Activities, Adaptation, & Aging, 11,* 1, 1988:31–47.

Becker, Howard S. *Outsiders: Studies in the Sociology of Deviance.* New York: Free Press, 1966.

Beckett, Paul. "Caste Away." *Wall Street Journal,* June 23, 2007.

Beeghley, Leonard. *The Structure of Social Stratification in the United States,* 5th ed. Boston: Allyn and Bacon, 2008.

Begley, Sharon. "Twins: Nazi and Jew." *Newsweek, 94,* December 3, 1979:139.

Belkin, Lisa. "The Feminine Critique." *New York Times,* November 1, 2007.

Bell, Daniel. *The Coming of Post-Industrial Society: A Venture in Social Forecasting.* New York: Basic Books, 1973.

Bell, David A. "An American Success Story: The Triumph of Asian-Americans." In *Sociological Footprints: Introductory Readings in Sociology,* 5th ed., Leonard Cargan and Jeanne H. Ballantine, eds. Belmont, Calif.: Wadsworth, 1991:308–316.

Bellah, Robert N. *Beyond Belief.* New York: Harper & Row, 1970.

Belluck, Pam. "Prosecutors Say Greed Drove Pharmacist to Dilute Drugs." *New York Times,* August 18, 2001.

Belsky, Jay. "Early Child Care and Early Child Development: Major Findings of the NICHD Study of Early Child Care." *European Journal of Developmental Psychology, 3,* 1, 2006:95–110.

Belsky, Jay, Deborah Lowe Vandell, Margaret Burchinall, K. Alison Clarke-Stewart, Kathleen McCartney, and Margaret Tresch Owen. "Are There Long-Term Effects of Early Child Care?" *Child Development, 78,* 2, March/April 2007:681–701.

Benet, Sula. "Why They Live to Be 100, or Even Older, in Abkhasia." *New York Times Magazine, 26,* December 1971.

Benford, Robert D. "The College Sports Reform Movement: Reframing the 'Educational' Industry." *The Sociological Quarterly, 48,* 2007:1–28.

Bennet, James. "Palestinian Mob Attacks Pollster Over Study on 'Right to Return.'" *New York Times,* July 14, 2003.

Benson, Herbert, Jeffrey A. Dusek, Jane B. Sherwood, et al. "Study of the Therapeutic Effects of Intercessory Prayer (STP) in Cardiac Bypass Patients: A Multicenter Randomized Trial of Uncertainty and Certainty of Receiving Intercessory Prayer." *American Heart Journal, 151,* 2006:934–942.

Bergen, Raquel Kennedy. *Wife Rape: Understanding the Response of Survivors and Service Providers.* Newbury Park, Calif.: Sage, 1996.

Berger, Arthur Asa. *Video Games: A Popular Culture Phenomenon.* New Brunswick, N.J.: Transaction Publishers, 2002.

Berger, Jeffrey T., Fred Rasner, and Eric J. Cassell. "Ethics of Practicing Medical Procedures on Newly Dead and Nearly Dead Patients." *Journal of General Internal Medicine, 17,* 2002:774–778.

Berger, Joseph. "Family Ties and the Entanglements of Caste." *New York Times,* October 24, 2004.

Berger, Peter. "Invitation to Sociology." In *Down to Earth Sociology: Introductory Readings,* 14th ed., James M. Henslin, ed. New York: The Free Press, 2007. First published in 1963.

Berger, Peter L. *The Capitalist Revolution: Fifty Propositions About Prosperity, Equality, and Liberty.* New York: Basic Books, 1991.

Berger, Peter L. *Invitation to Sociology: A Humanistic Perspective.* New York: Doubleday, 1963.

Bergmann, Barbara R. "The Future of Child Care." Paper presented at the 1995 meetings of the American Sociological Association.

Bergström, Hans. "Pressures Behind the Swedish Health Reforms." *Viewpoint Sweden, 12,* July 1992:1–5.

Berk, Richard A. *Collective Behavior.* Dubuque, Iowa: Brown, 1974.

Berle, Adolf, Jr., and Gardiner C. Means. *The Modern Corporation and Private Property.* New York: Harcourt, Brace and World, 1932. As cited in Useem 1980:44.

Bernard, Jessie. "The Good-Provider Role." In *Marriage and Family in a Changing Society,* 4th ed., James M. Henslin, ed. New York: Free Press, 1992:275–285.

Bernard, Viola W., Perry Ottenberg, and Fritz Redl. "Dehumanization: A Composite Psychological Defense in Relation to Modern War." In *The Triple Revolution Emerging: Social Problems in Depth,* Robert Perucci and Marc Pilisuk, eds. Boston: Little, Brown, 1971:17–34.

Bernstein, Elizabeth. "More Prayer, Less Hassle." *Wall Street Journal,* June 27, 2003:W3, W4.

Bernstein, Nina., "Taking the War Out of a Child Soldier." *New York Times,* May 13, 2007.

Bernstein, Robert, and Mike Bergman. "Hispanic Population Reaches All-Time High of 38.8 Million, New Census Bureau Estimates Show." *U.S. Department of Commerce News,* June 18, 2003.

Bertrand, Marianne, and Sendhil Mullainathan. "Are Emily and Brendan More Employable than Lakish and Jamal? A Field Experiment on Labor Market Discrimination." Unpublished paper, November 18, 2002.

Best, Joel. *Flavor of the Month: Why Smart People Fall for Fads.* Berkeley: University of California Press, 2006.

Bhagwati, Jagdish. "Made in China." *New York Times,* February 18, 2007.

Bialik, Carl. "The Numbers Guy.' Ambitious Homeless Count Fills a Void, But Has Limitations." *Wall Street Journal,* March 3, 2006.

Bianchi, Suzanne M., and Lynne M. Casper. "American Families." *Population Bulletin, 55,* 4, December 2000:1–42.

Bianchi, Suzanne M., John P. Robinson, and Melissa A. Milkie. *Changing Rhythms of American Family Life.* New York: Russell Sage Foundation, 2006.

Binyon, Michael. "The Graveyard of Invading Armies." *The Times,* September 14, 2001.

Bird, Chloe E., and Patricia P. Rieker. "Gender Matters: An Integrated Model for Understanding Men's and Women's Health." *Social Science and Medicine, 48,* 6, March 1999:745–755.

Bishop, Jerry E. "Study Finds Doctors Tend to Postpone Heart Surgery for Women, Raising Risk." *Wall Street Journal,* April 16, 1990:B4.

Bjerklie, David, Andrea Dorfman, Wendy Cole, Jeanne DeQuine, Helen Gibson, David S. Jackson, Leora Moldofsky, Timothy Roche, Chris Taylor, Cathy Booth Thomas, and Dick Thompson. "Baby, It's You: And You, and You . . . " *Time,* February 19, 2001:47–57.

Blankstein, Andrew, and Richard Winton. "Paraplegic Allegedly 'Dumped' on Skid Row." *Los Angeles Times,* February 9, 2007.

Blassi, Joseph, and Michael Conte. "Employee Stock Ownership and Corporate Performance Among Public Companies." *Industrial and Labor Relations Review, 50,* 1, October 1996:60–79.

Blau, David M. "The Production of Quality in Child-Care Centers: Another Look." *Applied Developmental Science, 4,* 3, 2000:136–148.

Blau, Peter M., and Otis Dudley Duncan. *The American Occupational Structure.* New York: John Wiley, 1967.

Blauner, Robert. "Death and Social Structure." *Psychiatry, 29,* 1966:378–394.

Blee, Kathleen M. "Inside Organized Racism." In *Life in Society: Readings to Accompany Sociology A Down-to-Earth Approach, Seventh Edition,* James M. Henslin, ed. Boston: Allyn and Bacon, 2005:46–57.

Blomfield, Adrian. "Putin Vows to Aim Nukes at Europe." *London Daily Telegraph,* June 4, 2007.

Blumer, Herbert George. "Collective Behavior." In *Principles of Sociology,* Robert E. Park, ed. New York: Barnes and Noble, 1939: 219–288.

Blumer, Herbert George. *Industrialization as an Agent of Social Change: A Critical Analysis,* David R. Maines and Thomas J. Morrione, eds. Hawthorne, N. Y.: Aldine de Gruyter, 1990.

Blumstein, Alfred, and Joel Wallman. "The Crime Drop and Beyond." *Annual Review of Law and Social Science, 2,* December 2006:125–146.

Blumstein, Philip, and Pepper Schwartz. *American Couples: Money, Work, Sex.* New York: Pocket Books, 1985.

Bond, Rod. "Group Size and Conformity." *Group Processes and Intergroup Relations, 8,* 4, 2005:331–354.

Bonow, Robert O., and Robert H. Eckel. "Diet, Obesity, and Cardiovascular Risk." *New England Journal of Medicine, 348,* 17, May 22, 2003:2057–2058.

Booth, Alan, and James M. Dabbs, Jr. "Testosterone and Men's Marriages." *Social Forces, 72,* 2, December 1993:463–477.

Booth, Alan, David R. Johnson, and Douglas A. Granger. "Testosterone, Marital Quality, and Role Overload." Paper presented at the 2004 meetings of the American Sociological Association.

Borjas, George J. "Making It in America: Social Mobility in the Immigrant Population." *National Bureau of Economic Research Working Paper* 12088, March 2006.

Borjas, George J. "The Labor Market Impact of High-Skill Immigration." *National Bureau of Economic Research Working Paper* 11217, March 2005.

Borjas, George J. "Increasing the Supply of Labor Through Immigration: Measuring the Impact on Native-born Workers." *Backgrounder,* May 2004:1–11.

Bosman, Ciska M., et al. "Business Success and Businesses' Beauty Capital." National Bureau of Economic Research Working Paper: 6083, July 1997.

Bosman, Julie. "New York Schools for Pregnant Girls Will Close." *New York Times,* May 24, 2007.

"The Boss's Pay." *Wall Street Journal,* April 7, 2007.

Boulding, Elise. *The Underside of History.* Boulder, Colo.: Westview Press, 1976.

Bower, Amanda. "The Semiprivate Checkup." *Time,* November 10, 2003.

Bowles, Samuel. "Unequal Education and the Reproduction of the Social Division of Labor." In *Power and Ideology in Education,* J. Karabel and A. H. Halsely, eds. NY: Oxford University Press, 1977.

Bowles, Samuel, and Herbert Gintis. "*Schooling in Capitalist America* Revisited." *Sociology of Education, 75,* 2002:1–18.

Bowles, Samuel, and Herbert Gintis. *Schooling in Capitalist America.* New York: Basic Books, 1976.

Boxer, Sarah. "When Emotion Worms Its Way Into Law." *New York Times,* April 7, 2001.

Boyle, Elizabeth Heger, Fortunata Songora, and Gail Foss. "International Discourse and Local Politics: Anti-Female-Genital-Cutting Laws in Egypt, Tanzania, and the United States," *Social Problems, 48,* 4, November 2001:524–544.

Bradford, Phillips Verner, and Harvey Blume. *Ota Benga: The Pygmy in the Zoo.* New York: Delta, 1992.

Bradsher, Keith. "As Asia Keeps Cool, Scientists Worry About the Ozone Layer." *New York Times,* February 23, 2007.

Bradsher, Keith. "China Enacting a High-Tech Plan to Track People." *New York Times,* August 12, 2007b.

Brajuha, Mario, and Lyle Hallowell. "Legal Intrusion and the Politics of Fieldwork: The Impact of the Brajuha Case." *Urban Life, 14,* 4, January 1986:454–478.

Bramlett, M. D., and W. D. Mosher. "Cohabitation, Marriage, Divorce, and Remarriage in the United States." Hyattsville, Md.: National Center for Health Statistics, Vital Health Statistics, Series 23, Number 22, July 2002.

Brannon, Linda. *Gender: Psychological Perspectives,* 2nd ed. Boston: Allyn and Bacon, 1999.

Brass, Paul R. *The Production of Hindu-Muslim Violence in Contemporary India.* Seattle: University of Washington Press, 2003.

Brauchli, Marcus W. "Wary of Education But Needing Brains, China Faces a Dilemma." *Wall Street Journal,* November 15, 1994:A1, A10.

Bray, Rosemary L. "Rosa Parks: A Legendary Moment, a Lifetime of Activism. *Ms., 6,* 3, November-December 1995:45–47.

"Brazil Arrests U.S. Pilot Over Obscene Gesture." Associated Press, January 15, 2004.

Brecher, Edward M., and the Editors of Consumer Reports. *Licit and Illicit Drugs.* Boston: Little, Brown, 1972.

Bretos, Miguel A. "Hispanics Face Institutional Exclusion." *Miami Herald,* May 22, 1994.

Bridgwater, William, ed. *The Columbia Viking Desk Encyclopedia.* New York: Viking Press, 1953.

Brilliant, Ashleigh E. *Social Effects of the Automobile in Southern Califronia during the 1920s.* Unpublished doctoral disertation University of California at Berkeley, 1964.

Brines, Julie, and Kara Joyner. "The Ties That Bind. Principles of Cohesion in Cohabitation and Marriage." *American Sociological Review, 64,* June 1999:333–355.

Brinkley, Joel. "U.S. Faults 4 Allies Over Forced Labor." *New York Times,* June 4, 2005.

Brinton, Crane. *The Anatomy of Revolution.* New York: Vintage Books, 1965.

Broad, William J. "The Shuttle Explodes." *New York Times,* January 29, 1986, A1, A5.

Broad, William J., and David E. Sanger. "With Eye on Iran, Rivals Also Want Nuclear Power." *New York Times,* April 15, 2007.

Brock, Dan. "Health Care Resource Prioritization and Rationing: Why Is It So Difficult?" Harvard Medical School, 2007.

Brockerhoff, Martin P. "An Urbanizing World." *Population Bulletin, 55,* 3, September 2000:1–44.

Broder, Michael S., David E. Kanouse, Brian S. Mittman, and Steven J. Bernstein. "The Appropriateness of Recommendations for Hysterectomy." *Obstetrics and Gynecology, 95,* 2, February 2000: 199–205.

Bromley, David G. "The Satanic Cult Scare." *Culture and Society,* May–June 1991:55–56.

Bronfenbrenner, Urie. "Principles for the Healthy Growth and Development of Children." In *Marriage and Family in a Changing Society,* 4th ed., James M. Henslin, ed. New York: Free Press, 1992:243–249.

Brooks-Gunn, Jeanne, Greg. J. Duncan, and Lawrence Aber, eds. *Neighborhood Poverty, Volume 1: Context and Consequences for Children.* New York: Russell Sage Foundation, 1997.

Brown, Patricia Leigh. "At New Rentals, the Aim Is to Age with Creativity." *Wall Street Journal,* September 10, 2006.

Browne, Andrew. "In China, Preventive Medicine Pits Doctor Against System." *Wall Street Journal,* January 16, 2007.

Browne, Andrew. "Chinese Doctors Tell Patients to Pay Upfront, or No Treatment." *Wall Street Journal,* December 5, 2005.

Browne, Beverly A. "Gender Stereotypes in Advertising on Children's Television in the 1990s: A Cross-National Analysis." *Journal of Advertising, 27,* 1, Spring 1998:83–96.

Browning, Christopher R. *Ordinary Men: Reserve Police Battalion 101 and the Final Solution in Poland.* New York: HarperPerennial, 1993.

Brunello, Giorgio, and Beatrice D'Hombres. "Does Body Weight Affect Wages? Evidence From Europe." *Economics and Human Biology, 5,* 2007:1–19.

Brunvand, Jan Harold. *Be Afraid, Be Very Afraid: The Book of Scary Urban Legends.* New York: W.W. Norton, 2004.

Brunvand, Jan Harold. *Encyclopedia of Urban Legends.* New York: Norton, 2003.

Brunvand, Jan Harold. *The Choking Doberman and Other "New" Urban Legends.* New York: Norton, 1984.

Brunvand, Jan Harold. *The Vanishing Hitchhiker: American Urban Legends and Their Meanings.* New York: Norton, 1981.

Bryant, Alyssa N. "Community College Students: Recent Findings and Trends." *Community College Review, 29,* 3, 2001:77–93.

Bryant, Chalandra M., Rand D. Conger, and Jennifer M. Meehan. "The Influence of In-Laws on Changes in Marital Success." *Journal of Marriage and the Family, 63, 3,* August 2001:614–626.

Brzezinksi, Matthew. "Where Cash Isn't King: Barter Lines Pockets in Ex-Soviet States." *Wall Street Journal,* May 1, 1997:A14.

Buckley, Frank, and Elizabeth Cohen. "Bush Orders Smallpox Vaccination for Military, Himself." CNN. Com, December 16, 2002.

Budrys, Grace. *Unequal Health: How Inequality Contributes to Health or Illness.* Lanham, Md.: Rowman and Littlefield, 2003.

Bumiller, Elisabeth. "First Comes Marriage—Then, Maybe, Love." In *Marriage and Family in a Changing Society,* 4th ed., James M. Henslin, ed. New York: Free Press, 1992:120–125.

Burawoy, Michael. "The Field of Sociology: Its Power and Its Promise." In *Public Sociology: Fifteen Eminent Sociologists Debate Politics and the Profession in the Twenty-first Century.* Berkeley: University of California Press, 2007:241–258.

Burgess, Ernest W. "The Growth of the City: An Introduction to a Research Project." In *The City,* Robert E. Park et al., eds. Chicago: University of Chicago Press, 1925:47–62.

Burgess, Ernest W., and Harvey J. Locke. *The Family: From Institution to Companionship.* New York: American Book, 1945.

Burnham, Walter Dean. *Democracy in the Making: American Government and Politics.* Englewood Cliffs, N.J.: Prentice Hall, 1983.

Burris, Val. "Interlocking Directorates and Political Cohesion Among Corporate Elites." *American Journal of Sociology, 111,* 1, 2005:249–283.

Burris, Val. "The Myth of Old Money Liberalism: The Politics of the *Forbes* 400 Richest Americans." *Social Problems, 47,* 3, August 2000:360–378.

Bus, David M., Todd K. Shakelford, Lee A. Kirkpatrick, and Randy L. Larsen. "A Half Century of Mate Preferences: The Cultural Evolution of Values." *Journal of Marriage and Family, 63,* May 2001:491–503.

Bush, Diane Mitsch, and Robert G. Simmons. "Socialization Processes Over the Life Course." In *Social Psychology: Sociological Perspectives,* eds. Morris Rosenberger and Ralph H. Turner. New Brunswick, N.J.:Transaction, 1990:133–164.

Butler, Robert N. "Ageism: Another Form of Bigotry." *Gerontologist, 9,* Winter 1980:243–246.

Butler, Robert N. *Why Survive? Being Old in America.* New York: Harper & Row, 1975.

Butterfield, Fox. "Prison Rates Among Blacks Reach a Peak, Report Finds." *New York Times,* April 7, 2003.

Bynum, Bill. "Discarded Diagnoses." *Lancet, 358,* 9294, November 17, 2001:1736.

Cadge, Wendy, and Courtney Bender. "Yoga and Rebirth in America: Asian Religions Are Here to Stay." *Contexts,* Winter 2004:45–51.

Callahan, Daniel. *Setting Limits: Medical Goals in an Aging Society.* New York: Simon & Schuster, 1987.

Calle, Eugenia E., and Rudolf Kaaks. "Overweight, Obesity and Cancer." *Nature Reviews Cancer, 4,* 2004:579–591.

Campbell, Colin. "Do Today's Sociologists Really Appreciate Weber's Essay *The Protestant Ethic and the Spirit of Capitalism?*" *The Sociological Review,* 2006:207–223.

Campbell, Karen E., and Holly J. McCammon. "Elizabeth Blackwell's Heirs: Women as Physicians in the U.S., 1880–1920." Unpublished paper, 2005.

Canavan, Margaret M., Walter J. Meyer, III, and Deborah C. Higgs. "The Female Experience of Sibling Incest." *Journal of Marital and Family Therapy, 18,* 2, 1992:129–142.

Canedy, Dana. "Critics of Graduation Exam Threaten Boycott in Florida." *New York Times,* May 13, 2003.

Cannon, Lou. *Official Negligence: How Rodney King and the Riots Changed Los Angeles and the LAPD.* New York: Times Books, 1998.

Cantril, Hadley. *The Psychology of Social Movements.* New York: Wiley, 1941.

Caproni, Paula J. "Work/Life Balance: You Can't Get There from Here." *Journal of Applied Behavioral Science, 40,* 2, June 2004:208–218.

Carey, Benedict. "In the Hospital, a Degrading Shift From Person to Patient." *New York Times,* August 16, 2005.

Carlson, Bonnie E., Katherine Maciol, and Joanne Schneider. "Sibling Incest: Reports from Forty-One Survivors." *Journal of Child Sexual Abuse, 15,* 4, 2006:19–34.

Carlson, Lewis H., and George A. Colburn. *In Their Place: White America Defines Her Minorities, 1850–1950.* New York: Wiley, 1972.

Carnevale, Anthony P., and Stephen J. Rose. "Socioeconomic Status, Race/Ethnicity, and Selective College Admissions." New York: The Century Foundation, March 2003.

Carpenito, Lynda Juall. "The Myths of Acquaintance Rape." *Nursing Forum, 34,* 4, October-December 1999:3.

Carpenter, Betsy. "Redwood Radicals." *U.S. News & World Report, 109,* 11, September 17, 1990:50–51.

Carper, James C. "Pluralism to Establishment to Dissent: The Religious and Educational Context of Home Schooling." *Peabody Journal of Education, 75,* 1–2, 2000:8–19.

Carr, Deborah. "Gender, Preloss Marital Dependence, and Older Adults' Adjustment to Widowhood." *Journal of Marriage and Family, 66,* February 2004:220–235.

Carr, Deborah, Carol D. Ryff, Burton Singer, and William J. Magee. "Bringing the 'Life' Back into Life Course Research: A 'Person-Centered' Approach to Studying the Life Course." Paper presented at the 1995 meetings of the American Sociological Association.

Carrington, Tim. "Developed Nations Want Poor Countries to Succeed on Trade, But Not Too Much." *Wall Street Journal,* September 20, 1993:A10.

Cartwright, Dorwin, and Alvin Zander, eds. *Group Dynamics,* 3rd ed. Evanston, Ill.: Peterson, 1968.

Case, Anne, and Christina Paxson. "Stature and Status: Height, Ability, and Labor Market Outcomes." Working Paper, August 2006.

Casper, Lynne M., and Loretta E. Bass. "Voting and Registration in the Election of November 1996." *Current Population Reports,* July 1998.

Casper, Monica J., ed. *Synthetic Planet: Chemical Politics and the Hazards of Modern Life.* New York: Taylor and Francis, 2003.

Casper, Monica J. *The Making of the Unborn Patient: A Social Anatomy of Fetal Surgery.* New Brunswick, N.J.: Rutgers University Press, 1998.

Caspi, Avshalom, HonaLee Harrington, Terrie E. Moffitt, Barry J. Milne, and Richie Poulton. "Socially Isolated Children 20 Years Later: The Risk of Cardiovascular Disease." *Archives of Pediatric Adolescent Medicine, 160,* August 2006:805–811.

Cassel, Russell N. "Examining the Basic Principles for Effective Leadership." *College Student Journal, 33,* 2, June 1999:288–301.

Castanzo, Emanuele, and Roger Giner-Sorolla. "Not Quite Human: Infrahumanization in Response to Collective Responsibility for Intergroup Killing." *Journal of Personality and Social Psychology, 90,* 15, 2006:804–818.

Cauce, Ana Mari, and Melanie Domenech-Rodriguez. "Latino Families: Myths and Realities." In *Latino Children and Families in the United States: Current Research and Future Directions,* Josefina M. Contreras,

Kathryn A. Kerns, and Angela M. Neal-Barnett, eds. Westport, Conn.: Praeger, 2002:3–25.

Cauthen, Nancy K., and James M. Jasper. "Culture, Politics, and Moral Panics." *Sociological Forum, 9,* 3, September 1994: 495–503.

Cava, Marco R. della. "Working Out of a 'Third Place.'" *USA Today,* October 5, 2006.

Center for American Women and Politics. "Women in Elective Office 2007." April 2007.

Centers for Disease Control and Prevention. "A Glance at the HIV/AIDS Epidemic." January 2007a.

Centers for Disease Control and Prevention. "Native American Suicides per 100,000, Ages 0–19, IHS Areas, 1989–1998." June 13, 2007b.

Centers for Disease Control and Prevention. "WISQARS Injury Mortality Reports, 1999–2004." Atlanta, GA: National Center for Injury Prevention and Control, 2006a.

Centers for Disease Control and Prevention. *HIV/AIDS Surveillance Report, 2005, 17,* 2006b.

Centers for Disease Control. "Fact Sheet: CDC Efforts to Reduce or Prevent Obesity." April 19, 2005d.

Centers for Disease Control. 2001 Surveillance Report. Divisions of HIV/AIDS Prevention, 2003.

Centers for Disease Control. *HIV/AIDS Surveillance Report,* 1997.

Cerulo, Karen A., and Janet M. Ruane. "Death Comes Alive: Technology and the Re-Conception of Death." In *Science as Culture,* 1996.

Chaddock, Gail Russell. "Math + Test = Trouble for U.S. Economy." *Christian Science Monitor,* December 7, 2004.

Chafetz, Janet Saltzman. *Gender Equity: An Integrated Theory of Stability and Change.* Newbury Park, Calif.: Sage, 1990.

Chafetz, Janet Saltzman. *Masculine/Feminine or Human? An Overview of the Sociology of Sex Roles.* Itasca, Ill: F. E. Peacock, 1974.

Chafetz, Janet Saltzman, and Anthony Gary Dworkin. *Female Revolt: Women's Movements in World and Historical Perspective.* Totowa, N.J.: Rowman & Allanheld, 1986.

Chagnon, Napoleon A. *Yanomamo: The Fierce People,* 2nd ed. New York: Holt, Rinehart and Winston, 1977.

Chaker, Anne Marie. "For Antidepressant Makers, Shopaholics Are New Market." *Wall Street Journal,* January 2, 2003a.

Chaker, Anne Marie. "A Backdoor Route to a College Dream." *Wall Street Journal,* June 26, 2003b.

Chaker, Anne Marie, and Hilary Stout. "After Years off, Women Struggle to Revive Careers." *Wall Street Journal,* May 6, 2004.

Chalfant, H. Paul. "Stepping to Redemption: Twelve-Step Groups as Implicit Religion." *Free Inquiry in Creative Sociology, 20,* 2, November 1992:115–120.

Chalkley, Kate. "Female Genital Mutilation: New Laws, Programs Try to End Practice." *Population Today, 25,* 10, October 1997:4–5.

Chambliss, Daniel F. "The World of the Hospital." In *Down to Earth Sociology: Introductory Readings,* 12th ed., James M. Henslin, ed. New York: The Free Press, 2003:434–446.

Chambliss, William J. "The Saints and the Roughnecks." In *Down to Earth Sociology: Introductory Readings,* 14th ed., James M. Henslin, ed. New York: The Free Press, 2007. First published in 1973.

Chambliss, William J. *Power, Politics, and Crime.* Boulder: Westview Press, 2000.

Chandler, Tertius, and Gerald Fox. *3000 Years of Urban Growth.* New York: Academic Press, 1974.

Chandra, Vibha P. "Fragmented Identities: The Social Construction of Ethnicity, 1885–1947." Unpublished paper, 1993a.

Chandra, Vibha P. "The Present Moment of the Past: The Metamorphosis." Unpublished paper, 1993b.

Chase, Marilyn. "Scientists Extend Life Span of Worms by Altering Genes." *Wall Street Journal,* October 24, 2003.

Chazman, Guy. "Murdered Regulator in Russia Made Plenty of Enemies." *Wall Street Journal,* September 22, 2006.

Chen, Edwin. "Twins Reared Apart: A Living Lab." *New York Times Magazine.* December 9, 1979:112.

Chen, Kathy. "China's Growth Places Strains on a Family's Ties." *Wall Street Journal,* April 13, 2005.

Cherlin, J. Andrew. "Remarriage as an Incomplete Institution." In *Marriage and Family in a Changing Society,* 3rd ed., James M. Henslin, ed. New York: Free Press, 1989:492–501.

Cherrier, Helene, and Jeff. B. Murray. "The Sociology of Consumption: The Hidden Facet of Marketing." *Journal of Marketing Management, 20,* 2004:509–525.

"Child Support for Custodial Mothers and Fathers." *Current Population Reports,* Series P60–187. Washington, D.C.: U.S. Bureau of the Census, 1995.

Chin, Nancy P., Alicia Monroe, and Kevin Fiscella. "Social Determinants of (Un)Healthy Behaviors." *Education for Health: Change in Learning and Practice, 13,* 3, November 2000:317–328.

Chivers, C. J. "Putin Urges Plan to Reverse Slide in the Birth Rate." *New York Times,* May 10, 2006.

Chivers, C. J. "Officer Resigns Before Hearing in D. W. I. Case." *New York Times,* August 29, 2001.

Chodorow, Nancy J. "What Is the Relation Between Psychoanalytic Feminism and the Psychoanalytic Psychology of Women?" In *Theoretical Perspectives on Sexual Difference,* Deborah L. Rhode, ed. New Haven, Conn.: Yale University Press, 1990:114–130.

Chung, He Len, and Laurence Steinberg. "Relations Between Neighborhood Factors, Parenting Behaviors, Peer Deviance, and Delinquency Among Serious Juvenile Offenders." *Developmental Psychology, 42,* 2, 2006:319–331.

Churchill, Ward. *A Little Matter of Genocide: Holocaust and Denial in the Americas, 1492 to the Present.* San Francisco: City Lights Books, 1997.

CIA World Factbook. Washington, D.C.: U.S. Government Printing Office, published annually.

Clair, Jeffrey Michael., David A. Karp, and William C. Yoels. *Experiencing the Life Cycle: A Social Psychology of Aging,* 2nd ed. Springfield, Ill.: Thomas, 1993.

Clark, Candace. *Misery and Company: Sympathy in Everyday Life.* Chicago: University of Chicago Press, 1997.

Clarke, Lee. "Panic: Myth or Reality?" *Contexts,* Fall 2002:21–26.

Clawson, Dan, Robert Zussman, Joya Misra, Naomi Gerstel, Randall Stokes, Douglas L. Andereton, and Michael Burawoy, eds. *Public Sociology: Fifteen Eminent Sociologists Debate Politics and the Profession in the Twenty-first Century.* Berkeley: University of California Press, 2007.

Clay, Jason W. "What's a Nation?" *Mother Jones,* November- December 1990:28, 30.

Cleeland, Nancy. "Slowdown's Silent Victims." *Los Angeles Times,* October 21, 2001.

Cloud, John. "For Better or Worse." *Time,* October 26, 1998:43–44.

Cloward, Richard A., and Lloyd E. Ohlin. *Delinquency and Opportunity: A Theory of Delinquent Gangs.* New York: Free Press, 1960.

Cockerham, William C. "Health Lifestyles and the Absence of the Russian Middle Class." *Sociology of Health and Illness, 29,* 3, 2007:457–473.

Cohen, Patricia. "Forget Lonely. Life Is Healthy at the Top." *New York Times,* May 15, 2004.

Cohen, Roger. "Europe's Shifting Role Poses Challenge to U.S." *New York Times,* February 11, 2001.

"Coke Adds Life, But It Cannot Always Explain It." *Lancet, 354,* 9174, July 17, 1999:173.

Colapinto, John. *As Nature Made Him: The Boy Who Was Raised as a Girl.* New York: HarperCollins, 2001.

Cole, Elizabeth R., and Safiya R. Omari. "Race, Class and the Dilemmas of Upward Mobility for African Americans." *Journal of Social Issues, 59,* 4, 2003:785–802.

Coleman, James S., and Thomas Hoffer. *Public and Private Schools: The Impact of Communities.* New York: Basic Books, 1987.

Coleman, James William. "Politics and the Abuse of Power." In *Down to Earth Sociology: Introductory Readings,* 8th ed., James M. Henslin, ed. New York: Free Press, 1995:442–450.

Coleman, Marilyn, Lawrence Ganong, and Mark Fine. "Reinvestigating Remarriage: Another Decade of Progress." *Journal of Marriage and the Family, 62,* 4, November 2000:1288–1307.

Collins, Randall. "Socially Unrecognized Cumulation." *American Sociologist, 30,* 2, Summer 1999:41–61.

Collins, Randall. *Theoretical Sociology.* San Diego, Calif.: Harcourt, Brace Jovanovich, 1988.

Collins, Randall. *The Credential Society: An Historical Sociology of Education.* New York: Academic Press, 1979.

Collins, Randall, Janet Saltzman Chafetz, Rae Lesser Blumberg, Scott Coltrane, and Jonathan H. Turner. "Toward an Integrated Theory of Gender Stratification." *Sociological Perspectives, 36,* 3, 1993:185–216.

Collymore, Yvette. "Conveying Concerns: Women Report on Gender-Based Violence." Washington, D.C.: Population Reference Bureau, 2000.

Conahan, Frank C. "Human Experimentation: An Overview on Cold War Era Programs." Washington, D.C.: U.S. General Accounting Office, September 28, 1994:1–11.

Conklin, John E. *Why Crime Rates Fell.* Boston: Allyn and Bacon, 2003.

Connors, L. "Gender of Infant Differences in Attachment: Associations with Temperament and Caregiving Experiences." Paper presented at the Annual Conference of the British Psychological Society, Oxford, England, 1996.

Conrad, Peter. "Public Eyes and Private Genes: Historical Frames, New Constructions, and Social Problems." *Social Problems, 44,* 2, May 1997:139–154.

Contreras, Josefina M., Kathryn A. Kerns, and Angela M. Neal-Barnett, eds. *Latino Children and Families in the United States: Current Research and Future Directions.* Westport, Conn.: Praeger, 2002.

Cook, Bradley J. "Islam and Egyptian Higher Education: Student Attitudes." *Comparative Education Review, 45,* 3, August 2001:379–403.

Cookson, Peter W., Jr., and Caroline Hodges Persell. "Preparing for Power: Cultural Capital and Elite Boarding Schools." In *Life in Society: Readings to Accompany Sociology A Down-to-Earth Approach, Seventh Edition,* James M. Henslin, ed. Boston: Allyn and Bacon, 2005:175–185.

Cooley, Charles Horton. *Social Organization.* New York: Schocken Books, 1962. First published by Scribner's, 1909.

Cooley, Charles Horton. *Human Nature and the Social Order.* New York: Scribner's, 1902.

Coontz, Stephanie. *The Way We Never Were: American Families and the Nostalgia Trap.* New York: Basic Books, 2000.

Cooper, Helene. "Offering Aerobics, Karate, Aquatics, Hospitals Stress Business of 'Wellness.'" *Wall Street Journal,* August 9, 1993:B1, B3.

Copeland, Libby. "Click Clique: Facebook's Online College Community." *Washington Post,* December 28, 2004.

Corcoran, Mary. "Mobility, Persistence, and Consequences of Poverty for Children: Child and Adult Outcomes." In *Understanding Poverty,* Sheldon H. Danziger and Robert H. Haveman, eds. New York: Russell Sage, 2001:127–161.

Cortese, Anthony. *Provocateur: Images of Women and Minorities in Advertising,* 2nd ed. Boulder, Colo: Rowman and Little Publishers, 2003.

Cose, Ellis. "Black Versus Brown." *Newsweek,* July 3, 2006:44–45.

Cose, Ellis. "What's White Anyway?" *Newsweek,* September 18, 2000:64–65.

Cose, Ellis. "The Good News About Black America." *Newsweek,* June 7, 1999:29–40.

Coser, Lewis A. *Masters of Sociological Thought: Ideas in Historical and Social Context,* 2nd ed. New York: Harcourt Brace Jovanovich, 1977.

Cottin, Lou. *Elders in Rebellion: A Guide to Senior Activism.* Garden City, N. Y.: Anchor Doubleday, 1979.

Coughlan, Sean. "If Your Face Fits." *BBC News Magazine,* June 2006.

Coughlin, Ellen K. "Studying Homelessness: The Difficulty of Tracking a Transient Population." *Chronicle of Higher Education,* October 19, 1988:A6-A12.

"Country Statistics at a Glance." World and News, Fact Monster, online, 2005.

Cousins, Albert N., and Hans Nagpaul. *Urban Man and Society: A Reader in Urban Sociology.* New York: McGraw-Hill, 1970.

Cowell, Alan. "4 Suspects in '94 Massacres of Rwanda Tutsi Are Held in London to Face Extradition." *New York Times,* November 30, 2006.

Cowen, Emory L., Judah Landes, and Donald E. Schaet. "The Effects of Mild Frustration on the Expression of Prejudiced Attitudes." *Journal of Abnormal and Social Psychology.* January 1959:33–38.

Cowgill, Donald. "The Aging of Populations and Societies." *Annals of the American Academy of Political and Social Science, 415,* 1974:1–18.

Cowley, Geoffrey. "Attention: Aging Men." *Newsweek,* November 16, 1996:66–75.

Cowley, Joyce. *Pioneers of Women's Liberation.* New York: Merit, 1969.

Crawford, Duane W., Renate M. Houts, Ted L. Huston, and Laura J. George. "Compatibility, Leisure, and Satisfaction in Marital Relationships." *Journal of Marriage and Family, 64,* May 2002:433–449.

Crosnoe, Robert, and Glen H. Elder, Jr. "Successful Adaptation in the Later Years: A Life Course Approach to Aging. "*Social Psychology Quarterly, 65,* 4, 2002:309–328.

Crossen, Cynthia. "How Pygmy Ota Benga Ended Up in Bronx Zoo as Darwinism Dawned." *Wall Street Journal,* February 6, 2006.

Crossen, Cynthia. "Before Social Security, Most Americans Faced Very Bleak Retirement." *Wall Street Journal,* September 15, 2004a.

Crossen, Cynthia. "Déjà Vu." *New York Times,* February 25, 2004b.

Crossen, Cynthia. "Deja Vu." *Wall Street Journal,* March 5, 2003.

Crossen, Cynthia. "Margin of Error: Studies Galore Support Products and Positions, But Are They Reliable?" *Wall Street Journal,* Nov 14, 1991:A1.

Crossette, Barbara. "Caste May Be India's Moral Achilles' Heel." *New York Times,* October 20, 1996.

Crossland, David. "Gas Dispute Has Europe Trembling." *Spiegel Online,* January 2, 2006.

Cumming, Elaine. "Further Thoughts on the Theory of Disengagement." In *Aging in America: Readings in Social Gerontology,* Cary S. Kart and Barbara B. Manard, eds. Sherman Oaks, Calif.: Alfred Publishing, 1976:19–41.

Cumming, Elaine, and William E. Henry. *Growing Old: The Process of Disengagement.* New York: Basic Books, 1961.

Dabbs, James M., Jr., and Robin Morris. "Testosterone, Social Class, and Antisocial Behavior in a Sample of 4,462 Men." *Psychological Science, 1,* 3, May 1990:209–211.

Dabbs, James M., Jr., Marian F. Hargrove, and Colleen Heusel. "Testosterone Differences Among College Fraternities: Well-Behaved vs. Rambunctious." *Personality and Individual Differences, 20,* 1996: 157–161.

Dabbs, James M., Jr., Timothy S. Carr, Robert L. Frady, and Jasmin K. Riad. "Testosterone, Crime, and Misbehavior Among 692 Male Prison Inmates." *Personality and Individual Differences, 18,* 1995:627–633.

Dahl, Robert A. *Dilemmas of Pluralist Democracy: Autonomy vs. Control.* New Haven, Conn.: Yale University Press, 1982.

Dahl, Robert A. *Who Governs?* New Haven, Conn.: Yale University Press, 1961.

Dao, James. "Instant Millions Can't Halt Winners' Grim Side." *New York Times,* December 5, 2005.

Darley, John M., and Bibb Latané. "Bystander Intervention in Emergencies: Diffusion of Responsibility." *Journal of Personality and Social Psychology, 8,* 4, 1968:377–383.

Darweesh, Suzanne. "Use Your Buying Power to Promote Ethics." *Los Angeles Times,* November 5, 2000.

Darwin, Charles. *The Origin of Species.* Chicago: Conley, 1859.

Dasgupta, Nilanjana, Debbie E. McGhee, Anthony G. Greenwald, and Mahzarin R. Banaji. "Automatic Preference for White Americans: Eliminating the Familiarity Explanation." *Journal of Experimental Social Psychology, 36,* 3, May 2000:316–328.

Davies, W. Martin. "Cognitive Contours: Recent Work on Cross-Cultural Psychology and Its Relevance for Education." *Studies in the Philosophy of Education, 26,* 2007:13–42.

Davis, Ann. "Artificial Reproduction Arrangers Are Ruled Child's Legal Parents." *Wall Street Journal,* March 11, 1998a:B2.

Davis, Ann. "High-Tech Births Spawn Legal Riddles." *Wall Street Journal,* January 26, 1998b:B1.

Davis, Ann, Joseph Pereira, and William M. Bulkeley. "Security Concerns Bring Focus on Translating Body Language." *Wall Street Journal,* August 15, 2002.

Davis, Donald R., and David E. Weinstein. "Technological Superiority and the Losses From Migration." Working Paper. National Bureau of Economic Research. June 2002.

Davis, Gerald F. "American Cronyism: How Executive Networks Inflated the Corporate Bubble." *Contexts, 2,* 3, Summer 2003:34–40.

Davis, Kingsley. "Extreme Isolation." In *Down to Earth Sociology: Introductory Readings,* fourteenth ed., James M. Henslin, ed. New York: The Free Press, 2007.

Davis, Kingsley, and Wilbert E. Moore. "Reply to Tumin." *American Sociological Review, 18,* 1953:394–396.

Davis, Kingsley, and Wilbert E. Moore. "Some Principles of Stratification." *American Sociological Review, 10,* 1945:242–249.

Davis, Kingsley. "Extreme Social Isolation of a Child." *American Journal of Sociology, 45,* 4 Jan. 1940:554–565.

Davis, Nancy J., and Robert V. Robinson. "Class Identification of Men and Women in the 1970s and 1980s." *American Sociological Review, 53,* February 1988:103–112.

Davis, Stan. *Lessons From the Future: Making Sense of a Blurred World.* New York: Capstone Publishers, 2001.

Dawley, Richard Lee. *Amish in Wisconsin.* New Berlin, Wis.: Amish Insight, 2003.

"The Dawn of Artificial Intelligence?: Prize-Winning George." *Strategic Direction, 23,* 2, 2007:34–36.

De May, J. "A Picture History of Kew Gardens, N. Y.—Kitty Genovese." Online. April 15, 2005.

Deaver, Michael V. "Democratizing Russian Higher Education." *Demokratizatsiya, 9,* 3, Summer 2001:350–366.

Deck, Leland P. "Buying Brains by the Inch." *Journal of the College and University Personnel Association, 19,* 1968:33–37.

DeCrow, Karen. Foreword to *Why Men Earn More* by Warren Farrell. New York: AMACOM, 2005:xi-xii.

Deegan, Mary Jo. "W. E. B. Du Bois and the Women of Hull-House, 1895–1899." *American Sociologist,* Winter 1988:301–311.

Deflem, Mathieu, ed. *Sociological Theory and Criminological Research: Views from Europe and the United States.* San Diego: JAI Press, 2006.

DeFrancis, Marc. "U.S. Elder Care Is in a Fragile State." *Population Today, 30,* 1, January 2002:1–3.

Deliege, Robert. *The Untouchables of India.* New York: Berg Publishers, 2001.

DeMartini, Joseph R. "Basic and Applied Sociological Work: Divergence, Convergence, or Peaceful Co-existence?" *The Journal of Applied Behavioral Science, 18,* 2, 1982:203–215.

DeMause, Lloyd. "Our Forebears Made Childhood a Nightmare." *Psychology Today 8,* 11, April 1975:85–88.

De May, J. "A Picture History of Kew Gardens, N.Y.—Kitty Genovese." Online. April 15, 2005.

Demidov, Vadim. "Ten Years of Rolling the Minicircles: RCA Assays in DNA Diagnostics." *Expert Review of Molecular Diagnostics, 5,* 4, July 2005:477–478. <http://www. future-drugs. com/ loi/ erm;jsessionid= o_3C1_i2Jnr-mGoATO>

Denney, Nancy W., and David Quadagno. *Human Sexuality,* 2nd ed. St. Louis: Mosby, 1992.

Denzin, Norman K. "The Suicide Machine." *Society,* July–August, 1992: 7–10.

Denzin, Norman K. *Symbolic Interactionism and Cultural Studies: The Politics of Interpretation.* Cambridge, Mass.: Blackwell 2007.

DeOilos, Ione Y., and Carolyn A. Kapinus. "Aging Childless Individuals and Couples: Suggestions for New Directions in Research." *Sociological Inquiry, 72,* 1, Winter 2002:72–80.

DeParle, Jason. "Report to Clinton Sees Vast Extent of Homelessness." *New York Times,* February 17, 1994:A1, A10.

Derne, Steve. "Arnold Schwarzenegger, Ally McBeal and Arranged Marriages: Globalization on the Ground in India." *Contexts,* Summer 2003:12–18.

Deutscher, Irwin. *Accommodating Diversity: National Policies that Prevent Ethnic Conflict.* Lanham, Md.: Lexington Books, 2002.

Diamond, Edwin, and Robert A. Silverman. *White House to Your House: Media and Politics in Virtual America.* Cambridge, Mass.: MIT Press, 1995.

Diamond, Milton, and Keith Sigmundson. "Sex Reassignment at Birth: Long-term Review and Clinical Implications." *Archives of Pediatric and Adolescent Medicine, 151,* March 1997:298–304.

Dickey, Christopher, and John Barry. "Iran: A Rummy Guide." *Newsweek,* May 8, 2006.

Dietz, Tracy L. "An Examination of Violence and Gender Role Portrayals in Video Games." *Women and Language, 23,* 2, Fall 2000:64–77.

Digest of Education Statistics. Washington, D.C.: National Center for Education Statistics, 2003.

Dillon, Sam. "Public Schools Begin to Offer Classes Online." *New York Times,* August 2, 2005a.

Dillon, Sam. "Students Ace State Tests, But Earn D's From U.S." *New York Times,* November 25, 2005b.

Dillon, Sam. "States Cut Test Standards to Avoid Sanctions." *New York Times,* May 21, 2003.

DiSilvestro, Roger L. *In the Shadow of Wounded Knee: The Untold Final Chapter of the Indian Wars.* New York: Walker & Co., 2006.

Doane, Ashley W., Jr. "Dominant Group Ethnic Identity in the United States: The Role of 'Hidden' Ethnicity in Intergroup Relations." *The Sociological Quarterly, 38,* 3, Summer 1997: 375–397.

Dobash, Russell P., R. Emerson Dobash, Margo Wilson, and Martin Daly. "The Myth of Sexual Symmetry in Marital Violence." *Social Problems, 39,* 1, February 1992:71–91.

Dobash, Russell P., R. Emerson Dobash, Margo Wilson, and Martin Daly. "Marital Violence Is Not Symmetrical: A Response to Campbell." *SSSP Newsletter, 24,* 3, Fall 1993:26–30.

Dobriner, William M. "The Football Team as Social Structure and Social System." In *Social Structures and Systems: A Sociological Overview.* Pacific Palisades, Calif.: Goodyear, 1969a:116–120.

Dobriner, William M. *Social Structures and Systems.* Pacific Palisades, California: Goodyear, 1969b.

Dobyns, Henry F. *Their Numbers Became Thinned: Native American Population Dynamics in Eastern North America.* Knoxville: University of Tennessee Press, 1983.

Dodds, Peter Sheridan, Roby Muhamad, and Duncan J. Watts. "An Experimental Study of Search in Global Social Networks." *Science, 301,* August 8, 2003:827–830.

Dollard, John, et al. *Frustration and Aggression.* New Haven, Conn.: Yale University Press, 1939.

Domhoff, G. William. *Who Rules America? Power, Politics, and Social Change,* 5th ed. New York: McGraw-Hill, 2006.

Domhoff, G. William. "The Bohemian Grove and Other Retreats." In *Down to Earth Sociology: Introductory Readings,* 10th ed., James M. Henslin, ed. New York: Free Press, 1999a:391–403.

Domhoff, G. William. "State and Ruling Class in Corporate America (1974): Reflections, Corrections, and New Directions." *Critical Sociology, 25,* 2–3, July 1999b:260–265.

Domhoff, G. William. *Who Rules America? Power and Politics in the Year 2000,* 3rd ed. Mountain View, Calif: Mayfield Publishing, 1998.

Domhoff, G. William. *The Power Elite and the State: How Policy Is Made in America.* Hawthorne, N. Y.: Aldine de Gruyter, 1990.

Donaldson, Stephen. "A Million Jockers, Punks, and Queens: Sex Among American Male Prisoners and Its Implications for Concepts of Sexual Orientation." February 4, 1993. Online.

Donlon, Margie M., Ori Ash, and Becca R. Levy. "Re-Vision of Older Television Characters: A Stereotype-Awareness Intervention." *Journal of Social Issues, 61,* 2, June 2005.

Douglas, Carol Anne, et al. "Kenya: FGM Increasingly Occurring in Hospitals." *Off Our Backs, 35,* January-February 2005:5.

Douthat, Ross. "The Truth About Harvard." *Atlantic Monthly,* March 2005.

Dove, Adrian. "Soul Folk 'Chitling' Test or the Dove Counterbalance Intelligence Test." no date. (Mimeo)

Dowd, Maureen. "The Knife Under the Tree." *New York Times,* December 5, 2002.

Drivonikou, G. V., P. Kay, T. Regler, R. B. Ivry, A. L. Gilbert, A. Franklin, and I. R. L. Davies. "Further Evidence That Whorfian Effects are Stronger in the Right Visual Field Than in the Left." *PNAS, 104,* 3, January 16, 2007:1097–1102.

Drucker, Peter F. "There's More Than One Kind of Team." *Wall Street Journal,* February 11, 1992:A16.

Du Bois, W. E. B. *Black Reconstruction in America: An Essay Toward a History of the Part Which Black Folk Played in the Attempt to Reconstruct Democracy in America, 1860–1880.* New York: Atheneum, 1992. First published in 1935.

Du Bois, W. E. B. *The Autobiography of W. E. B. Du Bois: A Soliloquy on Viewing My Life from the Last Decade of Its First Century.* New York: International, 1968.

Du Bois, W. E. B. *The Philadelphia Negro: A Social Study.* New York: Schocken Books, 1967. First published in 1899.

Du Bois, W. E. B. *The Souls of Black Folk: Essays and Sketches.* Chicago: McClurg, 1903.

Ducharme, Lori J., Hannah K. Knudsen, J. Aaron Johnson, and Paul M. Roman. "Work as Haven? Modeling the Work-Related Attitudes of Dual-Earner Parents." Paper presented at the 2004 meetings of the American Sociological Association.

Duff, Christina. "Superrich's Share of After-Tax Income Stopped Rising in Early '90s, Data Show." *Wall Street Journal,* November 22, 1995:A2.

Duffy, Michael. "Can This Machine Be Trusted?" *Time,* October 29, 2006.

Dugger, Celia W. "Abortion in India Is Tipping Scales Sharply Against Girls." *New York Times,* April 22, 2001.

Dugger, Celia W. "Wedding Vows Bind Old World and New." *New York Times,* July 20, 1998.

Duneier, Mitchell. *Sidewalk.* New York: Farrar, Straus and Giroux, 1999.

Dunlap, Riley E., and William R. Catton, Jr. "What Environmental Sociologists Have in Common Whether Concerned with 'Built' or 'Natural' Environments." *Sociological Inquiry, 53,* 2–3, 1983:113–135.

Dunlap, Riley E., and William R. Catton, Jr. "Environmental Sociology." *Annual Review of Sociology, 5,* 1979:243–273.

Durkheim, Emile. *Suicide: A Study in Sociology.* John A. Spaulding and George Simpson, trans. New York: Free Press, 1966. First published in 1897.

Durkheim, Emile. *The Elementary Forms of the Religious Life.* New York: Free Press, 1965. First published in 1912.

Durkheim, Emile. *The Rules of Sociological Method.* Sarah A. Solovay and John H. Mueller, trans. New York: Free Press, 1938, 1958, 1964. First published in 1895.

Durkheim, Emile. *The Division of Labor in Society.* George Simpson, trans. New York: Free Press, 1933. First published in 1893.

Durning, Alan. "Cradles of Life." In *Social Problems 90/91,* LeRoy W. Barnes, ed. Guilford, Conn.: Dushkin, 1990:231–241.

Dush, Claire M. Kamp, Catherine L. Cohan, and Paul R. Amato. "The Relationship Between Cohabitation and Marital Quality and Stability: Change Across Cohorts?" *Journal of Marriage and Family, 65,* 3, August 2003:539–549.

Dye, Jane Lawler. "Fertility of American Women, June 2004." U.S. Bureau of the Census. *Current Population Reports,* December 2005.

Dyer, Gwynne. "Anybody's Son Will Do." In *Down to Earth Sociology: Introductory Readings,* 14th ed., James M. Henslin, ed. New York: The Free Press, 2007.

Easley, Hema. "Indian Families Continue to Have Arranged Marriages." *The Journal News,* June 9, 2003.

Ebner, Johanna. "Fighting International Terrorism with Social Science Knowledge." *Footnotes,* February 2005.

Eckholm, Erik. "Desire for Sons Drives Use of Prenatal Scans in China." *New York Times,* June 21, 2002.

Eder, Donna. "On Becoming Female: Lessons Learned in School." In *Down to Earth Sociology: Introductory Readings,* 14th ed., James M. Henslin, ed. New York: The Free Press, 2007.

Eder, Donna. *School Talk: Gender and Adolescent Culture.* New Brunswick, N.J.: Rutgers University Press, 1995.

Eder, Klaus. "The Rise of Counter-Culture Movements Against Modernity: Nature as a New Field of Class Struggle." *Theory, Culture & Society, 7,* 1990:21–47.

Edgerton, Robert B. *Sick Societies: Challenging the Myth of Primitive Harmony.* New York: Free Press, 1992.

Edgerton, Robert B. *Deviance: A Cross-Cultural Perspective.* Menlo Park, Calif.: Benjamin/Cummings, 1976.

Egan, Timothy. "Many Seek Security in Private Communities." *New York Times,* September 3, 1995:1, 22.

Egan, Timothy, and Adam Liptak. "Fraught Issue, But Narrow Ruling in Oregon Suicide Case." *New York Times,* January 18, 2006.

Ehrenreich, Barbara, and Deidre English. *Witches, Midwives, and Nurses: A History of Women Healers.* Old Westbury, N. Y.: Feminist Press, 1973.

Ehrlich, Paul R., and Anne H. Ehrlich. "Humanity at the Crossroads." *Stanford Magazine,* Spring-Summer 1978:20–23.

Ehrlich, Paul R., and Anne H. Ehrlich. *Population, Resources, and Environment: Issues in Human Ecology,* 2nd ed. San Francisco: Freeman, 1972.

Eibl-Eibesfeldt, Irrenäus. *Ethology: The Biology of Behavior.* New York: Holt, Rinehart, and Winston, 1970.

Eisenhart, R. Wayne. "You Can't Hack It, Little Girl: A Discussion of the Covert Psychological Agenda of Modern Combat Training." *Journal of Social Issues, 31,* Fall 1975:13–23.

Ekman, Paul. *Faces of Man: Universal Expression in a New Guinea Village.* New York: Garland Press, 1980.

Ekman, Paul, Wallace V. Friesen, and John Bear. "The International Language of Gestures." *Psychology Today,* May 1984:64.

Elder, Glen H., Jr. *Children of the Great Depression: Social Change in Life Experience.* Boulder: Westview Press, 1999.

Elder, Glen H., Jr. "Age Differentiation and Life Course." *Annual Review of Sociology, 1,* 1975:165–190.

Elias, Paul. " 'Molecular Pharmers' Hope to Raise Human Proteins in Crop Plants." *St. Louis Post-Dispatch,* October 28, 2001:F7.

Elinson, Elaine. "Lifting the Veil on Government Surveillance." *ACLU News.* Spring 2004.

Elkins, Stanley M. *Slavery: A Problem in American Institutional and Intellectual Life,* 2nd ed. Chicago: University of Chicago Press, 1968.

Elliott, Joel. "Birth Control Allowed at Maine Middle School." *New York Times,* October 18, 2007.

Ellul, Jacques. *The Technological Society.* New York: Knopf, 1965.

Elson, Jean. *Am I Still a Woman? Hysterectomy and Gender Identity.* Philadelphia: Temple University Press, 2004.

England, Paula. "The Impact of Feminist Thought on Sociology." *Contemporary Sociology: A Journal of Reviews,* 2000:263–267.

Epstein, Cynthia Fuchs. "Great Divides: The Cultural, Cognitive, and Social Bases of the Global Subordination of Women." *American Sociological Review, 72,* February 2007:1–22.

Epstein, Cynthia. "Similarity and Difference: The Sociology of Gender Distinction." In *Handbook of the Sociology of Gender,* Janet Saltzman Chafetz, ed.. New York: Kluwer Academic/Plenum Publishers, 1999.

Epstein, Cynthia Fuchs. Letter to the author, January 26, 1989.

Epstein, Cynthia Fuchs. *Deceptive Distinctions: Sex, Gender, and the Social Order.* New Haven, Conn.: Yale University Press, 1988.

Ernst, Eldon G. "The Baptists." In *Encyclopedia of the American Religious Experience: Studies of Traditions and Movements,* Vol. 1, Charles H. Lippy and Peter W. Williams, eds. New York: Scribners, 1988: 555–577.

Escalante, Jaime, and Jack Dirmann. "The Jaime Escalante Math Program." *Journal of Negro Education, 59,* 3, Summer 1990: 407–423.

Eshleman, J. Ross. *The Family,* 9th ed. Boston: Allyn and Bacon, 2000.

Espinosa, Linda M., and James M. Laffey. "Urban Primary Teacher Perceptions of Children with Challenging Behaviors." *Journal of Children and Poverty, 9,* 2, 2003:135–156.

"Ethiopia: Fighting Female Circumcision at Local Level." African News Service, February 16, 2005.

Evans, Peter, and James E. Rauch. "Bureaucracy and Growth: A Cross-National Analysis of the Effects of 'Weberian' State Structures on Economic Growth." *American Sociological Review, 64,* October 1999: 748–765.

Ezekiel, Raphael S. *The Racist Mind: Portraits of American Neo-Nazis and Klansmen.* New York: Viking, 1995.

Fabrikant, Geraldine. "Old Nantucket Warily Meets the New." *New York Times,* June 5, 2005.

Fadiman, Anne. *The Spirit Catches You and You Fall Down.* Farrar, Straus and Giroux, 1997.

Fagot, Beverly I., Richard Hagan, Mary Driver Leinbach, and Sandra Kronsberg. "Differential Reactions to Assertive and Communicative Acts of Toddler Boys and Girls." *Child Development, 56,* 1985: 1499–1505.

Faris, Robert E. L., and Warren Dunham. *Mental Disorders in Urban Areas.* Chicago: University of Chicago Press, 1939.

Farkas, George. *Human Capital or Cultural Capital?: Ethnicity and Poverty Groups in an Urban School District.* New York: Walter DeGruyter, 1996.

Farkas, George, Robert P. Grobe, Daniel Sheehan, and Yuan Shuan. "Cultural Resources and School Success: Gender, Ethnicity, and Poverty Groups Within an Urban School District." *American Sociological Review, 55,* February 1990a:127–142.

Farkas, George, Daniel Sheehan, and Robert P. Grobe. "Coursework Mastery and School Success: Gender, Ethnicity, and Poverty Groups Within an Urban School District." *American Educational Research Journal, 27,* 4, Winter 1990b:807–827.

Farley, John E., and Gregory D. Squires. "Fences and Neighbors: Segregation in twenty first Century America." *Contexts,* Winter 2005:33–39.

Fattah, Hassan M. "After First Steps, Saudi Reformers See Efforts Stall." *New York Times,* April 26, 2007.

Faunce, William A. *Problems of an Industrial Society,* 2nd ed. New York: McGraw-Hill, 1981.

"FBI Director Defends Patriot Act." Associated Press, March 27, 2007.

FBI Uniform Crime Reports. Washington, D.C.: U.S. Government Printing Office, published annually.

Feagin, Joe R. "The Continuing Significance of Race: Antiblack Discrimination in Public Places." In *Majority and Minority: The Dynamics of Race and Ethnicity in American Life,* 6th ed., Norman R. Yetman, ed. Boston: Allyn and Bacon, 1999:384–399.

Feagin, Joe R., and Karyn D. McKinney. *The Many Costs of White Racism.* Lanham, Md.: Rowman and Littlefield, 2003.

Featherman, David L. "Opportunities Are Expanding." *Society, 13,* 1979:4–11.

Featherman, David L., and Robert M. Hauser. *Opportunity and Change.* New York: Academic Press, 1978.

Feder, Barnaby. "Billboards That Know You by Name." *New York Times,* January 29, 2007.

Feder, Barnaby J. "Services at the First Church of Cyberspace." *New York Times,* May 15, 2004.

Feldman, Saul D. "The Presentation of Shortness in Everyday Life— Height and Heightism in American Society: Toward a Sociology of Stature." Paper presented at the 1972 meetings of the American Sociological Association.

Felsenthal, Edward. "Maine Limits Liability for Doctors Who Meet Treatment Guidelines." *Wall Street Journal,* May 3, 1993:A1, A9.

Felsenthal, Edward. "Justices' Ruling Further Defines Sex Harassment." *Wall Street Journal,* March 5, 1998:B1, B2.

Felton, Lee Ann, Andrea Gumm, and David J. Pittenger. "The Recipients of Unwanted Sexual Encounters Among College Students." *College Student Journal, 35,* 1, March 2001:135–143.

Fendrich, James Max, and Kenneth L. Lovoy. "Back to the Future: Adult Political Behavior of Former Student Activists." In *Collective Behavior and Social Movements,* Russell L. Curtis, Jr., and Benigno E. Aguirre, eds. Boston: Allyn and Bacon, 1993:429–434.

Fernandez, Manny. "Study Finds Disparities in Mortgages by Race." *New York Times,* October 15, 2007.

Ferraro, Kathleen J. "Intimate Partner Violence." In *Social Problems,* 7th ed., by James M. Henslin. Upper Saddle River, N. J.: Prentice Hall, 2006:373.

Ferraro, Susan. "Future Fighters: How Military Technology is Advancing Medical Science." *Daily News,* July 11, 2001.

Feshbach, Murray. "Russia's Farms, Too Poisoned for the Plow." *Wall Street Journal,* May 14, 1992:A14.

Fessenden, Ford. "Subprime Mortgages Concentrated in City's Minority Neighborhoods." *New York Times,* October 15, 2007.

Fialka, John J. "A Dirty Discovery Over Indian Ocean Sets Off a Fight." *Wall Street Journal*, May 6, 2003:A1, A6.

Fields, Jason. "America's Families and Living Arrangements: 2003." *Current Population Reports*, November 2004.

Fine, Gary Alan, and Patricia A. Turner. *Whispers on the Color Line: Rumor and Race in America*. Berkeley: University of California Press, 2001.

Finer, Jonathan. "Faculty Group Rebukes Harvard President With Vote." *Washington Post*, March 16, 2005.

Finke, Roger, and Roger Stark. *The Churching of America, 1776–1990: Winners and Losers in Our Religious Economy*. New Brunswick, N.J.: Rutgers University Press, 1992.

Finkelhor, David, and Kersti Yllo. "Marital Rape: The Myth Versus the Reality." In *Marriage and Family in a Changing Society*, 3rd ed., James M. Henslin, ed. New York: Free Press, 1989:382–391.

Finkelhor, David, and Kersti Yllo. *License to Rape: Sexual Abuse of Wives*. New York: Henry Holt, 1985.

Fischer, Claude S. *The Urban Experience*. New York: Harcourt, 1976.

Fischer, Tamar F. C., Paul M. De Graaf, and Matthijs Kalmijn. "Friendly and Antagonistic Contact Between Former Spouses After Divorce." *Journal of Family Issues, 26*, 8, November 2005:1131–1163.

Fish, Jefferson M. "Mixed Blood." *Psychology Today, 28*, 6, November-December 1995:55–58, 60, 61, 76, 80.

Fisher, Ian. "Italian Premier Resigns After Losing Foreign Policy Vote." *New York Times*, February 22, 2007.

Fisher, Marla Jo. "California College Grapples with Title IX Compliance." *Community College Week, 14*, 20, May 13, 2002:18.

Fisher, Sue. *In the Patient's Best Interest: Women and the Politics of Medical Decisions*. New Brunswick, N.J.: Rutgers University Press, 1986.

Flanagan, William G. *Urban Sociology: Images and Structure*. Boston: Allyn and Bacon, 1990.

Flavel, John H., et al. *The Development of Role-Taking and Communication Skills in Children*. New York: Wiley, 1968.

Flavel, John, Patricia H. Miller, and Scott A. Miller. *Cognitive Development*, 4th ed. Upper Saddle River, N.J.: Prentice Hall, 2002.

Fletcher, June. "Address Envy: Fudging to Get the Best." *Wall Street Journal*, April 25, 1997:B10.

Fletcher, Martin. "Jolie Takes Up Plight of World's Refugees." *The Times*, August 28, 2001.

Flexner, Abraham. *Medical Education in the United States and Canada: A Report to the Carnegie Foundation for the Advancement of Teaching*. Bulletin No. 4. Boston: Merrymount Press, 1910.

Flexner, E. *Century of Struggle*. Cambridge, Mass.: Belknap, 1971. In Claire M. Renzetti and Daniel J. Curran, *Women, Men, and Society*, 4th ed. Boston: Allyn and Bacon, 1999.

Flink, James J., *The Automobile Age*. Cambridge, Mass.: MIT Press, 1990.

Flippen, Annette R. "Understanding Groupthink From a Self-Regulatory Perspective." *Small Group Research, 30*, 2, April 1999:139–165.

Foley, Douglas E. "The Great American Football Ritual." In *Society: Readings to Accompany Sociology: A Down-to-Earth Approach, Core Concepts*, James M. Henslin, ed. Boston: Allyn and Bacon, 2006: 64–76. First published in 1990.

Food and Agriculture Organization of the United Nations. "World and Regional Review: Facts and Figures." 2006.

Foote, Donna. "And Baby Makes One." *Newsweek*, February 2, 1998: 68–69.

Foote, Jennifer. "Trying to Take Back the Planet." *Newsweek, 115*, 6, February 5, 1990:24–25.

Forelle, Charles. "Ivy League Schools Begin to Offer Online Courses." *Wall Street Journal*, January 15, 2003.

Form, William. "Comparative Industrial Sociology and the Convergence Hypothesis." In *Annual Review of Sociology, 5*, 1, 1979, Alex Inkeles, James Coleman, and Ralph H. Turner, eds.

Foster, Andrea L. "Oxford, Stanford, and Yale End Venture to Provide Noncredit Online Courses." *Chronicle of Higher Education*, March 31, 2006.

Fountain, Henry. "Archaeological Site in Peru Is Called Oldest City in Americas." *New York Times*, April 27, 2001.

Fowler, Geoffrey A., and Amy Chozick. "Cartoon Characters Get Big Makeover for Overseas Fans." *Wall Street Journal*, October 16, 2007.

Fox, Elaine, and George E. Arquitt. "The VFW and the 'Iron Law of Oligarchy.' " In *Down to Earth Sociology*, 4th ed., James M. Henslin, ed. New York: Free Press, 1985:147–155.

Fox, Nicols. *Against the Machine: The Hidden Luddite Tradition in Literature, Art, and Individual Lives*. Washington: Island Press, 2004.

Franklin, John Hope, and John Whittington Franklin. *My Life and an Era: The Autobiography of Buck Colbert Franklin*. Baton Rouge: Louisiana State University, 1997.

Fraser, Graham. "Fox Denies Free Trade Exploiting the Poor in Mexico." *Toronto Star*, April 20, 2001.

Freedman, Jane. *Feminism*. Philadelphia: Open University Press, 2001.

Freidson, Eliot. *Professionalism: The Third Logic*. Chicago: University of Chicago Press, 2001.

Fremson, Ruth. "Dead Bachelors in Remote China Still Find Wives." *New York Times*, October 5, 2006.

French, Howard W. "Chinese Censors and Web Users Match Wits." *New York Times*, March 4, 2005.

French, Howard W. "As Girls 'Vanish,' Chinese City Battles Tide of Abortions." *New York Times*, April 14, 2004.

Freund, Charles Paul. "A Riot of Our Own." *Reason, 32*, 10, March 2001:10.

Frey, William H. "Migration to the South Brings U.S. Blacks Full Circle." *Population Today, 29*, 4, May-June 2001:1, 2.

Friedl, Ernestine. "Society and Sex Roles." In *Conformity and Conflict: Readings in Cultural Anthropology*, James P. Spradley and David W. McCurdy, eds. Glenview, Ill.: Scott, Foresman, 1990: 229–238.

Friedman, Thomas. *The World Is Flat: A Brief History of the Twenty-First Century*. New York: Farrar, Straus, and Giroux, 2005.

Fritz, Jan M. "The History of Clinical Sociology." *Sociological Practice, 7*, 1989:72–95.

Frumkin, Robert M. "Early English and American Sex Customs." In *Encyclopedia of Sexual Behavior*, Vol. 1. New York: Hawthorne Books, 1967.

Fuhrmans, Vanessa, and Carol Hymowitz. "WellPoint's CEO Takes the Reins, Facing Challenges." *Wall Street Journal*, June 6, 2007.

Fuller, Rex, and Richard Schoenberger. "The Gender Salary Gap: Do Academic Achievement, Internship Experience, and College Major Make a Difference?" *Social Science Quarterly, 72*, 4, December 1991:715–726.

Furstenberg, Frank F., Jr., and Kathleen Mullan Harris. "The Disappearing American Father? Divorce and the Waning Significance of Biological Fatherhood." In *The Changing American Family: Sociological and Demographic Perspectives*, Scott J. South and Stewart E. Tolnay, eds. Boulder, Colo.: Westview Press, 1992: 197–223.

Furstenberg, Frank F., Jr., Sheela Kennedy, Vonnie C. McLoyd, Ruben G. Rumbaut, and Richard A. Settersten, Jr. "Growing Up Is Harder to Do." *Contexts, 3*, 3, Summer 2004:33–41.

Galbraith, John Kenneth. *The Nature of Mass Poverty*. Cambridge Mass.: Harvard University Press, 1979.

Galliher, John F. *Deviant Behavior and Human Rights*. Englewood Cliffs, N.J.: Prentice Hall, 1991.

Galliher, John F., Wayne Brekus, and David P. Keys. *Laud Humphreys: Prophet of Homosexuality and Sociology*. Madison, Wisconsin: University of Wisconsin Press, 2004.

Gallmeier, Charles P. "Methodological Issues in Qualitative Sport Research: Participant Observation among Hockey Players." *Sociological Spectrum, 8*, 1988:213–235.

Gallup Poll. "Americans More Likely to Believe in God Than the Devil, Heaven More Than Hell." June 13, 2007.

Gallup Poll. "Religion and Social Trends." Princeton, N.J.: The Gallup Organization, 2005.

Gallup, George, Jr. *The Gallup Poll: Public Opinion 1989*. Wilmington, Dela.: Scholarly Resources, 1990.

Gans, Herbert J., "Public Sociologies: Reply to Hausknecht." *Footnotes*, January 2003:8.

Gans, Herbert J. *People, Plans, and Policies: Essays on Poverty, Racism, and Other National Urban Problems*. New York: Columbia University Press, 1991.

Gans, Herbert J. *People and Plans: Essays on Urban Problems and Solutions*. New York: Basic Books, 1968.

Gans, Herbert J. *The Urban Villagers*. New York: Free Press, 1962.

Garfinkel, Harold. *Studies in Ethnomethodology*. Englewood Cliffs, N.J.: Prentice Hall, 1967.

Garfinkel, Harold. "Conditions of Successful Degradation Ceremonies." *American Journal of Sociology, 61*, 2, March 1956: 420–424.

Garfinkel, Harold. *Ethnomethodology's Program: Working Out Durkheim's Aphorism*. Lanham, MD: Rowman & Littlefield, 2002.

Garrett, Michael Tlanusta. "Understanding the 'Medicine' of Native American Traditional Values: An Integrative Review." *Counseling and Values, 43*, 2, January 1999:84–98.

Gates, Eddie Faye. "The Oklahoma Commission to Study the Tulsa Race Riot of 1921." *Harvard Black Letter Law Journal, 20*, 2004:83–89.

Gatewood, Willard B. *Aristocrats of Color: The Black Elite, 1880–1920*. Bloomington, Ind.: Indiana University Press, 1990.

Gauch, Sarah. "In Egyptian Schools, A Push for Critical Thinking." *Christian Science Monitor*, February 9, 2006.

Gaufberg, Slava V. "Russia." E-Medicine, March 11, 2004.

Gautham S. "Coming Next: The Monsoon Divorce." *New Statesman, 131,* 4574, February 18, 2002:32–33.

Geis, Gilbert, Robert F. Meier, and Lawrence M. Salinger. *White-Collar Crime: Classic and Contemporary Views,* 3rd ed. New York: Free Press, 1995.

Genetski, Robert. "Privatize Social Security." *Wall Street Journal,* May 21, 1993.

Gerhard, Jane. "Revisiting 'The Myth of the Vaginal Orgasm': The Female Orgasm in American Sexual Thought and Second Wave Feminism." *Feminist Studies, 26,* 2, Fall 2000:449–477.

Gerson, Kathleen. *Hard Choices: How Women Decide about Work, Career, and Motherhood.* Berkeley: University of California Press, 1985.

Gerth, H. H., and C. Wright Mills. *From Max Weber: Essays in Sociology.* New York: Galaxy, 1958.

Gerth, Jeff. "Two Companies Pay Penalties for Improving China Rockets." *New York Times,* March 3, 2003.

Gewirtz, Sharon, and Alan Cribb. "What to Do About Values in Social Research: The Case for Ethical Reflexivity in the Sociology of Education." *British Journal of Sociology of Education, 27,* 2, April 2006:141–155.

Gibson, Margaret A., and Anne Rios Rojas. "Globalization, Immigration, and the Education of 'New' Immigrants in the 21st Century." *Current Issues in Education, 9,* 1, 2006:69–76.

Giele, Janet Zollinger. *Women and the Future: Changing Sex Roles in Modern America.* New York: Free Press, 1978.

Gilbert, Dennis L. *The American Class Structure in an Age of Growing Inequality,* 6th ed. Belmont, Calif.: Wadsworth Publishing, 2003.

Gilbert, Dennis, and Joseph A. Kahl. *The American Class Structure: A New Synthesis.* 4th ed. Belmont, Calif.: Wadsworth Publishing, 1998.

Gilligan, Carol. *The Birth of Pleasure.* New York: Knopf, 2002.

Gilligan, Carol. *Making Connections: The Relational World of Adolescent Girls at Emma Willard School.* Cambridge, Mass.: Harvard University Press, 1990.

Gilligan, Carol. *In a Different Voice: Psychological Theory and Women's Development.* Cambridge, Mass.: Harvard University Press, 1982.

Gillum, R. F. "Frequency of Attendance at Religious Services and Smoking: The Third National Health and Nutrition Examination Survey." *Preventive Medicine, 41,* 2005:607–613.

Gilman, Charlotte Perkins. *The Man-Made World or, Our Androcentric Culture.* New York: 1971. First published 1911.

Girshick, Lori B. *Woman-To-Woman Sexual Violence: Does She Call It Rape?* Boston: Northeastern University Press, 2002.

Gitlin, Todd. *The Twilight of Common Dreams: Why America Is Wracked by Culture Wars.* New York: Metropolitan Books, 1997.

Glascock, Jack. "Gender Roles on Prime-Time Network Television: Demographics and Behaviors." *Journal of Broadcasting and Electronic Media, 45,* Fall 2001:656–669.

Gleason, Carmen L. "Officials Emphasize Zero Tolerance of Sexual Assault." Army News Service, April 5, 2007.

Glenn, Evelyn Nakano. "Chinese American Families." In *Minority Families in the United States: A Multicultural Perspective,* Ronald L. Taylor, ed. Englewood Cliffs, N.J.: Prentice Hall, 1994:115–145.

Glenngård, Anna H., Frida Hjalte, Marianne Svensson, Anders Anell, and Valda Bankauskaite. *Health Systems in Transition: Sweden.* Copenhagen: WHO Regional Office for Europe, 2005.

Glick, Paul C., and S. Lin. "More Young Adults Are Living with Their Parents: Who Are They?" *Journal of Marriage and Family, 48,* 1986: 107–112.

"Global 2000." *Forbes,* March 29, 2007.

"Global 1000—Top World Companies." *Business Week.* July 2004.

Goetting, Ann. *Getting Out: Life Stories of Women Who Left Abusive Men.* New York: Columbia University Press, 2001.

Gofen, Anat. "Family Capital: How First-Generation Higher-Education Students Break the Intergenerational Cycle." Institute for Research on Poverty, Discussion Paper 1322–07, 2007.

Goffman, Erving. *Stigma: Notes on the Management of Spoiled Identity.* Englewood Cliffs, N.J.: Prentice Hall, 1963.

Goffman, Erving. *Asylums: Essays on the Social Situation of Mental Patients and Other Inmates.* Chicago: Aldine, 1961.

Gold, Ray. "Janitors Versus Tenants: A Status-Income Dilemma." *American Journal of Sociology, 58,* 1952:486–493.

Goldberg, Carey, and Sophia Kishkovsky. "Russia's Doctors Are Beggars at Work, Paupers at Home." *New York Times,* December 16, 2000.

Goldberg, Steven. *Fads and Fallacies in the Social Sciences.* Amherst, N. Y.: Humanity/Prometheus, 2003.

Goldberg, Steven. *Why Men Rule: A Theory of Male Dominance.* Chicago: Open Court, 1993.

Goldberg, Steven. "Reaffirming the Obvious." *Society,* September–October 1986:4–7.

Goldberg, Steven. *The Inevitability of Patriarchy,* rev. ed. New York: Morrow, 1974.

Goldberg, Susan, and Michael Lewis. "Play Behavior in the Year-Old Infant: Early Sex Differences." *Child Development, 40,* March 1969: 21–31.

Goldberg-Glen, Robin, Roberta G. Sands, Ralph D. Cole, and Carolyn Cristofalo. "Multigenerational Patterns and Internal Structures in Families in Which Grandparents Raise Grandchildren." *Families in Society: The Journal of Contemporary Human Services, 79,* 5, September 1998:477–489.

Goldman, Kevin. "Seniors Get Little Respect on Madison Avenue." *Wall Street Journal,* September 20, 1993:B6.

Goleman, Daniel. "Pollsters Enlist Psychologists in Quest for Unbiased Results." *New York Times,* September 7, 1993:C1, C11.

Gonzales, Alberto R. "Memorandum for Albert R. Gonzales, Counsel to the President: Re: Standards of Conduct for Interrogation Under *18 U.S.C. 2340–2340A.*" August 2, 2002.

Gonzalez, David. "A Sliver of a Storefront, a Faith on the Rise." *New York Times,* January 14, 2007.

Goode, Erica. "Study Says 20% of Girls Reported Abuse by a Date." *New York Times,* August 1, 2001.

Goode, William J. "Encroachment, Charlatanism, and the Emerging Profession: Psychology, Sociology, and Medicine." *American Sociological Review, 25,* 6, December 1960:902–914.

Goozen, Stephanie H. M. van, Graeme Fairchild, Heddeke Snoek, and Gordon T. Harold. "The Evidence for a Neurobiological Model of Childhood Antisocial Behavior." *Psychological Bulletin, 133,* 1, 2007: 149–182.

Gorman, Christine. "The Disease Detective." *Time,* January 6, 1997: 56–65.

Gorman, James. "High-Tech Daydreamers Investing in Immortality." *Wall Street Journal,* November 1, 2003.

Gorman, Peter. "A People at Risk: Vanishing Tribes of South America." *The World & I.* December 1991:678–689.

Gornick, Janet C., and Alexandra Heron. "The Regulation of Working Time as Work-Family Reconciliation Policy: Comparing Europe, Japan, and the United States." *Journal of Comparative Policy Analysis, 8,* 2, June 2006:149–166.

Gottfredson, Michael R., and Travis Hirschi. *A General Theory of Crime.* Stanford, Calif.: Stanford University Press, 1990.

Gottschalk, Peter, Sara McLanahan, and Gary Sandefur, "The Dynamics and Intergenerational Transmission of Poverty and Welfare Participation." In *Confronting Poverty: Prescriptions for Change,* Sheldon H. Danziger, Gary D. Sandefur, and Daniel H. Weinberg, eds. Cambridge, Mass.: Harvard University Press, 1994.

Gracey, Harry L. "Kindergarten as Academic Boot Camp." In *Down to Earth Sociology: Introductory Readings,* fourteenth ed., James M. Henslin, ed. New York: The Free Press, 2007. Also appeared in the 6th edition of this book; 1991: 377–390.

Grant, Peter. "Looking for Love (Or a Date) on Cable TV." *Wall Street Journal,* December 15, 2005.

Gray Panthers. "Age and Youth in Action." No date.

Greeley, Andrew M. "The Protestant Ethic: Time for a Moratorium." *Sociological Analysis, 25,* Spring 1964:20–33.

Greeley, Andrew M., and Michael Hout. "Americans' Increasing Belief in Life After Death: Religious Competition and Acculturation." *American Sociological Review, 64,* December 1999:813–835.

Greene, Jay P., and Marcus A. Winters. "Public High School Graduation and College-Readiness Rates, 1991–2002." Center for Civic Innovation at the Manhattan Institute. *Education Working Paper, 8,* 2005.

Greenhouse, Linda. "Justices Decline Case on 200-Year Sentence for Man Who Possessed Child Pornography." *New York Times,* February 27, 2007.

Greenhouse, Linda. "Justices Uphold Long Prison Terms in Repeat Crimes." *New York Times,* March 6, 2003.

Greenwald, Anthony G., and Linda Hamilton Krieger. "Implicit Bias: Scientific Foundations." *California Law Review,* July 2006.

Greider, William. "Pro Patria, Pro Mundus." *Nation, 273,* 15, November 12, 2001:22–24.

Grimmett, Richard F. "Conventional Arms Transfers to Developing Nations, 1997–2004." Washington, D.C.: Congressional Research Service, August 29, 2005.

Gross, Jan T. *Neighbors.* New Haven: Yale University Press, 2001.

Gross, Jane. "In the Quest for the Perfect Look, More Girls Choose the Scalpel." *New York Times,* November 29, 1998.

Guensburg, Carol. "Bully Factories." *American Journalism Review, 23,* 6, 2001:51–59.

Guessous, Fouad, Thorsten Juchem, and Norbert A. Hampp. In *Optical Security and Counterfeit Deterrence Techniques,* Rudolf L. van Renesse, ed. *Proceedings of the SPIE, 5310,* 2004.

Guice, Jon. "Sociologists Go to Work in High Technology." *Footnotes,* November 1999:8.

"Guilds." *Columbia Encyclopedia,* 6th ed. New York: Columbia University Press, 2005.

Gunther, Marc. "The Mosquito in the Tent." *Fortune, 149,* 11, May 31, 2004:158.

Gupta, Giri Raj. "Love, Arranged Marriage, and the Indian Social Structure." In *Cross-Cultural Perspectives of Mate Selection and Marriage,* George Kurian, ed. Westport, Conn.: Greenwood Press, 1979.

Guru, Gopal, and Shiraz Sidhva. "India's 'Hidden Apartheid.'" *UNESCO Courier,* September 2001:27.

Haas, Jack. "Binging: Educational Control Among High-Steel Iron Workers." *American Behavioral Scientist, 16,* 1972:27–34.

Haas, Jack, and William Shaffir. "The Cloak of Competence." In *Down to Earth Sociology: Introductory Readings,* 7th ed. New York: Free Press, 1993:432–441.

Hacker, Helen Mayer. "Women as a Minority Group." *Social Forces, 30,* October 1951:60–69.

Hafner, Katie. "Welding Kitchen Knives and Honing Office Skills." *New York Times,* January 13, 2007.

Hage, Dave. *Reforming Welfare by Rewarding Work.* Minneapolis: University of Minnesota Press, 2004.

Hall, Edward T. *The Hidden Dimension.* Garden City, N. Y.: Anchor Books, 1969.

Hall, Edward T. *The Silent Language.* New York: Doubleday, 1959.

Hall, Edward T., and Mildred R. Hall. "The Sounds of Silence." In *Down to Earth Sociology: Introductory Readings,* 14th ed., James M. Henslin, ed. New York: The Free Press, 2007.

Hall, G. Stanley. *Adolescence: Its Psychology and Its Relations to Physiology, Anthropology, Sociology, Sex, Crime, Religion, and Education.* New York: Appleton, 1904.

Hall, Richard H. "The Concept of Bureaucracy: An Empirical Assessment." *American Journal of Sociology, 69,* July 1963:32–40.

Hall, Ronald E. "The Tiger Woods Phenomenon: A Note on Biracial Identity." *The Social Science Journal, 38,* 2, April 2001: 333–337.

Hamermesh, Daniel S., and Jeff E. Biddle. "Beauty and the Labor Market." *American Economic Review, 84,* 5, December 1994:1174–1195.

Hamid, Shadi. "Between Orientalism and Postmodernism: The Changing Nature of Western Feminist Thought Towards the Middle East." *HAWWA, 4,* 1, 2006:76–92.

Hamilton, William L. "The New Nursing Home, Emphasis on Home." *New York Times,* April 23, 2005.

Hampson, Rick. "Studies: Gentrification a Boost for Everyone." *USA Today,* April 19, 2005.

Handbook on Women Workers. Washington D.C.: Women's Bureau of the U.S. Department of Labor, 1969.

Hardy, Dorcas. *Social Insecurity: The Crisis in America's Social Security and How to Plan Now for Your Own Financial Survival.* New York: Villard Books, 1991.

Harlow, Harry F., and Margaret K. Harlow. "The Affectional Systems." In *Behavior of Nonhuman Primates: Modern Research Trends,* Vol. 2, Allan M. Schrier, Harry F. Harlow, and Fred Stollnitz, eds. New York: Academic Press, 1965:287–334.

Harlow, Harry F., and Margaret K. Harlow. "Social Deprivation in Monkeys." *Scientific American, 207,* 1962:137–147.

Harper, Charles L., and Kevin T. Leicht. *Exploring Social Change: America and the World.* Upper Saddle River, N.J.: Prentice Hall, 2002.

Harrington, Michael. *The Vast Majority: A Journey to the World's Poor.* New York: Simon & Schuster, 1977.

Harrington, Michael. *The Other America: Poverty in the United States.* New York: Macmillan, 1962.

Harris, Chauncey D. "The Nature of Cities and Urban Geography in the Last Half Century." *Urban Geography, 18,* 1997.

Harris, Chauncey D., and Edward Ullman. "The Nature of Cities." *Annals of the American Academy of Political and Social Science, 242,* 1945:7–17.

Harris, Gardiner. "F.D.A. Says Bayer Failed to Reveal Drug Risk Study." *New York Times,* September 30, 2006.

Harris, Gardiner. "Drug Makers Are Still Giving Gifts to Doctors, F. D. A. Official Says." *New York Times,* March 4, 2005.

Harris, Kim, Dwight R. Sanders, Shaun Gress, and Nick Kuhns. "Starting Salaries for Agribusiness Graduates From an AASCARR Institution: The Case of Southern Illinois University." *Agribusiness, 21,* 1, 2005: 65–80.

Harris, Marvin. "Why Men Dominate Women." *New York Times Magazine,* November 13, 1977:46, 115, 117–123.

Harrison, Paige M., and Allen J. Beck. "Prison and Jail Inmates at Midyear 2004." Bureau of Justice Statistics. April 2005.

Harrison, Paul. *Inside the Third World: The Anatomy of Poverty,* 3rd ed. London: Penguin Books, 1993.

Hart, Charles W. M., and Arnold R. Pilling. *The Tiwi of North Australia,* Fieldwork Edition. New York: Holt, Rinehart and Winston, 1979.

Hart, Hornell. "Acceleration in Social Change." In *Technology and Social Change,* Francis R. Allen, Hornell Hart, Delbert C. Miller, William F. Ogburn, and Meyer F. Nimkoff. New York: Appleton, 1957:27–55.

Hart, Paul. "Groupthink, Risk-Taking and Recklessness: Quality of Process and Outcome in Policy Decision Making." *Politics and the Individual, 1,* 1, 1991:67–90.

Hartley, Eugene. *Problems in Prejudice.* New York: King's Crown Press, 1946.

Hartocollis, Anemona. "Harvard Faculty Votes to Put the Excellence Back in the A." *New York Times,* May 22, 2002.

Hatch, Laurie Russell. *Beyond Gender Differences: Adaptation to Aging in Life Course Perspective.* Amityville, N. Y.: Baywood Publishing Company, 2000.

Haub, Carl. "World Population Data Sheet." Washington, D.C.: Population Reference Bureau, 2006.

Haub, Carl. "World Population Data Sheet." Washington, D.C.: Population Reference Bureau, 2005.

Haub, Carl. "World Population Data Sheet." Washington, D.C.: Population Reference Bureau, 2004.

Haub, Carl. "Has Global Growth Reached Its Peak?" *Population Today, 30,* 6, August–September 2002:6.

Haub, Carl, and Nancy Yinger. "The U. N. Long-Range Population Projections: What They Tell Us." Washington, D.C.: Population Reference Bureau, 1994.

Hauser, Philip, and Leo Schnore, eds. *The Study of Urbanization.* New York: Wiley, 1965.

Hawkes, Nigel. "Asbestos-Related Diseases Will Rise for 20 Years." *The Times,* September 25, 2001.

Hawley, Amos H. *Urban Society: An Ecological Approach.* New York: Wiley, 1981.

Hayashi, Gina M., and Bonnie R. Strickland. "Long-Term Effects of Parental Divorce on Love Relationships: Divorce as Attachment Disruption." *Journal of Social and Personal Relationships, 15,* 1, February 1998, 23–38.

Hays, Constance L. "What Wal-Mart Knows About Customers' Habits." *New York Times,* November 14, 2004.

Heames, Joyce Thompson, Michael G. Harvey, and Darren Treadway. "Status Inconsistency: An Antecedent to Bullying Behavior in Groups." *International Journal of Human Resource Management, 17,* 2, February 2006:348–361.

Hechter, Michael. *Containing Nationalism.* New York: Oxford University Press, 2000.

Heilman, Madeline E. "Description and Prescription: How Gender Stereotypes Prevent Women's Ascent Up the Organizational Ladder." *Journal of Social Issues, 57,* 4, Winter 2001:657–674.

Helliker, Kevin. "Body and Spirit: Why Attending Religious Services May Benefit Health." *Wall Street Journal,* May 3, 2005.

Hellinger, Daniel, and Dennis R. Judd. *The Democratic Facade.* Pacific Grove, Calif.: Brooks/Cole, 1991.

Hemmings, Annette. "The 'Hidden' Corridor Curriculum." *High School Journal, 83,* December 1999:1–12.

Hendin, Herbert. "Suicide, Assisted Suicide, and Medical Illness." *Harvard Mental Health Letter, 16,* 7:January 2000: 4–7.

Hendin, Herbert. "Euthanasia and Physician-Assisted Suicide in the Netherlands." *New England Journal of Medicine, 336,* 19, May 8, 1997:1385–1387.

Hendrix, Lewellyn. "What Is Sexual Inequality? On the Definition and Range of Variation." *Gender and Society, 28,* 3, August 1994:287–307.

Henslin, James M. *Social Problems: A Down-to-Earth Approach,* 8th ed. Boston: Allyn and Bacon, 2008.

Henslin, James M., and Mae A. Biggs. "Behavior in Pubic Places: The Sociology of the Vaginal Examination." In *Down to Earth Sociology: Introductory Readings,* 14th ed., James M. Henslin, ed. New York: The Free Press, 2007.

Henslin, James M. "On Becoming Male: Reflections of a Sociologist on Childhood and Early Socialization." In *Down to Earth Sociology: Introductory Readings,* 14th ed., James M. Henslin, ed. New York: The Free Press, 2007.

Henslin, James M. "Author's File on a Divorce." 2005.

Hentoff, Nat. "Bush-Ashcroft Versus Homeland Security." *The Village Voice,* April 18, 2003.

Herrick, Thaddeus. "Aging Areas Around Cities Push Suburban Renewal." *New York Times,* January 31, 2007.

Hetherington, Mavis, and John Kelly. *For Better or For Worse: Divorce Reconsidered.* New York: W. W. Norton, 2003.

Hewitt Associates. *Worklife Benefits Provided by Major U.S. Employers, 2003–2004.* Lincolnshire, Ill.: Hewitt Associates, 2004.

Higginbotham, Elizabeth, and Lynn Weber. "Moving with Kin and Community: Upward Social Mobility for Black and White Women." *Gender and Society, 6,* 3, September 1992:416–440.

Hill, Andrew J. "Motivation for Eating Behaviour in Adolescent Girls: The Body Beautiful." *Proceedings of the Nutrition Society, 65,* 2006: 376–384.

Hill, Mark E. "Skin Color and the Perception of Attractiveness Among African Americans: Does Gender Make a Difference?" *Social Psychology Quarterly, 65,* 1, 2002:77–91.

Hilliard, Asa, III. "Do We Have the *Will* to Educate All Children?" *Educational Leadership, 49,* September 1991:31–36.

Hiltz, Starr Roxanne. "Widowhood." In *Marriage and Family in a Changing Society,* 3rd ed., James M. Henslin, ed. New York: Free Press, 1989:521–531.

Hipler, Fritz. Interview in a television documentary with Bill Moyers in *Propaganda,* in the series "Walk Through the 20th Century," 1987.

Hirschi, Travis. *Causes of Delinquency.* Berkeley: University of California Press, 1969.

Historical Statistics of the United States: From Colonial Times to the Present. New York: Basic Books, 1976.

Hitt, Jack. "The Next Battlefield May Be in Outer Space." *New York Times,* August 5, 2001.

Hochschild, Arlie. "When Work Becomes Home and Home Becomes Work." In *Society: Readings to Accompany Sociology: A Down-to-Earth Approach, Core Concepts,* James M. Henslin ed. Boston: Allyn and Bacon, 2006:182–191.

Hochschild, Arlie Russell. *The Time Bind: When Work Becomes Home and Home Becomes Work.* New York: Henry Holt, 1997.

Hochschild, Arlie Russell. *The Managed Heart: Commercialization of Human Feeling.* Chicago: University of Chicago Press, 1983.

Hochschild, Arlie Russell. "The Sociology of Feeling and Emotion: Selected Possibilities." In *Another Voice: Feminist Perspectives on Social Life and Social Science,* Marcia Millman and Rosabeth Moss Kanter, eds. Garden City, N. Y.: Anchor Books, 1975.

Hofferth, Sandra. "Did Welfare Reform Work? Implications for 2002 and Beyond." *Contexts,* Spring 2002:45–51.

Holder, Kelly. "Voting and Registration in the Election of November 2004." *Current Population Reports,* March 2006.

Holmwood, John. "Sociology as Public Discourse and Professional Practice: A Critique of Michael Burawoy." *Sociological Theory, 25,* 1, March 2007:46–66.

Holtzman, Abraham. *The Townsend Movement: A Political Study.* New York: Bookman, 1963.

Homblin, Dora Jane. *The First Cities.* Boston: Little, Brown, Time-Life Books, 1973.

Hommel M., and A. Jaillard. "Alcohol for Stroke Prevention?" *New England Journal of Medicine, 341,* 21, November 18, 1999: 1605–1606.

Honeycutt, Karen. "Disgusting, Pathetic, Bizarrely Beautiful: Representations of Weight in Popular Culture." Paper presented at the 1995 meetings of the American Sociological Association.

Hong, Lawrence. "Marriage in China." In *Til Death Do Us Part: A Multicultural Anthology on Marriage,* Sandra Lee Browning and R. Robin Miller, eds. Stamford, Conn.: JAI Press, 1999.

hooks, bell. *Where We Stand: Class Matters.* New York: Routledge, 2000.

Horn, James P. *Land As God Made It: Jamestown and the Birth of America.* New York: Basic Books, 2006.

Horowitz, Donald L. *The Deadly Ethnic Riot.* Berkeley: University of California Press, 2001.

Horowitz, Ruth. "Studying Violence Among the 'Lions.' " In James M. Henslin, *Social Problems.* Upper Saddle River, New Jersey: Prentice Hall, 2005:135.

Horowitz, Ruth. *Honor and the American Dream: Culture and Identity in a Chicano Community.* New Brunswick, N.J.: Rutgers University Press, 1983.

Hossfeld, Karen J. " 'Their Logic Against Them': Contradictions in Sex, Race, and Class in Silicon Valley." In *Gender Through the Prism of Difference,* 2nd ed., Maxine Baca Zinn, Pierrette Hondagneu-Sotelo, and Michael A. Messner, eds. Boston: Allyn and Bacon, 2000:388–400.

Hostetler, John A. *Amish Society,* 3rd ed. Baltimore: Johns Hopkins University Press, 1980.

Hotz, Robert Lee. "Most Science Studies Appear to Be Tainted by Sloppy Analysis." *Wall Street Journal,* September 14, 2007.

Hougham, Victoria. "Sociological Skills Used in the Capture of Saddam Hussein." *Footnotes,* July–August 2005.

"House Divided." *People Weekly,* May 24, 1999:126.

Houtman, Dick. "What Exactly Is a 'Social Class'?: On the Economic Liberalism and Cultural Conservatism of the 'Working Class'." Paper presented at the 1995 meetings of the American Sociological Association.

Howe, Henry, John Lyne, Alan Gross, Harro VanLente, Aire Rip, Richard Lewontin, Daniel McShea, Greg Myers, Ullica Segerstrale, Herbert W. Simons, and V. B. Smocovitis. "Gene Talk in Sociobiology." *Social Epistemology, 6,* 2, April-June 1992:109–163.

Howells, Lloyd T., and Selwyn W. Becker. "Seating Arrangement and Leadership Emergence." *Journal of Abnormal and Social Psychology, 64,* February 1962:148–150.

Hoyt, Homer. "Recent Distortions of the Classical Models of Urban Structure." In *Internal Structure of the City: Readings on Space and Environment,* Larry S. Bourne, ed. New York: Oxford University Press, 1971:84–96.

Hoyt, Homer. *The Structure and Growth of Residential Neighborhoods in American Cities.* Washington, D.C.: Federal Housing Administration, 1939.

Hsu, Francis L. K. *The Challenge of the American Dream: The Chinese in the United States.* Belmont, Calif.: Wadsworth, 1971.

Huber, Joan. "Micro-Macro Links in Gender Stratification." *American Sociological Review, 55,* February 1990:1–10.

Huddle, Donald. "The Net National Cost of Immigration." Washington, D.C.: Carrying Capacity Network, 1993.

Hudson, Valerie M., and Andrea M. den Boer. *Bare Branches: The Security Implications of Asia's Surplus Male Population.* Cambridge, Mass.: MIT Press, 2004.

Huffstutter, P. J. "God Is Everywhere on the Net." *Los Angeles Times,* December 14, 1998.

Huggins, Martha K. "Moral Universes of Brazilian Torturers." Lecture, April 11, 2004.

Huggins, Martha K., and Sandra Rodrigues. "Kids Working on Paulista Avenue." *Childhood, 11,* 2004:495–514.

Huggins, Martha K., Mika Haritos-Fatouros, and Philip G. Zimbardo. *Violence Workers: Police Torturers and Murderers Reconstruct Brazilian Atrocities.* Berkeley: University of California Press, 2002.

Hughes, Everett C. "Good People and Dirty Work." In *Life in Society: Readings to Accompany Sociology: A Down-to-Earth Approach, Seventh Edition,* James M. Henslin, ed. Boston: Allyn and Bacon, 2005: 125–134. Article originally published in 1962.

Hughes, H. Stuart. *Oswald Spengler: A Critical Estimate,* rev. ed. New York: Scribner's, 1962.

Hughes, Kathleen A. "Even Tiki Torches Don't Guarantee a Perfect Wedding." *Wall Street Journal,* February 20, 1990:A1, A16.

Humphreys, Laud. "Impersonal Sex and Perceived Satisfaction." In *Studies in the Sociology of Sex,* James M. Henslin, ed. New York: Appleton-Century-Crofts, 1971:351–374.

Humphreys, Laud. *Tearoom Trade: Impersonal Sex in Public Places,* enlarged ed. Chicago: Aldine, 1970, 1975.

Hundley, Greg. "Why Women Earn Less Than Men in Self-Employment." *Journal of Labor Research, 22,* 4, Fall 2001:817–827.

Hunt, Stephen. *The Life Course: A Sociological Introduction.* London: Palgrave Macmillan, 2005.

Hurtado, Aída, David E. Hayes-Bautista, R. Burciaga Valdez, and Anthony C. R. Hernández. *Redefining California: Latino Social Engagement in a Multicultural Society.* Los Angeles: UCLA Chicano Studies Research Center, 1992.

Huttenbach, Henry R. "The Roman *Porajmos:* The Nazi Genocide of Europe's Gypsies." *Nationalities Papers, 19,* 3, Winter 1991: 373–394.

Hutton, Will. *The Writing on the Wall: Why We Must Embrace China as a Partner or Face It as an Enemy.* New York: The Free Press, 2007.

Hutzler, Charles. "Yuppies in China Protest Via the Web—And Get Away With It." *Wall Street Journal,* March 19, 2004.

Hymowitz, Carol. "Raising Women to Be Leaders." *Wall Street Journal,* February 12, 2007.

Hymowitz, Carol. "Through the Glass Ceiling." *Wall Street Journal,* November 8, 2004.

Hyra, Derek S. "Racial Uplift? Intra-Racial Class Conflict and the Economic Revitalization of Harlem and Bronzeville." *City and Community, 5,* 1, March 2006:71–92.

"In Perspective: America's Conflicts." *New York Times,* April 20, 2003: B16.

Iori, Ron. "The Good, the Bad and the Useless." *Wall Street Journal,* June 10, 1988:18R.

Ismail, M. Asif. "The Clinton Top 100: Where Are They Now?" Washington, D.C.: The Center for Public Integrity, 2003.

Itard, Jean Marc Gospard. *The Wild Boy of Aveyron.* Translated by George and Muriel Humphrey. New York: Appleton-Century-Crofts, 1962.

Jacobs, Charles. "Money Talks." *The Boston Globe,* February 19, 1999.

Jacobs, Jerry A. "Detours on the Road to Equality: Women, Work and Higher Education." *Contexts,* Winter 2003:32–41.

Jacobs, Margaret A. " 'New Girl' Network Is Boon for Women Lawyers." *Wall Street Journal,* March 4, 1997:B1, B7.

Jaffee, Sara, and Janet Shibley Hyde. "Gender Differences in Moral Orientation: A Meta-Analysis." *Psychological Bulletin, 126,* 5, 2000: 703–726.

Jaffrelot, Christophe. "The Impact of Affirmative Action in India: More Political than Socioeconomic." *India Review, 5,* 2, April 2006:173–189.

Jaggar, Alison M. "Sexual Difference and Sexual Equality." In *Theoretical Perspectives on Sexual Difference,* Deborah L. Rhode, ed. New Haven, Conn.: Yale University Press, 1990:239–254.

Jamieson, Amie, Hyon B. Shin, and Jennifer Day. "Voting and Registration in the Election of November 2000." *Current Population Reports,* February 2002.

Janis, Irving. L. *Groupthink: Psychological Studies of Policy Decisions and Fiascoes.* Boston: Houghton Mifflin, 1982.

Janis, Irving L. *Victims of Groupthink.* Boston, Mass.: Houghton Mifflin, 1972.

Jankowiak, William R., and Edward F. Fischer. "A Cross-Cultural Perspective on Romantic Love." *Journal of Ethnology, 31,* 2, April 1992:149–155.

Jankowski, Martín Sánchez. *Islands in the Street: Gangs and American Urban Society.* Berkeley: University of California Press, 1991.

Jasper, James M. "Moral Dimensions of Social Movements." Paper presented at the annual meetings of the American Sociological Association, 1991.

Jasper, James M., and Dorothy Nelkin. *Animal Crusade.* New York: The Free Press, 1993.

Jasper, James M., and Jane D. Poulsen. "Recruiting Strangers and Friends: Moral Shocks and Social Networks in Animal Rights and Anti-Nuclear Protests." *Social Problems, 42,* 4, November 1995:493–512.

Jáuregui, Gurutz. "El poder y la soberana en la aldéa global." *El Pais.* July 19, 1996:11.

Jenkins, Philip. "The Next Christianity." *Atlantic Monthly,* October 2002:53–68.

Jerrome, Dorothy. *Good Company: An Anthropological Study of Old People in Groups.* Edinburgh, England: Edinburgh University Press, 1992.

Johansson, Perry. "Consuming the Other: The Fetish of the Western Woman in Chinese Advertising and Popular Culture." *Postcolonial Studies, 2,* 3, November 1999.

Johnson, Benton, "On Church and Sect." *American Sociological Review, 28,* 1963:539–549.

Johnson, Gail. "Time to Broaden Diversity." *Training, 41,* 19, September 2004, 16.

Johnson, Johna Till. "The Costs and Benefits of Remote Workers." *Network World,* December 20, 2004:24.

Johnson, Norris R. "Panic at 'The Who Concert Stampede': An Empirical Assessment." In *Collective Behavior and Social Movements,* Russell L. Curtis, Jr., and Benigno E. Aguirre, eds. Boston: Allyn and Bacon, 1993:113–122.

Johnson-Weiner, Karen. *Train Up a Child: Old Order Amish and Mennonite Schools.* Baltimore: Johns Hopkins University Press, 2007.

Johnston, David Cay. "Is Live Sex On-Demand Coming to Hotel TVs?" *New York Times,* January 17, 2007.

Johnston, Drue M., and Norris R. Johnson. "Role Extension in Disaster: Employee Behavior at the Beverly Hills Supper Club Fire." *Sociological Focus, 22,* 1, February 1989:39–51.

Johnston, Lloyd. D., Patrick M. O'Malley, Jerald J. Bachman, and John E. Schulenberg. *Monitoring the Future, National Results on Adolescent Drug Use: Overview of Key Findings, 2006.* Bethesda, MD: National Institute on Drug Abuse, May 2007.

Johnston, Lloyd. D., Patrick M. O'Malley, Jerald J. Bachman, and John E. Schulenberg. *Monitoring the Future, National Survey Results on Drug Use, 1975–2005, Volume II, College Students and Adults, Ages 19–45.* Bethesda, MD: National Institute on Drug Abuse, 2006.

Jones, Dale E., et al. "Religious Congregations and Membership in the United States 2000: An Enumeration by Region, State and County. Based on Data Reported by 149 Religious Bodies." Nashville, Tenn.: Glenmary Research Center, 2002.

Jones, James H. *Bad Blood: The Tuskegee Syphilis Experiment,* 2nd ed. New York: Free Press, 1993.

Jones, Steve. "Let the Games Begin: Gaming Technology and Entertainment Among College Students." Washington, D.C.: PEW Internet and American Life Project, 2003.

Jordan, Miriam. "Among Poor Villagers, Female Infanticide Still Flourishes in India." *Wall Street Journal,* May 9, 2000:A1, A12.

Josephson, Matthew. "The Robber Barons." In *John D. Rockefeller: Robber Baron or Industrial Statesman?,* Earl Latham, ed. Boston: Heath, 1949: 34–48.

"Judge Rules Against Ford in Discrimination Lawsuit." *New York Times,* March 17, 2005.

Judge, Timothy A., and Daniel M. Cable. "The Effect of Physical Height on Workplace Success and Income: Preliminary Test of a Theoretical Model." *Journal of Applied Psychology, 89,* 3, 2004:428–441.

Juergensmeyer, Mark. *Terror in the Mind of God: The Global Rise of Religious Violence.* Berkeley: University of California Press, 2000.

Jung, Jaehee, and Gordon B. Forbes. *Psychology of Women Quarterly, 31,* 4, December 2007:381–393.

Kaebnick, Gregory E. "On the Sanctity of Nature." *Hastings Center Report, 30,* 5, September-October 2000:16–23.

Kagan, Jerome. "The Idea of Emotions in Human Development." In *Emotions, Cognition, and Behavior,* Carroll E. Izard, Jerome Kagan, and Robert B. Zajonc, eds. New York: Cambridge University Press, 1984:38–72.

Kahn, Joseph. "China Shows Assertiveness in Weapons Test." *New York Times,* January 20, 2007a.

Kahn, Joseph. "Thousands Reportedly Riot in China." *International Herald-Tribune,* March 13, 2007b.

Kahn, Joseph. "China's Elite Learn to Flaunt It While the New Landless Weep." *New York Times,* December 25, 2004.

Kahn, Joseph. "Some Chinese See the Future, and It's Capitalist." *New York Times,* May 4, 2002.

Kalb, Claudia. "Faith and Healing." *Newsweek,* November 10, 2003: 44–56.

Kalberg, Stephen. *Introduction to Max Weber, The Protestant Ethic and the Spirit of Capitalism,* 3rd ed. Los Angeles: Roxbury Publishing, 2002.

Kalof, Linda. "Vulnerability to Sexual Coercion Among College Women: A Longitudinal Study." *Gender Issues, 18,* 4, Fall 2000:47–58.

Kanazawa, Satoshi, and Jody L. Kovar. "Why Beautiful People Are More Intelligent." *Intelligence, 32,* 2004:227–243.

Kane, Yukariitwatani, and Phred Dvorak. "Howard Stringer, Japanese CEO." *Wall Street Journal,* March 3, 2007.

Kanter, James, and Andrew C. Revkin. "Scientists Detail Climate Changes, Poles to Tropics." *New York Times,* April 7, 2007.

Kanter, Rosabeth Moss. *The Change Masters: Innovation and Entrepreneurship in the American Corporation.* New York: Simon & Schuster, 1983.

Kanter, Rosabeth Moss. *Men and Women of the Corporation.* New York: Basic Books, 1977.

Kanter, Rosabeth Moss, Fred Wiersema, and John J. Kao, eds. *Innovation: Breakthrough Thinking at 3M, DuPont, GE, Pfizer, and Rubbermaid.* New York: Harper, 1997.

Kantor, Jodi. "On the Job, Nursing Mothers Find a 2-Class System." *New York Times,* September 1, 2006.

Kaplan, Robert D. "A Tale of Two Colonies." *Atlantic Monthly,* April 2003.

Karp, David A., and William C. Yoels. "Sport and Urban Life." *Journal of Sport and Social Issues, 14,* 2, 1990:77–102.

Karp, David A., Gregory P. Stone, and William C. Yoels. *Being Urban: A Sociology of City Life,* 2nd ed. New York: Praeger, 1991.

Kart, Cary S. *The Realities of Aging: An Introduction to Gerontology,* 3rd ed. Boston: Allyn and Bacon, 1990.

Katz, Richard S. "Electoral Reform in Italy: Expectations and Results." *Acta Politica, 41,* 2006:285–299.

Katz, Sidney. "The Importance of Being Beautiful." In *Down to Earth Sociology: Introductory Readings,* 14th ed., James M. Henslin, ed. New York: The Free Press, 2007.

Kaufman, Joanne. "Married Maidens and Dilatory Domiciles." *Wall Street Journal,* May 7, 1996:A16.

Keans, Carl. "Socioenvironmental Determinants of Community Formation." *Environment and Behavior, 23,* 1, January 1991:27–46.

Keates, Nancy. "Alternative Care Crops Up At 'Traditional' Hospitals." *Wall Street Journal,* March 28, 2003.

Kefalas, Maria. "Looking for the Lower Middle Class." *City and Community, 6,* 1, March 2007:63–68.

Keith, Jennie. *Old People, New Lives: Community Creation in a Retirement Residence,* 2nd ed. Chicago: University of Chicago Press, 1982.

Kelly, Joan B. "How Adults React to Divorce." In *Marriage and Family in a Changing Society,* 4th ed., James M. Henslin, ed. New York: Free Press, 1992:410–423.

Kenchaiah, Satish, et. al. "Obesity and the Risk of Heart Failure." *New England Journal of Medicine, 347,* August 1, 2002:305–313.

Keniston, Kenneth. *Youth and Dissent: The Rise of a New Opposition.* New York: Harcourt, Brace, Jovanovich, 1971.

Kent, Mary, and Robert Lalasz. "In the News: Speaking English in the United States." Population Reference Bureau, January 18, 2007.

Kephart, William M., and William W. Zellner. *Extraordinary Groups: An Examination of Unconventional Life-Styles,* 7th ed. New York: Worth Publishing, 2001.

Kerr, Clark. *The Future of Industrialized Societies.* Cambridge, Mass.: Harvard University Press, 1983.

Khattak, Mizuko Ito. "Anime's 'Transnational Geekdom.'" UCLA's Asia Institute, January 23, 2007.

Kibria, Nazli. *Family Tightrope: The Changing Lives of Vietnamese Americans.* Princeton, N.J.: Princeton University Press, 1993.

Kifner, John. "Building Modernity on Desert Mirages." *New York Times,* February 7, 1999.

Kilbourne, Jean. "Beauty and the Beast of Advertising." In *Down to Earth Sociology: Introductory Readings,* 12th ed., James M. Henslin, ed. New York: The Free Press, 2003:421–424.

Kingston, Maxine Hong. *The Woman Warrior.* New York: Vintage Books, 1975:108. Quoted in Frank J. Zulke and Jacqueline P. Kirley. *Through the Eyes of Social Science,* 6th ed. Prospect Heights, Ill.: Waveland Press, 2002.

Kinsella, Kevin, and David R. Phillips. "Global Aging: The Challenge of Success." Washington, D.C.: Population Reference Bureau, 2005.

Klahanie Association Web site. http://www.klahanie.com/

Klandermans, Bert. The Social Psychology of Protest. Cambridge, Mass.: Blackwell, 1997.

Kleinfeld, Judith S. "Gender and Myth: Data about Student Performance." In *Through the Eyes of Social Science,* 6th ed., Frank J. Zulke and Jacqueline P. Kirley, eds. Prospect Heights, Ill.: Waveland Press, 2002a:380–393.

Kleinfeld, Judith S. "The Small World Problem." *Society,* January–February, 2002b:61–66.

Kluegel, James R., and Eliot R. Smith. *Beliefs About Inequality: America's Views of What Is and What Ought to Be.* Hawthorne, N. Y.: Aldine de Gruyter, 1986.

Knapp, Daniel. "What Happened When I Took My Sociological Imagination to the Dump." *Footnotes,* May–June, 2005:4.

Knauth, Donna G. "Predictors of Parental Sense of Competence for the Couple During the Transition to Parenthood." *Research in Nursing and Health, 23,* 2000:496–509.

Knickerbocker, Brad. "Firebrands of 'Ecoterrorism' Set Sights on Urban Sprawl." *Christian Science Monitor,* August 6, 2003.

Kohlberg, Lawrence. "A Current Statement on Some Theoretical Issues." In *Lawrence Kohlberg: Consensus and Controversy,* Sohan Modgil and Celia Modgil, eds. Philadelphia: Falmer Press, 1986:485–546.

Kohlberg, Lawrence. *The Psychology of Moral Development: Moral Stages and the Life Cycle.* San Francisco: Harper and Row, 1984.

Kohlberg, Lawrence. "Moral Education for a Society in Moral Transition." *Educational Leadership, 33,* 1975:46–54.

Kohlberg, Lawrence, and Carol Gilligan. "The Adolescent as a Philosopher: The Discovery of the Self in a Postconventional World." *Daedalus, 100,* 1971:1051–1086.

Kohn, Alfie. "Make Love, Not War." *Psychology Today,* June 1988: 35–38.

Kohn, Melvin L. *Class and Conformity: A Study in Values,* 2nd ed. Homewood, Ill.: Dorsey Press, 1977.

Kohn, Melvin L. "Occupational Structure and Alienation." *American Journal of Sociology, 82,* 1976:111–130.

Kohn, Melvin L., and Carmi Schooler. "Class, Occupation, and Orientation." *American Sociological Review, 34,* 1969:659–678.

Kohn, Melvin L. "Social Class and Parent-Child Relationships: An Interpretation." *American Journal of Sociology, 68,* 1963:471–480.

Kohn, Melvin L. "Social Class and Parental Values." *American Journal of Sociology, 64,* 1959:337–351.

Kohn, Melvin L., and Carmi Schooler. *Work and Personality: An Inquiry into the Impact of Social Stratification.* New York: Ablex Press, 1983.

Kohn, Melvin L., Kazimierz M. Slomczynski, and Carrie Schoenbach. "Social Stratification and the Transmission of Values in the Family: A Cross-National Assessment." *Sociological Forum, 1,* 1, 1986:73–102.

Kolata, Gina. "The Genesis of an Epidemic: Humans, Chimps and a Virus." *New York Times,* September 4, 2001.

Kontos, Louis, David Brotherton, and Luis Barrios, eds. *Gangs and Society: Alternative Perspectives.* New York: Columbia University Press, 2003.

Koppel, Ross, Joshua P. Metlay, Abigail Cohen, Brian Abaluck, A. Russell Localio, Stephen E. Kimmel, and Brian L. Strom. "Role of Computerized Order Entry Systems in Facilitating Medication Errors." *Journal of the American Medical Association, 293,* March 9, 2005:1197–1203.

Korda, Michael. *Male Chauvinism: How It Works.* New York: Random House, 1973.

Kornhauser, William. *The Politics of Mass Society.* New York: Free Press, 1959.

"Krakatoa Rumor Stokes Tsunami Fears." Reuters, May 17, 2005.

Kramer, Josea B. "Serving American Indian Elderly in Cities: An Invisible Minority." *Aging Magazine,* Winter-Spring 1992:48–51.

Krane, Vikki, Julie A. Stiles-Shipley, Jennifer Waldron, and Jennifer Michalenok. "Relationships Among Body Satisfaction, Social Physique Anxiety, and Eating Behaviors in Female Athletes and Exercisers." *Journal of Sport Behavior, 24,* 3, September 2001: 247–264.

Krause, Neal, and Christopher G. Ellison. "Forgiveness by God, Forgiveness of Others, and Psychological Well-Being in Late Life." *Journal for the Scientific Study of Religion, 42,* 1, 2003:77–93.

Krauss, Clifford. "Venture Capitalists Want to Put Some Algae in Your Tank." *New York Times,* March 7, 2007.

Kraybill, Donald B. *The Riddle of Amish Culture.* Revised edition. Baltimore, Md.: Johns Hopkins University Press, 2002.

Kristensen, Peer Hull, and Glenn Morgan. "Multinationals: Institutionalizing Agents and Institutionalized Agency." Copenhagen: International Center for Business and Politics, Working Paper 30, 2006.

Kristoff, Nicholas D. "Interview With a Humanoid." *New York Times,* July 23, 2002.

Kroeger, Brooke. "When a Dissertation Makes a Difference." *New York Times,* March 20, 2004.

Krueger, Alan B. "The Apple Falls Close to the Tree, Even in the Land of Opportunity." *New York Times,* November 14, 2002.

Krugman, Paul. "White Man's Burden." *New York Times,* September 24, 2002.

Kübler-Ross, Elisabeth. *Living with Death and Dying.* New York: Macmillan, 1981.

Kübler-Ross, Elisabeth. *On Death and Dying.* New York: Macmillan, 1969.

Kubrin, Charis E., and Ronald Weitzer. "Retaliatory Homicide: Concentrated Disadvantage and Neighborhood Culture." *Social Problems, 50,* 2, May 2003:157–180.

Kucukarslan, Suzan N., Michael Peters, Mark Mlynarek, and Daniel A. Nafziger. "Pharmacists on Rounding Teams Reduce Preventable Adverse Drug Events in Hospital General Medicine Units." *Archives of Internal Medicine, 163,* September 22, 2003:2014–2018.

Kuhn, Margaret E. "The Gray Panthers." In *Social Problems,* 2nd ed., James M. Henslin, Englewood Cliffs, N.J.: Prentice Hall, 1990:56–57.

Kurian, George Thomas. *Encyclopedia of the Third World,* Vols. 1, 2, 3. New York: Facts on File, 1992.

Kurian, George Thomas. *Encyclopedia of the Second World.* New York: Facts on File, 1991.

Kurian, George Thomas. *Encyclopedia of the First World,* Vols. 1, 2. New York: Facts on File, 1990.

Kurlantzick, Josh. "China's Future: A Nation of Single Men?" *Los Angeles Times,* October 21, 2007.

La Barre, Weston. *The Human Animal.* Chicago: University of Chicago Press, 1954.

Lacayo, Richard. "In the Grip of a Psychopath." *Time,* May 3, 1993a: 34–36, 39–43.

Lacayo, Richard. "The 'Cultural' Defense." *Time,* Fall 1993b:61.

Lacey, Marc. "Tijuana Journal: Cities Mesh Across Blurry Border, Despite Physical Barrier. *New York Times,* March 5, 2007.

LaFraniere, Sharon. "Africa's World of Forced Labor, in a 6-Year-Old's Eyes." *New York Times,* October 29, 2006.

LaFraniere, Sharon. "Health Workers Race to Block Deadly Virus in Angolan Town." *New York Times,* April 11, 2005.

Lambert, Bruce. "Manufacturer in $2 Million Accord With U.S. on Deficient Kevlar in Military Helmets." *Wall Street Journal,* February 6, 2008.

Lamptey, Peter R., Jami L. Johnson, and Marya Khan. "The Global Challenge of HIV and AIDS." *Population Bulletin, 61,* 1, March 2006: 1–24.

Landry, Brett J. L., Sathi Mahesh, and Sandra Hartman. "The Changing Nature of Work in the Age of E-Business." *Journal of Organizational Change Management, 18,* 2, 2005:132–144.

Landtman, Gunnar. *The Origin of the Inequality of the Social Classes.* New York: Greenwood Press, 1968. First published in 1938.

Lang, Iain, Robert B. Wallace, Felicia A. Huppert, and David Melzer. "Moderate Alcohol Consumption in Older Adults Is Associated With Better Cognition and Well-being Than Abstinence." *Age and Ageing, 36,* 2007:256–261.

Lang, Kurt, and Gladys E. Lang. *Collective Dynamics.* New York: Crowell, 1961.

Lareau, Annette. "Invisible Inequality: Social Class and Childrearing in Black Families and White Families." *American Sociological Review, 67,* October 2002:747–776.

Larsen, Elena. "CyberFaith: How Americans Pursue Religion Online." Washington, D.C.: Pew Internet and American Life Project., December 23, 2001.

Larson, Jeffry H. "The Marriage Quiz: College Students' Beliefs in Selected Myths About Marriage." *Family Relations,* January 1988:3–11.

Larson, Mary Strom. "Interactions, Activities and Gender in Children's Television Commercials: A Content Analysis." *Journal of Broadcasting and Electronic Media, 45,* Winter 2001:41–51.

Lasch, Christopher. *Haven in a Heartless World: The Family Besieged.* New York: Basic, 1977.

Lauer, Jeanette, and Robert Lauer. "Marriages Made to Last." In *Marriage and Family in a Changing Society,* 4th ed., James M. Henslin, ed. New York: Free Press, 1992:481–486.

Lawler, Steph. " 'Getting Out and Getting Away': Women's Narratives of Class Mobility." *Feminist Review,* 63, Autumn 1999:3–24.

Lazarsfeld, Paul F., and Jeffrey G. Reitz. "History of Applied Sociology." *Sociological Practice, 7,* 1989:43–52.

Leach, Darcy K., "The Iron Law of *What* Again? Conceptualizing Oligarchy Across Organizational Forms." *Sociological Theory, 23,* 3, September 2005:312–337.

Leacock, Eleanor. *Myths of Male Dominance.* New York: Monthly Review Press, 1981.

LeBon, Gustave. *Psychologie des Foules (The Psychology of the Crowd).* Paris: Alcan, 1895. Various editions in English.

LeDuff, Charlie. "Handling the Meltdowns of the Nuclear Family." *New York Times,* May 28, 2003.

Lee, Alfred McClung, and Elizabeth Briant Lee. *The Fine Art of Propaganda: A Study of Father Coughlin's Speeches.* New York: Harcourt Brace, 1939.

Lee, Nick. *Childhood and Society: Growing Up in an Age of Uncertainty.* Buckingham: Open University Press, 2001.

Lee, Raymond M. *Unobtrusive Methods in Social Research.* Philadelphia: Open University Press, 2000.

Lee, Sharon M., and Barry Edmonston. "New Marriages, New Families: U.S. Racial and Hispanic Intermarriage." *Population Bulletin, 60,* 2, June 2005:1–36.

Lee, Sharon M. "Asian Americans: Diverse and Growing." *Population Bulletin, 53,* 2, June 1998:1–39.

Lee, Sunmin, Graham Colditz, Lisa Berkman, and Ichiro Kawachi. "Caregiving to Children and Grandchildren and Risk of Coronary Heart Disease in Women." *American Journal of Public Health, 93,* November 2003:1939–1944.

Leland, John. "A New Harlem Gentry in Search of Its Latte." *New York Times,* August 7, 2003.

Leland, John, and Gregory Beals. "In Living Colors." *Newsweek,* May 5, 1997:58–60.

Lemann, Nicholas, "The Myth of Community Development." *New York Times Magazine,* January 9, 1994, p. 27.

Lenski, Gerhard. *Power and Privilege: A Theory of Social Stratification.* New York: McGraw-Hill, 1966.

Lenski, Gerhard. "Status Crystallization: A Nonvertical Dimension of Social Status." *American Sociological Review, 19,* 1954:405–413.

Lenski, Gerhard, and Jean Lenski. *Human Societies: An Introduction to Macrosociology,* 5th ed. New York: McGraw-Hill, 1987.

Lerner, Gerda. *The Creation of Patriarchy.* New York: Oxford, 1986.

Lerner, Gerda. *Black Women in White America: A Documentary History.* New York: Pantheon Books, 1972.

"Less Rote, More Variety: Reforming Japan's Schools." *The Economist,* December 16, 2000:8.

Lesser, Alexander. "War and the State." In *War: The Anthropology of Armed Conflict and Aggression,* Morton Fried, Marvin Harris, and Robert Murphy, eds. Garden City, N. Y.: Natural History, 1968:92–96.

Lester, David. "Adolescent Suicide from an International Perspective." *American Behavioral Scientist, 46,* 9, May 2003:1157–1170.

Letherby, Gayle. "Childless and Bereft? Stereotypes and Realities in Relation to 'Voluntary' and 'Involuntary' Childlessness and Womanhood." *Sociological Inquiry, 72,* 1, Winter 2002:7–20.

Levine, John M. "Solomon Asch's Legacy for Group Research." *Personality and Social Psychology Review, 3,* 4, 1999:358–364.

Levinson, D. J. *The Seasons of a Man's Life.* New York: Knopf, 1978.

Levinson, Wendy, and Nicole Lurie. "When Most Doctors Are Women: What Lies Ahead." *Annals of Internal Medicine, 141,* 2004:471–474.

Levy, Clifford J. "Doctor Admits He Did Needless Surgery on the Mentally Ill." *New York Times,* May 20, 2003.

Levy, Clifford J., and Michael Luo. "New York Medicaid Fraud May Reach into Billions." *New York Times,* July 18, 2005.

Levy, Marion J., Jr. "Confucianism and Modernization." *Society, 24,* 4, May-June 1992:15–18.

Lewin, Tamar. "Colleges Regroup After Voters Ban Race Preferences." *New York Times,* January 26, 2007.

Lewin, Tamar. "Little Sympathy or Remedy for Inmates Who Are Raped." *New York Times,* April 15, 2001b.

Lewis, Neil A. "Justice Dept. Toughens Rules on Torture." *New York Times,* January 1, 2005.

Lewis, Oscar. "The Culture of Poverty." *Scientific American, 115,* October 1966a:19–25.

Lewis, Oscar. *La Vida.* New York: Random House, 1966b.

Lewis, Richard S. *Challenger: The Final Voyage.* New York: Columbia University Press, 1988.

Li, Zheng. "China Faces Elderly Dilemma." *China Daily,* August 21, 2004.

Lichtblau, Eric. "Librarians Say Yes, Officials Do Quiz Them About Users." *New York Times,* June 20, 2005.

Lichter, Daniel T., and Martha L. Crowley. "Poverty in America: Beyond Welfare Reform." *Population Bulletin, 57,* 2, June 2002:1–36.

Lieberson, Stanley. *A Matter of Taste: How Names, Fashions, and Culture Change.* New Haven: Yale University Press, 2000.

Liebow, Elliott. *Tally's Corner: A Study of Negro Streetcorner Men.* Boston: Little, Brown, 1999. Originally published in 1967.

Light, Donald W. "Perestroika for Russian Health Care?" *Footnotes, 20,* 3, March 1992:7, 9.

Lightfoot-Klein, A. "Rites of Purification and Their Effects: Some Psychological Aspects of Female Genital Circumcision and Infibulation (Pharaonic Circumcision) in an Afro-Arab Society (Sudan)." *Journal of Psychological Human Sexuality, 2,* 1989:61–78.

Lind, Michael. *The Next American Nation: The New Nationalism and the Fourth American Revolution.* New York: Free Press, 1995.

Linden, Eugene. "Lost Tribes, Lost Knowledge." *Time,* September 23, 1991:46, 48, 50, 52, 54, 56.

Lines, Patricia M. "Homeschooling Comes of Age." *Public Interest,* Summer 2000:74–85.

Linton, Ralph. *The Study of Man.* New York: Appleton-Century-Crofts, 1936.

Linz, Daniel, Paul Bryant, et al. "An Examination of the Assumption that Adult Businesses Are Associated with Crime in Surrounding Areas: A Secondary Effects Study in Charlotte, North Carolina." *Law & Society, 38,* 1, March 2004:69–104.

Lippitt, Ronald, and Ralph K. White. "An Experimental Study of Leadership and Group Life." In *Readings in Social Psychology,* 3rd ed., Eleanor E. Maccoby, Theodore M. Newcomb, and Eugene L. Hartley, eds. New York: Holt, Rinehart and Winston, 1958: 340–365. (As summarized in Olmsted and Hare 1978:28–31.)

Lipset, Seymour Martin. "The Social Requisites of Democracy Revisited." Presidential address to the American Sociological Association, Boston, Massachusetts, 1993.

Lipset, Seymour Martin. "Democracy and Working-Class Authoritarianism." *American Sociological Review, 24,* 1959:482–502.

Liptak, Adam. "Prosecution of Midwife Casts Light on Home Births." *New York Times,* April 3, 2006.

Liu, Haiyong. "Growing Up Poor and Childhood Weight Problems." Institute for Research on Poverty, Discussion Paper. DP 1324-07, April 2007.

Liu, Yuanli. "China's Public Health-Care System: Facing the Challenges." *Bulletin of the World Health Organization, 82,* 7, July 2004:532–538.

Lleras-Muney, Adriana. "The Relationship Between Education and Adult Mortality in the United States." *Review of Economic Studies, 72,* 2005:189–221.

Lofland, John F. *Protest: Studies of Collective Behavior and Social Movements.* New Brunswick, New Jersey: Transaction Books, 1985.

Logue, John, and Jacquelyn Yates. "Modeling an Employee Ownership Sector." *Peace Review, 12,* 2, June 2000:243–249.

Lombroso, Cesare. *Crime: Its Causes and Remedies,* H. P. Horton, trans. Boston: Little, Brown, 1911.

Lorber, Judith. *Paradoxes of Gender.* New Haven, Conn.: Yale University Press, 1994.

Loucks, Cynthia. "But This Is My Mother!" In *Sociology: Windows on Society,* 6th ed., Robert H. Lauer and Jeanette C. Lauer, eds. Los Angeles: Roxbury Publishing Company, 2002:182–187.

Lublin, Joann S. "Living Well." *Wall Street Journal,* April 8, 1999.

Lublin, Joann S. "Women at Top Still Are Distant from CEO Jobs." *Wall Street Journal,* February 28, 1996:B1.

Lublin, Joann S. "Trying to Increase Worker Productivity, More Employers Alter Management Style." *Wall Street Journal,* February 13, 1991:B1, B7.

Lucas, Samuel Roundfield. *Tracking Inequality: Stratification and Mobility in American High Schools.* New York: Teachers College Press, 1999.

Luhnow, David. "As Jobs Move East, Plants in Mexico Retool to Compete." *Wall Street Journal,* March 5, 2004.

Luke, Timothy W. *Ideology and Soviet Industrialization.* Westport, Conn.: Greenwood Press, 1985.

Lunneborg, Patricia. *Chosen Lives of Childfree Men.* Westport, Conn.: Bergin and Garvey, 1999.

Lurie, Nicole, Jonathan Slater, Paul McGovern, Jacqueline Ekstrum, Lois Quam, and Karen Margolis. "Preventive Care for Women: Does the Sex of the Physician Matter?" *New England Journal of Medicine, 329,* August 12, 1993:478–482.

Mabry, Marcus. "The Price Tag on Freedom." *Newsweek,* May 3, 1999: 50–51.

Macartney, Jane. "China's Men Lack Millions of Brides." *The Australian,* January 15, 2007.

MacDonald, William L., and Alfred DeMaris. "Remarriage, Stepchildren, and Marital Conflict: Challenges to the Incomplete Institutionalization Hypothesis." *Journal of Marriage and the Family, 57,* May 1995: 387–398.

Mack, Raymond W., and Calvin P. Bradford. *Transforming America: Patterns of Social Change,* 2nd ed. New York: Random House, 1979.

Mackay, Charles. *Memories of Extraordinary Popular Delusions and the Madness of Crowds.* London: Office of the National Illustrated Library, 1852.

Madigan, Nick. "Judge Questions Long Sentence in Drug Case." *New York Times,* November 17, 2004.

Madslien, Jorn. "Nuclear Waste Poses Arctic Threat." *BBC News,* October 19, 2006.

Magnuson, E. "A Cold Soak, a Plume, a Fireball." *Time,* February 17, 1986:25.

Mahoney, John S., Jr., and Paul G. Kooistra. "Policing the Races: Structural Factors Enforcing Racial Purity in Virginia (1630–1930)." Paper presented at the 1995 meetings of the American Sociological Association.

Mahoney, Patricia. "High Rape Chronicity and Low Rates of Help-Seeking Among Wife Rape Survivors in a Nonclinical Sample: Implications for Research and Practice." *Violence Against Women, 5,* 9, September 1999:993–1016.

Maier, Mark. "Teaching from Tragedy: An Interdisciplinary Module on the Space Shuttle *Challenger.*" *T. H. E. Journal,* September 1993: 91–94.

Main, Jackson Turner. *The Social Structure of Revolutionary America.* Princeton, N.J.: Princeton University Press, 1965.

Malinowski, Bronislaw. *Sex and Repression in Savage Society.* Cleveland, Ohio: World, 1927.

Malson, Lucien. *Wolf Children and the Problem of Human Nature.* New York: Monthly Review Press, 1972.

Malthus, Thomas Robert. *First Essay on Population 1798.* London: Macmillan, 1926. Originally published in 1798.

Mamdani, Mahmood. "The Myth of Population Control: Family, Caste, and Class in an Urban Village." New York: Monthly Review Press, 1973.

Mander, Jerry. *In the Absence of the Sacred: The Failure of Technology and the Survival of the Indian Nations.* San Francisco, Calif.: Sierra Club Books, 1992.

Manheimer, Ronald J. "The Older Learner's Journey to an Ageless Society." *Journal of Transformative Education, 3,* 3, 2005.

Manno, Bruno V. "The Real Score on the SATs." *Wall Street Journal,* September 13, 1995:A14.

Manpower Report to the President. Washington, D.C.: U.S. Department of Labor, Manpower Administration, April 1971.

Manzo, Kathleen Kennedy. "History in the Making." *Community College Week, 13,* 15, March 5, 2001:6–8.

Marcus, Amy Dockser. "Mideast Minorities: Kurds Aren't Alone." *Wall Street Journal,* September 5, 1996:A12.

Mardell, Mark. "Europe in Khaki." *BBC News,* June 14, 2007.

"Marital History for People 15 Years Old and Over by Age, Sex, Race and Ethnicity: 2001." Annual Demographic Survey, Bureau of Labor Statistics and the Bureau of the Census. 2004.

Marolla, Joseph, and Diana Scully. "Attitudes Toward Women, Violence, and Rape: A Comparison of Convicted Rapists and Other Felons." *Deviant Behavior, 7,* 4, 1986:337–355.

Marquardt, Elizabeth. *Between Two Worlds: The Inner Lives of Children of Divorce.* New York: Crown Publishers, 2005.

Marshall, Samantha. "Vietnamese Women Are Kidnapped and Later Sold in China as Brides." *Wall Street Journal,* August 3, 1999.

Marshall, Samantha. "It's So Simple: Just Lather Up, Watch the Fat Go Down the Drain." *Wall Street Journal,* November 2, 1995:B1.

Martin, William G., and Mark Beittel. "Toward a Global Sociology: Evaluating Current Conceptions, Methods, and Practices." *Sociological Quarterly, 39,* 1, 1998:139–161.

Martineau, Harriet. *Society in America.* Garden City, N. Y.: Doubleday 1962. First published in 1837.

Marx, Gary T. "The Road to the Future." In *Triumph of Discovery: A Chronicle of Great Adventures in Science.* New York: Holt, 1995:63–65.

Marx, Gary T. "Thoughts On a Neglected Category of Social Movement Participant: The Agent Provocateur and the Informant." In *Collective Behavior and Social Movements,* Russell L. Curtis, Jr., and Benigno E. Aguirre, eds. Boston: Allyn and Bacon, 1993:242–258.

Marx, Karl, and Friedrich Engels. *Communist Manifesto.* New York: Pantheon, 1967. First published in 1848.

Marx, Karl. "Contribution to the Critique of Hegel's Philosophy of Right." In *Karl Marx: Early Writings,* T. B. Bottomore, ed. New York: McGraw-Hill, 1964:45. First published in 1844.

Masheter, Carol. "Postdivorce Relationships Between Ex-spouses: The Role of Attachment and Interpersonal Conflict." *Journal of Marriage and the Family, 53,* February 1991:103–110.

Massey, Douglas S., and Garvey Lundy. "Use of Black English and Racial Discrimination in Urban Housing Markets: New Methods and Findings." *Urban Affairs Review, 36,* 2001:451–468.

Mathews, Anna Wilde. "Fraud, Errors Taint Key Study of Widely Used Sanofi Drug." *Wall Street Journal,* May 1, 2006.

Mathews, T. J., and Brady E. Hamilton. "Mean Age of Mother, 1970–2000." *National Vital Statistics Report, 51,* 1, December 11, 2002.

Mauss, Armand. *Social Problems as Social Movements.* Philadelphia, Penn.: Lippincott, 1975.

Mayer, John D. *Personality: A Systems Approach.* Boston: Allyn and Bacon, 2007.

Mayo, Elton. *Human Problems of an Industrial Civilization.* New York: Viking, 1966.

McAdam, Doug, John D. McCarthy, and Mayer N. Zald. "Social Movements." In *Handbook of Sociology,* Neil J. Smelser, ed. Newbury Park, Calif.: Sage, 1988:695–737.

McCabe, J. Terrence, and James E. Ellis. "Pastoralism: Beating the Odds in Arid Africa." In *Conformity and Conflict: Readings in Cultural Anthropology,* James P. Spradley and David W. McCurdy, eds. Glenview, Ill.: Scott, Foresman, 1990:150–156.

McCall, Michael. "Who and Where Are the Artists?" In *Fieldwork Experience: Qualitative Approaches to Social Research,* William B. Shaffir, Robert A. Stebbins, and Allan Turowetz, eds. New York: St. Martin's, 1980:145–158.

McCarthy, John D., and Mark Wolfson. "Consensus Movements, Conflict Movements, and the Cooperation of Civic and State Infrastructures." In *Frontiers in Social Movement Theory,* Aldon D. Morris and Carol McClurg Mueller, eds. New Haven, Conn.: Yale University Press, 1992:273–297.

McCarthy, John D., and Mayer N. Zald. "Resource Mobilization and Social Movements: A Partial Theory." *American Journal of Sociology, 82,* 6, 1977:1212–1241.

McCarthy, Michael J. "Granbury, Texas, Isn't a Rural Town: It's a 'Micropolis.'" *Wall Street Journal,* June 3, 2004.

McCarthy, Michael J. "James Bond Hits the Supermarket: Stores Snoop on Shoppers' Habits to Boost Sales." *Wall Street Journal,* August 25, 1993:B1, B8.

McCormick, John. "Change Has Taken Place." *Newsweek,* June 7, 1999b:34.

McCormick, John. "The Sorry Side of Sears." *Newsweek,* February 22, 1999:36–39.

McDowell, Bart. "Mexico City: An Alarming Giant." *National Geographic, 166,* 1984:139–174.

McFalls, Joseph A., Jr. "Population: A Lively Introduction, 5th ed." *Population Bulletin, 62,* 1, March 2007:1–30.

McGee, Glenn. "Cloning, Sex, and New Kinds of Families." *Journal of Sex Research, 37,* 3, August 2000:266–272.

McGinn, Daniel, and Jason McLure. "Home School: The Ring." *Newsweek,* November 10, 2003:12.

McGlynn, Elizabeth A., Steven M. Asch, John Adams, Joan Keesley, Jennifer Hicks, Allison deCristofaro, and Eve A. Kerr. "The Quality of Health Care Delivered to Adults in the United States." *New England Journal of Medicine,* June 26, 2003:2635–2645.

McIntosh, Peggy. "White Privilege and Male Privilege: A Personal Account of Coming to See Correspondences through Work in Women's

Studies." Working Paper #189. Wellesley College Center for Research on Women, 1988.

McIntyre, Jamie. "Army Rape Case Renews Debate on Coed Training." April 30, 1997: CNN Internet article.

McKay, Jim. "Pittsburgh's iGate Wants to Go Beyond Back Office." *Pittsburgh Post-Gazette,* March 22, 2004.

McKenna, George. "On Abortion: A Lincolnian Position." *Atlantic Monthly,* September 1995:51–67.

McKeown, Thomas. *The Modern Rise of Population.* New York: Academic Press, 1977.

McKown, Clark, and Rhona S. Weinstein. "Modeling the Role of Child Ethnicity and Gender in Children's Differential Response to Teacher Expectations." *Journal of Applied Social Psychology, 32,* 1, 2002: 159–184.

McLanahan, Sara, and Gary Sandefur. *Growing Up with a Single Parent: What Hurts, What Helps.* Cambridge, Mass.: Harvard University Press, 1994.

McLanahan, Sara, and Dona Schwartz. "Life Without Father: What Happens to the Children?" *Contexts, 1,* 1, Spring 2002: 35–44.

McLemore, S. Dale. *Racial and Ethnic Relations in America.* Boston: Allyn and Bacon, 1994.

McNeil, Donald G., Jr. "Circumcision Halves H.I.V. Risk, U.S. Agency Finds." *New York Times,* December 14, 2006.

McNeill, William H. "How the Potato Changed the World's History." *Social Research, 66,* 1, Spring 1999:67–83.

McPhail, Clark. *The Myth of the Madding Crowd.* Hawthorne, N. Y.: Aldine de Gruyter, 1991.

McPhail, Clark. "Blumer's Theory of Collective Behavior: The Development of a Non-Symbolic Interaction Explanation." *Sociological Quarterly, 30,* 3, 1989:401–423.

McQueen, M. P. "The Road to Wellness Is Starting at the Office." *New York Times,* December 5, 2006.

McShane, Marilyn, and Frank P. Williams, III., eds. *Criminological Theory.* Upper Saddle River, N.J.: Prentice Hall, 2007.

McTague, Jim. "Going Underground: America's Shadow Economy." *Baron's,* January 6, 2005.

Mead, George Herbert. *Mind, Self and Society.* Chicago: University of Chicago Press, 1934.

Mead, Margaret. *Sex and Temperament in Three Primitive Societies.* New York: New American Library, 1950. First published in 1935.

Medlin, Richard G. "Home Schooling and the Question of Socialization." *Peabody Journal of Education, 75,* 1–2, 2000:107–123.

Meek, Anne. "On Creating 'Ganas': A Conversation with Jaime Escalante." *Educational Leadership, 46,* 5, February 1989:46–47.

Meese, Ruth Lyn. "A Few New Children: Postinstitutionalized Children of Intercountry Adoption." *Journal of Special Education, 39,* 3, 2005:157–167.

Meier, Barry. "Guidant Debated Device Peril." *New York Times,* January 20, 2006.

Meier, Barry. "Health Studies Suggest Asbestos Substitutes Also Pose Cancer Risk." *Wall Street Journal,* May 12, 1987:1, 21.

"Melee Breaks Out at Retirement Home." *The Daily News,* March 5, 2004.

Meltzer, Scott A. "Gender, Work, and Intimate Violence: Men's Occupational Spillover and Compensatory Violence." *Journal of Marriage and the Family, 64,* 2, November 2002:820–832.

Melucci, Alberto. *Nomads of the Present: Social Movements and Individual Needs in Contemporary Society.* Philadelphia: Temple University Press, 1989.

Menaghan, Elizabeth G., Lori Kowaleski-Jones, and Frank L. Mott. "The Intergenerational Costs of Parental Social Stressors: Academic and Social Difficulties in Early Adolescence for Children of Young Mothers." *Journal of Health and Social Behavior, 38,* March 1997:72–86.

Mende, Nazer, and Damien Lewis. *Slave: My True Story.* New York: Public Affairs, 2005.

Menzel, Peter. *Material World: A Global Family Portrait.* San Francisco: Sierra Club, 1994.

Mero, Jenny. "Fortune 500 Women CEOs." *CNN Money,* April 20, 2007.

Merton, Robert K. *Social Theory and Social Structure.* Glencoe, Ill.: Free Press, 1949, Enlarged ed., 1968.

Merton, Robert K. "The Social-Cultural Environment and *Anomie.*" In *New Perspectives for Research on Juvenile Delinquency,* Helen L. Witmer and Ruth Kotinsky, eds. Washington, D.C.: U.S. Department of Health, Education, and Welfare, 1956:24–50.

Merwine, Maynard H. "How Africa Understands Female Circumcision." *New York Times,* November 24, 1993.

Messner, Michael. "Boyhood, Organized Sports, and the Construction of Masculinities." *Journal of Contemporary Ethnography, 18,* 4, January 1990:416–444.

Messner, Michael A., Margaret Carlisle Duncan, and Cheryl Cooky. "Silence, Sports Bras, and Wrestling Porn." *Journal of Sport and Social Issues, 27,* 1, February 2003:38–51.

Meyers, Laurie. "Asian-American Mental Health." *APA Online,* February 2006.

Mezentseva, E. *Russian Social Science Review, 42,* 4, July-August 2001:4–21.

Michael, Robert T., John H. Gagnon, Edward O. Laumann, and Gina Kolata. "How Many Sexual Partners Do Americans Have?" In *Exploring Social Life: Readings to Accompany Essentials of Sociology: A Down-to-Earth Approach* 5th ed., James M. Henslin, ed. Boston: Allyn and Bacon, 2004:166–174.

Michels, Robert. *Political Parties.* Glencoe, Ill.: Free Press, 1949. First published in 1911.

Milbank, Dana. "Guarded by Greenbelts, Europe's Town Centers Thrive." *Wall Street Journal,* May 3, 1995:B1, B4.

Milgram, Stanley. "The Small World Problem." *Psychology Today, 1,* 1967:61–67.

Milgram, Stanley. "Some Conditions of Obedience and Disobedience to Authority." *Human Relations, 18,* February 1965: 57–76.

Milgram, Stanley. "Behavioral Study of Obedience." *Journal of Abnormal and Social Psychology, 67,* 4, 1963:371–378.

Milkie, Melissa A. "Social World Approach to Cultural Studies." *Journal of Contemporary Ethnography, 23,* 3, October 1994: 354–380.

Miller, Laura L. "Women in the Military." In *Down to Earth Sociology: Introductory Readings,* 14th ed., James M. Henslin, ed. New York: The Free Press, 2007. First published in 1997.

Miller, Lisa. "Son of Elijah Muhammad Preaches Gentler Islam in Tune With the Times." *Wall Street Journal,* July 9, 1999.

Miller, Walter B. "Lower Class Culture as a Generating Milieu of Gang Delinquency." *Journal of Social Issues, 14,* 3, 1958:5–19.

Miller-Loessi, Karen. "Toward Gender Integration in the Workplace: Issues at Multiple Levels." *Sociological Perspectives, 35,* 1, 1992:1–15.

Mills, C. Wright. *The Sociological Imagination.* New York: Oxford University Press, 1959.

Mills, C. Wright. *The Power Elite.* New York: Oxford University Press, 1956.

Mills, Karen M., and Thomas J. Palumbo. *A Statistical Portrait of Women in the United States: 1978.* U.S. Bureau of the Census, *Current Population Reports,* Series P-23, no. 100, 1980.

Miner, Horace. "Body Ritual Among the Nacirema." In *Down to Earth Sociology: Introductory Readings,* 14th ed., James M. Henslin, ed. New York: The Free Press, 2007. First published in 1956.

Minkler, Meredith, and Ann Robertson. "The Ideology of 'Age/Race Wars': Deconstructing a Social Problem." *Ageing and Society, 11,* 1, March 1991:1–22.

Mintz, Beth A., and Michael Schwartz. *The Power Structure of American Business.* Chicago: University of Chicago Press, 1985.

Mirola, William A. "Asking for Bread, Receiving a Stone: The Rise and Fall of Religious Ideologies in Chicago's Eight-Hour Movement." *Social Problems, 50,* 2, May 2003:273–293.

Mizruchi, Mark S., and Thomas Koenig. "Size, Concentration, and Corporate Networks: Determinants of Business Collective Action." *Social Science Quarterly, 72,* 2, June 1991:299–313.

Mohal, Paul, and Robin Saha. "Racial Inequalities in the Distribution of Hazardous Waste: A National-Level Reassessment." *Social Problems, 54,* 3, 2007:343–370.

Mohawk, John C. "Indian Economic Development: An Evolving Concept of Sovereignty." *Buffalo Law Review, 39,* 2, Spring 1991: 495–503.

Mol, Arthur P. *Globalization and Environmental Reform: The Ecological Modernization of the Global Economy.* Cambridge, Mass.: MIT Press, 2001.

Money, John, and Anke A. Ehrhardt. *Man and Woman, Boy and Girl.* Baltimore: Johns Hopkins University Press, 1972.

Monitoring the Future: A Continuing Study of American Youth. Ann Arbor: University of Michigan, October 2004a.

"'Monkey' Gives Delhi Claws for Alarm." *The Australian,* May 17, 2001.

Montagu, M. F. Ashley, ed. *Race and IQ: Expanded Edition.* New York: Oxford University Press, 1999.

Montagu, M. F. Ashley. *The Concept of Race.* New York: Free Press, 1964.

Montagu, M. F. Ashley. *Introduction to Physical Anthropology,* 3rd ed. Springfield, Ill.: Thomas, 1962.

Moore, Elizabeth S. *Advergaming and the Online Marketing of Food to Children.* Kaiser Family Foundation Report, July 2006.

Moore, Sarah, Leon Grunberg, and Edward Greenberg. "Are Female Supervisors Good for Employee Job Experiences, Health, and Well-Being?" *Women in Management Review, 20,* 2, 2005:86–96.

Moore, Stephen D., and Ron Winslow. "Health-Care Systems in 12 Countries Near Crisis, Drug Maker Study Says." *Wall Street Journal,* September 15, 1993:B6.

Morgan, Lewis Henry. *Ancient Society.* New York: Holt, 1877.

Morin, Monte. "$1.7 Million Awarded in Retirement Home Death." *Los Angeles Times,* October 17, 2001.

Morris, Aldon. "Black Southern Student Sit-In Movement: An Analysis of Internal Organization." In *Collective Behavior and Social Movements,* Russell L. Curtis, Jr., and Benigno E. Aguirre, eds. Boston: Allyn and Bacon, 1993:361–380.

Morris, Joan M., and Michael D. Grimes. "Moving Up from the Working Class." In *Down to Earth Sociology: Introductory Readings,* 13th ed., James M. Henslin, ed. New York: The Free Press, 2005:365–376.

Morrow, Betty Hearn. "Urban Families as Support after Disaster: The Case of Hurricane Andrew." Paper presented at the 1995 meetings of the American Sociological Association.

Mosca, Gaetano. *The Ruling Class.* New York: McGraw-Hill, 1939. First published in 1896.

Moscos, Charles, C., and Sydney Butler. *All That We Can Be: Black Leadership and Racial Integration the Army Way.* New York: Basic Books, 1997.

Mosher, Steven W. "China's One-Child Policy: Twenty-Five Years Later." *Human Life Review,* Winter 2006:76–101.

Mosher, Steven W. "Too Many People? Not by a Long Shot." *Wall Street Journal,* February 10, 1997:A18.

Mosher, Steven W. "Why Are Baby Girls Being Killed in China?" *Wall Street Journal,* July 25, 1983:9.

Mouawad, Jad. "Saudi Officials Seek to Temper the Price of Oil." *Bloomberg News,* January 27, 2007.

Mount, Ferdinand. *The Subversive Family: An Alternative History of Love and Marriage.* New York: Free Press, 1992.

Moynihan, Daniel Patrick. "Social Justice in the *Next* Century." *America,* September 14, 1991:132–137.

Mufti, Siraj. "Islamic Community in North America: Prospects and Problems." Muslim American Society online. November 23, 2004.

"Mujer Con Cabeza Humana Alega Religion en Defensa." AOL Online News, February 14, 2006.

"Mujer 'resucita' en España." BBC Mundo, February 17, 2006.

Mukamal, K. J., et al. "Roles of Drinking Pattern and Type of Alcohol Consumed in Coronary Heart Disease in Men." *New England Journal of Medicine, 348,* 2, January 9, 2003.

Murdock, George Peter. *Social Structure.* New York: Macmillan, 1949.

Murdock, George Peter. "The Common Denominator of Cultures." In *The Science of Man and the World Crisis,* Ralph Linton, ed. New York: Columbia University Press, 1945.

Murdock, George Peter. "Comparative Data on the Division of Labor by Sex." *Social Forces, 15,* 4, May 1937:551–553.

Murray, Christopher J. L., Sandeep C. Kulkarni, Catherine Michard, Niels Tomijima, Maria T. Bulzaccheili, Terrell J. Landiorio, and Majid Ezzati. "Eight Americas: Investigating Mortality Disparities across Races, Counties, and Race-Counties in the United States." *PLoS Medicine, 3,* 9, September 2006:1513–1524.

Murray, G. W. *Sons of Ishmael.* London: Routledge, 1935.

Muslim Americans: Middle Class and Mostly Mainstream. Washington, D.C.: Pew Research Center, May 22, 2007.

Mydens, Seth. "A Fervor of Capitalism Sweeps Vietnam." *International Herald Tribune,* April 26, 2006.

Nabhan, Gary Paul. *Cultures in Habitat: On Nature, Culture, and Story.* New York: Counterpoint, 1998.

Naik, Gautam. "Doing Hard Time in Greenland Isn't Really That Hard." *Wall Street Journal,* January 13, 2004.

Nakamura, Akemi. "Abe to Play Hardball with Soft Education System." *The Japan Times,* October 27, 2006.

Nakao, Keiko, and Judith Treas. "Occupational Prestige in the United States Revisited: Twenty-Five Years of Stability and Change." Paper presented at the annual meetings of the American Sociological Association, 1990. (As referenced in Kerbo, Harold R. Social Stratification and Inequality: *Class Conflict in Historical and Comparative Perspective,* 2nd ed. New York: McGraw-Hill, 1991:181.)

Nash, Gary B. *Red, White, and Black.* Englewood Cliffs, N.J.: Prentice Hall, 1974.

Nathan, John. *Sony: The Private Life.* New York: Houghton Mifflin, 1999.

National Center for Health Statistics. *Advance Data No. 351,* December 15, 2004.

National Center for Education Statistics. *Digest of Education Statistics.* Washington, D.C.: U.S. Government Printing Office, 1991.

National Center for Health Statistics. *Health: United States, 2005.*

National Institute of Child Health and Human Development. "Child Care and Mother-Child Interaction in the First 3 Years of Life." *Developmental Psychology, 35,* 6, November 1999: 1399–1413.

National Institute of Population and Social Security Research. "Population Statistics of Japan," 2006.

National Ombudsman Reporting System Data Tables. Washington, D.C.: U.S. Administration on Aging, 2003.

National School Safety Center. "School Associated Violent Deaths." Westlake Village, California, 2007.

National School Safety Center. "School Associated Violent Deaths: Westlake Village, Calif.: 2005.

National Women's Political Caucus. "Factsheet on Women's Political Progress." Washington, D.C., June 1998.

Nauta, André. "That They All May Be One: Can Denominationalism Die?" Paper presented at the annual meetings of the American Sociological Association, 1993.

Navarro, Mireya. "For New York's Black Latinos, a Growing Racial Awareness." *New York Times,* April 28, 2003.

Navarro, Vicente, ed. *The Political Economy of Social Inequalities: Consequences for Health and Quality of Life.* Amityville, N. Y.: Baywood Publishing, 2002.

Needham, Sarah E. "Grooming Women for the Top: Tips from Executive Coaches." *Wall Street Journal,* October 31, 2006.

Neeley, Mark E., Jr. *The Fate of Liberty: Abraham Lincoln and Civil Liberties.* New York: Oxford University Press, 1992.

Neikirk, William, and Glen Elsasser. "Ruling Weakens Abortion Right." *Chicago Tribune,* June 30, 1992:1, 8.

Neil, Martha. "New 'Big Brother' Software Will Monitor Workers' Facial Expressions." *ABA Journal,* January 16, 2008.

Nestar, Russell, and Robert Gregory. "Making the Undoable Doable: Milgram, the Holocaust, and Modern Government." *The American Review of Public Administration, 35,* December 1, 200:327–349.

Neugarten, Bernice L. "Personality and Aging." In *Handbook of the Psychology of Aging,* James E. Birren and K. Warren Schaie, eds. New York: Van Nostrand Reinhold, 1977:626–649.

Neugarten, Bernice L. "Middle Age and Aging." In *Growing Old in America,* Beth B. Hess, ed. New Brunswick, N.J.: Transaction, 1976: 180–197.

Neuman, W. Lawrence. *Social Research Methods: Qualitative and Quantitative Approaches,* 6th ed. Boston: Allyn and Bacon, 2006.

"New Report Provides In-Depth Analysis of Recent Commuting Trends." *News: The National Academies,* October 16, 2006.

Newman, Michael. "Class, State and Democracy: Laski, Miliband and the Search for a Synthesis." *Political Studies, 54,* 2006:328–348.

Niebuhr, Gustav. "Studies Suggest Lower Count for Number of U.S. Muslims." *New York Times,* October 25, 2001.

Niebuhr, H. Richard. *The Social Sources of Denominationalism.* New York: Holt, 1929.

Nisbett, Richard E. *The Geography of Thought: How Asians and Westerners Think Differently . . . and Why.* New York: The Free Press, 2003.

Noah, Timothy. "White House Forms Panel to Investigate Cold War Radiation Tests on Humans." *Wall Street Journal,* January 4, 1994:A12.

Nordland, Rod. "That Joke Is a Killer." *Newsweek,* May 19, 2003:10.

Nuland, Sherwin B. "The Debate Over Dying." *USA Weekend,* February 3–5, 1995:4–6.

Nusbaum, Marci Alboher. "New Kind of Snooping Arrives at the Office." *New York Times,* July 13, 2003.

Nussenbaum, Evelyn. "Video Game Makers Go Hollywood. Uh-Oh." *New York Times,* August 22, 2004.

O'Brien, John E. "Violence in Divorce-Prone Families." In *Violence in the Family,* Suzanne K. Steinmetz and Murray A. Straus, eds. New York: Dodd, Mead, 1975:65–75.

O'Brien, Timothy L. "Fed Assesses Citigroup Unit $70 Million in Loan Abuse." *New York Times,* May 28, 2004.

O'Connell, Vanessa. "Massachusetts Tries to Halt Sale of 'Sweet' Cigarettes." *Wall Street Journal,* May 20, 2004.

O'Hare, William P. "A New Look at Poverty in America." *Population Bulletin, 51,* 2, September 1996a:1–47.

O'Hare, William P. "U.S. Poverty Myths Explored: Many Poor Work Year-Round, Few Still Poor After Five Years." *Population Today: News, Numbers, and Analysis, 24,* 10, October 1996b:1–2.

Oberschall, Anthony. *Social Conflict and Social Movements.* Englewood Cliffs, N.J.: Prentice Hall, 1973.

Offen, Karen. "Feminism and Sexual Difference in Historical Perspective." In *Theoretical Perspectives on Sexual Difference,* Deborah L. Rhode, ed. New Haven, Conn.: Yale University Press, 1990:13–20.

Ogburn, William F. *On Culture and Social Change: Selected Papers,* Otis Dudley Duncan, ed. Chicago: University of Chicago Press, 1964.

Ogburn, William F. "The Hypothesis of Cultural Lag." In *Theories of Society: Foundations of Modern Sociological Theory,* Vol. 2, Talcott Parsons, Edward Shils, Kaspar D. Naegele, and Jesse R. Pitts, eds. New York: Free Press, 1961:1270–1273.

Ogburn, William F. "The Family and its Functions." In *Recent Social Trends in the United States: Report of the President's Research Committee on Social Trends.* New York: McGraw-Hill, 1933: 661–708.

Ogburn, William F. *Social Change with Respect to Culture and Human Nature.* New York: W. B. Huebsch, 1922. (Other editions by Viking in 1927, 1938, and 1950.)

Ohmae, Kenichi. *The End of the Nation State: The Rise of Regional Economies.* New York: Free Press, 1995.

Okamoto, Dina G., and Lynn Smith-Lovin. "Changing the Subject: Gender, Status, and the Dynamics of Topic Change." *American Sociological Review, 66,* 6, December 2001:852–873.

Olmsted, Michael S., and A. Paul Hare. *The Small Group,* 2nd ed. New York: Random House, 1978.

Olneck, Michael R., and David B. Bills. "What Makes Sammy Run? An Empirical Assessment of the Bowles-Gintis Correspondence Theory." *American Journal of Education, 89,* 1980:27–61.

Olshansky, S. Jay, Bruce Carnes, Richard G. Rogers, and Len Smith. "Infectious Diseases—New and Ancient Threats to World Health." *Population Bulletin, 52,* 2, July 1997:1–51.

"On History and Heritage: John K. Castle." *Penn Law Journal,* Fall 1999.

Ono, Hiroshi. "Who Goes to College? Features of Institutional Tracking in Japanese Higher Education." *American Journal of Education, 109,* 12, February 2001:161–195.

Ono, Yumiko. "By Dint of Promotion Japanese Entrepreneur Ignites a Soccer Frenzy." *Wall Street Journal,* September 17, 1993:A1, A6.

Orme, Nicholas. *Medieval Children.* New Haven: Yale University Press, 2002.

Orwell, George. *1984.* New York: Harcourt Brace, 1949.

Osborne, Lawrence. "Got Silk." *New York Times Magazine,* June 15, 2002.

Oster, Shai. "Illegal Power Plants, Coal Mines in China Pose Challenge for Beijing." *Wall Street Journal,* December 27, 2006.

Ouchi, William. "Decision-Making in Japanese Organizations." In *Down to Earth Sociology: Introductory Readings,* 7th ed., James M. Henslin, ed. New York: Free Press, 1993:503–507.

Ouchi, William. *Theory Z: How American Business Can Meet the Japanese Challenge.* Reading, Mass.: Addison-Wesley, 1981.

Padgett, Tim. "An Ivy Stepladder." *Time,* April 4, 2005.

Pagelow, Mildred Daley. "Adult Victims of Domestic Violence: Battered Women." *Journal of Interpersonal Violence, 7,* 1, March 1992:87–120.

Pager, Devah. "Blacks and Ex-Cons Need Not Apply." *Context, 2,* 3, Fall 2003:58–59.

Pager, Devah. "The Mark of a Criminal Record." *American Journal of Sociology, 108,* 5, March 2003:937–975.

Palen, John J. *The Urban World,* 7th ed. Boston: McGraw Hill, 2005.

Paluck, Elizabeth Levy. "Diversity Training and Intergroup Contact: A Call to Action Research." *Journal of Social Sciences, 62,* 3, 2006:577–595.

Parfit, Michael, "Earth First!ers Wield a Mean Monkey Wrench." *Smithsonian, 21,* 1, April 1990:184–204.

Park, Robert. *Masse und Publikum.* Berlin: Lack and Grunau, 1904.

Park, Robert Ezra. "Human Ecology." *American Journal of Sociology, 42,* 1, July 1936:1–15.

Park, Robert Ezra, and Ernest W. Burgess. *Human Ecology.* Chicago: University of Chicago Press, 1921.

Parsons, Talcott. "An Analytic Approach to the Theory of Social Stratification." *American Journal of Sociology, 45,* 1940:841–862.

Partington, Donald H. "The Incidence of the Death Penalty for Rape in Virginia." *Washington and Lee Law Review, 22,* 1965: 43–75.

Pascoe, C. J. "Multiple Masculinities? Teenage Boys Talk About Jocks and Gender." *American Behavioral Scientist, 46,* 10, June 2003:1423–1438.

Passell, Peter. "Race, Mortgages and Statistics." *New York Times,* May 10, 1996:D1, D4. Washington, D.C.: Pew Hispanic Center.

Patterson, Orlando. "The Root of the Problem." *Time,* April 26, 2007.

Pear, Robert. "Huge Billing Fraud Is Cited by Health Plans at California Clinics." *New York Times,* March 12, 2005.

Pear, Robert. "9 of 10 Nursing Homes Lack Adequate Staff, Study Finds." *New York Times,* February 18, 2002.

Pearlin, L. I., and Melvin L. Kohn. "Social Class, Occupation, and Parental Values: A Cross-National Study." *American Sociological Review, 31,* 1966:466–479.

Peart, Karen N. "Converts to the Faith." *Scholastic Update, 126,* 4, October 22, 1993:16–18.

Pedersen, R. P. "How We Got Here: It's Not How You Think." *Community College Week, 13,* 15, March 15, 2001:4–5.

Peña, Maria. "Patrullaje de voluntarios destaca urgencia de aprobar reforma." EFE. April 3, 2005.

Pennar, Karen, and Christopher Farrell. "Notes from the Underground Economy." *Business Week,* February 15, 1993:98–101.

Perrow, Charles. "A Society of Organizations." *Theory and Society, 20,* 6, December 1991:725–762.

Perry, Barbara. "Nobody Trusts Them! Under- and Over-Policing Native American Communities." *Critical Criminology, 14,* 2006:411–444.

Perry, William J., Ashton B. Carter, and Michael M. May. "After the Bomb." *New York Times,* June 12, 2007.

Peter, Laurence J., and Raymond Hull. *The Peter Principle: Why Things Always Go Wrong.* New York: Morrow, 1969.

Peters, Jeremy W., and Danny Hakim. "Ford's Lending Practices Challenged in a Lawsuit." *New York Times,* March 1, 2005.

Petersen, Melody. "Court Papers Suggest Scale of Drug's Use." *New York Times,* May 30, 2003.

Petersen, Melody. "Suit Says Company Promoted Drug in Exam Rooms." *New York Times,* May 15, 2002.

Peterson, Iver. "1993 Deal for Indian Casino Is Called a Model to Avoid." *New York Times,* June 30, 2003.

Peterson, Janice. "Welfare Reform and Inequality: The TANF and UI Programs." *Journal of Economic Issues, 34,* 2, June 2000: 517–526.

Pfann, Gerard A., et al. "Business Success and Businesses' Beauty Capital." *Economics Letters, 67,* 2, May 2000:201–207.

Phillips, Barbara D. "America's Forgotten Plague." *Wall Street Journal,* February 9, 1998:A15.

Phillips, Mary. "Midwives Versus Medics: A 17th-Century Professional Turf War." *Management and Organizational History, 2,* 1, 2007:27–44.

Piaget, Jean. *The Construction of Reality in the Child.* New York: Basic Books, 1954.

Piaget, Jean. *The Psychology of Intelligence.* London: Routledge & Kegan Paul, 1950.

Picker, David. "Blood, Sweat and Type O: Japan's Weird Science." *New York Times,* December 14, 2006.

"Piden en Holanda aplicar la eutanasia infantil." BBC Mundo. December 15, 2004.

Pillemer, Karl, and Beth Hudson. "A Model Abuse Prevention Program for Nursing Assistants." *Gerontologist, 33,* 1, 1993: 128–131.

Pillemer, Karl, and J. Jill Suitor. "Violence and Violent Feelings: What Causes Them Among Family Caregivers?" *Journal of Gerontology, 47,* 4, 1992:165–172.

Pillemer, Karl, and Rosalie S. Wolf. *Elder Abuse: Conflict in the Family.* Dover, Mass.: Auburn House, 1987.

Pilling, D., and M. Kellmer Pringle. *Controversial Issues in Child Development.* London: Paul Elek, 1978.

Pines, Maya. "The Civilizing of Genie." *Psychology Today, 15,* September 1981:28–34.

Piotrow, Phylis Tilson. *World Population Crisis: The United States' Response.* New York: Praeger, 1973.

Pohl, Otto. "Universities Exporting B. A. Programs Via the Internet." *New York Times,* March 26, 2003.

Polgreen, Lydia, and Marlise Simons. "Global Sludge Ends in Tragedy for Ivory Coast." *New York Times,* October 2, 2006.

Polsby, Nelson W. "Three Problems in the Analysis of Community Power." *American Sociological Review, 24,* 6, December 1959:796–803.

Pope, Liston. *Millhands and Preachers: A Study of Gastonia.* New Haven, Conn.: Yale University Press, 1942.

"Population Today." Washington, D.C.: Population Reference Bureau, 4, 5, September 1998.

Portés, Alejandro, and Ruben G. Rumbaut. *Immigrant America.* Berkeley: University of California Press, 1990.

Postman, Neil. *Technopoly: The Surrender of Culture to Technology.* New York: Knopf, 1992.

Powell, Lynda H., Leila Shahabi, and Carl E. Thoresen. "Religion and Spirituality: Linkages to Physical Health." *American Psychologist, 58,* 1, January 2003:36–52.

Pratt, Laura A., Achintya N. Dey, and Alan J. Cohen. "Characteristics of Adults with Serious Psychological Distress as Measured by the K6 Scale: United States, 2001–04." *Vital and Health Statistics, 382,* March 30 2007:1–18.

Presser, Stanley, and Linda Stinson. "Data Collection Mode and Social Desirability Bias in Self-Reported Religious Attendance." *American Sociological Review, 63,* February 1998:137–145.

Preston, Howard L. *Automobile Age Atlanta: the Making of a Southern Metropolis, 1900–1935.* Athens U. of Georgia Press, 1979.

Princiotta, Daniel, Stacey Bielick, and Chris Chapman. "1.1 Million Homeschooled Students in the United States in 2003." *Education Statistics Quarterly, 6,* 3, 2004:23–25.

Proctor, Robert N. *The Nazi War on Cancer.* Princeton, N.J.: Princeton University Press, 1999.

Prystay, Cris, and Geoffrey A. Fowler. "They Shun Hard-Body Look, Preferring Pills, Teas and Gels." *Wall Street Journal,* October 9, 2003.

Purdum, Todd S. "NATO Strikes Deal to Accept Russia in a Partnership." *New York Times,* May 15, 2002.

Quadagno, Jill. *Aging and the Life Course: An Introduction to Gerontology,* 4th ed. New York: McGraw-Hill, 2007.

Rafalovich, Adam. "Exploring Clinician Uncertainty in the Diagnosis and Treatment of Attention Deficit Hyperactivity Disorder." *Sociology of Health and Illness, 27,* 3, April 2005:305–323.

Raghunathan, V. K. "Millions of Baby Girls Killed in India." *The Straits Times,* February 8, 2003.

Rainwater, Lee, and Timothy M. Smeeding. *Poor Kids in a Rich Country: America's Children in Comparative Perspective.* New York: Russell Sage, 2003.

Raisfeld, Robin, and Rob Patronite. "Shirako Season." *New York Magazine,* December 25, 2006.

Ramos, Jorge. "Project Minuteman Is Meaningless." *Oakland Tribune.* April 10, 2005.

Rand, Michael, and Shannan Catalano. "Criminal Victimization, 2006." *Bureau of Justice Statistics Bulletin,* December 2007.

Ray, J. J. "Authoritarianism Is a Dodo: Comment on Scheepers, Felling and Peters." *European Sociological Review, 7,* 1, May 1991:73–75.

Reat, Noble Ross. *Buddhism: A History.* Berkeley, Calif: Asian Humanities Press, 1994.

Reckless, Walter C. *The Crime Problem,* 5th ed. New York: Appleton, 1973.

Reed, Susan, and Lorenzo Benet. "Ecowarrior Dave Foreman Will Do Whatever It Takes in His Fight to Save Mother Earth." *People Weekly, 33,* 15, April 16, 1990:113–116.

Regalado, Antonio. "Seoul Team Creates Custom Stem Cells from Cloned Embryos." *Wall Street Journal,* May 20, 2005.

Reibstein, Larry. "Managing Diversity." *Newsweek,* 1/2 5/96:50.

Reiman, Jeffrey. *The Rich Get Richer and the Poor Get Prison: Ideology, Class, and Criminal Justice,* 7th ed. Boston: Allyn and Bacon, 2004.

Reiser, Christa. *Reflections on Anger: Women and Men in a Changing Society.* Westport, Conn.: Praeger Publishers, 1999.

Reisman, Lonny. "Hospital Errors: The Tip of the Medical-Error Iceberg." *Managed Care Quarterly,* Spring 2003:36–38.

Rennison, Callie Marie. "Intimate Partner Violence, 1993–2001." Washington, D.C.: Bureau of Justice Statistics, February 2003.

Reskin, Barbara F. *The Realities of Affirmative Action in Employment.* Washington, D.C.: American Sociological Association, 1998.

Resnik, David B. "Financial Interests and Research Bias." *Perspectives on Science, 8,* 3, Fall 2000:255–283.

Reuters. "Fake Tiger Woods Gets 200-Years-To-Life in Prison." April 28, 2001.

Revkin, Andrew C., and Matthew L. Wald. "Material Shows Weakening of Climate Reports." *New York Times,* March 20, 2007.

Rhoads, Christopher. "Web Site to Holy Site: Israeli Firm Broadcasts Prayers for a Fee." *Wall Street Journal,* January 25, 2007.

Rhone, Nedra. "Widespread Violations Found at Care Homes." *Los Angeles Times,* April 18, 2001.

Richardson, Stacey, and Marita P. McCabe. "Parental Divorce During Adolescence and Adjustment in Early Adulthood." *Adolescence, 36,* Fall 2001:467–489.

Richman, Joe. "From the Belgian Congo to the Bronx Zoo." National Public Radio, September 8, 2006.

Richtel, Matt. "For Liars and Loafers, Cellphones Offer an Alibi." *New York Times,* June 26, 2004.

Ricks, Thomas E. "'New' Marines Illustrate Growing Gap Between Military and Society." *Wall Street Journal,* July 27, 1995:A1, A4.

Rideout, Victoria J., and Elizabeth A. Vandewater. "Zero to Six: Electronic Media in the Lives of Infants, Toddlers and Preschoolers." Kaiser Family Foundation, Fall 2003.

Rieker, Patricia P., Chloe E. Bird, Susan Bell, Jenny Ruducha, Rima E. Rudd, and S. M. Miller, "Violence and Women's Health: Toward a Society and Health Perspective." Unpublished paper, 1997.

Riessman, Catherine Kohler. "Women and Medicalization: A New Perspective." In *Dominant Issues in Medical Sociology,* 3rd ed., Howard D. Schwartz, ed. New York: McGraw-Hill, 1994: 190–211.

Rifkin, Jeremy. *The End of Work: The Decline of the Global Labor Force and the Dawn of the Post-Market Era.* New York: Putnam, 1995.

Riley, Nancy E. "China's Population: New Trends and Challenges." *Population Bulletin, 59,* 2, June 2004:3–36.

Risen, James, David Johnston, and Neil A. Lewis. "Harsh C. I. A. Methods Cited in Top Qaeda Interrogations." *New York Times,* May 13, 2004.

Rist, Ray C. "Student Social Class and Teacher Expectations: The Self-Fulfilling Prophecy in Ghetto Education." *Harvard Educational Review, 40,* 3, August 1970:411–451.

Ritzer, George. "The McDonaldization of Society." In *Down to Earth Sociology: Introductory Readings,* 11th ed., James M. Henslin, ed. New York: The Free Press, 2001:459–471.

Ritzer, George. *The McDonaldization Thesis: Explorations and Extensions.* Thousand Oaks, Calif.: Sage Publications, 1998.

Ritzer, George. *The McDonaldization of Society: An Investigation into the Changing Character of Contemporary Life.* Thousand Oaks, Calif.: Pine Forge Press, 1993.

Rivera, Sharon Werning, and David W. Rivera. "The Russian Elite Under Putin: Militocratic or Bourgeois?" *Post-Soviet Affairs, 22,* 2, 2006: 125–144.

Rivlin, Gary. "Beyond the Reservation." *New York Times,* September 22, 2007.

Robb, John. "The Coming Urban Terror." *City Journal,* Summer 2007. Online.

Robbins, John. *Healthy at 100.* New York: Random House, 2006.

Robertson, Ian. *Sociology,* 3rd ed. New York: Worth, 1987.

Rodash, Mary Flannery. "The College of Midwifery: A Sociological Study of the Decline of a Profession." Unpublished doctoral dissertation, Southern Illinois University at Carbondale, 1982.

"Rodney King." *Time,* April 25, 2007.

Rodriguez, Richard. "Searching for Roots in a Changing Society." In *Down to Earth Sociology: Introductory Readings,* 8th ed., James M. Henslin, ed. New York: Free Press, 1995:486–491.

Rodriguez, Richard. "Mixed Blood." *Harper's Magazine, 283,* November 1991:47–56.

Rodriguez, Richard. "The Late Victorians: San Francisco, AIDS, and the Homosexual Stereotype." *Harper's Magazine,* October 1990:57–66.

Rodriguez, Richard. *Hunger of Memory: The Education of Richard Rodriguez.* Boston: Godine, 1982.

Rodriguez, Richard. "The Education of Richard Rodriguez." *Saturday Review,* February 8, 1975:147–149.

Rodríguez, Victor M. "Los Angeles, U.S. A. 1992: 'A House Divided Against Itself . . .'?" *SSSP Newsletter,* Spring 1994:5–12.

Roediger, David R. *Colored White: Transcending the Racial Past.* Berkeley: University of California Press, 2002.

Roethlisberger, Fritz J., and William J. Dickson. *Management and the Worker.* Cambridge, Mass.: Harvard University Press, 1939.

Rogers, Joseph W. *Why Are You Not a Criminal?* Englewood Cliffs, N.J.: Prentice Hall, 1977.

Rogers, Stacy J., and Paul R. Amato. "Have Changes in Gender Relations Affected Marital Quality?" *Social Forces, 79,* December 2000:731–748.

Rohter, Larry. "Tracking the Sale of a Kidney on a Path of Poverty and Hope." *New York Times,* May 23, 2004.

Rohter, Larry. "For Chilean Coup, Kissinger Is Numbered Among the Hunted." *New York Times,* March 28, 2002.

Rohwedder, Cecilie. "London Parents Scramble for Edge in Preschool Wars." *Wall Street Journal,* February 12, 2007.

Roosevelt, Margot. "Choosing Their Time." *Time,* April 4, 2005:31–33.

Rosaldo, Michelle Zimbalist. "Women, Culture and Society: A Theoretical Overview." In *Women, Culture, and Society,* Michelle Zimbalist Rosaldo, and Louise Lamphere, eds. Stanford: Stanford University Press, 1974.

Rose, Frederick. "Los Angeles Tallies Losses; Curfew Is Lifted." *Wall Street Journal,* May 5, 1992:A3, A18.

Rosenbaum, David E. "U.S. Breaks a Ring That Smuggled in Thousands of Workers." *New York Times,* November 21, 1998.

Rosenberg, Charles E. *The Care of Strangers: The Rise of America's Hospital System.* New York: Basic Books, 1987.

Rosenfeld, Richard. "Crime Decline in Context." *Contexts, 1,* 1, Spring 2002:25–34.

Rosenthal, Elisabeth. "Cat Lovers Lining Up for No-Sneeze Kitties." *New York Times,* October 6, 2006.

Rosenthal, Elisabeth. "Harsh Chinese Reality Feeds a Black Market in Women." *New York Times,* June 25, 2001b.

Rosenthal, Elisabeth. "China's Chic Waistline: Convex to Concave." *New York Times,* December 9, 1999.

Rosenthal, Elisabeth, and Andrew C. Revkin. "Science Panel Calls Global Warming 'Unequivocal.'" *New York Times,* February 2, 2007.

Rosenthal, Robert, and Lenore Jacobson. *Pygmalion in the Classroom: Teacher Expectation and Pupils' Intellectual Development.* New York: Holt, Rinehart, and Winston, 1968.

Ross, Casey. "Jackpot Grandma Busy Eluding Moochers." *Boston Herald,* July 14, 2004:2.

Ross, Emma. "Social Life Helps Prevent Dementia." Associated Press, April 23, 2000.

Rossi, Alice S. "Gender and Parenthood." *American Sociological Review, 49,* 1984:1–18.

Rossi, Alice S. "A Biosocial Perspective on Parenting." *Daedalus, 106,* 1977:1–31.

Rossi, Peter H. "Half Truths with Real Consequences: Journalism, Research, and Public Policy." *Contemporary Sociology,* 1999:1–5.

Rossi, Peter H. "Going Along or Getting It Right?" *Journal of Applied Sociology, 8,* 1991:77–81.

Rossi, Peter H. *Down and Out in America: The Origins of Homelessness.* Chicago: University of Chicago Press, 1989.

Rossi, Peter H., Gene A. Fisher, and Georgianna Willis. *The Condition of the Homeless of Chicago.* Amherst: University of Massachusetts, September 1986.

Rossi, Peter H., James D. Wright, Gene A. Fisher, and Georgianna Willis. "The Urban Homeless: Estimating Composition and Size." *Science, 235,* March 13, 1987:1136–1140.

Rotello, Gabriel. "The Risk in a 'Cure' for AIDS." *New York Times,* July 14, 1996.

Roth, Louise Marie. "Selling Women Short: A Research Note on Gender Differences in Compensation on Wall Street." *Social Forces, 82,* 2, December 2003:783–802.

Rothman, Barbara Katz. "Midwives in Transition: The Structure of a Clinical Revolution." In *Dominant Issues in Medical Sociology,* 3rd ed. Howard D. Schwartz, ed. New York: McGraw-Hill, 1994:104–112.

Rothschild, Joyce, and J. Allen Whitt. *The Cooperative Workplace: Potentials and Dilemmas of Organizational Democracy and Participation.* Cambridge, England: Cambridge University Press, 1986.

Rotstein, Arthur H. "Minuteman Volunteers May Have Played Prank." Associated Press, April 7, 2005.

Rowe, S. Y., M. A. Olewe, D. G. Kleinbaum, et al. "The Influence of Observation and Setting on Community Health Workers' Practices." *International Journal for Quality in Health Care, 18,* 4, May 2006:299–305.

Rubin, Zick. "The Love Research." In *Marriage and Family in a Changing Society,* 2nd ed., James M. Henslin, ed. New York: Free Press, 1985.

Rudner, Lawrence M. "The Scholastic Achievement of Home School Students." *ERIC/AE Digest,* September 1, 1999.

Ruggles, Patricia. "Short and Long Term Poverty in the United States: Measuring the American 'Underclass.'" Washington, D.C.: Urban Institute, June 1989.

Rundle, Rhonda L. "Pay-as-You-Go M. D.: The Doctor Is In, But Insurance Is Out." *Wall Street Journal,* November 6, 2003.

Russell, Diana E. H. "Preliminary Report on Some Findings Relating to the Trauma and Long-Term Effects of Intrafamily Childhood Sexual Abuse." Unpublished paper.

Russell, Diana E. H. *Rape in Marriage.* Bloomington: Indiana University Press, 1990.

Russell, Nestar, and Robert Gregory. "Making the Undoable Doable: Milgram, the Holocaust, and Modern Government." *The American Review of Public Administration, 35,* 4, December 2005:327–349.

"Russia Sets Out to Fight Corruption in Education With a New Standardized Test." Associated Press, February 2, 2007.

Sadler, Anne G., Brenda M. Booth, Brian L. Cook, and Bradley N. Doebbeling. "Factors Associated With Women's Risk of Rape in the Military Environment." *American Journal of Industrial Medicine, 43,* 2003:252–273.

Saenz, Rogelio. "Latinos and the Changing Face of America." Washington, D.C.: Population Reference Bureau, 2004:1–28.

Saguy, Abigail. "Are We Eating Ourselves to Death?" *Contexts,* Spring 2006:11–13.

Sahlins, Marshall D. *Stone Age Economics.* Chicago: Aldine, 1972.

Sahlins, Marshall D., and Elman R. Service. *Evolution and Culture.* Ann Arbor: University of Michigan Press, 1960.

Sales, Leila. "Facebook Is the Greatest Thing Since Marx." *Chicago Maroon,* May 4, 2004.

Salopek, Paul. "Shattered Sudan: Drilling for Oil, Hoping for Peace." *National Geographic, 203,* 2, February 2003:30–66.

Samor, Geraldo, Cecilie Rohwedder, and Ann Zimmerman. "Innocents Abroad?" *Wall Street Journal,* May 5, 2006.

Sampson, Robert J., Jeffrey D. Morenoff, and Felton Earls. "Beyond Social Capital: Spatial Dynamics of Collective Efficacy for Children." *American Sociological Review, 64,* October 1999: 633–660.

Sampson, Robert J., Gregory D. Squires, and Min Zhou. *How Neighborhoods Matter: The Value of Investing at the Local Level.* Washington, D.C.: American Sociological Association, 2001.

Samuelson, Paul Anthony, and William D. Nordhaus. *Economics,* 18th ed. New York: McGraw Hill, 2005.

Samuelson, Robert J. "The Elderly Aren't Needy." *Newsweek,* March 21, 1988:68.

Sanchez, Juan I., and Nohora Medkik. "The Effects of Diversity Awareness Training on Differential Treatment." *Group and Organization Management, 29,* 4, August 2004:517–536.

Sanchez-Jankowski, Martin. "Gangs and Social Change." *Theoretical Criminology, 7,* 2, 2003:191–216.

Sanders, Peter. "Casinos Bet on Radio-ID Gambling Chips." *Wall Street Journal,* May 13, 2005.

Sapir, Edward. *Selected Writings of Edward Sapir in Language, Culture, and Personality.* David G. Mandelbaum, ed. Berkeley, Calif.: University of California Press, 1949.

Saranow, Jennifer. "The Snoop Next Door." *Wall Street Journal,* January 12, 2007.

Sayres, William. "What Is a Family Anyway?" In *Marriage and Family in a Changing Society,* 4th ed., James M. Henslin, ed. New York: Free Press, 1992:23–30.

Schackner, Bill. "How to Win New 'Friends' With a Click." *Pittsburgh Post-Gazette.* November 29, 2004.

Schaefer, Richard T. *Racial and Ethnic Groups,* 9th ed. Upper Saddle River, N.J.: Prentice Hall, 2004.

Scheff, Thomas J. *Being Mentally Ill: A Sociological Theory,* 3rd ed. New York: Aldine de Gruyter, 1999.

Schellenberg, James A. *Conflict Resolution: Theory, Research, and Practice.* Albany: New York University Press, 1996.

Schemo, Diana Jean. "When Students' Gains Help Teachers' Bottom Line." *New York Times,* May 9, 2004.

Schemo, Diana Jean. "Rate of Rape at Academy Is Put at 12% in Survey." *New York Times,* August 29, 2003b.

Schemo, Diana Jean. "Women at West Point Face Tough Choices on Assaults." *New York Times,* May 22, 2003a.

Schemo, Diana Jean. "Education Dept. Says States Have Lax Standard for Teachers." *New York Times,* June 13, 2002.

Schmiege, Cynthia J., Leslie N. Richards, and Anisa M. Zvonkovic. "Remarriage: For Love or Money?" *Journal of Divorce and Remarriage,* May-June 2001:123–141.

Schmitt, Eric. "Rapes Reported by Servicewomen in the Persian Gulf and Elsewhere." *New York Times,* February 26, 2004.

Schmitt, Eric. "How Army Sleuths Stalked the Adviser Who Led to Hussein." *New York Times,* December 20, 2003.

Schoenborn, Charlotte A. "Marital Status and Health: United States, 1999–2002." *Vital and Health Statistics, 351,* December 15, 2004: 1–32.

Schottland, Charles I. *The Social Security Plan in the U.S.* New York: Appleton, 1963.

Schwartz, Mildred A. *A Sociological Perspective on Politics.* Englewood Cliffs, N.J.: Prentice Hall, 1990.

Schulz, William F. "The Torturer's Apprentice: Civil Liberties in a Turbulent Age." *The Nation,* May 13, 2002.

Scommegna, Paola. "Increased Cohabitation Changing Children's Family Settings." *Population Today, 30,* 7, October 2002:3, 6.

Scott, Ellen Kaye. "How to Stop the Rapists: A Question of Strategy in Two Rape Crisis Centers." *Social Problems, 40,* 3, August 1993: 343–361.

Scott, Janny. "White Flight, This Time Toward Harlem." *New York Times,* February 25, 2001.

Scott, Monster Cody. *Monster: The Autobiography of an L. A. Gang Member.* New York: Penguin Books, 1994.

Scott, Susie. "The Medicalization of Shyness: From Social Misfits to Social Fitness." *Sociology of Health and Illness, 28,* 2, 2006:133–153.

Scully, Diana. "Negotiating to Do Surgery." In *Dominant Issues in Medical Sociology,* 3rd ed., Howard D. Schwartz, ed. New York: McGraw-Hill, 1994:146–152.

Scully, Diana. *Understanding Sexual Violence: A Study of Convicted Rapists.* Boston: Unwin Hyman, 1990.

Scully, Diana, and Joseph Marolla. "'Riding the Bull at Gilley's': Convicted Rapists Describe the Rewards of Rape." In *Down to Earth Sociology:*

Introductory Readings, 14th ed., James M. Henslin, ed. New York: The Free Press, 2007.

Scully, Diana, and Joseph Marolla. "Convicted Rapists' Vocabulary of Motive: Excuses and Justifications." *Social Problems, 31,* 5, June 1984: 530–544.

Segal, Nancy L., and Scott L. Hershberger. "Virtual Twins and Intelligence." *Personality and Individual Differences, 39,* 6, 2005:1061–1073.

Seib, Gerald F. *Wall Street Journal,* "Click Here for Democracy." *Wall Street Journal,* January 1, 2000:R45-R46.

Seltzer, Judith A. "Consequences of Marital Dissolution for Children." *Annual Review of Sociology, 20,* 1994:235–266.

Sengupta, Somini. "In the Ancient Streets of Najaf, Pledges of Martyrdom for Cleric." *New York Times,* July 10, 2004.

Sennett, Richard, and Jonathan Cobb. "Some Hidden Injuries of Class." In *Down to Earth Sociology: Introductory Readings,* 5th ed., James M. Henslin ed. New York: Free Press, 1988:278–288. Excerpts from Richard Sennett and Jonathan Cobb. *The Hidden Injuries of Class.* New York: Knopf, 1972.

Shane, Scott. "Through the Revolving Door, a Pot of Gold Still Awaits." *New York Times,* December 28, 2004.

Shanker, Thom. "U.S. Troops Were Subjected to a Wider Toxic Testing." *New York Times,* October 8, 2002.

Shapiro, Joseph P. "Euthanasia's Home." *U.S. News and World Report, 122,* 1, January 13, 1997:24–27.

Sharp, Deborah. "Miami's Language Gap Widens." *USA Today,* April 3, 1992:A1, A3.

Sharp, Lauriston. "Steel Axes for Stone-Age Australians." In *Down to Earth Sociology: Introductory Readings,* 8th ed., James M. Henslin, ed. New York: Free Press, 1995:453–462.

Sheets, Lawrence Scott, and William J. Broad. "Georgia Says It Blocked Smuggling of Arms-Grade Uranium." *New York Times,* January 25, 2007a.

Sheets, Lawrence Scott, and William J. Broad. "Smuggler's Plot Highlights Fear Over Uranium." *New York Times,* January 25, 2007b.

Shellenbarger, Sue. "Extreme Juggling: Parents Home-School the Kids While Holding Full-time Jobs." *Wall Street Journal,* September 14, 2006.

Shellenbarger, Sue. "When Caring for Aging Relatives Stirs Up Unwelcome Emotions." *New York Times,* July 17, 2003.

Shenon, Philip. "Arguments Conclude in Army Sex Hearing." *New York Times,* August 26, 1997.

Sherif, Muzafer, and Carolyn Sherif. *Groups in Harmony and Tension.* New York: Harper & Row, 1953.

Sherman, Spencer. "The Hmong in America." *National Geographic,* October 1988:586–610.

Shibutani, Tamotsu. *Improvised News: A Sociological Study of Rumor.* Indianapolis, Ind.: Bobbs-Merrill, 1966.

Shibutani, Tamotsu. "On the Personification of Adversaries." In *Human Nature and Collective Behavior,* Tamotsu Shibutani, ed. Englewood Cliffs, N.J.: Prentice Hall, 1970.

Shields, Stephanie A. *Speaking from the Heart: Gender and the Social Meaning of Emotion.* New York: Cambridge University Press, 2002.

Shively, JoEllen. "Cowboys and Indians: Perceptions of Western Films Among American Indians and Anglos." *American Sociological Review, 57,* December 1992:725–734.

Shively, JoEllen. "Cultural Compensation: The Popularity of Westerns Among American Indians," Paper presented at the annual meetings of the American Sociological Association, 1991.

"Sierra Leone: Female Circumcision Is a Vote Winner." African News Service, March 21, 2005.

Sills, David L. "Voluntary Associations: Sociological Aspects." In *International Encyclopedia of the Social Sciences, 16,* David L. Sills, ed. New York: Macmillan, 1968:362–379.

Sills, David L. *The Volunteers.* Glencoe, Ill.: Free Press, 1957.

Silverman, Eric K. "Anthropology and Circumcision." *Annual Review of Anthropology, 33,* 2004:419–445.

Simmel, Georg. *The Sociology of Georg Simmel,* Kurt H. Wolff, ed. and trans. Glencoe, Ill.: Free Press, 1950. First published between 1902 and 1917.

Simon, Julian L. "The Nativists Are Wrong." *Wall Street Journal,* August 4, 1993:A10.

Simon, Julian L. *Theory of Population and Economic Growth.* New York: Blackwell, 1986.

Simon, Julian L. *The Ultimate Resource.* Princeton, N.J.: PrincetonR University Press, 1981.

Simons, Andre B., and Jeannine Willie. "Runaway or Abduction. Assessment Tools for the First Responder." *FBI Law Enforcement Bulletin,* November 2000:1–7.

Simons, Marlise. "Social Change and Amazon Indians." In *Exploring Social Life: Readings to Accompany Essentials of Sociology: A Down-to-Earth Approach, Sixth Edition,* 2nd edition, James M. Henslin, ed. Boston: Allyn and Bacon, 2006:157–165.

Simpson, George Eaton, and J. Milton Yinger. *Racial and Cultural Minorities: An Analysis of Prejudice and Discrimination,* 4th ed. New York: Harper & Row, 1972.

Sindayen, Nelly. "I Once Was Lost. But Now I'm Wired." *Time, 157,* 22, June 4, 2001:80–83.

Skeels, H. M. *Adult Status of Children with Contrasting Early Life Experiences: A Follow-up Study.* Monograph of the Society for Research in Child Development, *31,* 3, 1966.

Skeels, H. M., and H. B. Dye. "A Study of the Effects of Differential Stimulation on Mentally Retarded Children." *Proceedings and Addresses of the American Association on Mental Deficiency, 44,* 1939:114–136.

Skinner, Jonathan, James N. Weinstein, Scott M. Sporer, and John E. Wennberg. "Racial, Ethnic, and Geographic Disparities in Rates of Knee Arthroplasty Among Medicare Patients." *New England Journal of Medicine, 349,* 14, October 2, 2003:1350–1359.

Sklair, Leslie. *Globalization: Capitalism and Its Alternatives,* 3rd ed. New York: Oxford: University Press, 2001.

Sloan, Allan. "A Lot of Trust, But No Funds." *Newsweek,* July 30, 2001:34.

Smart, Barry. "On the Disorder of Things: Sociology, Postmodernity and the 'End of the Social.'" *Sociology, 24,* 3, August 1990:397–416.

Smedley, Brian D., Adrienne Y. Stith, and Alan R. Nelson eds. *Unequal Treatment: Confronting Racial and Ethnic Disparities in Health Care.* Washington, D.C.: The National Academies Press, 2003.

Smith, Beverly A. "An Incest Case in an Early 20th-Century Rural Community." *Deviant Behavior, 13,* 1992:127–153.

Smith, Christian, and Robert Faris. "Socioeconomic Inequality in the American Religious System: An Update and Assessment." *Journal for the Scientific Study of Religion, 44,* 1, 2005:95–104.

Smith, Clark. "Oral History as 'Therapy': Combatants' Account of The Vietnam War." In *Strangers at Home: Vietnam Veterans Since the War,* Charles R. Figley and Seymore Leventman, eds. New York: Praeger, 1980:9–34.

Smith, Craig S. "Abduction, Often Violent, a Kyrgyz Wedding Rite." *New York Times,* April 30, 2005.

Smith, Craig S. "China Becomes Industrial Nations' Most Favored Dump." *Wall Street Journal,* October 9, 1995:B1.

Smith, Daniel Scott, and Michael Hindus. "Premarital Pregnancy in America, 1640–1971: An Overview and Interpretation." *Journal of Interdisciplinary History, 4,* Spring 1975:537–570.

Smith, Harold. "A Colossal Cover-Up." *Christianity Today,* December 12, 1986:16–17.

Smith, Jackie, Charles Chatfield, and Ron Pagnucco. *Transnational Social Movements and Global Policy: Solidarity Beyond the State.* Syracuse, N. Y.: Syracuse University Press, 1997.

Smith, Simon C. "The Making of a Neo-Colony? Anglo-Kuwaiti Relations in the Era of Decolonization." *Middle Eastern Studies, 37,* 1, January 2001:159–173.

Smith, Wesley J. "Dependency or Death? Oregonians Make a Chilling Choice." *Wall Street Journal,* February 25, 1999.

Smith-Lovin, Lynn, and Charles Brody. "Interruptions in Group Discussions: The Effects of Gender and Group Composition." *American Sociological Review, 54,* 1989:424–435.

Snow, David A., Louis A. Zurcher, Jr., and Sheldon Ekland-Olson. "Social Networks and Social Movements: A Microstructural Approach to Differential Recruitment." In *Collective Behavior and Social Movements,* Russell L. Curtis, Jr., and Benigno E. Aguirre, eds. Boston: Allyn and Bacon, 1993a:323–334.

Snyder, Mark. "Self-Fulfilling Stereotypes." In *Down to Earth Sociology: Introductory Readings,* 7th ed., James M. Henslin, ed. New York: Free Press, 1993:153–160.

"Social Darwinism in Sweden." *Report* (Alberta Edition), *28,* 14, July 9, 2001:4.

Solomon, Charlene Marmer. "Cracks in the Glass Ceiling." *Workforce, 79,* 9, September 2000:87–91.

Solomon, Jolie. "Companies Try Measuring Cost Savings from New Types of Corporate Benefits." *Wall Street Journal,* December 29, 1988:B1.

Sorokin, Pitirim A. *Social and Cultural Dynamics.* 4 vols. New York: American Book Company, 1937–1941.

Soss, Joe. "Lessons of Welfare: Policy Design, Political Learning, and Political Action." *American Political Science Review, 93,* 1999:363–380.

Sourcebook of Criminal Justice Statistics. Washington, D.C.: U.S. Government Printing Office, published annually.

South, Scott J. "Sociodemographic Differentials in Mate Selection Preferences." *Journal of Marriage and the Family, 53,* November 1991:928–940.

Specter, Michael. "Plunging Life Expectancy Puzzles Russians." *New York Times,* August 1, 1995.

Spector, Malcolm, and John Kitsuse. *Constructing Social Problems.* Menlo Park, Calif.: Cummings, 1977.

Spector, Tim. "Ageing Linked to Social Status." *BBC News,* March 29, 2007.

Spencer, Jane. "Shirk Ethic: How to Face a Hard Day at the Office." *Wall Street Journal,* May 15, 2003:D1, D3.

Spengler, Oswald. *The Decline of the West,* 2 vols. Charles F. Atkinson, trans. New York: Knopf, 1926–1928. First published in 1919–1922.

Spickard, P. R. S. *Mixed Blood: Intermarriage and Ethnic Identity in Twentieth Century America.* Madison: University of Wisconsin Press, 1989.

Spitzer, Steven. "Toward a Marxian Theory of Deviance." *Social Problems, 22,* June 1975:608–619.

Spivak, Gayatri Chakravorty. "Feminism 2000: One Step Beyond." *Feminist Review, 64,* Spring 2000:113.

Spragins, Ellyn E. "To Sue or Not to Sue?" *Newsweek,* December 9, 1996:50.

Sprecher, Susan, and Rachita Chandak. "Attitudes About Arranged Marriages and Dating Among Men and Women from India." *Free Inquiry in Creative Sociology, 20,* 1, May 1992:59–69.

Srole, Leo, et al. *Mental Health in the Metropolis: The Midtown Manhattan Study.* Albany, N. Y.: New York University Press, 1978.

Stack, Carol B. *All Our Kin: Strategies for Survival in a Black Community.* New York: Harper, 1974.

Stampp, Kenneth M. *The Peculiar Institution: Slavery in the Ante-Bellum South.* New York: Vintage Books, 1956.

Stanley, Scott M., Galena Kline Rhoads, and Howard J. Markman. "Sliding Versus Deciding: Inertia and the Premarital Cohabitation Effect." *Family Relations, 55,* October 2006:499–509.

Stark, Rodney. *Sociology,* 3rd ed. Belmont, Calif.: Wadsworth, 1989.

Starr, Paul. *The Social Transformation of American Medicine.* New York: Basic Books, 1982.

"State of the World's Children 2001." *Reading Today, 18,* 4, February–March 2001:24.

Statham, Anne, Eleanor M. Miller, and Hans O. Mauksch. "The Integration of Work: Second-Order Analysis of Qualitative Research." In *The Worth of Women's Work: A Qualitative Synthesis.* Statham, Anne, Eleanor M. Miller, and Hans O. Mauksch, eds. Albany, N. Y.: State University of New York Press, 1988:11–35.

Statistical Abstract of the United States. Washington D.C.: Bureau of the Census, published annually.

Stecklow, Steve. "SAT Scores Rise Strongly after Test Is Overhauled." *Wall Street Journal,* August 24, 1995:B1, B12.

Stein, Rob. "FDA Approves Implantable Identity Chip." *Washington Post,* October 14, 2004.

Steinberg, Jacques. "Student Failure Causes States to Retool Testing Programs." *New York Times,* December 22, 2000.

Steinberg, Laurence, Stanford Dornbusch, and Bradford Brown. *Beyond the Classroom.* New York: Simon & Shuster, 1996.

Steinhauer, Jennifer, and Ford Fessenden. "Medical Retreads: Doctor Punished by State But Prized at the Hospitals." *New York Times,* March 27, 2001.

Steinhauer, Jennifer. "So, the Tumor is on the Left, Right?" *New York Times,* April 1, 2001.

Steinhauer, Jennifer. "Angry at Managed Care, Doctors Start Fighting Back." *New York Times,* January 10, 1999.

Stenner, Karen. *The Authoritarian Dynamic.* New York: Cambridge University Press, 2005.

Stephens, Bret. "The Foreign Brides." *Wall Street Journal,* May 2, 2006.

Stevens, Amy, and Sarah Lubman. "Deciding Moment of the Trial May Have Been Five Months Ago." *Wall Street Journal,* May 1, 1992:A6.

Stevens, Mitchell L. *Kingdom of Children: Culture and Controversy in the Homeschooling Movement.* Princeton: Princeton University Press, 2001.

Stevenson, Richard W. "U.S. Debates Investing in Stock for Social Security." *New York Times,* July 27, 1998.

"Sticky Ticket: A New Jersey Mother Sues Her Son Over a Lottery Jackpot She Claims Belongs to Them Both." *People Weekly,* February 9, 1998:68.

Stiles, Daniel. "The Hunters Are the Hunted." *Geographical, 75,* June 2003:28–32.

Stinnett, Nicholas. "Strong Families." In *Marriage and Family in a Changing Society,* 4th ed., James M. Henslin, ed. New York: Free Press, 1992:496–507.

Stipp, David. "Himalayan Tree Could Serve as Source of Anti-cancer Drug Taxol, Team Says." *Wall Street Journal,* April 20, 1992:B4.

Stockard, Jean, and Miriam M. Johnson. *Sex Roles: Sex Inequality and Sex Role Development.* Englewood Cliffs, N.J.: Prentice Hall, 1980.

Stockwell, John. "The Dark Side of U.S. Foreign Policy." *Zeta Magazine,* February 1989:36–48.

Stodgill, Ralph M. *Handbook of Leadership: A Survey of Theory and Research.* New York: Free Press, 1974.

Stolberg, Sheryl Gay. "Blacks Found on Short End of Heart Attack Procedure." *New York Times,* May 10, 2001.

Stouffer, Samuel A., Arthur A. Lumsdaine, Marion Harper Lumsdaine, Robin M. Williams, Jr., M. Brewster Smith, Irving L. Janis, Shirley A. Star, and Leonard S. Cottrell, Jr. *The American Soldier: Combat and Its Aftermath,* Vol. 2. New York: Wiley, 1949.

Stout, David. "Pentagon Toughens Policy on Sexual Assault." *New York Times,* January 5, 2005.

Strang, David, and Michael W. Macy. "In Search of Excellence: Fads, Success Stories, and Adaptive Emulation." *American Journal of Sociology, 197,* 1, July 2001:147–182.

Strangleman, Tim. "The Nostalgia for Permanence at Work?: The End of Work and Its Commentators." *The Sociological Review, 55,* 1, 2007:82–103.

Strategic Energy Policy: Challenges for the 21st Century. New York: Council on Foreign Relations, 2001.

Straus, Murray A. "Explaining Family Violence." In *Marriage and Family in a Changing Society,* 4th ed., James M. Henslin, ed. New York: Free Press, 1992:344–356.

Straus, Murray A., and Richard J. Gelles. "Violence in American Families: How Much Is There and Why Does It Occur?" In *Troubled Relationships,* Elam W. Nunnally, Catherine S. Chilman, and Fred M. Cox, eds. Newbury Park, Calif.: Sage, 1988:141–162.

Straus, Roger A. "The Sociologist as a Marketing Research Consultant." *Journal of Applied Sociology, 8,* 1991:65–75.

Stryker, Sheldon. "Symbolic Interactionism: Themes and Variations." In *Social Psychology: Sociological Perspectives,* Morris Rosenberg and Ralph H. Turner, eds. New Brunswick, N.J.: Transaction, 1990.

Suizzo, Marie-Anne. "The Social-Emotional and Cultural Contexts of Cognitive Development: Neo-Piagetian Perspectives." *Child Development, 71,* 4, August 2000:846–849.

Sullivan, Andrew. "What's So Bad about Hate?" *New York Times Magazine,* September 26, 1999.

Sullivan, Andrew. "What We Look Up to Now." *New York Times,* November 15, 1998.

Sulloway, Frank J. *Born to Rebel: Birth Order, Family Dynamics, and Creative Lives.* New York: Vintage Books, 1997.

Sullum, Jacob. "Curing the Therapeutic State: Thomas Szasz on the Medicalization of American Life." *Reasonline,* July 2000.

Sumner, William Graham. *Folkways: A Study in the Sociological Importance of Usages, Manners, Customs, Mores, and Morals.* New York: Ginn, 1906.

Sun, Lena H. "China Seeks Ways to Protect Elderly." *Washington Post,* October 23, 1990:A1.

Surgeon General of the United States. *The Surgeon General's Annual Report: Health Consequences of Smoking.* Washington, D.C.: Centers for Disease Control, 2005.

Surgeon General of the United States. *The Health Consequences of Involuntary Exposure to Tobacco Smoke.* Washington, D.C.: Centers for Disease Control and Prevention, *2006.*

Surowiecki, James. *The Wisdom of Crowds.* New York: Anchor Books, 2005.

Sutherland, Edwin H. *White Collar Crime.* New York: Dryden Press, 1949.

Sutherland, Edwin H. *Principles of Criminology,* 4th ed. Philadelphia: Lippincott, 1947.

Sutherland, Edwin H. *Criminology.* Philadelphia: Lippincott, 1924.

Sutherland, Edwin H., Donald R. Cressey, and David F. Luckenbill. *Principles of Criminology,* 11th ed. Dix Hills, N. Y.: General Hall, 1992.

Sutton, Paul D., and T. J. Matthews. "Trends in Characteristics of Births by State: United States, 1990, 1995, and 2000–2002." *National Vital Statistics Reports, 52,* 19, May 10, 2004:1–150.

Suzuki, Bob H. "Asian-American Families." In *Marriage and Family in a Changing Society,* 2nd ed., James M. Henslin, ed. New York: Free Press, 1985:104–119.

Swarns, Rachel. "Growing Unease for Some Blacks on Immigration." *New York Times,* May 4, 2006.

Swatos, William H., Jr., and Lutz Kaelber, eds. *The Protestant Ethic Turns 100: Essays on the Centenary of the Weber Thesis.* Boulder, CO.: Paradigm Publishers, 2005.

"Swedish Health Care in the 1990s." Stockholm: Federation of Swedish County Councils, July 2002.

Sweeney, Megan M. "Remarriage and the Nature of Divorce: Does It Matter Which Spouse Chose to Leave?" *Journal of Family Issues, 23,* 3, April 2002:410–440.

Sykes, Gresham M., and David Matza. "Techniques of Neutralization." In *Down to Earth Sociology: Introductory Readings,* 5th ed., James M. Henslin, ed. New York: Free Press, 1988: 225–231. First published in 1957.

Szasz, Thomas S. *Cruel Compassion: Psychiatric Control of Society's Unwanted.* Syracuse: Syracuse University Press, 1998.

Szasz, Thomas S. "Mental Illness Is Still a Myth." In *Deviant Behavior 96/97,* Lawrence M. Salinger, ed. Guilford, Conn.: Dushkin, 1996:200–205.

Szasz, Thomas S. *The Myth of Mental Illness,* rev. ed. New York: Harper & Row, 1986.

Tach, Laura, and George Farkas. "Ability Grouping and Educational Stratification in the Early School Years." Unpublished paper, 2003.

Tafoya, Sonya M., Hans Johnson, and Laura E. Hill. "Who Chooses to Choose Two?" Washington, D.C.: Population Reference Bureau, 2005.

Taneja, V., S. Sriram, R. S. Beri, V. Sreenivas, R. Aggarwal, R. Kaur, and J. M. Puliyel. " 'Not by Bread Alone': Impact of a Structured 90-Minute Play Session on Development of Children in an Orphanage." *Child Care, Health & Development, 28,* 1, 2002: 95–100.

Tannen, Deborah. " 'But What Do You Mean?' Women and Men in Conversation." In *Down to Earth Sociology: Introductory Readings,* 14th ed., James M. Henslin, ed. New York: The Free Press, 2007.

Tannen, Deborah. *You Just Don't Understand: Women and Men in Conversation.* New York: Morrow, 1990.

Tapia, Andres. "Churches Wary of Inner-City Islamic Inroads." *Christianity Today, 38,* 1, January 10, 1994:36–38.

Tappan, Mark B. "Moral Function as Mediated Action." *Journal of Moral Education, 35,* 1, March 2006:1–18.

Taylor, Chris. "The Man Behind Lara Croft." *Time,* December 6, 1999:78.

Taylor, Howard F. "The Structure of a National Black Leadership Network: Preliminary Findings." Unpublished manuscript, 1992. As cited in Margaret L. Andersen and Howard F. Taylor, *Sociology: Understanding a Diverse Society.* Belmont, Calif.: Wadsworth, 2000.

Taylor, Monique M. *Harlem: Between Heaven and Hell.* Minneapolis: University of Minnesota Press, 2002.

Terhune, Chad. "Pepsi, Vowing Diversity Isn't Just Image Polish, Seeks Inclusive Culture." *Wall Street Journal,* April 19, 2005.

Thau, Richard. "Are We Heading for Intergenerational War?" *Across the Board, 38,* 4, July/August, 2001:70–74.

Thayer, Stephen. "Encounters." *Psychology Today,* March 1988: 31–36.

The Statistical History of the United States: From Colonial Times to the Present. New York: Basic Books, 1976.

"The World of the Child 6 Billion." Population Reference Bureau, 2000.

Thomas, Paulette. "Boston Fed Finds Racial Discrimination in Mortgage Lending Is Still Widespread." *Wall Street Journal,* October 9, 1992:A3.

Thomas, Paulette. "U.S. Examiners Will Scrutinize Banks with Poor Minority-Lending Histories." *Wall Street Journal,* October 22, 1991:A2.

Thomas, W. I., and Dorothy Swaine Thomas. *The Child in America: Behavior Problems and Programs.* New York: Alfred A. Knopf, 1928.

Thompson, Ginger. "Chasing Mexico's Dream into Squalor." *New York Times,* February 11, 2001.

Thompson, William. "Handling the Stigma of Handling the Dead." In *Down to Earth Sociology: Introductory Readings,* 14th ed., James M. Henslin, ed. New York: The Free Press, 2007.

Thomson, Irene Tavis. "The Theory That Won't Die: From Mass Society to the Decline of Social Capital." *Sociological Forum, 20,* 3, September 2005:421–448.

Thornton, Russell. *American Indian Holocaust and Survival: A Population History Since 1492.* Norman: University of Oklahoma Press, 1987.

Thurow, Roger. "Farms Destroyed, Stricken Sudan Faces Food Crisis." *Wall Street Journal,* February 7, 2005.

Tilly, Charles. *Social Movements, 1768–2004.* Boulder Colo.: Paradigm Publishers, 2004.

Timasheff, Nicholas S. *War and Revolution.* Joseph F. Scheuer, ed. New York: Sheed & Ward, 1965.

Tobias, Andrew. "The 'Don't Be Ridiculous' Law." *Wall Street Journal,* May 31, 1995:A14.

Tocqueville, Alexis de. *Democracy in America,* J. P. Mayer and Max Lerner, eds. New York: Harper & Row, 1966. First published in 1835.

Tocqueville, Alexis de. *The Old Regime and the French Revolution.* Stuart Gilbert, trans. Garden City, N. Y.: Doubleday Anchor, 1955. First published in 1856.

Todosijevic, Jelica, Esther D. Rothblum, and Sondra E. Solomon. "Relationship Satisfaction, Affectivity, and Specific Stressors in Same-Sex Couples Joined in Civil Unions." *Psychology of Women Quarterly, 29,* 2005:158–166.

Tokoro, Masabumi. "The Shift Towards American-style Human Resource Management Systems and the Transformation of Workers' Attitudes at Japanese Firms." *Asian Business and Management, 4,* 2005:23–44.

Tolchin, Martin. "Surgeon General Asserts Smoking Is an Addiction." *New York Times,* May 17, 1988:A1, C4.

Tönnies, Ferdinand. *Community and Society (Gemeinschaft und Gesellschaft),* with a new introduction by John Samples. New Brunswick, N.J.: Transaction, 1988. First published in 1887.

Torres, Jose B., V. Scott H. Solberg, and Aaron H. Carlstrom. "The Myth of Sameness Among Latino Men and Their Machismo." *American Journal of Orthopsychiatry, 72,* 2, 2002:163–181.

Toynbee, Arnold. *A Study of History,* D. C. Somervell, abridger and ed. New York: Oxford University Press, 1946.

Tracy, Jon. "Sometimes in War, You Can Put a Price on Life." *New York Times,* May 16, 2007.

Treiman, Donald J. *Occupational Prestige in Comparative Perspective.* New York: Academic Press, 1977.

Tresniowski, Alex. "Payday Or Mayday?" *People Weekly,* May 17, 1999: 128–131.

Trice, Harrison M., and Janice M. Beyer. "Cultural Leadership in Organization." *Organization Science, 2,* 2, May 1991:149–169.

Troeltsch, Ernst. *The Social Teachings of the Christian Churches.* New York: Macmillan, 1931.

Troiano, R. P. "Physical Activity Among Young People." *New England Journal of Medicine, 347,* September 5, 2002:706–707.

"Tsunami Deaths Over 283,000." *News 24.com,* January 27, 2005.

Tuhus-Dubrow, Rebecca. "Rites and Wrongs." *Boston Globe,* February 11, 2007.

Tumin, Melvin M. "Some Principles of Social Stratification: A Critical Analysis." *American Sociological Review 18,* August 1953:394.

Turner, Bryan S. "Outline of a Theory of Citizenship." *Sociology, 24,* 2, May 1990:189–217.

Turner, Jonathan H. *The Structure of Sociological Theory.* Homewood, Ill.: Dorsey, 1978.

Turner, Ralph H. "Collective Behavior." In *Handbook of Modern Sociology,* Robert E. L. Faris, ed. Chicago: Rand McNally, 1964: 382–425.

Turner, Ralph H., and Lewis M. Killian. *Collective Behavior,* 2nd ed. Englewood Cliffs, N.J.: Prentice Hall, 1987.

Twenge, Jean M., W. Keith Campbell, and Craig A. Foster. "Parenthood and Marital Satisfaction: A Meta-Analytical Review." *Journal of Marriage and Family, 65,* August 2003:574–583.

Tyler, Patrick E. "A New Life for NATO? But It's Sidelined for Now." *New York Times,* November 20, 2002.

Tyre, Peg. "Professor in Your Pocket." *Newsweek,* November 28, 2005: 46–47.

U.S. Bureau of the Census. *Statistical Abstract of the United States: The National Data Book.* Washington, D.C.: U.S. Government Printing Office. Published annually.

U.S. Bureau of the Census. "Annual Social and Economic Supplement to Current Population Survey." Washington, D.C.: U.S. Government Printing Office, 2006.

U.S. Bureau of the Census. Current Population Survey, November 2004. May 26, 2005.

U.S. Bureau of the Census. *Historical Statistics of the United States, Colonial Times to 1970, Bicentennial Edition.* Washington, D.C.: U.S. Government Printing Office, 1975.

U.S. Department of Education, Institute of Education Sciences, National Center for Education Statistics. *The Condition of Education, 2007.*

U.S. Department of Energy, Advisory Committee on Human Radiation Experiments. Final Report, 1995. Washington, D.C.: U.S. Government Printing Office, 1995.

U.S. Department of Labor. "President Bush's Prisoner Re-Entry Initiative: Protecting Communities by Helping Returning Inmates Find Work." Washington, D.C.: U.S. Government Printing Office, January 16, 2007.

U.S. Department of State. "World Military Expenditures and Arms Transfers." February 6, 2003.

Uchitelle, Louis. "How to Define Poverty? Let Us Count the Ways." *New York Times,* May 28, 2001.

Udry, J. Richard. "Biological Limits of Gender Construction." *American Sociological Review, 65,* June 2000:443–457.

Udy, Stanley H., Jr. "Bureaucracy and Rationality in Weber's Organizational Theory: An Empirical Study." *American Sociological Review, 24,* December 1959:791–795.

Ullman, Edward, and Chauncey Harris. "The Nature of Cities." In *Urban Man and Society: A Reader in Urban Ecology,* Albert N. Cousins and Hans Nagpaul, eds. New York: Knopf, 1970:91–100.

UNAIDS. *Aids Epidemic Update,* December 2006.

UNESCO. *Education for All Global Monitoring Report, 2006.*

UNESCO Institute for Statistics. "World Illiteracy Rates." 2005.

UNESCO: Institute for Statistics, 2000.

UNICEF. *The State of the World's Children.* New York: Oxford University Press, 1995.

Uniform Crime Reports. Washington D.C.: FBI, published annually.

United Nations. "Global Summary of the HIV/AIDS Epidemic." December 2004.

United Nations. "Agriculture: Towards 2015/30." Technical Interim Report, Food and Agriculture Organization (FAO) of the United Nations, Economic and Social Department. April 2000.

Urban Institute. "A Decade of Welfare Reform: Facts and Figures." June 2006.

Usdansky, Margaret L. "English a Problem for Half of Miami." *USA Today,* April 3, 1992:A1, A3, A30.

Useem, Michael. *The Inner Circle: Large Corporations and the Rise of Business Political Activity in the U.S. and U. K.* New York: Oxford University Press, 1984.

Van Marsh, Alphonso. "South Africans: 'Leave' Is No Answer to Violence." *CNN,* July 3, 2006.

Vanderburg, David. "The Story of Semco: The Company that Humanized Work." *Bulletin of Science, Technology & Society, 24,* 5, October 2004: 430–434.

Varese, Federico. *The Russian Mafia: Private Protection in a New Market Economy.* Oxford: Oxford University Press, 2005.

Vartabedian, Ralph, and Scott Gold. "New Questions on Shuttle Tile Safety Raised." *Los Angeles Times,* February 27, 2003.

Vaughan, Diane. "Uncoupling: The Social Construction of Divorce." In *Marriage and Family in a Changing Society,* 2nd ed., James M. Henslin, ed. New York: Free Press, 1985:429–439.

Veblen, Thorstein. *The Theory of the Leisure Class.* New York: Macmillan, 1912.

Vega, William A. "Hispanic Families in the 1980s: A Decade of Research." *Journal of Marriage and the Family, 52,* November 1990:1015–1024.

Venkatesh, Sudhir Alladi. *Off the Books: The Underground Economy of the Urban Poor.* Cambridge: Harvard University Press, 2006.

Vincent, John A. "Ageing Contested: Anti-ageing Science and the Cultural Construction of Old Age" *Sociology, 40,* 2006.

Vital and Health Statistics, Series 10, Number 217, December 2003.

Volti, Rudi. *Society and Technological Change,* 3rd ed. New York: St. Martin's Press, 1995.

Von Hoffman, Nicholas. "Sociological Snoopers." *Transaction 7,* May 1970:4, 6.

Wade, Nicholas. "In Dusty Archives, a Theory of Affluence." *New York Times,* August 7, 2007.

Wagley, Charles, and Marvin Harris. *Minorities in the New World.* New York: Columbia University Press, 1958.

Wald, Matthew L., and John Schwartz. "Alerts Were Lacking, NASA Shuttle Manager Says." *New York Times,* July 23, 2003.

Waldholz, Michael. "Major Hospitals Use Trances for Fractures, Cancer, Burns; Speeding Surgery Recoveries." *Wall Street Journal,* October 7, 2003.

Waldrop, Deborah P., and Joseph A. Weber. "From Grandparent to Caregiver: The Stress and Satisfaction of Raising Grandchildren." *Families in Society: The Journal of Contemporary Human Services,* 2001:461–472.

Walker, Alice, and Pratibha Parmar. *Warrior Marks: Female Genital Mutilation and the Sexual Blinding of Women.* New York: Harcourt Brace, 1993.

Wallace, Anthony F. C. *Religion: An Anthropological View.* New York: Random House, 1966.

Wallace, John M., Ryoko Yamaguchi, Jerald G. Bachman, Patrick M. O'Malley, John E. Schulenberg, and Lloyd D. Johnston. "Religiosity and Adolescent Substance Use: The Role of Individual and Contextual Influences." *Social Problems, 54,* 2, 2007:308–327.

Wallerstein, Immanuel. "Culture as the Ideological Battleground of the Modern World-System." In *Global Culture: Nationalism, Globalization, and Modernity,* Mike Featherstone, ed. London: Sage, 1990:31–55.

Wallerstein, Immanuel. *The Capitalist World-Economy.* New York: Cambridge University Press, 1979.

Wallerstein, Immanuel. *The Modern World System: Capitalist Agriculture and the Origins of the European World-Economy in the Sixteenth Century.* New York: Academic Press, 1974.

Wallerstein, Judith S., Sandra Blakeslee, and Julia M. Lewis. *The Unexpected Legacy of Divorce: A 25-Year Landmark Study.* Concord, N. H.: Hyperion Press, 2001.

Walsh, Catherine. "The Life and Legacy of Lawrence Kohlberg." *Society, 37,* 2, January-February 2000:38–44.

Walter, Lynn. *Women's Rights: A Global View.* Westport, Conn.: Greenwood Press, 2001.

Walters, Alan. "Let More Earnings Go to Shareholders." *Wall Street Journal,* October 31, 1995:A23.

Wang, Hongyu, and Paul R. Amato. "Predictors of Divorce Adjustment: Stressors, Resources, and Definitions." *Journal of Marriage and the Family, 62,* 3, August 2000:655–668.

Wang, Yong, and Carl W. Roberts. "*Schadenfreude:* A Case Study of Emotion as Situated Discursive Display." *Comparative Sociology, 5,* 1, 2006:45–63.

Wanzer, Sidney. "'Dr. Death' Served Us All With Time in Prison." *USA Today,* June 6, 2007.

Wark, Gillian R., and Dennis L. Krebs. "Gender and Dilemma Differences in Real-Life Moral Judgment." *Developmental Psychology, 32,* 1996:220–230.

Watson, J. Mark. "Outlaw Motorcyclists." In *Society: Readings to Accompany Sociology: A Down-to-Earth Approach, Core Concepts,* James M. Henslin ed. Boston: Allyn and Bacon, 2006:105–114. First published in 1980 in *Deviant Behavior, 2,* 1.

Wayne, Julie Holliday, Christine M. Riordan, and Kecia M. Thomas. "Is All Sexual Harassment Viewed the Same? Mock Juror Decisions in Same- and Cross-Gender Cases." *Journal of Applied Psychology, 86,* 2, April 2001:179–187.

Wayne, Leslie. "Lucrative Lobbying Jobs Await Many Leaving Government Service." *New York Times,* December 16, 2000.

Weber, Max. *Economy and Society,* G. Roth and C. Wittich, eds. Berkeley: University of California Press, 1978. First published in 1922.

Weber, Max. *The Protestant Ethic and the Spirit of Capitalism.* New York: Scribner's, 1958. First published in 1904–1905.

Weber, Max. *The Theory of Social and Economic Organization,* A. M. Henderson and Talcott Parsons, trans., Talcott Parsons, ed. Glencoe, Ill.: Free Press, 1947. First published in 1913.

Weber, Max. *From Max Weber: Essays in Sociology.* Hans Gerth and C. Wright Mills, trans. and ed. New York: Oxford University Press, 1946.

Weiner, Tim. "A New Model Army Soldier Rolls Closer to Battle." *New York Times,* February 16, 2005.

Weiner, Tim. "Air Force Seeks Bush's Approval for Space Weapons Programs." *New York Times,* May 18, 2005.

Weiner, Tim. "Pentagon Envisioning a Costly Internet for War." *New York Times,* November 13, 2004.

Weiss, Rick. "Mature Human Embryos Cloned." *Washington Post,* February 12, 2004:A1.

Weitoft, Gunilla Ringback, Anders Hjern, Bengt Haglund, and Mans Rosen. "Mortality, Severe Morbidity, and Injury in Children Living with Single Parents in Sweden: A Population-Based Study." *Lancet, 361,* January 25, 2003:289–295.

Werbner, Pnina. "Veiled Interventions in Pure Space: Honour, Shame and Embodied Struggles among Muslims in Britain and France." *Theory, Culture, Society, 24,* 2007:161–186.

Werner, Erica. "Indian Casinos Gross $25 Billion in 2006." Associated Press, June 5, 2007.

Wertz, Richard W., and Dorothy C. Wertz. "Notes on the Decline of Midwives and the Rise of Medical Obstetricians." In *The Sociology of Health and Illness: Critical Perspectives,* Peter Conrad and Rochelle Kern, eds. New York: St. Martin's Press, 1981: 165–183.

West, Candace, and Angela Garcia. "Conversational Shift Work: A Study of Topical Transitions Between Women and Men." *Social Problems, 35,* 1988:551–575.

"What Scares Doctors? Being the Patient." *Time,* May 1, 2006.

Wheaton, Blair, and Philippa Clarke. "Space Meets Time: Integrating Temporal and Contextual Influences on Mental Health in Early Adulthood." *American Sociological Review, 68,* 2003:680–706.

White, Emily. "School Away from School." *New York Times,* December 7, 2003.

White, Jack E. "Forgive Us Our Sins." *Time,* July 3, 1995:29.

White, James A. "When Employees Own Big Stake, It's a Buy Signal for Investors." *Wall Street Journal,* February 13, 1991:C1, C19.

White, Joseph B., Stephen Power, and Timothy Aeppel. "Death Count Linked to Failures of Firestone Tires Rises to 203." *Wall Street Journal,* June 19, 2001:A4.

White, Richard D., Jr. "Are Women More Ethical? Recent Findings on the Effects of Gender Upon Moral Development." *Journal of Public Administration Research and Theory, 9*, 3, July 1999: 459–471.

Whitehead, Barbara Dafoe, and David Popenoe. "The Marrying Kind: Which Men Marry and Why." Rutgers University: The State of Our Unions: The Social Health of Marriage in America, 2004.

Whorf, Benjamin. *Language, Thought, and Reality,* J. B. Carroll, ed. Cambridge, MA: MIT Press, 1956.

Whyte, William Foote. "Street Corner Society." In *Down to Earth Sociology: Introductory Readings,* 11th ed., James M. Henslin, ed. New York: The Free Press, 2001:61–69.

Whyte, William H. *The City: Rediscovering the Center.* New York: Doubleday, 1989.

Wilford, John Noble. "In Maya Ruins, Scholars See Evidence of Urban Sprawl." *New York Times,* December 19, 2000.

Williams, Christine L. *Still a Man's World: Men Who Do Women's Work.* Berkeley: University of California Press, 1995.

Williams, Rhys H. "Constructing the Public Good: Social Movements and Cultural Resources." *Social Problems, 42,* 1, February 1995:124–144.

Williams, Robin M., Jr. *American Society: A Sociological Interpretation,* 2nd ed. New York: Knopf, 1965.

Williams, Thomas D. "The Year of Tolerance." Rome: Anteneo Pontificio, 2003.

Willie, Charles Vert. "Caste, Class, and Family Life Experiences." *Research in Race and Ethnic Relations, 6,* 1991:65–84.

Willie, Charles Vert, and Richard J. Reddick. *A New Look at Black Families,* 5th ed. Walnut Creek, Calif.: AltaMira Press, 2003.

Wilson, Edward O. *Sociobiology: The New Synthesis.* Cambridge, Mass.: Harvard University Press, 1975.

Wilson, James Q., and Richard J. Herrnstein. *Crime and Human Nature.* New York: Simon & Schuster, 1985.

Wilson, William Julius. *The Bridge over the Racial Divide: Rising Inequality and Coalition Politics.* Berkeley: University of California Press, 2000.

Wilson, William Julius. *When Work Disappears: The World of the New Urban Poor.* Chicago: University of Chicago Press, 1996.

Wilson, William Julius. *The Truly Disadvantaged: The Inner City, the Underclass, and Public Policy.* Chicago: University of Chicago Press, 1987.

Wilson, William Julius. *The Declining Significance of Race: Blacks and Changing American Institutions.* Chicago: University of Chicago Press, 1978.

Wilson, William Julius, and Richard P. Taub. *There Goes the Neighborhood: Racial, Ethnic, and Class Tensions in Four Chicago Neighborhoods and Their Meaning for America.* New York: Knopf, 2006.

Wines, Michael. "Virulent TB in South Africa May Imperil Millions." *Wall Street Journal,* January 28, 2007.

Wines, Michael. "Africa Adds to Miserable Ranks of Child Workers." *New York Times,* August 24, 2006a.

Wines, Michael. "How Bad Is Inflation in Zimbabwe?" *Wall Street Journal,* May 2, 2006b.

"Winner, Dumbest Moment, Marketing." CNN, February 1, 2006.

Wirth, Louis. "The Problem of Minority Groups." In *The Science of Man in the World Crisis,* Ralph Linton, ed. New York: Columbia University Press, 1945.

Wirth, Louis. "Urbanism as a Way of Life." *American Journal of Sociology, 44,* July 1938:1–24.

Wise, Raul Delgado, and James M. Cypher. "The Strategic Role of Mexican Labor Under NAFTA: Critical Perspectives on Current Economic Integration." *Annals of the American Academy of Political and Social Science, 610,* March 2007:120–142.

Wolfensohn, James D., and Kathryn S. Fuller. "Making Common Cause: Seeing the Forest for the Trees." *International Herald Tribune,* May 27, 1998:11.

Wolfinger, Nicholas H. "Family Structure Homogamy: The Effects of Parental Divorce on Partner Selection and Marital Stability." *Social Science Research, 32,* 2003:80–97.

Wolinsky, Frederic D., Timothy E. Stump, and Christopher M. Callahan. "Does Being Placed in a Nursing Home Make You Sicker and More Likely to Die?" In *Societal Mechanisms for Maintaining Competence in Old Age,* Sherry L. Willis, K. Warner Schaie, and Mark Hayward, eds. New York: Springer Publishing Company, 1997:94–130.

Womack, James P., Daniel T. Jones, and Daniel Roos. *The Machine That Changed the World: The Story of Lean Production.* New York: Harper Perrenial, 1991.

"Women in Politics: 60 Years in Retrospect." Geneva, Switzerland: Inter-Parliamentary Union, 2006.

"Women of Our World." Washington, D.C.: Population Reference Bureau, 2002.

Wonacott, Peter. "India's Skewed Sex Ratio Puts GE Sales in Spotlight." *Wall Street Journal,* April 18, 2007.

Wood, Daniel B., "Latinos Redefine What It Means to Be Manly." *Christian Science Monitor, 93,* 161, July 16, 2001.

Wood, Scott Small. "The Price Professors Pay for Teaching at Public Universities." *Chronicle of Higher Education, 2001, 46,* 32, A18-A24.

Woodward, Kenneth L. "Heaven." *Newsweek, 113,* 13, March 27, 1989:52–55.

World Health Organization. *Constitution of the World Health Organization.* New York: World Health Organization. Washington, D.C.: Interim Commission, 1946.

Worsley, Peter. *The Trumpet Shall Sound.* London: MacGibbon and Kee, 1957.

Wright, Erik Olin. *Class.* London: Verso, 1985.

"The WSJ 350: A Survey of CEO Compensation." *Wall Street Journal,* April 10, 2006.

Wright, Lawrence. "Double Mystery." *New Yorker,* August 7, 1995:45–62.

Wright, Lawrence. "One Drop of Blood." *New Yorker,* July 25, 1994: 46–50, 52–55.

Wyatt, Edward. "City Plans to Let Company Run Some Public Schools in a First." *New York Times,* December 21, 2000.

Xie, Yu, and Kimberly A. Goyette. "A Demographic Portrait of Asian Americans." Washington, D.C.: Population Reference Bureau, 2004:1–32.

Yamaguchi, Kazuo. "Subjective Rationality of Initiators and of Threshold-Theoretical Behavior of Followers in Collective Action." *Rationality and Society, 12,* 2, May 2000:185–225.

Yan, Yunxiang. *Private Life Under Socialism: Love, Intimacy, and Family Change in a Chinese Village, 1949–1999.* Stanford, Calif.: Stanford University Press, 2003.

Yardley, Jim. "Married for the Afterlife in China." *International Herald Tribune,* October 4, 2006.

Yardley, Jim. "Faces of Abortion in China: A Young, Single Woman." *New York Times,* May 13, 2007.

Yinger, J. Milton. *The Scientific Study of Religion.* New York: Macmillan, 1970.

Yinger, J. Milton. *Toward a Field Theory of Behavior: Personality and Social Structure.* New York: McGraw-Hill, 1965.

Yonas, Michael A., Patricia O'Campo, Jessica G. Burke, and Andrea C. Gielen. "Neighborhood-Level Factors and Youth Violence: Giving Voice to the Perception of Prominent Neighborhood Individuals." *Health, Education, and Behavior OnlineFirst,* July 21, 2006.

Young, Laurie E. "The Overlooked Contributions of Women to the Development of American Sociology: An Examination of AJS Articles from 1895–1926." Paper presented at the 1995 meetings of the American Sociological Association.

Zachary, G. Pascal. "Behind Stocks' Surge Is an Economy in Which Big U.S. Firms Thrive." *Wall Street Journal,* November 22, 1995: A1, A5.

Zald, Mayer N. "Looking Backward to Look Forward: Reflections on the Past and the Future of the Resource Mobilization Research Program." In *Frontiers in Social Movement Theory,* Aldon D. Morris and Carol McClurg Mueller, eds. New Haven, Conn.: Yale University Press, 1992:326–348.

Zald, Mayer N., and John D. McCarthy, eds. *Social Movements in an Organizational Society.* New Brunswick, N.J.: Transaction, 1987.

Zamiska, Nicholas. "Pressed to Do Well on Admissions Tests, Students Take Drugs." *Wall Street Journal,* November 8, 2004.

Zaslow, Jeffrey. "A New Generation Gap: Differences Emerge Among Women in the Workplace." *Wall Street Journal,* May 4, 2006.

Zaslow, Jeffrey. "Will You Still Need Me When I'm . . . 84? More Couples Divorce After Decades." *Wall Street Journal,* June 17, 2003:D1.

Zellner, William W. *Countercultures: A Sociological Analysis.* New York: St. Martin's, 1995.

Zeng, Douglas Zhihua, and Shuilin Wang. "China and the Knowledge Economy: Challenges and Opportunity." World Bank Policy Research Working Paper 4223, May 2007.

Zernike, Kate. "The Harvard Guide to Happiness." *New York Times,* April 8, 2001.

Zerubavel, Eviatar. *The Fine Line: Making Distinctions in Everyday Life.* New York: Free Press, 1991.

Zhang, Yuanting, and Franklin W. Goza. "Who Will Care for the Elderly in China?" Center for Family and Demographic Research, Bowling Green, OH: May 2007.

Zhao, Zhongwei. "Income Inequality, Unequal Health Care Access, and Mortality in China." *Population and Development Review, 32,* 3, September 2006:461–483.

Zhuravskaya, Ekaterina. "Whither Russia? A Review of Andrei Shleifer's *A Normal Country." Journal of Economic Literature, 45,* March 2007: 127–146.

Zielbauer, Paul. "Study Finds Pequot Businesses Lift Economy." *New York Times,* November 29, 2000.

Zoepf, Katherine. "A Dishonorable Affair." *New York Times,* September 23, 2007.

Zola, Irving K. *Socio-Medical Inquiries.* Philadelphia: Temple University Press, 1983.

Zuboff. Shoshanna. "New Worlds of Computer-Mediated Work." In *Down to Earth Sociology: Introductory Readings,* 6th edition, James M. Henslin, ed. New York: The Free Press, 1991: 476–485.

Zuckerman, Laurence. "Management Employee-Ownership Experiment Unravels at United." *New York Times,* March 14, 2001.

Zweigenhaft, R. L., and G. William Domhoff. *Diversity in the Power Elite: How It Happened, Why It Matters.* New York: Rowman and Littlefield, 2006.

Subject Index

political system of, 408
population policy of, 600, 602
profiteering in, 204
and technology, 263
urban renewal in, 620
Chinese Americans. *See* Asian
   Americans
Chinese Exclusion Act of 1882, 361
Christian Solidarity International,
   239
Christianity, 537–38, 542–43.
   See also specific denominations
Chromosomes: "XYY" theory, 208
Chukwu septuplets, 479
CIA (Central Intelligence
   Agency), 416, 451
Cigarettes, 580–81
Cinco de Mayo, 355
Circular reaction, 625
Circumcision
   accidental, 303–4
   and AIDS transmission, 577
   female, 313
   male, 536, 577
Cities. *See also* Inner city;
   Urbanization
   and the automobile, 662
   development of, 603–10
   edge cities, 608
   fastest and slowest growing,
      608
   and industrialization, 603, 606
   life in, 612–16
   megacities, 607
   models of growth of, 610–12
   revitalization of, 608, 609,
      618–20
   suburbanization, 608–9,
      617–18, 662
   world's largest, 607
Citigroup, 217
Citizenship, as a social invention,
   436–37, 658
City-states, 436
Civil religion, 529
Civil rights, threats to, 453
Civil Rights Act of 1964, 357
Civil Rights Act of 1968, 357
Civil rights movement
   brief history of, 357
   participants in, 644
   photos of, 357, 624
   and relative deprivation, 644
   and religion, 529
Civilization, natural cycles of,
   656–57
Class. *See* Social class
Class conflict, 11, 29, 220–21,
   244, 247–48, 446–47
Class consciousness, 244, 247
Classless state, 657
Clique, 163
Cloning, 158
Closed-ended questions, 134, 136
Clothing, 206, 433, 434, 544, 655
Coalition governments, 429
Coalitions, 166–67
Coca-Cola, 406, 632
Coercion, 432
Cohabitation, 481–83
   and commitment, 8, 9, 482,
      483
   and divorce, 482
   and marriage, 482, 483
   meaning of, 483
   trends in, 482
Cold War, 407, 582

Cold War experiments, 582
Collective behavior, 623–36
   defined, 624
   emergent norms in, 626–27
   explanations/theories of,
      624–27
   fads and fashions, 195, 634–35
   mobs, 623, 625–26
   moral panics, 633–34
   panics, 629–33
   protests, 135
   riots, 357, 627–28, 630
   rumors, 628–29, 631, 634
   urban legends, 635–36
Collective mind, 624
College. *See also* Education;
   Schools
   attendance, by family income,
      512
   attendance, by gender, 315–18
   as bureaucracies, 177–78, 181
   community, 501, 502
   drug/alcohol use, 579–80
   graduation statistics, 356, 501
   online degrees, 517, 518
   and SATs, 503, 516–18
   types of, and race-ethnicity,
      512–13
Cologne, Germany, 603
Colombia, 209, 602, 604–5
Colonialism, 258–59, 261, 348
Colony, The, 395
Colored Baptist Ministers'
   Conference, 346
Columbia, space shuttle, 173
Columbine High School, 520
Commitment
   in marriage *vs.* cohabitation,
      482, 483
   to religion, 547
   to a social movement, 644–45
Common sense
   and ethnomethodology, 118
   language and perception, 48
   and race, 337
   and sociology, 8, 128, 147
Communication. *See also*
   Language; Mass media
   by body language, 113, 424
   and cultural leveling, 61–62,
      425
   electronic, 438, 439
   gender and conversation,
      319–20
   gestures in, 44–45
   global, 666
   by language, 45–48, 67
   and nonmaterial culture, 60
   problems in bureaucracies,
      185–86
Communism, 11, 250–51, 408,
   529–30, 638
Communist Party, 250, 409, 410
Community. *See also*
   Gemeinschaft; "Moral
   community"
   building of, 609, 618–20
   in cities, 609, 614
   compared with alienation,
      612–14, 615–16
   and elder care, 390–91
   electronic, 165
   gated, 616
   and religion, 528, 529, 531,
      533, 550
   significance of, 372
Community colleges, 501, 502

Compartmentalization, 347
Competition, 87, 406, 412,
   416–17
Computers
   and Big Brother, 664
   in business and finance, 666
   in education, 665
   in medicine, 61, 568–69, 664
   and social inequality, 666
   in war and terrorism, 667
   and work, 195–96, 197,
      655–56
Concentric zone model,
   610–11
Concrete operational stage, 73
Conflict perspective
   chart summarizing, 30
   explained, 29–30, 30
   and feminists, 29, 107
   as macrosociology, 98
Conflict perspective on
   aging, 382–87
   capitalism, 195, 413–18
   class conflict, 11, 29–30,
      220–21, 244, 247–48,
      446–47
   crime and criminal justice
      system, 208, 219–21
   divorce, 29–30
   ecosabotage, 671–72
   education, 86, 508–13
   the elderly, 382–87
   family size, 596
   gendered violence, 328
   global birth control, 598
   globalization of capitalism,
      247, 413–18
   health care, 560–62
   the homeless, 31
   marriage and family, 29–30,
      466
   the mass media, 104–5
   medicalization, 560
   midwives, defeat of, 564
   politics in U.S., 446–47
   power, 98, 220–21, 247–48,
      657
   power elite, 21, 220, 446–47
   prejudice, 344–45, 348
   religion, 533–34
   reproduction, 596
   resources, 247–48, 593
   social institutions, 106–7
   Social Security, 382–87
   social stratification, 247–48,
      268
   welfare, 294
   work, 195, 243–45, 247, 324,
      657
Conformity, 89, 170–71, 215
Confucianism, 541
Congress, U.S., 444–46, 446–47,
   529, 667
Conspicuous consumption, 401,
   661
Construction of reality. *See* Reality,
   social construction of
Continuity theory, 382
Contradictory class locations, 274,
   276
Control groups, 138
Control theory, 210–11
Controversy in social research
   in Cold War experiments, 582
   in counting the homeless,
      141–44
   deception, 145–46, 171–73

due to manipulating the
   subjects, 171–73
due to protecting the subjects,
   145
in marketing research, 142
Convergence theory, 409
Conversation, and gender
   inequality, 319–20
Coors Brewery, 192
Core nations, 259
Cornell University, 177–78
Corporate capitalism, 412,
   413–18
"Corporate cook-offs," 195
Corporate crime, 216–17, 219
Corporate culture, 191–92, 195,
   421
Corporate welfare, 669
Corporations, 191–99. *See also*
   Bureaucracies; Multinational
   corporations
   boards of directors, 412, 416–17
   CEOs, 270–71, 323, 416, 485
   consumer research by, 134
   and crime, 216–17
   and day care, 194, 485
   defined, 412
   diversity in, 191, 192–93
   and economic colonies, 258
   and elder care, 485
   in Japan, 167, 196–99
   and marketing research, 142
   and "sandwich generation,"
      485
   stockholders' revolt in, 412
   transforming the workplace,
      495
   women in management of,
      194, 323
Correlations, 139
Correspondence principle,
   511–12
"Corridor curriculum," 86
Cosmology, 532
Cosmopolites, 615
Countercultures, 52
Courtship, 468–70, 663
"Covering up," 371
Cowboys, 56, 82
Credential society/credentialing,
   506, 507
Credit cards, 404
Crime. *See also* Criminal justice
   system; Delinquents;
   Deviance; Mafia; Murder;
   Rape
   and capitalism, 216–17
   conflict perspective on, 219–21
   corporate, 216–17, 219
   decline of, 224
   defined, 204
   distribution of in U.S., 218
   functionalist perspective on,
      208, 213–19, 224
   and gangs, 151–52, 210, 217
   and gender, 218–19, 223, 225,
      227, 228, 302
   hate as a, 220, 228–29
   and illegitimate opportunity,
      216–19
   and police discretion, 229
   relativity of, 204, 228
   and social class, 208–9,
      212–13, 216–19,
      219–21, 223, 225, 229,
      283–84
   statistics on, 218, 229

Crime *(continued)*
street, 208, 216, 217–18, 221–24, 232
symbolic interactionist perspective on, 209–13, 229
white-collar, 216–17, 219, 232
Criminal justice system
conflict perspective on, 219–21
prisons, 88, 221–24, 327
reaction to deviance, 221–32
and social class, 219–21, 225, 283–84
"three strikes" laws, 223–24
women in, 218–19, 225, 226, 227, 228, 327
Criminal records, and discrimination, 32
Crips, the, 151–52, 161
Crowds. *See* Collective behavior
Crusades, the, 530
Crying, 45
Cuban Americans, 353, 355, 356. *See also* Latinos
Cueva Indians, 673
Cults, 525, 541, 542–43, 637
Cultural diffusion, 61, 658
Cultural diversity. *See* Diversity
Cultural evolution, 656
Cultural goals, 215
Cultural icons, 425
Cultural lag, 61, 658–59
Cultural leveling, 61–62, 425
Cultural privilege, 352
Cultural relativism, 41–42, 93, 205, 207–8
Cultural transmission of values, 506
Cultural universals, 59
Culture, 36–63. *See also*
Countercultures; Subcultures
and beauty, 43, 116–17, 301, 307
and biological explanations, 300–305, 307–8
and body image, 116–17
and business, 191–92, 411, 421
and childhood, 89–91
of corporations, 191–92, 195
defined, 38, 39
in education, 61, 503
and emotions, 76–77
evolution of, 656
and gestures, 44–45
and global capitalism, 411, 425
health, views on, 558
hidden, 191–92, 421
ideal, 58–59, 205
internalization of, 39–41, 41
and IQ testing, 510
and language, 45–48, 67
mainstream, 52–53, 56–57
male, 421
material, 38, 60, 61
and morality, 39, 41
and New Technology, 60–62
nonmaterial, 38, 44–51, 60, 61
and privilege, 352
real, 58–59, 205
and religious beliefs, 542, 544–45
secularization of, 531
as social structure, 100–101
symbolic, 44–51
and taken-for-granted assumptions, 39–41
and values, 52–53, 56–59, 504, 506

Culture clash (or conflict), 58, 544–45
Culture lag, 61
Culture of poverty, 261, 292, 295
Culture shock, 39, 40
Culture wars, 58
Cyberloafing, 197
Cybersleuthing, 197
Cycle of poverty, 292

Danza Teocalt, 355
Dating, online, 465
Day care
in corporations, 194, 485
effects on children, 84
and the Internet, 472
moral panic about, 633–34
numbers of children in, 473
quality of, 472
and schools, 507–8
Death. *See also* Murder
adjusting to, 392–93, 394, 474
in agricultural societies, 92
from AIDS, 561, 575–76
contemplating, 92
and the family, 28
and HMOs, 573
and industrialization, 392
infant mortality, 561, 586
leading causes of, 561, 565, 568–69
and medical errors, 568–69
in nursing homes, 390
process of, 392–93
and racism, 623, 624, 625–26
and religion, 528
at school, 520
and sexism, 315, 371
and social class, 281
sociology of, 392–94
stages of, 392–93
by suicide, 8, 9, 12–13, 15, 363, 394, 571–72
and technology, 392
from tobacco, 580
from unsafe products, 217
in wars, 449
Death penalty, 204, 225–28, 432, 640–41
Death rates, 592, 593, 599
Death row, 228
Death squads, 254–55
Debit cards, 404
Debts of poor nations, 261–62, 263
Declining Significance of Race, The (Wilson), 359
Deferred gratification, 294
Definition of the situation. *See* Reality, social construction of; Thomas theorem
Degradation ceremony, 88, 206–7, 230
Dehumanization, 346, 347, 389–90, 449–50, 451
Deindustrialization, 618
Delinquents
and differential association, 209–10
and labeling, 211–12, 212–13
and social class, 121, 124, 212–13, 229
and techniques of neutralization, 211–12
and testosterone levels, 304–5

Democracy, 436–46
authority in, 434
as a core value, 53
defined, 436
direct, 437, 438
in Europe, 440–41
and the mass media, 438
representative, 437
Democracy in America (de Tocqueville), 188
Democratic façade, 271
Democratic leaders, 169, 170
Democratic socialism, 407
Democrats, 409, 439–40
Demographic equation, basic, 600
Demographic transition, 592, 653
Demographic variables, 598–600
Demography, defined, 590
Denominations, 544
Department of Homeland Security, 107, 249, 453
Dependency, of the elderly, 388–92
Dependency ratio, 385
Dependent variable, 138
Depersonalization, 569
Deposit receipts, 403
Descent, reckoning, 464
Desert Storm. *See* Gulf Wars
Deviance, 202–33. *See also* Crime; Social control
conflict perspective on, 219–21
control theory of, 210–11
and differential association, 209–10
explanations of, 208–9
and the family, 209
and friends, neighborhoods, 209–10
functionalist perspective on, 213–19
functions of, 213–14
and the homeless, 231
and honor, 210, 312
humane approach to, 232
labeling theory of, 211–13
mainstreaming of, 211
medicalization of, 230–31
and mental illness, 230–31
and moral holidays, 49–50
and neighborhoods, 209–10
neutralization of, 211–12
and peers, 209–10
and pornography, 214, 553
reactions to, 221–32
relativity of, 204, 208, 209, 214
sexual, 205, 206, 207–8, 214, 226–27
and social change, 214
and social class, 121, 124, 208–9, 212–13, 219–21, 229
sociological perspective on, 209–21
symbolic interactionist perspective on, 204, 208, 209–13, 214, 229
theories of, 209–13
and values, 214–16
Dialectical process of history, 657
Dictatorships, 437–39
Differential association theory, 209–10
Diffusion
of culture, 60–62, 657, 658
of ideas, 657, 658

of inventions, 657, 658
of responsibility, 168, 616
Dinka tribe, 239
"Dirty work," 161, 345, 449
Disabilities, people with, 102, 507, 658–59
Disabling environments, 581
Disasters, 185, 595
Disasters, coping with, 122–23
Discovery, 657, 658
Discrimination. *See also* Prejudice; Racism; Social inequality; *specific racial-ethnic groups*
anti-Semitism, 161, 343, 344, 537
in car loans, 342
and criminal records, 32
and day laborers, 349
defined, 340
ethnic cleansing, 334, 335, 655
as an everyday burden, 359–60
and gender, 155, 166, 243, 302, 305–12, 315–20, 324, 360, 371, 419–21
and hate crimes, 220, 228–29
in health care, 315, 342
and the homeless, 231
individual and institutional, 341–42
and in-/out-groups, 344
and intelligence (IQ) tests, 510–11
in mortgages, 342
and out-groups, 161
in rental market, 360
and segregation, 357
and stereotypes, 345
unintentional, 166, 342
and women, 155, 166, 243, 302, 305–12, 315, 319–20, 324, 360, 371, 419–21
Disease, globalization of, 582–83
Disengagement theory, 381
Disinvestment, 618
Disney film rumors, 628–29
Distance learning, 516, 517, 655
"Distance zones," 112
Diversity. *See also* Race-ethnicity
among Asian Americans, 361
and contradictory standards, 162
in the corporation, 191, 192–93
among Latinos, 355
among Native Americans, 362
and religious groups, 546
in U.S. families, 474–80
Diversity training, 192–93
Divine right of kings, 248, 534
Division of labor
in bureaucracies, 182
defined, 107
and gender, 153, 155, 308–9, 310–11, 466–68
on a global scale, 410–11
in hunting and gathering societies, 153
modern/traditional comparison, 179
in pastoral and horticultural societies, 154–55, 400
in social movement organizations, 646
and social solidarity, 107

Homicide. *See* Murder
Homogamy, 470
Homosexuals
  and access to power, 220
  and families, 480
  and the "gay gene," 60
  and marriage, 462–63, 480
  and religion, 550–51
  sexual harassment of, 324
  as victims of hate crimes, 229
Honor, and killing, 210
"Honor killings," 309
Hopi, the, 48
Horatio Alger myth, 294–95
Horticultural societies, 154–55
Hospices, 393–94
Households, defined, 462
Housework, 8, 9, 92, 466–68, 663
Housing, segregation in, 342,
  349, 359, 360
Hualapi, the, 363–64
Hughes Electronics, 219
Hula hoops, 635
Hull-House, 18, 19
Human ecology, 610
Human genome, decoding of,
  157, 187, 401
Human heads, in religion, 542
Human nature, 65–70
Human sexuality, 28, 205, 303–4,
  468–70
Humanitarianism, as a value, 53
Humanizing the work setting,
  193–95
Hunting and gathering societies,
  153–54, 302, 400, 423, 500,
  658
Hurricane Katrina, 185
Hutus, 334, 347
Hygiene, 37–38, 119–20, 203
Hypothesis, 129–30
Hysterectomies, 316

Id, defined, 73–74
Ideal types
  of authority, 435
  defined, 183
Identity. *See also* Self, the
  and initiation rites, 91
  and labels, 49
  national, 506–7
  personal identity kit, 88
  racial-ethnic, 336, 337, 339
  and religion, 533
  and roles, 117–18
  and sports, 87
  and voluntary associations, 189
  and work, 87, 186, 275, 424
Ideology
  of capitalism and socialism,
    407, 660
  commitment to, 644–45
  defined, 238
  and education, 248
  of equality, 271
  to justify slavery, 238
  to justify stratification, 238,
    248–49
  of opportunity, 294–95
  and power, 271–72
  and work, 660–61
Ifaluk (of Micronesia), 76–77
Illegitimate opportunity,
  216–19
Illiteracy
  functional, 518
  and gender, 243, 309

Illness. *See* Health and health care
Immigrants
  assimilation of, 40, 47, 348,
    351–52, 362, 442, 501,
    506, 529
  birthplace of, 600
  Chinese, 361
  costs of, 599–600
  on Ellis Island, 442
  and health, 442
  and Hull-House, 18
  illegal, 353, 354, 422, 442,
    599–600
  Irish, 442
  Latinos, 47, 85, 349, 548
  marriage and culture clash,
    207–8
  politics of, 442, 506
  push and pull factors of, 599
  and racial-ethnic mix in U.S.,
    365, 366
  socialization of, 85, 506
Imperialism, 9, 655
Implicit Association Test, 341–42
Impression management, 113–18
Incarceration, 221–24
Incas, 437
Incest and incest taboo, 59, 464,
  466, 493
Income. *See also* Poverty; Wealth
  and attractiveness, 111, 117
  of CEOs, 270–71
  defined, 268
  distribution of, 252–53,
    268–71, 427
  and divorce, 487, 490
  and education, 246, 277, 283,
    290, 519
  and gender, 8, 9, 243, 290,
    309, 318, 320–23
  and illness, 567
  inequality of, 245–46, 268–71
  and inflation, 422–23
  of Native Americans, 364
  and race-ethnicity, 288, 356,
    359
  and religious affiliation, 545,
    546
  of teachers, 519, 521
  in underground economy, 422
  and voting patterns, 441, 443
Incompetence
  in bureaucracies, 187
  in medicine, 568–69
Indentured service, 238
Independent variables, 138
India
  as arms buyer, 452
  British rule of, 338
  caste system in, 240–41, 242,
    261, 348, 534
  child labor in, 240, 402
  and cultural diffusion, 62
  infanticide in, 601
  marriage in, 468, 469
  mass hysteria in, 632
  megacity in, 607
  as a nuclear power, 657
  orphanages in, 68–69
  photos taken in, 45, 181, 204,
    240, 241, 255, 310–11,
    468, 469, 526, 558
  population growth in, 595
  religion in, 261, 534, 539–40,
    542, 599
  and technology, 263
  terrorism in, 531

Individualism, 53, 58
Individualistic *vs.* structural
  explanations of poverty, 292,
  294–95
Indonesia, 91, 437, 595, 631
Industrial Revolution. *See also*
  Industrialization
  and adolescence, 91
  and cities, 603, 606
  effects on society, 155–56, 181,
    401
  and origin of sociology, 9
Industrialization. *See also*
  Industrial Revolution
  and aging/elderly, 372–73, 378,
    379
  and birth rate, 601–2
  and capitalism/modernization,
    179–80, 652–53
  and childhood, 90, 91, 254–55
  and cities, 613
  development of, 258
  and development of sociology, 9
  and dying, 392
  and education, 500–502
  and the environment, 668–71,
    674
  and the family, 27, 90, 91
  and global stratification,
    654–56
  and health, 560–61
  and leisure, 423–24
  and medium of exchange,
    403–4
  and pollution, 668–71
  and production, 179
  and rationality, 178–80
  and relationships, 178–79, 410
  and religion, 535–36, 653
  traditional authority in,
    433–34, 535–36
  and types of society, 652–53
  and urbanization, 613
Industrializing Nations. *See also*
  Least Industrialized Nations;
  Most Industrialized Nations
  distribution of land, income,
    population, 252, 254
  education in, 503–4
  environmental problems in,
    260, 670–71
  health care in, 585
  map of, 252–53
Inequality. *See* Social inequality
Infant mortality, 561, 586
Infanticide, 572, 601
Inflation, 403–4, 422–23
Information societies.
  See Postindustrial societies
In-groups, 161, 344
Inheritance, 464
Initiation rites, 91
Inner circle, 190–91, 413, 416
Inner city
  and disinvestment, 618
  and poverty, 288, 359, 608,
    609
  schools in, 510, 521–22
Inquisition, the, 530
Insider trading, 216
Institutionalized means, 215
Instrumental leaders, 169
Instrumental relationships, 87
Insurance, health, 573–74
Intelligence, 67–69
Intelligence (IQ) tests, 510
Interaction. *See* Social interaction

Intergenerational conflict, 383
Intergenerational mobility, 284,
  285–86
Intergroup relations, global
  patterns of, 345–49
Interlocking directorates, 416–17
Internal colonialism, 345, 348
International Telephone and
  Telegraph (IT&T), 416
Internet
  and day care, 472
  Donor Sibling Registry, 479
  and education, 516, 665
  electronic communities on, 165
  and flash mobs, 634
  and global communication, 666
  interaction on, 108
  and mate selection, 465
  in politics, 438
  pornography on, 214, 553
  religion on, 553
  and rumors, 631
  shaming sites, 206
  and social inequality, 666
  social networks on, 164
  and voting, 438
Interracial marriage
  and endogamy, 463–64
  forbidden in U.S., 241, 336,
    348
  patterns in U.S., 362, 470–71
Interracial student organizations,
  336
Interviewer bias, 135, 144
Interviews, 135–36
Intimacy, in marriage, 24
Intimacy rape, 493
Invasion-succession cycle, 611
Inventions. *See also* New
  technology; Social inventions
  diffusion of, 657, 658
  mediums of exchange, 404–5
  microchip, 156–57, 195–96,
    652, 664–66
  of plow, 153, 155, 400, 652
  and social change, 104, 156–57,
    400–401, 657–59
  and social revolutions, 153,
    155–58, 652
  of steam engine, 153, 155–56
Investments, global, 417–18,
  425
Invisible knapsack, 352
IQ tests, 510
Iran, 435, 449, 452, 455, 603
Iraq, 23, 174, 258, 439, 449, 451,
  455, 631
Iraqi immigrants, 207
"Iron law of oligarchy," 190–91,
  191
Iroquois, the, 362, 436–37
Islam, 108, 538–39, 543, 638
Isolation, 559
Israel, 338, 455, 562
Italy, 441, 452, 455, 638

Japan
  body image in, 117
  capitalism in, 425
  and China, 438
  corporations in, 167, 196–99
  cultural leveling in, 62
  culture of, 167, 196–99, 411
  education in, 503, 506
  emperor as a god, 534
  group identity in, 167
  megacity in, 607

and perception, 74
socialization of children in, 81
and suicide, 8, 9
teamwork in, 167, 196, 403
wealth and poverty in, 250, 261
Japanese Americans. *See* Asian Americans
Jews. *See also* Holocaust
as an out-group, 161
anti-Semitism, 161, 340, 343, 344, 537
and education in the past, 500
of Ethiopia, 338
as ethnic group, 337–38
genocide/Holocaust, 161, 172, 334, 335, 347, 537
and hate crimes, 228, 229
Nazis creating prejudice against, 343–44
as patients of Nazis, 450
and religion, 531, 536–37, 545
Jim Crow laws, 357
Joe Camel, 581
Judaism, 536–37

Kayapo Indians, 673
Kennedy Space Center, 651
Kenya, 205, 313, 576, 577
Khmer Rouge, 67
Kindergarten, 510, 513–14
Klahanie, Washington, 616
"Knowledge work," 401
Koran (Qur'an), 538, 539
Kosovo, 239, 347–48
Ku Klux Klan, 162, 340, 341, 645
Kurds, 457
Kuwait, 258
Kyrgystan, 208

Labeling
and delinquents, 121, 124, 211–12, 212–13
and deviance, 211–13
in education, 513–15
and growing old, 377
and perception, 345
and prejudice, 345, 347
race and self-labeling, 49
and teacher expectations, 513–15
Labor. *See* Work
Laissez-faire capitalism, 405
Laissez-faire leaders, 169, 170
Lake of the Ozarks, Missouri, 49–50
Land, income and population distribution, 251–58
Language, 45–48
body language, 113, 424
and culture, 45–48, 67
and day care, 84
defined, 45
"English only" movement, 354
and ethnic relations, 47
feminine terms as insults, 319
functions of, 45–48, 72
and perception, 48
and social class, 250, 508, 510
Spanish in U.S., 47, 85, 354, 442
Laser weapons, 667
Latinos, 352–55. *See also*
Race-ethnicity
and AIDS, 578
car culture, 57
comparative well-being of, 356

and culture, 57, 85
defined, 352
discrimination against, 349
diversity among, 355
and education, 85, 290, 317, 355, 356, 513, 521–22
and ethnic work, 355
family structure of, 475, 476
and housing, 349, 356
income of, 356
learning a new culture, 85
and mortgages, 342
numbers of, 350, 353, 366
and politics, 355, 440, 441, 443, 444
and poverty, 288, 290, 291, 356
and religion, 548
residence patterns of, 353
and social class, 355
and Spanish language, 47, 85, 354
statistics on, 356
terms for, 349–50, 352
and undocumented workers, 353, 354, 422, 442
Law. *See also* Crime; Criminal justice system
conflict perspective on, 220–21
mandatory education, 501
and oppression, 220–21
as social institution, 105
unintended consequences of, 223–24
unusual laws, 228
Leaders. *See also* Authority
African-American networks, 166
authoritarian, 169, 170
charismatic, 434–35, 542
defined, 168
democratic, 169, 170
expressive, 169
and groupthink, 173–74
instrumental, 169
laissez faire, 169, 170
transition of, 435–35
Leadership, 168–70, 190–91, 248, 341, 434–36, 436.
See also Authority; Leaders
Leadership styles, 169
Least Industrialized Nations.
See also Industrializing
Nations; Most Industrialized
Nations
child labor in, 402, 589, 596, 597
children in, 589, 596–97
cities in, 603, 604–5, 606, 612, 613
and colonialism, 258–59
and debt, 261–62, 263
defined, 255
distribution of land, income, population, 252–53, 255
education in, 504–5
elites of, 262
environmental problems in, 670–71
food in, 593–94
and global stratification, 252–53, 255
health care in, 560–61, 585
map of, 252–53
megacities in, 607
migration from, 599–600
population growth in, 563, 591–600

poverty in, 255, 256–57, 261, 589
resources of, 262–63
symbolic interactionist perspective on births in, 595–602
and the U.N., 598
urbanization in, 602, 604–5, 613
Legal system, 219–21
Leisure, 57, 154, 423–24, 426
Lesbians. *See* Homosexuals
Liason Agency Network, 239
Liberia, 454
Libraries, and revealing information on users, 453
Life chances, 236, 263, 268, 280–84
Life course, 88–93, 474
Life expectancy
of Abkhasians, 372
in China, 379
by country, 375, 561, 586
and education, 508
in Ethiopia, 235
in Mexico, 236
of Native Americans, 363
and pollution in Russia, 671
in U.S., 236, 374–76
Life span, 376, 395–96
Lifestyles
and health, 22, 281, 528, 583–84
of the super-rich, 271, 272, 410
Lion King, The, 628
Little Mermaid, The, 628
Living together. *See* Cohabitation
Loans, 342
Lobbyists, 444–45
Longevity, 395–96
Looking-glass self, 70
Los Angeles, 355, 357, 440, 627–28, 668
Lottery winners, 275
Louisiana, 669
Love
in India, 469
and marriage, 24–26, 53, 468–70
research on attraction, 470
Lower middle class, 279, 280, 284
Loyalty, 161
Luddites, 659
Lumpenproletariat, 244
Lutheranism, as ecclesia, 544
Lynching, 623, 624, 625–26

Machismo, 476, 596
Macro level of sociology, 30–31, 98–109, 121, 124
Macropolitics, 432
Macrosociological perspective
and culture, 100–101
and microsociology, 30, 98–99, 110–24
and social class, 101
and social status, 101–3
and social structure, 98–109, 121, 124
Macy's, 217
Mafia, 210, 251
Mainstreaming
defined, 507
of deviance, 211
of people with disabilities, 507
Malthus theorem, 590
Malthusians
anti-Malthusians, 495, 592–93

new-Malthusians, 590–91, 592–93, 594
Mandatory education laws, 501
Maquiladoras, 259–61, 263
Marburg virus, 583
March of Dimes, 187, 188
Mardi Gras, 49
Marginal working class, 219, 220
Marietta College, 326
Marines, U.S., 89, 145
Market forces, 406, 409
Marketing research, 142
Marriage. *See also* Cohabitation;
Courtship; Divorce;
Families; Mate selection
age at, 93, 481
arranged, 469
buying brides, 307
and caste, 240, 241, 469
changing meanings of, 24–26
child care responsibilities, 466–68
childless, 478
children, effect on, 471
and commitment, 482, 483
companionate, 24
conflict perspective on, 29–30, 466
cultural themes of, 463–64, 469
of dead sons in China, 463
defined, 463
and empty nest, 474
functionalist perspective on, 464, 466
future of, 494
and gender roles, 466–68
among the Hmong, 207
and housework, 8, 9, 92, 466–68
and incest, 59
interracial, 241, 336, 348, 362, 362, 463–64, 470–71
and intimacy, 24
and love, 24, 53, 468–70
monogamy and polygamy, 52, 462, 537, 539
postponing, 481
rape in, 207–8, 493
and remarriage, 490–91
in the 1800s, 17
same-sex, 462–63, 480
and "second shift," 466–68
sexual norms in, 205
and social class, 282, 469, 472–73
spouse abuse, 127–41, 491, 492, 493
successful, 493–94
symbolic interactionist perspective on, 24–26, 93
and testosterone levels, 304–5
two-paycheck, 466–68
and women in labor force, 420–21
Martians, 629–31
Marxism, Marx on, 11
Masculinities, 300
Masculinity, 80, 81, 87, 210, 303, 319, 466
Mass hysteria, 632
Mass media. *See also* Advertising
and body image, 116–17, 408
conflict perspective on, 104–5
and consumption, 408
control of, 104–5, 249, 276, 642

Mass Media (continued)
and debts of poor nations, 263
defined, 80
and democracy, 438
and the elderly, 378, 380
functionalist perspective on, 104
and gender, 80–81, 82
in Japan, 81, 411
and moral panics, 634
movies, 56, 628–29
and Native Americans, 56
and panics, 629–31
and pornography, 214, 553
and propaganda, 643
and religion, 547, 549, 553
and school shootings, 520
and slavery today, 238
sleazy newsmagazines, 104
as a social institution, 104–5
and social movements, 639, 642
and stereotypes, 80–81, 380
television, 80–81, 82, 91, 408
video games as, 81, 82
and voting, 438
Mass society theory, 642, 644
Master status, 102–3, 204, 300
Matchmaking, 465, 508
Mate selection. *See also* Marriage
bride stealing, 307
changes in, 24–26, 465
as cultural theme, 463–64
and love, 465, 468–70
polygyny, 462, 537, 539
in schools, 508
and social class, 282
Material culture, 38, 60, 61, 659
Math and gender, 306
Math education, 516–17, 521–22
Matriarchy, 303, 464
Matrilineal system of descent, 464
Mattel Toys, 62
"Maximum-security society," 196
Mazda, 199, 662
McDonaldization of society, 184
McDonald's, 62, 184
McMinnville, Tennessee, 632
Means, explained, 133
Means of production.
See Production
Mechanical solidarity, 107, 108, 410
Medellin, Colombia, 602, 604–5
Medians, explained, 133
Medicaid, 386, 563–64
Medical accidents, 303–4
Medical experiments, 333, 581
Medical insurance, 573–74
Medicalization
of deviance, 230–31
of society, 571
Medicare, 386, 563–64, 575
Medicine. *See also* Health and health care
alternative, 584
and American Medical Association, 563
black market in, 562
cesarean section births, 15
and computers, 61
conflict of interest in, 569
and cultural lag, 61
defensive, 567–68
defined, 558
diagnosis-related groups, 574
fraud in, 569–70

gender in, 315, 316, 317, 560, 564, 571
group care in, 574
gynecological examinations, 120–21
HMOs, 573–74
incompetence in, 568–69
and indigenous peoples, 673
malpractice suits, 567–68
and midwives, 309, 564
monopoly of, 563–64
pay-as-you-go programs, 574
plastic surgery, 117
and population explosion, 563
professionalization of, 562–63
racism in, 333, 581–82
rationing of, 574–75
sexism in, 315, 316, 564, 571
and the sick role, 559–60
as a social institution, 105
socialized, 563, 585
as a subculture, 51
and suicide, 571–72
Mediums of exchange, 403–5
Megacities, 606, 607
Megalopolis, 606
Melanesian Islands, 637
Melting pot, 339
Menstruation, 315
Mental illness
and the homeless, 231, 557
myth of, 230–31
in present *vs.* past, 565
of rapists, 8, 9
and religion, 528
and social class, 281–82, 566–67
Mercy killing, 571–72
Meritocracy, 246
Metaformative social movements, 638
Methodists, 550
Metropolis, 606
Metropolitan statistical areas (MSAs), 607
Mexican Americans, 353, 355, 356. *See also* Latinos
Mexico, 44, 205, 235–36, 259–61, 339, 340, 354, 422, 589, 596–98, 607, 613
Miami, 47
Mickey Mouse, 629
Microchip, effects on society, 156–57, 195–96, 652, 664–66. *See also* Computers
Microlevel of sociology, 30, 110–24
Micropolis, 609
Micropolitics, 432
Microsociological perspective
and background assumptions, 118–19
described, 98–99
and macrosociology, 30–31, 98–99, 121, 124
and presentation of self, 113–18
and social construction of reality, 119–21
and symbolic interaction, 110–13
Microsoft Corporation, 277
Middle age, 91–92
Middle class, 83, 212–13, 229, 359, 472–73, 474–75
Midwives, 309, 564

Migration, 339, 599–600, 606–10, 613
Milgram experiments, 163–65, 171–73
Military
as a bureaucracy, 181
and Cold War experiments, 582
and computers, 667
and corporations, 262
and groupthink, 174
LSD experiments, 145
rape in, 324–25
and resocialization, 89
sexual harassment in, 324–25
as a social institution, 105
soldiers, 304–5, 319, 324–25, 450, 451, 454–55
and space wars, 667
Militias, 645
Millenarian social movements, 637
Milling, 626
Mind, development of, 70–73
Minimax strategy, 626
Minority group(s). *See also*
Race-ethnicity; *specific groups*
and access to power, 220
distribution in U.S., 351
and dominant groups, 338–39
emergence of, 338–39
numbers of, 350
shared characteristics of, 338–39
women as, 305–8, 338
Minutemen (border patrol), 353
"Miss Rivers' Lodge," 333
Mobs, 623, 625–26. *See also*
Collective behavior
Model T, 661, 662
Modernization, 535, 551, 652–53
Modes, 133
Monarchies, 436
Money. *See also* Income; Property; Wealth
currency, 403, 456
digitized, 404, 666
e-cash, 404
history of, 403–5
Mongolia, 306
Monkeys, 42, 69–70, 79
Monogamy, 52
Monopolies, 406, 563–64
Monotheism, 537
"Moral community," 526, 532, 533
Moral holidays, 49–50
Moral panics, 633–34
Morality
development of, 75–76
and gender, 75–76, 483
and science, 26, 208, 214, 552
and social movements, 644–45
and war, 449
Mores, defined, 50, 51
Mormons, 52, 58, 545, 583
Morocco, culture of, 37–38, 119–20
Mortgage loans, 342, 618
Most Industrialized Nations.
See also G-8; Industrializing Nations; Least Industrialized Nations
and Africa/geopolitics, 655–56
defined, 251

distribution of land, income, population, 251, 252, 254
dominance of, 654–56
education in, 503
elderly in, 92, 372–76
environmental problems in, 668–70
food in, 594
and global stratification, 251–54, 258–59, 655–56
health care in, 585, 586
map of, 252–53
migration to, 599–600
population growth of, 593, 596, 599, 600, 602
power of, 261–63, 592–93, 654–56
and the U.N., 598
Motherhood, 596
Motorcyclists, 52, 54.
See also Bikers
Movies, 56, 628–29
Multiculturalism, 345, 348, 367
Multinational corporations.
See also Globalization of capitalism
and energy shortage, 669–70
and funny business failures, 411
and global domination, 262–63, 424–25, 667
ownership *vs.* management of, 412, 416–18
and pollution, 669
power of, 262–63, 413, 416–18
and social stratification, 262–63, 425
world's largest, 413
Multiple-nuclei model, 611–12
Murder. *See also* Genocide
of African Americans, 357, 358, 623, 625–26
and alienation in cities, 612–14
by an abused wife, 127
of Brazilian children, 254–55
of Cueva Indians, 673
of Deletha Word, 614
and gangs, 151–52
honor and killing, 210
"honor killings," 309
infanticide, 572, 601
of Kitty Genovese, 612–13, 616
by Mafia, 210, 251
prison *vs.* parole for, 327
rates in South Africa, 241
school shootings, 520
serial, 226–27
sex of victims and killers, 326–27
Muslims, 531, 533, 553.
See also Islam
Myths
about rape, 147–48
about school shootings, 520
about social mobility, 294–95
about the poor, 288
about welfare, 8, 9, 288
of an idyllic past, 565
of corporations, 198, 199
of equality in law, 219–21
Horatio Alger, 294–95
of mental illness, 230–31
of race, 334–35
of the small world phenomenon, 164–65

and death, 623, 624, 625–26
defined, 340
and diversity training, 192–93
learning, 340–41
and lynchings, 623, 624,
625–26
in medicine, 333, 571
in the rental market, 360
and Tuskegee experiment, 333,
581–82
as a value, 53, 56–57
Racist Mind, The (Ezekiel), 341
Radio, 661
Rainforests, 671, 673
Rammadan, 533
Random sample, 132–33
Rape, 493
acquaintance, 326
and conquest, 237
cultural constructions of,
207–8
and death penalty, 227
and ethnic cleansing, 348
marital (intimacy), 478
and mental illness, 8, 9,
147–48
in the military, 324–25
myths about, 8, 9, 147–48
and power, 147
in prison, 326
rate in U.S., 326
relationship of victim to
rapist, 326
research on and rapport, 136
research on in prisons, 8, 9,
144, 147–48
and serial murder, 226–27
stopping, 639
Rapists, 8, 9, 144, 147–48, 221,
326, 639
Rapport, 136
Rationalization of society, 178–80
Rational-legal authority, 434, 435
Reactive social movements, 636
Reality, social construction of
and abortion, 647–48
aging, 372, 376–80, 392
defined, 120
germs, 119–20
gynecological examinations,
120–21
health and illness, 558
and marriage or rape, 207–8
and medicalization of human
conditions, 564, 571
multiple realities, 642
pregnancy and childbirth, 564
and race, 335
and social movements, 639,
642, 647–48
through language, 48
Reasoning, development of,
72–73
Recidivism rate, 224–25
Recreation, as function of the
family, 28
Red tape, 185–86
Redemptive social movements,
637
Redlining, 618
Redwoods, 57, 671–72
Reference groups, 162, 163
Reform. *See* Social reform
Reform Party, 440
Reformation. *See* Protestant
Reformation

Reformative social movements,
637
Refugees, 457
Reincarnation, 540
Relative deprivation, 644
Reliability (of data), 130
Religion, 525–55
as agent of socialization, 84
Amish, 109
and capitalism, 13–14, 180,
535–36
and caste in India, 240–41
and charismatic leaders, 434,
435
and community, 531, 533, 550
conflict perspective on, 533–34
and death, 528
defined, 526
and divorce, 487
dysfunctions of, 530
electronic church, 547, 549
functional perspective on, 106,
527–30
fundamentalism in, 108,
538–39, 547
future of, 552–53
and hate crimes, 228, 229
and health, 528
and ideology, 248
and industrialization, 535–36,
563
and Internet, 553
membership statistics, 539,
547, 549
and poverty, 261
and prayer, 528
secularization of, 549–51
and social class, 283
and social control, 526
as a social institution, 105
and social mobility, 545, 550
and spirit of capitalism, 13–14,
180, 535–36
symbolic interactionist
perspective on, 530,
532–33
and technology, 547, 549, 553
and terrorism, 530, 531
toleration of, 542, 547
types of groups in, 541–45
in U.S., 539, 545–51
and values, 53, 84
world's largest, 536–41
Religious experience, 532–33
Religious groups, types of, 541–45
Relocation camps, 347, 361
Remarriage, 490–91
Replication, 14, 130, 165
Reproduction of humans
by cloning, 158
conflict perspective on, 596
social control of, 28
and technology, 158, 479
women's reproductive organs,
medical attack on, 316
Reproduction of social structure,
86, 248–49, 508–13
Republicans, 409, 439–40
Research, 126–49. *See also*
Experiment(s); *specific topics*
on aggression and testosterone,
304–5
analysis of results, 130, 134,
137
and bias, 14, 133, 134, 135,
144, 147

causation and correlation
in, 139
and common sense, 128
and controversy, 141–44, 145,
171–73, 581, 582
on education, 510, 513–15
ethics in, 141, 145–46
and gender, 140, 144, 147
on the homeless, 141, 142–43
interviewer effect in, 547
levels of analysis, 98–99
methods of (design), 126–41
misunderstanding subjects,134
model, 128–30
ownership of results of, 130,
142
on peer pressure, 170–71
on rapists, 144, 147–48
replication of, 14
tables summarizing, 132
and theory, 146–48
valid topics, 128
and values, 14, 142
vs. reform, 31–33
women in studies of social
mobility, 285
Reserve labor force, 294, 344
Resocialization, 87–88
Resource mobilization, 646
Resources, conflict perspective on,
247–48, 382–87, 593, 657
Retirement, 381–82. *See also*
Social Security
Revolution(s)
agricultural, 153, 155
and authority, 433
biotech, 153, 157–58
defined, 433
deprivation theory, 644
domestication, 153, 154–55
French, 9, 10, 11
Industrial *See* (Industrial
Revolution)
information, 153, 156–57
and liberty, 437
and relative deprivation, 644
and rising expectations, 357
Russian, 250
social, 152–58, 652
as social movements, 638
"the quiet," 420
Thomas Jefferson on rebellion,
437
of workers, 244, 247, 660
Riddle of Amish Culture, The
(Kraybill), 109
Rights. *See* Civil rights
Riots, 357, 627–28, 630
Rising expectations, defined, 357
Rites of passage, 91, 94
Ritual pollution, 240
Ritualism, 215
Rituals, 91, 94, 526, 532, 542
Robot soldiers, 667
"Rods from God," 667
Roe v. Wade, 647, 648
Role conflict, 114, 115
Role confusion, 466
Role exit, 117–18
Role extension, 633
Role performance, 114–15
Role strain, 114, 115
Role taking, 71–72
Roles, 103–4, 113–18, 559–60
Roman Catholic Church
and capitalism, 13–14

charismatic leaders, 434, 435
as ecclesia, 544
and Internet, 553
member characteristics, 545,
546
as political power, 242, 248
school system of, 521
Romance, 53, 468–70
Romania, orphans in, 68
"Roughnecks," the, 121, 124,
212–13
Routinization of charisma, 436
Ruling class, 447. *See also* Power
elite
Rumors, 628–29, 631, 634
Rural patterns, 606, 607, 610, 662
Rural poor, 289
Rural rebound, 610
Russia
capitalism in, 251, 409, 504
in Chechnya, 457
crime in, 251
economy of, 251, 408, 409
education in, 503–4
ethnic relations in, 655
and G-8, 455, 654–55
health care in, 585
homelessness in, 143
in NATO, 187, 458
pollution in, 585, 671
population, 600
power realignment, 655
and religious persecution,
529–30
revolution in, 250, 409
social stratification in, 250–51
and transfer of power, 436
and U.S. missiles planned for
Poland, 655
and wars, 448, 457
Rwanda, 334, 347, 655

Sacred, defined, 526
"Saints," the, 121, 124, 212–13
Same-sex marriage, 462–63, 480
Samples, 131–33, 134, 143, 147
Sanctions, 48, 206
"Sandwich generation," 92, 485
Saneros, 542
Sapir-Whorf hypothesis, 48
SARS (Severe Acute Respiratory
Syndrome), 583
Satanists, 52, 634
SATs, 503, 516–18
Saudi Arabia, 262, 452
Scapegoats, 343–44
Schools. *See also* College;
Education
as agent of socialization, 84–86
and caste in India, 240–41
class rings, 509
correspondence principle of,
512–13
"corridor curriculum" in, 86
and cultural lag, 61
functions of, 84–86
funding of, 511, 512
and gender, 86–87
"hidden curriculum" in, 86,
508, 510
in inner city, 510, 521–22
and mate selection, 508
parental involvement in, 509,
521
preschools, 283
private, 283, 513, 521

Streetcorner men, 97, 98–99, 100, 294. *See also* Homeless
Structural mobility, 285
Structured interviews, 136
Students. *See also* Education; Schools
  and alcohol/drug use, 579, 580
  and subcultures, 518
Studied nonobservance, 116
Subcultures, 51–52, 54–55
  of children, 86–87, 91
  of deviance, 147–48, 209–10, 211–12
  ethnic groups as, 55
  explained, 50, 51–52
  military, 89
  photo essay on, 54–55
  in sports, 55
  of students, 518
  of terrorists, 531
Subjective meanings, 15
Suburban flight, 617
Suburbanization, 608–9, 617–18, 662
Sudan, 42, 239, 313
Suicide
  of adolescents, 394
  of the elderly, 15, 394
  in Europe, 12
  medically assisted, 571–72
  methods of, 13
  of Native Americans, 363
  and race-ethnicity, 13
  and social integration, 12–13
  of soldiers, 450
  of students in Japan *vs.* U.S., 8, 9
Suicide bombers, 452, 531
Sun Microsystems, 409
Superego, defined, 74
Superiority, 53, 161
Super-rich, the, 272, 276–78
Surgery, 316, 384, 450, 562, 568, 570, 571, 575, 582, 585
Surveillance, 141, 195–96, 249, 453, 664, 666
Surveys, 131–36, 142
"Survival of the fittest," 10
Survivalists, 52
Sustainable environment, 668
Sweden, 407, 544, 585, 586, 631
Symbolic culture, 44–51, 659
Symbolic interactionism
  chart summarizing, 30
  explained, 23–26, 30
  and fossils, 552
  as microsociology, 30, 98, 110–13
  and social construction of reality, 119–21
Symbolic interactionist perspective on
  aging, 376–80
  births in Least Industrialized Nations, 595–602
  deviance, 204, 208, 209–13, 214, 229
  divorce, 24–26, 30
  ecosabotage, 671–72
  education, 513–15
  eye contact, 112–13
  gender, 466–68
  gendered violence, 327–28
  health and health care, 564, 571
  the homeless, 30
  marketing research, 152

marriage and family, 24–26, 93, 466–68
  medicalization, 571
  micropolitics, 432
  midwives, defeat of, 564
  population growth, 595–602
  prejudice, 345
  religion, 530, 532–33
  and self concept, 161
  sexual harassment, 324
  statistics, 494
Symbols
  defined, 23–24
  religious, 530, 532
Syphilis experiments, 333, 581–82
System of descent, 464

Tables, how to read, 132
Taboo
  defined, 50
  incest, 59, 466
Tact, 116
Taken-for-granted assumptions. *See* Background assumptions
Taking the role of the other, 71–72
Tarantism, 632
Tari Huli dancer, 673
Tartars, 656
Tasmania, 61, 347
Tattooing, 55, 130, 206
Teacher expectations, 513–15, 521–22
Teamwork, 115, 194, 196
"Tearooms," 146
Technological life, 392
Technology. *See also* New technology
  and control of workers, 156, 195–96
  as a core value, 53
  and cultural leveling, 61–62
  and death, 392
  defined, 60, 660
  and divorce, 661
  and the elderly, 392, 395–96
  and the environment, 674
  and the family, 479
  and gender, 60, 658
  and global domination, 263
  and global inequality, 263, 425–27
  and global stratification, 654
  and the homeless, 284
  and ideology, 660–61
  and life span, 395–96
  and nursing homes, 390
  and religion, 547, 549, 553
  and social change, 60–62, 156–58, 183, 657–59, 660–67
  and social class, 284
  and social organization, 660
  and social relationships, 661, 666
  and surveillance, 195–96, 249, 664
  and values, 659, 660–61
  and war and terrorism, 452, 667
Telecommuting, 424, 666
Telephone operators, 183
Television, 80–81, 91, 380, 408
Televoting, 438
Teleworking, 424

Terror(ism)
  and Al-Qaeda, 638, 657
  bioterrorism, 411
  and body language, 113
  defined, 450, 452
  as dysfunction of religion, 530
  and the future, 452, 455
  and global inequalities, 425, 655
  international, 452, 638
  and nationalism, 457
  and NATO, 187
  and religion, 530, 531
  school drills for, 519
  as subculture, 54
  suicide, 452, 531
  and technology, 452, 667
Testimonials, 643
Testosterone, 304–5
Thailand, 595
Theory. *See also* Conflict, Functionalist, and Symbolic interactionist perspectives
  defined, 23
  reform *vs.*, 20–21
  in sociology, 20–31
Thesis and antithesis, 657
Thinness, 116–17, 579
Third estate, 242
Third parties, 440
Thomas theorem, 119
"Three-strikes" laws, 223–24
Tiwi, the, 371, 373, 390
Tobacco, 580–81
Torah, the, 537
Tornado photo essay, 122–23
Torture, 161, 174, 449–50, 451
"Torture warrants," 161
Total institutions, 88
Totalitarianism, 104, 438–39
Touching, 112
Toyota, 199
Toys, 62, 78, 79
Tracking in schools, 507, 513–14
Trading blocs, 412, 455–56, 457
Tradition and science, 8–10
Traditional authority
  and charismatic authority, 435
  and industrialization, 433–34, 535, 653, 654
  and rationalization, 178–80
Traditional orientation, 178
Traditional societies, 175, 179–80, 468, 469, 654
Trail of Tears, 363
Transformative social movements, 637, 638
Transitional adulthood, 91, 92
Transnational social movements, 637–38
Transplants, 562
Triads, 166–67, 168
Tsunami, the, 595
Tulsa, Oklahoma, 630
Tunisia, 299
Turkish marriage customs, 208
Tuskegee syphilis experiment, 333, 581–82
Tuskegee University, 333
Tutsis, 334, 347, 655
Twin studies, 66

"U"-Curve of leisure, 424
Unabomber, the, 659
Underclass, 279–80, 284, 341. *See also* Homeless
Underground economy, 422

Unemployment, 356, 508
Union Bank of Monterey, 194
United Airlines, 194–95
United Arab Emirates, 632
United Fruit Company, 262
United Nations, 593, 598
Universal citizenship, 437
University of Chicago, 18, 517, 610, 625
University of Georgia, 515
University of Michigan, 367
University of Phoenix, 517
Unobtrusive measures, 140–40
Unstructured interviews, 136
Upper middle class, 278, 280, 284
Upward social mobility, 284–85, 287
Urban flight, 617–18
Urban legends, 635–36
Urban renewal, 518, 618–20
Urban sprawl, 612, 662
Urban Villagers, The (Gans), 614
Urbanization, 602–20. *See also* Cities
  and industrialization, 613
  in the Least Industrialized Nations, 602, 604–5, 613
  process of, 606
  in U.S., 606–9
U.S. Department of Transportation, 193
U.S. Justice Department, 174
U.S. Postal Service, 183
U.S. Public Health Service, 333, 335, 581–82
U.S. Steel, 425
Utah, 583

Vaginal examinations, 120–21
Validity, 130, 143
Value clusters, 56
Value contradictions, 56–57
Value free sociology, 14
Value judgments, and sociology, 14, 214
Values, 52–59
  of the Amish, 109
  as blinders, 58
  Confucian, 477
  contradictions in, 56–57
  core, 52–53, 503, 506
  cultural transmission of, 506
  defined, 48
  and deviance, 214–16
  and education, 53, 501, 503, 504, 506
  emerging, 57–58
  and the environment, 57–58
  and health, 583–84
  and home schooling, 509
  and individualism, 53, 58
  and religion, 84
  in research, 14, 142
  in social institutions, 105
  and subcultures, 54
  and technology, 659, 660–61
  transformation of, 660–61
  universal, 59
  in U.S., 52–53, 56–59
  and work, 314
Variables, 129–30, 138, 139
Verstehen, 15–16
VFW (Veterans of Foreign Wars), 190
Video games, 81, 82
Vietnam, 173, 407, 409, 449, 450
Vietnam Veterans Study, 304–5

Violence. *See also* Murder
  and authority, 432–33
  "cage fighting," 210
  in the family, 127–41, 327,
    491–93
  and feminists, 327–28
  and gangs, 151–52, 210, 217
  and husband's achievement, 132
  and male identity, 80, 210
  in nursing homes, 390, 391
  and religion, 530, 531
  riots, 357, 627–28, 630
  in schools, 8, 9, 109, 518–19,
    520
  against women, 226–27, 307,
    309, 312, 313, 324–28,
    491, 492, 493, 601
  by women, 127, 218–19, 226
Voice Response Units (VRU),
  425–26
Volkswagen, 424
Voluntary associations, 188–91
Voodoo, 542
Voting
  and alienation, 441
  and apathy, 441
  in early democracies, 436–37
  in early U.S., 437
  electronic/Internet, 438
  and employment, 441, 443
  and gender, 17, 312, 443, 444
  and ideology, 271
  patterns in U.S., 441–44
  and race-ethnicity, 355, 357,
    441, 443, 444
  and social class, 271, 283, 441,
    443
Voting Rights Act of 1965, 357

Waco, Texas, 525
Walkman, the, 198
War, 447–55. *See also* Genocide;
  Soldiers
  and arms sales, 452, 457
  child soldiers, 454–55
  and computers, 667
  costs of, 449
  defined, 447
  and dehumanization, 449–50,
    451
  as dysfunction of religion, 530
  and ethnic conflicts, 457, 655
  and the future, 452, 455
  and groupthink, 173, 174
  Gulf Wars I and II, 62, 258,
    262, 449
  and politics, 447–55
  reasons for, 448, 457
  and slavery, 237
  in space, 667
  and starvation, 594
  and technology, 452, 455, 667
  universality of, 448
War of the Worlds (Wells), 629–31,
  632
Warfighter I, 667

Washington, D.C., 97
WASPs, defined, 351
"Water boarding," 451
Wealth, 244, 268–71, 275,
  276–78, 410
Webster v. Reproductive Services,
  647–48
Weight, body, 116–17, 578–79
Welfare
  conflict perspective on, 294
  corporate, 669
  myths about, 8, 9, 288
  reform of, 293–94
  Welfare socialism, 407
Welfare (state) capitalism, 405–6,
  407
"Wellness," 584
Western Electric Company, 140
Western Wall, 553
Westerns, 56
Whales, 674
White ethnics, 350, 351–52
White-collar crime, 216–17, 219,
  232
Whites, 356. *See also* Race-
  ethnicity
  and AIDS, 578
  background assumptions, 352
  and education, 290, 317, 356,
    513
  ethnic background of, 350,
    351–52
  family structure of, 475
  interracial marriage of, 470–71
  numbers of, 350, 366
  and poverty, 288, 289–90, 291,
    356
  statistics on, 346
  and voting, 443, 444
  WASPs, defined, 351
  well-being compared to other
    groups, 356
Widowhood and widows, 388,
  433, 434, 474, 540
Wilberforce University, 19
Witches, 530
Women. *See also* Gender; Sexism;
  Single mothers
  and abortion, 647–48
  and AIDS, 577–78
  births to, 483–84
  circumcision of, 313
  in criminal justice system, 225,
    226, 227, 228, 327
  and death penalty, 225, 227,
    228
  discrimination against, 305–8,
    308–12, 315–19,
    319–20, 371, 421
  in early sociology, 16–17, 18
  and education, 16, 315–19,
    514–15
  elderly, among the Tiwi, 371
  in the estate system, 242
  female infanticide, 601

  and gynecology, 120–21
  health care of, 316, 571, 573
  impression management for
    executives, 118
  in the military, 324–25
  as a minority group, 305–8,
    338
  and networking, 166
  and pay gap, 309, 318, 320–23
  in politics, 328–29
  in poverty, 290, 392
  and power, 247
  in prostitution, 299, 307
  and the "quiet revolution," 420
  social mobility of, 285, 286
  social stratification of, 243
  and stereotypes, 16–17, 80–81,
    82, 111, 314, 315, 323,
    327
  violence against, 226–27, 307,
    309, 312, 313, 324–28,
    491, 492, 493, 601
  violence by, 127, 218–19, 226
  and voting, 17, 443, 444
  and work, 118, 183, 308–9,
    310–11, 320–25
Women's movement, 312, 314,
  639. *See also* Feminism;
  Women
Woolworth's, 357
Work and workers. *See also*
  Division of labor
  capitalists, thinking of selves as,
    244
  children (*See* Child labor)
  conflict perspective on, 195,
    243–45, 247, 261, 294,
    324, 344–45
  control of, 156, 195–96,
    344–45
  in the corporation, 191–99
  discrimination in, 32
  and diversity, 191–93
  exploitation of, 11, 244, 247,
    407, 660
  and gender, 306, 307, 308–9,
    308, 314, 320–25,
    419–21, 564
  gender as social control, 324
  global division of labor, 410–11
  and globalization, 260, 261, 412
  and identity, 87, 186, 275, 424
  and illness, 567
  and Industrial Revolution, 9,
    155–56
  in Japan *vs.* U.S., 196–99
  and leisure, 423–24
  maquiladoras, 259–61
  motivation of, 245–46
  prestige of, 272–74, 308–9,
    545, 546
  reserve labor force, 294,
    344–45
  restructuring of, 425–27
  revolution of, 244, 247, 660
  and social class, 83

  social control of, 195–96, 261,
    324, 344–45
  and socialization, 87
  and split labor market, 261,
    344–45
  and struggle for rights, 156
  teleworking, 424
  in types of society, 400–402
  in underground economy, 422
  in U.S. society, 418–24, 495
  work becoming home, 495
Work teams, 194
Working class. *See also* Work and
  workers
  and child rearing, 282–83,
    472–73
  defined, 220, 276, 279, 280
  and deviance, 212–13, 216,
    229
  exploitation of, 11, 244,
    247–48, 344–45, 657, 660
  marginal, 219, 220
  Marx on, 11, 243–44, 247,
    274, 276
  and prestige of work, 273
  and socialization of children,
    83, 86, 282–83, 472
Working poor, the, 235, 279,
  284
Workplace
  alienation/isolation, 186–87,
    194, 660
  and anticipatory socialization,
    87
  becoming home, 495
  computers in, 195–96,
    655–56
  cyberslacking, 197
  cybersleuthing, 197
  gender inequality, 320–25
  humanizing of, 193–95
  and new technology, 195–96,
    197, 284
  racial-ethnic diversity, 192–93,
    344–45
  sexual harassment in, 324–25
World Bank, 671
World Court, 456
World system theory, 259, 654
World Trade Center, 422, 452,
  531, 633, 634
World Trade Organization, 456
World Wars I and II, 449
World's Fair, 346
Wounded Knee, 363
Wrestling, 152

"XYY" theory, 208

Yanomamo Indians, 4, 203
Youthfulness, as a value, 57
Yugoslavia, 347–48, 655

Zapotec Indians, 205
Zero population growth, 602
Zimbabwe, inflation in, 403–4

Photo Credits

left: ©Dale Berman/Corbis Outline; **p. 282, right:** ©Alison Wright/Corbis; **p. 285:** UPI/Bettmann/Corbis; **p. 287:** David Deas/DK Stock/Getty Images; **p. 289:** By permission of Johnny Hart and Creators Syndicate. **(on page credit); p. 290:** Jean-Yves Rabeuf/The Image Works.

Chapter 11: p. 299: ©J. L. Bulcão/Corbis; **p. 301:** Mexico: Tony Anderson/Getty Images; Jordan: Dave Bartruff/Corbis; Kenya: ©Doug Scott/AgeFotostock; Ethiopia: Art Wolfe/Photo Researchers, Inc.; Brazil: ©Reuters/ Corbis; Chile: ©Owen Franken/Stock, Boston; India: ©Steven Vidler/ Eurasia Press/Corbis; Tibet: ©Panorama Images/The Image Works; **p. 302:** Photo by John Sheretz, courtesy of CASBS; **p. 303:** Courtesy of Steven Goldberg; **p. 305:** ©Bettmann/Corbis; **p. 306, top:** ©Marilyn Humphries/ The Image Works; **p. 306, bottom:** ©Hamid Sardar/Corbis; **p. 307, top:** View Stock China/Alamy; **p. 307, bottom:** Alon Reininger/Contact Press Images; **p. 308:** ©Alison Wright/The Image Works; **p. 309:** REUTERS/Ge Gong/Landov; **p. 310-11:** ©James M. Henslin; **p. 312:** Bettman/Corbis; **p. 313:** ©Sven Torfinn/Panos; **p. 316:** image100/Alamy Images Royalty Free; **p. 318:** ©EMPICS/Topham/The Image Works; **p. 325:** AP Images/ Jacquelyn Martin; **p. 328:** Molly Riley/Reuters.

Chapter 12: p. 333: ©Ben Shahn/Corbis; **p. 334, left:** ©Robert Mora/Getty Images; **p. 334, right:** ©Reuters/Landov; **p. 335, left:** ©Time Life Pictures/Getty Images; **p. 335, right:** AP Images; **p. 336:** REUTERS/Mike Blake/Landov; **p. 337:** David R. Frazier/Photo Researchers, Inc.; **p. 338:** ©Jim Hollander/Reuters/Landov; **p. 340:** AP Images; **p. 346:** ©Wildlife Conservation Society; **p. 347:** AP Images; **p. 349:** AP Images/Kathy Willens; **p. 350:** Digital Vision Ltd./SuperStock Royalty Free; **p. 352:** ©Adrianne Starnes/Landov LLC; **p. 353:** ©Jack Kurtz/The Image Works; **p. 354:** REUTERS/Carlos Barria/Landov; **p. 355:** AP Images/Lynn Hermosa; **p. 357:** Fred Blackwell; **p. 358:** ©Bob Daemmrich/The Image Works; **p. 359:** Courtesy of William Julius Wilson. Jon Chase/Harvard News Office; **p. 361:** AP Images/Xinhua; **p. 363:** Zogbaum/North Wind Picture Archives; **p. 365:** ©Sidney Harris; **p. 367:** ©Hans Neleman/Getty Images.

Chapter 13: p. 371: ©Joyce Fincher, Photo International/Alamy; **p. 372:** ©John Launois/Black Star; **p. 377:** AP Images/Kyodo News; **p. 378:** ©James M. Henslin; **p. 378:** PEANUTS ® Charles M. Schulz; **p. 379:** ©Panorama Images/The Image Works; **p. 380:** ©Lisa O'Connor/Corbis; **p. 381:** ©Joe McBride/Getty Images; **p. 384:** Courtesy of Pfizer Corporation; **p. 389:** ©Robert Harbison; **p. 390:** ©Bob Daemmrich/The Image Works; **p. 391, top:** Justin Sullivan/Getty Images; **p. 391, bottom:** Chuck Savage/Corbis; **p. 395:** ©Roy McMahon/Corbis.

Chapter 14: p. 399: ©Yang Liu/Corbis; **p. 400:** ©Tibor Bognár/Corbis; **p. 402:** Lewis Hine/Bettmann/Corbis; **p. 404:** ©James M. Henslin; **p. 406:** The Granger Collection, New York; **p. 407:** ©Hubert Boesl/dpa/Corbis; **p. 408, top:** Philip Silcock/Riser/Getty Images Rights Ready; **p. 408, bottom:** AKG London; **p. 409:** Guang Niu/Getty Images; **p. 410:** ©Catherine Panchout/Corbis; **p. 411:** Issei Kato/Reuters Limited; **p. 414–15:** ©James M. Henslin; **p. 421:** Jenny Acheson/Riser/Getty Images Rights Ready; **p. 425:** ©Tatsuyuki Tayama/Fujifotos/The Image Works; **p. 426:** ©Edy Purnomo/ The Image Works.

Chapter 15: p. 431: ©David Ball/Stone/Getty Images; **p. 432:** Brown Brothers; **p. 433:** Marion Kaplan/Alamy; **p. 434:** Jean-Auguste-Dominique Ingres, Jeanne d'Arc. 1854. Musee du Louvre, Paris. Photo AKG London; **p. 435:** AKG London; **p. 436:** JIM WATSON/AFP/Getty Images; **p. 437:** AP Images; **p. 438:** Judith Miller/Dorling Kindersley/Lights, Camera, Action; **p. 440:** A. Ramey/PhotoEdit, Inc.; **p. 441:** Gary Markstein ©Milwaukee Journal Sentinal **(On page credit); p. 442:** ©Bettmann/Corbis; **p. 450:** AP Images/Charles Dharapak; **p. 451:** Photo courtesy of Washington Post via Getty Images; **p. 453:** ©The New Yorker Collection, 2002 Robert Mankoff from cartoonbank.com. All Rights Reserved **(On page credit); p. 454:** Michael Kamber/Polaris; **p. 456, left:** ©Swim Ink 2, LLC/Corbis; **p. 456, right:** Library of Congress, #LC-USZC2-985; **p. 457:** AP Images.

Chapter 16: p. 461: ©DP Clark/The Image Bank/Getty Images; **p. 462:** Courtesy of the National Parenting Association (NPA), N.Y. copyright 1994 by the NPA; **p. 465:** ©Tribune Media Services, Inc. All rights Reserved. Reprinted with Permission; **p. 468:** ©James M. Henslin; **p. 469:** ©James M. Henslin; **p. 471:** ©Chuck Savage/Corbis; **p. 475:** ©Jeff Greenberg/Alamy; **p. 476:** Spencer Grant/PhotoEdit, Inc.; **p. 477:** ©Marilyn Angel Wynn/ Nativestock Pictures/Corbis; **p. 479:** Copyright 2006 Darren Modricker/ Willow Street Pictures; **p. 480:** Tim Boyle/Getty Images; **p. 487:** Peter Dazeley/Photographer's Choices/Getty Images; **p. 488:** ©Ford Smith/Corbis; **p. 489:** Courtesy of the National Parenting Association (NPA); **p. 490:** ©Sidney Harris; **p. 492:** ©James W. Porter/Corbis; **p. 495:** ©2002 by King Features Syndicate, Inc. World Rights Reserved **(On page credit)**.

Chapter 17: p. 499: Tannen Maury/Landov; **p. 500:** ©Peter Johnson/Corbis; **p. 501:** ©Bettmann/Corbis; **p. 502:** ©Rachel Epstein/The Image Works; **p. 505, top:** ©A. Perigot/Hoa-Qui/Photo Researchers, Inc.; **p. 505, bottom:** Courtesy of Lisa Pearce; **p. 506:** ©The New Yorker Collection, 2001 Robert Mankoff from cartoonbank.com. All Rights Reserved. **(On page credit); p. 507:** Michael Ventura/PhotoEdit, Inc.; **p. 508:** AP Images/Mark Duncan; **p. 509:** ©Jostens, Inc. All rights Reserved; **p. 510:** Myrleen Ferguson Cate/PhotoEdit, Inc.; **p. 514:** ©The Art Archive/Corbis; **p. 516:** ©Najlah Feanny/Corbis; **p. 517:** UPI Photo/Art Foxall/Landov; **p. 520:** AP Images; **p. 521:** ©Peter Hvizdak/The Image Works; **p. 522:** ©David Butow/Corbis SABA.

Chapter 18: p. 525: Time Magazine, Copyright Time Inc./Time & Life Pictures/Getty Images; **p. 526:** ©James M. Henslin; **p. 527:** ©David H. Wells/Corbis; **p. 528:** ©Barry Lewis/Corbis; **p. 529:** ©Bob Henriques/ Magnum Photos; **p. 530:** ©Scala/Art Resource, NY; **p. 531:** HIP/Art Resource, NY; **p. 532:** ©James Estrin/The New York Times; **p. 533:** ©Stapleton Collection/Corbis; **p. 536, top:** ©The New Yorker Collection, 2000 Robert Mankoff from cartoonbank.com. All rights Reserved **(On page credit); p. 536, bottom:** AP Images; **p. 540:** ©Redlink/Corbis; **p. 542:** ©Reuters/Corbis; **p. 544:** ©James M. Henslin; **p. 548:** Angel Franco/The New York Times; **p. 550:** PEANUTS ® by Charles M. Schulz **(On page credit); p. 552:** National Museum of Kenya/Visuals Unlimited; **p. 553:** ©Israel images/Alamy.

Chapter 19: p. 557: ©Jeff Greenberg/Alamy; **p. 558:** ©James M. Henslin; **p. 559:** Frank Siteman Photography; **p. 561:** Jean Chung/WpN; **p. 562:** Will & Deni McIntyre/Photo Researchers, Inc.; **p. 564:** NNS/Birmingham News/Landov; **p. 568:** ©Anthony Bolante/Reuters/Corbis; **p. 570:** AP Images/Marta Lavandier; **p. 572:** ©Reuters/Corbis; **p. 573: On page credit; p. 575:** ©Cristian Baitg Creative Collection/Alamy; **p. 576:** ©Sven Torfinn/ Panos; **p. 579:** ©Enigma/Alamy; **p. 581, top:** David Young-Wolff/PhotoEdit; **p. 581, bottom:** ©Shuji Kobayashi/Stone/Getty Images; **p. 584:** ©GARO/ PHANIE/Photo Researchers, Inc.

Chapter 20: p. 589: ©Barry Lewis/Alamy; **p. 590:** ©Corbis; **p. 593, left:** ©Reuters/Landov; **p. 593, right:** ©David Paul Morris/Getty Images; **p. 595:** ©John Russell/AFP/Getty Images; **p. 599:** ©A. Ramey/Woodfin Camp & Associates; **p. 601:** RAVEENDRAN/AFP/Getty Images; **p. 602:** ©Wolfgang Kaehler/Corbis; **p. 603:** ©Roger-Viollet/The Image Works; **p. 604-5:** ©James M. Henslin; **p. 609:** ©Lee Snider/The Image Works; **p. 613:** Mariana Bazo/Reuters/Corbis; **p. 614:** ©Lee Snider/The Image Works; **p. 615:** Jeff Greenberg/PhotoEdit, Inc.; **p. 616:** ©Jeff Greenberg/The Image Works; **p. 617:** Copyright OMA; **p. 619:** Cameron Davidson/Stone/Getty Images; **p. 620:** Xinhua/Landov.

Chapter 21: p. 623: ©Corbis; **p. 624:** ©Bettmann/Corbis; **p. 628:** ©Peter Turnley/Corbis; **p. 629:** SEBASTIAN D'SOUZA/AFP/Getty Images; **p. 630:** ©Corbis; **p. 631:** ©John Henley/Corbis; **p. 632:** ©Bettmann/Corbis; **p. 634:** REUTERS/Shannon Stapleton/Landov; **p. 635:** ©Al Campanie/Syracuse Newspapers/The Image Works; **p. 636:** AP Images; **p. 639:** ©Cesar Rangel/AFP/Getty Images; **p. 640-1:** ©James M. Henslin; **p. 642:** EM-PICS/Landov; **p. 643:** Bill Aron/PhotoEdit Inc.; **p. 645:** ©Mark Peterson/Corbis; **p. 647:** Mark Wilson/Getty Images.

Chapter 22: p. 651: ©Bettmann/Corbis; **p. 652:** ©Roger-Viollet/The Image Works; **p. 653:** Erich Lessing/Art Resource, NY; **p. 654:** ©Jim Young/Reuters/Corbis; **p. 656:** ©Transit Leipzig/Sovfoto; **p. 658:** ©Penny Tweedie/Alamy; **p. 659:** ©Tom Treick, The Oregonian/Corbis Sygma; **p. 661:** ©Bettmann/Corbis; **p. 662, left:** Hulton Collection/Liaison/Getty Images; **p. 662, right:** ©Car Culture/Corbis; **p. 664:** Courtesy The Computer Museum History Center/Model Photo Dennis Bourke; **p. 665:** AP Images; **p. 667:** ©Mike Agliolo/Photo Researchers, Inc.; **p. 668, top left:** ©Klein/Hubert-Bios/Peter Arnold, Inc.; **p. 668, top right:** ©Terry Whittaker/Photo Researchers, Inc.; **p. 668, bottom left:** ©Tom McHugh/Photo Researchers, Inc.; **p. 668, bottom right:** ©Anup Shah/Animals Animals; **p. 669:** Copyright 2001 by Greenpeace, Newscom TagID: zumalive588025/ Newcom; **p. 672:** Copyright 1998 by Shaun Walker (Newscom TagID: zumaphotos003379/Newscom; **p. 673:** ©Wolfgang Kaehler/Alamy; **p. 674:** ©REUTERS/Bruno Domingos/Landov.